THE AMERICAN PSYCHIATRIC PRESS

# TEXTBOOK OF SUBSTANCE ABUSE TREATMENT

*Second Edition*

THE AMERICAN PSYCHIATRIC PRESS

# TEXTBOOK OF
# SUBSTANCE ABUSE TREATMENT

*Second Edition*

Edited by

Marc Galanter, M.D.
Herbert D. Kleber, M.D.

American Psychiatric Press, Inc.

Washington, DC
London, England

**Note:** The authors have worked to ensure that all information in this book concerning drug dosages, schedules, and routes of administration is accurate as of the time of publication and consistent with standards set by the U.S. Food and Drug Administration and the general medical community. As medical research and practice advance, however, therapeutic standards may change. For this reason and because human and mechanical errors sometimes occur, we recommend that readers follow the advice of a physician who is directly involved in their care or the care of a member of their family.

Books published by the American Psychiatric Press, Inc., represent the views and opinions of the individual authors and do not necessarily represent the policies and opinions of the Press or the American Psychiatric Association.

Manufactured in the United States of America on acid-free paper
02  01  00  99     4  3  2  1
Second Edition

American Psychiatric Press, Inc.
1400 K Street, N.W., Washington, DC   20005
www.appi.org

**Library of Congress Cataloging-in-Publication Data**
The American Psychiatric Press textbook of substance abuse treatment /
    edited by Marc Galanter, Herbert D. Kleber. — 2nd ed.
        p.   cm.
    Includes bibliographical references and index.
    ISBN 0-88048-820-4
    1. Substance abuse—Treatment.     I. Galanter, Marc.     II. Kleber,
Herbert D.   III. Title: Textbook of substance abuse treatment.
    [DNLM: 1. Substance-Related Disorders—therapy.     WM 270 A5107
1999]
RC564.A525   1999
616.86′06—dc21
DNLM/DLC
for Library of Congress
                                                                                                98-32242
                                                                                                      CIP

**British Library Cataloguing in Publication Data**
A CIP record is available from the British Library.

Cover design: Anne Friedman
Cover illustration: Improvisation: The Deluge, Wassily Kandinsky
Credit: Stadtische Gallery in Lenbachhaus, Munich, Germany/SuperStock

# Contents

Contributors . . . . . . . . . . . . . . . . . . . . . . . . ix

Preface . . . . . . . . . . . . . . . . . . . . . . . . . . xiii

---

## Section 1  The Nature of Addiction

*1*  Neurobiology of Alcohol . . . . . . . . . . . . . . . . . 3
    *Boris Tabakoff, Ph.D., Paula L. Hoffman, Ph.D.*

*2*  Neurobiology of Opiates/Opioids . . . . . . . . . . . . . 11
    *Jerome H. Jaffe, M.D., Ari B. Jaffe, M.D.*

*3*  Neurobiology of Stimulants . . . . . . . . . . . . . . . . 21
    *Marian W. Fischman, Ph.D., Margaret Haney, Ph.D.*

*4*  Neurobiology of Hallucinogens . . . . . . . . . . . . . . 33
    *Richard A. Glennon, Ph.D.*

*5*  Neurobiology of Marijuana . . . . . . . . . . . . . . . . 39
    *Billy R. Martin, Ph.D.*

*6*  Epidemiology of Drug Dependence . . . . . . . . . . . . . 47
    *James C. Anthony, Ph.D.*

*7*  Genetics of Substance Abuse . . . . . . . . . . . . . . . 59
    *C. Robert Cloninger, M.D.*

*8*  Principles of Learning in the Study and Treatment of Substance Abuse:
    Applying What We've Learned . . . . . . . . . . . . . . . 67
    *Stephen T. Higgins, Ph.D.*

*9*  Cross-Cultural Aspects of Substance Abuse . . . . . . . . 75
    *Joseph Westermeyer, M.D., M.P.H., Ph.D.*

## Section 2 Overview of Treatment

**10** Goals of Treatment. . . . . . . . . . . . . . . 89
*Marc A. Schuckit, M.D.*

**11** Typologies of Addiction . . . . . . . . . . . . . 97
*Michael J. Bohn, M.D., Roger E. Meyer, M.D.*

**12** Assessment of the Patient . . . . . . . . . . . . 109
*Richard S. Schottenfeld, M.D., Michael V. Pantalon, Ph.D.*

**13** Patient Placement Criteria . . . . . . . . . . . . 121
*David R. Gastfriend, M.D.*

**14** Outcome Research: Alcoholism . . . . . . . . . . . 129
*Theresa Moyers, Ph.D., Reid K. Hester, Ph.D.*

**15** Outcome Research: Drug Abuse . . . . . . . . . . . 135
*Dean R. Gerstein, Ph.D.*

## Section 3 Treatment for Specific Drugs of Abuse

**16** Alcohol . . . . . . . . . . . . . . . . . . 151
*Don Gallant, M.D.*

**17** Cannabis . . . . . . . . . . . . . . . . . . 165
*Mark S. Gold, M.D., Michelle Tullis, Ph.D. candidate*

**18** Stimulants . . . . . . . . . . . . . . . . . 183
*Thomas R. Kosten, M.D., Amrita K. Singha, Ph.D.*

**19** Hallucinogens . . . . . . . . . . . . . . . . 195
*J. Thomas Ungerleider, M.D., Robert N. Pechnick, Ph.D.*

**20** Phencyclidine . . . . . . . . . . . . . . . . 205
*Sidney H. Schnoll, M.D., Ph.D., Michael F. Weaver, M.D.*

**21** Tobacco. . . . . . . . . . . . . . . . . . . 215
*Judith K. Ockene, Ph.D., Jean L. Kristeller, Ph.D., Gary Donnelly, M.P.H.*

**22** Benzodiazepines and Other Sedative-Hypnotics . . . . . . . 239
*David E. Smith, M.D., Donald R. Wesson, M.D.*

**23** Opioids: Detoxification . . . . . . . . . . . . . 251
*Herbert D. Kleber, M.D.*

**24**  Opioids: Methadone Maintenance . . . . . . . . . . . . . . . 271
*Edward C. Senay, M.D.*

**25**  Opioids: Antagonists and Partial Agonists . . . . . . . . . . . . 281
*Charles P. O'Brien, M.D., Ph.D., James W. Cornish, M.D.*

**26**  MDMA, Ketamine, GHB, and the "Club Drug" Scene . . . . . . . 295
*David M. McDowell, M.D.*

## Section 4  Treatment Modalities

**27**  Psychodynamics . . . . . . . . . . . . . . . . . . . . . . . . 309
*Richard Frances, M.D., Jenny Frances, B.A., John Franklin, M.D., Lisa Borg, M.D.*

**28**  Network Therapy . . . . . . . . . . . . . . . . . . . . . . . 323
*Marc Galanter, M.D.*

**29**  Individual Psychotherapy: Alcohol . . . . . . . . . . . . . . . 335
*Sheldon Zimberg, M.D., M.S.*

**30**  Individual Psychotherapy: Other Drugs . . . . . . . . . . . . . 343
*George E. Woody, M.D., Delinda Mercer, Ph.D., Lester Luborsky, Ph.D.*

**31**  Relapse Prevention . . . . . . . . . . . . . . . . . . . . . . 353
*G. Alan Marlatt, Ph.D., Kimberly Barrett, Ed.D., Dennis C. Daley, M.S.W.*

**32**  Group Therapy . . . . . . . . . . . . . . . . . . . . . . . . 367
*Edward J. Khantzian, M.D., Sarah J. Golden, Ph.D., William E. McAuliffe, Ph.D.*

**33**  Family Therapy: Alcohol . . . . . . . . . . . . . . . . . . . . 379
*Peter Steinglass, M.D.*

**34**  Family Therapy: Other Drugs . . . . . . . . . . . . . . . . . . 389
*Edward Kaufman, M.D.*

## Section 5  Special Approaches and Treatment Programs

**35**  Alcoholics Anonymous and Other 12-Step Groups . . . . . . . . 403
*Chad D. Emrick, Ph.D.*

**36**  Inpatient Treatment . . . . . . . . . . . . . . . . . . . . . . 413
*Roger D. Weiss, M.D.*

**37** Employee Assistance Programs and Other Workplace Interventions . . . . . . . . 423
Paul M. Roman, Ph.D., Terry C. Blum, Ph.D.

**38** Community-Based Treatment . . . . . . . . . . . . . . . . . . . . . . 437
Jonathan I. Ritvo, M.D., James H. Shore, M.D.

**39** Therapeutic Communities . . . . . . . . . . . . . . . . . . . . . . . 447
George De Leon, Ph.D.

## Section 6   Special Populations

**40** Adolescent Substance Abuse . . . . . . . . . . . . . . . . . . . . . . 465
Yifrah Kaminer, M.D., Ralph E. Tarter, Ph.D.

**41** Dual Diagnosis . . . . . . . . . . . . . . . . . . . . . . . . . . . 475
Kathleen T. Brady, M.D., Ph.D., Patricia Halligan, M.D., Robert J. Malcolm, M.D.

**42** Addiction in Women . . . . . . . . . . . . . . . . . . . . . . . . . 485
Sheila B. Blume, M.D., C.A.C.

**43** Perinatal Substance Use . . . . . . . . . . . . . . . . . . . . . . . 491
Beth Glover Reed, Ph.D.

**44** HIV/AIDS and Substance Use Disorders . . . . . . . . . . . . . . . . . 503
Steven L. Batki, M.D., Kalpana I. Nathan, M.D.

**45** Treatment of Pain in Drug-Addicted Persons . . . . . . . . . . . . . . . 511
Barry Stimmel, M.D.

## Section 7   Special Topics

**46** Diagnostic Testing—Laboratory and Psychological . . . . . . . . . . . . . 521
Robert L. DuPont, M.D.

**47** Medical Education . . . . . . . . . . . . . . . . . . . . . . . . . . 529
John N. Chappel, M.D., David C. Lewis, M.D.

**48** Prevention . . . . . . . . . . . . . . . . . . . . . . . . . . . . . 535
Mary Anne Pentz, Ph.D.

**49** Substance Abuse Treatment Under Managed Care: A Provider Perspective . . . . . 545
Arnold M. Washton, Ph.D., Richard A. Rawson, Ph.D.

Index . . . . . . . . . . . . . . . . . . . . . . . . . . . . . . . 553

# Contributors

James C. Anthony, Ph.D.
Professor, Johns Hopkins University School of Hygiene and Public Health, Department of Mental Hygiene, Baltimore, Maryland

Kimberly Barrett, Ed.D.
Western Psychiatric Institute and Clinic, Pittsburgh, Pennsylvania

Steven L. Batki, M.D.
Clinical Professor of Psychiatry, University of California, San Francisco, School of Medicine; and Director, Division of Substance Abuse and Addiction Medicine, San Francisco General Hospital, San Francisco, California

Terry C. Blum, Ph.D.
School of Management, Georgia Institute of Technology, Atlanta

Sheila B. Blume, M.D., C.A.C.
Sayville, New York; Former Medical Director, Alcoholism, Chemical Dependency, and Compulsive Gambling Programs, South Oaks Hospital; and Clinical Professor of Psychiatry, State University of New York at Stony Brook

Michael J. Bohn, M.D.
Assistant Clinical Professor of Psychiatry, University of Wisconsin Medical School, Madison; and Gateway Recovery, Madison, Wisconsin

Lisa Borg, M.D.
Guest Investigator and Associate Physician, Laboratory on the Biology of Addictive Diseases, The Rockefeller University; and Clinical Instructor in Psychiatry, Department of Medicine, The Joan & Sanford I. Weill Medical College of Cornell University, New York City

Kathleen T. Brady, M.D., Ph.D.
Professor of Psychiatry, Department of Psychiatry and Behavioral Sciences, Center for Drug and Alcohol Programs, The Medical University of South Carolina, Charleston

John N. Chappel, M.D.
Professor of Psychiatry, University of Nevada—Reno; and Medical Director of the Addiction Programs, West Hill Hospital, Reno, Nevada

C. Robert Cloninger, M.D.
Wallace Renard Professor of Psychiatry, Department of Psychiatry, Washington University School of Medicine, St. Louis, Missouri

James W. Cornish, M.D.
Assistant Professor of Psychiatry and Director, Division of Pharmacotherapy, Treatment Research Center, University of Pennsylvania, Department of Veterans Affairs Medical Center, Philadelphia, Pennsylvania

Dennis C. Daley, M.S.W.
Associate Professor of Psychiatry and Chief, Drug and Alcohol Services, Western Psychiatric Institute and Clinic, Pittsburgh, Pennsylvania

George De Leon, Ph.D.
Director, Center for Therapeutic Community Research, New York City

Gary Donnelly, M.P.H.
Associate Director of Market Development, Health and Business Division, Channing L. Bete, Co., Inc., South Deerfield, Massachusetts

Robert L. DuPont, M.D.
President, Institute for Behavior and Health, Inc., Rockville, Maryland; and Clinical Professor of Psychiatry, Georgetown University School of Medicine, Washington, D.C.

Chad D. Emrick, Ph.D.
Department of Psychiatry, University of Colorado Health Sciences Center, Denver

Marian W. Fischman, Ph.D.
Professor of Behavioral Biology, Department of Psychiatry, College of Physicians and Surgeons of Columbia University and New York State Psychiatric Institute, New York City

Jenny Frances, B.A.
The Joan & Sanford I. Weill Medical College and
Graduate School of Medical Sciences of Cornell
University, New York City

Richard Frances, M.D.
Silver Hill Hospital, New Canaan, Connecticut; and
Department of Psychiatry, New York University
Medical School, New York City

John Franklin, M.D.
Department of Psychiatry and Behavioral Science,
Northwestern Medical Faculty Foundation, Chicago,
Illinois

Marc Galanter, M.D.
Professor of Psychiatry and Director of the Division of
Alcoholism and Drug Abuse, New York University
School of Medicine, New York City

Don Gallant, M.D.
Professor Emeritus, Department of Psychiatry and
Neurology, Tulane Medical School, New Orleans,
Louisiana

David R. Gastfriend, M.D.
Director, Addiction Services, Massachusetts General
Hospital; and Associate Professor of Psychiatry,
Harvard Medical School, Boston, Massachusetts

Dean R. Gerstein, Ph.D.
Senior Research Vice President, National Opinion
Research Center at the University of Chicago,
Washington Office, Washington, D.C.

Richard A. Glennon, Ph.D.
Professor of Medicinal Chemistry, Department of
Medicinal Chemistry, School of Pharmacy, Medical
College of Virginia, Virginia Commonwealth
University, Richmond

Mark S. Gold, M.D.
Professor, Departments of Psychiatry, Neuroscience,
Community Health and Family Medicine, University
of Florida Brain Institute, Gainesville

Sarah J. Golden, Ph.D.
Associate Director of Psychology, Department of
Psychiatry, Beth Israel Deaconess Medical Center; and
Instructor in Psychology, Harvard Medical School,
Boston, Massachusetts

Patricia Halligan, M.D.
Assistant Professor of Psychiatry, Department of
Psychiatry and Behavioral Sciences, Center for Drug
and Alcohol Problems, The Medical University of
South Carolina, Charleston

Margaret Haney, Ph.D.
Assistant Professor of Behavioral Biology, Department
of Psychiatry, College of Physicians and Surgeons of
Columbia University and New York State Psychiatric
Institute, New York City

Reid K. Hester, Ph.D.
Behavior Therapy Associates, Albuquerque,
New Mexico

Stephen T. Higgins, Ph.D.
Professor, Departments of Psychiatry and Psychology,
University of Vermont, Burlington

Paula L. Hoffman, Ph.D.
Professor, University of Colorado Health Sciences
Center, Department of Pharmacology, Denver,
Colorado

Ari B. Jaffe, M.D.
Resident in Psychiatry, New York University, New
York City

Jerome H. Jaffe, M.D.
Clinical Professor of Psychiatry, University of
Maryland, Baltimore

Yifrah Kaminer, M.D.
Associate Professor of Psychiatry, Department of
Psychiatry, Alcohol Research Center, University of
Connecticut Health Center, Farmington

Edward Kaufman, M.D.
Clinical Professor of Psychiatry, Department of
Psychiatry and Human Behavior, University of
California at Irvine, College of Medicine, Irvine,
California

Edward J. Khantzian, M.D.
Clinical Professor of Psychiatry, Harvard Medical
School at The Cambridge Hospital; and Associate
Chief of Psychiatry, Tewksbury Hospital, Tewksbury,
Massachusetts

Herbert D. Kleber, M.D.
Professor of Psychiatry and Director of the Division on
Substance Abuse, New York State Psychiatric
Institute and Columbia University College of
Physicians and Surgeons, New York City

Thomas R. Kosten, M.D.
Professor and Chief of Psychiatry, Yale University
School of Medicine, VA Connecticut Health Care
System, Department of Psychiatry, West Haven,
Connecticut

Jean L. Kristeller, Ph.D.
Professor of Psychology and Director, Wather Cancer Research Program, Indiana State University, Terre Haute

David C. Lewis, M.D.
Director, Center for Alcohol and Addiction Studies, Brown University; and Professor of Medicine and Community Health, and Donald G. Millar Professor of Alcohol and Addiction Studies, Brown University, Providence, Rhode Island

Lester Luborsky, Ph.D.
Professor of Psychology in Psychiatry, Department of Psychiatry, University of Pennsylvania, Philadelphia

Robert J. Malcolm, M.D.
Professor of Psychiatry, Department of Psychiatry and Behavioral Sciences; and Medical Director, Center for Drug and Alcohol Problems, The Medical University of South Carolina, Charleston

G. Alan Marlatt, Ph.D.
Addictive Behaviors Research Center, Department of Psychology, University of Washington, Seattle

Billy R. Martin, Ph.D.
Louis and Ruth Harris Professor, Department of Pharmacology and Toxicology, Medical College of Virginia, Virginia Commonwealth University, Richmond

William E. McAuliffe, Ph.D.
Director, National Technical Center, North Charles Research and Planning Group; and Associate Professor, Department of Psychiatry, Harvard Medical School, Boston, Massachusetts

David M. McDowell, M.D.
Medical Director, Substance Treatment and Research Service; and Assistant Clinical Professor of Psychiatry, Columbia University College of Physicians and Surgeons, Division on Substance Abuse, New York Psychiatric Institute, New York City

Delinda Mercer, Ph.D.
Instructor, Department of Psychiatry, University of Pennsylvania, Philadelphia

Roger E. Meyer, M.D.
Division of Biomedical and Health Sciences, Association of American Medical Colleges, Washington, D.C.

Theresa Moyers, Ph.D.
Veterans Administration Medical Center, Albuquerque, New Mexico

Kalpana I. Nathan, M.D.
Director, Transition Program, Palo Alto Veterans Affairs Health Care System, Menlo Park, California

Charles P. O'Brien, M.D., Ph.D.
Kenneth E. Appel Professor and Vice-Chair of Psychiatry, University of Pennsylvania; and Chief of Psychiatry, Department of Veterans Affairs Medical Center, Philadelphia, Pennsylvania

Judith K. Ockene, Ph.D.
Professor and Director, Division of Preventive and Behavioral Medicine, Department of Medicine, University of Massachusetts Medical School, Worcester

Michael V. Pantalon, Ph.D.
Assistant Professor of Psychology (in Psychiatry), Department of Psychiatry, Substance Abuse Treatment Unit, Yale University School of Medicine, New Haven, Connecticut

Robert N. Pechnick, Ph.D.
Associate Professor of Pharmacology and Neuroscience, Louisiana State University Medical Center, New Orleans

Mary Anne Pentz, Ph.D.
Professor and Director, Center for Prevention Policy Research, Institute for Prevention Research, University of Southern California, Los Angeles

Richard A. Rawson, Ph.D.
Executive Director, Matrix Institute on Addictions, Los Angeles, California; and Deputy Director, Alcoholism and Addiction Medicine Service, University of California at Los Angeles School of Medicine

Beth Glover Reed, Ph.D.
Professor, School of Social Work, University of Michigan, Ann Arbor

Jonathan I. Ritvo, M.D.
Clinical Associate Professor of Psychiatry and Training Director, Addiction Psychiatry Program, Denver Health Medical Center, University of Colorado Health Sciences Center, Denver

Paul M. Roman, Ph.D.
Center for Research on Deviance and Behavioral Health, Institute for Behavioral Research, and Department of Sociology, University of Georgia, Athens

Sidney H. Schnoll, M.D., Ph.D.
Chairman, Division of Addiction Medicine; and
Professor, Departments of Internal Medicine and
Psychiatry, Medical College of Virginia, Virginia
Commonwealth University, Richmond

Richard S. Schottenfeld, M.D.
Professor of Psychiatry, Department of Psychiatry,
Substance Abuse Treatment Unit, Yale University
School of Medicine, New Haven, Connecticut

Marc A. Schuckit, M.D.
Professor of Psychiatry, University of California at San
Diego School of Medicine, and San Diego Veterans
Hospital, San Diego, California

Edward C. Senay, M.D.
Department of Psychiatry, University of Chicago
School of Medicine, Chicago, Illinois

James H. Shore, M.D.
Professor and Chair, Department of Psychiatry,
School of Medicine, University of Colorado Health
Sciences Center, Denver

Amrita K. Singha, Ph.D.
Research Fellow, Yale University School of Medicine,
VA Connecticut Healthcare System, Department of
Psychiatry, West Haven, Connecticut

David E. Smith, M.D.
Founder and Medical Director, Haight Ashbury Free
Clinics, San Francisco, California; and Professor,
University of California, San Francisco

Peter Steinglass, M.D.
Executive Director, Ackerman Institute for the
Family; and Clinical Professor of Psychiatry, Cornell
University Medical College, New York City

Barry Stimmel, M.D.
Katherine and Clifford Goldsmith Professor of
Medicine and Professor of Medical Education, Mount
Sinai School of Medicine, New York City

Boris Tabakoff, Ph.D.
Professor and Chair, University of Colorado Health
Sciences Center, Department of Pharmacology,
Denver, Colorado

Ralph E. Tarter, Ph.D.
Professor, Department of Psychiatry, Western
Psychiatric Institute and Clinic, Pittsburgh,
Pennsylvania

Michelle Tullis, Ph.D. candidate
Research Associate, Department of Psychiatry,
University of Florida Brain Institute, Gainesville

J. Thomas Ungerleider, M.D.
Professor Emeritus, Department of Psychiatry and
Biobehavioral Sciences, University of California at Los
Angeles School of Medicine

Arnold M. Washton, Ph.D.
Private practice of addiction psychology, New York
City; and Clinical Professor of Psychiatry, New York
University School of Medicine, New York City

Michael F. Weaver, M.D.
Assistant Professor of Internal Medicine and
Psychiatry, Division of Addiction Medicine, Medical
College of Virginia, Virginia Commonwealth
University, Richmond

Roger D. Weiss, M.D.
Clinical Director, Alcohol and Drug Abuse Program,
McLean Hospital, Belmont, Massachusetts; and
Associate Professor of Psychiatry, Harvard Medical
School, Boston, Massachusetts

Donald R. Wesson, M.D.
Scientific Director, Friends Research Associates,
Berkeley, California

Joseph Westermeyer, M.D., M.P.H., Ph.D.
Chief, Psychiatry Services, Minneapolis Veteran
Affairs Medical Center and St. Cloud Veteran Affairs
Medical Center; and Professor of Psychiatry and
Adjunct Professor of Anthropology, University of
Minnesota, Minneapolis

George E. Woody, M.D.
Chief, Substance Abuse Treatment, Department of
Psychiatry, Veteran Affairs Medical Center; and
Clinical Professor, Department of Psychiatry,
University of Pennsylvania, Philadelphia

Sheldon Zimberg, M.D., M.S.
Clinical Professor of Psychiatry, Columbia University
College of Physicians and Surgeons, New York City

# Preface

Substance abuse is one of the major public health issues confronting the United States today and is a worldwide problem of major dimension. In the United States, 18% of the population experience a substance use disorder at some point in their lives. The cost of addictive illness to Americans is currently $144 billion per year in health care and job loss. Furthermore, an average of 20% of patients in general medical facilities and 35% in general psychiatric units present with substance use disorders—in some settings, many more. When the sequelae of addiction, such as cirrhosis, psychopathology, trauma, and infection, are present, they generally receive proper medical attention; patients' primary addictive problems, however, often go untreated.

Nonetheless, we stand on the threshold of important opportunities in the addiction field, with many advances in receptor mechanisms, membrane chemistry, and patterns of genetic transmission emerging in recent years. Public awareness of the need for greater research and treatment resources has been aroused as well, and substance-abusing individuals now seek help earlier, at a point when treatment can be administered more effectively. Furthermore, the health community has been alerted to the need for early diagnosis and provision of comprehensive care. New treatment concepts, both pharmacological and psychosocial, have made recovery a possibility for most alcohol- and drug-abusing patients.

The first edition of this volume emerged from a growing commitment of psychiatry to address the problem of substance abuse. In 1982, the American Psychiatric Association (APA) established a Task Force on Treatment of Psychiatric Disorders, consisting of 26 panels. We served as chairpersons of the panels on psychoactive substance use disorders, alcohol, and other drugs, respectively. In response to this APA initiative, we brought together a group of experts who could provide a carefully drawn perspective on addiction treatment, perhaps the most comprehensive one to date. After several years' work, our panels developed reports for the Task Force that were published by the APA in 1989 in the four-volume set, *Treatments of Psychiatric Disorders*.

Soon after the appearance of these volumes, we decided that it was important to update and amplify the substance abuse treatment information. In addition, we wanted to focus on the most recent developments in biological and psychosocial therapies and the problems of specific populations. Over 2 years, we brought together the authors of the original volume, along with additional experts, to produce the first edition of this volume. We had hoped that it would offer the field a well-organized review on the best and most effective modalities currently available for managing substance abuse.

The scope of the current edition has been broadened considerably. The initial volume focused on issues related directly to treatment. We felt it was now important to expand the contents to address several topics essential to the mechanisms underlying addictive illness and the scientific basis of treatment. For example, a major section has been added on the nature of addiction. It includes five new chapters on the neurobiology of alcohol, opiates, stimulants, hallucinogens, and marijuana as well as chapters on epidemiology, genetics, cross-cultural issues, and the psychology of addiction.

We have included other new chapters on diagnostic procedures, prevention, and treatment outcome research. Two new chapters deal with issues specifically related to women. Chapters on certain medical problems—the treatment of pain, AIDS, and addiction—and on medical education also have been added. Finally, a chapter analyzing strategic issues in the area of managed care has been included.

Of course, the material from the first edition has been extensively revised to include new research and clinical findings. This volume now represents the best of our current understanding of addictive illness, its management, and its place in a research and social perspective.

Most important to the development of the first and current editions was the maturation of the substance abuse field itself. As recently as the mid-1980s, American departments of psychiatry, as well as academic programs for other health professionals, paid little heed to the importance of training for substance use treatment.

Although the medical addiction community had been vocal in expressing the need for better care over the previous two decades, investment in addiction training was relatively small and had only a limited association with academic teaching centers. This situation has changed dramatically in recent years. Substance abuse training is now an integral part of undergraduate curricula in most medical schools and a component of most psychiatry residency training programs. Courses are also taught in graduate psychology and social work programs. Postresidency fellowships in addiction psychiatry and general medicine now number over 50. They are showing great vitality and are playing an influential role in ensuring quality treatment for the future. The federal institutes on drug and alcohol abuse are becoming more aware of the need for research training and are working closely with organizations in the addiction field to promote growth in clinical teaching as well.

We have designed this volume to serve clinicians in practice and researchers concerned with addiction, as well as trainees in psychiatry, general medicine, and other health professions. We therefore hope that this book can serve as a definitive, valuable treatment resource for any health care professional concerned with the problems posed by the issue of substance abuse.

*Marc Galanter, M.D.*
*Herbert D. Kleber, M.D.*

# 1 The Nature of Addiction

*1*

# Neurobiology of Alcohol

Boris Tabakoff, Ph.D.
Paula L. Hoffman, Ph.D.

Ethanol, or beverage alcohol, is an organic molecule composed of two carbon atoms, six hydrogen atoms, and one oxygen atom. This molecule seemingly carries little chemical information in its structure but generates myriad effects in the central nervous system (CNS) and in peripheral organs of mammals and other organisms. The chronic ingestion of ethanol can result in the alterations of CNS function observed in the alcohol dependence syndrome (American Psychiatric Association 1994; World Health Organization 1992). These alterations are manifested by tolerance, physical dependence, and craving (i.e., compulsion to drink and inability to stop drinking).

## Acute Effects of Ethanol

Ethanol is considered to be a CNS depressant; however, in particular individuals and within certain dosage ranges (i.e., blood alcohol levels of 25–150 mg%), ethanol produces euphoriant and behavioral activating effects (Phillips and Shen 1996). Other important components of the nonanesthetic, acute actions of ethanol include the drug's anxiolytic and stress-reducing effects (Eckardt et al. 1998). A popular explanation of ethanol's acute actions within the CNS has focused on a rather nonspecific interaction of ethanol with neuronal membrane lipids (Goldstein et al. 1982). The intercalation of ethanol into the lipids of neuronal membranes has been proposed to result in a disorganization of the lipid bilayer and to translate into altered function of the proteins (e.g., receptors, enzymes, ion channels) that reside in the neuronal membrane. Although the membrane hypothesis of ethanol's actions (Goldstein et al. 1982; Taraschi et al. 1986) may remain viable as an explanation of the high-dosage anesthetic effects of ethanol (but even that hypothesis has been challenged [Franks and Lieb 1997; Peters and Lambert 1997]), the lower-dosage effects (i.e., reinforcement, anxiolysis, incoordination, euphoria, and cognitive actions) are not easily explained by ethanol-induced perturbation of membrane lipids.

A critical experiment in ascertaining whether membrane lipid perturbation determines biological sensitivity to ethanol would start with a protein that has been mutagenically or genetically modified in its primary structure. Such a protein and its unmodified counterpart would be placed in an identical membrane lipid environment. If the two proteins display identical functional characteristics in the absence of ethanol but differ in their response to ethanol, one could conjecture that the primary structure of the protein, rather than the lipid environment, determines the observed differential sensitivity to ethanol. Such experiments have been performed examining the effects of ethanol on $\gamma$-aminobutyric acid$_A$ (GABA$_A$) receptor function. Subunits of this receptor that differ in primary structure (i.e., $\gamma_2$ short and $\gamma_2$ long, which are splice variants of the $\gamma_2$ subunit) were expressed with the other GABA$_A$ receptor subunits in *Xenopus* oocytes. One can assume that the membrane lipid composition of a group of oocytes is intrinsically similar. Yet the sensitivity of the

The authors' work is supported by the National Institute on Alcohol Abuse and Alcoholism and the Banbury Fund.

expressed GABA$_A$ receptor to ethanol differed depending on which $\gamma_2$ splice variant was expressed in the oocytes (i.e., ethanol had little effect on receptors containing the $\gamma_2$ short isoform, whereas it had significant effects on those containing the $\gamma_2$ long isoform) (Wafford et al. 1991).

More recently, similar studies were performed with glycine receptor proteins, the primary structure of which was modified using mutagenic techniques (Mihic et al. 1997). A modification of one amino acid (the substitution of a serine with isoleucine at amino acid 267 of the glycine receptor $\alpha_1$ subunit) produced a receptor complex that was completely resistant to the effects of ethanol, even though the mutant protein was expressed in the identical cells used for studies of the wild-type (i.e., normal) protein. Ethanol significantly potentiated the function of the wild-type glycine receptor, and although the mutation eliminated the glycine receptor's response to ethanol, it did not significantly alter the characteristics of the mutant glycine receptor response to the classic agonists or antagonists of this receptor.

These experiments call into question the membrane lipid perturbation hypothesis as a full explanation of ethanol's actions and suggest that particular proteins may play an important role in differential sensitivity of biological systems to ethanol. Ethanol at moderate and even high dosages seems to direct its effects at proteins that are subunits of multisubunit systems and to alter protein-protein interactions through conformational changes in the subunit protein structure. Most of the ethanol-sensitive systems described in this chapter are either multisubunit systems (e.g., the GABA$_A$ receptor system, the $N$-methyl-D-aspartate [NMDA] receptor system, or the nicotinic cholinergic receptor system) or multicomponent systems, such as the receptor-coupled adenylyl cyclase system, which consists of various receptors (e.g., dopamine receptors) coupled through the guanine nucleotide–binding proteins (G proteins) to the catalytic unit of adenylyl cyclase.

## GABA Receptor System

GABA is the major inhibitory neurotransmitter in brain tissue. For many years, the CNS depressant actions of ethanol were hypothesized to result from ethanol's interactions with GABA-mediated neurotransmission. Benzodiazepines and barbiturates can potentiate the actions of GABA at the GABA$_A$ receptor by their interactions with receptor sites for these compounds on the

GABA$_A$ receptor complex (DeLorey and Olsen 1992). Researchers suggested that the sedative, anticonvulsant, anxiolytic, and incoordinating effects of ethanol could be explained by ethanol's interactions with the GABA$_A$ receptor because the spectrum of effects produced by the benzodiazepines and barbiturates resembled the spectrum of ethanol's actions. However, it was the demonstration that a benzodiazepine partial inverse agonist (Ro 15-4513) could antagonize the hypnotic, anxiolytic, locomotor- impairing, amnestic, anticonvulsant, and discriminative stimulus properties of ethanol (Prunell et al. 1994; Suzdak et al. 1988) that gave greater credence to the suggested interactions of ethanol with the GABA$_A$ receptor. An important caveat in interpreting the results of studies with Ro 15-4513 is that this drug, as a partial inverse agonist, has intrinsic actions that would, in an algebraic fashion, counter ethanol's actions. For instance, Ro 15-4513 has proconvulsant and anxiogenic properties, and controversy has arisen over whether Ro 15-4513 is a true antagonist of ethanol's actions or whether the intrinsic effects of Ro 15-4513 are simply algebraically additive with those of ethanol (e.g., anxiogenic properties of Ro 15-4513 countering the anxiolytic properties of ethanol). Of note is the observation that a more "pure" antagonist of the benzodiazepine receptor (i.e., flumazenil) does not reverse the CNS depressant actions of ethanol (Barrett et al. 1985). Furthermore, Ro 15-4513 does not counteract all of ethanol's actions, and the locomotor-activating and hypothermic effects of ethanol are unperturbed by coadministration of Ro 15-4513. Thus studies with Ro 15-4513 have been suggestive of the involvement of the GABA$_A$ receptor in a spectrum of ethanol's acute effects, but they have not been conclusive.

Molecular biological and electrophysiological studies have further implicated the GABA$_A$ receptor system in certain actions of ethanol and have brought a greater understanding of the variables that contribute to ethanol's interactions with the GABA$_A$ receptor. Electrophysiological assessment of the interactions of ethanol and GABA on single neurons has uncovered a discordance in observation (for reviews, see Mihic and Harris 1996; Tabakoff and Hoffman 1996b). For example, with the use of whole cell patch-clamp recording, ethanol was reported to enhance the response of neurons of the dorsal root ganglion to GABA in one study but not in another. In studies using slices of hippocampus, ethanol had little or no effect on GABA actions, but when the levels of ATP were more carefully preserved in the cells of the hippocampal slices, ethanol significantly potentiated GABA's effects. In the cerebellum, ethanol had little effect on GABA's actions on cerebellar Purkinje cells unless cyclic adenosine monophosphate (cAMP) levels in these cells were increased simultaneously with the administration of ethanol. Systemic administration of ethanol, coupled with iontophoretic administration of GABA, demonstrated that ethanol could potentiate GABA inhibition of cell firing in the medial septal area of the brain but not in the lateral septum. These studies demonstrated that neurons in different brain areas and under different metabolic conditions respond differentially to ethanol with regard to ethanol's interactions with GABA at the $GABA_A$ receptor.

The $GABA_A$ receptor is composed of a pentameric array of subunits. The subunits composing this array have been classified into groups based on similarities in the primary structure of these proteins. Six types of α subunits ($α_1$–$α_6$), four β subunits ($β_1$–$β_4$), three γ subunits ($γ_1$–$γ_3$), and δ, ε, σ, and ζ subunits have been identified (Sieghart 1992). The native $GABA_A$ receptor can be composed of different combinations of these subunits, and the pharmacological profile (i.e., the response of the receptor to various compounds) depends on the receptor's subunit composition (Sieghart 1992). The $GABA_A$ receptor's subunit composition in various areas of mammalian brain differs in a defined manner and contributes to region-specific sensitivity to particular drugs, including ethanol. For example, zolpidem's actions seem to be concentrated on brain areas possessing $GABA_A$ receptors containing $α_1$ subunits.

Studies of regional sensitivity of the $GABA_A$ receptor to ethanol seem to indicate that ethanol sensitivity follows the brain distribution of the $GABA_A$ receptor $α_1$ subunit (Criswell et al. 1993). As already noted, when different $GABA_A$ receptor γ subunits were expressed in *Xenopus* oocytes, the presence of the $γ_2$ long splice variant imparted ethanol sensitivity on the expressed $GABA_A$ receptor. This phenomenon was explained by the fact that the $γ_2$ long subunit of the $GABA_A$ receptor has a phosphorylation site for protein kinase C (PKC) that is absent in the $γ_2$ short variant. The phosphorylation by PKC of the $γ_2$ long subunit was deemed to be important in imparting sensitivity to ethanol (Weiner et al. 1994). This proposal was further strengthened by studies with mice in which the brain-specific γ isoform of PKC was knocked out. The mice deficient in PKC γ were resistant to the hypnotic effects of ethanol, and their $GABA_A$ receptor function was also less sensitive to ethanol compared with wild-type mice (Harris et al. 1995).

The sensitivity of the $GABA_A$ receptor to ethanol in certain brain areas is also controlled by the activity of adenylyl cyclase, cAMP, and protein kinase A (PKA). Purkinje cell $GABA_A$ receptors are insensitive to ethanol unless adenylyl cyclase is activated concomitantly with the administration of ethanol (Lin et al. 1993). The lack of evidence for such interactions in other parts of the brain may result from the particular subunit composition of the $GABA_A$ receptors in the cerebellum (Sieghart 1992) and from the presence of an ethanol-sensitive adenylyl cyclase in cerebellar Purkinje cells (Mons et al. 1998; Yoshimura and Tabakoff 1995). In Purkinje cells, ethanol can act in a "feed forward" manner by activating the ethanol-sensitive adenylyl cyclase, which generates cAMP and activates PKA. The activated PKA can then modify Purkinje cell $GABA_A$ receptors to increase their sensitivity to ethanol.

Cerebellar Purkinje cells are intimately involved in maintenance of body positioning in space and in coordinated motion. The inhibition of Purkinje cell function by ethanol—through its enhancement of the actions of GABA on the cells—would lead to increased body sway and incoordination. Individuals who are considered to be predisposed to alcoholism because they are offspring of alcoholic fathers (Schuckit 1994) are resistant to increases in body sway and incoordination induced by ingested ethanol. Although the characteristics of the $GABA_A$ receptor and/or the adenylyl cyclase in the cerebellum of such individuals have not been determined, such individuals appear to have a lower activity of the ethanol-sensitive isoform of adenylyl cyclase, at least in other cells of their body (e.g., their platelets) (Tabakoff and Hoffman 1998).

Thus ethanol's direct and indirect interactions with the $GABA_A$ receptor may mediate certain acute actions of ethanol (i.e., incoordination, anxiolysis). The sensitivity of the $GABA_A$ receptor to ethanol may be controlled by genetically determined characteristics of the receptor in different brain areas and by the activity of second-messenger signaling systems (e.g., PKC, adenylyl cyclase, PKA). The interactions of ethanol with the $GABA_A$ receptor system in the brain take on added importance with recent demonstrations that an animal's level of alcohol intake can be controlled with brain site–specific injections of $GABA_A$ receptor agonists and antagonists. The competitive $GABA_A$ receptor antagonist SR-95531 significantly reduced ethanol consumption by rats when injected at low dosages into the central amygdaloid nucleus and at higher dosages into the stria terminalis and the shell of the nucleus accumbens (Hyytiä and Koob 1995).

# NMDA Receptor System

The NMDA subtype of glutamate receptor has similarities to the $GABA_A$ receptor. For example, it is a multisubunit, receptor-gated ion channel that has binding sites for several psychoactive drugs. The glutamatergic system is the major excitatory system of the brain, and activation of the NMDA receptor by glutamate and its coagonist glycine produces neuronal membrane depolarization by increasing the permeability of the membrane to sodium, potassium, and calcium ions. The entry of calcium into the neuron through the activated NMDA receptor not only adds to the membrane depolarization but also contributes to significant alterations in the intracellular homeostasis of the neuron (i.e., calcium acts as an intracellular second messenger and activator of several important signaling cascades within the neuron). The NMDA receptor has an important role in the initial stages of memory formation, in neural excitability and seizures, in excitotoxic brain damage, and in neural development (Choi 1992; Collingridge and Lester 1989).

Ethanol is a potent inhibitor of NMDA receptor function when the receptor is acutely exposed to ethanol at concentrations as low as 10 mM (approximately 50 mg%) (for reviews, see Tabakoff and Hoffman 1996a, 1996c). The effects of ethanol, in the presence of saturating levels of the neurotransmitter glutamate, are selective for the NMDA receptor in comparison with the other subtypes of ionotropic or metabotropic glutamate receptors. At lower concentrations of glutamate, however, ethanol also has effects on the kainate/α-amino-3-hydroxy-5-methyl-4-isoxazolepropionate (AMPA) subtypes of glutamate receptors. Ethanol's actions on the NMDA receptor seem to be less dependent on the subunit composition of this receptor than are ethanol's actions on the $GABA_A$ receptor, but phosphorylation of the NMDA receptor may play an important role in determining the receptor's sensitivity to ethanol. In cerebellar granule cells, phorbol esters, which activate the serine/threonine kinase PKC, inhibit NMDA receptor function in a manner similar to the inhibition produced by ethanol, and inhibitors of PKC block the inhibition of the NMDA receptor produced by phorbol esters and the inhibition produced by ethanol.

Tyrosine kinases also phosphorylate NMDA receptors. The role of one of the tyrosine kinases, Fyn kinase, in the actions of ethanol was investigated in knockout mice deficient in Fyn (Fyn-negative mice) and in mice in which Fyn was functional (Fyn-positive mice)

(Miyakawa et al. 1997). Ethanol stimulated the phosphorylation of the NMDA receptor (NMDAR-2B subunit) in the brains of the Fyn-positive mice, whereas no such ethanol-induced phosphorylation was evident in the Fyn-negative mice. The Fyn-negative mice were also significantly more sensitive to the hypnotic actions of ethanol and did not acquire the acute tolerance to ethanol that the Fyn-positive mice acquired. Work on ethanol's acute actions on the NMDA receptor indicates that certain of the sedative, amnestic, and anxiolytic effects of ethanol may be mediated by inhibition of the NMDA system and by ethanol's actions on the $GABA_A$ receptor. Thus ethanol can be considered to be an inhibitor of a component of the major excitatory system in the brain (i.e., the NMDA receptor) and a potentiator of the major inhibitory system in the brain (i.e., the $GABA_A$ receptor). In both cases, ethanol's actions seem to be intimately involved with phosphorylation events influencing these receptors.

# 5-HT₃ Receptors and Other Receptor-Gated Ion Channels

Ethanol modulates the activity of two other receptor-gated ion channels. Concentrations of ethanol that produce moderate intoxication (i.e., 25 mM) potentiate the effects of serotonin (5-HT) at the 5-HT₃ subtype of the serotonin receptor and of acetylcholine at the nicotinic cholinergic receptor system (Aracava et al. 1991; Lovinger and Zhou 1994). The 5-HT₃ receptor is the only serotonin receptor subtype that is a receptor-gated ion channel. Interestingly, ethanol has direct actions at only this serotonin receptor, although other serotonin receptor subtypes (the G protein–coupled subtypes) may be affected secondarily by ethanol-induced increases in brain serotonin release and turnover (for review, see Tabakoff and Hoffman 1996b).

Evidence indicates that the G protein–coupled 5-HT₁B receptor, although not directly affected by ethanol, may be important in mediating ethanol preference in mammals. Mice lacking the 5-HT₁B receptor (5-HT₁B knockout mice) displayed an elevated preference for ethanol compared with their wild-type counterparts (Crabbe et al. 1996). The use of serotonergic drugs for reducing alcohol intake and preventing relapse in humans may have a rationale, given the possible involvement of serotonergic systems in the actions of ethanol. The 5-HT₃ receptor antagonists (e.g., zimeldine, ondansetron) reduce alcohol consumption in humans (Sellers et al. 1994), and selective serotonin reuptake inhibitors (SSRIs) and buspirone, which acts as a partial agonist at $5\text{-HT}_{1A}$ receptors, have been used with partial success in reducing alcohol intake and preventing relapse in alcohol-dependent individuals (Litten et al. 1996).

## Role of Receptor-Gated Ion Channels in the Reinforcing Properties of Ethanol

Although the pleasurable and reinforcing properties of ethanol are part of a spectrum of ethanol's actions in many humans, not all humans or other mammals experience the drug's reinforcing properties. Selective breeding studies with rats have demonstrated that ethanol's reinforcing properties and other actions may be under genetic control to a significant extent (Li et al. 1993). The dopaminergic neuron systems that project from the brain stem to the nucleus accumbens, frontal cortex, and other limbic areas (i.e., the mesolimbic dopamine systems) are activated by administered or ingested ethanol in experimental animals (Di Chiara and Imperato 1988; Gessa et al. 1985), and this action of ethanol may be more efficacious in animals selectively bred for alcohol preference (Li and McBride 1995).

Similar activation of the mesolimbic dopamine system is evident with administration of cocaine, morphine, nicotine, and other drugs (Di Chiara and Imperato 1988). The increased firing of the mesolimbic dopamine neurons produced by ethanol leads to increased release of dopamine in the nucleus accumbens, an event associated with the presence of several other motivational stimuli (Di Chiara 1995). The molecular process by which ethanol activates the mesolimbic dopamine system is poorly understood, but ethanol's actions at the NMDA and $5\text{-HT}_3$ receptor systems may be the initiating factors in ethanol's activation of this system (Di Chiara et al. 1994; Wozniak et al. 1990). The $5\text{-HT}_3$ receptor antagonist tropisetron (ICS 205-930) blocks the ethanol-induced enhancement of dopamine release in the nucleus accumbens, and NMDA antagonists, which inhibit NMDA receptor function, increase the release of dopamine in the nucleus accumbens.

Not only do the $5\text{-HT}_3$ antagonist and NMDA receptor blockers antagonize or mimic actions of ethanol on dopaminergic neurotransmission, but they also influence the discriminative stimulus properties of ethanol. In animals trained to distinguish ethanol from other fluids, $5\text{-HT}_3$ receptor antagonists block ethanol's discriminative stimulus properties (Grant 1995). In contrast, NMDA receptor antagonists can generalize to the ethanol cue (Grant and Colombo 1993). In other words,

the trained animals' response to NMDA antagonists indicates that the animals perceive the NMDA antagonists to be like ethanol in some of their physiological actions.

Other receptors may synergize with $5\text{-HT}_3$ and NMDA receptors in mediating ethanol's actions on the mesolimbic dopamine neurons. Low to moderate ($\leq 50$ mM) concentrations of ethanol promote the binding of opioid agonists to $\mu$ opioid receptors (Tabakoff and Hoffman 1983). The $\mu$ opioid receptors are present on the cell bodies of the dopaminergic neurons in the ventral tegmental area, and activation of these receptors promotes the firing of dopaminergic neurons and the release of dopamine in the nucleus accumbens. Thus, it is of some interest that the opioid receptor antagonist naltrexone can reverse the dopamine-releasing effects of ethanol in rats and that, when administered to human ethanol-dependent subjects, naltrexone reduces relapse (O'Brien et al. 1996). The limited effectiveness of naltrexone in human alcoholic patients (Volpicelli et al. 1995) may indicate that actions of ethanol at receptors other than the opioid receptors (e.g., NMDA, $5\text{-HT}_3$) contribute significantly to the positive reinforcing effects of ethanol.

## Neuroadaptive Phenomena Associated With Alcohol Dependence

The chronic administration of ethanol to animals for periods sufficient to produce functional tolerance and signs of physical dependence results in changes in the subunit characteristics and functions of the $\text{GABA}_A$ and NMDA receptor systems in the brain (for reviews, see Mihic and Harris 1996; Tabakoff and Hoffman 1996a, 1996c). Neuroadaptive changes in voltage-sensitive calcium channels (VSCC), exemplified by increases in the binding of nitrendipine, an L-type VSCC blocker, are also evident (Dolin et al. 1987). Although changes in the quantities of several $\text{GABA}_A$ receptor subunits have been observed in the brains of ethanol-dependent animals (i.e., increases in $\beta$ and $\alpha_6$ subunits, decreases in $\alpha_2$ subunits), the most consistent changes have been significant decreases in $\alpha_1$ subunits. As noted earlier, $\text{GABA}_A$ receptors with a particular subunit composition (i.e., those containing the $\alpha_1$ subunits [Criswell et al. 1993]) may be selectively sensitive to ethanol, and investigations of brain synaptoneurosomes obtained from chronically alcohol-treated animals demonstrated a reduced effect of ethanol in potentiating GABA-mediated chloride flux through the GABA_A receptor/channel complex (i.e., the system had become tolerant to ethanol's actions).

Substantial evidence also indicates upregulation of the NMDA receptor complex in the brains of humans and other animals after chronic ethanol ingestion. This upregulation is observed as an increase in the binding of ligands specific for the NMDA receptor (i.e., receptor upregulation) and an increase in NMDA receptor–mediated influx of calcium into neurons that have been chronically exposed to ethanol. Tabakoff and Hoffman (1996a) suggested that the increase in NMDA receptor number and function may lead to neuronal hyperexcitability, which is responsible for some signs and symptoms of ethanol withdrawal (e.g., seizures, sleep disturbances, anxiety). NMDA receptor–induced neuronal excitability during ethanol withdrawal predisposes neurons to glutamate-induced excitotoxicity and neuronal death (for review, see Hoffman et al. 1995; Tabakoff and Hoffman 1996c). NMDA receptor antagonists, although not available for use in humans, effectively alleviate alcohol withdrawal signs in animals. The benzodiazepines, acting as potentiators of GABA effects at the GABA_A receptor, are also effective in the treatment of alcohol withdrawal signs. However, the more severe signs (i.e., seizures, convulsions) may not be the result of GABA_A receptor changes observed after chronic ethanol ingestion. Electrophysiological studies of brain slices from ethanol-dependent animals suggested that ethanol withdrawal seizures resulted from a synergistic effect of increased NMDA receptor and VSCC function rather than from changes in the function of GABA_A receptors (Ripley et al. 1996). The effectiveness of benzodiazepines in controlling alcohol withdrawal seizures and convulsions may be the result of the general anticonvulsant properties of the benzodiazepines rather than specific actions of benzodiazepines on the molecular systems initiating withdrawal-induced neuronal hyperexcitability.

The termination of alcohol consumption by an alcohol-dependent individual usually generates a state of anhedonia as well as initiating the spectrum of withdrawal hyperexcitability mentioned earlier. Withdrawal from ethanol generates a decrease in the firing of dopaminergic neurons in the ventral tegmental area of the brain and a decrease in the release of dopamine from these neurons (Rossetti et al. 1991). This phenomenon is opposite to the increased dopaminergic activity observed after acute administration of ethanol to animals. NMDA receptors may exert a tonic inhibitory control over the firing of the mesolimbic dopamine neurons (Rossetti et al. 1992). The upregulated NMDA receptor system, which has been noted in alcohol-dependent animals, could thus generate an increase in this tonic inhibitory control. The increased inhibitory control would result in the decreased dopaminergic neuron activity and decreased dopamine release observed after alcohol withdrawal (Rossetti et al. 1991, 1992).

Congruent with the proposal of NMDA receptor–mediated inhibitory control of dopaminergic neurons is the observation that an NMDA receptor antagonist reversed the decreased dopamine release associated with alcohol withdrawal (Rossetti et al. 1991). Systemic administration of alcohol also reversed the decreased release of dopamine in the nucleus accumbens of alcohol-withdrawn animals (Diana et al. 1993). Because the decreased mesolimbic dopaminergic transmission is believed to be an important contributor to the negative affect associated with alcohol and other drug withdrawal, the increased NMDA receptor function noted during withdrawal could underlie both the glutamate-mediated neuroexcitation that promotes seizures and excitotoxicity and the decreased dopaminergic function that results in an affective state that increases the compulsion to drink alcohol.

It must be emphasized, however, that several neuronal systems, including the GABA_A receptor system, interact with dopaminergic neurotransmission to generate control or loss of control over alcohol intake. Alcohol-dependent rats increase their responding for ethanol during a period of alcohol withdrawal, but the injection of the GABA_A receptor agonist muscimol into the amygdala of these animals attenuated their increased ethanol intake (Roberts et al. 1996). Experiments in which muscimol was administered into the nucleus accumbens further demonstrated that the GABA_A receptor may be intimately involved in the early termination of alcohol self-administration, whereas the dopaminergic systems are more focused on the initiation or maintenance of alcohol-reinforced responding in animals (Hodge et al. 1995).

## Conclusion

Overall, the selective potency of ethanol's actions on receptor-gated ion channels may contribute significantly to the acute and chronic neurobiological effects of ethanol. The neuroadaptation of the receptor-gated ion channels, as observed with the NMDA and GABA_A receptors, and the neuroadaptive events taking place within other systems (e.g., VSCCs) may contribute to the development of alcohol tolerance and physical dependence and play an integral role in increasing the compulsion to drink in the alcohol-dependent individual.

# References

American Psychiatric Association: Diagnostic and Statistical Manual of Mental Disorders, 4th Edition. Washington, DC, American Psychiatric Association, 1994

Aracava Y, Fróes-Ferráo MM, Pereira EFR, et al: Sensitivity of N-methyl-D-aspartate (NMDA) and nicotinic acetylcholine receptors to ethanol and pyrazole. Ann N Y Acad Sci 625:451–472, 1991

Barrett JE, Brady LS, Witkin JM: Behavioral studies with anxiolytic drugs, I: interactions of the benzodiazepine antagonist Ro15-1788 with chlordiazepoxide, pentobarbital and ethanol. J Pharmacol Exp Ther 233:554–559, 1985

Choi DW: Excitotoxic cell death. J Neurobiol 23:1261–1276, 1992

Collingridge GL, Lester RAJ: Excitatory amino acid receptors in the vertebrate central nervous system. Pharmacol Rev 40:143–210, 1989

Crabbe JC, Phillips TJ, Feller DJ, et al: Elevated alcohol consumption in null mutant mice lacking 5-HT$_{1B}$ serotonin receptors. Nat Genet 14:98–101, 1996

Criswell HE, Simson PE, Duncan GE, et al: Molecular basis for regionally specific action of ethanol on γ-aminobutyric acid$_A$ receptors: generalization to other ligand-gated ion channels. J Pharmacol Exp Ther 267:522–537, 1993

DeLorey TM, Olsen RW: γ-Aminobutyric acid$_A$ receptor structure and function. J Biol Chem 267:16747–16750, 1992

Diana M, Pistis M, Carboni S, et al: Profound decrement of mesolimbic dopaminergic neuronal activity during ethanol withdrawal syndrome in rats: electrophysiological and biochemical evidence. Proc Natl Acad Sci U S A 90: 7966–7969, 1993

Di Chiara G: The role of dopamine in drug abuse viewed from the perspective of its role in motivation. Drug Alcohol Depend 38:95–137, 1995

Di Chiara G, Imperato A: Drugs abused by humans preferentially increase synaptic dopamine concentrations in the mesolimbic system of freely moving rats. Proc Natl Acad Sci U S A 85:5274–5278, 1988

Di Chiara G, Morelli M, Consolo S: Modulatory functions of neurotransmitters in the striatum: ACh/dopamine/ NMDA interactions. Trends Neurosci 17:228–233, 1994

Dolin SJ, Little HJ, Hudspith M, et al: Increased dihydropyridine sensitive calcium channels in rat brain may underlie ethanol physical dependence. Neuropharmacology 26:275–279, 1987

Eckardt MJ, File SE, Gessa GL, et al: The effects of moderate alcohol consumption on the central nervous system. Alcohol Clin Exp Res 22:998–1040, 1998

Franks NP, Lieb WR: Anaesthetics set their sites on ion channels. Nature 389:334–335, 1997

Gessa GL, Montoni F, Collu M, et al: Low doses of ethanol activate dopaminergic neurons in the ventral tegmental area. Brain Res 348:201–203, 1985

Goldstein DB, Chin JH, Lyon RC: Ethanol disordering of spin-labeled mouse brain membranes—correlation with genetically determined ethanol sensitivity of mice. Proc Natl Acad Sci U S A 79:4231–4233, 1982

Grant KA: The role of 5-HT$_3$ receptors in drug dependence. Drug Alcohol Depend 38:155–171, 1995

Grant KA, Colombo G: Discriminative stimulus effects of ethanol: effect of training dose on the substitution of N-methyl-D-aspartate antagonists. J Pharmacol Exp Ther 264:1241–1247, 1993

Harris RA, McQuilkin SJ, Paylor R, et al: PKCγ null mutant mice show decreased behavioral actions of ethanol and altered GABA$_A$ receptor function. Proc Natl Acad Sci U S A 92:3633–3635, 1995

Hodge CW, Chappelle AM, Samson HH: GABAergic transmission in the nucleus accumbens is involved in the termination of ethanol self-administration in rats. Alcohol Clin Exp Res 19:1486–1493, 1995

Hoffman PL, Iorio KR, Snell LD, et al: Attenuation of glutamate-induced neurotoxicity in chronically ethanol-exposed cerebellar granule cells by NMDA receptor antagonists and ganglioside GM$_1$. Alcohol Clin Exp Res 19:721–726, 1995

Hyytiä P, Koob GF: GABA$_A$ receptor antagonism in the extended amygdala decreases ethanol self-administration in rats. Eur J Pharmacol 283:151–159, 1995

Li T-K, McBride WJ: Pharmacogenetic models of alcoholism. Clin Neurosci 3:182–188, 1995

Li T-K, Lumeng L, Doolittle DP: Selective breeding for alcohol preference and associated responses. Behav Genet 23:163–170, 1993

Lin AMY, Freund RK, Palmer MR: Sensitization of γ-aminobutyric acid–induced depressions of cerebellar Purkinje neurons to the potentiative effects of ethanol by *beta* adrenergic mechanisms in rat brain. J Pharmacol Exp Ther 265:426–432, 1993

Litten RZ, Allen J, Fertig J: Pharmacotherapies for alcohol problems: a review of research with focus on developments since 1991. Alcohol Clin Exp Res 20:859–876, 1996

Lovinger DM, Zhou Q: Alcohols potentiate ion current mediated by recombinant 5-HT$_3$RA receptors expressed in a mammalian cell line. Neuropharmacology 33:1567–1572, 1994

Mihic SJ, Harris RA: Alcohol actions at the GABA$_A$ receptor/chloride channel complex, in Pharmacological Effects of Ethanol on the Nervous System. Edited by Deitrich RA, Erwin VG. Boca Raton, FL, CRC Press, 1996, pp 51–72

Mihic SJ, Ye Q, Wick MJ, et al: Sites of alcohol and volatile anaesthetic action on GABA$_A$ and glycine receptors. Nature 389:385–389, 1997

Miyakawa T, Yagi T, Kitazawa H, et al: Fyn-kinase as a determinant of ethanol sensitivity: relation to NMDA-receptor function. Science 278:698–701, 1997

Mons N, Yoshimura M, Ikeda H, et al: Immunological assessment of the distribution of type VII adenylyl cyclase in brain. Brain Res 788:251–261, 1998

O'Brien CP, Volpicelli LA, Volpicelli JR: Naltrexone in the treatment of alcoholism: a clinical review. Alcohol 13:35–39, 1996

Peters JA, Lambert JJ: Anaesthetics in a bind? Trends Pharmacol Sci 18:454–455, 1997

Phillips TJ, Shen EH: Neurochemical bases of locomotion and ethanol stimulant effects. Int Rev Neurobiol 39:243–282, 1996

Prunell M, Escorihuela RM, Fernandez-Teruel A, et al: Differential interactions between ethanol and Ro15-4513 on two anxiety tests in rats. Pharmacol Biochem Behav 47:147–151, 1994

Ripley TL, Whittington MA, Butterworth AR, et al: Ethanol withdrawal hyperexcitability *in vivo* and in isolated mouse hippocampal slices. Alcohol Alcohol 31:347–357, 1996

Roberts AJ, Cole M, Koob GF: Intra-amygdala muscimol decreases operant ethanol self-administration in dependent rats. Alcohol Clin Exp Res 20:1289–1298, 1996

Rossetti ZL, Melis F, Carboni S, et al: Marked decrease of extraneuronal dopamine after alcohol withdrawal in rats: reversal by MK-801. Eur J Pharmacol 200:371–372, 1991

Rossetti ZL, Hmaidan Y, Gessa GL: Marked inhibition of mesolimbic dopamine release: a common feature of ethanol, morphine, cocaine and amphetamine abstinence in rats. Eur J Pharmacol 221:227–234, 1992

Schuckit MA: Low level of response to alcohol as a predictor of future alcoholism. Am J Psychiatry 155:184–189, 1994

Sellers EM, Toneatto T, Romach MK, et al: Clinical efficacy of the 5-HT$_3$ antagonist ondansetron in alcohol abuse and dependence. Alcohol Clin Exp Res 18:879–885, 1994

Sieghart W: GABA$_A$ receptors: ligand-gated Cl$^-$ ion channels modulated by multiple drug-binding sites. Trends Pharmacol 13:446–450, 1992

Suzdak PD, Glowa JR, Crawley JN, et al: Is ethanol antagonist Ro15-4513 selective for ethanol? Science 239:648–650, 1988

Tabakoff B, Hoffman PL: Alcohol interactions with brain opiate receptors. Life Sci 32:197–204, 1983

Tabakoff B, Hoffman PL: Alcohol addiction: an enigma among us. Neuron 16:909–912, 1996a

Tabakoff B, Hoffman PL: Effect of alcohol on neurotransmitters and their receptors and enzymes, in The Pharmacology of Alcohol and Alcohol Dependence. Edited by Begleiter H, Kissin B. New York, Oxford University Press, 1996b, pp 356–430

Tabakoff B, Hoffman PL: Ethanol and glutamate receptors, in Pharmacological Effects of Ethanol on the Nervous System. Edited by Deitrich RA, Erwin VG. Boca Raton, FL, CRC Press, 1996c, pp 73–93

Tabakoff B, Hoffman PL: Adenylyl cyclases and alcohol, in Advances in Second Messenger and Phosphoprotein Research, Vol 32. Edited by Cooper DMF. Philadelphia, PA, Lippincott-Raven Publishers, 1998, pp 173–193

Taraschi RF, Ellingson JS, Wu A, et al: Phosphatidylinositol from ethanol-fed rats confers membrane tolerance to ethanol. Proc Natl Acad Sci U S A 83:9398–9402, 1986

Volpicelli JR, Volpicelli LA, O'Brien CP: Medical management of alcohol dependence: clinical use and limitations of naltrexone treatment. Alcohol Alcohol 30:789–798, 1995

Wafford KA, Burnett DM, Leidenheimer NJ, et al: Ethanol sensitivity of the GABA$_A$ receptor expressed in *Xenopus* oocytes requires eight amino acids contained in the $\gamma_{2L}$ subunit. Neuron 7:27–33, 1991

Weiner JL, Zhang L, Carlen PL: Potentiation of GABA$_A$-mediated synaptic current by ethanol in hippocampal CA1 neurons: possible role of protein kinase C. J Pharmacol Exp Ther 268:1388–1395, 1994

World Health Organization: International Statistical Classification of Diseases and Related Health Problems, 10th Revision. Geneva, Switzerland, World Health Organization, 1992

Wozniak KM, Pert A, Linnoila M: Antagonism of 5-HT$_3$ receptors attenuates the effects of ethanol on extracellular dopamine. Eur J Pharmacol 187:287–289, 1990

Yoshimura M, Tabakoff B: Selective effects of ethanol on the generation of cAMP by particular members of the adenylyl cyclase family. Alcohol Clin Exp Res 19:1435–1440, 1995

# 2

# Neurobiology of Opiates/Opioids

Jerome H. Jaffe, M.D.
Ari B. Jaffe, M.D.

The term *opioid* refers to the opiates morphine and codeine (which occur naturally in opium), the semisynthetic drugs produced by modifying morphine and codeine, and a variety of totally synthetic drugs with actions that resemble those of morphine. Our understanding of opioid actions has expanded dramatically with the landmark discoveries of several families of specific receptors for opioids and of endogenous ligands for these receptors. More recent discoveries of how opioid receptors are linked to second and third messenger systems within the cell, and how these systems are linked to adaptive mechanisms and to gene expression, have been equally remarkable. Those discoveries, along with advances in behavioral and neurophysiological studies of how opioids alter hedonic tone, have provided a greater understanding of how opioids gain control of behavior and of the complex syndrome of opioid dependence. In this chapter, intended for the psychiatrist or physician who specializes in problems of drug abuse and dependence, I discuss the clinical neurobiology of opioid dependence. In most instances, the references cited are major review articles rather than the original research studies.

portant roles in modulating responses to stress and pain; in regulating temperature, respiration, endocrine and gastrointestinal activity, and mood and motivation; and in other functions (Reisine and Pasternak 1995). When opioid receptors are activated by an agonist (either endogenous or exogenous), a cascade of intracellular changes involving second and third messenger systems is set in motion. These changes not only produce immediate changes in the responsiveness of the receptor-bearing neurons but also lead to a number of intracellular adaptive changes involving intracellular messenger systems and protein phosphorylation and changes in gene expression. Some of these intracellular changes are related to the development of tolerance (decreased responsiveness to the same concentration of the opioid at the receptor) and altered excitability (withdrawal) when the agonist is removed after a period of receptor occupancy. In the intact organism, the opioid withdrawal syndrome represents changes within the opioid-receptor-bearing neurons themselves and altered activity in other neuronal systems affected less directly by opioid actions in the CNS (Koob and Bloom 1988; Nestler 1997; Nestler and Aghajanian 1997).

## Opioid Actions

Opioid drugs act by binding to specific receptors on neurons distributed throughout the central nervous system (CNS) and peripheral nervous system. Several types of opioid receptors exist; drugs that bind to these receptor types can act as agonists, partial agonists, or antagonists. These opioid receptors are the binding sites for three families of endogenous peptides that play im-

## Opioid Receptors

Three major types of opioid receptors have been identified and cloned: $\mu$, $\kappa$, and $\delta$. These receptors belong to a larger superfamily of receptors that have seven transmembrane $\alpha$ helices and are coupled to guanine nucleotide–binding proteins (G proteins). Based on binding-affinity studies in neural material, researchers have proposed additional receptor types and subtypes of the three major types of opioid receptors. Although the endogenous peptide ligands and the currently available opioids bind preferentially to one or more subtypes of receptor, they are not as highly selective in their binding characteristics as some recently developed synthetic ligands. Selective antagonists for each of the three receptor types have also been developed. Each of the major receptor types has a distinct distribution in the CNS and the peripheral nervous system. μ and δ receptor activation produce generally similar actions that are quite distinct from those resulting from κ receptor activation.

## Opioid Drugs: Agonists, Partial Antagonists, Antagonists, Mixed Agonist/Antagonists

More than 20 clinically available drugs exert actions at opioid receptors. Most of these drugs, such as morphine, are prototypical μ agonists: they produce analgesia, altered mood (often euphoria), decreased anxiety, respiratory depression, inhibition of certain spinal polysynaptic reflexes, inhibition of gastrointestinal motility, suppression of cough, suppression of corticotropin-releasing factor and adrenocorticotropic hormone release, and miosis (pinpoint pupils); they can also produce pruritus, nausea, and vomiting. When brain levels rise rapidly, which occurs when opioid drugs are injected intravenously or inhaled, users may experience a brief, intense, usually pleasurable sensation called a *rush* or *thrill*. This is followed by a longer-lasting period of altered feeling state—the *high*. Most of the μ agonists are full agonists, able to produce maximal responses in opioid responsive systems. In clinical dosages, few agonists have any significant actions at the δ or κ receptors. Some μ agonist opioids, such as codeine, are essentially prodrugs and act at the μ receptor only after biotransformation to morphine. When any μ agonist is used chronically, tolerance and physical dependence develop (Jaffe 1990; Jaffe et al. 1997; Reisine and Pasternak 1995).

Several opioid antagonists (e.g., naloxone, naltrexone, nalmefene) are now available. These drugs bind primarily to the μ receptor, but in higher dosages they can bind to δ and κ receptors. Also available are several drugs that are often described as mixed agonist/antagonists. They bind to several receptor types, usually acting as antagonists or partial agonists at the μ receptor, while having agonist actions at the κ receptor. Drugs in this group include pentazocine, nalbuphine, butorphanol,

and dezocine (Jaffe et al. 1997; Reisine and Pasternak 1995).

The drug buprenorphine is best described as a partial μ agonist, although in animals it also has κ antagonist activity. Buprenorphine produces typical μ agonist effects; however, as the dosage is increased, the response intensity plateaus, reaching a ceiling comparable to about 20–30 mg of morphine parenterally. Thus buprenorphine is far less likely to produce the severe respiratory depression observed with high dosages of full μ agonists. Like other μ agonists, buprenorphine produces tolerance and physical dependence, but withdrawal is less intense because of the ceiling effect and possibly because it binds quite tightly to the receptor. Buprenorphine exhibits cross-tolerance and cross-dependence with other μ agonists, except that when it is substituted for a full μ agonist that has been given at high dosage it can replace the full μ agonist effects with partial effects and thereby induce some opioid withdrawal. At low to modest levels of opioid dependence, buprenorphine can substitute for other μ agonists and has been used for detoxification and as a maintenance drug. Because of its ceiling effect, very large doses of buprenorphine can be used to extend its duration of action. Given at such high dosages, it can suppress opioid withdrawal for more than 72 hours (Bickel and Amass 1995; Reisine and Pasternak 1995).

Virtually all of the opioids that are abused are prototypical μ agonists. Diacetylmorphine, or heroin, is the most widely used illicit opioid. Heroin is, in part, a prodrug, metabolized within minutes to 6-monoacetylmorphine and to morphine. However, it is more lipid soluble than morphine, passing more rapidly into the brain.

The likelihood of a μ agonist drug being misused (abused) depends in part on its pharmacokinetics and the route by which it is administered. Drugs with short half-lives used intravenously (e.g., heroin, morphine, hydromorphone, fentanyl) produce behavioral syndromes characterized by a brief period of intoxication (i.e., the high) followed within hours by a period of relative withdrawal, drug-seeking behavior, or the administration of more drug. Drugs with long half-lives, for example, methadone or L-α-acetylmethadol (LAAM), given orally, can allow a relatively stable pattern of behavior; once tolerance has developed, there is minimal or no impairment of mood, judgment, or psychomotor performance (see Senay, Chapter 24, in this volume).

There are sporadic cases of abuse and dependence involving mixed agonist/antagonists, but there is virtually no abuse of κ agonists. Although they can produce analgesia, κ agonists also typically produce dysphoria and a distinct form of physical dependence. There is no cross-dependence between μ and κ agonists.

## Endogenous Opioid Peptides

Three genetically distinct families of endogenous opioid peptides have been well defined: proenkephalin, prodynorphin, and proopiomelanocortin (POMC) peptides. Each of the precursor proteins for these peptides can be processed to produce a number of active peptides with varying affinities for the three major types of opioid receptors. There are at least 10 proenkephalin peptides, 11 prodynorphin peptides, and 2 POMC peptides—β-endorphin 1-31 and β-endorphin 1-27.

The first two endogenous opioid peptides to be described were the two pentapeptides: met-enkephalin (tyr-gly gly phe-met) and leu-enkephalin (tyr-gly gly phe-leu). The core opioid sequence tyr-gly gly phe-, found in the three well-defined major families of endogenous opioid peptides (sometimes called the *message*), ensures that the peptide binds to an opioid receptor. The extension beyond this core (the *address*) determines the selectivity. As a generalization, the enkephalin peptides are δ receptor preferring, the dynorphin principal peptides are κ receptor preferring, and the endorphins show about comparable affinity for μ and δ receptors (Akil et al. 1997, 1998).

Posttranslational processing of the endogenous peptides can substantially alter their receptor affinities and preferences. For example, met-enkephalin binds preferentially to δ receptors, whereas two of the other proenkephalin peptides bind equally or preferentially at κ receptors. Most of the prodynorphin peptides bind preferentially to κ receptors, but Dyn 1-6 also shows about equivalent binding at μ and δ. Some smaller dynorphin peptides can have nonopioid actions. Further, some processing produces peptides that still have affinity for the opioid receptors but act functionally as antagonists. For example, although β-endorphin 1-31 is a potent agonist at μ and δ receptors, β-endorphin 1-27 has one-tenth the activity and can antagonize the actions of β-endorphin 1-31 (Akil et al. 1997).

A fourth family of receptors and neuropeptides with considerable homology to the opioid systems has been identified. Despite high homology, the receptor does not bind to the known endogenous or exogenous ligands and was designated the opioid *orphan receptor*. The endogenous ligand subsequently discovered almost simultaneously by two groups was named orphanin FQ by one and nociceptin by the other. The peptide does not interact with the opioid receptors, and it has a distinct behavioral profile producing neither place preference nor aversion. The orphanin neuropeptide system has a distinct anatomical distribution (Akil et al. 1997, 1998).

Most recently, another distinct family of opioid peptides was identified. Termed *endomorphins*, these peptides appear to have a high affinity and specificity for the μ receptor, and like other μ agonists, they produce analgesia in mammals (Akil et al. 1998; Zadina et al. 1997).

## Opioids, Reinforcement, and Hedonic Regulation

The two brain regions most often identified as mediating reinforcing properties of drugs are the ventral tegmentum and the nucleus accumbens. In animal models, direct stimulation of the nucleus accumbens and microinjection of dopamine agonists into the region are reinforcing. μ and δ opioid agonists increase activity of dopaminergic neurons originating in the ventral tegmentum by inhibiting the γ-aminobutyric acid$_A$ (GABA$_A$)–ergic interneurons that normally exert a tonic inhibitory effect on them. These dopaminergic neurons project fibers into the nucleus accumbens. Neurons in the nucleus accumbens express all three types of opioid receptors, and there are direct reinforcing actions of μ and δ agonists in the nucleus accumbens that do not depend on dopamine (Nestler 1997). Currently available κ agonists decrease activity of dopaminergic neurons in the ventral tegmentum and produce aversive effects (Akil et al. 1997; Di Chiara and Imperato 1988). Interestingly, endogenous κ-preferring peptides, such as dynorphin 1-13, do not appear to produce dysphoria (Kreek 1997).

Although the action of dopamine in the nucleus accumbens and other structures is widely believed to play a critical role in the reinforcing effects of opioids and several other classes of psychoactive drugs, some argument exists over how dopamine release engenders drug-seeking behavior. The current controversy focuses on whether dopamine release acts as a signal of potential reward, acts as a sensitizer of reward, or is the mechanism of reward in itself. Much evidence suggests that the rise in dopamine levels in the nucleus accumbens is directly reinforcing and produces an effect experienced as pleasure or intense euphoria (Koob and Le Moal 1997; Koob and Bloom 1988; Wise 1998). But recent interpretations of the evidence have suggested that dopamine release, rather than acting directly or solely to cause pleasure and reinforce behavior, may act to focus the organism's attention on the stimuli and events leading to its release and thus help the organism to recognize and repeat the behavior that produced the rewarding effects (Nesse and Berridge 1997; White 1996). Repeated bursts of dopamine may sensitize motivational systems to increase the interest in (e.g., wanting or craving) the reward (Robinson and Berridge 1993). Such an interpretation is consistent with the observation that stimuli that signal pleasurable events such as food or sex (or merely important events) also cause dopamine to rise in these pathways. It is worth noting that the reinforcing effects of opioids cannot fully explain the clinical phenomena of opioid dependence, and it is generally accepted that avoidance of withdrawal also contributes to the observed syndrome (see section "Tolerance and Physical Dependence" later in this chapter).

## Vulnerability Factors/Genetics

It is generally accepted that not everyone who tries opioids continues to use them or does so to the point at which dependence develops. In the National Comorbidity Survey, only 7.5% of those respondents who had ever tried any opioid for nonmedical purposes developed opioid dependence. Of those who had used heroin, 23% had a lifetime history of opioid dependence, whereas 16.7% of those who had ever used cocaine became cocaine dependent (Anthony et al. 1994). What is known about vulnerability factors for opioid dependence is based on clinical, epidemiological, and animal studies. There appear to be significant differences in the way $\mu$ agonists such as morphine are experienced: former addicts generally report euphoria, whereas nonaddicted subjects are more likely to report mental clouding and dysphoria.

There is evidence that genetic factors play a role in vulnerability to opioid dependence. Animal studies show that marked differences exist between strains of rodents in the rapidity and enthusiasm with which they learn to self-administer opioid drugs and in their sensitivity to them. In a study population of Vietnam era veterans, monozygotic twins were more likely than dizygotic twins to be concordant for heroin dependence. Multivariate biometric modeling showed that there are common vulnerability factors underlying the abuse of a variety of drugs (influenced by genetic and

environmental factors), as well as genetic influences that appear to be substance specific. Heroin abuse had a greater specific genetic influence than marijuana, stimulants, or sedatives (Tsuang et al. 1996, 1998). Overall, evidence suggests that in males genetic factors are at least as important in opioid dependence as they are in the genesis of alcoholism. Certain behavioral syndromes in childhood (e.g., conduct disorder) and certain psychiatric disorders in adulthood (especially antisocial personality disorder) also increase the likelihood of drug use and dependence, including opioid dependence. These syndromes have both biological and environmental roots (Cadoret et al. 1995; Gershon 1995; Kendler 1995; Lyons et al. 1995).

Environmental stressors or the administration of corticosteroids can sensitize animals to the effects of drugs and increase their tendency to self-administer drugs; stress can also trigger reinitiation of drug self-administration after a period of extinction. This stress response is an object of intense study. An important brain mediator of environmental stress, corticotropin-releasing factor (CRF) appears to stimulate heroin-seeking behavior in dependent animals, and intracerebral injections of CRF antagonists can partially reduce stress-induced relapse. One mechanism by which stress may reinitiate drug-seeking behavior appears to be activation of excitatory projections from the prefrontal cortex to the ventral tegmentum. There, the dopamine projections from the ventral tegmentum to the nucleus accumbens are activated, and drug self-administration is stimulated by the release of dopamine in the nucleus accumbens, as described earlier. Moreover, systemic stress hormones (i.e., corticosteroids) appear to increase the sensitivity of the ventral tegmentum neurons to excitatory inputs, further potentiating the stress-induced release of dopamine in the nucleus accumbens. Blocking the glucocorticoid response to stress eliminates the enhanced behavioral sensitivity to morphine and amphetamine that is induced by stress (Schulteis et al. 1997; Self and Nestler 1998).

Individuals who are addicted to heroin exhibit high levels of glucocorticoids during withdrawal, and their hypothalamic-pituitary-adrenal (HPA) function is deranged. Rises in adrenocorticotropic hormone (ACTH) and $\beta$-endorphin precede the onset of other signs and symptoms of opioid withdrawal, and HPA axis activation can be induced by exposure to doses of opioid antagonists too small to result in the appearance of subjective withdrawal. Function is also abnormal in abstinent heroin users. This latter group shows hyperresponsiveness (an excess secretion of the POMC gene products

ACTH and β-endorphin) in response to stress chemically induced by a single large dose of metyrapone, a blocker of cortisol synthesis that causes feedback upregulation of brain CRF, ACTH, and β-endorphin. This hyperresponsiveness to stress may be related to relapse. In stabilized methadone-maintained patients, classical signs of opioid withdrawal could be elicited by the administration of metyrapone, suggesting that activation of the HPA axis (e.g., increased CRF and ACTH) may serve as an internal cue of opioid withdrawal (Kreek 1997; Kreek and Koob 1998). This stimulation of withdrawal is one example of how withdrawal symptoms and craving can become conditioned to internal and external stimuli so that these stimuli (e.g., the sight of drugs or paraphernalia, or stress) can trigger withdrawal-like symptoms and craving.

## Tolerance and Physical Dependence

### The Phenomena in Brief

With repeated use, tolerance develops to most of the actions of μ agonist drugs, but it does not develop with equal rapidity in all systems. For example, tolerance develops to the miotic and constipating effects far more slowly than to the euphoriant and respiratory depressant effects. Patients stably maintained on methadone for years may continue to complain of excessive sweating (Jaffe 1990; Kreek 1997).

Some degree of physical dependence on near-clinical dosages of μ agonist drugs develops quite rapidly, and some symptoms of withdrawal (e.g., yawning, rhinorrhea, dysphoria, and nausea) can be elicited by administration of a large dose of naloxone 12–24 hours after a single dose of morphine (Jaffe 1990; Jaffe et al. 1997). The μ agonist withdrawal syndrome consists of a number of physiological disturbances that can be thought of as rebound hyperactivity in those biological systems that the agonists suppressed. Thus, instead of analgesia, euphoria, tranquillity, dampened sympathetic activity, miosis, depressed spinal reflexes, and decreased gastrointestinal motility, individuals experience hyperalgesia, dysphoria, anxiety, muscle aches and bone pain, spinal reflex hyperactivity that causes kicking movements ("kicking the habit"), dilated pupils, cramps, and diarrhea. They also experience yawning, sweating, and rhinorrhea. The intensity of the syndrome is generally proportional to the opioid dosage and duration of use. The onset and duration of the syndrome is closely

correlated with the rate at which the drug is cleared from the receptors. With short-acting drugs such as heroin the onset of early symptoms occurs at about 8 hours, and the peak of the syndrome is at about 48–72 hours. Once significant physical dependence has developed, the effort to avoid withdrawal becomes a powerful new motive for continued drug taking. With longer-acting opioids such as methadone and LAAM, 24–72 hours may elapse before the onset of withdrawal; peak intensity, which is typically not as severe as with short-acting drugs, may not be reached until the fifth or sixth day. Although at its peak, withdrawal from longer-acting opioids may be less severe than occurs with comparable doses of short-acting drugs, the prolonged discomfort and hypophoria may be experienced as less tolerable. The acute withdrawal syndrome from short-acting drugs such as morphine or heroin largely subsides within 5–7 days, but with drugs such as methadone it may persist in milder form for 14–21 days. In both situations, the acute phase of withdrawal may be followed by a longer-lasting period characterized by decreased self-esteem, unstable mood, and dysphoria (Jaffe 1990; Reisine and Pasternak 1995). It is not clear whether this protracted abstinence represents a later manifestation of opioid-induced biological changes or the emergence of one of several varieties of mood disorders that commonly co-occur among heroin addicts (Brooner et al. 1997).

The general principle that intense opioid withdrawal is relatively short lived and that slower withdrawal is less intense but more protracted led to efforts to shorten the duration of withdrawal by using small doses of antagonists to precipitate withdrawal. Benzodiazepines and, later, benzodiazepines plus clonidine were used to make the experience more tolerable (Kleber et al. 1987). That technique has now been extended to using large doses of antagonists to induce opioid withdrawal during anesthesia. In this way, the duration of the acute phase can be shortened to 24–48 hours, although some milder discomfort may persist for several more days (Brewer 1997). (A more complete description of the opioid withdrawal syndrome is found in Kleber, Chapter 23, in this volume.)

### Mechanisms of Tolerance and Dependence

Tolerance to opioids involves several mechanisms. Acutely, all three types of opioid receptor (μ, κ, and δ) agonists produce an inhibition of adenylyl cyclase and a decrease in intracellular cyclic adenosine monophosphate (cAMP) levels. There are also Gi and/or Go protein–mediated changes in conductance of an inhibitory $K^+$ ion channel (see Figure 2–1).

A type of acute tolerance that develops over minutes may be mediated by protein kinase C (PKC) phosphorylation of the µ and δ receptors (Akil et al. 1997). The tolerance that develops more gradually with chronic drug exposure involves a compensatory upregulation of the cAMP pathway, probably by upregulation of several forms of adenylyl cyclase, an internalization of µ and δ opioid receptors, and adaptive changes in other neural systems that interact with those directly influenced by the opioids. Still another mechanism might involve a decrease in the abundance of the G proteins that couple the opioid receptors to the second messengers and ion channels (Akil et al. 1997, 1998; Nestler 1997; Nestler and Aghajanian 1997).

The upregulation of adenylyl cyclase is mediated by the transcription factor cAMP response element binding protein (CREB). CREB is probably also involved in longer-lasting cellular adaptations that include the accumulation of distinct and stable Fos-like proteins. These novel transcription elements are thought to play a role in the adaptation involved in tolerance (Nestler and Aghajanian 1997).

The upregulation of cAMP occurs in a number of neural systems affected by opioids, including the locus coeruleus (LC), nucleus accumbens, ventral tegmentum, and periaqueductal gray (PAG). The excessive activity seen in these systems when opioid actions are terminated during withdrawal is caused not only by the rebound increase in levels of cAMP within the opioid receptor–bearing neurons but also by effects on other neurotransmitter systems. In the LC, for example, the increased activity results also from increased excitatory glutaminergic inputs (Nestler and Aghajanian 1997).

The LC has the largest concentration of noradrenergic neurons in the brain, with extensive connections to other brain structures. Activity of these neurons generates feelings of anxiety and many of the autonomic symptoms—for example, increased blood pressure, nausea, sweating, gastrointestinal distress—that emerge during opioid withdrawal. The role of LC hyperactivity during opioid withdrawal is of particular clinical relevance because LC neurons express not only receptors for µ and δ opioids but also receptors for $\alpha_2$ adrenergic receptors. The $\alpha_2$ adrenergic agonists, such as clonidine or lofexidine, can suppress some of the symptoms of opioid withdrawal (Jaffe et al. 1997; Kleber et al. 1987; Reisine and Pasternak 1995).

The upregulation of cAMP in the ventral tegmentum and PAG regions, and particularly within the

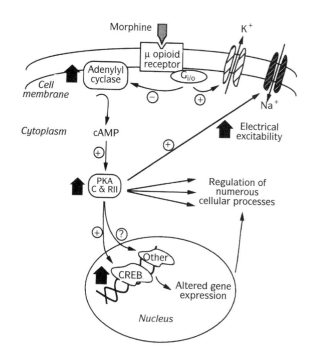

**Figure 2–1.**    Scheme illustrating opiate actions in the locus coeruleus (LC). Opiates acutely inhibit LC neurons by increasing the conductance of a $K^+$ channel (light crosshatch) via coupling with subtypes Gi and/or Go and by decreasing a $Na^+$-dependent inward current (dark crosshatch) via coupling with Gi/o and the consequent inhibition of adenylyl cyclase. Reduced levels of cyclic adenosine monophosphate (cAMP) decrease protein kinase A (PKA) activity and the phosphorylation of the responsible channel or pump. Inhibition of the cAMP pathway also decreases phosphorylation of numerous other proteins and thereby affects many additional processes in the neuron. For example, it reduces the phosphorylation state of cAMP response element binding protein (CREB), which may initiate some of the longer-term changes in LC function. Upward bold arrows summarize effects of chronic morphine in the LC. Chronic morphine increases levels of adenylyl cyclase, PKA, and several phosphoproteins, including CREB. These changes contribute to the altered phenotype of the drug-addicted state. For example, the intrinsic excitability of LC neurons is increased via enhanced activity of the cAMP pathway and $Na^+$-dependent inward current, which contributes to the tolerance, dependence, and withdrawal exhibited by these neurons. This altered phenotypic state appears to be maintained in part by upregulation of CREB expression. *Source.*   Reprinted from Nestler EJ: "Molecular Mechanisms Underlying Opiate Addiction: Implications for Medications Development." *Seminars in Neurosciences* 9:84–93, 1997. Copyright 1997, Academic Press. Used with permission.

GABAergic neurons that innervate these areas, could explain some of the phenomena seen during opioid withdrawal. For example, increased activity in GABAergic neurons that normally inhibit dopaminergic neurons in the ventral tegmentum would result in reduced dopamine release at the nucleus accumbens—an action consistent with the states of dysphoria, depression, and anhedonia observed during clinical withdrawal (Koob and Bloom 1988; Koob and Le Moal 1997; Nestler 1997). However, as is the case with altered function within the LC, multiple changes in the ventral tegmentum could account for dysphoria during acute withdrawal and perhaps for hypophoria during protracted withdrawal. These changes include upregulation of subunits of α-amino-3-hydroxy-5-methyl-4-isoxazolepropionate (AMPA) and *N*-methyl-D-aspartate (NMDA) glutamate receptors and structural adaptations in dopaminergic neurons. Chronic opioid use reduces neurofilament proteins and the average size of dopamine neurons in the ventral tegmentum, changes that may be associated with functional hypoactivity following a period of exposure (Nestler 1997).

Drug-induced changes in the endogenous opioid systems might also be relevant to postwithdrawal functioning, protracted abstinence, and relapse. Studies of chronic exposure to μ and κ agonists and μ antagonists on levels of endogenous peptides or on activity of opioid precursor genes, manifested as changes in mRNA, have not produced consistent results. Some studies have shown an increase in mRNA for dynorphin (Trujillo et al. 1995). Such a finding would be consistent with an adaptive change if, as is proposed, κ agonists act at κ autoreceptors on presynaptic terminals of dopaminergic neurons, dampening dopaminergic activity (Hyman and Nestler 1996). Given that the opioid drugs of abuse are typically μ agonists, similar studies are needed to assess the effects of chronic opioid use on the newly discovered endomorphin system.

Some studies have found decreased affinity and density of opioid receptors after chronic exposure to opioid agonists, but others have found no significant change in the number of opioid receptors. Conversely, chronic treatment with opioid antagonists produces upregulation of receptor density. In rodents, this upregulation of opioid receptors appears to contribute to a hyperresponsiveness to μ opioid agonists when antagonist administration is stopped. These findings in animal models have raised some concern that patients who relapse to opioid use following a period of treatment with antagonists might be more vulnerable to opioid toxicity.

Some neurons expressing opioid receptors also express receptors for one or more glutamatergic (Glu) receptors, and evidence indicates that these Glu receptors play a role in the development of opioid tolerance and dependence. NMDA agonists open a membrane calcium channel that can initiate a calcium-calmodulin activation of nitric oxide (NO) synthase resulting in increased levels of NO. The mechanism for this interaction between the μ receptor and the NMDA receptor appears to involve activation of PKC, which phosphorylates the NMDA receptor, resulting in calcium influx and NO formation in the presence of glutamate. The development of opioid tolerance and dependence can be influenced by agents that act at various points in the pathway from the NMDA receptor to the rise in NO. In rodents, agents that block the NMDA receptor or inhibit NO synthase activity can attenuate or prevent the development of opioid tolerance and dependence. Such agents include MK801, phencyclidine (PCP), and dextrorphan (a metabolite of the widely used antitussive agent dextromethorphan), which are noncompetitive NMDA receptor antagonists (Inturrisi 1997; Wiesenfeld-Hallin 1998).

It is of interest that the D-isomer of racemic methadone has no analgesic activity but exerts noncompetitive blocking action at the NMDA receptor (Inturrisi 1997). This effect at the NMDA receptor may partly explain why tolerance develops so slowly to racemic methadone used as an analgesic or in opioid maintenance therapy, but it would not explain why physical dependence is not also attenuated. A combination product of morphine and dextromethorphan is being marketed as an analgesic. Glutamate also appears to be involved in sensitization to the actions of other psychoactive drugs such as amphetamine and cocaine, and glutamate blockers prevent the development of this sensitization. If sensitization is related to the obsessive interest in (i.e., craving for) drugs, glutamate blockers may be useful as therapeutic agents.

## Opioid Toxicity

Most opioids given by mouth are relatively nontoxic, and drugs such as methadone have been used over prolonged periods with little or no significant organ damage (see Senay, Chapter 24, in this volume). However, a range of toxic effects have been associated with the use of injected or inhaled opioids. The etiology of the toxic effects is not always apparent.

The most dramatic of the toxic effects are acute opioid overdoses characterized by stupor or coma, depressed respiration, and typically extreme miosis. Pulmonary edema may also occur. If respiratory depression persists, anoxia may lead to hypotension and dilated pupils. Overdoses with a more gradual onset but similar clinical picture have been observed in nontolerant opioid users who are given methadone.

After a patent airway has been established and ventilation started, opioid antagonists such as naloxone or nalmefene given intravenously will reverse the respiratory depression, but pulmonary edema may require positive pressure ventilation. To prevent the precipitation of severe withdrawal in patients who are opioid dependent, naloxone should be given in incremental doses starting at about 0.5 mg; the response to naloxone usually occurs within 1–2 minutes. Generally, 5–10 mg is adequate even for severe opioid overdoses. However, buprenorphine overdoses may require larger doses because buprenorphine binds more tightly to the opioid receptors than most other available opioids.

When an overdose involves a longer-acting drug such as methadone or LAAM, naloxone, a short-acting antagonist, only displaces the drug from the opioid receptors. Opioid toxicity may recur when the naloxone is metabolized, and the long-acting agonist reoccupies the receptors. Patients must be observed until it is clear that additional naloxone is not required.

Injection use of illicit opioids has also been associated with neurological lesions, such as necrosis of spinal gray matter and degeneration of globus pallidus (found at autopsy); transverse myelitis; amblyopia; and plexitis. Inhaled opioids have also been associated with neurological damage such as spongiform encephalopathy (Strang et al. 1997). The role of contaminants in these syndromes is not clear—cases of toxicity associated with inhaled opioids involved inhaling vapors from a mixture heated on aluminum foil. A known contaminant in the illicit manufacture of meperidine, MPTP (1-methyl, 4 phenyl, 1,2,3,6-tetrahydropyridine), causes destruction of dopaminergic neurons and is responsible for several cases of severe parkinsonism seen among drug users. Intramuscular injection of meperidine and certain other opioids, such as pentazocine, can produce long-lasting induration and sclerosis of muscle tissues. Some infectious disorders (e.g., human immunodeficiency virus, hepatitis, subacute bacterial endocarditis, skin ulcers) are found in opioid users who do not use sterile techniques or who share injection equipment.

There are a few exceptions to the general rule about the safety of opioids. Some opioids have toxic metabolites. For example, normeperidine, a metabolite of meperidine, can produce seizures and confused delir-

ium. Normeperidine accumulates if it is given frequently in high dosages (as may be seen in physician addicts) and may do so in ordinary dosages when renal function is impaired. Certain drug interactions may also lead to an accumulation of normeperidine.

## Future Directions and Implications for Therapy

Twenty years ago, the only pharmacological agents available for the treatment of opioid dependence were other opioids (i.e., substitution therapies). Recent advances in the understanding of the neurobiology of opioids have provided new options in the treatment of opioid dependence and withdrawal. Some of these options, such as the use of clonidine to attenuate the severity of opioid withdrawal, have been in use for quite some time. The future may bring treatments based on more specific targeting of opioid receptor subtypes, on second and third messenger systems downstream of the opioid receptor itself, or on allied neurotransmitter systems, such as dopamine and NMDA, whose role in initiating and maintaining opioid dependence is now becoming better understood.

## References

Akil H, Meng F, Devine DP, et al: Molecular and neuroanatomical properties of the endogenous opioid system: implications for treatment of opiate addiction. Seminars in Neuroscience 9:70–83, 1997

Akil H, Owens C, Gutstein H, et al: Endogenous opioids: overview and current issues. Drug Alcohol Depend 51:127–140, 1998

Anthony JC, Warner LA, Kessler RC: Comparative epidemiology of dependence on tobacco, alcohol, controlled substances, and inhalants: basic findings from the National Comorbidity Survey. Exp Clin Psychopharmacol 2:244–268, 1994

Bickel W, Amass L: Buprenorphine treatment of opioid dependence: a review. Exp Clin Psychopharmacol 3:477–489, 1995

Brewer C: Ultra-rapid, antagonist-precipitated opiate detoxification under general anaesthesia or sedation. Addiction Biology 2:291–302, 1997

Brooner RK, King VL, Kidorf M, et al: Psychiatric and substance use comorbidity among treatment-seeking opioid abusers. Arch Gen Psychiatry 54:71–80, 1997

Cadoret RJ, Yates WR, Troughton E, et al: Genetic-environmental interaction in the genesis of aggressivity and conduct disorders. Arch Gen Psychiatry 52:916–924, 1995

Di Chiara G, Imperato A: Opposite effects of mu and kappa opiate agonists on dopamine release in the nucleus accumbens and in the dorsal caudate of freely moving rats. J Pharmacol Exp Ther 244:1067–1080, 1988

Gershon ES: Antisocial behavior. Arch Gen Psychiatry 52:900–901, 1995

Hyman SE, Nestler EJ: Initiation and adaptation: a paradigm for understanding psychotropic drug action. Am J Psychiatry 153:151–162, 1996

Inturrisi CE: Preclinical evidence for a role of glutamatergic systems in opioid tolerance and dependence. Seminars in Neuroscience 9:110–119, 1997

Jaffe JH: Drug addiction and drug abuse, in Goodman and Gilman's The Pharmacological Basis of Therapeutics, 8th Edition. Edited by Gilman AG, Rall TW, Nies AS, et al. New York, Pergamon, 1990, pp 522–573

Jaffe JH, Knapp CM, Ciraulo DA: Opiates: clinical aspects, in Substance Abuse: A Comprehensive Textbook, 3rd Edition. Edited by Lowinson JH, Ruiz P, Millman RB, et al. Baltimore, MD, Williams & Wilkins, 1997, pp 158–166

Kendler KS: Genetic epidemiology in psychiatry: taking both genes and environment seriously. Arch Gen Psychiatry 52:895–899, 1995

Kleber HD, Topazian M, Gaspari J, et al: Clinical utility of rapid clonidine-naltrexone detoxification for opioid abusers. Am J Drug Alcohol Abuse 13:1–8, 1987

Koob GF, Bloom FE: Cellular and molecular mechanisms of drug dependence. Science 242:715–723, 1988

Koob GF, Le Moal M: Drug abuse: hedonic homeostatic dysregulation. Science 278:52–57, 1997

Kreek MJ: Clinical update of opioid agonist and partial agonist medications for the maintenance treatment of opioid addiction. Seminars in Neuroscience 9:140–157, 1997

Kreek MJ, Koob GF: Drug dependence: stress and dysregulation of brain reward pathways. Drug Alcohol Depend 51:23–47, 1998

Lyons MJ, True WR, Eisen SA, et al: Differential heritability of adult and juvenile antisocial traits. Arch Gen Psychiatry 52:906–915, 1995

Nesse RM, Berridge KC: Psychoactive drug use in evolutionary perspective. Science 278:63–65, 1997

Nestler EJ: Molecular mechanisms underlying opiate addiction: implications for medications development. Seminars in Neuroscience 9:84–93, 1997

Nestler EJ, Aghajanian GK: Molecular and cellular basis of addiction. Science 278:58–63, 1997

Reisine T, Pasternak G: Opioid analgesics and antagonists, in Goodman and Gilman's The Pharmacological Basis of Therapeutics, 9th Edition. Edited by Harman JG, Limbird LE, Molinoff RW, et al. New York, McGraw-Hill, 1995, pp 521–555

Robinson TW, Berridge KC: The neural basis of drug craving: an incentive-sensitization theory of addiction. Brain Research Reviews 18:241–291, 1993

Schulteis G, Gold LH, Koob GF: Preclinical behavioral models for addressing unmet needs in opiate addiction. Seminars in Neuroscience 9:94–109, 1997

Self DW, Nestler EJ: Relapse to drug-seeking: neural and molecular mechanisms. Drug Alcohol Depend 51:49–60, 1998

Strang J, Griffiths P, Gossop M: Heroin smoking by "chasing the dragon": origins and history. Addiction 92:673–683, 1997

Trujillo KA, Bronstein DM, Sanchez IO, et al: Effects of chronic opiate and opioid antagonist treatment on striatal opioid peptides. Brain Res 698:69–78, 1995

Tsuang MT, Lyons MJ, Eisen SA, et al: Genetic influences on DSM-III-R drug abuse and dependence: a study of 3,372 twin pairs. Am J Med Genet 67:473–477, 1996

Tsuang MT, Lyons MJ, Meyer JM, et al: Co-occurrence of abuse of different drugs in men. Arch Gen Psychiatry 55:967–972, 1998

White NM: Addictive drugs as reinforcers: multiple partial actions on memory systems. Addiction 91:921–949, 1996

Wiesenfeld-Hallin Z: Combined opioid-NMDA antagonist therapies. Drugs 55:1–4, 1998

Wise R: Drug-activation of brain reward pathways. Drug Alcohol Depend 51:13–22, 1998

Zadina JE, Hackler L, Ge L-J, et al: A potent and selective endogenous agonist for the mu-opiate receptor. Nature 386:499–502, 1997

# Neurobiology of Stimulants

Marian W. Fischman, Ph.D.
Margaret Haney, Ph.D.

Cycles of cocaine or amphetamine abuse have occurred throughout the world for more than 100 years. The two most commonly abused illicit stimulants in the United States are cocaine and methamphetamine. In California, the number of individuals entering treatment for methamphetamine abuse rose from approximately 900 in 1984 to 29,000 in 1994. Similarly, emergency room mentions of methamphetamine have more than doubled from 1991 to 1993 (Pearce 1993). Although recent data suggest that the number of individuals who occasionally use cocaine has decreased, arrest statistics, drug treatment records, and emergency room mentions suggest that those who are using cocaine are using it very heavily (National Drug Control Strategy 1997). No effective pharmacotherapy is available to treat cocaine or amphetamine dependence. Continued progress in our understanding of the mechanism of cocaine and amphetamine action and of the consequences of their chronic use will be important in the development of compounds to treat dependence and to improve changes in brain function that may occur as a consequence of chronic use.

## Mechanism of Action

Cocaine's behavioral effects are mediated primarily by its binding to the dopamine transporter and inhibiting the reuptake of synaptic dopamine (Ritz et al. 1987). Given that reuptake is the primary mechanism of terminating dopamine transmission, cocaine administration results in dose-dependent increases in extracellular levels of dopamine in various brain regions (Hurd et al. 1990; Wise et al. 1995). Cocaine also blocks the reuptake of norepinephrine and serotonin. The affinity of cocaine for serotonin-binding sites is greater than its affinity for dopamine-binding sites (Koe 1976).

Amphetamine has a more complex mechanism of action than cocaine, both blocking dopamine reuptake and promoting dopamine release via the dopamine transporter (Jaber et al. 1997). Although methamphetamine is the primary type of amphetamine that is abused, laboratory studies have often used dextroamphetamine (*d*-amphetamine), which has similar behavioral and dopaminergic effects as methamphetamine but a different pattern of effects on serotonin and norepinephrine, particularly following repeated administration (Kuczenski et al. 1995). Thus we present laboratory data on methamphetamine when available.

## Subjective and Discriminative Stimulus Effects

Among the most important behavioral effects of cocaine and methamphetamine are their mood-altering properties (see Johanson and Fischman 1989). Both cocaine and amphetamine dose-dependently increase questionnaire scores considered to measure euphoria and decrease scores considered to measure sedative-like effects (Foltin and Fischman 1991a; Martin et al. 1971). Behavioral methods have been developed to obtain information from laboratory animals on the discriminative stimuli of drugs of abuse. In a typical drug discrimination experiment, laboratory animals are trained to make a particular behavioral response when they receive an active dose of a drug and to emit another behavioral response when they receive a placebo. Specifically, after receiving a training dose of a drug, making a drug-appropriate behavioral response results in *reinforcer delivery*, whereas making a placebo-appropriate response does not result in reinforcer delivery.

Once animals have been trained, drugs from the

same or different pharmacological classes can be administered, and the behavioral response the animals make provides information as to how similar or different the test drug is from the training drug. In studies with animals trained with either cocaine or amphetamine, generalization tests have shown that the discriminative stimulus properties of these two drugs are similar. That is, if trained to discriminate cocaine from saline, animals respond on the cocaine-appropriate lever when given amphetamine, and vice versa (de la Garza and Johanson 1986).

## Reinforcing Effects

Drugs that maintain behavior leading to their administration are classified as reinforcers. The most salient feature of drug dependence is repeated drug use, indicating that these drugs are reinforcers. Much research has focused on the reinforcing effects of stimulant drugs because of the substantial use and abuse of these substances. The primary method used to determine if a drug functions as a reinforcer is the *self-administration paradigm*, in which the drug is delivered after a specific behavioral response is emitted. The robust reinforcing effects of cocaine and amphetamine are thought to result from their effects on the mesolimbic/mesocortical dopaminergic neuronal systems, including the ventral tegmental area (VTA), nucleus accumbens, ventral pallidum, and medial prefrontal cortex (Koob and Bloom 1988). The belief that dopamine has a primary role in the reinforcing effects of psychostimulant drugs is supported by the following data (see Fischman and Johanson 1996):

- Dopamine receptor antagonists decrease the reinforcing effects of cocaine and amphetamine (Bergman et al. 1990; Davis and Smith 1975).
- A depletion of dopamine produced by the injection of neurotoxin into these dopaminergic pathways attenuates cocaine and amphetamine self-administration (Caine and Koob 1994; Lyness et al. 1979).
- The potency of cocaine and related compounds as dopamine reuptake blockers is correlated positively with their ability to maintain self-administration behavior (Bergman et al. 1989; Ritz et al. 1987).
- The amount of cocaine self-administered is correlated positively with extracellular dopamine levels in the nucleus accumbens (Pettit and Justice 1991).
- The magnitude of the self-reported "high" in humans

correlates with the occupancy of the dopamine transporter by cocaine, and the time course for these ratings parallels cocaine concentrations in the striatum (Volkow et al. 1997).

Neither norepinephrine nor serotonin appears to specifically mediate the reinforcing effects of cocaine or amphetamine (de Wit and Wise 1977; Roberts et al. 1977). Although pharmacologically increasing or decreasing serotonin activity alters cocaine or amphetamine self-administration, food-maintained behavior is also affected, suggesting that the effects are not specific (Kleven and Woolverton 1993; Leccese and Lyness 1984). Other neurotransmitters may influence cocaine or amphetamine self-administration by modulating dopamine indirectly. For instance, glutamate projects to dopaminergic neurons in the nucleus accumbens, and injections of selective N-methyl-D-aspartate (NMDA) receptor antagonists into the nucleus accumbens block both the dopaminergic effects of psychostimulants (Pap and Bradberry 1995) and their reinforcing effects (Schenk et al. 1993b). The inhibitory neurotransmitter γ-aminobutyric acid (GABA) also interacts with dopamine neurons in the nucleus accumbens and the VTA, and pharmacological manipulation of GABA alters both dopamine activity (Klitenick et al. 1992) and cocaine self-administration (Roberts et al. 1996). Finally, opioids, which also modulate dopaminergic activity, alter cocaine self-administration (Mello et al. 1990).

These data demonstrate that dopamine plays a primary role in mediating the reinforcing effects of cocaine and amphetamine. However, because of the intricate interactions between dopamine and other neurotransmitters and neuromodulators, a range of nondopaminergic agents influence cocaine and amphetamine use.

## Consequences of Repeated Stimulant Exposure

Stimulant drugs are generally abused in repeated dose bouts, called *binge-crash cycles*. The consequences of repeated stimulant exposure depend on the schedule of repeated dosing. With intermittent dose exposure, the motor-activating effects of stimulant drugs increase in magnitude, and chronic intoxication in humans can result in a stimulant psychosis. In contrast, chronic dose exposure can result in decreased sensitivity, or tolerance, to many of the effects of stimulant drugs. The development of tolerance depends on the dosage and patterning of cocaine or amphetamine use.

## Sensitization

Description.   Repeated, intermittent administration of cocaine or amphetamine to laboratory animals results in a gradual but persistent increase in sensitivity to the motoric effects of these drugs (Robinson and Becker 1986). Conditioning processes appear to play an important role in the development of sensitization. In laboratory animals, sensitization is more apparent if drug administration occurs in the environment associated with drug administration. Thus, even though repeated exposure to psychostimulant drugs produces demonstrable adaptations in the nervous system (described later in this chapter), whether these adaptations are expressed behaviorally depends on the circumstances surrounding drug administration (Robinson et al. 1998).

Other behavioral effects may also become sensitized. For example, exposure to repeated doses of cocaine renders rats more sensitive to its convulsant effects, suggesting that sensitization may increase the likelihood of cocaine-induced lethality. In humans and nonhuman primates, a significant consequence of chronic cocaine or amphetamine abuse is the development of behavioral pathology (see Johanson and Fischman 1989). In its most extreme, this pathology can include psychosis characterized by paranoia; impaired reality testing; and vivid visual, auditory, and tactile hallucinations (Post and Kopanda 1976). Methamphetamine-related psychosis may last as long as several days or weeks, whereas cocaine-related psychosis tends to have a briefer duration (Jackson 1989). Amphetamine psychosis has been replicated reliably in drug-free volunteers who were given small but frequent doses of the drug over the course of several days (Griffith et al. 1972). Chronic cocaine or methamphetamine users who have experienced drug-induced psychosis report that this paranoid state readily recurs with readministration of even a small dose of the drug (Satel et al. 1991; Sato et al. 1983), but these reports have not been replicated in the laboratory. The data on increased sensitivity to stimulants after repeated intermittent use suggest that sensitization may play a role in the behaviorally toxic consequences of psychostimulant abuse.

Some evidence indicates that sensitization to the reinforcing effects of cocaine and amphetamine also may occur. Dosages of amphetamine or cocaine that were subthreshold for maintaining self-administration in animals (Piazza et al. 1989; Schenk and Partridge 1997) maintained the behavior if the animals were preexposed to the dosages. Robinson and Berridge (1993) argued that the neuroadaptations underlying sensitization may contribute to psychostimulant abuse. Specifically, they argued that the compulsion to use stimulants in addicted individuals reflects sensitization to the intense desire or craving for cocaine. The long-lasting nature of sensitization may explain how drug-related stimuli can trigger a relapse, even in detoxified, "recovered" addicted individuals. However, others point out that in humans it is difficult to dissociate behaviors that appear to become sensitized from those that are the result of a learned association between drug cues or contextual cues and the positive motivational properties of the drugs (DiChiara 1995).

Neurochemical basis.   Most stimuli that are capable of inducing behavioral sensitization stimulate dopamine transmission either directly or indirectly. The neuroanatomical loci mediating the initiation of sensitization are distinct from the loci mediating the expression of sensitization. It appears that the initiation of sensitization to both cocaine and amphetamine occurs in the VTA, where dopamine cell bodies (A10) that project to the nucleus accumbens are located, whereas the expression of sensitization is mediated in the nucleus accumbens (Kalivas and Duffy 1993). Dopamine receptors are classified as $D_1$ or $D_2$ receptors. In the initial phases of sensitization, the firing rate of dopamine neurons originating in the VTA increases, as a result of a decrease in sensitivity of the inhibitory, impulse-regulating $D_2$ autoreceptors. This subsensitivity in the $D_2$ autoreceptors is not maintained for long, supporting the idea that the VTA is important in initiating but not maintaining sensitization. In the nucleus accumbens, where sensitization is expressed, $D_1$ receptors become supersensitive to the effects of extracellular dopamine, and the time course of behavioral sensitization corresponds with increased $D_1$ receptor sensitivity in the nucleus accumbens (Henry and White 1991, 1992). $D_1$ but not $D_2$ antagonists block the development of sensitization (Stewart and Vezina 1989). Thus, sensitization may in part reflect decreased sensitivity to $D_2$ autoreceptors in the VTA, resulting in increased dopamine release, and increased sensitivity to postsynaptic $D_1$ receptors in the nucleus accumbens.

Other neurotransmitters and neuromodulators also influence the development and expression of sensitization, often through their effects on dopamine. In rats with no prior cocaine exposure, cocaine decreases spontaneous serotonin neuronal firing in the dorsal raphe nucleus, whereas in sensitized rats, the inhibition of the serotonin firing rate in response to cocaine is augmented. A decreased release of serotonin in projections to areas such as the VTA and the nucleus accumbens would diminish the inhibitory influence of serotonin, thereby increasing dopamine neurotransmission (Cunningham et al. 1992). Coadministering serotonin antagonists with cocaine blocks the development of sensitization (King et al. 1997) without blocking cocaine's reinforcing or discriminative stimulus effects (Peltier and Schenk 1991), providing further evidence for a role of serotonin in stimulant sensitization.

Evidence suggests that NMDA-receptor activation is also essential for the development of stimulant sensitization (Segal et al. 1995). The coadministration of NMDA-receptor antagonists with cocaine or methamphetamine prevents the development of sensitization to their locomotor and reinforcing effects (Ohmori et al. 1996; Schenk et al. 1993a). In sensitized rats, NMDA antagonists block changes in mesoaccumbens dopamine (i.e., $D_2$ autoreceptor subsensitivity in the VTA and postsynaptic $D_1$ receptor supersensitivity in the nucleus accumbens) (Wolf et al. 1994). Repeated administration of cocaine or amphetamine results in an enhanced responsiveness to glutamate's excitatory effects on dopaminergic neurons in the VTA (White et al. 1995); this effect is not present 14 days later, indicating that excitatory amino acids are involved in the initiation but not the maintenance of sensitization (Zhang et al. 1997). Finally, amphetamine-sensitized rats have increases in dendritic surface and in the number of dendritic spines in the nucleus accumbens and prefrontal cortex, which is where dopamine modulates glutaminergic inputs (Robinson and Kolb 1997). These neuroanatomical studies suggest a potential mechanism for a glutamate role in stimulant sensitization.

Nitric oxide (NO), which is produced following NMDA-receptor activation, is also thought to play a role in the enhancement of presynaptic dopamine release in sensitized rats (Pudiak and Bozarth 1993). NO synthesis inhibitors administered during cocaine administration prevented the development of sensitization, whereas the same drugs administered during methamphetamine administration attenuated but did not abolish the development of sensitization (Itzhak 1997). These data suggest that the role of NO in sensitization to methamphetamine appears to be modulatory rather than critical.

Finally, opioid drugs also appear to influence psychostimulant sensitization, perhaps by acting on the enkephalin neurons in the nucleus accumbens that modulate dopamine release. Coadministration of μ, κ, or σ agonists, or δ antagonists, with methamphetamine or cocaine attenuates the development of sensitization

(Toyoshi et al. 1996; Ujike et al. 1992, 1996). Sensitized rats are more sensitive to the excitatory effects of a μ agonist on dopamine release and less sensitive to the inhibitory effects of a κ agonist on dopamine release than are control subjects (Yokoo et al. 1994). These data suggest that sensitization may be partly mediated by alterations in opioid input on dopamine neurons.

## Tolerance

Description.    Depending on the dosage and temporal pattern of dose administration, repeated exposure to cocaine or amphetamine can also result in tolerance to certain measures, in which larger doses are needed to achieve the same effect as the original dose. For example, large cocaine doses administered frequently to rats can result in tolerance to cocaine's motoric effects, whereas frequent administration of small doses produces locomotor sensitization (Sarnyai et al. 1992). Some researchers have argued that tolerance to cocaine's reinforcing effects can also be demonstrated when chronic large-dose cocaine exposure is maintained (see Hammer et al. 1997). This tolerance is defined as a decrease in the maximal amount of responding an animal will make in order to obtain a dose of cocaine or a faster rate of cocaine self-administration compared with control conditions (Emmett-Oglesby et al. 1993).

The notion of tolerance to cocaine's reinforcing effects is not accepted universally. The effects are often transient, occur only at certain dosages, and occur only in a subset of animals. Tolerance may develop to cocaine's rate-limiting effects rather than to its reinforcing effects (Katz et al. 1993). It has also been argued that chronic large-dose exposure to psychostimulants results in a generalized decrease in sensitivity to the endogenous reinforcement system rather than specific tolerance to cocaine (Schenk and Partridge 1997). The threshold of intracranial self-stimulation, thought to reflect endogenous reinforcement pathways, is increased after administrations of large quantities of cocaine or d-amphetamine, suggesting that sensitivity to a range of reinforcers may be attenuated after a stimulant binge (Wise and Munn 1995).

Although daily cocaine users report that they develop tolerance to cocaine's positive rewarding effects (Trinkoff et al. 1990), this tolerance was not demonstrated in a controlled laboratory study comparing cocaine's subjective and reinforcing effects over the course of a 2- to 3-day cocaine binge (Ward et al. 1997). However, acute tolerance to the cardiovascular and subjective effects of smoked, snorted, or inhaled cocaine develops in humans during a single episode of cocaine use. That is, the first dose administration produces larger cardiovascular and subjective effects than do subsequent doses, despite sustained elevations in cocaine plasma levels (Foltin and Fischman 1991a).

**Neurochemical basis.**   Individuals who abuse cocaine have shown neurochemical alterations that could provide a basis for tolerance: decreases in the dopamine transporter (Hitri et al. 1994) and decreased levels of $D_2$ receptors in the dorsal striatum (Volkow et al. 1990). However, these data are correlative, and their functional significance remains to be determined.

## Toxicity

**Description.**   An additional consequence of chronic exposure to psychostimulants, particularly amphetamine, is neurotoxicity. Repeated administration of large doses of *d*-amphetamine or methamphetamine is associated with decreased tissue concentrations of dopamine and serotonin, decreases in dopamine-uptake sites, and an inhibition of tyrosine hydroxylase and tryptophan hydroxylase (see Seiden and Sabol 1996). Postmortem analysis of human methamphetamine abusers has found decreased levels of striatal dopamine, tyrosine hydroxylase, and dopamine transporters compared with control subjects, although it is not clear if this finding reflects methamphetamine's direct effects or its neurotoxic effects (Wilson et al. 1996).

The occurrence of neurotoxicity may depend on how rapidly high-dosage administration is achieved. When doses of *d*-amphetamine are escalated gradually, the neurotoxicity in the neostriatal dopamine and serotonin system is attenuated or prevented compared with the repeated administration of large doses (Robinson and Camp 1987; Schmidt et al. 1985). The persistence of amphetamine's neurotoxic effects is also unclear. Some studies in nonhuman primates show that methamphetamine-induced dopamine damage persists for up to 3 years (Woolverton et al. 1989), whereas other studies suggest that dopamine levels may recover over time (Melega et al. 1997). Rats treated with a neurotoxic regimen of methamphetamine had persistent decreases in striatal dopamine transporters but showed recovery of cortical NMDA receptors (Eisch et al. 1996). Thus the precise behavioral and physiological consequences of methamphetamine's neurotoxic effects remain to be determined.

Cocaine has not been shown to produce the same degree of dopaminergic neurotoxicity as methamphetamine. In animal studies comparing doses of cocaine and *d*-amphetamine that produced comparable levels of weight loss, behavioral activation, and lethality, amphetamine resulted in axonal degeneration in the neostriatum and frontal cortex but cocaine did not (Ryan et al. 1988). There is also little evidence of toxicity to dopaminergic nerve terminals in human cocaine overdose patients compared with drug-free and age-matched control subjects (Staley et al. 1997). Cocaine may have neurotoxic effects outside of dopamine pathways. Chronic cocaine administration has been shown to produce axonal degeneration in the lateral habenula, which may have relevance to cocaine-induced psychosis (see Ellison 1994). Finally, cocaine abusers (who often abuse other drugs as well) also tend to show deficits in cerebral blood perfusion and cerebral glucose metabolism that persist after detoxification from cocaine. These abnormalities, which mimic certain neurological disorders, may play a role in cocaine's behavioral toxicity (see Majewska 1996).

**Neurochemical basis.**   Dopamine plays an essential role in mediating the neurotoxic effects of methamphetamine. Destruction of both serotonin and dopamine neurons is reduced or prevented if the following steps are taken prior to methamphetamine administration: 1) dopamine reuptake blockers are administered, 2) dopamine synthesis inhibitors or dopamine antagonists are administered, or 3) brain dopamine levels are depleted (see Seiden and Sabol 1996). The magnitude of dopamine release correlates with the amount of neurotoxicity (O'Dell et al. 1991). Methamphetamine's neurotoxic effects may be mediated by the formation of dopamine auto-oxidation products. That is, methamphetamine-induced release of dopamine is auto-oxidized to 6-hydroxydopamine, which is taken up into the dopaminergic terminals, resulting in neurodegeneration (Pu et al. 1994). Oxidative conditions are also thought to affect serotonin neurons (Fleckenstein et al. 1997), which are even more sensitive to the neurotoxic effects of methamphetamine than dopamine neurons (Hotchkiss and Gibb 1980). The role of auto-oxidation is supported by the demonstration that antioxidants protect dopamine from damage induced by methamphetamine (Wagner et al. 1986).

Neurotoxicity with repeated methamphetamine administration may also be partly the result of increased glutamate release, which appears to underlie the neuron-damaging effects of a range of central nervous system insults (Nash and Yamamoto 1992). Toxic doses of methamphetamine increase glutamate efflux in the striatum, where neurotoxicity occurs, but not in the nucleus accumbens, where neurotoxicity does not occur (Abekawa et al. 1994). NMDA antagonists prevent both dopaminergic and serotonergic neurotoxicity (Johnson et al. 1989; Ohmori et al. 1996), although it is not clear if this effect is mediated by blocking methamphetamine-induced hyperthermia or by specifically blocking glutamate's effects (Boireau et al. 1995).

## Pharmacotherapy

Understanding the neurobiological consequences of stimulant use can provide useful information about potential targets for pharmacotherapy. Such medications could modify stimulant abuse by decreasing craving, initiating or prolonging abstinence, or blocking the acute stimulant effects of the drug being abused. Pharmacotherapeutic interventions likely will not cure a chronic, relapsing disorder such as stimulant abuse. Rather, given that the problem of stimulant abuse is a behavioral one, the hope is that pharmacotherapy will provide a window of opportunity during which behavioral and psychosocial interventions can be applied (see Johanson and Fischman 1989).

In the following sections, we discuss laboratory investigations of potential medications for treating stimulant abuse. Data are limited to investigations on cocaine because few studies have been conducted on potential medications for methamphetamine abuse.

### Dopaminergic Agents

The possibility that cocaine abuse is characterized by dopamine dysfunction has provided the basis for investigating dopaminergic agonists and antagonists as potential treatment medications, much as opiate agonists and antagonists have been used in the treatment of opiate abuse (Fischman and Johanson 1996). The medications that have been tested have shown little promise so far. The $D_2$ receptor agonist bromocriptine failed to block the subjective and physiological effects of either experimentally administered cocaine (Preston et al. 1992) or cocaine-related cues (Kranzler and Bauer 1992). Bromocriptine also produced side effects, such as nausea and fainting, which often preclude its clinical application (see Kleber 1995). In a laboratory study of intravenous cocaine self-administration, the dopamine agonist pergolide mesylate, at a dose presumed to be selective for $D_2$ receptors, increased self-reported craving

for cocaine in non-treatment-seeking cocaine users (Haney et al. 1998); in a treatment setting, pergolide appeared to impair rather than facilitate treatment compliance, compared with placebo maintenance (Levin et al., in press; Malcolm et al., in preparation), supporting the reported increase in craving seen in the laboratory context. A recent investigation of the full $D_1$ agonist, ABT-431, on smoked cocaine self-administration in humans showed that ABT-431 did not affect the number of times participants chose to smoke each dose of cocaine, but it produced significant dose-dependent decreases in the subjective effects of cocaine (e.g., high, stimulated, dose liking, quality, and potency). There was a near-significant trend for ABT-431 to decrease cocaine craving (Haney et al., in press). These findings support data from laboratory animals (Self et al. 1996) indicating the $D_1$ agonists may have utility as medications for treating cocaine abuse.

In terms of dopaminergic antagonists, maintenance on the $D_1/D_2$ receptor antagonist flupenthixol did not alter the pattern of cocaine self-administration compared with maintenance on placebo. During the 2-week outpatient phase in this study, almost all subjects reported continued cocaine use regardless of maintenance drug (S. M. Evans et al., unpublished data, December 1998). Thus maintenance on flupenthixol does not appear to be an effective strategy for reducing cocaine use.

A recent finding with important implications for the development of medications for treating cocaine abuse is that cocaine binds to a separate area of the dopamine transporter molecule than does dopamine (Hitri et al. 1994), thus making it possible to design drugs that block cocaine without inhibiting dopamine uptake. Animal data suggest that a drug that antagonizes both the dopamine autoreceptor and the postsynaptic dopamine receptors shows promise as a treatment medication because blocking the autoreceptor increases dopamine activity, whereas blocking postsynaptic receptors limits dopamine activity (Richardson et al. 1993).

### Opiates

In laboratory studies investigating the effects of buprenorphine on cocaine self-administration in both opioid-dependent and non-opioid-dependent research volunteers, buprenorphine significantly decreased the self-administration of relatively large cocaine doses. However, subjective-effects ratings showed that participants were clearly intoxicated from a drug combination that mimicked a cocaine-heroin (i.e., *speedball*) effect. Buprenorphine did not affect ratings of cocaine craving or ratings of cocaine liking, which suggests that buprenorphine's effects on cocaine self-administration reflect its opiate agonist rather than its antagonist effects (Foltin and Fischman 1994). Controlled clinical trials with buprenorphine maintenance of heroin abusers also suggest that buprenorphine has little clinical utility for cocaine abuse (Schottenfeld et al. 1997).

## Antidepressants

The rationale for using antidepressants to treat cocaine abuse is to reverse the neurochemical changes produced by chronic exposure to cocaine. In a human self-administration study, the tricyclic antidepressant desipramine decreased cocaine craving and some of cocaine's stimulant-related effects, although cocaine self-administration was not affected (Fischman et al. 1990). Desipramine has shown promise in some clinical investigations, although the effects appear to be limited to the subpopulation of cocaine users who are depressed and are not coabusing opioids. These data support the idea that pharmacological interventions for the treatment of cocaine abuse may have to be targeted to specific subpopulations of users (Fischman and Johanson 1996).

Maintenance on the selective serotonin reuptake inhibitor fluoxetine reduced reported liking for cocaine and the magnitude of the drug effect in a laboratory study of cocaine's subjective effects (Walsh et al. 1994). In another laboratory study (M. Mayr, unpublished data, 1998), fluoxetine did not decrease cocaine use and appeared to have some cardiovascular toxicity in combination with cocaine. Clinical trials also provide little evidence for the effectiveness of fluoxetine in treating cocaine abuse (Grabowski et al. 1995).

## Final Comment

Cocaine and amphetamine share a number of important features. Acutely, both drugs have similar discriminative stimulus effects, and repeated exposure results in sensitization to certain effects and tolerance to others, depending on the dosage and patterning of drug administration. Some important distinctions exist between cocaine and amphetamine. First, cocaine's effects are relatively short lasting, often resulting in a pattern of more frequent self-administration over a shorter time than is the case with amphetamine. Second, the neurochemical effects of cocaine and amphetamine are distinct, which may explain differences in their neuro-

toxicities. Cocaine inhibits the reuptake of dopamine, whereas amphetamine also promotes dopamine release. The enhancement of dopamine release renders amphetamine more neurotoxic to dopaminergic neurons than is cocaine.

The substantial advances in our understanding of the complex neuroadaptations following cocaine or amphetamine use have formed the basis for studies attempting to reverse or treat the consequences of chronic drug use with medications. The far-reaching effects of psychostimulant abuse on a range of neurochemical systems illustrate the difficulty of this task, because finding a compound that acts specifically is difficult. For example, NMDA antagonists appeared promising because they can block cocaine's reinforcing effects and cocaine sensitization. Yet other studies have shown that NMDA antagonists alone are reinforcing (Nestler and Aghajanian 1997), produce sensitization (Wolf et al. 1993), and impair associative learning (Stewart and Druhan 1993), suggesting that their effects may be problematic for the treatment of stimulant abuse. It is hoped that continued efforts at the preclinical level, combined with human laboratory investigations to detail prospective medications' mechanisms of action, will lead to an effective treatment for cocaine or methamphetamine abuse.

## References

Abekawa T, Ohmori T, Koyama T: Effects of repeated administration of a high dose of methamphetamine on dopamine and glutamate release in rat striatum and nucleus accumbens. Brain Res 643:276–281, 1994

Bergman J, Madras BK, Johnson SE, et al: Effects of cocaine and related drugs in nonhuman primates; III: self-administration by squirrel monkeys. J Pharmacol Exp Ther 251:150–155, 1989

Bergman J, Kamien JB, Spealman RD: Antagonism of cocaine self-administration by selective dopamine $D_1$ and $D_2$ antagonists. Behav Pharmacol 1:355–363, 1990

Boireau A, Bordier F, Dubedat P, et al: Methamphetamine and dopamine neurotoxicity: differential effects of agents interfering with glutamatergic transmission. Neurosci Lett 195:9–12, 1995

Caine SB, Koob GF: Effects of mesolimbic dopamine depletion on responding maintained by cocaine and food. J Exp Anal Behav 61:213–221, 1994

Cunningham KA, Paris JM, Goeders NE: Serotonin neurotransmission in cocaine sensitization. Ann N Y Acad Sci 654:117–127, 1992

Davis WM, Smith SG: Effect of haloperidol on (+)-amphetamine self-administration. J Pharm Pharmacol 27:540–542, 1975

de la Garza R, Johanson C-E: The discriminative stimulus properties of cocaine and d-amphetamine: the effects of three routes of administration. Pharmacol Biochem Behav 24:765–768, 1986

de Wit H, Wise RA: Blockade of cocaine reinforcement in rats with the dopamine receptor blocker pimozide, but not with the noradrenergic blockers phentolamine and phenoxybenzamine. Can J Psychiatry 31:195–203, 1977

DiChiara G: The role of dopamine in drug abuse viewed from the perspective of its role in motivation. Drug Alcohol Depend 38:95–137, 1995

Eisch AJ, O'Dell SJ, Marshall JF: Striatal and cortical NMDA receptors are altered by a neurotoxic regimen of methamphetamine. Synapse 22:217–225, 1996

Ellison G: Stimulant-induced psychosis, the dopamine theory of schizophrenia, and the habenula. Brain Res Rev 19:223–239, 1994

Emmett-Oglesby MW, Peltier RL, Depoortere RY, et al: Tolerance to self-administration of cocaine in rats: time-course and dose-response determination using a multi-dose method. Drug Alcohol Depend 32:247–256, 1993

Fischman MW, Johanson CE: Toward an integrated neurobehavioral approach, in Handbook of Experimental Pharmacology, Pharmacological Aspects of Drug Dependence: Toward an Integrated Neurobehavioral Approach. Edited by Schuster CR, Gust S, Kuhar MJ. Heidelberg, Germany, Springer-Verlag, 1996, pp 159–195

Fischman MW, Foltin RW, Nestadt G, et al: Effects of desipramine maintenance on cocaine self-administration by humans. J Pharmacol Exp Ther 253:760–770, 1990

Fleckenstein AE, Metzger RR, Wilkins DG, et al: Rapid and reversible effects of methamphetamine on dopamine transporters. J Pharmacol Exp Ther 282:834–838, 1997

Foltin RW, Fischman MW: Smoked and intravenous cocaine in humans: acute tolerance, cardiovascular and subjective effects. J Pharmacol Exp Ther 257:247–261, 1991a

Foltin RW, Fischman MW: Self-administration of cocaine by humans: choice between smoked and intravenous cocaine. J Pharmacol Exp Ther 261:841–849, 1991b

Foltin RW, Fischman MW: Effects of buprenorphine on the self-administration of cocaine by humans. Behav Pharmacol 5:79–89, 1994

Grabowski J, Rhoades H, Elk R, et al: Fluoxetine is ineffective for treatment of cocaine dependence or concurrent opiate and cocaine dependence: two placebo-controlled, double-blind trails. J Clin Psychopharmacol 15:163–174, 1995

Griffith JD, Cavanaugh J, Held J, et al: Dextro-amphetamine: evaluation of psychotomimetic properties in man. Arch Gen Psychol 26:97–100, 1972

Hammer RP Jr, Egilmez Y, Emmett-Oglesby MW: Neural mechanisms of tolerance to the effects of cocaine. Behav Brain Res 84:225–239, 1997

Haney M, Fischman MW, Foltin RW: Effects of pergolide on cocaine self-administration in men and women. Psychopharmacology 137:15–24, 1998

Haney M, Collins ED, Ward AS, et al: Effects of a selective dopamine D1 agonist (ABT-431) on smoked cocaine self-administration in humans. Psychopharmacology (in press)

Henry DJ, White FJ: Repeated cocaine administration causes persistent enhancement of $D_1$ dopamine receptor sensitivity within the rat nucleus accumbens. J Pharmacol Exp Ther 258:882–890, 1991

Henry DJ, White FJ: Electrophysiological correlates of psychomotor stimulant-induced sensitization, in The Neurobiology of Drug and Alcohol Addiction. Edited by Kalivas PW, Samson HH. New York, New York Academy of Sciences, 1992, pp 47–59

Hitri A, Casanova MF, Kleinman JE, et al: Fewer dopamine transporter receptors in the prefrontal cortex of cocaine users. Am J Psychiatry 151:1074–1076, 1994

Hotchkiss AJ, Gibb JW: Long-term effects of multiple doses of methamphetamine on tryptophan hydroxylase and tyrosine hydroxylase activity on rat brain. J Pharmacol Exp Ther 214:257–262, 1980

Hurd YL, Weiss F, Koob GF, et al: The influence of cocaine self-administration on in vivo dopamine and acetylcholine neurotransmission in rat caudate-putamen. Neurosci Lett 109:227–233, 1990

Itzhak Y: Modulation of cocaine- and methamphetamine-induced behavioral sensitization by inhibition of brain nitric oxide synthase. J Pharmacol Exp Ther 282:521–527, 1997

Jaber M, Jones S, Giros B, et al: The dopamine transporter: a crucial component regulating dopamine transmission. Mov Disord 12:629–633, 1997

Jackson JG: Hazards of smokable methamphetamine (letter). New Engl J Med 321:907, 1989

Johanson CE, Fischman MW: The pharmacology of cocaine related to its abuse. Pharmacol Rev 41:3–52, 1989

Johnson M, Hanson GR, Gibb JW: Effect of MK-801 on decrease in tryptophan hydroxylase induced by methamphetamine and its methylenedioxy analog. Eur J Pharmacol 165:315–318, 1989

Kalivas PW, Duffy P: Time course of extracellular dopamine and behavioral sensitization to cocaine, I: dopamine axon terminals. J Neurosci 13:266–275, 1993

Katz JL, Griffiths JW, Sharpe LG, et al: Cocaine tolerance and cross-tolerance. J Pharmacol Exp Ther 264:183–192, 1993

King GR, Xiong Z, Ellinwood EH Jr: Blockade of cocaine sensitization and tolerance by the co-administration of odansetron, a 5-HT$_3$ receptor antagonist, and cocaine. Psychopharmacology 130:159–165, 1997

Kleber HD: Pharmacotherapy, current and potential, for the treatment of cocaine dependence. Clin Neuropharmacol 18:S96–S109, 1995

Kleven MS, Woolverton WL: Effects of three monoamine uptake inhibitors on behavior maintained by cocaine or food presentation in rhesus monkeys. Drug Alcohol Depend 31:149–158, 1993

Klitenick MA, Dewitte P, Kalivas PW: Regulation of somatodendritic dopamine release in the ventral tegmental area by opioids and GABA: an in vivo microdialysis study. J Neurosci 12:2623–2632, 1992

Koe BK: Molecular geometry of inhibitors of the uptake of catecholamines and serotonin in synaptosomal preparations of rat brain. J Pharmacol Exp Ther 199:649–661, 1976

Koob GF, Bloom FE: Cellular and molecular mechanisms of drug dependence. Science 242:715–723, 1988

Kranzler HR, Bauer LO: Bromocriptine and cocaine cue reactivity in cocaine-dependent patients. Br J Addict 87:1537–1548, 1992

Kuczenski R, Segal DS, Cho AK, et al: Hippocampus norepinephrine, caudate dopamine and serotonin, and behavioral responses to the stereoisomers of amphetamine and methamphetamine. Neuroscience 15:1308–1317, 1995

Leccese AP, Lyness WH: The effects of putative 5-hydroxytryptamine receptor active agents on *d*-amphetamine self-administration in controls and rats with 5,7-dihydroxytryptamine median forebrain bundle lesions. Brain Res 303:153–162, 1984

Levin FR, McDowell DM, Evans SM, et al: Pergolide mesylate for cocaine abuse: a controlled preliminary trial. American Journal on Addictions (in press)

Lyness WH, Friedle NM, Moore KE: Destruction of dopaminergic nerve terminals in nucleus accumbens: effect on *d*-amphetamine self-administration. Pharmacol Biochem Behav 11:553–556, 1979

Majewska MD: Cocaine addiction as a disorder: implications for treatment, in Neurotoxicity and Neuropathology Associated With Cocaine Abuse (NIDA Res Monogr 163). Edited by Majewska MD. Rockville, MD, National Institute on Drug Abuse, 1996, pp 1–27

Martin WR, Sloan JW, Sapira JD, et al: Physiologic, subjective and behavioral effects of amphetamine, ephedrine, phenmetrazine, and methylphenidate in man. Clin Pharmacol Ther 12:245–258, 1971

Melega WP, Raleigh MJ, Stout DB, et al: Recovery of striatal dopamine function after acute amphetamine- and methamphetamine-induced neurotoxicity in the vervet monkey. Brain Res 766:113–120, 1997

Mello NK, Mendelson JH, Bree MP, et al: Buprenorphine and naltrexone effects on cocaine self-administration by rhesus monkeys. J Pharmacol Exp Ther 254:926–939, 1990

Nash JF, Yamamoto BK: Methamphetamine neurotoxicity and striatal glutamate release: comparison to 3,4-methylenedioxymethamphetamine. Brain Res 581:237–243, 1992

National Drug Control Strategy: 1997. Washington, DC, U.S. Government Printing Office, 1997

Nestler JE, Aghajanian GK: Molecular and cellular basis of addiction. Science 278:58–63, 1997

O'Dell SJ, Weihmuller FB, Marshall JF: Multiple methamphetamine injections induce marked increases in extracellular striatal dopamine which correlate with subsequent neurotoxicity. Brain Res 564:256–260, 1991

Ohmori T, Abekawa T, Koyama T: The role of glutamate in behavioral and neurotoxic effects of methamphetamine. Neurochem Int 29:301–307, 1996

Pap A, Bradberry CW: Excitatory amino acid antagonists attenuate the effects of cocaine on extracellular dopamine in the nucleus accumbens. J Pharmacol Exp Ther 274:127–133, 1995

Pearce B: Methamphetamine: Findings From the Literature and Various Data Sets. Rockville, MD, T. Head & Company, 1993

Peltier RL, Schenk S: GR38032F, a serotonin 5-HT3 antagonist, fails to alter cocaine self-administration in rats. Pharmacol Biochem Behav 39:133–136, 1991

Pettit HO, Justice JB Jr: Effect of dose on cocaine self-administration behavior and dopamine levels in the nucleus accumbens. Brain Res 539:94–102, 1991

Piazza PV, Deminiere JM, Le Moal M, et al: Factors that predict individual vulnerability to amphetamine self-administration. Science 245:1511–1513, 1989

Post RM, Kopanda RT: Cocaine, kindling and psychosis. Am J Psychiatry 133:627–634, 1976

Preston KL, Sullivan JT, Strain EC, et al: Effects of cocaine alone and in combination with bromocriptine in human cocaine abusers. J Pharmacol Exp Ther 262:279–291, 1992

Pu C, Fisher EJ, Cappon GD, et al: The effects of amfonelic acid, a dopamine uptake inhibitor, on methamphetamine-induced dopaminergic terminal degeneration and astrocytic in rat striatum. Brain Res 649:217–224, 1994

Pudiak CM, Bozarth MA: L-NAME and MK-801 attenuate sensitization to the locomotor-stimulating effect of cocaine. Life Sci 53:1517–1521, 1993

Richardson NR, Piercey MF, Svensson K, et al: Antagonism of cocaine self-administration by the preferential dopamine autoreceptor antagonist, (+)-AJ 76. Brain Res 619:15–21, 1993

Ritz MC, Lamb RJ, Goldberg SR, et al: Cocaine receptors on dopamine transporters are related to self-administration of cocaine. Science 237:1219–1223, 1987

Roberts DCS, Corcoran ME, Fibiger HC: On the role of ascending catecholaminergic systems in intravenous self-administration of cocaine. Pharmacol Biochem Behav 6:615–620, 1977

Roberts DCS, Andrews MM, Vickers GJ: Baclofen attenuates the reinforcing effects of cocaine in rats. Neuropsychopharmacology 15:417–423, 1996

Robinson TE, Becker JB: Enduring changes in brain and behavior produced by chronic amphetamine administration: a review and evaluation of animal models of amphetamine psychosis. Brain Res Rev 11:157–198, 1986

Robinson TE, Berridge KC: The neural basis of drug craving: an incentive-sensitization theory of addiction. Brain Res Rev 18:247–291, 1993

Robinson TE, Camp DM: Long-lasting effects of escalating doses of d-amphetamine on brain monoamines, amphetamine-induced stereotyped behavior and spontaneous nocturnal locomotion. Pharmacol Biochem Behav 26:821–827, 1987

Robinson TE, Kolb B: Persistent structural modifications in nucleus accumbens and prefrontal cortex neurons produced by previous experience with amphetamine. J Neurosci 17:8491–8497, 1997

Robinson TE, Browman KE, Crombag HS, et al: Modulation of the induction or expression of psychostimulant sensitization by the circumstances surrounding drug administration. Neurosci Biobehav Rev 22:347–354, 1998

Ryan LJ, Martone ME, Linder JC, et al: Cocaine, in contrast to D-amphetamine, does not cause axonal degeneration in neostriatum and agranular frontal cortex of Long-Evans rats. Life Sci 43:1403–1409, 1988

Sarnyai Z, Bíró E, Babarczy E, et al: Oxytocin modulates behavioral adaptation to repeated treatment with cocaine in rats. Neuropharmacology 31:593–598, 1992

Satel SL, Southwick SM, Gawin FH: Clinical features of cocaine-induced paranoia. Am J Psychiatry 148:495–498, 1991

Sato M, Chen C-C, Akiyama K, et al: Acute exacerbation of paranoid psychotic state after long-term abstinence in patients with previous methamphetamine psychosis. Biol Psychiatry 18:429–440, 1983

Schenk S, Partridge B: Sensitization and tolerance in psychostimulant self-administration. Pharmacol Biochem Behav 57:543–550, 1997

Schenk S, Valadez A, McNamara C, et al: Development and expression of sensitization to cocaine's reinforcing properties: role of NMDA receptors. Psychopharmacology 111:332–338, 1993a

Schenk S, Valadez A, Worley CM, et al: Blockade of the acquisition of cocaine self-administration by the NMDA antagonist MK-801 (dizocilpine). Behav Pharmacol 4:652–659, 1993b

Schmidt CJ, Sonsalla PK, Hanson GR, et al: Methamphetamine-induced depression of monoamine synthesis in the rat: development of tolerance. J Neurochem 44:852–855, 1985

Schottenfeld RS, Pakes JR, Oliverto A, et al: Buprenorphine vs methadone maintenance treatment for concurrent opioid dependence and cocaine abuse. Arch Gen Psychiatry 54:713–720, 1997

Segal DS, Kuczenski R, Florin SM: Does dizocilpine (MK-801) selectively block the enhanced responsiveness to repeated amphetamine administration? Behav Neurosci 109:532–546, 1995

Seiden LS, Sabol KE: Methamphetamine and methylenedioxymethamphetamine neurotoxicity: possible mechanisms of cell destruction, in Neurotoxicity and Neuropathology Associated With Cocaine Abuse (NIDA Res Monogr 163). Edited by Majewska MD. Rockville, MD, National Institute on Drug Abuse, 1996, pp 251–276

Self DW, Barnhart WJ, Lehman DA, et al: Opposite modulation of cocaine-seeking behavior by $D_1$- and $D_2$-like dopamine receptor agonists. Science 271:1586–1589, 1996

Staley JK, Talbot JZ, Ciliax J, et al: Radioligand binding and immunoautoradiographic evidence for a lack of toxicity to dopaminergic nerve terminals in human cocaine overdose victims. Brain Res 747:219–229, 1997

Stewart J, Druhan JP: Development of both conditioning and sensitization to behavioral activating effects of amphetamine is blocked by the non-competitive NMDA receptor antagonist MK-801. Psychopharmacology 110:125–132, 1993

Stewart J, Vezina P: Microinjections of SCH-23390 into the ventral tegmental area and substantia nigra pars reticulata attenuate the development of sensitization to the locomotor activating effects of systemic amphetamine. Brain Res 495:401–406, 1989

Toyoshi T, Ukai M, Kameyama T: Opioid receptor agonists selective for μ and κ receptors attenuate methamphetamine-induced behavioral sensitization in the mouse. Biol Pharm Bull 19:369–374, 1996

Trinkoff AM, Ritter C, Anthony JC: The prevalence and self-reported consequences of cocaine use: an exploratory and descriptive analysis. Drug Alcohol Depend 26:217–225, 1990

Ujike H, Kanzaki A, Okumura K, et al: Sigma (σ) antagonist BMY 14802 prevents methamphetamine-induced sensitization. Life Sci 50:PL129–PL134, 1992

Ujike H, Kuroda S, Otsuki S: Receptor antagonists block the development of sensitization to cocaine. Eur J Pharmacol 296:123–128, 1996

Volkow ND, Fowler JS, Wolf AP, et al: Effects of chronic cocaine abuse on postsynaptic dopamine receptors. Am J Psychiatry 147:719–724, 1990

Volkow ND, Wang GJ, Fischman MW, et al: Relationship between subjective effects of cocaine and dopamine transporter occupancy. Nature 386:827–839, 1997

Wagner GC, Carelli RM, Jarvis MF: Ascorbate acid reduces the dopamine depletion induced by methamphetamine and the 1-methyl-4-phenyl pyridinium ion. Neuropharmacology 25:559–561, 1986

Walsh SL, Preston KL, Sullivan JT, et al: Fluoxetine alters the effects of intravenous cocaine in humans. J Clin Psychopharmacol 14:396–407, 1994

Ward AS, Haney M, Fischman MW, et al: Binge cocaine self-administration in humans: intravenous cocaine. Psychopharmacology 132:375–381, 1997

White FJ, Hu X-T, Zhang X-F, et al: Repeated administration of cocaine or amphetamine alters neuronal responses to glutamate in the mesoaccumbens dopamine system. J Pharmacol Exp Ther 273:445–454, 1995

Wilson JM, Kalasinsky KS, Levey AI, et al: Striatal dopamine nerve terminal markers in human, chronic methamphetamine users. Nat Med 2:699–703, 1996

Wise RA, Munn E: Withdrawal from chronic amphetamine elevates baseline intracranial self-stimulation thresholds. Psychopharmacology 117:130–136, 1995

Wise RA, Newton P, Leeb K, et al: Fluctuations in nucleus accumbens dopamine concentration during intravenous cocaine self-administration in rats. Psychopharmacology 120:10–20, 1995

Wolf ME, White FJ, Hu X-T: Behavioral sensitization to MK-801 (dizocilipine): neurochemical and electrophysiological correlates in the mesoaccumbens dopamine system. Behav Pharmacol 4:429–442, 1993

Wolf ME, White FJ, Hu XT: MK-801 prevents alterations in the mesoaccumbens dopamine system associated with behavioral sensitization to amphetamine. J Neurosci 14:1735–1745, 1994

Woolverton WL, Ricaurte GA, Forno LS, et al: Long-term effects of chronic methadone administration in rhesus monkeys. Brain Res 486:73–78, 1989

Yokoo H, Yamada S, Yoshida M, et al: Effect of opioid peptides on dopamine release from nucleus accumbens after repeated treatment with methamphetamine. Eur J Pharmacol 256:335–338, 1994

Zhang XF, Hu XT, White FJ, et al: Increased responsiveness of ventral tegmental area dopamine neurons to glutamate after repeated administration of cocaine or amphetamine is transient and selectively involves AMPA receptors. J Pharmacol Exp Ther 281:699–706, 1997

# 4

# Neurobiology of Hallucinogens

## Richard A. Glennon, Ph.D.

Hallucinogenic agents represent an old and very large class of drugs. Nearly every major civilization throughout history has had a preferred drug of abuse, and in many instances these agents were hallucinogens or hallucinogen-related agents or plant products. What constitutes a hallucinogen? Various agents can produce hallucinogenic episodes, and terms used to describe such agents include *hallucinogens, psychotomimetics, psychedelics, inebriants,* and *intoxicants.* Many agents have been included in this general class of psychoactive agents. Do agents as structurally diverse as (+)lysergic acid diethylamide (LSD), phencyclidine (PCP, Angel Dust), tetrahydrocannabinol (THC; a constituent of marijuana), amphetamine, and mescaline all produce the same (or a common) effect? Do they all work via a common pharmacological mechanism? Studies over the past several decades suggest that they do not. Hollister wrote that "one can scarcely get any agreement upon the term used to describe this class of drugs" (1968, p. 18). How, then, do we define *hallucinogen?* Hollister (1968) attempted to define these agents on the basis of their pharmacological effects:

- In proportion to other effects, changes in thought, perception, and mood should predominate.
- Intellectual or memory impairment should be minimal at dosages that produce the above effects.
- Stupor, narcosis, or excessive stimulation should not be an integral effect.
- Autonomic nervous system side effects should be neither disabling nor severely disconcerting.
- Addictive craving should be minimal.

Although these criteria allowed the classification of certain agents by a process of elimination, they still al-

lowed inclusion of a rather wide variety of pharmacologically distinct agents. Hallucinogenic agents do not appear to represent a behaviorally homogeneous class of agents. Evidence indicates that agents once included in the single general category of hallucinogenic/ psychotomimetic agents should be further subclassified. For example, psychotomimetic PCP-related agents likely produce many of their actions via interaction at PCP receptors, cannabinoid receptors may account for some of the actions of various cannabinoids, and amphetamine psychosis likely involves dopaminergic receptors. Many agents remain, and none of the previously mentioned categories would accommodate hallucinogens such as LSD or mescaline. The term *classical hallucinogen* has evolved to account for some of these agents (Glennon 1998; Lin and Glennon 1994).

## Classical Hallucinogens: Classification

Although no formal definition has been provided for the classical hallucinogens, perhaps the best working definition is an agent that meets the Hollister criteria and that 1) binds at serotonin type 2 receptors ($5\text{-HT}_2$) and 2) is recognized by animals trained to discriminate 1-(2,5-dimethoxy-4-methylphenyl)-2-aminopropane (DOM) from nondrug, or vehicle, in tests of stimulus generalization (Glennon 1996). These criteria may account for many of the remaining agents.

Although a significant amount of human data are available (Brimblecombe and Pinder 1975; Hoffer and Osmond 1967; Jacob and Shulgin 1994; Lin and Glennon 1994; Shulgin and Shulgin 1991; Siva Sankar 1975), many putative hallucinogens have been poorly investigated in humans, if at all. Some results are from animal studies; however, no reliable animal model of hallucinogenic activity has been developed (Glennon 1992). As a result, animal data must be interpreted cautiously.

Nevertheless, a procedure that has become widely accepted for classifying centrally acting agents is the *drug discrimination paradigm*, usually with rats, pigeons, or monkeys as test subjects (Glennon 1994). Using a typical operant behavior paradigm, researchers can train animals to respond in one manner (e.g., to press one of two levers) under a given set of conditions and to respond in a different manner (e.g., to press the opposite of the two levers) under a different set of conditions. Thus animals can be reliably trained to discriminate administration of a centrally acting agent from vehicle. Typically, the drug stimulus is reliable, robust, and replicable from laboratory to laboratory.

Once animals are trained to discriminate a given training drug from vehicle, several types of studies can be conducted. Two of the most useful and widely used studies are tests of stimulus generalization and tests of stimulus antagonism. In the former, challenge drugs are administered intermittently to the trained animals to determine whether the agents produce stimulus effects similar to those of the training drug. Results are both qualitative and quantitative; that is, the method allows classification of the type of action produced and also provides information about the potency of the challenge drugs relative to the training drug. In tests of

stimulus antagonism, the training drug's mechanism of action can be explored by attempting to antagonize the stimulus effects of the drug with various neurotransmitter antagonists. Although such studies are not limited to the investigation of hallucinogenic agents and have been used more for the investigation of nonhallucinogens than for hallucinogens, they have provided a wealth of information regarding the classification and mechanism of action of hallucinogenic agents. Furthermore, results obtained from such studies can be compared with results of human studies in which data are available to corroborate the findings.

The strength of the drug discrimination paradigm is that stimulus generalization does not occur between agents that do not produce common stimulus effects. For example, animals trained to discriminate (+)LSD do not recognize PCP or THC, animals trained to discriminate (+)amphetamine do not recognize mescaline, and so on. Using this procedure, several classical hallucinogens have been used as training drugs, including (+)LSD, DOM, mescaline, and 5-methoxy-*N,N*-dimethyltryptamine (Glennon 1996). Moreover, animals trained to one of these agents recognize each of the other agents, further attesting to the similarity of their stimulus effects. Several hundred agents have been examined in rats trained to discriminate DOM from vehicle, and this has aided their classification. Table 4–1 shows categories and examples of classical hallucinogens. Figure 4–1 shows chemical structures of

**Table 4–1.**    Categories and examples of classical hallucinogens

| Category | Subcategory | Examples |
|---|---|---|
| Indolealkylamines | Tryptamines | *N,N*-Dimethyltryptamine (DMT) |
| | | *N,N*-Diethyltryptamine (DET) |
| | | 4-Hydroxy-DMT (Psilocin) |
| | | 5-Methoxy-DMT |
| | α-Alkyltryptamines | α-Methyltryptamine (α-MeT) |
| | | 5-Methoxy-α-MeT |
| | Lysergamides | Lysergic acid diethylamide (LSD) |
| | β-Carbolines | Harmaline |
| Phenylalkylamines | Phenylethylamines | Mescaline |
| | | 2-(4-Bromo-2,5-dimethoxyphenyl)-1-aminoethane (Nexus) |
| | Phenylisopropylamines | α-Methylmescaline (3,4,5-TMA) |
| | | 1-(2,5-Dimethoxy-4-methylphenyl)-2-aminopropane (DOM) |
| | | 1-(4-Bromo-2,5-dimethoxyphenyl)-2-aminopropane (DOB) |
| | | 1-(2,5-Dimethoxy-4-iodophenyl)-2-aminopropane (DOI) |
| | | 1-(3,4-Methylenedioxyphenyl)-2-aminopropane (MDA; Love Drug) |

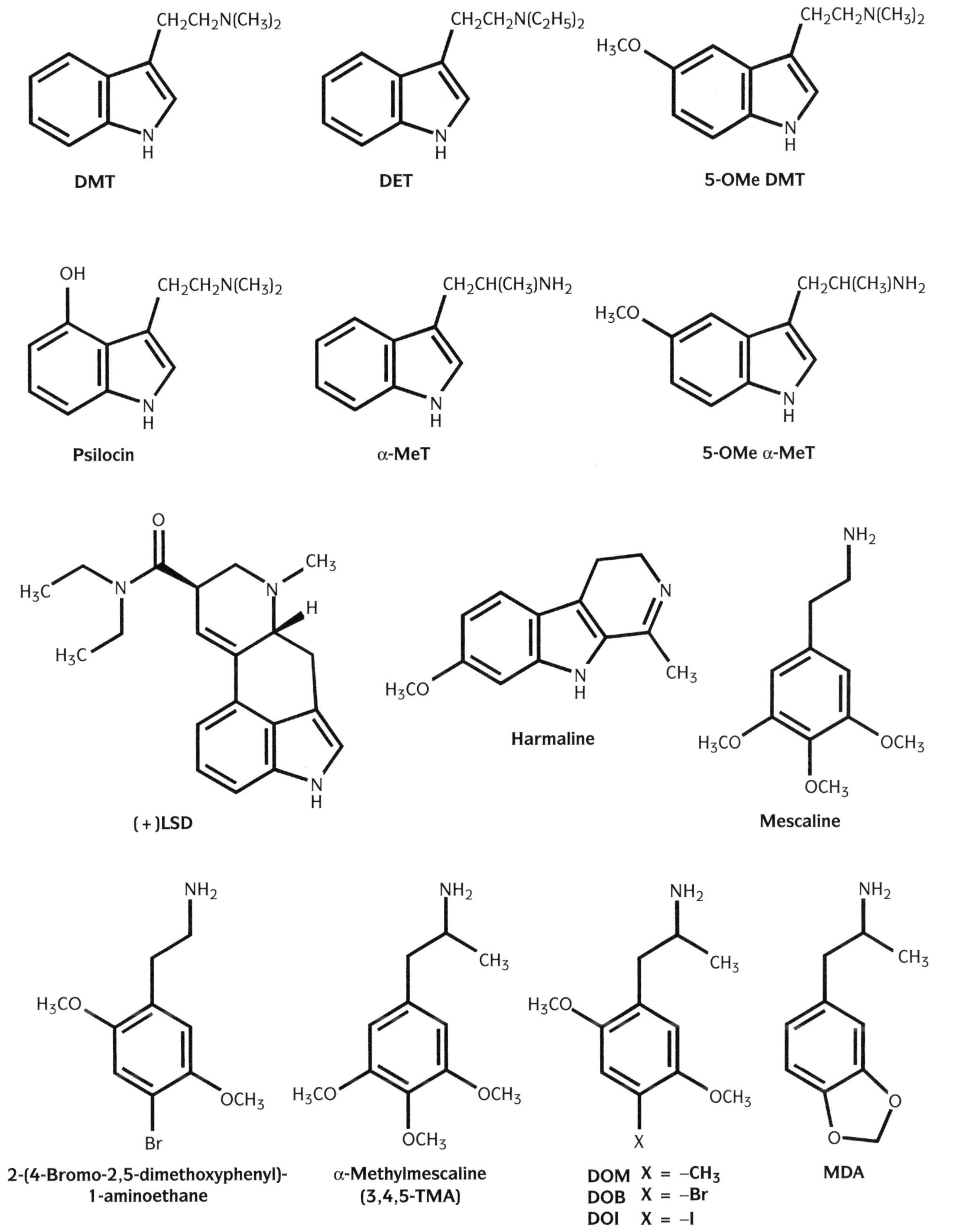

**Figure 4–1.** Structures of examples of hallucinogenic agents listed in Table 4–1.

selected examples. The agents in Table 4–1 seem to share a common component of action in that they are recognized by DOM-trained animals.

## Classical Hallucinogens: Mechanism of Action

Tests of stimulus antagonism have been conducted with various neurotransmitter antagonists. Researchers have shown that serotonin antagonists can antagonize the effects of hallucinogens. Ketanserin, pirenperone, and other antagonists with affinity for a particular population of serotonin receptors (i.e., 5-HT$_2$ receptors) are the most effective in blocking the stimulus effects of the classical hallucinogens, leading to the concept that classical hallucinogens may act as 5-HT$_2$ agonists. Subsequently, the 5-HT$_2$ receptor affinities of various hallucinogens were measured, and a significant correlation was found between any two of the following parameters: 1) drug discrimination–derived potencies, 2) human hallucinogenic potencies, and 3) 5-HT$_2$ receptor affinities. It would appear, then, that hallucinogens act as 5-HT$_2$ receptor agonists. This theory has become known as the *5-HT$_2$ hypothesis of classical hallucinogen action* (Glennon 1994). This hypothesis does not preclude a role for other populations of receptors in the actions of hallucinogens. Indeed, hallucinogens can display widely varying binding profiles. Nevertheless, 5-HT$_2$ receptor affinity is the one feature that all classical hallucinogens have in common.

Three populations of 5-HT$_2$ receptors (5-HT$_{2A}$, 5-HT$_{2B}$, and 5-HT$_{2C}$) have been identified since the 5-HT$_2$ hypothesis was proposed. Although hallucinogens bind at all three subpopulations (Nelson et al. 1994), work from several laboratories suggests that hallucinogens may act primarily via a 5-HT$_{2A}$ mechanism (Fiorella et al. 1995; Ismaiel et al. 1993; Schreiber et al. 1994).

## Hallucinogen-Related Designer Drugs

*Designer drugs*, or controlled substance analogs, are structural variants of known drugs of abuse. For example, the designer drug Nexus (see Table 4–1) is a mescaline-like analog of DOB [1-(4-bromo-2,5-dimethoxyphenyl)-2-aminopropane] and is a hallucinogen. The phenylisopropylamines (PIAs) represent one of the largest categories of hallucinogens, and a wealth of human data are available about them (Shulgin and

Shulgin 1991). Amphetamine, a nonhallucinogen central stimulant that can produce hallucinations (called *amphetamine psychosis*) upon chronic administration of high dosages, is also a PIA, and some PIAs are amphetamine-like central stimulants rather than hallucinogens. Methcathinone is an example of a designer drug with stimulant activity. Other PIAs produce an empathogenic effects (i.e., increased empathy, talkativeness, and openness); and an agent with this activity is the N-methyl analog of MDA (i.e., MDMA; "XTC," "Ecstasy") (Nichols and Oberlender 1989). Thus minor structural alterations of a PIA can result in agents with central stimulant, hallucinogenic, or other actions (see Figure 4–2). A PIA might have more than one such action depending on its specific chemical structure, which may explain the difficulty in classifying various PIAs with respect to their observed clinical effects (Glennon et al. 1997). This possibility may also explain why certain PIAs are self-administered by animals, whereas others are not. Such a classification scheme may also extend to indolealkylamine hallucinogens.

## Summary

Hallucinogens/psychotomimetics represent a diverse group of agents that are perhaps best understood by subdividing them into several categories (e.g., PCP-like psychotomimetics, cannabinoids, cholinergic hallucino-

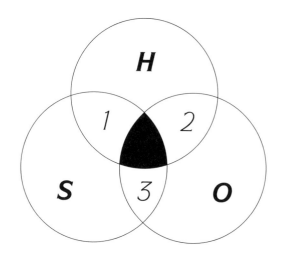

**Figure 4–2.**    Venn diagram representing possible overlapping activities or behavioral similarities among the psychoactive phenylisopropylamines. H = hallucinogenic, S = central stimulant, and O = other activity. The agent (±)MDA seems to represent the common (shaded) intersect in that it produces all three actions. See Glennon et al. (1997) for further discussion.

gens). The agents that generally come to mind when one hears the term *hallucinogen,* such as LSD and mescaline, may be best termed *classical hallucinogens.* Although the agents in this class do not necessarily produce identical effects, they do seem to produce a common effect that may represent the activation of $5\text{-HT}_2$ receptors in the brain. Structural modification of these agents modulates their potency and action. That is, certain classical hallucinogens may produce central stimulant and other actions in addition to their hallucinogenic effects, and these effects may need to be considered when addressing or treating hallucinogen abuse.

## References

Brimblecombe RW, Pinder RM: Hallucinogenic Agents. Bristol, England, Wright-Scientechnica, 1975

Fiorella D, Rabin RA, Winter JC: The role of $5\text{-HT}_{2A}$ and $5\text{-HT}_{2C}$ receptors in the stimulus effects of hallucinogenic drugs, I: antagonist correlation analysis. Psychopharmacology 121:347–356, 1995

Glennon RA: Animal models for assessing classical hallucinogens, in Animal Models for the Assessment of Psychoactive Drugs. Edited by Boulton AA, Baker GB, Wu PH. Clifton, NJ, Humana Press, 1992, pp 345–381

Glennon RA: Classical hallucinogens: an introductory overview, in Hallucinogens: An Update. Edited by Lin GC, Glennon RA. Washington DC, U.S. Department of Health and Human Services, 1994, pp 4–32

Glennon RA: Classical hallucinogens, in Pharmacological Aspects of Drug Dependence. Edited by Schuster CR, Kuhar MJ. Berlin, Germany, Springer, 1996, pp 343–372

Glennon RA: Hallucinogens: pharmacology, in Sourcebook on Substance Use and Abuse. Edited by Tarter RE, Ammerman RT, Ott PJ. Needham, MA, Allyn & Bacon, 1998, pp 217–227

Glennon RA, Young R, Dukat M, et al: Initial characterization of PMMA as a discriminative stimulus. Pharmacol Biochem Behav 57:151–158, 1997

Hoffer A, Osmond H: The Hallucinogens. New York, Academic Press, 1967

Hollister LE: Chemical Psychoses. Springfield, IL, Charles C Thomas, 1968

Ismaiel AM, De Los Angeles J, Teitler M, et al: Antagonism of the 1-(2,5-dimethoxy-4-methylphenyl)-2-aminopropane stimulus with a newly identified $5\text{-HT}_2$- versus $5\text{-HT}_{1C}$-selective antagonist. J Med Chem 36:2519–2525, 1993

Jacob P III, Shulgin AT: Structure-activity relationships of the classical hallucinogens and their analogs, in Hallucinogens: An Update. Edited by Lin GC, Glennon RA. Washington, DC, U.S. Department of Health and Human Services, 1994, pp 74–91

Lin GC, Glennon RA (eds): Hallucinogens: An Update. Washington, DC, U.S. Department of Health and Human Services, 1994

Nelson DL, Glennon RA, Wainscott DB: Comparison of the affinities of hallucinogenic phenylalkylamines at the cloned human $5\text{-HT}_{2A,\ 2B}$ and $_{2C}$ receptors (Abstract No 120). Paper presented at the 3rd IUPHAR Satellite Meeting on Serotonin, Chicago, IL, July 30–August 3, 1994, p 116

Nichols DE, Oberlender R: Structure-activity relationships of MDMA-like substances, in Pharmacology and Toxicology of Amphetamine and Related Designer Drugs. Edited by Ashgar K, De Souza EB. Washington, DC, U.S. Government Printing Office, 1989, pp 1–29

Schreiber R, Brocco M, Millan MJ: Blockade of the discriminative stimulus effects of DOI by MDL 100,907, and the atypical antipsychotics clozapine and risperidone. Eur J Pharmacol 264:99–102, 1994

Shulgin A, Shulgin A: Pihkal. Berkeley, CA, Transform Press, 1991

Siva Sankar DV: LSD—A Total Study. Westbury, NY, PJD Publications, 1975

# Chapter 5

# Neurobiology of Marijuana

Billy R. Martin, Ph.D.

Marijuana, the common name for the plant *Cannabis sativa*, is the most widely used illicit drug today; it has been used for centuries for its therapeutic and its mood-altering properties. Marijuana has prominent effects on the central nervous system (CNS) and has numerous peripheral effects. Acutely, marijuana produces an altered state of consciousness characterized by mild euphoria, relaxation, perceptual alterations including time distortion, and the enhancement of ordinary sensory experiences (Hall et al. 1994). Cognitive effects such as impaired short-term memory are also marked. Motor skills and reaction time are also impaired, so that various types of skilled activities are frequently disrupted (Hall et al. 1994). The cannabinoids have several potential therapeutic effects, including antiemesis, analgesia, anticonvulsant action, and lowered intraocular pressure (Hollister 1986).

The positive identification of $\Delta^9$-tetrahydrocannabinol (THC) as the psychoactive constituent in marijuana provided the first significant breakthrough in the systematic pharmacological evaluation of the cannabinoids. The structural elucidation of THC and its availability to the scientific community came at a propitious time in that recreational use of marijuana peaked during the early 1970s. The sudden emergence of marijuana as a major substance of abuse was accompanied by intense interest in understanding the mechanism by which it produced its centrally mediated effects and, more important, the biological consequences of its acute and chronic use.

Early attempts to define the neurobiological actions of cannabinoids were fraught with difficulties. First, few cannabinoids were available as investigational probes. As a result, almost all research was based on the actions of $\Delta^9$-THC, $\Delta^8$-THC, cannabinol (CBN), and cannabidiol (CBD). Both $\Delta^8$-THC and CBN were pharmacologically similar to but slightly less potent than $\Delta^9$-THC, whereas CBD was used as the negative control because of its lack of cannabinoid activity. The high water-insolubility of cannabinoids made it difficult to conduct in vivo and in vitro experiments. It became apparent that high concentrations of THC were effective in altering numerous biochemical processes in vitro (Martin 1986). The difficulty arose in attempts to establish the pharmacological relevance of these findings. Because THC affected a wide range of biochemical processes, from enzymatic activity to neurotransmitter uptake, and because relatively high concentrations of THC were required, researchers continued to speculate that cannabinoids produced at least some of their actions through nonselective perturbation of membranes. However, progress during the past 10–15 years has clarified the existence of an endogenous cannabinoid system that includes specific receptors, signal transduction systems, and endogenous ligands.

## Receptors

One of the first indications of receptor involvement in drug action is often enantioselectivity and/or structure-activity relationships. Even the earliest research provided strong indications of structural requirements for cannabinoid activity before Edery et al. (1971) described the influence of systematic alteration of THC structure. Initial studies revealed rather low enantioselectivity, which Mechoulam et al. (1991) attributed to low purity of THC. The synthesis of potent THC derivatives that could be crystallized led to the isolation of highly pure stereoisomers that were highly enantioselective in vivo (Little et al. 1989). Extensive structure-activity relationship studies have shown that subtle structural alterations in the THC molecule have profound effects on its pharmacological potency (Razdan 1986).

The development of novel synthetic analogs of $\Delta^9$-THC played a major role in the characterization and cloning of the cannabinoid $CB_1$ receptor. One of these analogs was CP 55,940, a highly potent cannabinoid agonist that when radiolabeled was used to characterize cannabinoid-binding sites in the brain (Devane et al. 1988). These sites exhibit high affinity for cannabinoids but not for the other centrally active compounds. These binding sites are also present in high quantities and are distributed widely throughout the brain (Herkenham et al. 1990). Receptor cloning proved the existence of this $CB_1$ receptor. The $CB_1$ receptor cDNA was isolated from a rat brain library by a homology screen for guanine nucleotide–binding protein (G protein)–coupled receptors, and its identity was confirmed by transfecting the clone into CHO cells and demonstrating cannabinoid-mediated inhibition of adenylyl cyclase (Matsuda et al. 1990). Initial identification of the ligand for this *orphan receptor* involved the screening of many candidate ligands, including opioids, neurotensin, angiotensin, substance P, and neuropeptide Y, until cannabinoids were found to act via this molecule. The $CB_1$ receptor is a seven-transmembrane protein with characteristics similar to G protein–coupled receptors. Gérard et al. (1991) isolated a human $CB_1$ receptor cDNA. The rat and human receptors are highly conserved, with 93% identity at the nucleic acid level and 97% at the amino acid level.

A second cannabinoid receptor clone, $CB_2$, which has a different sequence but a similar binding profile to the $CB_1$ clone, was discovered by a polymerase chain reaction–based strategy designed to isolate G protein–coupled receptors in differentiated myeloid cells (Munro et al. 1993). The $CB_2$ receptor, which has been found in the spleen and in the cells of the immune system, has 44% amino acid identity with the brain clone and thus represents a receptor subtype. The affinities for several cannabinoids are comparable to the brain receptor, with the exception of CBN, which is only weakly cannabimimetic and binds the brain receptor with 10-fold less affinity than THC, yet CBN and $\Delta^9$-THC have similar affinities for the expressed $CB_2$ receptor. Several analogs have been developed that have some selectivity for $CB_1$ and $CB_2$ receptors (Showalter et al. 1996). The most notable examples are the $CB_2$-selective analogs that lack a phenolic hydroxyl group and an aminoalkylindole derivative (Showalter et al. 1996).

Although the $CB_2$ receptor appears to be localized exclusively in the periphery (based on its presence in the spleen), in hematopoietic cell lines (Munro et al. 1993), and in mast cells (Facci et al. 1995), evidence indicates that mRNA for the $CB_2$ receptor is present in the brain.

## Signal Transduction

The primary candidate for a cannabinoid second messenger has been cyclic adenosine monophosphate (cAMP). Considerable effort has been devoted to establishing cAMP's role in mediating the effects of THC (for reviews, see Childers et al. 1992; Martin et al. 1994). The ability of a series of cannabinoid analogs to inhibit cAMP accumulation correlates with the analogs' affinity for cannabinoid-receptor binding (Howlett and Fleming 1984; Matsuda et al. 1990). The identity of a cDNA clone as the cannabinoid receptor was confirmed by transfecting the clone into CHO cells and demonstrating cannabinoid-mediated inhibition of adenylyl cyclase (Matsuda et al. 1990). However, manipulation of adenylyl cyclase in vivo has not been very effective in modulating the effects of cannabinoids (Cook et al. 1995). In vivo studies are likely to be complicated by their inability to selectively alter adenylyl cyclase associated with the cannabinoid receptor and the receptor reserve. The report that ligand–cannabinoid receptor interactions result in G protein activation through measurement of the GTPγS binding provides additional evidence for adenylyl cyclase involvement (Selley et al. 1996). However, other researchers have demonstrated a G protein–mediated inhibition of calcium channels that was not cAMP dependent (Felder et al. 1993; Mackie and Hille 1992). When the $CB_2$ receptor was transfected into AtT20 cells, cannabinoid-mediated inhibition of adenylyl cyclase activity was conferred, but modulation of calcium or potassium channels was not (Felder et al. 1995).

Other possible second messenger systems for cannabinoids have been investigated. Prostaglandins may play a role in cannabinoid action, as cannabinoids can either stimulate or inhibit arachidonic acid release (Burstein 1987). However, definitive evidence that eicosanoids play a direct role in the actions of cannabinoids has been elusive. The identification of an arachidonic acid derivative as an endogenous cannabinoid ligand (discussed later in this chapter) has renewed interest in this area.

Cannabinoid agonists have effects on intracellular

calcium (Harris and Stokes 1982). In CHO cells, cannabinoid agonists induced a nonspecific release of intracellular calcium (Felder et al. 1995). Both the untransfected and the $CB_1$- and $CB_2$-transfected CHO cells were able to release calcium when both pharmacologically active and inactive cannabinoids were used as agonists. The authors concluded that transfected cannabinoid receptor clones do not mediate these effects. Rather, these effects are the result of non-receptor-mediated events.

Investigations of tertiary messenger systems for the cannabinoids have also been described. When administered to rats, the cannabinoid agonist CP 55,940 induced expression of the immediate early gene *krox*-24 in striosomes (Glass and Dragunow 1995). Stimulation of the $CB_1$ receptor also induced expression of *krox*-24 in human astrocytoma cells (Bouaboula et al. 1995). This effect appears to be receptor mediated in that it was blocked by the cannabinoid receptor antagonist carboximide hydrochloride (SR141716A). In addition, these researchers examined expression of several other immediate early genes and found that *jun*-B and *krox*-20 were also induced by cannabinoids, but c-*fos* was not. They showed that induction of *krox*-24 expression was mediated by a pertussis toxin–sensitive G protein but probably not via cAMP. Whether activation of the $CB_2$ receptor leads to induction of immediate early genes remains to be determined. These researchers provided further evidence that the $CB_1$ receptor is functionally linked to the mitogen-activated protein kinase cascade and postulated that this pathway provided the critical link between the $CB_1$ receptor and regulation of *krox*-24. Bouaboula et al. (1996) also reported that the signaling pathway associated with stimulation of the $CB_2$ receptor involves mitogen-activated protein kinase and induction of *krox*-24 expression.

## Endogenous Ligands

After definitive evidence for a cannabinoid receptor was found, identification of an endogenous ligand became a high priority. Devane et al. (1992) successfully isolated a substance from porcine brain that bound to the cannabinoid receptor and inhibited electrically stimulated contractions of murine vas deferens. The structure of this compound was established by mass spectrometry to be arachidonic acid ethanolamide and was named anandamide. The pharmacological properties of anandamide are consistent with its initial identification as an endogenous ligand for the cannabinoid receptor. Anandamide produces many of the same pharmacological effects as the classical cannabinoid ligands, including hypomotility, antinociception, catalepsy, and hypothermia (Fride and Mechoulam 1993; Smith et al. 1994). However, it is 4- to 20-fold less potent than $\Delta^9$-THC in producing these pharmacological effects, and it has a shorter duration of action. In addition, rats trained to discriminate between $\Delta^9$-THC and vehicle identified anandamide as $\Delta^9$-THC-like (Wiley et al. 1995a). Wickens and Pertwee (1993) reported similarities between $\Delta^9$-THC and anandamide in that both compounds enhanced the ability of muscimol to induce catalepsy when administered into the globus pallidus of rats. Other researchers have proposed that the nigrostriatal dopaminergic system is involved in the motor effects of $\Delta^9$-THC and anandamide (Romero et al. 1995).

Although this evidence provides ample support that anandamide produces cannabinoid effects, some differences exist between $\Delta^9$-THC and anandamide. For instance, $\kappa$ opioid antagonists block the spinal analgesic effects of $\Delta^9$-THC but not those of anandamide (Smith et al. 1994). In several instances, anandamide has failed to exert full agonist effects (Mechoulam and Fride 1995).

Anandamide's ability to bind to the brain cannabinoid receptor provided the first evidence that it was an endogenous ligand. Structure-activity relationship studies also led to the development of stable and potent anandamide analogs (Abadji et al. 1994; Adams et al. 1995). Anandamide binds to both the $CB_1$ and the $CB_2$ receptors, as has been demonstrated in membrane preparations from brain and in transfected cells. The initial study suggested that anandamide's affinity for the $CB_2$ receptor was considerably less than that for the $CB_1$ receptor (Munro et al. 1993), and subsequent studies have demonstrated that anandamide's affinity for the $CB_2$ receptor is approximately fourfold less than that for the $CB_1$ receptor in stably transfected cells.

The synthetic and degradative pathways for anandamide appear to be present in the CNS. The most plausible synthetic pathway involves phosphodiesterase-mediated cleavage of N-arachidonyl-phosphatidylethanolamine (Di Marzo et al. 1994). However, the stimulus that activates this synthetic process is unknown. Degradation occurs readily by hydrolytic cleavage to form arachidonic acid and ethanolamine, a process blocked by the enzyme inhibitor phenymethylsulfonyl fluoride (PMSF) (Deutsch and Chin 1993). Inactivation may also occur through a putative active reuptake mechanism (Beltramo et al. 1997).

Additionally, anandamide may only be representative of a family of endogenous compounds. Mechoulam et al. (1995) identified a monoglycerol derivative of arachidonic acid (2-arachidonyl glycerol), which they isolated from canine gut and found to have weak cannabinoid activity. This derivative binds to both the $CB_1$ and the $CB_2$ receptors, inhibits adenylyl cyclase activity in mouse splenocytes, and exhibits pharmacological effects similar to those of $\Delta^9$-THC.

## Functional Significance of the Endogenous System

### Relationship Between Pharmacological Effects and Receptor Activation

The fundamental question is, What role does this endogenous system play in the mediation of the central effects of cannabinoids? Devane et al. (1988) were the first to report that an excellent correlation exists between antinociceptive potency and $CB_1$ receptor affinity. Later, this correlation was extended to include a large number of cannabinoids and several behavioral measures, and the results revealed a high correlation between receptor affinity and in vivo potency in the mouse (Compton et al. 1993). An excellent correlation also exists between $CB_1$ receptor affinity and pharmacological activity in humans (Balster and Prescott 1992). Thus this receptor appears to mediate many of the known pharmacological effects of cannabinoids. No other cannabinoid receptor subtype has been identified in the brain.

### Cannabinoid Receptor Antagonist

The development of SR141716A provided an additional strategy for assessing receptor function (Rinaldi-Carmona et al. 1994). SR141716A antagonizes in a highly selective manner the inhibitory effects of cannabinoid receptor agonists on vas deferens contractions and adenylyl cyclase activity in mice. In vivo, SR141716A antagonizes the hypothermia, antinociception, catalepsy, and drug discrimination produced by cannabinoids (Rinaldi-Carmona et al. 1994; Wiley et al. 1995b).

### Receptor Distribution in Brain

The distribution of the cannabinoid receptor was carefully mapped in the rat brain (Herkenham et al. 1990).

The highest densities were found in the basal ganglia (substantia nigra pars reticulata, globus pallidus, entopeduncular nucleus, and lateral caudate putamen) and in the molecular layer of the cerebellum. Receptor localization in these regions most likely explains cannabinoid interference with movement. Intermediate levels of binding were found in the CA pyramidal cell layers of the hippocampus, the dentate gyrus, and layers I and VI of the cortex, observations consistent with $\Delta^9$-THC disruption of short-term memory in humans. Cannabinoid effects on memory and cognition are consistent with receptor localization in the hippocampus and cortex. The presence of cannabinoid receptors in regions associated with mediating brain reward (e.g., ventromedial striatum and nucleus accumbens) suggests an association with dopamine neurons. Sparse receptor levels were detected in the brain stem, hypothalamus, corpus callosum, and deep cerebellum nuclei. Low levels of receptors in brain stem areas controlling cardiovascular and respiratory functions is also consistent with the lack of lethality of marijuana. The $CB_2$ receptor is the most abundantly expressed cannabinoid receptor subtype in the immune system.

The high correlation between pharmacological potency and $CB_1$ receptor affinity, the isolation of an endogenous substance with cannabinoid pharmacological properties, the antagonism of cannabinoid effects by a selective $CB_1$ antagonist, and the discrete localization of receptors in the brain all point to a major role for the cannabinoid receptors in mediation of cannabinoid effects.

## Regulation of Receptor Expression

The $CB_1$ receptor is expressed as early as postnatal day 3 in rat brain; that is, $CB_1$ receptor mRNA and binding sites can be detected (McLaughlin and Abood 1993). Relative $CB_1$ mRNA expression increases steadily in the cerebellum and brain stem until postnatal days 18–21, whereas expression in the forebrain does not change (McLaughlin and Abood 1993). In addition to these studies using Northern blot analysis, in situ hybridization data also suggest that regional differences in the relative expression of $CB_1$ mRNA may parallel cerebellar proliferation and organization or may reflect unique tissue-specific expression of the cannabinoid receptor.

Cannabinoid receptor mRNA levels have been manipulated by several agents that influence CNS function. Adrenalectomy increased $CB_1$ mRNA levels in the striatum of rats, an effect that could be prevented with glucocorticoid treatment (Mailleux and Vanderhaeghen 1993b). This finding suggested glucocorticoid downregulation of cannabinoid receptor gene expression in the striatum. Studies in which unilateral 6-hydroxydopamine lesions were associated with an increase in mRNA levels in the ipsilateral side suggested a negative dopaminergic influence on $CB_1$ gene expression. Furthermore, treatment with dopamine receptor antagonists mimicked the effect (Mailleux and Vanderhaeghen 1993a). Previous experiments had documented the disappearance of CP 55,940 binding after ibotenic acid lesioning of the striatum but not after 6-hydroxydopamine lesioning, indicating that cannabinoid receptors are not colocalized with dopamine-containing neurons but are probably on axonal terminals of striatal intrinsic neurons (Herkenham et al. 1991). Glutamatergic regulation of cannabinoid receptor mRNA levels in the striatum has also been reported (Mailleux and Vanderhaeghen 1994). Unilateral cerebral decortication and treatment with the N-methyl-D-aspartate (NMDA) receptor antagonist MK-801 resulted in decreases in mRNA levels, suggesting that an NMDA receptor activation elevates or maintains cannabinoid receptor mRNA levels. The mechanisms by which these changes occur are not known.

Alterations in $CB_1$ receptor expression have also been examined after chronic exposure to cannabinoids as a logical explanation for the development of tolerance. Tolerance develops readily to most pharmacological effects of $\Delta^9$-THC after a period of chronic exposure in laboratory animals (Compton et al. 1990). These effects include anticonvulsant activity, catalepsy, depression of locomotor activity, hypothermia, hypotension, immunosuppression, and static ataxia. Tolerance develops not only to $\Delta^9$-THC but also to other psychoactive cannabinoids.

Cannabinoid tolerance develops in the absence of pharmacokinetic changes (Compton et al. 1990); therefore, biochemical and/or cellular changes are responsible for this adaptation. One hypothesis for tolerance development is that receptors lose function during chronic agonist treatment, leading to diminished biological responses. Mice tolerant to CP 55,940 exhibit cannabinoid receptor downregulation in cerebellum concomitant with increased levels of receptor mRNA (Fan et al. 1996). Similarly, development of tolerance to $\Delta^9$-THC and CP 55,940 in rats was accompanied by decreases in receptor density in striatum (Oviedo et al. 1993). Rodriguez de Fonseca et al. (1994) also observed region-specific differences in rats made tolerant

to $\Delta^9$-THC; receptor downregulation was observed in striatum and limbic forebrain but not in ventral mesencephalon.

Alterations in receptors should be accompanied by similar changes in the signal transduction pathways. In N18TG2 cells exposed to $\Delta^9$-THC for 24 hours, cannabinoid-inhibited adenylyl cyclase activity was attenuated (Dill and Howlett 1988). However, cerebella from mice chronically treated with CP 55,940 exhibited receptor downregulation without evidence of any change in adenylyl cyclase activity (Fan et al. 1996). However, other investigators demonstrated that GTPase activity was attenuated in cannabinoid tolerance, which may be a better reflection of functional activity than is measurement of forskolin-stimulated adenylyl cyclase activity (Sim et al. 1996).

The consequences of changes in receptor function that arise from chronic drug exposure have not been defined fully. Dependence develops after chronic marijuana exposure in humans and laboratory animals. Indeed, SR141716A can precipitate physical withdrawal symptoms in rodents made tolerant to $\Delta^9$-THC (Aceto et al. 1995; Tsou et al. 1995). Furthermore, evidence indicates that precipitated withdrawal in cannabinoid-dependent rats results in activation of the corticotropin-releasing hormone in the limbic system (Rodriguez de Fonseca et al. 1997). The characteristics of this withdrawal syndrome suggest activation of the autonomic nervous system. It will be important to establish the relationship between the cannabinoid system and other endogenous systems.

## ■ Summary

The major challenge facing researchers is to elucidate the physiological role of the endogenous cannabinoid system. An understanding of this system may provide insight into the mechanism by which cannabinoids produce their unique behavioral effects. One of the most fundamental questions is whether the cannabinoid system is an integral part of cognitive processes. Evidence indicates that the cannabinoids are involved directly in cognitive processes. Likewise, it will be important to determine the relationship between the cannabinoid system and central control of motor function. A critical question is whether the endogenous ligands act as neurotransmitters or neuromodulators. Elucidation of synthesis, degradation, storage, and stimulated release should clarify this issue. At this point, methods for quantitation of endogenous anandamides release in vivo are not available. Another approach to determining the role of the endogenous cannabinoid system is via the chronic administration of receptor agonists or antagonists, the construction of knockout transgenic mouse models, or pharmacological "knockouts" of the receptors using antisense oligonucleotides. These approaches may lead to an understanding of the pathological consequences of a dysfunctional cannabinoid system and, consequently, to novel therapies.

# References

Abadji V, Lin S, Taha G, et al: (R)-Methanandamide: a chiral novel anandamide possessing higher potency and metabolic stability. J Med Chem 37:1889–1893, 1994

Aceto M, Scates S, Lowe J, et al: Cannabinoid precipitated withdrawal by the selective cannabinoid receptor antagonist, SR141716A. Eur J Pharmacol 282:R1–R2, 1995

Adams IB, Ryan W, Singer M, et al: Evaluation of cannabinoid receptor binding and in vivo activities for anandamide analogs. J Pharmacol Exp Ther 273:1172–1181, 1995

Balster RL, Prescott WR: $\Delta^9$-tetrahydrocannabinol discrimination in rats as a model for cannabis intoxication. Neurosci Biobehav Rev 16:55–62, 1992

Beltramo M, Stella N, Calignano A, et al: Functional role of high-affinity anandamide transport. Science 277:1094–1097, 1997

Bouaboula M, Bourrié B, Rinaldi-Carmona M, et al: Stimulation of cannabinoid receptor CB1 induces *krox*-24 expression in human astrocytoma cells. J Biol Chem 270:13973–13980, 1995

Bouaboula M, Poinot-Chazel C, Marchand J, et al: Signaling pathway associated with stimulation of CB2 peripheral cannabinoid receptor involvement of both mitogen-activated protein kinase and induction of *krox*-24 expression. Eur J Biochem 237:704–711, 1996

Burstein SH: Inhibitory and stimulatory effects of cannabinoids on eicosanoid synthesis, in Structure-Activity Relationships of the Cannabinoids. Edited by Rapaka RA, Makriyannis A. Washington, DC, U.S. Government Printing Office, 1987, pp 158–172

Childers SR, Fleming L, Konkoy C, et al: Opioid and cannabinoid receptor inhibition of adenylyl cyclase in brain. Ann N Y Acad Sci 654:33–51, 1992

Compton DR, Dewey WL, Martin BR: Cannabis dependence and tolerance production, in Addiction Potential of Abused Drugs and Drug Classes. Edited by Erickson CK, Javors MA, Morgan WW. Binghamton, NY, Hayworth, 1990, pp 129–147

Compton DR, Rice KC, De Costa BR, et al: Cannabinoid structure-activity relationships: correlation of receptor binding and in vivo activities. J Pharmacol Exp Ther 265:218–226, 1993

Cook SA, Welch SP, Lichtman AH, et al: Evaluation of cAMP involvement in cannabinoid-induced antinociception. Life Sci 56:2049–2056, 1995

Deutsch DG, Chin SA: Enzymatic synthesis and degradation of anandamide, a cannabinoid receptor agonist. Biochem Pharmacol 46:791–796, 1993

Devane WA, Dysarz FA, Johnson MR, et al: Determination and characterization of a cannabinoid receptor in rat brain. Mol Pharmacol 34:605–613, 1988

Devane WA, Hanus L, Breuer A, et al: Isolation and structure of a brain constituent that binds to the cannabinoid receptor. Science 258:1946–1949, 1992

Dill JA, Howlett AC: Regulation of adenylate cyclase by chronic exposure to cannabimimetic drugs. J Pharmacol Exp Ther 244:1157–1163, 1988

Di Marzo V, Fontana A, Cadas H, et al: Formation and inactivation of endogenous cannabinoid anandamide in central neurons. Nature 372:686–691, 1994

Edery H, Grunfeld Y, Ben-Zvi Z, et al: Structural requirements for cannabinoid activity. Ann N Y Acad Sci 191:40–53, 1971

Facci L, Dal Tosa R, Romanello S, et al: Mast cells express a peripheral cannabinoid receptor with differential sensitivity to anandamide and palmitoylethanolamide. Proc Natl Acad Sci U S A 92:3376–3380, 1995

Fan F, Tao Q, Abood M, et al: Cannabinoid receptor down-regulation without alteration of the inhibitory effect of CP 55,940 on adenylyl cyclase in the cerebellum of CP 55,940-tolerant mice. Brain Res 706:13–20, 1996

Felder CC, Briley EM, Axelrod J, et al: Anandamide, an endogenous cannabimimetic eicosanoid, binds to the cloned human cannabinoid receptor and stimulates receptor-mediated signal transduction. Proc Natl Acad Sci U S A 90:7656–7660, 1993

Felder CC, Joyce K, Briley EM, et al: Comparison of the pharmacology and signal transduction of the human cannabinoid CB1 and CB2 receptors. Mol Pharmacol 48:443–450, 1995

Fride E, Mechoulam R: Pharmacological activity of the cannabinoid receptor agonist, anandamide, a brain constituent. Eur J Pharmacol 231:313–314, 1993

Gérard CM, Mollereau C, Vassart G, et al: Molecular cloning of a human cannabinoid receptor which is also expressed in testis. Biochem J 279:129–134, 1991

Glass M, Dragunow M: Induction of the krox 24 transcription factor in striosomes by a cannabinoid agonist. Neuroreport 6:241–244, 1995

Hall W, Solowij N, Lemon J: The health and psychological consequences of cannabis use. National Drug Strategy Monograph Series No 25, Australian Government Publication Service, Canberra, 1994, p 210

Harris RA, Stokes JA: Cannabinoids inhibit calcium uptake by brain synaptosomes. J Neurosci 2:443–447, 1982

Herkenham M, Lynn AB, Little MD, et al: Cannabinoid receptor localization in the brain. Proc Natl Acad Sci U S A 87:1932–1936, 1990

Herkenham M, Lynn AB, DeCosta BR, et al: Neuronal localization of cannabinoid receptors in the basal ganglia of the rat. Brain Res 547:267–274, 1991

Hollister LE: Health aspects of cannabis. Pharmacol Rev 38:1–20, 1986

Howlett AC, Fleming RM: Cannabinoid inhibition of adenylate cyclase: pharmacology of the response in neuroblastoma cell membranes. Mol Pharmacol 26:532–538, 1984

Little PJ, Compton DR, Mechoulam R, et al: Stereochemical effects of 11-OH-dimethylheptyl-$\Delta^8$-tetrahydrocannabinol. Pharmacol Biochem Behav 32:661–666, 1989

Mackie K, Hille B: Cannabinoids inhibit N-type calcium channels in neuroblastoma-glioma cells. Proc Natl Acad Sci U S A 89:3825–3829, 1992

Mailleux P, Vanderhaeghen J: Dopaminergic regulation of cannabinoid receptor mRNA levels in the rat caudate-putamen: an in situ hybridization study. J Neurochem 61:1705–1712, 1993a

Mailleux P, Vanderhaeghen JJ: Glucocorticoid regulation of cannabinoid receptor messenger RNA levels in the rat caudate-putamen; an in situ hybridization study. Neurosci Lett 156:51–53, 1993b

Mailleux P, Vanderhaeghen JJ: Glutamatergic regulation of cannabinoid receptor gene expression in the caudate-putamen. Eur J Pharmacol 266:193–196, 1994

Martin BR: Cellular effects of cannabinoids. Pharmacol Rev 38:45–74, 1986

Martin BR, Welch SP, Abood M: Progress toward understanding the cannabinoid receptor and its second messenger systems, in Advances in Pharmacology. Edited by August JT, Anders MW, Murad F. San Diego, CA, Academic Press, 1994, pp 341–397

Matsuda LA, Lolait SJ, Brownstein MJ, et al: Structure of a cannabinoid receptor and functional expression of the cloned cDNA. Nature 346:561–564, 1990

McLaughlin CR, Abood ME: Developmental expression of cannabinoid receptor messenger RNA. Dev Brain Res 76:75–78, 1993

Mechoulam R, Fride E: The unpaved road to the endogenous cannabinoid ligand anandamide, in Cannabinoids. Edited by Pertwee RG. London, Academic Press, 1995, pp 233–258

Mechoulam R, Devane WA, Breuer A, et al: A random walk through a cannabis field. Pharmacol Biochem Behav 40:461–464, 1991

Mechoulam R, Ben-Shabat S, Hanus L, et al: Identification of an endogenous 2-monoglyceride, present in canine gut, that binds to cannabinoid receptors. Biochem Pharmacol 50:83–90, 1995

Munro S, Thomas KL, Abu-Shaar M: Molecular characterization of a peripheral receptor for cannabinoids. Nature 365:61–64, 1993

Oviedo A, Glowa J, Herkenham M: Chronic cannabinoid administration alters cannabinoid receptor binding in rat brain: a quantitative autoradiographic study. Brain Res 616:293–302, 1993

Razdan RK: Structure-activity relationships in cannabinoids. Pharmacol Rev 38:75–149, 1986

Rinaldi-Carmona M, Barth F, Héaulme M, et al: SR141716A, a potent and selective antagonist of the brain cannabinoid receptor. FEBS Lett 350:240–244, 1994

Rodriguez de Fonseca F, Gorriti M, Fernandez RJJ, et al: Downregulation of rat brain cannabinoid binding sites after chronic $\Delta^9$-tetrahydrocannabinol treatment. Pharmacol Biochem Behav 47:33–40, 1994

Rodriguez de Fonseca F, Carrera M, Navarro M, et al: Activation of corticotropin-releasing factor in the limbic system during cannabinoid withdrawal. Science 276:2050–2054, 1997

Romero J, de Miguel R, García-Palomero E, et al: Time-course of the effects of anandamide, the putative endogenous cannabinoid receptor ligand, on extrapyramidal function. Brain Res 694:223–232, 1995

Selley DE, Stark S, Sim LJ, et al: Cannabinoid receptor stimulation of guanosine-5′-0-(3-[$^{35}$S]thio) triphosphate binding in rat brain membranes. Life Sci 59:659–668, 1996

Showalter V, Compton DR, Martin BR, et al: Evaluation of binding in a transfected cell line expressing a peripheral cannabinoid receptor (CB$_2$): identification of cannabinoid receptor subtype selective ligands. J Pharmacol Exp Ther 278:989–999, 1996

Sim LJ, Hampson RE, Deadwyler SA, et al: Effects of chronic treatment with D$^9$-tetrahydrocannabinol on cannabinoid-stimulated [$^{35}$]GTPγS autoradiography in rat brain. J Neurosci 16:8057–8066, 1996

Smith PB, Compton DR, Welch SP, et al: The pharmacological activity of anandamide, a putative endogenous cannabinoid, in mice. J Pharmacol Exp Ther 270:219–227, 1994

Tsou K, Patrick S, Walker JM: Physical withdrawal in rats tolerant to $\Delta^9$-tetrahydrocannabinol precipitated by a cannabinoid receptor antagonist. Eur J Pharmacol 280:R13–R15, 1995

Wickens AP, Pertwee RG: $\Delta^9$-Tetrahydrocannabinol and anandamide enhance the ability of muscimol to induce catalepsy in the globus pallidus of rats. Eur J Pharmacol 250:205–208, 1993

Wiley J, Balster R, Martin B: Discriminative stimulus effects of anandamide in rats. Eur J Pharmacol 276:49–54, 1995a

Wiley J, Lowe J, Balster R, et al: Antagonism of the discriminative stimulus effects of $\Delta^9$-tetrahydrocannabinol in rats and rhesus monkeys. J Pharmacol Exp Ther 275:1–6, 1995b

# 6

# Epidemiology of Drug Dependence

## James C. Anthony, Ph.D.

In drug dependence epidemiology as in all main branches of epidemiology in public health, the main point of departure is a clinical concept of disease, disorder, or syndrome. Epidemiologists now can orient their work with respect to a reasonably well-measured concept of drug dependence as a clinically meaningful biobehavioral syndrome (i.e., a syndrome with observable manifestations akin to signs and symptoms that run together and cohere to a degree beyond that of chance co-occurrence).

For practitioners who treat drug dependence in clinical settings, epidemiology can be used as a lens to help look beyond the clinic's threshold, out toward the population from which the drug-dependent patients have surfaced. Epidemiologists have grown fond of depicting the ratio of treated to untreated cases in terms of an iceberg (see Figure 6–1). According to recent epidemiological field survey estimates, for every treated case of drug dependence surfacing from the population, at least three cases with a similar profile of signs and symptoms are untreated (Anthony and Helzer 1991; Grant 1997a).

Anyone charged with responsibility for the health of a population must pay attention to both the treated and the untreated cases. Public health work is especially difficult and complex when the goal is to increase the number of treated cases relative to the number of untreated cases and to reduce the total occurrence of cases in a population. This work becomes even more complex when one case begets others, as in contagious person-to-person spread or diffusion. Some drug users,

inadvertently or deliberately, introduce others to drug-taking practices, whereas individuals whose drug dependence has been treated effectively tend not to do so. Hence, population– or public health–oriented initiatives to prevent drug dependence rely on effective intervention programs to reach untreated cases of drug dependence or anyone else responsible for the person-to-person spread of drug taking.

Epidemiology also has another, more ambitious agenda. It seeks basic evidence that will form a solid foundation for comprehensive prevention and intervention programming. In its search for evidence, drug dependence epidemiology has five main rubrics, expressed in the following questions:

1. In the community at large, how many people are affected by drug dependence?
2. Where are the affected people more likely to be found?
3. Why do some people in the community become drug dependent while others do not?
4. What linkages of states and processes influence who becomes and who remains drug dependent?
5. What can be done to prevent and intervene in drug dependence?

Anthony and Van Etten (1998) offer a detailed review of these rubrics with respect to psychiatric epidemiology in general. In this chapter, I introduce these rubrics using selected examples and evidence from epidemiological studies of dependence on alcoholic bever-

Preparation of this chapter was supported in part by National Institute on Drug Abuse Grant R01DA09897.

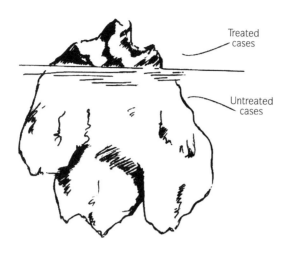

Treated cases

Untreated cases

**Figure 6–1.** The "iceberg" phenomenon of treated and untreated cases. (Graphics: Patricia J. Anthony, 1998, for this publication.)

ages and/or the internationally regulated controlled drugs such as marijuana and cocaine. I also present selected estimates for tobacco and caffeine dependence.

## A Question of Quantity

*In the Community at Large,
How Many People Are Affected?*

Epidemiology's quest to learn the population frequency and occurrence of mental and behavioral disturbances began more than 150 years ago as part of national census-taking and local field surveys. For example, in the 1840 United States census, the local census-takers were to enumerate every citizen and resident, free and enslaved. They also had to ask knowledgeable informants within each household and area about residents who might be characterized as "insane" or as "idiots." Later in the nineteenth century, the scope of this census inquiry was enlarged to encompass chronic inebriates (Wines 1888).

For the 1880 United States census, nearly 100,000 doctors in all parts of the country were contacted, furnished with blank forms, and asked to report to the Census Office all so-called idiots and mentally disordered persons "within the sphere of their personal knowledge" (Wines 1888). In several local area surveys concerning habitual use of opium-containing preparations of that era, druggists and apothecaries were asked to serve as key informants knowledgeable about the citizenry's drug store purchases.

A more formal and rigorous approach to epidemiological field surveys of drug dependence and psychiatric

disturbances emerged early in the twentieth century (e.g., see Rosanoff 1917). By 1980, it had become customary to adopt a set of standard diagnostic criteria, such as those published in DSM-III (American Psychiatric Association 1980), and to translate these criteria into interview measurements for standardized field surveys with general population samples, as was done for the Epidemiologic Catchment Area (ECA) surveys. From surveys of this type, completed since 1979, we have more complete evidence about the frequency and occurrence of drug dependence in the population. DSM-III prevalences cited in this chapter are from Anthony and Helzer (1991, 1995); DSM-IV estimates are from Grant (1995, 1997b).

### Lifetime Prevalence: Having Developed Dependence

According to surveys based on DSM-III criteria, an estimated 8% of adults in the United States are dependent on alcohol; DSM-IV criteria yield an estimate of about 13% (American Psychiatric Association 1994). With respect to dependence on marijuana, cocaine, and/or other controlled drugs, DSM-III and DSM-IV lifetime prevalence estimates are 3%–4% and about 3%, respectively. Of course, alcohol dependence often coexists with other drug dependence.

### Annual Incidence: Risk of Developing Dependence

Virtually all retrospectively oriented population surveys can produce lifetime prevalence estimates of how many individuals have become affected by drug dependence. The much more difficult task of completing a prospective or longitudinal study is necessary to produce a direct estimate of the risk of developing dependence for the first time in one's life. The first-time risk of developing dependence is conventionally estimated during a 1-year interval, giving the *annual incidence rate*. According to the ECA surveys, our most recently completed prospective investigation of an adult household sample in the United States, the estimated annual incidence (based on DSM-III) of alcohol dependence and/or abuse is 1.8%; the estimated annual incidence of controlled-drug dependence and/or abuse is 1.1%. That is, the risk of developing an adult-onset case of alcohol abuse and/or dependence during a 1-year follow-up interval is about 1 in 55. The corresponding 1-year risk estimate for controlled drugs is about 1 in 90 (Eaton et al. 1989). To date, we have no prospectively measured

DSM-III-R (American Psychiatric Association 1987) or DSM-IV estimates for annual incidence or risk of becoming a case of alcohol or other drug dependence.

## Prevalence of Recently Active Drug Dependence: Being an Active Case

The standard *lifetime prevalence proportion* reflects the "probability of having become a case during one's lifetime," up to and including the date of assessment. The standard *incidence rate* reflects "the probability of becoming a case for the first time during some fixed interval of time," such as 1 year (as in an *annual incidence rate*).

In contrast with incidence rates (which convey the probability of becoming something, or change per unit time), all prevalence estimates are proportions, assessed as of some point in time. In standard form, these proportions reflect "the probability of being an active case as of some point in time, with at least one active clinical manifestation or symptom during some fixed prior interval of time." For example, in a 1-year prevalence proportion, the numerator counts not only the people who recently have become cases for the first time but also previously developed cases with symptom manifestations during the year prior to cross-sectional assessment.

Based on DSM-III criteria, the estimated prevalence of being a recently active case of alcohol dependence in the United States is about 4%. An additional 3% qualify as recently active cases of alcohol abuse but did not qualify as cases of alcohol dependence. The corresponding DSM-IV estimates are roughly the same.

With respect to marijuana and other controlled drugs, an estimated 1%–2% of United States adults qualify as recently active cases of drug dependence according to DSM-III criteria, and an additional 1% qualify as recently active cases of DSM-III drug abuse but not dependence. The corresponding DSM-IV estimates are 0.5% and 1.1%, respectively.

The DSM-III values reported in this section are estimates based on Diagnostic Interview Schedule (DIS) assessments, administered by lay interviewers for the ECA surveys. Standardized clinical examinations conducted for the ECA surveys by board-eligible psychiatrists yielded slightly higher DSM-III estimates for alcohol and other drug disorders. The difference seems to have depended largely on the clinicians' cross-examination of subjects, which secured evidence of more recent alcohol and drug-related pathologies (Anthony et al. 1985).

To place these estimates for alcohol and controlled drug use into perspective, according to the National Comorbidity Survey (NCS), an estimated one in four 15- to 54-year-old United States residents (24%) has met DSM-III-R criteria for tobacco dependence (Anthony et al. 1994); a majority remain active daily smokers. An estimated one in five to six (15%–20%) drinks at least five cups of coffee per day (Anthony and Arria, in press).

## ■ A Question of Location

### *Where Are the Affected People More Likely to Be Found?*

It is a short step from the first rubric of epidemiology to its second rubric. Here, *location* can refer to placement in time and geography (e.g., as reflected in time trends, space-time clustering, or variation within and between geopolitical boundaries). Location also refers to characteristics of the person (i.e., most traditionally, age, sex, and race or ethnic status).

One striking observation from the ECA surveys of psychiatric disturbances was that drug dependence, and most other DSM-III disorders, was more likely to be found among persons age 18–54 years. Except for cognitive impairments, these disorders were quite infrequent among persons age 55 years or older. This was true for both incidence and prevalence estimates (Anthony and Helzer 1991; Eaton et al. 1989).

Building from the foundation created by the ECA surveys, one research group argued successfully in favor of a nationally representative sample survey of United States community residents age 15–54 years in 1990–1992 (Kessler et al. 1994). The resulting survey, the NCS, has provided a sharper focus on the prevalence of drug dependence in the United States, specific for individual categories of psychoactive drugs, and specific for age.

Based on the NCS, an estimated 92% of 15- to 54-year-old United States residents have consumed alcoholic beverages. Among these drinkers, an estimated 15% have become alcohol dependent. The resulting estimated lifetime prevalence of alcohol dependence in the population is 14%. Males were more likely to have become dependent than were females (Anthony et al. 1994).

Fewer 15- to 54-year-old United States residents have smoked tobacco than have consumed alcoholic beverages, but the estimated prevalence of dependence among users is greater for tobacco than for any of the other drugs studied. For example, an estimated 32% of tobacco smokers have developed tobacco dependence. In comparison, an estimated 9.1% of marijuana smokers have developed marijuana dependence, and an estimated 16.7% of cocaine users have developed cocaine dependence. Again, males were more likely to be dependent on these drugs than were females (Anthony et al. 1994).

When limited to studying the location of cases in the population, epidemiologists do not seek to draw causal inferences. Rather, they attempt to discern the patterned occurrence of health conditions within and between populations. The detection of these disease patterns might have a pragmatic implication for the delivery of prevention or intervention services. These patterns also are important guides to more probing causal research.

To illustrate, as noted earlier in this section, evidence highlights a male excess in the frequency and occurrence of drug dependence for most drug categories. These descriptive estimates do not address the cause of the male excess, but they confirm a need for treatment services and outreach for both men and women who have become drug dependent. Furthermore, these estimates highlight the importance of a policy debate about existing outreach and treatment programs: given that women are underrepresented in drug dependence treatment, should we expand outreach and treatment services for women until the male-to-female ratio of treated cases is approximately equivalent to the ratio observed in epidemiological studies?

When epidemiologists investigate the location of cases in the population, they define location broadly to encompass geographical differences and variation over time. For example, the two parts of Figure 6–2 depict geographic variation in the prevalence of recently active alcohol and illicit drug dependence, based on state-by-state estimates from recent government-sponsored National Household Surveys on Drug Abuse (NHSDA). Here the analysts sought to disclose variation but were not able to explain the evidence, including an interesting observation that higher prevalence values tended to be observed in states west of Missouri, Arkansas, and Louisiana (Folsom and Judkins 1997).

Cross-national comparisons provoke the same impulses as do these cross-state comparisons. For example, a nationally representative sample survey of mental disorders in the United Kingdom recently applied a drug dependence assessment similar to assessment procedures used in recent United States surveys. The United Kingdom prevalence estimate for recently active drug dependence is 2.2%, somewhat higher than has been observed in the United States surveys. It is tempting to give a substantive interpretation to this difference; however, because drug dependence case definitions and assessment procedures were not identical in the United States and United Kingdom studies, this interpretation is premature (Meltzer et al. 1994). Procedure-related variations might well account for observed differences (as was true in United States–United Kingdom comparative studies on schizophrenia and the mood disorders).

These considerations do not undercut the value of epidemiological surveys that serve a mainly descriptive function in disclosing variations in frequency and occurrence of drug dependence within and across populations and time periods. Studies of the location of affected cases represent an important scientific step toward studies of causes, mechanisms of causal action, prevention, and intervention (as demonstrated by the history of psychiatric epidemiology and epidemiology generally) (Anthony and Van Etten 1998).

## A Question of Causes

### Why Do Some People in the Community Become Drug Dependent While Others Do Not?

Twin studies have played an important role in research on the genetics of alcohol and drug dependence (see Cloninger, Chapter 7, in this volume). Some of these studies were clinically oriented in that recruitment of twin pairs began with identification of treated index cases or probands, with later follow-back to untreated siblings. Other studies are more epidemiological in orientation, in that sampling and recruitment are from population registries of twin pairs, uninfluenced by treatment status of a proband.

Twin studies have provided the strongest evidence for the importance of experiential and environmental conditions and processes that influence the risk of developing dependence on alcohol and other drugs. Estimates of *heritability* for alcohol dependence and drug dependence tend to fall between 25% and 65%, depending on the sex of the twins under study, ascertainment methods, and other factors. Nevertheless, these estimates leave considerable room for the influence of noninherited characteristics in the etiology of the drug dependence syndromes.

Recognition of experiential and environmental conditions in drug dependence often starts with an appreci-

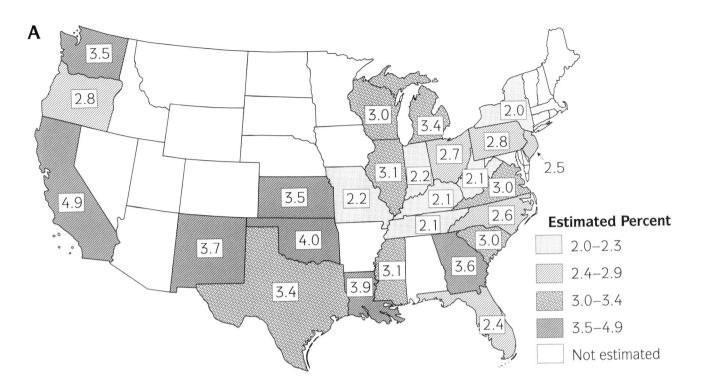

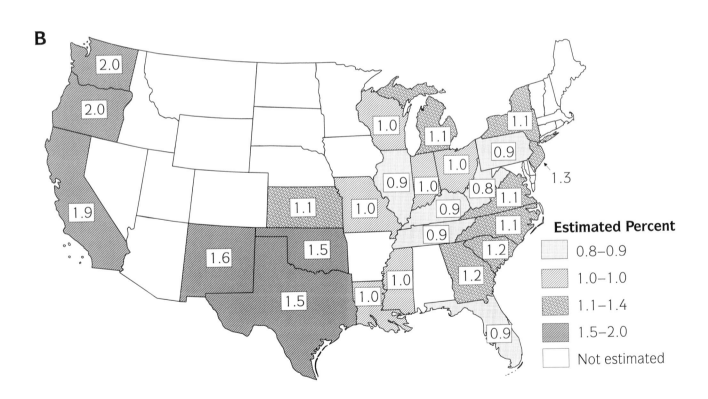

**Figure 6–2.** Geographical variation in state-specific population prevalence estimates for recently active alcohol dependence **(A)** and active illicit drug dependence **(B)** in the United States (Folsom and Judkins 1997). Data are from the National Household Surveys on Drug Abuse conducted between 1991 and 1993. Estimates were not made for states left unshaded. (Graphics: Scott Hubbard, 1998, for this publication.)

ation that drug dependence cannot develop until *effective contact* has occurred between the drug and a vulnerable individual. Here, effective contact can be measured by a biomarker such as immune response to the drug-antigen. Or, as is more typical in epidemiological studies, effective contact is measured by a *verbomarker* (i.e., a response to either a survey questionnaire or an interview).

Processes governing effective contact are central in the epidemiological study of drug dependence, including the contagious person-to-person diffusion of drug-taking practices and the variation in availability of drugs. For example, estimates of heritability from twin studies generally do not take into account that one twin might be the source of a drug for the other twin. To the extent that monozygotic twins are more likely to share drugs with each other, as compared with dizygotic twins, heritability estimates for drug dependence would be inflated, unless opportunities to use drugs are measured and controlled in the analysis.

Natural experiments of variation in drug availability are critical in the epidemiological study of experiences and environments that promote the risk of drug dependence. The paradigmatic example of epidemiological research in this tradition involves a Vietnam veteran study in which almost 20% of veterans in the epidemiological sample had become dependent on heroin and other opioid drugs while in Vietnam, a high-availability zone for these compounds (Helzer 1985). However, when reassessed within a few years after their return to the United States from Vietnam, less than 5% had remained opioid dependent or returned to opioid dependence. Adding to this natural experiment, the researchers found that the probability of returning to opioid dependence was associated with living in a metropolitan area. That is, veterans returning to lower-availability nonmetropolitan areas were at extremely low risk for becoming readdicted; the relative risk of readdiction was greater for veterans who had returned to higher-availability metropolitan areas (Helzer 1985).

In attempting to understand why metropolitan area residents might be more likely to become or remain opioid dependent, we can entertain both social causation and social selection hypotheses. That is, greater drug availability or other conditions of city life might promote drug dependence processes. Alternatively, individuals vulnerable to drug dependence might be selective in their choice of residence and might migrate to metropolitan areas in order to gain more ready access to their drugs of choice.

The contending hypotheses of social selection and social causation cannot be investigated with randomized experiments. Instead, epidemiologists must turn to specialized research tactics, typically learned in doctoral or postdoctoral research training. For example, in a formal experiment, randomization can be used as a tactic for efficient control of potentially distorting variables. Randomization helps an investigator balance the array of potentially distorting influences that might otherwise complicate causal inferences. If randomization cannot or does not balance these distorting influences, then alternative tactics must be used. For example, matching and stratification can be used during or after sampling of subjects for an epidemiological study. As an alternative or in addition to matching and/or stratification, statistical modeling can be used to constrain potentially distorting influences during data analysis.

Dohrenwend et al.'s (1992) study of Sephardic and Ashkenazi Jews living in Israel is an excellent illustration of how nonexperimental tactics can be applied to study social causation versus social selection processes in the etiology of drug dependence and other psychiatric disturbances. The researchers worked from a premise that the Sephardic Jews were at higher social disadvantage by virtue of a more prominent African family heritage, physical appearance, and ethnicity. Assessing the Sephardic and Ashkenazi Jews' lifetime histories of mental disorders, the research team plotted the frequency and occurrence of drug dependence and other disorders in relation to their research subjects' achieved levels of education. Using a mix of stratification and statistical modeling, the team expressed the occurrence of different types of mental disorders in the two groups as a function of acquired education and social status. The result was a pattern of association consistent with a more prominent influence of social selection in relation to disorders such as schizophrenia and was consistent with a more prominent influence of social causation in relation to disorders such as dependence on alcohol and other drugs (Dohrenwend et al. 1992). This study shows how epidemiological studies can shed light on important scientific issues of causation that are difficult, if not impossible, to study within the framework of randomized controlled trials.

## The Human Envirome Project

Using tactics such as matching, stratification, and statistical modeling, epidemiological investigators have searched for an array of life experience and environmental conditions and processes that might promote or reduce an individual's risk of drug dependence. This search is a central mission for psychiatric epidemiology generally and for drug dependence epidemiology specifically. In brief, epidemiology now is responsible for a longer-term Human Envirome Project, running parallel with the more rapidly evolving National Institutes of Health (NIH) Human Genome Project. Just as the Human Genome Project seeks to map the total ensemble of human genes, with a special NIH focus on genes that impinge on human health, the Human Envirome Project must seek a map of the total ensemble of environmental conditions that impinge on human health, including gene-environment interactions that provoke drug dependence (Anthony et al. 1995).

Candidate conditions within the Human Envirome Project can be specified developmentally along a maturational time line from conception to death. For example, one might suppose that maternal exposure to tobacco smoking yields an increased risk of teen smoking among genetically vulnerable offspring, but this is an inference for which there is but limited epidemiological evidence. A more substantial argument based on epidemiological evidence can be made for a childhood environment of especially inept parental monitoring and supervision of children. For example, deficient parental monitoring in the home environment seems to influence the risk of early-onset drug taking (e.g., Chilcoat and Anthony 1996; Duncan et al. 1998), which is linked to a later increased risk of drug problems associated with drug dependence (e.g., see Anthony and Petronis 1995).

Youths' affiliation with misbehaving and deviant peers represents a strong candidate environment for promotion of risk of drug use and drug dependence in childhood, adolescence, and adulthood. By adding social reinforcers, affiliation with deviant peers might promote deviant attitudes and otherwise enhance the pharmacologically based reinforcing functions of drug taking (Newcomb and Bentler 1988).

Affiliation with deviant peers in adolescence is important but is not the only characteristic that must be considered in relation to the risk of drug taking. For example, the occurrence of LSD ingestion and other psychedelic drug use shows a sharp peak in the late teen years and the early 20s. This location of psychedelic drug use in relation to the personal characteristic of age (in years) does not settle the issue of causation, but it points strongly toward linkages between late high school and early college experiences and critical social environments that promote initiation and persistence of the use of these drugs.

It would be a mistake to conclude that environmen-

tal conditions and processes make no difference in the risk of drug dependence after the adolescent years. To illustrate, Muntaner et al. (1995) and Crum et al. (1995) have identified conditions in the psychosocial work environment that seem to enhance the risk of adult-onset drug and alcohol dependence syndromes. The strongest evidence from Muntaner's research implicated risk-increasing aspects of physically hazardous work environments that allow little room for decision making. Crum's research found that the risk of alcohol dependence syndromes also varies in relation to aspects of job strain in the adult work environment.

## Individual Vulnerabilities and Their Consequences

Although the epidemiological perspective tends to be oriented toward the more malleable experiential and environmental conditions and processes leading toward drug-taking behavior and drug dependence, important advances are being made in the individual temperament, personality, and constitutional characteristics that might influence an individual's risk of drug dependence. When more fixed characteristics such as a specific gene or an early established trait are brought into focus, the disposition in epidemiology is to search for experiential or environmental conditions under which these predispositions are expressed or not expressed.

Perhaps as early manifestations of gene expression and gene-environment interactions, individual vulnerabilities in the form of temperament, personality, and behavior are among the suspected causal determinants of drug involvement. For example, prenatal and perinatal obstetric complications such as hypoxia might be associated with later reduced risk of drug involvement, perhaps as a result of more careful parental supervision of vulnerable youths (Buka et al. 1993). Kellam et al. (1980) implicated a mixture of early shyness or socially withdrawn behavior with aggressiveness and acting out in primary school, and Blackson et al. (1994) suggested that irritability or difficult temperament is an early trait that accounts for excess adolescent drug involvement.

As summarized elsewhere, later in life, an individual's social attachment to parents or bonding to conventional social institutions such as school have theoretically compelling links to a reduced risk of youthful drug involvement (Brook et al. 1990). In this context, poor school performance also has been associated with both reduced and excess risk of teen drug involvement (Boyle et al. 1993; Duncan et al. 1998; Fleming et al.

1982). The increased risk sometimes observed in relation to precocious school readiness might be associated with novelty-seeking or openness to experience. Elsewhere, these characteristics have been investigated as personality traits that modulate vulnerability to drug use and drug dependence (Wills et al. 1994).

Dropout during the high school and college years also has been studied as a consequence of earlier drug taking and is a suspected cause of later drug dependence. Experimental trials likely will be needed to sort out this network of relationships (Crum et al. 1993; Kasen et al. 1998).

One of the most robust indicators of later risk of drug involvement, at least for boys, is early deviance and conduct problems in childhood and antisocial personality traits later in life (Robins 1966). To some extent, these characteristics reflect lower degrees of social bonding and attachment to parents and to conventional social norms. Among males, this suspected causal linkage is supported by prospective and longitudinal studies and by experimental trials in which primary school interventions have been used to modify levels of early misbehavior in school (Kellam and Anthony 1998; O'Donnell et al. 1995).

## A Question of Mechanisms

*What Linkages of States and Processes Influence Who Becomes and Who Remains Drug Dependent?*

The study of mechanisms in drug dependence epidemiology encompasses research on the natural history of these syndromes as they develop without early intervention or treatment, their clinical course during and after interventions, and the precursor and prodromal processes. The topics investigated include *stepping-stone* and *gateway* hypotheses about linked progressions from one drug to the next in a developmental sequence (Chen and Kandel 1995) and insights gained by making daily rounds with untreated drug users and drug-dependent individuals (e.g., see Schick et al. 1978). Whereas the natural history of diseases generally has been learned by astute clinicians who observed the progress of signs and symptoms during eras of no effective treatments, much of the natural history of drug dependence has been learned by anthropologists and ethnographers who have looked into the population for drug users who never came into contact with treatment services (Kaplan and Lambert 1995). Many valuable results from this population research into mechanisms and early stages of drug dependence beyond the clinical threshold have been integrated into professional practice in the form of outreach, treatment, and prevention programs (Agar 1997; Carlson et al. 1995).

The history of epidemiology also has illustrated that firm knowledge of causes and causal mechanisms is unnecessary for effective prevention and intervention. Many current methods of preventing and treating disease were discovered decades before anyone sorted out the underlying causal mechanisms; however, our knowledge base for effective prevention and intervention will be improved when we know more about causal mechanisms. Each firmly identified mechanism highlights new targets for intervention (Anthony and Van Etten 1998).

At a very simplistic level, we can decompose the process or causal mechanisms for becoming drug dependent into a linked sequence of stages or transitions, with intermediate dimensional progression within these stages. On the way toward drug dependence, the earliest stage of drug involvement occurs before drug taking begins; its start is marked by the first age or time at which an individual has an opportunity to try a given drug such as marijuana. The next stage occurs when drug taking begins. A subsequent stage occurs when drug dependence has developed (Anthony and Helzer 1995). The four parts of Figure 6–3 are based on epidemiological data related to the use of marijuana, cocaine, psychedelic drugs (e.g., LSD, Ecstasy), and heroin. The figure shows the estimated proportions of the population (at various age ranges) that had an opportunity to try the drugs (*opportunity to use*), the proportion that tried them (*history of use*), and the proportion that developed dependence on them (*history of dependence*).

From this figure, we can discern that a possible mechanism underlying generally lower risk of drug dependence among older adults is that there formerly was a lower probability of having an opportunity to try these drugs. Similarly, if the experience of late adolescents during the 1990s rings true with that of their older brothers and sisters, then the observed data suggest an increased prevalence of drug dependence in the early twenty-first century (because of greater opportunities for young people to try these drugs in the waning years of the twentieth century).

There are more challenging examples of how causal mechanisms are being examined in epidemiological field studies, with implications for prevention. For example, Duncan et al. (1998) described the Oregon Social Learning Center model for antisocial behavior and adapted it to drug taking:

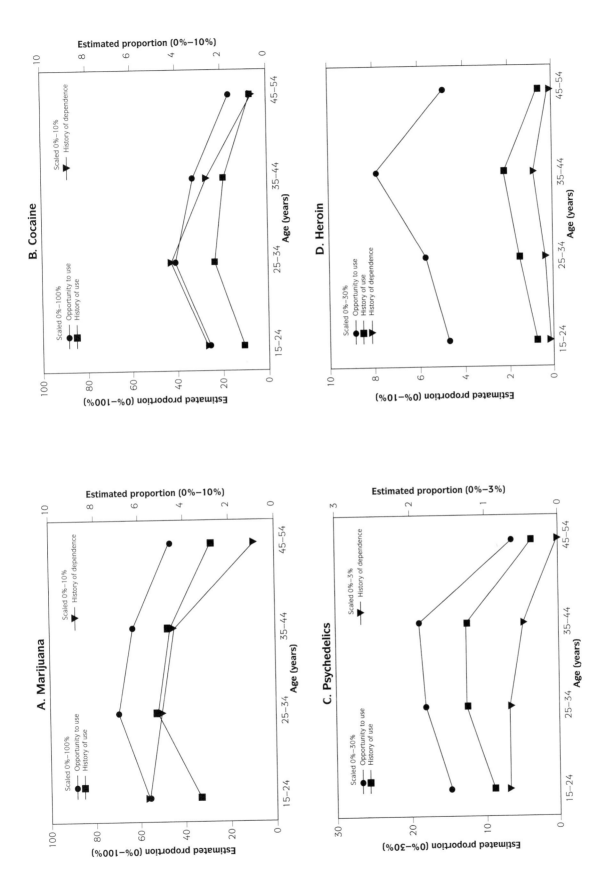

**Figure 6–3.** Age-specific estimates for drug involvement for marijuana (**A**), cocaine (**B**), psychedelic drugs (**C**), and heroin (**D**). *Opportunity to use* data are from the National Household Surveys on Drug Abuse; *history of use* and *history of dependence* data are from the National Comorbidity Survey, United States, 1990–1992.

*Source.* Anthony et al. 1994; Van Etten and Anthony, in press. (Graphics: Scott Hubbard, 1998, for this publication.)

According to this model, parental mismanagement of early oppositional and aggressive behavior shapes further aggressive behavior which leads to a pattern of coercive interactions and conflict between parents and children. Parental attempts at discipline are inconsistent and [are] met with the child's aggression. Seeking to avoid these aversive interactions, parents become increasingly inconsistent in their parenting practices and become less involved with their children. The child's aggressive behavior and non-compliance then become well-established. . . . [T]his pattern of non-compliance and aggressive behavior is extended to the school environment and often places the child on a trajectory that includes rejection by normal peers and academic failure in the classroom. These outcomes contribute to a drift toward other rejected, aggressive peers by early adolescence, where further problematic behavior is shaped and reinforced. Continued association with this deviant peer group places the child at high risk for developing a consistent pattern of antisocial and delinquent behavior. Thus, this model accounts for delinquent and antisocial behavior in adolescents through proximal peer influence, but suggests that poor family management practices (especially conflict and poor parental monitoring) explain the adolescent's subsequent engagement with deviant peers. (Duncan et al. 1998, p. 58)

This type of developmental causal model can be tested only with epidemiological sampling of children early in life and with multiple longitudinal observations through the years of schooling and beyond. To the extent that these hypothesized mechanisms are confirmed, they become targets for preventive intervention with respect to early-onset drug taking and later risk of drug dependence.

## A Question of Prevention and Intervention

### What Can Be Done to Prevent and Intervene in Drug Dependence?

Although epidemiologists can fill satisfying careers with important nonexperimental and strictly observational studies, the search for a solid foundation of evidence has led many epidemiologists to enter the experimental world of randomized controlled intervention and prevention trials. This search explains, for example, why our research group has undertaken long-term randomized preventive trials to test the previously mentioned hypotheses about causal mechanisms linking early childhood aggression and later risk of early-onset drug taking (Kellam and Anthony 1998).

Hence, the fifth main rubric for drug dependence epidemiology is expressed in relation to prevention or intervention. When successful, randomized preventive trials not only clarify which programs merit widespread dissemination and which do not but also marshal important evidence about causal hypotheses and suspected causal mechanisms. Pentz (Chapter 48, in this volume) examines prevention in more detail.

## Prospects for the Future

Looking to the future, ongoing epidemiological field surveys are projected to expand, including a much-increased sample size for the NHSDA and a new prospective elaboration of the ECA survey and NCS data gathering. Nonetheless, the most exciting new evidence from drug dependence epidemiology is more likely to come when the Human Genome Project intersects with the Human Envirome Project in a deliberate effort to find gene-environment interactions that influence the risk of drug dependence in adolescence and early adulthood. This clarification of causes and causal mechanisms will forge a new generation of experimental intervention and prevention trials with epidemiological samples of sufficient size to yield definitive evidence—as we now are gaining the benefit of large-sample trials in cancer and cardiovascular disease epidemiology.

## References

Agar MH: Ethnography: an overview. Subst Use Misuse 32:1155–1173, 1997

American Psychiatric Association: Diagnostic and Statistical Manual of Mental Disorders, 3rd Edition. Washington, DC, American Psychiatric Association, 1980

American Psychiatric Association: Diagnostic and Statistical Manual of Mental Disorders, 3rd Edition, Revised. Washington, DC, American Psychiatric Association, 1987

American Psychiatric Association: Diagnostic and Statistical Manual of Mental Disorders, 4th Edition. Washington, DC, American Psychiatric Association, 1994

Anthony JC, Arria AM: Epidemiology of psychoactive drug dependence in adulthood, in Sourcebook on Substance Abuse. Edited by Tarter RE, Ammerman RT, Ott PJ. Needham Heights, MA, Allyn & Bacon (in press)

Anthony JC, Helzei JE: Syndromes of drug abuse and dependence, in Psychiatric Disorders in America. Edited by obins LN, Regier DE. New York, Free Press, 1991, pp 116–154

Anthony JC, Helzer JE: Epidemiology of drug dependence, in Textbook in Psychiatric Epidemiology. Edited by Tsuang MT, Tohen M, Zahner GEP. New York, Wiley-Liss, 1995, pp 361–406

Anthony JC, Petronis KR: Early onset drug use and risk of later drug problems. Drug Alcohol Depend 40:9–15, 1995

Anthony JC, Van Etten ML: Epidemiology and its rubrics, in Comprehensive Clinical Psychology, Vol 1. Edited by Bellack A, Hersen M. Oxford, England, Elsevier, 1998, pp 355–390

Anthony JC, Folstein MF, Romanoski AJ, et al: Comparison of the lay Diagnostic Interview Schedule and a standardized psychiatric diagnosis: experience in Eastern Baltimore. Arch Gen Psychiatry 42:667–675, 1985

Anthony JC, Warner LA, Kessler RC: Comparative epidemiology of dependence on tobacco, alcohol, controlled substances, and inhalants: basic findings from the National Comorbidity Survey. Exp Clin Psychopharmacol 2:244–268, 1994

Anthony JC, Eaton WW, Henderson AS: Looking to the future. Epidemiol Rev 17:1–8, 1995

Blackson TC, Tarter RE, Martin CS, et al: Temperament-induced father-son family dysfunction: etiological implications for child behavior problems and substance abuse. Am J Orthopsychiatry 64:280–292, 1994

Boyle MH, Offord DR, Racine YA, et al: Predicting substance use in early adolescence based on parent and teacher assessments of childhood psychiatric disorder. J Child Psychol Psychiatry 34:535–544, 1993

Brook JS, Brook DW, Whiteman M, et al: The psychosocial etiology of adolescent drug use: a family interactional approach. Genet Soc Gen Psychol Monogr 116:113–267, 1990

Buka SL, Tsuang MT, Lipsitt LP: Pregnancy/delivery complications and psychiatric diagnosis. Arch Gen Psychiatry 50:151–156, 1993

Carlson RG, Siegal HA, Falck RS. Qualitative research methods in drug and AIDS prevention research: an overview, in Qualitative Methods in Drug Abuse and HIV Research (NIDA Res Monogr 57). Edited by Lambert EY, Ashery RS, Needle RH. Rockville, MD, U.S. Department of Health and Human Services, 1995, pp 6–26

Chen K, Kandel DB: The natural history of drug use from adolescence to the mid-thirties in a general population sample. Am J Public Health 85:41–47, 1995

Chilcoat HD, Anthony JC: Impact of parent monitoring on initiation of drug use through late childhood. J Am Acad Child Adolesc Psychiatry 35:91–100, 1996

Crum RM, Helzer JE, Anthony JC: Level of education and alcohol abuse and dependence in adulthood. Am J Public Health 83:830–837, 1993

Crum RM, Muntaner C, Eaton WW, et al: Occupational stress and the risk of alcohol abuse and dependence. Alcohol Clin Exp Res 19:647–655, 1995

Dohrenwend BP, Levav I, Shrout PE, et al: Socioeconomic status and psychiatric disorders. Science 255:946–952, 1992

Duncan SC, Duncan TE, Biglan A, et al: Contributions of the social context to the development of adolescent substance use. Drug Alcohol Depend 50:57–71, 1998

Eaton WW, Kramer M, Anthony JC, et al: The incidence of specific DIS/DSM-III mental disorders. Acta Psychiatr Scand 79:163–178, 1989

Fleming JP, Kellam SG, Brown CH: Early predictors of age at first use of alcohol, marijuana, and cigarettes. Drug Alcohol Depend 9:285–303, 1982

Folsom RE, Judkins DR: Substance abuse in states and metropolitan areas: model-based estimates from the 1991–1993 National Household Surveys on Drug Abuse. Methodological Series M-1. Rockville, MD, Substance Abuse and Mental Health Services Administration, Office of Applied Studies, 1997

Grant BF: Comorbidity between DSM-IV drug use disorders and major depression. J Subst Abuse 7:481–497, 1995

Grant BF: Barriers to alcoholism treatment. J Stud Alcohol 58:365–371, 1997a

Grant BF: Prevalence and correlates of alcohol use and DSM-IV alcohol dependence in the United States. J Stud Alcohol 58:464–473, 1997b

Helzer JE: Specification of predictors of narcotic use versus addiction, in Studying Drug Abuse. Edited by Robins LN. New Brunswick, NJ, Rutgers University Press, 1985, pp 173–197

Kaplan CD, Lambert EY: The daily life of heroin-addicted persons, in Qualitative Methods in Drug Abuse and HIV Research (NIDA Res Monogr 57). Edited by Lambert EY, Ashery RS, Needle RH. Rockville, MD, U.S. Department of Health and Human Services, 1995, pp 100–116

Kasen S, Cohen P, Brook JS: Adolescent school experiences and dropout, adolescent pregnancy, and young adult deviant behavior. Journal of Adolescence Research 13:49–72, 1998

Kellam SG, Anthony JC: Targeting early antecedents to prevent tobacco smoking: findings from an epidemiologically based randomized field trial. Am J Public Health 88:1490–1495, 1998

Kellam SG, Ensminger ME, Simon MB: Mental health in first grade and teenage drug, alcohol, and cigarette use. Drug Alcohol Depend 5:273–304, 1980

Kessler RC, McGonagle KA, Shanyang Z, et al: Lifetime and 12-month prevalence of DSM-III-R psychiatric disorders in the United States. Arch Gen Psychiatry 51:8–19, 1994

Meltzer H, Gill B, Petticrew M, et al: The prevalence of psychiatric morbidity among adults living in private households. OPCS Surveys of Psychiatric Morbidity in Great Britain. Report 1. London, Her Majesty's Stationery Office, 1994

Muntaner C, Anthony JC, Crum R, et al: Psychosocial dimensions of work and the risk of drug dependence among adults. Am J Epidemiol 142:183–190, 1995

Newcomb, MD, Bentler PM: The impact of family context, deviant attitudes, and emotional distress on adolescent drug use: longitudinal latent-variable analyses of mothers and their children. Journal of Research in Personality 22:154–176, 1988

O'Donnell J, Hawkins JD, Catalano RF, et al: Preventing school failure, drug use, and delinquency among low-income children: long-term intervention in elementary schools. Am J Orthopsychiatry 65:87–100, 1995

Robins LN: Deviant Children Grown Up. Baltimore, MD, Williams & Wilkins, 1966

Rosanoff AJ: Survey of mental disorders: in Nassau County, New York; July–Oct., 1916. Psychiatr Bull 2:1–73, 1917

Schick JF, Dorus W, Hughes PH: Adolescent drug using groups in Chicago parks. Drug Alcohol Depend 3:199–210, 1978

Van Etten ML, Anthony JC: Comparative epidemiology of initial drug opportunities. Drug Alcohol Depend (in press)

Wills TA, Vaccaro D, McNamara G: Novelty seeking, risk taking, and related constructs as predictors of adolescent substance use. J Subst Abuse 6:1–20, 1994

Wines FH: Report on the Defective, Dependent, and Delinquent Classes of the Population of the United States as Returned at the Tenth Census (June 1, 1880). Washington, DC, U.S. Government Printing Office, 1888

# 7

# Genetics of Substance Abuse

## C. Robert Cloninger, M.D.

Recent studies have identified genetic risk factors predisposing individuals to substance abuse and dependence, and in some cases, these studies have mapped specific genes that influence susceptibility to substance abuse and dependence (Kotler et al. 1997). Specifically, linkage and association studies have identified several chromosomal regions and possibly specific genes that influence the risk of some forms of substance abuse and dependence, such as opiate dependence (Kotler et al. 1997). Other studies have identified chromosomal regions and specific genes underlying variation in personality traits that influence susceptibility to substance abuse and dependence. Large-scale genome scans have been carried out in familial cases of alcohol dependence, leading to the identification of chromosomal regions influencing severe alcoholism. Such severe, early-onset cases of alcoholism usually involve polysubstance abuse.

## Genetic Epidemiology of Substance Abuse

Family studies of individuals who abuse cocaine, opiates, marijuana, or alcohol have found that individuals exhibit much polysubstance abuse, and members of the same family may abuse different types of drugs. Much of this work has relied on the family history to assess relatives rather than interviewing the individual relatives directly. In contrast, a recent study of alcoholic probands with a variety of comorbid substance abuse found evidence of partial familial specificity in aggrega-tion (Bierut et al. 1995). However, even in this study, individual probands and their siblings exhibited much comorbidity among different forms of substance abuse. Therefore, some genetic risk factors predispose individuals to drug abuse in a nonspecific manner, whereas other risk factors may be more specific to a particular type of drug. The nonspecific predisposition explains the frequency of polysubstance abuse and extensive comorbidity for different types of drug abuse within individuals and within families. The more specific risk factors explain the affinities for a single drug in some individuals and some families.

One large-scale twin study indicated that the heritability of any drug abuse is about 34% (see Table 7–1) (Tsuang et al. 1996). Similar heritability estimates were obtained for marijuana, stimulants, opiates, and any drug. Such similarity may reflect the frequency of polysubstance abuse. Polysubstance abuse is frequently associated with strong familial aggregation of substance abuse, childhood conduct disorder, teenage onset of substance abuse, and in adulthood, antisocial personality disorder, low adaptive functioning, and severity of dependence, as is typical of type 2 alcoholic individuals (Sigvardsson et al. 1996). Further analyses are needed to unravel the influence of multiple risk factors, such as personality traits, on drug abuse.

The importance of genetic influences on drug abuse is also supported by the only small adoption study in this area (see Table 7–2) (Cadoret et al. 1995). Adoptees at high risk for drug abuse were selected if a biological parent had substance abuse or antisocial personality disorder. Most biological parents were alco-

Supported in part by National Institutes of Health Grants MH31302, AA08401, AA08402, and AA08403.

**Table 7–1.**    Heritability of substance abuse or dependence in 1,874 pairs of monozygotic (MZ) twins and 1,498 pairs of dizygotic (DZ) twins in the Vietnam Era Twin Registry

| Illicit substance | Heritability | Tetrachoric correlation MZ/DZ | Pairwise concordance MZ/DZ (%) |
|---|---|---|---|
| Marijuana | .33[a] | .62/.46 | 22/15[a] |
| Stimulants | .44[a] | .53/.24 | 14/5[a] |
| Sedatives | .38 | .44/.25 | 6/3 |
| Opiates | .43[a] | .67/.29 | 13/3 |
| Phencyclidine/psychedelics | .25 | .44/.32 | 5/3 |
| Any drug abuse | .34[a] | .63/.44 | 26/17[a] |

[a]Heritability estimate or concordance difference significant, $P < 0.05$.
*Source.*    Adapted from Tsuang et al. 1996.

**Table 7–2.**    Increased risk of substance abuse in adopted-away children of biological parents with substance abuse and/or antisocial personality (experimental group) compared with other adoptees (control group)

| Adoptee diagnosis | Experimental group (n = 46) (%) | Control group (n = 49) (%) |
|---|---|---|
| Alcohol abuse/ dependence | 70 | 55 |
| Other drug abuse/ dependence | 54* | 33 |
| Total (alcohol or drugs) | 76 | 61 |
| Antisocial personality disorder | 33 | 16 |

*$\chi^2$, df = 4.55, $P = 0.033$; other contrasts not significant.
*Source.*    Reanalysis of data presented by Cadoret et al. 1995.

holic. Adoptees at low risk had no biological parent with any identified record of such psychopathology. The adopted-away children at putative high risk had an excess of drug abuse other than alcoholism compared with control subjects. Additional multivariate analysis suggested that two developmental pathways to drug abuse exist: direct transmission of risk to the adoptee from the alcoholic biological parent, and indirect transmission of risk via early impulsive-aggressive behavior in the adoptee from similar personality traits in the biological parent.

Although this adoption study of drug abuse was small, such findings are consistent with much other data about alcoholic subtypes (Cloninger et al. 1988). In particular, other studies have shown that impulsive-aggressive personality traits in childhood and adolescence predict early onset of substance abuse (Cloninger et al. 1988). The only prospective study was a study of the onset of alcoholism before age 28 years (Cloninger et al. 1988). The association of teenage onset of criminality with type 2 alcoholism and other personality studies of patients with early-onset alcoholism suggested that traits related to antisocial personality disorder would be predictive of type 2 alcoholism. According to Cloninger's (1987) personality model, antisocial personality disorder is characterized by high novelty-seeking (i.e., impulsivity), low harm-avoidance (i.e., risk taking), and low reward-dependence (i.e., aloofness). The explosive (borderline) personality disorder, which is also associated with much criminality, is like the antisocial profile except that harm-avoidance is high (i.e., these individuals are anxiety prone). A study of 431 children who had been assessed at age 11 years showed that personality ratings at that age were predictive of alcohol abuse at age 27 years (Cloninger et al. 1988). As predicted, high novelty-seeking and low harm-avoidance were most strongly predictive of early-onset alcohol abuse. When high novelty-seeking was combined with extreme scores on the other two dimensions, increased risk of early-onset alcohol abuse was present. For example, early-onset substance abuse was frequent in boys with antisocial or explosive (borderline) temperaments. This observation has been confirmed in subsequent longitudinal and descriptive studies for adolescent-onset alcohol and drug abuse.

Howard et al. (1997) reviewed more than 30 studies of alcoholic subtypes, other substance abuse, and personality as measured by the Tridimensional Personality Questionnaire (TPQ) or the more comprehensive Temperament and Character Inventory (TCI). They concluded that novelty-seeking predicts early-onset alcoholism, criminality, and other substance abuse and that it discriminates alcoholic individuals who have antisocial behavior and persons with antisocial personality disorder from their nonantisocial counterparts. Sher et al. (1991) has shown that children of alcoholic parents are significantly higher in novelty-seeking and lower in reward-dependence than are children of nonalcoholic parents and that high novelty-seeking is correlated consistently with substance use and abuse (Howard et al. 1997). High novelty-seeking has also been associated with stimulant abuse. Compared with novelty-seeking, findings from the harm-avoidance and reward-dependence scales are less consistent, possibly because their influence depends on the individual's overall temperament configuration, intelligence, and social adversity, which interact to influence character development. Nonlinear interactions among the personality dimensions are significant in their influence on the individual's risk of conduct disorder and substance use.

Several features other than personality emerge repeatedly as robust indicators of phenotypic heterogeneity associated with differences in heritability of substance abuse (see Table 7–3). These features include

**Table 7–3.** Clinical observations guiding candidate gene searches in polysubstance abusers (type 2 substance abuse)

| Variable | Observed characteristic |
|---|---|
| Heritability | Greater than in abusers of single substances |
| Age at onset | Early—usually in teens |
| Criminality | Frequent antisocial conduct (child and adult) |
| Severity | Greater than in abusers of single substances (i.e., more abuse problems, withdrawal) |
| Number of drugs | More than one drug class |
| Temperament | Explosive: more novelty seeking, more harm avoidance, less reward dependence |
| Character | Immature: less self-directed, less cooperative |
| Axis II diagnosis | Most often Cluster B (borderline or antisocial) |
| Global adaptive functioning (GAF) score | Lower general adaptive functioning |
| Evoked potentials | Lower P300 amplitude |

age at onset, gender, presence of childhood conduct disorder, presence of antisocial personality disorder, severity of dependence, presence of polysubstance abuse, and global adaptive functioning (GAF). Each of these variables, except GAF, has been advocated as the preferred basis for subgrouping alcoholic patients. However, the overlap among such univariate subdivisions is imperfect, and no consensus exists on the optimal criterion (perhaps based on etiology or treatment response) for calibrating a multivariate classification.

Cloninger and colleagues derived their classification from a multivariate analysis of genetic transmission in adoptees (Sigvardsson et al. 1996). Others have produced similar classifications based on cluster analyses of phenotypic data in abusers of alcohol and cocaine. The cluster classifications agree well with those defined by Cloninger's personality model. Schuckit et al. (1995), using data from the Collaborative Study of the Genetics of Alcoholism (COGA), found that 5 variables were nearly as effective as a more detailed classification scheme using 17 features of alcohol abuse and dependence: 1) ounces of alcohol consumed, 2) relief drinking (i.e., drinking to relieve withdrawal symptoms), 3) medical conditions, 4) physical consequences, and 5) social consequences. Brown et al. (1994) found that an efficient set of discriminators were 5 other variables: 1) lifetime severity, as measured by total Michigan Alcohol Screening Test score; 2) number of medical problems; 3) number of antisocial personality disorder symptoms; 4) childhood behavior problems such as hyperactivity or conduct disorder; and 5) dependence severity.

The analyses of COGA have made a valuable contribution to our understanding of the role of other substance abuse to alcoholic subtypes. The COGA investigators found that the cluster assignments resulted in differences in many other variables that had not been used in the classification, such as number of illicit drugs used, socioeconomic status, early onset of regular drinking or problems, and GAF scores. Type 2 alcoholism was associated on average with the use of more drugs (3.6 vs. 1.6 in men, and 3.4 vs. 1.3 in women), lower adaptive function (62 vs. 71), lower socioeconomic status, and earlier onset of regular drinking (age 16 vs. age 18) or problems (age 22 vs. age 26).

Such observations are consistent and show that subdivisions account for a substantial but minor part of the variability in symptoms. No individual feature or set of features such as age at onset, antisocial personality, or severity of dependence separates alcoholic individuals or substance abusers in general into mutually exclusive groups. Yet the consistent differences indicate that the motivational processes underlying the development of alcoholism are different in the prototypic groups such as Type I (or A) or Type II (or B) alcoholism. Therefore, studies of the genetics of substance abuse are using complementary strategies, including studies of the genetics of heritable personality traits, of heritable neurophysiological traits (such as P300), and of subtypes of abusers divided according to severity. In this way, the processes underlying development of substance abuse can be understood as interactions among multiple heritable risk factors leading to heterogeneity in substance abuse.

## Personality Antecedents of Substance Abuse

It is well established that substance abuse is associated with antisocial personality traits, but genetic studies must measure personality in ways that can help to guide the choice of candidate genes (Table 7–3). This has been done using the TCI in COGA for severe alcohol dependence (as defined by ICD-10 criteria), which is usually associated with polysubstance abuse (Table 7–4). Substance abusers differ significantly from others in six TCI dimensions, with the largest effects being the associations of dependence with high novelty-seeking (effect size = +.79) and immature development in two character dimensions: self-directedness and cooperativeness. In other words, severe substance dependence is associated with impulsive personality disorders (Cluster B). The development of alcoholism is most strongly associated with low self-directedness (effect size = −.85), which is characterized by a tendency to

deny responsibility and difficulty in impulse control and goal-directed discipline.

The personality correlates of substance abusers also depend on the social context for the use of the substance. This issue can be seen most clearly for cigarette smoking, which has been available consistently but is subject to changing social attitudes. Cigarette smoking is legal, enhances cognitive function, and does not lead to intoxication or interfere directly with general psychosocial adaptive functioning such as occupational achievement. Consequently, its use is influenced substantially by voluntary responses to social expectations that have differed between men and women and between different birth cohorts (see Table 7–5). In one survey, TCI novelty-seeking was correlated positively with three behaviors: ever smoking, daily smoking, and current smoking (defined as any in the past 6 months), although this correlation varied in magnitude and significance by age and gender (see also Downey et al. 1996). TCI harm-avoidance was not correlated significantly with smoking behavior but was correlated with endorsement of symptoms of nicotine dependence in young women ($r = .18$).

For men born before 1950 (older than 45), smoking behavior, especially daily smoking and number of DSM-IV symptoms of dependence (American Psychiatric Association 1994), was correlated positively with cooperativeness. In other words, if you were a man born before 1950, smoking was a prosocial behavior associated with social confidence and maturity in character. In contrast, for women born before 1950, smoking was a mildly antisocial behavior associated with low cooperativeness ($r = -.17$ with daily smoking and −.22 with number of dependence symptoms). For men and

**Table 7–4.**    Temperament and Character Inventory (TCI) scores distinguishing severe alcoholic subjects from other subjects in the Collaborative Study of the Genetics of Alcoholism

| TCI dimension | Mean TCI scores | | d/s | P |
|---|---|---|---|---|
| | Alcoholic subjects ($n = 138$) | Other subjects ($n = 580$) | | |
| Novelty-seeking | $22.8 \pm 6.1$ | $17.9 \pm 6.3$ | +.79 | 0.0001 |
| Harm-avoidance | $14.4 \pm 7.0$ | $13.7 \pm 6.8$ | +.11 | 0.2560 |
| Reward-dependence | $15.5 \pm 3.9$ | $16.7 \pm 3.8$ | −.32 | 0.0012 |
| Persistence | $5.2 \pm 2.0$ | $5.3 \pm 1.9$ | −.03 | 0.7722 |
| Self-directedness | $27.1 \pm 8.6$ | $33.9 \pm 7.5$ | −.85 | 0.0001 |
| Cooperativeness | $31.8 \pm 6.9$ | $36.2 \pm 4.6$ | −.79 | 0.0001 |
| Self-transcendence | $17.1 \pm 6.1$ | $15.8 \pm 5.8$ | +.23 | 0.0191 |

*Note.*    d/s = effect size (difference of means/standard deviation).

**Table 7–5.** Effects of gender and birth cohort on personality correlates of cigarette smoking in 1995 St. Louis Health Survey

| Behavior | Birth cohort | Gender | Personality correlation (×100) | | | |
|---|---|---|---|---|---|---|
| | | | NS | HA | SD | CO |
| Ever smoked | 1950 and later | Men | 17 | 2 | –4 | –3 |
| | | Women | 15* | 5 | –15* | –3 |
| | Before 1950 | Men | 13 | –6 | 5 | 10 |
| | | Women | 10 | 12 | –13 | –11 |
| Daily smoker | 1950 and later | Men | 8 | 4 | –18 | –8 |
| | | Women | 6 | 12 | –23* | –1 |
| | Before 1950 | Men | 17* | –16 | 7 | 21* |
| | | Women | 18* | 10 | –11 | –17* |
| Current smoker | 1950 and later | Men | 0 | 8 | –19* | –9 |
| | | Women | 16* | 8 | –19* | –12 |
| | Before 1950 | Men | 10 | 3 | 0 | 14 |
| | | Women | 10 | 2 | –10 | –11 |
| Dependent symptoms (DSM-IV) | 1950 and later | Men | 2 | 7 | –25* | –19 |
| | | Women | –7 | 18* | –25* | 1 |
| | Before 1950 | Men | –10 | 3 | 2 | 21* |
| | | Women | 17 | 13 | –28* | –22* |

*Note.* Sample size: 107 men and 182 women born in 1950 and later; 136 men and 165 women born before 1950. NS = novelty-seeking; HA = harm-avoidance; SD = self-directedness; CO = cooperativeness.
*Correlations significant at $P < 0.05$.

women born after 1950, continuing to smoke was associated with low self-directedness ($r = -.19$), that is, poor impulse control, consistent with prior reports that self-efficacy is the strongest predictor of smoking cessation. For women born after 1950, ever smoking and daily smoking were also associated significantly with low self-directedness.

These differences reflect changing social attitudes toward smoking. Originally men but not women were encouraged to smoke, and individuals born after 1950 were discouraged from smoking regardless of gender. Individuals born after 1950 reached midadolescence after the release of the United States surgeon general's report (1964) warning about the health risks of cigarette smoking. Thus, the same behavior has different psychobiological correlates depending on changes in social context. Accordingly, genetic research must focus on the underlying psychobiological traits from which behaviors such as substance abuse emerge, recognizing that substance dependence is the result of complex interactions among multiple genetic and environmental factors.

# Candidate Gene Approaches to Substance Abuse

Candidate gene approaches to substance abuse were encouraged by the consistently replicated findings of a protective effect of genetic polymorphisms of the alcohol-metabolizing enzymes alcohol dehydrogenase and aldehyde dehydrogenase in Asian populations. However, susceptibility to substance abuse genes is not influenced much by heritable differences in receptor affinity or metabolism of other abused substances, possibly because familial cases of substance abuse are nonspecific patterns of antisocial behavior involving multiple drugs taken on the basis of availability and social pressures.

Nevertheless, polysubstance abuse is most consistently associated with the personality trait of novelty-seeking, which is a heritable temperament trait related to pleasure and thrill-seeking behaviors that show little or no variation across culture or birth cohort. The heritability of novelty-seeking is about 50%, according to twin studies (Stallings et al. 1996). Its heritability, quantifiable across generations and birth cohorts, and its putative relationship to brain reward mechanisms have stimulated research on the genetics and psychobiology of novelty-seeking in general and in substance abusers in particular. Available data on the genetics and psychobiology of novelty-seeking have been reviewed in detail elsewhere (Cloninger 1998) and are summarized in Table 7–6. Novelty-seeking quantifies individual differences in approach behavior to novelty or cues to reward, as regulated in medial prefrontal cortex and other regions shown in Table 7–6. Based on animal models, dopaminergic mechanisms were hypothesized to play a key role in the modulation of novelty-seeking, which has been supported by findings of associations with striatal dopaminergic activity and genetic associations with genes regulating dopamine neurotransmission. These genes include the dopamine transporter and $D_2$ and $D_4$ dopamine receptors.

Two studies have confirmed the expected associations between substance abuse and genes related to novelty-seeking. Novelty-seeking and the number of drugs abused were increased in cocaine abusers who carried the A2 allele of the Taq1 polymorphism on chromosome 11q of the $D_2$ dopamine receptor (Compton et al. 1996) (see Table 7–7). This polymorphism has been associated with, but not linked with, susceptibility to substance abuse and to severe alcoholism in several studies.

Several studies have been carried out on a polymorphism in the $D_4$ dopamine receptor (D4DR), which is expressed largely in limbic regions regulating brain reward. First, using a test that is a robust indicator of genetic transmission, researchers found an association between long-repeat variants of D4DR on chromosome 11 and novelty-seeking in the general population and in families (Benjamin et al. 1996). This association has been supported by several studies of children with attention-deficit disorder but not in all studies of personality in the general population (see Table 7–6). The same repeat polymorphism has been associated with opiate dependence (Table 7–8).

These association studies demonstrate the sensitivity of association for detecting the effects of genes with small to moderate effects on a trait. The D4DR gene explains about 4% of the total variance in novelty-seeking, which is approximately 10% of its total genetic variance. Other associations, such as those between the serotonin transporter and harm-avoidance, also account only for small effects and are unlikely to be detected consistently when tested for association with a heterogeneous categorical diagnosis such as alcoholism or substance abuse.

**Table 7–6.**    Genetic and neurobiological correlates of novelty seeking, a heritable risk factor for substance abuse

| Variable | Effect |
|---|---|
| Neuroanatomy (positron-emission tomography/ single photon emission computed tomography) | |
| Prefrontal (left) | Decreased activity (behavioral disinhibition) |
| Cingulate | Increased activity (behavioral activation) |
| Caudate (left) | Increased activity (behavioral activation) |
| Neuropsychology | |
| Reaction time | Slower to respond if not reinforced (neutral stimuli, $r = -.4$) |
| Stimulus intensity (N1/P2 ERP) | Augmentation of intensity of cortical responses to novel auditory stimuli ($r = .5$) |
| Sedation threshold | More easily sedated by diazepam (lower threshold, $r = -.3$) |
| Rey word list memory | Deterioration of verbal memory when excited (after ingesting amphetamine, $r = .6$) |
| Neurogenetics | |
| $D_2$ dopamine receptor | Association with Taq1-A2 allele |
| $D_4$ dopamine receptor | Association with long exon III variants |
| Dopamine transporter | Association with increased reuptake |

*Note.*    N1 = first negative wave of evoked reaction potential (ERP); P2 = second positive wave of ERP.
*Source.*    Cloninger 1998.

**Table 7–7.** Clinical correlates of $D_2$ dopamine receptor polymorphism in cocaine abusers carrying Taq1-A1 allele versus A2 allele

| Variable | Mean | | P |
| --- | --- | --- | --- |
| | A1 allele | A2 allele | |
| Severity (number of drugs used ever) | 6.5 | 7.4 | 0.04 |
| Personality (novelty-seeking) | 17.6 | 20.9 | 0.01 |

*Source.* Compton et al. 1996.

**Table 7–8.** Association of $D_4$ dopamine receptor exon III 7-repeat allele in patients with opiate dependence in Israel

| Subjects | Opiate dependent | Control group |
| --- | --- | --- |
| Sephardic Jews | 29.0% ($n = 107$) | 13.0% ($n = 54$) |
| Israeli Arabs | 29.4% ($n = 34$) | 10.7% ($n = 56$) |
| Combined total | 29.1% ($n = 141$) | 10.9% ($n = 110$) |

*Note.* Each group differs significantly ($P < 0.05$), and when combined, the difference is highly significant ($P < 0.01$).
*Source.* Kotler et al. 1997.

## Genome Scans for Detecting Linkage

Another strategy for detecting genes that contribute to substance abuse involves carrying out a genome-wide scan with many markers to detect chromosomal regions containing genes linked to susceptibility to the disorder or to related quantitative traits. This strategy has been used in COGA for the diagnosis of alcoholism, for related personality traits, and for related evoked potential measures.

The results for temperament are summarized in Table 7–9. Each temperament dimension was linked to multiple loci, which interacted in a nonadditive manner. This linkage suggests that even at the level of temperament the genetic systems influencing substance abuse are complex, involving several genes that act in different ways depending on the way they are combined.

The results for P300 voltage (amplitude) and for diagnosis of alcoholism are summarized in Table 7–10. The data suggested that the genes contributing to low risk of any abuse (i.e., having a protective effect) are different from those contributing to high risk. Likewise, different genes were linked to susceptibility to mild al-

**Table 7–9.** Multilocus epistatic interactions in linkage analysis of human personality in the Collaborative Study of the Genetics of Alcoholism

| Temperament trait | Locus | LOD score | P | Explained variance |
| --- | --- | --- | --- | --- |
| Harm-avoidance | 8:17 21:62 | 5.1 | 0.000007 | 66% |
| Reward-dependence | 2:4 2:116 16:15 | 5.3 | 0.0005 | 53% |
| Novelty-seeking | 10:88 15:65 | 2.8 | 0.02 | 50% |
| Persistence | 2:158 3:220 | 2.5 | 0.01 | 45% |

cohol dependence, based on DSM-III-R criteria for alcoholism (American Psychiatric Association 1987), and to severe alcohol dependence, based on ICD-10 criteria (World Health Organization 1992) and latent class analyses. The locus linked to a protective effect is in the vicinity of the gene encoding alcohol dehydrogenase 3, which was previously known to have a protective effect against alcoholism in Asians. These results will be tested in a larger replication sample in the near future in order to evaluate the reproducibility of the linkage results.

## Conclusion

Impressive progress has been made in understanding the genetics of substance abuse. Twin and adoption studies confirm the heritability of substance abuse. Heritable personality traits underlying impulsive (i.e., Cluster B) personality disorders predict risk of substance abuse. This prediction primarily involves an association between novelty-seeking and early-onset, severe forms of polysubstance abuse. Genome-wide scans have identified chromosomal regions containing genes linked to high risk and low risk for alcohol and other substance dependence. Association studies of genes influencing dopamine neurotransmission have been associated with substance abuse and related traits such as novelty-seeking and attention-deficit disorder. Future work is needed to confirm the replicability of these results and to clarify the nonlinear interactions among multiple genetic and environmental risk factors in the pathways leading to substance abuse.

**Table 7–10.**    Multipoint linkage findings in genome-wide scans of alcoholism-related traits in the Collaborative Study of the Genetics of Alcoholism

| Alcoholic trait | Chromosome | Nearby markers | LOD score |
|---|---|---|---|
| Low risk for any abuse | 4 | ADH3 | 2.5 |
| High risk for mild dependence | 7 | D7S1793 | 3.4 |
| | 1 | D1S1588 | 2.9 |
| High risk for severe dependence | 16 | D16S475 | 4.0 |
| | | D16S675 | |
| P300 voltage | | | |
| O$^2$ | 2q35-qter | D2S425 | 3.3 |
| Cz | 6q22.3 | GATA30/D6S1007 | 3.4 |

# References

American Psychiatric Association: Diagnostic and Statistical Manual of Mental Disorders, 3rd Edition, Revised. Washington, DC, American Psychiatric Association, 1987

American Psychiatric Association: Diagnostic and Statistical Manual of Mental Disorders, 4th Edition. Washington, DC, American Psychiatric Association, 1994

Benjamin J, Greenberg B, Murphy DL, et al: Mapping personality traits to genes: population and family association between the D4 dopamine receptor and measures of novelty seeking. Nat Genet 12:81–84, 1996

Bierut LJ, Dinwiddie SH, Begleiter H, et al: Familial transmission of substance dependence: alcohol, marijuana, and cocaine. Presented at the annual meeting of the Research Society on Alcoholism, Steamboat Springs, CO, June 1995

Brown J, Babor TF, Litt MD, et al: The type A/type B distinction; subtyping alcoholics according to indicators of vulnerability and severity. Ann N Y Acad Sci 708:23–33, 1994

Cadoret RJ, Yates WR, Troughton E, et al: Adoption study demonstrating two genetic pathways to drug abuse. Arch Gen Psychiatry 52:42–52, 1995

Cloninger CR: Neurogenetic adaptive mechanisms in alcoholism. Science 236:410–416, 1987

Cloninger CR: Genetics and psychobiology of the seven factor model of personality, in Biology of Personality Disorders. Edited by Silk KR. Washington, DC, American Psychiatric Press, 1998

Cloninger CR, Sigvardsson S, Bohman M: Childhood personality predicts alcohol abuse in young adults. Alcohol Clin Exp Res 12:494–504, 1988

Compton PA, Anglin MD, Khalsa-Denison ME, et al: The D2 dopamine receptor gene, addiction, and personality: clinical correlates in cocaine abusers. Biol Psychiatry 39:302–304, 1996

Downey KK, Pomerleau CS, Pomerleau OF: Personality differences related to smoking and adult attention deficit hyperactivity disorder. J Subst Abuse 8:129–135, 1996

Howard MO, Kivlahan D, Walker RD: Cloninger's tridimensional theory of personality and psychopathology: applications to substance use disorders. J Stud Alcohol 58:48–66, 1997

Kotler M, Cohen H, Segman R, et al: Excess dopamine D4 receptor (D4DR) exon III seven repeat allele in opioid-dependent subjects. Mol Psychiatry 2:251–254, 1997

Schuckit MA, Tipp JE, Smith TL, et al: An evaluation of type A and B alcoholics. Addiction 90:1189–1203, 1995

Sher KJ, Walitzer KS, Wood PK, et al: Characteristics of children of alcoholics: putative risk factors, substance use and abuse, and psychopathology. J Abnorm Psychol 100:427–448, 1991

Sigvardsson S, Bohman M, Cloninger CR: Replication of the Stockholm Adoption Study of Alcoholism: confirmatory cross-fostering analysis. Arch Gen Psychiatry 53:681–687, 1996

Stallings MC, Hewitt JK, Cloninger CR, et al: Genetic and environmental structure of the Tridimensional Personality Questionnaire: three or four temperament dimensions? J Pers Soc Psychol 70:127–140, 1996

Tsuang MT, Lyons MJ, Eisen SA, et al: Genetic influences on DSM-III-R drug abuse and dependence: a study of 3,372 twin pairs. Am J Med Genet 67:473–477, 1996

United States Surgeon General: Smoking and health (Public Health Service Publ No 1103). Washington, DC, U.S. Government Printing Office, 1964

World Health Organization: International Statistical Classification of Diseases and Related Health Problems, 10th Revision. Geneva, Switzerland, World Health Organization, 1992

# Principles of Learning in the Study and Treatment of Substance Abuse

*Applying What We've Learned*[1]

Stephen T. Higgins, Ph.D.

Psychology has contributed to the study and treatment of substance use disorders in many important ways (Miller and Brown 1997). In this chapter, I provide a detailed discussion of research from experimental and clinical psychology demonstrating that drugs promote repeated drug use for nonmedical purposes, in part, through operant conditioning and social learning processes.[2] This knowledge has provided a valuable and widely used set of theoretical concepts and experimental methods for studying substance use disorders in preclinical and clinical settings. Perhaps most important, this work has elucidated fundamental behavioral mechanisms of action (e.g., reinforcement) that have significant scientific and practical implications for understanding substance use disorders.

This information has been well integrated into basic-science and clinical research practices in the area of substance use disorders, but less well into treatment and policy arenas. For example, books on the treatment of substance use disorders sometimes fail to mention the reinforcing effects of abused drugs, and clinicians or policy makers sometimes discuss substance use disorders exclusively in terms of physical dependence and withdrawal or underlying psychopathology. Although those processes and concepts have an important role in a comprehensive account of substance use disorders,

they do not completely explain it. They ignore fundamental contributions of operant conditioning and social learning to the genesis and maintenance of substance use disorders and to its remediation. In this chapter, I attempt to illustrate how a broader appreciation for the importance of these learning processes can improve efforts to reduce substance use disorders.

## Drugs as Reinforcers

Beginning in the 1940s, experimental psychologists developed methods for studying voluntary drug self-administration in laboratory animals (Spragg 1940). Initial studies often used animals that were first made physically dependent on drugs via experimenter-administered drug exposure (e.g., Thompson and Schuster 1964). The animals learned an arbitrary response that resulted in the delivery of a drug injection. These studies were important because of the methodology they introduced, but the effects observed were easily integrated with extant theories that posited substance use disorders to be driven by physical dependence and withdrawal. Shortly thereafter, however, studies using this new methodology showed that rats and monkeys who were not physically dependent

[1]Preparation of this chapter was supported by National Institute on Drug Abuse Research Grants RO1-DA09378 and RO1-DA08076.

[2]Readers are referred elsewhere (see O'Brien et al. 1986; Robinson and Berridge 1993) for coverage of the important contributions of respondent conditioning to understanding and treating substance use disorders.

would similarly learn to self-administer commonly abused drugs such as morphine, amphetamine, or cocaine (e.g., Deneau et al. 1969). Experimental variations of parameters such as the scheduled relationship between the learned response and the drug administration, the drug dosage, and the presence of stimuli signaling drug availability influenced the response in the same manner as when comparable manipulations were made using food, sex, and other unconditioned reinforcers as behavioral consequences (Young and Herling 1986). These findings provided an empirical foundation for concluding that, like food, water, and sex, abused drugs had the capacity to function as unconditioned positive reinforcers and that drug seeking and use conformed to the principles of operant conditioning.

Operant conditioning is a basic form of learning in which the future probability of voluntary behavior is controlled by its consequences (Catania 1998). Several decades of experimental research demonstrated that drug self-administration conformed to the principles of operant conditioning and that laboratory animals voluntarily consumed most of the same drugs that humans abuse (Henningfield et al. 1986). Psychomotor stimulants, ethanol, nicotine, opioids, and sedatives function as reinforcers and promote voluntary drug self-administration in a variety of species (Young and Herling 1986). Physical dependence, tolerance, and withdrawal could be established and shown to influence patterns of drug consumption in these self-administration arrangements, but the evidence showed that those were consequences of repeated drug use and not necessary conditions for drug self-administration to be established and maintained. When given unconstrained access to drugs of abuse such as cocaine and opiates, laboratory animals sometimes consumed lethal doses of the drugs or engaged in repeated drug use to the exclusion of basic sustenance, thereby demonstrating that even these most extreme characteristics of substance abuse and dependence were not exclusively human phenomena (e.g., Aigner and Balster 1978; Deneau et al. 1969).

## Social Learning Factors

During this period of intensive research on drugs as reinforcers, theoretically related research on drug dependence as learned behavior was examining the influence of social factors on the behavioral action of drugs in humans. An important advance in this area extended to human drug use the social learning concepts of modeling and imitation. For example, alcoholic individuals imitate the rates and patterns of alcohol ingestion modeled by others drinking in their presence (e.g., Caudill and Lipscomb 1980).

In another set of experimental studies, prototypical drugs of abuse shared a common effect of facilitating social interaction (see Stitzer et al. 1981). For example, when under the acute influence of alcohol or other abused drugs, individuals would forgo opportunities to earn money in order to interact socially with other research volunteers (Griffiths et al. 1975; Higgins et al. 1989). These studies illustrated that in addition to the unconditioned reinforcing effects of abused drugs, repeated drug use also might be supported via drug-produced enhancement of social interaction.

Another series of rigorous experimental studies demonstrated that drinking by alcoholic persons was sensitive to social consequences (see Griffiths et al. 1978). For example, drinking decreased significantly when hospitalized alcoholic patients had to forgo either social interaction with other alcoholic patients on the ward or visitation privileges with a romantic partner as a consequence of drinking.

As a final example, a series of studies demonstrated that the behavioral effects of drugs were influenced significantly by what drug users were told or believed about the drugs they consumed as opposed to the pharmacological effects of the substances per se. Instructing subjects that the substance they consumed was an active drug was a more important determinant of outcome than the pharmacological content of the substance (see Wilson 1978). For example, whether social drinkers or nonabstinent alcoholic individuals consumed relatively large amounts of a beverage in a taste-testing procedure was determined by whether they were told the beverage contained alcohol rather than by the alcohol content of the drink (Marlatt et al. 1973). Alcohol dosages were typically on the low side in these studies (0.5 g/kg), and there seems little doubt that higher dosages would reveal a greater influence of pharmacological factors. That point notwithstanding, these findings illustrated a striking influence of nonpharmacological factors on behavioral effects of ethanol that heretofore had been attributed to the direct pharmacological effects of the drug.

## Theoretical Implications

These advances regarding the role of learning in drug use and its behavioral consequences had important theoretical implications. First, theories of substance use disorders couched exclusively in terms of physiological and pharmacological processes of tolerance and withdrawal (Jellinek 1960), even those that included conditioned tolerance and withdrawal (Wikler 1980), were incomplete. This advance in our conceptual understanding of substance use disorders is discernible, for example, across consecutive editions of the psychoactive substance use disorder syndromes section of DSM. In DSM-III (American Psychiatric Association 1980), the psychoactive substance use disorder syndromes were defined exclusively in terms of tolerance and withdrawal. In DSM-III-R (American Psychiatric Association 1987), tolerance and withdrawal were reduced to four of the nine symptoms, and the remaining five addressed behavioral symptoms. In DSM-IV (American Psychiatric Association 1994), tolerance and withdrawal were retained and in some ways made more prominent than in DSM-III-R, but they represented only two of the seven symptoms and were explicitly noted to be neither necessary nor sufficient for a diagnosis of dependence.

Second, this body of scientific evidence contradicted self-medication theories that personality disorders or other psychiatric disturbances were necessary conditions for substance use disorders. The drug self-administration literature provided compelling scientific evidence that repeated substance use is a product of normal learning processes that are an integral part of the evolutionary history of humans and other species. As such, any physically intact human is deemed to possess the necessary neurobiological systems to experience drug-produced reinforcement and hence the potential to develop a substance use disorder given appropriate opportunity and supporting environmental circumstances. In brief, psychopathology is a factor that can significantly increase the probability of substance use disorders (Regier et al. 1990), but it is not a necessary condition for them to emerge.

Third, studies on instructions and beliefs as determinants of the behavioral actions of alcohol provided the impetus for current theoretical and clinical interests in cognitive and expectancy factors in substance use disorders (see Marlatt et al., Chapter 31, in this volume). Humans bring complex histories to drug-using situations, often involving years of direct and vicarious experience with drug use and years assimilating peer influence and other cultural views about reasons for and consequences of substance use. Those rich histories influence substance consumption practices and the consequences of substance use, and they provide therapeutic targets for treatment interventions.

## A Learning-Based Conceptual Framework

This learning-based approach raises an important question: if all biologically intact humans possess the basic prerequisites for a substance use disorder, and drug use for recreational purposes is quite prevalent, why is the prevalence of these disorders not higher? A complete answer to this question is not available, but several decades of behavioral research have revealed a number of determinants of substance use, abuse, and dependence that have important clinical and policy implications.

First, cost is an important determinant of substance use by recreational users and dependent individuals (see Chaloupka et al., in press; Edwards et al. 1994). Cost is used broadly here to subsume 1) monetary price; 2) the degree of effort required to search out and obtain substances; 3) the frequency and intensity of aversive events encountered while obtaining, using, and recovering from substance use; and 4) what is forfeited by choosing to allocate time to substance consumption rather than existing alternatives.

Second, environmental context is an important determinant of substance use. Contexts lacking alternative sources of nonpharmacological reinforcement, for example, can promote the acquisition and maintenance of drug use (Higgins 1997). Similarly, individuals lacking skills or resources necessary to find available sources of alternative reinforcement are likely to be at greater risk for substance use disorders (cf. Schuster 1986). Such skill deficits likely contribute to the higher prevalence rates of these disorders observed, for example, among individuals who have severe mental illness, among those who have lower educational achievement, and among those who are unemployed (Substance Abuse and Mental Health Services Administration 1996). Also, as I noted earlier, social or peer influence can modulate risk for substance use disorders, likely via modeling of abusive or risky consumption patterns and social reinforcement of deviant behavior (Hawkins et al. 1992). Family context also influences risk for substance use disorders not only via the substance use practices and views of the parents but also via family behavior-management practices, interpersonal conflict, and the degree of parent monitoring of child behavior (Hawkins et al. 1992). Finally, neighborhoods can influence risk through the number of substance-using opportunities afforded to youths and probably through other social-learning processes (Chilcoat and Johanson 1998).

Third, individual differences must be considered.

Genetics significantly influence risk for alcoholism, smoking, and other substance use disorders (see Cloninger, Chapter 7, in this volume). How such genetic differences in risk are expressed is not well understood. Variations in individual sensitivity to drug-produced reinforcement and related learning factors discussed in this chapter have been well demonstrated in preclinical studies and offer a reasonable possibility that is being pursued by researchers in behavioral genetics (Elmer et al. 1998).

## Preclinical and Clinical Practices

Knowledge regarding the role of operant conditioning and social learning processes in substance use disorders has important practical applications.

### Preclinical Applications

As was noted earlier in this chapter, the notion that substance use and abuse are products of reinforcement and related conditioning processes is well integrated into basic-science research on substance abuse. For example, this knowledge provided an important impetus for examining whether drugs of abuse from different pharmacological classes share common neurochemical and neuroanatomical mechanisms of action that might account for their common reinforcing functions (Wise 1996). The emerging picture is a dynamic one, but evidence suggests that abused drugs share common actions on mesocorticolimbic dopamine efferent and afferent pathways, the same pathways that are involved in the motivating actions of other nonpharmacological reinforcers (Wise 1996).

As another example, animal self-administration concepts and methods have become a mainstay in preclinical efforts to elucidate the basic pharmacology of abused drugs and to develop pharmacotherapies for substance use disorders. The quest to develop a pharmacotherapy for cocaine dependence, for example, depends heavily on animal self-administration models to screen new potential treatment agents (Winger 1998). Studies on possible vaccines against cocaine abuse have used the drug self-administration preparation as a measure of efficacy (Fox et al. 1996), as did the seminal study that introduced the notion of vaccines against drug abuse (Bonese et al. 1974).

At a still more practical level, the concordance between the drugs that laboratory animals self-administer and the drugs that humans abuse is sufficiently strong

that self-administration testing in nonhumans and humans has become a core component of abuse liability testing used by the Food and Drug Administration, the Drug Enforcement Agency, and other regulatory agencies in approving and scheduling new compounds (Fischman and Mello 1989).

### Clinical Applications

Perhaps most important, knowledge regarding the reinforcing effects of drugs and the fundamental role of social learning in the development and maintenance of substance use disorders has led to the development of efficacious treatments (Stitzer and Higgins 1995).

Contingency management.    Much of the research reviewed in this chapter underscored the operant nature of drug use. As such, it follows logically that the probability that patients will successfully abstain from substance use during and after treatment should be modifiable via frequent, systematic delivery of reinforcing consequences for abstinence. Interventions designed to provide such systematic reinforcement are termed *contingency-management interventions* and are typically used as adjuncts to broader-focused therapies. In controlled trials, contingency-management interventions have reduced most forms of substance use, especially illicit drug abuse (Higgins and Silverman, in press; Stitzer and Higgins 1995). Contingency-management interventions are the only treatment shown in controlled clinical trials to reliably reduce cocaine use in dependent outpatients (Higgins et al. 1994; Silverman et al. 1996).

Skills training.    The skill levels of many substance abusers are sufficiently limited to preclude participation in important activities that could function as alternatives to substance abuse and to make managing the challenges of everyday life stressful. Efficacious skills-training interventions, developed by learning-based therapists, reduce those skill deficits and improve substance-abuse treatment outcomes, including coping- and social-skills training (Monti et al. 1995), relapse-prevention training (Marlatt et al., Chapter 31, in this volume), and behavioral-marriage therapy using positive communication skills (O'Farrell 1995).

Community reinforcement approach.    Participation in communities that reinforce a healthy lifestyle is considered by many experts in substance abuse to be important to successful recovery. Learning-based therapists have developed interventions designed to systematically rearrange significant aspects of local communities to differentially support an abstinent lifestyle. For example, the community reinforcement approach (CRA) attempts to increase alternatives to a substance-abusing lifestyle through improved family and marital relations and through vocational and social/recreational activities (Hunt and Azrin 1973). To the extent possible, participation in these alternatives is contingent on abstinence from substance abuse. In a series of controlled trials, CRA produced impressive treatment outcomes with severely and less-impaired alcoholic individuals (Meyers and Smith 1995) and, when used in combination with voucher-based incentives, with cocaine-dependent and opioid-dependent outpatients (Bickel et al. 1997; Higgins et al. 1994). Clinician manuals are available for using CRA in the treatment of alcoholism (Meyers and Smith 1995) and cocaine dependence (Budney and Higgins 1998).

**Brief interventions.** Learning-based therapists have been leaders in the development of efficacious, cost-effective, brief interventions that can be delivered in primary care and other medical settings and through other community agencies (see Fiore et al. 1990; Heather 1995). These interventions are used with problem drinkers, usually at an early point in their history of problem drinking, and with cigarette smokers. To my knowledge, there are no reports of their use with illicit-drug abusers. Treatment content and duration vary depending on the population, settings, and other factors, but treatment typically involves problem identification and assessment, a specific recommendation for reducing or discontinuing problematic substance use, and follow-up visits to assess change, with treatment sessions lasting as little as 10–15 minutes. Despite these relatively modest characteristics, brief interventions have achieved impressive reductions in substance abuse and related problems.

**Learning-based treatments and comorbidity.** Recognition of the importance of offering integrated substance abuse and mental health services in the treatment of individuals with comorbid substance abuse and other mental illness is growing (Onken et al. 1997). Learning-based interventions for substance use disorders are conceptually consistent and thus easily integrated with many efficacious treatments for other psychiatric disorders. For example, behavioral treatments for anxiety disorders, depression, and insomnia are included as components of CRA treatment for cocaine dependence (Budney and Higgins 1998). Combining

pharmacotherapies with learning-based treatments for substance use disorders is common (e.g., Onken et al. 1995) and is likely to meet with fewer philosophical objections to psychopharmacology than is sometimes the case with more traditional substance-abuse treatment approaches.

## Conclusion

Substance use disorders result from a complex interplay of many factors. Operant and social learning are important psychological factors that contribute to the genesis, maintenance, and recovery from these disorders. These psychological factors and their related methods certainly are not the elusive magic bullet that can alleviate substance use disorders. Rather, they represent a thoroughly researched set of scientific concepts, principles, and practices that can improve efforts to reduce substance use disorders if better disseminated and applied. Those of us trained in the health sciences are probably the best source for the dissemination of such scientific information into community settings and practices.

## References

Aigner TG, Balster RL: Choice behavior in rhesus monkeys: cocaine versus food. Science 201:534–535, 1978

American Psychiatric Association: Diagnostic and Statistical Manual of Mental Disorders, 3rd Edition. Washington, DC, American Psychiatric Association, 1980

American Psychiatric Association: Diagnostic and Statistical Manual of Mental Disorders, 3rd Edition, Revised. Washington, DC, American Psychiatric Association, 1987

American Psychiatric Association: Diagnostic and Statistical Manual of Mental Disorders, 4th Edition. Washington, DC, American Psychiatric Association, 1994

Bickel WK, Amass L, Higgins ST, et al: Effects of adding behavioral treatment to opioid detoxification with buprenorphine. J Consult Clin Psychol 65:803–810, 1997

Bonese KF, Wainer BH, Fitch FW, et al: Changes in heroin self-administration by a rhesus monkey after morphine immunization. Nature 252:708–710, 1974

Budney AJ, Higgins ST: Treating Cocaine Dependence: A Community Reinforcement Plus Vouchers Approach. Rockville, MD, National Institute on Drug Abuse, 1998

Catania AC: Learning, 4th Edition. Upper Saddle River, NJ, Prentice-Hall, 1998

Caudill BD, Lipscomb TR: Modeling influences on alcoholics' rates of alcohol consumption. J Appl Behav Anal 13:355–365, 1980

Chaloupka FJ, Bickel WK, Grossman M, et al (eds): The Economic Analysis of Substance Use and Abuse: An Integration of Econometric and Behavioral Economic Research. Chicago, IL, University of Chicago Press (in press)

Chilcoat H, Johanson C-E: Vulnerability to cocaine abuse, in Cocaine Abuse Research: Behavior, Pharmacology, and Clinical Applications. Edited by Higgins ST, Katz JL. San Diego, CA, Academic Press, 1998, pp 313–341

Deneau G, Yanagita T, Seevers MH: Self-administration of psychoactive substances by the monkey. Psychopharmacologia 16:30–48, 1969

Edwards G, Anderson P, Babor TF, et al: Alcohol Policy and the Public Good. New York, Oxford University Press, 1994

Elmer GI, Miner LL, Pickens RW: The contributions of genetic factors in cocaine and other drug abuse, in Cocaine Abuse Research: Behavior, Pharmacology, and Clinical Applications. Edited by Higgins ST, Katz JL. San Diego, CA, Academic Press, 1998, pp 289–311

Fiore MC, Pierce JP, Remington PL, et al: Cigarette smoking: the clinician's role in cessation, prevention, and public health. Dis Mon 35:183–242, 1990

Fischman MW, Mello NK (eds): Testing for Abuse Liability of Drugs (NIDA Res Monogr 92; DHHS Publ No ADM-89-1613). Rockville, MD, National Institute on Drug Abuse, 1989

Fox BS, Kantak KM, Edwards MA, et al: Efficacy of a therapeutic cocaine vaccine in rodent models. Nat Med 2:1129–1132, 1996

Griffiths RR, Bigelow G, Liebson I: Effect of ethanol self-administration on choice behavior: money vs. socializing. Pharmacol Biochem Behav 3:443–446, 1975

Griffiths RR, Bigelow GE, Liebson IA: Relationship of social factors to ethanol self-administration in alcoholics, in Alcoholism: New Directions in Behavioral Research and Treatment. Edited by Nathan PE, Marlatt GA, Loberg TT. New York, Plenum, 1978, pp 351–379

Hawkins JD, Catalano RF, Miller JY: Risk and protective factors for alcohol and other drug problems in adolescence and early adulthood: implications for substance abuse prevention. Psychol Bull 112:64–105, 1992

Heather N: Brief intervention strategies, in Handbook of Alcoholism Treatment Approaches: Effective Alternatives, 2nd Edition. Edited by Hester RK, Miller WR. Boston, MA, Allyn & Bacon, 1995, pp 105–122

Henningfield JE, Lukas SE, Bigelow GE: Human studies of drugs as reinforcers, in Behavioral Analysis of Drug Dependence. Edited by Goldberg SR, Stolerman IP. Orlando, FL, Academic Press, 1986, pp 69–122

Higgins ST: The influence of alternative reinforcers on cocaine use and abuse: a brief review. Pharmacol Biochem Behav 57:419–427, 1997

Higgins ST, Silverman K (eds): Motivating Behavior Change in Illicit-Drug Abusers: Research on Contingency-Management Interventions. Washington, DC, American Psychological Association (in press)

Higgins ST, Hughes JR, Bickel WK: Effects of d-amphetamine on choice of social versus monetary reinforcement: a discrete-trial test. Pharmacol Biochem Behav 34:297–301, 1989

Higgins ST, Budney AJ, Bickel WK, et al: Incentives improve outcome in outpatient treatment of cocaine dependence. Arch Gen Psychiatry 51:568–576, 1994

Hunt GM, Azrin NH: A community reinforcement approach to alcoholism. Behav Res Ther 11:91–104, 1973

Jellinek EM: The Disease Concept of Alcoholism. New Brunswick, NJ, Hillhouse Press, 1960

Marlatt GA, Deming B, Reid J: Loss of control drinking in alcoholics. J Abnorm Psychol 81:233–241, 1973

Meyers RJ, Smith JE: Clinical Guide to Alcohol Treatment: The Community Reinforcement Approach. New York, Guilford, 1995

Miller WR, Brown SA: Why psychologists should treat alcohol and drug problems. Am Psychol 52:1269–1279, 1997

Monti PM, Rohsenow DJ, Colby SM, et al: Coping and social skills training, in Handbook of Alcoholism Treatment Approaches: Effective Alternatives, 2nd Edition. Edited by Hester RK, Miller WR. Boston, MA, Allyn & Bacon, 1995, pp 221–241

O'Brien CP, Ehrman RN, Ternes JW: Classical conditioning in human opioid dependence, in Behavioral Analysis of Drug Dependence. Edited by Goldberg SR, Stolerman IP. Orlando, FL, Academic Press, 1986, pp 329–356

O'Farrell TJ: Marital and family therapy, in Handbook of Alcoholism Treatment Approaches: Effective Alternatives, 2nd Edition. Edited by Hester RK, Miller WR. Boston, MA, Allyn & Bacon, 1995, pp 195–220

Onken LS, Blaine JD, Boren JJ (eds): Integrating Behavioral Therapies With Medications in the Treatment of Drug Dependence (NIDA Res Monogr 150; NIH Publ No 95-3899). Rockville, MD, National Institute on Drug Abuse, 1995

Onken LS, Blaine JD, Genser S, et al (eds): Treatment of Drug-Dependent Individuals With Comorbid Mental Disorders (NIDA Res Monogr 172; NIH Publ No 97-4172). Rockville, MD, National Institute on Drug Abuse, 1997

Regier DA, Farmer ME, Rae DS, et al: Comorbidity of mental disorders with alcohol and other drug abuse. JAMA 264:2511–2518, 1990

Robinson TE, Berridge KC: The neural basis of drug craving: an incentive-sensitization theory of addiction. Brain Res Rev 18:247–291, 1993

Schuster CR: Implications of laboratory research for the treatment of drug dependence, in Behavioral Analysis of Drug Dependence. Edited by Goldberg SR, Stolerman IP. Orlando, FL, Academic Press, 1986, pp 357–385

Silverman K, Higgins ST, Brooner RK, et al: Sustained cocaine abstinence in methadone maintenance patients through voucher-based reinforcement therapy. Arch Gen Psychiatry 53:409–415, 1996

Spragg SDS: Morphine addiction in chimpanzees, in Comparative Psychology Monographs, Vol 15. Baltimore, MD, Johns Hopkins University Press, 1940, pp 1–172

Stitzer ML, Griffiths RR, Bigelow GE, et al: Social stimulus factors in drug effects in human subjects, in Behavioral Pharmacology of Drug Dependence (NIDA Res Monogr 37; DHHS ADM-81-1137). Edited by Thompson T, Johanson CE. Washington, DC, U.S. Government Printing Office, 1981, pp 130–154

Stitzer ML, Higgins ST: Behavioral treatment of drug and alcohol abuse, in Psychopharmacology: The Fourth Generation of Progress. Edited by Bloom FE, Kupfer DL. New York, Raven, 1995, pp 1807–1819

Substance Abuse and Mental Health Services Administration (SAMHSA): National Household Survey on Drug Abuse; Main Findings 1994 (DHHS Publ No SMA96-3085). Rockville, MD, SAMHSA, Office of Applied Studies, 1996

Thompson T, Schuster CR: Morphine self-administration, food-reinforced, and avoidance behaviors in rhesus monkeys. Psychopharmacologia 5:87–94, 1964

Wikler A: Opioid Dependence. New York, Plenum, 1980

Wilson GT: Booze, beliefs, and behavior: cognitive processes in alcohol use and abuse, in Alcoholism: New Directions in Behavioral Research and Treatment. Edited by Nathan PE, Marlatt GA, Loberg T. New York, Plenum, 1978, pp 315–339

Winger G: Preclinical evaluation of pharmacotherapies for cocaine abuse, in Cocaine Abuse Research: Behavior, Pharmacology, and Clinical Applications. Edited by Higgins ST, Katz JL. San Diego, CA, Academic Press, 1998, pp 135–158

Wise RA: Neurobiology of addiction. Curr Opin Neurobiol 6:243–251, 1996

Young AM, Herling S: Drugs as reinforcers: studies in laboratory animals, in Behavioral Analysis of Drug Dependence. Edited by Goldberg SR, Stolerman IP. Orlando, FL, Academic Press, 1986, pp 9–67

# Chapter 9

# Cross-Cultural Aspects of Substance Abuse

Joseph Westermeyer, M.D., M.P.H., Ph.D.

*Culture* consists of the sum total of a group's life-ways, including the group's material culture, world view, social organization, symbols, status, child raising, language, technology, and citizenship. *Ethnicity*, as applied to multiethnic societies, applies to peoples from diverse cultural backgrounds who share a common national culture. Such distinctive characteristics include identity with a national origin, religious practice, language besides English spoken in the home or neighborhood, dress, diet, nonnational holidays or ceremonial events, traditional family rituals, and use of disposable income and free time (Keyes 1976). *Subculture* refers to groups within a culture that have distinctive cultural characteristics but that cannot exist independent of the group. Substance use, abuse, or commerce can foster highly cohesive and distinctive subcultures, such as *tavern culture, cocktail lounge culture, opium den culture,* and the *sidewalk ashram culture* of a few decades ago (Deutsch 1975; Dumont 1967; Westermeyer 1974a). *Cross-cultural* can refer to the comparison of psychosocial characteristics across two or more culture groups or, in the medical context, treatment in which the clinician and the patient belong to different cultures (Comas-Diaz and Jacobsen 1991). Comparisons across cultures are often termed *etic*, whereas noncomparable, culture-specific elements are termed *emic* (Lefley and Pedersen 1986).

## Prehistory

The development of psychoactive substances began millennia before written records (Westermeyer 1988). The people of Africa, Asia, and Europe prepared alcohol from fruits, grains, tubers, and mammalian milk. They also grew opium, cannabis, and some stimulant plant compounds, such as khat in the Red Sea area, kola in other parts of Africa, and kratom in Thailand (Getahun and Krikorias 1973). Farmers across South Asia, Southeast Asia, and Oceania consumed betel nut in preparation for laborious tasks under difficult climatic and topographical circumstance (Ahluwalia and Ponnampalam 1968; Burton-Bradley 1977).

The champions of psychoactive substance invention were the peoples of the Americas. Before A.D. 1500, they developed several hundred stimulant and hallucinogenic compounds, including tobacco, cocaine, coffee, and peyote (DuToit 1977). American Aztecs and Papago prepared beverage alcohol from cactus and other plants—methods still used commercially today.

## Routes of Administration

People in Africa, Asia, and Europe consumed psychoactive substances primarily by ingesting them. They also chewed some, for example, betel nut and khat (Getahun and Krikorias 1973). Again, the peoples of the Americas prior to A.D. 1500 were the undisputed champions in developing innovative means for consuming drugs. They developed several other routes of administration, besides swallowing and chewing (Negrete 1978), that are still used widely today (i.e., snuffing, smoking, and rectal clysis) (Furst and Coe 1977). Smoking and snuffing avoided first-pass metabolism in the liver and provided rapid onset of effect.

## Social Controls

Laws regarding substance use and abuse appeared in the earliest codes of law (Anawalt and Berdan 1992). The

Aztecs had laws governing the occasions and amounts of alcohol that could be imbibed, depending on one's social status, role, and age; the punishments for breaking the laws ranged up to and included death (Anawalt and Berdan 1992). Typical patterns of informal social control have included the following:

- Substance use restricted to ceremonies or holidays
- Substance use restricted to large group or extended family events
- Proscription of taboo substances by certain groups (e.g., alcohol use by Muslims)

## History

### Descriptions of Substance-Related Pathology

The peoples of Asia, literate and illiterate, developed lay terms synonymous with *opium addiction* in English (Chopra 1928). Several centuries ago, the English described the untoward fetal, family, and social concomitants of chronic, heavy alcohol use (Rodin 1981).

Before A.D. 1500, wine, tobacco, and probably other substances were traded widely. However, no known dramatic changes in substance use or abuse accompanied these early empires and commercial routes (Westermeyer 1988).

The post–A.D. 1500 world, following the rediscovery of the New World by Columbus, produced two momentous substance abuse epidemics, one in Asia and one in Europe. It could be argued that alcohol and volatile inhalant abuse among the aboriginal peoples of the Americas and Australia comprise a third epidemic (Brady 1992; Brod 1975; Manson et al. 1992). Around A.D. 1500, improved methods of shipbuilding and new navigation technology led to safer and less expensive commerce. These changes resulted in the exchange of psychoactive substances across thousands of miles.

Substance abuse epidemics first became apparent in far eastern Asia and western Europe. Tobacco smoking, which spread rapidly around the world, reached the China Sea during the 1500s. Smokers consumed it in tobacco houses, the meeting places of the day. Tobacco houses became associated with sedition and were outlawed. Tobacco raising and smoking went underground and continued. Around the same time, opium—previously known as a herbal medication—began to be smoked in social settings. By the 1600s, the Asian opium epidemic was well under way (Chopra 1928; Fields and Tararin 1970; Merrill 1942; Park 1899;

Terry and Pellens 1928). Attempts at reducing opium use included antiopium laws, establishment of government ministries charged with eliminating opium production and commerce, and private antiopium societies that aided addicted people trying to quit opium and warned the general public against using opium. By the mid-1900s, when the Communist regime in China succeeded in eliminating opium use, an estimated 18 million Chinese were addicted to opium. Democratic, leftist, and rightist governments in Japan, both Koreas, and Taiwan also reversed their opium endemic around the same time (i.e., the 1950s and 1960s). The Asian opiate endemic continues in Thailand, Laos, Burma, Malaysia, Bangladesh, Pakistan, India, Afghanistan, Iran, and several countries of the Middle East.

The gin epidemic in England also began around the 1600s and continued for almost two centuries, with some vestiges remaining into the 1900s. It involved imported rum and gin, which were used as ballast in ships returning from commercial voyages. Although mead had been drunk traditionally in England, the population had limited experience with distilled beverage alcohol. During the development of the gin epidemic, the Industrial Revolution was also under way, with a massive shift of the population from farms and small towns to industrial towns of various sizes. Because a calorie of alcohol cost less than a calorie of bread, potent economic forces favored the use of gin and rum as food. Because workers were thought to perform better after moderate drinking, taverns were open briefly in the morning and again at noon so that workers could imbibe before and during work (Rodin 1981; Thurn 1978).

Public and private efforts gradually brought the gin epidemic under control in the seventeenth and eighteenth centuries. An import duty on beverages reduced economic incentives to drink. Small eight-page booklets detailed the family, health, and social consequences of excessive drinking. Around this time, abstinence-oriented Christian religions developed, leading eventually to the founding of Alcoholics Anonymous in the twentieth century (Aaron and Musto 1981).

The first pandemic of youthful drug abuse began in the mid-1900s and involved all continents (Cameron 1968). During World War II, tens of millions of young men were transported long distances from home and exposed to years of combat. This tremendous undertaking affected not only the combatants but many civilian populations in Asia. In addition to beverage alcohol, combatants were exposed to opiates and other drugs not familiar in their native lands. Returning home to high unemployment, lost youth, and devastated countries, many combatants used nontraditional forms of psychoactive substances. A *youth culture* with its own nontraditional dress, music, mores, morals, and drugs appeared simultaneously in many countries during the 1950s and 1960s (Deutsch 1975; Gfroerer and DeLa-Rosa 1993; Maddahian et al. 1986; Needle et al. 1988; Smart and Adlaf 1986). Some researchers have argued that the resurgence of fundamentalist (and absti-nence-oriented) Buddhist, Christian, and Islamic sects across the globe has its roots in societal responses to youth culture, including youthful drug use and abuse (Galanter and Buckley 1978; Galanter and Wester-meyer 1980; Hippler 1973; Kearny 1970; Westermeyer and Walzer 1975).

## From Cottage Industry to High-Tech Industry

Before the 1800s, much of the production and distribu-tion of drugs of abuse depended on high-labor/low-technology methods. Substances such as opium and alcohol were produced in agricultural settings, us-ing human and animal power. Rapid, efficient intercon-tinental sailing ships and navigation technology had stimulated intercontinental trade in substances, but local distribution depended largely on human and ani-mal transport. Because the technology of the day was widely known and available to virtually anyone, alcohol and drugs were produced and distributed mostly on a small scale to meet local needs. Distribution was ef-fected through local barter and small shopkeepers. Un-til the opium and gin epidemics, few producers, ship-pers, or retailers depended solely on alcohol or drugs for their livelihoods. As cottage industry techniques gave way to myriad technological advances, new substance-focused occupations and even industries evolved. Along with these advances, new social and health problems also appeared (Westermeyer 1988).

Since the early 1800s, advancing technology has re-sulted in more efficient and rapid means of drug admin-istration. The first advancement was the syringe and hollow needle, which permitted the user to avoid the first-pass effect of the liver and consume the entire drug dose. Cigarette production fostered all-day to-bacco smoking and dependence. Some new substances can now be administered by skin patches. These new methods of administration have resulted in new medi-cal and public health challenges (Davoli et al. 1997; Harding et al. 1992). Parenteral drug administration has produced epidemics of drug-related maladies

(e.g., AIDS, hepatitis), which have led to increased drug smoking and snuffing in recent years (Perez-Jimenez and Robert 1997; Strang et al. 1997).

## Concentration of Traditional Substances

During the 1800s, concentrates of opium (morphine and heroin) and coca leaves (cocaine) were developed. These concentrates facilitated the use of these sub-stances by nasal insufflation, smoking, and parenteral injection. Whereas crude plant compounds had a lim-ited shelf life and were bulky, odoriferous, and easily detected, heroin and cocaine had long shelf lives and were highly compact and much less odoriferous. These new compounds lent themselves to prolonged storage, smuggling, and secretive retail commerce (Wester-meyer 1982).

## Synthetic Psychoactive Substances

In the 1800s, synthetic psychoactive substances began to be produced. Soon after their development, recre-ational users began using the gaseous analgesics and an-esthetics nitrous oxide, chloroform, and ether. Early abusers were principally medical and pharmaceutical workers. Development of the petroleum industry dur-ing the later 1800s and early 1900s led to inexpensive, readily available industrial, cleaning, and fuel com-pounds that could produce relaxation or an altered state of consciousness. Abusers of petroleum chemicals have included industrial workers, gas station workers, me-chanics, unemployed workers, children and adoles-cents, alcoholic and addicted prisoners, and military in-ductees in basic training or on bivouac (Beauvais et al. 1985; Eastwell 1979; Teck-Hong 1986; Westermeyer 1987a).

In the early 1900s, invention of synthetic sedatives and stimulants brought the newly developing pharma-ceutical industry into the picture as a producer of ad-dictive drugs. By the 1930s, barbiturate addiction was appearing in industrialized countries. Sporadic cases of amphetamine abuse were known before World War II, but the use of these drugs by the military catapulted them into widespread use in some countries, producing the first amphetamine epidemics after the war. In prep-aration for World War II, various pharmaceutical houses developed synthetic opioid drugs, anticipating that raw opium might not be available during conflict. This process led to the development of many synthetic opioids with various durations of action—from metha-done and L-α-acetylmethadol (LAAM) at one extreme, to fentanyl at the other extreme. In the later 1900s, "outlaw" chemists synthesized new compounds with psychoactive properties, the so-called *designer drugs* that were supposed to target desirable effects.

## Smuggling

Smuggling relies on individuals sophisticated in operating illegally at one or more national boundaries. World War II, which displaced millions of people, and refugee movements since that time have provided a huge reservoir of such persons in many countries around the world. Although the vast majority of these people are law abiding, a sufficient number are drawn by the drug trade, keeping it not only viable but active and largely successful. Small airplanes, high-speed "cigarette boats," and extensive truck traffic have enabled the transportation of illicit substances over great distances with relative ease.

Community-level retail distribution of illicit substances remains a cottage industry around the world. Its features include the following:

- Low capital investment for starting up (e.g., a storefront or car, a gun, a day's or a week's supply of drugs)
- A relationship and/or shared identity between buyer and seller
- Multiple distribution and sales points (so that inactivation of one point does not undermine the trade)
- High profits relative to investment
- Reduced risk through corruption of police and elected officials

## Ethnic Identity and Substance Use

*Culturally prescribed use*, in which an individual must use a psychoactive substance under certain cultural circumstances, exists among many ethnic groups in the United States (Smith 1965). Examples include wine at Jewish Passover seders and at Catholic masses. Peyote chewing at ceremonies of the pan-Indian Native American Church continues actively today (LaBarre 1964). Prescribed use subserves religious and social ends. Duration of use and dosages are also prescribed. Failure to imbibe might be considered unfriendly.

Proscribed or *taboo use* exists for some substances in all societies (Westermeyer 1987b). Some substances are totally forbidden under any circumstances. Examples include heroin in the United States, alcohol in

Saudi Arabia, or coffee among Mormons. Taboo tends to work well as long as the individual remains affiliated with the ethnic group proscribing the use; separation from the group tends to erode the taboo. Because no society can enculturate its members into the safe, healthful use of all available substances, most substances are forbidden or available only under specific circumstances (e.g., medical prescriptions).

Substances have taken on symbolic meaning in some instances. Psychoactive substances have come to represent certain values, attitudes, identities, or characteristics. One form of symbolism is ethnic identity (Carstairs 1954). Among many Jewish people, the image of drunkenness or alcoholism is seen as non-Jewish. Many Muslims consider any use of alcohol to be sinful (Chafetz 1964). Throughout history, substances have at times possessed political symbolism. For example, the Irish long distilled illicit poteen as a means of avoiding English taxation and English beverage alcohol (Connell 1961). Cannabis has been a symbol of youthful rebellion against established order worldwide in recent decades (Cameron 1968).

Substance use has also served as a social bridge. In parts of Latin America, drinking establishments have provided a meeting place for persons of differing class and ethnic backgrounds (Comas-Diaz and Jacobsen 1991). Likewise, in parts of Africa, beer gardens have served as an egalitarian social venue for people of different races and tribes (Wolcott 1974).

## Cultural Risk Factors

*Lack of prescription or proscription*, in which the culture or ethnic group neither requires nor forbids use of a substance, leaves the decision to the individual (Baasher 1981). This in-between area most predisposes individuals to substance abuse and dependence, especially for addictive substances such as alcohol and tobacco. *Norm conflict* occurs when ideal norms and behavioral norms differ in a culture. Ideal norms in a culture or ethnic group may forbid use of a substance, whereas the behavioral norms may expect use as a normative behavior. The greater the gap between ideal and behavioral norms, the greater the presumed conflict. Norm conflicts occur because individuals rather than entire societies make the choices regarding substance use.

*Pathogenic use patterns* can occur as a behavioral norm, especially in groups with norm conflict regarding substance use. An example of such a pathogenic use pattern is the heavy binge use of alcohol around the clock for an entire holiday weekend or over a 1- or 2-week vacation. This pattern exists among some northern European groups, some Native American tribes, and various European ethnic groups in the United States. It is likely to lead to pathological use of alcohol in vulnerable persons in as many as half of adult males in some groups (Boehnlein et al. 1993).

Technological changes can render a traditional use pattern unsafe. This is especially true in societies that at one time accepted very heavy episodic intoxication at ceremonial times or that permitted alcohol or drug use during certain types of work. For example, a heavy drinker riding home from a New Year celebration on an ox cart may be relatively safe and is unlikely to harm others. The same person riding a bicycle or a motorcycle, or driving a car or truck, poses a serious risk of harming self and others. Intoxicated mariners today risk the lives of hundreds of people (e.g., on a ferry boat) or risk damaging an entire ecosystem (e.g., on an oil tanker).

Inadequate *ensocialization* occurs if the prescriptions and proscriptions regarding a substance are not taught to developing children. To be effective, these aspects of culture must be taught during infancy, childhood, and adolescence. Some ethnic groups do an excellent job of ensocializing their children into appropriate prescriptions and proscriptions regarding substances (Bennett and Ames 1985). Individuals who leave the group are at risk for substance abuse (Eaton and Weil 1955).

Disenfranchised groups can play major roles in the drug trade—a common feature around the world. Examples include the Chiu Cheow minority in Hong Kong, Hmong and Iu Mien minorities in Laos and Thailand, Corsican French and Sicilian Italians in Europe, and Lebanese refugees and immigrants in parts of Latin America.

Generational change can influence the forms of psychoactive substance use within a given culture (Keaulana and Whitney 1990; Markides 1988; Westermeyer 1982). This often involves the replacement of traditional cottage industry substances (e.g., locally grown tobacco, locally produced beer or wine) with industry-produced substances (e.g., manufactured cigarettes, imported beer or spirits). In some situations, young people have used substances completely unfamiliar to earlier generations (Bennett and Ames 1985). Secular use then replaces ritual or ceremonial use, individual choice replaces group decision-making, and untried patterns replace patterns that had evolved over centuries (Westermeyer 1982).

*Anomie*, the loss of a positive ethnic identity, is apt to occur in traditional peoples whose technological culture has been rapidly and extensively undermined by the sudden influx of foreign influences. Rapid and fundamental changes in technological bases of a culture provoke tremendous changes in social organization, family relationships, cultural symbols, and other aspects of culture (Caetano et al. 1983). Conquest by a foreign power with dramatically different values and mores can also precipitate cultural tumult (Wallace 1970). Examples of substance abuse accompanying anomie have included an amphetamine epidemic in postwar Japan (Tamura 1989) and abuse of alcohol and inhalants among aboriginal peoples of the Americas, Australia, and Oceania (Waddell and Everett 1980; Walker et al. 1985).

## Factors Affecting Ethnic Distribution of Substance Use

Imported drugs, such as cocaine and heroin, have long dominated in commercial areas, such as the coastal United States. By dint of geographic location, various ethnic groups become associated with the drug trade (Westermeyer 1982). Mafia members, Hispanic refugees and immigrants, and urban African Americans have been highly identified with the coastal, urban-centered heroin and cocaine drug trade in recent decades. Locally grown drugs, especially cannabis, hold much greater sway in the middle of the United States. In several states, cannabis is a common cash crop grown in rural areas. Cannabis agroeconomics have been largely identified with the Euroamerican ethnic groups that have inhabited rural small-farm areas of the Carolinas, Tennessee, Kentucky, Arkansas, Missouri, eastern Oklahoma, Kansas, and some of the western states. In each of these ecological niches, community leaders may be accepting, even supportive of the drug trade as a necessary evil that brings jobs and wealth into the community. Successful drug trade requires a *shadow government*, whose key members may share ethnic identity, kinship, and community affiliation.

*Status conflict* may be involved in the decision to choose an occupation in the illicit drug trade. The distance between a person's perceived or aspired status and his or her actual status in the community constitutes the individual's status conflict. Status conflict can be a source of motivation, driving the individual to work or strive harder. An overwhelming degree of status conflict, with no possible resolution, can motivate an individual to accept the inherent risks of an illicit trade.

Availability, access, and acceptance of illicit drugs are central features of an active drug trade within a small neighborhood or community. An illicit drug may be geographically available in a community, but all ethnic groups may not have equal access to the drug. Access involves factors such as knowing when and where drugs can be purchased, from whom they can be purchased, and how to effect a purchase. On the retail level, safety in conducting illicit sales lies in knowing one's clientele. Unfamiliar customers pose a potential risk. This risk may be ameliorated by restricting sales to identifiable members of one's own ethnic group. Thus, to gain access to an illicit substance, the potential buyer must be accepted by the retailer. This same analogy holds in gaining access to the wholesale trade. As one gains access to higher levels of wholesale trade, the profits mount and the severity of the punishments (although not necessarily the risk of punishment) may also increase. In addition, the risk of theft, robbery, or violent takeover of a lucrative trade also exists. Trust can develop across cultures and ethnicities, but it is more difficult to achieve.

Smuggling can thrive under the following community circumstances:

- A national boundary that lends itself to secret movement (e.g., a remote seacoast, roadless mountains or deserts)
- Occupation of the boundary region by a group that is economically disadvantaged, relative to its fellow citizens
- Boundary occupation by a distinct ethnic group that is sociopolitically disenfranchised
- Differing national laws or economics across the boundary, so that smuggling pays handsome profits

In order to be successful and stable, smuggling must achieve social support. To accomplish this, the local people must accept it morally, at least as a necessary evil if not as an honorable trade. Those who engage in smuggling as an occupation typically have other seasonal occupations, such as farming, fishing, trading, or crafting.

## Consequences of Addiction on Ethnicity

Decline in ethnic affiliation among addicted individuals accompanies reduced activities that reinforce ethnic identity and support ethnic organizations. Examples include declining participation in extended family gatherings, religious rituals, ethnic celebrations, and other community activities. Disposable income goes to alcohol or drugs rather than to institutions representing community development (Westermeyer and Neider 1988). Addicted individuals who are parents contribute to anomie by not ensocializing their children to the norms and values of their ethnic group.

Social role conflicts ensue as addicted individuals cannot meet social expectations and responsibilities (e.g., parenting, working, and otherwise meeting community obligations) as a result of their addiction. Inability to discharge the responsibilities of a social role leads to social role conflict, with reduced social status.

Addicted individuals can become alienated and isolated from their ethnic group in two ways: 1) the addicted individual over time becomes alienated from his or her family, social network, and community; or 2) some alienated people seek solace in substance abuse (Holmgren et al. 1983). Regardless of cause, the effect of increasing social distance is a reduction in the universal taboo against harming one's own family or ethnic group. Thus addicts may steal from relatives and former friends, or they may use resources meant for the family to purchase drugs or alcohol. Alienation from the family produces a downward spiral into further substance abuse, because of the diminished family support to deal with loss or stress. During recovery, the regaining of trust among family and former friends always takes many months and may require years.

## Ethnicity and Treatment

Treatment access, like access to drugs, requires more than availability in the community. For example, Kane (1981) found that a particular ethnic group did not seek alcohol-drug treatment from a local program because the program staff did not include any members of the ethnic group. As a consequence, the program was not sensitive to the social aspects of addiction in that ethnic group. With regard to health care in general, having staff members from the ethnic community is a key feature in making treatment accessible (Westermeyer et al. 1974). An element of acceptance lies in the staff's appreciating and perhaps employing the models of healing and changing preferred by a particular ethnic group (Keene and Raynor 1993). Many examples of ethnic-sensitive or ethnic-specific programs have been described in the literature (Albaugh and Anderson 1974; Argeriou 1978; Ferguson 1976; Jilek 1982; J. Red

Horse 1982; Y. Red Horse 1982; Shore and Von Fumetti 1972; Walker 1981; Westermeyer and Bourne 1978; Westermeyer et al. 1974).

*Cultural recovery* involves regaining a viable ethnic identity; a functional social network committed to the person's recovery; a religious, spiritual, or moral recommitment; recreational or avocational activities; and a social role in the recovering community, in the society at large, or in both (Westermeyer 1992). Individuals who fail to make a satisfactory cultural recovery are at risk for readdiction (Westermeyer and Neider 1984). Most recovering people return to their culture of origin (or ethnic group of origin). Old conflicts, aversions, and rejections related to the culture of origin may make recovery in that culture impossible. Thus some people are able to recover in another culture or ethnic group besides their own. Recovering as an adult in a foreign culture or ethnic group is not a simple, easy, or brief task, as individuals are best ensocialized into a culture during infancy, childhood, or adolescence.

Some persons who have recovered outside of their ethnic group have later provided support to their ethnic peers by helping others get treatment, by serving as a sponsor, or by hiring a recovering person.

*Recovery subcultures* are substitute social groups and networks that can foster early recovery (Lieberman and Borman 1976). Such subcultures may have their own jargon, values, customs, symbols, status markers, and/or social organizations. A subculture of therapists, therapy groups, and self-help groups can guide the individual toward health and stability. These recovery subcultures can provide support as needed, can confront or challenge the recovering person according to the situation, and can guide the person in avoiding dangerous situations that might precipitate relapse. The recovering person's family and friends may not be able to do this in so nearly a skilled fashion.

In some cases, the recovery group may attempt to dominate the recovering person and keep him or her away from outside influences, even when the person is ready to cope with such influences. Likewise, people who find recovery in religious cults may find their further progress stifled by isolation in the group. Or some individuals may not be able to recover sufficiently to cope with the world as it is. Consequently, some recovering people remain tied to the recovery group.

*Cultural reentry* occurs when the recovering person reaches a point at which further progress involves branching out from the recovery subculture. Reentry may grow out of a desire for additional education, a new occupation, or a new hobby or avocation. This movement into new groups involves risks (e.g., exposure to alcohol or drugs, loss or failure at a new enterprise, rejection by those biased against former alcoholic or addicted individuals). If the recovery subculture has done its work well, the recovering person should be prepared for this step.

## Special Issues

### Ethnic Minority Patients

Recovery among ethnic minority patients may require dealing with identity issues. Substance abuse may have given these patients a means for coping psychologically and socially with their feelings about minority status and/or the majority society (Lampkin 1971). During recovery, such people may find themselves consumed with ethnic issues (Westermeyer 1990). One type of problem can be a negative ethnic self-identity. Another problem is an overwhelming hostility toward the majority society. Ideally, early attempts at resolving these ethnic issues should take place with a therapist or peers who are from the same ethnic group as the recovering person. After recovery is well established, work with therapists or peers of other ethnic groups may not be a problem; it may even provide a means for working on cross-ethnic issues involving trust, projection, demonization of the other, and so forth. Work at a legitimate occupation can enhance the individual's self-esteem and increase his or her chances for recovery (Stead et al. 1990).

### Travelers, Foreign Students, Immigrants, and Refugees

*Going geographic*, long known among substance abuse subcultures, consists of an addicted person's use of travel or relocation as a means of coping with a problem, when alcohol or drugs can no longer do so. This tactic is generally seen as a symptom of substance abuse rather than a means of dealing with it (Kimura et al. 1975). In some cases, however, relocation may be used to promote early recovery efforts. Maddux and Desmond (1981) first described the utility of this method among those whose repeated return to the same family, friends, work, or neighborhood precipitated relapses into substance abuse. Relocation to a different school, neighborhood, or even town can have a salutary effect, especially if accompanied by treatment, including family counseling. When returning home, the recovering person should plan carefully, considering alternatives and support systems, reentry into treatment, and other protective measures (Westermeyer 1989).

## Victimized Persons

Refugees, combat veterans, and individuals who have been raped may find that substance abuse can stifle or even temporarily ameliorate posttraumatic stress symptoms. In some cases, the individuals may progress to posttraumatic stress disorder (PTSD), which can complicate recovery (Westermeyer and Wahmenholm 1989). Substance abuse at the time of victimization or loss may also predispose the individuals to PTSD by compromising their ability to adapt to victimization, integrate the experience, and recover from it (Green et al. 1992). Studying refugees in Australia, Krupinski et al. (1973) observed a window in time—several years to a decade after relocation—when refugees are at greatest risk for developing substance abuse.

## Prevention

Prevention of substance abuse lies in creating communities safe from licit and illicit drugs—a difficult, lengthy, expensive task if substance abuse is already established (Fleming 1992; May 1992; Smart 1982). It requires the ability of the community to assume responsibility for itself, to develop leadership that can establish and ensure responsible use of licit substances and eradicate illicit substances (Beauvais 1992). This complex task involves close and active collaboration among public and private leaders, including those responsible for the public's health, education, and security. Reliance on outside agencies (e.g., the state or national government) or on any one profession (e.g., clinicians, the police, teachers) or any one sector of the population (e.g., parents, youths, workers) is doomed to failure. Moreover, once a community safe from substance abuse has been established, relapse to widespread substance abuse still poses a risk if vigilance is suspended. Local eradication of highly prevalent substance abuse has occurred in Asian villages, Native American communities, and elsewhere (Kato 1990; May 1986; Medicine 1982; Popham et al. 1975; J. Red Horse 1982; Y. Red Horse 1982; Smart et al. 1988).

National prevention is also feasible but not easily, rapidly, or cheaply accomplished. Simply passing anti-addiction legislation without undertaking intensive health and social programs can exacerbate rather than reduce substance-related problems (Westermeyer 1974b). Many countries in the Americas, Asia, and Europe display continued, recurrent, or increasing alcoholism and opiate and/or stimulant abuse and addiction (Hughes et al. 1972; Okruhlica 1997; Tamura 1989).

# References

Aaron P, Musto D: Temperance and prohibition in America: a historical overview, in Alcohol and Public Policy: Beyond the Shadow of Prohibition. Edited by Moore M, Gerstein D. Washington, DC, National Academy Press, 1981

Ahluwalia HS, Ponnampalam JT: The socioeconomic aspects of betel-nut chewing. Journal of Tropical Medical Hygiene 71:48–50, 1968

Albaugh B, Anderson P: Peyote in the treatment of alcoholism among American Indians. Am J Psychiatry 131:1247–1256, 1974

Anawalt PR, Berdan FF: The Codex Mendoza. Sci Am June:70–79, 1992

Argeriou M: Reaching problem-drinking blacks: the unheralded potential of the drinking driver programs. International Journal of the Addictions 13:443–459, 1978

Baasher T: The use of drugs in the Islamic world. Br J Addiction 76:233–243, 1981

Beauvais F: The need for community consensus as a condition of policy implementation in the reduction of alcohol abuse on Indian reservations. American Indian and Alaska Native Mental Health Research 4:77–81, 1992

Beauvais F, Oetting ER, Edward RW: Trends in the use of inhalants among American Indian adolescents. White Cloud Journal 3:3, 1985

Bennett LA, Ames GM: The American Experience With Alcohol: Contrasting Cultural Perspectives. New York, Plenum, 1985

Boehnlein JK, Kinzie JD, Leung PK, et al: The natural history of medical and psychiatric disorder in an American Indian community. Cult Med Psychiatry 16:543–554, 1993

Brady M: Ethnography and understandings of Aborigine drinking. Journal Drug Issues 22:699–712, 1992

Brod TM: Alcoholism as a mental health problem of Native Americans. Arch Gen Psychiatry 32:1385–1391, 1975

Burton-Bradley BG: Some implications of betel chewing. Med J Aust 2:744–746, 1977

Caetano R, Suzman RM, Rosen DG, et al: The Shetland Islands: longitudinal changes in alcohol consumption in a changing environment. British Journal of Addiction 78:21–36, 1983

Cameron DC: Youth and drugs: a world view. JAMA 206:1267–1271, 1968

Carstairs GM: Daru and bhang: cultural factors in the choice of intoxicant. Q J Stud Alcohol 15:220–237, 1954

Chafetz ME: Consumption of alcohol in the Far and Middle East. N Engl J Med 271:297–301, 1964

Chopra RN: The present position of the opium habit in India. Indian J Med Res 16:389–439, 1928

Comas-Diaz L, Jacobsen FM: Ethno-cultural transference and countertransference in the therapeutic dyad. Am J Orthopsychiatry 61:392–402, 1991

Connell KH: Illicit distillation: an Irish peasant industry. Historical Studies of Ireland 3:58–91, 1961

Davoli M, Perucci CA, Rapiti E, et al: A persistent rise in mortality among injection drug users in Rome, 1980 through 1992. Am J Public Health 87:851–853, 1997

Deutsch A: Observations of a sidewalk ashram. Arch Gen Psychiatry 32:166–175, 1975

Dumont M: Tavern culture: the sustenance of homeless men. Am J Orthopsychiatry 37:938–945, 1967

DuToit BM: Drugs, Rituals and Altered States of Consciousness. Rotterdam, The Netherlands, Balkema, 1977

Eastwell HD: Petrol-inhalation in aboriginal towns. Med J Aust 2:221–224, 1979

Eaton JW, Weil RJ: Culture and Mental Disorders. Glencoe, IL, Free Press, 1955

Ferguson F: Stake theory as an explanatory device in Navajo alcoholism response. Human Organization 35:65–78, 1976

Fields A, Tararin PA: Opium in China. British Journal of Addiction 64:371–382, 1970

Fleming CM: The next twenty years of prevention in Indian country: visionary, complex, and practical. American Indian and Alaska Native Mental Health Research 4:85–88, 1992

Furst PT, Coe MD: Ritual enemas. Natural History 86:88–91, 1977

Galanter M, Buckley P: Evangelical religion and meditation: psychotherapeutic effects. J Nerv Ment Dis 166:685–691, 1978

Galanter M, Westermeyer J: Charismatic religious experience and large-group psychology. Am J Psychiatry 137:1550–1552, 1980

Getahun A, Krikorias AD: Chat: coffee's rival from Hirar, Ethiopia. Economic Botany 27:353–389, 1973

Gfroerer J, DeLaRosa M: Protective and risk factors associated with drug use among Hispanic youth. J Addict Dis 12:87–107, 1993

Green BL, Lindy JD, Grace MC, et al: Chronic posttraumatic stress disorder and diagnostic comorbidity in a disaster sample. J Nerv Ment Dis 180:760–766, 1992

Harding R, Helgerson SD, Damrow T: Hepatitis B and injecting-drug use among American Indians—Montana, 1989–1990. MMWR Morb Mortal Wkly Rep 41:13–14, 1992

Hippler AE: Fundamentalist Christianity: an Alaskan Athabascan technique for overcoming alcohol abuse. Transcultural Psychiatric Research Review 10:173–179, 1973

Holmgren C, Fitzgerald BJ, Carmen RS: Alienation and alcohol use by American Indian and Caucasian high school students. Journal of School Psychology 120:139–140, 1983

Hughes PH, Braker NW, Crawford HA: The natural history of a heroin epidemic. Am J Public Health 62:995–1001, 1972

Jilek WG: Indian Healing: Shamanistic Ceremonialism in the Pacific Northwest Today. Surrey, Canada, Hancock House, 1982

Kane G: Inner City Alcoholism: An Ecological and Cross-Cultural Study. New York, Human Science Press, 1981

Kato M: Brief history of control, prevention and treatment of drug dependence in Japan. Drug Alcohol Depend 25:213–214, 1990

Kearny M: Drunkenness and religious conversion in a Mexican village. Q J Stud Alcohol 31:248–249, 1970

Keaulana KA, Whitney S: Ka wai kau mai o Maleka "Water from America": the intoxication of the Hawai'ian people. Contemporary Drug Problems Summer:161–194, 1990

Keene J, Raynor P: Addiction as a "soul sickness": the influence of client and therapist beliefs. Addiction Research 1:77–87, 1993

Keyes CF: Towards a new formulation of the concept of ethnic group. Ethnicity 3:202–212, 1976

Kimura SD, Mikolashek PI, Kirk SA: Madness in paradise: psychiatric crises among newcomers in Honolulu. Hawaii Medical Journal 34:275–278, 1975

Krupinski J, Stoller A, Wallace L: Psychiatric disorders in Eastern European refugees now in Australia. Soc Sci Med 7:31–45, 1973

LaBarre W: The Peyote Cult. Hamden, CT, Shoe String Press, 1964

Lampkin LC: Alienation as a coping mechanism, in Crisis of Family Disorganization. Edited by Parrenstedt E, Bernard W. New York, Behavioral Publications, 1971

Lefley HP, Pedersen PB: Cross-Cultural Training for Mental Health Professionals. Springfield, IL, Charles C Thomas, 1986

Lieberman MA, Borman LD: Self-help groups. J Appl Behav Sci 12:261–303, 1976

Maddahian E, Newcomb MD, Bentler PM: Adolescents' substance use: impact of ethnicity, income, and availability. Advances in Alcohol and Substance Abuse 5:63–79, 1986

Maddux JF, Desmond DP: Careers of Opioid Users. New York, Praeger, 1981

Manson SM, Shore JH, Baron AE, et al: Alcohol abuse and dependence among American Indians, in Alcoholism in North America, Europe, and Asia. Edited by Helzer JE, Canino GJ. Oxford, England, Oxford University Press, 1992

Markides KS: Acculturation and alcohol consumption among Mexican Americans: a three-generation study. Am J Public Health 78:1178–1181, 1988

May PA: Alcohol and drug misuse prevention programs for American Indians: needs and opportunities. J Stud Alcohol 47:187–195, 1986

May P: Alcohol policy considerations for Indian reservations and bordertown communities. American Indian and Alaska Native Mental Health Research 4:55–59, 1992

Medicine B: New roads to coping—Siouan sobriety, in New Directions in Prevention Among American Indian and Alaska Native Communities. Edited by Manson SM. Portland, Oregon Health Sciences University, 1982, pp 189–212

Merrill TF: Japan and the Opium Menace. New York, Institute of Pacific Relations, 1942

Needle R, Brown P, Lavee Y, et al: Costs and consequences of drug use: a comparison of health care utilization and social-psychological consequences for clinical and non-clinical adolescents and their families. International Journal of the Addictions 23:1125–1143, 1988

Negrete JC: Coca leaf chewing: a public health assessment. British Journal of Addiction 73:283–290, 1978

Okruhlica L: Epidemic of heroin use in Slovakia. Addiction Research 3:83–86, 1997

Park WH: Opinions of 100 Physicians on the Use of Opium in China. Shanghai, China, American Presbyterian Mission Press, 1899

Perez-Jimenez JP, Robert MS: Transitions in the route of heroin use. Addiction Research 3:93–98, 1997

Popham RE, Schmidt W, DeLint J: The prevention of alcoholism: epidemiological studies of the effects of government control measures. British Journal of Addiction 70:125–144, 1975

Red Horse J: American Indian community mental health: a primary prevention strategy, in New Directions in Prevention Among American Indian and Alaska Native Communities. Edited by Manson SM. Portland, Oregon Health Sciences University, 1982, pp 217–230

Red Horse Y: A cultural network model: perspectives for adolescent services and para-professional training, in New Directions in Prevention Among American Indian and Alaska Native Communities. Edited by Manson SM. Portland, Oregon Health Sciences University, 1982, pp 173–184

Rodin AE: Infants and gin mania in 18th century London. JAMA 245:1237–1239, 1981

Shore JH, Von Fumetti B: Three alcohol programs for American Indians. Am J Psychiatry 128:1450–1454, 1972

Smart RG: The impact of prevention legislation: an examination of research findings, in Legislative Approaches to Prevention of Alcohol-Related Problems. Edited by Kaplan AK. Washington, DC, Institute of Medicine, 1982

Smart R, Adlaf E: Patterns of drug use among adolescents: the past decade. Soc Sci Med 23:717–719, 1986

Smart R, Murray GF, Arif A: Drug abuse and prevention programs in 29 countries. International Journal of the Addictions 23:1–17, 1988

Smith WR: Sacrifice among the Semites, Reader in Comparative Religion. Edited by Lessa WA, Vogt EZ. New York, Harper & Row, 1965, pp 39–48

Stead P, Rozynko V, Berman S: The SHARP carwash: a community-oriented work program for substance abuse patients. Soc Work 35:79–80, 1990

Strang J, Griffiths P, Gossop M: Heroin smoking by "chasing the dragon": origins and history. Addiction 92:673–683, 1997

Tamura M: Japan: stimulant epidemics past and present. United Nations Bulletin of Narcotics 41:81–93, 1989

Teck-Hong O: Inhalant abuse in Singapore. International Journal of the Addictions 21:955–960, 1986

Terry CE, Pellens M: The Opium Problem. Montclair, NJ, Patterson Smith, 1928

Thurn RJ: The gin plague. Minn Med 61:241–243, 1978

Waddell JO, Everett MW: Drinking Behavior Among Southwestern Indians. Tucson, University of Arizona Press, 1980

Walker RD: Treatment strategies in an urban Indian alcoholism treatment program. J Stud Alcohol 9:171–184, 1981

Walker RD, Benjamin GA, Kivlahan D, et al: American Indian alcohol misuse and treatment outcome, in Alcohol Use Among U.S. Ethnic Minorities. Edited by Spiegler DL, Tate DA, Aitken SS, et al. Washington, DC, Department of Health and Human Services, 1985, pp 301–311

Wallace AFC: The Death and Rebirth of the Seneca. New York, Alfred Knopf, 1970

Westermeyer J: Opium dens: a social resource for addicts in Laos. Arch Gen Psychiatry 31:237–240, 1974a

Westermeyer J: The pro-heroin effects of anti-opium laws in Asia. Arch Gen Psychiatry 33:1135–1139, 1974b

Westermeyer J: Poppies, Pipes and People: Opium and Its Use in Laos. Berkeley, University of California Press, 1982

Westermeyer J: The psychiatrist and solvent-inhalant abuse: recognition, assessment, and treatment. Am J Psychiatry 144:903–907, 1987a

Westermeyer J: Cultural patterns of drug and alcohol use: an analysis of host and agent in the cultural environment. United Nations Bulletin of Narcotics 39:11–27, 1987b

Westermeyer J: The pursuit of intoxication: our 100 century-old romance with psychoactive substances. Am J Drug Alcohol Abuse 14:175–187, 1988

Westermeyer J: Mental Health for Refugees and Other Migrants: Social and Preventative Approaches. Springfield, IL, Charles C Thomas, 1989

Westermeyer J: Treatment for psychoactive substance use disorder in special populations: issues in strategic planning. Advances in Alcohol and Substance Abuse 8:1–8, 1990

Westermeyer J: The sociocultural environment in the genesis and amelioration of opium dependence, in Anthropological Research: Process and Application. Edited by Pogge J. New York, State University of New York Press, 1992, pp 115–132

Westermeyer J, Bourne P: Treatment outcome and the role of the community in narcotic addition. J Nerv Ment Dis 166:51–58, 1978

Westermeyer J, Neider J: Predicting treatment outcome after ten years among American Indian alcoholics. Alcohol Clin Exp Res 8:179–184, 1984

Westermeyer J, Neider J: Social network and psychopathology among substance abusers. Am J Psychiatry 145:1265–1269, 1988

Westermeyer J, Wahmenholm K: Assessing the victimized psychiatric patient. Hosp Community Psychiatry 40:245–249, 1989

Westermeyer J, Walzer V: Drug usage: an alternative to religion? Dis Nerv Syst 36:492–495, 1975

Westermeyer J, Tanner R, Smelker J: Change in health care services: for Indian Americans. Minn Med 57:732–734, 1974

Wolcott HF: African Beer Garden of Bulawayo: Integrated Drinking in a Segregated Society. New Brunswick, NJ, Rutgers Center of Alcoholism Studies, 1974

# 2

# Overview of Treatment

# *10* Goals of Treatment

Marc A. Schuckit, M.D.

This chapter focuses on the need of clinicians in the field of substance use disorders to make decisions about specific treatment goals to be applied in the day-to-day situations in which we, the clinicians, function. The first section examines the components incorporated in our desire to help our patients function at an optimal level (Schuckit 1995, 1998a). The next section discusses the administrative and programmatic objectives that must be considered in our efforts to meet our patients' needs. This section is followed by an overview of some of the goals that may be less appropriate (and at times inappropriate) in substance dependence treatment programs. Finally, these thoughts are pulled together in a clinically oriented summary.

## Patient-Oriented Goals

Several decades ago, treatment programs focused mostly on the achievement and maintenance of abstinence. However, we have learned that being substance free, although an essential step, does not by itself guarantee optimal life functioning (Committee 1990). Thus we can divide, somewhat arbitrarily, patient-oriented goals into those aimed at helping patients to achieve a substance-free lifestyle, those aimed at maximizing multiple aspects of life functioning, and those aimed at relapse prevention.

### Helping to Achieve a Substance-Free Lifestyle

There are at least two components to achieving a substance-free lifestyle (Schuckit 1995). The first involves enhancing motivation for abstinence, and the second relates to teaching patients how to rebuild their lives after redirecting the focus of their activities away from substance use.

*Maximizing motivation for abstinence.* Substance dependence is, essentially, a condition in which the use of alcohol or other drugs has become such a central part of an individual's life that he or she is willing to give up important activities to continue to use the substance or resume substance intake (Babor 1996). The usual clinical course of substance-related problems often involves temporary periods of controlled substance intake, established through rules regarding particular situations, times of day, or other conditions in which substances will be taken but "kept under control" (Schuckit et al. 1997c; Vaillant 1995). Unfortunately, men and women with a history of severe substance-related life impairment are likely to discover that rules can be bent, which leads to an escalation in intake and the development of a crisis. There then follows a new, intense resolve to stop taking the drug, "at least for a while," after which use begins again, efforts of control are instituted, and new crises develop (Ludwig 1985; Schuckit et al. 1995).

In recognition of this pattern of repeated efforts at "controlled substance use," with the high likelihood (some would say almost certainty) of progression to the point of problems once use resumes, most programs dealing with substance-dependent individuals make abstinence a clear goal. However, some men and women with substance dependence at least initially refuse to try to meet a goal of abstinence. In the field of alcohol research, some clinicians and researchers have thus attempted to develop experimental programs aimed at teaching *controlled use* to those who refuse to give up their substance (Sobell and Sobell 1984). Unfortunately, these programs generally have been small in scope, follow-ups have tended to be incomplete (Pendery et al. 1982), and results have been inconsistent. Thus at least for alcohol-dependent individuals, most clinicians and scientists view efforts at teaching controlled use as worthy of investigation but not appropriate for inclusion in the usual treatment program. At the same time, however, some researchers have reported promising results regarding teaching control of alcohol use to individuals who have not met criteria for dependence but who have expressed concerns over their occasional heavy intake of alcohol and refuse to totally abstain.

For substance-dependent men and women, various maneuvers are appropriate for attempting to maximize the motivation for abstinence (Schuckit 1995), including lectures, counseling sessions, self-help groups, and videotapes. The goal is to educate the individual and his or her family about the dangers of substance use, the usual clinical course of substance use disorders, and the responsibility of the individual for his or her own actions. Thus, any return to substance use is likely to set off a series of events that lead to a fairly predictable group of severe life problems. On the other hand, the individual should be taught that abstinence is achievable, life patterns can change, and there is a high level of hope for success.

Teaching how to rebuild a substance-free life.    Staff in most programs admit to their patients that giving up all substance use is not easy. Patients are likely to have undergone years of heavy substance intake and to have developed a life pattern in which a good deal of their time and most of their friends are involved with heavy, repeated substance intake. Even substance-free relatives and friends are likely to have developed expectations about the individual's behaviors and to have subtly, or even blatantly, communicated these expectations to the individual, sometimes producing an almost scripted style of interaction. Thus, an important part of helping an individual develop a substance-free lifestyle is helping him or her to discover ways of dealing with free time, to develop relationships with substance-free friends, to adjust to day-to-day living in which the crisis-upon-crisis lifestyle associated with substance use is absent, and to reestablish rewarding relationships with family members.

## Helping to Maximize Multiple Aspects of Life Functioning

Although becoming substance free is an essential first step in rebuilding one's life, this achievement alone is rarely sufficient to optimize functioning. Thus, most treatment programs attempt to address essential elements of day-to-day living.

Optimizing medical functioning.    The heavy use of alcohol and other drugs is likely to damage body systems, increase the risk for physical trauma through accidents, and (in the case of depressants, stimulants, and opioids) produce clinically relevant levels of physical dependence (Schuckit 1995, 1998a). Therefore, it is hard to conceive of an effective program that would ignore the importance of a careful physical examination, neglect emergent physical difficulties, fail to deal with the appropriate treatment of withdrawal when needed, and make no effort to prevent future medical difficulties. These steps not only are essential parts of the responsibility assumed by a treatment program but also are important for optimizing the patient's ability to participate fully in rehabilitation.

Identifying and treating psychiatric symptoms and disorders.    During intoxication and withdrawal from substances, as many as 80% of substance-dependent individuals have psychiatric symptoms (Regier et al. 1990). For example, perhaps as many as two-thirds of alcohol-dependent individuals experience social phobic-like symptoms or panic attacks during withdrawal, whereas a similar proportion of actively drinking alcoholic individuals and persons undergoing withdrawal from stimulants such as cocaine or amphetamines have serious depressive symptoms that can last from 2 to 4 weeks or more (Brown and Schuckit 1988; Brown et al. 1991; Schuckit 1990; Schuckit et al. 1997a). Treatment program staff must be aware of these temporary conditions, carefully evaluate their patients for the presence of independent psychiatric disorders, and take appropriate steps to deal with the clinical symptoms, even when the symptoms are only temporary and part of the substance-use pattern. In this latter instance, education, reassurance, and evaluations to determine whether there is a need for suicide precautions, along with cognitive, supportive, or behavioral counseling techniques, may be appropriate (Schuckit 1995, 1998a). The intense depression and anxiety related to intoxication or withdrawal improve fairly quickly, although some low-grade symptoms can linger for several months, as part of a protracted abstinence syndrome (Satel et al. 1993).

In addition to these fairly common substance-related temporary conditions, individuals with substance use disorders have at least as high a risk for independent psychiatric disorders as the general population has. Therefore, at least 5% of men and 10% of women might have major depressive disorders, and as many as 10% of both men and women could be expected to have one of the anxiety disorders (Regier et al. 1988; Schuckit et al. 1997a, 1997b). However, men and women with bipolar disorder, schizophrenia, antisocial personality disorder, or possibly panic disorder have higher risks for subsequent substance-related problems than does the general population (Hesselbrock et al. 1986; Salloum et al. 1991). Therefore, most treatment programs incorporate a careful history-gathering procedure that obtains information from both the patient and at least one knowledgeable friend or relative. This helps determine whether psychiatric syndromes that meet criteria for severe disorders were apparent either before the onset of severe life problems caused by substance use or during a period of perhaps several months or more when the individual was totally abstinent (Schuckit et al. 1997a). Programs also are likely to incorporate procedures for observing the persistence of intense psychiatric symptomatology remaining approximately 6 weeks after abstinence, which is documented as indicative of potentially important independent disorders.

After a diagnosis of an independent psychiatric syndrome has been established, through a careful history taking or observation of individuals over time after abstinence, appropriate treatments must be instituted. Thus, the relatively small proportion of men and women who have both substance dependence and independent major depressive disorders are candidates for intense cognitive therapy and/or antidepressant medications, the 1%–4% of substance-dependent men and women who actually have bipolar disorder may require lithium, and the 1%–2% of patients who have both substance dependence and schizophrenia are almost certain to require antipsychotic medications (Schuckit 1995). Recognizing and appropriately treating these independent psychiatric disorders in the minority of our patients is as important a part of our goals for substance-related treatment as carrying out steps to optimize medical functioning.

**Dealing with marital and other family issues.** Reestablishing and maintaining close relationships with their spouses, their children, and other family members is a demanding task for our patients. Further, the behaviors likely to be exhibited by individuals with substance use problems are apt to jeopardize these relationships. Thus, most treatment programs in the field of substance use disorders have made attempts to reach out to family members by establishing couples and family counseling sessions and incorporating as many family members and friends as appropriate into relevant aspects of rehabilitation efforts. These steps not only

make good sense but also increase the probability of long-term abstinence in our patients (Higgins et al. 1994; O'Farrell et al. 1996).

**Enriching job functioning and financial management.** Most men and women who come to alcohol- and other substance-related programs have multiple financial problems. They are likely to have difficulty holding a job, to spend too much money on substance use, and to have developed a pattern of responding to financial crises, rather than of planning ahead. An important part of helping individuals to optimize their life functioning is helping them to find jobs that are not as closely intertwined in their minds with substance use and helping them to develop patterns of financial planning that will keep food on the table. Thus, financial management guidance along with vocational education efforts are important parts of therapeutic interventions (Spittle 1991).

**Addressing relevant spiritual issues.** Many treatment programs have grown out of the Alcoholics Anonymous tradition and emphasize that reconstituting one's life involves recognizing the importance of a supreme being or at least the need to address the care and nurturing of one's soul (Galanter et al. 1990). Although there is debate over whether spirituality is an *essential* aspect of treatment (Ellis and Schoenfeld 1990), most clinicians in the field agree that issues of religiosity or spirituality are worth exploring with patients who are attempting to rebuild their lives free of substance-related problems.

**Dealing with homelessness.** The issue of homelessness used to apply only to central-city, "skid-row" programs. However, in most current treatment programs that attempt to optimize functioning of their patients, staff must take the time to find out about the stability of their patients' current living situations (Segal 1991). An important part of treatment is determining appropriate placement. Thus, it is worth the time and effort not only to scan present living situations but also to consider the likelihood of the need for help in the near future.

## Preventing Relapse

Many of the programmatic goals discussed later in this chapter emphasize the necessity of recognizing the limitation of financial resources. Because of this limitation, in part, the amount of time allowed for the intensive intervention phase in either an inpatient or an outpatient mode has been considerably reduced in recent years. Therefore, an important aspect of treatment is helping to prevent relapses.

An integral part of helping individuals to function is raising their awareness of the need to develop high levels of vigilance against potential relapses and helping them to produce a plan of action to follow should they find themselves in situations in which relapse is highly likely or should a temporary resumption of substance use (a "slip") occur (Carroll 1996). Most treatment programs use the intensive phase of care to teach about relapse prevention, a subject that is emphasized even more in aftercare groups. Ways to minimize the risk of returning to substance use are taught through lectures, group discussions, and individual counseling sessions. Likely to be covered are how to recognize situations in which craving is apt to increase, the individual's responsibility for avoiding exposure to stressful situations in which substances are freely available, how to develop a scenario of what to do and whom to contact if problems begin, and how to avoid allowing the occurrence of a temporary resumption of substance use to be used as an excuse for escalating intake even further.

## Programmatic Goals

Because resources are needed to develop a treatment program, clinicians should recognize that the goals for patients outlined previously are not enough to develop and maintain a program. The "institution" formed by individuals attempting to reach out to men and women with substance-related problems must itself function in relation to a number of goals. These can be summarized as the steps required to develop an atmosphere that is optimally conducive to helping patients with substance-related problems.

### Goal 1: To Consider Fiscal and Political Realities

Comparing the amount of monies available with the number of patients seeking care helps to determine things such as the type of facility that will be used (e.g., inpatient vs. outpatient, freestanding vs. affiliated with a medical institution), the therapeutic regimen (e.g., more vs. less emphasis on physician care), the number of staff, the length of contact with patients, and the number of hours that the facility will be open. The source of funding also has an effect on treatment

goals. For instance, for a city-funded skid-row facility, the probable low 1-year rate of absolute abstinence for homeless drug- and alcohol-dependent individuals entering rehabilitation makes it unwise to judge the program solely on the number of patients who abstained over long periods (Powell et al. 1985; Schuckit 1995). The funding agencies (including insurers) might consider that a more appropriate immediate goal would be dealing with severe medical problems that require active treatment because efforts here can be lifesaving and outcomes more easily documented. This can, of course, occur in the context of efforts to help patients achieve and maintain abstinence. However, as discussed elsewhere, most studies support the need for a broad spectrum of services, including inpatient programs (Schuckit 1998b).

### Goal 2: To Carefully Use Financial and Staff Resources

In general, to achieve the goal of carefully using financial and staff resources, treatment approaches must be kept as simple as possible. Potentially expensive or potentially dangerous additions to a standard regimen must not be made until controlled studies have demonstrated that these more costly approaches are justified.

### Goal 3: To Clearly State the Philosophy of the Staff

In the field of substance use disorders, it is not clear that one theoretical approach is likely to be more effective than another. Thus, after the realities of financial and staff resources are considered, different programs are likely to demonstrate different theoretical biases, without any one being apparently superior. The specific theoretical bent of a program is probably as much of a result of chance and the training of the director as of any solid literature review. In any event, staff members who want to function optimally while reaching out to patients must develop a level of comfort with one another. This, in turn, often requires that the philosophy of the program (be it eclectic or committed to any specific model) be clearly stated and understood.

### Goal 4: To Remember That No Treatment Is Totally Safe

Patients can have adverse reactions to medications, may develop complications of diagnostic procedures, might act on bad advice, and run the risk of exhausting their scarce resources of time and money. Therefore, all programs should have the goal of doing the most good possible while exposing their patients to the least possible number of risks (Goodwin and Guze 1996). This cost-benefit ratio depends on knowledge of the usual course of alcohol- and drug-related problems in order to be certain that the intervention poses less risk to the patient than the clinical course likely to be observed in the subsequent months.

One way to predict the probable course of problems likely to be observed over time with or without treatment is to carefully establish the diagnosis of abuse or dependence (Goodwin and Guze 1996; Schuckit 1995, 1998a). Once it is certain that actual dependence has developed, the risks and costs of most of the usual substance-related rehabilitation efforts are likely to be outweighed by the benefits of such treatments. At the same time, documenting isolated problems or showing that an individual fulfills criteria for abuse (in the absence of dependence) indicates that a confrontation is likely to be beneficial and that some form of intervention is justified (Schuckit 1995). However, the lower level of intensity of the future course (assuming dependence does not subsequently develop) might not be sufficient to justify a several-week inpatient rehabilitation program or assignment of a patient to a long-term halfway or recovery home.

### Goal 5: To Determine That the Treatment Approaches Being Considered Are More Effective Than No Treatment At All

Substance abuse problems fluctuate in intensity (Schuckit et al. 1997c; Vaillant 1995). Patients are likely to participate in a treatment program at the time of most intense problems. With the passage of time and in the absence of aggressive treatment, individuals are likely to continue to experience a waxing and waning of symptom intensity. Therefore, the fact that an individual shows improvement in functioning 6 months after intervention $x$ was used in that patient does not prove that the intervention was responsible for any improved level of functioning after care. Only through careful studies can we be sure that any intervention is useful.

Ideally, all treatment efforts in medicine and in the behavioral sciences should be the subjects of careful studies to determine that intervention is superior to the passage of time alone. Because of the costs involved in such studies, however, most clinicians in most programs have a basic treatment approach that they accept as potentially beneficial and that is rarely tested. This approach often includes the efforts described previously for increasing motivation for abstinence and helping people to rebuild their lives without the substance. On the other hand, addition of any intervention beyond the basic program should require documentation, through carefully controlled research, that the additional approach substantially improves outcome. Therefore, it is not wise to add a medication or additional therapy time or to change the length of treatment without carefully considering whether patients will benefit adequately from the altered approach.

## Potentially Inappropriate Goals

Sometimes the things we do not do are as important as the things we do. It is valuable to recognize goals that are potentially inappropriate in dealing with substance-related problems.

For example, while attempting to help a patient achieve and maintain abstinence as well as to develop a lifestyle free of substance use, it is unwise to use medications to treat insomnia, anxiety, or depression observed only during intoxication or withdrawal (Litten and Allen 1991; Schuckit 1995). In the case of physically addicting drugs (i.e., depressants, stimulants, and opioids), withdrawal-related psychological symptoms can be expected to be most intense during the first several weeks, with a great deal of improvement occurring over the subsequent weeks (Brown and Schuckit 1988; Schuckit 1995). However, it is likely that the body will not reach its optimal level of functioning in a substance-free environment until perhaps 3–6 months after abstinence (Satel et al. 1993). Counseling, cognitive therapy, and behavioral approaches can help these men and women deal with their temporary but troubling problems (e.g., insomnia, mood swings, and nervousness) that are apt to plague their existence in an off-again, on-again fashion during the early months of recovery.

There are two exceptions to this general prohibition against medications for substance-related anxiety or depression. The first exception is the use of medications to deal with acute withdrawal, especially for depressant- and opioid-type drugs (Schuckit 1995). The second exception relates to those individuals who have been documented as having an independent major psychiatric disorder and who thus require lithium for their bipolar disorder, antidepressant medication for their severe major depressive disorder, or antipsychotic drugs for schizophrenia.

There is also a need to distinguish between treatments that might *possibly enhance* recovery rates and those that have been demonstrated through careful study to be worth the risks involved. When this approach is taken, few medications are found to be justified for use on a routine basis in persons with substance use problems. The exceptions include methadone for severely impaired opioid-dependent individuals (Ball and Ross 1991) and possibly disulfiram (Antabuse) for alcohol-dependent individuals (Fuller et al. 1986). Two additional medications with promising data regarding treatment of alcoholism are naltrexone and acamprosate, as discussed elsewhere (O'Malley et al. 1992; Sass et al. 1996; Volpicelli et al. 1992). Although many other potential drugs currently are being evaluated for efficacy in treatment of substance use disorders, few if any of these drugs have been subject to enough carefully controlled studies to justify their routine use.

Another potentially inappropriate goal is the goal of changing long-standing personality characteristics during substance-dependence rehabilitation. There are few convincing data that a specific personality profile, other than antisocial personality disorder, is an important cause of substance dependence (Hesselbrock et al. 1986; Irwin et al. 1990). Even if such data existed, financial and staff resources of a usual treatment program are not likely to be adequate for including intensive efforts to alter personality styles as an integral part of treatment.

## Conclusion

At first glance, the goals of treatment for substance use disorders appear obvious. Few would disagree that maximizing motivation for abstinence and teaching patients how to develop a substance-free lifestyle are the central goals of almost all treatment efforts with substance-dependent individuals.

This chapter was written to demonstrate that the implementation of these general goals requires the recognition of many realities regarding our patients and the political and fiscal environments in which we work. Thus, the manner in which we go about attempting to achieve our more global objectives is likely to have a marked influence on the survival of both our patients and our programs.

The general goals of treatment, however, should be placed in proper perspective. Because they are general in nature, some individual goals will not apply to specific programs. Nonetheless, it is hoped that the thoughts offered here will serve as a base of reference for many of the subsequent chapters. Perhaps some of these issues might also be of use in developing new programs and in optimizing existing ones.

## References

Babor TF: Reliability of the ethanol dependence syndrome scale. Psychology of Addictive Behavior 10:97–103, 1996

Ball J, Ross A: The Effectiveness of Methadone Maintenance Treatments. New York, Springer-Verlag New York, 1991

Brown SA, Schuckit MA: Changes in depression among abstinent alcoholics. J Stud Alcohol 49:412–417, 1988

Brown SA, Irwin M, Schuckit MA: Changes in anxiety among abstinent male alcoholics. J Stud Alcohol 52:55–61, 1991

Carroll KM: Relapse prevention as a psychosocial treatment: a review of controlled clinical trials. Experimental and Clinical Psychopharmacology 4:46–54, 1996

Committee for the Study of Treatment and Rehabilitation Services for Alcoholism and Alcohol Abuse: Broadening the Base of Treatment for Alcohol Problems. Washington, DC, National Academy Press, 1990, pp 23–183

Ellis A, Schoenfeld E: Divine intervention and the treatment of chemical dependency (editorial). J Subst Abuse Treat 2:459–468, 1990

Fuller RK, Branchey L, Brightwell DR, et al: Disulfiram treatment of alcoholism. JAMA 256:1449–1455, 1986

Galanter M, Talbott D, Gallegos K, et al: Combined Alcoholics Anonymous and professional care for addicted physicians. Am J Psychiatry 147:64–68, 1990

Goodwin DW, Guze SB: Psychiatric Diagnosis, 5th Edition. New York, Oxford University Press, 1996

Hesselbrock VM, Hesselbrock MN, Workman-Daniels KL: Effects of major depression and antisocial personality on alcoholism: course and motivational patterns. J Stud Alcohol 47:207–212, 1986

Higgins ST, Budney AJ, Bickel WK, et al: Participation of significant others in outpatient behavioral treatment predicts greater cocaine abstinence. Am J Drug Alcohol Abuse 20:47–56, 1994

Irwin M, Schuckit MA, Smith TL: Clinical importance of age at onset in Type 1 and Type 2 primary alcoholics. Arch Gen Psychiatry 47:320–324, 1990

Litten RZ, Allen JP: Pharmacotherapies for alcoholism: promising agents and clinical issues. Alcohol Clin Exp Res 15:620–633, 1991

Ludwig AM: Cognitive processes associated with "spontaneous" recovery from alcoholism. J Stud Alcohol 46:53–58, 1985

O'Farrell TJ, Choquette KA, Cutter HSG, et al: Cost-benefit and cost-effectiveness analyses of behavioral marital therapy as an addition to outpatient alcoholism treatment. J Subst Abuse 8:145–166, 1996

O'Malley SS, Jaffe AJ, Chang G, et al: Naltrexone and coping skills therapy for alcohol dependence: a controlled study. Arch Gen Psychiatry 49:881–887, 1992

Pendery ML, Maltzman IM, West LJ: Controlled drinking by alcoholics? New findings and a reevaluation of a major affirmative study. Science 217:169–175, 1982

Powell BJ, Penick EC, Read MR, et al: Comparison of three outpatient treatment interventions: a twelve-month follow-up of men alcoholics. J Stud Alcohol 46:309–312, 1985

Regier DA, Boyd JH, Burke JD, et al: One-month prevalence of mental disorders in the United States. Arch Gen Psychiatry 45:977–986, 1988

Regier DA, Farmer ME, Rae DS, et al: Comorbidity of mental disorders with alcohol and other drug abuse. JAMA 264:2511–2518, 1990

Salloum IM, Moss HB, Daley DC: Substance abuse and schizophrenia: impediments to optimal care. Am J Drug Alcohol Abuse 17:321–336, 1991

Sass H, Soyka M, Mann K, et al: Relapse prevention by acamprosate: results from a placebo-controlled study on alcohol dependence. Arch Gen Psychiatry 53:673–680, 1996

Satel SL, Kosten TR, Schuckit MA, et al: Should protracted withdrawal from drugs be included in DSM-IV? Am J Psychiatry 150:695–704, 1993

Schuckit MA: Treatment of anxiety in patients who abuse alcohol and drugs, in Handbook of Anxiety, Vol 4: The Treatment of Anxiety. Edited by Noyes R, Roth M, Burrows GD. New York, Elsevier, 1990, pp 461–481

Schuckit MA: Drug and Alcohol Abuse: A Clinical Guide to Diagnosis and Treatment, 4th Edition. New York, Plenum, 1995

Schuckit MA: Educating Yourself About Alcohol and Drugs: A People's Primer. New York, Plenum, 1998a

Schuckit MA: Penny-wise, ton-foolish? The recent movement to abolish inpatient alcohol and drug treatment (editorial). J Stud Alcohol 59:5–7, 1998b

Schuckit MA, Anthenelli RM, Bucholz KK, et al: The time course of development of alcohol-related problems in men and women. J Stud Alcohol 56:218–225, 1995

Schuckit MA, Tipp JE, Bergman M, et al: A comparison of induced and independent major depressive disorders in 2,945 alcoholics. Am J Psychiatry 154:948–957, 1997a

Schuckit MA, Tipp JE, Bucholz KK, et al: The life-time rates of three major mood disorders and four major anxiety disorders in alcoholics and controls. Addiction 92:1289–1304, 1997b

Schuckit MA, Tipp JE, Smith TL, et al: Periods of abstinence following the onset of alcohol dependence in 2,230 men and women. J Stud Alcohol 58:581–589, 1997c

Segal B: Homelessness and drinking. Drugs and Society 5:1–150, 1991

Sobell MB, Sobell LC: The aftermath of heresy: a response to Pendery et al.'s (1982) critique of "individualized behavior therapy for alcoholics." Behav Res Ther 22:413–440, 1984

Spittle B: The effect of financial management of alcohol-related hospitalization. Am J Psychiatry 148:221–223, 1991

Vaillant G: The Natural History of Alcoholism Revisited. Cambridge, MA, Harvard University Press, 1995

Volpicelli JR, Alterman AI, Hayashida M, et al: Naltrexone in the treatment of alcohol dependence. Arch Gen Psychiatry 49:876–880, 1992

# Chapter

## 11 Typologies of Addiction

Michael J. Bohn, M.D.
Roger E. Meyer, M.D.

Although substance use disorders have been defined categorically in the DSM-III, DSM-III-R, DSM-IV, and ICD-10 systems (American Psychiatric Association 1980, 1987, 1994; World Health Organization 1992), there is abundant evidence that individuals with substance use disorders present with many dissimilar clinical characteristics. Subtypes of substance-abusing individuals might be related to distinct heritable characteristics and/or prognostic features. The vast majority of typologies of substance-abusing individuals have focused on persons with alcoholism. In this chapter we attempt to summarize both early and recent work on alcoholism and drug abuse typologies, including efforts to apply typologies to patient-treatment–matching strategies. Several recent clinical trials have sought to determine whether subgroups of alcoholic individuals respond differentially to different psychosocial treatment modalities (Finney and Moos 1986; Institute of Medicine 1990; Kadden et al. 1989; Litt et al. 1992; Project MATCH Research Group 1997a, 1997b) and/or different pharmacotherapies (Kranzler et al. 1996; Powell et al. 1995).

## Historical Overview

Attempts to classify meaningfully subtypes of alcoholic persons date from the Ebers Papyrus and include several schemes developed in the nineteenth century (Babor and Lauerman 1986). When the psychiatrist Karl Bowman and the biometrician E. M. Jellinek summarized the extant alcoholic typologies in 1941, they identified 39 classifications of abnormal drinkers (Bowman and Jellinek 1941). Jellinek (1960) later proposed a five-way alcoholism typology using etiological elements; alcoholism process elements such as dependence; and physical, mental, and socioeconomic damage elements. His formulation was based on data obtained from members of Alcoholics Anonymous. Two of Jellinek's types, gamma alcoholic individuals and delta alcoholic individuals, met his concept of a disease (Jellinek 1960). Gamma alcoholic individuals were characterized by "loss of control" drinking; whereas delta alcoholic individuals, under the strong influence of sociocultural and economic factors, were unable to abstain. Despite the heuristic and clinical appeal of Jellinek's multidimensional typology, little empirical research has been conducted to assess its ability to predict the longitudinal course or posttreatment outcomes of alcoholic subjects (Babor and Dolinsky 1988). Walton et al. (1966) found no significant differences in outcome status between groups of gamma and delta alcoholic subjects. More recently, Kahler et al. (1995) systematically examined the presence or absence of loss of control and inability to abstain in a sample of 97 alcoholic men. In their sample, these features were highly correlated, which suggests that a unitary dimension of "impaired control" described alcohol dependence better than did two distinct dimensions or subtypes of drinkers.

## Unidimensional Typologies

Since the 1960s, theoretically based models have been applied to classify alcoholic individuals and drug abusers along a single dimension or characteristic. For alcoholic individuals, unidimensional criteria have related to drinking history (Cahalan et al. 1969), drinking pattern (Tarter et al. 1977), severity of dependence (Skinner 1980), family history of alcoholism (V. M. Hesselbrock et al. 1982; Penick et al. 1978), gender

97

(Rimmer et al. 1971; Schuckit 1969), personality style (Conley 1981; Nerviano and Gross 1983), primary or secondary psychopathology (Winokur et al. 1971), cognitive impairment (Eckhardt 1981; Shelly and Goldstein 1976), and sociopathy (Cadoret et al. 1985; M. N. Hesselbrock et al. 1984). The prognostic utility of a number of these typologies has been explored (Babor et al. 1992b; Meyer 1989). As described in this chapter, dependence severity and comorbid psychopathology have emerged as useful prognostic factors and have been incorporated into distinct unidimensional typologies. In our judgment, the field has not established clear guidelines for what constitutes an etiological or prognostic factor and what defines a unidimensional typology.

## Dependence Severity as Typology

The diagnostic criteria for substance dependence disorder in DSM-III-R and DSM-IV are based on the behaviorally defined alcohol dependence syndrome described by Edwards and Gross (1976). These authors proposed that alcohol dependence and disabilities be viewed along separate continua of severity. As applied to all substance dependence disorders in DSM-III-R and DSM-IV, the dependence syndrome is characterized by diminished capacity for control over psychoactive substance intake, salience of substance use, tolerance, withdrawal syndrome, and use of the substance to relieve withdrawal symptoms. Several reports have provided empirical evidence in support of the concept of a unitary dependence syndrome for alcohol (Babor et al. 1987; Hodgson et al. 1979; Skinner 1980, 1981; Skinner and Allen 1982) and other drugs (Kosten et al. 1987). For alcohol, several research instruments have been developed to quantify the severity of dependence (Chick 1980; M. N. Hesselbrock et al. 1985; Skinner and Allen 1982; Stockwell et al. 1979). Most patients with alcohol use disorders who enter inpatient treatment are in fact alcohol dependent (M. N. Hesselbrock et al. 1985).

A number of studies have highlighted the prognostic significance of alcohol dependence severity in clinical samples. The latter predicts attendance at a treatment clinic (Skinner and Allen 1982), craving for alcohol after a drink (Hodgson et al. 1979), response to alcohol and placebo alcohol cues (Kaplan et al. 1983), relapse to problem drinking (Polich et al. 1980), and reinstatement of dependence after a period of abstinence (Babor et al. 1987). Severity of alcohol dependence is positively related to the quantity and frequency of alcohol

consumption but not to psychopathology (M. N. Hesselbrock et al. 1985), whereas alcohol-related psychosocial disabilities are associated with a lifetime prevalence of psychopathology (including antisocial personality disorder [ASPD], major depression, and obsessive-compulsive disorder) and/or sociocultural factors.

## Psychopathology as Typology

The presence or absence of coexisting psychopathology has been used to distinguish subgroups of substance-abusing individuals. Several studies have found high rates of coexisting personality disorders and other major psychiatric disorders in substance-abusing patients (M. N. Hesselbrock et al. 1985; Ross et al. 1988; Rounsaville et al. 1982, 1991; Weiss et al. 1986) and in substance abusers identified in community surveys (Helzer and Pryzbeck 1988; Kessler et al. 1997; Warner et al. 1995). Penick et al. (1978) studied the prevalence of psychiatric syndromes and age at onset in 565 alcoholic men in five Veterans Administration (VA) treatment programs. Only 37% of the subjects met criteria for alcoholism alone; 63% had at least two syndromes, and the mean number of psychiatric syndromes was 2.4. Depression (42%), mania (22%), and ASPD (20%) were the most frequent disorders, followed by drug abuse, panic attacks, phobia, and obsessive-compulsive disorder (10%–15% each). Other conditions occurred in fewer than 5% of the subjects. Alcoholic subjects with at least one other disorder in addition to alcoholism reported a significantly earlier onset of problem drinking than did those patients who had no comorbid psychopathology.

Winokur et al. (1971) was one of the first of the modern descriptive psychiatrists to differentiate between primary and secondary alcoholism; he applied the term *secondary alcoholism* to individuals whose comorbid psychopathology antedated the onset of alcoholism. He reserved the term *primary alcoholism* for those individuals without other psychopathology or in whom the comorbid disorder followed the onset of alcohol dependence. Men with secondary alcoholism and primary depression had more depressive symptoms, less drug misuse, and longer periods of abstinence than did men with primary alcoholism (Schuckit 1985). In alcoholic men, secondary depression was more common than primary depression with secondary alcoholism. In contrast, alcoholic women with depression more often had a primary depression that antedated the onset of alcohol dependence (M. N. Hesselbrock et al. 1985;

Schuckit 1969; Schuckit and Winokur 1972).

Schuckit (1985) emphasized the prognostic significance of the primary/secondary distinction in the relationship between alcoholism and comorbid psychopathology. He hypothesized that individuals with secondary alcoholism are less likely to relapse to heavy drinking after treatment of their primary mood or anxiety disorder. Rounsaville et al. (1987) reported that depression in alcoholic women (which is usually primary) was a good prognostic sign, whereas depression in alcoholic men (which is usually secondary to the alcoholism) was not associated with a better prognosis. Three placebo-controlled clinical trials appear to support the utility of antidepressant treatment in depressed alcoholic individuals, but the primary/secondary distinction was not systematically compared in these three studies of imipramine (McGrath et al. 1992), desipramine (Mason et al. 1996), and fluoxetine (Cornelius et al. 1997) treatment. Similarly, Woody et al. (1984) reported that doxepin was an important adjunct to methadone treatment in a group of opioid addicts with depression (the depression was not further classified as primary or secondary).

Addictive disorder with ASPD may represent another subtype of addictive disorder, with major implications for research, prevention, and treatment. ASPD is one of the most prevalent associated psychiatric disorders among alcoholic individuals and drug abusers. Frequencies of ASPD reported in samples of alcoholic patients have ranged from 16% to 49%. Somewhat higher rates have been detected among opioid- and other drug-abusing populations. The frequency of occurrence of ASPD varies depending on the type of sample and the diagnostic criteria used (M. N. Hesselbrock et al. 1985; Rounsaville et al. 1983). The higher reported prevalence rates of ASPD among substance-dependent patients since 1980 (compared with the rates in the earlier literature) are likely a function of the broad diagnostic criteria applied to this disorder by DSM-III, DSM-III-R, and DSM-IV, rather than of a real change in the patient population.

The DSM-III and DSM-IV diagnostic criteria for ASPD require that conduct disorder be present before age 15 years and that antisocial behaviors be maintained into adulthood. These criteria are consistent with the longitudinal-study findings of Robins (1966) and of Jessor and Jessor (1975). The latter noted that adolescents who later became problem drinkers tended to be more rebellious and impulsive in childhood, and the former reported that childhood antisocial behavior is a risk factor for adult antisocial behavior, drug abuse, and

alcoholism. Epidemiological data suggest that antisocial behavior is most clearly a risk factor for the development of alcoholism and drug abuse in those societies in which the substance use (or heavy use) is not normative (Helzer et al. 1990; Robins 1978).

Although the DSM-III–DSM-IV classification of ASPD does not differentiate subtypes, several groups of investigators have suggested that distinct subtypes can be identified based on the presence or absence of a history of aggression and violence and/or a lack of remorse (Alterman and Cacciola 1991; Cottler et al. 1995; Harpur et al. 1989; V. M. Hesselbrock et al. 1992). At this juncture, subtyping of ASPD has not been systematically applied to studies of differential risk, course, symptom picture, and/or treatment prognosis in alcohol- or drug-dependent patients with ASPD. On the other hand, it was found that a history of violent or aggressive behavior in childhood tended to predict violence or aggression associated with adult ASPD and the substance use disorder (Buydens-Branchey et al. 1989a; Jaffe et al. 1988).

M. N. Hesselbrock et al. (1984, 1985) found that the presence of ASPD in alcoholic subjects affected the age at onset, course, and symptoms of their alcoholism. Both men and women with ASPD began drinking at a much earlier age, progressed to regular drinking at a much earlier age, and progressed from regular drinking to alcoholism much faster than did subjects without ASPD. Alcoholic individuals with ASPD also reported substantially greater psychosocial disability symptoms than did subjects without ASPD. More than any other psychiatric diagnosis, ASPD had a significant adverse effect on the pretreatment course of drinking problems among North American (M. N. Hesselbrock et al. 1984, 1985; Penick et al. 1978) and French (Babor et al. 1974) alcoholic persons.

Substance-abusing and substance-dependent patients with ASPD have disproportionately high rates of treatment failure (Caster and Parsons 1977; Mandell 1981; Rounsaville et al. 1987; Schuckit 1985). Treatment failure has been attributed to the fact that these individuals have poor social support networks, have difficulty learning new behaviors, are typically impulsive, and are slow to learn from punishment and other negative experiences. They are interpersonally insensitive and lack trust in others, particularly in matters requiring a substantial degree of intimacy. Several groups of investigators have advocated highly structured treatments that foster the development of social skills that may help to control impulsive urges for alcohol or drugs, anger, and anxiety (Cooney et al. 1991; Kadden et al. 1989; Rounsaville et al. 1986; Woody et al. 1985). Cooney et al. (1991) and Kadden et al. (1989) tested the usefulness of this form of cognitive-behavior (coping skills) therapy in a patient-treatment–matching study. They found that drinking outcomes after alcoholism treatment were superior among subjects with ASPD randomized to receive group coping skills treatment, whereas alcoholic subjects low on measures of ASPD had superior outcomes when randomized to receive group interactional therapy. Similarly, Woody et al. (1985) and Gerstley et al. (1989) found that an insight-oriented psychotherapy, similar to the group interactional therapy used by Kadden and Cooney, resulted in poorer drug-use outcomes in methadone-maintained opioid-addicted subjects with ASPD than in comparable subjects without ASPD.

Kadden et al. (1989) found that the global measure of psychiatric severity derived from the Addiction Severity Index (McLellan et al. 1983b) was as useful as a specific measure of "sociopathy" in their treatment-matching study. This report, plus the earlier report of McLellan et al. (1983a), suggests that a global measure of psychiatric severity (which groups together symptoms of depression, anxiety, psychosis, and cognitive function) may be sufficient to characterize the essential prognostic features of a unidimensional psychopathologically based typology of substance abusers in treatment. As noted previously, one problem with unidimensional typologies developed from treatment samples is that it is unclear what differentiates such a typology from a prognostic factor.

### Shortcomings of Unidimensional Typologies

Babor and colleagues identified several shortcomings of unidimensional typologies of alcoholic patients (Babor and Dolinsky 1988; Babor et al. 1992b). They noted considerable overlap among unidimensional classifications based on sex, family history, primary versus secondary alcoholism, personality types, and/or the gamma-delta distinction. In their analysis of data on 321 alcoholic inpatients, they found that sociopathy, familial alcoholism, and impulsive personality traits tended to cluster in alcoholic men (Babor et al. 1992b). None of the single elements, whether based on risk (e.g., family history of alcoholism) or recent functioning (e.g., drinking pattern), proved uniquely powerful in predicting future drinking, alcohol-associated problems, psychological functioning, and/or medical status at follow-up. Significant discriminations for each typology were generally limited to areas closely related to

the defining characteristics of that particular typology. Thus, it appears that unidimensional typologies offer limited potential for differentiating alcoholic individuals according to etiology, global clinical status, and/or posttreatment outcomes. We know of no similar studies among pure populations of drug-abusing individuals or among mixed alcohol- and drug-abusing populations.

Until fairly recently, researchers interested in clinical typologies in the field of substance abuse disorders generally developed their typologies from data gathered in clinical populations, and they sought to validate the typologies using data from patients entering treatment and in relation to differential treatment outcomes. Apart from the distinction between presence and absence of family history, data on family history were not generally used as a tool to validate typologies. With the rapid development of genomic science, this situation is changing. As in the case of typologies in other areas of clinical medicine (e.g., type I and type II diabetes), it should be possible to validate clinically derived typologies using the new methods of human genetics. Conversely, the power of molecular genetic analyses depends on the identification of well-characterized phenotypes that cluster in informative pedigrees. Researchers on the genetics of alcoholism and researchers on predictors of alcoholism-treatment response have begun to examine the connections between their work (Meyer 1994).

## Typologies Based on Familial Substance Abuse

Cloninger and colleagues (Cloninger 1987; Cloninger et al. 1988, 1989) were among the first groups to use family history data to classify alcoholic patients into distinct subtypes using methods of genetic epidemiology. Studies of the long-term alcohol-related outcomes of Swedish adoptees, classified according to the presence or absence of alcoholism in biological and nonbiological parents, led these investigators to propose two subtypes of alcoholism. *Type 1* or *milieu-limited* alcoholism affected both men and women, had onset after age 25, and had a variable course of alcohol-related symptoms. The severity of alcoholism among Type 1 alcoholic individuals appeared to be influenced by the adoptive home environment. A family environment marked by disruptiveness was associated with more severe alcohol problems in adult adoptee children genetically at risk for alcoholism. Fathers of Type 1 alcoholic patients tended not to have a history of criminality, and the adoptees rarely engaged in fights or were arrested when drinking. *Type 2* or *male-limited* alcoholism occurred only in men and was characterized by an inability to abstain from alcohol and by heavy consumption rates. Alcohol dependence generally began before age 25 and was associated with severe, recurrent medical and social consequences of alcoholism. Type 2 alcoholism appeared to be highly heritable and not significantly influenced by the postnatal environment. Typically, both the Type 2 alcoholic individual and his father had histories of criminality, including fighting and arrests while intoxicated.

Cloninger (1987) proposed that personality traits accounted for the inheritance of these two types of alcoholism. Whereas high degrees of reward dependence and harm avoidance and low degrees of novelty seeking were found in Type 1 alcoholic individuals, Type 2 alcoholic patients were characterized by high degrees of novelty seeking and low degrees of reward dependence and harm avoidance.[1] Cloninger (1987) speculated that differences in brain neurotransmitter systems account for alcoholism-associated personality traits.

In a Finnish study, low levels of cerebrospinal fluid 5-hydroxyindoleacetic acid (5-HIAA) were found in a group of alcoholic individuals with criminal histories (Linnoila et al. 1989). Cerebrospinal fluid 5-HIAA is believed to serve as a marker for basal levels of serotonin in the brain. Buydens-Branchey et al. (1989b) reported that alcoholic individuals with histories of violence had low plasma ratios of the serotonin precursor tryptophan relative to other neutral amino acids. George et al. (1992) reported that persons with early-onset alcoholism (often linked to Type 2 alcoholism) were more likely than individuals with late-onset alcoholism to experience alcohol-like effects from a serotonergic agonist (*m*-chlorophenylpiperazine). Fishbein et al. (1989) observed that self-reported aggressiveness and impulsiveness increased after administration of the indirect serotonergic agonist fenfluramine among a group of impulsive and violent polysubstance-abusing subjects (including some with histories of alcohol abuse or dependence).

The Cloninger typology shows greatest promise in accounting for differences in the pattern of inheritance of alcoholism (Gilligan et al. 1988). In one study (Nordstrom and Berglund 1987), the typology also predicted posttreatment outcome: treated patients considered to have Type 2 alcoholism (compared with patients with Type 1 alcoholism) had lower frequencies of abstinence and social drinking over two decades after an index treatment episode.

Several variations on the Cloninger model have been proposed by different groups of investigators in the United States and Europe. In a study of alcoholic families in western Pennsylvania, each of which included two alcoholic brothers, Hill (1992) replicated the Cloninger typology and also described a third type of heritable alcoholism. This type was similar to the Cloninger Type 2 but included no paternal sociopathy. Zucker's (1987) fourfold alcoholism typology, based primarily on a synthesis of the alcoholism natural history literature, is also consistent with the Cloninger typology. In Zucker's construct, antisocial alcoholism is characterized as having a genetic basis, with early onset of alcohol problems and antisocial activity. This form of alcoholism occurs more frequently in men and carries a poor prognosis. Developmentally cumulative alcoholism occurs in both men and women, evolving as a cumulative extension of adolescent problem drinking and delinquency. Environmental features are more prominent in modulating genetic predisposition in developmentally cumulative alcoholism than in antisocial alcoholism, and familial aggression is less prominent. Developmentally limited alcoholism, typified by frequent heavy drinking at times of increased autonomy during early adulthood, infrequently results in treatment entry and tends to remit to social drinking after successful adjustment to adult family and career roles. Finally, negative-affect alcoholism occurs primarily in women with a family history of depression. Individuals drink heavily to enhance relationships and modulate mood.

Age at onset of alcohol problems, one of the defining characteristics of the Cloninger typology, has been the specific focus of typological classification in the work of L. von Knorring et al. (1985) in Sweden and Buydens-Branchey et al. (1989a) in the United States. L. von Knorring and colleagues (1985) divided their subjects into a group with onset before age 25 (Type II alcoholic subjects) and a group with onset after age 25 (Type I alcoholic subjects). Like the Type 2 alcoholic individuals of the Cloninger model, the subjects with early-onset

---

[1]Cloninger (1987) defined novelty seeking as "a heritable tendency toward frequent exploratory activity and intense exhilaration in response to novel or appetitive stimuli" (pp. 413–414). Harm avoidance was defined as a heritable tendency to respond intensely to aversive stimuli and their conditioned signals, thereby facilitating learning to inhibit behavior in order to avoid punishment or negative consequences. Reward dependence was considered to be characterized by a need for succor and support by significant others.

alcoholism had higher rates of aggressiveness, criminality, drug abuse, and familial alcoholism than did the Type I alcoholic subjects. They were also more extroverted and scored higher on measures of impulsiveness and thrill and adventure seeking. They had more severe anxiety and guilt, and they scored significantly lower on measures of platelet monoamine oxidase activity (A.-L. von Knorring et al. 1985; L. von Knorring et al. 1985, 1987). Using slightly different onset criteria (i.e., heavy drinking before or after age 20), Buydens-Branchey et al. (1989a) found that men in treatment for early-onset alcoholism had higher rates of depression, suicide attempts, and violent crimes than did men with late-onset alcoholism. These subjects with early-onset alcoholism also reported higher rates of paternal alcoholism than did subjects with late-onset alcoholism. Among a group of 171 alcoholic men in the San Diego, CA, area, Irwin et al. (1990) found that early onset (i.e., a history of alcohol problems before age 25) was superior to the Type 1/Type 2 features of the Cloninger model in discriminating alcoholic individuals with early criminality, drug use and associated problems, and high severity of alcohol problems. Roy et al. (1991) also reported that subjects with early-onset alcoholism had greater lifetime rates of ASPD, drug abuse, bipolar disorder, suicide attempts, and panic disorder, as well as greater rates of paternal alcoholism, than did a group of subjects with late-onset alcoholism. Although Cloninger and colleagues (Cloninger 1987; Cloninger et al. 1988, 1989) did not find Type 2 alcoholism in women, Glenn and Nixon (1991) reported the Type 1/Type 2 characteristics among alcoholic women. At this juncture, data collected from community samples, from patients entering treatment, and from genetic epidemiological studies all point to the existence of at least two types of alcoholism characterized by differences in age at onset, the presence or absence of impulsive (frequently antisocial) personality characteristics, and/or the presence or absence of depressed mood and/or anxiety.

## Statistical Approaches to Classification of Subtypes

Given the aforementioned associations among a set of variables that characterize etiologically and prognostically distinct subgroups of substance abusers, many researchers have attempted to identify empirically similar subgroups using correlational methods. Skinner (1982) applied cluster analysis and other modern statistical classification methods to produce typologies based on multivariate assessments. Cluster analyses divide subjects into groups based on their differences from (and similarities to) the subject group mean scores. The process continues by iteration until a minimum number of subject clusters is found. Individuals within each cluster are more similar to each other than they are to individuals in other clusters. Although clustering procedures do produce distinct and relatively homogeneous groups, they do not ensure that all subjects assigned to one cluster manifest similar scores on all of the assessed attributes.

Like Cloninger and colleagues (Cloninger 1987; Cloninger et al. 1988, 1989), who analyzed personality and clinical data from Swedish adoptees, researchers first applied cluster analysis to personality measures obtained from clinical samples of alcoholic patients. Goldstein and Linden (1969) divided 513 alcoholic men into neurotic (depressive/anxiety) and personality disorder (psychopathic) groups based on cluster analysis of Minnesota Multiphasic Personality Inventory (MMPI) data. O'Leary et al. (1979) and Morey and Blashfield (1981) reviewed studies that used cluster analysis of MMPI data to categorize alcoholic patients. They found consistent support for the existence of one or more subtypes scoring high on psychopathic personality, a second and distinct passive-dependent personality type, and a third more depressed-anxious group. Because these study subject samples consisted primarily of middle-aged men recruited from state and VA hospital treatment settings, the external validity of these findings was suspect. Subsequently, Morey et al. (1984) performed a cluster analysis on data from a more heterogeneous population of 725 treatment-seeking urban drinkers who had completed an assessment of their personality, drinking history, drinking-related measures, alcohol-associated problems, and other drug use. Three clusters of subjects emerged: early-stage problem drinkers, affiliative dependent drinkers, and schizoid dependent drinkers. Early-stage problem drinkers had the lowest levels of psychological disturbance and aggression, the highest levels of social stability, and the most defensive response style. Affiliative dependent drinkers were more likely to drink on a daily basis, be socially oriented, and have moderate dependence. Schizoid dependent drinkers were socially isolated, drank in binges, had the highest levels of aggression and impulsiveness, and had severe alcohol dependence. Roberts and Morey (1985) derived a comparable three-cluster typology using similar assessment instruments in a population of 334 VA patients. Differences in the treatment response or posttreatment course of individuals in these three clusters were not reported in any of these early studies.

Babor et al. (1992a) applied cluster analysis to the multidimensional baseline data from a sample of 321 alcoholic men and women. These investigators identified two types of alcoholic individuals who differed consistently on 17 defining characteristics. The first group, labeled Type A alcoholic individuals, had fewer childhood risk factors for alcoholism, later onset of problem drinking, fewer alcohol-related problems, less sociopathy and other psychopathology, and less severe alcohol dependence. By contrast, Type B alcoholic individuals had more childhood risk factors, earlier onset of problem drinking, more sociopathy and other psychopathology, more alcohol-related problems, and more severe dependence. Outcomes measured prospectively 12 and 36 months after treatment indicated the prognostic validity of this typology. Type A alcoholic persons experienced longer intervals before returning to heavy drinking, had less distress, and used illicit drugs less often than did Type B alcoholic individuals over the 3-year interval. The A/B typology has been replicated among male (Litt et al. 1992) and mixed-gender groups of alcoholic inpatients and outpatients (Brown et al. 1994), among alcoholic probands and their family members (Schuckit et al. 1995), and among alcoholic persons assessed in epidemiological surveys (M. J. Bohn, unpublished data, February 1998). Similar A and B types have been identified among inpatients and outpatients with cocaine, cannabinoid, and opiate use (Ball et al. 1995; Feingold et al. 1996); among drug addicts assessed in epidemiological surveys (M. J. Bohn, unpublished data, February 1998); and among mixed groups of alcoholic individuals and drug addicts assessed with the use of self-report questionnaires (M. J. Bohn, unpublished data, February 1998).

## Typologies and Patient-Treatment Matching

Litt and colleagues' (1992) replication of the Type A/Type B typology was conducted in a sample of men enrolled in a randomized trial comparing coping skills and interactional group treatments after inpatient alcoholism rehabilitation. Although neither the patient type nor the therapy type predicted the rate of abstinence, number of heavy-drinking days, or presence of alcohol-related problems in an 18-month, posttreatment follow-up period, the match of patient type and therapy type did predict these three outcome measures. When these

drinking outcomes were measured during the 2 years after treatment, Type A alcoholic individuals fared better with interactional treatment and more poorly with coping skills treatment. Conversely, Type B alcoholic individuals had superior outcomes after coping skills treatment and inferior outcomes after interactional treatment. In this typology, sociopathy contributed strongly to subtype membership. Importantly, sociopathy alone predicted drinking outcomes as well as the more complex A/B typology did.

The possibility that the A/B type would serve as a patient-level characteristic that predicted differential response to distinct psychosocial treatments was assessed in the recently completed Project MATCH multicenter clinical trial (Project MATCH Research Group 1997a, 1997b). In this study, coordinated by the National Institute on Alcohol Abuse and Alcoholism, 1,726 patients were randomly assigned to one of three psychosocial treatments: coping skills (CS), motivational enhancement (MET), and twelve-step facilitation (TSF) treatments. Approximately 55% of subjects received outpatient therapy at one of five sites, and 45% received aftercare therapy after inpatient or outpatient hospital treatment at one of five sites. More than 20 patient characteristics, determined in previous research (Finney and Moos 1986; Institute of Medicine 1990; McLellan et al. 1983a; Miller and Hester 1986; Skinner 1981), were evaluated as potential treatment-matching variables. These included several domains relevant to the aforementioned typologies, including alcohol involvement, conceptual level (a measure of abstraction ability), gender, sociopathy, multidimensional A/B typological classification, psychiatric diagnosis, ASPD, and anger. All three treatment modalities were highly effective in enabling patients to improve their drinking behavior and their functioning in a variety of life areas and to an approximately equivalent degree. The matching results were surprising and challenged the role of patient-treatment matching for treatment of alcohol use disorders. Although TSF treatment produced statistically significant differences in drinking outcomes among outpatients with low levels of psychopathology, none of the treatments was superior in treatment of subjects with high levels of psychopathology. In the aftercare sample, low dependence severity predicted more improvement with CS treatment, whereas higher dependence severity predicted more improvement with TSF treatment. Among the a priori matching variables specified, the A/B type membership did not interact with any of the three psychosocial treatment methods to yield statistically significant differences in drinking outcomes during the 12-month posttreatment assessment period. Thus, the results of Project MATCH (Project MATCH Research Group 1997a, 1997b) indicate that differential psychosocial treatment assignment based on the A/B or other typological characteristics may not improve overall treatment outcomes. Post hoc analyses may reveal the presence of new subtypes of alcoholic individuals who did respond differentially to the different treatment modalities. Clinical trials involving the combination of selected psychotherapies and one or more pharmacological agents will provide additional tests of the validity of multivariate typologies of substance use disorders.

## Conclusion

The preceding sections of this chapter highlight the similarity between typologies developed from assessments of treatment-seeking alcoholic patients and typologies based on family/genetic epidemiological databases. This similarity is particularly the case for early-onset alcoholism. The latter frequently presents with coexisting psychiatric problems, such as impulsiveness, aggressive tendencies, criminality, and other antisocial behaviors. Jellinek's gamma, Cloninger model Type 2, von Knorring model Type II, Zucker's antisocial, and Babor model Type B alcoholic individuals display many of these characteristics. This alcoholism type has a severe course and is poorly responsive to many traditional alcoholism treatments. Arguments that cognitive-behavioral treatment should be more useful for these patients than TSF or MET treatments (Cooney et al. 1991; Litt et al. 1992) were not supported in Project MATCH (Project MATCH Research Group 1997a, 1997b). The latter study failed to demonstrate a specific treatment-matching effect, despite the heuristic appeal of a therapy focused on social skills enhancement and on tools for coping with alcohol urges, negative affects, and boredom during abstinence for patients with very specific needs in these areas.

A more heterogeneous group of alcoholic subjects is demonstrated in Jellinek's delta alcoholic individuals, the affiliative dependent drinkers of Morey et al., Cloninger model Type 1 and von Knorring model Type I alcoholic individuals, Zucker's developmentally cumulative alcoholic individuals, and Babor model Type A alcoholic individuals. Affective and anxiety disorders may be comorbid conditions in these patients. Although Project MATCH (Project MATCH Research Group 1997a, 1997b) failed to confirm specific patient/

psychotherapy-matching strategies for these patients, the patients may be responsive to anxiolytic and/or antidepressant pharmacotherapy (Cornelius et al. 1997; Kranzler et al. 1994; Mason et al. 1996; McGrath et al. 1992).

There is a third group of problem drinkers, consisting of persons whose drinking problems are relatively mild and who are often recognized during young adulthood. Such socially stable problem drinkers have minimal coexisting psychopathology but are often ambivalent and defensive about altering their drinking habits. These features are found in Morey model early-stage problem drinkers and Zucker's developmentally limited alcoholism type. For such drinkers, brief counseling techniques such as motivational interviewing (Miller and Rollnick 1991) appear particularly useful in mobilizing the patient's ambivalence, negotiating reduced levels of alcohol intake or abstinence, and providing feedback and encouragement to reduce drinking so that the patient can complete other more productive tasks. However, the degree to which motivational interviewing techniques, compared with nonspecific therapist characteristics such as empathy and warmth, are therapeutically active ingredients for such early-stage problem drinkers is unclear. Although Project MATCH (Project MATCH Research Group 1997a, 1997b) results did not support the superiority of MET (compared with CS and TSF therapies) for subjects with low degrees of alcohol problem severity, the skill of the study's therapists was high, a factor that may have moderated a specific treatment effect. For motivated early-stage problem drinkers, prophylactic and targeted use of short-acting antidipsotropic medications, such as calcium carbimide or naltrexone, before occasions when heavy drinking is anticipated may facilitate a reduction in alcohol intake (Annis and Peachey 1992; Kranzler et al. 1997).

Typological studies should focus on large, representative samples, including samples with subjects not seeking professional treatment. If the typological study is based on patients in treatment, one would predict greater dependence, a history of treatment episodes, and greater prevalence of comorbid psychopathology than in community samples (Berkson 1946). Treatment samples drawn from VA hospitals include a higher proportion of male subjects than in most treatment samples. Typological studies should enroll adequate numbers of substance-abusing women, to avoid missing potentially important gender differences in prognosis and treatment response.

Methodological issues aside, modern medicine has

been built on classification schemes that could be validated by differential treatment responses. In the last century, Robert Koch's system for obtaining pure cultures of bacteria enabled microbiologists eventually to identify the heritable factors and growth conditions that confer virulence. Effective strategies for primary prevention of infection, identification of host conditions favorable to infection and contagion, and treatment of infected individuals also flowed from this discovery. At this stage of development, typologies in the field of alcohol research do not convey ramifications for prevention or treatment. And although the early-onset alcoholism described by several different research groups may suggest a relatively robust phenotypic variant of alcoholism, there is room for doubt. Schuckit (1985), for one, has argued that rather than being a typology of alcoholism, alcoholism with ASPD is really a variant of ASPD.

Finally, it is important to place the recent interest in typologies in the field of substance abuse disorders into the context of the reemergence of descriptive psychiatry in DSM-III, DSM-III-R, and DSM-IV. During the past 20 years, typology researchers in the field have attempted to validate their models in treatment-matching and genetic epidemiological studies, while psychiatric researchers have been trying to validate categorical diagnoses using pharmacological challenge strategies (with biochemical markers), brain imaging studies, and human and molecular genetic studies. Replication has been a frequent problem. At this juncture, one can speculate that the next generation of psychiatric diagnoses and of substance abuse typologies will necessarily emerge from multigenerational longitudinal databases of informative pedigrees. If valid typologies exist, they will emerge from the more systematic genetic, developmental, and environmental data within these informative pedigrees. As in the rest of medicine, the identification of these typologies should have significant ramifications for future prevention and treatment in the field of substance abuse disorders.

# References

Alterman AI, Cacciola JS: The antisocial personality disorder diagnosis in substance abusers: problems and issues. J Nerv Ment Dis 179:401–409, 1991

American Psychiatric Association: Diagnostic and Statistical Manual of Mental Disorders, 3rd Edition. Washington, DC, American Psychiatric Association, 1980

American Psychiatric Association: Diagnostic and Statistical Manual of Mental Disorders, 3rd Edition, Revised. Washington, DC, American Psychiatric Association, 1987

American Psychiatric Association: Diagnostic and Statistical Manual of Mental Disorders, 4th Edition. Washington, DC, American Psychiatric Association, 1994

Annis HM, Peachey JE: The use of calcium carbimide in relapse prevention counselling: results of a randomized controlled trial. British Journal of Addiction 87:63–72, 1992

Babor TF, Dolinsky ZS: Alcoholic typologies: historical evolution and empirical evaluation of some common classification schemes, in Alcoholism: Origins and Outcome. Edited by Rose RM, Barrett J. New York, Raven, 1988, pp 245–266

Babor TF, Lauerman R: Classification and forms of inebriety: historical antecedents of alcoholic typologies, in Recent Developments in Alcoholism, Vol 5. Edited by Galanter M. New York, Plenum, 1986, pp 113–114

Babor TF, McCabe T, Mansanes P, et al: Patterns of alcoholism in France and America: a comparative study, in Alcoholism: A Multilevel Problem. Edited by Chafetz ME. Washington, DC, National Institute on Alcohol Abuse and Alcoholism, 1974, pp 113–128

Babor TF, Cooney NL, Lauerman R: The dependence syndrome concept as a psychological theory of relapse behaviour: an empirical evaluation of alcoholic and opiate addicts. British Journal of Addiction 82:393–405, 1987

Babor TF, Hoffman M, DelBoca FK, et al: Types of alcoholics, I: evidence for an empirically derived typology based on indicators of vulnerability and severity. Arch Gen Psychiatry 49:599–608, 1992a

Babor TF, Dolinsky ZS, Meyer RE, et al: Types of alcoholics: concurrent and predictive validity of some common classification schemes. British Journal of Addiction 87:1415–1431, 1992b

Ball SA, Carroll KM, Babor TF, et al: Subtypes of cocaine abusers: support for a type A–type B distinction. J Consult Clin Psychol 63:115–124, 1995

Berkson J: Limitations of the application of four-fold tables to hospital data. Biometric Bulletin 2:47–53, 1946

Bowman KM, Jellinek EM: Alcohol addiction and its treatment. Quarterly Journal of Studies on Alcohol 2:98–176, 1941

Brown J, Babor TF, Litt MD, et al: The type A/type B distinction: subtyping alcoholics according to indicators of vulnerability and severity. Ann N Y Acad Sci 708:23–33, 1994

Buydens-Branchey L, Branchey MJ, Noumair D: Age of alcoholism onset, I: relationship to psychopathology. Arch Gen Psychiatry 46:225–230, 1989a

Buydens-Branchey L, Branchey MJ, Noumair D, et al: Age of alcoholism onset, II: relationship to susceptibility to serotonin precursor availability. Arch Gen Psychiatry 46:231–236, 1989b

Cadoret RJ, O'Gorman TW, Troughton E, et al: Alcoholism and antisocial personality: interrelationships, genetic and environmental factors. Arch Gen Psychiatry 42:161–167, 1985

Cahalan D, Cisin IH, Crossley H: American Drinking Practices. New Brunswick, NJ, Rutgers Center for Alcohol Studies, 1969

Caster DV, Parsons OA: Relationship of depression, sociopathy, and locus of control to treatment outcome in alcoholics. J Consult Clin Psychol 45:751–756, 1977

Chick J: Alcohol dependence: methodological issues in its measurement: reliability of the criteria. British Journal of Addiction 75:175–186, 1980

Cloninger CR: Neurogenetic adaptive mechanisms in alcoholism. Science 236:410–416, 1987

Cloninger CR, Sigvardsson S, Bohman M: Childhood personality predicts alcohol abuse in young adults. Alcohol Clin Exp Res 12:494–505, 1988

Cloninger CR, Dinwiddie SH, Reich T: Epidemiology and genetics of alcoholism, in American Psychiatric Press Review of Psychiatry, Vol 8. Edited by Tasman A, Hales RE, Frances AJ. Washington, DC, American Psychiatric Press, 1989, pp 293–308

Conley JJ: An MMPI typology of male alcoholics: admission, discharge, and outcome comparison. J Pers Assess 45:33–39, 1981

Cooney NL, Kadden RM, Litt MD, et al: Matching alcoholics to coping skills or interactional therapies: two-year follow-up results. J Consult Clin Psychol 59:598–601, 1991

Cornelius JR, Salloum IM, Ehler JG, et al: Fluoxetine in depressed alcoholics: a double blind, placebo-controlled trial. Arch Gen Psychiatry 54:700–705, 1997

Cottler LB, Price RK, Compton WM, et al: Subtypes of adult antisocial behavior among drug abusers. J Nerv Ment Dis 183:154–161, 1995

Eckhardt M: Central nervous system impairment in the alcoholic: a research and clinical perspective, in Evaluation of the Alcoholic: Implications for Research, Theory, and Treatment (NIAAA Monogr No 5). Edited by Meyer RE, Babor TF, Glueck BC, et al. Rockville, MD, Alcohol, Drug Abuse, and Mental Health Administration, 1981, pp 349–368

Edwards G, Gross MM: Alcohol dependence: provisional description of a clinical syndrome. BMJ 1:1058–1061, 1976

Feingold A, Ball SA, Kranzler HR, et al: Generalizability of the type A/type B distinction across different psychoactive substances. Am J Drug Alcohol Abuse 22:449–462, 1996

Finney JW, Moos RH: Matching patient with treatments: conceptual and methodological issues. J Stud Alcohol 47:122–134, 1986

Fishbein DH, Lozovsky D, Jaffe JH: Impulsivity, aggression, and neuroendocrine responses to serotonergic stimulation in substance abusers. Biol Psychiatry 25:1049–1066, 1989

George DT, Wozniak K, Linnoila M: Basic and clinical studies on serotonin, alcohol, and alcoholism, in Novel Pharmacological Interventions for Alcoholism. Edited by Naranjo CA, Sellers EM. New York, Springer-Verlag New York, 1992, pp 92–104

Gerstley L, McLellan AT, Alterman AI, et al: Ability to form an alliance with the therapist: a possible marker of prognosis for patients with antisocial personality disorder. Am J Psychiatry 146:508–512, 1989

Gilligan SB, Reich T, Cloninger CR: Alcohol-related symptoms in heterogeneous families of hospitalized alcoholics. Alcohol Clin Exp Res 12:671–678, 1988

Glenn SW, Nixon SJ: Applications of Cloninger's subtypes in a female alcoholic sample. Alcohol Clin Exp Res 15:851–857, 1991

Goldstein SG, Linden JD: Multivariate classification of alcoholics by means of the MMPI. J Abnorm Psychol 74:661–669, 1969

Harpur TJ, Hare RD, Hakstian AR: Two-factor conceptualization of psychopathy: construct validity and assessment implications. Psychological Assessment 1:6–17, 1989

Helzer JE, Pryzbeck TR: The co-occurrence of alcoholism with other psychiatric disorders in the general population and its impact on treatment. J Stud Alcohol 49:219–224, 1988

Helzer JE, Canino GJ, Yeh E-K, et al: Alcoholism—North America and Asia. Arch Gen Psychiatry 47:313–319, 1990

Hesselbrock MN, Hesselbrock VM, Babor TF, et al: Antisocial behavior, psychopathology and problem drinking in the natural history of alcoholism, in Longitudinal Research in Alcoholism. Edited by Goodwin DW, VanDusen KT, Mednick SA. Boston, MA, Kluwer-Nijhoff, 1984, pp 197–214

Hesselbrock MN, Meyer RE, Keener JJ: Psychopathology in hospitalized alcoholics. Arch Gen Psychiatry 42:1050–1055, 1985

Hesselbrock VM, Stabenau JR, Hesselbrock MN, et al: The nature of alcoholism in patients with different family histories for alcoholism. Prog Neuropsychopharmacol Biol Psychiatry 6:607–614, 1982

Hesselbrock VM, Meyer RE, Hesselbrock MN: Psychopathology and addictive disorders: the specific case of antisocial personality disorder, in Addictive States. Edited by O'Brien CP, Jaffe JH. New York, Raven, 1992, pp 179–191

Hill SY: Absence of paternal sociopathy in the etiology of severe alcoholism: is there a Type III alcoholism? J Stud Alcohol 53:161–169, 1992

Hodgson RJ, Rankin JJ, Stockwell TR: Alcohol dependence and the priming effect. Behav Res Ther 17:379–387, 1979

Institute of Medicine: Broadening the Base of Treatment for Alcohol Problems. Washington, DC, National Academy Press, 1990

Irwin M, Schuckit M, Smith TL: Clinical importance of age at onset in type 1 and type 2 primary alcoholics. Arch Gen Psychiatry 47:320–324, 1990

Jaffe JH, Babor TF, Fishbein DH: Alcoholics, aggression and antisocial personality. J Stud Alcohol 49:211–218, 1988

Jellinek EM: Alcoholism: a genus and some of its species. Can Med Assoc J 83:1341–1345, 1960

Jessor R, Jessor SL: Adolescent development and the onset of drinking: a longitudinal study. J Stud Alcohol 36:27–51, 1975

Kadden RM, Cooney NL, Getter H, et al: Matching alcoholics to coping skills or interactional therapies: posttreatment results. J Consult Clin Psychol 57:698–704, 1989

Kahler CW, Epstein EE, McCrady BS: Loss of control and inability to abstain: the measurement of and the relationship between two constructs of male alcoholism. Addiction 90:1025–1036, 1995

Kaplan RF, Meyer RE, Stroebel CF: Alcohol dependence and responsivity to an ethanol stimulus as predictors of alcohol consumption. British Journal of Addiction 78:259–267, 1983

Kessler RC, Crum RM, Warner LA, et al: Lifetime co-occurrence of DSM-III-R alcohol abuse and dependence with other psychiatric disorders in the National Comorbidity Survey. Arch Gen Psychiatry 54:313–321, 1997

Kosten TR, Rounsaville BJ, Babor TF, et al: Substance use disorders in DSM-III-R: evidence for the dependence syndrome across different psychoactive substances. Br J Psychiatry 151:834–843, 1987

Kranzler HR, Burleson JA, Del Boca FK, et al: Buspirone treatment of anxious alcoholics: a placebo-controlled trial. Arch Gen Psychiatry 51:720–731, 1994

Kranzler HR, Burleson JA, Brown J, et al: Fluoxetine treatment seems to reduce the beneficial effects of cognitive-behavioral therapy in type B alcoholics. Alcohol Clin Exp Res 20:1534–1541, 1996

Kranzler HR, Tennen H, Penta C, et al: Targeted naltrexone treatment of early problem drinkers. Addictive Behavior 22:431–436, 1997

Linnoila M, DeJong J, Virkkunen M: Family history of alcoholism in violent offenders and impulsive fire setters. Arch Gen Psychiatry 46:613–616, 1989

Litt MD, Babor TF, DelBoca FK, et al: Types of alcoholics: application of an empirically derived typology to treatment matching. Arch Gen Psychiatry 49:609–614, 1992

Mandell W: Sociopathic alcoholics: matching treatment and patients, in Matching Patient Needs and Treatment Methods in Alcoholism and Drug Abuse. Edited by Gottheil E, McLellan AT, Druley KA. Springfield, IL, Charles C Thomas, 1981, pp 325–369

Mason BJ, Kocsis JH, Ritvo EC, et al: A double-blind, placebo-controlled trial of desipramine for primary alcohol dependence stratified on the presence or absence of major depression. JAMA 275:761–767, 1996

McGrath PJ, Nunes E, Quitkin FM: Imipramine in alcoholics with primary depression. Paper presented at the annual meeting of the American Psychiatric Association, Washington, DC, May 2–7, 1992

McLellan AT, Woody GE, Luborsky L, et al: Increased effectiveness of substance abuse treatment: a prospective study of patient-treatment matching. J Nerv Ment Dis 171:597–605, 1983a

McLellan AT, Luborsky L, Woody GE, et al: Predicting response to alcohol and drug abuse treatments: role of psychiatric severity. Arch Gen Psychiatry 40:620–625, 1983b

Meyer R: Typologies, in Treatments of Psychiatric Disorders: A Task Force Report of the American Psychiatric Association, Vol 2. Washington, DC, American Psychiatric Association, 1989, pp 1065–1071

Meyer RE: Toward a comprehensive theory of alcoholism. Ann N Y Acad Sci 708:238–250, 1994

Miller WR, Hester RK: Matching problem drinkers with optimal treatments, in Treating Addictive Behaviors: Processes of Change. Edited by Miller WR, Heather N. New York, Plenum, 1986, pp 175–203

Miller WR, Rollnick S: Motivational Interviewing: Preparing People to Change Addictive Behavior. New York, Guilford, 1991

Morey LC, Blashfield RK: Empirical classifications of alcoholism. J Stud Alcohol 42:925–937, 1981

Morey LC, Skinner HA, Blashfield RK: A typology of alcohol abusers: correlates and implications. J Abnorm Psychol 93:408–417, 1984

Nerviano VJ, Gross HW: Personality types of alcoholics on objective inventories. J Stud Alcohol 44:837–851, 1983

Nordstrom G, Berglund M: Type 1 and Type 2 alcoholics (Cloninger and Bohman) have different patterns of successful long-term adjustment. British Journal of Addiction 82:761–769, 1987

O'Leary M, Donovan DM, Chaney EF, et al: Cognitive impairment and treatment outcome with alcoholics: preliminary findings. J Clin Psychiatry 40:397–398, 1979

Penick E, Reed MR, Crawley PA, et al: Differentiation of alcoholics by family history. J Stud Alcohol 39:19–44, 1978

Polich JM, Armor DJ, Braiker HB: The Course of Alcoholism: Four Years After Treatment. Santa Monica, CA, Rand Corporation, 1980

Powell BJ, Campbell JL, Landon JF, et al: A double-blind, placebo-controlled study of nortriptyline and bromocriptine in male alcoholics subtyped by comorbid psychiatric disorders. Alcohol Clin Exp Res 19:462–468, 1995

Project MATCH Research Group: Matching alcoholism treatments to client heterogeneity: Project MATCH posttreatment drinking outcomes. J Stud Alcohol 58:7–29, 1997a

Project MATCH Research Group: Project MATCH secondary a priori hypotheses. Addiction 92:1671–1698, 1997b

Rimmer J, Pitts F, Reich T, et al: Alcoholism, II: sex, socio-economic status and race in two hospitalized samples. Quarterly Journal of Studies on Alcohol 32:942–952, 1971

Roberts WR, Morey LC: Convergent validation of a typology of alcohol abusers. Bulletin of the Society of Psychologists in Addictive Behaviors 4:226–233, 1985

Robins LN: Deviant Children Grown Up: A Sociologic and Psychiatric Study of the Sociopathic Personality. Baltimore, MD, Williams & Wilkins, 1966

Robins LN: Sturdy childhood predictors of adult anti-social behavior: replication from longitudinal studies. Psychol Med 8:611–622, 1978

Ross HE, Glaser FB, Germanson T: The prevalence of psychiatric disorders in patients with alcohol and other drug problems. Arch Gen Psychiatry 45:1023–1031, 1988

Rounsaville BJ, Weissman MM, Kleber HD, et al: Heterogeneity of psychiatric diagnosis in treated opiate addicts. Arch Gen Psychiatry 39:161–166, 1982

Rounsaville BJ, Eyre SL, Weissman MM, et al: The antisocial opiate addict. Advances in Alcohol and Substance Abuse 2:29–42, 1983

Rounsaville BJ, Kosten TR, Weissman MM, et al: Prognostic significance of psychopathology in treated opiate addicts: a 2.5-year follow-up study. Arch Gen Psychiatry 43:739–745, 1986

Rounsaville BJ, Dolinsky ZS, Babor TF, et al: Psychopathology as a predictor of treatment outcome in alcoholics. Arch Gen Psychiatry 44:505–513, 1987

Rounsaville BJ, Anton SF, Carroll K, et al: Psychiatric diagnoses of treatment-seeking cocaine abusers. Arch Gen Psychiatry 48:43–51, 1991

Roy A, DeJong J, Lamparski D, et al: Mental disorders among alcoholics: relationship to age of onset and cerebrospinal fluid neuropeptides. Arch Gen Psychiatry 48:423–427, 1991

Schuckit MA: Alcoholism: two types of alcoholism in women. Arch Environ Health 20:301–306, 1969

Schuckit MA: The clinical implications of primary diagnostic groups among alcoholics. Arch Gen Psychiatry 42:1043–1049, 1985

Schuckit MA, Winokur G: A short-term follow-up of women alcoholics. Diseases of the Nervous System 33:672–678, 1972

Schuckit MA, Tipp JE, Smith TL, et al: An evaluation of type A and B alcoholics. Addiction 90:1189–1203, 1995

Shelly CH, Goldstein G: An empirically derived typology of hospitalized alcoholics, in Empirical Studies of Alcoholism. Edited by Goldstein D, Heuringer CC. New York, Ballinger, 1976, pp 243–262

Skinner HA: Factor analysis and studies on alcohol: a methodological review. J Stud Alcohol 41:1091–1101, 1980

Skinner HA: Different strokes for different folks: differential treatment for alcohol abuse, in Evaluation of the Alcoholic: Implications for Research, Theory, and Treatment (NIAAA Monogr No 5). Edited by Meyer RE, Babor TF, Glueck BC, et al. Rockville, MD, Alcohol, Drug Abuse, and Mental Health Administration, 1981, pp 349–368

Skinner HA: Statistical approaches to the classification of alcohol and drug addiction. British Journal of Addiction 77:259–273, 1982

Skinner HA, Allen BA: Alcohol dependence syndrome: measurement and validation. J Abnorm Psychol 91:199–209, 1982

Stockwell T, Hodgson R, Edwards G, et al: The development of a questionnaire to measure severity of alcohol dependence. British Journal of Addiction 74:79–87, 1979

Tarter RE, McBride H, Buonpane N, et al: Differentiation of alcoholics: childhood history of minimal brain dysfunction, family history and drinking pattern. Arch Gen Psychiatry 34:761–768, 1977

von Knorring A-L, Bohman M, von Knorring L: Platelet MAO-activity as a biological marker in subgroups of alcoholism. Acta Psychiatr Scand 72:51–58, 1985

von Knorring L, Palm V, Andersson HE: Relationship between treatment outcome and subtype of alcoholism in men. J Stud Alcohol 46:388–391, 1985

von Knorring L, von Knorring A-L, Smigan L, et al: Personality traits in subtypes of alcoholics. J Stud Alcohol 48:523–527, 1987

Walton HJ, Ritson EB, Kennedy RI: Response of alcoholics to clinic treatment. BMJ 2:1171–1174, 1966

Warner LA, Kessler RC, Hughes M, et al: Prevalence and correlates of drug use and dependence in the United States: results from the National Comorbidity Survey. Arch Gen Psychiatry 52:219–229, 1995

Weiss RD, Mirin SM, Michael JL, et al: Psychopathology in chronic cocaine abusers. Am J Drug Alcohol Abuse 12:17–29, 1986

Winokur G, Rimmer J, Reich T: Alcoholism, IV: is there more than one type of alcoholism? Br J Psychiatry 118:525–531, 1971

Woody GE, McLellan AT, Luborsky L, et al: Severity of psychiatric symptoms as a predictor of benefits from psychotherapy: the VA-Penn study. Am J Psychiatry 141:1172–1177, 1984

Woody GE, McLellan AT, Luborsky L, et al: Sociopathy and psychotherapy outcome. Arch Gen Psychiatry 42:1081–1086, 1985

World Health Organization: Mental and behavioural disorders, in International Statistical Classification of Diseases and Related Health Problems, 10th Revision. Geneva, World Health Organization, 1992, pp 311–387

Zucker RA: The four alcoholisms: a developmental account of the etiologic process, in Alcohol and Addictive Behavior. Edited by Rivers PC. Lincoln, University of Nebraska Press, 1987, pp 27–83

# Chapter 12

# Assessment of the Patient

Richard S. Schottenfeld, M.D.
Michael V. Pantalon, Ph.D.

The primary goals of the substance abuse clinical evaluation are 1) to make an accurate diagnostic assessment of substance abuse or dependence and of the relation of substance use to other psychiatric and medical disorders, 2) to plan and initiate effective interventions and treatment where indicated, and 3) to enhance the patient's motivation for treatment.

The clinical assessment of substance use and substance-related disorders should be considered a routine part of all psychiatric or medical evaluations. Rates of substance use, abuse, and dependence vary depending on sociodemographic factors (i.e., age, social class, race or ethnicity, occupation, and gender), with, for example, higher rates more often found in men than in women. However, limiting assessment only to patients for whom there is an initial high level of suspicion will lead to failure to detect clinically important substance use disorders in many patients (Cyr and Wartman 1988). Several studies have documented that overall rates of routine detection of substance use disorders in medical and psychiatric practice are low and that physicians are even less likely to detect substance abuse in patients who are employed, married, white, insured, or female (Clark 1981; Cleary et al. 1988; Moore et al. 1989; Wolf et al. 1965). Needless to say, failure to diagnose substance abuse or dependence precludes effective intervention or treatment and contributes to continued and more severe problems.

Accurate diagnosis of a substance-related disorder is often made more difficult by the characteristic defenses of patients with these disorders (e.g., minimization, denial, projection, grandiosity) and the reluctance of the patient's family, friends, or co-workers to confront the patient or disclose information to the patient's

physician about these sensitive issues (Nace 1987). Covert and overt attitudes of physicians about drug and alcohol dependence—such as reluctance to recognize the harmful effects of a patient's substance use because of the physician's own pattern of alcohol or drug intake, a tendency to view these disorders as moral shortcomings of the patient rather than valid psychiatric disorders, or concerns about "labeling" a patient and the patient's potential angry response—may also interfere with timely diagnosis and treatment (Clark 1981; Lisansky 1975). Far from stigmatizing the patient, however, accurately diagnosing a substance use disorder and clearly labeling the patient's problems as resulting from alcohol or drug use are critical steps in motivating behavioral change and commitment to treatment.

In this chapter, we review the concept of the dependence syndrome and the diagnostic features of substance-related disorders and then discuss ways of eliciting an accurate history and observing signs of substance use disorders during the interview process. The utility of commonly used screening questionnaires and structured interviews is reviewed. In addition to the diagnostic interview with the patient and the mental status examination, a complete evaluation needs to include a review of the patient's medical records and results of the physical examination and laboratory studies; use of reports from family members, friends, co-workers, or supervisors; and monitoring of breath alcohol concentration and urine for toxicological evidence of drug use. Special attention is given to diagnostic issues regarding comorbid substance use and other psychiatric disorders. Finally, we review methods for assessing the patient's motivation for ending substance-related problems and discuss the application of motivational interviewing (Miller and Rollnick 1991) to patients who present with varying degrees of motivation for treatment during the assessment session.

On the basis of a thorough clinical assessment, the physician will be in a position to document the relationship between the patient's substance use and the patient's other psychiatric symptoms and experience of current or past life problems, including medical, family, occupational, social, and legal difficulties. A complete assessment will help determine the level or intensity of care required; the need for specific treatments, such as hospitalization or a medically supervised withdrawal; the necessary components of the overall treatment plan; and optimal patient-treatment–matching strategies. In addition, the assessment information is helpful in planning motivational strategies that can potentially increase the patient's readiness for treatment and compliance with treatment recommendations.

## Diagnosis of Substance-Related Disorders

In DSM-IV (American Psychiatric Association 1994), the category of substance-related disorders encompasses two groups of disorders: substance use disorders (substance dependence and substance abuse) and substance-induced disorders (substance intoxication, substance withdrawal, and a variety of other substance-induced mental disorders, such as substance-induced delirium, dementia, sexual dysfunction, or amnestic, psychotic, mood, anxiety, or sleep disorders). Eleven classes of psychoactive substances are identified: 1) alcohol, 2) amphetamine and related substances, 3) caffeine, 4) cannabis, 5) cocaine, 6) hallucinogens, 7) inhalants, 8) nicotine, 9) opioids, 10) phencyclidine (PCP) and related substances, and 11) sedatives, hypnotics, and anxiolytics. Because of their shared physiological and psychological effects, some of these substances can be grouped into two general categories: 1) central nervous system depressants, including alcohol and sedatives, anxiolytics, and hypnotics; and 2) stimulants, including cocaine and amphetamines and similarly acting sympathomimetics.

DSM-IV criteria for substance dependence reflect a consensus that dependence is best conceptualized as a biobehavioral construct characterized by compulsive use of a substance that may or may not be accompanied by physiological changes, including tolerance and withdrawal. Viewed in this fashion, the concept of dependence can be applied to the pathological use of sub-

stances, such as hallucinogens, that do not produce signs of physical dependence. Further, in the absence of symptoms of compulsive use, physical dependence is not considered indicative of substance dependence.

In DSM-IV, substance dependence and substance abuse are defined as maladaptive patterns of substance use, leading to clinically significant impairment or distress over a 12-month period. Substance dependence is manifested by at least three of seven possible symptoms. The first two symptoms indicate physical dependence or physiological dependence: 1) tolerance (need for increased amounts to obtain desired effects, or diminished effects with continued use of the same amount) and 2) withdrawal symptoms after discontinuation of use or abstinence, or use of the substance or a closely related substance to prevent or relieve withdrawal. The next two symptoms indicate impaired control of substance use: 3) taking the drug in larger amounts or over longer periods than originally intended and 4) persistent desire or unsuccessful efforts to control or cut down use. The final three symptoms indicate preoccupation with the substance and the salience of persistent or continued drug use to the person: 5) spending a great deal of time acquiring or using the substance or recovering from substance use; 6) reducing or giving up important social, occupational, or recreational activities because of substance use; and 7) continued use despite knowledge of having a persistent or recurrent physical or psychological problem that is caused or exacerbated by use of the substance.

Substance abuse can be diagnosed only in individuals who have never met criteria for substance dependence for the same class of substance. Substance abuse is manifested by at least one of four possible symptoms, occurring within a 12-month period: 1) recurrent use resulting in failure to fulfill important role obligations at work, school, or home; 2) recurrent use in situations in which use is physically hazardous; 3) recurrent substance-related legal problems; and 4) continued use despite the existence of persistent or recurrent interpersonal or social problems caused or exacerbated by substance use.

DSM-III-R (American Psychiatric Association 1987) included uniform criteria for rating the severity of substance dependence. Severity criteria are not included in DSM-IV, but ratings of the severity of dependence on specific substances (e.g., nicotine dependence scores on the Fagerstrom Test) may be helpful in planning or sequencing interventions. In DSM-IV, remission is characterized as either full (no symptoms) or partial (one or two symptoms but criteria for current dependence not met) and as either early (occurring in the past 1–12 months) or sustained (occurring for more than 12 months). Remissions associated with agonist therapy (e.g., methadone or L-α-acetylmethadol [LAAM] maintenance) or with living in a controlled environment (where access to the substance is restricted) should be classified as "on agonist therapy" or "in a controlled environment."

Despite the uniformity of the overall nomenclature used with regard to all 11 classes of substances, the specific syndromes and symptoms associated with each of the classes may vary. With the exception of caffeine, substance dependence can occur with use of any of the classes of substances either alone or in combination (polysubstance dependence), whereas substance abuse is not associated with either nicotine or caffeine but may occur with any of the 9 remaining classes either alone or in combination. There is even greater variability, however, with regard to the specific signs and symptoms of intoxication or withdrawal or the occurrence of other substance-induced mental disorders associated with each of the classes of substances. Withdrawal delirium, for example, is typically found only after discontinuation of use of central nervous system depressants (alcohol or sedatives, hypnotics, and anxiolytics). Withdrawal syndromes involving clinically significant distress or impairment are defined for alcohol, amphetamines, cocaine, nicotine, opioids, and sedatives, hypnotics, and anxiolytics but not for caffeine, cannabis, hallucinogens, inhalants, or PCP. With the exception of caffeine and nicotine, all classes of substances may cause delirium and psychotic disorders during intoxication and variable patterns of mood or anxiety disorders with intoxication or after withdrawal.

## Eliciting the Patient's History

Regardless of the care and sensitivity of the interviewer, patients with substance use disorders may not easily or invariably give a reliable report. One of the diagnostic hallmarks of a substance use disorder is that continued use of the substance becomes extraordinarily important to the patient, often even at the expense of the patient's health, safety, or social functioning. It should not be surprising, therefore, that patients will attempt to protect their ability to continue to use by minimizing, denying, or even lying about the extent of their use and the problems resulting from it. Rationalization and projection are also common. One woman, for example, attributed a broken leg (caused by her walking down the

street intoxicated) to her usual clumsiness and thus completely forgot to mention this problem during the evaluation. Many other patients blame others for all of their relationship, vocational, or legal problems rather than recognize these problems as resulting from their own drug use.

In eliciting the history, the psychiatrist needs to be alert to these characteristic defenses and to take note of what the patient is trying to hide. It is also necessary to make use of independent reports and objective measures in the assessment. It goes without saying that patients who are intoxicated or delirious at the time of assessment cannot give an accurate history.

With these caveats in mind, several specific strategies and approaches to history taking can be recommended. As in all aspects of the psychiatric interview, a straightforward, nonjudgmental approach is most likely to elicit accurate information. As noted by some authorities, history taking is facilitated by questions beginning with *how* (e.g., "How did that affect you?") rather than *why* (e.g., "Why did you smoke crack then?"). Not surprisingly, the latter approach is often perceived as judgmental and tends to evoke defensiveness (Kaufman and Reoux 1988).

When eliciting the history, the psychiatrist should directly address the patient's concerns about disclosure of information to family members, employers, legal authorities, or licensing boards. Sometimes the patient's reluctance to disclose sensitive information is lessened by a frank discussion about why this information is important, how the information will be used, and what measures can and will be taken to safeguard the patient's confidentiality. Because confidentiality regulations are set by both state and federal authorities and differ from one jurisdiction to another (and according to whether the patient is an adult or minor), physicians need to be informed about the specific reporting requirements and confidentiality statutes affecting their practices (Senay 1997).

One general strategy for eliciting the history is to avoid, at least initially, questions that are most likely to make patients with substance use disorders particularly defensive. Thus, it is often useful first to review the patient's life history, including successes and problems experienced at work and in school, in the family, and in friendships, as well as medical, legal, and psychological and emotional problems, without necessarily linking any of these problems to the patient's use of alcohol or other drugs. After this general overview, a parallel chronology of the patient's use of alcohol and drugs can be obtained, and, finally, specific inquiry can be made into the relationship between alcohol or drug use and the patient's life problems. This strategy may reveal a correlation between substance use and the patient's life problems that has not previously been recognized by the patient.

Although sensitivity to the patient's defensiveness is necessary, it is essential to obtain a complete history of the patient's use of alcohol and of all other drugs. Thus, specific questions need to be asked about each category of psychoactive substances. The major categories include nicotine (cigarettes, cigars, chewing tobacco), caffeine (coffee, tea, and other caffeinated beverages, food products, and medications), alcohol (beer, wine, and distilled spirits, such as whiskey, vodka, and gin), cannabinoids (marijuana, hashish), stimulants (cocaine, amphetamines), opioids (heroin, morphine, hydromorphone hydrochloride [Dilaudid], methadone, oxycodone), sedative-hypnotics and anxiolytics (barbiturates, benzodiazepines), psychomimetics and hallucinogens (PCP, LSD, mescaline), and inhalants (glue, paint thinners, solvents). Inquiry should be made into a history of lifetime ("Have you ever used . . . ?") and recent use of substances from each of the categories. For drugs that can be prescribed for medical purposes, it is also essential to determine whether these drugs were taken only for the prescribed purpose and whether the patient ever exceeded the prescribed dose or duration. When inquiring about use of drugs in each of the categories, it is useful to ask about the general category and then name specific substances, using generic, brand, and street names as examples (e.g., "Have you ever used any opioid or opiate-like drugs, such as morphine, Demerol, Dilaudid, methadone, or Percodan?" "What about heroin, P-dope, smack, or horse?").

As part of the evaluation for each of the drug categories, patients should be asked about their lifetime use, recent or current use, and periods of heaviest use. Age and circumstances of first use, how the person reacted initially, who was there, and how soon he or she used it again are often of diagnostic and therapeutic import.

Specific questions should be asked regarding tolerance and withdrawal, the pattern of use during each period of use, how drug use was supported, and what circumstances or personal efforts help to curtail or control use. Recognition of tolerance and withdrawal requires familiarity with the symptoms of intoxication and withdrawal specific to each of the 11 classes of substances. Tolerance to nicotine, for example, may be indicated by the absence of symptoms of nausea or dizziness after substantial nicotine use. Nicotine withdrawal may be manifested by dysphoric mood, insomnia, restlessness,

irritability, anxiety, difficulty concentrating, decreased heart rate, or increased appetite or weight gain. More detailed descriptions of the withdrawal syndromes specific to each class of substance are provided elsewhere in this volume and in the diagnostic criteria for the withdrawal syndrome listed in DSM-IV.

Pattern of use refers to quantity used per occasion (average and maximum), frequency (how often used), duration of episodes of use, route of administration, and expense. The interviewer needs to be alert to early and subtle indications of problematic use. With regard to alcohol, for example, these indications may include relief drinking, surreptitious drinking, anticipatory drinking, and gulping of drinks. Rationalization of drinking, protection of supply, geographic escapes to facilitate drinking, and regular morning drinking are later occurrences and indicate greater problem severity (Farr et al. 1980). Changes in the pattern of alcohol or other drug use, including reduction of the patient's alcohol or drug repertoire, may also be a clue to a diagnosis of dependence. Patients often provide evidence of impaired control when they attempt to demonstrate that substance use is not a problem for them. For example, patient reports of "I never drink before five o'clock," "I never drink alone," or "I never drink spirits, only beer" may indicate some difficulty and attempt at controlling use.

Finally, attention needs to be directed to any medical, psychological or emotional, and social complications of use; to the patient's history of treatment for a substance-related disorder; and to any family history of substance-related or other psychiatric disorders. The evaluator's familiarity with the details of how substance use affects these areas and his or her willingness to ask specific questions about them are likely to lead to the most complete disclosure. This approach facilitates recognition of early and later signs of problematic alcohol or drug use. Early indicators may include blackouts, accidental overdoses, behavior changes, driving or engaging in other dangerous or aggressive activities while intoxicated, or feeling guilty about behaviors engaged in while using. Later sequelae include loss of nonusing friends; loss of interest in non-drug-related activities; impaired relationships with family, friends, and coworkers; disruptions of occupational or social functioning; and medical or legal problems.

Pattison (1986) identified 10 components of an alcohol-related history, and these components serve as a useful summary of the areas that need to be addressed in the patient's substance use history. In addition to 1) quantity/frequency measures; 2) assessment of tolerance and withdrawal; and assessment of adverse 3) medical, 4) interpersonal, 5) vocational, 6) social, and 7) legal consequences; components include assessment of 8) the behaviors engaged in when the patient is drinking or using drugs, 9) personality changes associated with drinking or drug use; and 10) emotional consequences (such as shame, diminished self-esteem, paranoid ideation, anxiety, and dissociative states) of drinking or drug use.

## Physical and Mental Status Examination

The physical and mental status examination provides critical information for diagnosis, management, and treatment of substance use disorders. Careful physical examination is essential because of the wide range of medical disorders associated with tobacco, alcohol, or other drug use (Lieber 1995; O'Connor and Schottenfeld 1998; O'Connor et al. 1994). Although psychiatrists and other mental health and substance abuse treatment professionals may prefer to refer patients to primary care or internal medicine physicians for a complete physical examination, assessment of the patient's vital signs and a brief physical assessment, in combination with the mental status examination, may reveal evidence of recent or current use, intoxication, withdrawal, or potentially life-threatening medical sequelae of substance use disorders. Because many excellent references on the mental status examination in psychiatry are available, we focus discussion in this chapter on elements that are of particular importance with regard to substance use disorders.

A brief physical assessment should be performed to look for evidence of recent or past intravenous drug use (e.g., track marks, abscesses) or of chronic use of drugs by insufflation (e.g., nasal discharge, ulcers, perforated septum). Drug overdose may be signaled by depressed respiration and marked somnolence. Signs of sepsis (fever, pallor, hypotension) or of nutritional deficiency (wasted appearance, gingivitis, cheilosis or ulceration of the skin at the corners of the mouth) associated with alcohol or other drug dependence can also be noted during a brief physical assessment.

The physical and mental status examination also should be directed at detecting signs of acute intoxication, withdrawal, or delirium. Signs of alcohol, sedative, or anxiolytic intoxication, for example, include slurred speech, incoordination, unsteady gait, nystagmus, impaired attention or memory, and (in the case of alcohol

intoxication) a flushed face. Signs of stimulant intoxication (including caffeine intoxication) include tachycardia, pupillary dilation, diaphoresis, restlessness, nervousness, excitement, a flushed face, muscle twitching, psychomotor agitation, and pressured or rambling speech. Evidence of opioid intoxication includes pupillary constriction, drowsiness, slurred speech, and impaired attention or memory. Cannabis intoxication may be indicated by conjunctival injection, increased appetite, dry mouth, and tachycardia.

Physical signs of opioid withdrawal include lacrimation, rhinorrhea, pupillary dilation, diaphoresis, fever, piloerection, and yawning. Signs of withdrawal from alcohol, sedatives, or anxiolytics include tachycardia, elevated blood pressure, and tremulousness. Signs of delirium, which may result from intoxication with stimulants, cannabis, PCP, and hallucinogens or withdrawal from alcohol, sedatives, or anxiolytics, include reduced ability to attend to external stimuli, disorganized thinking, disorientation, perceptual disturbances, memory impairment, psychomotor agitation or retardation, and reduced level of consciousness.

A careful mental status examination, including assessment of cognitive functioning, is also essential for accurate diagnosis of substance dependence, comorbid psychiatric disorders, and cognitive dysfunction. Major sequelae of substance abuse disorders that can be documented in the mental status examination include transient or persistent hallucinatory phenomena, mood and affective disturbances (panic, anxiety, depression, guilt, shame, diminished self-esteem), and paranoid, suicidal, or violent ideation or behavior. Assessment of cognitive function should include evaluation of attention and concentration, recent and remote memory, abstract reasoning, and problem-solving ability. All of these functions may be impaired by recent alcohol, sedative, anxiolytic, stimulant, or polydrug use. At least in the case of central nervous system depressants and inhalants and as documented more recently, cocaine, memory deficits, and other cognitive impairments may be persistent or permanent (Grant 1987; O'Malley et al. 1992).

Both obvious manifestations and more subtle signs and symptoms of substance-related disorders documented in a careful mental status examination may provide critical information for diagnosis and treatment. Affective instability or lability, irritability, anxiety, and depressed mood can be signs of current substance use (intoxication), withdrawal, or dependence. Sleep and appetite disturbances are also caused by alcohol and other central nervous system depressants, caffeine, and other stimulants and opioids. Many alcohol-dependent patients, for example, will report difficulty falling asleep and/or interrupted sleep after attempts to self-medicate with alcohol. They may be completely unaware that these problems are actually a result of or exacerbated by their alcohol use. The presence of any of these abnormalities on mental status examination provides presumptive evidence of problematic substance use in patients who otherwise report "controlled" or nonproblematic use of alcohol or other drugs. Confronting patients with this evidence of problems related to substance use, in an empathic and nonthreatening manner, may help to overcome their denial and increase recognition of the need to abstain.

The mental status examination should also document evidence, when present, of comorbid psychiatric disorders, including schizophrenia, bipolar disorder, depression, and anxiety disorders. These comorbid disorders occur frequently, affect prognosis, and have important treatment implications, as discussed in this volume.

## Screening Instruments and Structured Interviews

A number of short, self-report questionnaires are available to aid in the detection of alcohol abuse and dependence. The four-question CAGE questionnaire (Mayfield et al. 1974) ("Have you ever 1) attempted to Cut back on alcohol? 2) been Annoyed by comments made about your drinking? 3) felt Guilty about drinking? 4) had an Eye-opener first thing in the morning to steady your nerves?") has been found to improve detection rates in primary care and medical settings (Clark 1981). Modified versions of the CAGE questionnaire, including the four-item T-ACE (Sokol et al. 1989) and five-item TWEAK (Russell et al. 1991) questionnaires, which include items assessing alcohol tolerance, appear to have even greater sensitivity and specificity than the CAGE questionnaire has for assessing lifetime alcohol abuse or dependence (Chan et al. 1993; O'Connor and Schottenfeld 1998). These questionnaires can be supplemented by standardized questions regarding quantity and frequency of drinking, such as those included in the Alcohol Use Disorders Identification Test (AUDIT; Saunders et al. 1993), to improve their sensitivity in detecting current disorders. More detailed questionnaires, such as various versions of the Michigan Alcoholism Screening Test (MAST; Selzer 1971) or the Alcohol Dependence Scale (Skinner and Horn 1984), may also

help to elicit information necessary to make a diagnosis of abuse or dependence.

Use of structured interviews is a reliable way to elicit diagnostic information and decrease the chance of omitting questions about important signs or symptoms. Two of these interviews merit special attention. The Structured Clinical Interview for DSM-IV (SCID; First et al. 1995) is a clinically based interview that facilitates definitive diagnosis of DSM-IV substance-related and other psychiatric disorders. The Addiction Severity Index (ASI; McLellan et al. 1980, 1992) facilitates a multidimensional assessment of patients with substance use disorders by evaluating alcohol and drug problem severity and the severity of medical, psychiatric, social, legal, and occupational problems experienced by the patient. Initial ASI ratings of problem severity are highly correlated with treatment outcome and can be used to determine the need for specialized psychiatric, vocational, or medical interventions (McLellan et al. 1997). The ASI can also be used to monitor the effects of treatment and changes in the patient's functioning.

## Interviews With Significant Others

Whenever possible, evaluation should include an interview with family members or other people who know and have had contact with the patient in a variety of other settings. Ideally, these individuals should not themselves have problems with alcohol or drugs. Use of multiple informants can substantially increase the validity of the evaluation. The reliability of self-reports is often increased when the patient knows that others will be asked about his or her alcohol or drug use. Although family members may not be aware of all of the details of the patient's substance use, such as quantity, frequency, or variety of drugs used, they may be in a position to provide critical information regarding the patient's behavioral changes or problems experienced as a direct result of alcohol or other drug use. Involvement of family members in the initial stages of the evaluation will also facilitate family-based interventions, limit setting, and long-term family support of treatment goals.

## Laboratory Examination

Toxicology testing of blood, urine, or hair is an essential component of the substance abuse evaluation and plays an important role in the monitoring of recovery. Blood or urine toxicology testing is critical in cases of suspected or possible drug overdose and should be included in the routine evaluation of patients with acute changes in mental status or with any indication of suspected alcohol or drug problems. For the minority of patients with substance use disorders who persistently deny alcohol or drug use, toxicology testing of hair or urine may be the only way to document the problem and to confront the patient's drug use effectively. Even for patients who acknowledge drug problems, toxicology testing often yields surprising results. Patients may openly admit to using one substance that has become a problem for them (e.g., heroin) while continuing to deny their current use of other substances (e.g., cocaine, benzodiazepines, alcohol, cannabis) that they do not recognize or acknowledge as causing them problems.

The clinical utility of drug testing is enhanced by a thorough understanding of the methodologies that are used in the testing procedures (immunoassay, thin-layer chromatography, and gas chromatography/mass spectrometry), the sensitivity and specificity of the assays used, and the substances that can be detected by the assays (Chiang and Hawks 1986; Hawks and Chiang 1986; Manno 1986). Knowledge of the maximum length of time after last use that the drug or its metabolite can still be detected in blood, urine, or hair is also essential for accurate interpretation of negative results. A patient with a cocaine problem characterized by a pattern of weekend binges may have a negative drug screen on a urine sample collected on Friday morning, for example, because cocaine metabolites can be detected reliably only for a few days after last use. On the other hand, many drugs of abuse can be detected in hair samples months after last use. This prolonged detection period, however, makes toxicology testing of hair less useful than urine toxicology testing as a means of monitoring recovery or abstinence. Use of a Breathalyzer is a convenient, reliable and inexpensive way to determine current alcohol intoxication or recent use. Urine testing for alcohol is more expensive than Breathalyzer testing and does not substantially increase the detection period because alcohol usually can be detected in urine only up to 8–12 hours after use.

Testing is performed for a variety of biochemical substances that serve as markers of harmful alcohol use, but the value of such markers is limited by problems with sensitivity and specificity. Sensitivity and specificity of biochemical markers may be increased by the use of combinations of measures (e.g., measures of serum γ-glutamyltransferase or aspartate aminotransferase in conjunction with measures of increased red blood cell size [mean corpuscular volume]). Carbohydrate-deficient transferrin is currently the most sensitive and specific marker of heavy drinking and may be particularly useful in monitoring abstinence during treatment (Allen et al. 1994; Anton 1996).

Laboratory evaluation of patients with substance use disorders should also be used to detect adverse medical consequences of alcohol and other drug use. In addition to a complete physical examination, a thorough initial evaluation of a patient with a substance use disorder should include a urinalysis, a complete blood count, blood chemistry studies, liver enzyme determinations, serology (Venereal Disease Research Laboratory test, hepatitis antibodies and antigens), and testing for tuberculosis (purified protein derivative). After appropriate counseling, testing for HIV infection is also indicated, given the high rates of infection not only in intravenous drug users but also among users of freebase or crack cocaine and among alcoholics.

## Assessment of Comorbid Psychiatric Disorders

Acute and chronic use of psychoactive substances can have profound effects on cognitive functioning, mood, thought processes, and personality functioning. In the absence of a history of substance use, many of these effects may be indistinguishable, on the basis of signs and symptoms alone, from other Axis I psychiatric disorders. Although these syndromes should be classified as substance-induced mental disorders, accurate diagnosis is made problematic because patients with substance use disorders also experience high rates of primary psychiatric disorders (i.e., disorders unrelated to substance use or medical conditions). Common diagnostic dilemmas faced by clinicians include 1) differentiation of alcohol- and alcohol withdrawal–related depression and affective lability from unipolar and bipolar depression and anxiety disorders and 2) differentiation of cocaine-induced paranoid delusional states from schizophrenia.

Several guidelines for distinguishing primary psychiatric disorders from substance-induced disorders have been proposed. In general, a diagnosis of a primary psychiatric disorder is more likely if the onset of the disorder preceded the initial onset of substance use, the disorder persisted during past periods of abstinence, or the disorder continues after 4 weeks of abstinence. Waiting at least 4 weeks before beginning pharmacological treatment of depression or anxiety may be particularly advisable in treating patients with alcohol dependence, because the very high rates of anxiety and depressive symptoms after detoxification tend to resolve spontaneously during this period and because premature diagnosis and pharmacological treatment of a presumed underlying primary psychiatric disorder may complicate treatment of alcohol dependence. Delaying diagnosis and implementation of pharmacological treatment may be problematic, however, for patients who are unable to maintain abstinence for 4 weeks, and failure to treat an underlying psychiatric disorder may contribute to relapse (Rounsaville and Kranzler 1989). Consequently, some experts recommend using clinical features to differentiate primary from substance-induced disorders and shortening the period of abstinence required for making a diagnosis to 10 days to 2 weeks. This approach is clearly more risky in that there is an increased likelihood that patients will mix alcohol or other drugs with prescribed medications. Clinical features that may indicate a primary rather than a substance-induced mental disorder include a family history of the mental disorder or symptoms that are not typically associated with the substance or the doses used. Atypical presentations of primary psychiatric disorders in the context of substance use, such as a first manic episode late in life, suggest a substance-induced disorder. Shortening the period of abstinence required for making a diagnosis may also be more appropriate for patients dependent on opioids or other substances that may be less likely than alcohol or cocaine directly to cause affective disturbances.

Regardless of the decision rules followed in diagnosing comorbid psychiatric disorders and the exact timing of implementation of treatment for underlying psychiatric disorders, a diagnosis of comorbid psychiatric disorders has important prognostic and clinical implications. The occurrence of comorbid psychiatric disorders, with the exception of depression among alcoholic women, usually confers a poorer treatment prognosis (Rounsaville et al. 1986, 1987). Psychiatric treatment of underlying psychiatric disorders, however, has been shown to improve treatment outcome for both opioid-dependent patients and alcoholic patients (Rounsaville et al. 1985). Patient-treatment matching, based on assessment of comorbid psychiatric disorders, may also improve treatment outcome (McLellan et al. 1983, 1997). Kadden et al. (1989) and Litt et al. (1992), for example, documented that sociopathic alcoholic patients have improved treatment outcomes when treated in structured group settings providing coping skills training, whereas interactional group therapy was more effective for less sociopathic alcoholic patients.

# Enhancing Motivation

The assessment also affords the physician a unique opportunity to enhance the patient's motivation for treatment, if any treatment is indicated. Motivational strategies are critical, because resistance and ambivalence are often at their highest at the time of initial assessment and patients may not be ready even to talk about or acknowledge their problems, much less agree to treatment recommendations.

Five general principles of motivational interviewing can be applied during the assessment to facilitate behavioral change (Miller and Rollnick 1991). These principles include 1) expression of empathy (e.g., through reflective listening), 2) noting of discrepancies between current and desired behaviors (e.g., long-term goals), 3) avoidance of argumentation, 4) abstention from directly confronting resistance, and 5) support of self-efficacy or the patient's perception that he or she always has the ability to change. The specific motivational strategies used with a patient should be based on an assessment of the patient's level of motivation or stage of change at the time of the initial evaluation.

Assessing the patient's motivation for change involves gaining an understanding of the patient's goals and reasons for seeking consultation at this particular point in time and of the patient's understanding of the positive as well as negative consequences of substance use. The role of external coercion (e.g., parent, partner, or legal pressure) should also be explored. The patient's stage of change may be classified along a continuum from precontemplation (when patients do not think they have a problem) to contemplation (when patients are considering that they might have a problem but are not taking steps to change), to determination (when patients have made a decision to change but have yet to act on it), to action (when patients are actively taking steps to change), to maintenance (when patients are trying to maintain a current level of change by preventing relapse). Assessment of the patient's stage of change can often be made on the basis of information received during the assessment (Samet et al. 1996). Such assessment may also be facilitated by use of standardized questionnaires, such as the University of Rhode Island Change Assessment (URICA; Prochaska and DiClemente 1985) or the Contemplation Ladder (Beiner and Abrams 1991). A stage-of-change algorithm can be used to facilitate assessment as well. The algorithm of DiClemente et al. (1991) requires the patient to select the appropriate answer from the following responses to the physician's presumed inquiry about the patient's substance use: 1) "Yes, I quit more than 6 months ago" (maintenance); 2) "Yes, I quit less than 6 months ago" (action); 3) "No, but I intend to quit in the next 6 months" (contemplation); 4) "No, but I intend to quit in the next 30 days" (determination); or 5) "No, and I do not intend to quit in the next 6 months" (precontemplation). Simply describing each stage and then asking the patient to select which he or she believes most appropriately describes him or her at the time of evaluation may also be helpful in priming the patient for motivational interviewing (Pantalon and Swanson 1997).

Rather than directly confront denial in the patient who is in the precontemplation stage, the clinician can note discrepancies between the patient's current life situation or emotional state and the patient's ideal or desired situation. The assessment provides an opportunity to identify these discrepancies and to elicit from the patient self-motivating statements that point to the patient's ambivalence and interest in change. Thus, for example, the clinician might comment, basing remarks on the patient's statements, that although the patient experiences most of his or her best times (e.g., times when the patient feels the happiest, most energetic, or relaxed) when using, the patient is also concerned that some of his or her important relationships are imperiled because of other people's concerns about the patient's use. Once a patient begins to identify some negative consequences of use and begins to contemplate curtailing use, reflective listening can be used to identify the impediments to change experienced by the patient and to support the patient's sense of self-efficacy about making a change. The clinician might note, for example, that the patient seems concerned that curtailing substance use would eliminate all opportunities for fun, sex, pleasure, or relaxation, and then the clinician might ask the patient to think of alternative ways of achieving these same goals. Exploration of the patient's history of attempts to curtail or control use may also provide an opportunity for identifying appropriate treatment options and reasons the patient might now be successful in making and sustaining a change.

Other motivational techniques include 1) emphasizing the patient's personal choice and responsibility for treatment decisions; 2) frequently checking for the patient's agreement on goals and methods; 3) eliciting change strategies from the patient rather than directly telling the patient what course of action to take; 4) highlighting the patient's concerns about continued drug use; 5) asking about obstacles to change, both internal (e.g., lack of confidence) and external (e.g., lack of transportation to treatment facility); 6) accepting the patient's current level of motivation or commitment to treatment; 7) weighing the pros and cons of change; 8) offering a menu of change options (e.g., 12-step programs, cognitive-behavior therapy, medications); and 9) giving a motivational summary, which involves summarizing the patient's (not the physician's) reasons for change and ways to achieve change, regardless of how much the patient was committed to changing.

## Summary

In this chapter, we have discussed methods for conducting an assessment of substance abuse in an effort to make an accurate diagnosis, to delineate the effect of substance use on other medical and psychiatric disorders, to plan treatment interventions, and to increase the patient's motivation or readiness for initiating such treatment. The information obtained during the assessment will enable the clinician to determine the patient's need to make changes with regard to substance use and to recommend or plan appropriate treatment based on current practice guidelines (e.g., "Practice Guideline for Treatment of Patients With Substance Use Disorders" [American Psychiatric Association 1995]). A carefully conducted assessment will also increase the patient's interest in and capability of initiating and maintaining change.

## References

Allen JP, Litten RZ, Anton RF, et al: Carbohydrate-deficient transferrin as a measure of immoderate drinking: remaining issues. Alcohol Clin Exp Res 18:799–812, 1994

American Psychiatric Association: Diagnostic and Statistical Manual of Mental Disorders, 3rd Edition, Revised. Washington, DC, American Psychiatric Association, 1987

American Psychiatric Association: Diagnostic and Statistical Manual of Mental Disorders, 4th Edition. Washington, DC, American Psychiatric Association, 1994

American Psychiatric Association: Practice Guideline for Treatment of Patients With Substance Use Disorders. Washington, DC, American Psychiatric Association, 1995

Anton RF: The use of carbohydrate deficient transferrin as an indicator of alcohol consumption during treatment and follow-up. Alcohol Clin Exp Res 20 (suppl 8):54A–56A, 1996

Beiner L, Abrams DB: The Contemplation Ladder: validation of a measure of readiness to consider smoking cessation. Health Psychol 10:360–365, 1991

Chan AWK, Pristach EA, Welte JW, et al: Use of the TWEAK test in screening for alcoholism/heavy drinking in three populations. Alcohol Clin Exp Res 17:1188–1192, 1993

Chiang CN, Hawks RL: Implications of drug levels in body fluids: basic concepts, in Urine Testing for Drugs of Abuse (NIDA Res Monogr No 73). Edited by Hawks RL, Chiang CN. Rockville, MD, Department of Health and Human Services, 1986, pp 62–83

Clark WD: Alcoholism: blocks to diagnosis and treatment. Am J Med 71:275–285, 1981

Cleary PD, Miller M, Bush BT, et al: Prevalence and recognition of alcohol abuse in a primary care population. Am J Med 85:466–471, 1988

Cyr MG, Wartman SA: The effectiveness of routine screening questions in the detection of alcoholism. JAMA 259:51–54, 1988

DiClemente CC, Prochaska JO, Fairhurst SK, et al: The process of smoking cessation: an analysis of precontemplation, contemplation, and preparation stages of change. J Consult Clin Psychol 59:295–304, 1991

Farr WE, Karacan I, Pokorny AD, et al (eds): Phenomenology and Treatment of Alcoholism. New York, SP Medical & Scientific Books, 1980

First MB, Spitzer RL, Gibbon M, et al: Structured Clinical Interview for DSM-IV Axis I Disorders—Patient Version 2.0 (SCID-I/P). New York, New York State Psychiatric Institute, 1995

Grant I: Alcohol and the brain: neuropsychological correlates. J Consult Clin Psychol 55:310–314, 1987

Hawks RL, Chiang CN: Examples of specific drug assays, in Urine Testing for Drugs of Abuse (NIDA Res Monogr No 73). Edited by Hawks RL, Chiang CN. Rockville, MD, Department of Health and Human Services, 1986, pp 84–112

Kadden RM, Cooney NL, Getter H, et al: Matching alcoholics to coping skills or interactional therapies: posttreatment results. J Consult Clin Psychol 57:698–704, 1989

Kaufman E, Reoux J: Guidelines for the successful psychotherapy of substance abusers. Am J Drug Alcohol Abuse 14:199–209, 1988

Lieber CS: Medical disorders of alcoholism. N Engl J Med 333:1058–1065, 1995

Lisansky ET: Why physicians avoid early diagnosis of alcoholism. New York State Journal of Medicine 75:1788–1792, 1975

Litt MD, Babor TF, DelBoca FK, et al: Types of alcoholics, II: application of an empirically derived typology to treatment matching. Arch Gen Psychiatry 49:609–614, 1992

Manno JE: Specimen collection and handling, in Urine Testing for Drugs of Abuse (NIDA Res Monogr No 73). Edited by Hawks RL, Chiang CN. Rockville, MD, Department of Health and Human Services, 1986, pp 24–29

Mayfield D, McLeod G, Hall P: The CAGE questionnaire: validation of a new alcoholism screening instrument. Am J Psychiatry 131:1121–1123, 1974

McLellan AT, Luborsky L, Woody GE, et al: An improved diagnostic evaluation instrument for substance abuse patients: the Addiction Severity Index. J Nerv Ment Dis 168:26–33, 1980

McLellan AT, Luborsky L, Woody GE, et al: Predicting response to alcohol and drug abuse treatments. Alcohol and Drug Abuse 40:620–625, 1983

McLellan AT, Cacciola J, Kushner H, et al: The fifth edition of the Addition Severity Index: cautions, additions, and normative data. J Subst Abuse Treat 9:261–275, 1992

McLellan AT, Grissom GR, Zanis D, et al: Problem-service 'matching' in addiction treatment. Arch Gen Psychiatry 54:730–735, 1997

Miller WR, Rollnick S: Motivational Interviewing: Preparing People to Change Addictive Behavior. New York, Guilford, 1991

Moore RD, Bone LR, Geller G, et al: Prevalence, detection, and treatment of alcoholism in hospitalized patients. JAMA 261:403–407, 1989

Nace EP: The Treatment of Alcoholism. New York, Brunner/Mazel, 1987

O'Connor PG, Schottenfeld RS: Patients with alcohol problems. N Engl J Med 338:592–602, 1998

O'Connor PG, Selwin PA, Schottenfeld RS: Medical care for injection drug users with human immunodeficiency virus infection. N Engl J Med 331:451–459, 1994

O'Malley S, Adamse M, Heaton RK, et al: Neuropsychological impairment in chronic cocaine abusers. Am J Drug Alcohol Abuse 18:131–144, 1992

Pantalon MV, Swanson AJ: Motivational interviewing and treatment adherence among psychiatric and dually diagnosed patients. Poster presented at the annual convention of the Association for the Advancement of Behavior Therapy, Miami, FL, November, 1997

Pattison EM: Clinical approaches to the alcoholic patient. Psychosomatics 27:762–767, 1986

Prochaska JO, DiClemente CC: Common processes of change in smoking, weight control and psychological distress, in Coping and Substance Abuse. Edited by Shiffman S, Wills TA. New York, Academic Press, 1985, pp 345–363

Rounsaville BJ, Kranzler HR: The DSM-III-R diagnosis of alcoholism, in the American Psychiatric Press Review of Psychiatry, Vol 8. Edited by Tasman A, Hales RE, Frances AJ. Washington, DC, American Psychiatric Press, 1989, pp 323–340

Rounsaville BJ, Kosten TR, Weissman, et al: Evaluating and Treating Depressive Disorders in Opiate Addicts (NIDA Res Monogr Series, DHHS Publ No ADM-85-1406). Washington, DC, National Institute on Drug Abuse, 1985, pp 1–80

Rounsaville BJ, Kosten TR, Weissman MM, et al: Prognostic significance of psychiatric disorders in opiate addicts. Arch Gen Psychiatry 43:739–745, 1986

Rounsaville BJ, Dolinsky ZS, Babor TF, et al: Psychopathology as a predictor of treatment outcome in alcoholics. Arch Gen Psychiatry 44:505–513, 1987

Russell M, Martier SS, Sokol RJ, et al: Screening for pregnancy risk drinking: TWEAK-ing the tests (abstract). Alcohol Clin Exp Res 15:368, 1991

Samet JH, Rollnick S, Barnes H: Beyond CAGE: a brief clinical approach after detection of substance abuse. Arch Intern Med 156:2287–2293, 1996

Saunders JB, Aasland OG, Babor TF, et al: Development of the Alcohol Use Disorders Identification Test (AUDIT): WHO Collaborative Project on Early Detection of Persons With Harmful Alcohol Consumption, II. Addiction 88:791–804, 1993

Selzer ML: The Michigan Alcoholism Screening Test: the quest for a new diagnostic instrument. Am J Psychiatry 27:1653–1658, 1971

Senay EC: Diagnostic interview and mental status examination, in Substance Abuse: A Comprehensive Textbook, 3rd Edition. Edited by Lowinson JH, Ruiz P, Millman RB, et al. Baltimore, MD, Williams & Wilkins, 1997, pp 364–369

Skinner HA, Horn JL: Alcohol Dependence Scale (ADS) User's Guide. Toronto, Ontario, Canada, Addiction Research Foundation, 1984

Sokol RJ, Martier SS, Ager JW: The T-ACE questions: practical prenatal detection of risk-drinking. Am J Obstet Gynecol 160:863–868, 1989

Wolf I, Chafetz ME, Blane HT, et al: Social factors in the diagnosis of alcoholism: attitudes of Physicians. Quarterly Journal of Studies on Alcohol 26:72–79, 1965

# Chapter

## 13 Patient Placement Criteria

### David R. Gastfriend, M.D.

Patient placement criteria are decision rules that standardize treatment for optimal clinical efficacy and cost-effectiveness. Research demonstrates that substance abuse treatments reduce alcohol and drug use and relieve associated medical conditions and social, family, and psychological problems. Nevertheless, treatment is not effective in every case and programs vary widely in effectiveness. Beginning in the latter half of the 1980s, cost containment and managed care brought pressure on providers to justify treatment referrals for each patient. Despite the first call for treatment-matching principles more than half a century ago, protocols have only recently become available to practitioners.

Substance use disorders are heterogeneous and cause diverse biopsychosocial problems that vary by population. Standardized assessment might increase treatment effectiveness by helping to individualize treatment; however, this assumption remains to be proven.

In general, reviews of the treatment outcome literature lead to the conclusion that no single approach is superior, and principles for matching modalities of treatment to the specific needs of patients have not been easily validated. This state of affairs is, at the least, an annoyance, given the fact that multiple analyses indicate cost-effectiveness of treatment for addictions to be suboptimal (Institute of Medicine 1990a, 1990b; Miller and Hester 1986). Furthermore, when treatment components do gain some degree of research-based support, such components often fail to be adopted in for-profit treatment programs. These challenges have been driv-

ing studies in patient-treatment matching and cost-effectiveness research.

## Rationale for Patient Placement Criteria

Level-of-care matching is the basis for cost-effective patient placement criteria. If rules for level-of-care matching are valid and a continuum of settings is available, a managed care network has its best opportunity for clinical and cost optimization. In contrast to treatment modalities, levels of care are placement options or settings that offer discrete treatment intensities, structure, and restrictiveness. The typical levels of care have important cost implications; typical levels in decreasing order of expense are hospital, nonhospital inpatient (or residential), day treatment, and outpatient care.

Figure 13–1 outlines the original four levels of care of the American Society of Addiction Medicine (ASAM) Patient Placement Criteria for the Treatment of Psychoactive Substance Use Disorders (Hoffmann et al. 1991). Theoretically, certain levels of care might be expected to yield better cost savings than others. However, outcome studies have not conclusively shown inpatient rehabilitation or detoxification to be more cost-effective than outpatient rehabilitation or detoxification (Annis 1988; Hayashida et al. 1989; Litt et al. 1989; Miller and Hester 1986). In fact, there has been a consistent failure to prove that more intensive treatment settings offer patients better outcomes than less intensive ones. Managed care entities have used this

Supported by National Institute on Drug Abuse Grant DA08781.

121

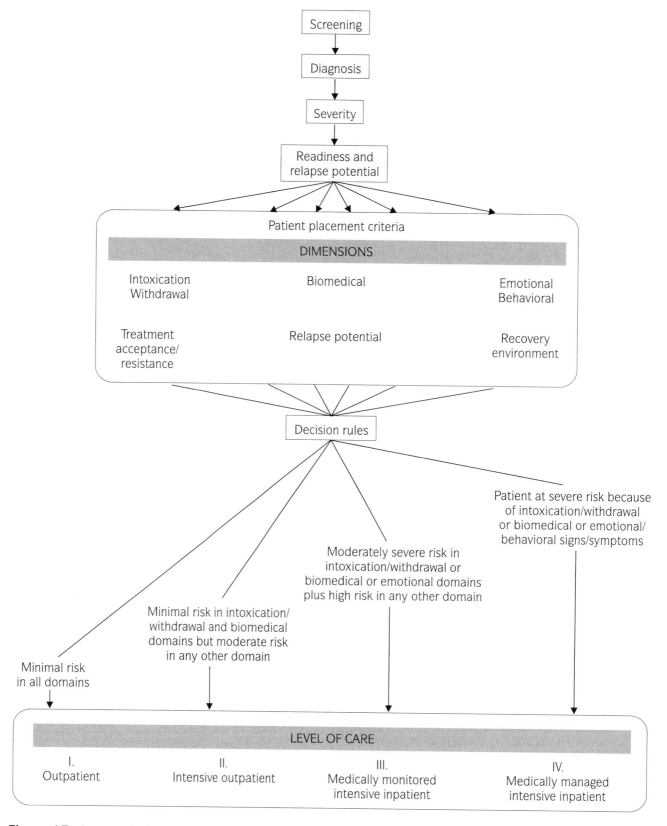

**Figure 13–1.**    Level-of-care treatment matching according to American Society of Addiction Medicine Patient Placement Criteria for the Treatment of Psychoactive Substance Use Disorders.

*Source.*    Reprinted from Gastfriend DR, McLellan AT: "Treatment Matching: Theoretic Basis and Practical Implications." *Medical Clinics of North America* 81:945–966, 1997. Used with permission.

pattern to justify eliminating higher levels of care such as hospital-based detoxification and rehabilitation. A critical point, however, is that these studies did not attempt to distinguish which patients experience the best outcomes from which level of care.

## Origins of Patient Placement Criteria

Managed care cost pressures prompted the development of 40–50 sets of addiction treatment–matching protocols during the 1980s, many of which were proprietary and conflicting. A haphazard, confusing system arose that frustrated providers who sought admission for their patients. Among nonprofit professional provider organizations, parallel efforts arose with important differences between placement criteria. These included the Cleveland Criteria (Hoffmann et al. 1987), developed for the Northern Ohio Chemical Dependency Treatment Directors Association, and the National Association of Addiction Treatment Providers (NAATP) Patient Placement Criteria (unpublished data). Despite the poor predictive validity of the Cleveland Criteria, these guidelines nonetheless became recognized as a substantial contribution to the field of treatment matching. Work groups of experts from the areas of internal medicine, adult and child psychiatry, pediatrics, psychology, social work, and addiction counseling subsequently critiqued the Cleveland Criteria and NAATP Patient Placement Criteria and revised them to form a single, new system.

The result of these consensus reviews was the first edition of the ASAM criteria (Hoffmann et al. 1991). This volume described four levels of care for adult and adolescent treatment. Levels of care were distinguished by the degree to which they provided medical management, structure, security, and treatment intensity. The ASAM criteria specified rules for treatment matching at three time points: admission, continued-stay review, and discharge. To place a patient, the evaluator was required to screen, diagnose, and then assess patient characteristics in six dimensions. Figure 13–1 is a schematic representation of this process.

Patients can be evaluated along these domains most effectively through the use of structured interviews (Gastfriend et al. 1994). The ASAM-NAATP work groups recommended the use of some standardized instruments such as the Clinical Institute Withdrawal Assessment for Alcohol Scale (Sullivan et al. 1989) or the Narcotic Withdrawal Scale (Fudala et al. 1991) for di-

mension 1 (acute intoxication and/or withdrawal). A simplified decision tree was created in which most treatment decisions could be based on a semistructured clinical interview, the Recovery Attitude and Treatment Evaluation (RAATE) (Mee-Lee et al. 1992). The RAATE was jointly developed by N. G. Hoffmann and D. Mee-Lee, members of the ASAM criteria work group, to facilitate use of the criteria. Typical items from the RAATE include the following (Mee-Lee et al. 1992): "Does the patient demonstrate a commitment to seeking help or treatment?" "Does the patient realize that recovery is an ongoing process requiring personal responsibility?" "Does the patient have a chronic physical condition or disability which interferes with treatment or recovery efforts?" "Is the patient able to focus on addiction treatment even if he/she has psychiatric/psychological symptoms, and is the work/school system accommodating or supportive of the treatment/recovery program?" Predictive validity was later found by Gastfriend et al. (1995) in a hospital detoxification sample, in which the 10% of patients who left prematurely against medical advice had statistically significantly higher initial RAATE scores. Interrater reliability was established at 0.88 (Najavits et al. 1997).

Publication of these nonproprietary matching criteria raised considerable interest and resulted in a range of responses, from continuing education courses across the United States to adoption by managed care entities and 16 American states. However, no process of field trial testing preceded publication of these criteria. Their predecessors, the NAATP Patient Placement Criteria and the Cleveland Criteria, had undergone little or no testing as well. McKay et al. (1997) retrospectively tested the psychosocial dimensions of the original ASAM criteria through an incomplete implementation of the criteria. This study suggested there were some areas of validity but highlighted a need for further revision. The Boston Target Cities Project used a version of the ASAM criteria in a large, urban, public population (Plough et al. 1996). In that project, patients who were referred through centralized intake centers, using standardized assessment with a coarse implementation of the ASAM criteria, were 38% more likely to begin longitudinal treatment within 30 days (i.e., outpatient care after detoxification) than were patients who underwent direct self-referred admission to treatment programs (odds ratio = 1.55, $P < 0.005$) (Plough et al. 1996). Further, patients referred through centralized intake centers also were statistically significantly less likely to return for detoxification within 90 days (odds ratio = 0.57, $P < 0.005$) (Plough et al. 1996). In part because of these findings, ASAM decided to revise its original document.

## Revision: Second Edition of the American Society of Addiction Medicine Criteria

The way in which services were grouped or "bundled" in the original ASAM criteria did not allow for great flexibility to meet individual needs of patients. In 1994–1995, the Coalition for National Treatment Criteria recognized that the ASAM criteria required revision. The coalition took a more inclusive approach than previous ASAM criteria workgroups had and addressed, in particular, criticism of the ASAM criteria from the field of managed care. Specifically, the ASAM criteria were criticized for the recognition of only four levels of care, the absence of criteria for methadone, and the required association of detoxification with inpatient care, among other points (Book et al. 1995). Most critically needed, according to the coalition, was a method for separating the levels of care into their component services.

The revised ASAM criteria addressed many of these needs (American Society of Addiction Medicine 1996). Pharmacotherapies such as detoxification and opioid maintenance therapy (e.g., methadone therapy) were separated from rehabilitation services, and multilevel criteria were created for outpatient and inpatient settings. New criteria distinguished between evening care or day treatment programs (level III.1) and partial hospitalization (level III.5), in the case of intensive outpatient care; and between halfway-house care (level III.1) and therapeutic community care (level III.5), in the case of residential inpatient care. Criteria were added for a new level of care (level 0.5, early intervention), defined as professional services for individuals who are at risk for developing substance-related problems but may not yet qualify for a diagnosis.

The following example is an illustration of the distinctions now being made: A patient with a history of withdrawal seizures but only mild medical conditions would be matched to level III.7 care (medically monitored inpatient detoxification). After 3–7 days without complications, the patient would be matched to level III.5 care (therapeutic community care) if he or she had problems such as poor compliance, difficulty postponing gratification, criminal behavior, and drug-oriented relationships. Thus, the patient would receive care in the least restrictive and least costly settings in which the patient's

needs in both phases of treatment could be met.

These changes in the ASAM criteria were widely welcomed in the United States and resulted in adoption by payers, state substance abuse agencies, and state Medicaid programs. In 1997, the revised ASAM criteria were adopted by the U.S. Department of Defense for worldwide use and by the U.S. Veterans Administration for its 171 hospitals nationwide. Yet, in the revised ASAM criteria a desirable continuum of care is recognized that is only in the planning stages in many regions. For example, halfway-house residents in many regions do not have access to methadone, and office detoxification programs are not offered everywhere. Nevertheless, these criteria are useful guides, particularly for capitated systems, for improving quality of care and reducing costs. These criteria should also serve as guidelines for health care networks in program development and acquisition, despite the fact that further methodological work and field trials regarding efficacy and effectiveness are needed (Longabaugh et al. 1994).

## Needs-to-Services Matching

Even the revised ASAM criteria orient treatment matching according to fixed levels of care. Patients being matched to treatment must be assigned to these predefined levels of care. But grouping patients by level of care leads to heterogeneous groups of patients with a range of needs. It may be more advantageous to orient placement criteria toward meeting patient needs rather than fitting program requirements (Longabaugh et al. 1995; McLellan et al. 1997). Needs-to-services matching, as this approach is called, is clinically useful whether performed formally in a research setting or informally in the clinic. Needs-to-service matching involves 1) consideration on many dimensions of the patient's range of needs and 2) provision of services to meet those needs. McLellan et al. (1993b) showed that matching clinical services according to patient needs generally yields the best outcomes in that distinct problem area (e.g., psychiatric or family/social).

In addition to substance use severity itself, several other dimensions of severity have been identified as having an effect on prognosis and requiring treatment attention (Gerstein and Harwood 1990; Institute of Medicine 1990b). McLellan et al. (1983b), using the Addiction Severity Index (ASI; McLellan et al. 1985, 1992), showed that alcohol- and drug-dependent subjects who were matched to specific treatments for dimensions showing high severity had outcomes that were 27% better than the outcomes of subjects who were not matched, with a $3,700 average savings in treatment costs per matched patient. Subsequently, in a prospective study, 130 alcohol- and 256 drug-dependent patients were randomly matched or conventionally treated without needs matching in two inpatient and two outpatient public and private-sector programs (McLellan et al. 1983a). Matched patients received more family, employment, and psychiatric services, according to their needs, resulting in greater treatment retention and 6-month outcomes that were 19% better than the outcomes of patients who only received substance abuse counseling. Similar results were reported in a study of patients receiving methadone (McLellan et al. 1993a). Multidimensional treatment yielded substantially better outcomes than did basic methadone treatment or methadone treatment plus drug counseling alone.

In a study of 198 employed, insured adults with mixed substance dependence, inpatient or outpatient level of care was not associated with differential outcomes but provision of psychiatric, family, and employment counseling was (McLellan et al. 1993b). In cocaine-dependent patients as well, combined psychiatric, family, and employment problems proved to be major predictors of outcome (McLellan et al. 1994). These results are consistent with earlier findings by Joe et al. (1991), who studied public drug dependence treatment programs; by Moos and Finney (1995), who studied residential alcohol treatment programs; and by Ball and Ross (1991), who studied methadone maintenance programs. This body of work indicates that needs-to-services matching has both face and predictive validity.

But although needs-to-services treatment matching is a logical starting point for a new model of care planning, it is still necessary to consider the setting within which or the level of care at which services can best be provided. A highly flexible, individualized approach to assignment to level of care seems essential for clinical quality and cost efficiency. Gastfriend (1994) proposed to the National Coalition on Placement Criteria the Cumulative Block Increment (CBI) Model. Based on the concept of small service units as building blocks (e.g., hourly units of care), this approach recommended a high-resolution assessment of individual clinical needs, followed by a grouping of these needs to determine the best setting for the constellation of necessary services. With use of the CBI Model, services could be designed to taper more incrementally in an individualized fashion. This model would integrate level of care consideration with needs-to-services matching. Al-

though the CBI Model appears to offer face validity as did earlier patient placement criteria models, it too awaits empirical validation.

## Coping With Complex Criteria Through Use of Automation

Matching guidelines have become complex and can be unreliable. Morey (1996) used a computerized algorithm in adapting the ASAM criteria to data from the National Household Survey. Researchers in the Addiction Services of Massachusetts General Hospital implemented the ASAM criteria in a comprehensive computerized interview. This real-time, laptop-based form of addiction treatment matching yielded a satisfactory degree of interrater reliability for the level of care assignment (intraclass correlation coefficient [ICC] = .77, $P \leq 0.01$). This level of reliability is promising for research and standardization across clinical systems and compares favorably with the level of reliability of diagnosis and severity rating (Endicott et al. 1976; Hall 1995; Regier et al. 1994).

## Summary

Psychiatrists, physicians, and other providers can address patients' substance use problems with the help of published patient placement criteria. Adoption of formal rules such as the ASAM criteria is under way in numerous states and by managed care entities, professional provider societies, and provider groups. Currently, such criteria rely more heavily on consensus recommendations than on empirical matching data. The technology for conducting psychosocial treatment–matching studies is rapidly becoming more sophisticated and has been demonstrated to yield adequate reliability. Although predictive validity has not yet been fully demonstrated, the national research portfolio on placement criteria is expanding. There is a public health need for further research in this area, given recent dramatic cost pressures, if addiction services are to continue to grow in quality and availability.

## References

American Society of Addiction Medicine: Patient Placement Criteria for the Treatment of Substance-Related Disorders. Chevy Chase, MD, American Society of Addiction Medicine, 1996

Annis H: Patient-Treatment Matching in the Management of Alcoholism (NIDA Res Monogr No 90). Rockville, MD, National Institute on Drug Abuse, 1988, pp 152–161

Ball J, Ross A: The Effectiveness of Methadone Maintenance Treatment. New York, Springer-Verlag, 1991

Book J, Harbim H, Marques C, et al: The ASAM's and Green Spring's alcohol and drug detoxification and rehabilitation criteria for utilization review. Am J Addict 4:187–197, 1995

Endicott J, Spitzer RL, Fleiss JL, et al: The Global Assessment Scale: a procedure for measuring overall severity of psychiatric disturbance. Arch Gen Psychiatry 33:766–771, 1976

Fudala PJ, Berkow LC, Fralich JL, et al: Use of naloxone in the assessment of opiate dependence. Life Sci 49:1809–1814, 1991

Gastfriend DR: Anticipated Problems Facing ASAM Patient Placement Criteria: Cumulative Increment Block Model. Report to Treatment Improvement Protocol Panel of the Center for Substance Abuse Treatment, Rockville, MD, April 21, 1994

Gastfriend D, Najavits L, Reif S: Assessment instruments, in Principles of Addiction Medicine. Edited by Miller N, Doot M. Chevy Chase, MD, American Society of Association Medicine, 1994, pp 1–8

Gastfriend DR, Filstead WJ, Rief S, et al: Validity of assessing treatment readiness in patients with substance use disorders. Am J Addict 4:254–260, 1995

Gerstein DR, Harwood HJ: Treating Drug Problems. Washington, DC, National Academy Press, 1990

Hall R: Global assessment of functioning: a modified scale. Psychosomatics 36:267–275, 1995

Hayashida M, Alterman AI, McLellan AT, et al: Comparative effectiveness and costs of inpatient and outpatient detoxification of patients with mild-to-moderate alcohol withdrawal syndrome. N Engl J Med 320:358–365, 1989

Hoffmann N, Halikas J, Mee-Lee D: The Cleveland Admission, Discharge and Transfer Criteria: Model for Chemical Dependency Treatment Programs. Cleveland, Northern Ohio Chemical Dependency Treatment Consortium, 1987

Hoffmann NG, Halikas JA, Mee-Lee D, et al: Patient Placement Criteria for the Treatment of Psychoactive Substance Use Disorders. Chevy Chase, MD, American Society of Addiction Medicine, 1991

Institute of Medicine: Broadening the Base of Treatment for Alcohol Problems: A Report of a Study by a Committee of the Institute of Medicine, Division of Mental Health and Behavioral Medicine. Washington, DC, National Academy Press, 1990a

Institute of Medicine: Treating Drug Problems. Washington, DC, National Academy Press, 1990b

Joe GW, Simpson DD, Hubbard RL: Treatment predictors of tenure in methadone maintenance. J Subst Abuse 3:73–84, 1991

Litt M, DelBoca F, Cooney NL: Matching Alcoholics to Aftercare Treatment by Empirical Clustering. Farmington, University of Connecticut Health Center, 1989

Longabaugh R, Wirtz PW, DiClemente CC, et al: Issues in the development of client-treatment matching hypotheses. J Stud Alcohol Suppl 12:46–59, 1994

Longabaugh R, Wirtz PW, Beattie MC, et al: Matching treatment focus to patient social investment and support: 18-month follow-up results. J Consult Clin Psychol 63:296–307, 1995

McKay JR, Cacciola JS, McLellan AT, et al: An initial evaluation of the psychosocial dimensions of the American Society of Addiction Medicine criteria for inpatient versus intensive outpatient substance abuse rehabilitation. J Stud Alcohol 58:239–252, 1997

McLellan AT, Woody GE, Luborsky L, et al: Increased effectiveness of substance abuse treatment: a prospective study of patient-treatment "matching." J Nerv Ment Dis 171:597–605, 1983a

McLellan AT, Luborsky L, Woody GE, et al: Predicting response to alcohol and drug abuse treatments: role of psychiatric severity. Arch Gen Psychiatry 40:620–625, 1983b

McLellan AT, Luborsky L, Cacciola J, et al: New data from the Addiction Severity Index: reliability and validity in three centers. J Nerv Ment Dis 173:412–423, 1985

McLellan AT, Kushner H, Metzger D, et al: The Fifth Edition of the Addiction Severity Index. J Subst Abuse Treat 9:199–213, 1992

McLellan AT, Arndt IO, Metzger DS, et al: The effects of psychosocial services in substance abuse treatment. JAMA 269:1953–1959, 1993a

McLellan AT, Grissom GR, Brill P, et al: Private substance abuse treatments: are some programs more effective than others? J Subst Abuse Treat 10:243–254, 1993b

McLellan AT, Alterman AI, Metzger DS, et al: Similarity of outcome predictors across opiate, cocaine, and alcohol treatments: role of treatment services. J Clin Consult Psychol 62:1141–1158, 1994

McLellan AT, Grissom GR, Zanis D, et al: Problem-service 'matching' in addiction treatment: a prospective study in 4 programs. Arch Gen Psychiatry 54:730–735, 1997

Mee-Lee D, Hoffmann NG, Smith MB: Recovery Attitude and Treatment Evaluator (RAATE) Manual. St. Paul, MN, CATOR/New Standards, 1992

Miller W, Hester R: Matching problem drinkers with optimal treatments, in Treating Addictive Behaviors: Processes of Change. Edited by Miller W, Heather NH. New York, Plenum, 1986, pp 175–203

Moos RH, Finney JW: Substance abuse treatment programs and processes: linkages to patients' needs and outcomes. J Subst Abuse 7:1–8, 1995

Morey L: Patient placement criteria: linking typologies to managed care. Alcohol Health and Research World 20:36–44, 1996

Najavits LM, Gastfriend DR, Nakayama EY, et al: A measure of readiness for substance abuse treatment: psychometric properties of the RAATE research interview. Am J Addict 6:74–82, 1997

Plough A, Shirley L, Zaremba N, et al: CSAT Target Cities Demonstration: Final Evaluation Report. Boston, MA, Boston Office for Treatment Improvement, 1996

Regier DA, Kaelber CT, Roper MT, et al: The ICD-10 clinical field trial for mental and behavioral disorders: results in Canada and the United States. Am J Psychiatry 151: 1340–1350, 1994

Sullivan JT, Sykora K, Schneiderman J, et al: Assessment of alcohol withdrawal: the revised Clinical Institute Withdrawal Assessment for Alcohol Scale. British Journal of Addiction 84:1353–1357, 1989

# 14 Outcome Research: Alcoholism

Theresa Moyers, Ph.D.
Reid K. Hester, Ph.D.

Treatments for alcohol abuse and dependence have advanced substantially in the last decade, and the scope of effective treatments offers hope with regard to these troubling problems. This chapter is a review of the current research in treatment of alcohol problems. Instead of the term *alcoholism*, which implies a unitary condition, we use the phrase *alcohol problems*. We assume that alcohol problems lie on a continuum and that effective treatments benefit many more individuals than the relatively small group at the far end of the spectrum.

A comprehensive and historical investigation of all alcohol treatments is beyond the scope of this chapter, so we focus primarily on current treatments that have the best empirical support. Treatments absent from this chapter are not necessarily ineffective; rather, such treatments have not undergone the careful study that the treatments considered here have. Later in the chapter, we briefly discuss treatments that controlled research has shown to be ineffective. Also covered is the concept of matching patients to treatments.

The value of controlled trials in investigating effectiveness of treatments for alcohol problems cannot be overstated. Historically, this field has been vulnerable to the introduction of exciting new treatments that are shown in subsequent controlled trials to have marginal or no importance for this population.

In our review, we use a rating system for treatments that was developed by W. R. Miller and colleagues (1995, 1998) for evaluating controlled studies. This rating system generates an overall score, the Cumulative Evidence Score (CES), which is a product of the methodological quality and strength of outcomes for a particular treatment approach. (See W. R. Miller et al. 1998 for full details of the CES for each treatment.)

## Evidence of Effectiveness: What Research Reveals

### Strong Evidence of Effectiveness

For the following interventions, which are ranked by CES, evidence of effectiveness is considered to be strong (i.e., three or more published studies exist, appropriate methodological designs were used, and outcomes were positive) (W. R. Miller et al. 1998):

- Brief interventions
- Motivational enhancement therapies
- Social skills training
- Community reinforcement approach
- γ-Aminobutyric acid (GABA) agonist therapy
- Opioid antagonist therapy
- Behavior contracting
- Patient-centered therapy
- Nausea aversion therapy
- Behavioral marital therapy
- Behavioral self-control training
- Cognitive therapy
- Apnea aversion therapy
- Covert sensitization
- Disulfiram (an antidipsotropic medication) therapy
- Self-help manual

The treatments listed here have been consistently supported by controlled research. Indeed, the community reinforcement approach, GABA agonist therapy, and opioid antagonist therapy all have perfect track records.

Brief interventions hold great promise for affecting

the drinking behaviors of individuals with alcohol-related problems. Such interventions, however, need not be conducted only by alcohol treatment programs. The Institute of Medicine (1990) concluded that brief interventions are appropriate interventions of health care providers outside the specialized treatment sector (e.g., internists or psychiatrists in general practice).

Although a variety of different brief interventions have been developed, the components have common features. The typical elements can be represented by the acronym FRAMES: Feedback regarding a patient's drinking that is individualized and objective; Responsibility that is placed on the patient for deciding what to do regarding drinking; clear Advice to change; a Menu of interventions and options for change; Empathic counseling; and an emphasis on Self-efficacy (W. R. Miller and Sanchez 1994).

The time involved in conducting a comprehensive assessment and providing the patient with one or two brief feedback sessions is minimal, especially relative to the time involved in comprehensive inpatient and outpatient programs. In outcome studies in which brief interventions were compared with more extensive interventions, differences between groups are usually small (e.g., Edwards et al. 1977). (For more about brief interventions, see Heather 1995 and W. R. Miller and Rollnick 1991.)

Motivational enhancement therapies are similar to brief interventions, but their primary goal is the enhancement of the patient's intrinsic energy for change. *Patient-centered therapies* are similar to brief motivational interventions and motivational enhancement therapies but seem to take a less directive approach.

Social skills training involves teaching patients how to form and maintain interpersonal relationships. This form of intervention often includes training in communication skills, listening skills, problem solving, and assertiveness skills. Social skills training has been considered an adjunct to treatment, not a stand-alone treatment, and has usually been conducted in groups. In studies in which its effectiveness has been evaluated, patients have typically, but not always, been selected for inclusion on the basis of patient deficiency in some aspect of social skills. Effectiveness has been evaluated in 17 studies to date. Adding this intervention has been found to improve outcomes in 11 of these studies. Some of those studies in which a difference in outcome was not found involved less severely dependent patients. An excellent manual is available for clinicians interested in learning how to provide this type of training (Monti et al. 1995).

The *community reinforcement approach* (CRA) focuses on altering contingencies in the patient's environment to reinforce abstinence. Drinking results in a time-out from those reinforcers. Working collaboratively, the therapist and patient rank the patient's alcohol-related problems and choose strategies from a menu of alternatives designed to address these problems. The menu includes 1) sobriety sampling, 2) a behavioral compliance program to take disulfiram, 3) job-finding training (if the patient is unemployed), 4) behaviorally oriented marital counseling, 5) problem-solving skills training, and 6) involvement in sober leisure-time activities. The CRA was originally developed and tested in the early 1970s. In these early studies, positive outcomes in patients, compared with control groups, were reported. Its impact on the field of alcohol treatment has been relatively minor until about the last 5 years. Recently, however, the CRA has received more attention and is becoming more popular in both the United States and Europe. Meyers and Smith (1995) wrote an extensive therapist manual for clinicians interested in this approach.

Previous investigations of medication to improve outcomes for alcohol problems have yielded only one effective drug with empirical support: *disulfiram*. This medication induces severe nausea and other unpleasant physical symptoms when the patient drinks alcohol and functions as a deterrent to further drinking when patients wish to abstain. The efficacy of this drug is dependent on the patient's desire to avoid the unpleasant side effects it produces. Studies show that disulfiram improves outcome in patients when the drug is used as a component of behavioral treatment and when patients faithfully take their doses (Fuller 1995). The placebo effect of the drug is substantial, and it is unclear if any further benefit is derived from the physical symptoms induced by the drug.

In the last decade, there has been an increase in the number of new medications for the treatment of alcohol problems. Two new drugs, *acamprosate* (a GABA analogue) and *naltrexone* (an opioid antagonist), appear to work by reducing the craving of abstinent patients for alcohol. Animal models indicate that the effect of these medications is mediated through the gluta-minergic and opioid systems, perhaps by reducing the reinforcing value of alcohol. Clinical trials clearly show that these medications reduce relapse to heavy drinking as well as craving in patients with drinking problems when they are used as part of a treatment program.

Finally, evidence indicates that medications that increase availability of the neurotransmitter serotonin are helpful in regulating alcohol abuse. Initial clinical trials involving several serotonergic drugs, including sertraline, ondansetron, and buspirone, indicate modest reductions in alcohol consumption by treated patients, reductions that appear to be independent of the antidepressant and anxiolytic effects of these medications.

It is clear that pharmacological interventions will be an important component of future treatments for problem drinking. Newer medications are more effective, are better tolerated by patients, and generally pose less risk in overdose because they do not potentiate the effects of alcohol. Each of these medications has been evaluated as an adjunct to ongoing treatment for problem drinking. Their effectiveness as stand-alone agents has not been evaluated. Furthermore, each of these medications may be contraindicated for a variety of physical problems, especially liver impairment, that are common in patients with drinking problems.

In *behavior contracting*, the therapist, patient, and often significant others set up clear contingencies for behaviors related to drinking and sobriety. A written contract specifies what kinds of reinforcers will be provided to the patient if he or she remains sober. Drinking behaviors result in a loss of those reinforcers. Although this form of contingency management seems to be more widespread in the treatment of drug abuse, controlled trials have demonstrated its potential for use with alcohol problems (P. M. Miller 1975).

Behavioral marital therapy emphasizes the improvement of communication skills and problem solving between partners. It also strives to increase the frequency of positive reinforcement each spouse gives the other. Treatment has usually been provided on a conjoint basis, with one couple meeting with a therapist, but groups have also been used. Results have been positive in seven studies. A number of therapist manuals are available for interested clinicians, including a primer (O'Farrell 1995) and more advanced manuals and clinical case studies (McCrady 1982, O'Farrell 1993).

Behavioral self-control training involves teaching patients a set of self-management skills that can be used either to moderate consumption to nonproblematic levels or to become and remain abstinent. The most common elements of self-control training are goal setting, self-monitoring, rate control and reduction, self-reinforcement of progress and goal attainment, functional analysis, and learning alternative coping skills. Controlled comparisons have indicated that self-control training can be provided effectively in either therapist-directed or self-help formats (e.g., Harris and Miller 1990). Several therapist manuals are available for clini-

cians interested in learning how to provide this intervention (see Hester and Delaney 1997 and Hester and Miller 1995 for information on these manuals).

Cognitive therapy for alcohol abuse stresses the importance of managing maladaptive thoughts about alcohol that spring from core beliefs of the individual. Patients are taught to replace irrational thoughts that lead to craving and relapse with more adaptive ones. For example, anticipatory beliefs about the pleasure of drinking, relief-oriented beliefs about escaping from uncomfortable emotions, and permissive beliefs that facilitate drinking behavior are explored in detail. Patients are also taught to recognize stimuli that provoke such maladaptive thoughts, as well as specific behaviors that reduce opportunities for drinking (Beck et al. 1993).

We have chosen not to discuss nausea and apnea aversion therapies and covert sensitization because of space limitations and for the following reasons: Although nausea aversion therapy is effective, it is currently practiced in only one hospital in the United States. Apnea aversion therapy was abandoned a number of years ago because of safety concerns. Proper administration of covert sensitization requires a very careful adherence to a relatively complex treatment protocol. These therapies are complicated and are typically not used by most treatment providers.

## Indeterminate Evidence of Effectiveness

A wide variety of treatments have been tested in controlled trials and have not been found to yield results that are superior to those for control groups. The treatments include the following:

- Electrical aversion therapy
- Nonbehavioral marital therapies
- Placebo therapy
- Stress management
- Lithium therapy
- Functional analysis
- Relapse prevention
- Self-monitoring
- Selective serotonin reuptake inhibitor (SSRI) antidepressant therapy

Those treatments of greatest interest to the reader are discussed.

Nonbehavioral marital therapies include structural and strategic approaches. Although the terms used in this form of therapy are quite different from those used in behavioral marital therapy, in practice the two treatments seem similar. Conversely, the difficulties in operationally defining terms and strategies in nonbehavioral marital therapy may have hindered research on these approaches and contributed to equivocal outcomes.

Stress management teaches individuals how to reduce tension and manage stress. A broad-based approach usually includes relaxation strategies, systematic desensitization, and cognitive strategies. The patient learns not only how to manage his or her responses to stressful situations but also how to make changes in the external environment. Stress management training is typically considered an adjunctive treatment rather than a stand-alone treatment. To date, adding this treatment has been found to improve outcome in six studies and not to improve outcome in four studies. Stockwell (1995) has published a primer for clinicians interested in learning more about how to provide these interventions.

Studies in which acupuncture was used as an addition to treatment for alcohol problems show mixed results. The methodological difficulties of standardizing the acupuncture intervention may have precluded consistent outcomes.

The *relapse prevention* protocols of Marlatt and Gordon (1985) and Annis (1986) were designed to help patients maintain gains they had made in the first few months of treatment. Both protocols are cognitive-behavioral and address situations in which there is high risk for relapse. The protocol of Marlatt and Gordon (1985) also emphasizes achieving a balance in life between what one must do (responsibilities) and what one likes to do. Although the notion of directly addressing the prevention of relapse makes clinical sense, there have been more clinical trials to date in which outcomes were not improved than trials in which outcomes were improved.

## Insufficient Evidence of Effectiveness

The following treatments have consistently not been found to improve outcomes:

- Hypnosis
- Psychedelic medication therapy
- Calcium carbimide (an antidipsotropic medication) therapy
- Non-SSRI antidepressant therapy
- Standard treatment
- Milieu therapy
- Anxiolytic agent therapy

- Mandated attendance at Alcoholics Anonymous (AA) meetings
- Metronidazole therapy
- Relaxation training
- Confrontational counseling
- Psychotherapy
- General alcoholism counseling
- Educational lectures/films

The effect of tricyclic antidepressant therapy on drinking behaviors and depression was the focus of research from the mid-1960s to the early 1970s. The evidence of these antidepressants' effect on drinking behaviors per se is modest. On the other hand, there is more evidence of its effect on mood. However, although the incidence of affective disorders is relatively high among patients at the time of admission to alcohol treatment programs, the rate of spontaneous remission of these disorders is also high during the first few weeks of sobriety. This situation suggests that clinicians should not begin medication treatment regimens unless there is either a clear history of affective disorders predating the development of alcohol problems or a persistence of depression into sobriety.

Readers may be surprised that mandated attendance at AA meetings falls in this category. Requiring patients to attend AA meetings has been found to be effective in one study and ineffective in four studies. One conclusion of these studies is that judges should not treat mandatory attendance at AA meetings as an alternative to legal sanctions. In the original writings of AA, mandatory attendance was opposed and the importance of voluntary participation was stressed. Twelve-step facilitation (TSF) therapy with noncoerced patients is discussed in the section on matching patients to treatments.

In addition to these interventions, videotape self-confrontation has been shown to have negative outcomes with alcohol-abusing patients. The intervention involves taping the patient when he or she is intoxicated (usually on admission to a hospital emergency room or a treatment program) and then playing it back when the patient is sober. However, in a number of the studies, dropout rates increased among patients who underwent videotape self-confrontation. This highlights the notion that not all therapies are benign.

This list of treatments might come as a surprise to clinicians familiar with treatment services in the United States. Informal discussions with colleagues in substance abuse programs reveal that some of these interventions (e.g., educational lectures and films) are quite common and are thought to have great impact by the clinicians providing them. This discrepancy between clinicians' beliefs and the findings of controlled clinical research illustrates the pitfalls of relying solely on personal experience to draw conclusions about the effectiveness of particular treatments.

## Potential Effectiveness

Three treatments are promising and merit further research. For each of the following treatments, outcomes have been positive in two studies and negative in none.

- Sensory deprivation
- Biofeedback
- Cue exposure

 ## Additional Factors Affecting Treatment Outcome

### Therapist Characteristics

In retrospective analyses as well as prospective studies, therapist empathy has been found to contribute positively to outcomes. Conversely, evidence is mounting that when therapists confront patients in an aggressive manner, outcomes suffer.

Being empathic does not mean being nondirective or nonconfrontative. An effective therapist can be directive, confrontative, and empathic at the same time. An approach that incorporates these elements has come to be known as *motivational interviewing* (W. R. Miller and Rollnick 1991).

### Matching Patients to Treatments

One of the most surprising developments in the area of treatment outcomes concerns the results of the Project MATCH trial (Project MATCH Research Group 1997). This experiment was designed to test the hypothesis that patients receiving alcohol treatment would respond differentially depending on the goodness of fit between certain of their own characteristics and the kind of treatments offered. The three treatments selected for investigation were cognitive-behavioral therapy, motivational enhancement therapy, and TSF therapy. Patient-matching characteristics included severity of dependence, conceptual level, meaning-seeking by the patient, social support for drinking in the patient's life, and severity of psychiatric problems. Patient characteristics were found not to influence re-

sponse to treatment, regardless of the kind of treatment received. The hypothesis that outcomes would improve if patients were matched to optimal treatments was not supported, indicating that the kind of theoretical perspective used to guide treatment is less important than previously supposed. However, it was found that patients without major psychiatric problems had fewer drinking days in the follow-up period when treated with TSF therapy than did patients receiving other treatments. This finding supports conventional wisdom that a 12-step approach can be successfully integrated into professional treatment. Perhaps most gratifying, Project MATCH findings provide evidence that all three types of treatment produced substantial improvements in patients with severe alcohol problems. Paradoxically, the excellent design and careful execution of this study, which included 8 hours of pretreatment assessment, may have favorably influenced patient outcomes and thereby obscured any differences that might otherwise have been observed between the treatments.

 ## Conclusion

Several conclusions can be drawn from the research literature on treatments for alcohol problems. First, the data indicate that no one treatment is more effective than all others. Rather, there is fair to good evidence of effectiveness for a number of interventions. Therefore, it would make sense for programs to offer a variety of different treatments rather than a single treatment for all patients. Second, therapist characteristics, particularly empathy, appear to have a substantial influence on outcomes. Third, Project MATCH results indicate that clinicians who adhere closely to either cognitive-behavior, motivational enhancement, or TSF therapy protocols can improve patient outcomes. It is clear that there is more than one true path to recovery.

## References

Annis HM: A relapse prevention model for treatment of alcoholics, in Treating Addictive Behaviors: Processes of Change. Edited by Miller WR, Heather NH. New York, Plenum, 1986, pp 407–433

Beck A, Wright F, Newman C, et al: Cognitive Therapy of Substance Abuse. New York, Guilford, 1993

Edwards G, Orford J, Egert S, et al: Alcoholism: a controlled trial of "treatment" and "advice." J Stud Alcohol 38: 1004–1031, 1977

Fuller RK: Antidipsotropic medications, in Handbook of Alcoholism Treatment: Effective Approaches, 2nd Edition. Edited by Hester RK, Miller WR. Needham Heights, MA, Allyn & Bacon, 1995, pp 123–133

Harris KB, Miller WR: Behavioral self-control training for problem drinkers: components of efficacy. Psychology of Addictive Behaviors 4:82–90, 1990

Heather N: Brief intervention strategies, in Handbook of Alcoholism Treatment: Effective Alternatives, 2nd Edition. Edited by Hester RK, Miller WR. Needham Heights, MA, Allyn & Bacon, 1995, pp 105–122

Hester RK, Delaney HD: Behavioral Self-Control Program for Windows: results of a controlled clinical trial. J Consult Clin Psychol 65:686–693, 1997

Hester RK, Miller WR: Self-control training, in Handbook of Alcoholism Treatment: Effective Alternatives, 2nd Edition. Edited by Hester RK, Miller WR. Needham Heights, MA, Allyn & Bacon, 1995, pp 148–159

Institute of Medicine: Prevention and Treatment of Alcohol Problems: Research Opportunities. Washington, DC, National Academy Press, 1990

Marlatt GA, Gordon JR: Relapse Prevention: Maintenance Strategies in the Treatment of Addictive Behaviors. New York, Guilford, 1985

McCrady BS: Conjoint behavioral treatment of an alcoholic and his spouse, in Clinical Case Studies in the Behavioral Treatment of Alcoholism. Edited by Hay WM, Nathan PE. New York, Plenum, 1982, pp 127–156

Meyers RJ, Smith JE: Clinical Guide to Alcohol Treatment: The Community Reinforcement Approach. New York, Guilford, 1995

Miller PM: A behavioral intervention program for chronic public drunkenness offenders. Arch Gen Psychiatry 32:915–918, 1975

Miller WR, Rollnick S: Motivational Interviewing. New York, Guilford, 1991

Miller WR, Sanchez VC: Motivating young adults for treatment and lifestyle change, in Alcohol Use and Misuse by Young Adults. Edited by Howard G, Nathan PE. Notre Dame, IN, Notre Dame Press, 1994, pp 55–81

Miller WR, Brown JM, Simpson TL, et al: What works? A methodological analysis of the alcohol treatment outcome literature, in Handbook of Alcoholism Treatment Approaches: Effective Alternatives, 2nd Edition. Edited by Hester RK, Miller WR. Needham Heights, MA, Allyn & Bacon, 1995, pp 12–44

Miller WR, Andrews NR, Wilbourne P, et al: A wealth of alternatives: effective treatments for alcohol problems, in Treating Addictive Behaviors: Processes of Change, 2nd Edition. Edited by Miller WR, Heather N. New York, Plenum, 1998, pp 203–216

Monti PM, Rohsenow DJ, Colby SM, et al: Coping and social skills training, in Handbook of Alcoholism Treatment: Effective Alternatives, 2nd Edition. Edited by Hester RK, Miller WR. Needham Heights, MA, Allyn & Bacon, 1995, pp 221–241

O'Farrell TJ (ed): Treating Alcohol Problems: Marital and Family Interactions. New York, Guilford, 1993

O'Farrell TJ: Marital and family therapy, in Handbook of Alcoholism Treatment Approaches: Effective Alternatives, 2nd Edition. Edited by Hester RK, Miller WR. Needham Heights, MA, Allyn & Bacon, 1995, pp 195–220

Project MATCH Research Group: Matching alcohol treatments to client heterogeneity: Project MATCH posttreatment drinking outcomes. J Stud Alcohol 58:7–29, 1997

Stockwell T: Anxiety and stress management, in Handbook of Alcoholism Treatment Approaches: Effective Alternatives, 2nd Edition. Edited by Hester RK, Miller WR. Needham Heights, MA, Allyn & Bacon, 1995, pp 242–250

# Chapter 15

# Outcome Research: Drug Abuse

Dean R. Gerstein, Ph.D.

P atient outcomes of treatment for drug dependence have been studied in light of the chronic, relapsing nature of the disorders, that is, not in terms of cure versus failure to cure during the course of treatment but in terms of extent of remission and degrees of improvement over time. Because the mechanisms of drug dependence are complex and treatment approaches vary widely, an iterative presentation is needed to convey the results of outcome studies. In this chapter, current knowledge about treatment outcomes is summarized in a three-part paradigm, repeated for each treatment modality:

- *What are the concepts behind the treatment?* That is, what is the theoretical rationale for each mode of treatment, what specific types of drug problems or population groups are being addressed, and what is the expected and observed efficacy at follow-up under trial conditions?
- *How well does each modality work in practice?* How adequate is the methodology to evaluate nonexperimental programs, and what do the best of these evaluations reveal?
- *Why do nonexperimental outcomes fall short of trial results?* To what extent is the problem poor implementation, unsuitable diagnosis (patient selection),

high prevalence of complications, noncompliance, or adverse environmental effects?

The major modalities of drug treatment considered here are methadone maintenance (MM), long-term residential treatment (LRT), outpatient nonmethadone treatment (ONT), and short-term inpatient treatment (SIT). Some methods of treatment diverge from these general types. In particular, two well-known types of treatment are not covered here, for different reasons. Independent self-help fellowship groups such as Narcotics Anonymous (NA), Cocaine Anonymous (CA), or the Oxford Houses are not discussed, because there are virtually no data to answer the above-mentioned three critical questions. Although the ideas underlying the Anonymous fellowships were incorporated at the outset into the clinical approaches of therapeutic communities and chemical dependency programs (in fact, the 12 steps of the Anonymous creed are so fundamental to the chemical dependency modality that the latter has been referred to as the "professionalization of Alcoholics Anonymous [AA]"), the fellowships have shied away from formal evaluation.

The second exclusion is detoxification, or medically supervised withdrawal. Detoxification *without subsequent treatment* has consistently been found to have no

This chapter is a shortened and updated version of "The Effectiveness of Drug Treatment" (Gerstein 1992). For this chapter, I drew extensively on work carried out under the auspices of the Institute of Medicine's Substance Abuse Coverage Study (Gerstein and Harwood 1990, 1992), supported by National Institute on Drug Abuse Contract 283-88-0009(SA). I am indebted to M. Douglas Anglin, John C. Ball, David T. Courtwright, David A. Deitch, Henrick J. Harwood, Robert L. Hubbard, Herbert D. Kleber, and Lawrence S. Lewin for their insights and their comments on the earlier versions.

effects (in terms of reducing subsequent drug use behavior and especially relapse to dependence) that are discernibly superior to those achieved by untreated withdrawal (Cole et al. 1981; Moffet et al. 1973; Newman 1983; Resnick 1983; Sheffet et al. 1976). There has been substantial success in the management of cocaine withdrawal symptoms and craving in ambulatory clinical trials (Dackis et al. 1987; Gawin et al. 1989a, 1989b; Tennant and Sagherian 1987), but dropout rates in the programs in which trials have been conducted range from 30% to 70%.

A special topic concluding the main section of the chapter is treatment in correctional institutions. A specialized literature on correctional treatment has arisen, and the vast growth in imprisoned populations makes this topic especially important.

## Methadone Maintenance

### What Is Methadone Maintenance?

MM is a treatment specifically designed for dependence on narcotic analgesics, particularly the narcotic of greatest concern in the United States, heroin. The controversy surrounding MM has made it the subject of hundreds of studies, including a number of clinical trials, from which good evidence has accumulated about the safety and efficacy of methadone.

At the base of MM is the empirical observation, made before the biological reasons for it were well understood, that all narcotic analgesics may be substituted for one another with sufficient adjustments in dose and route of administration. Methadone, however, has several unusual pharmacological properties that make it especially suited to a maintenance approach. The drug is effective orally, and because of its particular pattern of absorption and metabolism, a single dose within a train of level doses, in the typical maintenance range of 30–100 mg/day, has a gradual onset and yields a fairly even effect across a 24-hour period or longer. Methadone is thus suitable for a regimen of single daily maintenance doses, which eliminates dramatic subjective or behavioral changes and makes it easy for the clinician and patient to fit into a routine clinic schedule. This pattern is different from the shorter action and more dramatic highs and lows of heroin, morphine, and most other opioids.

The long-term toxic side effects of methadone, as of other opioids if taken in hygienic conditions in controlled doses, are notably benign. Since the mid-1960s,

about 2 million person-years of MM have accumulated in the United States. The accumulated clinical experience, confirmed by thousands of carefully documented research cases, yields a well-supported conclusion that is epitomized by the following:

> [P]hysiological and biochemical alterations occur, but there are minimal side effects that are clinically detectable in patients during chronic MM treatment. Toxicity related to methadone during chronic treatment is extraordinarily rare. The most important medical consequence of methadone during chronic treatment, in fact, is the marked improvement in general health and nutritional status observed in patients compared with their status at the time of admission to treatment. (Kreek 1983, p. 474)

MM may be offered only within especially licensed programs (Rettig and Yarmolinsky 1995). These programs are largely ambulatory, involving daily visits to swallow doses under clinical observation. After several months of "clean" drug testing and compliance with other program requirements such as attendance of counseling sessions, patients may regularly take home 1 or more days' doses between every-other-day, twice-weekly, or even weekly visits—a revocable privilege. Some patients undergoing MM voluntarily taper their doses to abstinence and conclude treatment, others continue MM indefinitely, and others have their doses tapered and are discharged from MM programs because of poor response or compliance.

MM programs include numerous monitoring and adjustment features that stress the need for patients to wean themselves away from street-drug seeking. Program clinics have specific hours for dispensing, counseling, and medical appointments. There are codes of proscribed behavior (e.g., no violence or threats of violence), and monitored drug tests are conducted at random intervals—at least monthly and as often as weekly—although the cost of the tests has led financially strained programs to cut them back to a minimum number. Counseling includes the assessment of patient attitudes and appearance (important in themselves and as clues to drug behavior) and the gathering of information about employment, family, and criminal activities; counselors offer psychotherapy and individualized social assistance and recognition, depending on their caseloads and their training for such tasks.

There was extensive research from the late 1960s to the late 1970s on a longer-acting methadone congener, L-α-acetylmethadol (LAAM), that requires less frequent doses (i.e., every 2–3 days instead of daily). LAAM has been studied in a series of phased clinical trials, and its safety and freedom from toxic side effects appear similar to those of methadone (Blaine et al. 1981; Ling et al. 1978; Savage et al. 1976). A substantial percentage—although by no means all—of opiate-dependent patients in MM programs find LAAM superior to methadone and LAAM therapy easy to comply with because of the less demanding dosing requirements (Goldstein 1976). LAAM has recently been approved for clinical use (Rettig and Yarmolinsky 1995).

## How Well Does Methadone Maintenance Work?

Early trials of MM in New York (Dole and Nyswander 1965, 1967; Dole et al. 1966, 1968, 1969) had two striking findings: 1) most patients remained in treatment for as long as it was available to them, in marked contrast to the usual experience in outpatient psychotherapy; and 2) MM substantially improved the condition of patients, as revealed by studies that considered behavior in the community for periods of several months to several years. Although there was some use of other drugs, including heroin, especially in the first few weeks after admission, such use generally decreased over time, a sharp contrast to the increasing return over time to heroin dependence that was the norm after detoxification or other typical medical or psychiatric treatments. The steadiness of employment increased somewhat, but a more dramatic change was the sustained reduction in criminal behavior, especially in the form of drug trafficking crimes.

The most convincing results concerning the capacity of MM to induce patient changes, independent of initial selection or motivational effects, come from a handful of widely separated randomized clinical trials by Dole et al. (1969) in New York, Newman and Whitehill (1978) in Hong Kong, and Gunne and Gronbladh (1984) in Sweden. The latter may be taken as representative. Thirty-four heroin-dependent individuals applied for admission to the only methadone clinic in a Swedish community; 17 were randomly assigned to MM, and 17 were assigned to ONT (these individuals could not apply for admission to the methadone clinic again for 24 months). After 2 years, 71% of patients taking methadone were doing well, compared with 6% of control patients. After 5 years, 13 of the patients taking methadone remained in treatment and were still not using heroin, and 4 had been denied treatment because of unremitting drug problems. Among the control pa-

tients, 9 had applied for admission and had entered the MM program; of these, 8 patients were not using drugs and were socially productive. Of the 8 control patients who did not apply for methadone when eligible, it was reported that "five are dead (allegedly from overdose), two in prison, and one is still drug free" (Gunne and Gronbladh 1984, p. 211).

Similar results have been reported in a number of California cities that abruptly closed publicly supported MM programs for fiscal and political reasons. In cities where methadone became much less accessible as a result of such closures, former patients as a whole were doing appreciably less well at 2-year follow-up (in terms of heroin use, other criminal behavior, and, to a lesser degree, employment) than were comparison groups in locations where there was continued access to treatment. In cities where public programs closed but private ones opened, those who transferred to the alternative MM programs did much better (in terms of staying free of drugs and out of crime) than those who did not or could not continue treatment (Anglin et al. 1989; McGlothlin and Anglin 1981; McGlothlin et al. 1977).

In all of the studies cited and in later multisite studies (Gerstein et al. 1994; Hubbard et al. 1989; Simpson and Curry 1997; Simpson et al. 1979), retention in MM as opposed to attrition, particularly very early attrition, was associated with much better results as measured by reduced heroin use and other criminal activity, even net of baseline conditions and covariates.

## Why Do the Results of Methadone Maintenance Vary?

An appreciable proportion of patients in MM programs do not respond well to treatment for a variety of reasons relating to the patients themselves and to the programs. This proportion averages about one in four, although there is wide variation from program to program (Ball et al. 1988; Gerstein et al. 1994; Hubbard et al. 1989; Simpson and Curry 1997; Simpson et al. 1979). Some patients enter MM programs for purposes other than pursuing recovery; such patients are not compliant or responsive and are most likely to leave MM programs after short periods. It is easier to identify these patients after the fact than at the time of entrance into a program.

The largest group of patients performs at least moderately well in response to MM and would do poorly without it, even when other kinds of treatment are available. There is compelling evidence that program factors such as methadone-dosing policies and counselor characteristics affect patient behavior beyond any initial differences in motivation or severity of problems. Program performance (in terms of patient retention and continued use of drugs by patients) varies greatly across programs. The multisite Treatment Outcome Prospective Study (TOPS), for example, showed a large degree of variation in clinically important patient outcomes across nine MM programs (Hubbard et al. 1989). Twelve-month retention rates averaged 34% of admissions; five programs had rates of 7%–25%, and two programs had rates greater than 50%. Regular heroin use by patients at follow-up (approximately 3 years later) was reported by 21% of the entire follow-up sample; two programs had rates greater than 30%, and three had rates of 11%–14%. In the multisite Drug Abuse Treatment Outcome Study (DATOS) programs, comparably large variations were observed in retention in treatment in 10 MM programs, with 12-month retention rates ranging from 15% to 76%; these variations could not be explained by variations in patient characteristics, and there were marginal indications that greater frequency of counseling contributed to higher retention (Simpson et al. 1997).

Variation in performance has been linked most strongly to variations in methadone dosing policies. Programs that are committed to the maintaining of low average doses (30–50 mg/day) as a virtual goal of treatment—because of therapeutic philosophy or because state regulators strongly discourage administration of higher doses—are less tolerant of occasional patient drug use, missed counseling appointments, and other such treatment lapses and have markedly lower patient retention rates than do more tolerant, higher-dose programs. This lower tolerance does not, however, act as a stimulant to better patient behavior or as a conveyor to move poorly responding patients out and bring in or keep better responders. There is solid, experimentally grounded evidence (Hargreaves 1983; Rettig and Yarmolinsky 1995) that higher dose levels are fundamentally more successful than lower ones in controlling a patient's illicit drug consumption during treatment. MM programs in which average doses of 60–120 mg/day are prescribed have consistently better results than do programs involving lower average doses (Ball and Ross 1991; Ball et al. 1988; Dole 1989). Doses in excess of 120 mg/day are seldom needed. Knowledge of and sensitivity to the clinical importance of appropriate dose levels are probably one notable element in a constellation of clinical competencies and strategies that contribute to the greater or lesser effectiveness of MM programs. Few research efforts have focused on the

area of competence, appropriate training, and different service arrangements in the clinical management of patients in MM programs (McLellan et al. 1988, 1993).

## Long-Term Residential Treatment

### What Is Long-Term Residential Treatment?

The prototype of LRT for drug dependence was the therapeutic community (TC), and virtually all LRT programs consider themselves to be TCs or modified TCs. Drug-focused TCs were designed initially (ca. 1960) to treat the same problem that MM programs treat: the "hard-core" heroin-dependent criminal. The original drug TCs, including Synanon in California and Daytop Village and Phoenix House in New York, and their lineal descendants throughout the United States, have had a broader perspective than MM programs have had, treating individuals who are severely dependent on any illicitly obtained drug or combination of drugs and whose social adjustment to conventional family and occupational responsibilities is severely compromised as a result of drug seeking (although in most cases, social adjustment was compromised before drug seeking entered the picture). In the 1980s, cocaine dependence overtook heroin dependence in the LRT population; patients receiving LRT have also been younger than the predominantly heroin-dependent MM population (Gerstein et al. 1994; Hubbard et al. 1989; Simpson and Curry 1997).

LRT's group-centered methods (described in greater detail elsewhere in this volume) encompass the following elements, all grounded in an interdependent social environment, with a direct link to a specific historical foundation:

- Firm behavioral norms across a wide range of proscriptions and specifications
- Reality-oriented group and individual psychotherapy that extends to lengthy encounter sessions focusing on current living issues or more deep-seated emotional problems
- A system of clearly specified rewards and punishments within a communal economy
- A hierarchy of responsibilities, privileges, and esteem achieved by working up a "ladder" of tasks from admission to graduation
- A degree of mobility from patient to staff status

The modifications from older TC practices now common in LRT include accelerated (shorter) treatment plans, sharpened boundaries between patient and staff roles, and more catholic use of therapeutic imports such as psychopharmacological support and 12-step procedures. To a significant extent LRT simulates and enforces a model family environment that the patient lacked during developmentally critical preadolescent and adolescent years. LRT attempts to make up for lost years in a relatively short time; there are approximately 6–12 months of residential envelopment and an additional 6–12 months of gradual reentry to the outside community before "graduation." Continued involvement after graduation is encouraged because graduates serve as role models for new residents and gain recognition and reinforcement and because such involvement provides psychological and financial support for the program.

## How Well Does Long-Term Residential Treatment Work?

Conclusions about the effectiveness of LRT are limited by the difficulties in maintaining randomized clinical trial protocols in a highly interactive treatment milieu and a population resistant to following instructions. The most notable attempt to use a randomized design to evaluate the effectiveness of LRT compared with no treatment or other treatments was conducted in California by Bale et al. (1980). The subjects were 585 heroin-addicted male veterans who sought and gained entry to the Veterans Administration (VA) Medical Center in Palo Alto, CA, for a 5-day opioid detoxification program during an 18-month intake period in the mid-1970s. The subjects also met the study's requirements of no pending felony charges or major psychiatric complications. About one-fifth of the subjects denied any interest in transferring to a VA drug treatment program after detoxification (some later changed their minds). Those interested were randomly assigned to one of two MM clinics or one of three TCs.

The clinical staff invested a substantial amount of time in trying to enlist every subject in his assigned program, and the overall rate of transfers from detoxification to VA programs doubled as a result. Nevertheless, the random-assignment design was thoroughly compromised. Less than half of the randomly assigned subjects entered and spent as long as 1 week in any of the VA treatment programs, and only half of those subjects entered the specific programs to which they had been assigned (the other men waited out exclusion periods of

at least 30 days to enter their preferred programs). Altogether, 42% of the total study cohort did not enter any kind of treatment during the follow-up year, approximately 28% entered one of the VA TCs, 12% entered a VA methadone clinic, and 19% entered a non-VA program.

The lack of compliance affected the study so profoundly that research analysts (who were independent of the clinical staff) were obliged to use multivariate statistical procedures to control for initial differences in age, ethnicity, prior treatment, drug use patterns, and criminal history among treatment and nontreatment groups. About 13% of the patients stayed less than 1 week (these individuals were considered *no treatment* subjects), 57% dropped out within 7 weeks, and 85% left treatment before 6 months. In contrast, approximately 65% of patients entering MM programs were continuously in treatment for the follow-up year. The TC group was therefore divided at the median length of stay (for all admitted men who had remained longer than a week), which was 50 days. On average, the short-term group stayed in treatment approximately 3 weeks, the long-term group stayed approximately 20 weeks, and the methadone group stayed approximately 40 weeks.

At 1-year follow-up, those subjects who had been recontacted (all but 7%) were divided among the no-treatment (41%), non-VA treatment (21%), short-term TC (14%), long-term TC (14%), and MM (11%) categories. Controlling for pretreatment characteristics, the combined long-term TC and MM groups, compared with the combined no-treatment, non-VA treatment, and short-term TC groups, were

- One-third less likely to have used heroin in the past month (41% vs. 64%)
- Two-fifths less likely to have been convicted during the year (22% vs. 37%)
- Two-thirds less likely to be incarcerated at year's end (7% vs. 19%)
- One and one-half times more likely to be at work or in school at year's end (59% vs. 40%)

The long-term TC group ranked somewhat better than the total MM group on each measure, but the differences were not large enough to be statistically significant in a sample of this size.

Beyond the efforts of Bale et al. (1980), there is a substantial amount of controlled observational literature on LRT. The bulk of these studies have focused on patients admitted to particular programs such as Phoenix House and Daytop Village in New York; in addition, TOPS and the Drug Abuse Reporting Program (DARP) separately examined patients who were admitted to about 10 TCs.

The most extensive outcome evaluations from a single program come from Phoenix House. De Leon et al. (1982) studied a sample of 230 graduates and dropouts and found that before admission the two groups were similar with respect to criminal activity and drug use but that dropouts had somewhat greater employment. After treatment, the status of both groups was better than before, but graduates had dramatically superior posttreatment outcomes compared with dropouts.

In a smaller study that is notable for its careful execution, a random sample of graduates and dropouts from a Connecticut TC were followed in an 18- to 24-month treatment plan (Romond et al. 1975). The authors found few pretreatment differences between the graduate and dropout groups except that women were much less likely than men to graduate. All 20 graduates in the sample were contacted, 10 of 31 dropouts in the sample were not located, and 1 dropout refused an interview; therefore, there were 20 contacts for each group. Graduates had spent on average 21 months in treatment, compared with 5.7 months for dropouts (range, 10 days to 16 months). Interview data were corroborated through formal and informal community networks.

Graduates had consistently better outcomes. Only 1 of 20 graduates relapsed to dependence for some part of the follow-up period, another 5 sometimes used nonopioid drugs, and 14 remained drug free throughout the interval. Altogether, graduates spent 0.5% of the follow-up period dependent. Of the 20 dropouts interviewed, 14 relapsed to dependence for some of the follow-up period, 2 used nonopioids occasionally, 1 was incarcerated for the entire period, and 3 had used no drugs; 35% of the dropouts' posttreatment time was spent as drug dependent. For 94% of the posttreatment time, graduates were enrolled in school or employed; dropouts were employed or in school only 40% of the posttreatment time.

DARP, TOPS, and DATOS provided further important controlled observational findings across three decades about the effectiveness of LRT (Hubbard et al. 1989; Sells 1974a, 1974b; Simpson and Curry 1997; Simpson et al. 1979). The mean and median lengths of stay in the traditional TCs involved in DARP were close to 7 months, well below the average treatment length of 16 months, and the ultimate graduation rate was 23%. By most of the DARP outcome measures (i.e., daily opioid use, daily nonopioid use, arrests, incarceration), outcome 1 year after discharge was significantly better for patients in TCs than for patients who underwent detoxification only and patients who made no contact after program entry. As in the study of Bale et al. (1980), the multivariate-adjusted outcomes for patients in LRT programs and patients in MM programs (matched for time since admission) on daily opioid use, nonopioid use, employment, and a composite index were similar. The length of stay in treatment was a positive, robust, statistically significant predictor of posttreatment outcomes (i.e., drug use, employment, and crime). Among patients who stayed in treatment for more than 90 days, there was a positive and linear relationship between outcome and retention. The outcomes among patients who stayed in treatment for less than 90 days were indistinguishable from outcomes among patients who underwent detoxification only and patients who did not make any contact after program entry.

The analysis of TOPS and DATOS data on LRT (Hubbard et al. 1989; Simpson and Curry 1997) used multivariate logistical regression and hierarchical linear modeling to control for pretreatment demographics, drug use, and criminality and to compare individual-level and program-level factors. These studies found a strong positive relationship between length of stay and drug-use outcomes. Progressively longer durations of LRT were significantly related to reduced cocaine, marijuana, and alcohol use; predatory crime; and unemployment 12 months after treatment. In DATOS, the odds of using cocaine, for example, were about one-tenth as great for patients who stayed in treatment 12 months or longer as for patients who received treatment for less than 3 months, and the odds of having a job nearly doubled for longer-term subjects. Patients with longer lengths of stay were more likely than those with shorter time in treatment to report at follow-up that they had a good relationship with a primary counselor, had attended education classes during treatment, and participated in aftercare following LRT.

In summary, even in the absence of successful clinical trials, it is difficult to credit any explanation of the multisite and single-site LRT research findings other than that LRT strongly affects the behavior of many of the drug-dependent individuals who receive it and time in treatment is strongly related to improved outcomes as measured by drug and alcohol consumption, predatory criminal activity, and economically productive behavior.

## Why Do the Results of Long-Term Residential Treatment Vary?

There are wide variations in outcome indicators across programs. In DATOS, 90-day retention in treatment ranged from 21% to 65% across 19 LRT programs. Patient profile differences contributed somewhat to these differences in retention; programs with older patients and a more alcohol-dependent mix of patients tended to retain patients longer. However, substantial differences in outcome by program remain, net of baseline patient differences, and there has been virtually no revealing research on the programmatic determinants of patient success and failure in LRT. It is plausible that the results of treatment depend on three primary elements: patient motivation, quality (and quantity) of staffing, and the psychosocial organization and therapeutic design of the program. LRT staffing has been particularly problematic because of constant budget pressures and rising competition for credentialed, experienced staff. Yet virtually no studies have investigated the relationship between LRT staffing and treatment effectiveness.

## Outpatient Nonmethadone Treatment

### What Is Outpatient Nonmethadone Treatment?

ONT ranges from one session of assessment/referral to virtual board-out LRT with daily psychotherapy, milieu therapy, and counseling for 1 year or longer (Kleber and Slobetz 1979). In between lie the vast majority of programs, which have treatment plans involving one to two weekly visits for 3–6 months and use a panoply of therapeutic approaches from psychiatry, counseling psychology, social work, TCs, and the 12-step paradigm. Some ONT programs contract extensively with probation departments, offering limited therapeutic services but monitoring compliance with probation conditions, particularly through administration of drug tests.

In some ONT programs, medications are prescribed by staff psychiatrists or other physicians. These drugs include ameliorants for acute withdrawal symptoms, maintenance antagonists to prevent intoxication (e.g., naltrexone), medications to control drug cravings after withdrawal, and drugs for treatment of psychiatric comorbidities (e.g., depression, mood disorders, schizophrenia). Programs with the requisite resources may deliver or link their patients to organizations offering formal education, vocational training, health care (e.g., AIDS testing or treatment), housing assistance (especially for homeless patients), support for battered spouses and children, or other social services.

The diversity of ONT approaches defies easy summary and is matched by the heterogeneity of ONT populations. These populations generally are not abusing opioids, are somewhat less likely than patients in LRT or MM programs to be involved in the criminal justice system, and include substantial proportions of abusing rather than dependent individuals—differing in all these respects from typical patients in MM programs and in TCs.

### How Well Does Outpatient Treatment Work?

The major observation about ONT is familiar: the longer patients remain in treatment, the better the outcomes are at follow-up. These conclusions are based on multivariate results (statistically controlled for baseline covariates of outcome) of the major multisite evaluations, DARP and TOPS (Hubbard et al. 1989; Sells 1974a, 1974b; Simpson and Curry 1997; Simpson et al. 1979). Patients receiving ONT in DARP exhibited statistically significant follow-up improvements relative to pretreatment in terms of employment and consumption of opioids and nonopioids but not in terms of arrest rates, which were lower before treatment than they were in patients in TCs or MM programs. The DARP comparison groups (patients in detoxification programs and patients who made no contact after program entry) reported no major pretreatment to posttreatment changes except in opioid consumption (Simpson et al. 1979).

In TOPS (Hubbard et al. 1989), data were collected on 1,600 patients receiving ONT in a total of 10 programs. Patients reported better performance during and after treatment than before admission, and multivariate analyses strongly related posttreatment outcomes to length of stay in treatment, using multivariate logistical regression to adjust for patient drug use histories and sociodemographic characteristics at admission. The analysis suggested that the critical retention threshold may be 6 months, but only 17% of patients in TOPS who underwent ONT were retained this long. ONT dropout rates were significantly higher than for patients in MM programs or patients in TCs. Similar relationships were evident in DATOS, although the median length of stay in ONT had increased to 3 months, which was similar to the length of stay in LRT. Reductions in heroin use, cocaine use, criminal behavior, and AIDS risk behaviors were more substantial at lengths of stay above rather than below this median.

## Why Do the Results of Outpatient Nonmethadone Treatment Vary?

There is no good answer to the question of why ONT results vary. Evidence of wide variation in program retention rates exists, with rates in DATOS ranging from 16% to 76% for stays in treatment of more than 90 days. But DATOS results offer little guidance about what components of ONT lead to these variations. One can only speculate that the same factors that are beginning to emerge from MM and TC research—in particular, staff quality and program design—may prove equally important here.

## Short-Term Inpatient Treatment

### What Is Short-Term Inpatient Treatment?

SIT is also called chemical dependency, Minnesota Model, 12-step, or Hazelden-type treatment. SIT is the predominant therapeutic approach in inpatient and residential programs that are oriented heavily toward insured populations. Virtually all of these programs were originally oriented toward alcohol problems but have increasingly served patients who use illicit drugs. Cook (1988a, 1988b) provided a concise historical review of the development of the Minnesota Model. He noted the similarities between the underlying theories that shape SIT and TC treatment but observed that they developed almost completely independently of each other.

SIT is usually an intensive, highly structured 3- to 6-week inpatient regimen. Patients begin with an in-depth psychiatric and psychosocial evaluation and are actively engaged in developing and implementing a recovery plan, which is patterned on the "step work" (working through the 12 steps of recovery) of AA. Self-help is a large part of therapy; patients work with one another and are generally required to attend AA/CA/NA meetings. Virtually all SIT programs incorporate daily classroom-type lectures plus two to three meetings per week in small task-oriented groups to teach patients about the disease concept of dependence, with the focus being on the harmful medical and psychosocial effects of illicit drugs and excessive alco-

hol consumption. There is also an individual track for each patient, meetings twice a week with a focal counselor, and appointments with other professionals if medical, psychiatric, or family services are needed. Recently, there has been increasing emphasis on family or codependent therapy.

Aftercare is considered important in SIT, but relatively few program resources are devoted to it. Patients are urged to continue an intensive schedule of AA/CA/NA meetings through the follow-up period of 3 months to 2 years, with continued contacts thereafter at a lower rate. Some programs follow up with monthly telephone calls, weekly group therapy, or individual counseling as needed.

SIT has some elements in common with the TC approach, but there are noteworthy differences. The inpatient or residential phase of the SIT plan is shorter, and the aftercare phase is seldom a strongly integrated program element. Patients in SIT programs are not required to perform housekeeping duties, so there is more time available for psychotherapy and educational tasks; in the TC process, however, performance of housekeeping and other program maintenance duties is an integral component of treatment. SIT program staff, like TC staff, are a mixture of stable, recovering (from alcohol or drug dependence) individuals and treatment professionals. SIT programs are especially attractive to patients with greater initial functional and social resources, who can afford the better facilities and amenities; indeed, the prototypical patient in a SIT program used to be approximately 40 years old, middle class, employed, white, and dependent on alcohol, whereas patients in TCs have almost always had massive functional and social deficits. Today, although the SIT population is more diversified (programs are now serving more patients with combined cocaine/alcohol problems, as well as a segment of adolescents with both psychiatric and drug diagnoses), these origins continue to shape the SIT approach.

### How Well Does Short-Term Inpatient Treatment Work?

Research data on SIT for illicit drug problems are weaker than for the other modalities. There are no relevant random-assignment trials or quasi-experimental studies. Only one observational study of an SIT program includes an untreated comparison group (Rawson et al. 1986), and none have included in analysis patients with short lengths of stay. There is practically no use of multivariate statistical methods. No SIT programs were in the DARP or TOPS samples, too few were in DATOS for more detailed analyses to be performed, and SIT-type programs in the California Drug and Alcohol Treatment Assessment were restricted to California's "social model" treatment of alcoholism (Gerstein et al. 1994).

During the 1980s, patients in SIT programs who presented with drug problems had poorer outcomes at posttreatment follow-up than did patients with alcohol problems (with no illicit drug consumption) in the same programs. This finding was consistent across studies by the CareUnit system (Comprehensive Care Corporation 1988), the Chemical Abuse/Addiction Treatment Outcome Registry follow-up service, and the Hazelden center in Minnesota (Gilmore 1985; Laundergan 1982).

SIT programs changed rapidly during the 1990s because of behavioral-health managed care protocols. Many such programs disappeared or were replaced by ONT programs. DATOS results indicated that there were minimal differences between results for alcohol, cocaine, and marijuana use. Because of the short duration of treatment, length-of-stay analyses were unproductive.

## Why Do the Results of Short-Term Inpatient Treatment Vary?

No currently published studies distinguish why some patients in SIT programs do well and others do not. As with other treatments, patient motivation and program staff quality are suspected factors. But there is no readily available information on variations in outcomes of drug-dependent patient across SIT programs or any successful attempts to relate such differences to systematic variations among patients or in the therapeutic approach.

## Correctional Treatment Programs

The context for research on prison-based drug treatment programs is the largely null-difference results of most therapeutic treatment offered to prisoners in hopes of reducing their recidivism (Besteman 1992; Chaiken 1989; Vaillant 1988). Yet Falkin et al. (1992) sounded an optimistic note that has led to the resumption of correctional treatment approaches in the 1990s, promising a renewed basis for evaluation research.

Falkin et al. (1992) listed the elements necessary for a successful prison drug treatment program:

- A competent and committed staff
- Adequate administrative and material support by correctional authorities
- Separation from the general prison population
- Incorporation of self-help principles and ex-offender aid
- Comprehensive, intensive therapy aimed at the entire lifestyle of the patient and not just the substance abuse aspects
- Continuity of care into the parole period—an absolute essential

Three moderately well designed evaluations of prison-based programs that incorporate these criteria currently exist. The most influential study (Falkin et al. 1992; Frohling 1989) is of Stay'n Out, a prison program in New York. Stay'n Out is based on the social organization of Phoenix House, a TC, which was adapted to the prison setting, with community-based TCs extending treatment contact after release. Stay'n Out patients from 1977 to 1984 ($n = 682$) were compared with prisoner groups either receiving regular drug abuse counseling ($n = 576$), receiving milieu therapy ($n = 364$), or waiting for Stay'n Out admission and paroled without treatment for lack of an opening during the 6- to 12-month window before their release date ($n = 197$). All groups were followed for 2–9 years (average, more than 4 years) after release from prison.

The TC group was arrested significantly less often than the control subjects were, with differences of 8–14 percentage points (which represent 22%–35% reductions in rearrest rates) for men and 6–12 percentage points (25%–40% reductions) for women. For every arrest, such individuals have generally committed hundreds of crimes (Ball et al. 1981; Johnson et al. 1985; Speckart and Anglin 1986). The authors indicated, however, that intergroup differences at follow-up in rates of reincarceration, rapidity of rearrest, and parole revocation were statistically or substantively negligible, except that significantly more Stay'n Out–treated women than untreated women completed parole.

Field (1984, 1989) reported results of a controlled observational study on Cornerstone, a modified TC program (a mixture of milieu therapy and TC principles) at Oregon State Hospital in Salem. Cornerstone is designed for state prisoners in their last year before parole eligibility; after release, parolees move to a halfway house. In this study, Cornerstone participants were convicted substantially less often in the 3 years after release than were comparable parolees, and program graduates were more crime-free at follow-up than were participants who dropped out early from the program. In the Stay'n Out study, and in several other well-regarded, well-studied voluntary correctional programs (Falkin et al. 1992), length of stay in treatment correlated strongly with nonrecidivism, the same result seen in community-based programs. The fact that individuals who drop out early from prison programs are even more likely to relapse, by every measure, than are untreated control subjects suggests that prison-based TCs may be more efficient than community-based programs at sorting out and excluding (or encouraging self-exclusion by) the poorest responders.

California's Civil Addict Program (CAP), which began in 1961 (Anglin 1988; Anglin and McGlothlin 1984; McGlothlin et al. 1977), was the most comprehensive and best-studied example of a correctional treatment program combining treatment in a penal institution (ONT-like therapy) with specialized parole supervision, including access to a variety of community-based treatments. CAP operated as designed for only 8 years, after which much of its original character was lost because of changing correctional policies and systemic overcrowding. Two similar civil commitment programs, one federal and one operated by the state of New York, fell far short of their design goals, ended fairly quickly, and were roundly regarded as failures (Besteman 1978, 1992; Inciardi 1988).

CAP permitted adjudication of heroin-dependent felons through a civil commitment procedure (rather than regular criminal sentencing) to a 7-year term of supervision, three-fourths of which, on average, was spent on parole. The first (repeatable) stop for CAP participants was a term in a medium-security prison with a large staff of psychotherapists. Community supervision was carried out by a specially trained cadre of parole officers with unusually small caseloads (30 parolees) and through weekly drug testing (Anglin 1988).

The civil commitment law was complex enough that legal-procedural errors were made in committing at least half of the early CAP participants. In such cases the commitments were challenged by writs of habeas corpus, and the individuals were released from CAP and returned to regular adjudication. The released group differed from those persons who continued in that many released individuals had less serious offenses for which the 7-year CAP commitment was longer than the sentence they would probably otherwise have served; virtually all of the CAP group would probably have had longer sentences without CAP. The researchers therefore used matching procedures to select from within the released group a comparison sample that was

as similar as possible to the continuing group on 15 criteria, including criminal and drug histories and demographics.

Under CAP, heroin use and total criminality while not incarcerated decreased to levels that were half or less than half those reported for the comparison group. These reductions became apparent immediately after the CAP parolees' release into the community, and the reductions were sustained. The difference between CAP parolees and control subjects narrowed over the next several years as more control subjects reduced their heroin use and other criminal behavior. By the time the continuing CAP group's paroles ended, the control group was at a more nearly similar level, especially considering pretreatment (baseline) differences. The subsequent recovery paths of the two groups remained parallel. The residential and community supervision components of CAP were evidently effective in accelerating the recovery of a substantial percentage (at least 50%) of those treated.

## Conclusions About Treatment Effectiveness

Research on MM has demonstrated the following:

- On average, heroin-dependent (or other opioid-dependent) individuals have better outcomes in terms of illicit drug consumption and other criminal behavior when they are maintained on methadone than when they are not treated at all, when they are simply detoxified and released, or when methadone is tapered and treatment is terminated arbitrarily.
- Methadone clinics have substantially higher rates of retention of opioid-dependent patients than do other treatment modalities.
- Patients assessed after discontinuation of MM who continued MM longer have better outcomes than do patients likewise assessed who discontinued MM earlier.
- Methadone doses need to be clinically monitored and individually optimized. Patients do better, generally, when they are stabilized on doses in the range of 60–120 mg/day. Program characteristics such as inadequate methadone dose levels and differences between counselors (which are not yet fully defined) are significantly related to differences in patient performance during treatment.

The results of research on the effects of LRT are as follows:

- LRT patients end virtually all illicit drug taking and other criminal behavior while in residence and perform better (in terms of reduced drug taking and other criminal activity and increased social productivity) after discharge than before admission. The length of stay is the strongest predictor of outcomes at follow-up, with graduates having the best outcomes at that point.
- TC attrition is typically high—above the rates for MM programs but below the rates for ONT programs.
- The minimum retention necessary to yield improvement in long-term outcomes seems to be several months, which covers one-third to one-half of a typical program's admissions. Improvements continue to become more substantial for treatment durations of 1 year and more.

Despite the heterogeneity of ONT programs and program participants, the limited number of outcome evaluations of ONT programs has generated conclusions qualitatively similar to those from studies of TCs. Patients who receive ONT exhibit better behavior during and after treatment than before treatment. Those patients who are actually admitted to programs have better outcomes than patients who contact but do not enter programs (and patients who undergo detoxification only). Outcome at follow-up is positively related to length of stay in treatment, and those who complete treatment have better outcomes than those who drop out.

Before the 1990s, SIT programs focused primarily on alcohol problems and were not adequately evaluated for treatment of drug problems. SIT programs were shrinking and redefining themselves so rapidly during the 1990s, chiefly because of the conviction in managed care that "the only good patient is an outpatient," that even well-developed results cannot be confidently generalized.

Results of a small number of well-designed controlled studies, involving in-prison LRT with strong linkages to community-based supervision and/or treatment programs, indicate that prison-initiated treatment can reduce the treated group's rate of rearrest by one-fourth to one-half; clear correlations are observed between positive outcome rates and length of time in treatment, just as in studies of entirely community-based modalities. The results have some anomalies, and there have been difficulties in sustaining the integrity of prison-based treatment programs, but the results support the concept that these programs should be encouraged and research continued.

There is no single treatment that is effective for the majority of the individuals who seek treatment. Each of the treatment modalities for which there is a baseline of adequate studies can fairly be said to be effective for many of the people who seek that treatment; enough of these individuals do find the right treatment and continue it long enough to make the current aggregate of treatment programs worthwhile.

# References

Anglin MD: The efficacy of civil commitment in treating narcotic addiction, in Compulsory Treatment of Drug Abuse: Research and Clinical Practice (NIDA Res Monogr 86). Edited by Leukefeld CG, Tims FM. Rockville, MD, National Institute on Drug Abuse, 1988, pp 8–34

Anglin MD, McGlothlin WH: Outcome of narcotic addict treatment in California, in Drug Abuse Treatment Evaluation: Strategies, Progress, and Prospects (NIDA Res Monogr 5). Edited by Tims FM, Ludford JP. Rockville, MD, National Institute on Drug Abuse, 1984, pp 106–128

Anglin MD, Speckart GS, Booth MW, et al: Consequences and costs of shutting off methadone. Addict Behav 14:307–326, 1989

Bale RN, Van Stone WW, Kuldau JM, et al: Therapeutic communities vs. methadone maintenance: a prospective controlled study of narcotic addiction treatment: design and one-year follow-up. Arch Gen Psychiatry 37:179–193, 1980

Ball JC, Ross A: The Effectiveness of Methadone Maintenance. New York, Springer-Verlag New York, 1991

Ball JC, Rosen L, Flueck JA, et al: The criminality of heroin addicts when addicted and when off opiates, in The Drugs-Crime Connection. Edited by Inciardi JA. Beverly Hills, CA, Sage, 1981, pp 39–65

Ball JC, Lange WR, Meyers CP, et al: Reducing the risk of AIDS through methadone maintenance treatment. J Health Soc Behav 29:214–226, 1988

Besteman KJ: The NARA program, in Drug Addiction and the U.S. Public Health Service. Edited by Martin WR, Isbell H. Rockville, MD, National Institute on Drug Abuse, 1978, pp 274–280

Besteman KJ: Federal leadership in building the national drug treatment system, in Treating Drug Abuse, Vol 2. Edited by Gerstein DR, Harwood, HJ. Washington, DC, National Academy Press, 1992, pp 63–88

Blaine JD, Thomas DB, Barnett G, et al: Levo-alpha acetylmethadol (LAAM): clinical utility and pharmaceutical development, in Substance Abuse: Clinical Problems and Perspectives. Edited by Lowinson JH, Ruiz P. Baltimore, MD, Williams & Wilkins, 1981, pp 360–388

Chaiken MR: Prison Programs for Drug-Involved Offenders: Department of Justice Research in Action (NCJ 118316). Washington, DC, U.S. Department of Justice, 1989

Cole SG, Lehman WE, Cole EA, et al: Inpatient vs outpatient treatment of alcohol and drug abusers. Am J Drug Alcohol Abuse 8:329–345, 1981

Comprehensive Care Corporation: Evaluation of Treatment Outcome. Irvine, CA, Comprehensive Care Corporation, 1988

Cook CCH: The Minnesota Model in the management of drug and alcohol dependency: miracle, method or myth? Part I: the philosophy and the programme. British Journal of Addiction 83:625–634, 1988a

Cook CCH: The Minnesota Model in the management of drug and alcohol dependency: miracle, method or myth? Part II: evidence and conclusions. British Journal of Addiction 83:735–748, 1988b

Dackis C, Gold MS, Sweeney D, et al: Single dose bromocriptine reverses cocaine craving. Psychiatry Res 20:261–264, 1987

De Leon G, Wexler HK, Jainchill N: The therapeutic community: success and improvement rates 5 years after treatment. International Journal of the Addictions 17:703–747, 1982

Dole VP: Methadone treatment and the acquired immunodeficiency syndrome epidemic. JAMA 262:1681–1682, 1989

Dole VP, Nyswander M: A medical treatment for diacetylmorphine (heroin) addiction: a clinical trial with methadone hydrochloride. JAMA 193:80–84, 1965

Dole VP, Nyswander M: Rehabilitation of the street addict. Arch Environ Health 14:477–480, 1967

Dole VP, Nyswander M, Kreek MJ: Narcotic blockade. Arch Intern Med 118:304–309, 1966

Dole VP, Nyswander M, Warner A: Successful treatment of 750 criminal addicts. JAMA 206:2708–2711, 1968

Dole VP, Robinson JW, Orraga J, et al: Methadone treatment of randomly selected criminal addicts. N Engl J Med 280:1372–1375, 1969

Falkin GP, Wexler HK, Lipton DS: Drug treatment in state prisons, in Treating Drug Abuse, Vol 2. Edited by Gerstein DR, Harwood HJ. Washington, DC, National Academy Press, 1992, pp 89–132

Field G: The Cornerstone program: a client outcome study. Federal Probation 48:50–55, 1984

Field G: The effects of intensive treatment on reducing the criminal recidivism of addicted offenders. Federal Probation 53:51–72, 1989

Frohling R: Promising Approaches to Drug Treatment in Correctional Settings. Washington, DC, National Conference of State Legislatures, 1989

Gawin FH, Kleber HD, Byck R, et al: Desipramine facilitation of initial cocaine abstinence. Arch Gen Psychiatry 46:117–121, 1989a

Gawin FH, Allen D, Humblestone B: Outpatient treatment of "crack" cocaine smoking with flupenthixol decanoate: a preliminary report. Arch Gen Psychiatry 46:322–325, 1989b

Gerstein DR: The effectiveness of drug treatment, in Addictive States. Edited by O'Brien CP, Jaffe JH. New York, Raven, 1992, pp 253–282

Gerstein DR, Harwood HJ (eds): Treating Drug Problems, Vol 1. Washington, DC, National Academy Press, 1990

Gerstein DR, Harwood HJ (eds): Treating Drug Problems, Vol 2. Washington, DC, National Academy Press, 1992

Gerstein DR, Johnson RA, Harwood HJ, et al: Evaluating Recovery Services: the California Drug and Alcohol Treatment Assessment (CALDATA): General Report. Sacramento, CA, State of California Department of Alcohol and Drug Programs, 1994

Gilmore KM: Hazelden Primary Residential Treatment Program: Profile and Patient Outcome. Center City, MN, Hazelden, 1985

Goldstein A: A clinical experience with LAAM, in Rx LAAM: 3×/Week: LAAM Alternative to Methadone (NIDA Res Monogr 8). Edited by Blaine JD, Renault PF. Rockville, MD, National Institute on Drug Abuse, 1976, pp 115–117

Gunne L, Gronbladh L: The Swedish methadone maintenance program, in The Social and Medical Aspects of Drug Abuse. Edited by Serban G. Jamaica, NY, Spectrum, 1984, pp 205–213

Hargreaves WA: Methadone dose and duration for methadone treatment, in Research on the Treatment of Narcotic Addiction: State of the Art (NIDA Treatment Res Monogr, DHHS Publ No ADM-83-1281). Edited by Cooper JR, Altman F, Brown BS, et al. Rockville, MD, National Institute on Drug Abuse, 1983, pp 19–79

Hubbard RL, Marsden ME, Rachal JV, et al: Drug Abuse Treatment: A National Study of Effectiveness. Chapel Hill, University of North Carolina Press, 1989

Inciardi JA: Some considerations on the clinical efficacy of compulsory treatment: reviewing the New York experience, in Compulsory Treatment of Drug Abuse: Research and Clinical Practice (NIDA Res Monogr 86). Edited by Leukefeld CG, Tims FM. Rockville, MD, National Institute on Drug Abuse, 1988, pp 126–138

Johnson BD, Goldstein PJ, Preble E, et al: Taking Care of Business: The Economics of Crime by Heroin Abusers. Lexington, MA, Lexington Books, 1985

Kleber HD, Slobetz F: Outpatient drug-free treatment, in Handbook on Drug Abuse. Edited by Dupont RL, Goldstein A, O'Donnell J. Rockville, MD, National Institute on Drug Abuse, 1979, pp 31–38

Kreek MJ: Health consequences associated with the use of methadone, in Research on the Treatment of Narcotic Addiction: State of the Art (NIDA Treatment Res Monogr, DHHS Publ No ADM-83-1281). Edited by Cooper JR, Altman F, Brown BS, et al. Rockville, MD, National Institute on Drug Abuse, 1983, pp 456–482

Laundergan JC: Easy Does It! Alcoholism Treatment Outcomes, Hazelden and the Minnesota Model. Center City, MN, Hazelden, 1982

Ling W, Klett CJ, Gillis RD: A cooperative clinical study of methadyl acetate. Arch Gen Psychiatry 35:345–353, 1978

McGlothlin WH, Anglin MD: Shutting off methadone: costs and benefits. Arch Gen Psychiatry 38:885–892, 1981

McGlothlin WH, Anglin MD, Wilson BD: An Evaluation of the California Civil Addict Program (Services Res Monogr). Rockville, MD, National Institute on Drug Abuse, 1977

McLellan AT, Luborsky L, Woody G, et al: Counselor differences in methadone treatment, in Problems of Drug Dependence, 1987 (NIDA Res Monogr 81). Edited by Harris LS. Rockville, MD, National Institute on Drug Abuse, 1988, pp 243–250

McLellan AT, Arndt IO, Metzger DS, et al: The effects of psychosocial services in substance abuse treatment. JAMA 269:1953–1966, 1993

Moffet AD, Soloway IH, Glick MX: Post-treatment behavior following ambulatory detoxification, in Methadone: Experience and Issues. Edited by Chambers CD, Brill L. New York, Behavioral Publications, 1973, pp 215–227

Newman RG: Critique, in Research on the Treatment of Narcotic Addiction: State of the Art (NIDA Treatment Res Monogr, DHHS Publ No ADM-83-1281). Edited by Cooper JR, Altman F, Brown BS, et al. Rockville, MD, National Institute on Drug Abuse, 1983, pp 168–171

Newman RG, Whitehill WB: Double-blind comparison of methadone and placebo maintenance treatment of narcotic addicts in Hong Kong. Lancet 2:485–488, 1978

Rawson RA, Obert JL, McCann MJ, et al: Cocaine treatment outcome: cocaine use following inpatient, outpatient, and no treatment, in Problems of Drug Dependence, 1985 (NIDA Res Monogr 67). Edited by Harris LS. Rockville, MD, National Institute on Drug Abuse, 1986, pp 271–277

Resnick R: Methadone detoxification from illicit opiates and methadone maintenance, in Research on the Treatment of Narcotic Addiction: State of the Art (NIDA Treatment Res Monogr, DHHS Publ No ADM-83-1281). Edited by Cooper RJ, Altman F, Brown BS, et al. Rockville, MD, National Institute on Drug Abuse, 1983, pp 160–178

Rettig RR, Yarmolinsky A (eds): Federal Regulation of Methadone. Washington, DC, National Academy Press, 1995

Romond AM, Forrest CK, Kleber HD: Follow-up of participants in a drug dependence therapeutic community. Arch Gen Psychiatry 32:369–374, 1975

Savage C, Karp EG, Curran SF, et al: Methadone/LAAM maintenance: a comparison study. Compr Psychiatry 17:415–424, 1976

Sells SB (ed): Studies of the Effectiveness of Treatments for Drug Abuse, Vol 1: Evaluation of Treatments. Cambridge, MA, Ballinger, 1974a

Sells SB (ed): Studies of the Effectiveness of Treatments for Drug Abuse, Vol 2: Research on Patients, Treatments and Outcomes. Cambridge, MA, Ballinger, 1974b

Sheffet A, Quinones M, Lavenhar MA, et al: An evaluation of detoxification as an initial step in the treatment of heroin addiction. Am J Psychiatry 133:337–340, 1976

Simpson DD, Curry SJ (eds): Drug Abuse Treatment Outcome Study (DATOS). Psychology of Addictive Behaviors 11 (special issue):211–338, 1997

Simpson DD, Savage LJ, Lloyd MR: Follow-up evaluation of treatment of drug abuse during 1969 to 1972. Arch Gen Psychiatry 36:772–780, 1979

Simpson DD, Joe GW, Broome KM, et al: Program diversity and treatment retention rates in the Drug Abuse Treatment Outcome Study (DATOS). Psychology of Addictive Behaviors 11:279–293, 1997

Speckart GR, Anglin MD: Narcotics and crime: a causal modeling approach. Journal of Quantitative Criminology 2:3–28, 1986

Tennant FS, Sagherian AA: Double-blind comparison of amantadine and bromocriptine for ambulatory withdrawal for cocaine dependence. Arch Intern Med 147:109–112, 1987

Vaillant GE: What can long-term follow-up teach us about relapse and prevention of relapse in addiction? British Journal of Addiction 83:1147–1157, 1988

# 3 Treatment for Specific Drugs of Abuse

# Chapter 16

# Alcohol

## Don Gallant, M.D.

Great strides have been made in basic and clinical alcoholism research during the past two decades. Recent findings on the treatment of the alcohol withdrawal syndromes; pharmacotherapy and behavioral therapy for the abstinence phase, including treatment of comorbid conditions; and psychosocial interventions are presented in this chapter. These findings should influence how alcoholic individuals are treated at each stage of the illness. However, a problem still exists in transmitting the clinical research findings to the practicing physician. Another problem in treatment is that despite the availability of easily administered, effective screening diagnostic instruments, the diagnosis of alcoholism during the early course of the illness is frequently missed by the physician or social worker (Gallant 1987). An equally important problem to be solved is the selection of the appropriate abstinence treatment modality for the specific subtype of alcoholic patient described by investigators such as Cloninger et al. (1996) and Babor et al. (1992). Cloninger and colleagues described the Type II alcoholic patient as having a primarily genetic background, usually being male, having illness onset before age 25, presenting antisocial behavior with high novelty seeking, and drinking to induce euphoria, which resembles Babor and colleagues' description of the Type B alcoholism patient who presents with a family history of alcoholism, early onset with childhood risk factors, and some antisocial traits associated with polydrug use. Some overlap of Type I and Type A is also seen as described in these previously cited references.

Promising data for treatment matching do exist (Litt et al. 1992). In a 2-year study, a group of alcoholic patients labeled Type B (resembling Cloninger and colleagues' Type II alcoholic individuals with antisocial traits) showed better treatment outcomes with coping skills treatment and worse outcomes with interactional psychotherapy, whereas the converse was true for the Type A group (resembling Cloninger and colleagues' mild form of Type I) (Cloninger et al. 1996). Because other research attempts at treatment matching of patient subgroups for specific treatment modalities have been unsuccessful, it is important that the study results be replicated (Project MATCH Research Group 1997). It may be interesting to note that the antisocial characteristics in the Type II alcoholic individuals described by Cloninger et al. and the Type B alcoholic patients described by Litt et al. resemble the "underarousal criminal types" studied in a 9-year prospective neurophysiological evaluation of central and autonomic measures of arousal in 101 Caucasian schoolboys that was initiated when the children were ages 14–16 years (Raine et al. 1990).

It should also be mentioned that the recent increase in patients with combined alcohol and cocaine addiction not only requires modification of treatment procedures originally devised for the "pure" alcoholic patient or drug addict but also presents more complicated hepatotoxicity problems (Boyer and Petersen 1990).

## Detoxification

It should be stressed that quantitative criteria measures are a necessary part of clinical management. The revised Clinical Institute Withdrawal Assessment for Alcohol

The author thanks W.W. Norton and Co. for permission to publish several excerpts from his book, *Alcoholism: A Guide to Diagnosis, Intervention and Treatment,* and Williams and Wilkins for permission to publish excerpts from several review articles that he wrote for their journal *Alcoholism: Clinical and Experimental Research* by the Research Society on Alcoholism.

Scale (CIWA-Ar), a 10-item scale; the 6-item Alcohol Withdrawal Scale (AWS); and the Modified Selective Severity Assessment Scale (MSSA) contain objective and subjective criteria that enable the clinician to make a decision about the use of pharmacological medication (Benzer and Cushman 1980; Cushman et al. 1985; Sullivan et al. 1989). One of these short-form scales should be administered routinely to all patients admitted to detoxification units. The CIWA-Ar is a practical clinical instrument derived from the 15-item CIWA-A Scale with no loss of clinical validity or reliability, and it offers an increase in acceptance by ward personnel. The items include sweating, anxiety, tremor, auditory disturbances, agitation, nausea, tactile disturbances, headache, and orientation, with all of the items except orientation (0–4) weighted equally on a scale of 0–7. If the patient scores less than 10 on the scale, then pharmacological treatment usually is not indicated; the patient's condition may be managed with supportive care alone (Sullivan et al. 1989). In one study (Sullivan et al. 1991) using the guideline of instituting psychopharmacological medication only if the score was greater than 10, the results showed that patients scoring high on the scale with a greater degree of physical dependence received higher doses of benzodiazepines, whereas those scoring in the lower part of the scale received lower doses of benzodiazepines.

In a prospective randomized, double-blind, controlled evaluation of "symptom-triggered therapy" (S-TT) compared with a standard treatment regimen based on the CIWA-Ar, S-TT decreased both the total amount of benzodiazepine dosage used and the treatment duration (Saitz et al. 1994). Thus, use of the CIWA-Ar minimizes inadequate dosing of benzodiazepines for patients experiencing moderate to severe withdrawal and decreases overmedicating with benzodiazepines in those alcoholic patients who are undergoing only mild withdrawal. However, the clinician must be extremely careful not to undertreat those patients who have experienced repeated withdrawal because some investigators (Ballenger and Post 1978) believe that repeated inadequately treated withdrawal episodes could produce future withdrawal syndromes of increased severity with possible permanent central nervous system (CNS) changes. These clinical observations correlate with an adult male mouse model of alcohol withdrawal (kindling), which showed that repeated episodes of alcohol withdrawal potentiate the severity of subsequent withdrawal seizures (Becker and Hale 1993).

The treatment of alcohol withdrawal syndromes has two primary goals: 1) to help a patient achieve detoxification in as safe and as comfortable a way as possible and 2) to foster the patient's motivation to enter rehabilitation therapy. Recent advances in the treatment of alcohol withdrawal syndromes, particularly those regimens that use a standardized alcohol withdrawal scale with S-TT, promise improvements in our ability to realize both goals.

## Mild to Moderate Alcohol Withdrawal

Outpatient treatment may be sufficient for a significant number of patients with alcohol withdrawal syndrome. In addition to use of the CIWA-Ar or AWS, the blood alcohol level (BAL) can be used as another guideline to decide whether to place the patient in a social detoxification unit, to refer him or her to a medical ward for more intensive treatment of severe withdrawal symptoms, or to follow up the patient at home with proper supervision. For example, if the BAL is 250–300 mg% and the patient appears to be alert and not dysarthric, then the physician should be on guard for possible moderate to severe withdrawal symptoms as the BAL decreases. In this situation, the tolerance for alcohol is too high, and the patient may have a predisposition to develop marked withdrawal symptoms when he or she stops drinking.

Successful outpatient treatment in patients with mild to moderate alcohol withdrawal symptoms has been described in several studies (Hyashida et al. 1989; Pattison 1977; Whitfield 1980). However, the patients in these studies are not representative of all alcoholic individuals who develop withdrawal symptomatology because individuals with symptoms of delirium or convulsions could not be included in these investigations. In addition, some of the studies reporting successful outpatient treatment in these patient populations did not use specific criteria that delineated the subgroup of individuals who were selected for outpatient therapy. However, the clinician may feel relatively safe in treating an outpatient with alcohol withdrawal symptoms if the CIWA-Ar score is less than 10 and if the patient has no history of alcohol-related convulsions or delirium. These patients may be helped to decrease the intake of alcohol with family support and the use of a short-acting hypnotic for sleep in association with moderate doses of benzodiazepines for daytime anxiety. The use of short-acting benzodiazepines such as oxazepam (30 mg four times a day) or lorazepam (1 mg three or four times a day) in association with a short-acting hypnotic (e.g., chloral hydrate) will enable the patient to withdraw from alcohol comfortably over a period of

4–7 days. In this manner, the clinician avoids over-sedating the patient with long-acting compounds, which can interfere with the patient's compliance and can cause accidents secondary to interference with cognition or manual dexterity. Of course, the patient must have a family member or friend available to accompany him or her to the clinic on a daily basis. Adequate screening, program-supported housing if no residence is available, psychosocial therapy, and use of a standardized assessment scale for withdrawal symptomatology can result in an impressive therapeutic outcome. Thiamine (50–100 mg/day) should be used to avoid potential future CNS damage, such as Wernicke's encephalopathy, a rapidly advancing organic mental syndrome that may be difficult to diagnose. The alcoholic patient who has adequate nutrition and abstinence usually does not require extraordinary doses of minerals or vitamins, and hydration is best accomplished by oral fluids, which will significantly decrease the possibility of iatrogenic illnesses such as overhydration or electrolyte imbalance.

Introduction of the β-blockers propranolol and atenolol and of an α-adrenergic receptor agonist, clonidine, has improved treatment of mild to moderate alcohol withdrawal syndromes by replacing more sedating medications (Kraus et al. 1985; Manhem et al. 1985; Sellers et al. 1977). However, β-blockers present a possible problem: they may potentiate hypoglycemia in the first 36 hours after ingestion of large amounts of alcohol by malnourished alcoholic subjects (Gallant 1982). Because alcoholic individuals seem to have an increased incidence of chronic obstructive pulmonary disease as well as alcoholic cardiomyopathy, precautions about the use of β-blockers should be further emphasized. Clonidine and guanabenz, both α-adrenergic agonists, have also been effective in suppressing the symptoms and signs of alcohol withdrawal (Baumgartner and Rowen 1988).

If a patient continues to drink sporadically during outpatient treatment of the mild to moderate alcohol withdrawal syndrome, inpatient detoxification may be required even though severe withdrawal symptoms are not present. From a therapeutic viewpoint, it may be necessary to interrupt the self-destructive cycle of heavy drinking followed by withdrawal symptoms that are then relieved through resumption of alcohol intake. In addition, if the patient has other serious medical problems accompanying the alcohol withdrawal syndrome, such as uncontrolled diabetes or a blood pressure that is considered to be dangerously high, then hospitalization is indicated. Other medical illnesses not only can complicate the symptomatology of the withdrawal syndrome but also may worsen if not carefully monitored in an inpatient setting.

## Severe Alcohol Withdrawal (Alcohol Withdrawal Delirium)

Criteria for alcohol withdrawal delirium include a clouding of consciousness, difficulty in sustaining attention, disorientation to present circumstances, autonomic hyperactivity associated with tachycardia, excessive sweating, and elevated blood pressure. On the CIWA-Ar, the patient's score is usually higher than 20. These symptoms occur within the first week after cessation or reduction of heavy alcohol ingestion. With adequate treatment, these symptoms should disappear by the end of the first week and surely by no later than the beginning of the second week (Gallant 1987). This diagnosis warrants immediate hospitalization because it infers that the patient is unable to care for himself or herself and is seriously ill. The use of benzodiazepines may be of considerable help in alcoholic patients who have experienced recent alcohol withdrawal convulsions because these compounds have anticonvulsant activity. If the patient is suspected of having a moderate amount of liver damage, the most appropriate benzodiazepines may be oxazepam or lorazepam because these drugs do not require metabolism by the liver and, therefore, do not accumulate. The dosage range for benzodiazepines should vary with the quantity of the alcohol consumption prior to withdrawal, the weight of the patient, and the severity of the presenting symptomatology such as a very high score on the CIWA-Ar. Although patients who present with high BALs usually experience more severe withdrawal symptoms than do patients with relatively low BALs, these observations are not consistent. Exceptions may include patients who have experienced severe withdrawal symptoms following previous drinking episodes or those who have developed intercurrent illnesses during the present withdrawal stage. In severe cases of alcohol withdrawal syndrome with delirium, dosages as high as 60 mg four times a day of oxazepam or 1–2 mg four times a day of lorazepam or 20 mg four times a day of diazepam may be needed. Diazepam-loading regimens (e.g., dosages of 40 mg at bedtime) have also been successfully used (Romach and Sellers 1991). In a recent paper that summarized a meta-analysis of English-language medical articles on treatment of ethanol withdrawal published before July 1, 1995, the benzodiazepines were reported to be the most suitable agents (Mayo-Smith 1997).

The clinician should be aware that intramuscular

benzodiazepine compounds such as chlordiazepoxide and diazepam are poorly absorbed. If the patient is vomiting profusely and unable to tolerate oral medication, then the use of intramuscular lorazepam would be indicated because this compound absorbs quite readily after intramuscular administration. Prochlorperazine, 25 mg, as a suppository can be used temporarily to inhibit the emesis. Intravenous infusions should be used *only* in patients who are definitely dehydrated from excessive vomiting or diarrhea. Even in these cases, the clinician must be cautious with glycogen-depleted patients who may be thiamine deficient because the patient may develop Wernicke's encephalopathy if a glucose infusion is administered without additional thiamine. These patients should be weighed daily to evaluate their hydration state.

During the past decade, encouraging results in the treatment of severe alcohol withdrawal syndromes have been reported. One published double-blind, controlled evaluation of carbamazepine compared with oxazepam for the treatment of alcohol withdrawal confirmed the results of previous evaluations of the efficacy of carbamazepine (Malcolm et al. 1989). To be included in this trial, patients had to meet DSM-III (American Psychiatric Association 1980) criteria for alcohol dependence and had to score 20 or higher on the CIWA-A. Eighty-six subjects were randomly assigned to either the carbamazepine (200 mg four times a day with gradual reduction) group or the oxazepam (30 mg four times a day) group. The CIWA-A, physiological measures, and neurological examinations were administered twice daily, 1 hour after medication was administered. The clinical measures in both treatment groups showed that maximal reduction of symptoms was achieved between days 4 and 5. There were no significant differences between groups on the CIWA-A or on the other measures except that the global distress score of the Symptom Checklist-90—Revised (SCL-90-R) at the end of the study indicated significantly less psychological distress in the carbamazepine group than in the oxazepam group. This short-term carbamazepine treatment regimen appears to be quite safe. Ataxia appears to be the most uncomfortable side effect.

Alcoholic patients who have made multiple attempts at alcohol withdrawal are likely to experience seizures and to develop long-term neurological and psychiatric disabilities. If these sequelae are associated with *kindlinglike* changes in the limbic areas, then the *antikindling* effects of carbamazepine may offer future protection against this type of CNS damage as well as ameliorate the acute phase of the withdrawal syndrome. The finding that carbamazepine was significantly more effective than oxazepam in reducing psychiatric symptoms and the relatively minimal sedative side effects of this compound are important features of carbamazepine withdrawal methodology. The findings suggest a potential use for a compound such as carbamazepine in the long-term pharmacological management of alcoholic patients. In a controlled evaluation of carbamazepine versus placebo in 29 alcoholic patients, the carbamazepine group showed fewer drinking days and fewer drinks per day during a 6-month follow-up period (Mueller et al. 1995). However, these findings require additional controlled research investigations with larger numbers of patients.

The European journals report other compounds that show promise for the treatment of moderate to severe alcohol withdrawal symptomatology. In one double-blind study of γ-hydroxybutyric acid (GHB), a constituent of the mammalian brain that may act as a neuromodulator of γ-aminobutyric acid (GABA), GHB administration produced a prompt reduction of withdrawal symptoms, including tremors, sweating, nausea, anxiety, and restlessness (Gallimberti et al. 1989). The only side effect noted in the administration of this compound was dizziness. It is interesting that in rats, GHB not only suppresses ethanol withdrawal symptoms but also inhibits voluntary alcohol consumption. Other European journal publications have reported that clomethiazole, a compound structurally related to thiamine, is quite effective for the treatment of withdrawal symptoms (Schuckit 1990). Not only does clomethiazole appear to be comparable to the benzodiazepines in alleviating the withdrawal symptoms, but administration of this medication also appears to be associated with less severe gastrointestinal side effects.

The combined alcohol-benzodiazepine withdrawal syndrome appears to be different from the classical alcohol withdrawal syndrome. These withdrawal symptoms can start anywhere from 2 to 10 days after abrupt discontinuation of drugs and are characterized by more psychomotor and autonomic nervous system signs than are usually seen in alcohol withdrawal (Benzer and Cushman 1980). The clinician may use carbamazepine, which should be effective for the combined alcohol-benzodiazepine addictions, particularly because carbamazepine has been shown to be effective for both alcohol and benzodiazepine withdrawal (Ries et al. 1989; Schweizer et al. 1991). However, the treatment regimen for benzodiazepine withdrawal, as compared with alcohol withdrawal, should be extended for a period of approximately 2 weeks while the benzodiazepine is tapered rather than discontinued abruptly because initiation of carbamazepine may temporarily induce metabolism of some benzodiazepines. In the study by Schweizer et al., more subjects in the carbamazepine group as compared with the placebo group remained benzodiazepine-free after the benzodiazepine taper regimen was completed.

## Pharmacotherapy During the Abstinence Phase

### Disulfiram

The efficacy of disulfiram has been demonstrated in a number of studies by different authors (Fuller and Williford 1980; Gerrein et al. 1973; Sereny et al. 1986). In one well-designed controlled evaluation of disulfiram in a Veterans Administration (VA) hospital, a life-table analysis showed that the use of this compound significantly increased the number of abstinent months compared with a placebo group. Both groups of patients had requested disulfiram at the outset of the study, thus negating the variable of motivation for taking the medication. Although the 12-month endpoint of the study showed no significant differences in total abstinence rates between the groups, the evaluation of the effect of disulfiram on abstinence over time provided information about the number of additional months of abstinence before the 12-month endpoint. These additional months of abstinence may delay or possibly prevent the occurrence of alcohol-induced tissue damage to various organs (Fuller and Williford 1980). In other studies (Gerrein et al. 1973; Sereny et al. 1986), supervised disulfiram maintenance has been significantly superior to voluntary disulfiram therapy in keeping patients in treatment. In fact, administration of disulfiram to patients by spouses or cohabitants who had received positive reinforcement counseling with social skills training for administering the disulfiram resulted in even more therapeutic gains compared with patients receiving disulfiram on a routine basis from the cohabitant without positive reinforcement (Azrin et al. 1982). All of these studies have shown that disulfiram as an addition to other treatment modalities helps to increase the abstinence rate and is only rarely associated with serious side effects (Gallant 1991b).

Disulfiram can be used not only as an aversive agent for alcohol ingestion but also as a symbol of the patient's commitment to treatment. If the patient agrees to take disulfiram and then discontinues the medication either overtly or covertly, without notifying his or her cohabitant or the physician, this action points out the patient's strong denial and/or lack of motivation for abstinence. Disulfiram compliance can be determined by testing the urine for diethylamine, a metabolite of disulfiram.

Because disulfiram inhibits dopamine-$\beta$-hydroxylase activity, it should be used only in small doses (e.g., 125 mg/day) and with caution in alcoholic patients who have a comorbid diagnosis of schizophrenia. In such patients, it may be advisable to prescribe an adequate dopamine-blocking agent, such as a high-potency neuroleptic, during administration of disulfiram. Published reports (Berlin 1989) indicate definite problems with disulfiram-induced hepatotoxicity. Although only about 30 cases of disulfiram-induced liver damage have been reported in the world medical literature, the physician is obligated to monitor hepatic transaminases with a warning to the patient that if any clinical symptoms of hepatitis occur, the patient should immediately contact a physician and discontinue the disulfiram. If the $\gamma$-glutamyltransferase (GGT) increases two to three times over normal baseline values, disulfiram should be discontinued. In most cases, a mild GGT increase is only transient and will return to normal values without stopping the disulfiram administration.

### Naltrexone

In a 12-week double-blind, placebo-controlled evaluation of naltrexone, 50 mg/day, in 70 alcoholic patients involved in outpatient group therapy, the naltrexone group had a significantly lower relapse rate and showed a decrease in subsequent drinking in subjects who had at least one drink (Volpicelli et al. 1992). In the evaluation of those patients who had "sampled" alcohol, 95% of the placebo patients and only 40% of the naltrexone patients lost control of their drinking and met the criteria for relapse. The authors suggested that the initial drink stimulates alcohol craving in some subjects by increasing the activity of the opioid system, and blocking of this system by naltrexone dampens the alcohol craving. In another 12-week controlled study of naltrexone (O'Malley et al. 1992), 50 mg/day, and psychotherapy with specific guidelines, 97 alcoholic patients were divided into four treatment groups: naltrexone with coping skills, naltrexone with supportive therapy, placebo with coping skills, and placebo with supportive therapy. The naltrexone group was superior to the placebo subjects in abstention rate, severity of alcohol-related problems, number of drinking days, and relapse. Although the overall rate of abstinence was highest in the patient group receiving naltrexone with supportive therapy, the authors observed that those patients who received naltrexone and coping skills therapy were the least likely to relapse to heavy drinking after an initial lapse or drinking episode. Another controlled evaluation of naltrexone that used the Obsessive Compulsive Drinking Scale (Anton et al. 1995) showed a significant correlation between degree of craving and abstinence success in the naltrexone group, thus offering a possible guide as to which subgroup of alcoholic patients might be more likely to benefit from naltrexone treatment (Chick 1996). Continued treatment beyond the 12 weeks may be advisable because a 6-month follow-up "off-treatment" evaluation showed that naltrexone therapy abstinence rates had persisted only through the first month after cessation of naltrexone (O'Malley et al. 1996). Naltrexone appears to be a relatively safe compound without serious long-term side effects.

## Other Pharmacological Approaches for Reducing Alcohol Intake

The importance of the brain GABA system in relation to ethanol effects has been known for more than three decades. A more recent investigation in alcohol-preferring rats has shown a significant increase in GABA terminals in the nucleus accumbens (NA) of both alcohol-preferring and high alcohol–drinking rats as compared with control rats (Hwang et al. 1990). These basic laboratory data relate to an evaluation of GHB (a metabolite of GABA that was described in the earlier section, "Severe Alcohol Withdrawal [Alcohol Withdrawal Delirium]") in a more recent double-blind investigation for the treatment of alcohol dependence (Gallimberti et al. 1989, 1992). In this 3-month controlled evaluation of GHB (50 mg/kg/day in black cherry syrup) versus placebo, abstinence significantly increased and control drinking in the GHB group significantly improved as compared with the control group. Side effects with GHB were mild and transient.

Acamprosate (calcium acetyl homotaurinate) at oral dosages of 2,000 mg/day in controlled trials was significantly superior to placebo in terms of abstinence (Moore and Libert 1991; Sass et al. 1996). The value of two of these studies is emphasized by the length of the trials, which were of 1 and 2 years' duration (Sass et al. 1996). Acamprosate resembles L-glutamate and may indirectly block the reinforcing effects of alcohol. This compound has not yet been approved by the U.S. Food and Drug Administration (FDA) for clinical use, al-

though it is available in Europe. It should be emphasized that medications for the abstinence phase, such as disulfiram, naltrexone, GHB, and acamprosate, should be used only as part of a psychosocial-behavioral treatment program. If these drugs are used alone without such a program, the dropout rate is likely to be extremely high, and the potential value of these medications will not be realized.

At present, I am unaware of any adequately controlled studies that show lithium to be significantly superior to placebo in those alcoholic patients who do not have a comorbid diagnosis (Gallant 1985).

Clinicians should remember that not all of the answers to the treatment of alcoholic patients depend solely on psychopharmacological agents. In one very interesting controlled trial of acupuncture in severely alcoholic patients, with control patients treated at ear points ≤5 mm from the specific points of treatment, 21 of 40 patients in the treatment group completed the program compared with only 1 of 40 control patients (Bullock et al. 1989). Not only was there a significant difference between the groups in completion of the treatment program, but also more of the control patients expressed a moderate to strong need for alcohol and had more than twice the number of drinking episodes and admissions to detoxification centers as the active treatment group. These significant treatment effects persisted at the end of a 6-month follow-up. One important shortcoming of this study was that a breath analyzer was not used to monitor drinking episodes; also, no systematic attempt was made to obtain confirmatory reports of the alcoholic patients' abstinence periods by cohabitants. Nonetheless, these data are impressive enough to warrant further research to evaluate the efficacy of the specific type of acupuncture used in this study.

Although a variety of treatment methodologies are available for the alcoholic patient, no one pharmacological or psychosocial innovation will ever be significantly effective during abstinence for most of these patients seen in clinical settings despite the publicity and, at times, exaggerated importance that each new medical event receives. Each pharmacological advance requires additional psychological, behavioral, social, vocational, and sometimes legal treatment in varying degrees for each patient with a substance abuse problem. Without such support systems, even the most specific pharmacological treatment modality would be useless when the patient decides to discontinue the medication (e.g., in the multisite naltrexone study in opiate-dependent individuals; National Research Council Committee Report 1978). Although excellent environmental treatment modalities were available in the research studies detailed in this paper (e.g., O'Malley et al. 1992; Volpicelli et al. 1992), such staffing resources with individual attention to each patient are not available in many outpatient substance abuse programs and are particularly absent in primary care settings where most substance abuse patients are seen.

## Medications for Comorbid Disorders Associated With Alcoholism

Before considering the various uses of psychopharmacological agents in the treatment of coexisting psychiatric disorders in alcoholic patients, it is necessary to discuss the protracted withdrawal symptoms experienced by alcoholic individuals following cessation of alcohol intake. Some of the symptoms of protracted withdrawal syndrome (PWS) have been listed under other clinical terms such as *protracted abstinence syndrome* or *alcoholism-induced subacute organic mental disorders* (Grant et al. 1979, 1984; Schuckit 1991). Between the resolution of the acute alcohol withdrawal symptomatology and the plateau of improvement that may continue for 1 year or more following the cessation of alcohol, a slowly resolving alcohol-related PWS was described in several articles during the late 1970s (Grant et al. 1979; Kissin 1979).

Symptoms attributable to PWS include physiological variations such as changes in sleep latency and frequency of awakening; increases in respiratory rate, body temperature, blood pressure, and pulse; decrease in cold-stress response; persistence of tolerance to sedative effects; and tremor (Gallant 1982; Kissin 1979; Schuckit 1991). These patients may show frustration and irritability resulting from deficits in problem-solving, symptoms of spontaneous anxiety, and depressive episodes for no apparent reason (Gallant 1982; Grant et al. 1979, 1984). Some patients may become easily discouraged by these symptoms and resort to alcohol use in an attempt to alleviate such discomfort.

Inappropriate use of psychopharmacological agents during these periods may cause additional discomfort from anticholinergic or sedative side effects, further confusing the patient. A sensible therapeutic approach to this problem is a fully detailed explanation to the patient and the family, which will enable them to accept these symptoms as a *normal part of the withdrawal phase of alcohol*. This approach may help the patient accommodate the discomfort and maintain abstinence. The patient should realize that these symptoms are not a sign of relapse or psychological illness and that they will gradually resolve. The current literature does not contain any well-controlled evaluations of psychopharmacological medications that can alleviate the symptoms of PWS. Before the clinician diagnoses this syndrome, he or she should be sure the patient did not have a combination of such symptoms prior to alcohol abstinence and should rule out all other possible metabolic, physiological, and psychological causes for these behavioral and emotional abnormalities.

Use of antidepressant agents.   The delineation of primary versus secondary affective disorder in patients presenting the syndrome of alcoholism may be one of the most difficult diagnostic problems in psychiatry. Some patients have a history of alcoholism and affective disorder starting at approximately the same age, and it is often quite difficult to determine whether the excessive use of alcohol resulted in depression or the patient was self-medicating the depression with alcohol. Certain biographical and clinical data help the clinician to diagnose a primary major depressive disorder (or bipolar disorder): 1) affective disorder preceding the onset of alcoholism or a history of an affective disorder occurring during sustained periods of abstinence; 2) early childhood history of separation anxiety, phobic behavior, or neurasthenia; 3) occurrence of a hypomanic or manic reaction to antidepressant medication; 4) family history of bipolar illness; 5) family history of affective illness in two or more consecutive generations; and 6) a positive dexamethasone suppression test after the patient has been abstinent for 4 weeks or more (Gallant 1987). However, inadequate histories presented by some alcoholic patients create difficulties in dating the initial onset of loss of control of alcohol and the development of the affective disorder. If the affective symptomatology is secondary to excessive alcohol intake and the accompanying life failures, then the affective disorder should resolve within a period of several weeks as abstinence continues. These patients usually do not require specific psychopharmacological intervention for their affective symptomatology. However, if this secondary affective illness persists for more than 4–5 weeks despite psychotherapeutic attempts to alleviate the discomfort, then initiation of psychopharmacological therapy may be worthwhile to avoid an alcoholic relapse or suicide attempt secondary to painful affective symptomatology.

The importance of diagnosing and treating depression in alcoholic patients is emphasized by studies showing not only that depressive affect increases desire for alcohol when cues are present but also that depressed alcoholic men may be more likely to seek treatment, leading to reduction in consumption (Greeley et al. 1992).

Some of the antidepressant agents that are capable of producing sedative side effects, such as doxepin, amitriptyline, and trazodone, can be used for hypnotic purposes in alcoholic patients without fear of habituation. The sedative side effects of these antidepressants, used at relatively low doses between 25 and 100 mg at bedtime, can be quite helpful in some alcoholic patients who have a history of chronic insomnia. A controlled trial of trazodone (Nirenberg et al. 1991), 50–100 mg at bedtime, compared with placebo was conducted in 10 inpatients who were receiving nonsedating antidepressants and complaining of persistent insomnia. In a 4-day crossover study of this group, all of the trazodone patients showed significant improvement on the sleep measures compared with the placebo group. They were able to distinguish the active drug from the placebo and wanted to continue treatment with trazodone. These medications, which are not habit-forming, are easily discontinued after the patient has developed adequate sleep habits.

Use of anxiolytics.    In the treatment of generalized anxiety disorder, panic disorder, or other anxiety-related disorders in alcoholic patients, the ideal anxiolytic agent should not interfere with the patient's cognitive processes or manual dexterity or with the recovery of the patient who may be likely to abuse a habit-forming drug. The compound should be suitable, if necessary, for prolonged use without any undue risks and therefore should produce neither high-dose tolerance nor normal-dose dependence withdrawal symptoms. Only a relatively small number of well-conducted clinical trials of anxiolytic drug treatment have been done in patients with alcoholism.

Outpatient studies usually have a high dropout rate as well as deficiencies in markers of alcohol intake and abstinence. When these studies are conducted on inpatient treatment units that emphasize psychotherapy and 12-step programs, the placebo and control group therapeutic gains may be so significant that they obscure the anxiolytic efficacy of the active drug (McFarlain et al. 1976). Anxiety reduction resulting from the extensive therapy available to alcoholic patients in a carefully planned ward milieu could mask additional therapeutic gains from pharmacotherapy. In this particular environment, it may be impossible to draw any conclusions from an anxiolytic investigation unless the study includes a *very large number of patients.*

The use of benzodiazepines for anxiety reduction in alcoholic patients during their maintenance phase of abstinence is somewhat controversial. In controlled placebo studies, benzodiazepines such as diazepam and alprazolam have been shown to cause a significant increase in symptoms of euphoria not only in alcoholic men but also in the adult male offspring of alcoholic men; these offspring had not yet developed alcoholism (Ciraulo et al. 1989). If the clinician finds it necessary to use a benzodiazepine in an alcoholic patient, a good rule of thumb is to plan the duration of therapy for no more than 4–6 weeks, using that time to instruct the patient on the use of cognitive and behavior therapies to reduce the anxiety. If the alcoholic patient has a history of abusing other drugs, the use of mild to moderate doses of some antidepressant medications may be of help (Gallant et al. 1969). In one controlled evaluation of doxepin compared with diazepam in 100 abstinent chronic alcoholic inpatients who had the target symptomatology of anxiety and tension (Gallant et al. 1969), an average dose of doxepin (100–150 mg/day) appeared to be just as effective as 15–30 mg of diazepam, and this tricyclic compound lacks the habituating properties of diazepam. In addition to the potential habituation problems that benzodiazepines pose for the alcoholic patient, the side effects of decrease in performance of cognitive tasks and manual dexterity as well as the appearance of anterograde amnesia may interfere with the patient's recovery phase.

Patients with panic disorder, especially those with agoraphobia, show relatively good therapeutic responses to monoamine oxidase inhibitors (MAOIs), particularly when administered in conjunction with behavior modification techniques. In studies of social phobia, a frequent comorbid diagnosis in alcoholic patients, phenelzine has been shown to be significantly superior to both atenolol and placebo (Liebowitz et al. 1990). Hepatotoxicity has been associated with MAOIs, but the incidence appears to be relatively low in alcoholic individuals without previous severe liver pathology (Gallant 1987).

It is not unusual for a patient with adult attention-deficit/hyperactivity disorder (ADHD) to develop a problem with alcohol or drug abuse. Adult ADHD can be diagnosed only in patients who 1) have a childhood history of definite hyperactivity and attention problems and 2) have present symptoms of adult hyperactivity and difficulty with attention in addition to "two of the following five characteristics: 1) affective lability, 2) disorganization and inability to complete tasks,

3) hot temper, 4) impulsivity, and 5) stress intolerance" (Wender and Reimherr 1990, p. 1019). Concern about alcoholic individuals abusing drugs such as methylphenidate or amphetamines has made many clinicians hesitant to use these compounds, which have definite efficacy in reducing the hyperactivity of this syndrome. However, no valid data indicate that patients with this comorbid diagnosis do abuse these drugs. This ambivalence may be partially resolved by a report of bupropion treatment (an effective antidepressant) of ADHD in adults (Wender and Reimherr 1990). Caution is advised with the use of bupropion in alcoholic patients who have had a history of withdrawal seizures. Bupropion, as noted with other antidepressant drugs, tends to lower seizure threshold as the dosage is increased.

Use of neuroleptic medications.    The degree of psychopathology appears to be a predictor of treatment outcome in alcoholic patients (Rounsaville et al. 1987). Therefore, appropriate pharmacological treatment with neuroleptic drugs and supportive therapy are absolutely necessary for alcoholic patients with a comorbid diagnosis of schizophrenia. However, before making a definitive diagnosis of schizophrenia, the clinician must rule out an alcohol-induced psychotic disorder, with hallucinations and/or delusions, a syndrome that can occur within a month of alcohol withdrawal (American Psychiatric Association 1994). Patients with this disorder have delusional thought processes and/or hallucinations accompanied by a clear sensorium. Exclusion criteria of other diagnoses include no history of a primary major psychiatric disorder before the development of the alcoholism or during sustained periods of abstinence.

In one study, alcohol-induced psychotic disorder, with hallucinations and/or delusions, was reported by approximately 10% of 220 patients consecutively admitted to an inpatient alcohol treatment center. The psychotic symptoms cleared within several weeks and were not linked to a risk of schizophrenia (Schuckit 1982).

The clinician must exercise caution in the dosage regimen for these schizophrenic patients. It may well be that some of the schizophrenic patients who are abusing alcohol may actually be self-medicating one of their neuroleptic-induced side effects such as akathisia. Therefore, one must seek the minimal optimal dosage of the neuroleptic that alleviates the psychotic symptomatology but is associated with minimal to absent extrapyramidal side effects, particularly akathisia. Even though high-potency neuroleptics are usually preferable for schizophrenic patients with alcoholism because these drugs are less likely to cause uncomfortable sedation and orthostatic hypotension, it may be necessary to change the medication to a low-potency neuroleptic or one of the atypical neuroleptics, such as risperidone or olanzapine, if the akathisia cannot be controlled by a β-blocker, propranolol, or one of the standard antiparkinsonian drugs. If the patient has a history of self-medication with alcohol secondary to neuroleptic-induced akathisia, then prophylactic use of propranolol may be indicated when reinstituting a high-potency neuroleptic drug or switching to an atypical neuroleptic.

If disulfiram is added to the regimen after a neuroleptic has been initiated, the patient should be seen more frequently for close observation of possible exacerbation of psychotic symptoms (secondary to inhibition of dopamine-β-hydroxylase), which would necessitate immediate increase of the neuroleptic dosage.

The clinician should be aware that the problem of neuroleptic-induced tardive dyskinesia may be more frequent in neuroleptic-treated psychiatric patients with alcoholism than in "pure" schizophrenia. In one sample of 284 psychiatric patients who chronically abused street drugs and received neuroleptic treatment for an average of $10.5 \pm 5.8$ years, the overall incidence of tardive dyskinesia was 15.9% (Olivera et al. 1990). In those groups of psychiatric patients who abused alcohol alone or in combination with cannabis, the incidence of tardive dyskinesia was *highest:* 25.4% and 26.7%, respectively. Chronic alcohol intake may be associated with structural or chemical changes that provide a substrate for development of tardive dyskinesia when neuroleptic drugs are administered over a relatively long time. Because the use of alcohol and other drugs of abuse by psychiatric patients has increased, it is essential that future psychopharmacological investigations evaluate the effects of these psychoactive substances on the development of tardive dyskinesia in patients receiving neuroleptic therapy. In the meantime, psychiatric patients receiving neuroleptic drugs should be informed of the present data concerning the possible enhancement of neuroleptic-induced side effects by alcohol.

Use of vitamins.    It is not unusual for alcoholic patients to have one or more nutritional deficiencies such as of magnesium, zinc, and various vitamins. It is generally agreed that supplemental thiamine should be administered to all patients who have a history of chronic alcoholism. In severely symptomatic patients with alcoholic delirium presenting with hallucinations, higher oral dosages of thiamine should be considered (≥200 mg/day) because it has been shown that these individuals have a lower thiamine absorption rate than patients without hallucinations (Holzbach 1996). Thiamine administration is the recommended treatment for Wernicke's encephalopathy (Gallant 1987). Another disease that may benefit from supplemental thiamine therapy is alcoholic amblyopia, characterized by blurring of vision caused by central scotomas, which can develop into optic atrophy if untreated (Edmondson 1980). Improvement of alcoholic amblyopia has been reported in association with vitamin B supplements, but no controlled studies have been done in this area. Controlled data are similarly lacking in most of the other areas involving vitamin therapy for alcohol-related diseases. A significant percentage of alcoholic individuals have peripheral neuropathies; chronic thiamine deficiency, as well as pantothenic acid and pyridoxine deficiency, may be responsible for development of this syndrome (Gallant 1987). However, it is not known whether one or several of these vitamin deficiencies are specific causes of the development of this syndrome; it is also uncertain as to what part direct alcohol toxicity plays in producing this pathology. Multiple mega-B therapy is recommended for these patients. Thiamine therapy, vitamin A, and zinc supplements have been recommended by some clinicians for alcoholic patients who complain about night blindness. If the patient does not show any significant neurological or hematological problems secondary to chronic excessive alcohol intake, routine orders should include only thiamine, 100 mg/day, and a multivitamin supplement.

### Pharmacotherapy for organ damage secondary to chronic excessive intake of ethanol.

Concerning the available data on prophylactic therapy for large esophageal varices and recurrent bleeding from severe portal hypertensive gastropathy in men with chronic liver disease, propranolol administration appears to be the safest and most effective treatment at this time.

Other encouraging results in patients with chronic alcoholic liver disease have been reported with the use of propylthiouracil. In a long-term, double-blind randomized clinical trial of 310 alcoholic patients with mild to severe liver disease, the group receiving propylthiouracil (300 mg/day) had a mortality rate at the end of the 2-year study that was half that of the entire group receiving placebo ($P < 0.05$) and less than half that of the placebo subgroup of severely ill patients.

There even have been successful attempts by neuropsychopharmacological researchers to reverse the supposedly terminal syndrome of hepatic encephalopathy with flumazenil, a selective benzodiazepine receptor antagonist.

Other reports on alcohol-induced organ damage contain some optimistic data. In a 5-year follow-up study of liver transplantation in 147 patients with alcoholic liver disease, those patients with alcoholic hepatitis plus cirrhosis had a survival rate similar to those patients with cirrhosis alone (80% versus 84%), so a brief period of abstention was not a contraindication to surgery (Bonet et al. 1993). It should also be noted that the reduced osteoblastic activity occurring with normal osteoclastic function that is associated with alcoholic osteoporosis has the potential of being reversed by alendronate, which inhibits osteoclastic activity.

In summary, we now see serious efforts devoted not only to the treatment of alcoholism before permanent liver and CNS damage develop but also to the maintenance of patients who have already developed permanent organ damage that can shorten their lives unless pharmacological and surgical steps are taken in association with their sobriety.

## Specific Psychosocial Interventions

### Psychological and Behavioral-Biochemical Interventions

Psychological interventions.    The classical interpersonal intervention technique was originally described in 1973 (Johnson 1973). A number of modifications of this technique have been published since that time (Gallant 1987, pp. 66–68, 82–84). Early intervention with the alcoholic (or drug-abusing) individual compresses past crises caused by the misuse of alcohol into one dramatic confrontation. This confrontation helps to brush aside the denial mechanism so that the patient will agree to get help. This therapeutic maneuver is designed to help the patient immediately. The alternative is to wait interminably for the alcoholic patient to "hit bottom" and/or lose or destroy his or her family, health, or job. If the family, friends, and employer wait until the patient hits bottom, it may be far too late. Early intervention, when used with adequate preparation and sensitivity, may save the patient and the family many years of suffering and, in some cases, prevent total loss of the patient's human support systems. Adequate preparation, interpersonal sensitivity, and experience are required for this therapeutic intervention.

Behavioral interventions with biofeedback measures. Other psychological-behavioral techniques include a variety of laboratory and clinical measures undertaken to interrupt the course of alcohol abuse or dependence before inpatient hospitalization becomes necessary. In addition to the use of clinical instruments such as the Michigan Alcohol Screening Test (MAST) or CAGE questionnaire, some laboratory measures can be of help for an intervention with the alcoholic patient. In one 5-year study of 8,859 men, patients in the top 10% of the GGT distribution were requested to return for repeat analyses within 3 weeks to validate their elevated GGT values (Kristenson et al. 1983). Heavy drinking (more than 40 g of alcohol daily) was determined in 54% of the high GGT group. Patients were randomly assigned to either the intervention group or a control group. The intervention group had follow-up consultations with the same physician every third month and monthly GGT tests with positive reinforcing contacts with the same nurse, with the goal of reducing GGT levels. Instead of using a rigid goal of total abstinence, counseling with the nurse focused mainly on living habits, with the goal of reducing ethanol intake to decrease GGT values. Moderate drinking was tolerated as long as GGT values continued to decrease as the study progressed. The control subjects were informed by letter that their liver tests had revealed some damage and were told to restrict their intake of alcoholic beverages. They were also informed that they would be invited for follow-up liver tests every year. The intervention group showed significantly greater improvement than the control group in the following areas: 50% lower mortality rate, 60% fewer hospitalization days, and 80% fewer days sick or absent from work.

Even routine laboratory measures such as obtaining BALs on all emergency room patients may provide data for early intervention. Studies of positive BALs among emergency room patients have shown that up to 25% have BALs and 16% have readings above 0.10%, which is the legal intoxication limit in most states (Teplin et al. 1989).

## Social Interventions

I believe that all physicians should be aware of the primary and secondary prevention measures that involve legal as well as laboratory procedures to intervene early in the course of this widespread illness and that they have a moral responsibility to play an active role in their community for preventing alcohol-related deaths.

Legal approaches. One legal approach for detecting early cases of alcohol and/or drug abuse is screening the driving records of individuals convicted of driving under the influence of alcohol (DUI). The DUI records have shown that the average time interval between DUI convictions decreases with each subsequent arrest and conviction (Maisto et al. 1979). After an initial DUI conviction, recommendation by the court for compulsory treatment and/or education on alcoholism can provide an opportunity for a therapeutic intervention with family and friends as well as by the court. Compulsory treatment of such traffic violators may be helpful if the duration of the sentence is long enough to work out the subject's initial anger when the sentence provides harsh penalties for noncompliance (Gallant et al. 1968).

Another type of legal intervention approach involves compulsory treatment of paroled *criminal alcoholics* (Gallant et al. 1968). The findings in this study suggested that enforced clinic attendance is a valuable parole technique for follow-up treatment of the criminal alcoholic patient after release from prison.

Taxing alcoholic beverages to reduce per capita consumption, a form of public health intervention, is a politically sensitive subject (Cook 1982). Many researchers in the field of alcoholism believe that a significant increase in alcohol taxes may have a much greater impact than expensive national education efforts and treatment services to reduce alcohol-related morbidity and mortality. In an excellent review, Cook (1982) used cirrhosis mortality rates (a good indicator of heavy drinking during the previous one to two decades) to show that 30 states that raised their liquor tax during the years 1960–1974 had a significantly greater reduction in cirrhosis mortality than other states during the same years. In this study, the states' cirrhosis mortality rates were reduced by 1.97% for each $1 tax increase for each proof gallon of liquor. Using a parametric statistical method for these data, it was predicted that doubling the United States federal alcohol tax would reduce the nation's cirrhotic mortality rate by at least 20%. A beneficial side effect would be reduction of the United States budget deficit.

Educational approaches. Studies suggest that incorporation of a peer-led cognitive-behavioral intervention within the school curricula may have some effect on dissuading adolescents from using alcohol and other drugs (Botvin et al. 1990). The results of this study indicated that the *peer booster condition* (older student leaders) produced significantly fewer users of alcohol, tobacco, and marijuana than did the teacher-led program. Surprisingly, the teacher-led program produced results that were no better and, in some instances, even worse than control conditions. Some of the shortcomings of the study included the use of a select student population with an absence of urban or central city schools and the disappointing failure of most of the teachers to implement the intervention according to the research protocol. The results of this study are still extremely promising, and the peer-condition cognitive-behavioral approaches described in this investigation should be evaluated in other school populations, particularly because this effective technique is less expensive in personnel time than teacher-led programs. The most obviously difficult and serious challenge is the alcohol and drug abuse problem among school dropouts in poverty areas, a problem that will probably not significantly decrease without accompanying immense social and economic changes in addition to treatment intervention strategies (Gallant 1991a).

In families with histories of child abuse, spouse battery, or other types of extreme violence such as rape or assault, it is not uncommon to find the problem of alcoholism (Gallant 1987). The tragic consequences of alcohol abuse and alcoholism do provide opportunities for specific social interventions in these cycles of abuse. Identification of the alcoholic offender and assurance that this individual receives follow-up treatment to avoid future violence are the moral responsibility of all medical personnel.

The specific psychosocial intervention measures described in this section of the chapter should be considered as only several of many potential intervention measures that are available and as only the initial steps to reduce the morbidity and mortality rates caused by the devastating illness of alcoholism, which affects all segments of society.

# References

American Psychiatric Association: Diagnostic and Statistical Manual of Mental Disorders, 3rd Edition. Washington, DC, American Psychiatric Association, 1980

American Psychiatric Association: Diagnostic and Statistical Manual of Mental Disorders, 4th Edition. Washington, DC, American Psychiatric Association, 1994

Anton RF, Moak DH, Latham P: The Obsessive Compulsive Drinking Scale: a self-rated instrument for the quantification of thoughts about alcohol and drinking behavior. Alcohol Clin Exp Res 19:92–99, 1995

Azrin WH, Sisson RW, Meyers R, et al: Alcoholism treatment by disulfiram and community reinforcement therapy. J Behav Ther Exp Psychiatry 13:105–112, 1982

Babor TF, Hoffman M, Del Boca FK, et al: Types of alcoholics, I: evidence for an empirically derived typology based on indicators of vulnerability and severity. Arch Gen Psychiatry 49:599–608, 1992

Ballenger JC, Post RM: Kindling as a model for alcohol withdrawal syndromes. Br J Psychiatry 133:1–14, 1978

Baumgartner GR, Rowen RC: Follow-up cross-over comparison of clonidine with chlordiazepoxide in alcohol withdrawal management. Journal of Psychiatry and Neurology 1:5–6, 1988

Becker HC, Hales RL: Repeated episodes of ethanol withdrawal potentiate the severity of subsequent withdrawal seizures: an animal model of alcohol withdrawal "kindling." Alcohol Clin Exp Res 4:243–247, 1993

Benzer D, Cushman P Jr: Alcohol and benzodiazepines: withdrawal syndromes. Alcohol Clin Exp Res 4:243–247, 1980

Berlin RG: Disulfiram toxicity: a consideration of biochemical mechanism and clinical spectrum. Alcohol Alcohol 24:241–246, 1989

Bonet H, Kramer D, Wright HI, et al: Liver transplantation for alcoholic liver disease: survival of patients transplanted with alcoholic hepatitis. Alcohol Clin Exp Res 17:1102–1106, 1993

Botvin GJ, Baker E, Filazzola AD, et al: A cognitive-behavioral approach to substance abuse prevention: one year follow-up. Addict Behav 15:47–63, 1990

Boyer CS, Petersen DR: Potentiation of cocaine-induced hepatotoxicity by acute and chronic ethanol. Alcohol Clin Exp Res 14:28–31, 1990

Bullock ML, Culliton PD, Olander RT: Controlled trial of acupuncture for severe recidivist alcoholism. Lancet 1:1435–1438, 1989

Chick S: New insights into alcoholism treatment. Paper presented at the annual meeting of the American Psychiatric Association, New York, May 1996

Ciraulo DA, Barnhill JG, Ciraulo AM, et al: Parental alcoholism as a risk factor in benzodiazepine abuse: a pilot study. Am J Psychiatry 146:1333–1335, 1989

Cloninger CR, Sigvardsson S, Bohman M: Type I and Type II alcoholism: an update. Alcohol Health Res World 20:18–23, 1996

Cook PJ: Alcohol taxes as a public health measure. British Journal of Addiction 77:244–250, 1982

Cushman P, Forbes R, Lerner W, et al: Alcohol withdrawal syndromes: clinical management with lofexidine. Alcohol Clin Exp Res 9:103–108, 1985

Edmondson HA: Pathology of alcoholism. Am J Clin Pathol 74:725–742, 1980

Fuller RD, Williford WO: Life-table analysis of abstinence in a study evaluating the efficacy of disulfiram. Alcohol Clin Exp Res 4:298–301, 1980

Gallant DM: Psychiatric aspects of alcohol intoxication, withdrawal, and organic brain syndromes, in Alcoholism and Clinical Psychiatry. Edited by Solomon J. New York, Plenum, 1982, pp 73–93

Gallant DM: Does lithium have value in the treatment of alcoholism? Alcohol Clin Exp Res 9:297–298, 1985

Gallant DM: Alcoholism: A Guide to Diagnosis, Intervention and Treatment. New York, WW Norton, 1987, pp XII–XIII

Gallant DM: Alcohol and drug abuse prevention in adolescents. Alcohol Clin Exp Res 15:308–309, 1991a

Gallant DM: Recent advances in research and treatment of alcoholism and drug abuse, in ASAM Review Course Manual. Edited by Geller A. New York, ASAM, 1991b, pp 589–618

Gallant DM, Faulkner M, Stoy B, et al: Enforced clinical treatment of paroled criminal alcoholics. Quarterly Journal of Studies on Alcohol 29:77–83, 1968

Gallant DM, Bishop MP, Guerrero-Figueroa R: Doxepin versus diazepam: a controlled evaluation in 100 chronic alcoholic patients. J Clin Pharmacol 9:57–61, 1969

Gallimberti L, Gentile N, Canton G, et al: Gamma-hydroxybutyric acid for treatment of alcohol withdrawal syndrome. Lancet 2:787–789, 1989

Gallimberti L, Ferrara SD, Fadda F, et al: Gamma-hydroxybutyric acid in the treatment of alcohol dependence: a double-blind trial. Alcohol Clin Exp Res 16:673–676, 1992

Gerrein JR, Rosenberg C, Manohar V: Disulfiram maintenance in outpatient treatment of alcoholism. Arch Gen Psychiatry 28:798–802, 1973

Grant I, Adams KM, Reed R: Neuropsychological abilities of alcoholic men in their late thirties. Am J Psychiatry 136:1263–1268, 1979

Grant I, Adams KM, Reed R: Aging, abstinence, and medical risk factors in the prediction of neuropsychologic deficit among long-term alcoholics. Arch Gen Psychiatry 41:710–718, 1984

Greeley J, Swift W, Heather N: Depressed affect as a predictor of increased desire for alcohol in current drinkers of alcohol. British Journal of Addiction 87:1005–1012, 1992

Holzbach E: Thiamine absorption in alcoholic delirium patients. J Stud Alcohol 57:581–584, 1996

Hwang BH, Lumeng L, Jang-Yen W, et al: Increased number of GABAergic terminals in the nucleus accumbens is associated with alcohol preference in rats. Alcohol Clin Exp Res 14:503–507, 1990

Hyashida M, Alterman AI, McClellan AT, et al: Comparative effectiveness and costs of inpatient and outpatient detoxification of patients with mild to moderate withdrawal syndrome. N Engl J Med 320:358–365, 1989

Johnson V: I'll Quit Tomorrow. New York, Harper & Row, 1973

Kissin B: Biological investigations in alcohol research. J Stud Alcohol 8:146–181, 1979

Kraus ML, Gottlieb LD, Horwitz RI, et al: Randomized clinical trial of atenolol in patients with alcohol withdrawal. N Engl J Med 313:905–909, 1985

Kristenson H, Ohlin H, Hulten-Nosslin M-J, et al: Identification and intervention of heavy drinking in middle-aged men: results of follow-up of 24–60 months of long-term study with randomized controls. Alcohol Clin Exp Res 7:203–209, 1983

Liebowitz MR, Schneir F, Campeas R, et al: Phenelzine and atenolol in social phobia. Psychopharmacol Bull 26:123–125, 1990

Litt MD, Babor TF, DelBoca FK, et al: Types of alcoholics, II: application of an empirically derived typology to treatment matching. Arch Gen Psychiatry 49:609–614, 1992

Maisto SA, Sobell LC, Zelhart PF, et al: Driving records of persons convicted of driving under the influence of alcohol. J Stud Alcohol 40:70–77, 1979

Malcolm R, Ballenger JC, Sturgis ET, et al: Double-blind controlled trial comparing carbamazepine to oxazepam treatment of alcohol withdrawal. Am J Psychiatry 146:617–621, 1989

Manhem P, Nilsson LH, Moberg AL, et al: Alcohol withdrawal: effects of clonidine treatment on sympathetic activity, the renin-aldosterone system, and clinical symptoms. Alcohol Clin Exp Res 9:238–243, 1985

Mayo-Smith MF: Pharmacological management of alcohol withdrawal. JAMA 278:144–151, 1997

McFarlain RA, Mielke DH, Gallant DM: Comparison of muscle relaxation with placebo medication for anxiety reduction in alcoholic inpatients. Current Therapeutic Research 20:173–176, 1976

Moore N, Libert C: Acamprosate, citalopram, and alcoholism (letter). Lancet 1:1228, 1991

Mueller TI, Stout R, Rudden S, et al: A pilot study of carbamazepine treatment of alcohol dependence. Abstract presented at the annual meeting of the American College of Neuropsychopharmacology, San Juan, PR, 1995

National Research Council Committee Report (CENA): Clinical evaluation of naltrexone treatment of opiate-dependent individuals. Arch Gen Psychiatry 35:335–340, 1978

Nirenberg AA, Adler LA, Peselow E, et al: A controlled trial of trazodone in antidepressant-associated insomnia. Abstract presented at the annual meeting of the American College of Neuropsychopharmacology, San Juan, PR, December 11–15, 1991

Olivera AA, Kiefer MW, Manley NK: Tardive dyskinesia in psychiatric patients with substance use disorders. Am J Drug Alcohol Abuse 16:57–66, 1990

O'Malley SS, Jaffe AJ, Chang G, et al: Naltrexone and coping skills therapy for alcohol dependence: a controlled study. Arch Gen Psychiatry 49:881–887, 1992

O'Malley SS, Jaffe AJ, Chang G, et al: Six-month follow-up of naltrexone and psychotherapy for alcohol dependence. Arch Gen Psychiatry 53:217–224, 1996

Pattison ME: Management of alcoholism in medical practice. Med Clin North Am 61:797–809, 1977

Project MATCH Research Group: Matching alcoholism treatments to client heterogeneity: Project MATCH posttreatment outcomes. J Stud Alcohol 58:7–29, 1997

Raine A, Venables PH, Williams M: Relationships between central and autonomic measures of arousal at 15 years and criminality at age of 24 years. Arch Gen Psychiatry 47:1003–1007, 1990

Ries RK, Roy-Byrne PP, Ward NG, et al: Carbamazepine treatment for benzodiazepine withdrawal. Am J Psychiatry 146:536–537, 1989

Romach MK, Sellers EM: Management of the alcohol withdrawal syndrome, in Annual Review of Medicine. Edited by Creger WP, Coggins CH, Hancock EW. Palo Alto, CA, Annual Reviews Inc, 1991, pp 323–339

Rounsaville BJ, Dolinsky ZS, Babor TF, et al: Psychopathology as a predictor of treatment outcome in alcoholics. Arch Gen Psychiatry 44:505–513, 1987

Saitz R, Mayo-Smith MF, Roberts MJ, et al: Individualized treatment for alcohol withdrawal. JAMA 272:519–523, 1994

Sass H, Soyka M, Mann K, et al: Relapse prevention by acamprosate: results from a placebo-controlled study on alcohol dependence. Arch Gen Psychiatry 53:673–680, 1996

Schuckit MA: The history of psychotic symptoms in alcoholics. J Clin Psychiatry 43:53–57, 1982

Schuckit MA: Chlormethiazole (Heminevrin): a drug for alcohol withdrawal? Drug Abuse Alcohol News 19:1–3, 1990

Schuckit MA: Is there a protracted abstinence syndrome with drugs? Drug Abuse Alcohol News 20:1–3, 1991

Schweizer E, Rickels K, Case WG, et al: Carbamazepine treatment in patients discontinuing long-term benzodiazepine therapy: efects on withdrawal severity and outcome. Arch Gen Psychiatry 48:448–452, 1991

Sellers EM, Zilm DH, Degani NC: Comparative efficacy of propranolol and chlordiazepoxide in alcohol withdrawal. J Stud Alcohol 38:2096–2108, 1977

Sereny G, Sharma V, Holt J, et al: Mandatory supervised Antabuse therapy in an outpatient alcoholism program: a pilot study. Alcohol Clin Exp Res 10:290–292, 1986

Sullivan JT, Sykora K, Schneiderman J, et al: Assessment of alcohol withdrawal: the revised Clinical Institute Withdrawal Assessment for Alcohol Scale (CIWA-Ar). British Journal of Addiction 84:1353–1357, 1989

Sullivan JT, Swift RM, Lewis DC: Benzodiazepine requirements during alcohol withdrawal syndrome: clinical implications of using a standardized withdrawal scale. J Clin Psychopharmacol 11:291–295, 1991

Teplin LA, Ebram KM, Michael SK: Blood alcohol level among emergency room patients; a multivariate analysis. J Stud Alcohol 50:441–447, 1989

Volpicelli JR, Alterman AI, Hyashida M, et al: Naltrexone in the treatment of alcohol dependence. Arch Gen Psychiatry 48:876–880, 1992

Wender PH, Reimherr FW: Bupropion treatment of attention-deficit hyperactivity disorder in adults. Am J Psychiatry 147:1018–1020, 1990

Whitfield CL: Nondrug detoxification, in Phenomenology and Treatment of Alcoholism. Edited by Whitfield C. New York, Spectrum Press, 1980

# 17 Cannabis

Mark S. Gold, M.D.
Michelle Tullis, Ph.D. candidate

**M**arijuana is the second most commonly smoked drug and the most frequently used illicit drug in the United States. Its use sharply increased among America's youth and college students in the late 1960s and the 1970s. Use declined in the 1980s and is now on the rise again. The University of Michigan's Monitoring the Future Study (Johnston 1998), which assesses drug and alcohol use among American youth, reported substantial increases in use among eighth, tenth, and twelfth graders from 1992 through 1996. While the Institute of Medicine conducts a risk-benefit study of the potential for cannabis and cannabis derivatives in medicine, Americans are spending more than $15 billion a year for marijuana for nonmedicinal purposes (Chalsma and Boyum 1994).

Why do people smoke marijuana? This question is complex, but it appears that no one smokes marijuana to produce a cough, bronchitis, memory problems, hoarseness, paranoia, or performance problems. The simple answer is that they smoke to obtain the euphoria that marijuana produces. Although, an increasing number of people claim that they smoke marijuana for relief of a diverse range of symptoms. People generally smoke for the positive reinforcement, which makes self-administration possible and likely. Laboratory animals *will* self-administer tetrahydrocannabinol (THC), like other drugs of abuse, and receive neurochemical effects on the putative reward neuroanatomy similar to those of other drugs of abuse (Childers and Breivogel 1998; Gardner and Lowinson 1991; Tanda et al. 1997). These drugs are usually taken for the state they produce rather than the abstinence state they reverse. In this sense, the drive for marijuana intoxication is similar to that for cocaine or alcohol.

The relative risk of marijuana use is approximately equal for men and women; therefore, the historical assumption of male predominance of substance abuse does not apply to cannabis (Kendler and Prescott 1998). Women appear to develop drug dependence more rapidly than do men, and there is the additional concern for women who use drugs during pregnancy and while nursing. Both male and female use of marijuana is age related. Use increases throughout the teens, peaks in the early 20s, and declines thereafter. Marijuana use decreases sharply in users in their 20s (Bachman et al. 1997).

## Forms and Types of Marijuana

Marijuana, the combined leaves, stems, and flowering tops of *Cannabis sativa*, can be used in a variety of forms. It is most commonly smoked via a rolled cigarette or in a pipe or bong (water pipe). Oral ingestion is less common; however, marijuana is sometimes baked in brownies. According to the National Institute on Drug Abuse (NIDA), marijuana potency varies considerably—from 1% to 15% or more—with most ordinary marijuana containing an average of 3% THC. Sinsemilla, the buds and flowering tops of female plants, has an average THC concentration of 7.5%, although it can be as high as 24%. Hashish, or hash, is the resin obtained from the female plant flowers and has an average of 2%–8% THC and can contain up to 20% THC. It is prepared by collecting the resin on the cannabis leaves or by boiling the plant. Hashish oil is even more potent, containing up to 30% THC, and involves distilling the plant in organic solvents (Gold 1989).

There is a lot of controversy over what marijuana smoke actually is and does. In comparisons between ingestion of dronabinol (Marinol), the oral form of

$\Delta^9$-THC, and inhalation of cannabis, THC produced antinociception, catalepsy, anticonvulsive activity, hypothermia, hyperexcitability, and depression of motor activity through interaction with a specific cannabinoid receptor. However, the slower onset of dronabinol made it less reinforcing than the smoked marijuana (Beal et al. 1995; Stimmel 1995). The marijuana plant contains more than 400 compounds, not all of which have been characterized. Therefore, extrapolations from THC to smoking are tenuous. Cannabis potency is related to agricultural factors such as light and soil, genetic strains, and how the leaves are handled after harvesting. Cannabis growing in hotter, dryer climates produces more of the resin containing the psychoactive ingredients, whereas cannabis grown in temperate climates produces more fibrous stalk.

## History

C. sativa is Latin for planted hemp. Historically, cannabis use can be traced to prehistoric times when it was hailed "the father of Chinese medicine" during China's Nung dynasty in 2327 B.C. It was also a staple in India in 2000 B.C. and throughout the Arab world since the tenth century. Cannabis may be the earliest non-food-bearing plant cultivated by humans (Abel 1980).

By the mid-nineteenth century, cannabis was prescribed for everything from gonorrhea to tetanus, but after it was recognized as a drug of abuse, the 1937 Marijuana Tax Act banned its use. Widespread cultivation and use preceded the discovery that THC, the prototypical cannabinoid, exerts many of its central effects by binding to cannabinoid-1 receptors in the peripheral and central nervous system and by binding to cannabinoid-2 receptors on immune cells (Pertwee 1998).

## Epidemiology

Marijuana is the most commonly used and the most controversial illicit drug in America. Although only 2% of all Americans had ever tried an illicit drug in the early 1960s, recent data suggest that marijuana use is an alarming fact of preteen and teenage life in America. We reported evidence of a reversal in the trend of decreasing illicit drug use each year from 1985 to 1992 (Gold et al. 1993); subsequently, marijuana smoking, cigarette smoking, and use of other illicit drugs increased in all ages of school-age children studied (Gold and Gleaton 1994). By 1994, 4%–5% of the general

population and 15%–20% of high school seniors had used marijuana at least once a month. According to the 1998 National Household Survey on Drug Abuse, 13.9 million Americans age 12 and older used illicit drugs in 1997. For youth ages 12–13, the rate of current use of cigarettes increased significantly from 7.3% in 1996 to 9.7% in 1997. Marijuana was the most frequently used illicit drug, with 60% of all illicit drug users reporting use of marijuana only and another 20% using marijuana and another illicit drug. For young people ages 12–17 years, the survey found an increase in current use of drugs, primarily marijuana. The rate of marijuana use increased from 7.1% in 1996 to 9.4% in 1997. A 1994 report by the National Center on Addiction and Substance Abuse found that youth between ages 12 and 17 years who use marijuana are 17–85 times more likely to use cocaine than youth who abstain from marijuana. The range is dependent on age at onset and frequency of use.

The rise in marijuana use has also been confirmed by the Monitoring the Future Study reported by the University of Michigan and NIDA (see Figure 17–1).

Figure 17–1 shows that marijuana smoking among eighth graders increased from 12% in 1991 to 22% in 1997. Consistent with this increased use, the National Association of State Drug and Alcohol Directors reported that 137,564 American received treatment for marijuana abuse in 1994 (Rueshe 1997).

## Patterns of Use and Abuse

Varying patterns of use and abuse are associated with marijuana. The level of abuse appears to be indigenous to the individual, but the following variables should be considered:

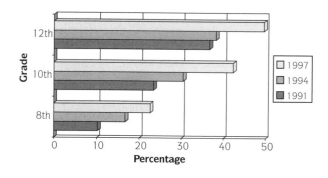

**Figure 17–1.** Lifetime marijuana use in eighth, tenth, and twelfth graders. *Source.* Johnston L: *Monitoring the Future Study, University of Michigan.* National Institute on Drug Abuse, 1998.

- Demographics: age, sex, geographic location
- Social factors: multicultural issues, socioeconomic status, parental influence, education
- Individual factors: psychological, physiological, and emotional status

The continuum of use includes the experimental, occasional, daily, and chronic user. The chronic user is compulsive to the point of smoking the first marijuana joint on awakening and throughout the day. Typical users smoke marijuana on the weekend to "relax" or "socialize." These individuals often smoke in social settings.

Much more is known about the factors associated with adolescents' initiation into drug use than about the factors associated with cessation. Aging is a potent predictor of cessation. Maturity is associated with different interests, needs, and attitudes, including decreased risk-taking and increased conformity. Teen characteristics for use, such as risk-taking, delinquent activities, low religiosity, depression, and low self-esteem, are less likely to appear in adults. There appears to be a relative incompatibility between using illicit drugs and participation in conventional roles of adulthood (Chen and Kandel 1998). Chen and Kandel's recent study suggested that controlling for all other factors, the two most important predictors of stopping marijuana use were frequency of use and age. Infrequent users and those in their late 20s were most likely to stop using. Frequent users were more persistent in their use, and many became dependent. Using for social reasons accelerated cessation, whereas using to enhance positive feelings and reduce negative feelings was associated with persistence of use. Many of these smokers "grow out" of their marijuana use as a result of maturity, family, education, and employment.

Marijuana use is often related to social context and the acceptability of marijuana among peers. Interactions with drugs and drug users are a persistent risk factor. Social role participation is related to discontinuation; for example, when illicit drug users assume an expected social role, such as getting married or becoming pregnant, they are more likely to stop using a drug.

## Factors Associated With Marijuana Use

Numerous variables have been studied to explain adolescent marijuana use. For example, high school students who are academic achievers, are involved in athletics or school activities, are strongly religious, work few hours outside of school, and spend few evenings out during the week are less likely to use marijuana. An adolescent who has frequent interactions with marijuana and marijuana users is persistently at risk.

Recent data suggest that unhealthy behaviors such as fasting and other weight control measures are also associated with teenage marijuana and alcohol use (Neumark-Sztainer et al. 1998). Many weight-conscious young women would rather smoke marijuana than drink alcohol because of the caloric properties inherent in alcohol. Although genetic factors appear to have a minimal effect on the probability of using marijuana, genetics do affect the likelihood of abuse and dependence. Another possible reason for teen use may be related to THC's function in modifying brain function and hormones. More research is needed, but it cannot be a coincidence that marijuana use is associated with puberty (Asch et al. 1981).

Students who graduated from high school in 1992 were at far less risk of using marijuana than those who graduate today. Some experts blame the proponents of legalization for the resurgence in marijuana use (Dupont and Voth 1995). Proponents of legalization try to minimize the consequences of drugs, particularly smoking marijuana, to support their political goals. The debate regarding medicinal use of marijuana also may play a role. Just as a physician would not tell a patient with ulcerative colitis to smoke tobacco cigarettes, even though nicotine has a beneficial effect on the natural history of the disease, smoking marijuana leaves is unlikely to emerge as a "medical treatment." The outcome of controlled cannabinoid research will likely be a series of important new compounds that use cannabinoid systems to exert their effects but that are administered orally, inhaled in their pure form, or administered rectally and produce little or no euphoria. As with other potent chemicals, decisions as to their availability for medical use should remain with the U.S. Food and Drug Administration (FDA), which can weigh the risk-benefit ratios, rather than with a referendum process.

Changes in what teenagers smoke have continued since the 1960s, along with changes in marijuana importation, domestic production, hydroponics, and selective breeding. The THC content of marijuana continues to change and may play a role in the increase in teen smoking. Marijuana is usually sold by a "brand" name that correlates roughly to THC concentration. From Gainesville Green, to KGB, to Krippie, the price of marijuana and its THC content increase respectively. THC content has risen dramatically. In the 1960s, a typical marijuana cigarette contained 0.6% THC, whereas today, a wide range of strengths is available, some as high as

50%. Users can select the "type" and length of high they want for a particular situation. In controlled studies, the higher the THC content, the more users prefer and self-administer it (Kelly et al. 1994).

Increase in marijuana use by teens also may be a result of changes in perception of the danger associated with marijuana use (Bachman et al. 1998). Investigators attribute increases to a decrease in cost, low rate of peer disapproval, decrease in perceived danger, and the connection with the resurgence of cigarette smoking. The media has played a role in glamorizing marijuana in movies, television, and so on. These changes in perceived danger (see Figure 17–2) have persisted as marijuana use has continued to increase.

High school seniors who perceived marijuana use as dangerous and who disapproved of use among their friends were much less likely to use marijuana. Yet, the sharpest national decline in perceived drug danger has been reported for marijuana. In 1991, 79% of twelfth graders thought that regular marijuana users were at great risk for harming themselves. But by 1995, only 61% held that opinion. Peer disapproval rates continue to decline: only 57% now disapprove of experimenting with marijuana. Interestingly, marijuana availability, which has been relatively constant for the last 20 years, does *not* correlate with the changes in use. However, others have shown that for users there appears to be a separation between acknowledging the harmfulness of marijuana and using it. Attitudes toward marijuana use affect initiation but not cessation. Simply changing users' attitudes on perceived harmfulness of a drug may not be sufficient to enable cessation of substance use.

Of today's high school seniors, 4.6% currently smoke marijuana daily compared with 2.9% of tenth graders. In some high schools, smoking marijuana every day is now more common than drinking alcohol. Even though marijuana use has shown the sharpest increase, the use of other illicit drugs, including lysergic acid diethylamide (LSD), hallucinogens other than LSD, amphet-

amines, stimulants, and inhalants, has also continued to increase. This finding suggests that the increases are attributable, at least in part, to cultural influences that minimize the danger and/or glamorize drug taking. In fact, 41% of teens and 53% of their parents state that American culture glamorizes the use of illegal drugs (National Center on Addiction and Substance Abuse 1996). Paradoxically, today's teens are hearing and seeing less about the dangers and consequences of drug use while receiving more encouragement to use and hearing more about the positive aspects of drug use. Many rap bands, alternative groups, and rock musicians exploit marijuana and other drug themes in their lyrics. The net result is mixed messages. Drugs are not only being touted as safe, but a subliminal message is being sent that it is okay to use drugs. Survey data regarding parental expectations support this hypothesis. In a study published in 1996, the Center for Addiction and Substance Abuse at Columbia University found that 65% of baby boomer parents who had used marijuana regularly expected their own children to use, compared with only 29% of baby boomer parents who had never used. Consequently, parental attitudes and expectations regarding the risks of drug use are contributing and validating factors in the growing acceptance of marijuana use among teens.

## Learning How to Smoke

Cigarette and marijuana smoking are strongly correlated, with cigarette smoking historically preceding onset of marijuana use. In order to smoke marijuana, one must learn to take smoke into the lungs; this is not a normal behavior for any species. To inhale and hold toxic smoke in the lung long enough for the psychoactive constituents to be absorbed require the user to resist the primal, biological urge to cough. Once the brain and lungs are trained via cigarettes, it becomes much more natural to smoke marijuana, crack, or heroin. In our recent survey of university students, virtually no one had smoked crack, heroin, or methamphetamine without smoking cigarettes or marijuana as a precursor (Gold et al., in press).

## The Tobacco/Marijuana Connection

Smoking manipulates the effects of marijuana. Our data (Gold et al., in press) from a random sample of university students suggested that curiosity is the primary reason for initial marijuana use. Concurrent use with tobacco or alternating use appears to make mari-

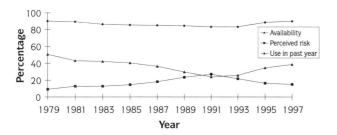

**Figure 17–2.**    Trends in availability, perceived risk, and use of marijuana for twelfth graders.

juana more inviting. Cigarettes may boost and sustain the marijuana high and may also reverse some of the more negative effects of marijuana, such as decreased arousal and attention.

Cigarette smoking has typically initiated marijuana smoking behavior, but recent data from the University of Florida (Gold et al., in press) are showing not only a reversal in this trend but also the concurrent initiation of tobacco and marijuana smoking in some students 2–3 years later than those students smoking only tobacco. It appears that teens are smoking marijuana, then rapidly initiating tobacco smoking because of the discovery that nicotine not only sustains, but also enhances, the marijuana high.

According to the 1998 National Household Survey on Drug Abuse, an estimated 64 million Americans (30%) reported smoking tobacco within 30 days prior to the interview. Approximately 4.5 million youths ages 12–17 (19.9%) had smoked cigarettes in the past month in 1997. For those youth ages 12–13, the increase in past month cigarette use was statistically significant (from 7.3% in 1996 to 9.7% in 1997).

Historically, marijuana use has been linked to prior and current use of legal drugs available to adults, specifically, alcohol and tobacco (Kandel 1975). This progression of drug involvement from legal to illegal drugs, also termed the *gateway theory*, has been reported for decades (Adler and Kandel 1981), although the mechanism for this progression is debated. Recent experience, however, suggests that alcohol is not always a precursor to marijuana and that marijuana use nearly always precedes use of cocaine, crack, and heroin. With the growing prevalence of marijuana use, the importance of alcohol as a gateway to marijuana appears to have declined. However, marijuana use as a preview to both legal and illegal drug use appears to have increased (Golub and Johnson 1994).

## Clinical Psychopharmacology

### Administration

Marijuana can be ingested orally, but the most common mode of administration is by smoking and inhalation. Smoking is a method of cannabinoid and smoke delivery that appears to be quite reinforcing in teens and young adults. The principal psychoactive constituents $\Delta^8$-THC and $\Delta^9$-THC were isolated in the 1960s (Gaoni and Mechoulam 1964). Marijuana smoke contains more than 400 compounds in addition to the major psychoactive component, $\Delta^9$-THC. Many of the cannabinoids

and other complex organic compounds appear to have psychoactive properties, and most have not been tested for long- or short-term safety in animals or humans. $\Delta^9$-THC is more prevalent in marijuana and more potent than $\Delta^8$-THC; therefore, most of the psychoactivity is attributed to $\Delta^9$-THC. The lack of precise correlation between peak high and $\Delta^9$-THC has suggested the importance of THC metabolism in the high. Smoking delivers THC to the brain in seconds, thereby being one of the quickest routes of administration. Intensity of central brain rewarding effects is usually correlated with the rapidity of hitting the brain. Marijuana is rapidly absorbed from the lungs, and THC and major metabolites can be traced throughout the body and brain. Up to 59% of smoked THC is absorbed, compared with only 3% when taken orally. Reports are now surfacing that marijuana users are dipping their joints and cigars ("blunts") into embalming fluid, a compound composed of formaldehyde, methanol, ethanol, and other solvents. Users believe these cigarettes burn more slowly, thereby slowing the rate of absorption. "Fry," the street name for this technique, is sometimes laced with phencyclidine (PCP) and appears to be an adolescent trend (Khun et al. 1997). (For more detailed discussion of marijuana neurobiology, see Martin, Chapter 5, in this volume.)

### Intoxication

According to DSM-IV (American Psychiatric Association 1994), acute marijuana intoxication begins with a "high" feeling followed by symptoms described in Table 17–1. In addition to euphoria, users report an increase in hunger and a state of relaxation. Individual differences in intoxication are explained on the basis of THC concentration, frequency of use, smoking abilities of the user, and genetic and psychiatric risks. Intoxication develops within minutes if smoked but usually takes at least 30 minutes if ingested orally. "The effects usually last 3–4 hours, the duration being somewhat longer when the substance is ingested orally. The magnitude of the behavioral and physiological changes depends on the dose, the method of administration, and the individual characteristics of the person using the substance, such as rate of absorption, tolerance, and sensitivity to the effects of the substance" (American Psychiatric Association 1994, p. 217).

Motor performance, ability to drive a car or an airplane, concentration, and alertness may be affected for hours to days. Because most cannabinoids, including $\Delta^9$-THC, are fat soluble, the effects of cannabis or hash-

**Table 17–1.**   DSM-IV diagnostic criteria for cannabis intoxication

A.   Recent use of cannabis.

B.   Clinically significant maladaptive behavioral or psychological changes (e.g., impaired motor coordination, euphoria, anxiety, sensation of slowed time, impaired judgment, social withdrawal) that developed during, or shortly after, cannabis use.

C.   Two (or more) of the following signs, developing within 2 hours of cannabis use:

    (1)   conjunctival injection
    (2)   increased appetite
    (3)   dry mouth
    (4)   tachycardia

D.   The symptoms are not due to a general medical condition and are not better accounted for by another mental disorder.

ish may occasionally persist or recur for 12–24 hours because of a slow release of psychoactive substances from fatty tissue or to enterohepatic circulation (Naditch 1974). Visual distortions, including object size and distance (Isbell et al. 1967), decrease in color discrimination, and decrease in ocular motor tracking (Adams et al. 1975), have been reported. Decreased recognition and analysis of peripheral visual field light stimuli have also been reported (Moskowitz et al. 1972).

These visual distortions and perceptual problems are especially troublesome for the marijuana-intoxicated driver or worker. Motor performance is further compromised by the drug intoxication state that can result in a pleasurable sense of floating, the loss or distortion of the sense of time, and failure to calculate proper braking time. In our experience, these persons believe that they are able to drive and may even volunteer as a "safe ride" for an alcohol-impaired friend. Fatal traffic accidents occur more often in individuals who test positive for cannabinoids than in the general population. THC is second to ethanol as the drug most frequently detected in the blood of drivers cited for impaired driving. State police used a rapid urine test to identify reckless drivers who may be under the influence of cocaine or marijuana; of 150 subjects who were stopped and provided a urine sample, 59% tested positive. Intoxicated drivers were difficult to characterize because of many differences in driving, behavior, and appearance. Toxicological screening at the roadside is a practical means of identifying drivers under the influence of drugs and as an adjunct to standard roadside sobriety testing (Brookoff et al. 1994).

In addition, in tests of flying, using the simulated flying paradigm, the marijuana-related loss of motor and complex analysis skills and judgment decreases the pilots' ability to land safely (Janowsky et al. 1976).

Concurrent use of tobacco cigarettes or crack appears to extend the normal course of marijuana-induced effects. Marijuana-induced vasodilation of the nasal mucosa attenuates the vasoconstrictive effects of cocaine and thus increases absorption (Lukas et al. 1994). Marijuana also impairs the emesis normally produced by acute alcohol poisoning and can be associated with youth alcohol toxicity. However, acute marijuana intoxication alone rarely results in a medical emergency. Occasionally, acute intoxication can cause psychological distress to the point that the user complains and seeks help for the unpleasant and negative affect, fearfulness, anxiety, or depression.

## Adverse Psychiatric Reactions

Marijuana smoking experience, mood, dose, and route of administration determine whether the smoker becomes euphoric or dysphoric. Dysphoria occurs more commonly when marijuana is eaten, probably because of the facility of dose titration when marijuana is smoked rather than swallowed. Cannabis that is taken in high doses or is extremely potent has psychoactive effects that can cause emergency presentations that are difficult to differentiate from those of hallucinogens such as LSD. Paranoid ideation and persistent paranoia ranging from suspiciousness to frank delusions also may be associated with use. We have seen college students with marijuana-related ideas of reference, depersonalization, and derealization.

Panic, anxiety, nausea, dizziness, and a general difficulty in expressing even simple thoughts in words may be associated with marijuana use. Marijuana usually does not cause psychiatric disorders, but in an individual who is predisposed to a psychiatric illness, marijuana use may trigger episodes of panic attacks, paranoia, anxiety, and even psychoses (Novak 1980). These episodes are not necessarily indicative of a psychiatric diagnosis because the symptoms typically reside after the user "comes down" from the high. However, patients with schizophrenia have relapsed to psychotic behavior after smoking marijuana. In their most extreme forms, psychiatric manifestations of marijuana intoxication may result in emergency room or student health service presentations. Naive users, especially older individuals, or those exposed to high-potency marijuana tend to be the most common groups seeking treatment.

Effects of cannabis and $\Delta^9$-THC in humans include disruption of short-term memory, cognitive impairment, a sense of time distortion, and enhanced body awareness. Sometimes marijuana's effects may be at odds with the individual's personality and goals, leading to extremely negative reactions. For students focused on grades and time, the loss of time or time perception distortion may provoke negative affect and other reactions not generally seen in others. These idiosyncratic reactions may be caused by the particular type of marijuana smoked, the setting, or the individual's biological blueprint. In other cases, laboratory analysis of the substance (e.g., looking for PCP), interviewing those who smoked with the patient, and assessing for family history of substance abuse or other psychiatric disorders will help the psychiatrist to determine the causative factors. In these instances, there is almost always a "teachable moment," and even the addicted person can be receptive to medical counseling.

## Clinical Syndromes

### Dependence

Studies (Warner et al. 1995) suggest that 9.2% of those who ever use marijuana will eventually meet DSM-IV criteria for dependence. Another study (Hall 1994) suggested that 20% of individuals who smoke several times will meet these criteria. An increasing number of college students in the United States are presenting for treatment of their marijuana use, complaining of loss of control of use, preoccupation, inability to stop despite adverse consequences, narrowing of interests, and an uneasy feeling that they may be addicted. Users report selling everything from furniture to football tickets to obtain the most potent marijuana. Marijuana acquisition and use become primary, and school, work, or recreational activities become secondary. Clinicians are evaluating and treating more marijuana-dependent patients than ever before. These patients typically establish a pattern of chronic use that gradually increases in both frequency and amount, and according to researchers at the Center for Psychosocial Studies in New York, users believed marijuana improved their self-awareness and overall functioning. They also appeared to use marijuana to avoid stress-inducing situations (National Institute on Drug Abuse 1997).

Chronic use sometimes results in a diminished or complete loss of the pleasurable effects of marijuana, which establishes a pattern of tolerance to the drug.

Marijuana-dependent patients report that they repeatedly fail at attempts to cut down, ration, or limit their use and that they are easily angered by questions relating to their marijuana use. They often smoke their first marijuana cigarette on awakening and report feelings of guilt about their use and the consequences. Many of these patients have had losses of career, family, and friends. Some addicted persons report that they grow their own marijuana and smoke throughout the day, maintaining a personal relationship with their plants and paraphernalia. Addiction does not end when the drug is removed from the body (detoxification) or when the acute post-drug-taking illness dissipates (withdrawal). Rather, the disorder can persist and produce a tendency to relapse. Individuals with cannabis dependence, like other addictions, are compulsive users.

### Tolerance

Chronic exposure to cannabinoids must be carefully studied for addiction and withdrawal syndrome in humans. Decreased cerebellar metabolic rates in habitual marijuana users may reflect neuroadaptive changes and also marijuana's effects on motor coordination, learning, and proprioception (Gatley and Volkow 1998). Chronic administration of cannabinoids to animals results in tolerance to many acute effects, including locomotor changes (Abood et al. 1993; Oveido et al. 1993). Tolerance to $\Delta^9$-THC develops quickly and continues long term after cessation of treatment (Fride 1995). Tolerance develops to anandamide (arachidonyl ethanol-amide; ANA), a naturally occurring compound in the brain that binds with cannabinoid receptors, and cross-tolerance develops between THC and ANA. Tolerance in humans has also been reported (Hollister 1986) and usually appears with doses of at least 3 mg/kg/day. Withdrawal can be readily produced after chronic cannabis administration (Aceto et al. 1995; Rodriquez de Fonseca et al. 1997; Tsou et al. 1995). Dependence and tolerance develop simultaneously and for some drugs are related to the severity of withdrawal symptomatology.

### Withdrawal

Recent studies (Wickelgren 1997) suggest that marijuana influences the brain's stress and reward systems in the same way as opiates, nicotine, and cocaine. The neural substrates responsible for the reinforcement of drug seeking, as well as the emotional stress of withdrawal noted in individuals addicted to cocaine and heroin, are identical. Withdrawal from cocaine, alcohol, and opiates increases intracellular corticotropin-releasing factor (CRF), producing concomitant anxiety and stress. Researchers at the Scripps Institute hastened THC withdrawal in rats with a cannabinoid antagonist, which produced increases in CRF, anxiety, and stress. These results provide a neurochemical model for marijuana withdrawal that is consistent with the current understanding of drug withdrawal and the emotional symptoms commonly observed in marijuana users who abruptly discontinue use.

The slow release of THC and active metabolites from lipid stores and other areas may explain the so-called carryover effects on driving and other reports of behavioral changes over time. THC and possibly other psychoactive ingredients accumulate in the brain and other fat-rich areas and form what has been described by N. Volkow (personal communication, June 1998) as a depot. This may explain the slow excretion and minimal acute withdrawal signs on abrupt discontinuation and also the effects on T cells and other immunological cells. Although acute withdrawal complaints are rarely reported, thoughts and dreams about marijuana smoking, mental cloudiness, irritability, and other behavioral signs are commonly reported for months after discontinuation of chronic marijuana smoking. It is logical to assume that brain cannabinoids decrease after prolonged marijuana smoking, as has been suggested in recent studies (Romero et al. 1997). Dependence is easily demonstrated though cannabinoids are not avidly self-administered (Dewey 1986). Like nicotine and cocaine, cannabinoids increase dopamine levels in the mesolimbic system (Tanda et al. 1997).

## Overdose

Marijuana overdose is rare, and no deaths have been reported. However, the inhibition of the vomiting reflex may be associated with toxic and potentially lethal consequences caused by the combination of alcohol and marijuana. Marijuana is generally used with other drugs and alcohol and can alter the typical presentation of drug withdrawal and intoxication. College students are infamous for failure to report drug problems from emergencies to overdoses. They cite fear of legal consequences, academic expulsion, and even using parental insurance as reasons for not seeking medical assistance. Additionally, most college students are underage and use a wide range of substances to obtain a "high." Thus, users are often unable to communicate to peers exactly what they have ingested. At rave parties, other attendees may be afraid to get involved.

The identification and localization of the cannabinoid receptor in the brain has greatly advanced the knowledge of molecular mechanisms of marijuana. A receptor with a unique and specific distribution has been shown to have the most dense binding in the outflow nuclei of the basal ganglia. These areas—the forebrain and cerebellum—may have a function in the cognition and movement changes experienced with cannabinoid intoxication. The paucity of receptors in the brain stem could explain why large doses of marijuana do not lethally suppress cardiovascular and respiratory function (Herenham et al. 1990).

Some advances have been made in identifying and testing an antagonist in animals, but little progress has been made in determining which drugs activate the cannabinoid system indirectly by inhibiting the tissue uptake or metabolism of endogenous cannabinoids. Interestingly, new data suggest that nonsteroidal anti-inflammatory drugs inhibit ANA hydrolysis; therefore, ibuprofen may cause special problems when used by marijuana smokers (Pertwee 1998). Eventually, the availability of novel THC antagonists will allow us not only to treat overdoses but also to identify those patients who are physiologically dependent on marijuana. Precipitated withdrawal with a selective antagonist in rats chronically treated with $\Delta^9$-THC was unequivocally shown for the first time in a recent report (Aceto et al. 1995).

 ## Medical Implications

### Respiratory

The effects of marijuana smoking on human health have been studied since the 1970s and are similar to the effects of tobacco smoking on the respiratory system. Chronic marijuana smoking (at least 4 days a week for 6–8 weeks) results in mild airway obstruction that may not be reversed, even with continued abstinence. Marijuana smoking can also cause decreased exercise tolerance, chronic cough, bronchitis, and decreased pulmonary function (Tashkin et al. 1976; Tilles et al. 1986). Lung function decreases even more significantly with concurrent use of tobacco cigarettes. Both marijuana and tobacco increase the number of inflammatory cells in the lung, but they differentially affect the activation of these inflammatory cells, possibly leading to differential effects on lung injury and physiological consequences, including altered alveolar epithelial permeability (Kelp et al. 1995). Cannabis smoke is highly irritating to the nasopharynx and bronchial lining and thus increases the risk for chronic cough and other signs and symptoms of nasopharyngeal pathology. Sinusitis, pharyngitis, bronchitis, emphysema, and pulmonary dysplasia may occur with chronic, heavy use.

Much of the risk of smoked marijuana comes from the products of combustion; however, some risk may be directly attributed to the process of smoking marijuana (i.e., deep inhalation and long breath holding). Several cases of pneumothorax have been reported among marijuana smokers and attributed to this form of inhalation (Feldman et al. 1993). The risks related to products of combustion of marijuana are also comparable to those of tobacco smoke. Smoked tobacco delivers more than 3,000 chemicals, including cyanide and other toxins, directly to the lungs via carbon monoxide gas. Regular cigarettes contain 15 mg of tar each, whereas low-tar cigarettes contain 7 mg. Marijuana smoke contains 3.8 times more tar than tobacco smoke and 50% more carcinogenic hydrocarbons (Wu et al. 1988). Smoking marijuana produces a fivefold greater increase in blood carboxyhemoglobin levels compared with smoking tobacco (Tashkin et al. 1988a).

Although THC is thought to have bronchodilatory properties, work by Tashkin and colleagues (1977, 1988b) identified large airway bronchoconstriction following marijuana smoking similar to the effects seen in reactive airway disease. Long-term effects include lung immune system dysfunction, as evidenced by studies on pulmonary macrophages (Baldwin et al. 1997).

## Immunology

Animal studies have clearly established that marijuana and synthetic and endogenous cannabinoids change the natural function of immune cells (Klein et al. 1998). Cannabinoids are immunomodulators altering immune system homeostasis. Cannabinoid receptors are found on white blood cells, but whether marijuana increases a nonimmunosuppressed or an immunosuppressed person's risk of acquiring an infection has yet to be proven. Even at low doses, marijuana suppresses natural killer cell activity and may also suppress cytotoxic T lymphocytes and macrophages. Although human studies are contradictory, several showed that marijuana use impairs the immune system; animal studies provide firmer evidence of immune system impairment. Both marijuana and THC contribute to acute phase response. THC decreases signals to helper T cells and interferes with macrophage antigen processing. Long-term impairment of the immune system may increase the risk of cancer.

## Cancer

No discussion of the risks associated with marijuana smoking is complete without mention of its carcinogenic potential. Epidemiological evidence strongly implicates cigarette smoking as a causative factor in pulmonary malignancy. Barsky et al. (1998) recently reported that marijuana appears to cause molecular damage to the lungs similar to that of cigarettes. Smoking both marijuana and tobacco puts the smoker at greater risk for cancer than either alone. Marijuana smoke contains even larger amounts of known carcinogens than does tobacco, and heavy use may increase the risk of developing malignant disease. Risk of cancer of the respiratory system from lips, mouth, pharynx, larynx, trachea, bronchi, and lung is significantly increased in smokers. Evidence correlates marijuana smoking with earlier onset and greater dysplastic changes in several types of head and neck malignancies (Barsky et al. 1998; Denissenko et al. 1996; Fligiel et al. 1997; Matthias et al. 1997).

## Cardiovascular

There is a causal relationship between cardiac and pulmonary vascular diseases and smoking marijuana and tobacco (Wu et al. 1988). In fact, right heart disease and pulmonary hypertension may be more common and/or severe in marijuana smokers than nonsmokers. Marijuana smoking almost immediately produces a significant increase in heart rate (Stillman et al. 1976), with inversion or flattening of the T wave on electrocardiogram (ECG), elevation of the ST segment, and increase in the amplitude of the P wave with occasional premature ventricular contractions. These cardiovascular effects can aggravate existing cardiac conditions or hypertension. The tachycardia associated with marijuana use appears to result from parasympathetic and sympathetic stimulation of the cardiac pacemaker; however, it is not clear whether β-adrenergic stimulation is involved (Beaconsfield et al. 1972). Fortunately, these changes in cardiac function can usually be reversed by abstinence.

## Sexual Dysfunction and Related Issues

Initiation of marijuana smoking is occurring among younger populations. Naturally, the toxic effects of marijuana are greater on developing than on developed organisms. THC also modifies sexual hormone function and rhythm at a crucial developmental stage. THC has mainly inhibitory effects on pituitary luteinizing hormone (LH), prolactin, and growth hormone (GH) and has little or no effect on follicle-stimulating hormone (FSH) secretion. Recently, the purification and availability of the putative endogenous ligand for the cannabinoid receptor, ANA, have provided the opportunity to compare the effects of THC and ANA on the female neuroendocrine system in ovariectomized rats. Both THC and ANA decrease serum LH level, although THC to a higher degree. No significant differences were observed in serum FSH level. Both drugs decreased serum prolactin. Serum GH was increased after THC administration and significantly decreased after ANA administration. The results indicate that THC and ANA alter pituitary hormone secretion mainly by inhibitory action (Wenger et al. 1995).

Marijuana is reported to decrease plasma testosterone, sperm count, and sperm motility (Kolodny et al. 1974). Marijuana is antiandrogenic, and many of its components, including $\Delta^9$-THC, bind to androgen receptors. Whether these antiandrogenic effects result in decreased libido or impaired fertility is not clear (Dupont and Voth 1995). Marijuana use can disrupt the female reproductive system; women who use marijuana four or more times a week have shorter menstrual cycles, elevated prolactin levels, and depressed testosterone levels, with galactorrhea occurring in as many as 20% of these patients (Cohen 1985). Animal studies also show a suppression of ovarian function, interference with gonadotropin and estrogenic activity, and amenorrhea associated with marijuana use.

Women who smoke marijuana during pregnancy often have babies with low birth weights, and those with the highest consumption of marijuana have the lowest birth-weight babies. One study found numerous abnormal responses, including increased startle reflex, tremors, poor self-quieting, and failure to habituate to light, in newborns whose mothers used marijuana during pregnancy (Jones and Chernoff 1984). In addition, THC has been shown to cross the placental barrier, and it accumulates in mothers' milk (Fehr and Kalant 1983).

## Effects on College Students and Adolescents

### Neuropsychological

In college students who heavily smoke marijuana, long-lasting and demonstrable neuropsychological defi-

cits, including problems in executive functioning, attention, new-word learning, and verbal fluency that persisted beyond intoxication, have been reported (Pope and Yurgelun-Todd 1996). In our recent survey (Gold et al., in press), marijuana users had significantly lower grade point averages than nonusers. In addition to these studies, Lundavist (1995) studied approximately 400 cannabis users (use from 6 months to 25 years) over a 10-year period. Lundavist described a cannabis-state-dependent set of cognitive processes. Participants who used marijuana had weak analytic and synthetic skills, difficulty sorting and classifying information correctly, poor concentration, and weak psychospatial skills such as differentiating time and space. These changes were observed in individuals who used cannabis regularly or more than once every 6 weeks (the approximate elimination time of THC) for more than 2 years. These data suggest that cannabis-induced cognitive processes result from temporary prefrontal dysfunction because the symptom pattern is similar to that of prefrontal syndrome. This hypothesis is further supported by the greater density of cannabinoid receptors in the forebrain than in the hindbrain. The effects of marijuana on memory, cognition, coordination, and judgment remain long after the subjective feelings of the "high" have subsided.

### Behavioral

Multiple brain systems are affected by marijuana use. Cerebral blood flow and cerebral metabolism are tightly coupled to brain function and used as indices of brain activity. In a recent study (Matthew et al. 1998), cerebral blood flow response to THC showed a marked increase in bilateral frontal regions, insula, and cingulate gyrus of the right hemisphere, peaking 30–60 minutes after intravenous infusion. Marijuana users also had decreased cerebral metabolism at baseline. Marijuana intoxication impairs time perception. A positron-emission tomography study showed an increase in cortical and cerebral blood flow following THC administration. Cerebral blood flow was decreased in those patients with a significantly altered time sense (Matthew et al. 1998). Additional studies may ultimately suggest that the most profound effects occur on brain structures where survival drives and emotions are centered and in the prefrontal regions, which sustain attention, shift focus, and promote adaptation to environmental change and new learning. The effects are often illusive and disguised by other addictive behaviors. For example, we noted that individuals who regularly use marijuana are vastly underemployed in positions that require less cognitive challenge or technological acuity. In one study, heavy users were significantly more impaired than light users when attempting attentional and executive functions. These cognitive differences remained after the researchers controlled for levels of premorbid functioning and other substance use (Pope and Yurgelun-Todd 1996). This ultimately results in a general lowering of life's goals and decreased ability to attain or even establish goals, now called the *chronic cannabis syndrome* and formerly referred to as *amotivational syndrome.*

For the millions of teens who use marijuana, the cumulative effects on their developing intellect and character will leave many woefully unprepared for the challenges of adulthood. Consider the educational and employment potential for a young person who has a compromised memory, limited ability to handle multiple stimuli, and lapses in motivation. The loss of human potential and the subsequent cost to society will continue to be substantial.

# Treatment

## Marijuana Treatment Research

Although little research has been done in the area of marijuana dependence treatment, contrary to popular belief, marijuana dependence does not always present in the context of polydrug abuse. Treatment for other drugs of abuse does not always recognize or effectively treat marijuana abuse (Budney et al. 1997). Relapse prevention appears to play a key role in the success rate of treatment. The ritualistic and behavioral components inherent in marijuana users, like tobacco smokers, raise unique concerns for the treatment provider. Issues related to environmental cues, the frequency with which the drug is dosed, and the culture surrounding marijuana use should be incorporated into any treatment protocol.

Self-efficacy, a judgment about one's ability to perform a specific behavior in a specific context, is also a consideration according to Stephens et al. (1995). Marijuana users seeking treatment appear to be motivated, and self-empowerment encourages the belief that they can live successfully without smoking marijuana. Marlatt and Gordon (as cited in Stephens et al. 1995) suggested that the availability of an alternative coping response in a high-risk situation would increase self-efficacy even more.

## Presentation for Treatment

In the current cohort of college students we observed, treatment was sought after decompensation of academic, social, and physical performance. Although changes are typically subtle, problems are usually first recognized by teachers, significant others, and friends. The student often fails to make the association between their marijuana use and their social, academic, and health problems. Early manifestations are behavioral: non-drug-using friends feel estranged, rigorous activities are dropped, interests are narrowed, and preoccupation with acquiring and using marijuana and socializing in places where marijuana is used is common. Friends and loved ones may instigate a visit to a health care provider as a direct result of poor classroom attendance, confrontations with the university judicial system, poor grades, or concomitant psychiatric disorders.

Drug testing may be a major reason that marijuana-smoking students seek treatment. Positive test results lead to a referral, but students also want and ask for help in quitting before an interview or a test with a major national employer. Testing fears appear to be a new major concern, and according to our recent survey (Gold et al., in press), many students seeking internships, employment, or admittance to higher education face the prospect of failing the pre-employment drug test. They are afraid that they cannot stop using marijuana for 1 week or 1 month to obtain a job. Fear of a positive drug screen can alter their career path significantly, inhibiting application for employment or termination of employment after a positive screen. Marijuana counseling should be facilitated with an open, non-judgmental attitude and patience while the student goes through the process of accepting the loss of his or her current lifestyle.

## Diagnosis of Marijuana Dependence

Diagnosis of marijuana dependence is not specifically addressed in DSM-IV. Diagnosis of cannabis intoxication (see Table 17–1) does not immediately suggest dependence in the same way that acute alcohol intoxication does not prove dependence. However, marijuana dependence is more likely to be identified in smokers and those with recent marijuana use. To diagnose marijuana dependence, we have proposed using quick office-based assessments similar to those commonly used to diagnose alcohol dependence. The following quick and reliable test (CAGE) can be administered easily in the physician's office:

1. C—Have you felt the need to Cut down on your marijuana use?
2. A—Are you easily Angered when questioned about your drug use?
3. G—Do you feel Guilty about your marijuana use?
4. E—Do you smoke first thing in the morning (Eye opener)?

Pathological attachment, despite adverse consequences, and loss of control are hallmarks of marijuana dependence. However, *when* loss of control actually occurs is a question that most addicted persons cannot answer. Avoidance of activities that do not include marijuana is a good indicator though. This avoidance is shown by changes in friends, sports, and school interests and initiation of amotivational behavior. Lack of clear thought processes, dreaming, and preoccupation with drug use provide the clinician an opportunity for intervention and treatment. These early signs are not pathognomonic and mistakes can be made, but early intervention is crucial. Urine samples can confirm evidence of recent use.

Diagnosing the use and abuse of marijuana by a clinical interview alone is often difficult. Interviews with parents and significant others combined with laboratory results will assist in the diagnosis. The user may be brought for evaluation based on marijuana use or change in motivation, behavior, and/or performance. Less often, users may come in themselves to seek a diagnosis. Finally, drug use may lead to involvement with the criminal justice system through drug courts, accidents, criminal activity, or a random drug test. Regardless, most marijuana-dependent individuals eventually come to medical attention and can then be evaluated after a positive urine sample.

Drug testing.    Urine tests generally identify cannabinoid metabolites. Because these substances are fat soluble, they persist in bodily fluids for extended periods and are excreted slowly. Routine urine tests for cannabinoids in individuals who casually use cannabis can be positive for 7–10 days; urine tests in individuals who heavily use cannabis may be positive for 2–4 weeks. With marijuana use on the rise, both governmental and private workplaces have implemented pre-employment drug testing. Millions of people are being tested for the use of marijuana and other drugs of abuse. Most test sites collect urine specimens and send them to large laboratories for results. Recently, self-contained urine drug testing kits have been marketed and used for fast results. Although the validity of these "home" tests compared with their predecessors has been questioned, they do seem to produce results consistent with gas chromatography/mass spectrometry at higher THC levels (Jenkins et al. 1995).

## General Overview of Treatment Process

Treatment of marijuana dependence, as with that for other drugs, must be individualized for the highest probability of success. Addictions are chronic disorders, not acute conditions like a broken leg. Detoxification does not address the underlying disorder and thus is not adequate treatment (O'Brian and McLellan 1996). Many chronic marijuana smokers successfully stopped using for short periods, only to start again for no apparent reason. It is hard to imagine that physical dependence is driving this addictive behavior, but similar patterns are seen with other drugs, including alcohol, nicotine, cocaine, and heroin.

Before actual treatment begins, an accurate history is essential, and all dependencies must be recognized. The 12-step programs based on the principles of Alcoholics Anonymous are at the core of most treatments.

The treatment of marijuana addiction has three general phases, all of which revolve around the addicted person's pathological attachment to the drug:

1. *The process of developing the willingness to enter treatment or what Alcoholics Anonymous calls the desire to stop using.* The first phase of treatment includes many important tasks, such as decreasing social tolerance for the use of marijuana, alcohol, and other drugs. The modern structured intervention is an organized approach to overcoming the most basic stages of denial to get addicted people into treatment. In this phase, the clinician must approach the patient in an accepting and caring manner, yet confrontation may be necessary at this time to break through denial.
2. *The process of stopping use.* The second phase of treatment can be done on either an inpatient or an outpatient basis. Patients manifesting acute medical symptoms should be admitted and assessed for additional diagnoses. Inpatient treatment is also essential for suicidal patients. Most marijuana-dependent patients, however, can receive outpatient treatment. During this phase, patients often grieve the loss of their drug and use defense mechanisms to resist treatment. Emotional support is paramount at this point.

3. *The process of staying clean and sober.* The third phase of treatment is when relapse prevention and the 12-step programs—Alcoholics Anonymous, Narcotics Anonymous, Al-Anon, and other programs built on the foundation of Alcoholics Anonymous—play their biggest role.

## Crisis Intervention

Many addicted persons will seek treatment in response to a crisis, be it physical, emotional, or drug-induced panic. The clinician should be able to respond to these individuals with crisis intervention skills. A Rogerian approach of genuine concern is recommended. The clinician should be calm and reassuring on the basis of his or her experience with marijuana-related crisis. After assessment for suicidal ideation, a drug screen should be administered. Patients typically minimize their drug use, and the results will prove helpful even after the crisis is over. Many users admit to the least "offensive" drug, often describing recent alcohol, cigarette, and marijuana use and failing to mention the heroin they have been sniffing or methylenedioxymethamphetamine (MDMA) they have been taking. After an initial assessment, admission to an inpatient treatment facility or detoxification unit may be needed if other drugs or significant medical or psychiatric problems are involved. If the patient is medically stable, the clinician should give immediate attention to the problem that initiated the patient's desire for help. Using listening skills and allowing the patient to talk through the crisis will often diffuse the situation. Reassurance that "this too shall pass" and use of cognitive and behavioral skills may be particularly effective.

## Inpatient Treatment

The least restrictive environment is generally recommended when patients are first attempting to stop using drugs. However, the patient's mental state, impulsivity, history, and safety must remain primary concerns. Outpatient treatment has the advantage of enabling addicted patients or drug abusers to incorporate and confront the everyday problems they will encounter without the use of drugs. Inpatient treatment, an intense program involving residential treatment or hospitalization, is appropriate when the patient has

- Continuing drug use after outpatient treatment
- Medical and/or psychiatric complications
- A limited support system at home

- An intent to harm self or others
- A dual diagnosis requiring expertise in dealing with multiple issues

## Group Therapy

"Group therapy has become the most frequently used modality for all classes of drug abusers" (Millman and Beeder 1994, p. 105). This approach is extremely effective in helping those patients who are isolated from nonusers, who are in denial, and who have limited experience with detoxification and long-term abstinence. A viable peer group can be a part of the group process and provide a major positive in the recovering person's life at a time when giving up marijuana is perceived as such an overwhelming loss. Peers can provide a template for recovery through their own lives and experiences. Cathartic sharing coupled with confrontation allow users to recognize their typical defense mechanisms. Gestalt techniques are useful as well, enabling patients to "talk" to their drug-using friends, parents, or other people they may have difficulty with. A great deal of shame is often involved with drug use and consequent behavior. A group setting will offer support and validation of feelings.

## Individual and Family Psychotherapy

Treatment with either relapse prevention or social support paradigms has been the outpatient approach used by many clinicians because both are associated with substantial reductions in frequency of marijuana use and problems. However, treatment appears to be the most successful for those who smoke the least (Budney et al. 1997). In a study of 161 men and 51 women seeking treatment for marijuana use (Stephens et al. 1995), cognitive-behavioral relapse prevention treatment resulted in greater self-efficacy and a decrease in post-treatment marijuana use. Acknowledging the dangers of using marijuana had no effect on cessation. Overcoming denial is relevant to accepting the possibility that treatment has anything to offer. However, even though attitudes toward marijuana use affect tobacco smoking initiation, these attitudes do not appear relevant to successful cessation of tobacco use.

Individual and family psychotherapy may be particularly effective in helping patients accept the loss of time and goals, reconcile their ambitions, and plan for the future. Individual work can help with the anger the addicted person directs at self and the developmental and cognitive issues that a sober 20-year-old will need to address after spending adolescence and college under the influence. Individual sessions should address

- Issues too painful to share in group therapy
- Goal-setting
- Behavioral contracts, if needed
- Identification of problems specific to patient
- Issues related to dual diagnosis, if relevant
- Discussion of feelings about group process

Family psychotherapy can be a useful adjunct to individual and group counseling, especially if the patient has issues specific to the family. Often the patient is the only one who receives treatment, and family members are left to deal with the pain on their own. A therapeutic environment is essential for all participants when addressing family issues, such as trust and anger, because these feelings have been anesthetized for so long in the marijuana user. A skilled clinician will be able to uncover the problems and facilitate growth among all participants.

## Prevention and Intervention

While researchers question the respective causes and effects to explain the current escalation in marijuana smoking, others have tried to summarize what is known and describe marijuana use and risk factors that might be more protective (Bachman et al. 1998) (Table 17–2). Recent studies support the conclusion that youths do pay attention to credible information about the dangers of drug use and that the reduction in demand that occurred during the 1980s was a result of this approach (Bachman et al. 1997).

All physicians, especially pediatricians, should be cognizant of the possibility of drug use in their patients and of the importance of providing sound medical information to their patients, patients' family, and community. Physicians should stress the importance of how parental attitudes about drugs, not just illicit drugs, can influence their offspring. All annual physical examinations and hospital or office visits should also establish smoking (tobacco, marijuana) status. Simply including smoking status among the vital signs gathered at a routine physical examination may elicit important information and establish smoking prevention as an integral part of the examination. Prevention and early intervention with initiation and maintenance of abstinence are effective treatments that can be applied by all physicians.

Physicians should also recognize that adolescent attitudes can be used to help prevent drug abuse. For example,

- Almost half of the teenagers who use marijuana regularly fear being caught by law enforcement. An even greater number fear getting caught by parents or school authorities.
- About 4 out of 10 adolescents fear that their drug use will negatively influence siblings.
- One teenager in three is afraid of obtaining impure marijuana; twice that number fear impure cocaine or crack.
- Nearly 6 out of 10 teenagers fear that cocaine use will lead to physical or psychological damage; half of them fear becoming dependent on the drug (Black 1988).

Prevention of smoking is the first priority. If that fails, postponing onset into marijuana use, reducing the extensiveness of use, increasing commitment to conventional social roles, and reducing delinquent participation are important interventions that appear likely to shorten any marijuana use, which, as long as use remains illegal, is most likely to stop by the 30s.

**Table 17–2.**    Protective and risk factors associated with marijuana abstinence and use

| Protective factors associated with decreased marijuana use | Risk factors associated with increased marijuana use |
| --- | --- |
| Increased parental presence in the home | Easy access to illicit drugs |
| Student focus on school and grades | Cigarette smoking |
| Teens who are very "connected" to their parents | Peers who smoke cigarettes or marijuana |
| Personal importance placed on religion and prayer | Working 20 or more hours/week (ninth to twelfth graders) |
| Few nights out with peers | Appearing older |
| High self-esteem | Low grade point average |
| High levels of school "connectedness" | Sexually deviant behavior |
| Disapproval and avoidance of peers who smoke | Perceived risk of untimely death |

# Conclusion

Marijuana is an important drug of abuse associated with numerous physical and psychological consequences. Marijuana is usually smoked and thus serves as a potential "gateway" to other smokeable drugs. Regardless of whether progression to other drug use occurs, however, the subtlety of symptoms and user denial can create substantial problems. Predicting or measuring the loss of drive, memory, and motivation and altered quality of human relationships is difficult. Pathological attachment to marijuana forms the basis of the marijuana dependence diagnosis. To the casual observer, marijuana, like alcohol, is perceived as another choice of the smorgasbord of recreational experience. For family members and concerned others, marijuana is the focus of considerable anxiety, and they experience it as a robber of family life, relationships, motivation, potential, time, and quality of life.

# References

Abel EL: Marijuana: The First Twelve Thousand Years. New York, Plenum, 1980

Abood ME, Sauss C, Fan F, et al: Development of behavioral tolerance to delta-9-THC without alteration of cannabinoid receptor binding or mRNA levels in whole brain. Pharmacol Biochem Behav 46:575–579, 1993

Aceto MD, Scates SM, Lowe JA, et al: Cannabinoid precipitated withdrawal by the selective cannabinoid receptor antagonist SR 141716A. Eur J Pharmacol 282:R1–R2, 1995

Adams AJ, Brown B, Flom ME, et al: Alcohol and marijuana effects on static visual acuity. American Journal of Optometry and Physiological Optics 52:729–735, 1975

Adler I, Kandel DB: Cross-cultural perspectives on developmental stages in adolescent drug use. J Stud Alcohol 42:701–715, 1981

American Psychiatric Association: Diagnostic and Statistical Manual of Mental Disorders, 4th Edition. Washington, DC, American Psychiatric Association, 1994

Asch RH, Smith CG, Siler-Khodor TM, et al: Effects of delta-9-tetrahydrocannabinol during the follicular phase of the rhesus monkey (Macaca mulatta). J Clin Endocrinol Metab 52:50–55, 1981

Bachman JG, Wadsworth KN, O'Malley PM, et al: Smoking, Drinking, and Drug Use in Young Adulthood: The Impacts of New Freedoms and New Responsibilities. Mahwah, NJ, Lawrence Earlbaum Associates, 1997

Bachman JG, Johnston LD, O'Malley PM: Explaining recent increases in students' marijuana use: impacts of perceived risks and disapproval, 1976 through 1996. Am J Public Health 88:887–892, 1998

Baldwin GC, Taskin DP, Buckley DP, et al: Marijuana and cocaine impair alveolar macrophage function and cytokine production. Am J Respir Crit Care Med 156:1606–1613, 1997

Barsky SH, Roth MD, Kleerup EC, et al: Histopathologic and molecular alterations in bronchial epithelium in habitual smokers of marijuana, cocaine, and/or tobacco. J Natl Cancer Inst 90:1198–1205, 1998

Beaconsfield P, Ginsburg J, Rainsbury R: Marijuana smoking: cardiovascular effects in man and possible mechanisms. N Engl J Med 287:209–212, 1972

Beal JE, Olson R, Laubenstein KL, et al: Dronabinol as a treatment for anorexia associated with weight loss in patients with AIDS. J Pain Symptom Manage 10:89–97, 1995

Black GS: Changing attitudes toward drug use. Reports from The Media-Advertising Partnership for a Drug-Free America, Inc. New York, The Gordon S Black Corporation, 1988

Brookoff D, Cook CS, Williams C, et al: Testing reckless drivers for cocaine and marijuana. N Engl J Med 331: 518–522, 1994

Budney AJ, Kande DB, Cherek DR, et al: Marijuana use and dependence. Drug Alcohol Depend 45:1–11, 1997

Chalsma AL, Boyum D: It is not abuse (ONDCCD Publication). Washington, DC, Marijuana Situation Assessment Office of National Drug Control Policy, 1994

Chen K, Kandel DB: Predictors of cessation of marijuana use: an event history analysis. Drug Alcohol Depend 50:109–121, 1998

Childers SR, Breivogel CS: Cannabis and endogenous cannabinoid systems. Drug Alcohol Depend 51:173–187, 1998

Cohen S: Marijuana and reproductive functions. Drug Abuse and Alcoholism News 13:1, 1985

Denissenko MF, Pao A, Tang M, et al: Preferential formation of benzo(a)pyrene adducts at lung cancer mutational hotspots in P53. Science 274:430–432, 1996

Dewey WL: Cannabinoid pharmacology. Pharmacol Rev 38:151–178, 1986

Dupont RL, Voth EA: Legalization, harm reduction and drug policy. Ann Intern Med 123:461–465, 1995

Fehr KO, Kalant H (eds): Addiction Research Foundations. World Health Organization Meeting on Adverse Health and Behavioral Consequences of Cannabis Use. Toronto, Ontario, Addiction Research Foundation, May 1983

Feldman AL, Sullivan JT, Passero MA, et al: Pneumothorax in poly-substance abusing marijuana and tobacco smokers: three cases. J Subst Abuse 5:183–186, 1993

Fligiel SE, Roth MD, Kleerup EC, et al: Tracheobronchial histopathology in habitual smokers of cocaine, marijuana, and/or tobacco. Chest 112:319–326, 1997

Fride E: Anandamides: tolerance and cross-tolerance to delta-9-THC. Brain Res 697:83–90, 1995

Gaoni Y, Mechoulam R: Isolation, structure, and partial synthesis of an active constituent of hashish. Journal of American Chemistry Society 86:1646–1647, 1964

Gardner EL, Lowinson JH: Marijuana's interaction with the brain reward systems: update 1991. Pharmacol Biochem Behav 40:571–580, 1991

Gatley SJ, Volkow ND: Addiction and imaging of the human living brain. Drug Alcohol Depend 51:97–108, 1998

Gold MS: Drugs of Abuse: A Comprehensive Series for Clinicians: Marijuana. New York, Plenum, 1989

Gold MS, Gleaton TJ: Marked increases in USA marijuana and LSD: results of annual junior and senior high school survey (abstract). Biol Psychiatry 35:694, 1994

Gold MS, Schuchard K, Gleaton T: LSD in the USA: déjà vu again (abstract)? Biol Psychiatry 33:431, 1993

Gold MS, Tullis LM, Miller MD: Tobacco and marijuana smoking: a connection? Biol Psychiatry (in press)

Golub A, Johnson BD: The shifting importance of alcohol and marijuana as gateway substances among serious drug users. J Stud Alcohol 55:607–614, 1994

Hall W: Health and Psychological Consequences of Cannabis Use (Monogr Series 25). Canbinn, Australian Government Publishing Service, 1994

Herenham M, Lynn AB, Little MD, et al: Canabinoid receptor localization in the brain. Proc Natl Acad Sci U S A 87:1932–1936, 1990

Hollister LE: Health aspects of cannabis. Pharmacol Rev 38:1–20, 1986

Isbell H, Gorodetzsky CW, Jasinski DR, et al: Effect of (-)trans-tetrahydrocannabinol in man. Psychopharmacologia 11:184–188, 1967

Janowsky DS, Meacham MP, Blaine JD, et al: Marijuana effects on simulated flying ability. Am J Psychiatry 133:384–388, 1976

Jenkins AJ, Darwin WD, Huestis MA, et al: Validity testing of the accupinch THC test. J Anal Toxicol 19:5–12, 1995

Johnston L: Monitoring the Future Study, University of Michigan. Ann Arbor, MI, National Institute on Drug Abuse, 1998

Jones KL, Chernoff GF: Effects of chemical and environmental agents, in Maternal Fetal Medicine. Edited by Creasy RK, Resnik R. Philadelphia, PA, WB Saunders, 1984

Kandel D: Stages in adolescent involvement in drug use. Science 190:912–914, 1975

Kelly TH, Foltin RW, Emurian CS, et al: Effects of delta-9-THC on marijuana smoking, drug choice and verbal reports of drug liking. Journal of Experimental Analysis of Behavior 61:203–211, 1994

Kelp E, Webber M, Taskin DP: Acute and chronic effects of marijuana smoking on pulmonary alveolar permeability. Life Sci 56:2193–2199, 1995

Kendler KS, Prescott CA: Cannabis use, abuse, and dependence in a population-based sample of female twins. Am J Psychiatry 155:1016–1022, 1998

Khun C, Scott S, Wilson W: Buzzed: The Straight Facts About the Most Used and Abused Drugs From Alcohol to Ecstasy. New York, WW Norton, 1997

Klein TW, Friedman H, Specter S: Marijuana, immunity and infection. J Neuroimmunol 83:102–115, 1998

Kolodny RC, Masters WH, Kolodner RM, et al: Depression of plasma testosterone levels after chronic intensive marijuana use. N Engl J Med 290:872–874, 1974

Lukas SE, Sholar M, Kouri E, et al: Marijuana smoking increases plasma cocaine levels and subjective reports of euphoria in male volunteers. Pharmacol Biochem Behav 48:715–721, 1994

Lundavist T: Specific thought patterns in chronic cannabis smokers observed during treatment. Life Sci 56:2141–2144, 1995

Matthew RJ, Wilson WH, Turkington TG, et al: Cerebellar activity and disturbed time sense after THC. Brain Res 797:183–189, 1998

Matthias P, Tashkin DP, Marques-Magallanes JA, et al: Effects of varying marijuana potency on deposition of tar and delta-9-THC in the lung during smoking. Pharmacol Biochem Behav 58:1145–1150, 1997

Millman RB, Beeder AB: Cannabis, in The American Psychiatric Press Textbook of Substance Abuse Treatment. Edited by Galanter M, Kleber HD. Washington, DC, American Psychiatric Press, 1994, pp 91–109

Moskowitz H, Sharma SM, McGlothin W: Effects of marihuana upon peripheral vision and function of the information processing demands in central vision. Percept Mot Skills 35:875–882, 1972

Naditch MP: Acute adverse reactions to psychoactive drugs, drug usage and psychopathology. J Abnorm Psychol 83:394–403, 1974

National Center on Addiction and Substance Abuse at Columbia University (CASA): Cigarettes, Alcohol, Marijuana: Gateway to Illicit Drug Use. New York, The National Center on Addiction and Substance Abuse at Columbia University (CASA), October 27, 1994

National Center on Addiction and Substance Abuse at Columbia University (CASA): Quarterly Update, 1996. Available at: http://www.casacolumbia.org

National Household Survey on Drug Abuse: CDC's TIPS. August 1998. Available at: http://www.cdc.gov

National Institute on Drug Abuse: NIDA Capsule Series (C-88-06) [Revised September 1997], Rockville, MD, National Institute on Drug Abuse, 1997

Neumark-Sztainer D, Story M, Dixon LB, et al: Adolescents engaging in unhealthy weight control behaviors: are they at risk for other health-compromising behaviors? Am J Public Health 88:952–955, 1998

Novak W: High Culture: Marijuana in the Lives of Americans. New York, Alfred A Knopf, 1980

O'Brian CP, McLellan AT: Myths about the treatment of addiction. Lancet 347:237–240, 1996

Oveido A, Glowa J, Herkenham M: Chronic cannabinoid administration alters cannabinoid receptor binding in rat brain: a quantitative autoradiographic study. Brain Res 616:293–302, 1993

Pertwee RG: Pharmacological, physiological and clinical implications of the discovery of cannabinoid receptors. Biochem Soc Trans 26:267–272, 1998

Pope HG, Yurgelun-Todd D: The residual cognitive effects of heavy marijuana use in college students. JAMA 275:521–527, 1996

Rueshe S: National Families in Action. Available at: http://www.emery.edu/NFIA 10, 1997

Rodriquez de Fonseca F, Carrera MRA, Navarro M, et al: Activation of corticotropin-releasing factor in the limbic system during cannabinoid withdrawal. Science 276:2050–2054, 1997

Romero J, Garcia-Palormero E, Castro JG, et al: Effects of chronic exposure to delta-9-THC on cannabinoid receptor binding and mRNA levels in several rat brain regions. Mol Brain Res 46:100–108, 1997

Stephens RS, Wertz JS, Roffman RA: Self-efficacy and marijuana cessation: a construct validity analysis. J Consult Clin Psychol 63:1022–1031, 1995

Stillman R, Galanter M, Lemberger L, et al: Tetrahydrocannabinol (THC): metabolism and subjective effects. Life Sci 19:569–576, 1976

Stimmel B: Medical marijuana: to prescribe or not to prescribe: that is the question. J Addict Dis 14:1–4, 1995

Tanda G, Pontieri FE, DiChiara G: Cannabinoid and heroin activation of mesolimbic dopamine transmission by a common mu1 opioid receptor mechanism. Science 276:2048–2050, 1997

Tashkin DP: Bronchial effects of aerosolized delta 9 THC in healthy and asthmatic subjects. Am Rev Respir Dis 115:57–65, 1977

Tashkin DP, Shapiro BJ, Lee EY, et al: Subacute effects of heavy marijuana smoking on pulmonary function in healthy young males. N Engl J Med 294:125–129, 1976

Tashkin DP, Wu TC, Djahed B, et al: Acute and chronic effects of marijuana smoking compared with tobacco smoking on blood carboxyhemoglobin levels. J Psychoactive Drugs 20:27–31, 1988a

Tashkin DP, Simmins M, Clark V, et al: Effects of habitual smoking of marijuana alone and with tobacco on nonspecific airway hyperactivity. J Psychoactive Drugs 20:221–225, 1988b

Tilles DS, Goldenheim PD, Johnson DC, et al: Marijuana smoking as cause of reduction in single-breath carbon monoxide diffusing capacity. Am J Med 80:601–606, 1986

Tsou K, Patrick SL, Walker JM: Physical withdrawal in rats tolerant to delta-9-THC precipitated by a cannabinoid receptor antagonist. Eur J Pharmacol 280:R13–R15, 1995

Warner LA, Kessler RC, Hughes M, et al: Prevalence and correlates of drug use and dependence in the United States: results from the National Comorbidity Survey. Arch Gen Psychiatry 52:219–229, 1995

Wenger T, Toth BE, Martin BR: Effects of anandamide (endogenous cannabinoid) on the anterior pituitary hormone secretion in adult ovariectomized rats. Life Sci 56:2057–2063, 1995

Wickelgren I: Marijuana: harder than we thought? Science 276 (5321):1967–1968, 1997

Wu TC, Tashkin DP, Djahed B, et al: Pulmonary hazards of smoking marijuana as compared with tobacco. N Engl J Med 318:347–351, 1988

# 18 Stimulants

Thomas R. Kosten, M.D.
Amrita K. Singha, Ph.D.

Cocaine and amphetamine are psychoactive agents that increase central nervous system (CNS) activity and produce powerful reinforcing effects (e.g., euphoria, elevated mood, high) that contribute to their high abuse liability. Since the peak of the cocaine epidemic in the mid 1980s, addiction to this stimulant has been a major public health concern. Recently, localized epidemics of amphetamine abuse have been developing, particularly in the western United States. The dangers associated with stimulant use are enormous and include increased risk of human immunodeficiency virus (HIV) infection, detrimental effects on the unborn and newborn, increased crime and violence, as well as medical, financial, and psychological problems. Because of these consequences, the task of identifying, characterizing, and developing treatments is more important than ever.

Progress has been made in identifying and developing pharmacological and behavioral treatments for stimulant addiction. In this chapter, we provide a brief understanding of the biological basis underlying stimulant reinforcement, describe the clinical characteristics resulting from stimulant use, and discuss the pharmacological and behavioral treatment approaches for stimulant abuse. We conclude by providing specific treatment guidelines for managing stimulant abuse. (The neurobiology of stimulants, which provides the foundation for possible clinical interventions, is discussed in more detail in Fischman and Haney, Chapter 3, in this volume.)

## ■ Neurochemical Actions Mediating Stimulant Reward

A vast behavioral and pharmacological literature demonstrates that the rewarding effects of stimulants are mediated through the mesocorticolimbic dopamine (DA) system, which consists of DA neurons of the ventral tegmental area and their target projections, including the nucleus accumbens and prefrontal cortex (for reviews, see Johanson and Fischman 1989; Koob 1992). The reinforcing properties of cocaine and amphetamine are associated with their ability to increase synaptic DA levels. Cocaine increases DA by binding to the dopamine transporter (DAT) and inhibiting its activity (Ritz et al. 1987), whereas amphetamine increases synaptic DA concentrations by causing its release into synapses (Bunney and Aghajanian 1978). Cocaine and amphetamine also have actions on norepinephrine and serotonin neurons (Chiueh and Moore 1974; Ritz et al. 1987). However, behavioral and neurochemical studies indicate that DA is the critical neurotransmitter mediating the reinforcing effects of these stimulants. For instance, laboratory animals will readily self-administer DA agonists with an intake pattern resembling cocaine and amphetamine self-administration (e.g., Baxter et al. 1974; Woolverton et al. 1984; Yokel and Wise 1978), and DA receptor antagonists increase self-administration of amphetamine and cocaine in animals (Davis and Smith 1975; DeWit and Wise 1977); the increase in

Supported by National Institute on Drug Abuse Grants P50-DA04060 and P50-DA09250-02.

self-administration is believed to reflect a blockade of the rewarding effects of stimulants. Administration of serotonergic and adrenergic antagonists do not alter self-administration behavior of cocaine and amphetamine (DeWit and Wise 1977; Lacosta and Roberts 1993). Moreover, selective lesions of the DA neurons produce extinction-like responding in cocaine and amphetamine self-administration (Lyness et al. 1979; Roberts and Koob 1982). However, selective lesions of noradrenergic systems fail to alter self-administration for cocaine (Roberts et al. 1977). Finally, binding studies show a significant correlation between the binding affinities of cocaine and related drugs to the DAT and their efficacies in maintaining self-administration (Ritz et al. 1987). Thus, these behavioral and pharmacological studies support the theory that the rewarding effects of cocaine and amphetamine are mediated through the DA neural system.

## Neurobiological Effects of Chronic Stimulant Abuse

In addition to the acute reinforcing effects, chronic stimulant use can produce a constellation of neurochemical, physiological, and neuropsychological impairments. Studies examining DA receptor function show both decreased (Farfel et al. 1992; Peris et al. 1990; Volkow et al. 1990) and increased DA postsynaptic levels, as well as autoreceptors, following chronic cocaine use (Henry et al. 1989; Pierce et al. 1995). In addition, chronic administration of cocaine increases the number of DAT sites in the caudate nucleus (Aloyo et al. 1995) and prefrontal cortex (Hitri and Wyatt 1993) in laboratory animals. Also, studies measuring prolactin and growth hormone, as a measure of DA and serotonin activity, have reported increases (Dackis and Gold 1985; Kranzler and Wallington 1989) or no change (Gawin and Ellinwood 1988; Swartz et al. 1990) in cocaine-addicted persons.

Additional evidence of neurochemical and physiological alterations comes from single photon emission computed tomography (SPECT) and positron-emission tomography (PET) studies, which show increased DAT sites in acutely abstinent cocaine abusers (Malison et al. 1998), decreased DA D$_2$ receptor binding in detoxified cocaine abusers (Volkow et al. 1990, 1996), and reduced cerebral blood flow (rCBF) and cortical perfusion among chronic cocaine users (Holman et al. 1991, 1993; Levin et al. 1994, 1995; Strickland et al. 1993; Volkow et al. 1988, 1991; Weber et al. 1993) relative

to control subjects (Holman et al. 1991; Levin et al. 1994; Volkow et al. 1988). Treatment with buprenorphine improved the rCBF in cocaine-dependent individuals (Holman et al. 1993), suggesting that drug-induced alterations may be reversed to some extent. Stimulant administration has also altered glucose metabolism. During early withdrawal, tests show increased glucose metabolism among cocaine users relative to control subjects (Volkow et al. 1991), but during late withdrawal, metabolic activity decreases among cocaine-addicted persons (Volkow et al. 1992). Such reductions in glucose metabolism also have been observed after acute administration of cocaine (London et al. 1990) and amphetamine (Wolkin et al. 1987).

Given the evidence of disturbances in brain structure and function following stimulant use, it is not surprising that individuals with histories of cocaine abuse also show cognitive deficits. In fact, impairments in verbal learning, memory, and attention have been well documented in cocaine-abusing individuals (Ardila et al. 1991; Beatty et al. 1995; Berry et al. 1993; Hoff et al. 1991; O'Malley and Gawin 1990), and these neuropsychological deficits have been shown to correlate with reductions in blood flow among cocaine users (Woods et al. 1991). Thus, chronic cocaine use produces not only neurochemical and physiological alterations but also cognitive impairments.

## Clinical Aspects of Stimulant Use

The rewarding effects of cocaine and amphetamine are influenced by the route of administration, because some routes (e.g., intravenous administration) produce more immediate onset of euphoria. The preferred method of self-administering cocaine has been snorting and, more recently, smoking. The effects of snorted cocaine generally occur within 15–20 minutes, whereas the effects of intravenously injected cocaine can be felt within 1 or 2 minutes. A smokable form of cocaine (crack cocaine), which changes cocaine hydrochloride into a free base by using baking soda and water, produces euphoria within seconds. Amphetamines come in a variety of forms (e.g., pill, liquid, or powder) but are usually taken orally or intravenously. A smokable version of amphetamine (ice amphetamine), similar to cocaine, is also available. Because of its long duration of action, it can produce euphoria lasting 12–24 hours.

Stimulant use may range from low to high dose and from infrequent to chronic or binge patterns. Depending on the dosage, pattern, and duration of use, stimulants can produce several drug-induced states with different clinical characteristics. Moderate to high doses of stimulants can produce stimulant intoxication that may or may not be pleasant. The intoxicated person may show signs of hyperawareness, hypersexuality, hypervigilance, and psychomotor agitation. Often, the symptoms of stimulant-induced intoxication resemble mania. The intoxicated person should be monitored by the medical staff until the symptoms of intoxication diminish. If the intoxication does not return to baseline level within 24 hours, mania may be present, and treatment for manic disorder may be required (Gawin et al. 1994).

With increased dosage and duration of administration, stimulants can also produce a state of mental confusion and excitement known as *stimulant delirium.* Delirium is associated with becoming disoriented and confused as well as anxious and fearful. Extreme medical caution is needed when treating delirium because such symptoms may indicate stimulant overdose. For instance, patients addicted to crack cocaine who overdose need careful monitoring for seizures, cardiac arrhythmias, stroke, and pulmonary complications. Overdose management has been reviewed in detail (see Gay 1982), but more recently a syndrome of hyperthermia and agitation has been described that resembles neuroleptic malignant syndrome (Kosten and Kleber 1988; Mittleman and Wetli 1984). Standard pharmacological management of overdose includes neuroleptics, but high doses of benzodiazepines may be safer alternatives for controlling the delirium and agitation because neuroleptics will worsen the hyperthermia in some cases of overdose and lead to fatality. Acute use of benzodiazepines can also help minimize the need for physical restraints.

During high-dose stimulant use, often seen during binge episodes, individuals can experience stimulant-induced psychosis characterized by delusions, paranoid thinking, and stereotyped compulsive behavior. Delusional patients require close clinical monitoring and may need short-term treatment with neuroleptics to ameliorate the psychosis. Psychosis is induced more commonly by amphetamine than by cocaine, perhaps because it is difficult to maintain high chronic levels of cocaine in the body (King and Ellinwood 1997). Also, stimulant-induced psychosis in humans is related to the dose and duration of administration of amphetamine (Bell 1970) and cocaine (Satel et al. 1991) rather than psychiatric predisposition.

Stimulant withdrawal, which occurs following cessation of chronic cocaine or amphetamine use, can produce a wide range of dysphoric symptoms:

- Following binge use, individuals may initially experience a "crash" period, which is characterized by symptoms of depression, anxiety, agitation, and intense drug craving (Gawin and Ellinwood 1988; Gawin and Kleber 1986).
- During the intermediate withdrawal phase, individuals may experience fatigue, a loss of physical and mental energy, and decreased interest in the surrounding environment (Gawin and Ellinwood 1988; Weddington et al. 1990).
- During the late withdrawal phase, individuals may experience brief periods of intense drug craving, such that objects and people in the addicted person's life can become a conditioned trigger for craving and relapse.

These withdrawal symptoms may be a target for pharmacological agents (see subsection, "Dopaminergic Agents," below).

## Treatment of Stimulant Abuse

Although a great deal has been learned about the reward mechanisms underlying stimulant abuse, the development of effective treatment has lagged behind. Virtually no controlled treatment literature exists for amphetamine abuse, partly because amphetamine use has not been as popular as cocaine use for the last decade. However, epidemics of amphetamine abuse are on the rise, especially in the western United States. The pharmacological and behavioral treatment approaches used for cocaine abuse appear to be applicable to the treatment of amphetamine abuse.

### Pharmacotherapy

No agent has been approved by the U.S. Food and Drug Administration (FDA) for cocaine dependence, but two major classes of medications have been investigated: 1) dopaminergic agonists and 2) antidepressants. Studies have been relatively brief for both types of agents and have focused on abstinence initiation rather than on relapse prevention. In addition to dopaminergic agents and antidepressants, other compounds have been examined as potential treatments of cocaine dependence.

**Dopaminergic agents.** Based on the theory that chronic cocaine use reduces the efficiency of central

DA neurotransmission, several dopaminergic compounds, including amantadine, bromocriptine, mazindol, and methylphenidate, have been examined as treatments for cocaine abuse. Investigators thought that these dopaminergic agents, which have a fast onset of action, would correct the DA dysregulation and alleviate the withdrawal symptoms that often follow cessation of stimulant use.

A number of studies have found amantadine to be effective in attenuating cocaine craving and use. For instance, in cocaine-abusing methadone-maintained patients, Handelsman et al. (1988) reported decreased urine cocaine metabolite levels and self-reported cocaine use following amantadine treatment, and Alterman et al. (1992) found that patients who were given amantadine had significantly greater rates of cocaine abstinence than did individuals who were given placebo. In a double-blind comparison of amantadine and bromocriptine for the treatment of acute cocaine withdrawal, Tennant and Sagherian (1987) found that amantadine was superior to bromocriptine. However, a placebo-controlled study comparing amantadine and placebo observed no differences between the treatment groups (Weddington et al. 1991). Amantadine has also been compared with desipramine and placebo. In methadone-maintained patients, no differences were found among the three groups in treatment retention, cocaine craving, and cocaine-free urine samples, but attainment of 2 weeks of cocaine abstinence was significantly greater in the amantadine treatment group relative to the desipramine or placebo group (Kosten et al. 1992b). Thus, these studies suggest that amantadine may be effective in reducing cocaine withdrawal symptoms and initial attainment of cocaine abstinence.

The DA $D_2$ agonist bromocriptine also has been examined in the treatment of cocaine dependence. In a double-blind, placebo-controlled study with cocaine-dependent individuals, Giannini et al. (1987) found that compared with placebo, bromocriptine significantly reduced cocaine craving, and Tennant and Sagherian (1987) noted that bromocriptine blocked the euphorigenic effects of cocaine in several addicted patients. Despite these positive results, bromocriptine has been reported to produce side effects such as headache, nausea, hypotension, and psychosis (Dackis et al. 1987; Turner et al. 1984), which makes this agent a poor treatment choice.

Mazindol, a catecholamine reuptake inhibitor, was initially associated with reduced cocaine use (Berger et al. 1989; Seibyl et al. 1992), but more recent studies failed to show significant therapeutic effects. For instance, in a 1-week crossover study, mazindol did not reduce cocaine use or craving (Kosten et al. 1993), and in double-blind studies, no differences were observed between mazindol and placebo treatment groups in self-report ratings, rates of relapse, or cocaine use (Margolin et al. 1995a; Stine et al. 1995).

Methylphenidate, a stimulant, has been examined for treatment of cocaine dependence because of its low abuse liability relative to cocaine or amphetamine, rapid onset of action relative to antidepressants, and long duration of action relative to cocaine (Kosten and McCance-Katz 1995). Methylphenidate has been reported to produce beneficial effects in cocaine-dependent individuals with attention-deficit/hyperactivity disorder (ADHD) (Khantzian et al. 1984). However, others have found that methylphenidate results in a mild sense of stimulation that evokes an increased desire for cocaine in persons without ADHD (Gawin et al. 1985). Furthermore, a recent double-blind, placebo-controlled study found no difference in cocaine use between methylphenidate and placebo treatment groups (Grabowski et al. 1997).

Overall, these studies indicate that the rewarding effects and withdrawal symptoms induced by cocaine may be attenuated by fast-acting dopaminergic agents. However, more controlled studies are needed to better characterize the therapeutic efficacy of these agents and to assess additional compounds, including DA antagonists (e.g., flupentixol).

**Antidepressants.** The second class of medications used to treat cocaine dependence—antidepressants—are thought to downregulate synaptic catecholamine receptors, an action opposite to the presynaptic upregulation caused by chronic stimulant use (Gawin and Ellinwood 1988). Although antidepressants have a relatively benign side-effect profile, good patient compliance rates, and lack of abuse liability, they have a delayed onset of action ranging from 10 to 20 days (Kosten and McCance-Katz 1995). Therefore, the physician may consider beginning antidepressant treatment during early withdrawal and continuing for weeks or longer as clinically indicated.

The tricyclic antidepressant desipramine has been studied most extensively as a treatment of cocaine dependence. Early studies of desipramine to treat cocaine dependence showed positive results (Gawin et al. 1989; Tennant and Rawson 1982), but placebo-controlled trials have not produced impressive findings. A meta-analysis of placebo-controlled studies by Levin and Lehman (1991) showed that although desipramine did not improve retention in treatment, it did produce greater cocaine abstinence relative to placebo. Treatment with desipramine has induced "early tricyclic jitteriness syndrome" and cocaine craving, as well as relapse to cocaine use in some patients (Weiss 1988). Thus, desipramine as pharmacotherapy for stimulant dependence should be used with caution.

Imipramine, another tricyclic antidepressant, also has been used as pharmacotherapy for cocaine dependence. Treatment with imipramine in cocaine-using subjects showed cocaine abstinence in 80% of the subjects, but because participants were also given tyrosine and tryptophan, the contribution of imipramine's effects is unclear (Rosecan 1983). In a double-blind, placebo-controlled study with cocaine users, cocaine craving and high decreased significantly in the imipramine group relative to placebo; however, urine specimens for cocaine did not differ between the groups (Nunes et al. 1991). Moreover, secondary analyses of studies with imipramine and desipramine have suggested that depressed cocaine abusers are more likely to show significant reductions in cocaine abuse (Nunes et al. 1991; Ziedonis and Kosten 1991) than nondepressed cocaine abusers. Hence, the therapeutic efficacy of imipramine to treat stimulant dependence needs further assessment, particularly in depressed patients who are addicted to cocaine.

Several other antidepressants, including fluoxetine, sertraline, and trazodone hydrochloride, that work predominantly through serotonergic mechanisms also have been used as pharmacotherapy for cocaine dependence. Although some reports indicated that treatment with fluoxetine reduced cocaine craving and use in cocaine-abusing heroin addicts (Batki et al. 1993; Pollack and Rosenbaum 1991), other investigators have not found fluoxetine to be an effective agent for cocaine abuse (e.g., Covi et al. 1994; Grabowski et al. 1991; Oliveto et al. 1995). Only open studies of trazodone and sertraline have shown them to be effective in attenuating cocaine use and withdrawal symptoms (Kosten et al. 1992a; Small and Purcell 1985).

Bupropion, a "second-generation" antidepressant, has been studied as pharmacotherapy for cocaine dependence. In an open pilot study, treatment with bupropion reduced cocaine use (Margolin et al. 1991) and attenuated several cocaine-induced positive subjective ratings during laboratory cocaine administration (Singha et al. 1997). However, a multisite placebo-controlled study failed to show that bupropion produced greater efficacy than placebo for reducing cocaine's effects (Margolin et al. 1995b).

**Other treatment agents and approaches.** In addition to the dopaminergic agents and antidepressants, several miscellaneous agents, including carbamazepine, disulfiram, and buprenorphine, have been examined as pharmacotherapy for cocaine dependence. Although carbamazepine showed efficacy in reducing cocaine use (Halikas et al. 1991, 1992), other studies have been unable to replicate therapeutic effects of this compound (Cornish et al. 1995; Kranzler et al. 1995; Montoya et al. 1995). Disulfiram, which is used in the treatment of alcoholism, has been effective in treatment of comorbid cocaine and alcohol dependence (Carroll et al. 1993; McCance-Katz et al. 1993). Buprenorphine has had more negative than positive findings supporting its efficacy in treating cocaine-abusing opiate addicts (Fudala et al. 1991; Johnson et al. 1992; Kosten et al. 1989; Oliveto et al. 1994). Clearly, more studies are needed to fully understand the efficacy of these agents for managing stimulant dependence.

Recent advances in the molecular biology of DA neuronal systems have led to innovative approaches for understanding cocaine's biochemical and behavioral effects. Giros and colleagues (1996) showed that rats, lacking DAT encoding gene, do not respond to cocaine biochemically or behaviorally. Moreover, a study by Carrera et al. (1995) suggested that animals injected with a protein-conjugated analogue of cocaine, which triggers the immune system to produce cocaine antibodies, had reduced cocaine concentrations in striatal tissue and lower psychomotor responses to stimulants than did nonimmunized animals. Finally, Fox and colleagues (1996) reported that a cocaine vaccine reduced cocaine self-administration in rats and decreased cocaine levels in the brains of immunized mice. These findings are exciting and suggest that vaccinations against cocaine's effects are possible. Future studies are needed to assess how these molecular approaches may be used to treat stimulant addiction in humans.

## Behavioral Therapy

In addition to pharmacotherapy, a behavioral approach to relapse prevention has been used to manage cocaine and amphetamine abuse (Anker and Crowley 1982; Boudin 1972; Higgins et al. 1991, 1993, 1994). The goal of this approach has been to decrease behavior maintained by drug reinforcers and increase behavior maintained by nondrug reinforcers by presenting rewards contingent on documented drug abstinence (positive contingencies) and withdrawing privileges contingent on documented drug use (negative contingencies).

Anker and Crowley (1982) reported that more than 80% of the participants involved in the negative contingency contract procedure were cocaine-free for the duration of their contract, which averaged 3 months. However, more than 50% of these patients relapsed at the completion of the contract. The investigators also found that more than 90% of the individuals who did not enter the contract (instead received psychotherapy) dropped out of therapy or resumed cocaine use within 2–4 weeks.

A series of studies have shown that positive contingency management procedures in combination with a community reinforcement approach facilitate initial abstinence in cocaine-dependent persons. In the first 12-week study (Higgins et al. 1991), the contingency management procedure consisted of vouchers with a monetary value that were presented upon evidence of drug abstinence (i.e., cocaine-free urine). The vouchers increased in value for every consecutive drug-free urine sample and could be exchanged for retail items and activities that the patient and therapist agreed on. The community reinforcement approach consisted of reciprocal relationship counseling with a significant other, including engaging in activities that were purchased with vouchers for drug-free urine samples. Other components of the counseling included instructions on recognizing antecedents and consequences of drug use and changing the patient's behavior to increase the probability of drug abstinence (e.g., assistance with employment/career goals, development of new nondrug-related recreational activities). Treatment retention was significantly higher in the behavioral treatment than in the standard drug counseling group, and 85% of the patients receiving the behavioral treatment achieved at least 3 weeks of abstinence as compared with 33% of the patients receiving standard drug abuse counseling.

In the second 24-week study (Higgins et al. 1993), the contingency management procedure was modified to include vouchers that could be exchanged for goods and services in weeks 1–12 and lottery tickets during weeks 13–24. It was expected that a more intensive reward system (i.e., vouchers) could facilitate initial drug abstinence, and a less intensive reward system (i.e., lottery tickets) could maintain sustained drug abstinence. As in the previous study, treatment retention was significantly higher in the behavioral treatment compared with the standard drug counseling group. Similarly, 68% and 42% of the patients in the behavioral treatment group achieved at least 8 and 16 weeks, respec-

tively, of continuous cocaine abstinence as opposed to 11% and 5% in the standard drug abuse counseling group. Moreover, cocaine abstinence did not precipitously decline when lottery tickets were substituted at week 13.

In the third 24-week study (Higgins et al. 1994), cocaine-dependent individuals were randomized to receive either behavioral treatment without incentives or behavioral treatment with incentives (i.e., vouchers that could be exchanged for goods and services) during weeks 1–12. During weeks 13–24, patients in both groups received a $1 lottery ticket for every drug-free urine in addition to behavioral treatment. The group that received the incentives showed significantly greater treatment retention and longer duration of continuous abstinence than the group not receiving the incentives.

Recently, this voucher system was examined in a 12-week clinical trial among methadone-maintained cocaine abusers (Silverman et al. 1995). Relative to control subjects, the contingency group achieved significantly longer duration of sustained cocaine abstinence. Overall, these findings suggest that incentives contingent on drug abstinence can be a powerful intervention tool for facilitating cocaine abstinence in cocaine abusers and methadone-maintained cocaine abusers.

## Psychiatric Comorbidity

The rates of comorbid psychiatric disorders in stimulant abusers are significantly higher than community rates of depression, ADHD, and antisocial personality disorders (Gawin and Kleber 1984; Rounsaville et al. 1991; Weiss et al. 1986; Ziedonis and Kosten 1991). Because psychiatric disorders may increase the risk for drug use (e.g., individuals may self-medicate to ease psychiatric symptomology), treatment must address both the stimulant addiction and the comorbid disorder. Certain pharmacotherapies may be particularly useful for stimulant abusers with comorbid psychiatric disorders. For instance, treatment with antidepressants has reduced depressive symptoms, cocaine use, and craving in depressed cocaine addicts (Nunes et al. 1990, 1991; Ziedonis and Kosten 1991). Also, methylphenidate and lithium have been reported to be effective in treating cocaine addicts with ADHD (Khantzian et al. 1984) and cyclothymia (Gawin 1986; Nunes et al. 1990), respectively. Unfortunately, psychiatric comorbidity has not yet shown a specific prognostic significance for behavioral therapies.

# Treatment Guidelines for Stimulant Abuse

Treatment of stimulant abuse requires a comprehensive assessment of the patient's psychological, medical, forensic, and drug use history. Moreover, because information obtained from chemically dependent persons may be incomplete or unreliable, it is important that patients receive a thorough physical examination, including blood and supervised urine samples for analysis. The clinician must be aware that polydrug abuse is common. Patients may ingest large amounts of one or more drugs at potentially lethal doses; therefore, the physician must be aware of the dangers of possible drug combinations, such as cocaine and alcohol or heroin (Goldsmith 1996).

Pharmacological intervention may be necessary during stimulant-induced drug states. For example, neuroleptics may be useful in controlling stimulant-induced psychosis or delirium, and anticraving agents with a fast onset of action may be helpful during the early withdrawal period. During the late withdrawal phase, when depression may be present, antidepressants may be an appropriate choice for treatment. Treatment medications can be given on an inpatient or outpatient basis. However, if medications are used for outpatient treatment, the clinician must warn the patient of the potential adverse interactions between cocaine and the prescribed medication. For instance, high blood pressure could result from the release of epinephrine by cocaine combined with the reuptake blockade by the tricyclic (Fischman et al. 1976), although later in the course of treatment, tricyclics decrease the sensitivity of the postsynaptic adrenergic receptors (Charney et al. 1981).

# Summary

DA neural systems appear to mediate the reinforcing effects of cocaine and amphetamine. The powerful rewarding effects make stimulants addictive and dangerous, creating a range of psychological, social, economic, and medical problems. To date, no effective treatment is available for stimulant dependence, although progress has been made in the development of pharmacological and behavioral techniques for cocaine and amphetamine addiction. Dopaminergic agents and antidepressants have shown some promise for reducing drug craving and preventing relapse. Behavioral techniques aimed at maintaining drug abstinence and preventing relapse have also shown favorable results. Although both pharmacological and behavioral interventions may be useful in treating addiction, Kosten (1989) suggested that individuals with significant medical risks, psychiatric comorbidity, and neuroadaptation from heavy stimulant use are particularly likely to benefit from pharmacological treatment. Further research is needed to address this issue and identify other effective ways to treat, manage, and prevent stimulant use.

# References

Aloyo VJ, Pazdalski PS, Kirifides AL, et al: Behavioral sensitization, behavioral tolerance, and increased [3H]WIN 35,428 binding in rabbit caudate nucleus after repeated injections of cocaine. Pharmacol Biochem Behav 52:335–340, 1995

Alterman AI, Droba M, Antelo RE, et al: Amantadine may facilitate detoxification of cocaine addicts. Drug Alcohol Depend 31:19–29, 1992

Anker AL, Crowley TJ: Use of contingency contracts in specialty clinics for cocaine abuse, in Problems of Drug Dependence (NIDA Res Monogr 42). Edited by Harris LS. Washington, DC, U.S. Government Printing Office, 1982, pp 452–459

Ardila A, Rosselli M, Strumwasser S: Neuropsychological deficits in chronic cocaine abusers. Int J Neurosci 57:73–79, 1991

Batki SL, Manfredi LB, Jacob P, et al: Fluoxetine for cocaine dependence in methadone maintenance: quantitative plasma and urine cocaine/benzoylecognine concentration. J Clin Psychopharmacol 13:243–250, 1993

Baxter BL, Gluckman MI, Stein L, et al: Self-injection of apomorphine in the rat. Pharmacol Biochem Behav 2:387–391, 1974

Beatty WW, Katzung VM, Moreland VJ, et al: Neuropsychological performance of recently abstinent alcoholics and cocaine abusers. Drug Alcohol Depend 37:247–253, 1995

Bell DS: The experimental reproduction of amphetamine psychosis. Arch Gen Psychiatry 127:1170–1175, 1970

Berger P, Gawin F, Kosten TR: Treatment of cocaine abuse with mazindol (letter). Lancet 1:283, 1989

Berry J, van Gorp WG, Herzberg DS, et al: Neuropsychological deficits in abstinent cocaine abusers: preliminary findings after two weeks of abstinence. Drug Alcohol Depend 32:231–237, 1993

Boudin HM: Contingency contracting as a therapeutic tool in the deceleration of amphetamine use. Behav Res Ther 3:604–608, 1972

Bunney BS, Aghajanian GK: d-Amphetamine-induced depression of central dopamine neurons: evidence for mediation by both autoreceptors and a striato-nigral feedback pathway. Naunyn Schmiedebergs Arch Pharmacol 304:255–261, 1978

Carrera MR, Ashley JA, Parsons LH, et al: Suppression of psychoactive effects of cocaine by active immunization. Nature 378(6558):727–730, 1995

Carroll K, Ziedonis D, O'Malley S, et al: Pharmacological interventions for alcohol- and cocaine-abusing individuals. Am J Addict 2:77–79, 1993

Charney DS, Menkes DB, Heninger GR: Receptor sensitivity and the mechanism of action of antidepressant treatment. Arch Gen Psychiatry 38:1160–1180, 1981

Chiueh CC, Moore KE: In vivo evoked release of endogenously synthesized catecholamines from the cat brain evoked by electrical stimulation and d-amphetamine. J Neurochem 23:159–168, 1974

Cornish JW, Maany I, Fudala PJ, et al: Carbamazepine treatment for cocaine dependence. Drug Alcohol Depend 38:221–227, 1995

Covi L, Hess JM, Kreiter NA, et al: Three models for the analysis of a fluoxetine controlled treatment in cocaine abuse, in Problems of Drug Dependence, 1993 (NIDA Res Monogr 141). Edited by Harris LS. Washington, DC, U.S. Government Printing Office, 1994, p 138

Dackis CA, Gold MS: New concepts in cocaine addiction: the dopamine depletion hypothesis. Neurosci Biobehav Rev 9:469–477, 1985

Dackis CA, Gold MS, Sweeny DR, et al: Single-dose bromocriptine reverses cocaine craving. Psychiatry Res 20:261–264, 1987

Davis WM, Smith SG: Effect of haloperidol on (+)-amphetamine self-administration. J Pharm Pharmacol 27:540–542, 1975

DeWit H, Wise RA: Blockade of cocaine reinforcement in rats with the dopamine receptor blocker pimozide, but not with the noradrenergic blockers phentolamine or phenoxybenzamine. Canadian Journal of Psychology 31:195–203, 1977

Farfel GM, Kleven MS, Woolverton WL, et al: Effects of repeated injections of cocaine on catecholamine receptor binding sites, dopamine transporter binding sites and behavior in rhesus monkeys. Brain Res 578:235–243, 1992

Fischman MW, Schuster CR, Resnekov I, et al: Cardiovascular and subject effects of intravenous cocaine administration in humans. Arch Gen Psychiatry 10:535–546, 1976

Fox BS, Kantak KM, Edwards MA, et al: Efficacy of a therapeutic cocaine vaccine in rodent models. Nat Med 2:1129–1132, 1996

Fudala PJ, Johnson RE, Jaffe JH: Outpatient comparison of buprenorphine and methadone maintenance, II: effects on cocaine usage, retention time in study, and missed clinic visits, in Committee on Problems of Drug Dependence (NIDA Res Monogr 105). Edited by Harris LS. Washington, DC, U.S. Government Printing Office, 1991, pp 576–588

Gawin FH: New uses of antidepressants in cocaine abuse. Psychosomatics 27 (suppl):24–29, 1986

Gawin FH, Ellinwood EH: Cocaine and other stimulants: actions, abuse, and treatments. N Engl J Med 318:1173–1182, 1988

Gawin FH, Kleber HD: Cocaine abuse treatments: an open pilot trial with lithium and desipramine. Arch Gen Psychiatry 41:903–910, 1984

Gawin FH, Kleber HD: Abstinence symptomology and psychiatric diagnosis in chronic cocaine abusers. Arch Gen Psychiatry 43:107–113, 1986

Gawin FH, Riordan CA, Kleber HD: Methylphenidate treatment of cocaine abusers without attention deficit disorder: a negative study. Am J Drug Alcohol Abuse 11:193–197, 1985

Gawin FH, Kleber HD, Byck R, et al: Desipramine facilitation of initial cocaine abstinence. Arch Gen Psychiatry 46:117–121, 1989

Gawin FH, Khalsa ME, Ellinwood E: Stimulants, in The American Psychiatric Press Textbook of Substance Abuse Treatment. Edited by Galanter M, Kleber HD. Washington, DC, American Psychiatric Press, 1994, pp 111–139

Gay GR: Clinical management of acute and chronic cocaine poisoning. Ann Emerg Med 11:562–572, 1982

Giannini AJ, Baumgartel P, Dimarzio LR: Bromocriptine therapy in cocaine withdrawal. J Clin Pharmacol 27:267–270, 1987

Giros B, Jaber M, Jones SR, et al: Hyperlocomotion and indifference to cocaine and amphetamine in mice lacking the dopamine transporter. Nature 379:606–612, 1996

Goldsmith RJ: The elements of contemporary treatment, in The Principles and Practice of Addictions in Psychiatry. Edited by Miller NS. Philadelphia, PA, WB Saunders, 1996, pp 392–399

Grabowski J, Elk R, Kirby K, et al: Fluoxetine and behavioral factors in treatment of cocaine dependence, in Problems of Drug Dependence, 1991 (NIDA Res Monogr 119). Edited by Harris LS. Washington, DC, U.S. Government Printing Office, 1991, p 362

Grabowski J, Roache J, Schmitz J, et al: Replacement medication for cocaine dependence: methylphenidate. J Clin Psychopharmacol 17:485–488, 1997

Halikas JA, Crosby RD, Carlson GA, et al: Cocaine reduction in unmotivated crack users using carbamazepine versus placebo in a short-term, double-blind crossover design. Clin Pharmacol Ther 50:81–95, 1991

Halikas J, Kuhn K, Carlson G, et al: The effect of carbamazepine on cocaine use. Am J Addict 1:129–139, 1992

Handelsman L, Chordia PL, Escovar IM, et al: Amantadine for treatment of cocaine dependence in methadone-maintained patients (letter). Am J Psychiatry 145:533, 1988

Henry DJ, Green MA, White FJ: Electrophysiological effects of cocaine in the mesoaccumbens dopamine system: repeated administration. J Pharmacol Exp Ther 251:833–839, 1989

Higgins ST, Delaney DD, Budney AJ, et al: A behavioral approach to achieving initial cocaine abstinence. Am J Psychiatry 148:1218–1224, 1991

Higgins ST, Budney AJ, Bickel WK, et al: Achieving cocaine abstinence with a behavioral approach. Am J Psychiatry 150:763–769, 1993

Higgins ST, Budney AJ, Bickel WK, et al: Incentives improve outcome in outpatient behavioral treatment of cocaine dependence. Arch Gen Psychiatry 51:568–576, 1994

Hitri A, Wyatt RJ: Regional differences in rat brain dopamine transporter binding: function of time after chronic cocaine. Clin Neuropharmacol 16:525–539, 1993

Hoff AL, Riordan H, Alpert R, et al: Cognitive function in chronic cocaine abusers. J Clin Exp Neuropsychol 13:60–72, 1991

Holman BL, Carvalo PA, Mendelson J, et al: Brain perfusion is abnormal in cocaine dependent polydrug users. J Nucl Med 32:1206–1210, 1991

Holman BL, Mendelson J, Garda B, et al: Regional cerebral blood flow improves with treatment in chronic cocaine polydrug users. J Nucl Med 34:723–727, 1993

Johanson CE, Fischman MM: The pharmacology of cocaine related to its abuse. Pharmacol Rev 41:3–52, 1989

Johnson RE, Jaffe JH, Fudala PJ: A controlled trial of buprenorphine treatment for opioid dependence. JAMA 267:2750–2755, 1992

Khantzian EJ, Gawin F, Kleber HD, et al: Methylphenidate (Ritalin) treatment of cocaine dependence: a preliminary report. J Subst Abuse Treat 1:107–112, 1984

King GR, Ellinwood EH: Amphetamines and other stimulants, in Substance Abuse: A Comprehensive Textbook, 3rd Edition. Edited by Lowinson JH, Ruiz P, Millman RB, et al. Baltimore, MD, Williams & Wilkins, 1997, pp 207–223

Koob GF: Drugs of abuse: anatomy, pharmacology and function of reward pathways. Trends Pharmacol Sci 13:177–184, 1992

Kosten TR: Pharmacotherapeutic interventions for cocaine abuse: matching patients to treatment. J Nerv Ment Dis 177:379–389, 1989

Kosten TR, Kleber TR: Rapid death during cocaine abuse: variant of the neuroleptic malignant syndrome? Am J Drug Alcohol Abuse 14:335–346, 1988

Kosten TR, McCance-Katz E: New pharmacotherapies, in American Psychiatric Press Review of Psychiatry, Vol 14. Edited by Oldham JM, Riba MB. Washington, DC, American Psychiatric Press, 1995, pp 105–126

Kosten TR, Kleber TR, Morgan CM: Treatment of cocaine abuse using buprenorphine. Biol Psychiatry 26:637–639, 1989

Kosten TR, Kosten TA, Gawin FH, et al: An open trial of sertraline for cocaine abuse. Am J Addict 1:349–353, 1992a

Kosten TR, Morgan CM, Falcioni J, et al: Pharmacotherapy for cocaine-abusing methadone-maintained patients using amantadine or desipramine. Arch Gen Psychiatry 49:894–899, 1992b

Kosten TR, Steinberg M, Diakogiannis IA: Cross-over trial of mazindol for cocaine dependence. Am J Addict 2:161–164, 1993

Kranzler HR, Wallington DJ: Prolactin, cocaine dependence and treatment (NR199), in 1989 New Research Program and Abstracts, American Psychiatric Association 142nd Annual Meeting, San Francisco, CA, May 6–11, 1989. Washington, DC, American Psychiatric Association, 1989

Kranzler HR, Bauer LO, Hersh D, et al: Carbamazepine treatment of cocaine dependence: a placebo-controlled trial. Drug Alcohol Depend 38:203–211, 1995

Lacosta S, Roberts D: MDL 72222, ketanserin, and methysergide pretreatments fail to alter breaking points on a progressive ratio reinforced by intravenous cocaine. Pharmacol Biochem Behav 44:161–165, 1993

Levin FR, Lehman AF: Meta-analysis of desipramine: an adjunct in the treatment of cocaine addiction. J Clin Pharmacol 11:374–378, 1991

Levin JM, Holman BL, Mendelson JH, et al: Gender differences in cerebral perfusion in cocaine abuse: technetium-99m-HMPAO SPECT study of drug abusing women. J Nucl Med 35:1902–1909, 1994

Levin JM, Mendelson JH, Holman BL, et al: Improved regional cerebral blood flow in chronic cocaine polydrug users treated with buprenorphine. J Nucl Med 36:1211–1215, 1995

London ED, Cascella NG, Wong DF, et al: Cocaine-induced reduction of glucose utilization in human brain: a study using positron emission tomography and [fluorine18]fluorodeoxyglucose. Arch Gen Psychiatry 47:567–574, 1990

Lyness WH, Friedle NM, Moore KE: Destruction of dopaminergic nerve terminals in nucleus accumbens: effect on d-amphetamine self-administration. Pharmacol Biochem Behav 11:553–556, 1979

Malison RT, Best SE, van Dyck CH, et al: Elevated striatal dopamine transporters during acute cocaine abstinence as measured by [$^{123}$I]β-CIT SPECT. Am J Psychiatry 155:832–834, 1998

Margolin A, Kosten TR, Petrakis I, et al: Bupropion reduces cocaine abuse in methadone-maintained patients (letter). Arch Gen Psychiatry 48:87, 1991

Margolin A, Avants SK, Kosten TR: Mazindol for relapse prevention to cocaine abuse in methadone-maintained patients. Am J Drug Alcohol Abuse 21:469–481, 1995a

Margolin A, Kosten TR, Avants SK, et al: A multicenter trial of bupropion for cocaine dependence in methadone-maintained patients. Drug Alcohol Depend 49:125–131, 1995b

McCance-Katz EF, Price LH, Kosten TR, et al: Concurrent cocaine and ethanol ingestion in humans: pharmacology, physiology and role of coethelylene. Psychopharmacology 111:39–46, 1993

Mittleman R, Wetli CV: Death caused by recreational cocaine use. JAMA 252:1889–1892, 1984

Montoya ID, Levin FR, Fudala PJ, et al: Double-blind comparison of carbamazepine and placebo for treatment of cocaine dependence. Drug Alcohol Depend 38:213–219, 1995

Nunes EV, McGrath PJ, Wager S, et al: Lithium treatment for cocaine abusers with bipolar disorders. Am J Psychiatry 147:655–657, 1990

Nunes EV, Quitkin FM, Brady R, et al: Imipramine treatment of methadone maintenance patients with affective disorder and illicit drug use. Am J Psychiatry 148:667–669, 1991

Oliveto AH, Kosten TR, Schottenfeld RS, et al: A comparison of cocaine use in buprenorphine and methadone-maintained cocaine users. Am J Addict 3:43–48, 1994

Oliveto AH, Kosten TR, Schottenfeld RS, et al: Desipramine, amantadine, or fluoxetine in buprenorphine-maintained cocaine users. J Subst Abuse Treat 12:423–428, 1995

O'Malley SS, Gawin FH: Abstinence symptomology and neuropsychological impairments in chronic cocaine abusers, in Residual Effects of Abused Drugs on Behavior (NIDA Res Monogr 101). Edited by Spencer JW, Boren JJ. Rockville, MD, U.S. Department of Health and Human Services, 1990, pp 179–190

Peris J, Boyson SJ, Cass WA, et al: Persistence of neurochemical changes in dopamine systems after repeated cocaine administration. J Pharmacol Exp Ther 253:38–44, 1990

Pierce RC, Duffy P, Kalivas PW: Sensitization to cocaine and dopamine autoreceptor subsensitivity in the nucleus accumbens. Synapse 20:33–36, 1995

Pollack MH, Rosenbaum JF: Fluoxetine treatment of cocaine abuse in heroin addicts. J Clin Psychiatry 52:31–33, 1991

Ritz MC, Lamb RJ, Goldberg SR, et al: Cocaine receptors on dopamine transporters are related to self-administration of cocaine. Science 237:1219–1223, 1987

Roberts DCS, Koob GF: Disruption of cocaine self-administration following 6-hydroxydopamine lesions of the ventral tegmental area in rats. Pharmacol Biochem Behav 17:901–904, 1982

Roberts DCS, Corcoran ME, Fibiger HC: On the role of ascending catecholaminergic system in intravenous self-administration of cocaine. Pharmacol Biochem Behav 6:615–620, 1977

Rosecan J: The treatment of cocaine abuse with imipramine, L-tyrosine, and L-tryptophan. Presented at the 7th World Congress of Psychiatry, Vienna, Austria, July 14–19, 1983

Rounsaville BJ, Anton SF, Carroll KM, et al: Psychiatric diagnosis of treatment seeking cocaine abusers. Arch Gen Psychiatry 18:43–51, 1991

Satel SL, Southwick SM, Gawin FH, et al: Clinical features of cocaine-induced paranoia. Am J Psychiatry 148:495–498, 1991

Seibyl JP, Brenner L, Krystal JH, et al: Mazindol and cocaine addiction in schizophrenia (letter). Biol Psychiatry 31:1179–1181, 1992

Silverman K, Brooner RK, Montoya I, et al: Differential reinforcement of sustained cocaine abstinence in intravenous polydrug abusers, in Problems of Drug Dependence (NIDA Res Monogr 153). Edited by Harris LS. Rockville, MD, U.S. Department of Health and Human Services, 1995, p 212

Singha A, Oliveto A, McCance E, et al: Effects of cocaine prior to and during bupropion maintenance in cocaine abusers. Paper presented at the 59th Annual Scientific Meeting of the College on Problems of Drug Dependence. Nashville, TN, June 14–19, 1997

Small GW, Purcell JJ: Trazodone and cocaine abuse (letter). Arch Gen Psychiatry 42:524, 1985

Stine SM, Krystal JH, Kosten TR, et al: Mazindol treatment for cocaine dependence. Drug Alcohol Depend 39:245–252, 1995

Strickland TL, Mena I, Vilanueva-Myers J, et al: Cerebral perfusion and neuropsychological consequences of chronic cocaine use. J Neuropsychiatry Clin Neurosci 5:419–427, 1993

Swartz CM, Breen K, Leone F: Serum prolactin levels during extended cocaine abstinence. Am J Psychiatry 147:777–779, 1990

Tennant FS, Rawson RA: Cocaine and amphetamine dependence treated with desipramine, in Problems of Drug Dependence (NIDA Res Monogr 43). Edited by Harris LS. Rockville, MD, U.S. Department of Health and Human Services, 1982, pp 351–355

Tennant FS, Sagherian AA: Double-blind comparison of amantadine and bromocriptine for ambulatory withdrawal from cocaine dependence. Arch Intern Med 147:109–112, 1987

Turner TH, Cookson JC, Wass JAH, et al: Psychotic reactions during treatment of pituitary tumors with dopamine agonists. BMJ 289:1101–1103, 1984

Volkow ND, Mullani N, Gould KL, et al: Cerebral blood flow in chronic cocaine users: a study with positron emission tomography. Br J Psychiatry 152:641–648, 1988

Volkow ND, Fowler JS, Wolf AP, et al: Effect of chronic cocaine abuse on postsynaptic dopamine receptors. Am J Psychiatry 147:719–724, 1990

Volkow ND, Hitzemnn R, Fowler JS, et al: Regional brain metabolic activity during different stages of cocaine withdrawal. J Nucl Med 32:960–972, 1991

Volkow ND, Hitzemann R, Wang GH, et al: Long-term frontal brain metabolic changes in cocaine abusers. Synapse 11:184–190, 1992

Volkow ND, Wang GJ, Fowler JS, et al: Cocaine uptake is decreased in the brain of detoxified cocaine abusers. Neuropsychopharmacology 14:159–168, 1996

Weber DA, Franceschi D, Ivanovic M, et al: SPECT and planar brain imaging in crack abuse: iodine-123-iodamphetamine uptake and localization. J Nucl Med 34:899–907, 1993

Weddington WW, Brown BS, Haertzen CA, et al: Changes in mood, craving, and sleep during short-term abstinence reported by male cocaine addicts: a controlled, residential study. Arch Gen Psychiatry 47:861–868, 1990

Weddington WW Jr, Brown BS, Haertzen CA, et al: Comparison of amantadine and desipramine combined with psychotherapy for treatment of cocaine dependence. Am J Drug Alcohol Abuse 17:137–152, 1991

Weiss RD: Relapse to cocaine after initiating desipramine treatment. JAMA 260:2545–2546, 1988

Weiss RD, Mirin SM, Michael JL, et al: Psychopathology in chronic cocaine abusers. Am J Drug Alcohol Abuse 12:17–29, 1986

Wolkin A, Angrist B, Wolf A, et al: Effects of amphetamine on local cerebral metabolism in normal and schizophrenic subjects as determined by positron emission tomography. Psychopharmacology 92:241–246, 1987

Woods SW, O'Malley SS, Martini BL, et al: SPECT regional cerebral blood flow and neuropsychological testing in non-demented HIV-positive drug abusers. Prog Neuropsychopharmacol Biol Psychiatry 15:649–662, 1991

Woolverton WL, Goldberg LI, Ginos JZ: Intravenous self-administration of dopamine receptor agonists by rhesus monkeys. J Pharmacol Exp Ther 230:678–683, 1984

Yokel RA, Wise RA: Amphetamine-type reinforcement by dopaminergic agonists in the rat. Psychopharmacology 58:282–296, 1978

Ziedonis DM, Kosten TR: Pharmacotherapy improves treatment outcome in depressed cocaine addicts. J Psychoactive Drugs 23:417–425, 1991

# Chapter 19

# Hallucinogens

J. Thomas Ungerleider, M.D.
Robert N. Pechnick, Ph.D.

Hallucinogens that are likely to be abused include the ergot hallucinogen lysergic acid diethylamide (LSD), which is the prototype of these drugs of abuse; other indolealkylamines such as psilocybin ("magic mushrooms") and dimethyltryptamine (DMT); and the phenalkylamines, including mescaline and dimethoxymethylamphetamine (DOM or "STP"). Other drugs with hallucinogenic activity, marijuana, phencyclidine (PCP), ketamine, and the so-called *stimulant-hallucinogens*, methylenedioxyamphetamine (MDA), and methylenedioxymethamphetamine (MDMA, "Ecstasy," or "X"), are covered elsewhere. The hallucinogens, called *psychotomimetics* or *psychedelics* (mind-manifesting), are a group of drugs that produce thought, mood, and perceptual disorders. Depending on dosage, expectation (set), and environment (setting), they also can induce euphoria and a state similar to a transcendental experience.

The term *hallucinogen* means "producer of hallucinations." Many drugs can cause auditory and/or visual hallucinations. These hallucinations may be present as part of a delirium, accompanied by disturbances in judgment, orientation, intellect, memory, and emotion (e.g., an organic brain syndrome). Such delirium also may result from drug withdrawal (e.g., sedative-hypnotic withdrawal or delirium tremens in alcohol withdrawal). When referring to substance abuse, however, the term *hallucinogens* generally refers to a group of compounds that alter consciousness without delirium, sedation, excessive stimulation, or impairment of intellect or memory. The label *hallucinogen* actually is inaccurate because true LSD-induced hallucinations are rare. What are commonly seen are illusory phenomena. An illusion is a perceptual distortion of an actual stimulus in the environment. To "see" someone's face melt-ing is an illusion; to "see" a melting face when no one is present is a hallucination. Consequently, some have called these drugs *illusionogenic*. Those who use the terms *psychedelic* or *mind-manifesting* for hallucinogens (a term coined in 1957 by Osmond) have been criticized as being "prodrug" much as those who use the term *hallucinogen* have been accused of being "antidrug" (Osmond 1957). The term *psychotomimetic*, meaning a producer of psychosis, also has been widely used.

Peyote, containing mescaline, is the only hallucinogen that can be legally used in the United States, and even this practice has been challenged. Members of Native American religious communities have used it during certain ceremonies in a number of states and in Canada for many years.

In the last few years, there have been a number of interesting developments with respect to the use of hallucinogens. In general, the focus of illicit drug use shifted away from those drugs that were once used in an attempt to enhance self-awareness. The focus turned to drugs that were thought to elevate mood and increase work output, such as cocaine. However, data now indicate that the use of hallucinogens is on the rise, especially among adolescents. Thus, the trend of decreased use of the hallucinogens from the mid-1970s through the 1980s has begun to reverse.

Another new development is that although during the previous decade little research was conducted on hallucinogen administration to humans, over the last few years, there has been a resurgence of clinical studies carried out under highly controlled conditions (Hermle et al. 1992; Strassman 1995; Strassman and Qualls 1994; Strassman et al. 1994). The results obtained from controlled clinical studies should provide important and unbiased information, in contrast to some of the clinical data that have come from anecdotal information obtained from limited first-person accounts (Shulgin and Shulgin 1991), "street pharmacologists," or hospital emergency room records. The resurgence in clinical research has taken place at the same time as the major advances in the possible mechanisms of action of the hallucinogens. We may be reaching a point at which we can begin to develop a unified conceptual framework regarding the fundamental mechanisms underlying pharmacological effects of hallucinogens in humans, which might lead to advances in the pharmacological treatment of some adverse effects of these drugs.

The annual prevalence of use of hallucinogens declined from the mid-1970s through the 1980s. College students, followed up 1–4 years beyond high school, showed an annual prevalence rate for LSD that steadily dropped from 6% in 1980 to 3.4% in 1989 (Johnston 1990). The estimated availability of LSD also decreased fairly steadily from 1975 to 1989 (Johnston 1990). However, during the early 1990s, the indications were that LSD has been making a comeback (Johnston et al. 1996; R. H. Schwartz 1995). The Washington, D.C., Board of the Drug Enforcement Administration confiscated 14 doses of LSD in 1990 and 5,600 doses in 1991. The annual survey of high school seniors found that in 1990 and 1991, for the first time since 1976, more seniors had used LSD than cocaine in the previous 12 months (Nagy 1992; Seligmann et al. 1992). In 1992, the prevalence of the use of LSD increased in school-age children and young adults, but there are indications that since that time increases have continued only in high school students (Johnston et al. 1996). In 1994, the annual prevalence rates for LSD use were 7% in high school students and 5% in college students, and the lifetime prevalence rates for LSD and hallucinogen use were 3.7% and 2.2%, respectively, for students in the eighth grade and 13.8% and 7.4%, respectively, in young adults (Johnston et al. 1996). Other studies have shown even higher rates of hallucinogen use. For example, a random survey of Tulane University undergraduates in 1990 indicated that the number of students reporting having tried LSD was more than 17% (Cuomo et al. 1994). There are ethnic differences in the use of hallucinogens; in the twelfth grade, whites have the highest use of LSD and hallucinogens compared with blacks and Hispanics (Johnston et al. 1996).

Hallucinogens appear to be readily available on the street. In 1994, more than 24% of 18-year-olds said that they had been "exposed" (friends using drug or around people using drug) to LSD, whereas 14% said that they had been "exposed" to other hallucinogens

(Johnston et al. 1996). Aside from increases in prevalence and use of hallucinogens, there also have been changes in attitudes toward their use. The proportions of high school students disapproving LSD use and associating risk with its use have decreased; in contrast, older groups are more likely to perceive LSD as dangerous (Johnston et al. 1996). These changes in attitude are likely linked to the increase in use in those younger age groups.

LSD initially was used in the 1960s primarily by those interested in its ability to alter perceptual experiences (i.e., sight, sound, and taste). Much attention was paid to "set," the expectation of what the drug experience would be like, and "setting," the environment in which the drug was used. Thus, the early drug missionaries promulgated the erroneous notion that only good LSD "trips" would result if the prospective user ensured a number of preconditions for his or her drug experience, including a guide. In more recent times, users have attended concerts, films (particularly psychedelic or brightly colored ones), or "rave" parties during the drug experience. Users rarely indulge more than once weekly because tolerance to LSD occurs so rapidly.

No abstinence syndrome occurs after repeated use of hallucinogens. Thus, no detoxification for the chronic effects of the hallucinogens and little direct pharmacotherapy for toxic effects are required. We therefore focus on the acute and chronic effects of these drugs and the psychosocial interventions necessary to treat the adverse reactions. LSD is discussed as the prototypical hallucinogen.

## Physiological Effects

Hallucinogens such as LSD produce significant autonomic activity. They can dilate the pupils, increase the heart rate, and produce slight hypertension and hyperthermia. While under the influence, the face may flush, and the deep tendon reflexes quicken. On occasion, piloerection, salivation, nausea, a fine tremor, and lacrimation may be noted. In addition, a minor degree of incoordination, restlessness, and visual blurring can occur. A stress response with elevation of 17-hydroxycorticoids may be present.

DMT also increases heart rate, pupil diameter, and body temperature, and DMT and MDMA elevate plasma levels of adrenocorticotropic hormone (ACTH), cortisol, and prolactin (Grob et al. 1996; Strassman and Qualls 1994). Some of these autonomic effects of the hallucinogens are variable and may be due, in part, to the anxiety state of the user. LSD also can cause nausea;

nausea and sometimes vomiting are especially noteworthy after the ingestion of mescaline.

In terms of adverse physiological effects, LSD has a very high *therapeutic* index. The lethal dose in humans has not been determined, and fatalities that have been reported usually are secondary to perceptual distortions with resultant accidental death. Overdose with the psychotomimetic drugs is rare. Instances are known of people surviving 10,000 mg of LSD, 100 times the average dose. Hemiplegia has been reported after taking LSD, possibly a result of the production of vasospasm (Sobel et al. 1971). There is no generally accepted evidence of brain cell damage, chromosomal abnormalities, or teratogenic effects after the use of the indole-type hallucinogens and mescaline (Strassman 1984).

Drug interactions involving the hallucinogens do not appear to be an important source of adverse reactions. In some reports, the effects of LSD are reduced after the chronic administration of monoamine oxidase inhibitors or selective serotonin reuptake inhibitor antidepressants such as fluoxetine, whereas the effects of LSD are increased after the chronic administration of lithium or tricyclic antidepressants (Bonson and Murphy 1996; Bonson et al. 1996; Resnick et al. 1964; Strassman 1992).

## Psychological Effects

When the hallucinogens are taken orally, the psychic phenomena noted vary considerably, depending on the amount consumed and the set and the setting of both the subject and the observer. The overall psychological effects of the hallucinogens are quite similar; however, the rate of onset, duration of action, and absolute intensity of the effects can differ. Both Hofmann (1961) and Hollister (1978) described the effects of LSD in great detail. The absorption of LSD from the gastrointestinal tract and other mucous membranes occurs rapidly, with drug diffusion to all tissues, including the brain and across the placenta to the fetus. The onset of psychological and behavioral effects occurs approximately 30–60 minutes after oral administration and peaks at 2–4 hours after administration, with a gradual return to the predrug state in 8–12 hours. DMT produces similar effects but is inactive after oral administration and must be injected, sniffed, or smoked. It has a very rapid onset and short duration of action (60–120 minutes) (Strassman and Qualls 1994; Strassman et al. 1994). Thus, DMT previously was known as the "businessman's LSD" (i.e., one could have a psychedelic experience over the lunch hour and be back at work in the af-

ternoon). In contrast, the effects of DOM have been reported to last for longer than 24 hours.

The various hallucinogens also differ widely in potency and slope of the dose-response curve. Thus, some of the apparent qualitative differences between hallucinogens may be due, in part, to the amount of drug ingested relative to its specific dose-response characteristics. LSD is one of the most potent hallucinogens known, with behavioral effects occurring in some individuals after doses as low as 20 µg. Typical street doses range from 70 to 300 µg. Because of its high potency, LSD can be applied to paper blotters or to the backs of postage stamps. Some anecdotal evidence indicates that today's street LSD is less potent than that available in the 1960s, 20–80 µg versus 150–250 µg. It should be pointed out that the reported street dose is often highly inaccurate. The current cost of one street dose is about $5 versus $70 for ¼ ounce of marijuana and $50 for ½ gram of cocaine in powder form (Seligmann et al. 1992).

Perceptual alterations are notable with the hallucinogens; the initial subjective effect may be a colorful display of geometric patterns appearing before one's closed eyes. Distorted human, animal, or other forms may be projected onto the visual fields. With the eyes open, the color of perceived objects intensifies. Afterimages are remarkably prolonged; fixed objects may undulate and flow. Such illusions are common and may be given personal or idiosyncratic meaning. Auditory hallucinations are seldom described, but hyperacusis is commonly reported. Greater sensitivity to touch is regularly noticed, and sometimes taste and smell are altered. Synesthesia is frequently described with an overflow from one sense modality into another; colors are "heard," and sounds are "seen." Subjective time is frequently affected; users often feel that time is standing still. Hypersuggestibility and distractibility are notable, perhaps because the critical functions of the ego become diminished or are absent.

The emotional responses to the hallucinogens can vary markedly. Initial apprehension or mild anxiety is common, but the most frequent response is one of euphoria. Elation and a "blissful calm" also have been described. Less frequently, tension and anxiety culminating in panic have occurred. The mood is labile, shifting easily from happiness to depression and back. Prolonged laughter or tears may seem inappropriate emotional responses to any situation. Complete withdrawal (catatonic states) (Perera et al. 1995) and severe paranoid reactions have been encountered. An alternating intensification and fading out of the experience is present, with the subject going deeply in and out of the in-toxicated state.

Performance on tests involving attention, concentration, and motivation is impaired. Thought processes are significantly altered under the influence of hallucinogenic drugs. A loosening of associations is regularly noted. Thoughts are nonlogical and fantasy laden. Thoughts flood consciousness; on the other hand, a complete absence of thought occurs on occasion. Intelligence test scores drop, but this may be due to a lack of motivation to perform or a preoccupation with the unusual experiences. Orientation is ordinarily not impaired, but judgments are not reliable. Paranoid grandiosity and, less frequently, persecutory ideation are common.

Changes in ego functioning may be imperceptible at the lower dosage ranges; however, the ego can be completely disrupted when large amounts of hallucinogens have been ingested. At first one observes the ego's usual defense mechanisms operating to cope with these perceptions. Eventually, the ego may become overwhelmed to the point that depersonalization occurs. Current external events may not be differentiated from remote memories. The body image is frequently distorted, and the parts of the body may seem to become larger, smaller, or to disappear completely.

Chronic personality changes with a shift in attitudes and evidence of magical thinking also can occur after the use of hallucinogens. An atypical schizophrenic-like state may persist, but whether the use of hallucinogens causes or only unmasks a predisposition to this condition is unclear. There is always the associated risk that self-destructive behavior may occur during both the acute and the chronic reaction (e.g., thinking one can fly and jumping out of a window). In addition, the hallucinogenic drugs interact in various nonspecific ways with the personality, which may particularly impair the developing adolescent (D. Miller 1973). Today, many chronic LSD users eventually come to use a variety of drugs (polydrug or multiple drug use), particularly the sedative-hypnotics and stimulants. This is a marked departure from the LSD users seen in the 1960s, whose entire lifestyle was organized around the use of hallucinogens and involvement in the psychedelic subculture, adopting the motto "turn on, tune in, drop out."

## Diagnosis

The diagnosis of hallucinogen exposure is normally made from the patient's or an accompanying individual's report. The diagnosis can be made clinically when an individual is actively hallucinating, is having delusions, and is describing illusions, changes in body size or shape, slowing of time, and a waxing and waning of these and related symptoms. Ordinarily, the individual is able to report having taken a substance prior to the acute onset of the symptoms. The presence of dilated pupils, tachycardia, and quickened deep tendon reflexes increases the possibility that a hallucinogen has been consumed.

The routine clinical drug screen does not include testing for the hallucinogens in body fluids. However, they can be detected in the research laboratory in blood, and for longer periods in urine, by thin-layer chromatography, gas chromatography, fluorometry, or gas chromatography–mass spectrometry (Basalt 1982). A radioimmunoassay for LSD is also available. Shifts in body metabolism from hallucinogen ingestion are insufficient to induce specific abnormalities in blood chemistries, blood counts, or urine analyses.

The differential diagnosis of the psychotomimetic state includes consumption of delirium-inducing drugs such as the atropine-like agents or the atypical hallucinogens PCP and tetrahydrocannabinol (THC) in marijuana. Many drugs can produce a toxic psychosis, but this state can readily be differentiated from the psychotomimetic picture. In a toxic psychosis, confusion and loss of some aspects of orientation are present, whereas with hallucinogens, the perceptual changes occur with a clear sensorium, intact orientation, and retention of recent and remote memory. In addition, the hallucinogens produce electroencephalographic (EEG) arousal, whereas drugs that cause delirium result in slowing of the EEG (Fink and Itil 1968). Atropine poisoning can be differentiated by the presence of prominent anticholinergic effects such as dry mouth and blurred vision. The THC psychosis frequently occurs with drowsiness rather than with the hyperalertness characteristic of the LSD state. PCP psychosis is accompanied by marked neurological signs (e.g., vertical nystagmus, ataxia) and more pronounced autonomic effects than are seen with the psychotomimetics. Patients with amphetamine psychoses often fail to differentiate their perceptual distortions from reality, whereas LSD users are usually aware of the difference.

The differential diagnosis also must distinguish between an acute schizophrenic reaction and a hallucinogen-induced (or other drug-induced) psychosis. The differentiation is not always easily made. It should be recalled that initial research interest in LSD arose because of the possibility that it might provide an artificially induced model of schizophrenia. The notion that

LSD induces a *model psychosis* similar to schizophrenia has several serious shortcomings, and investigators who used single photon emission computed tomography (SPECT) found that the administration of mescaline to control subjects produced a "hyperfrontal" pattern, whereas "hypofrontality" has been observed in schizophrenic patients (Hermle et al. 1992). However, the use of the potent hallucinogens may have a variety of effects on the individual who is predisposed to schizophrenia: 1) they may cause the psychosis to become manifest at an earlier age, 2) they may produce a psychosis that would have remained dormant if drugs had not been used, or 3) they may cause relapse in an individual who has had a psychotic disorder (Bowers 1987).

It has also become more difficult to distinguish between LSD psychosis and paranoid schizophrenia, particularly because patients who are in fact paranoid often now complain of being poisoned with LSD, much as they once felt they were being talked about on radio or on television programs. Hallucinations in schizophrenic psychosis are usually auditory in contrast to the hallucinations from psychotomimetics, which are predominantly visual. A history of mental illness; a psychiatric examination that indicates the absence of an intact, observing ego; auditory (rather than visual) hallucinations; and the lack of development of drug tolerance all suggest schizophrenia. An organic brain syndrome in general speaks against LSD, especially if obtunded consciousness is also present. The brief reactive schizophrenic psychosis is of sudden onset but usually follows psychosocial stressors and is associated with emotional turmoil.

## Intervention

### Intervention With the Acute Adverse Reactions

Once commonly reported by medical facilities (Ungerleider et al. 1968b), acute adverse LSD reactions are rarely seen today. The paucity of users seeking emergency medical treatment may reflect increased knowledge of how to deal with such situations on the part of the drug-using community. An individual's experience of the effects of the drug may be either pleasant or unpleasant; a perceptual distortion or illusion may provide intense anxiety in one individual and be a pleasant interlude for another. Social factors, media presentations, and public fear have all shaped perceptions of the drug's effects. Individuals who place a premium on self-control, planning, and impulse restriction

may do particularly poorly on LSD. Prediction of who will have an adverse reaction is unreliable (Ungerleider et al. 1968a). The occurrence of multiple previous good LSD experiences renders no immunity from an adverse reaction. Traumatic and stressful external events can precipitate an adverse reaction (e.g., being arrested and read one's rights in the middle of a pleasant experience may precipitate an anxiety reaction). Thus, acute adverse behavioral reactions generally are not dose-related but are a function of personal predisposition, set, and setting. Adverse reactions have occurred after doses of LSD as low as 40 μg, and no effects have been reported from using 2,000 μg, although in general the hallucinogenic effects are proportional to dosage levels.

Acute dysphoric reactions are commonly known as "bummers" or "bad trips." These reactions are caused by loss of control, the inability to cope with ego dissolution, and/or marked environmental dissonance. The result is anxiety and, in some instances, panic. The acute anxiety/panic reactions usually wear off before medical intervention is sought. Symptoms of these acute reactions are best managed by using the hypersuggestibility of the hallucinogenic state to calm and reassure the individual that he or she will be protected and that the condition will soon subside. Thus, the use years ago of a "guide, sitter, or baby-sitter" prevented marked anxiety from developing. Most LSD is metabolized and excreted within 24 hours, and most panic reactions are usually over within this time frame.

*Acute paranoid states* are adverse responses resulting from the hypervigilant state, overreading of external cues, and the unusual thoughts that occur in the course of the hallucinogenic experience. Although likely to be grandiose or megalomaniacal, they sometimes are manifested by suspiciousness and persecutory thoughts. Occasionally a confusional state (organic brain syndrome) can occur (Ungerleider 1972), and depression with suicidal ideation can develop several days after drug use (Madden 1994). Some of the adverse reactions that occur after the ingestion of hallucinogens can be caused by other contaminants in the product, such as strychnine, PCP, and amphetamine.

Treatment of the acute adverse reactions to hallucinogens first must be directed toward preventing the patient from physically harming himself or herself or others. Because the anxiety and paranoid reactions from hallucinogens may last for an hour or for a few days, the patient may require unobtrusive protection for an extended time. Reassurance and support, or the *talkdown*, is done in a quiet, pleasant environment, usually in a homelike setting. Because closing the eyes intensifies the state, the patient should sit up or walk about. Reminding the patient that a drug has produced the extraordinary ideas and feelings and that they will soon disappear may be helpful. The time sense distortion that makes minutes seem like hours also should be explained.

If drugs are needed for continuing panicky feelings, a benzodiazepine such as lorazepam can be given. Such medication can be administered orally in mildly agitated patients; however, it can be difficult to convince severely agitated and/or paranoid patients to swallow a pill, in which case parenteral administration might be necessary. Severely agitated patients who do not respond to a benzodiazepine may be given a neuroleptic agent. Caution must be used in administering neuroleptics because they can lower the seizure threshold and elicit seizures, especially if the hallucinogen has been cut with an agent that has convulsant activity, such as strychnine. Phenothiazines, such as chlorpromazine, given orally or intramuscularly can end an LSD trip and have been effective in treating LSD-induced psychosis (Cohen 1978; Dewhurst and Hatrick 1972; D. Miller 1973; Neff 1973). Because anticholinergic crises can develop with chlorpromazine in combination with other drugs with anticholinergic activity (PCP and DOM), haloperidol is a safer drug to use when the true nature of the drug ingested is unknown. Moreover, paradoxical reactions have been reported with an increase in anxiety after the administration of phenothiazines (C. J. Schwartz 1968). It has been suggested that a combination of intramuscular haloperidol and lorazepam is particularly effective in treating acute adverse reactions (P. L. Miller et al. 1992). Theoretically, selective serotonin type 2A receptor (5-HT$_{2A}$) antagonists should block the acute effects of hallucinogens; however, other drugs with significant 5-HT$_{2A}$ antagonist activity (clozapine, olanzapine, and risperidone) also might be effective (Aghajanian 1994). However, there is some indication that risperidone might exacerbate flashbacks (Abraham and Mamen 1996; Morehead 1997).

## Intervention With the Chronic Adverse Reactions

Chronic adverse reactions include psychoses, depressive reactions, acting out, paranoid states, and flashbacks (Fisher 1972). The effects of the chronic use of LSD must be differentiated from the clinical picture seen with personality disorders, particularly in those who use a variety of drugs in polydrug abuse–type patterns. Personality changes that result from LSD use may occur after a single experience, unlike that with

other classes of drugs—PCP, perhaps, excepted (Fisher 1972). In some individuals with well-integrated personalities and no psychiatric history, chronic personality changes also have resulted from repeated LSD use. In addition, the hallucinogenic drugs interact in various nonspecific ways with the personality, which may particularly impair the developing adolescent (D. Miller 1973). The suggestibility that may come from many experiences with LSD may be reinforced by the social values of a particular subculture in which the drug is used. For instance, if some of these subcultures embrace withdrawal from society and a noncompetitive approach toward life, the person who withdraws after the LSD experience(s) may be enduring a side effect that represents more of a change in social values than a physiological drug effect. Use of hallucinogens can lead to a diminution in a variety of acceptable social behaviors.

Schizophreniform reactions lasting from weeks to years have followed the psychotomimetic experience. Closely following a dysphoric experience or developing shortly after a positive one, the manifestations of psychosis may emerge and persist. Although these reactions are most likely to be precipitated in characterologically predisposed individuals who have decompensated after the upsurge of repressed material overwhelms their ego defenses, it is unclear whether hallucinogen use can "cause" long-term psychosis or if it has a role in precipitating the onset of illness (Hekimian and Gershon 1968). Although some evidence indicates that prolonged psychotic reactions tend to occur in individuals with poor premorbid adjustment, a history of psychiatric illness, and/or repeated use of hallucinogens, severe and prolonged illness has been reported in individuals without such a history (Strassman 1984). The management of these prolonged psychotic reactions does not differ from that of schizophrenia. Neuroleptics are used, sometimes in a residential setting when behavioral dysfunction makes it necessary. These patients often attempt self-medication, and serious polydrug abuse patterns have been seen (Wesson and Smith 1978). The prognosis of these psychotic states is usually favorable; however, a few remain recalcitrant to treatment.

Chronic anxiety and depressive states.   It is evident that to some individuals (perhaps to everyone under adverse circumstances) the LSD experience can be an unsettling one. In general, the psyche is capable of reconstituting itself surprisingly well within a reasonable period. Anxiety and depression continue for unusually long periods in a few individuals, however, and they may attribute these feelings to whatever psychoto-mimetic they took. It is difficult to know how much of the state that sometimes occurs is caused by a disruption of psychological homeostasis and how much is caused by a fragile personality that was exposed to it. At any rate, the anxiety and depression may persist despite psychiatric therapy and antianxiety and/or antidepressant medication.

Nondrug antianxiety techniques such as relaxation exercises and behavioral therapy may be helpful. The clinician should not accede to the magical thinking of the patient that maybe another psychedelic session (or doubling the dose) might reshuffle the psychological fragments back into their premorbid pattern.

Flashbacks. A well-publicized adverse reaction unique to the hallucinogens is the *flashback*. Flashbacks have been renamed *hallucinogen persisting perception disorder* and have specific diagnostic criteria (American Psychiatric Association 1994). In the past, the use of variable definitions of what constitutes a flashback was a major problem (Frankel 1994), and it is hoped that the establishment of specific diagnostic criteria will facilitate studying and understanding this problem. Flashbacks are the apparently spontaneous recrudescence of the same effects that were experienced during the psychotomimetic state. These effects are usually brief visual, temporal, or emotional recurrences, complete with perceptive (time) and reality distortion, that may first appear days or months after the last drug exposure. They do not appear to be dose-related and can develop after a single exposure to the drug (Levi and Miller 1990), and they can continue to recur spontaneously several weeks or months after the original drug experience. Because flashbacks appear suddenly, unexpectedly, and inappropriately, the emotional response to them may be one of dread. Even a previously pleasant drug experience may be accompanied by anxiety when the person realizes there is no way to control its recurrence. Fear of insanity may arise because no external cause for the strange, often recurrent, phenomena is apparent. However, some seem to enjoy the experience. Only a small proportion of LSD and other hallucinogen users experience flashbacks (Shick and Smith 1970). Flashbacks may or may not be precipitated by stressors, fatigue, or subsequent use of another psychedelic such as psilocybin or marijuana. The administration of selective serotonin reuptake inhibitor antidepressants has been reported to initiate or exacerbate flashbacks in individuals with a history of LSD use (Markel et al. 1994).

The exact mechanism underlying flashbacks remains obscure. These recurrences may represent a response learned during a state of hyperarousal (Cohen 1981). LSD users have been shown to have long-term changes in visual function (Abraham 1982; Abraham and Aldridge 1993; Abraham and Wolf 1988). For example, a visual disturbance consisting of prolonged afterimages (palinopsia) has been found in individuals several years after the last reported use of LSD (Kawasaki and Purvin 1996). Such changes in visual function might underlie flashbacks. Individuals with flashbacks appear to have a high lifetime incidence of affective disorder compared with non-LSD-abusing substance abusers (Abraham and Aldridge 1994). Flashbacks can usually be handled with psychotherapy. In time, flashbacks usually decrease in intensity, frequency, and duration (although initially they often last only a few seconds), whether treated (with anxiolytics and/or reassurance) or not.

Treatment of chronic hallucinogen abuse usually involves long-term psychotherapy to determine—*after* cessation of use—what needs are being fulfilled by the long-term use of the drug for this particular person. Support in the form of 12-step program meetings and family involvement also is crucial to reinforce the decision to remain abstinent. The most important aspect of treatment consists of reassurance that the condition will pass, that the brain is not damaged, and that the hallucinogen is not retained in the brain. If the patient is agitated because of repeated flashbacks, an anxiolytic drug is indicated. The patient's physical and mental status should improve with the appropriate hygienic measures, and all substances with hallucinogenic activity, including marijuana, must be avoided. If no flashbacks have occurred during the 1–2 years since the last ingestion of the hallucinogen, it is unlikely that any more will occur.

# Summary

We have discussed the psychotropic drugs called hallucinogens from several perspectives, including the acute and chronic adverse effects of these drugs, their patterns of abuse, and their relation to mental illness. Diagnostic and treatment issues have been considered. We have emphasized the prototype hallucinogen LSD.

# References

Abraham HD: A chronic impairment of colour vision in users of LSD. Br J Psychiatry 140:518–520, 1982

Abraham HD, Aldridge AM: Adverse consequences of lysergic acid diethylamide. Addiction 88:1327–1334, 1993

Abraham HD, Aldridge AM: LSD: a point well taken. Addiction 89:762–763, 1994

Abraham HD, Mamen A: LSD-like panic from risperidone in post-LSD visual disorder. J Clin Psychopharmacol 16:238–241, 1996

Abraham HD, Wolf E: Visual function in past users of LSD: psychophysical findings. J Abnorm Psychol 97:443–447, 1988

Aghajanian GK: Serotonin and the action of LSD in the brain. Psychiatric Annals 24:137–141, 1994

American Psychiatric Association: Diagnostic and Statistical Manual of Mental Disorders, 4th Edition. Washington, DC, American Psychiatric Association, 1994

Basalt RC: Disposition of Toxic Drugs and Chemicals in Man. Davis, CA, Biomedical Publications, 1982

Bonson KR, Murphy DL: Alterations in responses to LSD in humans associated with chronic administration of tricyclic antidepressants, monoamine oxidase inhibitors or lithium. Behav Brain Res 73:229–233, 1996

Bonson KR, Buckholtz JW, Murphy DL: Chronic administration of serotonergic antidepressants attenuates the subjective effects of LSD in humans. Neuropsychopharmacology 14:425–437, 1996

Bowers MB Jr: The role of drugs in the production of schizophreniform psychoses and related disorders, in Psychopharmacology: The Third Generation of Progress. Edited by Meltzer HY. New York, Raven, 1987, pp 819–828

Cohen S: Psychotomimetics (hallucinogens) and cannabis, in Principles of Psychopharmacology. Edited by Clark WG, del Gudice J. New York, Academic Press, 1978, pp 357–371

Cohen S: The Substance Abuse Problems. New York, Haworth, 1981

Cuomo MJ, Dyment PG, Gamino VM: Increasing use of "ecstasy" (MDMA) and other hallucinogens on a college campus. J Am Coll Health 42:271–274, 1994

Dewhurst K, Hatrick JA: Differential diagnosis and treatment of lysergic acid diethylamide-induced psychosis. Practitioner 209:327–332, 1972

Fink M, Itil TM: Neurophysiology of phantastica: EEG and behavioral relations in man, in Psychopharmacology: A Review of Progress, 1957–1967. Edited by Efrom DH. Washington, DC, U.S. Department of Health, Education, and Welfare, 1968, pp 1231–1239

Fisher DD: The chronic side effects from LSD, in The Problems and Prospects of LSD. Edited by Ungerleider JT. Springfield, IL, Charles C Thomas, 1972, pp 69–80

Frankel FH: The concept of flashbacks in historical perspective. Int J Clin Exp Hypn 42:321–335, 1994

Grob CS, Poland RE, Chang C, et al: Psychobiologic effects of 3,4-methylenedioxymethamphetamine in humans: methodological considerations and preliminary observations. Behav Brain Res 73:103–107, 1996

Hekimian LJ, Gershon S: Characteristics of drug abusers admitted to a psychiatric hospital. JAMA 205:75–80, 1968

Hermle L, Fünfgeld M, Oepen G, et al: Mescaline-induced psychopathological, neuropsychological, and neurometabolic effects in normal subjects: experimental psychosis as a tool for psychiatric research. Biol Psychiatry 32:976–991, 1992

Hofmann A: Chemical, pharmacological, and medical aspects of psychotomimetics. Journal of Experimental Medical Sciences 5:31–51, 1961

Hollister LE: Psychotomimetic drugs in man, in Handbook of Psychopharmacology, Vol II. Edited by Iversen LL, Iversen SD, Snyder SH. New York, Plenum, 1978, pp 389–424

Johnston L: Monitoring the Future: The National High School Senior Survey. Rockville, MD, National Institute on Drug Abuse, 1990

Johnston LD, O'Malley PM, Bachman JG: National Survey Results on Drug Use From the Monitoring the Future Study, 1975–1994, Vol II: College Students and Young Adults (NIH Publ No 96-4027). Rockville, MD, National Institute on Drug Abuse, 1996

Kawasaki A, Purvin V: Persistent palinopsia following ingestion of lysergic acid diethylamide (LSD). Arch Ophthalmol 114:47–50, 1996

Levi L, Miller NR: Visual illusions associated with previous drug abuse. J Neuroophthalmol 10:103–110, 1990

Madden JS: LSD and post-hallucinogenic perceptual disorder. Addiction 86:762–763, 1994

Markel H, Lee A, Holmes RD, et al: LSD flashback syndrome exacerbated by selective serotonin reuptake inhibitor antidepressants in adolescents. J Pediatr 125:817–819, 1994

Miller D: The drug dependent adolescent, in Adolescent Psychiatry, Vol 2. Edited by Feinstein SC, Giovachini P. New York, Basic Books, 1973, pp 70–97

Miller PL, Gay GR, Ferris KC, et al: Treatment of acute, adverse reactions: "I've tripped and I can't get down." J Psychoactive Drugs 24:277–279, 1992

Morehead DB: Exacerbation of hallucinogen-persisting perception disorder with risperidone. J Clin Psychopharmacol 17:327–328, 1997

Nagy J: A Comparison of Drug Use Among 8th, 10th, and 12th Graders From NIDA's High School Senior Survey. Rockville, MD, National Institute on Drug Abuse, 1992

Neff L: Chemicals and their effects on the adolescent ego, in Adolescent Psychiatry, Vol 1. Edited by Feinstein S, Giovachini P, Miller A. New York, Basic Books, 1973, pp 108–120

Osmond H: A review of the clinical effects of psychotomimetic agents. Ann N Y Acad Sci 66:418–434, 1957

Perera KMH, Ferraro A, Pinto MRM: Catatonia LSD induced? Aust N Z J Psychiatry 29:324–327, 1995

Resnick O, Krus DM, Raskin M: LSD-25 action in normal subjects treated with a monoamine oxidase inhibitor. Life Sci 3:1207–1214, 1964

Schwartz CJ: The complications of LSD: a review of the literature. J Nerv Ment Dis 146:174–186, 1968

Schwartz RH: LSD: its rise, fall, and renewed popularity among high school students. Pediatr Clin North Am 42:403–413, 1995

Seligmann J, Mason M, Annin P, et al: The New Age of Aquarius. Newsweek, February 3, 1992, pp 66–67

Shick JFE, Smith DE: An analysis of the LSD flashback. Journal of Psychedelic Drugs 3:13–19, 1970

Shulgin A, Shulgin A: PIKHAL: A Chemical Love Story. Berkeley, CA, Transform Press, 1991

Sobel J, Espinas O, Friedman S: Carotid artery obstruction following LSD capsule ingestion. Arch Intern Med 127:290–291, 1971

Strassman RJ: Adverse reactions to psychedelic drugs: a review of the literature. J Nerv Ment Dis 172:577–595, 1984

Strassman RJ: Human hallucinogen interactions with drugs affecting serotonergic neurotransmission. Neuropsychopharmacology 7:241–243, 1992

Strassman RJ: Hallucinogenic drugs in psychiatric research and treatment; perspectives and prospects. J Nerv Ment Dis 183:127–138, 1995

Strassman RJ, Qualls CR: Dose-response study of N,N-dimethyltryptamine in humans, I: neuroendocrine, autonomic and cardiovascular effects. Arch Gen Psychiatry 51:85–87, 1994

Strassman RJ, Qualls CR, Uhlenhuth EH, et al: Dose-response study of N,N-dimethyltryptamine in humans, II: subjective effects and preliminary results of a new rating scale. Arch Gen Psychiatry 51:98–108, 1994

Ungerleider JT: The acute side effects from LSD, in The Problems and Prospects of LSD. Edited by Ungerleider JT. Springfield, IL, Charles C Thomas, 1972, pp 61–68

Ungerleider JT, Fisher DD, Fuller MC, et al: The bad trip: the etiology of the adverse LSD reaction. Am J Psychiatry 125:1483–1490, 1968a

Ungerleider JT, Fisher DD, Goldsmith SR, et al: A statistical survey of adverse reactions to LSD in Los Angeles County. Am J Psychiatry 125:352–357, 1968b

Wesson DR, Smith DE: Psychedelics in Treatment Aspects of Drug Dependence. West Palm Beach, FL, CRC Press, 1978

# 20 Phencyclidine

Sidney H. Schnoll, M.D., Ph.D.
Michael F. Weaver, M.D.

Phencyclidine (1-[1-phencyclohexyl]piperidine monohydrochloride; PCP) was synthesized in the late 1950s. It is an arylcyclohexylamine that was the first of a new class of general anesthetics known as cataleptoid anesthetics or dissociative anesthetics. PCP can be manufactured easily in unsophisticated laboratories from simple materials. Other arylcyclohexylamines include N-ethyl-1-phencyclohexalamine (PCE), 1-(1-2-thienyl-cyclohexyl)piperidine (TCP), 1-(1-phencyclohexyl)pyrrolidine (PHP), and 1-piperidino-cyclohexane carbonitrile (PCC). These products have been found as contaminants in samples of PCP sold on the street (Schnoll 1980). Ketamine, an arylcycloalkylamine related to PCP, is less potent and shorter acting and is still used as a dissociative anesthetic in humans (Chen et al. 1959) and illicitly as a drug of abuse.

PCP was originally described as a drug of abuse in both New York and San Francisco in the mid-1960s but rapidly disappeared as a popular drug of abuse because of the unexpected reactions that often occurred following its use. In the late 1960s and early 1970s, PCP emerged as a frequent contaminant of other drugs sold on the illicit market, most often in samples of hallucinogens and tetrahydrocannabinol, because it is relatively easy to manufacture chemically compared with processing of tetrahydrocannabinol. In the past few years, PCP has once again become a sought-after drug of abuse and a contaminant in other drugs of abuse. Data suggest that PCP abuse is not widespread in the United States but has become concentrated among post-high-school-age black males in a limited number of cities (Thombs 1989). In some urban settings in the United States, PCP abuse was rivaled only by crack cocaine in popularity (Johnson and Jones 1990). However, the Monitoring the Future Study by the National Institute on Drug Abuse showed that use of PCP by high school seniors has declined steadily since 1979, when 7% had used PCP in the preceding year (Johnston et al. 1993); in 1995, only 1.8% had used PCP in the preceding year. Patterns of PCP use vary with time and location. It is seen primarily in large cities in the United States, and its popularity tends to wax and wane.

PCP can be taken through several routes of administration: oral, intravenous, smoking, or snorting. As a frequent contaminant of street drugs, it is often used in conjunction with other drugs. PCP is well absorbed, and its effects are felt in a few minutes to a half-hour (Baldridge and Besson 1990) by most routes, including percutaneously (Bailey 1980). Although the absorption with oral administration usually takes more than 1 hour, the effect is almost immediate after smoking. Smoking is becoming the most popular route of administration among drug users, and inhalation produces a similar pharmacological profile to intravenous administration (Meng et al. 1996). This crystalline, water-soluble, lipophilic substance penetrates easily into fat stores and other cells and accumulates in adipose tissue and in the brain (Misra et al. 1979). Its half-life is 21–24 hours, depending on the route of administration (Hurlbut 1991). PCP is one of the longest acting drugs of abuse, and intoxication may take up to 6 weeks to clear (Schuckit 1984). Metabolism takes place primarily in the liver by oxidation, hydroxylation, and conjugation with glucuronic acid (Wong and Biemann 1976). Only a small amount of the active drug is excreted directly in the urine.

For some time, it was unclear how PCP worked in the central nervous system (CNS). It had been proposed that PCP interacted with numerous CNS neurotransmitters, including 5-hydroxytryptamine, norepinephrine, acetylcholine, dopamine, and glutamic acid. PCP and analogs such as ketamine have multiple effects on the CNS. They selectively reduce the excitatory actions of glutamate on CNS neurons mediated by the N-methyl-D-aspartate (NMDA) receptor complex (Anis et al. 1983). NMDA receptors mediate ion flux through channels permeable to sodium, potassium, and calcium and are involved in synaptic transmission, long-term potentiation, seizure induction, ischemic brain damage, and perhaps neuronal plasticity. But the behavioral effects of PCP are not simply the result of interaction with the NMDA-operated ion channel (Johnson and Jones 1990). PCP affects both σ and μ opioid receptors (Giannini et al. 1984), blocks uptake of dopamine equipotent to amphetamine (Bowyer et al. 1984), and inhibits serotonin uptake (R. C. Smith et al. 1977). The binding at the NMDA site may be responsible for PCP's behavioral effects, although drugs that bind to the σ opioid site are known to produce dysphoria and hallucinations. Further elucidation of PCP's action at these binding sites may play an important role in our understanding of its effects and potential benefits.

Clinically, PCP's CNS effects result in a rise in blood pressure, heart rate, and respiratory rate. These catecholamine-mediated actions may be related to panic reactions sometimes observed in users. PCP's effect on reflexes probably leads to muscle rigidity, and its cholinergic effects lead to increased CNS acetylcholine activity, with resulting sweating, flushing, drooling, and pupillary constriction. Its serotonergic effects cause dizziness, incoordination, slurred speech, and nystagmus. PCP has been shown to bind to specific receptors in the liver, kidney, lung, heart, and brain (Weinstein et al. 1981).

PCP produces brief dissociative psychotic reactions similar to schizophrenic psychoses. These reactions are characterized by changes in body image, thought disorder, depersonalization, and autism. At higher dosages, subjects have great difficulty differentiating between themselves and their surroundings. Other users will experience hostility, paranoia, violence, and preoccupation with death. While intoxicated, users may also have religious experiences such as feelings of meeting God or impending death (D. A. Gorelick et al. 1986). Differences in the response to PCP may be dose related or based on the individual response of the user (National Institute on Drug Abuse 1979). The PCP experience is regarded as pleasant only half the time and negative or aversive the other half, but many chronic users report that the unpredictability of the drug's effect is one of its attractive features (Carroll 1985).

Interest has been increasing in the use of PCP as a model to study schizophrenia. As opposed to amphetamines, PCP-induced psychosis incorporates both the positive symptoms of schizophrenia (e.g., hallucinations, paranoia) and the negative symptoms (e.g., emotional withdrawal, motor retardation) (Javitt and Zukin 1991). Other researchers have investigated positron-emission tomography of PCP-using patients as a possible drug model of schizophrenia (Wu et al. 1991).

PCP is used primarily by adolescents and young adults. First use is usually between ages 13 and 15 years. Chronic PCP use does occur outside the adolescent/young adult age group and is not rare among psychiatric patients (D. A. Gorelick et al. 1986). PCP users are usually polydrug abusers; more than 90% of PCP users report use of other substances, mainly marijuana and alcohol. In the past, PCP was often found as a contaminant in other street drugs; however, samples of PCP are now often contaminated by other drugs. The lack of knowledge of PCP's interactions with other drugs has led to problems in treating PCP reactions (Schnoll 1980).

On the street, PCP has been known by many names including angel dust. The abundance of street names for this substance is probably related to the initial lack of popularity of the oral route of PCP use. It has been suggested that a new drug that has a bizarre name and is smoked or snorted can be assumed to be PCP until proven otherwise.

## Phencyclidine Intoxication

Diagnosis of PCP or similarly acting arylcyclohexylamine intoxication is based on behavioral changes that occur following ingestion of the drug, including belligerence, assaultiveness, impulsiveness, unpredictability, psychomotor agitation, impaired judgment, and impaired social and occupational functioning. Physical findings may include horizontal and/or vertical nystagmus, hypertension, tachycardia, diminished pain sensation, ataxia, dysarthria, muscle rigidity, seizures, and hyperacusis. Low-dose intoxication (5–10 mg orally, by snorting or inhaling) induces agitation, excitement, catalepsy, and mutism (Burns and Lerner 1976). Patients with severe PCP intoxication are generally unresponsive and comatose yet their eyes are open (Pearlson 1981). A diagnosis of PCP intoxication should be confirmed with toxicological analysis of blood or urine. Without this confirmation, the diagnosis can be only presumptive at best.

Although not discrete from one another, three stages for PCP intoxication have been described depending on the dosage taken (Rappolt et al. 1980): behavioral toxicity, stuporous stage, and comatose stage (see Table 20–1). The patient may fluctuate between the stuporous stage and behavioral toxicity in 1- to 2-hour periods. The comatose stage may last 1–4 days, depending on the dosage of PCP taken and the rate of excretion of the drug. The electroencephalogram shows delta wave activity followed by theta wave activity.

The differential diagnosis for PCP intoxication should include head trauma, schizophrenia or acute psychosis, organic brain syndrome, mania, cerebro-

**Table 20–1.**  Stages of phencyclidine intoxication

|  | Stage I<br>Behavioral toxicity | Stage II<br>Stuporous stage | Stage III<br>Comatose stage |
|---|---|---|---|
| Ingested dose (mg) | 2–5 (snort/smoke) | 5–20 | > 25 (oral) |
| Serum level (ng/mL) | 20–30 | 90–300 | > 300 |
| Duration | 1–2 hours | 1–2 hours | 1–4 days |
| Mental status | Loss of concentration, illogical speech, agitation | Stupor with open eyes and wakeful appearance, seizures on stimulation | Deep coma, status epilepticus |
| Eye findings |  |  |  |
|   Gaze | Blank stare | Disconjugate, roving eyes or fixed stare | Disconjugate |
|   Pupils | Variable, often miotic | Midposition, reactive | ↑ dilatation |
|   Nystagmus | Horizontal<br>Vertical (late) | Any direction | Any direction |
| Vital signs |  |  |  |
|   Temperature | ↑ (98–101°F, 36.6–38.3°C) | ↑↑ (101–103°F, 38.3–39.4°C) | ↑↑↑ (103–108°F, 39.4–42.2°C; malignant hyperthermia) |
|   Blood pressure and heart rate | ↑ | ↑↑ (25% above normal) | ↑↑↑ (twice normal) |
|   Respiration | ↑ | ↑↑ (25% above normal) | Periodic respiration, apnea |
| Reflexes |  |  |  |
|   Deep tendon reflexes | ↑, clonus | ↑↑, crossed limb reflexes | Absent |
|   Gag | ↑ | ↓, repetitive swallowing, retching | Absent |
|   Corneal |  | Absent | Absent |
| Pain response | ↓ pinprick | Deep pain response intact | Deep pain response absent |
| Motor system | Muscle rigidity and spasm, ataxia, dysarthria, repetitive movements, grimacing, bruxism | Rigidity and twitching, myoclonus, spasticity | Opisthotonos, myoclonus |
| Autonomic system | Nausea, vomiting, flushing, diaphoresis, lacrimation, drooling | ↑ | ↑↑, profuse sweating |
| Electroencephalogram |  | Delta waves | Theta waves |

*Note.*  ↑ = slight increase; ↑↑ = moderate increase; ↑↑↑ = dangerous increase; ↓ = decrease.

vascular accident, and stupor and/or coma (of metabolic origin, from drug overdose, or from other unexplained etiology).

The clinical picture that should lead the physician to consider the possibility of PCP abuse in patients presenting with an unusual behavior includes cerebellar symptoms (e.g., nystagmus, "Groucho eyes," ataxia, and dysarthria), elevation of pulse and blood pressure, reduced sensitivity to pain, increased deep tendon reflexes, excessive salivation, and nausea. These signs and symptoms together with urine and blood toxicology should be used to differentiate PCP intoxication from acute psychosis or schizophrenia.

To help clinicians make an accurate diagnosis, emergency rooms should have laboratory techniques available to detect the presence of PCP in body fluids. The body fluids of arrested individuals whose arrests were associated with impulsive bizarre behavior or unexplained assaultive acts should also be tested for PCP. As in all instances of toxicological analysis, a positive urine test for PCP should be verified by using a second analytical technique.

The presence of ataxia and nystagmus and the absence of dilated pupils are useful in ruling out the CNS stimulants and lysergic acid diethylamide (LSD) when evaluating acutely agitated and confused patients. PCP is the only drug of abuse that causes a characteristic vertical nystagmus, although it can also cause horizontal or rotary nystagmus. The presence of hyperreflexia and hypertension differentiate PCP intoxication from sedative-hypnotic intoxication (National Institute on Drug Abuse 1979), although these signs may be present in acute withdrawal from sedative-hypnotic medications or ethanol.

## Management of Phencyclidine Intoxication

Because of poor judgment, the patient usually will require supervision in a nonstimulating environment that should include protection from self-injury. When possible, a careful history should be taken, including drugs taken, duration of use, time of last dose, adverse reactions to drugs, and psychiatric history. History obtained from companions or family members may be useful. Belongings should be searched carefully for the presence of drugs or paraphernalia, which should be analyzed to assist in making the diagnosis.

A thorough physical and neurological examination should be performed. Vital signs need to be monitored for laryngeal stridor or respiratory depression, and a res-

pirator may be required. Restraints should be avoided; Lahmeyer and Stock (1983) reported that the use of restraints may cause rhabdomyolysis with resultant acute renal failure, and Mercy et al. (1990) identified PCP as a major factor associated with the death of prisoners who were restrained by police. If required, the preferred method of physical restraint for combative patients is total body immobilization by rolling the patient in a sheet (Aronow et al. 1980). Although the *talking-down* technique has been used to treat acute hallucinogen reactions, this approach should be avoided in PCP-intoxicated patients because it may intensify agitation.

To establish the diagnosis, other types of altered mental status should be ruled out. Naloxone may be given to rule out opioid intoxication. Toxicology screen on samples of blood (10 mL) and urine (50 mL) is important, although reliance on blood levels is hazardous because the active substance may be released repeatedly from fat stores. The serum concentration of PCP is a less accurate indicator of a patient's level of intoxication than is a fat biopsy. PCP can also be detected in hair samples from chronic users (Slawson et al. 1996).

Most patients who have mild to moderate symptoms of acute PCP intoxication will improve rapidly. Intoxicated patients should be observed until their mental status has remained normal for several hours (Baldridge and Bessen 1990). If symptoms continue to diminish and no cognitive impairment is present after 12 hours, the patient may be discharged from the emergency department (Woolf et al. 1980).

There is no specific antagonist for PCP. If PCP is taken orally, a gastric lavage performed with a liter or more of half normal saline can be done. In cases of coma secondary to acute PCP intoxication, residual drug should be removed from the stomach and sent for analysis. The patient then may be placed on intermittent gastric suction using a nasogastric tube. An alternative to gastric lavage is the administration of activated charcoal to adsorb the PCP that is secreted into the acid environment of the stomach. Dialysis is ineffective in removing PCP from the body (Rappolt et al. 1980).

The concentration of PCP in the body fluids and tissues is influenced profoundly by pH. Some PCP is retained in fatty tissues and in the brain, where it escapes hepatic metabolism. Acidification of urine increases the excretion rate of PCP roughly 100-fold because the drug is a weak base. Urine acidification is controversial, and the risks and benefits to the individual patient must be weighed before acidification is begun. If acidification is done prior to toxicological screens of urine and blood for the presence of other drugs, excretion and analysis for other drugs (e.g., barbiturates or salicylates) may be affected adversely. Urine acidification is contraindicated in the presence of myoglobinuria, renal insufficiency, severe liver disease, or concomitant abuse of barbiturates or salicylates (Woolf et al. 1980).

One approach to urine acidification is to administer vitamin C (ascorbic acid) with intravenous fluids at the rate of 2 g in 500 mL every 6 hours. Another approach is to use ammonium chloride 2.75 mEq/kg dissolved in 60 mL of saline given through the nasogastric tube every 6 hours until the urine pH is 5.5 or less. Urine pH needs to be checked two to four times each day. When the pH is 5.5, diuresis should be forced by using furosemide 20–40 mg intravenously. After consciousness returns, urine acidification should continue for 1 week, by giving cranberry juice along with ammonium chloride, 500 mg orally four times a day, or ascorbic acid, 1 g orally three times a day. Ammonium chloride should be used with caution because ammonia breakdown products may burden a damaged liver (Rappolt et al. 1980). Throughout the initial treatment, electrolytes should be maintained within the normal range, and blood gases should be monitored periodically.

Medication other than acidifying agents should be avoided in the patient who is comatose from PCP intoxication. The exception to this rule is a patient who is hypertensive secondary to PCP. In this case, antihypertensive medications should be administered to reduce blood pressure. If the patient is severely agitated and poses a potential threat to self or others, haloperidol is effective in controlling the agitation. When there is doubt about the drug the individual has taken or when a combination of drugs may be present, diazepam 5–20 mg intravenously slowly or orally can be used. Studies indicate that barbiturates may be more efficacious in treating the psychotomimetic effects of PCP-like drugs (Olney et al. 1991).

## Complications of Phencyclidine Intoxication

1. *Undetected PCP overdose.* This complication usually follows oral ingestion of the compound or a compound in which PCP was a contaminant. Adding to the confusion is the late onset of action of the orally ingested form. This should be suspected in children and in patients who fail to improve after 3 hours of observation or in those whose level of confusion seems to increase rather than decrease with time. Whenever PCP ingestion is suspected, urine, blood, or gastric contents should be collected and sent for toxicological analysis to confirm or rule out the diagnosis of PCP intoxication.

2. *Seizure and status epilepticus.* The association of seizure with PCP use has been well documented (Alldredge et al. 1989). No medication is necessary to treat a single seizure; however, if repeated seizures occur or if the patient is in status epilepticus, diazepam, 10–20 mg intravenously, or lorazepam, 2–4 mg intravenously, should be used as needed.

3. *Hypertension.* Hydralazine or phentolamine intravenous drip (2–5 mg over 5–10 minutes) should be given.

4. *Hyperthermia.* Hypothermic blankets or ice should be used.

5. *Opisthotonos and acute dystonia.* This complication usually clears as blood levels of the drug decrease. If the problem persists, intravenous diazepam or lorazepam is often effective for relaxing the musculature.

6. *Cardiac arrhythmia.* In the case of a severe arrhythmia that does not clear, a cardiology consultation should be called.

7. *Rhabdomyolysis, myoglobinuria, and acute renal failure.* A urine sample should be obtained from the patient to evaluate for myoglobinuria, and serum should be obtained to test for elevated creatine phosphokinase levels to diagnose rhabdomyolysis, which may induce acute renal failure. Acidification of the urine is contraindicated in the presence of rhabdomyolysis or renal failure (either acute or chronic). When acute renal failure is present, a nephrology consultation should be called.

8. *PCP psychosis.* See section "Phencyclidine Delirium" below.

9. *Stroke.* Ischemic and hemorrhagic strokes have been reported in association with PCP (P. B. Gorelick 1990; Sloan et al. 1991).

10. *Obstetric complications.* Infants exposed to PCP in utero may have intrauterine growth retardation and prolonged hospitalizations. They are less likely than cocaine-exposed infants to be born prematurely (Tabor et al. 1990).

## Phencyclidine Delirium

Acute PCP delirium is the most common psychiatric syndrome that brings users to medical attention. The acute episode usually lasts 3–8 hours, but duration and severity are dose related. PCP delirium is characterized by clouded consciousness that frequently waxes and wanes, which may be attributable to periodic gastric secretion with enteric reabsorption of the drug (Hurlbut 1991). The clinical picture is dominated by insomnia, restlessness, and behavior that is purposeless, hyperactive, bizarre, aggressive, or agitated. The patient's mental state may fluctuate to include paranoia, mania, grandiosity, rapid thought and speech, and emotional lability.

Intravenous PCP has produced schizophrenic-like symptoms in subjects with no history of psychotic behavior (Gallant 1981). Initially, alterations of body image occur, with a loss of body boundaries and a sense of unreality. Feelings of estrangement and loneliness follow, sometimes associated with an intensification of dependency needs. Progressive disorganization of thought, negativism, and hostility can also develop. Some subjects become catatonic with dreamlike experiences. Distortion of body image and depersonalization are universal reactions, and attention and cognitive deficits are often present.

Three phases for PCP psychosis have been described, each lasting approximately 5 days: 1) agitated phase, 2) mixed phase, and 3) resolution phase. Factors reported to influence the duration of each phase are individual susceptibility, degree of exposure to the drug, dosage of antipsychotic, and urine acidification. The psychosis may persist in some individuals anywhere from 24 hours to several months or even years after the cessation of active PCP use. Whether this is a direct effect of PCP or the drug exacerbating an underlying psychotic disorder is not clear; administration of PCP to schizophrenic patients has been reported to acutely exacerbate schizophrenic-psychotic symptoms.

A PCP psychosis in the presence of a clear sensorium is rare. The patient should be examined for the presence of horizontal or vertical nystagmus, ataxia, or slurred speech. These signs indicate PCP intoxication rather than PCP psychosis. Preexisting psychiatric disorders should be ruled out. Daghestani (1987) emphasized the importance of a thorough diagnostic workup with all patients who present with acute psychotic decompensation. Anticholinergic drug intoxication must be ruled out before initiating treatment with an antipsychotic agent.

Luisada and Brown (1976) observed that "about one-fourth of the patients originally treated for phencyclidine psychosis return about 1 year later with schizophrenia in the absence of drug use. These later episodes have lacked the characteristic violence of the phencyclidine-induced psychosis, and they respond quickly to antipsychotic drugs" (p. 544).

## Management of Phencyclidine Delirium

The guidelines for management of PCP intoxication also apply to PCP delirium to a large extent. The goals of treatment should include prevention of injury, facilitation of the excretion of PCP through urine, and the amelioration of psychosis. The patient should be hospitalized in a closed psychiatric unit and assigned to a quiet room. If agitated, the patient should be restrained by trained personnel. All efforts should be made to avoid physical restraints. Because of the intense physical exertion often associated with the agitation observed in PCP delirium, the patient should be given adequate hydration.

The principles of urine acidification discussed earlier in this chapter apply here, although the acidifying agents should be given orally: cranberry juice (8–16 oz four times a day), ascorbic acid (1 g four times a day), or ammonium chloride (liquid solution 500 mg/5 mL, with an initial loading dose of 15–20 mL of ammonium chloride followed by 10 mL four times a day).

Once the urine pH is 5.5 or less, diuresis may be encouraged by the administration of furosemide 40 mg twice a day. Oral potassium supplementation will be necessary to avoid potassium depletion, and serum electrolytes should be monitored daily. Improvement may be expected 6–8 hours after diuresis. Urine acidification should continue for at least 3 days after all evidence of psychosis has disappeared, and most patients will require a 3- to 10-day course of acidification. The use of antacids, which act as alkalinizing agents, should be avoided while attempts are being made to enhance excretion of PCP by acidifying the urine. Antacids significantly reduce the ability of ammonium chloride and other acidifying drugs to lower the urine pH, resulting in retention of PCP in the serum.

The use of psychotherapeutic drugs should be undertaken carefully and judiciously. Benzodiazepines and haloperidol have been described as being useful in the treatment of delirium caused by PCP. Pitts (1984) suggested that a standard dose of a benzodiazepine, a neuroleptic, and a β-blocker given together will resolve the delirious psychotic state within minutes. This approach is based on the premise of the multiple receptor effects of PCP. It was thought that blockers or competitors would blunt the responses observed in these patients. According to Pitts, few patients who maintain confusional symptoms will require long-term therapy. There have been no subsequent reports verifying the effectiveness of this approach.

Electroconvulsive therapy has been tried successfully

in psychotic patients who have used PCP if they fail to respond to antipsychotic medications after 1 week of inpatient treatment (Grover et al. 1986; Rosen et al. 1984). Following the resolution of the acute confusional psychotic state, a referral to long-term therapy is important.

## Phencyclidine Organic Mental Disorder

Phencyclidine organic mental disorder is a chronic mental impairment believed to result from chronic PCP use. The condition is characterized by memory deficits and a state of confusion or decreased intellectual functioning with associated assaultiveness. There are also visual disturbances and speech difficulty, such as *blocking* (inability to retrieve the proper words). A differential diagnosis should rule out other causes of organicity. The course of the disorder may be quite variable. The reasons for this variability are not clear but may be related to the release of residual drug from adipose tissues of the chronic user. The confusional state may last 4–6 weeks. The patient's condition may improve with time if PCP exposure does not recur and if residual PCP is excreted by acidifying the patient's urine.

### Management of Phencyclidine Organic Mental Disorder

The basic management plan is that of protecting the patient from injury and helping him or her deal with disorientation by using a simple, structured, and supportive approach. Sensory input and stimuli should be kept to a minimum. A nonthreatening environment and nonjudgmental staff are of paramount importance. Excessive stimulation can result in agitation and violent, aggressive behavior.

## Phencyclidine Abuse and Phencyclidine Dependence

The diagnostic criteria for PCP or similarly acting arylcyclohexylamine abuse include the following:

1. Pattern of pathological use: intoxication throughout the day; episodes of PCP or similarly acting arylcyclohexylamine delirium or mixed organic mental disorder
2. Impairment in social or occupational functioning due to substance use, for example, fights, loss of

friends, absence from work, loss of job, or legal difficulties (other than those due to a single arrest for possession, purchase, or sale of the substance)
3. Duration of disturbance of at least 1 month.

These criteria should be supported by the presence of PCP or other arylcyclohexylamines in the blood or urine.

In addition to these criteria, D. E. Smith and Wesson (1978) reported that a significant number of individuals experience profound depression from chronic use of PCP. Physical dependence on PCP may develop but probably requires long-term regular exposure to relatively high levels of the drug (D. A. Gorelick et al. 1986). Tolerance to the disruptive effects of PCP on operant behavior has been reported. A PCP withdrawal syndrome in humans has not been clearly characterized (Carroll 1990). PCP withdrawal has been observed in animals within 4–8 hours after the drug is discontinued. Because of PCP's longer half-life in humans, withdrawal may not be seen for several days, if at all. Tennant and colleagues (1981) identified symptoms of depression, drug craving, increased appetite, laziness, and increased need for sleep occurring 1 week to 1 month after termination of drug use. Increased neuromuscular activity and bruxism are common. Diarrhea and abdominal pain have also been described (Balster and Woolverton 1981).

### Management of Phencyclidine Abuse and Dependence

Treatment of PCP abuse is often difficult because of patients' strong psychological dependence on the drug (D. A. Gorelick et al. 1986). Therapists should be aware that PCP users display a wide range of behaviors, including flattened affect, belligerence, depression, and anxiety. Difficulties of treating PCP abusers include impaired attention span and concentration, emotional lability, impulsiveness, poor group interaction, and low tolerance for confrontation (Bolter 1980). PCP abusers are often unable to cope with the demands and expectations of the structured, intensive, confrontational environment of the type often found in some residential treatment programs. Bolter (1980) suggested that the following management strategies may be effective at the beginning of treatment: 1) establish clear ground rules that are enforced, 2) keep decision making to a minimum, 3) accept some absentmindedness initially—directions may have to be repeated, 4) develop a short list of tasks with a regular routine, 5) avoid stressful situations, and 6) set realistic consequences for both positive and negative behavior and be consistent in the application of these consequences.

Because of the cognitive impairments associated with PCP abuse, the treatment environment should provide a supportive structure. All staff members must be aware of the treatment plan to prevent the patient from playing one staff member against another (splitting). Staff should be well trained in the effects of PCP so that they can work effectively with the types of problems presented. There are some differences between long-term narcotic-dependent individuals and chronic PCP-abusing individuals, making the therapeutic community approach inappropriate for those individuals needing long-term treatment for chronic PCP abuse. PCP-abusing individuals tend to be younger, more immature, and unable to tolerate the usual confrontation techniques used in therapeutic communities (De Angelis and Goldstein 1978). Chronic PCP-abusing individuals have characteristics similar to children with learning disabilities. They generally show emotional lability, social incompetence, overt impulsiveness, poor social judgment, poor attention span and concentration, poor interpersonal relationships, and social maladjustment. These characteristics may be reversible if PCP use stops and appropriate treatment is provided.

The following considerations are important when structuring a program responsive to PCP-abusing patients:

1. There should be minimal confrontation or hostility-provoking behavior by staff.
2. Patients should be provided with a nonthreatening, supportive environment in which they can begin to feel comfortable.
3. Minimal patient involvement in specific therapeutic interventions should be anticipated initially.

Caracci et al. (1983) recommended hospitalization for treatment of PCP-induced depression with suicidal potential in patients difficult to engage.

During the course of outpatient therapy, educational and nutritional awareness will enhance the patient's level of self-care. Vocational counseling and training may be beneficial in enhancing self-esteem. Outpatient follow-up treatment is aimed at keeping the patient from resuming drug use. It is important to assist staff in being realistic about their expectations for treatment.

Self-help groups have become an established and essential part of any successful treatment of PCP and other drug dependence. Narcotics Anonymous (NA) groups have begun to gain increasing acceptance of PCP users, and many patients have been able to use NA as part of a recovery program. PCP-abusing patients may not initially join extensively in group therapy, individual therapy, or school or recreation programs. They may be belligerent toward treatment, especially on program entry. However, mixing PCP abusers with other substance abusers appears to make clinical sense, because most PCP abusers and users also abuse other drugs (D. A. Gorelick and Wilkins 1989).

De Angelis and Goldstein (1978) found that chronic PCP-abusing patients stay in treatment longer than do individuals who use PCP occasionally. D. A. Gorelick et al. (1989) found that older patients and those referred by the criminal justice system tended to stay in treatment longer. Individual, family, couples, and group therapies have been used with some success. Body awareness therapy, yoga, and progressive relaxation techniques help patients to focus and help to improve their attention span and concentration. Many PCP-abusing individuals have a sense of loss of contact with their bodies. These exercises can be helpful in restoring a healthy body image. Consistent with this approach, patients should be encouraged to seek out athletic activities.

Treatment of PCP abuse and dependence, like all other chemical dependence problems, requires long-term treatment. Persistence and patience on the part of staff are necessary to achieve a satisfactory outcome.

# References

Alldredge BK, Lowenstein DH, Simon RP: Seizures associated with recreational drug abuse. Neurology 39:1037–1039, 1989

Anis NA, Berry SC, Burton N, et al: The dissociative anesthetics ketamine and phencyclidine selectively reduce excitation of central mammalian neurons by $N$-methyl-aspartate. Br J Pharmacol 79:565–575, 1983

Aronow R, Miceli JN, Done AK: A therapeutic approach to the acutely overdosed PCP patient. J Psychedelic Drugs 12:259–267, 1980

Bailey DN: Percutaneous absorption of phencyclidine hydrochloride in vivo. Research Communications in Substances of Abuse 1:443–450, 1980

Baldridge EB, Besson HA: Phencyclidine. Emerg Med Clin North Am 8:541–550, 1990

Balster RH, Woolverton WH: Tolerance and dependence to phencyclidine, in Phencyclidine (PCP): Historical and Current Perspectives. Edited by Domino EF. Ann Arbor, MI, NPP Books, 1981, pp 293–306

Bolter A: Issues for inpatient treatment of chronic PCP abuse. J Psychedelic Drugs 12:287–288, 1980

Bowyer JF, Spuhler KP, Weiner N: Effects of phencyclidine, amphetamine and related compounds on dopamine release from and uptake into striatal synaptosomes. J Pharmacol Exp Ther 229:671–680, 1984

Burns RS, Lerner SE: Perspectives: acute phencyclidine intoxication. Clin Toxicol 9:477–501, 1976

Caracci G, Migoni P, Mukherjee S: Phencyclidine abuse and depression. Psychosomatics 24:932–933, 1983

Carroll ME: PCP, the dangerous angel, in The Encyclopedia of Psychoactive Drugs. Edited by Snyder SH. New York, Chelsea House, 1985

Carroll ME: PCP and hallucinogens. Adv Alcohol Subst Abuse 9:167–190, 1990

Chen G, Ensor CR, Russell D, et al: The pharmacology of 1-(1-phenylcyclohexyl) piperidine HCl. J Pharmacol Exp Ther 127:241–250, 1959

Daghestani AN: Phencyclidine-associated psychosis (letter). J Clin Psychiatry 48:386, 1987

De Angelis GG, Goldstein E: Treatment of adolescent phencyclidine (PCP) abusers. Am J Drug Alcohol Abuse 5:399–414, 1978

Gallant D: Phencyclidine: clinical and laboratory diagnostic problems, in Phencyclidine (PCP): Historical and Current Perspectives. Edited by Domino EF. Ann Arbor, MI, NPP Books, 1981, pp 437–447

Giannini AJ, Loiselle RH, Giannini MC, et al: Phencyclidine and the dissociatives. Psychiatr Med 3:197–217, 1984

Gorelick DA, Wilkins JN: Inpatient treatment of PCP abusers and users. Am J Drug Alcohol Abuse 15:1–12, 1989

Gorelick DA, Wilkins JN, Wong C: Diagnosis and treatment of chronic phencyclidine (PCP) abuse, in Phencyclidine: An Update (NIDA Res Monogr E64). Edited by Clouet DH. Rockville, MD, National Institute on Drug Abuse, 1986, pp 218–228

Gorelick DA, Wilkins JN, Wong C: Outpatient treatment of PCP abusers. Am J Drug Alcohol Abuse 15:367–374, 1989

Gorelick PB: Stroke from alcohol and drug abuse: a current social peril. Postgrad Med 88:171–174, 177–178, 1990

Grover D, Yeragani VK, Keshanan MS: Improvement of phencyclidine: associated psychosis with ECT. J Clin Psychiatry 47:477–478, 1986

Hurlbut KM: Drug-induced psychoses. Emerg Med Clin North Am 9:31–52, 1991

Javitt DC, Zukin SR: Recent advances in the phencyclidine model of schizophrenia. Am J Psychiatry 148:1301–1308, 1991

Johnson KM, Jones SM: Neuropharmacology of phencyclidine: basic mechanisms and therapeutic potential. Annu Rev Pharmacol Toxicol 30:707–750, 1990

Johnston LD, O'Malley PM, Bachman JG: National Survey Results on Drug Use From the Monitoring the Future Study, 1975–1992, Vol 2 (NIH Publ No 93-3598). Rockville, MD, National Institute on Drug Abuse, 1993, p 10

Lahmeyer HW, Stock PG: Phencyclidine intoxication, physical restraints, and acute renal failure: case report. J Clin Psychiatry 44:184–185, 1983

Luisada P, Brown B: Clinical management of phencyclidine psychosis. Clin Toxicol 9:539–545, 1976

Meng Y, Lichtman AH, Bridgen DT, et al: pharmacological potency and biodisposition of phencyclidine via inhalation exposure in mice. Drug Alcohol Depend 43:13–22, 1996

Mercy JA, Heath CW Jr, Rosenberg ML: Mortality associated with the use of upper-body control holds by police. Violence Vict 5:215–222, 1990

Misra AL, Pontani RB, Bartolomeo J: Persistence of phencyclidine (PCP) and metabolites in brain and adipose tissue and implications for long-lasting behavioral effects. Res Commun Chem Pathol Pharmacol 24:431–445, 1979

National Institute on Drug Abuse: Diagnosis and Treatment of Phencyclidine (PCP) Toxicity. Rockville, MD, National Institute on Drug Abuse, 1979

Olney JW, Labruyere J, Wang G, et al: NMDA antagonist neurotoxicity: mechanism and prevention. Science 254:1515–1518, 1991

Pearlson GD: Psychiatric and medical syndromes associated with phencyclidine (PCP) abuse. Johns Hopkins Med J 148:25–33, 1981

Pitts FN Jr: Pharmacological therapies for PCP abuse called fairly effective. Clinical Psychiatry News 12:17, 1984

Rappolt RT Sr, Gay GR, Farris RD: Phencyclidine (PCP) intoxication: diagnosis in stages and algorithms of treatment. Clin Toxicol 16:509–529, 1980

Rosen AM, Mukherjee S, Shinbach K: The efficacy of ECT in phencyclidine-induced psychosis. J Clin Psychiatry 45:220–222, 1984

Schnoll SH: Street PCP scene: issues on synthesis and contamination. J Psychedelic Drugs 12:229–233, 1980

Schuckit MA: Drug and Alcohol Abuse: A Clinical Guide to Diagnosis and Treatment, 2nd Edition. New York, Plenum, 1984, pp 152–160

Slawson MH, Wilkins DG, Foltz RL, et al: Quantitative determination of phencyclidine in pigmented and nonpigmented hair by ion-trap mass spectrometry. J Anal Toxicol 20:350–354, 1996

Sloan MA, Kittner SJ, Rigamonti D, et al: Occurrence of stroke associated with use/abuse of drugs. Neurology 41:1358–1364, 1991

Smith DE, Wesson DR: Barbiturate and other sedative hypnotics, in Treatment Aspects of Drug Dependence. Edited by Schecter A. New York, CRC Press, 1978, pp 117–130

Smith RC, Meltzer HY, Arora RC, et al: Effect of phencyclidine on $^3$H-catecholamine and $^3$H-serotonin uptake in synaptosomal preparations from rat brain. Biochem Pharmacol 26:1435–1439, 1977

Tabor BL, Smith-Wallace T, Yonekura ML: Perinatal outcome associated with PCP versus cocaine use. Am J Drug Alcohol Abuse 16:337–348, 1990

Tennant FS, Rawson RA, McCann M: Withdrawal from chronic phencyclidine (PCP) dependence with desipramine. Am J Psychiatry 138:845–847, 1981

Thombs DL: A review of PCP abuse trends and perceptions. Public Health Reports, University of Maryland 104:325–328, 1989

Weinstein H, Maayuni S, Glick S, et al: Integrated studies on the biochemical, behavioral and molecular pharmacology of phencyclidine: a progress report, in Phencyclidine (PCP): Historical and Current Perspectives. Edited by Domino EF. Ann Arbor, MI, NPP Books, 1981, pp 131–175

Wong LK, Biemann K: Metabolites of phencyclidine. Clin Toxicol 9:583–591, 1976

Woolf DS, Vourakis C, Bennett G: Guidelines for management of acute phencyclidine intoxication. Critical Care Update 7:16–24, 1980

Wu JC, Buchsbaum MS, Bunney WE: Positron emission tomography study of phencyclidine users as a possible drug model of schizophrenia. Yakubutsu Seishin Kodo 11:47–48, 1991

# 21 Tobacco

Judith K. Ockene, Ph.D.
Jean L. Kristeller, Ph.D.
Gary Donnelly, M.P.H.

The incontrovertible evidence linking cigarette smoking with serious illness and premature death has placed increasing demands on the medical and mental health community to intervene with smokers. Viewed as an addictive behavior, cigarette smoking can be treated from psychosocial, behavioral, and pharmacological perspectives. A mental health professional in a clinical setting can play an important role in preventing and treating this psychological and/or physiological addiction.

DSM-IV (American Psychiatric Association 1994) and the World Health Organization (1978) recognize nicotine dependence as an addiction. Tobacco use deserves attention as a serious problem not only because of the health risks involved but also because nicotine is a psychoactive substance that may control significant aspects of an individual's behavior. Tobacco shares a number of common factors with the other recognized addictive agents (i.e., cocaine, opioids, and alcohol): it produces centrally mediated effects on mood and feeling states, it is a reinforcer for animals, it leads to drug-seeking behavior with deprivation, and it shows similar patterns of social mediation and persistence in the face of evidence that it is damaging (Benowitz 1985; Fagerstrom 1991; Henningfield 1984). Within the neuropsychiatric patient population, evidence is increasing that nicotine can profoundly affect central nervous system processes (Newhouse and Hughes 1991). Individual variability in the intensity of the dependence is wide, and despite the large number of smokers who successfully quit on their own, many others can and do

benefit from a variety of interventions. As with any behavior change process, patients will have individual needs requiring different approaches to achieve maximum effect during treatment.

In this chapter, we examine the current strategies available to physicians and mental health professionals and offer guidelines for initial and long-term intervention.

## Effect of Cigarette Smoking: Why Should People Stop?

Unlike the other addictions considered in this book, heavy use of tobacco has not been widely recognized as producing significant psychological disturbance, other than craving and difficulty in stopping. Only in the last 10 years has the powerful addictive nature of nicotine been more thoroughly investigated and better understood (U.S. Department of Health and Human Services 1988). Jaffe and Kranzler (1979) noted in a review of the psychiatric literature that prior to the publication of DSM-III in 1980 (American Psychiatric Association 1980), virtually no attention had been paid to excessive tobacco use as a psychological problem worthy of treatment. In 1996, the American Psychiatric Association published practice guidelines for the treatment of patients with nicotine dependence. In the last decade, social disapproval and even legal sanctions have become factors in curbing tobacco use, increasing pressure on individuals to seek treatment. The medical problems arising from cigarette smoking have led to the need to take smoking seriously as an addictive disorder; thus, it is appropriate to review first the health risks of smoking. Since the first Surgeon General's Report on Smoking and Health (U.S. Department of Health, Education, and Welfare 1964), smoking has been recognized as a serious medical problem and, in the last 20 years, has been linked irrefutably to many serious diseases, including cancer, heart disease, lung disease, complications of diabetes, and ulcers. Comprehensive discussions of health risks of smoking and benefits of quitting are available in various surgeon general's reports, with the 1989 surgeon general's report (U.S. Department of Health and Human Services 1989) celebrating the 25 years of progress since the 1964 report and the 1990 report (U.S. Department of Health and Human Services 1990) presenting the benefits of cessation.

## Physiological Effects of Cigarette Smoke

### Carbon Monoxide and Other Gases

The health consequences and symptoms of smoking have been attributed to the many noxious substances found in cigarette smoke, including carbon monoxide and other toxic gases. Carbon monoxide develops a strong bond with hemoglobin, causing smokers to lose as much as 15% of the oxygen-carrying capacity of their red blood cells, a possible significant causal factor for the increased risk of coronary heart disease (CHD) in cigarette smokers.

Other toxic gases such as hydrogen cyanide, ammonia, hydrogen oxide, and nitrogen oxide have been shown to produce toxic effects. These gases are most immediately responsible for coughing and narrowing of the bronchial tubes and, over time, paralysis of the cilia, thickening of the mucus-secreting membranes, and eventually chronic obstructive pulmonary disease (COPD).

### Tar

Tar is a toxic particulate of cigarette smoke and is considered a *complete carcinogen*, not only causing but also promoting malignant changes. In cigarettes manufactured in the United States over the last three decades, tar yield has decreased from an average of 37 mg per cigarette to 12 mg (Federal Trade Commission 1997). Tar yields increase when filter vents are blocked. Among the many toxic organic compounds found in the tar phase are nonvolatile N-nitrosamines and aromatic amines, both known human carcinogens. The smoke

from the burning end of the cigarette, *sidestream* smoke, contains considerably higher amounts of the carcinogenic aromatic amines than does *mainstream* smoke and has been shown to have a negative effect on the health of individuals who do not smoke themselves but are in the smoker's environment (passive smoking or involuntary smoking; Glantz and Parmley 1991; U.S. Environmental Protection Agency 1992).

### Nicotine

Various forms of tobacco contain differing amounts of nicotine. Approximately 8 mg of nicotine is contained in the tobacco used for cigarettes. This is true for all brands of cigarettes, even those that are advertised as "low yield." The amount of nicotine delivered to the smoker varies widely among the brand types (i.e., 0.1–1.9 mg/cigarette) (Henningfield et al. 1993).

Nicotine causes the release of catecholamines, epinephrine, and norepinephrine, which increases heart rate, blood pressure, cardiac output, oxygen consumption, coronary blood flow, arrhythmias, peripheral vasoconstriction, and mobilization and utilization of free fatty acids. Nicotine is thought to contribute to heart disease through the acute strain placed on the cardiovascular system while smoking and, over time, as an irritant in the blood vessels, increasing the buildup of plaque and promoting arteriosclerosis. Thus, nicotine and carbon monoxide appear to produce the major adverse effects leading to CHD. In the diabetic patient, nicotine is a factor in both acute and chronic reduction of blood flow to the limbs, contributing to death of tissue and amputation.

### Medical Impact

The effect of cigarette smoking on morbidity and mortality from chronic disease is great. The development of lung cancer is 10 times more likely for smokers than nonsmokers and 15–25 times greater for heavy smokers (2 or more packs/day). Smokers have 2–4 times greater risk of dying from CHD than nonsmokers, depending on their rate of smoking (U.S. Department of Health and Human Services 1983). Even among men and women older than 60, those who smoke have significantly more CHD-related events than do nonsmokers (Frost et al. 1996; LaCroix et al. 1991). Of as much concern is smoking's effect on major respiratory ailments; it accounts for 90% of the development of chronic bronchitis and emphysema (Fielding 1985; U.S. Department of Health and Human Services 1989). Babies of smoking mothers weigh less at birth compared with those of nonsmoking mothers and are at higher risk for stillbirth and neonatal death, possibly through absorption of lead, cadmium, and cyanide from cigarette smoke (Kleinman et al. 1988; Sexton and Hebel 1984). Of more immediate concern to many smokers are troublesome symptoms such as morning cough; shortness of breath; fatigue; sputum production; hoarseness; increased pulse; skin and teeth stains; and increased incidence, severity, and duration of colds.

Assessment of a smoking patient also necessitates a consideration of other risk factors that act synergistically to cause CHD, COPD, and cancer. The risk for individuals with hypercholesterolemia and hypertension is greater than just the additive effect of each risk factor. Similarly, smoking, when coupled with exposure to asbestos and other occupationally encountered substances, greatly increases the smoker's risk of cancer of the lung when compared with smokers who are not so exposed. Attention also has been given to the synergistic effect of smoking and alcohol use on mortality (Hughes 1993).

Smokers sometimes believe that the damage caused by smoking has already been done and that quitting has little value. It is important to inform patients that for many diseases this is not so. Of note is that the 1990 surgeon general's report, *The Health Benefits of Smoking Cessation* (U.S. Department of Health and Human Services 1990), addresses the benefits of stopping rather than the risks of continuing to smoke. From an interventional perspective, such an approach is very valuable. A major conclusion of this report was that "smoking cessation has major and immediate health benefits for men and women of all ages. Benefits apply to persons with and without smoking-related disease" (p. 8). For example, patients who stop smoking after the diagnosis of CHD compared with those who continue to smoke have reduced risks of reinfarction, sudden cardiac death, and total mortality, resulting in a longer life expectancy. The risk of heart disease attributable to smoking drops to that of never smokers after several years of abstinence. Similarly, with certain lung diseases and circulation problems, cessation of smoking greatly improves the prognosis; symptoms may reverse quickly following cessation, although risk of mortality does not drop as quickly as for heart disease.

The provider's knowledge of these health risks and benefits of cessation is important and must be used skillfully to educate patients without giving them unrealistic expectations and without frightening them unnecessarily, which is counterproductive if it leads to increased denial or resistance.

# Factors Supporting Smoking Behavior

## Etiology and Stages of Smoking

Cigarette smoking is a complex behavior pattern that is affected by many psychosocial factors and goes through a sequence of phases and stages. During the initiation phase, individuals start experimenting with cigarettes, generally before age 20 years, and then move into the transition phase, in which environmental and psychological factors influence their becoming smokers or nonsmokers. Smokers then develop and maintain their smoking habit or attempt cessation. Stopping smoking is a long-term process and proceeds in stages: 1) precontemplation, 2) contemplation, 3) readiness for action, 4) taking action or steps toward quitting, and 5) (often) several relapses before long-term cessation is maintained (DiClemente et al. 1991). Those who relapse may go back to any of the preceding stages, and strategies can be used to facilitate a successful cessation.

Initiation of smoking is strongly associated with social forces or forces extrinsic to the individual (e.g., peer pressure, social network) and with psychological variables (e.g., self-esteem, status needs, depression, other personal needs). The sociological variables that are so important during the formation of the habit seem to play a minor role in the maintenance stage once smoking has become part of the lifestyle of the individual. As the habit continues, it becomes more and more tied to psychological and physiological needs and becomes an intrinsic part of the person's life, having many functions. Cessation and maintenance of cessation are affected by a combination of social, psychological, and physiological variables acting on and within the individual (Leventhal and Cleary 1980; Ockene and Ockene 1992). One study (Salber et al. 1968) suggested that 85%–90% of those who smoke four cigarettes become regular smokers, making smoking as highly addictive in this respect as other substances such as heroin or cocaine. However, even teenage smokers may express a desire to quit (Stone and Kristeller 1992). By use of DSM-III-R (American Psychiatric Association 1987) criteria, 50% of self-quitters fulfill criteria for nicotine withdrawal (Hughes et al. 1990), making it likely that this group is physiologically addicted. In comparison, 78%–86% of the smokers who enter treatment for cessation experience withdrawal symptoms that are sufficient to fulfill DSM-III-R criteria (Hughes et al. 1991).

Thus, most smokers, unlike users of alcohol, can be considered biochemically addicted.

## Physiological Factors

As evidence currently stands, cigarette smoking is likely maintained by at least three physiological processes: 1) avoidance of nicotine withdrawal effects, 2) desire for the immediate peripheral and central effects of nicotine, and 3) anticipation of the conditioned reinforcement consequences associated with smoking (O. Pomerleau and Pomerleau 1984; U.S. Department of Health and Human Services 1988). The first process largely interferes with immediate attempts to withdraw from cigarettes. The second process involves active effects of nicotine, such as the anorexic effect, arousal from norepinephrine activity, increased improvement in concentration, and euphoriant effects possibly mediated by β-endorphin release. The third process, the conditioning of these effects, is probably responsible for relapse under stress during the maintenance phase of cessation. The extent of the physiological addiction is most easily indirectly quantified in a clinical setting with the Fagerstrom Test for Nicotine Dependence (FTND; Heatherton et al. 1991), which is discussed more fully later in this chapter. The FTND is sensitive to amount of nicotine intake and to smoking to avoid immediate withdrawal effects (e.g., smoking immediately on awakening); lower scores tend to predict greater ability to stop smoking (Fagerstrom and Schneider 1989).

Although pharmacological and physiological factors play a role in smoking behavior change, they fail to explain the great variability observed in individual responses. The likelihood is greater that lighter smokers will be more successful at cessation than heavy smokers, but some light smokers cannot stop just as some heavy smokers can quit easily.

## Psychological Factors

Smoking, like other behaviors, is maintained because it provides a way of minimizing negative affects (e.g., distress, anger, fear, shame, contempt) and evokes the positive affects of excitement, enjoyment, and surprise. For reasons that are likely related to the psychoactive effects of nicotine, individuals with current or past history of significant psychiatric problems, including depression, schizophrenia, and alcoholism, are much more likely to be smokers than are people in the general population and may have a particularly difficult time stop-

ping smoking. For example, about 15%–20% of heavy smokers have alcohol problems, and 80% of alcohol/drug abusers in treatment are smokers (American Psychiatric Association 1996). Both current and past major depression are also strongly associated with smoking and predict lower quit rates and higher relapse rates (Breslau et al. 1993, 1994; Glassman 1993). Laboratory studies have supported the conclusion that smoking significantly reduces fluctuations or changes in mood or affect during stress (C. Pomerleau and Pomerleau 1987; O. Pomerleau and Pomerleau 1991). In relation to effects on depression and negative affect, nicotine may act by increasing firing rates in central dopaminergic nuclei involved in mediation of reward (Vaughan 1990) or by increasing norepinephrine release at the locus coeruleus (O. Pomerleau and Rosecrans 1989). For many individuals, smoking also becomes a habitual pattern with little conscious forethought.

Smokers who experience more stress in their lives or who have few resources for handling the stress have greater difficulty in the process of smoking cessation and in the maintenance of recently initiated nonsmoking behavior than do those who have less stress or more effective resources. Many smokers use cigarettes functionally as a way to provide a sanctioned "break" in their routine. The more addictive smoking patterns—which embrace a craving or compulsion, a need to control or prevent high levels of negative affect, or a belief that the cigarette can help control or stabilize troublesome situations—seem well outside the realm of conscious control. Thus, some smokers' behavior fits the description of addiction as obsessive behavior centered around obtaining and using a substance. Heavier smokers generally experience more feelings of negative affect and more withdrawal symptoms than do lighter smokers (Ockene et al. 1981).

Individuals who have had positive past experience with regard to behavior change have the ability to develop good resources for dealing with stress, have an expectation that they can stop smoking, and have a greater likelihood of successful cessation than those individuals with negative experiences (Yates and Thain 1985).

## Social, Demographic, and Medical Factors

The social and cultural environments of smokers also have been shown to affect their ability to stop smoking. Individuals who receive more social support for cessation and have fewer smokers in their environment are more successful at cessation attempts (Ockene et al. 1982). Likewise, smokers who are older, better educated, and at a higher occupational level are more likely to be able to stop smoking than the younger, less educated smoker who is at the lower end of the occupational scale (U.S. Department of Health and Human Services 1989). Work-site and hospital-based smoking intervention programs offer the promise of creating a more favorable environment and support for nonsmokers while providing the smoker with skills and resources necessary to become and remain a nonsmoker. Work-site programs can increase participation through various types of incentives (Glasgow et al. 1993; Matson et al. 1993), and comprehensive services, such as social support, stepped-care models, and group-augmented programs, may produce both increased movement through stages of quitting and extended abstinence. Individuals who present with more severe disease, at least with regard to CHD, have shown a greater likelihood of cessation (Ockene et al. 1992). In summary, individuals who have been most successful in cigarette smoking cessation are those who are more educated, have good personal resources to help them mediate and implement change, and receive support for the change from individuals in their environment; among ill individuals, those with more severe diseases are likely to stop smoking.

## General Issues in Treating Smoking in a Mental Health Facility

Treatment for smoking cessation is available from many sources. Mental health professionals who offer such treatment have a responsibility to recognize that other psychiatric problems may coexist with the presenting problems and that the addiction to smoking, both physiological and psychological, may require additional professional attention (Breslau et al. 1993; Covey et al. 1997; Glassman 1993). These responsibilities may be summarized as follows:

1. Assess psychiatric problems that may be present, particularly depression (e.g., current status; history; use of other addictive substances, especially alcohol, marijuana, and prescription medications) and recognize the potential role of smoking in the management of mental illness.
2. Evaluate the effect of these other problems on the patient's ability to stop smoking. Other problems may seriously complicate the course of the patient's ability to stop smoking or to maintain abstinence, resulting in a decision to treat them either

prior to or concurrently with smoking. Conversely, the best professional recommendation may be that, despite other problems, the patient can pursue a smoking cessation program because the smoking appears dissociated from the other difficulties.
3. Offer treatment or make appropriate referrals for other problems that may become apparent. If a mental health facility or hospital offers a smoking cessation program, patients may use their smoking as a safer and more acceptable route through which to gain help for other problems.
4. Be familiar with the physiological processes to which smoking is related, the physiological aspects of nicotine addiction, and the appropriate use of nicotine replacement therapy (NRT) and non-nicotine pharmacological therapy.
5. Provide treatment sensitive to the patient's needs, which may mean a range of treatment from offering self-help materials to using brief counseling plus follow-up to formal smoking intervention programs.

## Diagnosis and Assessment

Most of the evaluation of a smoker is assessment- rather than diagnosis-oriented. Two important diagnostic questions, however, are to what extent nicotine addiction is present and whether other addictive or psychiatric problems coexist. Often, a medical diagnosis has led to the urgency of treatment. In such an instance, the practitioner would benefit by communicating with the treating physician, with the patient's permission; if the patient is complaining of physical symptoms (e.g., shortness of breath, chest pain) that have not been evaluated, arranging a medical referral is necessary.

The assessment covers the three areas outlined earlier: physiological components of addiction, psychological components, and social factors.

The comprehensiveness of the evaluation depends on the setting, the apparent needs of the patient, and the types of treatment available. In some settings, patients may be asked to complete a standardized assessment battery prior to the initial interview, including material related to smoking patterns; screening for psychiatric difficulties with a self-report questionnaire, such as the Symptom Checklist-90—Revised (SCL-90-R; Derogatis 1977); and any other special requirements, such as the evaluation of the patient as a subject for hypnosis. Any areas of special concern can be followed up in that interview or in a subsequent one.

A standardized assessment might be appropriate when large numbers of individuals are being screened for a standard group treatment in a clinical setting or at a work-site treatment program. If the treatment offered is individual sessions, then the assessment process can be incorporated more appropriately into the initial session.

The distinction between assessment and intervention is usually blurred within a cognitive-behavioral framework; gathering information about the external contingencies supporting smoking or about cognitions related to motivation increases self-awareness in a way that facilitates behavior change. Figure 21–1 is a flowchart of the major assessment issues in the following discussion in relation to possible treatment choices.

## Assessment of Physiological Addiction

There are three primary ways to evaluate the extent of nicotine addiction and the likelihood that the individual will need special assistance during the withdrawal phase. One of the best indications is the reported difficulty of previous cessation attempts and the experience of withdrawal symptoms. The second is the score on the aforementioned FTND (Fagerstrom 1978; Fagerstrom and Schneider 1989; Heatherton et al. 1991), which is psychometrically more reliable and predictive of the value of NRTs (i.e., gum containing nicotine or transdermal nicotine patches) during treatment than the original Fagerstrom Tolerance Questionnaire (Fagerstrom 1978). This six-item test can be quickly administered and scored in a medical setting. An even briefer two-question version (Heatherton et al. 1989), which includes only number of cigarettes smoked and latency to first cigarette in the morning (Items 1 and 6), is the best predictor of biochemical measures of blood nicotine levels and is a clinically acceptable replacement for the full FTND. The third way is to ask if the smoker thinks that he or she is addicted to nicotine.

If the smoker reports having had intense withdrawal symptoms in the past, has a pattern of relapsing within a few hours or days, and scores high on the addiction scale, then nicotine addiction probably plays an important role in maintaining the behavior. Not all heavy smokers (more than 1 pack/day) report intense withdrawal symptoms, and some relatively light smokers appear more susceptible.

If nicotine addiction is a significant problem, several treatment options are available (discussed in more detail later in this chapter). Since the first publication of this textbook, a significant number of pharmaco-

therapies have become available to aid in smoking cessation. Currently these include transdermal nicotine patches, nicotine gum, nicotine nasal spray, nicotine inhaler, and bupropion (see Table 21–1). Nicotine gum and two brands of transdermal patches became available over-the-counter in 1996, enabling some consumer populations access to the products without going to their health care provider for a prescription. A nicotine inhaler also has received approval from a U.S. Food and Drug Administration (FDA) Advisory Panel and became available in June 1998. A "harm-reduction" option also has been considered (Marlatt and Tapert 1993; Warner et al. 1997) for smokers whose cessation seems unlikely. This approach uses safer NRTs long term in place of tobacco product use. However, because nicotine at any level is harmful, this is not an optimal alternative.

The degree of addiction, given identical nicotine intake, appears to be highly variable. Many ex-smokers or relapsed smokers report that withdrawal symptoms lasted longer than might be predicted from what is known of the pharmacology of nicotine, in which, for some individuals, psychological stimuli cue physiological reactions that mimic withdrawal symptoms (O. Pomerleau and Pomerleau 1984).

Finally, while evaluating nicotine addiction patterns, it is important to assess the use of other substances—in particular, alcohol, caffeine, marijuana, and anxiolytics.

## Psychological Assessment

### Assessment of Behavior

Much can be learned from a simple smoking history questionnaire. In addition to basic descriptive information, the smoker also should be asked about past attempts at quitting, resources that helped, factors that hindered, experience with other behavioral changes, factors that may have led to relapse, and highest- and lowest-"need" cigarettes.

In addition to the collection of this information, the smoker can be introduced to behavioral self-monitoring, which requires the smoker to record the time, place, mood, need, and thoughts associated with each cigarette smoked. This is best accomplished by the smoker carrying around a sheet of paper wrapped around a cigarette pack (a "wrap sheet") that the smoker is instructed to fill out before smoking each cigarette because delayed recall is very unreliable. After 1 week, the pattern of cigarettes smoked during the course of the week can be graphed. These records give

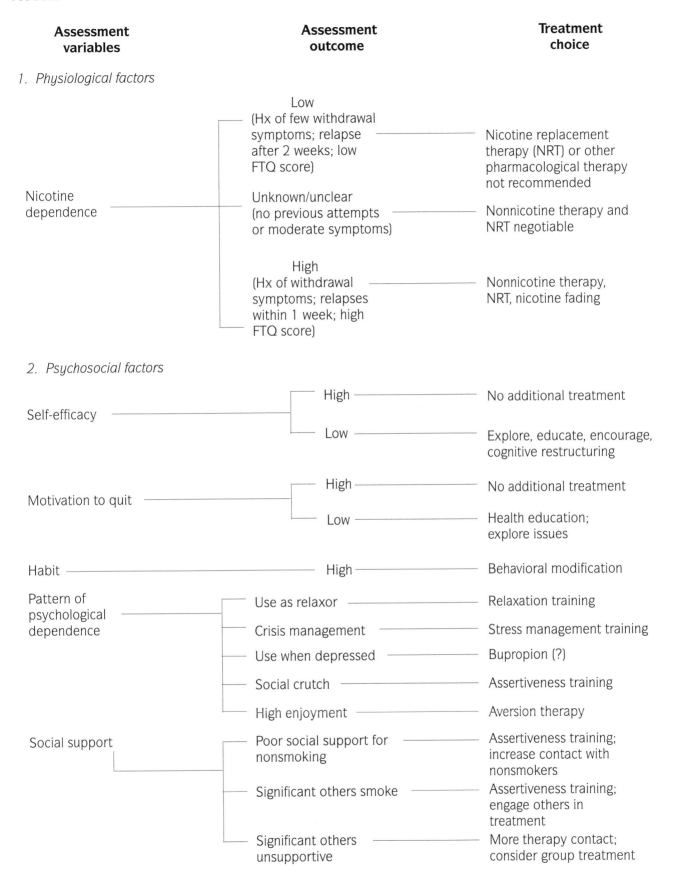

**Figure 21−1.** Flowchart of assessment outcome and treatment decisions. Hx = history; FTQ = Fagerstrom Tolerance Questionnaire.

**Table 21–1.** Comparison of current pharmacotherapy for smoking cessation

| | Transdermal nicotine (patch) | | | Nicotine polacrilex (gum) | Nicotine nasal spray | Nicotine inhaler | Bupropion hydrochloride |
|---|---|---|---|---|---|---|---|
| | Rx/OTC patches | | | | | | |
| | Nicotrol | Prostep | Nicoderm, NicoDerm CQ, Habitrol | Rx/OTC gum | Rx spray | Nicotrol Inhaler (Rx inhaler) | Nonnicotine sustained-release tablet |
| **Brand name** | | | | | | | |
| **Product strengths** | 15 mg | 22, 11 mg | 21, 14, 7 mg | 2, 4 mg | 10 mg/mL | 10 mg/cartridge (4 mg delivered) | 150 mg |
| **Initial dose** | 1 patch/16 hours | 1 patch/24 hours | 1 patch/24 or 16 hours | 1 piece every 1–2 hours | 1–2 doses/hour | 6–16 cartridges/day | 150 mg/day for 3 days, followed by increase to 300 mg/day |
| **Maximum dose** | Same | Same | Same | (2 mg: 24/day) (4 mg: 24/day) | (5 doses/hour or 40 doses/day) (1 dose is 2 sprays, 1 in each nostril) | 16 cartridges/day | 300 mg/day, given as 150 mg twice daily |
| **Time to peak plasma level** | 5–10 hours | 5–10 hours | 5–10 hours | 20–30 minutes | 5–7 minutes | 15 minutes | N/A |
| **Manufacturer's recommended treatment duration** | 6 weeks | 4 weeks | 10 weeks | 12 weeks | 3 months | 12 weeks initial treatment 6–12 weeks gradual reduction | 7–12 weeks |
| **Adverse reactions** | 50% of users experience mild skin reactions. Treat by rotating patch sites and applying steroid creams. Fewer than 5% of patients have to stop using the patch because of skin reactions. Some patients report vivid dreams and sleep disturbances while using the 24-hour patch. Treat by removing patch at night. | | | Mouth soreness, hiccups, dyspepsia, and jaw ache. Reactions are generally mild and transient. Reactions are often alleviated by correcting the patient's chewing technique. | Local transient irritation in the nose and throat, watering eyes, sneezing, and cough. Usually become less severe and more tolerable over time. | 40% experience mouth and throat irritation. Symptoms diminish with regular use. Upset stomach may also occur. | Most common: dry mouth and insomnia (sleep disturbances can be minimized by avoiding bedtime doses). Shakiness and skin rash also reported |

|  | | | | |
|---|---|---|---|---|
| **Contraindications** | Severe eczema, allergy to adhesive tape, or other skin disease that may be exacerbated by the patch. | Severe temporomandibular joint disease or other jaw problems may be exacerbated by gum chewing. Presence of dentures, dental appliances, or problems that would be affected adversely by gum chewing | Patients with asthma, rhinitis, nasal polyps, or sinusitis should not use the nasal spray. | Seizure disorder Current use of Wellbutrin, Wellbutrin SR, or other medications containing bupropion Patients with current or prior diagnosis of bulimia or anorexia nervosa Concurrent administration of bupropion and MAOIs Patients with allergic response to bupropion |
| **Cost** | Suggested retail price for OTC transdermal nicotine (starter box): approximately $4/day[a] | Suggested retail price for nicotine gum (starter box): approximately $5/day for lower usage (10–20 pieces) and up to $10/day for higher usage (20–30 pieces)[a] | Suggested retail price per bottle: approximately $5/day for lower usage (20 doses) and up to $10/day for maximum usage (40 doses)[a] | Average wholesale price: approximately $2.50/day[b] |

*Note.*   OTC = over the counter; N/A = not available; MAOIs = monoamine oxidase inhibitors.
[a]Retail prices quoted February 1997.
[b]Wholesale price quoted May 1997.

the patient and provider an understanding of what behaviors, cognitions, and environmental factors are related to smoking. Some patients are uncomfortable or resistant to keeping behavioral records and should not be unduly pressured to do so. An attempt at a 24-hour recall of cigarettes smoked can be a reasonable replacement for this, accompanied by focused questions such as "Which cigarettes tend to be 'automatic' ones you really wouldn't miss?" or "In what situations do you tend to smoke?"

If a patient is seen only once for an initial evaluation before referral to a treatment group, then self-monitoring can be incorporated into the early group sessions. Otherwise, self-monitoring between the first and second individual session is an effective way to gather more information, engage the patient immediately in the treatment process, and assess level of motivation. Monitoring in this way also assists many patients in cutting back, particularly on cigarettes smoked automatically.

### Assessment of Attitudes and Cognitions

The individual's reasons for smoking can be assessed with the Why Do You Smoke? self-test, consisting of 18 questions that assess the aspects of the smoking habit that predominate for that individual: stimulation, handling, accentuation of pleasure-relaxation, reduction of negative feelings, psychological addiction, and habit. The responses can be used quite effectively to introduce the need for a multicomponent approach to treatment. For example, suggestions for behavioral substitution can be tied specifically to those dimensions ranked highest.

More central to assessment of attitude is an evaluation of the patient's commitment to cessation and sense of self-efficacy in reaching a goal of abstinence. A 14-item self-efficacy questionnaire developed by Yates and Thain (1985) and derived from research by Condiotte and Lichtenstein (1981) predicted with a high degree of accuracy which patients would relapse by 6 months. A cognitive approach to behavior change emphasizes two types of self-efficacy expectations that mediate the decision to change and the eventual behavior change (Bandura 1977). The first type is a response-outcome expectancy that a given course of action will lead to a particular outcome. For example, how firmly does the patient expect that stopping will improve health? These cognitions must be favorable if the decision to change is to occur; understanding the effect of smoking on health has been shown to be a critical factor

in maintenance of cessation by post–myocardial infarction patients. If beliefs are not favorable, then intervention and education must begin at this level.

The second type of self-efficacy is based on an individual's belief in his or her ability to make the desired change—an expectation of success. A positive belief that one has the necessary tools and resources to live comfortably and effectively without cigarettes leads to a greater commitment to change and to a persistence of efforts. For smokers with little expectation of their ability to quit because of either perceived or actual deficits in personal skills or environmental supports, treatment will begin with enhancing mastery expectations or skills. Once treatment is initiated, expectations can be enhanced with the use of self-monitoring, successful performance accomplishments, cognitive restructuring, physiological feedback, and mastery of physiological or emotional arousal leads.

### Emotional Meaning of Cigarettes

In some cases, it may become apparent that for certain patients strong symbolic issues are related to smoking. This should be pursued, particularly if the smoker has made many unsuccessful attempts at quitting, if the smoker has serious health problems related to smoking, if the cigarettes appear closely tied to self-image, or if a family member has had severe health problems as a smoker. The use of cigarettes probably always had some special meaning to the individual. This meaning need not always be explored in an initial evaluation. In other cases, the smoker may be aware of the connection but needs encouragement to explore it fully. The clinician can also consider the effect of other issues in the smoker's life on his or her ability to stop smoking. In what way do other psychiatric issues appear to affect the ability to stop smoking? Are there any unusual life stressors occurring so that treatment for smoking might be more successful at another time? Stopping smoking during periods of moderate stress may help the patient realize that alternative coping strategies can be available and may protect against relapse at a future period of higher stress.

## Social Assessment

Three aspects of social support are important: 1) the number of smokers among the patient's friends, family, and co-workers; 2) the quality of support for cessation that can be expected by the smoker; and 3) the extent to which the smoker is able to be assertive in resisting social pressures to smoke. These can be assessed either in a questionnaire or in the assessment interview. The latter is preferable if time is available.

# Intervention

A wide variety of interventions have been shown to be effective in helping people stop smoking, and many interventions show long-term outcome at 6–12 months to be better than in an untreated comparison group. Treatments that incorporate behavioral and cognitive-behavioral approaches have been the most effective (Lichtenstein 1982). One of the most significant recent contributions to promoting smoking interventions, particularly within health care settings, has been the development by the Agency for Health Care Policy and Research (AHCPR 1996) of the "Smoking Cessation Clinical Practice Guideline" (Fiore et al. 1996; Pinney 1997). This guideline, based on a thorough review of the smoking intervention literature, endorses a range of behavioral interventions, in combination with NRT whenever appropriate. In addition to intensive group or individual therapy that uses standard cognitive-behavioral techniques, the guideline emphasizes the value of brief counseling delivered by health care professionals in primary care and inpatient settings. Pharmacological interventions for smoking cessation, including NRT and bupropion, have been successfully integrated with these cognitive-behavioral approaches (Fiore et al. 1996; Hurt et al. 1997; Tonnesen et al. 1991; Transdermal Nicotine Study Group 1992). The methods and treatment program proposed here are based on a cognitive-behavioral model of smoking behavior with incorporation of the physiological factors (see Figure 21–1 for selected treatment options and their relation to assessment outcomes).

Smoking cessation is a long-term process that proceeds in three major stages: 1) commitment to change and goal setting, 2) an action stage for making the change, and 3) maintenance of change. The second stage or period of action has tended to be the major focus of smoking treatment programs, although of late it has become increasingly evident that it is as important to attend to helping smokers to develop a commitment to change and to prevent relapse once change occurs. The clinician may feel less frustrated in attempts to promote change by recognizing that many smokers quit several times before successful cessation occurs. Strategies corresponding to the three noted stages of change are presented in the following sections. However, these strategies and stages are not always clearly separated and can blend into one another during treatment.

# Stage 1: Commitment to Change and Goal Setting

The ambivalent patient is the norm. The patient may be attempting to quit for the first time or may have a history of numerous frustrating attempts and relapses. He or she may be expecting the clinician to perform some magic to remove all ambivalence. Without offering such a promise, the clinician must help the patient become aware of, understand, and accept these mixed feelings. Before entering this stage, there may be a *precontemplation* period in which the smoker may not have thought about making a change in his or her smoking or may be actively resistant to new input that encourages change. For the former, the patient may only require more information, whereas the latter may need more help to uncover his or her barriers to being willing to initiate a change. The need to work with patients who are actively resistant may increase as social and medical pressures to stop smoking increase. Four steps that use the information gathered during the assessment process are suggested to help the provider work with the smoker in the process of developing a commitment to change:

1. Examine the risks of smoking and benefits of quitting in relation to the patient's medical, psychological, and social status. Results from the physical examination can be used effectively here. Smokers who already have experienced the onset of disease have a greater likelihood of quitting (Ockene et al. 1991; Pederson 1982). A positive response-outcome efficacy is necessary before the patient will be willing to initiate change. If this is lacking, the smoker may have a distorted or erroneous view of the effects of smoking and of cessation on his or her health or may be denying the seriousness of the disease. A pamphlet or other written material about the relation between smoking and disease can reinforce the verbal message to the patient. The National Cancer Institute (1993) pamphlet *Clearing the Air* has a list of useful suggestions. A pamphlet in Spanish, *Guia Para Dejar de Fumar* (*Guide for Quitting Smoking;* National Cancer Institute), and one tailored for African Americans, *Smoking Facts and Quitting Tips for African-Americans* (National Cancer Institute 1992), are also available. The clinician may have to help the

smoker explore other reasons for cessation that may be more important or personally relevant. For example, an individual may be more concerned about the effects of smoking on his or her children than on his or her own health.

2. Review past efforts at behavior change and current smoking patterns. It should be made clear to the patient that the pattern of repeated attempts leading to eventual success at smoking cessation is a common one. Focusing on a history of even short successes or of successful change in other behaviors can be used to help facilitate self-confidence. Relabeling of past cessation periods (no matter how short) as successes rather than failures is important.

3. Determine the patient's strengths and weaknesses that can help facilitate change or interfere with change. As previously noted, the following factors contribute to successful smoking cessation and maintained abstinence:

   A belief in the value of the change
   A belief in one's ability to change
   A strong sense of personal security
   A low level of stress or life changes
   Good social support
   Low levels of negative affect (e.g., depression, anger, anxiety)

The first two factors can be developed during the initial stages of intervention. Presence of the other factors (e.g., a weak sense of personal security, high levels of stress, poor social supports, or high levels of negative affect) may require interventions to decrease them. Changes in some of these may need to occur before an attempt at complete cessation is realistic.

4. Establish specific goals that are important to the patient and within the patient's current abilities. The three main alternatives for the patient are to make no immediate change in smoking, to reduce the amount smoked, or to quit. Some patients will need time to think over the information they have been given; others prefer to taper, going through a gradual retraining process in order to believe they are capable of making the desired change; and others may be ready to set a quit date at this point.

The aforementioned series of steps can be generally accomplished during the first visit with a smoker who does not have other psychological or substance abuse problems.

## Stage 2: Action Stage

Once the patient has made the commitment to stop smoking, a number of treatment options are available in the physiological, psychological, and social domains. In addition to the treatment modalities, other structural considerations must be made. These include number of sessions, individual versus group treatment, setting the quit date, cost of treatment, use of a written contract, and plans for follow-up.

The group protocol described here incorporates group support, NRT or bupropion or nicotine fading, behavioral management techniques, physiological feedback, contracting, relaxation training, and relapse prevention, with follow-up arranged on an individual basis. This program is illustrative rather than prescriptive, as many different types of treatment have been shown to be effective for both initial change and maintenance of change. Nicotine fading can be replaced with nicotine replacement or bupropion for those smokers who are suitable candidates. Much briefer versions of these intervention components provided in self-help manuals and by audiotape, and supplemented with telephone follow-up, also have been effective for many smokers.

With few exceptions, adequate evidence does not exist to recommend which approaches might be more effective for given patients. One exception is the better response of more highly addicted patients to treatment directly addressing nicotine addiction or withdrawal symptoms such as depression (i.e., use of NRT, bupropion, or nicotine fading). Adequate hypnotizability for hypnosis programs is another individual characteristic of significance.

### Techniques to Decrease Physiological Addiction

*NRT*

Nicotine-containing chewing gum.   In 1984, the FDA approved the use of nicotine-containing chewing gum as a prescription treatment for tobacco dependency to be used in combination with behavioral treatment. As mentioned earlier in this chapter, the gum is now available over-the-counter. More than 50 studies on the efficacy of nicotine-containing gum have been published; 4 of these are meta-analyses (Cepeda-Benito 1993; Lam et al. 1987; Silagy et al. 1994; Tang et al. 1994). Based on these reviews of the data, the AHCPR in its 1996 "Smoking Cessation Clinical Practice Guideline" concluded that nicotine gum improves smoking cessation rates by approximately 40%–60% compared with control interventions through 12 months of follow-up (Fiore et al. 1996). AHCPR recommended nicotine gum as an efficacious smoking treatment that patients should be encouraged to use.

The gum is usually used during the first few months of a quit attempt. Nicotine gum is available in 2- and 4-mg doses as an over-the-counter product. Patients using the 2-mg gum should not chew more than 24 pieces/day, and users of the 4-mg strength should not exceed 24 pieces/day (Fiore et al. 1996). The 4-mg gum is more efficacious than the 2-mg gum as an aid to highly dependent smokers (Fiore et al. 1996).

Nicotine gum can be used "on demand" to help cope with anticipated cravings. Although this method of dosing administration is still viable for some users, a more effective way to use the gum seems to be on a fixed schedule. This latter approach provides better insurance that the patient is getting enough nicotine to minimize withdrawal symptoms.

Understanding the role that pH plays in the absorption of nicotine in the buccal lining is important. The pH in the mouth is altered by eating or drinking liquids. This effect is most dramatic after ingestion of a cola drink because the pH levels rise in the mouth to a point that actually blocks the nicotine absorption. Other common errors in use of the gum include chewing too fast, using too few pieces, not "parking" it (i.e., letting the gum sit between the cheek and teeth for proper absorption), and using it for too short a time. The inadequate instruction offered by providers in the use of the gum in many instances also limits the efficacy of this approach.

Adherence problems with use of the gum also have been related to patient perceptions of social acceptability and unpleasant taste of the product.

Most patients can start reducing use of the gum after 3–4 weeks. Each week the daily amount of gum can be reduced by 1–2 pieces, or the patient may elect to switch from 4-mg to 2-mg gum as part of the weaning process (Orleans 1997).

Transdermal nicotine patch.   The transdermal nicotine patch, marketed by several pharmaceutical companies in slightly different formulations and delivery systems, also has been shown to be effective. Five meta-analyses of the efficacy of the nicotine patch were reviewed and reported on in the "Smoking Cessation Clinical Practice Guideline" (Fiore et al. 1994; Gourlay 1994; Po 1993; Silagy et al. 1994; Tang et al. 1994). The summarized study results indicate that transdermal nicotine approximately doubles 6- to 12-month abstinence rates over those produced by placebo interventions and that patients are more likely to comply with transdermal nicotine instructions than with nicotine gum instructions (Fiore et al. 1996). Based on this evidence, the guideline recommends that patients should be encouraged to use nicotine patches.

The transdermal nicotine system provides a more passive delivery system than the gum, thereby allowing for a more continuous administration. Peaks and troughs in nicotine delivery and the gastrointestinal and oral side effects associated with the gum are avoided.

Peak nicotine blood levels are reached within 4–9 hours after first use of the trandermal patches, which deliver between 15 and 22 mg/day of nicotine (Hughes 1996). Patches are available as prescription and over-the-counter products. Adherence to this regimen is usually better than with the gum, in part, because a patch is easier to use. A new patch is placed between the neck and waist on waking each day. Four of the transdermal systems (Habitrol, Nicoderm, NicoDerm CQ, Prostep[1]) may be left on for 24 hours, whereas one transdermal nicotine product (Nicotrol) is designed for use during 16-hour periods. With the 24-hour patches, users have reported vivid and sometimes disturbing dreams at night, giving rise to sleep disturbances. In these cases, the 24-hour patch can be removed at bedtime, or the patient can switch to the 16-hour patch. Up to 50% of patients using the nicotine patch have local skin reactions (Fiore et al. 1996). These irritations are usually mild and can be addressed by either rotating patch sites or using local treatment with hydrocortisone cream or triamcinolone cream (Fiore et al. 1996).

Treatment of 8 weeks or less has been shown to be as efficacious as longer treatment periods (Fiore et al. 1996). When weaning patients off the nicotine patch, the clinician should consider having them switch to a lower-dose patch about 2–4 weeks after quitting. The patient can switch more than once before discontinuing the patch (Orleans 1997). Some ex-smokers find that after discontinuation of the patch, occasional use of nicotine gum can help them cope with high-risk situations.

Nicotine nasal spray.   The main feature of the nicotine nasal spray is the reduction of nicotine craving

---

[1]Prostep is no longer available but remains FDA approved.

within several minutes of dosing. A clinical trial reported peak plasma concentrations of nicotine occurring at a speed comparable to that occurring when patients are smoking (Hjalmarson et al. 1994).

The spray is absorbed through the nasal mucosa, not through the sinuses as with other nasal sprays. Side effects are common with the spray but are tolerable and often subside after more frequent use. The most common effects are nasal irritation, runny nose, throat irritation, watering eyes, sneezing, and cough. Patients should be taught to administer the spray as follows:

1. Tilt head 30 degrees, and insert tip of the spray bottle into nostrils
2. Breathe only through the mouth
3. Spray once in each nostril, and refrain from sniffing or inhaling
4. Wait 2–3 minutes before blowing nose

Nicotine nasal spray was approved by the FDA as the AHCPR publication went to press; therefore, no recommendations were made in the "Smoking Cessation Clinical Practice Guideline." The FDA and AHCPR document that studies done with the nasal spray confirm its benefits compared with placebo interventions (Hjalmarson et al. 1994; Nicotrol NS Prescribing Information 1996; Sutherland et al. 1992). Smokers in these studies also showed that smokers treated with the nasal spray had more relief of the urge to smoke and fewer withdrawal symptoms compared with placebo-treated patients. Either individual or group counseling was provided to the study patients along with access to the nicotine nasal spray. In two of the trials, patients were permitted to continue to use the product for up to 1 year if they wished. Nicotine nasal spray has a greater dependence potential than the nicotine gum or patch (Hjalmarson et al. 1994).

An initial treatment is 6–8 weeks' duration. A maximum of 40 doses/day and 5 doses/hour are suggested (1 dose = 1 spray in each nostril). Maximum duration of treatment is 3 months. Because nicotine nasal spray use may involve a greater likelihood of dependency, it may be more difficult to wean patients from it than from the patch or gum. Some strategies that work are cutting the usual dose in half, using it less often, or switching to the patch or gum.

Nicotine inhaler.    The nicotine inhaler became available for sale in the United States in June 1998. Several studies have pointed to its utility as a short-term smoking cessation aid (Schneider et al. 1996; Tonnesen et al.

1993). The inhaler is unique in that the device provides some oral and handling reinforcement along with nicotine replacement. It consists of a mouthpiece, which is divided into two parts, and a porous nicotine cartridge. The smoker places the nicotine cartridge into the mouthpiece and pushes the two halves back together, breaking an aluminum seal on each end of the cartridge. The smoker inhales through the mouthpiece, and the air becomes saturated with nicotine, which is absorbed through the lining of the mouth (Schneider et al. 1996).

Underdosing has been a problem with the inhaler, partially because of the side effects during inhaler use. Gagging and chest irritation have been reported when smokers attempt to puff deeply. Precise instructions on dosing administration with the inhaler for patients will be essential.

### Nonnicotine Therapy

Bupropion.    Bupropion hydrochloride comes in the form of a sustained-release tablet and is the only nonnicotine agent for smoking cessation licensed by the FDA. Bupropion was initially developed and marketed as an antidepressant, but its chemical structure is unrelated to known antidepressant agents. The mechanism of action is unknown; however, bupropion is believed to work on the neurochemistry of nicotine addiction by

- Enhancing dopamine levels in the mesolimbic system
- Affecting noradrenergic neurons in the locus coeruleus (Ascher et al. 1995)

The efficacy of bupropion as a first-line agent for smoking cessation was shown in two placebo-controlled, double-blind studies in nondepressed chronic cigarette smokers (Hurt et al. 1997). Treatment with bupropion at both 150 and 300 mg/day was significantly more effective than placebo at 1-year follow-up. Treatment had no effect on depression scores as measured with the Beck Depression Inventory.

The recommended and maximum dose of bupropion as an aid in smoking cessation is 300 mg/day, given as 150 mg twice daily. Dosing should begin at 150 mg/day every day for the first 3 days, followed by a dose increase for most patients to the recommended usual dose of 300 mg/day. The patient should quit smoking 7–14 days after starting the drug. The most common observed adverse effects associated with the use of bupropion are dry mouth and insomnia.

## Health and Safety Risks

Specific contraindications and precautions for use of NRT products are as follows:

- Nicotine gum is contraindicated in patients with active temporomandibular joint disease.
- Transdermal nicotine patch is contraindicated in patients with hypersensitivity or allergy to nicotine or components of the therapeutic system (e.g., adhesive used to affix the patch to the skin).
- Nicotine nasal spray is contraindicated in patients with hypersensitivity or allergy to nicotine or a component of the product.
- Nicotine inhaler (see FDA product information, available June 1998).

The risks and benefits should be weighed before recommending or prescribing NRT for patients who are pregnant, are breast-feeding, and have a history of cardiovascular disease (e.g., recent heart attack, increasing angina, severe arrhythmia) (Fiore et al. 1996). Other conditions that may contraindicate NRT are

- Renal or hepatic insufficiency
- Poorly controlled insulin-dependent diabetes and other endocrine diseases
- Active peptic ulcer disease
- Accelerated hypertension
- Peripheral vascular disease

Bupropion is contraindicated in patients who

- Have a seizure disorder
- Have a current or prior diagnosis of bulimia or anorexia nervosa
- Are already being treated with Wellbutrin, Wellbutrin SR, or any other medications containing bupropion
- Have shown an allergic response to bupropion

Also, concurrent administration of bupropion and monoamine oxidase inhibitors is contraindicated. Some depressed patients treated with bupropion in depression trials have shown neuropsychiatric signs and symptoms, including delusions, hallucinations, psychosis, concentration disturbance, paranoia, and confusion. Clinicians also should be aware of the increased risk posed by use of the sustained-release formulation of bupropion for manic episodes in bipolar disorder patients during the depressed phase of their illness (Zyban Product Information 1997).

## Combined Therapy

Several trials on the combination of the nicotine patch and gum products have been reported and suggest that withdrawal can be reduced while abstinence is increased (Fagerstrom et al. 1993; Kornitzer et al. 1995; Puska et al. 1994). Another study conducted at four clinical centers included the combination of 300 mg/day of bupropion and 21 mg/day of nicotine patches but has not yet been published in the professional literature. In the bupropion/patch intervention, treatment with bupropion was initiated at 150 mg/day while the patient was still smoking and was increased after 3 days to 300 mg/day, given as 150 mg/day twice daily. Transdermal nicotine was added after 1 week when a target quit date was reached (unpublished data, Glaxo Wellcome, Inc.).

Further studies on combinations of nicotine and nonnicotine replacement products would be a welcome addition to the body of scientific literature on pharmacotherapy in smoking cessation. The pharmacological approach to treatment will need to become more comprehensive in the future to match the needs of the smoking population.

## Nicotine Maintenance

Nicotine maintenance, sometimes known as *harm reduction*, is an approach considered for some addicted smokers by providing them with less toxic nicotine delivery devices. This approach has been encouraged by several smoking researchers (Russell 1991; Slade et al. 1992). It has been cautioned that the adoption of a nicotine maintenance policy has many dangers as well as opportunities (Warner et al. 1997). Nicotine maintenance devices can include nicotine only, pharmaceuticals, or nicotine replacements. However, to compete successfully with cigarettes and other tobacco products, these pharmaceuticals may need to be made more attractive to consumers. A nicotine maintenance market may emerge from the present activity in development of innovative devices. The area of nicotine maintenance is a recent development given all of the nicotine replacement devices.

## Pharmacotherapy Among Alcohol and Drug Abusers

A paucity of data exists on the use of smoking cessation pharmacotherapy with alcohol and drug abusers. However, some findings suggest that smokers with a history of alcohol and drug abuse can benefit from nicotine replacement (Hughes 1993).

## Other Pharmacotherapies

In addition to the AHCPR "Smoking Cessation Clinical Practice Guideline," excellent reviews of pharmacotherapy for smoking cessation are available (Glassman and Covey 1990; Goldstein et al. 1991; Gourlay and McNeil 1990; Hughes 1996; Jarvik and Henningfield 1988, 1993; Lee and D'Alonzo 1993). Other pharmacotherapies include agents that make smoking aversive (e.g., silver acetate), clonidine, blocking agents (e.g., mecamylamine, naltrexone), and medications to decrease withdrawal problems or replace the positive effects of nicotine (e.g., anxiolytics, antidepressants, stimulants, anorectics). The $\alpha$-adrenergic agonists (e.g., clonidine) decrease both nicotine withdrawal symptoms and craving. Although some research (Covey and Glassman 1991; Glassman et al. 1988, 1990) suggests that the positive effect on cessation may be clearer for women, a meta-analysis of the research did not support this as clearly (Gourlay and Benowitz 1995). However, a role for clonidine may exist for those who can tolerate the side effects such as dry mouth, sedation, and constipation and for those who prefer not to use nicotine.

## Nicotine Fading

*Nicotine fading* (Foxx and Brown 1979) is an option for the highly nicotine-dependent smoker who may not be a candidate for NRT or bupropion. It has two components: switching to a cigarette brand with lower nicotine level and gradually reducing the number of cigarettes (tapering). Despite laboratory evidence that smokers will compensate for decreased nicotine content by puffing more heavily or more often (Benowitz 1985), brand switching in the context of a treatment program can be effective if patients are instructed to guard against such behavioral compensation. Encouraging patients to switch to a less preferred brand also helps to weaken pleasant associations attached to smoking. Tapering the number of cigarettes before quitting not only reduces the probability of severe withdrawal but also allows more dependent smokers to learn how to suppress smoking urges and to develop other skills that are helpful in quitting. However, the treatment provider must warn the smoker not to be lulled into a false sense of security and that cessation is the eventual goal. Smokers should not plan to taper to nothing but should plan to set a quit date after a level of 5–10 cigarettes per day has been reached. As numbers of cigarettes smoked decrease, carbon monoxide levels in expired air can be measured to provide feedback on dosage reduction.

## Techniques to Decrease Psychological Dependency

### Cognitive-Behavioral Treatment

Cognitive-behavioral treatment of smoking has been developed from treatment techniques used to intervene with a wide range of behavioral and addictive disorders. Rather than review these interventions extensively here, only illustrative examples are offered. The reader is directed to the discussions of behavioral treatment of smoking in Marlatt and Gordon (1985), Lichtenstein and Brown (1985), or Ockene and Ockene (1992) or to treatment manuals such as *Taking Charge of Your Smoking* (Nash 1981).

**Behavior change strategies.**    Patients can be helped to develop specific strategies to use to stop smoking. These strategies can be grouped under the following categories of behavioral methods:

- Avoiding specific situations or events that bring on a desire or urge to smoke
- Substituting alternative behaviors incompatible with smoking cigarettes when urges arise (e.g., use of deep muscle or mental relaxation, exercise, low-calorie snacking)
- Cognitive restructuring to help reduce positive associations with cigarettes; to develop alternative thought responses to stressful situations; or to develop the belief that other methods can help reduce anxiety, depression, or other uncomfortable affects
- Activating social support of friends, family, and/or co-workers

These strategies can be introduced in conjunction with review of the patient's self-monitoring form, which provides a means to identify higher- and lower-need cigarettes. The patient then begins to use behavior change strategies to eliminate first low-need cigarettes and then higher-need cigarettes.

**Rewards.**    Planning rewards throughout the change process will help sustain patient motivation over what may be a long road toward permanent cessation. The clinician should advise patients to plan periodic rewards not associated with smoking for successes in meeting goals for a week, a month, and so on (e.g., make a special purchase or a special telephone call, treat yourself to an evening out, set time aside for a hobby). Providers can reward signs of progress and reinforce the belief in the patient's ability to change.

Contracts.    A behavioral contract can serve as an aid to the provider and patient in establishing realistic goals and steps by which to accomplish them. The contract should include specific information about whether the patient will taper or stop smoking, a quit date, reasons for stopping, steps to follow in response to situational factors that could interfere with efforts to stop smoking, and a plan for follow-up. The contract's purpose is to make explicit the specific ways in which the patient will attempt to change the smoking behavior. The methods listed should be as specific as possible. For example, the patient who chooses exercise as a substitution activity for smoking should identify the type of activity, when it will be done, where it will be done, how it will be done, and with whom. Alternative strategies should be written down in case the first choice of coping methods cannot be accomplished (e.g., having sugarless candy in a pocket during a business meeting where it would be inappropriate to start physical activity). Written contracts seem to be more effective than verbal contracts in sealing commitment and are very effectively used in brief interventions.

Another aspect of contracting is to set weekly goals for specific changes, an exercise that can be particularly valuable in a group setting. Members can gain feedback on whether their goals are appropriate and support for achieving them.

## Aversive Techniques

The use of aversive stimuli to promote desired behavior change has a strong theoretical foundation in behavioral interventions (within both operant and classical conditioning models). These techniques have included electric shock, covert sensitization (aversive imagery), and aversive manipulation of smoke intake (i.e., rapid smoking, satiation smoking, and smoke holding). In addition, maintenance plans may include forfeiture of money (perhaps to a charity) if relapse occurs.

Most of these techniques appear to be relatively weak when used alone. Electric shock, in particular, appears to fail in generalizing to outside therapy (Pechacek 1979) and is not often used. Covert sensitization, the use of vivid imagery of unpleasant sensations (e.g., nausea) paired with the behavior of smoking, is one variation on imagery techniques. Use of cigarette smoke as the aversive stimulus is intuitively appealing. Aversion to the smoke itself characterizes many exsmokers. Rapid smoking (inhaling every 6 seconds) and satiation (doubling or tripling daily consumption) may help a smoker weaken a positive attachment to ciga-

rettes. Smoke holding (holding smoke in the mouth while continuing to breathe) is also promising because it contains aversive aspects without the medical risks of rapid smoking. It has been shown to be an effective adjunct in combination with other components (Lando and McGovern 1985), seems to have minimal side effects, but generally has been underused.

## Hypnosis

Broadly defined, the use of hypnosis in the treatment of smoking has two basic approaches. In the first, hypnosis is the focus of a single-session treatment, instructions are often standardized, and the therapy may be offered in a group format (Barabasz et al. 1986; Williams and Hall 1988). With a well-motivated patient group, this approach has produced 6-month abstinence rates in the range of 20%–40%, with higher success rates associated with individualized induction, greater clinical experience, and greater patient hypnotizability (Barabasz et al. 1986; Holroyd 1980; Spiegel 1970). In the second, hypnosis is used to explore individual motives more fully, is used to overcome resistance, and usually incorporates other adjunctive techniques as indicated. An excellent discussion of the use of hypnobehavioral and hypnoprojective techniques in treatment of smoking is found in Brown and Fromm (1987). When a multimodal approach is used that may include multiple sessions, self-hypnosis, hypnoprojective techniques, and follow-up, 6-month abstinence rates have been reported in the range of 50%–68% (e.g., Holroyd 1980). However, adequate clinical trials of the efficacy of hypnosis have not been conducted.

## Relaxation Techniques

Relaxation training can be a valuable adjunct to smoking cessation treatment. One of the most common reasons that patients give for relapse is an inability to handle stressful situations (Shiffman 1982). Habitual smokers may report having few, if any, alternative ways to manage stress (other than avoidance of it).

Certain types of relaxation training (e.g., deep breathing, brief meditation, visualization exercises) can serve as effective functional equivalents to smoking. Once well learned, they can be used for a few moments at a time, under almost any circumstances, and may provide two of the benefits associated with smoking: a brief break from ongoing activity and a physiologically active relaxation effect. Training in diaphragmatic breathing, a simple focused mantra meditation technique, or use of a personal positive relaxing image can be done relatively quickly and then strengthened with home practice and a few minutes of use in treatment sessions.

*Restricted environmental stimulation therapy* (REST) is an intervention related to both relaxation and hypnosis techniques and has been shown to be a promising treatment for smoking, with high maintenance rates when used in combination with self-management techniques (Best and Suedfeld 1982). A clinical follow-up of several hundred smoking patients found that a combination of hypnosis and REST produced high long-term abstinence rates (Barabasz et al. 1986). A more extensive review of the use of REST in behavioral medicine is found elsewhere (Suedfeld and Kristeller 1982).

## Social Support and Number of Contacts

Brief counseling, particularly in medical settings, provided by the physician (Ockene et al. 1988) or another health care professional, has shown effectiveness. For more intensive individual treatment, we have found weekly contact for approximately 4 weeks and then biweekly contact for another 4 weeks to be a reasonable frequency and one that provides the tapering of contact necessary for the patient to internalize control. This frequency allows the provider to give reinforcement directly and to alter the plan as needed. For the more dependent smoker or one who has other problems, a longer program may be indicated. A follow-up plan is important to help the patient maintain the changed behavior and allows the provider to detect the possibility of relapse. Minimal intervention protocols generally include weekly and then monthly telephone contact, for which patient acceptance is high, with the opportunity for an additional visit if desired or if relapse occurs (Ockene et al. 1992). The group protocol outlined here has eight weekly sessions, with a 2-week interval before the final eighth session to wean the participants from dependence on the group. One or more follow-up sessions are scheduled individually. Most relapse occurs within 3 months, although it continues at a slower rate thereafter (Ockene 1983). The smoking relapse curve appears to be similar to that of other addictive disorders (Hunt et al. 1971).

Some programs recommend very-high-frequency patient contact during the initial withdrawal period. The American Lung Association program uses 1 week of daily contact. Although this frequency of contact has been effective, it is usually not realistic for the patient or provider. However, recent use of proactive expert systems (e.g., Strecher et al. 1994) may be a reasonable alternative to provider contact. Interactive expert systems that use advances in computer technology can be a high-outreach intervention to assist smokers to stop smoking and can tailor assessment procedures based on information obtained during the assessment (Strecher et al. 1994).

Patients can be instructed to call a help line any time they have a problem in maintaining the smoking behavior change, but use of such lines is generally very low. Smokers can be helped and encouraged to build up social support systems of individuals in their natural environment. Supportive behaviors from a spouse facilitate quitting (e.g., Roski et al. 1996), whereas the presence of other smokers in the household predicts less success (Gourlay et al. 1994). Significant others also may be invited to participate in the intervention sessions if this seems appropriate. A patient who has a natural support system that is weak and cannot be strengthened may need more frequent contacts than a person with a strong support system.

## Other Structural Considerations

### Group Versus Individual Treatment

Group treatment has the advantage of social support and sharing of strategies and problems by group members. Group programs usually are cognitive-behavioral in orientation and should incorporate tapering or use of NRT, bupropion, or nicotine fading for the more dependent smoker. The American Cancer Society and American Lung Association sponsor such treatment programs, and they are often offered through clinics or work sites. Hypnosis also can be effectively offered in a group format, either as a single session (Holroyd 1980) or as part of a multimodal treatment program (Brown and Fromm 1987).

Individual treatment is more appropriate when a provider has few smokers in his or her practice, for patients who have other problems that complicate treatment, and for patients who refuse to participate in a group. In our experience and the experience of others, smokers often are not interested in groups (Ockene et al. 1992). Some techniques, such as acupuncture or hypnosis, are more commonly offered individually. All of the noted cognitive-behavioral techniques may be used either individually or in a group. Some clinicians who consider the use of NRT or other pharmacological interventions for selected patients have found it useful to insist that these patients attend a cognitive-behavioral group such as the one offered by the American Lung Association before prescribing the gum or patch. Individualized sessions can then be devoted to specialized problems. Brief individual treatment is also more appropriate when there is a desire or need to reach all smokers within a given population, such as on an inpatient cardiac service, in an outpatient medical clinic, in a prenatal care clinic, or on a psychiatric service.

### Setting the Quit Date

In group treatment, all patients are advised to use the same quit date. In the 8-week program we outline here, the quit date is set at the fifth session, providing a tapering phase before and a relapse prevention phase after. Other group programs may set it earlier or later. In any case, the patient should prepare for the quit date, removing environmental signals to smoke (e.g., cigarettes or ashtrays), and take social pressures into mind (the initial 3 days of withdrawal are the most difficult).

In individual treatment, more flexibility is possible. Some patients appear at the first session with plans to quit at that point and should not be discouraged from doing so if their decision is discussed and they are comfortable with it. The first session must then include a brief review of withdrawal symptoms and an initial development of strategies to be used in lieu of smoking. For the patient who plans to use NRT, the quit date may need to be week 1 instead of week 5. For smokers using bupropion, it may need to be week 3. Quitting immediately may need to be reconsidered, however, if an initial assessment indicates that the patient has an unrealistic view of what can be accomplished or appears to have few resources available. As mentioned above, other patients may hope to taper gradually to nothing, but such a plan is usually unrealistic, and further exploration of feelings of loss related to giving up cigarettes may be necessary.

## Stage 3: Maintenance of Nonsmoking—Monitoring and Evaluating Patient Progress

A major difficulty in smoking cessation, as with other substance abuse behaviors, is maintenance of the changed behavior. As many as 70% of those who stop smoking relapse within a year. Up to 65% of self-quitters relapse within the first week after cessation (Hughes and Hatsukami 1992). Changing smoking patterns takes time, and a focus on relapse prevention is necessary during the behavior change phase and the maintenance phase. Preparation for coping with with-

drawal symptoms may begin with the initial interview and then become more focused and personalized after the actual quit date (Shiffman et al. 1997). Most quitters who relapse have at least one symptom of nicotine withdrawal (Gritz et al. 1991; Hughes et al. 1991), and degree of dependence is highly related to likelihood and speed of relapse (Shiffman et al. 1996). The following strategies facilitating maintenance of nonsmoking behavior can be used in the last two sessions of a smoking intervention program as well as during follow-up.

### Coping With Withdrawal Effects

Almost all smokers who use a "cold turkey" approach to quitting cigarettes will experience some withdrawal distress (Gunn 1986; Hughes et al. 1991). Informing patients and preparing them to cope with some of the possible symptoms of withdrawal and side effects of cessation, as described in the DSM-IV tobacco withdrawal syndrome, can add to the success of the smoking intervention. The symptoms will begin within 24 hours and decrease quickly, and most will disappear within 1 month (Hughes et al. 1990). Craving, decreased heart rate, hunger, and weight gain may persist over a longer period. All withdrawal symptoms except decreased heart rate may be partly eased by exercise, relaxation, or the use of NRT or bupropion. Weight gain is commonly related to smoking cessation, partly because the metabolic rate increase caused by nicotine has been removed. The health significance of weight gained, 2–3 kg on average, is clearly outweighed by the health benefits of quitting, but fear of weight gain may need to be addressed. Learning to tolerate a modest weight gain may be important to preventing relapse (American Psychiatric Association 1996; Perkins 1993; Perkins et al. 1997). An additional symptom of nicotine withdrawal may be excess sputum production as the bronchial tubes regain their ability to clean out the lungs. Abstinence also has been shown to decrease performance on attention tasks (Hughes et al. 1990). This effect may be present for at least 1–10 days and is reversed by NRT (U.S. Department of Health and Human Services 1990).

### Relapse Prevention

Relapse prevention as a treatment technique was originally developed by Marlatt and Gordon (1980) to deal with preventing the relapse of alcohol abuse and has been extrapolated to use with smokers (Lichtenstein and Brown 1985). Smokers and ex-smokers who learn relapse prevention skills maintain cessation longer and smoke fewer cigarettes if they relapse than their counterparts who do not receive such training (Davis and Glaros 1986). An excellent discussion of relapse prevention from a self-management approach is presented by Shiffman and colleagues (1985) in a text on relapse prevention edited by Marlatt and Gordon and is discussed in Chapter 31, by Marlatt et al., in this volume.

## Summary of Treatment Recommendations

To stop smoking, a smoker must perceive this change as being beneficial; a smoking cessation program needs to be seen by the smoker as efficacious. The smoker thus must be helped to develop self-confidence and a belief that he or she can become a nonsmoker. From the behavioral perspective, the smoker must learn new skills or enhance old skills that can be used in place of cigarettes to deal with problems as they arise. The individual also needs to be able to attribute changes in smoking behavior to personal abilities and skills rather than to willpower or to the external aspects of treatment (Bandura 1977). From the pharmacological perspective, a smoker who has a high physiological dependency on nicotine would benefit from NRT, bupropion, or tapering. (See Table 21–1 for summary of pharmacological therapies.) This technique would allow him or her to work on the behavioral aspects without needing to deal with the physiological withdrawal at the same time. Finally, the patient will benefit from relapse prevention training and learning ways to respond to stressful situations and to recognize and manage resumptive thinking. In referring back to Figure 21–1, it becomes clearer how the assessment outcome may point the way toward different treatment choices, allowing the clinician to tailor a multicomponent treatment program to the needs of each patient.

## References

Agency for Health Care Policy and Research: Smoking cessation clinical practice guideline. JAMA 275:1270–1280, 1996

American Psychiatric Association: Diagnostic and Statistical Manual of Mental Disorders, 3rd Edition. Washington, DC, American Psychiatric Association, 1980

American Psychiatric Association: Diagnostic and Statistical Manual of Mental Disorders, 3rd Edition, Revised. Washington, DC, American Psychiatric Association, 1987

American Psychiatric Association: Diagnostic and Statistical Manual of Mental Disorders, 4th Edition. Washington, DC, American Psychiatric Association, 1994

American Psychiatric Association: Practice guideline for the treatment of patients with nicotine dependence. Am J Psychiatry 153 (10 suppl):1–31, 1996

Ascher JA, Cole JO, Colin JN, et al: Bupropion: a review of its mechanism of antidepressant activity. J Clin Psychiatry 56:395–401, 1995

Bandura A: Self-efficacy: toward a unifying theory of behavioral change. Psychol Rev 84:191–215, 1977

Barabasz A, Baer L, Sheehan D, et al: A three year clinical followup of hypnosis and REST for smoking: hypnotizability, absorption and depression. Int J Clin Exp Hypn 34:169–181, 1986

Benowitz N: The use of biologic fluid samples in assessing tobacco smoke consumption, in Measurement in the Analysis and Treatment of Smoking (NIDA Res Monogr 48). Edited by Grabowski J, Bell C. Rockville, MD, Department of Health and Human Services, 1985, pp 6–26

Best J, Suedfeld P: Restricted environmental stimulation therapy and behavioral self-management in smoking cessation. Journal of Applied Social Psychology 12:408–419, 1982

Breslau N, Kilbey MM, Andreski P: Nicotine dependence and major depression: new evidence from a prospective investigation. Arch Gen Psychiatry 50:31–35, 1993

Breslau N, Kilbey MM, Andreski P: DSM-III-R nicotine dependence in young adults: prevalence, correlates and associated psychiatric disorders. Addiction 89:743–754, 1994

Brown D, Fromm E: Hypnosis and Behavioral Medicine. Hillsdale, NJ, Lawrence Erlbaum, 1987

Cepeda-Benito A: A meta-analytic review of the efficacy of nicotine chewing gum in smoking treatment programs. J Consult Clin Psychol 61:822–830, 1993

Condiotte M, Lichtenstein E: Self-efficacy and relapse in smoking cessation programs. J Consult Clin Psychol 49:648–658, 1981

Covey L, Glassman A: A meta-analysis of double-blind placebo-controlled trials of clonidine for smoking cessation. British Journal of Addiction 86:991–998, 1991

Covey LS, Glassman AH, Stetner F: Major depression following smoking cessation. Am J Psychiatry 154:263–265, 1997

Davis J, Glaros A: Relapse prevention and smoking cessation. Addict Behav 11:105–114, 1986

Derogatis L: SCL-90-R: Administration Scoring and Procedures Manual I. Baltimore, MD, Clinical Psychometrics Research, 1977

DiClemente C, Prochaska J, Fairhurst S, et al: The process of smoking cessation: an analysis of precontemplation, contemplation, and preparation stages of change. J Consult Clin Psychol 59:295–304, 1991

Fagerstrom K: Measuring degree of physical dependency to tobacco smoking with reference to individualization of treatment. Addict Behav 3:235– 241, 1978

Fagerstrom K: Towards better diagnoses and more individual treatment of tobacco dependence (Special Issue: Future Directions in Tobacco Research). British Journal of Addiction 86:543–547, 1991

Fagerstrom K, Schneider N: Measuring nicotine dependence: a review of the Fagerstrom Tolerance Questionnaire. J Behav Med 12:159–182, 1989

Fagerstrom KO, Schneider NG, Lunell E: Effectiveness of nicotine patch and nicotine gum as individual versus combined treatments for tobacco withdrawal symptoms. Psychopharmacology 111:271–277, 1993

Federal Trade Commission: Tar, Nicotine, and Carbon Monoxide of the Smoke of 1206 Varieties of Domestic Cigarettes. Washington, DC, Federal Trade Commission, 1997

Fielding J: Smoking: health effects and control. N Engl J Med 313:491–498, 1985

Fiore MC, Smith SS, Jorenby DE, et al: The effectiveness of the nicotine patch for smoking cessation: a meta-analysis. JAMA 271:1940–1947, 1994

Fiore MC, Bailey WC, Cohen SJ, et al: Smoking cessation. Clinical Practice Guideline No 18 (AHCPR Publ No 96-0692). Rockville, MD, U.S. Department of Health and Human Services, Agency for Health Care Policy and Research, April 1996

Foxx R, Brown R: Nicotine fading and self-monitoring for cigarette abstinence or controlled smoking. J Appl Behav Anal 12:111–125, 1979

Frost PH, David BR, Burlando AJ, et al: Coronary heart disease risk factors in men and women aged 60 years and older: findings from the Systolic Hypertension in the Elderly Program (SHEP). Circulation 94:26–34, 1996

Glantz S, Parmley WW: Passive smoking and heart disease: epidemiology, physiology, and biochemistry. Circulation 83:1–12, 1991

Glasgow RE, Hollis JF, Ary DV, et al: Results of a year-long incentives-based worksite smoking cessation program. Addict Behav 18:455–464, 1993

Glassman AH: Cigarette smoking: implications for psychiatric illness. Am J Psychiatry 150:546–553, 1993

Glassman AH, Covey LS: Future trends in the pharmacological treatment of smoking cessation. Drugs 40:1–5, 1990

Glassman A, Stetner F, Walsh B, et al: Heavy smokers, smoking cessation and clonidine: results of a double-blind, randomized trial. JAMA 259:2863–2866, 1988

Glassman A, Helzer J, Covey L, et al: Smoking, smoking cessation, and major depression. JAMA 264:1546–1549, 1990

Goldstein MG, Niaura R, Abrams DB: Pharmacological and behavioral treatment of nicotine dependence: nicotine as a drug of abuse, in Medical-Psychiatric Practice. Edited by Stoudemire A, Fogel BS. Washington, DC, American Psychiatric Press, 1991, pp 541–596

Gourlay S: The pros and cons of transdermal nicotine therapy. Med J Aust 160:152–159, 1994

Gourlay SG, Benowitz NL: Is clonidine an effective smoking cessation therapy? Drugs 50:197–207, 1995

Gourlay SG, McNeil JJ: Antismoking products. Med J Aust 153:11–12, 1990

Gourlay SG, Forbes A, Marriner T, et al: Prospective study of factors predicting outcome of transdermal nicotine treatment in smoking cessation. BMJ 309:842–846, 1994

Gritz E, Carr C, Marcus A: The tobacco withdrawal syndrome in unaided quitters. British Journal of Addiction 86:57–69, 1991

Gunn R: Reactions to withdrawal symptoms and success in smoking cessation clinics. Addict Behav 11:49–53, 1986

Heatherton TF, Kozlowski LT, Frecker RC, et al: Measuring the heaviness of smoking: using self-reported time to the first cigarette of the day and number of cigarettes smoked per day. British Journal of Addiction 84:791–799, 1989

Heatherton T, Kozlowski L, Frecker R: The Fagerstrom Test for Nicotine Dependence: a revision of the Fagerstrom Tolerance Questionnaire. British Journal of Addiction 86:1119–1127, 1991

Henningfield J: Pharmacologic basis and treatment of cigarette smoking. J Clin Psychiatry 45:24–34, 1984

Henningfield JE, Cohen C, Pickworth WB: Psychopharmacology of nicotine, in Nicotine Addiction: Principles and Management. Edited by Orleans CT, Slade J. New York, Oxford University Press, 1993, pp 24–45

Hjalmarson A, Franzon M, Westin A, et al: Effect of nicotine nasal spray on smoking cessation. Arch Intern Med 154:2567–2572, 1994

Holroyd I: Hypnosis treatment for smoking: an evaluative review. Int J Clin Exp Hypn 23:341–357, 1980

Hughes J: Treatment of smoking cessation in smokers with past alcohol/drug problems. J Subst Abuse Treat 10:181–187, 1993

Hughes JR: Pharmacology of nicotine dependence, in Pharmacological Aspects of Drug Dependence: Toward an Integrative Neurobehavioral Approach (Handbook of Experimental Pharmacology Series). Edited by Schuster CR, Kuhar MJ. New York, Springer-Verlag, 1996, pp 599–626

Hughes J, Hatsukami D: The nicotine withdrawal syndrome: a brief review and update. International Journal of Smoking Cessation 1:21–26, 1992

Hughes J, Higgins S, Hatsukami D: Effects of abstinence from tobacco: a critical review, in Research Advances in Alcohol and Drug Problems, Vol 10. Edited by Kozlowski L, Annis H, Cappell HD, et al. New York, Plenum, 1990, pp 317–398

Hughes J, Gust S, Skoog K, et al: Symptoms of tobacco withdrawal: a replication and extension. Arch Gen Psychiatry 48:52–59, 1991

Hunt W, Barnett L, Branch L: Relapse rates in addiction programs. J Clin Psychol 27:455–456, 1971

Hurt RD, Sachs DPL, Glover ED, et al: A comparison of sustained-release bupropion and placebo for smoking cessation. N Engl J Med 337:1195–1202, 1997

Jaffe JH, Kranzler M: Smoking as an addictive disorder, in Research on Smoking Behavior (NIDA Res Monogr 23). Edited by Krasnegor NA. Rockville, MD, U.S. Department of Health, Education, and Welfare, Public Health Service, 1979, pp 4–23

Jarvik M, Henningfield J: Pharmacological treatment of tobacco dependence. Pharmacol Biochem Behav 30:279–294, 1988

Jarvik ME, Henningfield JE: Pharmacological adjuncts for the treatment of tobacco dependence, in Nicotine Addiction: Principles and Management. Edited by Orleans CT, Slade J. New York, Oxford University Press, 1993, pp 245–261

Kleinman J, Pierre M, Madans J, et al: The effects of maternal smoking on fetal and infant mortality. Am J Epidemiol 127:274–281, 1988

Kornitzer M, Boutsen M, Dramaix M, et al: Combined use of nicotine patch and gum in smoking cessation: a placebo-controlled clinical trial. Prev Med 24:41–47, 1995

LaCroix AZ, Lang J, Scheer P, et al: Smoking and morality among older men and women in three communities. N Engl J Med 324:1619–1625, 1991

Lam W, Sxe P, Sacks H, et al: Meta-analysis of randomized controlled trials of nicotine chewing gum. Lancet 2:27–29, 1987

Lando H, McGovern P: Nicotine fading as a nonaversive alternative in a broad-spectrum treatment for eliminating smoking. Addict Behav 10:153–161, 1985

Lee EW, D'Alonzo GE: Cigarette smoking, nicotine addiction, and its pharmacological treatment. Arch Intern Med 153:34–48, 1993

Leventhal H, Cleary P: The smoking problem: a review of the research and theory in behavioral risk modification. Psychol Bull 88:370–405, 1980

Lichtenstein E: The smoking problem: a behavioral perspective. J Consult Clin Psychol 50:804–819, 1982

Lichtenstein E, Brown A: Current trends in the modification of cigarette dependence, in International Handbook of Behavior Modification and Therapy. Edited by Bellack A, Hersen H, Kazdin A. New York, Plenum, 1985, pp 575–612

Marlatt GA, Gordon JR: Determinants of relapse: implications for the maintenance of behavior change, in Behavioral Medicine: Changing Health Lifestyles. Edited by Davidson PO, Davidson SM. New York, Brunner/Mazel, 1980, pp 410–452

Marlatt G, Gordon J (eds): Relapse Prevention. New York, Guilford, 1985

Marlatt GA, Tapert SF: Harm reduction: reducing the risks of addictive behaviors, in Addictive Behaviors Across the Lifespan. Edited by Baer JS, Marlatt GA, McMahon R. New York, Guilford, 1993, pp 243–273

Matson DM, Lee JW, Hopp JW: The impact of incentives and competitions on participation and quit rates in worksite smoking cessation programs. Prevention and Health Promotion 7:270–280, 1993

Nash J: Taking Charge of Your Smoking. Palo Alto, CA, Bull Publishing, 1981

National Cancer Institute: Guia Para Dejar de Fumar (Guide to Quitting Smoking) (NIH Publ No 88-3001). Washington, DC, U.S. Department of Health and Human Services, Public Health Service, National Institutes of Health, National Cancer Institute, June 1988

National Cancer Institute: Smoking Facts and Quitting Tips for African Americans (NIH Publ No 92-3345). Washington, DC, U.S. Department of Health and Human Services, Public Health Service, National Institutes of Health, National Cancer Institute, September 1992

National Cancer Institute: Clearing the Air (NIH Publ No 93-1647). Bethesda, MD, Office of Cancer Communications, September 1993

Newhouse P, Hughes J: The role of nicotine and nicotinic mechanisms in neuropsychiatric disease (Special Issue: Future Directions in Tobacco Research). British Journal of Addiction 86:521–525, 1991

Nicotrol NS Prescribing Information, McNeil Consumer Products, Fort Washington, PA, 1996

Ockene J: Changes in cigarette smoking behavior in clinical and community trials, in The Health Consequences of Smoking: Cardiovascular Disease: A Report of the Surgeon General. Washington, DC, U.S. Government Printing Office, 1983, pp 241–290

Ockene J, Ockene I: Helping patients to reduce their risk for coronary heart disease: an overview, in Prevention of Coronary Heart Disease. Edited by Ockene I, Ockene J. Boston, MA, Little, Brown, 1992, pp 173–199

Ockene J, Nutall R, Benfari R, et al: A psychosocial model of smoking cessation and maintenance of cessation. Prev Med 10:623–638, 1981

Ockene J, Benfari R, Hurwitz I, et al: Relationship of psychosocial factors to smoking behavior change in an intervention program. Prev Med 11:13–28, 1982

Ockene J, Quirk M, Goldberg R, et al: A resident's training program for the development of smoking intervention skills. Arch Intern Med 148:1039–1045, 1988

Ockene J, Kristeller J, Goldberg R, et al: Increasing the efficacy of physician-delivered smoking intervention: a randomized clinical trial. J Gen Intern Med 6:1–8, 1991

Ockene J, Kristeller J, Goldberg R, et al: Smoking cessation and severity of disease: the Coronary Artery Smoking Intervention Study. Health Psychol 11:119–126, 1992

Orleans T: Clear Horizons. Philadelphia, PA, Fox Chase Cancer Center, 1997, p 44

Pechacek T: Modification of smoking behavior, in Smoking and Health: A Report of the Surgeon General. Washington, DC, U.S. Government Printing Office, 1979, pp 5–63

Pederson L: Compliance with physician advice to quit smoking: a review of the literature. Prev Med 11:71–84, 1982

Perkins KA: Weight gain following smoking cessation. J Consult Clin Psychol 61:768–777, 1993

Perkins KA, Levine MD, Marcus MD, et al: Addressing women's concerns about weight gain due to smoking cessation. J Subst Abuse Treat 14:173–182, 1997

Pinney JM: AHCPR Smoking Cessation Guideline: Its Goals and Impact. Tob Control 6 (suppl 1), 1997

Po ALW: Transdermal nicotine in smoking cessation: a meta-analysis. Eur J Clin Pharmacol 45:519–528, 1993

Pomerleau C, Pomerleau O: The effects of a psychosocial stressor on cigarette smoking and subsequent behavioral and physiological responses. Psychophysiology 24:278–285, 1987

Pomerleau O, Pomerleau C: Neuroregulators and the reinforcement of smoking: towards a biobehavioral explanation. Neurosci Biobehav Rev 8:503–513, 1984

Pomerleau O, Pomerleau C: Research on stress and smoking: progress and problems. British Journal of Addiction 86:599–603, 1991

Pomerleau O, Rosecrans J: Neuroregulatory effects of nicotine. Psychoneuroendocrinology 14:407–423, 1989

Prochaska J, DiClemente C: Stages and processes of self-change of smoking: toward an integrative model of change. J Consult Clin Psychol 51:390–395, 1983

Puska P, Vartiainen E, Korhone H, et al: Combining patch and gum in nicotine replacement therapy: results of a double-blind study in North Karlia. Paper presented at the annual meeting of the Society of Behavioral Medicine. Boston, MA, April 1994

Roski J, Schmid LA, Lando HA: Long-term associations of helpful and harmful spousal behaviors with smoking cessation. Addict Behav 21:173–185, 1996

Russell MAH: The future of nicotine replacement. British Journal of Addiction 86:653–658, 1991

Salber E, Freeman H, Abelin T: Needed research on smoking: lessons from the Newton study, in Smoking, Health and Behavior. Edited by Borgatta E, Evans R. Chicago, IL, Aldine, 1968, pp 128–139

Schneider NG, Olmstead R, Nisson F, et al: Efficacy of a nicotine inhaler in smoking cessation: a placebo-controlled, double-blind trial. Addiction 91:1293–1306, 1996

Sexton M, Hebel J: A clinical trial of change in maternal smoking and its effect on birth weight. JAMA 251:911–915, 1984

Shiffman S: Relapse following smoking cessation: a situational analysis. J Consult Clin Psychol 50:71–86, 1982

Shiffman S, Read L, Maltese J, et al: Preventing relapse in ex-smokers: a self-management approach, in Relapse Prevention: Maintenance Strategies in Treatment of Addictive Behaviors. Edited by Marlatt G, Gordon J. New York, Guilford, 1985, pp 472–520

Shiffman S, Hickcox M, Paty JA, et al: Progression from a smoking lapse to relapse: prediction from abstinence violation effects, nicotine dependence, and lapse characteristics. J Consult Clin Psychol 64:993–1002, 1996

Shiffman S, Hickcox M, Paty JA, et al: Individual differences in the context of smoking lapse episodes. Addict Behav 22:797–811, 1997

Silagy C, Mant D, Fowler G, et al: Meta-analysis on efficacy of nicotine replacement therapies in smoking cessation. Lancet 343:139–142, 1994

Slade J, Connolly GN, David RM, et al: Report of the Tobacco Policy Research Study Group on adjunctive medications for managing nicotine dependence. Tob Control 1 (suppl):S10–S13, 1992

Spiegel H: A single-treatment method to stop smoking using ancillary self-hypnosis. Int J Clin Exp Hypn 18:235–250, 1970

Stone S, Kristeller J: Attitudes of adolescents towards smoking cessation. Am J Prev Med 8:221–225, 1992

Strecher VJ, Krueter M, Den Boer D, et al: The effects of computer-tailored smoking cessation messages in family practice settings. J Fam Pract 39:262–268, 1994

Suedfeld P, Kristeller J: Stimulus reduction as a technique in health psychology. Health Psychol 1:337–357, 1982

Sutherland G, Stapleton JA, Russell MA, et al: Randomised controlled trial of nasal nicotine spray in smoking cessation. Lancet 340:324–329, 1992

Tang JL, Law M, Wald N: How effective is nicotine replacement therapy in helping people stop smoking? BMJ 308:21–26, 1994

Tonnesen P, Norregaard J, Simonsen K, et al: A double-blind trial of a 16-hour transdermal nicotine patch in smoking cessation. N Engl J Med 325:311–315, 1991

Tonnesen P, Norregaard J, Mikkelsen K, et al: A double-blind trial of a nicotine inhaler for smoking cessation. JAMA 269:1268–1271, 1993

Transdermal Nicotine Study Group: Transdermal nicotine for smoking cessation. JAMA 266:3133–3138, 1992

U.S. Department of Health and Human Services: The Health Consequences of Smoking: Cardiovascular Disease: A Report of the Surgeon General. Washington, DC, U.S. Government Printing Office, 1983

U.S. Department of Health and Human Services: The Surgeon General's Report on Nutrition and Health. Washington, DC, U.S. Government Printing Office, 1988

U.S. Department of Health and Human Services: Reducing the Health Consequences of Smoking: 25 Years of Progress: A Report of the Surgeon General (CDC 89-8411). Washington, DC, Centers for Disease Control, Center for Chronic Disease Prevention and Health Promotion, Office of Smoking and Health, 1989

U.S. Department of Health and Human Services: The Health Benefits of Smoking Cessation: A Report of the Surgeon General (CDC Report 90-8416). Washington, DC, U.S. Government Printing Office, 1990

U.S. Department of Health, Education, and Welfare: Smoking and Health: Report of the Advisory Committee to the Surgeon General of the Public Health Service. Rockville, MD, Centers for Disease Control, 1964

U.S. Environmental Protection Agency: Respiratory Health Effects of Passive Smoking: Lung Cancer and Other Disorders (Review Draft). Washington, DC, Office of Research and Development, 1992

Vaughan DA: Frontiers in pharmacologic treatment of alcohol, cocaine, and nicotine dependence. Psychiatric Annals 20:695–710, 1990

Warner KE, Slade J, Sweanor DT: The emerging market for long-term nicotine maintenance. JAMA 278:1087–1092, 1997

Williams J, Hall D: Use of single session hypnosis for smoking cessation. Addict Behav 13:205–208, 1988

World Health Organization: Mental Disorders: Glossary and Guide to Their Classification, 9th Revision. Geneva, Switzerland, World Health Organization, 1978

Yates A, Thain J: Self-efficacy as a predictor of relapse following voluntary cessation of smoking. Addict Behav 10: 291–298, 1985

Zyban Product Information 1997, Glaxo Wellcome Inc, Research Triangle Park, NC

# 22 Benzodiazepines and Other Sedative-Hypnotics

David E. Smith, M.D.
Donald R. Wesson, M.D.

In this chapter, we focus on treatment of physical dependence on benzodiazepines and discuss other prescription sedative-hypnotics in terms of their similarities to or differences from benzodiazepines. Sedative-hypnotics are a chemically diverse group of compounds commonly prescribed to ameliorate symptoms of anxiety and insomnia. Although most benzodiazepines could also be classified as sedative-hypnotics, they are often grouped, as we have done here, by their chemical class name. All benzodiazepines currently marketed in the United States, except for the benzodiazepine antagonist flumazenil (Romazicon), share many pharmacological effects. Although clinically significant pharmacological differences exist among benzodiazepines (e.g., therapeutic indications, metabolic profile, receptor affinity, side effects, abuse potential), all benzodiazepine agonists produce little respiratory depression even in dosages much higher than those used to treat anxiety or insomnia. Even when a benzodiazepine is taken in an overdose of 50–100 times the usual therapeutic dose, fatality from respiratory depression is rare. The "safety" of benzodiazepines in the overdose situation is an important advantage of the benzodiazepines over the older sedative-hypnotics.

Benzodiazepines exert their physiological effects by attaching to a subunit of the $\gamma$-aminobutyric acid (GABA) receptor. GABA, the major inhibitory neurotransmitter in the brain and spinal cord, modulates the polarization of neurons. The GABA receptor is made up of an ion channel (an ionophore) and several subunits that bind to different drugs: one subunit binds GABA, another benzodiazepines, and another barbiturates.

Benzodiazepines that enhance the effect of GABA are designated *agonists*.

Attachment of an agonist at the benzodiazepine receptor facilitates the effect of GABA (i.e., opens the chloride channel). Opening the chloride channel allows more chloride ions to enter neurons. The influx of negatively charged chloride ions increases the electrical gradient across the cell membrane and makes the neuron less excitable. The clinical effects are anxiety reduction, sedation, and increased seizure threshold. Closing the channel decreases electrical polarization and makes the cell more excitable. Substances that attach to the benzodiazepine receptor and close the channel produce an opposite effect: they are anxiogenic and lower the seizure threshold. Compounds that produce the opposite effects from benzodiazepine agonists, such as betacarboline, are designated *inverse agonists*.

Some compounds attach to the benzodiazepine receptor but neither increase nor decrease the effect of GABA. In the absence of benzodiazepine agonists or inverse agonists, they are neutral ligands (i.e., they attach to the receptor and block the effects of both the agonist and the inverse agonist). Neutral agonists are designated *antagonists*. If the receptor is already occupied by an agonist or inverse agonist, the antagonist may displace the agonist or inverse agonist. Displacement of a benzodiazepine agonist has clinical utility. For example, the benzodiazepine antagonist flumazenil is used to reverse the sedation produced by a benzodiazepine.

The long-term interaction of benzodiazepine receptors with their ligands is extremely complex. Attachment of the ligands can alter the pharmacodynamics of the receptors (e.g., altering the number of receptors or changing the affinity of the ligands for the receptors).

## Benzodiazepine Abuse and Dependence

Benzodiazepines are not common primary drugs of abuse. Most people do not find the effects of benzodiazepines reinforcing or pleasurable (Chutuape and de Wit 1994; de Wit et al. 1984). Sedative-hypnotic abusers prefer pentobarbital to diazepam, even at high dosages (Griffiths et al. 1980). Benzodiazepines are commonly misused and abused among patients receiving methadone maintenance (Barnas et al. 1992; Iguchi et al. 1993).

Abuse of flunitrazepam (Rohypnol), a benzodiazepine not marketed in the United States, generated considerable media attention during the mid-1990s, particularly concerning its use as a "date rape drug" and as a drug of abuse by youth (Calhoun et al. 1996). In experimental studies of animals and non-drug-abusing human subjects, flunitrazepam is similar to most other benzodiazepines in its ability to produce drug-seeking behavior and in its capacity to produce physiological dependence (Woods and Winger 1997).

The imidazopyridines—another chemical class of sedative-hypnotics, which includes alpidem, zolpidem, and zopiclone—attach to the benzodiazepine receptor and are efficacious hypnotics. Their pharmacodynamics at the benzodiazepine receptor are controversial. Some researchers report preferential affinity of zolpidem at the omega 1 subtype of benzodiazepine receptor (Lloyd and Zivkovic 1988; Ruano et al. 1993; Sanger and Benavides 1993); others question the receptor subtype selectivity (Byrnes et al. 1992).

Zolpidem (Ambien) is prescribed extensively for treatment of insomnia. It is absorbed rapidly and has a short half-life ($T_{1/2} = 2.2$ hours). Its sedative effects are additive with alcohol. Few cases of zolpidem abuse or dependence have been reported. Some patients increased the dosage many times that prescribed, and it appears that at very high dosage levels zolpidem produces tolerance and a withdrawal syndrome similar to that of other sedative-hypnotics (Cavallaro et al. 1993).

Preclinical data relating to the issue of zolpidem tolerance are contradictory. Mice that were given 30 mg/kg of zolpidem or midazolam by gastric intubation for 10 days showed tolerance and a lowering of seizure threshold after drug discontinuation for midazolam but not zolpidem. The benzodiazepine antagonist flumaze-

nil precipitated withdrawal in the midazolam-treated animals but not in those treated with zolpidem (Perrault et al. 1992). Studies with baboons suggested that zolpidem is reinforcing and that it produces tolerance and physical dependence (Griffiths et al. 1992). The behavioral pharmacology of zolpidem has been reviewed recently (Rush 1998).

Patients who become physically dependent on benzodiazepines can generally be classified into one of three groups:

1. Street drug abusers who self-administer benzodiazepines as one of many in a pattern of polydrug abuse
2. Alcoholic individuals and prescription drug abusers who are prescribed benzodiazepines for treatment of chronic anxiety or insomnia
3. Non-drug-abusing patients with depression or panic disorders who are prescribed high dosages of benzodiazepines for long periods

Street drug abusers may take benzodiazepines to ameliorate the adverse effects of cocaine or methamphetamine, to self-medicate heroin or alcohol withdrawal, to enhance the effects of methadone, or to produce intoxication when other drugs are not available. Benzodiazepines are rarely their primary drug of abuse. Even if their use of benzodiazepines does not meet DSM-IV criteria for abuse (American Psychiatric Association 1994), most people would call the use of benzodiazepines by street drug abusers *abuse* because it falls outside the context of medical treatment and is part of a polydrug abuse pattern. Furthermore, the benzodiazepines are often obtained by such patients by street purchase, theft, or forged prescriptions. Benzodiazepine dependency occurring among such patients must be treated in a comprehensive drug treatment program.

Alcohol and prescription drug abusers who are receiving treatment for chronic anxiety or insomnia are at significant risk for developing benzodiazepine dependency. They may receive benzodiazepines for a long time, and they may be biologically predisposed to develop benzodiazepine dependency. A study of alprazolam (1 mg) in alcoholic and nonalcoholic men found that alprazolam produced positive mood effects in alcoholic men that were not reported by the nonalcoholic men (Ciraulo et al. 1988). The difference in subjective response may be genetic. The mood-elevating effects of alprazolam were found to be greater in daughters of alcoholic parents than in those without a history of parental alcohol dependence (Ciraulo et al. 1996). Similar results have been found in sons of alcoholic parents (Cowley et al. 1992, 1994).

Patients who have depression or panic disorders may be prescribed high dosages of benzodiazepines for long periods of time. Some of these patients will develop physiological dependency on the benzodiazepines. Physiological dependency arising in the context of medical treatment does not necessarily equate with a substance abuse disorder or contraindicate benzodiazepine treatment. A history of sedative-hypnotic abuse, alcoholism, or severe symptoms following benzodiazepine discontinuation is a relative contraindication.

## Other Sedative-Hypnotics

Short-acting sedative-hypnotics (e.g., secobarbital, pentobarbital) are primary drugs of abuse. Addicts take them alone by mouth or by injection to produce intoxication. Intoxication with sedative-hypnotics is similar to intoxication with alcohol, producing a state of disinhibition, in which mood is elevated; self-criticism, anxiety, and guilt are reduced; and energy and self-confidence are increased. During intoxication, the user's mood is often labile and may shift rapidly between euphoria and dysphoria. Users may also be irritable, hypochondriacal, anxious, or agitated, and they may have difficulty with memory. They may exhibit poor judgment, ataxia, slurred speech, and sustained vertical and horizontal nystagmus.

Buspirone appears to have minimal abuse potential and does not produce physical dependence. Buspirone is a serotonin 5-HT$_{1A}$ partial agonist (Taylor and Moon 1991). Its anxiolytic effects take from days to weeks to develop. Buspirone will not prevent sedative-hypnotic withdrawal (i.e., it is not cross-tolerant with benzodiazepines) nor will it effectively treat benzodiazepine withdrawal syndromes (Schweizer and Rickels 1986). Clinical observations suggest that patients with a history of benzodiazepine abuse are resistant to the anxiolytic effects of buspirone (Schweizer et al. 1986).

## Benzodiazepine and Other Sedative-Hypnotic Withdrawal Syndromes

The long-term use of benzodiazepines or sedative-hypnotics at dosages above the therapeutic dose range produces physical dependence, and both drug types have similar withdrawal syndromes that may be severe

and life threatening. Therapeutic doses of benzodiazepines taken daily for months to years may also produce physiological dependence.

## High-Dose Withdrawal Syndrome

Human studies have established that large doses of chlordiazepoxide (Hollister et al. 1961) and diazepam (Hollister et al. 1963), taken for 1 month or more, produce a sedative-hypnotic withdrawal syndrome. Other benzodiazepines have not been studied under such precise conditions, but case reports leave no doubt that they produce a similar withdrawal syndrome.

Signs and symptoms of sedative-hypnotic withdrawal include anxiety, tremors, nightmares, insomnia, anorexia, nausea, vomiting, postural hypotension, seizures, delirium, and hyperpyrexia. Abrupt discontinuation of sedative-hypnotics in patients who are severely physically dependent on them can result in serious medical complications and even death. The syndrome is qualitatively similar for all sedative-hypnotics; however, the time course and intensity of signs and symptoms may vary depending on the drug. With short-acting sedative-hypnotics (e.g., pentobarbital, secobarbital, meprobamate, and methaqualone) and short-acting benzodiazepines (e.g., oxazepam, alprazolam, and triazolam), withdrawal symptoms typically begin 12–24 hours after the last dose and peak in intensity between 24 and 72 hours. (Symptoms may develop more slowly in patients who have liver disease and in the elderly because of decreased drug metabolism.) With long-acting drugs (e.g., phenobarbital, diazepam, and chlordiazepoxide), withdrawal symptoms peak on the fifth to eighth day.

During untreated sedative-hypnotic withdrawal, the electroencephalogram may show paroxysmal bursts of high-voltage, slow-frequency activity that precedes the development of seizures. Withdrawal delirium may include confusion and visual and auditory hallucinations. Delirium generally follows a period of insomnia. Some patients may have only delirium, others only seizures, and some may have both.

## Low-Dose Benzodiazepine Withdrawal Syndrome

In the medical literature, the low-dose benzodiazepine withdrawal syndrome is variously referred to as *therapeutic-dose withdrawal, normal-dose withdrawal,* or *benzodiazepine discontinuation syndrome.*

Through the 1960s and early 1970s, it was generally

believed that benzodiazepines taken within the usual recommended therapeutic dose range did not produce physical dependence. The knowledge that some patients had a withdrawal syndrome emerged from clinical observations. In 1978, investigators at the Addiction Research Center in Lexington, Kentucky, published a detailed case study of an incarcerated 37-year-old man who had been prescribed 30–45 mg/day of diazepam for 20 months (Pevnick et al. 1978). Five days after the subject was crossed over to placebo, he reported muscle twitches, muscle cramps, facial numbness, and abdominal cramping. The patient lost weight and had an increased pulse rate. Symptoms occurred primarily between days 5 and 9 and had abated by day 16.

Winokur et al. (1980) reported a similar placebo crossover study of a 32-year-old man who had been taking 15–25 mg of diazepam for 6 years. Two days after crossover to placebo, the patient began complaining of anxiety, dizziness, blurred vision, constipation, and palpitations. During the next 2 days, he became increasingly anxious and irritable, diaphoretic, and grossly tremulous, and he had difficulty expressing his thoughts coherently. His auditory and olfactory senses were "at times so hypersensitive that normally unobtrusive sounds (a watch ticking) or odors (an orange peel) were acutely uncomfortable to him" (p. 103). He was also hypersensitive to tactile stimuli, to the point that he could not stand to have clothes on his body. His symptoms subsided over the next 30 days.

Standard medical texts prior to 1980 generally concurred that therapeutic doses of benzodiazepines produced minimal withdrawal. During the 1980s, additional clinical studies and case reports established that therapeutic doses of benzodiazepines could produce physical dependency (Lader 1991). Many patients experienced a transient increase in symptoms for 1–2 weeks after withdrawal. A few patients experienced a severe, protracted withdrawal syndrome that included symptoms, such as paresthesia and psychosis, that were not present before. The American Psychiatric Association formed a task force that reviewed the issues and published its report in book form (American Psychiatric Association 1990). The conclusions of the task force were unambiguous about therapeutic dose dependency:

> Physiological dependence on benzodiazepines, as indicated by the appearance of discontinuance symptoms, can develop with therapeutic doses. Duration of treatment determines the onset of dependence when typical therapeutic anxiolytic doses are used: clinically significant dependence indicated by the appearance of

discontinuance symptoms usually does not appear before four months of such daily dosing. Dependence may develop sooner when higher antipanic doses are taken daily. (p. 56)

The chronology of therapeutic dose dependency is important for medical-legal reasons. During the 1980s, some patients who developed therapeutic dose dependency sued their physicians for malpractice, claiming that their physicians were negligent in not warning them about the possibility of therapeutic dose dependency and in treating them with benzodiazepines for extended periods, often many years. Some of these patients were treated, however, during the 1960s and 1970s. During those decades, therapeutic dose dependency was not part of mainstream medical knowledge.

Some patients who have taken a benzodiazepine in therapeutic doses for months to years can abruptly discontinue it without developing withdrawal symptoms. Others, taking similar amounts of a benzodiazepine, develop symptoms ranging from mild to severe when the benzodiazepine is stopped or the dosage is reduced substantially. Characteristically, patients tolerate a gradual tapering of the benzodiazepine until they are at 10%–20% of the peak dosage. Further reduction in benzodiazepine dose causes patients to become increasingly symptomatic.

At least three reasons explain symptoms that emerge after benzodiazepine cessation. Two of these, *symptom rebound* and the *protracted withdrawal syndrome*, are the result of dependence; the other, *symptom reemergence*, is not.

## Symptom Rebound

Symptom rebound is an intensified return of the symptoms for which the benzodiazepine was prescribed (e.g., insomnia or anxiety). The term comes from sleep research in which rebound insomnia may occur after discontinuation of hypnotic use. Symptom rebound, the most common consequence of prolonged benzodiazepine use, may last a few days to weeks after discontinuation (American Psychiatric Association 1990, p. 16).

## Protracted Withdrawal From Benzodiazepines

Protracted withdrawal from benzodiazepines should be distinguished from the protracted withdrawal syndrome that has been described for most drugs, including alcohol (Geller 1991). The symptoms generally attributed to protracted withdrawal syndromes consist of relatively mild symptoms such as irritability, anxiety, insomnia, and mood instability. The protracted withdrawal syndrome from benzodiazepines can be severe and disabling, and it lasts many months.

Many symptoms are nonspecific, and they often mimic an obsessive-compulsive disorder with psychotic features. Symptoms such as increased sensitivity to sound, light, and touch and paresthesia are particularly suggestive of low-dose withdrawal.

The waxing-and-waning symptom intensity illustrated in the waviness of the line in the phase IV section of Figure 22–1 is characteristic of the low-dose protracted benzodiazepine withdrawal syndrome. Patients are sometimes asymptomatic for several days, then, without apparent reason, they become acutely anxious. Often concomitant physiological signs (e.g., dilated pupils, increased resting heart rate and blood pressure) are present.

Protracted benzodiazepine withdrawal has no pathognomonic signs or symptoms, and the broad range of nonspecific symptoms produced by the protracted benzodiazepine withdrawal syndrome also could be the result of agitated depression, generalized anxiety disorder, panic disorder, complex partial seizures, and schizophrenia. The time course of symptom resolution is the primary differentiating feature between the symptoms generated by withdrawal and symptom reemergence. The symptoms from withdrawal subside gradually with continued abstinence, whereas symptom reemergence and symptom sensitization do not.

### Symptom Reemergence (Recrudescence)

Patients' symptoms of anxiety, insomnia, or muscle tension abate during benzodiazepine treatment. When the benzodiazepine is stopped, symptoms return to the same level as before benzodiazepine therapy. A distinction is made between symptom rebound and symptom reemergence because symptom reemergence suggests underlying psychopathology, whereas symptom rebound suggests a withdrawal syndrome (American Psychiatric Association 1990, p. 17).

### Risk Factors for Low-Dose Withdrawal

Some drugs or medications may facilitate neuroadaptation by increasing the affinity of benzodiazepines for their receptors. Patients at increased risk for development of the low-dose withdrawal syndrome are those with a family or personal history of alcoholism, those who use alcohol daily, or those who concomitantly use other sedatives. Case-control studies suggest that patients with a history of addiction, particularly to other sedative-hypnotics, are at high risk for benzodiazepine dependence. The short-acting, high-milligram potency benzodiazepines appear to produce a more intense withdrawal syndrome (Rickels et al. 1990b).

## The Dependence/Withdrawal Cycle

When dependence arises during therapeutic treatment, a sequence of phases often occurs (see Figure 22–1). The clinical course described here most often occurs during long-term treatment of a generalized anxiety disorder, panic disorder, or severe insomnia.

### Pretreatment Phase

The first panel on Figure 22–1 represents the time before the patient was treated with benzodiazepines. Patients' symptoms generally vary in intensity from day to day depending on life stresses and the waxing and waning of their underlying disorder. For purposes of the illustration, the average symptom, shown by the horizontal dotted line, illustrates the patient's baseline level of symptoms.

### Therapeutic Phase

When treatment with a benzodiazepine is started, patients often have initial side effects, such as drowsiness, psychomotor impairment, or memory impairment. Tolerance to such side effects usually develops within a few days, and afterward the patient's overall level of symptoms decreases. The therapeutic phase, illustrated in phase II of Figure 22–1, may last for months to years.

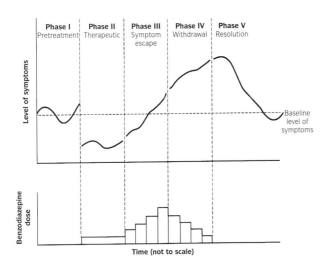

**Figure 22–1.**   The treatment-dependence cycle.

### Symptom Escape and Dosage Escalation Phase

During long-term treatment, benzodiazepines may suddenly lose their effectiveness in controlling symptoms. For some patients, the *symptom escape* coincides with a period of increased life stress; for others, no unusual psychological stressor is apparent. Patients are often aware that the medication "no longer works" or that its effect is qualitatively different. The increasing symptoms are represented by the ascending wavy line in phase III of Figure 22–1.

As the usual dosages of benzodiazepines lose effectiveness, patients may increase their benzodiazepine consumption hoping to regain symptom amelioration. As the daily dosage of benzodiazepine increases, patients may develop subtle neuropsychological impairment that is difficult to diagnose without psychometric assessment.

Benzodiazepine-induced memory impairment may be a common clinical problem that generally goes unrecognized. It has not received sufficient research attention. Although many studies have demonstrated that acute doses of benzodiazepines impair cognitive function, there has been little study of the effects of benzodiazepines with prolonged use. One psychometric study, which compared long-term benzodiazepine users with subjects who were benzodiazepine abstinent, found that the long-term benzodiazepine users performed poorly on tasks involving visual-spatial ability and sustained attention (Golombok et al. 1988). Patients may not be aware that their impairment is benzodiazepine induced. Coping skills that were previously bolstered by the benzodiazepine may become compromised. In a study with long-term benzodiazepine users who were taking 5–20 mg/day of diazepam, the neurocognitive effects of a 10-mg oral dose of diazepam had no measurable effect on psychomotor performance; however, it did produce measurable effects on memory. The author concluded that tolerance to the memory effects of benzodiazepines does not fully develop (Gorenstein et al. 1994).

The symptom escape phase is not an invariable consequence of long-term benzodiazepine treatment. Patients who have experienced symptom escape and dosage escalation may also be the most likely to have a protracted withdrawal syndrome.

### Withdrawal Phase

When patients stop taking the benzodiazepine or the daily dosage falls below 25% of the peak maintenance dosage, patients become increasingly symptomatic. The symptoms, represented by the ascending wavy line in phase IV of Figure 22–1, may be the result of symptom rebound, symptom reemergence, or the beginning of a protracted withdrawal syndrome. The symptoms that occur during this phase may be a mixture of symptoms that were present during the pretreatment phase and new symptoms. During the first few weeks, it is not possible to determine the exact cause of the symptoms or to accurately predict their duration. Symptoms of the same type that occurred during the pretreatment phase suggest symptom rebound or symptom reemergence. New symptoms, particularly alterations in sensory perception, suggest the beginning of a protracted withdrawal syndrome. Increasing the benzodiazepine dosage will reduce symptoms because benzodiazepines have not completely lost effectiveness and because the withdrawal syndrome is reversed; however, symptom reduction will not be as complete as during the initial therapeutic phase.

### Resolution Phase

The duration of the resolution phase is highly variable. Most patients will have only symptom rebound lasting a few weeks; others will have a severe, protracted abstinence syndrome lasting months to more than 1 year. During early abstinence, the patient's symptoms will generally vary in intensity from day to day. If abstinence from benzodiazepines is maintained, symptoms will gradually return to their baseline level. An encouraging finding of one discontinuation study was that "patients who were able to remain free of benzodiazepines for at least 5 weeks obtained lower levels of anxiety than before benzodiazepine discontinuation" (Rickels et al. 1990b, p. 899).

## Pharmacological Treatment of Benzodiazepine Withdrawal

The physician's response during the withdrawal phase is critical to achieving a satisfactory resolution of the physical dependency. One common response is to declare the patient "addicted to benzodiazepines" and refer him or her for chemical dependency treatment; however, referral to a chemical dependency program is not appropriate unless the patient has a substance abuse disorder. Some physicians interpret the patient's escalating symptoms as evidence of the patient's "need" for benzodiazepine treatment and reinstitute higher dosages of benzodiazepines or switch the patient to another benzodiazepine. Reinstitution of any benzodiazepine agonist usually does not achieve satisfactory symptom control and may prolong the recovery process. Benzodiazepine withdrawal, using one of the strategies described in this section, generally achieves the best long-term outcome.

The salient features of the various benzodiazepine withdrawal syndromes are summarized in Table 22–1. Benzodiazepine withdrawal strategies must be tailored to suit three possible dependency situations:

1. A high-dose withdrawal (i.e., doses greater than the recommended therapeutic doses for more than 1 month)
2. A low-dose withdrawal (i.e., doses below those in the upper range of Table 22–2)
3. A combined high-dose and low-dose withdrawal (i.e., following daily high dosages for more than 6 months, both a high-dose sedative-hypnotic withdrawal syndrome and a low-dose benzodiazepine withdrawal syndrome may occur)

## High-Dose Benzodiazepine Withdrawal

Four general strategies may be used for withdrawing patients from sedative-hypnotics, including benzodiazepines. The first is to use decreasing dosages of the agent of dependence. The second is to substitute phenobarbital or some other long-acting barbiturate for the addicting agent and gradually withdraw the substitute medication (Smith and Wesson 1970, 1971, 1983). The third, used for patients with a dependence on both alcohol and a benzodiazepine, is to substitute a long-acting benzodiazepine, such as chlordiazepoxide, and taper it over 1–2 weeks. Finally, valproate or carbamazepine may be prescribed. The method selected will depend on the particular benzodiazepine, the involvement of other drugs of dependence, and the clinical setting in which the detoxification program takes place.

### Phenobarbital Substitution

Phenobarbital substitution has the broadest use for all sedative-hypnotic drug dependencies. Substitution of phenobarbital can also be used to withdraw patients who have lost control of their benzodiazepine use or who are dependent on multiple sedative-hypnotics, including alcohol.

The pharmacological rationale for phenobarbital substitution is that phenobarbital is long acting, and little change in blood levels of phenobarbital occurs between doses. This allows the safe use of a progressively smaller daily dose. Phenobarbital is safer than the shorter-acting barbiturates; lethal doses of phenobarbital are many times higher than toxic doses, and the signs of toxicity (i.e., sustained nystagmus, slurred speech, and ataxia) are easy to observe. Phenobarbital has low abuse

**Table 22–1.** Characteristics of syndromes related to benzodiazepine withdrawal

| Syndrome | Signs and symptoms | Time course | Response to reinstitution of benzodiazepine |
|---|---|---|---|
| High-dose withdrawal | Anxiety, insomnia, nightmares, major motor seizures, psychosis, hyperpyrexia, death | Begins 1–2 days after a short-acting benzodiazepine is stopped; 3–8 days after a long-acting benzodiazepine is stopped | Signs and symptoms reverse 2–6 hours after a hypnotic dose of a benzodiazepine |
| Symptom rebound | Same symptoms that were present before treatment | Begins 1–2 days after a short-acting benzodiazepine is stopped; 3–8 days after a long-acting benzodiazepine is stopped; lasts 7–14 days | Signs and symptoms reverse 2–6 hours after a hypnotic dose of a benzodiazepine |
| Protracted, low-dose withdrawal | Anxiety, agitation, tachycardia, palpitations, anorexia, blurred vision, muscle cramps, insomnia, nightmares, confusion, muscle spasms, psychosis, increased sensitivity to sounds and light, paresthesia | Signs and symptoms emerge 1–7 days after a benzodiazepine is stopped or after a benzodiazepine is reduced to below the usual therapeutic dose | Signs and symptoms reverse 2–6 hours after a sedative dose of high-potency benzodiazepine |
| Symptom reemergence | Recurrence of the same symptoms that were present before taking a benzodiazepine (e.g., anxiety, insomnia) | Symptoms emerge when a benzodiazepine is stopped and continue unabated with time | Signs and symptoms reverse 2–6 hours after usual therapeutic dose of a benzodiazepine |

**Table 22–2.**    Benzodiazepines and their phenobarbital withdrawal equivalents

| Generic name | Trade name | Common therapeutic indication(s) | Therapeutic dose range (mg/day) | Dose equal to 30 mg phenobarbital for withdrawal (mg)[a] |
|---|---|---|---|---|
| Alprazolam | Xanax | Sedative, antipanic | 0.75–6 | 1 |
| Chlordiazepoxide | Librium | Sedative | 15–100 | 25 |
| Clonazepam | Klonopin | Anticonvulsant | 0.5–4 | 2 |
| Clorazepate | Tranxene | Sedative | 15–60 | 7.5 |
| Diazepam | Valium | Sedative | 4–40 | 10 |
| Estazolam | ProSom | Hypnotic | 1–2 | 1 |
| Flumazenil | Romazicon | Benzodiazepine antagonist | n/a | n/a |
| Flunitrazepam | Rohypnol[c] | Hypnotic | 0.5–1 | 0.5 |
| Flurazepam | Dalmane | Hypnotic | 15–30[b] | 15 |
| Halazepam | Paxipam | Sedative | 60–160 | 40 |
| Lorazepam | Ativan | Sedative | 1–6 | 2 |
| Midazolam | Versed | Intravenous sedation | 2.5–7 | 2.5 |
| Nitrazepam | Mogadon[c] | Hypnotic | 5–10 | 5 |
| Oxazepam | Serax | Sedative | 10–120 | 10 |
| Prazepam | Centrax | Sedative | 15–30 | 15 |
| Quazepam | Doral | Hypnotic | 15 | 15 |
| Temazepam | Restoril | Hypnotic | 15–30 | 15 |
| Triazolam | Halcion | Hypnotic | 0.125–0.50 | 0.25 |

*Note.*    n/a = not applicable.

[a]Phenobarbital withdrawal conversion equivalence is not the same as therapeutic dose equivalency. Withdrawal equivalence is the amount of the drug that 30 mg of phenobarbital will substitute for and prevent serious high-dose withdrawal signs and symptoms.

[b]Usual hypnotic dose.

[c]Although these benzodiazepines are not marketed in the United States, they are commonly used benzodiazepines in many countries.

potential (Griffiths and Roache 1985), and intoxication usually does not produce disinhibition. Most patients view phenobarbital as a medication not as a drug of abuse. Phenobarbital is excreted primarily by the kidneys, is not toxic to the liver, and can used in the presence of significant liver disease.

Stabilization phase.    The patient's history of drug use during the month before treatment is used to compute the stabilization dosage of phenobarbital. Although many addicted patients exaggerate the number of pills they are taking, patient history is the best guide to initiating pharmacotherapy. Patients who have overstated the amount of drug they are taking will become intoxicated during the first day or two of treatment. Intoxication is easily managed by omitting one or more doses of phenobarbital and recalculating the daily dosage.

The patient's average daily sedative-hypnotic dosage is converted to phenobarbital withdrawal equivalents, and the daily amount divided into three doses. (The conversion equivalents for various benzodiazepines are listed in Table 22–2 and for other sedative-hypnotics in Table 22–3.)

The computed daily phenobarbital dosage is given in divided doses three times daily. If the patient is using significant amounts of other sedative-hypnotics (including alcohol), the amounts of all the drugs are converted to phenobarbital equivalents and added together (30 cc of 100-proof alcohol is equated to 30 mg of phenobarbital for withdrawal purposes). The maximum starting phenobarbital dosage, however, is 500 mg/day.

**Table 22–3.** Sedative-hypnotics and their phenobarbital withdrawal equivalents

| Generic name | Trade name | Common therapeutic indication(s) | Therapeutic dose range (mg/day) | Dose equal to 30 mg phenobarbital for withdrawal (mg)[a] |
|---|---|---|---|---|
| Barbiturates | | | | |
| Amobarbital | Amytal | Sedative | 50–150 | 100 |
| Butabarbital | Butisol | Sedative | 45–120 | 100 |
| Butalbital | Fiorinal, Sedapap | Sedative/analgesic[b] | 100–300 | 100 |
| Pentobarbital | Nembutal | Hypnotic | 50–100[b] | 100 |
| Secobarbital | Seconal | Hypnotic | 50–100[b] | 100 |
| Other sedative-hypnotics | | | | |
| Buspirone | BuSpar | Sedative | 15–60 | NC |
| Chloral hydrate | Noctec | Hypnotic | 250–1,000 | 500 |
| Ethchlorvynol | Placidyl | Hypnotic | 500–1,000 | 500 |
| Glutethimide | Doriden | Hypnotic | 250–500 | 250 |
| Meprobamate | Miltown, Equanil, Equagesic, Deprol | Sedative | 1,200–1,600 | 400 |
| Methyprylon | Noludar | Hypnotic | 200–400 | 200 |

*Note.* NC = not cross-tolerant with barbiturates.

[a]Phenobarbital withdrawal conversion equivalence is not the same as therapeutic dose equivalency. Withdrawal equivalence is the amount of the drug that 30 mg of phenobarbital will substitute for and prevent serious high-dose withdrawal signs and symptoms.

[b]Butalbital is usually available in combination with opiate or nonopiate analgesics.

Before receiving each dose of phenobarbital, the patient is checked for signs of phenobarbital toxicity: sustained nystagmus, slurred speech, or ataxia. Sustained nystagmus is the most reliable sign of phenobarbital toxicity. If nystagmus is present, the scheduled dose of phenobarbital is withheld. If all three signs are present, the next two doses of phenobarbital are withheld, and the daily dosage of phenobarbital for the following day is halved.

If the patient is in acute withdrawal and has had or is in danger of having withdrawal seizures, the initial dose of phenobarbital is administered by intramuscular injection. If nystagmus and other signs of intoxication develop 1–2 hours after the intramuscular dosage, the patient is in no immediate danger from barbiturate withdrawal. Patients are maintained on the initial dosing schedule of phenobarbital for 2 days. If the patient has signs of neither withdrawal nor phenobarbital toxicity, then the patient enters the withdrawal phase of treatment.

Withdrawal phase. Unless the patient develops signs and symptoms of phenobarbital toxicity or sedative-hypnotic withdrawal, phenobarbital is decreased by 30 mg/day. Should signs of phenobarbital toxicity develop during withdrawal, the daily phenobarbital dose is decreased by 50%, and the 30 mg/day withdrawal is continued from the reduced phenobarbital dosage. Should the patient have objective signs of sedative-hypnotic withdrawal, the daily dosage is increased by 50%, and the patient is restabilized before continuing the withdrawal.

## Low-Dose Benzodiazepine Withdrawal

Most patients experience only mild to moderate symptom rebound that disappears after a few days to weeks. No special treatment is needed. During early abstinence, patients need support and reassurance that rebound symptoms are common and that with continued abstinence the symptoms will subside.

Some patients experience severe symptoms that may be quite unlike preexisting symptoms. The phenobarbital regimen described earlier will not suppress symptoms to tolerable levels, but increasing the phenobarbital dose to 200 mg/day and then tapering the phenobarbital over several months can be an effective protocol for treating low-dose withdrawal. There are others.

### Gradual Reduction of the Benzodiazepine

The gradual reduction of the benzodiazepine of dependence is used primarily for treatment of physiological dependence on long-acting benzodiazepines arising from treatment of an underlying condition. The patient must be cooperative and able to adhere to dosing regimens and must not be abusing alcohol or other drugs.

### Valproate and Carbamazepine

Medications used for treatment of seizure disorders have found clinical utility in treatment of mood and anxiety disorders (Keck et al. 1992) and in patients with comorbid anxiety and alcohol dependence (Brady et al. 1994). The medications most studied have been carbamazepine and valproate, although gabapentin (Neurontin) and lamotrigine (Lamictal) are receiving scrutiny. Carbamazepine and valproate enhance GABA function, seemingly by a different mechanism than the benzodiazepines. Neither carbamazepine nor valproate produce subjective effects that sedative-hypnotic abusers find desirable.

Valproate has received some clinical attention for treatment of alcohol withdrawal (Hammer and Brady 1996; Hillbom et al. 1989) and has been proposed for benzodiazepine withdrawal (Roy-Byrne et al. 1989). Clinical case reports of its use in benzodiazepine withdrawal have appeared (Apelt and Emrich 1990; McElroy et al. 1991). When used for low-dose benzodiazepine withdrawal, a dosage of 500–1,500 mg/day can be used. The most common side effect of valproate is gastrointestinal upset.

Carbamazepine is used widely in Europe for treatment of alcohol withdrawal. Case reports and controlled studies suggest its utility in treating benzodiazepine withdrawal (Klein et al. 1986; Lawlor 1987; Neppe and Sindorf 1991; Rickels et al. 1990a; Ries et al. 1989; Roy-Byrne et al. 1993; Schweizer et al. 1991). Withdrawal protocols use carbamazepine in a dosage of 200–800 mg/day.

In clinical experience with treating benzodiazepine withdrawal and in the controlled clinical trials in the treatment of epilepsy, valproate appears to be better tolerated than carbamazepine (Richens et al. 1994).

### Outpatient Treatment of Withdrawal

Although withdrawal from high dosages of barbiturates and other sedative-hypnotics should generally be done in a hospital, the realities of managed care often mean that many patients must be treated in part, if not exclusively, as outpatients. With patients who are withdrawing from therapeutic doses of benzodiazepines, a slow outpatient taper is a reasonable strategy and should be continued as long as the patient can tolerate withdrawal symptoms.

## Conclusion

Benzodiazepines have many therapeutic uses, and in the treatment of some conditions, such as panic disorder, benzodiazepine treatment for months or years is appropriate. Dependency is not always an avoidable complication. Physicians should discuss with patients before initiating a course of prolonged therapy the possibility of their developing new or intensified symptoms when the benzodiazepines are discontinued.

## References

American Psychiatric Association: Diagnostic and Statistical Manual of Mental Disorders, 4th Edition. Washington, DC, American Psychiatric Association, 1994

American Psychiatric Association Task Force on Benzodiazepine Dependency: Benzodiazepine Dependence, Toxicity, and Abuse. Washington, DC, American Psychiatric Association, 1990

Apelt S, Emrich HM: Sodium valproate in benzodiazepine withdrawal (letter). Am J Psychiatry 147:950–951, 1990

Barnas C, Rossmann M, Roessler H, et al: Benzodiazepines and other psychotropic drugs abused by patients in a methadone maintenance program: familiarity and preference. Clin Neuropharmacol 15 (suppl 1):110A–111A, 1992

Brady KT, Sonne S, Lydiard RB: Valproate treatment of comorbid panic disorder and affective disorders in two alcoholic patients (letter). J Clin Psychopharmacol 14:81–82, 1994

Byrnes JJ, Greenblatt DJ, Miller LG: Benzodiazepine receptor binding of nonbenzodiazepines in vivo: alpidem, zolpidem and zopiclone. Brain Res Bull 29:905–908, 1992

Calhoun SR, Wesson DR, Galloway GP, et al: Abuse of flunitrazepam (Rohypnol) and other benzodiazepines in Austin and south Texas. J Psychoactive Drugs 28:183–189, 1996

Cavallaro R, Regazzetti MG, Covelli G, et al: Tolerance and withdrawal with zolpidem (letter). Lancet 342:374–375, 1993

Chutuape MA, de Wit H: Relationship between subjective effects and drug preferences: ethanol and diazepam. Drug Alcohol Depend 34:243–251, 1994

Ciraulo DA, Barnhill JG, Greenblatt DJ, et al: Abuse liability and clinical pharmacokinetics of alprazolam in alcoholic men. J Clin Psychiatry 49:333–337, 1988

Ciraulo DA, Sarid-Segal O, Knapp C, et al: Liability to alprazolam abuse in daughters of alcoholics. Am J Psychiatry 153:956–958, 1996

Cowley DS, Roy-Byrne PP, Godon C, et al: Response to diazepam in sons of alcoholics. Alcohol Clin Exp Res 16:1057–1063, 1992

Cowley DS, Roy-Byrne PP, Radant A, et al: Eye movement effects of diazepam in sons of alcoholic fathers and male control subjects. Alcohol Clin Exp Res 18:324–332, 1994

de Wit H, Johanson CE, Uhlenhuth EH: Reinforcing properties of lorazepam in normal volunteers. Drug Alcohol Depend 13:31–41, 1984

Geller A: Protracted abstinence, in Comprehensive Handbook of Drug and Alcohol Addiction. Edited by Miller NS. New York, Marcel Dekker, 1991, pp 905–913

Golombok G, Moodley P, Lader M: Cognitive impairment in long-term benzodiazepine users. Psychol Med 18:365–374, 1988

Gorenstein C, Bernik MA, Pompeia S: Differential acute psychomotor and cognitive effects of diazepam on long-term benzodiazepine users. Int Clin Psychopharmacol 9:145–153, 1994

Griffiths R, Roache J: Abuse liability of benzodiazepines; a review of human studies evaluating subjective and/or reinforcing effects, in The Benzodiazepines: Current Standards for Medical Practice. Edited by Smith D, Wesson D. Hingham, MA, MTP Press, 1985

Griffiths RR, Bigelow GE, Leibson I, et al: Drug preference in humans: double-blind choice comparison of pentobarbital, diazepam, and placebo. J Pharmacol Exp Ther 215:649–661, 1980

Griffiths RR, Sannerud CA, Ator NA, et al: Zolpidem behavioral pharmacology in baboons: self-injection, discrimination, tolerance and withdrawal. J Pharmacol Exp Ther 260:1199–1208, 1992

Hammer BA, Brady KT: Valproate treatment of alcohol withdrawal and mania (letter). Am J Psychiatry 153:1232, 1996

Hillbom M, Tokola R, Kuusela V, et al: Prevention of alcohol withdrawal seizures with carbamazepine and valproic acid. Alcohol 6:223–226, 1989

Hollister LE, Motzenbecker FP, Degan RO: Withdrawal reactions from chlordiazepoxide (Librium). Psychopharmacology 2:63–68, 1961

Hollister LE, Bennett JL, Kimbell I, et al: Diazepam in newly admitted schizophrenics. Dis Nerv Syst 24:746–750, 1963

Iguchi MY, Handelsman L, Bickel WK, et al: Benzodiazepine and sedative use/abuse by methadone maintenance clients. Drug Alcohol Depend 32:257–266, 1993

Keck PE Jr, McElroy SL, Friedman LM: Valproate and carbamazepine in the treatment of panic and post-traumatic stress disorders, withdrawal states, and behavioral dyscontrol syndromes. J Clin Psychopharmacol 12 (suppl):36S–41S, 1992

Klein E, Uhde TW, Post RM: Preliminary evidence for the utility of carbamazepine in alprazolam withdrawal. Am J Psychiatry 143:235–236, 1986

Lader M: History of benzodiazepine dependence. J Subst Abuse Treat 8:53–59, 1991

Lawlor BA: Carbamazepine, alprazolam withdrawal, and panic disorder (letter). Am J Psychiatry 144:265–266, 1987

Lloyd KG, Zivkovic B: Specificity within the GABA$_A$ receptor supramolecular complex: a consideration of the new omega 1-receptor selective imidazopyridine hypnotic zolpidem. Pharmacol Biochem Behav 29:781–783, 1988

McElroy SL, Keck PE Jr, Lawrence JM: Treatment of panic disorder and benzodiazepine withdrawal with valproate (letter). J Neuropsychiatry Clin Neurosci 3:232–233, 1991

Neppe VM, Sindorf J: Carbamazepine for high-dose diazepam withdrawal in opiate users. J Nerv Ment Dis 179:234–235, 1991

Perrault G, Morel E, Sanger DJ, et al: Lack of tolerance and physical dependence upon repeated treatment with the novel hypnotic zolpidem. J Pharmacol Exp Ther 263:298–303, 1992

Pevnick JS, Jasinski DR, Haertzen CA: Abrupt withdrawal from therapeutically administered diazepam: report of a case. Arch Gen Psychiatry 35:995–998, 1978

Richens A, Davidson DL, Cartlidge NE, et al: A multicentre comparative trial of sodium valproate and carbamazepine in adult onset epilepsy. J Neurol Neurosurg Psychiatry 57:682–687, 1994

Rickels K, Case WG, Schweizer E, et al: Benzodiazepine dependence: management of discontinuation. Psychopharmacol Bull 26:63–68, 1990a

Rickels K, Schweizer E, Case WG, et al: Long-term therapeutic use of benzodiazepines; I: effects of abrupt discontinuation. Arch Gen Psychiatry 47:899–907, 1990b

Ries RK, Roy-Byrne PP, Ward NG, et al: Carbamazepine treatment for benzodiazepine withdrawal. Am J Psychiatry 146:536–537, 1989

Roy-Byrne PP, Ward NG, Donnelly P: Valproate in anxiety and withdrawal syndromes. J Clin Psychiatry 50:44–48, 1989

Roy-Byrne PP, Sullivan MD, Cowley DS, et al: Adjunctive treatment of benzodiazepine discontinuation syndromes: a review. J Psychiatr Res 27 (suppl 1):143–153, 1993

Ruano D, Benavides J, Machado A, et al: Regional differences in the enhancement by GABA of [$^3$H]zolpidem binding to omega 1 sites in rat brain membranes and sections. Brain Res 600:134–140, 1993

Sanger DJ, Benavides J: Discriminative stimulus effects of omega (BZ) receptor ligands: correlation with in vivo inhibition of [$^3$H]-flumazenil binding in different regions of the rat central nervous system. Psychopharmacology 111:315–322, 1993

Schweizer E, Rickels K: Failure of buspirone to manage benzodiazepine withdrawal. Am J Psychiatry 143:1590–1592, 1986

Schweizer E, Rickels K, Lucki I: Resistance to the anti-anxiety effect of buspirone in patients with a history of benzodiazepine use (letter). N Engl J Med 314:719–720, 1986

Schweizer E, Rickels K, Case WG, et al: Carbamazepine treatment in patients discontinuing long-term benzodiazepine therapy; effects on withdrawal severity and outcome. Arch Gen Psychiatry 48:448–452, 1991

Smith DE, Wesson DR: A new method for treatment of barbiturate dependence. JAMA 213:294–295, 1970

Smith DE, Wesson DR: Phenobarbital technique for treatment of barbiturate dependence. Arch Gen Psychiatry 24:56–60, 1971

Smith DE, Wesson DR: Benzodiazepine dependency syndromes. J Psychoactive Drugs 15:85–95, 1983

Taylor DP, Moon SL: Buspirone and related compounds as alternative anxiolytics. Neuropeptides 19 (suppl):15–19, 1991

Winokur A, Rickels K, Greenblatt DJ, et al: Withdrawal reaction from long-term, low-dosage administration of diazepam. Arch Gen Psychiatry 37:101–105, 1980

Woods JH, Winger G: Abuse liability of flunitrazepam. J Clin Psychopharmacol 17 (suppl 2):1S–57S, 1997

# Chapter 23

# Opioids: Detoxification

Herbert D. Kleber, M.D.

Patients from whom morphine is taken get well in spite of the treatment.

Kolb and Himmelsbach 1938

The availability and purity of heroin are higher than in decades and the cost per pure milligram lower. This increased purity has made it easier for individuals to begin heroin use by snorting or smoking, deluding themselves that if they are not injecting, they risk neither harm nor addiction. In New York City, as many as half of the heroin-addicted individuals seeking detoxification are not primarily injectors. Physicians who may have been seeing relatively few heroin-addicted patients will once again need to pay attention to this problem and the various treatment methods.

Before the advent of maintenance approaches to heroin addiction, such as methadone and more recently buprenorphine, detoxification with or without follow-up therapy was often the only treatment available to heroin-addicted patients. For many addicted individuals it is still a pretreatment route before the residential therapeutic community, narcotic antagonist maintenance, or outpatient drug-free treatment. Although drug detoxification is often the route into treatment, many patients who begin it do not complete it and many who complete it do not go on to more definitive treatment. Some patients enter detoxification only to lower their level of dependence and have an easier time supporting their habit, but others fully believe that detoxification is all they need to remain drug free. This is especially true with younger patients who have not yet had frequent relapses. Addicted individuals entering detoxification often describe themselves as tired of the drug life and indicate that the negative consequences —the legal problems, the large sums of money needed day in and day out, the health problems especially in this era of AIDS and tuberculosis, the family and social pressure, and the frequent withdrawal sickness—have begun to outweigh the pleasure from the drug-induced high.

## What Is Detoxification?

*Detoxification* refers to the process whereby an individual who is physically dependent on a drug is taken off that drug either abruptly or gradually (Kleber 1981). A variety of options are now available in the medications used to aid in detoxification: 1) the drug on which the individual is dependent, 2) other drugs that produce cross-tolerance, 3) medications to provide symptomatic relief, or 4) drugs that affect the mechanisms by which withdrawal is expressed. Settings for detoxification can include inpatient, residential, day, or outpatient programs.

In our current state of knowledge, detoxification should be able to be carried out safely, relatively quickly, and with a minimum of discomfort. However, the method chosen often depends more on what is available than on what would be ideal. This situation relates to factors such as physician or patient preference or bias, the availability of physicians trained in detoxification methods, federal and state regulations, insurance or other funding mechanisms, and the methods available in a given setting in a particular geographic area.

## Goals of Detoxification

1. Ridding the body of the acute physiological dependence associated with chronic daily narcotic use
2. Diminishing or eliminating the pain and discomfort that can occur during withdrawal

251

3. Providing a safe and humane treatment to help the individual over the initial hurdle of stopping narcotic use

4. Providing a situation conducive to a more long-range commitment to treatment and making appropriate referrals to these other treatment modalities

5. Treating any medical problems discovered or making appropriate referrals

6. Beginning the process of educating the patient about issues related to health and relapse prevention, and exploring issues such as family, vocational, and legal problems that may need referral

## When Is Detoxification Successful?

Because relatively few narcotic-addicted individuals discontinue their drug habit immediately after detoxification, detoxification is usually viewed as pretreatment or at best the first stage of treatment. It is unrealistic to expect to achieve the more ambitious goals for long-term treatment that include not just abstinence but other outcome measures relating to employment, criminality, interpersonal relationships, and general physical and psychological well-being. Success is a function of not just safety and minimal discomfort but also how many patients are retained and how many go on to longer-term treatment. This does not mean that detoxification is necessarily a failure if the person does not agree to go on to long-term treatment. Younger addicted patients often believe that detoxification is all they need to get rid of their habit and remain off drugs. They see no need for longer-term treatment. When they return for a second or third detoxification, they may be more realistic about what is involved in staying drug free and more willing to consider longer-term treatment. Because of the relapsing nature of the problem, formal detoxification usually occurs many times over the course of the disorder.

## Setting Choice

Detoxification can take place in an inpatient, partial hospitalization, or outpatient setting. Outpatient detoxification is the least expensive and enables the patient to remain at work or otherwise carry on his or her life. It forces the patient to cope with the home and/or work settings where he or she will be after becoming drug free; going from the protected inpatient setting to everyday reality is often accompanied by rapid relapse.

Disadvantages of outpatient detoxification include being surrounded by temptations when least able to handle them, more difficulty assessing and dealing with other medical conditions, and the possible need for detoxification to proceed more slowly in the unprotected environment.

During inpatient detoxification, access to drugs or to craving-inducing stimuli can be minimized, the patient can be observed more closely for medical problems or complications of withdrawal, and the withdrawal can be more rapid. If the program is a comprehensive one, more attention can be focused on other aspects of the patient's life—family, vocational, medical, and psychiatric issues. The disadvantages are primarily the cost but also the disruption of the patient's life and the need to be away from work and home.

Partial hospital programs are considerably less expensive than inpatient programs, and they have some of their advantages, but they are relatively uncommon. The clinician is usually forced to choose between inpatient and outpatient settings, and the decision is often made by other factors such as insurance coverage and availability of programs in the community. Now that managed care has become more prevalent, inpatient detoxification has become primarily for those patients who have serious medical or psychiatric problems or who have repeatedly failed outpatient detoxification. Although inpatient detoxification has a much higher completion rate (up to 80%) compared with outpatient programs (as low as 17%), long-term advantages related to relapse are less definite. Some patients need to receive inpatient treatment to achieve initial abstinence, and we need better ways to identify these patients.

## Historical Overview

In the past century, many treatments have been introduced for relieving the symptoms of opioid withdrawal. Many of these treatments have proven either more addicting than the drug being withdrawn from or more dangerous than untreated withdrawal. In a masterful review, Kolb and Himmelsbach (1938) looked back on 40 years of mostly futile attempts to treat narcotic withdrawal, including the use of autohemotherapy (injection of blood previously withdrawn from the patient), water balance therapy, and numerous often toxic chemicals, alone or in combination. Kleber and Riordan (1982) reviewed the earlier work by these writers and updated it with the techniques that had been used in the 40 years since their paper. Since that review, the most common approach—methadone substitution and gradual withdrawal—has declined in popularity, and the newer approaches we describe in this chapter have gained in favor.

## Clinical Characteristics of the Opioid (μ Agonist) Withdrawal Syndrome

Naturally occurring opiates such as opium, morphine, and codeine; derivatives such as heroin, hydromorphone, and dihydrocodeine; and synthetics such as methadone, meperidine, and fentanyl are capable of creating physical dependency and may require detoxification if they have been taken in sufficient quantities over time. In general, 2–3 weeks of daily administration are required to produce a clinically relevant withdrawal syndrome; this period is shorter in individuals who were previously addicted.

### Factors Influencing Symptom Severity

The nature and severity of withdrawal symptoms when opioid-type drugs are halted relate to a variety of factors:

- *Specific drug used.* Rapidly metabolized drugs such as heroin are generally associated with more severe withdrawal phenomena, whereas drugs that bind tightly to the receptor, such as buprenorphine, or that are slowly excreted from the body, such as methadone, have a slower onset with a less intense but also more protracted withdrawal syndrome. The general rule is the longer the duration of the drug, the less intense but longer lasting the withdrawal symptoms. Thus, the short-acting drug heroin has a more intense but shorter withdrawal period than the long-acting drug methadone.
- *Total daily amount used.* In general, the larger the daily amount of the drug, the more severe the withdrawal from that particular narcotic. However, some researchers have found that dosage did not correlate with severity of withdrawal symptoms (Gossop et al. 1987).
- *Duration and regularity of use.* Although some withdrawal can be seen when a single dose of morphine is followed a few hours later by a narcotic antagonist, clinically significant withdrawal usually requires daily use of an adequate amount for at least 2–3 weeks. In contrast, duration of use much beyond

2–3 months does not appear to be associated with any greater severity. The more intermittent the drug taking, the less likely severe withdrawal will result.
- *Psychological factors.* In general, the greater the patient's expectation that suffering will be relieved by medication becoming available, the more severe the withdrawal symptoms. Thus, if an individual is in a setting in which there is little hope of obtaining symptom relief, there seems to be a diminution in the intensity experienced. Individual sensitivity is also a factor. Some individuals experience abdominal cramps every time they kick an opioid habit, whereas other individuals experience primarily backaches or muscle aches. The patient's personality and state of mind can also influence withdrawal severity as can his or her general physical health and ability to handle stress. Anticipatory anxiety appears to increase withdrawal severity (Phillips et al. 1986).

### Signs and Symptoms of Opioid Withdrawal

The μ-agonist withdrawal syndrome can be conceptualized as rebound hyperactivity in the biological systems suppressed by the agonists. (For a more detailed description of the neurochemical mechanisms involved, see Jaffe and Jaffe, Chapter 2, in this volume.) Withdrawal phenomena are generally the opposite of the acute agonistic effects of the opioid (e.g., acute opioids cause constipation and pupillary constriction, whereas withdrawal is associated with diarrhea and pupillary dilatation). The clinical characteristics of opioid withdrawal may be described in several ways. Some authors separate purposive from nonpurposive symptoms, others separate objective signs from subjective symptoms, and still others separate signs and symptoms into grades on the basis of severity. None of these classifications is totally satisfactory.

Subjective symptoms, even under controlled conditions, are often more distressing than are the objective signs. It has also been shown experimentally that opioid-dependent patients may experience major withdrawal symptoms with minimal or no objective signs to confirm this discomfort. Table 23–1 lists the most common signs and symptoms, which are divided into two categories based on their approximate order of appearance.

When a short-acting opioid such as heroin has been taken chronically, the onset of withdrawal begins with anxiety and craving about 8–10 hours after the last dose (see Table 23–2). If the drug is not obtained, this pro-

**Table 23–1.** Signs and symptoms of opioid withdrawal

| Early to moderate | Moderate to advanced |
|---|---|
| Anorexia | Abdominal cramps |
| Anxiety | Broken sleep |
| Craving | Hot or cold flashes |
| Dysphoria | Increased blood pressure |
| Fatigue | Increased pulse |
| Headache | Low-grade fever |
| Increased respiratory rate | Muscle and bone pain |
| Irritability | Muscle spasm (hence the term *kicking the habit*) |
| Lacrimation | Mydriasis (with dilated fixed pupils at the peak) |
| Mydriasis (mild) | Nausea and vomiting |
| Perspiration | |
| Piloerection (goose flesh) | |
| Restlessness | |
| Rhinorrhea | |
| Yawning | |

gresses to dysphoria, yawning, lacrimation, rhinorrhea, perspiration, restlessness, and broken sleep. Later, there are waves of goose flesh, hot and cold flashes, aching of bones and muscles, nausea, vomiting, diarrhea, abdominal cramps, weight loss, and low-grade fever. An untreated addicted individual in withdrawal may be noted to lie in a fetal position (to ease the abdominal cramps) and to be covered with a blanket even on warm days (because of the hot and cold flashes). The individual's skin may be exquisitely sensitive to the touch. The heroin withdrawal syndrome reaches its peak typically between 36 and 72 hours after the last dose, and the

acute symptoms subside substantially within 5 days. With methadone withdrawal, in contrast, the peak occurs between days 4 and 6, and symptoms do not substantially subside until 14–21 days (Kleber 1996). With a drug that is shorter acting than heroin, such as meperidine, craving is intense, but the autonomic signs such as pupillary dilatation are not particularly prominent. Usually, little nausea, vomiting, or diarrhea occurs, but at peak intensity the muscle twitching, restlessness, and nervousness have been described as worse than during morphine withdrawal (Jaffe and Martin 1975). Regardless of which opioid is used, even after the acute symptoms have subsided, evidence indicates a more protracted abstinence syndrome with subtle disturbances of mood and sleep that can persist for 6–8 months (Martin and Jasinski 1969). Therefore, an addicted individual may not feel that he or she has returned to normal for months after the last ingestion of the drug. Fatigue, dysphoria, irritability, and insomnia may all lead to a state that increases the likelihood of relapse. Protracted abstinence may involve both conditioning and physiological factors (Satel et al. 1993).

## Evaluation and Diagnosis

When a patient is first seen by the clinician, he or she should be evaluated to determine whether detoxification is needed. Once this is determined and the patient is accepted for treatment, a more complete assessment is necessary to devise an individual treatment plan. Thus information needs to be gathered on a wider range of areas, including psychological, psychosocial, and physical status.

**Table 23–2.** Duration of effects and first appearance of withdrawal

| Drug | Effects wear off[a] | Appearance of nonpurposive withdrawal symptoms | Peak withdrawal effects | Majority of symptoms over |
|---|---|---|---|---|
| Meperidine | 2–3 hours | 4–6 hours | 8–12 hours | 4–5 days |
| Hydromorphone | 4–5 hours | 4–5 hours | Approximately the same as morphine | Approximately the same as morphine |
| Heroin | 4 hours[b] | 8–12 hours | 36–72 hours | 7–10 days |
| Morphine | 4–5 hours | 8–12 hours | 36–72 hours | 7–10 days |
| Codeine | 4 hours | Approximately the same as morphine | Approximately the same as morphine | Approximately the same as morphine |
| Methadone | 8–12 hours | 36–72 hours | 96–144 hours | 14–21 days |

[a]Duration may vary with chronic dosing.
[b]Usually taken two to four times per day.

## The Interview

While gathering the information below, especially the drug history, a nonjudgmental attitude is more likely to elicit the necessary data. Disdainful behavior is likely to create ongoing difficulties, produce false information, and even drive away the patient.

Drug history.   A review of current and past drug and alcohol use and abuse is necessary for adequate patient assessment. The following information should be obtained for each current substance or group of substances, with special emphasis on substance use during the past week:

- Name of drug used, length of time used, frequency of use
- Date or time of last use
- Route of administration
- Amount
- Cost
- Purpose (e.g., to get high, to relieve depression or boredom, to sleep, for energy, to relieve side effects of other drugs, to avoid withdrawal)
- For drugs previously used: name, age at which drug use started, length of time used, adverse effects
- Previous treatment experiences: where, what kind, outcome
- Prescription drugs currently used: name; reason for use; amount, frequency, and duration of use; last dose

Other medical history.   The medical history includes serious illnesses, accidents, and hospitalizations. In addition to the usual medical history, special attention should be given to the possible medical complications of drug abuse. The medical history also includes the existence of current symptoms in the various body systems. It is important to look for illnesses that may complicate withdrawal and those that may be ignored because of the patient's chaotic lifestyle.

Social functioning.   Information should be gathered on the following topics: 1) living arrangements (e.g., alone, with family); 2) marital status; 3) sexual orientation and functioning; 4) employment and/or educational status; 5) family members' (e.g., parents, siblings, spouse, other key members) occupations, education, psychological state, history of drug or alcohol problems; 6) friends (in particular, are there non-drug-using ones); 7) recreational and leisure-time activities; and

8) current and past legal status. The Addiction Severity Index is a useful instrument for gathering this information (McLellan et al. 1985).

The interviewer should try to get a feel for the emotional and factual aspects of the interview topics. For example: What is the patient's attitude toward his or her job and what type of job is it? What is the quality of the patient's marital or family relationships? How does the patient cope with spare time at nights and on weekends when relapse is most likely to occur? Such questioning can reveal the nature and degree of the patient's social supports and aid in planning for postdetoxification treatment. Prior attempts at withdrawal and factors associated with relapse should be especially explored.

Psychological status.   When carried out by a nonpsychiatrist, psychological evaluation may single out patients who need early psychiatric referral for possible psychosis, organic brain syndrome, serious depression, suicide, or being violence prone. The psychiatrist, in addition to evaluating factors that could complicate withdrawal, should look for conditions for which special treatments exist (e.g., lithium for mania). If possible, the evaluator should ascertain whether detectable psychiatric conditions predate or postdate the drug abuse. Some patients take drugs on a self-medicating basis to try to cope with dysphoric states of loneliness, depression, or anxiety or to control unacceptable aggressive or sexual drives. Conversely, continued use of certain drugs may lead to or exacerbate psychiatric states not previously evident. Opioids seem to have an ameliorating effect on psychosis in some patients, and withdrawal can lead to exacerbation or sudden appearance of psychotic symptoms.

As part of the psychological state evaluation, a mental status examination should be carried out and include orientation for place, person, and date; presence or absence of hallucinations, delusions, or suicidal ideation; memory; intelligence, mood, and affect; thought processes; preoccupations and behavior during interview; judgment; and insight.

## Physical Examination

Although there is no special physical examination for narcotic-addicted individuals, the clinician should remember that certain conditions can be either direct or indirect sequelae of drug abuse. Although some of these effects can be found in nonaddicted individuals, and some addicted individuals may have few or none of them, their presence helps in the diagnostic process.

**Cutaneous signs.** The following cutaneous signs may be directly or indirectly associated with drug abuse:

- *Needle puncture marks.* Needle marks are usually found over veins especially in the antecubital area, back of the hands, and forearms but can be found anywhere on the body where a vein is reachable, including the neck, tongue, and dorsal vein of the penis.
- *"Tracks."* Tracks are one of the most common and readily recognizable signs of chronic injectable drug abuse. They are scars located along veins and are usually hyperpigmented and linear. They result both from frequent unsterile injections and from the deposit of carbon black from attempts to sterilize the needle with a match. Tracks tend to lighten over time but may never totally disappear.
- *Tattoos.* Because tracks are such a well-known indication of drug abuse, addicted individuals may try to hide them with tattoos over the area.
- *Hand edema.* When addicted individuals run out of antecubital and forearm veins, they often turn to veins in the fingers and back of the hand, which can lead to hand edema. Such edema can persist for months.
- *Thrombophlebitis (blockage or inflammation of veins).* Thrombophlebitis is commonly found on the arms and legs of addicted individuals because of the unsterile nature of the injections and the irritating quality of some of the adulterants.
- *Abscesses and ulcers.* Abscesses and ulcers are particularly common among individuals who inject barbiturates because of the irritating quality of these chemicals. When secondary to narcotic injection, they are more likely to be septic and around veins.
- *Ulceration or perforation of the nasal septum.* Frequent snorting of heroin can lead to ulceration of the septum, whereas similar chronic use of cocaine can cause perforation secondary to the vasoconstriction and loss of blood supply.
- *Cigarette burns or scars from old burns.* Cigarette burns or scars can result from drug-induced drowsiness. Fresh burns are usually seen between the fingers, and old scars are often seen on the chest as a result of the cigarette falling out of the user's mouth. It has been estimated that more than 90% of drug-addicted and alcoholic individuals smoke.
- *Piloerection.* Piloerection, a sign of opioid withdrawal, is usually found on the arms and trunk.
- *Cheilosis (cracking of skin at corners of the mouth).* Cheilosis is especially seen in chronic am-

phetamine-using individuals and in opioid-addicted individuals prior to or during detoxification.
- *Contact dermatitis.* In solvent-abusing individuals, contact dermatitis is seen around the nose, mouth, and hands and is sometimes called *glue-sniffer's rash.* In other abusers, it may occur around areas of injection secondary to use of chemicals to cleanse the skin.
- *Jaundice.* Jaundice, due to hepatitis, is usually secondary to use of unsterilized shared needles and syringes. More than half of current heroin-addicted individuals are thought to be positive for hepatitis B or C.
- *Monilial infection.* Monilial infection, or thrush of the mouth, can be a sign of AIDS.

## Laboratory Tests

- Urine screen for drugs, including narcotics, barbiturates, amphetamines, cocaine, benzodiazepines, tricyclic antidepressants, phencyclidine, and marijuana
- Complete blood count and differential; leukocytosis is common, and white blood cell counts above 14,000 are not unusual
- Urinalysis
- Blood chemistry profile (e.g., sequential multiple analysis 20 with serum amylase and magnesium)
- Venereal Disease Research Laboratory test
- HIV test (permission from the patient is necessary in many states)
- Hepatitis antigen and antibody test
- Chest X ray
- Electrocardiogram in patients older than 40 years
- Pregnancy test in women (hold chest X ray until test is complete)
- Tuberculin skin test (PPD) plus antigen testing because HIV-positive individuals may give false-negative PPD
- Any other test suggested by the history or physical examination (e.g., failure to take in adequate food and fluids plus vomiting, sweating, and diarrhea can lead to weight loss, dehydration, ketosis, and disturbed acid-base balance)

## Methadone Technique of Withdrawal

The most common withdrawal method is methadone substitution and withdrawal, although this method is declining in popularity. Methadone is a long-acting orally effective synthetic narcotic. Because of cross-tolerance and cross-dependence between the various synthetic and natural narcotics, one could in theory use any of them to prevent withdrawal and gradually detoxify any individual who is dependent on any of the others. The historical advantages of methadone over other agents are as follows:

- It is orally effective (thus avoiding the risks associated with injection and avoiding continuing a needle habit).
- It is long acting (longer-acting opioids produce withdrawal syndromes that are milder though longer lasting, and they need to be given less often, producing smoother withdrawal).
- It is safe (the long experience with and ease of using methadone make it a safe method of opioid detoxification as long as certain precautions are followed regarding initial dosing).

In general, a more addictive drug should not be used to detoxify a patient from a less addictive one. In practice this means that although methadone can be used to withdraw patients from narcotics such as heroin, morphine, hydromorphone, or meperidine, it should be avoided for drugs such as propoxyphene or pentazocine, for which the withdrawal should be handled by gradually decreasing the dosage of the agent itself or by an agent such as clonidine. Codeine and oxycodone are in between these two groups, and clinicians differ as to whether to use methadone or the drugs themselves during their withdrawal.

U.S. Food and Drug Administration (FDA) guidelines for narcotic detoxification describe two types of detoxification: short term and long term. Short-term detoxification is for a period not more than 30 days; long-term detoxification is for a period not more than 180 days. Short-term detoxification is most likely to occur with individuals currently addicted to opioids other than methadone. Long-term detoxification is used for individuals already taking methadone and wishing to stop it, or in some programs, individuals are taken directly from heroin to long-term detoxification on methadone over a 6-month period. Prolonged detoxification avoids some of the withdrawal symptoms that occur in more rapid detoxification and provides a setting in which psychosocial rehabilitation can take place. However, the long-term effectiveness of this option, as opposed to shorter-term detoxification or methadone maintenance, has not been demonstrated.

## Initiation of Detoxification

If the patient has been taking narcotics for medical purposes, and the physician is reasonably sure about the amount being used, Table 23–3 can be used to convert the narcotic dosage into a methadone dosage. With illicit drug use, the picture is very different. Knowledge of the exact dosage is usually not available. The amount of narcotics in illegal "bags" can vary from dealer to dealer, week to week, city to city, and even from day to day. Under these circumstances, the physician must guess at the initial dosage. Given that the quality of heroin on the street has increased in the past few years, in some cities from as little as 5% to higher than 50% (but could just as easily turn down again), the choice of an initial dosage is an important one. It needs to be high enough to adequately suppress withdrawal symptoms so that the patient does not leave the program but low enough so that if the patient's habit was not as great as anticipated, the dosage would not be health or life threatening. Because 40 mg of methadone has proven to be a fatal dose in some individuals when given without adequate verification of prior habit, the initial dose must be substantially below that. One way to ensure the patient's safety is to start with a dose of 10–20 mg, large enough to control many if not most illicit habits yet small enough not to be particularly dangerous. The patient should be kept under observation so as to judge the effect of the dose. If withdrawal symptoms are present initially, the dose should suppress them within 30–60 minutes; if not, an additional 5–10 mg of methadone can be given. If withdrawal symptoms are not present, the patient should be observed for drowsiness or depressed respiration. When 10–20 mg is given as the initial dose, a similar amount may be given 12 hours later if necessary. This procedure is usually not practical in outpatient detoxification but is used sometimes in

**Table 23–3.**  Drug relationships for withdrawal

**Methadone 1 mg is equivalent to**

    Codeine 30 mg

    Dromoran 1 mg

    Heroin 1–2 mg

    Hydromorphone (Dilaudid) 0.5 mg

    Laudanum (opium tincture) 3 mL

    Levorphanol (Levo-Dromoran) 0.5 mg

    Meperidine (Demerol) 20 mg

    Morphine 3–4 mg

    Paregoric 7–8 mL

inpatient settings. Unless evidence of narcotic use in excess of 40 mg of methadone equivalent per day is documented, the initial dose should not exceed 30 mg, and the total 24-hour dose should not exceed 40 mg the first few days. A safe initial dose in a nontolerant individual can become dangerous if continued beyond 1 or 2 days because of rising blood levels. A dangerous dose manifests itself in drowsiness or signs of motor impairment.

Some clinicians disagree as to whether to start the withdrawal regimen in the absence of withdrawal signs and symptoms. It is usually difficult to know with certainty that an individual is currently physically addicted. The information gathered through the interview, physical examination, and laboratory tests does not usually prove the diagnosis of narcotic dependence sufficient to need withdrawal treatment, unless the clinician has observed the signs and symptoms of opioid withdrawal. The history of drug taking is not always reliable and can be altered, either by exaggerating to increase the amount of narcotic obtained or by minimizing to conceal a habit, not uncommon among addicted physicians and nurses. The drug history may be wrong even when the patient is trying to be honest because of the variable nature of illicitly obtained drugs. Physical signs such as tracks tell of past drug use not necessarily current use. Fresh needle marks say nothing about the frequency, nature, or amount of what was injected. Urinalyses positive for drugs suggest recent use but are not evidence of a duration long enough to require detoxification. Heroin, detected as morphine in the urine, can be found up to approximately 48 hours after the last use: quinine, a common diluent, can last 1 week or more.

Definitive evidence of physical dependence can be obtained through two methods: 1) wait until the patient develops withdrawal signs and symptoms or 2) run a naloxone provocative test. Parenteral naloxone can distinguish opioid-dependent from nondependent individuals through the severity of withdrawal related to the naloxone dose. A common method is to inject 0.2 mg of naloxone subcutaneously to be followed by 0.4 mg in 30 minutes if the results from the smaller dose are inconclusive. Some physicians recommend an initial dose of 0.6–0.8 mg to speed up the process and rule out false-negatives. Because of the possibility of fetal injury or induced abortion, the naloxone test should not be done if the patient is pregnant.

Whether the program is inpatient or outpatient, the availability of trained medical personnel will often determine whether the program will wait for withdrawal

signs to develop; use a naloxone challenge; or use the combined evidence of the history, physical, and urine screen as interpreted by experienced personnel to form a presumptive diagnosis. If the last approach is chosen (probably most often the case), the program should still be prepared to use one of the first two approaches in borderline or doubtful situations. Once a decision has been made that narcotic use is sufficient to require detoxification, decisions still have to be made regarding the setting, whether concurrent physical or emotional problems are present that may require separate treatment during withdrawal, and the choice of the specific method. When serious physical or emotional problems are present, it is not uncommon to delay withdrawal by temporarily maintaining the individual on methadone, attending to the acute problem, and then beginning withdrawal once some stability has been achieved in the other areas.

## Length of Withdrawal

The total methadone dosage necessary to stabilize a patient for the first 24 hours should be repeated on day 2, either in one dose for outpatients or in divided doses for inpatients. Corrections can then be made either up or down if the dosage is either too sedating or fails to adequately suppress the withdrawal syndrome. Revision to a higher dosage should preferably be made on the basis of objective signs of opioid withdrawal rather than on subjective complaints alone. This is not always easily done because certain signs, such as pupillary dilatation, may be modified by the dosage of methadone, but the patient may still be undermedicated. After the patient is stabilized, the dosage can then be withdrawn gradually. Two common approaches are either to decrease the methadone by 5 mg/day until zero dosage is reached (*linear withdrawal method*) or to decrease it by 10 mg/day until a dosage of 10 mg/day is reached, and then decrease it more slowly (e.g., by 2 mg/day) (*inverse exponential withdrawal method*). For individuals who have large initial habits, the linear method may be better, whereas in those with a starting dosage of less than 50 mg/day of methadone, the inverse exponential method led to more rapid passing of the withdrawal syndrome without any significant increase in withdrawal severity or dropout rate (Strang and Gossop 1990).

Inpatient withdrawal generally takes place over 5–10 days, whereas outpatient withdrawal may be stretched out longer to minimize symptoms even more and to decrease the likelihood of the patient leaving the program or reverting to opioid use. Some inpatient programs complete the process in as few as 4 or 5 days, whereas some outpatient programs may stretch on for months. Symptoms of insomnia, fatigue, and feelings of irritability or anxiety may linger for weeks or months. In terms of discharge from the detoxification program, if no objective signs of opioid withdrawal are present 48 hours after the last dose of methadone, the patient can be considered to be over the acute withdrawal phase.

## Withdrawal From Methadone Maintenance

For a patient withdrawing from a methadone maintenance program, the technique of withdrawal used tends to relate to why the patient is being withdrawn. Patients who are in good standing and desirous of trying to become drug free should be withdrawn slowly over a 3- to 6-month period. The most difficult period is when the dosage gets smaller than 25 mg/day because at that level methadone may not last the full 24 hours and some withdrawal symptoms may occur before the next dose. Split doses may help counter this problem, but they are not always possible or practical. Between 5 and 10 mg/week can be withdrawn from the established methadone dosage until the patient gets to 25 mg/day. At that point, a reduction of no more than 5 mg/week is often recommended. If the patient needs to be detoxified more rapidly because he or she is being discharged in bad standing, must leave the geographic area, or may be going to prison, then withdrawal usually takes place during a 10- to 30-day period. For example, the patient dosage may be decreased by 10 mg/day until a total dosage of 40 mg/day is reached, then it is decreased by 5 mg/day until the dosage of 5 mg/day is reached, at which point that dosage is given for 2–3 days. If the patient is on an inpatient or residential basis, divided doses are helpful, especially when the total dosage is below 25 mg/day.

## Other Drugs and Supportive Measures

Even with gradual withdrawal, all withdrawal symptoms may not be totally suppressed, and certain mild symptoms may persist sometimes for days after treatment has been completed. There is no consensus on the use of other drugs during these periods. Tranquilizers or bedtime sedation can help allay the patient's anxiety and minimize the craving for morphinelike drugs, but nonnarcotic medications are generally ineffective in relieving the specific symptoms of opioid abstinence, with the exception of certain $\alpha_2$-adrenergic agonists such as clonidine. If insomnia and other withdrawal symptoms are unusually severe, especially in older patients, an incremental increase in the next dose of methadone and, therefore, a slower withdrawal schedule can provide relief.

Insomnia can be one of the more debilitating withdrawal symptoms. It is difficult to tolerate in and of itself, and it also weakens the addicted individual's ability to deal with other withdrawal problems. Barbiturates, because of their dependence potential, should not be used to treat insomnia. Drugs that have been advocated include flurazepam, oxazepam, diphenhydramine, hydroxyzine, and antidepressants such as trazodone. Although these drugs have been used in withdrawal, objective comparisons are not available. Because many narcotic-addicted individuals also abuse benzodiazepine-type drugs, the choice of such agents needs to be made carefully.

Symptomatic medications used include nonsteroidal anti-inflammatory drugs, for example, ibuprofen 600–800 mg every 6–8 hours or ketorolac for muscle cramps or pain; dicyclomine 10 mg every 6 hours for abdominal cramps; and bismuth subsalicylate (Pepto Bismol) 30 cc after each loose stool.

Nonpharmaceutical supports can also play an important and useful role. A warm, kind, and reassuring attitude from the treatment staff is most helpful. Involvement of patients in their own detoxification schedule is of positive value in inpatient but not outpatient detoxification (Dawe et al. 1991). It is usually not necessary for an adversarial role to develop around the issue of medication dosing. Visitors, however, can be a problem, and a firm stand is necessary. Visitors should be limited to immediate family members (i.e., parents or spouse) who are known not to abuse drugs. Even parents have been known to smuggle in drugs under the pressure of a patient's entreaties that the staff does not understand his or her distress. A watchful presence is therefore necessary around all visitors. Such attempts at deception may be less likely to occur if family meetings are held.

Other advocated measures include warm baths, exercise (when the patient feels up to it), and various diets. Except when specific nutritional deficiencies are present, there is no evidence of the usefulness of a particular dietary regimen. Because addicted patients are often malnourished, general vitamin and mineral supplements should be given.

## Special Problems

### Seizures

Opioid withdrawal or intoxication usually does not lead to seizures; however, they may occasionally occur with intoxication from meperidine or propoxyphene. A seizure may signify undiagnosed sedative withdrawal, stimulant intoxication, another medical condition (e.g., head injury or epilepsy), or a faked or hysterical seizure. Because most addicted individuals are polydrug users, abuse of sedative-type drugs (including alcohol, barbiturates, and benzodiazepines) should be kept in mind when providing treatment. If a patient is suspected of this abuse, 200 mg of pentobarbital can be given. A nontolerant individual administered this dose will either be asleep in an hour or show coarse nystagmus, gross ataxia, positive Romberg's sign, and dysarthria. If these signs are lacking, addiction to one or more of these drugs should be presumed and treated correspondingly.

### Mixed Addictions

Sedative dependence can lead to serious hazards, including seizures, toxic psychosis, hyperthermia, and even death. Withdrawal from stimulant-type drugs is much less of a physical hazard, although it can be associated with severe depression and even suicide. If sedative dependence is present, it is often useful to maintain the patient on methadone, withdraw the sedative gradually, and then withdraw the methadone.

### Vomiting

Although vomiting can be a symptom of withdrawal, it can occur with no relation to the degree of physical abstinence and in spite of all kinds of support measures, including reintoxication with opioids. It can usually be handled by intramuscular injections of a drug such as trimethobenzamide or perphenazine. Patients sometimes vomit to receive repeat medication or intramuscular doses. Observation for 15–30 minutes after a dose usually eliminates this behavior.

### Intoxication

Dosing to intoxication is not necessary to prevent withdrawal symptoms and can complicate the safety and adequacy of care. If intoxication occurs, the next dose should be decreased sufficiently to prevent it at the next medication period. Smoking while intoxicated should not be permitted, and when patients are ambulatory, they should be assisted so as to avoid injury.

### Repetitive Withdrawal

Addicted individuals often have a characteristic withdrawal syndrome focused on a particular organ system. For one patient, withdrawal may involve the gastrointestinal system, with abdominal cramps the usual symptom; for another, it may involve the musculoskeletal system, in which aching in the bones will be typical. A supportive, reassuring, but firm approach usually helps patients with these symptoms. In the absence of psychosis, major tranquilizing drugs are usually not necessary.

### Other Medical Conditions

Opioid withdrawal is usually not accompanied by high fevers, although low-grade temperature elevation can occur. Acute febrile illnesses may temporarily increase the severity of withdrawal symptoms, thus necessitating more methadone. When serious medical or surgical problems are present, withdrawal should be very gradual to minimize the degree of stress. The patient should be brought to the point of tolerance, kept there for several days, and then slowly withdrawn. With certain illnesses (e.g., acute myocardial infarction, renal colic), the patient should be maintained on methadone until stable enough to permit withdrawal. The patient should also be evaluated carefully to see whether longer-term maintenance is indicated instead of withdrawal. When withdrawal does take place, giving methadone three or four times per day instead of once or twice can minimize the patient's discomfort and stress.

### Pregnancy

When pregnancy is complicated by heroin addiction, the patient and her physician are faced with the choice as to which of several undesirable alternatives is the least undesirable. The best circumstance would be for the woman to abstain totally from drugs, licit or illicit, during the pregnancy. Unfortunately, this is often not likely to occur. On an outpatient drug-free regimen, many patients cycle in and out of heroin use, subjecting the fetus to periods of intoxication and withdrawal and a risk of spontaneous abortion, stillbirth, prematurity, and anomalies. The drug effects are compounded by the patient's lifestyle, poor prenatal care, inadequate diet, and drug adulterants. Residential placement to ensure drug-free status is usually resisted, especially if other children are at home, or it may be hard to find, even if it is desired.

Narcotic antagonists have not been approved for maintenance during pregnancy. Methadone maintenance at the lowest dosage possible is left as the least undesirable option for most such patients. Dosing can be problematic because the increased metabolism of methadone during pregnancy can render the usual dosage inadequate and require an increased dosage rather than a decreased one. This can often be handled by split dosing during the day. The infant will be born addicted to methadone and will need to be withdrawn but should otherwise not have problems if the mother received adequate obstetrical care during the pregnancy. If withdrawal from methadone maintenance is necessary, it should be slow. The methadone should be reduced by no more than 5 mg/week, and withdrawal should take place during the mid-trimester. During the first trimester, withdrawal may be especially deleterious to fetal development; during the third trimester, withdrawal may trigger premature labor.

## Summary

Studies examining gradual methadone withdrawal suggest the following:

- Inpatient withdrawal has a significantly higher retention rate (about 80%) than short-term outpatient withdrawal (as low as 13%–17%).
- Although little evidence indicates that this initial higher rate is associated with better sustained abstinence 4–6 months later, more research is necessary to determine which patients need inpatient withdrawal.
- The success rate for short-term outpatient withdrawal appears about the same as reported by addicted individuals attempting self-withdrawal.
- The success rate for outpatient withdrawal appears to be improved substantially (up to 62%) if longer periods (e.g., 4–6 months) and higher dosages are used.
- Attention to psychosocial factors during outpatient withdrawal is associated with better retention and less use of heroin.
- Regardless of duration or dosage, once the methadone is stopped, a rebound in withdrawal symptoms lasting somewhat longer than 1 month occurs, and these symptoms are probably connected with the high postwithdrawal relapse rate.

## Other Detoxification Agents and Methods

### Clonidine

The $\alpha_2$-adrenergic agonist drug clonidine (Catapres), marketed as an antihypertensive, has been used to facilitate opioid withdrawal in both inpatient and outpatient settings (Charney et al. 1986; Gold et al. 1978; Kleber et al. 1985). Clonidine in doses of 0.6–2.0 mg/day reduces many of the autonomic components of the opioid withdrawal syndrome, although craving, lethargy, insomnia, restlessness, and muscle aches are not well suppressed (Charney et al. 1981; Jasinski et al. 1985). Clonidine is believed to exert its ameliorative actions by binding to $\alpha_2$ autoreceptors in the brain (e.g., locus coeruleus) and spinal cord. Both opioids and clonidine can suppress the activity of the locus coeruleus, which is hyperactive during opioid withdrawal.

Inpatients stabilized at 50 mg/day or less of methadone can be switched abruptly to clonidine. Dosages reaching 2.5 mg/day have been used. Sedation and hypotension have been the major side effects.

Clonidine has also been used for outpatient detoxification from either heroin or methadone maintenance. Patients maintained on 20 mg/day or less of methadone are about as successful after abrupt substitution of clonidine as after reduction of methadone by 1 mg/day (Kleber et al. 1985). With experienced personnel, street addicts can also be successfully withdrawn using clonidine. O'Connor et al. (1997) found that 65% of such patients completed withdrawal and entered the next phase of treatment. Although available as an antihypertensive agent, clonidine has not been given official FDA approval for use in controlling withdrawal, but it has been used so widely now, both in the United States and abroad, that it has become accepted as an alternative to gradual methadone reduction.

Although many of the clonidine studies were conducted by the group that originated the techniques, a number of both open and controlled studies have been published in the past 15 years (e.g., Cami et al. 1985; Gerra et al. 1995; Pini et al. 1991; San et al. 1990). Studies show that clonidine (or other $\alpha_2$-adrenergic agonists such as guanfacine or lofexidine) are about as effective as gradual methadone withdrawal with the following differences: 1) methadone detoxification has fewer symptoms early in withdrawal and more at the end; 2) clonidine has the opposite profile: dropouts are more likely to occur early with clonidine and later with methadone; 3) clonidine has more side effects, especially hypotension and sedation; and 4) clonidine is less likely to be associated with postwithdrawal rebound. It also appears that clonidine is more effective if given in the context of abrupt opioid withdrawal rather than as an adjunct during gradual methadone tapering (Ghodse et al. 1994)

Techniques of clonidine-aided detoxification.　On the day before clonidine detoxification is started, the usual dosage of opioid is given. The following day (day 1) the opioid is withdrawn completely, and clonidine is given in divided doses as shown in Table 23–4. Clonidine is to be used with caution in patients who have hypotension or who are taking antihypertensive medications. Use of tricyclic antidepressants within 3 weeks precludes use of clonidine because these agents render the $\alpha_2$ receptors hyposensitive to the clonidine. Other exclusions include pregnancy, history of psychosis, cardiac arrhythmias, or other medical conditions in which use of clonidine might aggravate the associated medical problems. Because clonidine can cause sedation, patients should be cautioned about driving and operating equipment.

When clonidine is used on an outpatient basis, it is usually advisable not to give the patient more than a 2-day supply at one time. The patient should not drive during the first few days. The patient's blood pressure should be checked at the next visit. If dizziness occurs, the clinician should instruct the patient to cut back on the dosage or to lie down.

Lower clonidine dosages are used on day 1 because narcotic withdrawal is less severe at that point, and the patient usually needs time to adjust to the sedative effects of clonidine. It is useful to give 0.1 mg of clonidine as the initial dose and observe the patient's reaction and blood pressure at least over the next hour. The total daily dosage should be divided into three doses given at 4- to 6-hour intervals. Unless the patient is either very thin or very obese, standard dosages are used rather than basing the dosage on body weight. The dosages from days 2–10 usually do not exceed 17 μg/kg/day (approximately 1.3 mg/day).

During withdrawal from long-acting opioids such as methadone, clonidine dosages can be increased gradually over several days. In treating withdrawal from short-acting opioids, however, dosages of clonidine are increased (i.e., titrated to symptoms) as rapidly as side effects permit because serious withdrawal symptoms appear earlier. However, the duration of clonidine dosing is shorter.

Antiwithdrawal effects usually begin within 30 minutes and peak at 2–3 hours. For inpatients, blood pressure should be checked before each dose; if it is 85/55 mm Hg or lower, subsequent doses should be withheld until the pressure stabilizes. Dizziness between doses is best handled by monitoring blood pressure and having the patient lie down. If the pressure is too low, the dosage should be reduced. Sedation is commonly experienced, especially within the first few days but usually remits by day 3 or 4. Dry mouth and facial pain are less common.

Insomnia is not usually a problem until day 3 or 4 of methadone withdrawal but occurs by day 2 or 3 with short-acting opioids. Paradoxically, clonidine may

---

**Table 23–4.**　Clonidine-aided detoxification

**Schedule for heroin, morphine, oxycodone, meperidine, and other short-acting opioids**

Outpatient/inpatient

　　Day 1: 0.1–0.2 mg orally every 4–6 hours up to 1 mg

　　Days 2–4: 0.2–0.4 mg orally every 4–6 hours up to 1.2 mg

　　Day 5 to completion: Reduce by 0.2 mg/day, given in two or three divided doses; the nighttime dose should be reduced last; or reduce total dosage by one-half each day, not to exceed 0.4 mg/day reduction

**Schedule for methadone-maintained patients (20–30 mg/day methadone)**

Day 1: 0.3 mg

Day 2: 0.4–0.6 mg

Day 3: 0.5–0.8 mg　　　Total daily dosage, given in divided doses every 4–6 hours

Day 4: 0.5–1.2 mg

Days 5–10: Maintain on above dosage

Day 11 to completion: Reduce by 0.2 mg/day, given in two or three divided doses; the nighttime dose should be reduced last; if the patient complains of side effects, the dosage can be reduced by one-half each day, not to exceed 0.4 mg/day reduction

worsen the insomnia associated with detoxification even while causing sedation during the day. Other withdrawal symptoms not relieved by clonidine are primarily muscle aches, nervousness, and irritability. Benzodiazepines may be used for both the muscle aches and the insomnia, but they should be given with caution because many addicted individuals abuse this class of drugs.

Clonidine is known to have mild analgesic effects. Thus, in withdrawing *medical opioid addicts*, analgesia may not be needed during the withdrawal period, even though the original painful condition persists to some extent. Pain usually returns 24–48 hours after the last clonidine dose; if naltrexone is to be used, pain needs to be treated with nonnarcotic analgesics.

Clonidine patches.   In some settings, clonidine is administered via transdermal patches (Spencer and Gregory 1989). The clonidine patch is a 0.2-mm square applied as a self-adhesive bandage. It comes in three sizes that deliver an amount of clonidine equal to daily dosing with 0.1, 0.2, or 0.3 mg of oral clonidine. The technique involves the following: Patients showing objective withdrawal signs are given 0.2 mg of oral clonidine every 6 hours during the first 24 hours. During the second 24 hours, the oral dose is halved. On day 1, patients are given one #2 patch if they weigh 100 pounds (0.2 mg in a 24-hour period), two #2 patches if they weigh 100–200 pounds, and three #2 patches if they weigh more than 200 pounds. The patch supplies clonidine for up to 7 days, is placed on a hairless area of the upper body, and is removed if systolic blood pressure falls below 80 mm Hg or diastolic blood pressure falls below 50 mm Hg. The patches are removed after the first week of treatment and replaced by half the dosage on another area of the upper body. The clonidine patches are removed after the second week of treatment or when the patient feels the patches are no longer effective.

Transdermal clonidine offers several advantages over the oral form:

- Patches can be applied by medical staff weekly; patients are not required to self-administer pills several times daily.
- Patients require fewer supplemental medications.
- The patches supply an even blood level of medication without peaks and troughs.
- The buildup of withdrawal symptoms during the night is prevented.
- Diversion and patient misuse is minimized.

Oral clonidine is given during the first 2 days because the steady-state levels of transdermal clonidine are not reached for 24–48 hours after application of the patch. The patches are used for 7 days for heroin withdrawal and 10 days or more for methadone withdrawal. To treat symptoms not relieved by clonidine, ibuprofen can be given for musculoskeletal pain, and other medications described earlier in this chapter can be given for insomnia.

Clonidine appears to be a safe and effective alternative to the gradual reduction of methadone for opioid detoxification. Its disadvantages include more side effects and less coverage of the spectrum of withdrawal symptoms. Its advantages include not being an opioid drug and, thus much less diversion potential, and more important, avoiding the long residual withdrawal symptoms that persist for weeks after methadone withdrawal. Use of the transdermal patch in selected patients might lead to smoother withdrawal, but the oral form must be used for the first 24–48 hours until a steady blood level is achieved.

## Lofexidine

Although clonidine can be an effective agent for opioid withdrawal, its usefulness is limited by its hypotensive effects. The $\alpha_2$-adrenergic agonist lofexidine, an analogue of clonidine, may be as effective as clonidine for opiate withdrawal but has fewer hypotensive side effects. The hypotension produced by clonidine at times limits its antiwithdrawal effect by making it difficult to use a high enough dosage. Three subtypes of the $\alpha_2$-adrenergic receptor have been cloned: A, B, and C. Herman and O'Brien (1997) suggested that although clonidine has equal affinity for all three subtypes, lofexidine has a higher affinity for A and thus has less hypotensive effects.

Although lofexidine was initially studied in the United States in the early 1980s for withdrawal, its lack of adequate hypotensive effect (the major desired indication) led its manufacturer to discontinue efforts for FDA approval. Since that time, the drug has been approved in England for opioid withdrawal, and it is estimated that more than 50,000 patients have received it to date. The controlled studies published so far suggest that it is approximately as efficacious as clonidine with less hypotension and sedation (Carnwath and Hardman 1998; Kahn et al. 1997). Bearn et al. (1996) found that at a maximum dosage of 2 mg/day, lofexidine was approximately equivalent to methadone detoxification as far as overall symptom relief, although the lofexidine group had slightly more severe self-rated withdrawal symptoms. Lofexidine is being studied by the National Institute on Drug Abuse's Medication Development Division for possible submission to FDA for opioid withdrawal.

## Clonidine-Naltrexone Ultrarapid Detoxification

Although clonidine can be an effective alternative to methadone for opioid withdrawal, it does not shorten substantially the time required for withdrawal. Furthermore, the success rate in outpatient withdrawal leaves much to be desired. To solve these two problems, researchers first combined clonidine and naloxone and then subsequently clonidine and naltrexone to provide a safe, effective, and rapid withdrawal for patients detoxifying from either heroin or methadone. The method uses the known ability of naltrexone to produce immediate withdrawal from opioids as it displaces the opioid from the endogenous receptor. By itself this would produce an immediate and severe withdrawal syndrome that would be unacceptable to most patients. When clonidine is used as pretreatment and after the naltrexone, symptoms are substantially relieved. For those symptoms not adequately controlled, other medications are used, such as oxazepam for muscle spasms and insomnia, and antiemetics for nausea and vomiting.

Vining et al. (1988) described the method in detail, and O'Connor et al. (1995) provided an update in a paper aimed at primary practitioners. The patient is premedicated with clonidine and oxazepam and then the naltrexone is started, starting at 12.5 mg on day 1, 25 mg on day 2, and 50 mg on day 3. Clonidine is given every 4 hours as needed and oxazepam every 4–6 hours as needed. Table 23–5 describes the method in detail. In the O'Connor study, 95% of the patients were able to successfully complete detoxification and move on to the next phase of treatment. By 1 month later, however, there was no difference in treatment retention between the clonidine-alone and the clonidine-naltrexone groups. The limitation of this method is the need to monitor patients for 8 hours on day 1 because of the potential severity of withdrawal that can occur after the first dose of naltrexone and because of the need for careful blood pressure monitoring during the detoxification procedure. Thus trained staff and appropriate space are necessary for this procedure. Other authors (Gerra et al. 1995; Senft 1991) have also successfully used this procedure.

An even more rapid version of the method was de-veloped for inpatient use (Brewer et al. 1988). By use of higher dosages of naltrexone and clonidine on day 1 and heavy doses of diazepam, the average withdrawal time was reduced from approximately 3 days to a little more than 2 days. It has been hypothesized that because the dosage of clonidine needed decreases after the first day, even though the dosage of naltrexone is increasing, naltrexone is rapidly normalizing the number and sensitivity of opioid receptors and reversing the opioid-induced central noradrenergic hypersensitivity (Kleber et al. 1987).

The clonidine-naltrexone ultrarapid withdrawal method appears to be a safe, effective, and economical alternative to either gradual methadone withdrawal or clonidine withdrawal. Its advantages in trained hands include a marked shortening of the time necessary to complete detoxification, high completion rates (e.g., 55%–95%), and ability to move rapidly to the next stage of rehabilitation with less lingering withdrawal symptoms. The shortened time frame also has economic advantages whether carried out inpatient or outpatient. Its disadvantages include the need for intensive monitoring by experienced staff, especially during the first day of inpatient or outpatient treatment, and adequate space for patients to remain the whole first day if the treatment is on an outpatient basis. The variations on this approach, while shortening the technique somewhat, tend to require hospitalization and do not appear to offer any significant advantage. There is no significant evidence that the technique is associated with any longer abstinence or retention on naltrexone. A recent review of 12 rapid clonidine-naltrexone studies found only 3 with outcome data after the acute detoxification (O'Connor and Kosten 1998).

## Ultrarapid Opioid Detoxification Under Anesthesia/Sedation

The rate-limiting factor of the clonidine-naltrexone method is the ability to find medications that adequately relieve the symptoms of the precipitated withdrawal in the awake patient. The procedure was later shortened and advanced by carrying it out under a general anesthetic (an ironic throwback to the hibernation therapy of 1941, in which the patient was kept asleep from 1 to 3 days) (Loimer et al. 1988). Over the next 10 years, the technique has been modified and improved (see Brewer 1997a for review). The current method commonly uses naltrexone, propofol anesthetic, the antiemetic ondansetron, the antidiarrheal octreotide, and clonidine and benzodiazepines for other

**Table 23–5.** Clonidine-naltrexone rapid detoxification

| Day | Time | Drug |
|---|---|---|
| 0 | | Use of heroin or methadone as usual |
| 1 | 9:00 A.M. | Clonidine, 0.2–0.4 mg orally |
| | | Oxazepam, 30–60 mg orally |
| | 10:00–11:00 A.M. | Naltrexone, 12.5 mg orally |
| | | Clonidine, 0.1–0.4 mg every 4–6 hours up to 1.2 mg |
| | | Oxazepam, 30–60 mg every 4–6 hours as needed |
| | Patient in clinic until 5:00 P.M. | |
| 2 | 9:00 A.M. | Clonidine, 0.1–0.2 mg orally (then every 4–6 hours as needed up to 1.2 mg) |
| | | Oxazepam, 30–60 mg (then every 4–6 hours as needed) |
| | 10:00 A.M. | Naltrexone, 25 mg orally |
| | Patient may leave 2 hours after naltrexone administration | |
| 3 | 9:00 A.M. | Clonidine, 0.1–0.2 mg (then every 4–6 hours as needed, tapering total dosage by 0.2–0.4 mg/day) |
| | | Oxazepam, 15–30 mg (then every 4–6 hours as needed) |
| | 10:00 A.M. | Naltrexone, 50 mg orally |
| | Patient may leave 1 hour after naltrexone administration | |
| After day 3[a] | | Clonidine, continue 0.1–0.2 mg every 4–6 hours as needed over next 2–3 days |
| | | Oxazepam, continue 15–30 mg every 4–6 hours as needed over next 2–3 days |
| | | Naltrexone, 50 mg/day orally |

[a]Adjuvant medications as needed. For muscle cramps: nonsteroidal anti-inflammatory drugs (NSAIDs; e.g., ibuprofen 600 mg orally every 6 hours or ketorolac 30 mg intramuscularly every 6 hours while on site); for nausea/vomiting: antiemetics (e.g., prochlorperazine 5 mg intramuscularly or 10 mg orally every 4–6 hours while on site or ondansetron 8 mg orally every 8 hours); for anxiety, insomnia, or muscle cramps: benzodiazepines (e.g., oxazepam 30–60 mg as needed, not to exceed 120 mg/day after day 1).

withdrawal symptoms. Heavy sedation via midazolam is sometimes used instead of anesthesia. Intubation is usually used with anesthesia but not with heavy sedation. Occasionally nalmefene is used instead of naltrexone. Some clinicians do the procedure on an inpatient basis, others on an outpatient basis; some encourage naltrexone maintenance and/or therapy after detoxification, others simply refer the patient to Narcotics Anonymous. What tends to be common is high price, usually ranging from $2,500 or more for the outpatient approach to $7,500 or more for the inpatient anesthesia method. Claims of high rates of abstinence months after detoxification have been made, but no objective verification has occurred, nor are the samples representative. Although some clinicians see these techniques as a

magic bullet or miracle breakthrough, others see them as exploitation of the addicted individual and the general public: use of a technique with potential serious morbidity and mortality for a condition, opiate withdrawal, that although painful is not associated with mortality. A recent review surveyed nine published anesthesia studies, and only two had outcome data beyond 7 days (O'Connor and Kosten 1998). The authors deplored the lack of randomized design or control groups, the short-term outcome studied, and the inadequate assessment of risks. Although at least four deaths occurred within 24 hours or so of the procedure, the exact number and cause is not clear (Brewer 1997b). More deaths could occur if the approach is extended to dual-dependent patients or those with cardiac or liver disease. Furthermore, postdetoxification symptoms have not been described adequately. Some patients have complained of major discomfort, such as prolonged vomiting or muscle cramps that persisted for days after the procedure (Brewer 1997a).

Lack of adequate studies precludes evaluation of the risk-benefit ratio for this method. Should the procedure show itself to be both adequately safe and effective in improving postdetoxification outcome, potential benefits could include reaching the subsets of addicted individuals who are fearful of opiate withdrawal and would welcome a short procedure while unconscious, and those who have failed to complete other methods. Furthermore, a technique that shortens and simplifies withdrawal from methadone maintenance could improve the likelihood that patients who have been socially and psychologically rehabilitated and wish to be totally abstinent could ultimately get off maintenance. Certainly induction onto naltrexone would be shortened and simplified. Until adequate control studies are carried out, however, the place for this technique in the spectrum of opioid detoxification procedures is unclear (Kleber 1998).

## Buprenorphine

Buprenorphine is a partial μ agonist (and in animals at least, a κ antagonist). Although introduced as a parenteral analgesic, it is being used in a variety of approaches for treatment of narcotic addiction, including as a maintenance agent itself, as a transition from full agonists such as methadone or heroin to a full antagonist such as naltrexone, and as a detoxification agent from an agonist such as methadone or heroin. The first step in detoxification is to transfer the patient from either heroin or methadone maintenance to buprenorphine. Detoxification can then be accomplished by gradual buprenorphine tapering, abrupt discontinuation, or discontinuation of buprenorphine and precipitation of withdrawal using naltrexone. In these methods, the patient is usually first stabilized on buprenorphine, which may be for as brief a period as 3 days on relatively low dosages of 2 or 3 mg/day sublingually or may involve longer-term maintenance of 6 months or more on dosages of up to 16 mg/day. The sublingual form of buprenorphine is being considered by the FDA as a detoxification agent and, in a combined form with a small dose of naloxone, as a maintenance agent. Because naloxone is 100 times more active by injection than orally, this small dose will not have an effect unless the sublingual tablet is dissolved and injected.

If buprenorphine is stopped abruptly, the withdrawal syndrome is mild, although in some patients it may be protracted. The literature is not clear on the exact duration of this withdrawal. Various periods have been reported, ranging from no signs of abstinence after being maintained for 10 days on 8 mg (Mello and Mendelson 1980); to mild symptoms after 2–3 days, which peaked at approximately 2 weeks after the last dose (Jasinski et al. 1978); to mild symptoms peaking at 3–5 days and going away after another 5 days (Fudala et al. 1990). Gradual tapering of buprenorphine appears to be less successful than abrupt discontinuation and has not been recommended (Bickel et al. 1988). At a dosage of 2 mg sublingually, buprenorphine was comparable to 30 mg of methadone in detoxification from buprenorphine or methadone maintenance (Bickel et al. 1988). Buprenorphine stabilization dosages may need to be adjusted in reference to the time course of the opioid being withdrawn. Because heroin's peak withdrawal effects occur in 1.5–3 days and methadone's peak withdrawal effects occur in 4–6 days, buprenorphine dosages need to be increased on day 2 of heroin withdrawal and day 4 of methadone withdrawal (Johnson et al. 1989). Variable dosages of buprenorphine (up to 0.9 mg im) were better than clonidine in withdrawing methadone-maintenance patients (Janiri et al. 1994).

As the dosage of buprenorphine is increased, a ceiling effect comparable to approximately 20–30 mg of parenteral morphine is reached. Buprenorphine is thus less likely to produce the severe respiratory depression found with full μ agonists. Withdrawal from buprenorphine is less intense, partially because of the ceiling effect and partially because it binds quite tightly to the μ receptor. Its long duration of action and slow dissociation from receptors may produce a self-tapering effect. Although buprenorphine exhibits cross-tolerance with other μ agonists when it is substituted for a full μ agonist used at high dosage, it replaces these full μ effects with partial effects and can therefore produce some opioid withdrawal. At lower dosages of opioid dependence, buprenorphine can substitute in full for other μ agonists and thus can be used for detoxification.

The possibility of using buprenorphine in rapid detoxification via naltrexone has also been studied. In one study, 23 patients maintained on buprenorphine for 1 month at a dosage of 3–6 mg were abruptly given increasing dosages of naltrexone over 4 days, starting 24 hours after the last buprenorphine dose (Kosten et al. 1991). Minimal withdrawal occurred, and 20 of the patients took the initial 6-mg naltrexone dose. However, only four patients continued the naltrexone at 50 mg/day beyond the 2 weeks. More recently, patients were given buprenorphine 3 mg/day sublingually for 3 days followed by 25 mg of clonidine-naltrexone on day 4 and 50 mg on day 5 (O'Connor et al. 1997). The individuals in the buprenorphine group had milder withdrawal and were more likely to complete detoxification (81%) than were those in the clonidine group (65%). The buprenorphine group was equal to the success of the clonidine-naltrexone comparison group (also 81%), but no difference in naltrexone retention was found at 8 days. Given the milder withdrawal from buprenorphine than from heroin or methadone, it would appear that a rapid detoxification method involving, first, transition to buprenorphine and, then, some variant of the clonidine-naltrexone approach will be ultimately least painful and produce the highest rate of success.

## Experimental Medications

A recent review suggested the possibility of other agents, none of which have been researched thoroughly enough to recommend or to discuss in depth but which may have some efficacy in the future (Herman and O'Brien 1997). These agents include low-affinity, noncompetitive *N*-methyl-D-aspartate (NMDA) receptor antagonists such as dextromethorphan and memantine; serotonergic agents such as the $5\text{-}HT_{1A}$ partial receptor agonist buspirone; and the neutral endopeptidase inhibitor acetorphan. In addition, some plant preparations, such as the West African hallucinogen ibogaine and the Vietnamese herbal mixture heanta, have developed enthusiastic followings, but adequate controlled studies of safety and efficacy have not been conducted.

## Acupuncture

Although acupuncture has been used for thousands of years in Chinese medicine to relieve pain, its use in the treatment of narcotic withdrawal is much more recent. Wen and Cheung (1973) reported more or less favorable results in 40 patients using acupuncture with electrical stimulation. A review 5 years later (Whitehead 1978) concluded that because the studies used inadequate controls, they did not prove that the procedure worked.

Acupuncture consists of the use of thin needles inserted subcutaneously at points on the body believed to be related to the body functions that need to be stimulated. For detoxification, points on the external ear are usually used. Electro-acupuncture involves applying small amounts of electricity to needles, which are inserted in those acupuncture points on the external ear believed to affect opioid withdrawal. Cranial electro-stimulation involves applying small amounts of electricity presumably to the central nervous system through electrodes applied to the skin surface over the cranium. Evidence from animal studies indicates that electro-acupuncture is mediated through the endorphin system, and its effects can be blocked by the use of naloxone. Although programs that use these methods tend to be enthusiastic about the results, published reviews tend to be more critical.

Research studies of these approaches have a number of methodological problems, including high dropout rates, inconsistent placement of electrodes, inconsistent electrical parameters, and problems in blinding patients and staff. Thus, we are not as far along as we should be since Whitehead (1978) concluded the existing evidence was inadequate.

Some studies or reviews have asserted that acupuncture or the other variants are effective, and others have asserted that they are not (e.g., Alling et al. 1990; Brewington 1994; National Council Against Health Fraud 1991; Riet et al. 1990; Ulett 1992). Studies have been flawed by the lack of random assignment or the lack of a placebo control. Although some studies suggest that acupuncture detoxification can be as effective as gradual methadone withdrawal in symptom alleviation, retention, and relapse rate, better controlled studies are needed to confirm this conclusion.

Even in the absence of definitive studies, however, the preponderance of reports suggests that some effect does occur, especially in reducing both the objective signs of withdrawal and the subjective discomfort. Thus acupuncture may be useful for some patients. The best technique to be used remains to be clarified. It also remains to be determined how acupuncture relates to other methods described earlier in this chapter, especially methadone detoxification and clonidine. For those who prefer not to use medications, clearly there is something appealing about a technique that relieves discomfort without involving medications. As Brumbaugh (1993, p. 36) noted, "Acupuncture is not a panacea, and it loses much of its efficacy . . . when practiced in isolation from the more traditional Western modalities of counseling, pharmaceutical therapies, 12-Step Programs, and urine testing. It is best seen as an adjunct or a complement to these other forms."

Thus, in addition to the need for better controlled trials, more attention needs to be paid to questions such as, What are the characteristics of individuals most likely to benefit from acupuncture during opioid withdrawal? For example, Washburn et al. (1993) suggested light heroin users stay in treatment longer than do heavy users. And what are the optimal circumstances and complements during the procedure?

## Conclusion

For most opioid-addicted individuals, detoxification from narcotics is only the first step in the long process of remaining abstinent from illicit drugs. Success is a function not just of how painless the procedure is but of the number of patients retained and the likelihood that they will go on to longer-term treatment. Whatever method is chosen, appropriate psychosocial interventions and education must be available to prepare the patient for this next step. More information is needed as to the best combinations of withdrawal techniques and patient characteristics. The ideal detoxification method would be relatively short, cheap, and painless; would be able to be done in an outpatient setting; and would leave the patient with a desire to seek longer-term help. Although none of the techniques reviewed in this chapter are perfect in these regards, we appear to be closing in on methods to deal with the pharmacological ramifications of opioid withdrawal and thus need to focus not just on better pharmacological methods but also on what approaches combined with them will most likely keep the patient in treatment for both detoxification and the next stage. Compared to 60 years ago, the current methods are more rapid and produce less discomfort. In the future, we may also find that some agents or combinations may decrease relapse by acting on the altered brain states related to protracted withdrawal and craving.

## References

Alling FA, Johnson BD, Elmoghazy E: Cranial electro stimulation (CES) use in the detoxification of opiate dependent patients. J Subst Abuse Treat 7:173–180, 1990

Bearn J, Gossop M, Strang J: Randomized double-blind comparison of lofexidine and methadone in the in-patient treatment of opiate withdrawal. Drug Alcohol Depend 43:87–91, 1996

Bickel WD, Stitzer ML, Bigelow GE, et al: A clinical trial of buprenorphine: comparison with methadone in the detoxification of heroin addicts. Clin Pharmacol Ther 43:72–78, 1988

Brewer C: Ultra-rapid antagonist precipitated opiate detoxification under general anesthesia or sedation. Addiction Biology 2:291–302, 1997a

Brewer C: The case for rapid detoxification under anesthesia (RODA): a reply to Gossop and Strang. British Journal of Intensive Care 7:137–143, 1997b

Brewer C, Rezae H, Bailey C: Opioid withdrawal and naltrexone induction in 48–72 hours with minimal dropout, using a modification of the naltrexone-clonidine technique. Br J Psychiatry 153:340–343, 1988

Brewington V, Smith M, Lipton D: Acupuncture as a detoxification treatment: an analysis of controlled research. J Subst Abuse Treat 11:289–307, 1994

Brumbaugh AG: Acupuncture: new perspectives in chemical dependency treatment. J Subst Abuse Treat 10:35–43, 1993

Cami J, De Torres S, San L, et al: Efficacy of clonidine and of methadone in the rapid detoxification of patients dependent on heroin. Clin Pharmacol Ther 38:336–341, 1985

Carnwath T, Hardman J: Randomized double-blind comparison of lofexidine and clonidine in the outpatient treatment of opiate withdrawal. Drug Alcohol Depend 50:251–254, 1998

Charney DS, Sternberg DE, Kleber HD, et al: The clinical use of clonidine in abrupt withdrawal from methadone. Arch Gen Psychiatry 38:1273–1277, 1981

Charney DS, Heninger GR, Kleber HD: The combined use of clonidine and naltrexone as a rapid, safe and effective treatment of abrupt withdrawal from methadone. Am J Psychiatry 143:831–837, 1986

Dawe S, Griffith P, Gossop M, et al: Should opiate addicts be involved in controlling their own detoxification? a comparison of fixed versus negotiable schedules. British Journal of Addiction 86:977–982, 1991

Fudala PJ, Jaffe JH, Dax EM, et al: Use of buprenorphine in the treatment of opioid addiction; II: physiologic and behavioral effects: effects of daily and alternate day administration and abrupt withdrawal. Clin Pharmacol Ther 47:525–534, 1990

Gerra G, Mercato A, Caccavari R, et al: Clonidine and receptor antagonists in the treatment of heroin addiction. J Subst Abuse Treat 12:35–41, 1995

Ghodse H, Myles J, Smith SE: Clonidine is not a useful adjunct to methadone gradual detoxification in opioid addiction. Br J Psychiatry 165:370–374, 1994

Gold MS, Redmond DE, Kleber HD: Clonidine blocks acute opiate withdrawal symptoms. Lancet 2:599, 1978

Gossop M, Bradley B, Phillips GT: An investigation of withdrawal symptoms shown by opiate addicts during and subsequent to a 21 day inpatient methadone detoxification procedure. Addict Behav 12:1–6, 1987

Herman BH, O'Brien CP: Clinical medications development for opiate addiction: focus on nonopioids and opioid antagonists for the amelioration of opiate withdrawal symptoms and relapse prevention. Seminars in Neuroscience 9:158–172, 1997

Jaffe JH, Martin WR: Narcotic analgesics and antagonists, in The Pharmacological Basis of Therapeutics, 5th Edition. Edited by Goodman LS, Gilman A. New York, Macmillan, 1975, pp 245–324

Janiri L, Mannelli P, Persico AM, et al: Opiate detoxification of methadone maintained patients using lofetamine, clonidine, and buprenorphine. Drug Alcohol Depend 36: 139–145, 1994

Jasinski DR, Pevnick JS, Griffith JD: Human pharmacology and abuse potential of the analgesic buprenorphine. Arch Gen Psychiatry 35:501–516, 1978

Jasinski DR, Johnson RE, Kocher TR: Clonidine in morphine withdrawal: differential effects on signs and symptoms. Arch Gen Psychiatry 42:1063–1066, 1985

Johnson RE, Cone EJ, Henningfield JE, et al: Use of buprenorphine in the treatment of opiate addiction, I: physiological and behavioral effects during a rapid dose induction. Clin Pharmacol Ther 46:335–343, 1989

Kahn A, Mumford JP, Rogers GA, et al: Double-blind study of lofexidine and clonidine in the detoxification of opiate addicts in hospital. Drug Alcohol Depend 44:57–61, 1997

Kleber HD: Detoxification from narcotics, in Substance Abuse: Clinical Issues and Perspectives. Edited by Lowinson JH, Ruiz P. Baltimore, MD, Williams & Wilkins, 1981, pp 317–339

Kleber HD: Outpatient detoxification from opiates. Primary Psychiatry 1:42–52, 1996

Kleber HD: Ultra-rapid opiate detoxification. Addiction 93:1629–1633, 1998

Kleber HD, Riordan CE: The treatment of narcotic withdrawal: a historical review. J Clin Psychiatry 43 (section 2):30–34, 1982

Kleber HD, Riordan CE, Rounsaville B, et al: Clonidine in outpatient detoxification from methadone maintenance. Arch Gen Psychiatry 42:391–394, 1985

Kleber HD, Topazian M, Gaspari J, et al: Clonidine and naltrexone in the outpatient treatment of heroin withdrawal. Am J Drug Alcohol Abuse 13:1–17, 1987

Kolb L, Himmelsbach CK: Clinical studies of drug addiction; III. a critical review of the withdrawal treatments with method of evaluating abstinence. Am J Psychiatry 94: 759–799, 1938

Kosten TR, Morgan C, Kleber HD: Treatment of heroin addicts using buprenorphine. Am J Drug Alcohol Abuse 17: 119–128, 1991

Loimer N, Schmid R, Presslich O, et al: Continuous naloxone administration suppresses opiate withdrawal in human opiate addicts during detoxification treatment. J Psychiatr Res 23:81–86, 1988

Martin WR, Jasinski DR: Physiological parameters of morphine dependence in man: tolerance, early abstinence, protracted abstinence. J Psychiatr Res 7:9–17, 1969

McLellan AT, Luborsky L, Cacciola J, et al: New data from the Addiction Severity Index: reliability and validity in three centers. J Nerv Ment Dis 173:412–423, 1985

Mello NK, Mendelson JH: Buprenorphine suppresses heroin use by heroin addicts. Science 207:657–659, 1980

National Council Against Health Fraud: Acupuncture: the position paper of the National Council Against Health Fraud. American Journal of Acupuncture 19:273–279, 1991

O'Connor PG, Kosten TR: Rapid and ultra-rapid opioid detoxification techniques. JAMA 279:229–234, 1998

O'Connor PG, Waugh ME, Carroll KM, et al: Primary care-based ambulatory opioid detoxification: the results of a clinical trial. J Gen Intern Med 10:255–260, 1995

O'Connor PG, Carroll KM, Shi JM, et al: Three methods of opioid detoxification in a primary care setting: a randomized trial. Am Intern Med 127:526–530, 1997

Phillips GT, Gossop M, Bradley B: The influence of psychological factors on the opiate withdrawal syndrome. Br J Psychiatry 149:235–238, 1986

Pini LA, Sternieri E, Ferretti C: Dapiprazole compared with clonidine and a placebo in detoxification of opiate addicts. Int J Clin Pharmacol Res 11:99–105, 1991

Riet GT, Kleijnen J, Knipschild P: A meta analysis of studies into the effect of acupuncture on addiction. Br J Psychiatry 40:379–382, 1990

San L, Cami J, Peri JM, et al: Efficacy of clonidine, guanfacine and methadone in the rapid detoxification of heroin addicts: a controlled clinical trial. British Journal of Addiction 85:141–147, 1990

Satel SL, Kosten TR, Schuckit MA, et al: Should protracted withdrawal from drugs be included in DSM-IV? Am J Psychiatry 150:695–704, 1993

Senft RA: Experience with clonidine-naltrexone for rapid opiate detoxification. J Subst Abuse Treat 8:257–259, 1991

Spencer L, Gregory M: Clonidine transdermal patches for use in outpatient opiate withdrawal. J Subst Abuse Treat 6: 113–117, 1989

Strang J, Gossop M: Comparisons of linear versus exponential methadone reduction curves in the detoxification of opiate addicts. Addict Behav 15:541–547, 1990

Ulett GA: Beyond Yin and Yang: How Acupuncture Really Works. St. Louis, MO, Warren H Green, 1992

Vining E, Kosten TR, Kleber HD: Clinical utility of rapid clonidine-naltrexone detoxification for opioid abuse. British Journal of Addiction 83:567–575, 1988

Washburn AM, Fullilove RE, Fullilove MT, et al: Acupuncture heroin detoxification: a single-blind clinical trial. J Subst Abuse Treat 10:345–351, 1993

Wen HL, Cheung SYC: Treatment of drug addiction by acupuncture and electrical stimulation. American Journal of Acupuncture 1:71–75, 1973

Whitehead PC: Acupuncture in the treatment of addiction: a review and analysis. International Journal of the Addictions 13:1–16, 1978

# 24 Opioids: Methadone Maintenance

## Edward C. Senay, M.D.

In almost all individuals who are dependent on opioids, properly prescribed methadone reduces and frequently eliminates use of nonprescribed opioids (Dole and Nyswander 1965; Newman and Whitehill 1979). Because many addicted individuals must commit crimes to pay for illegal opioids, an indirect effect of legal methadone is the reduction of associated crime (Ball et al. 1988a). Methadone has no direct effect on the array of social and psychological problems that complicate opioid dependence. A comprehensive program, in which methadone is prescribed as one of a number of services, may have desirable effects by changing the balance of forces on and in the addicted individual (e.g., the addicted individual with antisocial personality disorder has to steal less because of the methadone, thus avoiding arrests). These statements are supported by the largest scientific database ever gathered on any biopsychosocial problem. The only proper question to pose with respect to the clinical use of methadone is whether it is achieving the goal of reducing use of nonprescribed opioids.

Properly prescribed methadone is not intoxicating or sedating, is effective orally, suppresses narcotic withdrawal for 24–36 hours, and does not have effects that interfere with ordinary activities such as driving a car, reading a newspaper, or operating an industrial machine; thus it is not like "giving an alcoholic bourbon" as its critics contend. The methadone-maintenance (MM) patient who is intoxicated from the methadone, by definition, is getting improperly prescribed, poorly monitored doses of methadone. The successful MM patient has stopped centering his or her life on intoxication and has a daily lifestyle that has few, if any, differences from individuals not taking methadone.

Results from methadone programs are the familiar one-third do well, one-third vacillate between good and bad performance, and one-third show no change from a lifestyle centered on drugs and crime. The clinician needs to appreciate the subtle fact that before methadone there was no way to generate the one-third who do well or the successful periods of treatment for the one-third who vacillate. For most opioid-dependent individuals, methadone is not a cure, and to demean the substantial benefits that can flow from its proper use because they do not constitute a cure borders on the criminal in the age of HIV. Evidence indicates that methadone programs prevented many opioid injectors from getting HIV (Barthwell et al. 1989; Novick et al. 1990), and substantial evidence indicates that needle use and sharing are lessened when addicted individuals enter methadone programs (Ball et al. 1988b).

## Federal and State Eligibility Criteria for Methadone Maintenance

Methadone can be used for analgesia by any licensed physician. It cannot be used for the treatment of opioid dependence unless it is used by a physician working in a treatment facility licensed by a state. States can have criteria more stringent than those established for the United States by the U.S. Food and Drug Administration (FDA), but they cannot have less stringent criteria. States differ in eligibility criteria and in a variety of regulations on matters such as take-home methadone. By federal mandate, each state must have a single state agency that licenses and coordinates drug treatment and prevention programs. If questions arise about eligibility criteria, these single state agencies should be consulted. The FDA's eligibility criteria for MM, defined as the use of methadone for the treatment of narcotic dependence for more than 90 days, are as follows:

## Current Physiological Dependence on Opioids

A 1-year history of physiological dependence on opioids must be present together with current physiological dependence as demonstrated by positive urine screens for opioids, needle tracks, and signs and symptoms of opioid withdrawal. The regulations do not specify any particular subset of the foregoing criteria for current physiological dependence. Physiological dependence on opioids must have existed episodically or continuously for 1 year. If the addicted subject has a history of only 6–7 months of dependence, then the physician should consult with the single state agency before beginning a treatment regimen of MM.

## Individuals From Penal Institutions

A person who has been in a penal institution is eligible for MM after a period of incarceration without current physiological dependence on opioids if the individual's addiction met the criteria before entering the penal institution.

## Pregnant Patients

Pregnant patients can be placed on MM if currently physiologically dependent on opioids, or if dependent in the past, they may be started on MM if return to dependence is likely.

## Previously Treated Patients

For a 2-year period following an episode of MM, patients may be readmitted without evidence of current physiological dependence if the physician documents that return to opioid dependence is imminent.

## Individuals Under Age 18 Years

Individuals under age 18 years must have two documented attempts at drug detoxification or drug-free treatment with a 1-week period between treatment episodes, and they must show evidence of current physiological dependence on opioids to be eligible for MM. A parent, legal guardian, or responsible adult designated by state authority must also complete and sign *Form*

*FDA-2635 Consent to Methadone Treatment* to complete the eligibility criteria.

These criteria may vary in that a state can elect to be more stringent; for example, states can require 2 years of physiological dependence before MM is legal or they can make the rules for take-home methadone more stringent. FDA regulations permit programs to dispense one or two take-home doses of methadone after 3–6 months of good performance in treatment. Some states require longer periods of good performance, and some may not permit take-home doses at all.

If a patient is currently physiologically dependent on opioids but does not meet these criteria, then methadone can be used for detoxification for up to a 90-day period. This use is defined by FDA regulations as methadone detoxification. The previously described regulations are subject to periodic change, and there are current discussions about changing them again.

## Biotransformation of Methadone

Methadone is usually well absorbed from the stomach, and large concentrations appear in the plasma within minutes after oral administration. With chronic administration, pools of methadone are built up in body tissues, and methadone from these pools provides a steady blood concentration. After the first 3–4 weeks, methadone reaches a steady state, that is, a given daily dose does not cause a sharp increase in blood levels. This accounts for the drug's failure to produce sedation or intoxication and for the fact that methadone is not an effective analgesic in MM patients. Conversely, the pool level may not decrease much following omission of a daily dose, that is, omission of a daily dose may not produce withdrawal. Optimal blood levels in an MM patient are 150–600 ng/mL (Dole 1988). The optimal ratio of peak-to-trough levels during a 24-hour dosing period is 2:1.

Medically prescribed methadone is safe, and its routine use is remarkably free from serious problems. Common side effects are sedation, if the dosage is too high; constipation, which can be treated by increasing fluid intake and using stool softeners; occasional transient ankle edema in women; excessive sweating; and changes in libido. These side effects tend to improve with the passage of time, but they may require dosage reduction if they are very disturbing to the patient. The literature contains four recorded cases of severe edema in MM patients (O'Connor et al. 1991).

Daily administration of opioids increases the possibility of synergism with other psychoactive drugs. Patients in many United States clinics who develop alcohol problems while taking methadone may be required to take Breathalyzer tests before methadone is administered. If alcohol levels are 0.05 mg% or above, methadone is not administered until levels are below 0.05 mg% or perhaps until the next visit. Users of multiple drugs who are taking methadone are at risk for lethal overdose because of synergism.

Studies of the biotransformation of methadone indicate wide interindividual variability in blood levels following identical dosing regimens. This research suggests that poor responders to treatment may not absorb methadone from the gastrointestinal tract normally (Kelley et al. 1978). Liver and renal disease may account for some of the individual variations. Any stress (e.g., heavy alcohol or cocaine consumption; severe weather changes; marital discord; or pregnancy, particularly the third trimester) can speed the biotransformation of methadone with associated complaints, in a previously stable dosing pattern, of withdrawal toward the end of the 24-hour cycle. If testing for levels of methadone in a problem patient reveals that the individual is a rapid metabolizer (i.e., he or she has no or low levels at 24 hours), the single state agency may have to be petitioned to permit a dosage higher than current regulations allow.

A number of investigators have found that methadone does not interfere with reaction time (see Gritz et al. 1975 for review). MM patients do not appear to have memory deficits, but chronic administration of methadone differentiates performance of patients from that of control subjects in that subtle recall deficits appear on the more difficult tests (Gritz et al. 1975). Clinically these effects are not detectable. In a study of driving records, Maddox et al. (1977) found no evidence to restrict driving privileges of MM patients. MM clinics in large United States cities have patients from most, if not all, occupations necessary to the daily life of large urban centers.

Rifampin, barbiturates, and tricyclic antidepressants may induce liver enzymes, which speed the biotransformation of methadone. Patients taking these medications may need increases in the dosage of methadone to maintain stability. With close monitoring, methadone can be used concurrently with therapeutic doses of antidepressants, antipsychotics, anticonvulsants, anxiolytics, sedative-hypnotics, lithium, and disulfiram (Ling et al. 1983). Methadone and clonidine should not be used concurrently because of the danger of synergism of sedative effects.

 **Dose**

### Initial Dose

The initial dose of methadone must be individualized. If withdrawal is mild, an initial dose of 5–10 mg would be indicated. If there is obvious severe opioid withdrawal, as there may be in some communities in which high-potency heroin is being used, then an initial daily dose of 20–40 mg should be used. When the clinical situation is ambiguous, the clinician should err on the low side of dosing. Some patients entering treatment are not physiologically dependent even though they meet the criteria for physical dependence, including positive urine screens for morphine and positive signs of opioid withdrawal (Kanof et al. 1991; Senay and Schick 1978; Wang et al. 1974). A dose of 30–40 mg in nontolerant patients might induce a significant degree of sedation and could accumulate to toxic levels if given daily for as few as 2–3 days. If heroin, alcohol, and/or other drugs are used following the initial dose, as may occur when the addicted patient leaves the clinic, an overdose may occur.

It is good practice to observe the patient for a 1- to 2-hour period after the first dose to observe the effects of the dose on the signs of opioid withdrawal. Empirically, initial doses in hospitalized patients can be lower than is necessary in outpatient settings. Doses in hospitalized patients with medical-surgical problems can be split: for example, instead of prescribing a once-per-day dose of 30 mg of methadone, the clinician can prescribe 10 mg three times per day, with smooth control of withdrawal (i.e., control not marked by withdrawal at the end of the 24-hour dosing period, as may be the case with the once-per-day administration of 30 mg). If an MM patient is hospitalized, the maintenance dose should be continued throughout the hospital stay without change unless the associated stresses of medical-surgical conditions precipitate opioid withdrawal. In this case, an increase in methadone dose of 5–10 mg/day will usually stabilize the patient.

### Maintenance Dose

The maintenance dose of methadone also must be individualized. The clinician and/or the staff should observe the effects of a given dose with the following goals in mind: 1) suppression of narcotic withdrawal, 2) no induction of euphoria or sedation, and 3) reduction or elimination of narcotic use as measured by patient and other reports and from the results of random visually or temperature-monitored urine screens. Urine screens are particularly useful in the early phase of treatment and with relapsing patients, and they are critical in evaluating the success of programs.

Federal regulations prohibit doses above 120 mg/day without special permission from the FDA and/or state regulatory authorities. Most methadone clinics have patients who are successful at both ends of the dose spectrum as defined by federal regulations. Thus, some patients will do well on 20–50 mg/day, whereas others will require doses at the other end of the spectrum. There is no rationale for forcing patients at the lower end to higher doses if they are doing well because this will prolong and increase the severity of withdrawal if the patient wants to be withdrawn. If one examines a large number of addicted subjects from a national perspective, it appears that better results are achieved at doses in excess of 60 mg/day (Hargreaves 1983).

The clinician will encounter a spectrum in which the ends are defined by two different populations of dependent patients. One end of the spectrum will try to manipulate endlessly for higher and higher doses. The other end will resist higher doses because of fears that methadone habits are "worse than heroin habits," "methadone gets in your bones," and the like. Most addicted individuals will be between these two poles. With the former group, it is a good idea to observe the patient for signs of withdrawal such as dilated pupils, moist skin, runny nose, and tearing 24 hours after the last dose of methadone. The signs of withdrawal should bear some relation to the severity of complaints. The clinician can then decide whether to increase the dose. If dose increases appear to be indicated, then they may be made in increments of 5 or 10 mg/day depending on clinical judgment of the desired effects. For a patient who has severe complaints but no signs of withdrawal, the clinician might prescribe a 5-mg increment; for a patient who has positive signs and severe complaints, a 10-mg increment may be appropriate. The patient should be instructed that the differences between 30 and 60 mg/day are not pronounced (i.e., there is no simple linear relationship between dose level and severity of withdrawal), but the difference between 20 and 90 mg/day is clinically meaningful for at least some patients.

If urine screens for opioids are positive, the clinician should seriously consider raising the methadone dose because cessation of illegal opioid use is the first priority. Drug hunger bears no constant relationship to narcotic withdrawal, and although observation indicates few or no signs of withdrawal, an increase is justified to

attempt to stop illicit opioid use. Increments of 5 mg every few days should be used until illegal opioid use has diminished or stopped or legal ceilings have been reached. If the patient is willing, the clinician may request from the single state agency an exemption from the guidelines to bring the dosage higher than normally permitted, as the patient may be a rapid metabolizer of methadone.

The appropriate course of action when a patient is not doing well involves a number of considerations, including clinic policy, a clinical cost-benefit analysis, and pressure on the clinic for services. The challenge for the clinician is to find the factors responsible for the patient's continued drug use. A dependent individual whose family and extended family are involved in drug dealing may find family and neighborhood pressures too strong to overcome. In such a patient, a move to a new neighborhood may be the prescription. In others, a divorce, change of job, or entrance into a controlled environment such as a therapeutic community may be considered. Most addicted patients in MM programs will have to change friends if they want to get out of the drug culture.

In treatment failures, some clinics at the end of a 6- to 12-month period decrease the dosage of methadone by 1–3 mg for each positive urine screen so that the patient withdraws himself or herself out of the program by continued drug use. In the age of HIV, such policies need to be reconsidered because returning patients to needle use puts them at risk for contracting HIV. Evidence indicates that the clinician should explore dosage increases in failing patients rather than the reverse (see Cooper 1992 for review). Program policies that limit the duration of MM (e.g., to 2 years) are difficult to justify in the age of HIV. Attempts to force patients who do not want to be withdrawn from successful MM usually cause much suffering and occasionally may lead to incarceration and/or death for the patient.

There is no rationale for blind withdrawal of methadone from a legally competent adult patient without the patient's consent. In a blind withdrawal, the patient's dosing is changed in time and amounts, without the patient being aware of when and how much the dosage is being changed. This method is probably the best regimen for most dependent individuals who want to prepare to become drug free, but it is effective only when the patient has agreed to the contract. In blind withdrawal without the patient's consent, much suffering may be induced with little or no clinical gain. The legally competent patient has a right to know his or her dosage.

Current experience suggests that the addition of a mental health treatment capability and some ability to deliver elementary primary care would go a long way toward improving the fundamental treatment of drug problems. McLellan et al. (1993) compared three groups of randomly assigned patients: the first received methadone alone; the second received methadone plus counseling; and the third received methadone plus counseling, on-site medical, psychiatric, family therapy, and employment training. At 6 months a dosage-related improvement in outcome was clear: those receiving minimal services fared poorly, and the addition of service levels was associated with incremental major improvements in outcome. Kraft et al. (1997) carried out a cost analysis on the McLellan study. The results indicated that the intensive level of service with the best outcome also had a quite high cost and that the moderate degree of treatment was superior to the lower level and was the most cost-effective. Novick et al. (1988) and Senay et al. (1994) found that highly successful methadone patients could be cared for with minimal service levels with no diminution of the effectiveness of treatment, the so-called *medical maintenance model.*

Behavior modification techniques have clinical usefulness, although the clinic system has not had the resources to put these methods on line (Hall et al. 1991; O'Brien et al. 1991; Stitzer and Kirby 1991). Nolimal and Crowley (1990) discuss the difficulties in applying this technology. Kidorf et al. (in press) developed a contingency-based management program in which the behavior of the clinic patient determines status and dosage of treatment required. If the patient improves rapidly, then less treatment is required, but if urine screens continue to be positive and the patient is not attending required treatment sessions, he or she is discharged but can request reinstatement. Patient retention is surprisingly high in this model. Another novel feature of this model is that services for the poorest performing patients are delivered by the most senior staff.

## Methadone and Pregnancy

The pregnant opioid-dependent patient presents a dilemma because clinical experience indicates that attempts to withdraw her carry substantial risk of death for her fetus. The human adult rarely dies or has convulsions from opioid withdrawal, but this is a serious possibility for the human fetus/neonate. In the United States, several clinical centers have independently arrived at a policy of maintaining a pregnant opioid-dependent woman through her pregnancy and delivery on dosages of methadone as low as possible. This regimen avoids fetal death from withdrawal and also avoids the death of neonates from withdrawal if high dosages of methadone are used for maintenance throughout the pregnancy. Some centers will attempt slow withdrawal during pregnancy. With close monitoring it may be possible to lower the maintenance dosage of methadone, but even with sophisticated monitoring, success in safely reaching and maintaining zero dosage is not likely (Finnegan 1991).

Most neonates of MM patients will experience opioid withdrawal, but it will be mild and will not need treatment. Some neonates will have withdrawal severe enough to require treatment with paregoric and phenobarbital. The phenobarbital controls the hyperactivity and the threat of convulsions, whereas the paregoric controls the μ opioid withdrawal. Some centers use diazepam, chlorpromazine, and methadone in various combinations, but the paregoric and phenobarbital combination appears to be the most frequently used.

The fetus and neonate do not have enzyme systems mature enough to carry out the biotransformation and excretion of opioids. The result is that the onset of withdrawal in the fetus or neonate is frequently delayed in comparison with that of the adult; the neonatal opioid withdrawal syndrome can last many weeks and be more variant in its form. For example, it may manifest itself solely as hyperactivity or as failure to thrive. Common symptoms of opioid withdrawal in neonates are tremor, high-pitched cry, increased muscle tone, hyperactivity, poor sleep, poor feeding, sweating, mottling, excoriation, and yawning. Less common symptoms include convulsions, fever, vomiting, markedly hyperactive Moro reflex and flapping tremor; gastrointestinal symptoms of watery stools and/or vomiting may predominate. Some clinicians feel that sudden infant death syndrome is more frequent in opioid-dependent neonates than it is in non-drug-affected infants.

The analgesic needs of MM mothers will require usual opioid agonists in usual doses and in usual frequencies. As in other medical situations, maintenance methadone does not contribute to analgesic needs. In the event that a pregnant woman is delivering and has a heroin habit, methadone should be used to control the withdrawal symptoms. Here, as in other medical-surgical crises, clinicians should avoid unnecessary stresses on an individual. Opioid withdrawal is a major stress and should not be added to the stress of delivery.

Stress levels can be expected to be high in opioid-dependent women and will require psychological management (i.e., support, nonjudgmental attitudes, and recognition of the patient's suffering). Finnegan and Kaltenbach (1992) discuss additional principles of management of drug-dependent women.

The birth weights of the neonates of MM women are elevated compared with the offspring of heroin-dependent women, although they are not normal. If methadone has teratogenic effects or major developmental effects, they are not apparent in studies carried out to date.

## Methadone and Medical-Surgical Illness

Clinicians should try to avoid unnecessary stresses on opioid-dependent medical-surgical patients. In the event that a medical-surgical patient is on MM, the dosage used for maintenance should be continued throughout the medical-surgical crisis. If the opioid-addicted patient is a so-called street addict, then in most cases, smooth control can be achieved with methadone 10–30 mg/day. Control of withdrawal is usually possible with once-per-day administration, but if problems occur at the end of the 24-hour withdrawal, the total dosage can be split into two or three doses. During the medical-surgical treatment the problem of pain management may arise. The methadone-treated patient will not derive analgesic effects from the maintenance dosage of methadone and will need ordinary analgesics at ordinary dosages and frequencies in addition to the methadone. Obviously if anesthesia is necessary, the anesthesiologist should be told about the patient's current opioid dependence. Pentazocine or other mixed agonist-antagonists, such as buprenorphine, are contraindicated for analgesia because they may have antagonist actions and cause or worsen withdrawal.

Once the medical-surgical crisis has passed, a decision can be made about withdrawal. If a dependent patient wants to be withdrawn, referral to a drug abuse program should be the option of choice. Many patients will not want to be withdrawn and will want to return to heroin use in their customary surroundings. There may be no other option because drug abuse treatment programs in many areas of the United States have long waiting lists, and the option of withdrawal in medical-surgical wards is problematic. The staff of these wards are not equipped by training or experience to treat drug problems. More often than not, management

problems (e.g., drug use, intoxication, stealing) will occur. If a given patient was on MM on admission, the patient should be discharged back to his or her MM program without alteration of dosage.

In the occasional case of multiple simultaneous dependencies (e.g., heroin, alcohol), methadone may be used concurrently with other usual drugs to control withdrawal. For the patient who is physiologically dependent on alcohol and opioids, the clinician could combine methadone with benzodiazepines to stabilize the patient through the medical-surgical crisis. Once the crisis has passed, the methadone and the benzodiazepines can be withdrawn either sequentially or concurrently.

## Psychiatric Aspects of Methadone Treatment

The self-help movement defines the psychology of drug dependence as one of denial. Abundant observations support this view (Meyer 1986). However, in the population coming into treatment, therapists will see poles of healthy striving and of denial; that is, there is an intense ambivalence about the drug problem. Most dependent individuals are aware, both acutely and chronically, of the costs of the drug problem to themselves and to others, and they make repeated attempts to change. The therapist needs to identify the individually unique aspects of the healthy striving and support this pole of the ambivalence. Methadone appears to help by tilting the balance of the ambivalence toward the positive pole.

In addition to ambivalence, therapists will observe that drug seeking and drug taking have taken on the characteristics of a human or animal object relationship. This is reflected in the street terms for a drug habit (e.g., "I've got a Jones") or for a heroin habit (e.g., "I've got a monkey on my back"). One of the major tasks for the recovering dependent patient is to replace the drug with people.

The therapist needs to identify the recovering addicted patient's position on this dimension and work to complete the process of relating to people once again. In this regard, the therapist should recognize that the dependent patient has to mourn the loss of his or her drug object relationship and that this may take some time. In many successfully maintained patients, the therapist can observe that the subject of withdrawal is associated with phobic responses. The patient literally may not be able to think about withdrawal because of the intensity of arousal that automatically accompanies any attempt to reflect on the subject. Specific techniques are not available to treat this kind of phobia, but general techniques of behavior modification can be used.

Studies indicate that opioid-dependent populations have rates of depressive symptoms that are perhaps three times higher than that found in community-based samples (Ginzburg et al. 1984). The daily administration of methadone does not appear to improve or to worsen the depression. Patients studied appear to improve with respect to depression whether they stay in methadone treatment or drop out early (Dorus and Senay 1980). Anxiety disorders and antisocial personality disorders also appear to be more frequent in opioid-dependent populations than in the general population. Methadone has no effect on antisocial personality disorder, but if a patient who has this disorder is depressed, the depression may be treated and general functioning is improved. Some clinicians feel that methadone may have therapeutic effects on patients who have schizophrenia or bipolar affective disorder. In my experience, if such effects exist, they are quite variable from patient to patient and are not dramatic in any one patient.

McClellan (1986) studied both alcoholic and drug-addicted patients in six different treatments, including an MM clinic, and found that the patients with low psychiatric severity improved in every treatment program. Patients with high psychiatric severity showed virtually no improvement in any treatment. Patients with mid-range psychiatric severity (60% of the sample) showed outcome differences from treatment and especially from patient treatment matches. In these studies, psychiatric severity was measured by the psychiatric severity scale of the Addiction Severity Index (McLellan et al. 1980), which measures needs for treatment and services in a number of areas, including psychiatric.

## Alternatives to Methadone: Buprenorphine and L-α-Acetylmethadol

The narcotic agonist/antagonist buprenorphine is being studied for use both in withdrawal and in opioid maintenance because it may have less abuse potential, and buprenorphine withdrawal may be easier than methadone-assisted withdrawal. Buprenorphine is still an experimental drug.

L-α-Acetylmethadol (LAAM) is a long-acting conge-

ner of methadone now approved for use in legal substitution treatment (Marion 1995). In a LAAM regimen, most drug-dependent patients need to take the drug three times per week, usually on Monday, Wednesday, and Friday, with the Friday dose some 10%–15% higher than the Monday or Wednesday doses. The larger Friday dose is necessary, in most patients, to suppress withdrawal over the weekend. FDA regulations permit every-other-day dosing for the occasional patient who needs such a regimen. Results with LAAM are equal to those with methadone, although a different subset of addicted patients seems to be helped by LAAM.

### Pharmacology of LAAM

LAAM has two major metabolites, nor-LAAM and dinor-LAAM, both of which are active, as is the parent compound LAAM. Both nor-LAAM and dinor-LAAM are active for longer periods than LAAM itself, and they probably account for the long duration of withdrawal suppression achievable with this drug. The metabolites of LAAM form slowly with the consequence that onset of action is much delayed relative to methadone, and the time to reach steady state is longer for LAAM (8–20 days) than for methadone (5–8 days). Stabilization with LAAM takes longer and can be more problematic clinically.

LAAM is a congener of methadone and as such has μ agonist effects, including induction of analgesia, sedation, euphoria, constipation, pupillary constriction, and other classic morphinelike effects. Similarly, its withdrawal is associated with the classic opioid withdrawal syndrome. Some researchers believe that withdrawal from LAAM is slower but more tolerable than withdrawal from methadone. The definitive study on this point has not been carried out. The effects of LAAM have not been studied in the human fetus, and the drug is not approved for use in pregnant females.

The Monday and Wednesday doses are the same in the usual LAAM regimen, but the Friday dose is increased by 20%–40% to cover the weekend. When moving an MM patient to LAAM, the clinician multiplies the methadone dosage by 1.2 to 1.3 to arrive at the starting Monday and Wednesday dosages of LAAM, and when moving a LAAM-maintained patient to methadone, the clinician multiplies the LAAM dosage by .80. The usual starting dosage of LAAM is 20–40 mg/day with increases according to clinical need. Supplemental methadone doses, usually in the 5–20 mg/day range, may make the stabilization phase with LAAM much more tolerable. When LAAM-maintained patients miss a dose, a clinical decision has to be made according to the time elapsed since the missed dose and the patient's clinical condition. A supplemental dose of methadone may help the patient get on cycle again. The usual stabilization dosage is 60 mg of LAAM on Monday and Wednesday and 80–90 mg on Friday.

Patients with experience with both LAAM and methadone report that LAAM is "lighter" than methadone, and they prefer this effect. Others like the effects of methadone more than the effects of LAAM and will not want to go on LAAM maintenance.

Drug interactions with LAAM are similar to those of methadone. Stress increases the metabolism of LAAM, and if patients need analgesia when on LAAM maintenance they need ordinary analgesics in ordinary dosages at ordinary frequencies in addition to the LAAM. LAAM overdose requires a much longer period of monitoring than does a heroin overdose, as would be expected from its long duration of action.

## FDA Eligibility Criteria

Methadone and LAAM have the same eligibility criteria except for persons younger than 18 and females. Persons under 18 are not eligible for LAAM, whereas they may be eligible for methadone.

Females must have monthly pregnancy tests, and if positive they must be moved to methadone because there are not sufficient studies of the safety of LAAM in pregnancy. FDA regulations limit dosages for LAAM as they do for methadone, but the single state agency can be petitioned for exemptions when there is clinical need.

## Conclusion

One of the future tasks for legal opioid substitution treatment is to individualize treatment to meet the relatively unique mix of needs of different persons with opioid dependence. As the treatment-outcome prospective survey demonstrates, MM programs provide a wide range of services—legal, vocational, and social (Craddock et al. 1985), which are used and appreciated by patients, but treatment remains generic. As patients improve they sometimes need more and sometimes less support. Generic treatment is less and less appropriate for modern patients. Patterns of substance abuse are changing in the direction of abuse of multiple substances, in rotating fashion, with new intoxicants added constantly to the mix. However, opioids continue to be abused. A role for legal opioid substitution therapy seems assured because, despite its controversial status, the therapy appears to offer a unique service to a large number of addicted patients. It will be needed for the foreseeable future unless illicit opioid use is reduced dramatically.

## References

Ball JC, Corty E, Myers CP, et al: The Reduction of Intravenous Heroin Use, Non-Opiate Abuse and Crime During Methadone Maintenance Treatment: Further Findings (NIDA Res Monogr 81; DHHS Publ No ADM-88-1564). Rockville, MD, National Institute on Drug Abuse, 1988a

Ball JC, Lange WR, Myers E, et al: Reducing the risk of AIDS through methadone maintenance treatment. J Health Soc Behav 29:214–226, 1988b

Barthwell A, Senay E, Marks R, et al: Patients successfully maintained with methadone escaped human immunodeficiency virus infection (letter). Arch Gen Psychiatry 46:957, 1989

Cooper JR: Ineffective use of psychoactive drugs. JAMA 267:281–282, 1992

Craddock SG, Bray RM, Hubbard RL: Drug Use Before and During Drug Abuse Treatment: 1979–1981 Admission Cohorts (DHHS Publ No ADM-85-1387). Rockville, MD, National Institute on Drug Abuse, 1985

Dole VP: Implications of methadone maintenance for theories of narcotic addiction. JAMA 260:3025–3029, 1988

Dole VP, Nyswander ME: A medical treatment of diacetylmorphine (heroin) addiction. JAMA 193:646–650, 1965

Dorus W, Senay EC: Depression, demographics, and drug abuse. Am J Psychiatry 137:699–704, 1980

Finnegan LP: Perinatal substance abuse: comments and perspectives. Semin Perinatol 15:331–339, 1991

Finnegan LP, Kaltenbach K: Neonatal abstinence syndrome, in Primary Pediatric Care, 3rd Edition. Edited by Hoekelman RA, Friedman SB, Nelson NM, et al. St. Louis, MO, CV Mosby, 1992, pp 1367–1378

Ginzburg HM, Allison M, Hubbard RL: Depressive symptoms in drug abuse treatment clients: correlates, treatment and changes, in Problems of Drug Dependence 1983 (NIDA Res Monogr 49; DHHS Publ No ADM-84-1316). Edited by Harris LS. Washington, DC, U.S. Government Printing Office, 1984, pp 313–319

Gritz ER, Shiffman SM, Jarvik ME, et al: Physiological and psychological effects of methadone in man. Arch Gen Psychiatry 32:237–242, 1975

Hall SH, Wasserman DA, Havassy B: Relapse Prevention in Improving Drug Abuse Treatment (NIDA Res Monogr 106; DHHS Publ No ADM-91-1754). Edited by Pickens RW, Leukefeld CG, Schuster CR. Rockville, MD, Department of Health and Human Services, 1991

Hargreaves W: Methadone dosage and duration for maintenance treatment, in Research on the Treatment of Narcotic Addiction: State of the Art (DHHS Publ No ADM-83-1281). Edited by Cooper JA, Altman A, Brown B, et al. Washington, DC, U.S. Government Printing Office, 1983, pp 19–91

Kanof PD, Aronson MJ, Ness R, et al: Levels of opioid physical dependence in heroin addicts. Drug Alcohol Depend 27:253–262, 1991

Kelley D, Welch R, McKneely N, et al: Methadone maintenance; an assessment of potential fluctuations in behavior between doses. Int J Addict 13:1061–1068, 1978

Kidorf M, King V, Brooner R: Integrating psychosocial services with methadone treatment, in Treatment of Opioid Dependence and Alternative Medications. Edited by Strain E, Stitzer ML. Baltimore, MD, Johns Hopkins University Press (in press)

Kraft MK, Rothbard AB, Hadley TR: Are supplementary services provided during methadone maintenance really cost effective. Am J Psychiatry 154:1214–1219, 1997

Ling W, Weiss DG, Charuvastra VC, et al: Use of disulfiram for alcoholics in methadone maintenance programs. Arch Gen Psychiatry 40:851–854, 1983

Maddox JF, Williams TR, Ziegler DA, et al: Driving records before and during methadone maintenance. Am J Drug Alcohol Abuse 4:91–100, 1977

Marion IJ: LAAM in the Treatment of Opioid Addiction: Treatment Improvement Protocol TIP Series 22 (CSAT DHHS Publ No SMA 3052), 1995

McLellan AT: "Psychiatric severity" as a predictor of outcome from substance abuse treatments, in Psychopathology and Addictive Disorders. Edited by Meyer RE. New York, Guilford, 1986, pp 97–139

McLellan AT, Luborsky L, Woody GE, et al: An improved diagnostic evaluation instrument for substance abuse patients: the Addiction Severity Index. J Nerv Ment Dis 168:26–33, 1980

McLellan AT, Arndt IO, Metzger DS, et al: The effects of psychosocial services in substance abuse treatment. JAMA 269:1953–1959, 1993

Meyer RE (ed): Psychopathology and Addictive Disorders. New York, Guilford, 1986

Newman RG, Whitehill WB: Double-blind comparison of methadone and placebo maintenance treatments of narcotic addicts in Hong Kong. Lancet 11:485–488, 1979

Nolimal D, Crowley TJ: Difficulties in a clinical application of methadone-dose contingency contracting. J Subst Abuse Treat 7:219–224, 1990

Novick DM, Pascarelli EF, Joseph H, et al: Methadone patients in general medical practice. JAMA 259:3299–3302, 1988

Novick DM, Joseph H, Croxson TS, et al: Absence of antibody to human immunodeficiency virus in long-term, socially rehabilitated methadone maintenance patients. Arch Intern Med 150:97–99, 1990

O'Brien CP, Childress AR, McLellan AT: Conditioning factors may help to understand and prevent relapse in patients who are recovering from drug dependence, in Improving Drug Abuse Treatment (NIDA Res Monogr 106; DHHS Publ No ADM-91-1754). Edited by Pickens RW, Leukefeld CG, Schuster CR. Rockville, MD, Department of Health and Human Services, 1991, pp 293–312

O'Connor LM, Woody G, Yeh HS, et al: Methadone and edema. J Subst Abuse Treat 8:153–155, 1991

Senay EC, Shick JF: Pupillography responses to methadone challenge: aid to diagnosis of opioid dependence. Drug Alcohol Depend 3:133–138, 1978

Senay EC, Barthwell AG, Marks R, et al: Medical maintenance: an interim report. J Addict Dis 13:65–69, 1994

Stitzer ML, Kirby KC: Reducing illicit drug use among methadone patients, in Improving Drug Abuse Treatment (NIDA Res Monogr 106; DHHS Publ No ADM-91-1754). Edited by Pickens RW, Leukefeld CG, Schuster CR. Rockville, MD, Department of Health and Human Services, 1991, pp 178–203

Wang RIH, Wiesen RL, Sofian L, et al: Rating the presence and severity of opiate dependence. Clin Pharmacol Ther 16:653–658, 1974

# 25 Opioids: Antagonists and Partial Agonists

Charles P. O'Brien, M.D., Ph.D.
James W. Cornish, M.D.

Researchers have studied opioid drugs since the earliest days of pharmacology because of their importance in the treatment of pain. Over the past 25 years, this intense research produced discoveries in the endogenous opioid system that have increased knowledge about the way these drugs act. Our understanding of the biology of opioid effects including opioid dependence is well developed and probably more complete than our understanding of any other class of drugs of abuse (see O'Brien 1992). Although much remains to be learned about the chronic changes produced in opioid receptors and second messenger systems during dependence, considerable knowledge exists about the interaction between these receptors and both opiates (derivatives of the opium plant) and opioids (synthetic substances acting at opiate receptors). This knowledge has led to the classification of drugs according to their interactions with these receptors. The three basic categories are

1. *Agonists* (e.g., heroin, methadone), which activate specific opiate receptors
2. *Antagonists* (e.g., naloxone, naltrexone), which occupy opiate receptors but do not activate them; antagonists with high affinity may displace agonists in a dependent subject causing an immediate withdrawal syndrome
3. *Partial agonists* (e.g., buprenorphine), which occupy opiate receptors but activate them only in a limited way and may also block the occupation of receptors by full agonists with lesser affinity, thus producing both agonist and antagonist effects

Of all the medications used in the treatment of opioid dependence, methadone, a long-acting agonist at the μ subtype of the opioid receptor, has had the greatest impact (see Senay, Chapter 24, in this volume). Naltrexone, which became available for general use in 1985, is an antagonist and therefore offers a distinctly different treatment from methadone. Naltrexone specifically blocks opiate receptors. While this medication is present, readdiction to heroin and any other drug that acts via opiate receptors is prevented. Because it is so different from other available treatments, naltrexone is commonly misunderstood. Clinicians tend to confuse it with disulfiram (Antabuse) in the treatment of alcoholism or methadone for agonist maintenance of opioid-addicted patients. As an antagonist, naltrexone's mechanism of action is specific, and to use this tool effectively, clinicians should understand this mechanism completely.

Although pharmacologically distinctive, naltrexone does not change the fundamental requirements for good treatment of addiction. Rehabilitation requires a comprehensive treatment program with attention to the nonpharmacological variables that play a critical role in the complex problem of addiction. Thus the prescription of naltrexone alone will not work. It should be part of an overall treatment program that includes individual or group psychotherapy, family therapy, contingency contracting, and possibly behavioral extinction of drug-conditioned responses.

In considering this new treatment, it should be recognized that naltrexone will not appeal to most opioid-dependent individuals. Of all street-heroin-addicted subjects presenting for treatment, not more than 10%–15% show any interest in a drug that "keeps you from getting high" (Greenstein et al. 1984). The vast majority prefer methadone treatment, but for certain patients, naltrexone is an excellent alternative. Patients such as health care professionals, middle-class addicts, and former addicts given an early parole from prison may find naltrexone to be the treatment of choice. It may also be a form of "insurance" for patients who are graduating from a therapeutic community (see De Leon, Chapter 39, in this volume) and preparing to live in the "outside world," where heroin is readily available.

It should also be emphasized that naltrexone acts specifically only at opiate receptors. It does not block the effects of nonopioid drugs, although evidence indicates that it reduces the high from alcohol (discussed later in this chapter). Cocaine abuse in association with heroin became a common problem during the 1980s. Patients dependent on both opioids and cocaine may be treated with naltrexone, but they will need additional therapy to deal with their cocaine dependence.

## Receptor Interactions With Drugs

Opiates such as heroin and morphine and the synthetic opioids such as methadone and meperidine act through specific opiate receptors; these drugs are referred to as *agonists* (Reisine and Pasternak 1996). Antagonists such as naloxone or naltrexone also bind to these receptors, but they do not activate the receptor to initiate the chain of cellular events that produce so-called *opiate effects*. Naloxone and naltrexone are relatively pure antagonists in that they produce little or no agonist activity at usual doses. This is in contrast to mixed partial agonists, such as nalorphine or buprenorphine, which produce significant agonist effects. Not only do pure antagonists fail to produce opiate effects, but their presence at the receptor also prevents opiate agonists from binding to the receptor and producing opiate effects. Because the antagonist competes for a binding site with the agonist, the degree of blockade depends on the relative concentrations of each and their relative affinity for the receptor site. Naltrexone has high receptor affinity, and thus it can block virtually all the effects of the usual doses of opioids and opiates such as heroin. In the presence of naltrexone, there can be no opiate-induced euphoria, respiratory depression, pupillary construction, or any other opiate effect (Martin et al. 1973; O'Brien et al. 1975).

There are four categories of medical uses for opiate antagonists:

1. To reverse the effects of an opiate or opioid, particularly in the treatment of an opioid overdose. Naloxone is commonly used to reverse the effects of high-dose morphine anesthesia and to reverse opioid-induced respiratory depression in newborns whose mothers have received opioids during labor.
2. To diagnose physical dependence on opioid drugs. An antagonist such as naloxone will displace the opioid from the receptors in a dependent individual and produce an immediate withdrawal syndrome. Naloxone rather than naltrexone is typically used for this purpose because its brief duration of action will produce discomfort for only a short time. The absence of a withdrawal syndrome implies that the subject is not dependent on opioids, and thus it is safe to begin treatment with a long-acting antagonist such as naltrexone. Persons currently dependent on opioids are exquisitely sensitive to opioid antagonists. The degree of sensitivity depends on the time since the last dose of opioid and the size of the dose. Even a very small amount of naloxone or naltrexone can rapidly displace enough opioid from opiate receptors to precipitate a withdrawal syndrome. Therefore, in starting a patient on naltrexone, it is important to make certain that the opioid-dependent patient is fully detoxified prior to the initiation of antagonist treatment.
3. To prevent readdiction in an individual who has been detoxified from opioid drugs. This is the principal reason for the development of naltrexone and is discussed later in this chapter.
4. To block the effects of endogenous opioids when there is a disease state consisting of high levels of these substances (Myer et al. 1990). Blocking endogenous opioids is also the presumed mechanism of naltrexone in reducing the effects of alcohol (Benjamin et al. 1993)

## Effects of Antagonists

If a person not currently dependent on an opioid agonist receives an opioid antagonist, there are usually no obvious effects. Theoretically, something should happen because the antagonist blocks certain endogenous opioids (e.g., endorphins) that may regulate mood, pain perception, and various neuroendocrine and cardiovascular functions. Dysphoric reactions and endocrine changes have been reported in experimental subjects given naltrexone (Ellingboe et al. 1980; Mendelson et al. 1980). Spiegel et al. (1987) reported small decreases in appetite produced by naltrexone in human volunteers. Hollister et al. (1982) found adverse mood effects in normal volunteers given naltrexone. Crowley et al. (1985) noted similar effects in recently detoxified opioid-addicted subjects. These dysphoric effects of naltrexone were reported after brief treatment (1 day to 3 weeks), and the number of subjects was small. In contrast, another study of normal subjects reported no differences in mood effects between naltrexone and placebo (O'Brien et al. 1978). Moreover, most large-scale studies of recovering opioid-addicted patients have not found dysphoria or other mood changes to be a significant problem in the clinical use of naltrexone (Brahen et al. 1984; Greenstein et al. 1984; Tennant et al. 1984; Washton et al. 1984). Since 1995, larger numbers of alcoholic patients have received naltrexone, and up to 10% report dysphoric effects including nausea (O'Brien et al. 1996). A possible explanation is that the basal state of some patients includes relatively high levels of endogenous opioids whose access to receptors is blocked abruptly when naltrexone is taken. Such patients would likely comprise a significant portion of the early dropouts. Those who continue taking naltrexone for months or even years generally report no mood effects, although careful long-term studies of mood have not been conducted.

Among opiate-addicted patients, reduced drug craving has been reported in naltrexone-maintained patients (Sideroff et al. 1978), but it is not clear that this is a pharmacological effect. It may simply be a reduction in craving caused by the security that patients feel knowing that they are protected from the temptation to experience opioid effects (Meyer et al. 1975). Reduced craving for alcohol has also been reported among alcoholic patients receiving naltrexone under double-blind conditions (O'Malley et al. 1992; Volpicelli et al. 1992).

## Clinical Use of Naltrexone

### Naloxone Versus Naltrexone

Naloxone and naltrexone differ in several important ways. Naloxone is poorly absorbed from the gut; when given parenterally, it is metabolized rapidly. Naloxone, therefore, is useful only for the acute reversal of opioid effects as in the emergency treatment of opioid overdoses and in the diagnosis of physical dependence. If the presence of physical dependence is in question, a small (0.2–0.8 mg) injection of naloxone can be given. In a dependent individual, a withdrawal syndrome would occur immediately, but it would be short lived (i.e., 20–40 minutes).

In contrast to naloxone, naltrexone is well absorbed when given by mouth, and it has a long duration of action. Pharmacokinetic studies of naltrexone show a plasma half-life of the parent compound of 4 hours. An important active metabolite, 6-β-naltrexol has a plasma half-life of 12 hours. With chronic administration, both peak and trough levels of 6-β-naltrexol increase. The pharmacological duration of naltrexone is longer than might be predicted by the plasma kinetics. Double-blind studies showed antagonism of injected opioids up to 72 hours after a 150-mg dose, but the degree of antagonism was less than that seen at 24 and 48 hours (O'Brien et al. 1975). This observation is consistent with a positron-emission tomography study of naltrexone's occupation of brain μ receptors showing 80% blockade at 72 hours following a single dose (Lee et al. 1988).

Naltrexone could be used to reverse an opioid overdose, but it is more practical to use a short-acting drug such as naloxone administered by an intravenous drip that can be titrated as needed. In this way, an overdose can be reversed by a short-acting drug without the danger of giving too much antagonist and precipitating a withdrawal reaction in an opioid-dependent individual. However, a long-acting drug such as naltrexone is ideal for use in preventing relapse to opioid use. In the presence of naltrexone, heroin self-administration is no longer rewarding, and under experimental conditions, addicted individuals stop taking heroin even when it is available (Mello et al. 1981). Although daily ingestion of naltrexone would provide the most secure protection against opioid effects, naltrexone can be given as infrequently as two or three times per week, with adequate protection against readdiction to street heroin. The reduced frequency makes monitoring of the medication more practical over the long term. Tolerance does not appear to develop to the antagonism of opioid effects even after more than 1 year of regular naltrexone ingestion (Kleber et al. 1985).

### Benefits of Naltrexone

Naltrexone was approved by the U.S. Food and Drug Administration (FDA) on the basis of its clear pharmacological activity as an opioid antagonist. It has never been shown in large-scale double-blind trials to be more effective than placebo in the rehabilitation of opioid-addicted patients. In large-scale studies, the dropout rate is very high, just as it is in drug-free outpatient treatment of heroin addiction. Naltrexone is not effective when simply prescribed as a medication for street-heroin-addicted patients in the absence of a structured rehabilitation program. Within a structured program, naltrexone appears to be effective, particularly with specific motivated populations. A randomized controlled study conducted with federal probationers suggested that the impressions of efficacy can be confirmed by data collected in individuals who are at risk to return to prison (Cornish et al. 1997; Tilly et al. 1992). Naltrexone can permit recently detoxified addicted patients to return to their usual environments secure in the knowledge that they cannot succumb to an impulsive wish to get high. For many patients, this may be the first time in years that they have been able to exist outside of a hospital or prison in an opioid-free state. The subtle manifestations of the opioid withdrawal syndrome are known to persist for months (Martin and Jasinski 1969). During this protracted withdrawal syndrome, the patient's autonomic nervous system is unstable, and symptoms such as anxiety and sleep disturbances are common. Conditioned responses to environmental cues produced by previous drug use (O'Brien et al. 1986; Wikler 1965) also may contribute to relapse. Maintenance on naltrexone provides an ideal situation to extinguish these conditioned responses (O'Brien et al. 1980, 1984, 1992) and permit the protracted withdrawal syndrome to subside.

For someone recovering from addiction who works in a field such as nursing, pharmacy, or medicine, there is an added benefit to naltrexone maintenance: it reduces the concerns about relapse felt by colleagues who are aware of the person's history. Because these medical occupations often require individuals to work with opioid drugs, there is a daily temptation to resume drug use. Of course, return to work is very important to rehabilitation, but it presents problems in a medical setting. Colleagues tend to regard any hint of unusual behavior as a sign that relapse to addiction has occurred. However, with a program of verified naltrexone ingestion as part of a comprehensive treatment program, the professional can return to work. Physicians who are recovering from addiction often cite this reduction of suspicion from colleagues as an important reason to continue naltrexone, some for 5 years or more. Of course, the opioid-free period also permits the use of psychotherapy to deal with underlying or superimposed psychosocial problems.

## Comparison With Other Treatment Approaches

As with other treatments for addiction, naltrexone works best within a comprehensive program that deals with all aspects of the patient's problems (Resnick et al. 1979). Naltrexone is similar to methadone in this sense: both medications can reduce relapse to illicit drug use. There are significant differences, however. Methadone is an excellent treatment for most street heroin users because it satisfies their drug craving. Methadone also enables them to stop committing crimes because they no longer have an expensive drug habit to support. Former heroin users can thus stabilize their lives, take care of their families, and find legal employment. Methadone does not "block" heroin's effects, however. There is cross-tolerance between heroin and methadone, and because street heroin is relatively weak, the patient maintained on an adequate dosage of methadone will get little reward from the usual dosage of heroin. In addition to satisfying opioid craving, methadone may produce beneficial psychoactive effects.

In contrast to methadone, naltrexone cannot be given until all opioids have been metabolized and cleared from the body. Naltrexone does not produce opioid effects or any psychoactive benefits; patients are therefore without the feeling of opioids in their bodies. During the 24–72 hours of naltrexone's effects, it will effectively block the actions of any opioid drug; thus, if the patient decides to resume heroin use, he or she cannot experience euphoria or calming from the use of heroin as in the past.

Another important distinction between methadone and naltrexone is the absence of dependence on naltrexone. Naltrexone can be stopped abruptly at any time without concern for withdrawal symptoms. In a sense, this lack of physical dependence is a drawback to naltrexone in clinical practice because the patient perceives no direct drug effect as is the case with methadone. Thus, there is no built-in reward, and there is no immediate penalty for stopping. In an effort to provide an external reward, some clinicians have experimented with small monetary payments contingent on the patient ingesting naltrexone (Grabowski et al. 1979). Frequently, patients feel so good and overconfident at being opioid free that they may prematurely assume they no longer need naltrexone. They can stop naltrexone abruptly, but several days later they are again at risk for relapse to opioid use.

Another treatment strategy that is often confused with naltrexone is disulfiram. The medications are similar only in that both are taken to prevent relapse and both are nonaddicting. Disulfiram blocks the metabolism of alcohol, not its effects. If a person receiving disulfiram ingests alcohol, the normal degradation of alcohol is inhibited and acetaldehyde accumulates. Acetaldehyde produces flushing, nausea, and other noxious symptoms. These effects, of course, can be prevented by avoiding alcohol while taking disulfiram. In contrast, no such noxious effects result from the use of opioids in association with naltrexone treatment. The opioid effects are simply blocked or neutralized in an individual receiving naltrexone treatment.

## Target Populations

Health care professionals.   Health care professionals have generally done well in naltrexone treatment programs. For example, Ling and Wesson (1984) reported the use of naltrexone in the management of 60 health care professionals for an average of 8 months. Forty-seven were rated as "much improved" or "moderately improved" at follow-up. Washton et al. (1984) found that 74% of opioid-dependent physicians completed at least 6 months of treatment with naltrexone and were opioid free and practicing medicine at 1-year follow-up. These studies involved comprehensive treatment programs, with naltrexone providing a kind of structure around which psychotherapy was built.

The comprehensive treatment program should involve a full medical evaluation, detoxification, psychiatric evaluation, family evaluation, and provision for ongoing therapy along with confirmed regular ingestion of naltrexone. Ongoing therapy usually involves marital and individual therapy. By use of this approach, the physician, whose drug use may have been discovered during a crisis, can be detoxified, started on naltrexone, and back at work practicing medicine in as little as 2 weeks. Of course, therapy including naltrexone may continue for several years, but the disruption of family life and medical practice is minimized by avoiding a prolonged inpatient stay.

Employed individuals.   Studies of psychotherapy outcome consistently show that patients coming into treatment with the greatest psychosocial assets tend to respond best to treatment. Thus, it is not surprising that patients with a history of recent employment and good educational backgrounds do well on naltrexone. Some patients avoid methadone because of the required daily clinic visits, especially at the beginning of treatment. Because naltrexone is not a controlled substance,

greater flexibility is permitted. Although these patients may be strongly motivated to be drug free, they remain susceptible to impulsive drug use. Using naltrexone as a kind of insurance is often a very appealing idea.

Another practical reason that naltrexone has been successful in this population is that it can be prescribed by any licensed physician. Naltrexone use is not restricted to a special program for the treatment of addiction. Middle-class patients may object to coming to such a clinic. It is recommended, however, that naltrexone be prescribed only by physicians who are familiar with the psychodynamics and behavior patterns of the addicted individual. Patients may appreciate the opportunity for treatment by an experienced practitioner from a private office rather than being restricted to a drug treatment clinic.

Tennant et al. (1984) described a group of suburban practitioners treating opioid dependence in a wide range of socioeconomic groups in southern California. They reported on 160 addicted patients with an average history of opioid use of 10.5 years. The majority (63.8%) were employed, and all expressed a desire for abstinence-oriented treatment. Treatment was on an outpatient basis, and a naloxone challenge was given after completion of detoxification. After a graduated dosage increase, naltrexone was given three times per week. Patients paid a fee or had the treatment covered by insurance. Each week the patients were subjected to a urine screen for all drug classes and an alcohol breath test. Counseling sessions were held weekly.

The 160 patients remained in treatment a mean of 51 days with a range up to 635 days, but the majority were in short-term treatment. Only 27 (17%) remained longer than 90 days. Tests for illicit drug or alcohol use were only 1%–3% positive during treatment. Tennant et al. (1984) considered the program, which is still in operation, to be successful. However, it must be remembered that despite long remissions on naltrexone, relapse to opioid use can still occur after naltrexone is stopped. Based on follow-up results of naltrexone patients, Greenstein et al. (1983) found that although treatment with naltrexone tends to be short term, even as little as 30 days of treatment is associated with a significant improvement in overall rehabilitative status at 6-month follow-up.

A study of patients in a higher socioeconomic group predictably found even better results. Washton et al. (1984) reported on the treatment with naltrexone in 114 businessmen dependent for at least 2 years on heroin, methadone, or prescription opioids. They were mainly white men of about age 30 years, with a mean income of $42,000 per year in 1983 dollars. A critical feature of this group was that there was considerable external pressure for them to receive treatment, and almost half were in jeopardy of losing their jobs or suffering legal consequences.

The Washton et al. (1984) treatment program was oriented toward complete abstinence. It began with 4–10 weeks of inpatient treatment, during which detoxification and induction onto naltrexone was accomplished. Intensive individual psychotherapy and involvement in self-help groups was part of the program. The importance of the posthospital phase was stressed, and all patients signed a contract for aftercare treatment.

Of the 114 patients who began the program, all completed naltrexone induction; 61% remained on the medication for at least 6 months with no missed visits or positive urine tests. An additional 20% took naltrexone for less than 6 months but remained in the program with drug-free urine tests. Of the entire group, at 12- to 18-month follow-up, 64% were still opioid free. Those patients who had stipulated pressure from their employers to get treatment did significantly better than the group without a clear-cut risk of job loss.

Probationers in a work-release program.    It is a well-known fact that a large proportion of prison inmates throughout the country have been convicted of drug-related crimes. Of course, relapse to drug use and consequent crime is common among these prisoners after they are released. One way to approach this recidivism and perhaps also alleviate some of the overcrowding of our prison system is to use a work-release or halfway house program that enables prisoners to obtain an early release with the stipulation that they work in the community and live in a prison-supervised house. Naltrexone can be prescribed for those prisoners who are addicted to heroin. A pioneering model of such a program has been in existence in Nassau County, New York, since 1972.

Dr. Leonard Brahen, the founder and director of this program, has reported on the results of 691 former inmates whom he treated with naltrexone (Brahen et al. 1984). The treatment is set within a work-release program during which the members live in a transitional house outside the prison and obtain employment in the community. Prior to the introduction of naltrexone, the success of former opioid-addicted patients in the program was limited because of their high relapse rate when placed in an environment where drugs were freely available.

An inmate with a history of opioid addiction who wishes to volunteer for the program must first be stabilized on naltrexone. Random urine tests are also used to monitor the participants. Uncashed paychecks must be turned in as proof that attendance at work has been regular; a portion of the salary is applied to the cost of room and board. The participants are given supervision and counseling for problems that develop during this reentry period. Some try to use street heroin to get high despite the naltrexone, but because the heroin effects are blocked, they eventually abandon this behavior. Participants are also offered continued treatment after their sentences have been served.

Since the introduction of naltrexone, the rehabilitation success rate of the formerly addicted inmates is equal to that of inmates without a drug history. Although a controlled study with random assignment to naltrexone was not conducted, the staff of the work-release program were enthusiastic about the benefits of naltrexone. Follow-up data suggested that even after completing their terms and leaving the program, the individuals who received naltrexone had fewer drug arrests than did inmates with a history of opioid abuse who did not receive naltrexone treatment.

More recently, Cornish and colleagues (Cornish et al. 1997; Tilly et al. 1992) conducted a random assignment study among federal probationers convicted of drug-related crimes in Philadelphia, Pennsylvania. The probationers all received the same amount of parole counseling, but half were randomly selected to receive naltrexone. At follow-up 6 months after leaving prison, the group randomly selected for naltrexone had approximately half the reincarceration rate of the control group.

Heroin-addicted patients.    Although naltrexone can be used in the treatment of any opioid dependency, it appeals most to those patients who are strongly motivated to become drug free. Methadone, by contrast, requires much less motivation because treatment involves only a relatively small gradual shift from the state of daily heroin use to daily use of another opioid agonist, methadone. Naltrexone, in contrast, requires a much bigger change; the individual must genuinely wish to remain free of opioid effects. Unfortunately, most patients who assert strongly that they want to give up drugs have not really thought through the consequences of their assertions. Once they find themselves taking a medication that makes it physically impossible for them to get high on heroin, they often change their minds.

Most street-heroin-addicted individuals and participants in methadone-maintenance programs are generally not interested in naltrexone treatment after learning how effectively it antagonizes opioids. Studies of the use of naltrexone in public drug treatment clinics have found that no more than 10%–15% of patients are willing to try naltrexone, and most of these patients drop out during the first month of naltrexone treatment (Greenstein et al. 1983; Hollister 1978; Judson and Goldstein 1984; O'Brien et al. 1975).

Among street heroin users involved in crime to support their drug habit, it is difficult to predict who will respond well to treatment with naltrexone. Certainly the proportion of former heroin-using individuals currently being treated with naltrexone is low. One possible reason for this is that publicly funded treatment programs may be discouraged by the cost of naltrexone (currently about $5 per tablet). Of course, the main cost of the treatment is the counseling required to support patients after detoxification. Most programs that use naltrexone have focused on patients who are employed or who have good employment prospects, have a stable relationship with spouse or family, and express willingness to enter long-term psychotherapy or family therapy. As stated earlier in this chapter, even short-term (30 days or more) treatment with naltrexone has been associated with improved outcome at 6-month follow-up (Greenstein et al. 1983). Patients willing to continue taking the antagonist for 6–12 months generally do well, but it is difficult to know to what degree the success is influenced by the patient's strong motivation as evidenced by his or her remaining in treatment. A good outcome probably involves interaction of several factors, and any single factor might not have been adequate by itself.

## How to Use Naltrexone in a Comprehensive Treatment Program

### Detoxification

An abstinence-oriented program begins with detoxification. This process facilitates the performance of a complete medical evaluation and the determination of any additional health problems that may be present. Detoxification, which should be accomplished on an inpatient basis if possible, also allows for family and individual psychological evaluations.

Several pharmacological options are available for detoxification. Gradually reducing doses of methadone

for 5–10 days constitutes one approach. At the other end of the spectrum, a rapid clonidine-aided detoxification can ready the patient for naltrexone in as little as 48 hours after being opioid dependent (Kleber and Kosten 1984). The choice depends on the type of opioid agonist the patient was using (short acting versus long acting), the patient's motivation, and the need for speed in returning the patient to work. Ultrarapid detoxification under general anesthesia has been proposed as a means of starting naltrexone, but no published data show that this technique leads to a greater proportion of patients successfully stabilized on naltrexone. (See Kleber, Chapter 23, in this volume, for a discussion of the different types of detoxification techniques.)

### Naloxone Testing for Residual Dependence

Various methods are available for beginning treatment with naltrexone (Kleber and Kosten 1984). In all cases, there should be no residual physical dependence on opioid agonists. If the patient has been using a long-acting opioid such as methadone, it may be necessary to wait 7–10 days after the last dose before initiating treatment with naltrexone. With dependence on short-acting drugs such as heroin or hydromorphone, the time between detoxification and starting naltrexone can be much shorter. If naltrexone is started too soon, precipitated withdrawal will occur. Even mild withdrawal, consisting of only abdominal cramps or periods of nausea, may be enough to discourage the patient from further treatment. In contrast, the eagerness of some patients to be protected by naltrexone and to return to work results in their willingness to tolerate mild withdrawal symptoms.

Most clinicians who work with naltrexone have found it helpful to administer a naloxone test to determine whether the patient has any residual physical dependence before he or she is given the first dose of naltrexone. A positive test indicating physical dependence consists of symptoms of opioid withdrawal, such as perspiration, nausea, or cramps, that last for 20–40 minutes. A positive test indicates that the patient should wait at least another day before starting naltrexone. Naloxone can be given parenterally, 0.2–0.8 mg subcutaneously or intramuscularly. It can also be used intravenously if very rapid results are desired.

Some clinicians prefer to test for residual opioid dependence by using a very small oral dose of naltrexone rather than a naloxone injection. They recommend a half or a quarter of a tablet (12.5–25 mg) as a safe dosage (Greenstein et al. 1984). Certainly this approach is safe, but if even a mild withdrawal syndrome is precipitated, it will be of long duration (at least several hours and perhaps more than a day) and will possibly discourage the patient from further naltrexone treatment.

Generally, it is better to wait a longer time between the end of detoxification and the beginning of naltrexone rather than risk evoking a precipitated withdrawal reaction. This period is critical, however, because the patient is vulnerable to relapse, as yet unprotected by naltrexone. Therefore, the clinician must exercise judgment in balancing the benefits of a rapid transition to naltrexone against the risks of discouraging the patient with a recurrence of physical withdrawal symptoms. The rapid detoxification technique of using clonidine to treat withdrawal symptoms was developed because of this problem, but well-motivated patients are required for best results.

## Naltrexone to Prevent Relapse

When the naloxone challenge is negative, naltrexone can be started with an initial dose of 25 mg (one-half tablet). If no side effects occur within an hour, another 25 mg may be administered. The recommended dose subsequently is 50 mg/day. After the first 1–2 weeks, it is usually possible to graduate the patient to three doses per week (e.g., 100, 100, and 150 mg given on Monday, Wednesday, and Friday, respectively). It is critical that psychotherapy sessions be initiated early in treatment and that these sessions involve family members and other significant figures in the patient's life.

Naltrexone ingestion should be monitored. Confirmed dosing can occur in the clinic, but it is usually disruptive to the patient's rehabilitation to be required to come to the clinic for every dose. For this reason it is important to involve significant figures in the patient's life to observe the ingestion of naltrexone and to report periodically to the therapist. In the case of physicians, for example, a colleague may have already confronted the patient with his or her drug problem and helped steer the patient into therapy. This has sometimes been the chief of staff of the hospital where the patient works or the chairperson of the patient's department. A family member or coworker can also be enlisted after determining the existence of a constructive relationship.

Progress in treatment is determined by engagement in psychotherapy, performance on the job, and absence of drug abuse as confirmed by urine tests. The patient should be asked to agree to random urine tests arranged by telephoning the patient and asking him or her to

come in that day without prior notification. Patients who are doing well can eventually graduate to a schedule of only two doses of naltrexone per week, even though this would not provide full antagonist coverage over the entire interval between doses. However, the reduced frequency of visits reduces the patient's dependence on the therapist and decreases the treatment's interference with the patient's life. Although the degree of pharmacological blockade is reduced by the third or fourth day after receiving the drug, at this stage of therapy the patient is less likely to be testing limits by taking opioids. Moreover, the random urine testing should detect opioid use between naltrexone doses, which would necessitate a return to more frequent dosing. A slip should not be treated as a treatment failure but rather as a symptom to be examined in therapy (i.e., grist for the therapeutic mill).

In private practice, patients are often given a prescription for naltrexone that can be filled at a pharmacy. Patients can eventually be trusted to take doses of naltrexone at home, but it is best that some doses be taken in the physician's office under direct observation. If a patient is pretending to take naltrexone and is using opioids, a dose in the office would precipitate a withdrawal reaction. Also, the treating physician should keep a supply of naltrexone tablets in his or her office to administer to patients. Physician and pharmacist patients have been known to attempt to deactivate naltrexone tablets by treating them in a microwave oven. They could then appear to consume naltrexone in the presence of the treating physician or nurse, but they would be taking a relatively inert tablet.

## Side Effects

Considering that naltrexone is a very specific and potent drug that acts on opioid receptors throughout the body, it is surprising that it has so few side effects. Most patients report no symptoms at all; however, when the drug was first introduced in clinical trials, a variety of effects were reported. These effects included abdominal pain, headache, and mild increases in blood pressure. Many of these symptoms were probably related to precipitation of opioid withdrawal symptoms in recently detoxified heroin-addicted individuals. Because of the recognition of naltrexone's potency in producing withdrawal, these complaints have now become much less common.

Because naltrexone blocks endogenous opioid peptides in addition to injected opioid drugs, one would expect to find multiple symptoms related to blockage of the wide-ranging functions of the endorphin systems. Endocrine changes have been reported following naltrexone ingestion, although these changes are less dramatic than those produced by opioids themselves. For example, Ellingboe et al. (1980) reported a prompt rise in luteinizing hormone and a delayed rise in testosterone after naltrexone ingestion. The subjective effects probably depend on the baseline level of endogenous opioids. In babies with apparent excess endogenous opioids, naltrexone can be life saving (Myer et al. 1990).

Most former opioid-dependent patients do not report subjective effects that can be related to naltrexone. Of course, these patients have just discontinued heroin or a similar opioid that has altered for the past several years the normal patterns of endocrine function, libido, mood, and pain thresholds. They could be expected to experience some rebound phenomena simply because of the absence of heroin, to which they had been adapted. Some patients and their spouses report that the use of naltrexone increased the patient's sex drive, a finding that has also been observed in rodents. Some patients report decreased appetite, whereas others gain weight. Thus, the effects of naltrexone are probably confounded with those of protracted opioid withdrawal, and they are further influenced by the contrast with the patient's prior life on varying doses of opioids. Consistent subjective effects have been lacking even in patients who have been maintained on naltrexone for several years. Certainly the fear that long-term blocking of opioid receptors will inevitably lead to problems such as depression has not been realized.

## Effects on Opioid Receptors

Rodent studies have shown that repeated doses of naloxone or naltrexone produce upregulation of $\mu$ opioid receptors (Yoburn et al. 1985) and a transient increased sensitivity to morphine. If this phenomenon were present in humans treated with naltrexone, former opioid-addicted individuals would be at risk for overdose should they stop naltrexone, wait for the drug to be metabolized, and inject their usual dose of heroin. This question was addressed in an experiment by Cornish et al. (1993) that used nonaddicted volunteers. A dose of morphine depressed the brain stem and reduced the respiratory response to a $CO_2$ stimulus. The degree of depression was measured, and after 2 weeks of naltrexone at 50 mg/day, the subjects were retested. No change in morphine's effects were found at varying times after the last dose of naltrexone, indicating lack

of detectable change in receptor sensitivity. Thus, the theoretical risk of overdose based on upregulation of opioid receptors does not seem to present a clinical problem for the use of naltrexone in preventing relapse to opioid dependence.

## Effects on Blood Chemistry

Changes in laboratory tests have also been examined in more than 2,000 patients involved in clinical trials with naltrexone (Hollister 1978; Pfohl et al. 1986). Although addicted individuals are generally unhealthy to begin with, studies in addiction treatment programs have not turned up significant laboratory abnormalities resulting from naltrexone treatment (Brahen et al. 1988). Liver function tests are a matter of great concern because of the high frequency of hepatitis among addicted individuals. As many as 70%–80% of patients in methadone programs have some liver abnormalities, usually ascribed to past or present hepatitis.

Studies of patients given high-dose naltrexone for experimental treatment of conditions such as obesity have noted dose-related increments in transaminase levels that were all reversible when the drug was stopped. These subjects generally received 300 mg/day of naltrexone, or about six times the therapeutic dose for prevention of addiction relapse (Pfohl et al. 1986). This finding raises cautions in the treatment of addiction, although in practice, naltrexone-related transaminase elevations have not been observed at the lower dose levels used in recovering addicted patients (Arndt et al. 1986). Three recent naltrexone studies in different clinical patients were conducted to investigate the hepatic effects of the medication. Naltrexone, 50–300 mg/day, was used for periods between 10 and 36 months to treat dyskinesia in 10 patients with Huntington's disease and had no hepatic effects (Sax et al. 1994). Marrazzi and colleagues (1997) reported no adverse clinical or laboratory hepatic changes for subjects in a double-blind study of high-dose naltrexone, 200–400 mg/day, for the treatment of eating disorders. Naltrexone was also studied in 865 alcoholic patients; 570 patients received naltrexone, and 295 were in a reference group (Croop et al. 1997). The results from this large trial failed to show any hepatic toxicity related to naltrexone.

Opioid-addicted individuals in liver failure should not be given naltrexone, although those with minor abnormalities in liver function tests may receive naltrexone. Baseline laboratory tests must include a full battery of liver function studies, and monthly retesting should occur for the first 3 months. Assays for serum transaminases (e.g., serum glutamate transaminase [aspartate aminotransferase], serum glutamate pyruvate transaminase [alanine aminotransferase]) and serum γ-glutamyltransferase (GGT), total bilirubin, and uric acid are routinely used to assess damage to the liver from disease and heavy drinking. Caution should be exercised in using naltrexone with patients whose serum chemistry results are five times above normal. Because total bilirubin appears to be the most sensitive of these measures of naltrexone-induced hepatic toxicity, it can be used to evaluate and monitor the development of liver problems. This is particularly important in the use of naltrexone for alcoholic patients in whom alcohol-induced liver damage is frequent and treatment with naltrexone can spare the liver if it helps to reduce or eliminate drinking. In most cases, if no evidence of rising enzymes exists, the tests can be repeated at intervals of 2–6 months.

## Safety in Women and Children

Another set of issues regarding the safety of any new drug concerns its use in pregnant women and in children. There have been no clinical trials in these groups; thus, no definitive statements can be made. Studies of naltrexone in animals generally have not shown signs of potential risks for pregnant subjects at clinical doses (Christian 1984), but a teratogenic effect specific to humans is always possible.

## Drug Interactions

There have been no systematic studies of nonopioid drug interactions with naltrexone, but with more than 20 years of clinical trials and 15 years of postmarketing experience, much anecdotal information is available. Naltrexone has been used safely in combination with disulfiram, lithium, and tricyclic antidepressants; if these agents are indicated, they apparently can be used in their normal way at their usual doses.

An adverse interaction has been reported between thioridazine and naltrexone. Maany et al. (1987) reported that sedation occurred when naltrexone was added to the regimens of two patients stabilized on thioridazine. No thioridazine plasma levels were available, but a likely explanation is that naltrexone impaired the degradation of thioridazine, resulting in increased plasma levels and increased sedation. If a neuroleptic is required in combination with naltrexone, a nonsedating neuroleptic would be preferable.

## Treatment of Pain During Naltrexone Maintenance

Patients are expected to continue taking naltrexone for months or years to prevent relapse to opioid abuse. During this time, they may require surgery or treatment of trauma caused by an accident. The presence of naltrexone would not interfere with inhalation anesthesia, but the use of morphine during anesthesia would be affected. Also, opioids for immediate postoperative pain would be precluded in usual doses. If the surgery is elective, the naltrexone could be stopped several days before the date of the operation. For emergency surgery, nonopioid anesthesia and postoperative pain medication can be used. If opioid medication is necessary, high doses of a short-acting opioid could be used to override the competitive antagonism produced by naltrexone. As naltrexone and its active metabolites are metabolized, the problem would be resolved. In practice, this issue is rarely a problem because nonopioid alternatives can be used for these patients.

## New Therapeutic Prospects

### Depot Naltrexone

A major impediment to the more widespread use of naltrexone is the early dropout rate. Often patients express an apparently genuine desire for opioid-free treatment, but during the extremely vulnerable period within the first month after detoxification, they miss an appointment, act on an impulse, and take a dose of heroin. Stopping naltrexone does not produce withdrawal symptoms. Other patients simply become overconfident and feel that they do not need the protection of naltrexone. Even though the patient may later regret the sudden decision to stop naltrexone, the treatment process must start all over again with detoxification.

A delivery system for naltrexone that provides adequate antagonist protection for 30–60 days would take the patient through the period when relapse is most likely. Preclinical studies have been conducted using micronized spheres of naltrexone embedded in lactide polyglycolide, a substance that gradually dissolves, releasing the medication over time. Preliminary clinical testing of a subcutaneous injection of this form of naltrexone suggests that it is not irritating to the skin and that it provides a gradual release of naltrexone for up to 30 days (Kranzler et al. 1998). Much more testing is necessary, but this delivery system holds promise for increasing the efficacy of naltrexone in the rehabilitation of opioid-addicted patients.

## Buprenorphine: Qualities of Methadone and Naltrexone

Buprenorphine is a partial $\mu$ opioid agonist that is currently approved by the FDA in an injectable form to treat pain. As an agonist, it is 25–50 times more potent than morphine, but because it is a partial agonist, its opioid effects are limited. Unlike agonists such as morphine and methadone, higher dosages of buprenorphine do not produce progressively greater opioid effects, thus buprenorphine is less likely to produce an overdose.

In clinical trials, buprenorphine shows some of the features of methadone and naltrexone. The agonist properties of buprenorphine cause it to be attractive as a maintenance treatment for a large proportion of opioid-addicted patients. It blocks opioid withdrawal and satisfies craving for opioids. If buprenorphine is discontinued abruptly, the withdrawal syndrome is very mild. Heroin, in contrast, has an intense but short-lived withdrawal syndrome depending on the dose. The methadone withdrawal syndrome is milder than that of heroin but significantly longer in duration. In addition to these opioid agonist effects, buprenorphine antagonizes the effects of other opioids in a manner comparable to naltrexone. Buprenorphine has certain drawbacks. It is only one-fifteenth as potent by oral administration compared with subcutaneous injection (Jasinski et al. 1989). By sublingual administration, it is two-thirds as potent, and this is the delivery system used in clinical trials for addiction. Buprenorphine has been found to block craving for approximately 24 hours, but this means that patients are required to come to the clinic daily and hold the medication in their mouths without swallowing for at least 3 minutes. In busy treatment programs, this type of administration can be complicated.

Based on clinical trials to date (Bickel et al. 1988; Johnson et al. 1992), buprenorphine appears to be useful in the treatment of heroin addiction. Because of the benefits of making it available for prescription outside of methadone treatment programs, it is important to reduce the risk of abuse of this medication. It is currently being studied in a combination with naloxone that would block the $\mu$ effects of buprenorphine if injected, but because of the poor oral bioavailability of naloxone, it would not impair the sublingual administration of buprenorphine.

## Naltrexone in the Treatment of Alcoholism

We discuss here a recently approved use for naltrexone in the treatment of alcoholism because the mechanism is believed to involve the endogenous opioid system. Numerous animal studies show that alcohol drinking produces changes in the endogenous opioid system. Opioids have been reported to increase alcohol consumption in rodents (Hubbell et al. 1987; Reid and Hunter 1984), and opioid antagonists block or antagonize preference for alcohol (DeWitte 1984; Hubbell et al. 1986; Samson and Doyle 1985; Volpicelli et al. 1986). The mechanism of these effects is not clear, but blocking opioid receptors consistently tends to decrease the ingestion of alcohol by animals previously choosing to drink this substance. Alcohol increases dopamine levels in the nucleus accumbens, a structure involved in brain reward pathways. This effect of alcohol is blocked by naltrexone.

Although the effects of alcohol consumption on endogenous opioids appear to be quite complex and incompletely understood, experiments with naltrexone in alcoholic humans suggest a practical clinical application from this line of animal research. Volpicelli and colleagues (1990, 1992) found significant reductions in relapse to alcohol dependence in alcoholic outpatients treated with naltrexone after detoxification. The study was conducted under double-blind, placebo-controlled conditions, and all patients received intensive outpatient rehabilitation counseling in addition to the study medication. Naltrexone-treated patients had about as many small slips to alcohol use as the patients randomly assigned to placebo. However, significantly fewer of the naltrexone patients continued to drink and to relapse to alcohol dependence during the 3-month trial. Those who did drink alcohol while receiving naltrexone reported less pleasure than expected, an effect predicted by the animal research. One interpretation of these results is that alcohol activates endogenous opioids, which form part of the reinforcement of continued alcohol drinking. Because naltrexone blocks opioid receptors, the reinforcement via the opioid system would be attenuated, and the probability of continued alcohol drinking would be reduced. O'Malley and colleagues (1991, 1992) essentially replicated these results. Subsequent controlled trials (Anton, in press; Volpicelli et al. 1997) also reported positive results when naltrexone was added to alcohol treatment programs. Mason (1994) reported similar results with alcoholic patients using another opiate receptor antagonist, nalmefene. Our understanding of the mechanism is increasing because of laboratory research such as that of King et al. (1997) showing that naltrexone reduces the alcohol high in heavy drinkers who have a family history of alcoholism. As in the treatment of opioid dependence, medication alone would not be sufficient; rather, naltrexone requires a comprehensive treatment program including psychotherapy and attention to all facets of the alcohol dependence syndrome. Unfortunately, there remains a good deal of resistance to using a medication in the treatment of alcoholism; thus, naltrexone use is increasing slowly as word of its efficacy spreads among practitioners.

## Conclusion

Naltrexone is a specific opioid antagonist that has a relatively long duration of action such that it can be used in the prevention of relapse to opioid dependence. Naltrexone is safe and relatively nontoxic. The antagonist treatment option is important to make available to well-motivated opiate-addicted individuals who desire to become drug free. As with all medications in the treatment of addiction, naltrexone must be used within a comprehensive treatment program, including individual or family psychotherapy and urine testing for illicit drugs. Treatment should continue for at least 3 months after detoxification and in many cases longer because a significant risk of relapse continues for several years.

The National Institute on Drug Abuse is conducting an active program in medications development that will add several options for the treatment of opioid dependence in the next several years. The partial agonist buprenorphine combines features of methadone and naltrexone and will probably become available in several years. A depot form of naltrexone that gives protection against relapse for at least 30 days is under study. Controlled clinical trials in alcoholic patients show that naltrexone can reduce the frequency of relapse in patients engaged in an outpatient alcohol rehabilitation program.

## References

Anton R: Naltrexone and cognitive behavioral therapy in the treatment of alcoholics. Am J Psychiatry (in press)

Arndt IO, Cacciola JS, McLellan AT, et al: A re-evaluation of naltrexone toxicity in recovering opiate addicts, in Problems of Drug Dependence 1985 (NIDA Res Monogr 67; Publ No ADM-86-1448). Edited by Harris LS. Rockville, MD, U.S. Department of Health and Human Services, 1986, p 525

Benjamin D, Grant EF, Pohorecky LA: Naltrexone reverses ethanol-induced dopamine release in the nucleus accumbens in awake, freely moving rats. Brain Res 621:137–140, 1993

Bickel WK, Stitzer ML, Bigelow GE, et al: A clinical trial of buprenorphine: comparison with methadone in the detoxification of heroin addicts. Clin Pharmacol Ther 43:72–78, 1988

Brahen LS, Henderson RK, Copone T, et al: Naltrexone treatment in a jail work-release program. J Clin Psychiatry 45:49–52, 1984

Brahen L, Capone TJ, Capone DM: Naltrexone: lack of effect on hepatic enzymes. J Clin Pharmacol 28:64–70, 1988

Christian MA: Reproductive toxicity and teratology evaluation of naltrexone. J Clin Psychiatry 45:7–10, 1984

Cornish JW, Henson D, Levine S, et al: Naltrexone maintenance: effect on morphine sensitivity in normal volunteers. Am J Addict 2:34–38, 1993

Cornish JW, Metzger D, Woody GE, et al: Naltrexone pharmacotherapy for opioid dependent federal probationers. J Subst Abuse Treat 14:529–534, 1997

Croop RS, Faulkner EB, Labriola DF: The safety profile of naltrexone in the treatment of alcoholism: results from a multicenter usage study. The Naltrexone Usage Study Group. Arch Gen Psychiatry 54:1130–1135, 1997

Crowley T, Wagner J, Zerbe G, et al: Naltrexone-induced dysphoria in former opioid addicts. Am J Psychiatry 142:1081–1084, 1985

DeWitte P: Naloxone reduces alcohol intake in a free-choice procedure even when both drinking bottles contain saccharin sodium or quinine substances. Neuropsychobiology 12:73–77, 1984

Ellingboe J, Mendelson JH, Kuehnle JC: Effects of heroin and naltrexone on plasma prolactin levels in man. Pharmacol Biochem Behav 12:163–165, 1980

Grabowski J, O'Brien CP, Greenstein RA: Effects of contingent payment on compliance with a naltrexone regimen. Am J Drug Alcohol Abuse 6:355–365, 1979

Greenstein RA, Evans BD, McLellan AT, et al: Predictors of favorable outcome following naltrexone treatment. Drug Alcohol Depend 12:173–180, 1983

Greenstein RA, Arndt IC, McLellan AT, et al: Naltrexone: a clinical perspective. J Clin Psychiatry 45:25–28, 1984

Hollister L: Report of the national research council committee on clinical evaluation of narcotic antagonists: clinical evaluation of naltrexone treatment of dependent individuals. Arch Gen Psychiatry 33:335–340, 1978

Hollister L, Johnson K, Boukhabza D, et al: Aversive effects of naltrexone in subjects not dependent on opiates. Drug Alcohol Depend 8:37–42, 1982

Hubbell CL, Czirr SA, Hunter GA, et al: Consumption of ethanol solution is potentiated by morphine and attenuated by naloxone persistently across repeated daily administrations. Alcohol 3:39–54, 1986

Hubbell CL, Czirr SA, Reid LD: Persistence and specificity of small doses of morphine on intake of alcoholic beverages. Alcohol 4:149–156, 1987

Jasinski DR, Fudala PJ, Johnson RE: Sublingual versus subcutaneous buprenorphine in opiate abusers. Clin Pharmacol Ther 45:513–519, 1989

Johnson RE, Jaffe JH, Fudala PJ: A controlled trial of buprenorphine treatment for opioid dependence. JAMA 267:2750–2755, 1992

Judson BA, Goldstein A: Naltrexone treatment of heroin addiction: one year follow-up. Drug Alcohol Depend 13: 357–365, 1984

King AC, Volpicelli JR, Frazer A, et al: Effect of naltrexone on subjective alcohol response in subjects at high and low risk for future alcohol dependence. Psychopharmacology 129:15–22, 1997

Kleber HD, Kosten TR: Naltrexone induction: psychologic and pharmacologic strategies. J Clin Psychiatry 45:29–38, 1984

Kleber HD, Kosten TR, Gaspari J, et al: Nontolerance to the opioid antagonism of naltrexone. Biol Psychiatry 2:66–72, 1985

Kranzler HR, Modesto-Lowe V, Nuwayser ES: A sustained-release naltrexone preparation for treatment of alcohol dependence. Alcoholism: Clinical and Experimental Research 22:1074–1079, 1998

Lee MC, Wagner HN, Tanada S, et al: Duration of occupancy of opiate receptors by naltrexone. J Nucl Med 29:1207–1211, 1988

Ling W, Wesson DR: Naltrexone treatment for addicted health-care professionals: a collaborative private practice experience. J Clin Psychiatry 45:46–48, 1984

Maany I, O'Brien CP, Woody G: Interaction between thioridazine and naltrexone (letter). Am J Psychiatry 144:966, 1987

Marrazzi MA, Wroblewski JM, Kinzie J, et al: High-dose naltrexone and liver function safety. Am J Addict 6:21–29, 1997

Martin WR, Jasinski DR: Physiological parameters of morphine in man: tolerance, early abstinence, protracted abstinence. J Psychiatry Res 7:9–16, 1969

Martin W, Jasinski D, Mansky P: Naltrexone: an antagonist for the treatment of heroin dependence. Arch Gen Psychiatry 28:784–791, 1973

Mason BJ, Ritvo EC, Morgan RO, et al: A double-blind, placebo-controlled pilot study to evaluate the efficacy and safety of oral nalmefene HCl for alcohol dependence. Alcoholism: Clinical and Experimental Research 18: 1162–1167, 1994

Mello NK, Mendelson JH, Kuehnle JC, et al: Operant analysis of human heroin self-administration and the effects of naltrexone. J Pharmacol Exp Ther 216:45–54, 1981

Mendelson JH, Ellingboe J, Kuehnle JC, et al: Heroin and naltrexone effects of pituitary-gonadal hormones in man: interaction of steroid feedback effects, tolerance and supersensitivity. J Pharmacol Exp Ther 214:503–506, 1980

Meyer RE, Mirin SM, Altman JL: The clinical usefulness of narcotic antagonists: implications of behavioral research. Am J Drug Alcohol Abuse 2:417–432, 1975

Myer EC, Morris DL, Brase DA, et al: Naltrexone therapy of apnea in children with elevated cerebrospinal fluid beta-endorphin. Ann Neurol 27:75–80, 1990

O'Brien CP: Opioid addiction, in Handbook of Experimental Pharmacology. Edited by Herz A, Akil H, Simon EJ. Berlin, Springer-Verlag, 1992, pp 803–823

O'Brien CP, Greenstein R, Mintz J, et al: Clinical experience with naltrexone. Am J Drug Alcohol Abuse 2:365–377, 1975

O'Brien CP, Greenstein R, Ternes J, et al: Clinical pharmacology of narcotic antagonists. Ann N Y Acad Sci 311: 232–240, 1978

O'Brien CP, Greenstein R, Ternes J, et al: Unreinforced self-injections: effects on rituals and outcome in heroin addicts, in Proceedings of the 41st Annual Scientific Meeting, The Committee on Problems of Drug Dependence (NIDA Res Monogr 27; Publ No ADM-80-901). Edited by Harris LS. Washington, DC, U.S. Government Printing Office, 1980, pp 275–281

O'Brien CP, Childress AR, McLellan AT, et al: Use of naltrexone to extinguish opioid-conditioned responses. J Clin Psychiatry 45:53–56, 1984

O'Brien CP, Ehrman R, Ternes J: Classical conditioning in human opioid dependence, in Behavioral Analysis of Drug Dependence. Edited by Goldberg S, Stolerman I. San Diego, CA, Academic Press, 1986, pp 329–356

O'Brien CP, Childress AR, McLellan AT, et al: A learning model of addiction, in Addictive States, Vol 70. Edited by O'Brien CP, Jaffe J. New York, Raven, 1992, pp 157–177

O'Brien CP, Volpicelli LA, Volpicelli JR: Naltrexone in the treatment of alcoholism: a clinical review. Alcohol 13: 35–39, 1996

O'Malley SS, Jaffe A, Chang G, et al: Naltrexone in the treatment of alcohol dependence: preliminary findings, in Novel Pharmacological Interventions for Alcoholism. Edited by Naranjo CA, Sellers EM. New York, Springer-Verlag, 1991, pp 148–157

O'Malley SS, Jaffe A, Chang G, et al: Naltrexone and coping skills therapy for alcohol dependence: a controlled study. Arch Gen Psychiatry 49:881–887, 1992

Pfohl D, Allen J, Atkinson R, et al: Trexan (naltrexone hydrochloride): a review of hepatic toxicity at high dosage, in Problems of Drug Dependence 1985 (NIDA Res Monogr 67; Publ No ADM-86-1448). Edited by Harris LS. Rockville, MD, U.S. Department of Health and Human Services, 1986, pp 66–72

Reid LD, Hunter GA: Morphine and naloxone modulate intake of ethanol. Alcohol 1:33–37, 1984

Reisine T, Pasternak G: Opioid analgesics and antagonists, in The Pharmacological Basis of Therapeutics, 9th Edition. Edited by Hardman JG, Limbird LE. New York, McGraw-Hill, 1996, pp 521–555

Resnick RB, Schuyten-Resnick E, Washton AM: Narcotic antagonists in the treatment of opioid dependence: review and commentary. Compr Psychiatry 20:116–125, 1979

Samson HH, Doyle TF: Oral ethanol self-administration in the rat: effect of naloxone. Pharmacol Biochem Behav 22:91–99, 1985

Sax DS, Kornetsky C, Kim A: Lack of hepatotoxicity with naltrexone treatment. J Clin Pharmacol 34:898–901, 1994

Sideroff SI, Charuvastra VC, Jarvik ME: Craving in heroin addicts maintained on the opiate antagonist naltrexone. Am J Drug Alcohol Abuse 5:415–423, 1978

Spiegel F, Stunkard AJ, Shrager E, et al: Effect of naltrexone on food intake, hunger, and satiety in obese men. Physiol Behav 40:135–141, 1987

Tennant F, Rawson R, Cohen A, et al: A clinical experience with naltrexone in suburban opioid addicts. J Clin Psychiatry 45:42–45, 1984

Tilly J, O'Brien CP, McLellan AT, et al: Naltrexone in the treatment of federal probationers, in Proceedings of the 53rd Annual Scientific Meeting of the Committee on the Problems of Drug Dependence 1991 (NIDA Res Monogr 119; Publ No ADM-92-188). Edited by Harris L. Washington, DC, U.S. Government Printing Office, 1992, p 458

Volpicelli JR, Davis MA, Olgin JE: Naltrexone blocks the post-shock increase of ethanol consumption. Life Sci 38:841–847, 1986

Volpicelli JR, O'Brien CP, Alterman AI, et al: Naltrexone and the treatment of alcohol dependence: initial observations, in Opioids, Bulimia, and Alcohol Abuse and Alcoholism. Edited by Reid LB. New York, Springer-Verlag, 1990, pp 195–214

Volpicelli JR, Alterman AI, Hayashida M, et al: Naltrexone in the treatment of alcohol dependence. Arch Gen Psychiatry 49:876–880, 1992

Volpicelli JR, Rhines KC, Rhines JS, et al: Naltrexone and alcohol dependence. Arch Gen Psychiatry 54:737–742, 1997

Washton AM, Pottash AC, Gold MS: Naltrexone in addicted business executives and physicians. J Clin Psychiatry 45:39–41, 1984

Wikler A: Conditioning factors in opiate addiction and relapse, in Narcotics. Edited by Wilner DI, Kassebaum GG. New York, McGraw-Hill, 1965, pp 85–100

Yoburn BC, Goodman RR, Cohen AH, et al: Increased analgesic potency of morphine and increased brain opioid binding sites in the rat following chronic naltrexone treatment. Life Sci 36:2325–2332, 1985

# 26 MDMA, Ketamine, GHB, and the "Club Drug" Scene

David M. McDowell, M.D.

Methylenedioxymethamphetamine (MDMA), ketamine, and γ-hydroxybutyrate (GHB) are unique compounds, differing in terms of their pharmacological properties and their phenomenological effects. The common thread linking these disparate drugs is the people who use them. These substances are used throughout the world most frequently by a sophisticated, adolescent or 20-something constituency, and within a subculture of the gay community. The drugs are used and abused widely at urban social gatherings in both commercial and informal settings. They are most commonly used in nightclubs and all-night dance parties known as *raves* and at gay *circuit parties*. Attended primarily by affluent gay men, circuit parties are large social gatherings held in many different countries, usually on weekends and holidays. Both raves and circuit parties have become increasingly popular in recent years. Hence, these drugs, which we discuss extensively in this chapter, and several other drugs, which we describe more briefly, are widely known as *club drugs*.

In recent years, the popularity of the club drugs has been linked inextricably with the rise of the rave phenomenon. Anecdotal reports suggest that raves were "created" in Ibiza, an island off the coast of Spain. They first became popular in England during the late 1980s and have since spread to the United States and the rest of the world. In the early 1990s, raves were considered the "next big thing," a rising trend. Although their popularity has not grown dramatically, it has remained constant. Raves have remained a locus where young people use drugs.

At raves, groups of young people (typically in their teens) dance to rapid, electronically synthesized music that has no lyrics (called *techno*). These events traditionally take place in unregulated and unlicensed locations such as stadiums, abandoned warehouses, and other surreptitious places. Since the early 1990s, the venues have become increasingly mainstream. The club drugs are considered by teenagers and young adults as the perfect match for this scene. At some of these events, as many as 70% of rave participants are using MDMA, ketamine, GHB, or other drugs such as marijuana and lysergic acid diethylamide (LSD) (McDowell and Kleber 1994). A recent study done at a circuit party revealed that more than 80% of the participants had taken illicit drugs that day; the average participant was using three substances (S. Lee and D. McDowell, "The Pattern and Incidence of Drug Use at a 'Circuit Party,'" manuscript submitted for publication, 1999).

## MDMA

Do not get married within three weeks of doing Ecstasy.

Bumper sticker popular in
California during the 1980s

MDMA, better known as Ecstasy, has also been known as Adam, XTC, and X. A synthetic amphetamine analog with stimulant properties, the drug is easily distinguishable from chemically related substances in terms of its subjective effects (Hermle et al. 1993; Shulgin 1986). Recreational use of MDMA has been illegal since it was made a Schedule I drug on July 1, 1985. Despite its illegal status, the use of MDMA has skyrocketed in the past several years (Cohen 1998). This rise in use has been particularly marked among adolescents, and MDMA has been strongly linked to raves.

MDMA damages brain serotonin (5-HT) neurons in laboratory animals (McCann and Ricaurte 1993). Although it is not known definitively whether MDMA is neurotoxic to humans, the weight of current scientific evidence indicates that this is probably the case (Gold and Miller 1997; Sprague et al. 1998). MDMA's appeal rests primarily on its psychological effect, a dramatic and consistent ability to induce in the user a profound feeling of attachment and connection. The compound's street name is perhaps a misnomer; the Los Angeles drug dealer who coined the term *Ecstasy* wanted to call the drug Empathy but asked, "Who would know what that means?" (Eisner 1986).

## History

MDMA was patented in 1914 by Merck in Darmstadt, Germany (Shulgin 1990). MDMA was not, as is sometimes thought, intended as an appetite suppressant but was developed originally as an experimental compound. Except for a minor chemical modification in a patent in 1919, there is no other known historical record of MDMA until the 1950s. At that time, the United States Army experimented with MDMA. The resulting informational material was declassified and became available to the general public in the early 1970s. These findings consisted primarily of a number of LD$_{50}$ (median lethal dose) determinations for a variety of laboratory animals; the studies did not involve the use of the compound with humans.

MDMA was first used by humans probably in the late 1960s. It was discovered as a recreational drug by free-thinking pop aficionados (New Age seekers), people who liked its properties of inducing feelings of well-being and connection (Watson and Beck 1986). Given MDMA's capacity to induce feelings of warmth and openness, a number of practitioners and researchers interested in insight-oriented psychotherapy believed it would be an ideal agent to enhance the therapeutic process. The drug was introduced into clinical psychotherapy practice on the West Coast of the United States early in 1976, and on the East Coast about 6 months later (Shulgin 1990). Before the compound became illegal in 1985, it was used extensively for this purpose (Beck 1990).

In the early 1980s, MDMA became increasingly popular. In 1989, production reached at least 30,000 tablets per month. The drug's capacity to induce feelings of connection, and a psychomotor agitation that can be pleasurably relieved by dancing, made it the ideal "party drug." Despite widespread use during the early 1980s, the drug did not attract much attention from the media or from law enforcement officials.

This lack of widespread notoriety was changed by events that occurred in Texas. Until 1985, MDMA was not scheduled or regulated and was completely legal. A distribution network in Texas began an aggressive marketing campaign, and for a time, the drug was available over the counter at bars, at convenience stores, and even through a toll-free number. This widespread distribution attracted the attention of then–Texas Senator Lloyd Bentsen. He petitioned the U.S. Food and Drug Administration (FDA), and the compound was placed on Schedule I on an emergency basis as of July 1, 1985.

A series of three hearings was scheduled to determine MDMA's permanent status. FDA officials were reportedly surprised that a substantial number of people, including therapists and clergymen, supported a less restrictive categorization. The administrative judge recommended that the compound be placed on Schedule III. This recommendation was overruled. The compound's possible neurotoxicity, combined with concern about illicit drug use in general, resulted in MDMA's permanent placement on Schedule I. Its clinical use is prohibited, and because of the intense regulation of Schedule I compounds, research with MDMA is very difficult to execute. It remains on Schedule I today, and although some individuals believe the drug should be more widely available for research, its status will not likely change in the foreseeable future (Cohen 1998).

Synthesis of MDMA is relatively simple, and it is often made in illicit laboratories or even in domestic locations such as garages. In addition, it is often cut with other substances so that the purity varies substantially. In England, this impure MDMA is known as *Snide-E*. It currently sells in urban areas for about $25 for a 125-mg tablet, which produces the sought-after effect in most intermittent users (Green et al. 1995).

## Physiological Effects

MDMA is usually ingested orally. Other methods of administration are much less popular. The usual single dose is 100–150 mg. The onset of effect begins about 20–40 minutes after ingestion and is experienced as a sudden, amphetamine-like "rush." Nausea, usually mild, but sometimes severe enough to cause vomiting, often accompanies this initial feeling.

The plateau stage of drug effects lasts 3–4 hours. The principal desired effect, according to most users, is a profound feeling of relatedness to the rest of the world. Most users experience this feeling as a powerful connection to those around them, but this may include the larger world. In general, people taking the drug appear to be less aggressive and less impulsive. Users also experience a drastically altered perception of time and a decreased inclination to perform mental and physical tasks (Leister et al. 1992). Although the desire for sex can increase, the ability to achieve arousal and orgasm is greatly diminished in both men and women (Buffum and Moser 1986). MDMA has thus been termed a sensual, not a sexual, drug. In addition, people taking the drug experience mild psychomotor restlessness, bruxism, trismus, anorexia, diaphoresis, hot flashes, tremor, and piloerection (Peroutka et al. 1988). The array of physical effects and behaviors produced by MDMA is remarkably similar across mammalian species (Green et al. 1995).

Common aftereffects can be pronounced, sometimes lasting 24 hours or more. The most dramatic *hangover effect* is a sometimes-severe anhedonia. The hangover effects of MDMA share many similarities with amphetamine withdrawal. MDMA users can experience lethargy, anorexia, decreased motivation, sleepiness, depressed mood, and fatigue, occasionally lasting for days. In a few instances, more severe effects have been reported, including altered mental status, convulsions, hypo- or hyperthermia, severe changes in blood pressure, tachycardia, coagulopathy, acute renal failure, hepatotoxicity, and death (Demirkiran et al. 1996).

There are numerous case reports of a single dose of MDMA precipitating severe psychiatric illness. MDMA probably induces a range of depressive symptoms and anxiety in some individuals, and for that reason, people with affective illness should be specifically cautioned about the dangers of using MDMA (McCann et al. 1994). Many of these reports represent single cases, and there may be other explanations for these occurrences. Still, the growing number of such adverse events is cause for concern.

## Mechanism of Action

MDMA's primary mechanism of action is as an indirect serotonergic agonist (Ames and Wirshing 1993). However, MDMA is considered a "messy drug," because it affects serotonin- and dopamine-containing neurons and a host of other neurotransmitter systems (Rattray 1991).

MDMA is taken up by the serotonin cell through an active channel where it induces the release of serotonin stores. The drug also blocks reuptake of serotonin, contributing to its length of action. Although it inhibits the

synthesis of new serotonin, this is an aftereffect and does not contribute to the intoxication phase. It may, however, contribute to sustained feelings of depression reported by some users and to a diminished magnitude of subjective effects when the next dose is taken within a few days of the first dose. The drug's side effects, including anorexia, psychomotor agitation, difficulty in achieving orgasm, and profound feelings of empathy, can be explained as a result of the flooding of the serotonin system (Beck and Rosenbaum 1994).

People who use MDMA on a regular basis tend not to increase their use as time goes on (Peroutka 1990). Because the drug depletes serotonin stores and inhibits synthesis of new serotonin, subsequent doses produce a diminished high and a worsening of the drug's undesirable effects such as psychomotor restlessness and teeth gnashing. MDMA users quickly become aware of this consequence and adjust their usage patterns. Many users who are at first enamored with the drug subsequently lose interest, usually citing the substantial side effects. An adage about Ecstasy reported on college campuses captures this phenomenon: "Freshmen love it, sophomores like it, juniors are ambivalent, and seniors are afraid of it" (Eisner 1993). Those who continue to use the drug over longer periods of time usually tend to take the drug only periodically.

MDMA's effects can be characterized as short term (lasting less than 24 hours) and long term (lasting more than 24 hours) (McKenna and Peroutka 1990). The short-term effects presumably result from the acute release of serotonin and are associated with a decrease in serotonin and 5-hydoxyindoleacetic acid (5-HIAA), a decrease in tryptamine hydroxylase (TPH) activity, and recovery of 5-HIAA levels usually within 24 hours. The long-term effects are manifested by a persistent slow decrease in serotonin and 5-HIAA after initial recovery, persistently depressed TPH activity, and a decrease in serotonin terminal density (Demirkiran et al. 1996).

## MDMA and Neurotoxicity

In laboratory animals, the ingestion of MDMA causes a decrease in the serum and spinal fluid levels of 5-HIAA in a dose-dependent fashion (Shulgin 1990) and damages brain serotonin neurons (McCann and Ricaurte 1993). The dosage necessary to cause permanent damage to most rodent species is many times greater than that normally ingested by humans (Shulgin 1990). In nonhuman primates, the neurotoxic dosage approximates the recreational dosage taken by humans (McCann and Ricaurte 1993). Like its close structural relative methylenedioxyamphetamine (MDA or "Eve"), MDMA has been found to damage serotonin neurons in all animal species tested to date (McCann et al. 1996). The closer a given mammal is phylogenetically to humans, the less MDMA is required to induce this permanent damage.

Unequivocal data demonstrating that similar changes occur in the human brain do not exist, but the indirect clinical evidence is disconcerting (Green et al. 1995). For example, clear deficits and major neurotoxicity appear to be related to total cumulative dose in animals (Gold and Miller 1997). In addition, MDMA produces a 30%–35% drop in serotonin metabolism in humans (McCann et al. 1994). Even one dose of MDMA may cause lasting damage to the serotonin system. Furthermore, such damage might become apparent only with time or under conditions of stress. Users with no initial complications may manifest problems over time (McCann et al. 1996). There have been reports of individuals with lasting neuropsychiatric disturbances after MDMA use (Creighton et al. 1991; McCann and Ricaurte 1991; Schifano 1991).

The substantial acute side effects that limit the use of MDMA may also limit the number of permanent casualties. Also, the clinical effect of serotonergic damage is not clear because some animal data suggest that even significant destruction of serotonin neurons leads to little functional impairment (Robinson et al. 1993). Whether this holds true for humans is unclear. Until the full effect of widespread MDMA use is known, the risks must be taken seriously. The drug's potential neurotoxicity is the most significant concern about its use.

## Treatment

The treatment of MDMA abuse may be divided into the treatment of acute reactions to the drug and the treatment of chronic abuse.

As discussed earlier, dehydration, coupled with the direct effects of MDMA, may be life threatening. The clinical characteristics of acute MDMA reactions resemble a combination of the serotonin syndrome and neuroleptic malignant syndrome (NMS). It should therefore be treated in the emergency room as if the patient had both of these conditions. This is an uncommon but potentially fatal occurrence. The treatment recommendations that follow are adopted from the standard treatment given to patients with NMS (Bernstein et al. 1997; Kaplan and Sadock 1995).

Clinicians should be alert to the possibility of these syndromes in any patient who exhibits confusion or impaired sensorium, hyperthermia, muscle rigidity, and fever. If it can be established that a patient has been to a rave, or some clublike event, this should raise the clinician's suspicion that MDMA was ingested. Because this is a diagnosis of exclusion, other disorders first must be ruled out. These disorders include infections such as meningitis, trauma, and other drug intoxications. Management should include consultation with a trained neurologist and an arranged transfer to the intensive care unit as quickly as possible. Supportive measures such as effective hydration using intravenous fluids and lowering the temperature of the patient with cooling blankets or an ice bath are often necessary. Standard gastric lavage should be used. When other diagnoses have been excluded, the clinician should consider giving the patient the medications commonly used to treat both NMS and the serotonin syndrome.

Dantrolene sodium is a skeletal muscle relaxant that lessens rigidity and hyperthermia. This medication is given to the patient in a dose of 2–3 mg/kg intravenously three times per day. Daily dosages should not exceed 10 mg/kg/day because higher dosages are associated with hepatotoxicity. In patients who can tolerate oral medicine (an unlikely event), the treatment of choice is bromocriptine, a dopaminergic agonist, which may be used concurrently with dantrolene. Administration should be started at 5 mg orally three times per day. The patient's vital signs should be supported at all times, with whatever means are necessary. Benzodiazepines and anticonvulsants also may be used if clinically indicated. Caution should be used in adding neuroleptics for behavioral restraint, because these may exacerbate the syndrome. If the syndrome is treated aggressively and effectively, the patient usually recovers in a matter of days, although it may take longer; recovery is obviously impeded if more significant organ failure has occurred.

MDMA intoxication is associated with a number of psychiatric symptoms, particularly anxiety, panic, and depression. These symptoms are usually short-term sequelae and subside in a matter of days. Support and reassurance are often all that is needed to help the individual through this difficult time. If the symptoms are severe, brief pharmacotherapy, probably with benzodiazepines, is recommended.

Although physiological dependence on MDMA does not occur, some individuals use the drug compulsively and can be said to be dependent on it. For them, the standard approaches used in substance abuse treatment are recommended. These patients can be difficult to work with for many reasons. They are usually adolescents, and the many complications involved with this population must be considered (McDowell and Spitz 1999). Furthermore, they are more likely to be involved with the subculture that surrounds the drug, so that the very identity of the adolescent will need to be addressed in treatment. Healthy recreational alternatives need to be identified. Another complicating factor is that MDMA, as compared with other drugs, is often viewed as benign (Beck and Rosenbaum 1994). As a result, there is little urgency among the general public to eradicate MDMA as compared with other drugs that have more negative reputations.

In the summer of 1992 as many as 15 deaths occurring at raves in Great Britain were associated with the use of Ecstasy. These deaths appear to be similar to certain features of both the serotonin syndrome and the NMS (Ames and Wirshing 1993). The serotonin syndrome is a clinical phenomenon that occurs with an excess of serotonin and is characterized by confusion, restlessness, hyperthermia, diaphoresis, hyperreflexia, diarrhea, and myoclonus (Sternback 1991). NMS is associated with the use of antipsychotics (dopamine blockers) and dehydration, and it consists of mental status changes, hyperthermia, rigidity, elevated creatinine, and autonomic dysfunction (Guerra et al. 1992). Both syndromes exist on a spectrum of severity, but in their most severe form they may be life threatening.

Raves are often held in hot, crowded conditions. During the summer of 1992, some of the clubs turned off their water supplies in an effort to maximize profits by selling bottled water. The hot, crowded conditions; physical exertion; and subsequent dehydration combined with the drug effects certainly contributed to the deaths. After these incidents, the British government mandated an open water supply at all clubs; deaths of this kind appear to have since diminished, although they do still occur (Demirikiran et al. 1996). In Great Britain in recent years, one of the principal aims of the harm reduction efforts aimed at young people who take MDMA is to remind them that if they are going to take it, they must stay well-hydrated.

Although rare, there have been anecdotal reports of MDMA causing posthallucinogenic perception disorder (Creighton et al. 1991). This disorder is a prolonged, sometimes dramatic, but often low-grade, reexperience of the perceptual distortion produced during the MDMA high. Posthallucinogenic perceptual disorder can last for months, even years, and can be devastating. Although symptoms tend to diminish over time, there are no effective treatments for this disorder. The literature on this disorder is scant, but most reports indicate that the symptoms eventually diminish without treatment.

## Ketamine

> I remember dancing on the pier and looking way up at an apartment and thinking I could be there in five minutes and it wouldn't surprise me. It's like you're on a different plane. Anything seems possible.
>
> Ketamine user

Ketamine, also known as Special K, Super K, Vitamin K, or just plain K, was first manufactured in 1965 and is still legally manufactured, primarily for use by veterinarians and pediatric surgeons as a nonanalgesic anesthetic. It is often via these manufacturers and suppliers that illegal supplies are diverted to recreational users. Law enforcement officials have traditionally used fewer resources for regulating and monitoring medications intended for veterinary use, although there are indications that this trend is changing. The recreational use of ketamine probably began in the 1960s and was first described in detail by Lilly (1978). Since that time, its popularity has continued to rise (Cooper 1996; Dotson et al. 1995).

Ketamine is classified as a dissociative anesthetic. As its name implies, the drug causes a dose-dependent dissociative episode with feelings of fragmentation, detachment, and what one user described as "psychic/physical/spiritual scatter." It induces a lack of responsive awareness not only to pain but to the general environment, without a corresponding depression of autonomic reflexes and vital centers in the diencephalon.

### History

Ketamine was first manufactured in 1965 at the University of Michigan and was first marketed by Parke, Davis under the brand name Ketalar. Since that time it has been commercially available under various brand names. It is most commonly available in 10-mL (100 mg/mL) liquid-containing vials (Fort Dodge Laboratories 1997). It is a close chemical cousin of phencyclidine, also known as PCP or angel dust. PCP was the first of a new class of general anesthetics known as cataleptoid anesthetics or dissociative anesthetics. PCP had physiological properties that made it advantageous as an anesthetic, the most significant being that it was quite effective without a great risk of cardiac or respiratory depression typical of classical general anesthetic agents.

PCP also had a number of severe limitations as an anesthetic, most significantly that it caused a high degree of psychotic and violent reactions (National Institute on Drug Abuse 1979). At least half of the patients subjected to PCP anesthesia developed several perioperative reactions, including agitation and hallucinations. Some of these patients developed severe psychotic reactions that persisted for as long as 10 days (Crider 1986; Meyer et al. 1959). Ketamine produces minimal cardiac and respiratory effects, and its anesthetic and behavioral effects remit soon after administration (Moretti et al. 1984; Pandit et al. 1980). The medication has found a place in the pharmacopoeia, principally with children and animals.

Since the 1970s, ketamine has been popular with two types of users. The first type uses ketamine in a solitary fashion and seeks a paranormal experience or uses it to enhance a spiritual journey. The second type uses the drug socially. These are the young club-goers and "ravers." Ketamine is especially popular at circuit parties. Epidemiological evidence about the use of ketamine is difficult to obtain. Reports in the media, anecdotal evidence, and clinical observations by the author indicate that ketamine is quite popular in urban clubs and at raves. A very popular nightclub in New York City featured a three-story slide called the "K-hole," in a mocking gesture to the drug's popularity.

Ketamine is commercially available as a liquid. The liquid form is easily converted to a powder, the form in which it is most often sold. The drug is frequently mixed with vitamin B-12 in its illegal form. Ketamine can be administered in a variety of ways. In its most potent form, it is mixed with water and injected. Because of aversions to intravenous use, this probably is not the most popular form. At clubs, most people snort lines of the powder. Ketamine may also be dabbed on the tongue or mixed with a liquid and imbibed.

## Physiological Effects

Ketamine has been studied extensively in humans. Recreational users of ketamine report feeling anesthetized and sedated. This is clearly a dose-dependent phenomenon (Krystal et al. 1994). For example, ketamine can induce tangential thinking and ideas of reference. At higher dosages, it distorts perception of the body, the environment, and time. Ketamine can influence all modes of sensory function (Óye et al. 1992). At typical dosages, ketamine distorts sensory stimuli, producing illusions (Garfield et al. 1994). In higher than typical dosages, hallucinations and paranoid delusions can occur (Malhotra et al. 1996).

Ketamine substantially disrupts both attention and learning. Research volunteers using the drug fail to modify behavior in response to feedback. They take longer to learn initial tasks and do not apply strategy. The clinical literature does not indicate which memory function is affected by ketamine; retrieval, long-term recall, and the consolidation of memory are all altered (Krystal et al. 1994). Ketamine use produces decrements in free recall, recognition memory, and attention.

The recreational dosage is approximately 0.4 mg/kg, and the anesthetic dosage is almost double that. The $LD_{50}$ is nearly 30 times the anesthetic dosage. According to users, the minimal risk of overdosing is one of the drug's attractive properties.

Individuals injecting the drug recreationally begin to feel the effects in about 5 minutes. Intranasal users experience the effects of the drug in about 10 minutes. Chronic users develop tolerance. Although tingling sensations are present initially and mild effects occur almost immediately, the principal dissociative effect occurs about 10 minutes later. In the first half-hour after ingestion, the peak effects of the drug occur and then subside gradually. The bulk of the "trip" lasts about 1 hour (Delgarno and Shewan 1996). This is known as the *emergence state*, and it is here that the perception of time is significantly altered. Users describe a sense of "eternity" and a heightened capacity to discern causal connections in all things. The effects diminish gradually over another hour. Larger doses last longer and have a more intense effect (Malhotra et al. 1996). Flashbacks have been reported, and their incidence may be higher than with many other hallucinogens (Siegel 1984). Ketamine users report using the drug for the same reasons that users of hallucinogens report using: to achieve so-called higher forms of consciousness.

Someone who has recently used ketamine may exhibit catatonia, a flat face, an open mouth, fixed staring with dilated pupils, "sightless staring," and rigid posturing. At higher dosages, the user enters a catatonic state colloquially known as a *K-hole* and characterized by social withdrawal, autistic behavior, an inability to maintain a cognitive set, impoverished and idiosyncratic thought patterns, and bizarre responses. Motor impairment is a marked feature of this state, and people in a K-hole are found on the edge of the dance floor, staring blankly into space, appearing nondistressed but seemingly incapable of communication (GMHC 1997).

## Mechanism of Action

Molecular mechanisms underlying ketamine effects have been identified. Ketamine interferes with the actions of the excitatory amino acid neurotransmitters, especially glutamate and aspartate, the most prevalent excitatory neurotransmitters in the brain. These neurotransmitters regulate numerous functions of the central nervous system (CNS) and are particularly important in cortical-cortical and cortical-subcortical interactions (Cotman and Monaghan 1987). The excitatory amino acid receptor subtype to which ketamine binds with the most affinity is the *N*-methyl-D-aspartate (NMDA) receptor complex, which regulates calcium flow through its ion channel. Ketamine binds to the NMDA receptor complex on the same site as PCP, located inside the calcium channel. Therefore the direct action of ketamine is the blockade of calcium movement through this channel (Hampton et al. 1982).

Noncompetitive antagonism of NMDA receptors by the channel blockers induces changes of perception, memory, and cognition throughout the brain. In addition, the channel blockers affect dopaminergic transmission, inhibiting cocaine-induced increases in extracellular dopamine in the nucleus accumbens (Pap and Bradberry 1995). NMDA blockade causes an increase in dopamine release in the midbrain and prefrontal cortex (Bubser et al. 1992). NMDA blockade also causes activation of serotonin systems specifically targeting the 5-HT$_{1A}$ receptor (Loscher and Honack 1993). Agents such as ketamine work globally, directly or indirectly affecting numerous neurotransmitter systems. Nonetheless, the principal effects of ketamine appear to result from its actions as an NMDA antagonist.

## Treatment

Because of its high therapeutic index, only severe overdose presents substantial risk of significant morbidity and mortality and, as such, should be treated in the intensive care unit. Perhaps the most dangerous effects of ketamine are behavioral. Individuals may become withdrawn, paranoid, and very uncoordinated. In such cases, the physician must treat the overdose symptomatically. Calm reassurance and a low stimulation environment is usually most helpful. Clinical experience indicates that less stimulation is better. The patient should be placed in a part of the clinic or emergency room with the least amount of light and stimulation. Neuroleptics should be used in only the rarest of cases, because their side-effect profile may cause discomfort and therefore provoke the patient. If necessary, the patient may be given benzodiazepines to control the associated anxiety.

Ketamine is an addictive drug. It is reinforcing in the classical sense. Numerous reports exist of individuals who became dependent on the drug and use it daily (Galloway et al. 1997). Such dependence should be treated in the traditional manner. The clinician should evaluate the patient for any underlying psychiatric condition, and if such a condition is not found, then individual treatment should focus on the drug use issues.

## GHB

> I only meant to take a little, but when I woke up, I didn't remember what had happened.
>
> GHB user

GHB is sold as "liquid Ecstasy" and in Great Britain, as GBH, or "grievous bodily harm." It is found naturally in many mammalian cells. In the brain, the highest amounts are found in the hypothalamus and basal ganglia (Gallimberti et al. 1989). It may function as a neurotransmitter (Galloway et al. 1997). GHB is closely linked to γ-aminobutyric acid (GABA) and is both a precursor and a metabolite of GABA. GHB, however, does not act directly on GABA receptor sites (Chin et al. 1992).

In the 1970s, GHB was used with little fanfare as a sleep aid. It has some demonstrated therapeutic efficacy, particularly in the treatment of narcolepsy (Lammers et al. 1993; Scrima et al. 1990). In addition, bodybuilders sometimes use it, hoping it will promote muscle growth because it increases episodic secretion of growth hormone. In 1990, after reports indicated that GHB may have contributed to the hospitalization of several California youths, it was banned by the FDA. Because it has not been scheduled by the Drug Enforcement Agency as a drug, possession of it is legal. Manufacturing GHB for sale to laboratories for research purposes or for sale to the public is prohibited by law.

In some European countries, GHB is available by prescription. Most of the GHB sold in the United States is of the bootleg variety, manufactured by nonprofessional kitchen chemists. In fact, it is quite easy to manufacture, and several Internet sites are devoted to explaining the process. The unregulated nature of these operations arouses concern about the quality and safety of the GHB available for purchase.

GHB has an extremely small therapeutic index, and as little as double the euphorigenic dose may cause serious CNS depression. In recent years, it has been associated with several incidents of respiratory depression and coma. In the late 1990s, several deaths have been linked to GHB (Li et al. 1998).

## History

GHB was first synthesized about 30 years ago by Dr. H. Laborit, a French researcher interested in exploring the effects of GABA in the brain. Laborit was attempting to manufacture a GABA-like agent that would cross the blood-brain barrier (Vickers 1969). During the 1980s, GHB was widely available in health food stores. It came to the attention of authorities in the late 1980s as a drug of abuse, and the FDA banned it in 1990 after reports of several poisonings with the drug (Chin et al. 1992). In the past decade, it has become more widely known as a drug of abuse associated with nightclubs and raves.

## Physiological Effects

GHB is ingested orally, is absorbed rapidly, and reaches peak plasma concentrations in 20–60 minutes (Vickers 1969). The typical recreational dosage is 0.75–1.5 g; higher dosages result in increased effects. The high lasts for no more than 3 hours and reportedly has few lasting effects. Repeated use of the drug can prolong its effects.

Users of the drug report that GHB induces a pleasant state of relaxation and tranquility. Frequently reported effects are placidity, mild euphoria, and a tendency to verbalize. GHB, like MDMA, has also been described as a sensual drug. Its effects have been likened to alcohol, another GABA-like drug (McCabe et al. 1971). Users report a feeling of mild numbing and pleasant disinhibition. This disinhibition may account for the reports that GHB enhances the experience of sex. The dose-response curve for GHB is exceedingly steep. The recommended or intoxicating dosage can result in severe adverse effects. The $LD_{50}$ is estimated at perhaps only five times the intoxicating dosage (Vickers 1969). Furthermore, the drug has synergistic effects with alcohol and probably other drugs. Therefore, small increases in the amount ingested may lead to significant intensification of the effects and to the onset of CNS depression. Overdose is a real danger. Users drinking alcohol, which impairs judgment and with which synergy is likely, are at greater risk.

The most commonly experienced side effects of GHB are drowsiness, dizziness, nausea, and vomiting. Less common side effects include weakness, loss of peripheral vision, confusion, agitation, hallucinations, and bradycardia. The drug is a sedative and can produce ataxia and loss of coordination.

As doses increase, patients may experience loss of bladder control, temporary amnesia, and sleepwalking.

Clonus, seizures, and cardiopulmonary depression can occur. Coma and persistent vegetative states have been reported (Chin et al. 1992; Gallimberti et al. 1989; Takahara et al. 1977; Vickers 1969).

## Mechanism of Action

Several lines of evidence support the hypothesis that GHB is a neurotransmitter (Galloway et al. 1997). Specific high-affinity binding sites for GHB have been found in the rat brain (Hechler et al. 1992). GHB temporarily suppresses the release of dopamine in the mammalian brain. This is followed by a marked increase in dopamine release, especially in the nigrostriatal pathway, and is accompanied by the increased release of endogenous opioids (Hechler et al. 1992).

GHB also stimulates pituitary growth hormone (GH) release. One study (Takahara et al. 1977) reported 9-fold and 16-fold increases in GH 30 and 60 minutes, respectively, after intravenous administration of 2.5 g of GHB in six healthy adult men. GH levels were still 7-fold higher than baseline after 120 minutes. The mechanism by which GHB stimulates GH release is not known. Dopamine activity in the hypothalamus stimulates pituitary release of GH, but GHB inhibits dopamine release while it stimulates GH release. While GH is being released, serum prolactin levels also rise, in a similar time-dependent fashion. GHB has several different actions in the CNS, and some reports indicate it antagonizes the effects of marijuana (Galloway et al. 1997). The consequences of these physiological changes are unclear, as are the overall health consequences for individuals who use GHB.

## Treatment

Clinicians should remember to ask about GHB use, especially in younger people, for whom it has become a drug of choice. Because GHB is not detectable by routine drug screening, this history is that much more important. In cases of acute GHB intoxication, physicians should provide physiological support and maintain a high index of suspicion for intoxication with other drugs. A recent review (Li et al. 1998) suggested the following features for the management of GHB ingestion with a spontaneously breathing patient:

1. Maintain oxygen supplementation and intravenous access.
2. Maintain comprehensive physiological and cardiac monitoring.

3. Attempt to keep the patient stimulated.

4. Use atropine for persistent symptomatic bradycardia.

5. Admit the patient if he or she is still intoxicated after 6 hours.

6. Discharge the patient if he or she is clinically well in 6 hours.

Patients whose breathing is labored should be managed in the intensive care unit.

Often the most dangerous effects of GHB use have occurred with the use of other drugs. For example, concurrent use of sedatives or alcohol may increase the risk of vomiting, aspiration, or cardiopulmonary depression. For this reason, clinicians treating individuals who abuse or are dependent on GHB should be aware of its interactions with other drugs. The use of GHB and methamphetamine or cocaine may increase the risk of seizure. Most patients who overdose on GHB recover completely if they receive proper medical attention.

Some individuals have developed physiological dependence on GHB. The symptoms of withdrawal include anxiety, tremor, insomnia, and "feelings of doom," which may persist for several weeks after stopping the drug (Galloway et al. 1997). No studies have examined the treatment of GHB withdrawal. This complex of symptomatology suggests that benzodiazepines may be useful in treating GHB withdrawal. Because data are lacking, clinicians must exercise their most prudent judgment regarding what will be most helpful in a given situation. Health care professionals should be alert for this potentially dangerous drug.

## Conclusion

MDMA, ketamine, and GHB are by no means the only drugs found at clubs, raves, or circuit parties. They are, however, the most emblematic. Attendees also use more traditional drugs such as LSD and other hallucinogens. Marijuana is perennially popular, and alcohol use is also common. Some drug users have begun to experiment with flunitrazepam, a short-acting benzodiazepine better known by its street names, "Rohypnol," "Roofies," or "Ro." Because of the ability of this drug to interfere with short-term memory, it has become known in the media as the "date rape drug." Slipped into the drink of someone unsuspecting, it may indeed make the person feel very disinhibited and unable to remember much of what happened after ingestion. Furthermore, each week seems to bring a report of some "new" drug of abuse. Often this is just an older, well-known drug, packaged differently or with a new name.

These drugs are used at clubs, often in combination, and often by very young people. This is cause for concern for several reasons. The younger a person is when he or she begins to use drugs, and the more often he or she uses them, the more likely he or she is to develop serious problems with these or other substances. In the future we are likely to see more and more use of such drugs and the problems that come with their use.

## References

Ames D, Wirshing W: Ecstasy, the serotonin syndrome, and neuroleptic malignant syndrome—a possible link? JAMA 269:869–870, 1993

Beck J: The public health implications of MDMA use, in Ecstasy: the Clinical, Pharmacological and Neurotoxicological Effects of the Drug MDMA. Edited by Peroutka S. Boston, MA, Klewer Academic, 1990, pp 77–103

Beck J, Rosenbaum M: Pursuit of Ecstasy: The MDMA Experience. SUNY Series in New Social Studies on Alcohol and Drugs. New York, State University of New York Press, 1994

Bernstein C, Ladds B, Maloney A, et al: On Call Psychiatry. Philadelphia, PA, WB Saunders, 1997

Bubser M, Keseberg U, Notz PK, et al: Differential behavioral and neurochemical effects of competitive and noncompetitive NMDA receptor antagonists in rats. Eur J Pharmacol 229:75–82, 1992

Buffum J, Moser C: MDMA and human sexual function. J Psychoactive Drugs 18:355–359, 1986

Chin MY, Kreutzer RA, Dyer JE: Acute poisoning from gamma-hydroxybutyrate in California. West J Med 156: 380–384, 1992

Cohen R: The Love Drug: Marching to the Beat of Ecstasy. Binghamton, NY, Hayworth Press, 1998

Cooper M: "Special K:" rough catnip for clubgoers. The New York Times, January 28, 1996, p 6

Cotman CW, Monaghan DT: Chemistry and anatomy of excitatory amino acid systems, in Psychopharmacology: The Third Generation of Progress. Edited by Meltzer HY. New York, Raven, 1987, pp 194–210

Creighton F, Black D, Hyde C: Ecstasy psychosis and flashbacks. Br J Psychiatry 159:713–715, 1991

Crider R: Phencyclidine: Changing Abuse Patterns (NIDA Res Monogr 64). Rockville, MD, National Institute on Drug Abuse, 1986, pp 163–173

Delgarno PJ, Shewan D: Illicit use of ketamine in Scotland. J Psychoactive Drugs 28:191–199, 1996

Demirkiran M, Jankovic J, Dean J: Ecstasy intoxication: an overlap between serotonin syndrome and neuroleptic malignant syndrome. Clin Neuropharmacol 19:157–164, 1996

Dotson J, Ackerman D, West L: Ketamine abuse. Journal of Drug Issues 25:751–757, 1995

Eisner B: Ecstasy: The MDMA Story. Boston, MA, Little, Brown, 1986

Eisner B: Ecstasy: The MDMA Story, 2nd Expanded Edition. Berkeley, CA, Ronin Publishing, 1993

Fort Dodge Laboratories: Ketaset package insert. Fort Dodge, IA, Ketamine HCL INJ USP, 1997

Gallimberti L, Gentile N, Cibin M, et al: Gamma-hydroxybutyric acid for treatment of alcohol withdrawal syndrome. Lancet 30:787–789, 1989

Galloway GP, Frederick SL, Staggers FE, et al: Gamma-hydroxybutyrate: an emerging drug of abuse that causes physical dependence. Addiction 92:89–96, 1997

Garfield JM, Garfield FB, Stone JG, et al: A comparison of psychologic responses to ketamine and thiopental-nitrous oxide-halothane anesthesia. Anesthesiology 36:329–338, 1994

GMHC (McDowell D, consultant): Drugs in Partyland (educational brochure). New York, GMHC Press, 1997

Gold M, Miller N: Intoxication and withdrawal from marijuana, LSD, and MDMA, in Manual of Therapeutics for Addictions. Edited by Miller N, Gold M, Smith D. New York, Wiley, 1997, pp 71–89

Green A, Cross A, Goodwin G: Review of pharmacology and clinical pharmacology of 3,4-methylenedioxymethamphetamine (MDMA or "Ecstasy"). Psychopharmacology 119:247–260, 1995

Guerra R, Chang S, Romero J: A comparison of diagnostic criteria for neuroleptic malignant syndrome. J Clin Psychiatry 53:56–62, 1992

Hampton RY, Medzihradsky F, Woods JH, et al: Stereospecific binding of $^3$H phencyclidine in brain membranes. Life Sci 30:2147–2154, 1982

Hechler V, Goebaille S, Maitre M: Selective distribution pattern of gamma-hydroxybutyrate receptors in the rat forebrain and mid-brain as revealed by quantitative autoradiograph. Brain Res 572:345–348, 1992

Hermle L, Spitzer M, Borchardt K, et al: Psychological effects of MDE in normal subjects. Neuropsychopharmacology 8:171—176, 1993

Kaplan H, Sadock B (eds): The Comprehensive Textbook of Psychiatry, 6th Edition. Baltimore, MD, Williams & Wilkins, 1995

Krystal JH, Karper LP, Seityl JP, et al: Subanesthetic effects of the noncompetitive NMDA antagonist ketamine in humans. Arch Gen Psychiatry 51:199–214, 1994

Lammers GJ, Arends J, Deckerck AC, et al: Gamma-hydroxybutyrate and narcolepsy: a double blind placebo controlled study. Sleep 16:216–220, 1993

Leister M, Grob C, Bravo G, et al: Phenomenology and sequelae of 3,4-methylenedioxymethamphetamine use. J Nerv Ment Dis 180:345–354, 1992

Li J, Stokes S, Woeckener A: A tale of novel intoxication: a review of the effects of γ-hydroxybutyric acid with recommendations for management. Ann Emerg Med 31:729–736, 1998

Lilly JC: The Scientist: A Novel Autobiography. New York, JB Lippincott, 1978

Loscher W, Honack D: Effects of the novel 5-HT$_{1A}$ receptor antagonist, (+)-WAY 100135 on the stereotyped behavior induced by NMDA receptor antagonist dizocilpine in rats. Eur J Pharmacol 242:99–104, 1993

Malhotra AK, Pinals DA, Weingartner H, et al: NMDA receptor function and human cognition: the effects of ketamine in healthy volunteers. Neuropsychopharmacology 14:301–307, 1996

McCabe E, Layne E, Sayler D, et al: Synergy of ethanol and a natural soporific: gamma hydroxybutyrate. Science 171:404–406, 1971

McCann U, Ricaurte G: Lasting neuropsychiatric sequelae of methylenedioxymethamphetamine ("Ecstasy") in recreational users. J Clin Psychopharmacol 11:302–305, 1991

McCann U, Ricaurte G: Reinforcing subjective effects of 3,4-methylenedioxymethamphetamine ("Ecstasy") may be separable from its neurotoxic actions: clinical evidence. J Clin Psychopharmacol 13:214–217, 1993

McCann UD, Ridenour A, Shaham Y, et al: Serotonin neurotoxicity after (±)3,4-methylenedioxymethamphetamine (MDMA; "Ecstasy"): a controlled study in humans. Neuropsychopharmacology 10:129–138, 1994

McCann U, Slate S, Ricaurte G: Adverse reactions with 3,4-methylenedioxymethamphetamine (MDMA: "Ecstasy"). Drug Saf 15:107–115, 1996

McDowell D, Kleber H: MDMA, its history and pharmacology. Psychiatric Annals 24:127–130, 1994

McDowell D, Spitz H: Substance Abuse: From Principles to Practice. New York, Brunner/Mazel, 1999

McKenna D, Peroutka S: The neurochemistry and neurotoxicity of 3,4-methylenedioxymethamphetamine, "Ecstasy." J Neurochem 54:14–22, 1990

Meyer JS, Greifenstein F, DeVault M: A new drug causing symptoms of sensory depravation. J Nerv Ment Dis 129:54–61, 1959

Moretti RJ, Hassan SZ, Goodman LI, et al: Comparison of ketamine and thiopental in healthy volunteers: effects on mental status, mood, and personality. Anesth Analg 63:1087–1096, 1984

National Institute on Drug Abuse: Diagnosis and Treatment of Phencyclidine (PCP) Toxicity. Rockville, MD, National Institute on Drug Abuse, 1979

Óye N, Paulsen O, Maurset A: Effects of ketamine on sensory perception: evidence for a role of N-methyl D-aspartate receptors. J Pharmacol Exp Ther 260:1209–1213, 1992

Pandit SK, Kothary SP, Kumar SM: Low dose intravenous infusion technique with ketamine. Anesthesia 35:669–675, 1980

Pap A, Bradberry CW: Excitatory amino acid antagonists attenuate the effects of cocaine on extracellular dopamine in the nucleus accumbens. J Pharmacol Exp Ther 274: 127–133, 1995

Peroutka S: Ecstasy: the Clinical, Pharmacological and Neurotoxicological Effects of the Drug MDMA. Boston, MA, Klewer Academic, 1990

Peroutka S, Newman H, Harris H: Subjective effects of 3,4-MDMA in recreational abusers. Neuropsychopharmacology 11:273–277, 1988

Rattray M: Ecstasy: towards an understanding of the biochemical basis of the actions of MDMA. Essays Biochem 26:77–87, 1991

Robinson T, Casteneda E, Whishaw I: Effects of cortical serotonin depletion induced by 3,4-methylenedioxymethamphetamine (MDMA) on behavior, before and after additional cholinergic blockade. Neuropsychopharmacology 8:77–85, 1993

Schifano F: Chronic atypical psychosis associated with MDMA ("Ecstasy") abuse. Lancet 338:1335, 1991

Scrima L, Hartman P, Johnson F, et al: The effects of gamma-hydroxybutyrate on the sleep of narcolepsy patients: a double-blind study. Sleep 13:479–490, 1990

Shulgin A: The background and chemistry of MDMA. J Psychoactive Drugs 18:291–304, 1986

Shulgin A: History of MDMA, in Ecstasy: the Clinical, Pharmacological and Neurotoxicological Effects of the Drug MDMA. Edited by Peroutka S. Boston, MA, Klewer Academic, 1990, pp 1–20

Siegel RK: The natural history of hallucinogens, in Hallucinogens: Neurochemistry, Behavioral, and Clinical Perspectives. New York, Raven, 1984, pp 1–18

Sprague JE, Everman SL, Nichols DE: An integrated hypothesis for the serotonergic axonal loss induced by 3,4-methylenedioxymethamphetamine. Neurotoxicology 19: 427–441, 1998

Sternback H: The serotonin syndrome. Am J Psychiatry 148:705–713, 1991

Takahara J, Yunoki S, Yakushiji W, et al: Stimulatory effects of gamma-hydroxybutyric acid on growth hormone and prolactin release in humans. J Clin Endocrinol Metab 44: 1014, 1977

Vickers MD: Gamma-hydroxybutyric acid. Int Anaesthesia Clinic 71:75–89, 1969

Watson L, Beck J: New Age seekers: MDMA use as an adjunct to spiritual pursuit. J Psychoactive Drugs 23:261–270, 1986

# 4

# Treatment Modalities

# Chapter 27

**27 Psychodynamics**

Richard Frances, M.D.
Jenny Frances, B.A.
John Franklin, M.D.
Lisa Borg, M.D.

Psychodynamic theory, which has its roots in psychoanalysis, has had a wide effect on the practice of psychotherapy, and its principles have been applied to understanding a broad range of treatment issues, including addiction treatment. Whereas most of what is known about psychodynamic principles has evolved from clinical applications, it has been difficult to conduct good treatment outcome studies that clearly demonstrate the efficacy of these approaches to specific psychiatric disorders. A series of papers have demonstrated positive effects and cost-effectiveness for supportive-expressive psychotherapy of opioid-addicted persons in methadone maintenance programs (O'Brien 1997b). However, some investigators have argued that psychodynamic treatment has only a minor role in the treatment of substance abuse (Vaillant 1995). We believe that psychodynamic understanding can add depth to work with individuals and groups and to an understanding of the rehabilitation process (Dodes and Khantzian 1998; Frances et al. 1989; Khantzian 1997). Attempts have even been made to understand the usefulness of 12-step programs from this perspective (Dodes 1988). In this chapter, we develop a rationale for the application of dynamic concepts in addiction treatment, examine its indications and contraindications, and explore how psychodynamic theory can be used to enhance standard treatment techniques and deepen the understanding of addiction treatment.

phasis on resistance, defenses, and conflict; and the use of techniques such as free association, clarification, and interpretation are the basis of modern psychodynamic treatment. More recently, there has been a shift in attention from drives to ego psychology, object relations theory, self psychology, and the importance of affective states, and these developments have added to the applicability of psychodynamic ideas to addiction treatment.

Early psychoanalytic writers, including Freud (1905/1949), Abraham (1908/1960), and Rado (1984), emphasized oral cravings; regression toward infantile fixations, homosexual tendencies, and sexual and social inferiority; emotional immaturity; depressive tensions; and general insecurity (Lorand 1948). Freud (1930/1964) related the elation of intoxication, which he believed caused relaxation of the superego's repression, to manic states. Glover (1932/1956) emphasized the role of aggressive drives in substance use. Thus, early on, psychoanalysis emphasized alcohol's ability to cause regression in id, ego, and superego functions.

Bleuler (1911/1921) and Freud et al. (1993) took opposing positions on whether alcoholism causes or is caused by psychological conflict. Bleuler thought that drinking was more often the cause of neurotic disturbances and that clinicians should not be taken in by the "stupid excuses" of heavy drinkers. Freud et al. saw alcoholism as an "escape into narcosis" from underlying causes.

## Early Development

Freud's work in discovering the importance of unconscious phenomena; the development of a theory of the relationship between id, ego, and superego with an em-

## Recent Developments

Whereas early psychoanalytic theory centered around the drives, including libidinal and aggressive drives, oral wishes, and oral aggression, psychodynamic psychotherapists have focused more on developmental and structural deficits. The role of ego defenses, defense deficit, and affective experience have been connected to drug abuse and alcoholism. Krystal (1982) emphasized a defective stimulus barrier resulting from psychic trauma and the attempt to use substances to fortify against the onslaught of overwhelming affects. He described the inability of patients to label affects, which he called *alexithymia*, and the inability of addicted individuals to verbalize affective states.

Bean-Bayog (1988) described the addiction itself and the resultant loss of control as a sort of severe psychic trauma that results in characteristic defensive patterns. McDougall (1984) focused on drug use as a dispersion of affects into action. Wurmser (1984) and Meissner (1986) emphasized narcissistic collapse as a cause of substance use, compensating for a punctured grandiose or idealized self. According to Wurmser (1984), feelings of emptiness, boredom, rage, shame, depression, and guilt are symptoms of narcissistic wounds and superego regression, which prompt substance use. These authors stressed the severity of psychopathology underlying drug dependency. Lewis (1987) highlighted pathological shame, affecting one's core sense of self, as an affect associated with substance abuse. Silber (1974) emphasized the alcoholic individual's pathological identification with destructive or psychotic parents. According to Kohut and Wolf (1978), drugs serve as substitute idealized selfobjects that were missing developmentally in addicted individuals, and drug problems are considered to be *narcissistic behavior disorders*. Kernberg (1991) described addictive behavior as a reunion with a forgiving parent, an activation of "all good" selfobject images, and a gratification of instinctual needs. Kernberg (1991) identified subsets of addicted individuals with *malignant narcissism*, associated with strong antisocial features.

Theorists such as Wieder and Kaplan (1969), Milkman and Frosch (1973), and Khantzian (1997) discussed the importance of the specific effects of particular drugs on affect and the choice of a particular substance on the basis of specific sought-after effects. Khantzian (1997) highlighted this self-medication hypothesis in describing the use of opioids to assuage endpoint feelings of rage and aggression and the use of cocaine to counter feelings of depressive anergic restlessness or to augment grandiosity. Alcohol has been related to deep-seated fears of closeness, dependency, and intimacy, with the alcohol effect promoting toleration of loving or aggressive feelings.

Khantzian (1997) emphasized affect regulation; tolerance; and self-regulation of affect, self-esteem, need satisfaction, relationships, and self-care; he also related psychodynamic concepts to the total care of addicted patients, including a better understanding of how 12-step programs are helpful. He described substance-abusing individuals as lacking an internal, comforting sense of self-validation. These individuals also have difficulty obtaining nurturance and validation from others in a consistent, mature way. Self-care relates to the individual's developmental inability to anticipate danger or to worry about, anticipate, or consider the consequences of his or her actions, resulting in self-defeating and self-destructive behavior.

Dodes and Khantzian (1998) emphasized the addicted individual's sense of helplessness and powerlessness, often in the face of intolerable affects, and the need to restore through drug use a sense of power and control to which the individual feels entitled. Pharmacological control or change of one's affect state is the goal despite often unpredictable psychological, behavioral, or physiological drug or alcohol effects. Dodes suggested that addictions were in the same category as compulsions, and because compulsions have been seen as treatable with traditional psychodynamic psychotherapy, addictions should also be treatable by similar approaches.

Krystal (1982) described an inability in addicted individuals to take over the internal maternal functions that care for the self. Luborsky (1984) and Klerman et al. (1984) highlighted the importance of clarifying the role of drugs and the addicted individual in the context of one's interpersonal relationships.

Psychodynamics integrated with neurobiological models of addiction can give a fuller understanding of the patient. Scientists have clarified the neural circuits and pathways that involve every drug of abuse. Virtually all abusable drugs have common effects either directly or indirectly on a single pathway. The mesolimbic reward system extends from the ventral tegmental area to the nucleus accumbens, deep within the brain, and projects to the limbic system and the orbitofrontal cortex. Leshner (1997) pointed out that activity in this system keeps addicted individuals addicted, and although addiction is a brain disease, it is not just a brain disease. Rather, addiction is a consequence of fundamental changes in brain function leading to compulsive drug use, even in the face of negative health and social consequences. According to Leshner (1997), treatments should take into account not only the biology of addiction but also the psychological and social context in which it occurs. We believe that, in addition, the psychodynamic perspective should be integrated with current scientific understanding of brain mechanisms in relation to the etiology and treatment of addictions. Other chapters in this volume cover medications used to treat primary addiction and comorbidity, other treatment approaches, and public policy. In this chapter, we discuss how human motivation, including issues relating to child development, psychic trauma, conflict, ego psychology, and the unconscious, affects relapse.

Greater understanding of the addictive process and the psychology of addictions occurs through the process of dynamically oriented psychotherapy. This understanding may add to the development of treatment methods, such as improved cognitive-behavioral techniques (A. T. Beck et al. 1993), that take into account more complex human motivating factors and that may be tailored specifically to an individual's conflicts and defenses. In working with patients who have a *dual diagnosis*, a term most commonly used to define addiction plus another mental illness, an integrated mental illness and substance abuse treatment approach yields better results. The inclusion of psychodynamic understanding frequently enhances the treatment of anxiety disorders, depression, and personality disorders comorbid with substance abuse.

## Application of Psychodynamics to Treatment

Applied psychodynamic principles must be distinguished from psychoanalysis. Psychodynamic principles can be used to understand individual, group, rehabilitation, and other aspects of treatment, whereas psychoanalysis is a more specific technique that may be reserved for a small number of recovering addicted patients who are suitable for it. Most patients could not tolerate certain aspects of psychoanalysis, such as four to five meetings per week with the analyst providing relatively little feedback, being quite neutral, and providing little reassurance to the patient in order to allow frustration and permit regressive fantasies. The technical use of the couch is generally avoided, because it also facilitates regression. In contrast, psychodynamically oriented psychotherapy usually occurs one to two times per week, possibly in addition to group psychotherapy, and the patient sits up facing the therapist. A requirement of abstinence is an essential parameter for successful treatment. Vigilant efforts at relapse prevention and helping patients get back on track after relapse is very much a part of dynamic psychotherapy with ad-

dicted patients. Long-term maintenance of abstinence through combined 12-step mutual self-help approaches and psychotherapy is compatible.

Modern use of psychodynamic approaches tends to focus on current conflicts as they relate to the past rather than on childhood experience. The therapist, aware of the patient's characteristic defenses and particular ego weaknesses and strengths, more often takes an active confrontal and supportive role. The therapist-patient relationship is discussed openly in order to work through resistance and without an effort to foster further regression. Psychodynamic techniques aimed at increased self-awareness, growth, and working through of conflicts can be combined with cognitive approaches, suggestions, education, and provision of support and reassurance as indicated.

## Indications and Rationale for Dynamic Psychotherapy

Psychodynamic principles are applicable throughout psychiatry and are relevant to addiction treatment. Insight-oriented therapy may be especially sought out by individuals for whom this kind of approach represents a particularly good fit. Individual psychodynamic psychotherapy may be the sole treatment or may be combined with group, family, psychopharmacological, self-help, cognitive-behavioral, and other treatment approaches. It may be reserved for treatment-resistant cases, or it may be the treatment of choice because of patient factors. Some patients refuse group or self-help programs and seek out individual psychodynamic therapy because of a wish for privacy, confidentiality, and insight. Patients who have certain characteristics may especially seek out psychodynamic psychotherapy. Positive characteristics may include high intelligence, interest, and insight; psychological mindedness; a wish to understand or find meaning in behavior; a capacity for intimacy; identification with a therapist; time; money; and a wish to change aspects of self that are not acceptable.

As with most forms of psychotherapy, positive prognostic indicators are higher socioeconomic status, marital stability, less severe psychopathology, and minimal sociopathy (Woody et al. 1986). Some relatively negative characteristics for other treatments are social phobia with avoidance and fears that make Alcoholics Anonymous (AA) and Narcotics Anonymous (NA) attendance difficult. Factors that may lead some individuals to consider psychodynamic-oriented psychotherapy instead of other treatments include initial reactions of distaste toward spirituality, which may occur in some atheists; strong negative reactions to groups in general; unwillingness to take medication when indicated; and a lack of a "rational approach to the world," which might benefit from cognitive-behavioral treatment.

Adolescents and young adults sorting out identity issues, problems in individuation, and a need for independence may especially benefit from an insight-oriented approach. For patients in whom denial, projection, splitting, and projective identifications are prominent defenses, consistent interpretation of defenses may be needed to form a working alliance that then can be used to achieve sobriety and growth.

Patients who continue to be anxious, depressed, and troubled after detoxification are more likely to seek out additional psychotherapy. In many ways the patients who benefit from psychodynamic-oriented psychotherapy and have abused substances are very similar to those who benefit and have not abused substances. Many patients who have had failed psychodynamic psychotherapy when they were drinking find that they do benefit from this form of treatment when they are sober. Insight-oriented psychotherapy may be used to achieve or to maintain the benefits of abstinence and to prevent relapse.

Recovering addicted patients often have been survivors in families with heavy addictive behavior, and the danger of relapse is greater in those patients who have conflicts about enjoying and enhancing their success. Being more successful than an addicted parent or sibling may be feared, and insight into the sources of self-defeating behavior can be essential to prevent relapse.

For patients for whom self-care, self-destructiveness, suicidality, and masochism are major issues, an awareness of unconscious forces of self-destructive behavior can be useful to both patient and therapist. Many patients are not aware that their alcoholism may be what Menninger (1938) called "a slow form of suicide." Awareness of risk-taking aspects of behavior may help lead to greater cautions.

The rationale for using psychodynamic principles is frequently based on an in-depth clinical understanding of a particular patient's life situation. There is good evidence that alcoholism is influenced by genetic and environmental factors. Biological factors, such as the dopamine reward pathways and the mesolimbic reward system, have also enhanced our understanding of the brain basis of addiction (Koob et al. 1997; Leshner 1997; O'Brien 1997a, 1997b; Volkow et al. 1997). The study of temperament is leading to interesting treatment implications in psychiatry, including the addictions (Cloninger 1987). Psychodynamic understanding takes into account the patient's childhood history; temperament; existing conflicts at the oral, anal, phallic, or genital levels; development of defenses; and ego and superego development, including object relations and relationships with parents, siblings, and friends (Khantzian 1997).

Psychodynamics are used to deepen the patient's understanding of the rehabilitation process and group psychotherapy and to help him or her understand how self-help groups work (Frances et al. 1989). Awareness of the importance of an unconscious wish to return to drinking, especially during periods of stress, is used in treatment. When unconscious factors have repeatedly led to relapse, exploratory psychotherapy may be particularly useful (Dodes and Khantzian, in press). For example, a patient's association of a "lost weekend," a drunk dream, or a planned vacation to a location where there had been frequent relapses may be a warning sign of a possible relapse and can be used to help the patient to recognize that craving still exists and should be addressed.

An awareness of reasons not to drink and the strengthening of that side of the conflict may help, along with increased insight into the sources of the internal struggle. The greatest focus of attention has been on how substances may be used to self-medicate other psychiatric disorders or to self-regulate affect, and how their use may be a symptom of a deeper underlying problem (Khantzian 1997). Abused substances may be used to push away painful thoughts from consciousness and to numb feelings associated with painful knowledge, or they may be used to gain access to unconscious material and to facilitate experience or expression of angry and other feelings that may be avoided during sobriety. For patients for whom affect regulation is an issue, psychodynamic psychotherapy may be especially valuable. A patient who has an underlying dysthymia, depression, or affective disorder may need to understand how he or she has used substances to cope with unmanageable feelings. Given that alcohol or drugs invariably cause additional life difficulties, psychodynamic approaches may help the patient deal with the psychosocial effects associated with the toxic metabolic complications of substance use.

The application of psychodynamic theory to the treatment of comorbid psychiatric problems such as Axis II personality disorders (including borderline, narcissistic, and socially avoidant personality disorders) is important, especially because alcoholism and drug abuse are overrepresented in these patients. The literature on comorbidity of Axis I and Axis II disorders is extensive and beyond the scope of this chapter (see Kessler et al. 1997). It may be especially hard to identify the boundaries of temperament, acute substance-induced personality change, other Axis I disorders, secondary personality features, and independent personality disorders. Exploratory psychotherapy with borderline personality disorder patients who have a history of addiction must be informed by a good knowledge of addiction psychiatry and an emphasis on structure and limit setting in treatment, including the vital parameter of abstinence.

Kernberg (1991) discussed the deception and projection often seen in the initial therapeutic alliance with borderline and narcissistic personality disorder patients and the need to confront distorted views of reality in the therapeutic relationship. The use of insight in interpreting negative transference and acting out may deepen a positive transference and ultimately foster open expression. As a patient develops a clearer picture of his or her life through exploratory psychotherapy, the value of openness and honesty becomes apparent, and the tie to the therapist is cemented. Frequently, addicted patients have lied to themselves and others and are tired of feeling false and phony. The therapist's healthy ability to tolerate being conned by highly skilled, manipulative patients may minimize damaging countertransference reactions. If the therapist finds himself or herself doing something with a patient, either positive or negative, that is out of the ordinary, some examination of countertransference is warranted.

During early treatment it may be hard to tell whether personality change is resulting from a gradual return to better function because of physical, social, and psychological recovery from addiction effects; whether the initial diagnosis of personality disorder was correct; or whether psychodynamic and/or 12-step programs have effected personality change. Some patients experience a rebound "high" that is analogous to Mahler et al.'s (1975) practicing subphase of development in the second year of life, when there is a burst of autonomous development.

Many addicted patients who have narcissistic traits or personality disorder, and in whom the toxic effects of addiction heighten narcissism, feel a sense of specialness, entitlement, no empathy for others, an inability to allow gratification of dependency needs, and loneliness. The experience of rehabilitation for these patients often involves an acceptance of vulnerability and of being ordinary and similar to others with the same problem; a

reaching out for help; and an encouragement in developing a new humility. Whether this rehabilitation is achieved through 12-step programs, application of Beck's cognitive therapy (A. T. Beck et al. 1993; J. S. Beck and Liese 1998), or psychodynamic exploration of the narcissistic vulnerability, these issues should be dealt with in this substantial subpopulation.

A real danger of psychodynamic theory has been a tendency toward reductionism that tries to apply one theory or approach to every situation. A broad and flexible use of psychodynamic thinking takes into account the total range of structural issues including id, ego, and superego; conflict theory; self psychology; affect regulation; and cognitive deficits. Perry et al. (1987) clarified how three different models of psychodynamic theories—self psychology; object relations; and classical ego, id, and superego conflict theory—can flexibly be used to fit the metaphor most useful to a particular patient or dynamic history.

Evidence indicates that alcohol problems can either cause or result from anxiety disorders and that more often than not agoraphobia, social phobia, and obsessive-compulsive disorders may precede rather than follow an alcohol problem (Kushner et al. 1990). Although cognitive-behavioral and pharmacological approaches may be first-line treatment for panic disorder, agoraphobia, or social phobia, psychodynamic approaches are often used with patients who have been resistant to, or received only partially successful treatment with, other psychotherapies and medications (Frances and Borg 1993).

Partial (day) hospitals are increasingly being used after the patient has been stabilized and detoxified. In one series of papers, researchers found that day hospitals were as effective as inpatient treatment for substance abuse addiction (Alterman et al. 1994).

## Counterindications for Dynamic Psychotherapy

Counterindications for psychodynamic-oriented psychotherapy include active use of substances, severe organicity, psychosis, and for the most part, antisocial personality disorder. Some patients who regress too readily in individual therapy, develop psychotic transferences, or develop negative therapeutic reactions benefit from the diffusion of transference that takes place in group therapy. If the principal problem is marital, family therapy is the treatment of choice.

## Initiation of Treatment

Some authors recommend waiting 6 months to 1 year before beginning psychodynamic-oriented psychotherapy (Bean-Bayog 1988). We believe initiation of psychodynamic-oriented treatment can successfully occur early; however, timing should be tailored to the patient. The greatest opportunity to develop a treatment alliance is often early, while the patient is in crisis. Supportive elements, such as confrontation, clarification, support of defenses, and building on ego strengths, may be more prominent early in treatment. The therapist also should take into account state-related problems of organicity, physical illness, and affective vulnerability, all of which can lead to an inability to utilize interpretations. In their work on initiating treatment, Prochaska et al. (1992) discussed the stages in which patients develop awareness of their addiction problems. Focusing on motivational aspects of treatment and confronting denial of a need for help are essential elements in initiating the treatment process. Promoting an identification as a "recovering" person can boost self-esteem and provide stability. The dynamically oriented psychotherapist needs to consider the effects of intoxication, withdrawal, and the chronic organic effects of alcohol. However, during intoxication or withdrawal there are patients for whom psychodynamic-oriented interpretations are indicated from the very outset of treatment, regardless of the stage of addiction. Interpretations may help the patient work through resistances to accepting help. They may also provide a meaningful explanation for destructive patterns that can inspire a wish for change.

Timing of interpretations is crucial. A patient who may need to project blame and responsibility for his or her actions onto substances early in recovery may later be able to accept responsibility for those actions. For example, one patient later admitted that having an affair, embezzling money, and being abusive were things that he wanted to do anyway, and that he used alcohol and cocaine abuse as an excuse. The individual may not be ready to take full responsibility for his or her actions early into abstinence, but over time, these issues can be explored and pointed out, denial can be worked through, and acceptance of responsibility can be achieved. Defenses may need to be supported at first, including denial of affect related to some of the losses. Confrontation should concentrate initially on denial surrounding addictive behaviors. Clarification, confrontation, and interpretation of denial, lying, splitting, and projective defenses in other areas ultimately need to be expanded. However, in selected cases, with repeated treatment failure, an initial intervention may require active, across-the-board confrontation and interpretation of inconsistencies and denial in order to help the patient accept a need for change. In patients who have alexithymia and in patients who have constricted affect, interpretations are aimed at increasing the patient's awareness of feeling states and helping him or her connect thoughts and feelings without the use of substances.

## Frequency of Sessions, Setting, and Goals

Psychodynamic-oriented psychotherapy with alcoholic patients is usually given one to two times per week, it is often administered in conjunction with group psychotherapy, and it includes a parameter of abstinence and a long-term goal of sobriety. It can be done as part of an inpatient stay or as part of an organized outpatient or office practice, and it can be time limited and focused or long term.

It is foolhardy for psychotherapists to promise that once underlying causes of a "symptom of drinking" are dealt with, the patient will be able to return to controlled drinking. Similarly, it is unwise to promise that once a patient is fully treated with psychoanalytically oriented psychotherapy, he or she will never need additional help through 12-step programs or additional psychotherapy.

For most alcoholic individuals, shifting dependency from a chemical such as alcohol to a therapist, group, spiritual belief, or involvement with anything human is a major step in the direction of growth. Although issues of dependency may be worked through partially, an ongoing positive identification with a therapist, a sponsor, and/or recovering friends may be a major positive outcome of treatment. Active dialogue with the patient and an attitude of empathic concern and sharing on the part of the therapist are optimal. Issues of termination from individual therapy or graduation from phases of treatment may resurface earlier conflicts and trigger relapse. The goal of psychodynamic treatment for addicted patients is to help them maintain abstinence, provide them with a richer understanding and control of their inner life, and reduce psychological triggers for relapse. Indirectly, this goal helps improve patient self-esteem, self-care, and affect regulation (Khantzian 1997).

# General Technical Aspects of Treatment

Advances in object relations theory, ego psychology, and modern psychodynamic understanding of conflicts and affect regulation can be applied to addiction treatment. Psychodynamic principles are applied in conjunction with understanding the clinical exigencies of addiction treatment. Techniques need to be modified, especially those related to attaining and sustaining abstinence, and the effects of regression should be monitored carefully. However, well-established techniques and principles of brief and long-term psychodynamic treatment are generally maintained. The therapist listens for themes relating to the patient's intrapsychic conflicts, developmental impairments, and defenses with special attention to how they may relate to substance abuse and relapse potential. The therapist has some important objectives: obtaining a careful developmental history of the patient, with attention to achievement of milestones of ego development; evaluating temperament in the patient and significant caretakers; examining the patient's capacity to identify with and to separate from important figures of identification, including parents, siblings, or admired peers; and exploring the patient's affect regulation, especially in relation to substance use. The therapist's tools include the use of free association, "slips," and understanding of dreams to find meaning in the unconscious derivatives of behavior, such as an unconscious wish to drink expressed in a drunk dream.

# Treatment Parameters

Treatment parameters for patients with addictions, such as a need for structure, clear boundaries, and abstinence, are similar to those used effectively in treating borderline personality disorder. Structure and boundaries help the patient reestablish control and self-regulation and help him or her express feelings verbally rather than showing the therapist the problems by acting them out. The conventional practice of psychodynamic psychotherapy with limit setting is generally an aid in treatment, although on rare occasions a more active approach may be needed. For example, a therapist may need to actively mobilize a family to bring a suicidal alcoholic patient to the emergency room or to the physician's office after a relapse.

While the therapist works through the patient's resistance and defenses, he or she should be aware of how alcohol provides the patient with an escape, can numb or facilitate expression, and itself can alter defensive operations, especially heightening denial. The therapist should watch closely the interplay of ego function, feeling states, and chemical effects in the patient.

Abstinence is considered by most therapists in the addiction field to be necessary for psychotherapy to be effective. However, many therapists feel it is best to first develop a solid relationship with the patient and then gradually and progressively aim for abstinence (Dodes and Khantzian 1998). We believe that although flexibility is often needed for severely psychiatrically ill patients, for the most part psychiatric problems must be treated in synchrony with the addiction disorder, for which abstinence is vital. Unfortunately, sometimes a continuation of a psychodynamically oriented psychotherapy can enable the addicted patient to continue substance use. It can also raise conflicts that may lead to worsening of the addiction, and thus can be counterindicated. The following case illustrates such a situation:

> A 37-year-old successful journalist was in psychoanalysis 5 days per week for a severe alcohol addiction. He would frequently arrive at sessions intoxicated or miss them altogether. During years of analysis, his addiction to alcohol progressed. His family tried to convince him to seek consultation from an addiction psychiatrist. He protested that he had a good relationship with his analyst, thought he was being helped, and used this as a rationale to avoid effective treatment.

This patient had poor results in treatment because his psychoanalyst was not knowledgeable about addictions and was adhering to a technique that was wrong for this particular patient. The issue of abstinence was crucial here, but it was ignored.

# Other Treatment Tools

A combination of psychodynamic approaches such as clarification, interpretation, and genetic reconstruction may be used along with directive approaches such as assertiveness training, social skills training, self-efficacy groups, modeling, positive reinforcement, cognitive awareness, and suggestion. A sophisticated familiarity with typical problems that occur with alcoholic or drug-abusing individuals and their families and the use of psychoeducation about these issues help the therapist establish a positive alliance with his or her patient. The literature on adult children of alcoholic patients can be useful both for the therapist's understanding and in psychoeducation for patients and their families. The following case illustrates the use of combined approaches:

A 42-year-old recovering alcoholic woman who had panic attacks and agoraphobia had special problems when flying. Psychodynamic psychotherapy was useful when added to desensitization, relaxation therapy, exposure to flying, and closely monitored medication of panic attacks with imipramine and benzodiazepines 2 hours before airplane trips. The anxiety persisted at a significant level that frequently interfered with the patient's plans. Her fears of flying were related to childhood conflicts about having to take planes to visit her father after her parents divorced. She was the "apple of her father's eye" and had clearly won out over her mother, not without considerable guilt over her especially favored position. Her oedipal guilt persisted, contributing to difficulty reaching orgasm with her husband and feelings of guilt about enjoying her sexuality. The flights she currently fears most are those related to visits with her father or pleasure trips with her husband. Although none of the treatments have totally allayed her fears, she is able to travel without drinking and is better able to understand and cope with her fears of flying as a result of her enhanced insight into the roots of her fears. She is increasingly allowing herself to enjoy gradual steps toward success without relapsing.

## Initial Focus and Phases of Treatment

The phases of intervention include initial screening, evaluation and intervention, rehabilitation, and aftercare. The initial focus is often on conflicts related to the acceptance of addiction as a problem, the patient's reluctance to acknowledge dependency and the need for treatment, and conflicts resulting from the complications of alcoholism, including the loss of relationships, health, and jobs, and from missing alcohol itself. As emphasized earlier, the first goal is abstinence.

More often than is usually the case in insight-oriented psychotherapy, the patient may initially be forced into the consultation by an employer, probation officer, family member, or physician. Especially when coercion has occurred, the therapist must make considerable effort to develop trust and a working alliance with the patient. This is achieved through careful review of the patient's history and the ways in which addiction has interfered with family, work, and relationships or has caused legal problems, all of which have

contributed to pain and a need to escape it. The therapist's integrity, adherence to confidentiality, and ability to be helpful all contribute to the establishment of trust.

The patient is helped to accept a diagnosis and to accept a need for help, which may lead to positive transference. These steps are similar to the first two AA steps, in which patients admit their powerlessness over alcohol and accept their need for help or acknowledgment of their own dependency needs, which in AA is called *accepting a higher power*. A psychodynamic perspective may aid in the confrontation of denial and other defenses, and through interpretations patients achieve deeper understanding of certain destructive patterns that have led to the present problem. It is especially challenging to help the patient to acknowledge dependency needs that have been channeled into the addiction.

Therapy is the process in which a need for substances is shifted back into a need for people, including the therapist. Patients who abuse drugs often refuse medications because of their fears of using them in compulsive ways, being dependent on drugs for relief, and being dependent on the therapist to obtain these medications. From early in treatment, issues of trust, dependency, separation, loss, disappointment, and truthfulness are frequent themes.

In the later stages, the focus of treatment in exploratory psychotherapy should not be mechanically imposed from the outside, based on purely theoretical considerations. Rather, it should be targeted at the most pressing issue of the moment that may relate to the patient's drinking: a particular conflict; a relationship with a family member or employer; a problem with self-esteem, self-destructiveness, or self-medication of panic; or other painful affects.

Other major themes include specific conflicts over assertiveness, handling of aggression, and issues of control and inhibition. The disinhibiting role of addictions in allowing risk-taking behavior, including increased sexual activity, may be an issue. Alternatively, alcohol may play a role in distancing the individual from sexual life or it may substitute for sexual activity.

## Watch for Relapse

Patients need to be observed carefully for drinking or drug use behavior. Laboratory tests may be useful aids, and meeting with family and other sources of collateral information may be essential to get a true picture and to aid in confronting patients who dissimulate.

As mentioned earlier, psychodynamic therapy can help in relapse prevention. Consider the following case:

> A 47-year-old pediatric surgical nurse frequently relapses in her addiction to diazepam on evenings after she has had to deal with families whose child had a disastrous surgical result. As a child, she was traumatized by a younger sister's postoperative death due to a brain tumor. Her parents tried to protect her by never discussing her sister's death, and she had always found this to be strange. Her relapses were triggered by unresolved conflicts and grief regarding her dead sister, whom she envied, loved, and at self-destructive moments, wished to join in death. Her initial treatment plan involved detoxification, support, and an aim for abstinence. However, the effectiveness of relapse prevention was enhanced by psychodynamically oriented treatment that helped her mourn her sister and eliminate an important trigger for relapse.

## Acceptance of Self in Recovery

An important part of recovery is a change in self-awareness and self-perception. An enormous shift is in getting the patient to accept a diagnosis of alcoholism as an illness. This entails not only shifting from a moral model in which the patient sees himself or herself as weak, shameful, and bad for being alcoholic but also being aware that a problem exists about which a great deal is known, that it is treatable, and that it does not have to lead to hopelessness and despair. Sometimes this awareness leads to reaction formation in which the patient feels grateful for being alcoholic and turns a disability into an advantage. There may have been real advantages in terms of broadening of experience, overcoming a vulnerability, and developing a pride that can occur in any group that finds a way to overcome a stigma. The feeling of relief from no longer experiencing the consequences of alcoholism and addiction often leads to a rebound after initial abstinence that sometimes can approach euphoria. This euphoria can often be followed by a letdown when awareness of the multitude of problems that the addictions caused becomes apparent as denial wanes.

## An Ego Psychological Model of Rehabilitation

An assessment of ego function needs to include a search for strengths, talents, and positive qualities that can be used to help the patient. All too often, therapists miss opportunities to enhance self-esteem in those patients whose self-criticism leads them to overlook real and potential opportunities for growth. One way to combine positive insight with support is to help patients recall periods in which their values were in place and to give them hope for a return to a higher level of function. Even very damaged, impaired individuals in inner-city settings often have dreams in their lives that they have buried. Rekindled dreams can foster renewed hope and self-esteem. The stigma of the illness can also be lessened by discussing positive role models, such as Betty Ford, who have struggled with the same illness and have worked hard at recovery.

An ego psychological model can be applied to the biopsychosocial effects of addiction and a model of rehabilitation. Chemicals and psychosocial consequences have effects and may lead to regression and impairment of defenses, object relatedness, judgment, reality testing, and superego. It may take time and practice for good ego and superego function to return. The following case demonstrates recovery of function:

> A narcissistic 47-year-old man who drank heavily for 25 years had disuse atrophy of ego functions and was pushed to function better as part of rehabilitation. He thought of his wife only in terms of what she could do for him, as a part object or a need-satisfying object, and only with practice and with time sober could he relate to her in a more complex way as having needs of her own. He would idealize or devalue everyone and everything, and it took him a long time to relate to others as having both good and bad qualities. In order to develop friendships and break isolation, he had to practice relatedness in individual therapy, couples therapy, group therapy, and self-help groups. The superego had been dissolved in chemicals for years, and it took external structure and parameters to gradually awaken the sleeping policeman within, for the superego to start working again. The program requirements and the external norms of the groups helped him regain structure. His superego was initially inconsistent and vacillated from a lack of restraint and self-indulgence to a primitive punitive masochistic rigidity. Cognitive impairment, especially in the nondominant hemisphere functions of spatial and temporal relationships, was present and improved over time with abstinence.

The defenses initially encountered are usually the most primitive and include denial, rationalization, splitting, projection, and projective identification. With time and treatment, higher-level defenses such as intellectualization, reaction formation, repression, and sublimation may be more in the forefront. For example, instead of denying alcoholism and projecting poor self-esteem onto the group, a patient may feel grateful to have alcoholism and honored to have been part of a group that initially was perceived as being stigmatizing. Denial of alcohol's harmful effects on the liver, which can be addressed by a program of psychoeducation, can be replaced with curiosity and intellectualization about how liver damage occurs. Denial of losses related to addiction may over time be replaced with repression after grieving of the losses has occurred.

## Applications of Psychodynamics to Groups and Self-Help

The addition of group psychotherapy, AA, or NA is especially needed when individual therapy alone is not helping the patient maintain abstinence. Group treatments help diffuse some of the powerful negative transference that may be impossible to overcome early in treatment. Groups can focus on issues of self-care, self-esteem, affect regulation, sharing, and exposure to feared social situations. They can provide social support and models for identification and coping skills, and they can help patients work through family problems. They can be targeted to specific additional diagnoses such as anxiety disorders or to specific subpopulations such as the chronically mentally ill, those with medical complications, women, and adolescents. The focus of groups can be homogeneous (e.g., recovering physicians with anxiety disorders) or heterogeneous (e.g., all patients in a detoxification unit).

Khantzian (1997) described a model of modified dynamic group therapy for substance-abusing patients involving self-care, self-esteem, and affect regulation. Together the patient and the individual therapist can look at how the patient projects feelings toward other AA, NA, or group members who, for example, remind him or her of his or her alcoholic relatives. Character flaws can be actively worked on with immediate and multiple feedback from group members. If the individual therapist is also the group therapist, the individual work may be used to encourage the patient to try a new behavior in the group, and conversely, observation of conflicts in the group can be worked on individually.

Aspects of 12-step programs may readily lend themselves to incorporation with psychodynamic treatment. These aspects include accepting a diagnosis, accepting dependency needs, being aware that one cannot control drinking alone, taking a personal inventory (often discussed in terms of a higher power), working at change, dealing with sobriety one day at a time, accepting the structure of a treatment program, and enhancing self-esteem by helping others with the problem, thus living up to an ego ideal.

The 12-step programs provide education, auxiliary ego and superego support, and powerful role models for positive identification. Steps in AA that involve taking one's personal inventory and making amends can be used in conjunction with the psychotherapeutic process of self-exploration and insight aimed at behavioral change. The addition of AA is especially helpful during periods of relapse and during periods of separation in which the therapist is unavailable because either the patient or the therapist is away. Because alcoholism and drug abuse are often chronic relapsing illnesses, both the patient and the therapist must be prepared for the possibility of a relapse. The therapist should be both nonjudgmental and unafraid of confrontation when needed.

## The Patient-Therapist Relationship

Many of the problems related to working with addicted patients relate to the challenge of establishing a positive therapeutic relationship between the patient and the therapist. Frequently errors in treatment occur because of negative feelings and attitudes that therapists have toward addicted patients. Typical mistakes include providing inadequate empathy or overly identifying with patients. A major source of countertransference is that a clinician may uncritically accept roles projected onto him or her in the patient's transference.

In many cases, an understanding of the patient's specific transference that may either evoke countertransference problems or prevent compliance with treatment may be essential for good management and a successful alliance with the patient. Typical transference may result from growing up in a household in which the parents were addicted, inconsistent, and either overly harsh or indulgent. Children of alcoholic parents frequently have authority problems and will often trust siblings, peers, and fellow alcoholic individuals more readily than teachers, nurses, doctors, or police. When a patient describes a therapist as cold, neglectful, uninvolved, or detached, this may be transference to a parent who fits this description and may lead the therapist to behave in this way.

It is helpful for the therapist to be able to interpret

negative transference and to know how to manage and to appropriately use therapist countertransference. Alcoholic patients frequently will try to evoke in their therapists feelings of fear, anger, and despair and will reenact relationships with alcoholic parents, siblings, and spouses through the transference. They may project critical attitudes onto their therapists and keep secrets out of fear that the therapists will respond like a parent. When the patient feels the therapist is like a parent, sibling, or friend, this feeling may have been evoked for specific reasons. The greater the therapist's awareness of what is happening, the more this issue can be brought into the treatment in a constructive way.

A second major source of countertransference in treating addicted patients is therapists who have a weak knowledge base about addiction and its treatment. The more knowledgeable the therapist is about addiction psychiatry and about the patient, the less likely he or she is to project his or her own problems onto the patient. Attitudinal problems on the part of the therapist can be reduced by good training and an experience of having worked through issues related to stigma. The more the therapist is in command of a treatment armamentarium, the less frightened he or she is in the face of what can be a dreadful disease. Ultimately, patients are the best teachers. By listening carefully the therapist can gain knowledge about the addictive experience, practices, and street language.

A third source of countertransference is based on the mostly unconscious transference that the therapist may have toward the patient, related to the therapist's past or present problems. Transference may relate to a therapist's own attitudes about substances; present or past problems with addiction; or experience with a parent, spouse, or child with a substance use problem. The therapist's own envy, fear, hopes, and needs can adversely affect his or her prescribing practices and lead to overinvolvement, avoidance, hopelessness, jealousy, and burnout. Some clinicians who have chosen to work in the addiction field because of their wish to overcome personal problems related to addictions may have special difficulty dealing with patients' problems if they have not worked out their own. Frequent mistakes include excessive self-revelation of personal problems and a tendency not to see the specifics of the patients' problems clearly because of a need to see everyone as similar to the self. A recovering clinician might consider a patient's problem minor compared with his or her own. Alternatively, some clinicians see every problem only in relation to addictive problems. This results in misdiagnosis and overdiagnosis. The extreme of over-

involvement can include sexual or aggressive acting out with a vulnerable substance-abusing patient, which leads to disastrous consequences for both patient and therapist. Seeking out second opinions or supervision from experienced practitioners is advisable when working with difficult patients. The therapist's completion of a thorough self-exploration in personal therapy also helps. Clinicians with maturity, a good support system, and a secure personal life are better protected against countertransference problems. Additional protection is given by working in a team, where team members can point out one another's blind spots and assist in improving one another's technique. Feedback from patients and their families can be another source of supervision for the clinician who listens carefully. A wise clinician admits his or her mistakes, learns from them, and tries to avoid future mistakes (GAP Addiction Committee, in press).

 ## Beware of Myths and Pitfalls

This section includes a list of myths and pitfalls to avoid in dynamic psychotherapy.

### Myths

- One can first develop a therapeutic relationship and then gradually wean the patient off substances.
- Substance use will disappear with understanding.
- Once conflicts have been resolved, the patient can return safely to drinking.
- If the problem is narcotic addiction, alcohol is safer and legal.
- Addiction is always a symptom, not a primary problem.

### Pitfalls

- To believe a patient's explanation for drinking without awareness of rationalization and a patient's need for justifying his or her behavior.
- Not to check out the patient's story with collateral sources.
- To conduct treatment as if dynamic interpretations were "golden" and other interventions less valuable. The best mix of treatment and sequence should be selected on the basis of the patient's needs.
- Not to have a healthy respect for the patient's dependency needs and to have too high expectation for resolving these needs. It is better for the patient to depend on therapists or on AA than on substances,

and an endless relationship with AA is a desirable goal—not a compromise of a therapist's goal of self-reliance on the patient's part.

- To be overinvolved or overly distant. Therapists in recovery themselves sometimes have blind spots or may share with the patient more than the patient needs to know.
- Even moderate biases for one or another form of treatment and lack of flexibility both theoretical and practical can be a disservice to the patient.

## Usefulness of Treatment Outcome Research

The state of the art in addiction treatment involves being aware of the results of treatment outcome studies but also selecting a combination of treatment that takes into account current knowledge and patient characteristics. Treatment recommendations depend on a wide range of considerations, and trial results are only one factor. The American Psychiatric Association (1995) developed practice guidelines for the treatment of substance use disorder based on reviews of the literature on treatment and outcomes. These guidelines recommend individualizing treatment planning and include treatment of comorbid conditions. Woody et al. (1990) showed meaningful differences in efficacy between supportive-expressive psychotherapy in methadone-maintained patients. Carrol et al. (1994) pointed out that there is a delayed emergence of the effects of psychotherapy after cessation of short-term treatments in cocaine-dependent patients.

With managed care entering the arena of health care, studies of cost-effectiveness and outcomes are becoming increasingly important. Humphreys and Moos (1996) found reduced substance-related health care costs in a Veterans AA study. O'Brien (1997a) found favorable efficacy when comparing specific treatment approaches for addictive disorders with other chronic disorders such as diabetes and asthma. O'Brien (1997b) also pointed to studies that have shown a cost saving of $4–$12 for every dollar spent on substance abuse treatment.

It is too early in addiction outcome research to make hard-and-fast recommendations as to what treatments should be used. Treatment outcome studies discussed in this volume and treatment guidelines (that are and will be developed) provide useful information, but they are not definitive instructions to clinicians. Although clinicians agree in some areas (e.g., the usefulness of ab-

stinence as a goal; the pharmacotherapy of comorbid disorders such as panic attacks; the value of adding education, cognitive, and behavioral approaches), controlled study proof of the value of treatments such as 12-step programs and psychodynamic psychotherapy is not yet strong, although each treatment has a common-sense rationale. Where definite answers are still lacking, clinicians need to be aware of a growing literature of outcome studies, of the methodological problems in conducting good studies, and of the problems in reliability and validity in applying these results. Uncertainties as to the exact value of psychodynamic and combined treatments should not deter clinicians from using what has seemed useful, especially with patients who have specific favorable characteristics such as motivation and capacity for insight and destructive patterns amenable to interpretation. When definite conclusions about the effectiveness of treatment components are established, targeting of treatment will improve.

## Implications for Research

New research is needed to identify the patients for whom psychodynamic treatment is appropriate—specifically, which Axis I or Axis II disorders, which age group, what timing, which patient characteristics, combined with what other treatment, and which, among the broad range of psychodynamic interventions, are most useful. It is hard to find good databases of what are often clinically subjective material. Premature closure on any of these questions because of the challenge and expense of studying the particular area may lead to overly narrowly based, poorer-quality treatment approaches. It will take time, the pooling of large amounts of clinical data, and the collaboration of many clinician researchers to get these answers. Initially, nonrandomized, noncontrolled, and descriptive studies will be needed. Ultimately, randomized studies can best exclude even moderate biases, and with large numbers of patients studied, it will be possible to correct for both false-positive and false-negative results.

## Conclusion

Psychodynamic theory can have an important role in enriching and informing substance abuse treatment and improving the therapeutic relationship. Rigid application of psychoanalytic technique, however, has little place in substance abuse treatment and can be counterproductive. Application of psychodynamic understanding—including attending to the unconscious, child development, ego function, affect regulation, and efforts to enhance self-esteem and deal with shame and other narcissistic vulnerability—widens the range of patients that can be treated.

Definitive outcome studies of psychodynamic psychotherapy in substance-abusing patients will be difficult to achieve. However, a rich descriptive clinical experience in this area improves our understanding of addicted patients.

# References

Abraham K: The psychological relation between sexuality and alcoholism (1908), in Selected Papers of Karl Abraham. New York, Basic Books, 1960, pp 80–89

Alterman AI, O'Brien CP, McLellan AT, et al: Effectiveness and costs of inpatient versus day hospital cocaine rehabilitation. J Nerv Ment Dis 182:157–163, 1994

American Psychiatric Association: Practice guidelines for the treatment of patients with substance use disorder: alcohol, cocaine, opioids. Am J Psychiatry 152:5–59, 1995

Bean-Bayog M: Alcoholism as a cause of psychopathology. Hosp Community Psychiatry 39:352–354, 1988

Beck AT, Wright FD, Newman CF, et al: Cognitive Therapy of Substance Abuse. New York, Guilford, 1993

Beck JS, Liese BS: Cognitive therapy for substance abuse, in Clinical Textbook of Addictive Disorders, 2nd Edition. Edited by Frances RJ, Miller S. New York, Guilford, 1998, pp 547–574

Bleuler E: Alcohol and the neuroses (1911). Jahrbuch für Psychoanalytisch und Psychopathologische Forschungen; Jahrbuch der Psychoanalyse 3:848. Abstracted by Blungart L. Psychoanal Rev 8:443–444, 1921

Carrol KM, Rounsaville BJ, Nich C, et al: One-year follow-up of psychotherapy and pharmacotherapy for cocaine dependence. Arch Gen Psychiatry 51:989–997, 1994

Cloninger CR: A systematic method for clinical description and classification of personality variants: a proposal. Arch Gen Psychiatry 44:573–588, 1987

Dodes LM: The psychology of combining dynamic psychotherapy and Alcoholics Anonymous. Bull Menninger Clin 52:283–293, 1988

Dodes LM, Khantzian EJ: Individual psychodynamic psychotherapy, in Clinical Textbook of Addictive Disorders, 2nd Edition. Edited by Frances RJ, Miller SI. New York, Guilford, 1998, pp 479–496

Frances RJ, Borg L: The treatment of anxiety in patients with alcoholism. J Clin Psychiatry 54 (suppl):37–43, 1993

Frances RJ, Khantzian EJ, Tamerin JS: Psychodynamic psychotherapy, in Treatments of Psychiatric Disorders: A Task Force Report of the American Psychiatric Association, Vol 2. Washington, DC, American Psychiatric Association, 1989, pp 1103–1111

Freud S: Three essays on the theory of sexuality (1905), in The Standard Edition of the Complete Psychological Works of Sigmund Freud, Vol 7. Translated and edited by Strachey J. London, Hogarth Press, 1949, pp 125–245

Freud S: Civilization and Its Discontents (1930). New York, WW Norton, 1964

Freud S, Ferenczi S, Brabant E, et al: The Correspondence of Sigmund Freud and Sandor Ferenczi, Vol 1, 1908–1914. Cambridge, MA, Belknap Press/Harvard University Press, 1993

GAP Addiction Committee: The doctor-patient relationship. GAP Monograph, Chapter 6. Washington, DC, American Psychiatric Association (in press)

Glover E: On the etiology of drug addiction (1932), in Selected Papers of Psychoanalysis, Vol 1: On the Early Development of Mind. Edited by Glover E. New York, International Universities Press, 1956, pp 187–215

Humphreys K, Moos RH: Reduced substance-abuse-related health care costs among voluntary participants in Alcoholics Anonymous. Psychiatr Serv 47:709–713, 1996

Kernberg OF: Transference regression and psychoanalytic technique with infantile personalities. Int J Psychoanal 72:189–200, 1991

Kessler RC, Crum RM, Warner LA, et al: Lifetime co-occurrence of DSM-III-R alcohol abuse and dependence with other psychiatric disorders in the National Comorbidity Survey. Arch Gen Psychiatry 54:313–321, 1997

Khantzian EJ: The self medication hypothesis of substance use disorders: a reconsideration and recent applications. Harv Rev Psychiatry 4:231–244, 1997

Klerman GL, Weissman MM, Rounsaville BH, et al: The Theory and Practice of Interpersonal Psychotherapy for Depression. New York, Basic Books, 1984

Kohut H, Wolf ES: The disorders of the self and their treatment: an outline. Int J Psychoanal 59:413–425, 1978

Koob GF, Le Moal M: Drug abuse: hedonic homeostatic dysregulation. Science 278:52–57, 1997

Krystal H: Alexithymia and the effectiveness of psychoanalytic treatment. International Journal of Psychoanalytic Psychotherapy 9:353–388, 1982

Kushner MA, Sher KJ, Bertman BD: The relation between alcohol problems and anxiety disorders. Am J Psychiatry 147:685–695, 1990

Leshner AI: Addiction is a brain disease, and it matters. Science 278:45–47, 1997

Lewis HB: Shame and the narcissistic personality, in The Many Faces of Shame. Edited by Nathanson DL. New York, Guilford, 1987, pp 93–132

Lorand J: A summary of psychoanalytic literature on problems of alcoholism. Yearbook of Psychoanalysis 1:359–378, 1948

Luborsky L: Principles of Psychoanalytic Psychotherapy: A Manual for Supportive-Expressive Treatment. New York, Basic Books, 1984

Mahler M, Pine R, Bergman A: The Psychological Birth of the Human Infant: Symbiosis and Individuation. New York, Basic Books, 1975

McDougall J: The "dis-affected" patient: reflections on affect pathology. Psychoanal Q 53:366–409, 1984

Meissner WW: Psychotherapy and the Paranoid Process. New York, Jason Aronson, 1986

Menninger KA: Man Against Himself. New York, Harcourt Brace, 1938

Milkman H, Frosch WA: On the preferential abuse of heroin and amphetamine. J Nerv Ment Dis 156:242–248, 1973

O'Brien CP: Progress in the science of addiction. Am J Psychiatry 154:1195–1197, 1997a

O'Brien CP: A range of research-based pharmacotherapies for addiction. Science 278:66–69, 1997b

Perry S, Cooper A, Michels R: The psychodynamic formulation: its purpose, structure, and clinical application. Am J Psychiatry 144:543–550, 1987

Prochaska JO, Di Clemente CC, Norcross JC: In search of how people change: applications to addictive behavior. Am Psychol 47:1102–1114, 1992

Rado S: The psychoanalysis of pharmacothymia (drug addiction). J Subst Abuse Treat 1:59–68, 1984

Silber A: Rationale for the technique of psychotherapy with alcoholics. International Journal of Psychoanalytic Psychotherapy 3:28–47, 1974

Vaillant GE: The Natural History of Alcoholism Revisited. Cambridge, MA, Harvard University Press, 1995, pp 362–373

Volkow ND, Wang GJ, Fischman MW, et al: Relationship between subjective effects of cocaine and dopamine transporter occupancy. Nature 386:827–830, 1997

Wieder H, Kaplan EH: Drug use in adolescents. Psychoanal Study Child 24:399–431, 1969

Woody GE, McLellan AT, Luborsky L, et al: Psychotherapy for substance abuse. Psychiatr Clin North Am 9:547–562, 1986

Woody GE, Luborsky L, McLellan AT, et al: Corrections and revised analyses for psychotherapy in methadone maintenance patients (letter). Arch Gen Psychiatry 47:788–789, 1990

Wurmser L: The role of superego conflicts in substance abuse and their treatment. International Journal of Psychoanalytic Psychotherapy 10:227–258, 1984

# *28* Network Therapy

## Marc Galanter, M.D.

In this chapter, I define aspects of addiction relevant to ambulatory therapy and describe a treatment modality that was designed to address these aspects. This approach, called *network therapy* (Galanter 1993a), was developed specifically to bring addicted patients to a successful recovery, whereas conventional office therapy often fails in this task. Network therapy can be defined as an approach to rehabilitation in which specific family members and friends are enlisted to provide ongoing support and to promote attitude change. Network members are part of the therapist's working "team" and not subjects of treatment themselves. The goal of this approach is the prompt achievement of abstinence with relapse prevention and the development of a drug-free adaptation.

Most mental health professionals are ill-prepared to help alcoholic or drug-abusing individuals achieve recovery, even though addicted individuals and their families regularly turn to them for help. In one survey of general psychiatrists practicing primarily with psychiatric management alone, more than half reported no success with any alcoholic patients (Hayman 1956). Those who reported any success said that it occurred in no more than 10% of their patients. Furthermore, few alcoholic and addicted individuals are willing to go to 12-step programs such as Alcoholics Anonymous (AA) until they have endured their illness for a long time, and most drop out before becoming involved. A pointed question inevitably arises: how can we engage and treat these troubled individuals more effectively?

Furthermore, how can we make treatment more efficient? In recent years, inpatient rehabilitation facilities for substance-abusing patients have proliferated. These programs are useful in that they terminate the patient's access to drugs and create a safe environment for detoxification and education. Nonetheless, they require weeks of hospitalization and often disrupt family and social ties while patients are hospitalized. They also prevent patients from learning to deal with drinking cues while their treatment supports are greatest. It seems more reasonable to support a patient's rehabilitation by means of the social ties available in his or her own community.

This latter point is supported by the finding that augmentation of treatment by group and family therapy in the multimodality clinic setting has led to considerably more success in alcoholism treatment (Gallant et al. 1970). Groups such as AA also offer invaluable adjunctive support. A model for enhancing therapeutic intervention in the context of insight-oriented individual therapy would be of considerable value, given the potential role of the individual practitioner as primary therapist for many patients with addictive problems.

In enhancing the effectiveness of ambulatory therapy, an individual's immediate network might include his or her spouse, friends, or family of origin, and perhaps a friend from work. Components of the network are only parts of the natural support systems that usually operate without professional involvement, but if they can be brought to act in concert, the strength of their social influence can serve as a therapeutic device. The network can complement individual or group therapy and AA.

## Addressing the Problems of Relapse and Loss of Control

To frame a social therapy using network support, we must first define the target problem clearly and then consider how the network bears its influence. From a clinician's perspective, the problems of *relapse* and *loss of control*, embodied in the third and fourth criteria for substance dependence in DSM-IV (American Psychiatric Association 1994), are central to the difficulty of treating addiction. Because addicted patients are typically under pressure to relapse to ingestion of alcohol or drugs, they are seen as poor candidates for stable attendance in treatment and tend to drop out of treatment precipitously. *Loss of control* has been used to describe the addicted individual's inability to reliably limit consumption once an initial dose is taken (Gallant 1987).

These clinical phenomena are generally described anecdotally but can also be explained mechanistically by recourse to the model of conditioned withdrawal, which relates the psychopharmacology of dependency-producing drugs to the behaviors they produce. Wikler (1973), an early investigator of addiction pharmacology, developed this model to explain the spontaneous appearance of drug craving and relapse. He pointed out that drugs of dependence typically produce compensatory responses in the central nervous system at the same time that their direct pharmacological effects are felt, and these compensatory effects partly counter the drugs' direct actions. Thus when an opioid antagonist is administered to addicted subjects who are maintained on morphine, latent withdrawal phenomena are unmasked. Similar compensatory effects are observed in alcoholic subjects who are maintained on alcohol and who evidence evoked response patterns characteristic of withdrawal while still clinically intoxicated (Begleiter and Porjesz 1979).

In the laboratory, O'Brien et al. (1977) studied addicted subjects. They found that their subjects could be conditioned to experience opioid withdrawal responses to neutral stimuli such as sound and odor. This conditioning, produced in a laboratory setting, provided experimental corroboration of Wikler's hypothesis. Ludwig et al. (1974) demonstrated the direct behavioral correlates of such conditioned stimuli in relation to alcohol administration. They found that for the alcoholic subject, the alcohol dose itself might serve as a conditioned stimulus for enhancing craving, as could the appropriate drinking context.

Clinical interviews show that withdrawal feelings, and hence craving, could be elicited by cues previously associated with the addicted subject's use of the drug. Hence, exposure to the smell of liquor in a bar could precipitate the "need" to drink; seeing the "works" for injecting heroin, or going by a "shooting gallery," could lead a heroin-addicted individual to relapse.

The conditioned stimulus of a drug or environmental cue, or even the affective state regularly associated with

the drug, can lead directly to the behavioral response before the addicted individual consciously experiences withdrawal feelings. The individual may automatically seek out drugs on experiencing anxiety, depression, or narcissistic injury, all of which may have become conditioned stimuli.

Often modulations in mood state are the conditioned stimuli for drug seeking, and the substance-abusing individual can become vulnerable to relapse through reflexive response to a specific affective state. Such phenomena have been described clinically by Khantzian (1985) as *self-medication*. Such mood-related cues, however, are not necessarily mentioned spontaneously by the patient in a conventional therapy because the triggering feeling may not be associated with a memorable event, and the drug use may avert emergence of memorable distress.

More dramatic is the phenomenon of *affect regression*, which Wurmser (1977) observed among addicted patients studied in a psychoanalytic context. He pointed out that when addicted subjects sustain narcissistic injury, they are prone to a precipitous collapse of ego defenses and the consequent experience of intense and unmanageable affective flooding. In the face of such vulnerability, these subjects handle stress poorly and may turn to drugs for relief. This vulnerability can be considered in light of the model of conditioned withdrawal, whereby drug seeking can become an immediate reflexive response to stress, undermining the stability and effectiveness of a patient's coping mechanisms. This can occur quite suddenly in patients who have long associated drug use with their attempts to cope with stress, as illustrated in the following case:

> In the course of his therapy, an alcoholic lawyer found that his drinking had often been precipitated by situations that threatened his self-esteem. After 6 months of sobriety, he had a relapse that was later examined in a session as follows: immediately before his relapse he had received an erroneous report that his share of the partnership's profits would be cut back, which he took to be an evidence of failure. He reported feeling humiliated and then very anxious. Without weighing the consequences, he went out to purchase a bottle of liquor, returned to his office, and began drinking. He said that he had not thought to control this behavior at the time.

This model helps to explain why relapse is such a frequent and unanticipated aspect of addiction treatment. Exposure to conditioned cues, ones that were repeatedly associated with drug use, can precipitate reflexive drug craving during the course of therapy, and such cue exposure can also initiate a sequence of conditioned behaviors that lead addicted individuals to relapse unwittingly into drug use.

Loss of control can be the product of conditioned withdrawal, as described by Ludwig et al. (1978). The sensations associated with the ingestion of an addictive drug, such as the odor of alcohol or the euphoria produced by opioids, are temporally associated with the pharmacological elicitation of a compensatory response to that drug and can later produce drug-seeking behavior. For this reason, the first drink can serve as a conditioned cue for further drinking. These phenomena lead to patients who have very limited capacities to control consumption once a single dose of drug has been taken.

## Application to Treatment

What, then, will serve as a minimally noxious aversive stimulus that would be specific for the conditioned stimuli associated with drug craving, thereby providing a maximally useful learning experience? To answer this question, we may look at Wikler's (1971) initial conception of the implications of his conditioning theory:

> The user would become entangled in an interlocking web of self-perpetuating reinforcers, which perhaps explain the persistence of drug abuse, despite disastrous consequences for the user, and his imperviousness to psychotherapy which does not take such conditioning factors into account, because neither the subject nor the therapist is aware of their existence. (p. 611)

Since Wikler's time, specific techniques have been developed to overcome this problem. The model of conditioned drug seeking has been applied to training patients to recognize drug-related cues and avert relapse. Annis (1986), for example, used a self-report schedule to assist patients in identifying the cues, situations, and moods that are most likely to lead to alcohol craving. Marlatt evolved the approach he described as *relapse prevention* (Marlatt and Gordon 1985), whereby patients are taught strategies for avoiding the consequences of the alcohol-related cues they have identified, and a similar conception has been used to extinguish cocaine craving through cue exposure in a clinical laboratory (Childress et al. 1988).

These approaches can be introduced as part of a single-modality behavioral regimen, but they also can be used in expressive and family-oriented psychotherapy. For example, Ludwig et al. (1978) suggested the ap-

proach of *cognitive labeling*, in which drinking cues are associated with readily identified guideposts to aid the patient in consciously averting the consequences of prior conditioning. Similarly, Galanter (1983) described a process of guided recall to explore the sequence of antecedents of given episodes of craving or drinking "slips" that were not previously clear to a patient. These approaches can be applied concomitant with an examination of general adaptive problems in an exploratory therapy.

A problem exists in application, though. If a patient is committed to achieving abstinence from an addictive drug, but is in jeopardy of occasional slips, cognitive labeling can facilitate consolidation of an abstinent adaptation. Such an approach is less valuable, however, in the context of inadequate motivation for abstinence, fragile social supports, or compulsive substance abuse unmanageable by the patient in his or her usual social settings. Hospitalization or replacement therapy (e.g., with methadone) may be necessary in these situations because ambulatory stabilization through psychotherapeutic support is often not feasible. Under any circumstances, cognitive labeling is an adjunct to psychotherapy and not a replacement for group supports such as AA, family counseling, or ambulatory therapeutic community programs, where applicable.

## The Use of Network Therapy

Having examined the need for behavioral techniques in the ongoing treatment of addiction, we can now consider the model of network therapy for addiction. This model offers a pragmatic approach to augmenting conventional individual therapy that draws on the recent advances just described in order to enhance the effectiveness of office-based therapy.

This conception has been validated in general terms. In an evaluation of family treatment for alcohol problems, McCrady concluded that "research data support superior outcomes for family involved treatment, enough so that the modal approach should involve family members and carefully planned interventions" (Institute of Medicine 1990, p. 84). Indeed, the idea of the therapist intervening with the patient's family and friends to start treatment was introduced by Johnson (1986) as one of the early ambulatory techniques in the addiction field (Gallant 1987; Gitlow and Peyser 1980). More broadly, the availability of greater social support to patients is an important predictor of positive outcome in addiction (McLellan et al. 1983).

Galanter (1993b) reported a positive outcome for this approach in a clinical trial in a series of 60 patients treated in network therapy. The trial involved one network session per week for an initial month, with subsequent sessions held less frequently, typically on a bimonthly basis after 1 year of ambulatory care. Individual therapy was carried out concomitantly on a once- or twice-weekly basis. On average, the networks had 2.3 members, and the most frequent participants were mates, peers, parents, or siblings.

## The Couple as a Network

A cohabiting couple will provide an initial example of how natural affiliative ties can be used to develop a secure basis for rehabilitation. Couples' therapy for addiction has been described in both ambulatory and inpatient settings, and a favorable marital adjustment is associated with a diminished likelihood of dropout and a positive overall outcome (Kaufman and Kaufman 1979; McCrady et al. 1986; Stanton and Thomas 1982).

The use of disulfiram has yielded relatively little benefit overall in controlled trials when it is prescribed for patients to take on their own (Fuller and Williford 1980). This agent is only effective insofar as it is ingested as instructed, typically on a daily basis. Alcoholic patients who forget to take required doses will likely resume drinking in time. Such forgetting often reflects the initiation of a sequence of conditioned drug-seeking behaviors.

Although patient characteristics have not been shown to predict compliance with a disulfiram regimen (Schuckit 1985), changes in the format of patient management have been beneficial (Brubaker et al. 1987). For example, the involvement of a spouse in observing the patient's consumption of disulfiram yields a considerable improvement in outcome because this provides for introducing a system of monitoring (Azrin et al. 1982; Keane et al. 1984). Patients alerted to taking disulfiram each morning by this external reminder are less likely to experience conditioned drug seeking when exposed to addictive cues and are more likely to comply with the dosing regimen on subsequent days.

The technique also helps clearly define the roles in therapy of both the alcoholic patient and his or her spouse. The spouse does not need to monitor drinking behaviors he or she cannot control, nor does he or she actively remind the alcoholic patient to take each disulfiram dose. The spouse merely notifies the therapist if he or she does not observe the pill being ingested on a given day. Decisions on managing compliance are then allocated to the therapist, thereby avoiding entanglement of the couple in a dispute over the patient's attitude and the possibility of drinking in secret.

Other behavioral devices demonstrated to improve outcome can be incorporated into this couple's therapy format. For example, setting the first appointment as soon as possible after an initial telephone contact improves outcome by undercutting the possibility of an early loss of motivation (Stark et al. 1990). Spouses can also be engaged in history taking at the outset of treatment to minimize the introduction of denial into the patient's presentation of his or her illness (Liepman et al. 1989). The initiation of treatment with such a regimen is illustrated in the following case:

A 39-year-old alcoholic man was referred for treatment. The psychiatrist initially engaged both the patient and his wife in an exchange on the telephone, so that all three could plan for the patient to remain abstinent on the day of the first session. They agreed that the wife would meet the patient at his office at the end of the work day on the way to the appointment. This would ensure that cues presented by the patient's friends going out for a drink after work would not lead him to drink. In the session, an initial history was taken from the patient and his wife, allowing her to expand on ill consequences of the patient's drinking, thereby avoiding his minimizing the problem. A review of the patient's medical status revealed no evidence of relevant organ damage, and the option of initiating treatment with disulfiram at that time was discussed. The patient, with the encouragement of his wife, agreed to take his first dose that day and to continue under her observation. Subsequent sessions with the couple were dedicated to dealing with implementation of this plan, and concurrent individual therapy was initiated.

## The Network's Membership

Networks generally consist of a number of members. Once the patient has come for an appointment, establishment of a network is undertaken with active collaboration between the patient and the therapist. The two, aided by those parties who join the network initially, must search for the right balance of members. The therapist must carefully promote the choice of appropriate network members, however, just as the platoon leader selects those who will go into combat. The network will be crucial in determining the balance of the therapy. This process is not without problems, and the therapist must think strategically of the interactions that may occur among network members. The following case illustrates the nature of the therapist's task:

A 25-year-old graduate student had been abusing drugs since high school, in part drawing on funds from his affluent family, who lived in a remote city. At two points in the process of establishing his support network, the reactions of his live-in girlfriend were particularly important. They both agreed to bring in his 19-year-old sister, a freshman at a nearby college. He then mentioned a "friend" of his, a woman whom he had apparently found attractive, even though there was no history of an overt romantic involvement. The expression on his girlfriend's face suggested that she was uncomfortable with this option. The therapist deferred on the idea of the friend and moved on to evaluating the patient's uncle. Initially the patient was reluctant because he perceived the uncle as a potentially disapproving representative of the parental generation. The therapist and girlfriend nonetheless encouraged him to accept the uncle as a network member to round out the range of relationships within the group. The uncle was caring and supportive, particularly after he was helped to understand the nature of the addictive process.

## The Network's Task

The therapist's relationship to the network is one of a task-oriented team leader rather than a family therapist oriented toward restructuring relationships. The network is established to implement a straightforward task, that of aiding the therapist to sustain the patient's abstinence. It must be directed with the same clarity of purpose that a task force is directed in any effective organization. Competing and alternative goals must be suppressed or at least prevented from interfering with the primary task.

Unlike family members involved in traditional family therapy, network members are not led to expect symptom relief or self-realization for themselves. This approach prevents the development of competing goals for the network's meetings. It also protects the members from having their own motives scrutinized and thereby supports their continuing involvement without the threat of an assault on their psychological defenses. Because network members have kindly volunteered to participate, their motives must not be impugned. Their constructive behavior should be commended. Network members should be acknowledged for the contribution they are making to the therapy. Network members have a counterproductive tendency to minimize the value of their contribution. The network must, therefore, be structured as an effective working group with good morale.

A 45-year-old single woman served as an executive in a large family-held business, except when her alcohol problem led her into protracted binges. Her father, brother, and sister were prepared to banish her from the business but decided first to seek consultation. The father was a domineering figure who intruded in all aspects of the business, evoking angry outbursts from his children. The children typically reacted with petulance, provoking him in return. The situation came to a head when the patient's siblings angrily petitioned the therapist to exclude the father from the network, 2 months into the treatment. This presented a problem because the father's control over the business made his involvement important in securing the patient's compliance. The patient's relapse was still a real possibility. The father implied that he might compromise his son's role in the family business. The father's potentially coercive role, however, was an issue that the group could not easily deal with. The therapist supported the father's membership in the group, pointing out the constructive role he had played in getting the therapy started. It was clear to the therapist that the father could not deal with a situation where he was not accorded sufficient respect and that there was no real place in this network for addressing the father's character pathology directly. The children became less provocative themselves, as the group responded to the therapist's pleas for civil behavior.

## Some Specific Techniques

Yalom (1974) described anxiety-reducing tactics that he used in therapy groups with alcoholic patients in order to avert disruptions and promote cohesiveness. These tactics included setting an agenda for the session and using didactic instruction. In the network format, a cognitive framework can be provided for each session by starting out with the patient recounting events related to cue exposure or substance use since the last meeting. Network members are then expected to comment on this report to ensure that all members are engaged in a mutual task with correct, shared information. Their reactions to the patient's report are also addressed.

An alcoholic man began one of his early network sessions by reporting a minor lapse to drinking. His report was disrupted by an angry outburst from his older sister. She said that she had "had it up to here" with his frequent unfulfilled promises of sobriety. The psychiatrist addressed this source of conflict by explaining in a didactic manner how behavioral cues affect vulnerability to relapse. This didactic approach was adopted in order to defuse the assumption that relapse is easily controlled and to relieve consequent resentment. He then led members in planning concretely with the patient how he might avoid further drinking cues in the period preceding their next conjoint session.

Patients undergoing detoxification from chronic depressant medication often experience considerable anxiety, even when a gradual dose-reduction schedule is undertaken (American Psychiatric Association 1990). The expectancy of distress, coupled with conditioned withdrawal phenomena, may cause patients to balk at completing a detoxification regimen (Monti et al. 1988). In individual therapy alone, the psychiatrist would have little leverage on this point. When augmented with network therapy, however, the added support can be invaluable in securing compliance under these circumstances.

> A patient elected to undergo detoxification from chronic use of diazepam, approximately 60 mg/day. In network meetings with the patient, her husband, and a friend, the psychiatrist discussed the need for added support toward the end of her detoxification. As her daily dosage was brought to 2 mg three times daily, she became anxious, said that she had never intended to stop completely, and insisted on being maintained permanently on that low dose. Network members supportively but explicitly pointed out that this had not been the plan. She then relented to the original detoxification agreement, and the dose was reduced to zero over 6 weeks.

Contingency contracting as used in behavioral treatment stipulates that an unpalatable contingency will be applied should a patient carry out a prohibited symptomatic behavior (Hall et al. 1977). Crowley (1984) successfully applied this technique to rehabilitating cocaine-addicted patients by preparing a written contract with each patient that indicated a highly aversive consequence would be initiated for any use of the drug. For example, for an addicted physician, a signed letter admitting addiction was prepared for mailing to the state licensing board. This approach can also be adapted to the network setting.

Patients are strongly inclined to deny drinking problems during relapse. The network may be the only resource the psychiatrist has for communicating with a relapsing patient and for assisting in reestablishing abstinence.

> A patient relapsed to drinking after 6 months of abstinence. One of the network members consulted with

the psychiatrist and then stayed with the patient in his home for a day to ensure that he would not drink. He then brought the patient to the psychiatrist's office along with the other network members to reestablish a plan for abstinence.

## The Use of Alcoholics Anonymous

The use of AA is desirable whenever possible. For the alcoholic individual, certainly, participation in AA is strongly encouraged. Groups such as NA, Pills Anonymous, and Cocaine Anonymous are modeled after AA and play a similarly useful role for drug-abusing individuals. One approach is to tell the patient that he or she is expected to attend at least two AA meetings each week for at least 1 month so as to familiarize himself or herself with the program. If after 1 month the patient is quite reluctant to continue, and other aspects of the treatment are going well, his or her nonparticipation may have to be accepted.

Some patients are more easily convinced to attend AA meetings. Others may be less compliant. The therapist should mobilize the support network as appropriate in order to continue pressure for the patient's involvement with AA for a reasonable trial. It may take a considerable period of time, but ultimately a patient may experience something of a conversion wherein he or she adopts the group ethos and expresses a deep commitment to abstinence, a measure of commitment rarely observed in patients who experience psychotherapy alone. When this occurs, the therapist may assume a more passive role in monitoring the patient's abstinence and keep an eye on the patient's ongoing involvement in AA.

## Contrasts With Family Therapy

Like family and group therapy, network therapy brings several people together to address a psychological problem. Approaches vary among practitioners of group and family modalities, as therapists may focus on the individual patient or try to shape the family or group overall. In the network, in contrast, the focus is always on the individual patient and his or her addictive problem.

In network therapy, unlike family therapy, the practitioner avoids focusing on the patient's family history in the network sessions themselves because an involvement in family conflicts can be disruptive to the network's primary task of helping the therapist to maintain the patient's abstinence. Such a focus would establish an additional agenda and set of goals, potentially obliging the therapist to assume responsibility for resolving conflicts that are not necessarily tied to the addiction itself. Family and interpersonal dynamics can be addressed individually with the patient on his or her own.

> A patient brought his estranged wife and his brother in as network members as he embarked on treatment for prescription drug abuse. The tension between the patient and his spouse was considerable, as both were competitive and controlling in their own ways. She interrupted too often, offering her opinions, and he was dismissive of her and sat with his back to her. His brother tried his best to remain neutral. By listening with interest and respect to both husband and wife, letting each play a positive role in framing the treatment, the therapist could tap their initiative and their desire to "shine" in the session. This approach allowed the therapist to draw on the wife's knowledge of the patient's drug use and focused all three participants on the task of considering more members of this emerging network. The very traits that might have served as grist for a family therapist were not discussed.

A technique of family therapy that bears considerable similarity to the network format is the *strategic family approach* (Haley 1977). As in network therapy, this approach focuses directly on the current problem rather than the dynamics of the family system. Treatment is begun with a careful examination of the nature of the symptoms, their time course, and the events that take place as they emerge. As in other behaviorally oriented therapies, the focus is a relatively narrow one, and an understanding of behavioral sequences associated with the problematic situation is of primary importance. This identification of circumstances surrounding the problem's emergence can be likened to ferreting out conditioned cues that lead to the addicted subject's sequence of drug use. Both strategic family therapy and the behavioral approach assume that these circumstances will suggest options for bringing about the problem's resolution. Indeed, as he developed this strategic model, Haley observed that certain behaviors within a family can unintentionally promote the symptoms they are designed to suppress, similar to the conception of the alcoholic subject's spouse unwittingly serving as an enabler.

## Rules of Network Therapy: A Summary

At its heart, network therapy is meant to be straightforward and uncomplicated by theoretical bias. In this section, I summarize the main points to be observed in treatment.

### Who Needs Network Therapy?

- Network therapy is appropriate for individuals who cannot reliably control their intake of alcohol or drugs once they have taken their first dose, those who have tried to stop and relapsed, and those who have not been willing or able to stop.
- Individuals whose problems are too severe for the network approach in ambulatory care include those who cannot stop their drug use even for a day or comply with outpatient detoxification.
- Individuals who can be treated with conventional therapy and without a network include those who have demonstrated the ability to moderate their consumption without problems.

### Start a Network as Soon as Possible

- It is important to see the alcohol- or drug-abusing patient promptly because the window of opportunity for openness to treatment is generally brief.
- If the patient is married, the spouse should be engaged early on, preferably at the time of the first telephone call. The clinician should point out that addiction is a family problem. For most drugs, the therapist can enlist the spouse in ensuring that the patient arrives at the therapist's office with a day's sobriety.
- In the initial interview, the exchange should be framed so that a good case is built for the grave consequences of the patient's addiction, and this should be done before the patient can introduce a system of denial. That way the therapist does not put the spouse or other network members in the awkward position of having to contradict a close relation. Then the clinician must make it clear that the patient needs to be abstinent, starting now.
- When seeing an alcoholic patient for the first time, the clinician should prescribe disulfiram as soon as possible, in the office if possible. The patient should continue taking disulfiram under observation of a network member.
- At the first session, the clinician should make arrangements for a network to be assembled, generally involving a number of the patient's family members or close friends.
- From the first meeting, clinicians should consider whatever is necessary to ensure sobriety until the

next meeting, and that should be planned with the network. Initially, the plan might consist of the network's immediate company and a plan for daily AA attendance.

- People who are close to the patient, who have a long-standing relationship with him or her, and who are trusted should be included. Members with substance problems should be avoided because they will let you down when you need their unbiased support.
- The group should be balanced. A network composed solely of the parental generation, of younger people, or of people of the opposite sex should be avoided.
- The tone should be directive. The therapist must give explicit instructions to support and ensure abstinence.

## Three Priorities in Running the Ongoing Therapy

1. *Maintaining abstinence.*   The patient and the network members should report at the outset of each session any events related to the patient's exposure to alcohol and drugs. The patient and network members should be instructed on the nature of relapse and plan with the therapist how to sustain abstinence. Cues to conditioned drug seeking should be examined.
2. *Supporting the network's integrity.*   The patient is expected to make sure that network members keep their meeting appointments and stay involved. The therapist sets meeting times explicitly and summons the network for any emergency, such as relapse; he or she does whatever is necessary to secure membership stability if the patient is having trouble doing so.
3. *Securing future behavior.*   The therapist should combine any and all modalities necessary to ensure the patient's stability, such as a stable, drug-free residence; avoidance of substance-abusing friends; attendance at 12-step meetings; compliance in taking medications such as disulfiram or blocking agents; observed urinalysis; and ancillary psychiatric care.

Also, the patient should meet with the therapist as frequently as necessary to ensure abstinence, perhaps once a week for 1 month, every other week for the next few months, and every month or two by the end of 1 year. Individual sessions run concomitantly. Make sure that the mood of meetings is trusting and free of recrimination. Explain issues of conflict in terms of the

problems presented by addiction, rather than getting into personality conflicts. Once abstinence is stabilized, the network can help the patient plan for a new drug-free adaptation.

## Ending the Network Therapy

- Network sessions can be terminated after the patient has been stably abstinent for at least 6 months to 1 year. This should be done after discussion with the patient and network of the patient's readiness for handling sobriety.
- An understanding is established with the network members that they will contact the therapist at any point in the future if the patient is vulnerable to relapse. The members can also be summoned by the therapist. These points should be made clear to the patient before termination in the presence of the network, but they also apply throughout treatment.

## Research on Network Therapy

A treatment technique needs to be evaluated under controlled experimental conditions, even if it is based on a pragmatic approach to clinical management. To date, four studies carried out on network therapy have demonstrated its effectiveness in treatment and the feasibility of training in the approach as well. Each study addressed the technique's validation from a different perspective: a trial in office management; studies of its effectiveness in the training of psychiatric residents and of counselors who work with cocaine-addicted persons; and an evaluation of acceptance of the network approach in an Internet technology transfer course.

### An Office-Based Clinical Trial

A chart review was conducted on a series of 60 substance-dependent patients, with follow-up appointments scheduled through the period of treatment and up to 1 year thereafter (Galanter 1993b). For 27 patients, the primary drug of dependence was alcohol; for 23, it was cocaine; for 6, it was opiates; for 3, it was marijuana; and for 1, it was nicotine. In all but eight of the patients, networks were fully established. Of the 60 patients, 46 experienced full improvement (i.e., abstinence for at least 6 months) or major improvement (i.e., a marked decline in drug use to nonproblematic levels). The study demonstrated the viability of establishing networks and applying them in the practitioner's treatment setting. It also served as a basis for the ensuing developmental research supported by the National Institute on Drug Abuse.

## Treatment by Psychiatry Residents

We developed and implemented a network therapy training sequence in the New York University psychiatric residency program and then evaluated the clinical outcome of a group of cocaine-dependent patients treated by the residents. The psychiatric residency was chosen because of the growing importance of clinical training in the management of addiction in outpatient care in residency programs, in line with the standards set for specialty certification.

A training manual was prepared on the network technique, defining the specifics of the treatment in a manner allowing for uniformity in practice. It was developed for use as a training tool and then as a guide for the residents during the treatment phase. Network therapy tape segments drawn from a library of 130 videotaped sessions were used to illustrate typical therapy situations. A network therapy rating scale was developed to assess the technique's application, with items emphasizing key aspects of treatment (Keller et al. 1997). The scale was evaluated for its reliability in distinguishing between two contrasting addiction therapies, network therapy and systemic family therapy, both presented to faculty and residents on videotape. The internal consistency of responses for each of the techniques was high for both the faculty and the resident samples, and both groups consistently distinguished the two modalities. The scale was then used by clinical supervisors as a didactic aid for training and to monitor therapist adherence to the study treatment manual.

We trained 19 third-year psychiatry residents to apply the network therapy approach, with an emphasis placed on distinctions in technique between the treatment of addiction and of other major mental illness or personality disorder. The residents then worked with a sample of cocaine-addicted patients. The 24 patients were typically unemployed, unmarried white men who did not live alone. Of 262 random, observed urinalyses, 79% were negative for cocaine; 67% of patients produced three consecutive weekly urine samples free of cocaine at some point in treatment; and 42% of patients produced cocaine-free urine samples in their last three urine samples immediately before termination of our initial study (Galanter et al. 1997a).

These results were analyzed relative to reported findings on ambulatory treatment in comparable settings. The residents, inexperienced in drug treatment, achieved results similar to those reported for experienced professionals (Carroll et al. 1994; Higgins et al. 1993; Shoptaw et al. 1994). These comparisons supported the feasibility of successful training of psychiatry residents naive to addiction treatment and the efficacy of the treatment in their hands.

## Treatment by Addiction Counselors

This study was conducted in a community-based addictions treatment clinic, and the network therapy training sequence was essentially the same as the one applied to the psychiatry residents (Keller et al., in press). A cohort of 10 cocaine-dependent patients received treatment at the community program with a format that included network therapy, along with the clinic's usual package of modalities, and an additional 20 cocaine-dependent patients received treatment as usual and served as control subjects. The network therapy was found to enhance the outcome of the experimental patients. Of 107 urinalyses conducted on the network therapy patients, 88% were negative, but only 66% of the 82 urine samples from the control subjects were negative, a significantly lower proportion. The mean retention in treatment was 13.9 weeks for the network patients, reflecting a trend toward greater retention than the 10.7 weeks for control subjects.

The results of this study supported the feasibility of transferring the network technology into community-based settings with the potential for enhancing outcomes. Addiction counselors working in a typical outpatient rehabilitation setting were able to learn and then incorporate network therapy into their largely 12-step-oriented treatment regimens without undue difficulty and with improved outcome.

## Use of the Internet

We studied ways in which psychiatrists and other professionals could be offered training by a distance learning method using the Internet, a medium that offers the advantage of not being fixed in either time or location. An advertisement was placed in *Psychiatric News*, the newspaper of the American Psychiatric Association, offering an Internet course combining network therapy with the use of naltrexone for the treatment of alcoholism.

The sequence of material presented on the Internet was divided into three didactic "sessions," followed by a set of questions, with a hypertext link to download relevant references and a certificate of completion. The course took about 2 hours for the student to complete. Our assessment was based on 679 sequential counts, representing 240 unique respondents who went beyond the introductory Web page (Galanter et al. 1997b). Of these respondents, 154 were psychiatrists, who responded positively to the course. A majority responded "a good deal" or "very much" (a score of 3 or 4 on a 4-point scale) to the following statements: "It helped me understand the management of alcoholism treatment" (56%); "It helped me learn to use family or friends in network treatment for alcoholism" (75%); and "It improved my ability to use naltrexone in treating alcoholism" (64%). (More than 2,000 counts have now been recorded at this Web site as of this writing.)

The four studies described in this section support the use of network therapy as an effective treatment for addictive disorders. They are especially encouraging given the relative ease with which different types of clinicians were engaged and trained in the network approach. Because the approach combines a number of well-established clinical techniques that can be adapted to delivery in typical clinical settings, it is apparently suitable for use by general clinicians and addiction specialists.

## References

American Psychiatric Association: Diagnostic and Statistical Manual of Mental Disorders, 4th Edition. Washington, DC, American Psychiatric Association, 1994

American Psychiatric Association Task Force on Benzodiazepine Dependence, Toxicity, and Abuse: a Task Force Report of the American Psychiatric Association. Washington, DC, American Psychiatric Association, 1990

Annis HM: A relapse prevention model for treatment of alcoholics, in Treating Addictive Behaviors: Processes of Change. Edited by Miller WR, Heather NH. New York, Plenum, 1986, pp 407–434

Azrin NH, Sisson RW, Meyers R: Alcoholism treatment by disulfiram and community reinforcement therapy. J Behav Ther Exp Psychiatry 13:105–112, 1982

Begleiter H, Porjesz B: Persistence of a "subacute withdrawal syndrome" following chronic ethanol intake. Drug Alcohol Depend 4:353–357, 1979

Brubaker RG, Prue DM, Rychtarik RG: Determinants of disulfiram acceptance among alcohol patients: a test of the theory of reasoned action. Addict Behav 12:43–52, 1987

Carroll KM, Rounsaville BJ, Gordon LT, et al: Psychotherapy and pharmacotherapy for ambulatory cocaine abusers. Arch Gen Psychiatry 51:177–187, 1994

Childress AR, McLellan AT, Ehrman R, et al: Classically conditioned responses in opioid and cocaine dependence: a role in relapse? in Learning Factors in Substance Abuse (NIDA Res Monogr 84). Edited by Ray BA. Rockville, MD, U.S. Department of Health and Human Services, 1988, pp 25–43

Crowley TJ: Contingency contracting treatment of drug-abusing physicians, nurses, and dentists, in Behavioral Integration Techniques in Drug Abuse Treatment (NIDA Res Monogr 46). Edited by Grabowski J, Stitzer ML, Henningfeld JF. Rockville, MD, U.S. Department of Health and Human Services, 1984

Fuller RK, Williford WO: Life-table analysis of abstinence in a study evaluating the efficacy of disulfiram. Alcohol Clin Exp Res 4:298–301, 1980

Galanter M: Cognitive labeling: psychotherapy for alcohol and drug abuse: an approach based on learning theory. Journal of Substance Abuse Treatment and Evaluation 5:551–556, 1983

Galanter M: Network Therapy for Addiction: A New Approach. New York, Basic Books, 1993a

Galanter M: Network therapy for substance abuse: a clinical trial. Psychotherapy 30:251–258, 1993b

Galanter M, Keller DS, Dermatis H: Network therapy for addiction: assessment of the clinical outcome of training. Am J Drug Alcohol Abuse 23:335–368, 1997a

Galanter M, Keller DS, Dermatis H: Using the Internet for clinical training: a course on network therapy. URL: mednyu/substanceabuse/course. Psychiatr Serv 48:999, 1997b

Gallant DM: Alcoholism: A Guide to Diagnosis, Intervention, and Treatment. New York, WW Norton, 1987

Gallant DM, Rich A, Bey E, et al: Group psychotherapy with married couples: a successful technique in New Orleans alcoholism clinic patients. J La State Med Soc 122:41–44, 1970

Gitlow SE, Peyser HS (eds): Alcoholism: A Practical Treatment Guide. New York, Grune & Stratton, 1980

Haley J: Problem Solving Therapy. San Francisco, CA, Jossey-Bass, 1977

Hall SM, Cooper JL, Burmaster S, et al: Contingency contracting as a therapeutic tool with methadone maintenance clients. Behav Res Ther 15:438–441, 1977

Hayman M: Current attitudes to alcoholism of psychiatrists in Southern California. Am J Psychiatry 112:484–493, 1956

Higgins ST, Budney AJ, Bickel WK, et al: Achieving cocaine abstinence with a behavioral approach. Am J Psychiatry 150:763–769, 1993

Institute of Medicine: Broadening the Base of Treatment for Alcohol Problems. Washington, DC, National Academy Press, 1990

Johnson VE: Intervention: How To Help Someone Who Doesn't Want Help. Minneapolis, MN, Johnson Institute Books, 1986

Kaufman E, Kaufman PN: Family Therapy of Drugs and Alcohol Abuse. New York, Gardner, 1979

Keane TM, Foy DW, Nunn B, et al: Spouse contracting to increase Antabuse compliance in alcoholic veterans. J Clin Psychol 40:340–344, 1984

Keller D, Galanter M, Weinberg S: Validation of a scale for network therapy: a technique for systematic use of peer and family support in addiction treatment. Am J Drug Alcohol Abuse 23:115–127, 1997

Keller D, Galanter M, Dermatis H: Technology transfer of network therapy to community-based addiction counselors. J Subst Abuse Treat (in press)

Khantzian EJ: The self-medication hypothesis of addictive disorders: focus on heroin and cocaine dependence. Am J Psychiatry 142:1259–1264, 1985

Liepman MR, Nierenberg TD, Begin AM: Evaluation of a program designed to help family and significant others to motivate resistant alcoholics to recover. Am J Drug Alcohol Abuse 15:209–222, 1989

Ludwig AM, Wikler A, Stark LM: The first drink: psychobiological aspects of craving. Arch Gen Psychiatry 30:539–547, 1974

Ludwig AM, Bendfeldt F, Wikler A, et al: "Loss of control" in alcoholics. Arch Gen Psychiatry 35:370–373, 1978

Marlatt GA, Gordon J (eds): Relapse Prevention: Maintenance Strategies in the Treatment of Addictive Behaviors. New York, Guilford, 1985

McCrady BS, Noel NE, Abrams DB, et al: Comparative effectiveness of three types of spouse involvement in outpatient behavioral alcoholism treatment. J Stud Alcohol 47:459–467, 1986

McLellan AT, Woody GE, Luborsky L, et al: Increased effectiveness of substance abuse treatment: a prospective study of patient-treatment "matching." J Nerv Ment Dis 171:597–605, 1983

Monti PM, Rohsenow DJ, Abrams DB, et al: Social learning approaches to alcohol relapse: selected illustrations and implications, in Learning Factors in Substance Abuse (NIDA Res Monogr 84). Edited by Ray BA. Rockville, MD, U.S. Department of Health and Human Services, 1988, pp 141–159

O'Brien CP, Testa T, O'Brien TJ, et al: Conditioned narcotic withdrawal in humans. Science 195:1000–1002, 1977

Schuckit MA: A one-year follow-up of men alcoholics given disulfiram. J Stud Alcohol 46:191–195, 1985

Shoptaw S, Rawson RA, McCann MJ, et al: The Matrix Model of outpatient stimulant abuse treatment: evidence of efficacy. J Addict Dis 13:129–141, 1994

Stanton MD, Thomas TC (eds): The Family Therapy of Drug Abuse and Addiction. New York, Guilford, 1982

Stark MJ, Campbell BK, Brinkerhoff CV: "Hello, may we help you?" a study of attrition prevention at the time of the first phone contact with substance-abusing clients. Am J Drug Alcohol Abuse 16:67–76, 1990

Wikler A: Some implications of conditioning theory for problems of drug abuse. Behav Sci 16:92–97, 1971

Wikler A: Dynamics of drug dependence: implications of a conditioning theory for research and treatment. Arch Gen Psychiatry 28:611–616, 1973

Wurmser L: Mrs. Pecksniff's horse? Psychodynamics of compulsive drug use, in Psychodynamics of Drug Dependence (NIDA Res Monogr 12). Edited by Blaine JD, Julius DS. Rockville, MD, U.S. Government Printing Office, 1977, pp 36–72

Yalom ID: Group therapy and alcoholism. Ann N Y Acad Sci 233:85–103, 1974

# Chapter 29

# Individual Psychotherapy: Alcohol

### Sheldon Zimberg, M.D., M.S.

Most psychiatrists have considered psychotherapy for alcoholism to be ineffective because *psychoanalytic* psychotherapy for alcoholism has been largely a failure (Zimberg 1982). Also, the rationale for psychoanalysis has been the mistaken belief that alcoholism is always a symptom of underlying psychological disorders, and by uncovering these disorders and providing insight into their role in abusive drinking, the therapist could help end the patient's drinking problem. This has not proven to be the case because alcoholism has multiple causes, including biological (i.e., genetic), sociocultural, and psychological factors. The ineffectiveness of psychoanalysis and the psychodynamic rationale has resulted in psychotherapists' avoidance of alcoholic patients and a bias against psychiatry by those in the addictive disorders field and by many members of Alcoholics Anonymous (AA).

Many forms of psychotherapy other than psychoanalysis are available. Any form of verbal interaction between a therapist or counselor and a patient that is designed to change behavior and feelings can be called psychotherapy. The verbal process of AA is a form of psychotherapy.

Tiebout (1962) and Fox (1965) pioneered a modified form of psychodynamic psychotherapy in the treatment of alcoholism. They used a psychodynamic understanding of alcoholism in their approach to psychotherapy but avoided uncovering underlying psychological conflicts early in treatment and gave priority to the elimination of alcohol use as the first and necessary step in the psychotherapeutic approach.

Individual therapy is underutilized in the treatment of alcoholism, but it can be the most effective approach with individuals who are resistant to treatment or who have coexisting psychiatric disorders. The transference can develop into a dependent relationship with the therapist that can be used to influence the patient's drinking and to encourage changes in the self-perceptions and self-destructive behaviors characterizing the alcoholic individual's life. Individual therapy can be the preferred approach for those who feel uncomfortable in groups or who fear the disclosure of very sensitive information. Alcoholic individuals are a heterogeneous group, and no one treatment modality can be effective for all patients.

## Psychodynamics of Alcoholism

The psychological conflict observed in alcoholic individuals consists of low self-esteem along with feelings of worthlessness and inadequacy. These feelings are denied and repressed and lead to unconscious needs to be taken care of and to be accepted. Because these dependent needs cannot be met in reality, they lead to anxiety and compensatory needs for control, power, achievement, and elevated self-esteem. Denial of this conflict is present, and reactive grandiosity and excessive narcissism develop as defense mechanisms. Alcohol tranquilizes the anxiety, but more important, it creates pharmacologically induced feelings of power, omnipotence, and invulnerability in men (McClelland et al. 1972) and enhanced feelings of womanliness in women (Wilsnack 1976). When alcoholic individuals wake up after a drinking episode, they experience guilt and despair because they have not achieved anything more than before they drank and their problems remain. They have a primitive, punishing superego, and their feelings of worthlessness are intensified. The conflict continues in a vicious circle, often with a progressive downward spiral leading to psychological dependence and eventually addiction to alcohol.

Alcohol provides an artificial feeling state of power, control, and elevated self-esteem that cannot be achieved in reality. The act of producing this feeling of power at will feeds the alcoholic individual's conscious grandiose self-image.

An individual who has such a psychological conflict will become alcoholic if he or she has a genetic predisposition to alcoholism and if the individual lives in a society in which alcohol use is sanctioned as a way to feel better or in which there is considerable ambivalence regarding alcohol use. In any particular individual, one or more of these etiological factors may predominate and lead to alcoholism.

AA is effective because the alcoholic individual's narcissism is sublimated by the rescuing of other alcoholic individuals; therefore, the grandiosity becomes fulfilled and socially useful, and much of the alcoholic individual's dependent needs are met by the group's acceptance. AA members recognize that their support of other alcoholic individuals helps them maintain their own sobriety.

The central problem in the psychotherapy of alcoholism is in breaking through the reactive grandiosity that produces the patient's massive denial of profound feelings of inferiority and dependence, which permit the pattern of self-destructive drinking to continue. Alcoholic individuals destroy not only themselves but also their loved ones without perceiving their lack of control of their behavior pattern.

## Differential Diagnosis and Treatment of Coexisting Psychiatric Disorders

A cardinal rule for treating alcoholism is the recognition that alcoholic patients do not constitute a homogeneous group. Subpopulations of alcoholic individuals require specific treatment. No one treatment approach, even AA, will be successful for all alcoholic patients.

Among the subpopulations are problem drinkers with related developmental problems in which the abusive drinking is part of an adjustment reaction. Such groups include adolescent problem drinkers and the alcoholic elderly. The manifestation of alcoholism is different in these two groups, related to the adjustment problems in adolescents (Fischer 1985) or the stresses of aging in the alcoholic elderly (Zimberg 1990).

Another large subpopulation of alcoholic individuals

includes those with coexisting psychiatric disorders, called *dual-diagnosis patients* or *mentally ill chemical abusers* (MICA). The high prevalence of these disorders (Regier et al. 1990) and the difficulty in treating them has become apparent. Many alcoholic individuals also use other substances of abuse.

Successful treatment of alcoholism and identification of problems other than alcoholism require a complete psychiatric history, mental status examination, and developmental and family history as part of the initial evaluation.

Another cardinal rule in alcoholism therapy is that if signs and symptoms of a psychiatric disorder are present in an actively drinking alcoholic patient, the patient must be detoxified from alcohol and observed to be alcohol free for 3–6 weeks before a coexisting psychiatric disorder can be diagnosed effectively. This step is essential because the excessive use of alcohol can produce a large variety of organic and functional psychiatric symptoms. The understanding and treatment of these psychiatric complications are required for effective treatment of the alcoholism.

## Dual-Diagnosis Typology

A dual-diagnosis typology was developed, based on a study of 130 outpatients in mental health and substance abuse clinics, to facilitate the differential diagnosis and treatment of disorders in this complicated population (Hien et al. 1997). Type I patients have a primary psychiatric disorder and use substances only when psychiatrically symptomatic. Type II patients are primary substance abusers who develop substance-induced psychiatric symptoms that resolve with abstinence. Type III patients have long histories of psychiatric and substance use disorders that are not related temporally or in a cause-and-effect way. Type III represents the true dual-diagnosis or MICA patients. Hien et al. (1997) used a series of questions about current and past relationships between psychiatric disorders and substance use. This approach was reliable and valid in various clinical settings.

Therapists must be able to make an effective differential diagnosis and provide appropriate treatment for alcoholism that coexists with major psychiatric disorders. Most are primary alcoholic individuals and do not require psychiatric treatment. However, for those that do, such a multitreatment approach is essential if the alcoholic patient is to recover. Individual therapy is the most effective way to identify coexisting psychiatric disorders and provide appropriate treatment. If the therapist is a psychiatrist, he or she can provide medication and individual therapy. If the therapist is not a psychiatrist, he or she must refer the patient to a psychiatrist, who is knowledgeable about alcoholism, for psychiatric medication.

## Pharmacological Treatment of Alcoholism in Individual Therapy

Pharmacological interventions in the treatment of alcoholism include the use of benzodiazepines in detoxification and the use of psychiatric medications for coexisting psychiatric disorders. These medications are not designed to specifically treat the behavioral aspects of drinking behavior or the excessive consumption of alcohol.

Disulfiram has been used since the 1950s to modify some of the behavioral aspects of drinking, particularly impulsive drinking. This drug was introduced into the United States by Ruth Fox (1965), one of the early pioneers of the psychiatric treatment of alcoholism. Disulfiram inhibits the enzyme involved in ethyl alcohol metabolism in the liver at the stage of acetaldehyde. Acetaldehyde is a toxic substance that in sufficient quantity can produce the unpleasant physical consequences of a disulfiram-alcohol interaction. This interaction results in nausea, tachycardia, facial flushing, and dizziness and is subjectively unpleasant. The interaction is not life threatening if the dose of disulfiram is limited to 250–500 mg/day and the patient receives a medical examination before use to rule out cardiac problems and significant liver abnormalities.

Disulfiram can act as a deterrent to alcohol use early in treatment when the drinking has been impulsive without planning or conscious craving. It can be of particular use if given under supervision in an employee assistance program or by a spouse or significant other. The clinical effect takes several days to start after disulfiram therapy is initiated, and it lasts 4–7 days after the drug is stopped if the patient has been using it for 4–6 weeks. Such a prolonged response after spontaneously stopping disulfiram can encourage the patient to deal with his or her intention to drink in individual therapy, at AA meetings, or in a discussion with a sponsor. It can serve as an early warning sign to both the patient and the therapist. Although controlled studies of disulfiram use have had equivocal results, my clinical experience (Zimberg 1982) indicates that disulfiram is helpful in selected patients in the context of individual psychotherapy.

The drug naltrexone, a long-acting opiate antagonist, has been introduced into the treatment of alcoholism. Two controlled studies have shown that this drug can significantly reduce alcohol consumption and alcohol craving (O'Malley et al. 1992; Volpicelli et al. 1992) in long-term alcoholic patients. Those studies were done in different geographic locations and involved different treatment populations.

The use of naltrexone (at a dosage of 50 mg/day) has been a useful adjunct in the treatment of alcoholism where craving has been a significant clinical symptom. The only serious side effect can be liver toxicity, but this side effect is rare at the standard dosage. Initial liver chemistries should be obtained as a baseline before the drug is prescribed, and they should be monitored monthly for up to 6 months. (This is based on my experience in clinics and private practice.)

The initial positive findings of the value of naltrexone in alcoholism treatment have been substantiated in a recent review article (Weinrieb and O'Brien 1997) and in a recent clinical study (Jaffe et al. 1996). The mechanism of naltrexone on alcohol consumption is not clear, although most experts believe that this drug inhibits the effect of β-endorphin on the dopamine reward system (Terenius 1996).

Because naltrexone appears to be an effective drug, other opiate antagonists have been tried with some success. For example, nalmefene hydrochloride (Mason et al. 1994) and the anti-alcohol-craving compound L-camprosate (Spanagel et al. 1997) have been used experimentally. Clearly the use of such drugs along with psychotherapy and relapse prevention techniques will further improve alcoholism treatment outcomes.

Currently, I prescribe naltrexone for patients who have relapsed repeatedly and in whom craving appears to be a major factor in the relapses.

## Indications and Advantages of Individual Therapy

Individual therapy provides distinct advantages compared with the more commonly used modality of group therapy. These advantages include the ability to observe and scrutinize patients more closely to permit the differential diagnosis of coexisting psychiatric disorders. When such psychiatric disorders are present, the therapist must provide the necessary treatments or the patient will not recover.

Individual therapy can facilitate a dependent transference with the therapist. This dependent relationship can be useful for influencing the patient to change his or her drinking behavior and other maladaptive approaches to life and problems. Because the early stages of treatment require suggestions, guidance, advice, and role modeling for changes to occur, a dependent relationship will facilitate such approaches in individual therapy. The therapist is able to learn more about the patient more quickly, and this information enables the therapist to target intervention suggestions at a time when the patient may be receptive. Premature interventions can cause anger and avoidance and, in extreme situations, can cause the patient to leave therapy. The key to alcoholism psychotherapy that is active and interventionist is knowing when to intervene and when not to. This takes experience and a great deal of knowledge about the patient, which can come only in individual therapy. Knowledge of the patient is also important regarding cues or triggers that could lead to relapse drinking. Therefore, individual therapy can facilitate cognitive relapse prevention strategies specific for the patient, in contrast to the discussion of general principles, which occurs in groups.

Individual therapy can be more effective for individuals who fear groups and/or are unwilling to disclose very sensitive life traumas such as rape, incest, or illegal activities in a group setting. Individual therapy, however, cannot provide the peer support and identification with recovering alcoholic patients that occurs in group therapy if the group is made up of patients at various levels of recovery. However, the combination of individual therapy with AA participation can provide the peer support so helpful to recovery.

## Techniques of Individual Therapy

In this section, I focus on the techniques used in each stage of treatment: from early-, middle-, to late-stage treatment.

### Early Stage of Treatment

The basis of the early stage of treatment is *intervention* with regard to drinking. The therapeutic contract must establish that the goal of treatment is to achieve abstinence. Most patients in early-stage treatment will reluctantly agree to this goal because they believe they "cannot drink," although they will likely test it with slips or provocative drinking. This behavior must be confronted and used to help the patient see his or her inability to control the impulse to drink. The use of disulfiram should be introduced as a method for con-

trolling the impulse to drink. If the patient refuses such medication or the use of naltrexone, and craving is a major problem at this stage, a contract should be established indicating that if the patient can remain alcohol free, there is no problem; however, if the patient has one more slip, medication will be mandatory if treatment is to continue.

Patients should be encouraged to attend AA meetings. They should be helped to find meetings where they feel comfortable with other members, who should be their peers. The AA message and settings are similar from group to group, but the membership varies greatly. Although some alcoholic individuals can recover without AA, it can be extremely helpful for most individuals through its peer support, alcoholism education, opportunities to identify with recovering alcoholic individuals, and education on how to live without alcohol in our drinking society.

The family should be involved early and encouraged to attend Al-Anon. They should learn about their *enabling* behaviors, encourage the patient's sobriety with their support and interest, and avoid covering up or excusing the patient's drinking.

Thus, early in treatment a structure should be provided to the alcoholic patient in the form of *scaffolding*. The scaffolding erected around a building under renovation does not itself provide structural support for the building's foundation but enables workers to enter the building from different directions and make the renovations inside. The changes produced are from *outside in*. In psychoanalytic treatment, the changes occur through insight and are from *inside out*. The therapist, family involvement, AA participation, and use of medications specific for alcoholism provide the structural components of *scaffolding therapy*.

Verbal interactions involve the therapist providing direction, guidance, and cognitive suggestions to help the alcoholic patient learn to cope with unpleasant feelings, conflicts, problems, and stress without resorting to alcohol. Cognitive-behavioral suggestions are made to encourage the patient to avoid situations, interpersonal relationships, and places that have been triggers to drinking in the past. Because such triggers are unique to each individual, the therapist must learn about the unique drinking triggers in each patient. The more the therapist learns, the more effective this approach will be. This avoidance behavior is extremely useful early in therapy but can be modified at later stages as the patient has developed better coping skills and his or her attitude about the need for alcohol has changed. Anxiety and stress reduction techniques other than cognitive-behavioral approaches can be used early in therapy and can include meditation, self-hypnosis, biofeedback, and other relaxation techniques.

The major goals of scaffolding therapy are to help patients accept their problem with alcohol and learn to cope with their lives and its problems without using alcohol. In some patients, the absence of the anesthetic effects of alcohol will make the problems that were once neglected more apparent and more painful. Patients should be helped to recognize that only with sobriety can they successfully deal with their problems. In some patients, early sobriety can produce a feeling of euphoria and omnipotence (called the "pink cloud" in AA). Giving up alcohol successfully seems to suggest that they can do anything. Therapists should guide their patients through this reaction-formation defense by helping them recognize their limitations and the possibilities for feeling and functioning better without alcohol in the future if sobriety is maintained.

Defenses observed in patients and in the transference should not be interpreted at this stage of treatment but, if possible, should be utilized and redirected in the recovery process. Sublimation of the feelings of omnipotence with involvement in AA and helping others by qualifying to speak at AA meetings is an example of such redirection. Wallace (1985) gives an excellent discussion of managing the "preferred defense structure of the alcoholic."

This early stage of treatment, with its active intervention in relation to drinking and helping the alcoholic individual adapt to life and its problems without drinking, takes about 6 months to 1 year to produce stability. The overt conflict of whether to drink becomes internalized, and the alcoholic individual enters the next stage of treatment with the belief that "I won't drink."

## Middle Stage of Treatment

In the middle stage of treatment, the therapeutic effort should help the individual gain more independence, and the scaffolding system can be partially dismantled. Disulfiram or naltrexone can be discontinued but might be used intermittently when the patient anticipates some severe stress. The patient should be able to use these drugs when his or her control over the impulse to drink feels threatened by intense craving or other external or internal drink signals.

Attendance at AA should continue, but its frequency might diminish from daily to two to three times a week. Patients should be encouraged to actively speak at AA meetings to reinforce their determination to stay sober.

According to AA, "You can't keep it unless you give it away."

The therapeutic approach should be supportive, but the emphasis should shift to the patient's opportunities to change behavioral aspects that contributed to his or her drinking. Greater attention should be given to dealing with feelings such as anger and the need for control. Some interpretation of behavior and feelings could be made, but uncovering approaches and interpretation of the dependent transference should be avoided.

By helping the patient develop an ability to empathize, the therapist can help the patient become less egocentric and come to a more mature recognition of his or her limitations and the limitations of others to respond to all of the patient's needs. The patient will feel more anxiety, but he or she is usually able to cope without drinking because of stable internalized control over the impulse to drink. Drinking dreams and fantasies are common during this stage. Interpretation of these dreams and fantasies should deal with issues of controlling the impulse to drink.

After 1–1½ years in the middle stage, the alcoholic individual has generally established very good internalized controls over the impulse to drink. This is the stage that has been achieved by most successful AA members. These individuals will not have insight into the psychological sources of the dependency conflict or understanding of serious interpersonal problems or profound feelings of anger that may exist, but they have good sobriety.

## Late Stage of Treatment

Patients with severe anxiety, episodes of depression, or serious characterological problems are candidates for treatment in the late stage of treatment, in which "I don't have to drink" is the goal. This stage is not necessary to maintain sobriety but can produce longer-term, better outcomes through conflict resolution. At this stage, the focus of therapy is on uncovering and reconstruction and is less supportive, directive, and cognitive. The transition should be gradual because as the therapist becomes more passive and analytical, transference issues will surface that should be interpreted. Dreams and fantasies should be used to a greater degree, and memories and feelings from childhood should be examined as they relate to past and present behavior and feelings. Thus, a more traditional psychoanalytic approach can be used. The duration of this phase of treatment is indefinite but usually lasts an additional 1–2 years.

## Termination of Treatment

Drinking slips can occur in the middle and late stages of treatment but are usually of short duration and without serious consequences. If they occur in the middle stage, the issues of drinking cues and control issues are reviewed. If they occur in the late stage, the role of unconscious conflicts in the slips should be explored to produce insight and greater control of the impulse to drink with resolution of unconscious conflicts.

Successful termination can occur in the middle stage or in the late stage when the patient and the therapist mutually agree that the patient has good internalized controls over the impulse to drink and has experienced significant improvement in functioning. Because alcoholism is a lifelong condition and patients are never cured, the door to return to treatment should be left open. Patients involved in AA should be encouraged to maintain their involvement, and those not involved should be encouraged to consider trying again to observe role models of successful recovery.

## Transference and Countertransference

The transference relationship in individual therapy is intensified. It is usually based on dependent needs but with some mistrust and hostility based on previous rejections and is therefore ambivalent. The patient may test the therapeutic relationship by drinking early in therapy. If these episodes can be dealt with in an understanding and not a judgmental and punitive way, the transference can be shifted to the dependent relationship necessary for successful therapy. In a dependent transference, the patient is more receptive to guidance and suggestion as part of the scaffolding therapy.

A supportive and nonjudgmental, nonpunitive therapeutic relationship will produce a "corrective emotional experience" as described by Alexander (1946) and lead to the maintenance of long-term sobriety. After sobriety has been well stabilized up to 1–1½ years, the transference relationship can be regarded as part of the uncovering approaches used in the late stage of treatment. The late stage should be entered by mutual agreement, and the transition should be a slow process over weeks rather than an abrupt transition from support to insight-oriented therapy.

*Countertransference* is described as the therapist's reaction to the patient as if the patient were an important person in the therapist's life and/or as a reaction to the patient's behavior in relation to the therapist's feel-

ings, needs, and self-image. The patient's early and provocative drinking and later slips can cause the therapist to feel frustrated and angry because of his or her need for the gratification of successful treatment. This anger and frustration is very common in therapists and is the major reason that many therapists refuse to treat alcoholic patients.

The reality is that the therapist cannot force, control, or seduce patients into achieving abstinence but can only offer them tools to assist them in achieving abstinence for themselves. The therapist's omnipotent need for successful treatment cannot compete against the patient's unconscious psychological need for omnipotence and control or the treatment will fail. Only the patient can decide to work toward abstinence, using the therapist's help and guidance. Therapists who work with alcoholic patients must recognize their own limitations; otherwise, burnout, avoidance of alcoholic patients, and other adverse psychological reactions will result.

## Outcome Studies

Few controlled studies have compared outcomes of individual and group therapy of alcoholism. In a review of this subject, Solomon (1982) reported slightly better outcomes for group therapy. However, patient characteristics seemed more predictive of outcome than was the treatment modality. Woody et al. (1983) indicated the efficacy of individual therapy in opioid-addicted patients.

Clinical reports and my experience have indicated the value of individual therapy (Hoffman and Miller 1993; Kaufman 1989; Khantzian 1982; O'Malley and Carroll 1996; Wurmser 1984; Zimberg 1989). Group therapy is more widely practiced in alcoholism treatment, particularly in hospital- and institution-based programs, because group therapy, with its peer involvement, can be very effective, is generally more cost-efficient, and more closely resembles the group model of the self-help programs. However, the great heterogeneity of the alcoholic population suggests that no one modality of treatment can be the most effective for all patients. The literature suggests that different typologies of alcoholism require differing treatment approaches (Meyer 1989; Schuckit 1989). In this regard, individual therapy is neglected even though it can be extremely effective in selected patients. Often a combination of individual therapy with peer involvement in AA can be the most effective combination for many alcoholic patients.

Patients who drop out of group therapy or who do not respond to group therapy should not be considered treatment failures unless they have been given an opportunity for individual therapy in which a more profound patient-therapist attachment can be established. These patients, particularly those with coexisting major psychiatric disorders and those reluctant to disclose information about themselves in groups, are more likely to do better when treated in individual therapy.

# References

Alexander F, French TM: Psychoanalysis Therapy: Principles and Application. New York, Ronald Press, 1946

Fischer J: Psychotherapy of adolescent alcohol abusers, in Practical Approaches to Alcoholism Psychotherapy, 2nd Edition. Edited by Zimberg S, Wallace J, Blume SB. New York, Plenum, 1985, pp 295–313

Fox R: Psychiatric aspects of alcoholism. Am J Psychother 19:408–416, 1965

Hien D, Zimberg S, Weisman S, et al: Dual diagnosis subtypes in urban substance abuse and mental health clinics. Psychiatr Serv 48:1058–1063, 1997

Hoffman NG, Miller NS: Perspectives of effective treatment for alcohol and drug disorders. Psychiatr Clin North Am 16:127–140, 1993

Jaffe AJ, Rounsaville B, Chang G, et al: Naltrexone, relapse prevention, and supportive therapy matching with alcoholics: an analysis of patient treatment matching. J Consult Clin Psychol 64:1044–1053, 1996

Kaufman E: The psychotherapy of dually diagnosed patients. J Subst Abuse Treat 6:9–18, 1989

Khantzian EJ: Some treatment implications of the ego and self disturbance in alcoholism, in Dynamic Approaches to the Understanding and Treatment of Alcoholism. Edited by Bean MH, Zinberg NE. New York, Free Press, 1982, pp 103–188

Mason BJ, Ritvo EL, Morgan RO, et al: A double-blind, placebo controlled pilot study to evaluate the efficacy and safety of oral nalmefene HCl for alcohol dependence. Alcohol Clin Exp Res 18:1162–1167, 1994

McClelland DC, Davis WW, Kalin R, et al: The Drinking Man. New York, Free Press, 1972

Meyer R: Typologies, in Treatments of Psychiatric Disorders: a Task Force Report of the American Psychiatric Association, Vol 2. Washington, DC, American Psychiatric Association, 1989, pp 1065–1072

O'Malley SS, Carroll KM: Psychotherapeutic considerations in pharmacological trials. Alcohol Clin Exp Res 20 (suppl 7):17A–22A, 1996

O'Malley S, Jaffe AJ, Chang G, et al: Naltrexone and alcohol dependence: a controlled study. Arch Gen Psychiatry 49:881–887, 1992

Regier DA, Farmer ME, Rae DS, et al: Comorbidity of mental disorders with alcohol and other drug abuse. JAMA 264:2511–2518, 1990

Schuckit MA: Goals of treatment, in Treatments of Psychiatric Disorders: a Task Force Report of the American Psychiatric Association, Vol 2. Washington, DC, American Psychiatric Association, 1989, pp 1072–1076

Solomon SD: Individual versus group therapy: current status in the treatment of alcoholism. Advances in Alcohol and Substance Abuse 2:69–86, 1982

Spanagel R, Ziegigan S, Berger W: Anti-craving compounds for ethanol: new pharmacological tools to study addictive processes. Trends Pharmacol Sci 18:54–59, 1997

Terenius L: Alcohol addiction (alcoholism) and the opioid system. Alcohol 13:31–34, 1996

Tiebout HM: Intervention in psychotherapy. Am J Psychoanal 22:1–6, 1962

Volpicelli JR, Alterman AL, Hayashida M, et al: Naltrexone and the treatment of alcohol dependence. Arch Gen Psychiatry 49:876–880, 1992

Wallace J: Working with the preferred defense structure of the recovering alcoholic, in Practical Approaches to Alcoholism Psychotherapy, 2nd Edition. Edited by Zimberg S, Wallace J, Blume SB. New York, Plenum, 1985, pp 23–36

Weinrieb RM, O'Brien CP: Naltrexone in the treatment of alcoholism. Annu Rev Med 48:477–487, 1997

Wilsnack SC: The impact of sex roles and women's alcohol use and abuse, in Alcoholism Problems in Women and Children. Edited by Greenblat N, Schuckit MA. New York, Grune & Stratton, 1976

Woody GE, Luborsky L, McLellan AT, et al: Psychotherapy for opiate addicts: does it help? Arch Gen Psychiatry 40:639–645, 1983

Wurmser L: More respect for the neurotic process: comments on the problem of narcissism in severe psychopathology; especially the addictions. J Subst Abuse Treat 1:37–45, 1984

Zimberg S: The Clinical Management of Alcoholism. New York, Brunner/Mazel, 1982

Zimberg S: Individual management and psychotherapy, in Treatments of Psychiatric Disorders: a Task Force Report of the American Psychiatric Association, Vol 2. Washington, DC, American Psychiatric Association, 1989, pp 1093–1103

Zimberg S: Management of alcoholism in the elderly. Addiction Nursing Network 1:4–6, 1990

# Individual Psychotherapy: Other Drugs

## George E. Woody, M.D.
## Delinda Mercer, Ph.D.
## Lester Luborsky, Ph.D.

Psychotherapeutic treatments for substance use disorders are used widely. Individual therapy or drug counseling is available in about 99% of the drug-free, methadone-maintenance, and multiple-modality drug treatment units and about 97% of the detoxification units in the United States (National Drug and Alcoholism Treatment Unit Survey 1982). Often psychosocial interventions make up the entire program (Onken and Blaine 1990). There are numerous approaches to individual therapy, the most prominent of which are dynamic, interpersonal, cognitive and cognitive-behavioral, behavioral, contingency management, and motivational enhancement.

The many approaches to using psychotherapy in the treatment of substance use disorders, and the different orientations of the therapies themselves, make it difficult to write a brief yet comprehensive chapter on this topic. We have attempted to draw together significant contributions from clinical literature and our own experience and blend them with research findings to provide guidelines for practitioners who wish to use individual psychotherapy for the treatment of substance use disorders.

## Definitions of Psychotherapy and Counseling

Throughout this chapter, we use the term *psychotherapy* to describe a psychological treatment that aims to change problematic thoughts, feelings, and behaviors by creating a new understanding of the thoughts and feel-

ings that appear to be causally related to the problem(s). When psychotherapy is used to treat addiction, it must address the addictive behaviors and the thoughts and feelings that appear to promote, maintain, or occur as a result. Along with the goal of ceasing drug self-administration, psychotherapy addresses issues related to other problematic aspects of patients' lives, both past and present, under the assumption that some of these problems contribute to drug abuse.

Addiction counseling, rather than psychotherapy, is the most widely used psychosocial intervention in substance abuse treatment. In contrast to psychotherapy, counseling is much less focused on identifying and changing internal, intrapsychic processes and is much more focused on managing current problems related to drug use. *Counseling* can be defined as the regular management of addiction, primarily by giving support, providing structure, monitoring behavior, encouraging abstinence, and providing concrete services such as referrals for job counseling, medical services, or legal aid. This approach constantly addresses the addictive behavior, often using the language and concepts of the 12-step program developed by Alcoholics Anonymous.

## Rationale for Using Psychotherapy to Treat Substance Disorders

Psychotherapy has been used in the treatment of addiction because psychological and psychiatric problems may contribute to, or result from, chemical dependence. Also, many drugs of abuse appear to be abused because they temporarily reduce subjective distress, which might be treated more appropriately with psychotherapy. For example, opioids have potent sedative and analgesic effects, and benzodiazepines reduce anxiety. In this sense, psychological factors such as anxiety, anger, and depression may encourage drug use as an attempt to escape from painful subjective experiences (Khantzian 1985; Khantzian and Khantzian 1984).

A high level of comorbidity exists between substance use disorders and a wide range of psychiatric symptoms, many of which meet symptomatic and duration criteria for DSM-III-R or DSM-IV (American Psychiatric Association 1987, 1994) diagnoses (Kessler et al. 1996; Khantzian and Treece 1985; Rounsaville et al. 1982, 1991; Weiss et al. 1986; Woody et al. 1983, 1990a, 1990b). The syndromes most commonly comorbid with substance use disorders are major depression, dysthymia, and most anxiety disorders. Because chronic use of most drugs of abuse (with the exception of opioids and nicotine) will magnify or even produce psychiatric symptoms, it is often difficult to determine which symptoms and syndromes represent independent psychiatric disorders and which represent substance-induced conditions.

Whether symptoms are drug related or represent independent disorders, studies have shown that they have prognostic significance (Carroll et al. 1995; Woody et al. 1985, 1990a, 1990b). This finding is especially relevant to psychotherapeutic approaches for treating substance use disorders, because the psychotherapies were developed specifically to address psychiatric symptoms. When viewed in this way, the presence of psychiatric symptoms in the context of a substance use disorder identifies a subgroup of patients that may benefit from an approach that includes psychotherapy.

## General Factors Relevant to Providing Psychotherapy for Addiction

All therapists, regardless of their therapeutic approach or orientation, should have a basic knowledge of drugs of abuse and their effects, the defining features of addiction, typical lifestyles of drug-addicted individuals, and self-help groups including some knowledge of their philosophies and availability. Therapists also should be familiar with the various treatment options available to the patient.

## Treatment Settings

Psychotherapy and counseling are appropriate for use in almost any type of treatment setting. Substance abuse treatment is typically provided in six types of settings: 1) inpatient within psychiatric or general hospitals, 2) inpatient within penal institutions, 3) outpatient in clinics or private practice settings, 4) intensive day treatment programs, 5) halfway houses, and 6) therapeutic communities. The philosophy of treatment varies somewhat by treatment setting, and particular psychotherapeutic approaches may fit better into some programs than others.

Psychotherapy probably has the best chance to work in a setting in which it is integrated into an ongoing program that focuses directly on reducing or eliminating drug use but that also addresses psychiatric symptoms that may accompany the dependence. It is probably most effective when combined with the structure imposed by frequent urine testing. Urinalysis for the presence of drugs of abuse encourages honesty and helps hold the patient accountable for his or her behavior. Prompt feedback on drug-positive and drug-negative urine samples helps the patient feel that the therapist is concerned with and is monitoring his or her progress in recovery. In the case of any lapse to drug use, appropriate confrontation and analysis of what led to the use is important, whether it is discovered through urine testing or self-report. Positive feedback given for clean urine samples is a powerful reinforcer for abstinence.

Many clinicians have found that involvement of significant family members in the treatment process is also helpful. If family members are to be involved, they are usually informed of the nature and consequences of addiction and the treatment process, and their support may be enlisted through family meetings. It is usually helpful to pay attention to factors existing in the family that may undermine treatment, such as addiction in other family members or the development of family crises in response to the patient's improvement.

Drug treatment programs vary greatly in basic aspects of service delivery such as availability of psychiatric and medical services, control of behavior problems, level of illicit drug use, type of physical facilities, use of psychotropic drugs, level of staff morale, educational level of staff, and types of patients receiving treatment (Ball et al. 1986). These programmatic qualities may play a major role in the feasibility, efficacy, or relative importance that psychotherapy may have in different settings.

## Therapist Qualities

Therapist qualities appear to have an effect on success in therapy (Luborsky et al. 1985, 1986). In investigating crack- and cocaine-abusing subjects, Kleinman et al. (1990) found that therapist assignment was the strongest predictor of treatment retention, which has been associated with success in treatment. Despite the apparent significance of therapist differences in effectiveness, research has not identified certain "types" of therapists who tend to be more or less effective in treating addiction (Crits-Christoph et al. 1990). Perhaps one reason it has been difficult to identify therapist characteristics associated with successful outcome is that substance abusers are a very heterogeneous group.

Some guidelines can be offered from research that has examined therapist qualities as they relate to psychotherapy outcome in general. Three therapist qualities appear to be predictive of outcome: adjustment, skill, and interest in helping patients (Luborsky et al. 1985). Another related factor that predicts outcome in psychotherapy is the quality of the helping alliance, or the therapist-patient relationship.

## Therapeutic Alliance

In psychotherapy, therapists who from the beginning of treatment form a positive relationship that is perceived by the patient as "helping" appear to have a better chance of success than those who form less positive bonds (Luborsky et al. 1985). This relationship between alliance and outcome holds across different therapeutic modalities (Horvath and Symonds 1991) and for a variety of psychiatric problems, including substance abuse (Conners et al. 1997). Generally, patients' ratings of the therapeutic alliance are stronger predictors of outcome than are therapists' ratings (Horvath and Symonds 1991), but patient and therapist ratings are usually somewhat consistent.

Therapists' emotional reactions to substance abusers are theorized to be important determinants of outcome. This may be true to some extent in all psychotherapy, but it is considered to be more significant in the treatment of substance abuse because therapists' emotional responses are presumed to be more intense and negative and, thus, have a greater effect (Imhof 1991). In one study of alcoholism treatment (Milmoe et al. 1967), the more anger and anxiety in the clinician's voice in the initial session, the less likely the patient was to follow through on getting treatment.

According to recent data gathered as part of Project MATCH, a national multisite study of psychosocial treatments of alcoholism, among an outpatient sample ($N = 952$), the alliance—rated by the therapist or the patient—consistently predicted treatment participation, days abstinent, and drinks per drinking day (Conners et al. 1997). These changes were all in the expected direction, that is, a positive therapeutic alliance predicted greater participation in treatment and greater reduction in alcohol use. The study also looked at patients after discharge from inpatient rehabilitation ($N = 774$). In this sample, client ratings were not significant predictors of treatment participation or drinking-related outcomes, and therapist ratings of the alliance predicted only the percentage of days abstinent. The lack of an association between alliance and outcome in this group could be because patients who entered aftercare treatment following an inpatient stay were preselected in that they had already achieved some degree of abstinence and were compliant and/or motivated enough to continue treatment after discharge. It could also be that these aftercare patients established a positive alliance with members of their inpatient treatment staff, and it was the strength of this alliance (which was not studied) that promoted their continued treatment participation and recovery. Either of these possibilities would be consistent with Luborsky and colleagues' (1985) assertion that ratings of therapeutic alliance at early stages of treatment are more predictive of outcomes than are later ratings.

It seems reasonable that in treating substance use disorders, the therapist should be interested in and comfortable with addiction-related problems and behaviors. These include the manipulative, sociopathic, impulsive, or demanding behaviors that are sometimes observed, and the self-abusing aspect of the condition that may create negative countertransference feelings for some therapists. Simply stated, it is probably helpful to be interested in working with substance abusers and respect the severity of their problems (Woody et al. 1990a). Washton and Stone-Washton (1990) offered more specific suggestions. They recommended that therapists have a high degree of empathy, confidence, and hope, and a low wish to control the patient.

In clinical practice, therapists should refrain from being judgmental and should occasionally extend themselves a little more with addicted patients than with other types of adult psychiatric patients. The dependency needs of the patients often express themselves in the therapist-patient relationship, and occasional appropriate, concrete, supportive responses are probably useful, especially in the early phases of treatment. This therapeutic posture may consist of greeting the patient warmly on entering the office, actively seeking to reestablish contact when an appointment is missed, being generous with reinforcement for improvement, or seeing the patient occasionally at unscheduled times if necessary.

## Individual Psychotherapy for Substance Disorders

Many of the techniques and principles of psychotherapy used with substance-abusing patients are essentially the same as those used in psychotherapy with other patients. However, to treat addiction effectively, the therapist must combine competence in psychotherapy with a general knowledge of addiction. In modifying the supportive-expressive form of psychotherapy for use with substance-abusing patients, Luborsky et al. (1995) identified certain special emphases that are particularly important in treating substance use disorders. These emphases are also relevant for other orientations of psychotherapy.

1. The therapist must devote much time and energy to introducing the patient to treatment and to engaging him or her in it.
2. The treatment goals must be formulated early and kept in sight.
3. The therapist must give much attention to developing a positive relationship (i.e., therapeutic alliance) with and supporting the patient.
4. The therapist must keep abreast of the patient's compliance with the overall drug treatment program, which includes adherence to rules and avoidance of nonprescribed drugs. This information should come from the patient's self-report and urinalysis and may also be provided by family, friends, and other treatment staff.
5. If the patient is receiving methadone, the therapist should consider when the patient feels therapy is best—before or after the daily dose. Methadone is usually such a central part of the patient's life that establishing an agreed-on time for therapy around the dosing schedule could determine whether the patient engages in or drops out of therapy.

## Efficacy of Psychotherapy With Substance Abusers

The psychosocial components of drug abuse treatment have been the subject of formal research only in the past two decades. Most research on the efficacy of psychotherapy in the treatment of substance use disorders has concluded that psychotherapy can be an effective treatment (Carroll et al. 1991; Crits-Christoph and Siqueland 1997; Grenyer et al. 1996; Resnick et al. 1981; Stephens et al. 1994; Woody et al. 1983). These studies and reviews have examined individual and group psychotherapies in the treatment of opioid, cocaine, alcohol, and marijuana abuse and dependence. The comparison of specific models of therapy for substance use disorders has become the focus of much interest.

## Treatment of Opioid Dependence

Clinical experience with psychotherapy, in the absence of methadone-maintenance treatment, has shown that it is not effective in the treatment of opioid dependence (Nyswander et al. 1958). Dropout rates are extremely high, and few patients show meaningful benefits.

This conclusion changed significantly after the introduction of methadone, which reduces opioid use and keeps patients in treatment. One of the first controlled studies compared supportive-expressive psychotherapy and cognitive-behavioral therapy plus drug counseling with drug counseling alone for opioid-addicted methadone-maintenance patients in a Veterans Affairs treatment program (Woody et al. 1983). The professional psychotherapies in addition to the drug counseling benefited patients who had higher levels of psychopathology more than did the drug counseling alone; however, all patients improved, and drug counseling alone was equally helpful for patients with low levels of psychopathology. Neither of the two psychotherapy models was found to be superior to the other. A parallel study did not find a psychotherapy effect (Rounsaville et al. 1983). This difference in outcome may be the result of the low enrollment in the Rounsaville et al. study and programmatic differences (Woody et al. 1998). A recent study of three community-based methadone programs also showed that patients with high levels of psychiatric symptoms did better with counseling plus psychotherapy than with counseling alone (Woody et al. 1995). Other investigators have also found evidence for the efficacy of psychotherapy for opioid dependence when it is used in conjunction with methadone maintenance or naltrexone (Resnick et al. 1981). Thus a few controlled studies with heroin-addicted patients have found evidence that psychotherapy can be helpful when used in conjunction with pharmacotherapy, particularly for patients with high levels of psychiatric symptoms.

## Treatment of Cocaine Use Disorders

A large recently completed National Institute on Drug Abuse (NIDA) collaborative study investigated the efficacy of four psychosocial treatments when delivered in outpatient settings: 1) cognitive therapy plus group drug counseling, 2) supportive-expressive therapy plus group drug counseling, 3) individual drug counseling plus group drug counseling, and 4) group drug counseling alone (Crits-Christoph et al. 1997, in press). Four hundred eighty-seven patients were randomly assigned to one of these four manually guided treatments. Treatment was intensive, with 36 possible individual and 24 group sessions over 6 months. At admission to the study, patients were using cocaine about 10 days per month on average. Most had low levels of psychiatric symptoms, although there was a subgroup with higher symptom levels. Patients were assessed monthly during treatment and at 9 and 12 months after baseline. Although all groups showed substantial reductions in cocaine use in this intent-to-treat analysis, patients in the individual drug counseling plus group drug counseling condition reduced cocaine use to a greater degree than those in the other three groups. Patients with higher levels of psychiatric symptoms had poorer outcomes, but unlike the methadone studies and like the findings of Project MATCH, psychotherapy did not provide additional benefits to this more psychiatrically symptomatic group.

In an earlier smaller study, relapse prevention and interpersonal psychotherapy, provided once per week for 12 weeks, were compared in the treatment of cocaine abuse in ambulatory patients (Carroll et al. 1991). Fifty-seven percent of the relapse prevention subjects achieved greater than 3 weeks of abstinence during the 12 weeks, whereas only 33% of the interpersonal psychotherapy subjects met the same criterion. Overall, relapse prevention was more effective than interpersonal psychotherapy among patients with severe levels of cocaine dependence, although the research did not find statistically significant main effects between the two types of treatment.

Higgins et al. (1993) reported promising results in a comparison of community reinforcement, which included contingent behavioral reinforcers, with standard drug counseling. Treatment involved 12 weeks of twice-weekly sessions followed by 12 weeks of once-weekly sessions. Sixty-eight percent of patients in the community reinforcement condition achieved 8 weeks of abstinence compared with 11% of the standard drug counseling patients. A more recent study (Silverman et al. 1996) examined the effects of voucher-based reinforcement on cocaine abstinence in methadone-maintenance patients. The percentage of reinforcement patients who were abstinent from cocaine increased progressively during the voucher period to a level significantly higher than in the control group. In addition to being a relatively effective intervention for getting patients to achieve and sustain abstinence, behavioral reinforcement was a highly effective intervention for attendance and retention. In a related study, Iguchi et al. (1997) found that reinforcing treatment-plan-related tasks was even more effective in reducing drug use than was reinforcing drug-free urine samples.

Although psychotherapy and counseling alone have shown moderate efficacy, dropout rates have often been high, which has fostered interest in developing combined psychotherapy and pharmacotherapy approaches for treatment of cocaine dependence (Arndt et al. 1992; Gawin et al. 1989). The results of these studies are mixed, possibly because none of the medications studied has demonstrated clinically significant effects for cocaine dependence.

One study compared relapse prevention plus desipramine, clinical management plus desipramine, relapse prevention plus placebo, and clinical management plus placebo in the treatment of cocaine abuse in ambulatory patients (Carroll et al. 1994). All groups showed improvement, but there were no main effects for medication or psychotherapy. However, there was a significant interaction effect in that relapse prevention was associated with better outcomes for higher-severity cocaine users than was clinical management. Further analysis of these data (Carroll et al. 1995) suggests differential symptom reduction in depressed versus nondepressed cocaine patients. The depressed patients tended to have better retention and better cocaine outcomes than did the nondepressed patients. Desipramine was effective in reducing depressive symptoms but not in reducing cocaine use, which points to the importance of comprehensive evaluation of drug-dependent patients and psychiatric treatment in conjunction with drug treatment for those with dual diagnoses. Relapse prevention was more effective in reducing cocaine use than was clinical management among the depressed group, a finding consistent with the idea that it may be most effective to target the professional psychotherapies to the more psychiatrically severe patients. However, psychotherapy was not more effective than drug counseling in patients with high symptom levels in the recently completed NIDA study (Crits-Christoph et al., in press).

## Treatment of Alcohol Use Disorders

Project MATCH compared cognitive-behavioral therapy, 12-step facilitation therapy (Nowinski et al. 1992), and motivational enhancement therapy (Miller et al. 1992) for the treatment of alcohol dependence.[1] Patients decreased their alcohol use significantly and maintained improvement at 1-year posttreatment in all treatment conditions. There was no significant difference in outcome by type of treatment. Although higher levels of psychiatric severity were associated with worse outcome, the psychiatrically focused treatments did not alter this relationship.

## Treatment of Marijuana Use Disorders

Few studies have examined psychotherapy for marijuana abuse and dependence. Grenyer et al. (1996) compared a modification of supportive-expressive therapy (Grenyer et al. 1995) with a brief (one-session) intervention for treatment of marijuana dependence. The supportive-expressive therapy was offered for 16 weeks. At 16 weeks, the supportive-expressive group showed significantly larger decreases in marijuana use, depression, and anxiety and significantly larger increases in psychological health than did the brief intervention group.

In a study of group treatment of marijuana dependence (Stephens et al. 1994), patients were randomly assigned to either a relapse prevention (Marlatt and Gordon 1985) group or a social support group. All groups were conducted weekly for the first 8 weeks and then biweekly for the next four 4 weeks, for a total of ten 2-hour sessions. Patients in both treatments achieved and maintained reductions in marijuana use and related problems; however, outcomes did not differ between the two treatments.

## Frequency and Intensity of Psychotherapy

The "dose" of psychotherapy or counseling necessary to produce improvement is unclear. According to research on psychotherapy for methadone-maintained patients addicted to opioids, therapy has typically been offered once a week, but patients attend, on average, only once every 2 weeks (Woody et al. 1983). However, patients received daily doses of methadone, a potent pharmacotherapy for opioid dependence.

For cocaine-dependent outpatients, Kleinman et al. (1990) compared weekly family therapy, supportive-expressive psychodynamic therapy, and paraprofessionally led group therapy. Among the sample of mainly urban crack users, attrition was high and there was no evidence of a treatment effect for any of the modalities. Hoffman et al. (1991) combined individual, family, and group therapies at different frequencies for treatment of cocaine dependence. Results indicated that outcome was better in the group and individual conditions that provided intensive day treatment compared with weekly therapy, a finding consistent with the Kleinman et al. (1990) study. Alterman (1990) reported a 50%–60% abstinence rate at 6-month follow-up among cocaine-abusing patients receiving 12-step-oriented drug counseling treatment in either inpatient or intensive day treatment (5 days per week) for 1 month, followed by twice-weekly therapy. These studies suggest that for cocaine-dependent patients, participation in drug counseling should be relatively intense at least initially, and the intensity of treatment can decrease over time if the patient progresses.

Two controlled trials of psychotherapy for marijuana dependence, one studying group treatment (Stephens et al. 1994) and one individual treatment (Grenyer et al. 1996), found substantial reduction of marijuana use and related problems with once-weekly therapy in the individual treatment study and once-weekly decreasing to once every other week for the group treatment trial.

In Project MATCH, motivational enhancement therapy was offered only once a month and was still found to be effective for treating alcohol dependence. This result may imply that certain therapeutic approaches can be effective at relatively low doses, at least for some types of addiction (Project MATCH Research Group 1997).

Overall, these data suggest that the intensity of treatment needed probably varies with the specific drug, the severity of the dependence, and the nature of the patient's associated problems, particularly psychiatric problems. For most patients, opioid or cocaine dependence appears to require more intense treatment than does marijuana or alcohol dependence. In the methadone studies, psychotherapy was most useful for patients who had moderate to high levels of psychiatric

---

[1]Although we do not focus on alcohol research in this chapter, we mention Project MATCH here briefly because it is the largest controlled trial of psychotherapy for addiction.

symptoms in addition to their substance use disorders. In the two largest studies for other substance dependence (Crits-Christoph et al., in press; Project MATCH Research Group 1997), psychotherapy provided no advantage over drug counseling, even for patients with high levels of psychiatric symptoms.

However, other studies have shown that the mix of drug-focused treatments versus treatments that address associated problems may be important. These studies show that it is helpful to provide services that address associated problems, such as family, employment, and psychiatric, in addition to drug-focused treatments, and these services are especially important for patients with problems in these areas (McLellan et al. 1993, 1997).

## Implications for Treatment

Although the relative benefits of psychotherapy versus counseling vary in the studies reviewed here, most agree that psychotherapy can be effective in the treatment of substance abuse and addiction (Carroll et al. 1991; Crits-Christoph and Siqueland 1997; Resnick et al. 1981; Woody et al. 1983). However, it appears that other conditions must be met in order for positive outcomes to occur.

The chemically dependent patient usually requires more structure and greater frequency of visits than traditional psychotherapy provides. In the case of outpatient treatment for opioid dependence, methadone maintenance is essential for psychotherapy or counseling to be helpful. Thus psychotherapy appears to be most effective when combined with drug-focused treatment services, either within the context of a structured addiction treatment program or when organized as needed by the individual psychotherapist. The more traditional psychotherapies, such as cognitive-behavioral, supportive-expressive, and interpersonal, at least in the methadone studies, were primarily useful for patients experiencing clinically significant psychiatric symptoms in addition to their drug problems (Woody et al. 1985).

Thus far, research has not clearly indicated that one kind of psychotherapy is superior to any other for the treatment of addiction. This finding is consistent with much of the psychotherapy outcome research for other psychiatric disorders (Luborsky et al. 1975; Smith and Glass 1977). The therapist's qualities (specifically competence or skill), his or her ability to establish a positive therapeutic alliance with the patient, and the patient's qualities, including severity of the addiction and comorbid psychiatric symptoms and disorders, have a moderate influence on treatment outcome (Luborsky et al. 1985, 1986; McLellan et al. 1988).

The following guidelines may be helpful to the clinician who is interested in treating chemical dependence with psychotherapy:

- Be familiar with the pharmacology of abused drugs, the subculture of addiction, and self-help programs.
- Formulate clear goals early in treatment and keep abreast of the patient's success with abstinence and with compliance in other aspects of the treatment.
- Establish a positive, supportive therapeutic alliance with the patient.
- Incorporate direct, drug-focused interventions into the treatment program. In the outpatient treatment of heroin addiction, this includes methadone maintenance.
- Recognize that because the recovering addicted patient usually requires structure and treatment resources in addition to psychotherapy, therapy is most effective when it is provided within the context of a structured treatment program or when the individual therapist is prepared to refer the patient to other services as needed.
- Require frequent testing for the presence of drugs, through urinalysis, breathalyzer (for alcohol only), or other means and provide prompt feedback on the presence or absence of drugs.
- Understand that addiction is, for many, a chronic condition, and be pleased if the patient shows significant improvement, even if he or she is not "cured."
- Target the psychotherapy to patients with high levels of associated psychiatric or psychological problems, and address those difficulties in the therapy.

## References

Alterman AI: Day hospital versus inpatient cocaine dependence rehabilitation: an interim report, in Problems of Drug Dependence 1990 (NIDA Res Monogr 105). Edited by Harris L. Rockville, MD, U.S. Department of Health and Human Services, 1990, pp 363–364

American Psychiatric Association: Diagnostic and Statistical Manual of Mental Disorders, 3rd Edition, Revised. Washington, DC, American Psychiatric Association, 1987

American Psychiatric Association: Diagnostic and Statistical Manual of Mental Disorders, 4th Edition. Washington, DC, American Psychiatric Association, 1994

Arndt IO, Dorozynsky L, Woody GE, et al: Desipramine treatment of cocaine dependence in methadone maintained patients. Arch Gen Psychiatry 49:888–893, 1992

Ball JC, Corty E, Petroski SP, et al: Medical services provided to 2394 patients at methadone programs in three states. J Subst Abuse Treat 3:203–209, 1986

Carroll KM, Rounsaville BJ, Treece FH: A comparative trial of psychotherapies for ambulatory cocaine abusers: relapse prevention and interpersonal psychotherapy. Am J Drug Alcohol Abuse 17:229–247, 1991

Carroll KM, Rounsaville BJ, Gordon LT, et al: Psychotherapy and pharmacotherapy for ambulatory cocaine abusers. Arch Gen Psychiatry 51:177–187, 1994

Carroll KM, Niche C, Rounsaville BJ: Differential symptom reduction in depressed cocaine abusers treated with psychotherapy and pharmacotherapy. J Nerv Ment Dis 183:251–259, 1995

Conners GJ, Carroll KM, DiClemente CC: The therapeutic alliance and its relationship to alcoholism treatment participation and outcome. J Consult Clin Psychol 65:588–598, 1997

Crits-Christoph P, Siqueland L: Drug-use and associated outcomes of the pilot/training phase of the NIDA cocaine collaborative study. Presentation given at the Society for Psychotherapy Research, Geilo, Norway, June 26–29, 1997

Crits-Christoph P, Beebe KL, Connolly MB: Therapist effects in the treatment of drug dependence: implications for conducting comparative treatment studies, in Psychotherapy and Counseling in the Treatment of Drug Abuse (NIDA Res Monogr 104). Edited by Onken LS, Blaine JD. Rockville, MD, U.S. Department of Health and Human Services, 1990, pp 39–48

Crits-Christoph P, Siqueland L, Blaine J, et al: The National Institute on Drug Abuse Collaborative Cocaine Treatment Study: rationale and methods. Arch Gen Psychiatry 54:721–726, 1997

Crits-Christoph P, Siqueland L, Blaine J, et al: Psychosocial treatments for cocaine dependence: results of the NIDA Cocaine Collaborative Study. Arch Gen Psychiatry (in press)

Gawin FH, Kleber HD, Byck R, et al: Desipramine facilitation of initial cocaine abstinence. Arch Gen Psychiatry 46:117–121, 1989

Grenyer BFS, Luborsky L, Solowij N: Treatment manual for supportive-expressive dynamic therapy: special adaptation for treatment of cannabis (marijuana) dependence (Technical Report 26). Sydney, Australia, National Drug and Alcohol Research Centre, 1995

Grenyer BFS, Solowij N, Peters R: Psychotherapy for marijuana addiction: a randomized controlled trial of brief versus intensive treatment. Presentation given at the Society for Psychotherapy Research, Amelia Island, FL, June 19–23, 1996

Higgins ST, Budney AJ, Bickel WK, et al: Achieving cocaine abstinence with a behavioral approach. Am J Psychiatry 150:763–769, 1993

Hoffman JA, Caudill BD, Moolchan ET, et al: Effective treatments for cocaine abuse and HIV risk: the cocaine abuse treatment strategies (CATS) project. Plenary lecture given at 5th International Congress on Drug Abuse, "The Global Village" Research, Policies, and Community Action, Jerusalem, Israel, September 1–6, 1991

Horvath AO, Symonds BD: Relation between working alliance and outcome in psychotherapy: a meta-analysis. Journal of Counseling Psychology 38:139–149, 1991

Iguchi MY, Belding MA, Morral AR, et al: Reinforcing operants other than abstinence in drug abuse treatment: an effective alternative for reducing drug use. J Consult Clin Psychol 65:421–428, 1997

Imhof J: Countertransference issues in alcohol and drug addiction. Psychiatric Annals 21:292–306, 1991

Kessler RC, Nelson CB, McGonagle KA, et al: The epidemiology of co-occurring addictive and mental disorders: implications for prevention and service utilization. Am J Orthopsychiatry 66:17–31, 1996

Khantzian EJ: The self-medication hypothesis of addictive disorders: focus on heroin and cocaine dependence. Am J Psychiatry 142:1259–1264, 1985

Khantzian EJ, Khantzian NJ: Cocaine addiction: is there a psychological predisposition? Psychiatric Annals 14:753–759, 1984

Khantzian EJ, Treece C: DSM-III psychiatric diagnosis of narcotic addicts. Arch Gen Psychiatry 42:1067–1071, 1985

Kleinman PH, Woody GE, Todd TC, et al: Crack and cocaine abusers in outpatient psychotherapy, in Psychotherapy and Counseling in the Treatment of Drug Abuse (NIDA Res Monogr 104). Edited by Onken LS, Blaine JD. Rockville, MD, U.S. Department of Health and Human Services, 1990, pp 24–34

Luborsky L, Singer B, Luborsky L: Comparative studies of psychotherapies: is it true that "everyone has won and all must have prizes"? Arch Gen Psychiatry 32:995–1008, 1975

Luborsky L, McLellan AT, Woody GE, et al: Therapist success and its determinants. Arch Gen Psychiatry 42:602–611, 1985

Luborsky L, Crits-Christoph P, McLellan AT: Do therapists vary in their effectiveness? findings from four outcome studies. Am J Orthopsychiatry 66:501–512, 1986

Luborsky L, Woody GE, Hole A, et al: Supportive-expressive dynamic psychotherapy for opiate drug dependence, in Dynamic Therapies for Psychiatric Disorders. Edited by Barber J, Crits-Christoph P. New York, Basic Books, 1995, pp 131–160

Marlatt GA, Gordon J (eds): Relapse Prevention: Maintenance Strategies in the Treatment of Addictive Behaviors. New York, Guilford, 1985

McLellan AT, Woody GE, Luborsky L, et al: Is the counselor an "active ingredient" in methadone treatment? an examination of treatment success among four counselors. J Nerv Ment Dis 176:423–430, 1988

McLellan AT, Arndt IO, Metzger DS, et al: Are psychosocial services necessary in substance abuse treatment? JAMA 269:1953–1959, 1993

McLellan AT, Alterman A, Metzger DS, et al: Similarity of outcome predictors across opiate, cocaine, and alcohol treatments: role of treatment services. J Consult Clin Psychol 62:1141–1158, 1997

Miller WR, Zweben A, DiClemente CC, et al: Motivational Enhancement Therapy Manual: A Clinical Research Guide for Therapists Treating Individuals With Alcohol Abuse and Dependence, NIAAA Project MATCH Monograph, Vol 2 (DHHS Publ No ADM-92-1894). Washington, DC, U.S. Government Printing Office, 1992

Milmoe S, Rosenthal R, Blane H, et al: The doctor's voice: postdictor of successful referral of alcohol patients. J Abnorm Psychol 72:78–84, 1967

National Drug and Alcoholism Treatment Unit Survey (DHHS Publ No ADM-89-1626). Rockville, MD, U.S. Department of Health and Human Services, 1982

Nowinski J, Baker S, Carroll K: Twelve-Step Facilitation Therapy Manual: A Clinical Research Guide for Therapists Treating Individuals With Alcohol Abuse and Dependence, NIAAA Project MATCH Monograph, Vol 1 (DHHS Publ No ADM-92-1893). Washington, DC, U.S. Government Printing Office, 1992

Nyswander M, Winick C, Bernstein A, et al: The treatment of drug addicts as voluntary outpatients: a progress report. Am J Orthopsychiatry 28:714–729, 1958

Onken LS, Blaine JD: Psychotherapy and counseling research in drug abuse treatment: questions, problems, and solutions, in Psychotherapy and Counseling in the Treatment of Drug Abuse (NIDA Res Monogr 104). Edited by Onken LS, Blaine JD. Rockville, MD, U.S. Department of Health and Human Services, 1990, pp 1–5

Project MATCH Research Group: Matching alcoholism treatments to client heterogeneity: Project MATCH posttreatment drinking outcomes. J Stud Alcohol 58:7–29, 1997

Resnick RB, Washton AM, Stone-Washton N, et al: Psychotherapy and naltrexone in opioid dependence, in Problems of Drug Dependence (NIDA Res Monogr 34). Edited by Harris LS. Rockville, MD, U.S. Department of Health and Human Services, 1981, pp 109–115

Rounsaville BJ, Weissman MM, Kleber HD, et al: Heterogeneity of psychiatric diagnoses in treated opiate addicts. Arch Gen Psychiatry 39:161–166, 1982

Rounsaville BJ, Glazer W, Wilber CH, et al: Short-term interpersonal psychotherapy in methadone maintained opiate addicts. Arch Gen Psychiatry 40:629–636, 1983

Rounsaville BJ, Foley S, Carroll KM, et al: Psychiatric diagnoses of treatment-seeking cocaine abusers. Arch Gen Psychiatry 48:43–51, 1991

Silverman K, Higgins ST, Brooner RK, et al: Sustained cocaine abstinence in methadone maintenance patients through voucher-based reinforcement therapy. Arch Gen Psychiatry 53:409–415, 1996

Smith ML, Glass GV: Meta-analysis of psychotherapy outcome studies. Am Psychol 32:752–760, 1977

Stephens RS, Roffman RA, Simpson EE: Treating adult marijuana dependence: a test of the relapse prevention model. J Consult Clin Psychol 62:92–99, 1994

Washton A, Stone-Washton N: Abstinence and relapse in cocaine addicts. J Psychoactive Drugs 22:135–147, 1990

Weiss RD, Mirin SM, Michael JL, et al: Psychopathology in chronic cocaine abusers. Am J Drug Alcohol Abuse 12:17–29, 1986

Woody GE, Luborsky L, McLellan AT, et al: Psychotherapy for opiate addicts: does it help? Arch Gen Psychiatry 40:639–645, 1983

Woody GE, McLellan AT, Luborsky L, et al: Psychiatric severity as a predictor of benefits from psychotherapy. Am J Psychiatry 141:1172–1177, 1985

Woody GE, McLellan AT, Luborsky L, et al: Psychotherapy and counseling for methadone maintained opiate addicts: results of research studies (NIDA Research Monogr 104). Edited by Onken LS, Blaine JD. Rockville, MD, U.S. Department of Health and Human Services, 1990a, pp 9–23

Woody GE, McLellan AT, O'Brien CP: Research on psychopathology and addiction: treatment implications. Drug Alcohol Depend 25:121–123, 1990b

Woody GE, McLellan AT, Luborsky L, et al: Psychotherapy in community methadone programs: a validation study. Am J Psychiatry 152:1302–1308, 1995

Woody GE, McLellan AT, Luborsky L, et al: Psychotherapy with opioid-dependent patients. Psychiatric Times, November 1998

# Chapter 31

# Relapse Prevention

G. Alan Marlatt, Ph.D.
Kimberly Barrett, Ed.D.
Dennis C. Daley, M.S.W.

In this chapter, we present an overview of practical applications of the relapse prevention (RP) model of treatment for substance use disorders. Background research and theory leading to the development of this model and description of clinical applications of RP can be found in earlier publications on the RP approach (Daley 1989; Marlatt and Gordon 1985). Information on outcome studies, including those involving RP, can be found in other publications (Carroll 1996; Daley and Marlatt 1997a; Miller et al. 1995). Much of the material presented in this chapter is drawn from these sources.

## What Is Relapse Prevention?

*Relapse prevention* is a cognitive-behavioral treatment that combines behavioral skill-training procedures with cognitive intervention techniques to assist individuals in maintaining desired behavioral changes. Based in part on the principles of health psychology and social-cognitive theory, RP uses a psychoeducational self-management approach to substance abuse designed to teach patients new coping responses, to modify maladaptive beliefs and expectancies concerning substance use, and to change personal habits and lifestyles.

Initially, the RP model was developed as a behavioral maintenance program for use in the treatment of addictive behaviors. In the addictions, the typical treatment goals are either to refrain totally from performing a target behavior (i.e., *the abstinence model*) or to reduce the harm or risk of ongoing habits (i.e., *the harm-reduction model*) (Marlatt and Tapert 1993). Although the mate-

rial presented in this chapter is directed primarily toward substance use disorders, the RP model may be applicable to problems such as overeating, gambling, and high-risk sexual behaviors, which may be considered collectively as *addictive behaviors* (Donovan and Marlatt 1988). Addictive behaviors include those acts leading to a state of immediate reward. With many addictive behaviors (especially substance abuse), the experience of immediate reinforcement (i.e., the pleasure, "high," tension-reduction, or relief associated with the act itself) is followed by delayed negative consequences such as physical discomfort or disease, social disapproval, loss of significant relationships, occupational impairment, financial loss, and decreased self-esteem. Because many treatment programs for these kinds of problems have high recidivism rates, the RP model has been applied to an increasingly broad range of behaviors or problems including sexual deviance, eating disorders, chronic pain, marital disorders, psychiatric illness, and the dual disorders of psychiatric illness combined with substance abuse (Daley and Lis 1995; Wilson 1992).

## Treatment Goals and Treatment Philosophy

RP is one of several behavior therapy approaches to the treatment of addictive behaviors. Behavior therapists have been active in developing and evaluating a variety of empirically based techniques including aversion therapy, covert sensitization, and cue exposure (Childress et al. 1986); contingency contracting (Higgins et al. 1994); and community reinforcement methods (Meyers and Smith 1995).

The cornerstone of behavior therapy for substance abuse problems is skill training (Chaney et al. 1978; Kadden et al. 1995). In this approach, clients are taught behavioral and cognitive skills such as changing thoughts and beliefs; resisting social pressure; increasing assertiveness; developing relaxation and stress management techniques; and improving interpersonal communication.

RP procedures can be applied in prevention and treatment designed to prevent relapse, reduce relapse risk, or manage ongoing relapse problems. Maintenance strategies are designed both to anticipate and to prevent the occurrence of relapse following treatment and to help patients cope with relapse if it occurs in order to limit adverse effects on self and others. Because RP was designed as a posttreatment maintenance program, the methods can be applied regardless of the particular program or approach used during the initial stages of treatment. Once an alcoholic patient has stopped drinking, for example, RP methods can be applied toward the effective maintenance of abstinence, regardless of the methods used to initiate abstinence. RP can also be used to direct the substance-abusing patient to other useful treatment modes, such as family or couples therapy. One important goal of RP is to train the patient to become his or her own therapist and thus carry on the thrust of the initial treatment program after the formal therapeutic relationship terminates. Whether the initial treatment occurs in individual or group treatment, the RP model is fundamentally a self-control program in which patients are taught how to anticipate and cope effectively with addictive disorders or other problems as they arise during the posttreatment or follow-up period.

The RP model is also used to facilitate changes in personal habits and lifestyle to reduce the risk of physical disease or other harm associated with the addictive behavior. In this instance, the aim of the RP program is much broader in scope: to teach the individual how to reduce lifestyle health risks and prevent the formation of additional unhealthy habit patterns. The central motif of this approach is one of *moderation*, meaning a balanced lifestyle that is midway between the opposing extremes of behavioral excess and restraint. Viewed from this more global perspective, RP can be considered as a component of the developing public health model of *harm reduction*—behavior-change programs designed to reduce the risk of ongoing addictive behavior problems (Marlatt and Tapert 1993).

## Definition of Lapse and Relapse

Broadly considered, *relapse* is defined as any discrete violation of a self-imposed rule or set of rules governing the rate or pattern of a selected target behavior. Total abstinence, the most stringent rule one can adopt, is thus violated by a single instance of a target behavior (e.g., the first drink or use of a substance). Viewed from this absolute black-white perspective, a single *lapse* is equated with total relapse (see Figure 31–1). Although violation of the abstinence rule is the primary form of relapse we have studied in our research in substance abuse, other forms of relapse would also be included within the above definition. Violation of rules governing caloric intake imposed by a diet would constitute a relapse, as would exceeding alcohol-consumption limits imposed in a drinking moderation program. Within this general definition of relapse, we distinguish between the first violation of the rules (the initial lapse) and the subsequent secondary effects in which the behavior may increase toward the original pretreatment baseline level (a full-blown relapse). This distinction between lapse and relapse is shown in Figure 31–2, showing the gray area of a lapse experience.

In the RP approach, relapse is viewed as a transitional process rather than an outcome failure. The relapse process consists of a series of external and internal events that may or may not be followed by a return to pretreatment baseline levels of the target behavior. In clinical practice, a patient can be considered to be in a relapse process prior to ingesting alcohol or other drugs. Usually, the patient will show warning signs that indicate movement away from abstinence toward substance use (Daley and Marlatt 1997b). In conducting microanalyses of relapse episodes, the clinician often can help the patient identify obvious and subtle warning signs that preceded the lapse or relapse. It is possible to view the alcoholic individual who takes a single drink after a period of abstinence or the cocaine addict who ingests the drug one time as someone who has made a single excursion over the border between abstinence and relapse. Whether this excursion or lapse is followed by a return to abstinence depends in part on the expectations and attributions of the individual involved. One of the goals of RP is to provide an individual with the necessary skills and cognitive strategies to prevent a lapse from escalating into a total relapse. Rather than looking pessimistically on a lapse as a dead-end failure, the RP approach views each lapse as a fork in the road, one path returning to the former problem behavior (relapse) and the other continuing in the direction of posi-

**Figure 31–1.** Black-white model of abstinence versus relapse.

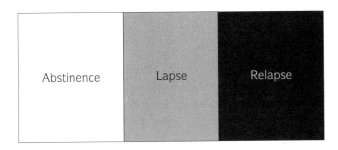

**Figure 31–2.** The "gray area" model of abstinence, lapse, and relapse.

tive change (see Figure 31–3). Instead of being viewed as an indication of failure, a lapse can be viewed more optimistically as a challenging mistake or error, an opportunity for new learning to occur. In clinical practice, lapses vary in terms of negative or positive effects on the patient. For example, a single lapse for a health care professional mandated to attend treatment who is closely monitored could have serious adverse consequences on this individual's career. Some patients report lapses as significant positive events in terms of increasing their motivation to change the way they cope with their substance use disorder.

## Overview of High-Risk Situations for Relapse

In the following overview, only the highlights of the RP model are presented. Further details on background research and theory leading to the assessment of high-risk situations can be found in Marlatt and Gordon (1985). Figure 31–4 shows a schematic representation of the relapse model.

To begin, we assume that the individual experiences a sense of perceived control while maintaining absti-

nence (or complying with other rules governing the target behavior). The target behavior is "under control" so long as it does not occur. For example, the longer the period of successful abstinence, the greater the individual's perception of self-control. This perceived control will continue until the individual encounters a *high-risk situation*, defined broadly as any situation that poses a threat to the individual's sense of control and increases the risk of potential relapse. In an analysis of 311 initial relapse episodes obtained from patients with a variety of problem behaviors (problem drinking, smoking, heroin addiction, compulsive gambling, and overeating), three primary high-risk situations were associated with almost 75% of all the relapses reported (Marlatt and Gordon 1985). A brief description of these three high-risk situations associated with the highest relapse rates follows.

1. *Negative emotional states* (35% of all relapses in the sample): situations in which the individual is experiencing a negative (or unpleasant) emotional state, mood, or feeling, such as frustration, anger, anxiety, depression, or boredom, prior to or occurring simultaneously with the first lapse. For example, a smoker in the sample gave the following description of a relapse episode:

   > It had been raining continually all week. Saturday I walked down to the basement to do laundry and I found the basement filled with a good 3 inches of water. To make things worse, as I went to turn on the light to see the extent of the damage, I got shocked from the light switch. Later that same day I was feeling real low and knew I had to have a cigarette after my neighbor, who is a contractor, assessed the damage at over $4,000. I went to the store and bought a pack.

   In some instances, negative emotional states may represent specific symptoms of a psychiatric disorder such as bipolar disorder, major depression, or one of the anxiety disorders. Research suggests that 37% of individuals with alcohol abuse or dependence and 53% of individuals with drug abuse or dependence will experience a psychiatric disorder at some point in their lives (Robins and Regier 1991).

2. *Interpersonal conflict* (16% of the relapses): situations involving an ongoing or relatively recent conflict associated with any interpersonal relationship such as with a spouse, friend, family member, employer, or employee. Arguments and interpersonal confrontations occur frequently in this category.

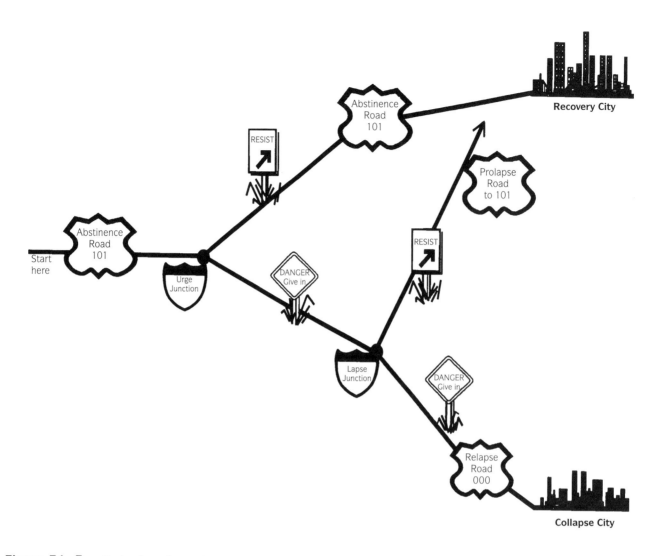

**Figure 31–3.** Forks along the road to recovery.

For example, a recovering alcoholic father confronts his teenage son about having stayed out all night with the car. His son then accuses him of being "on his case all the time." The son leaves the house slamming the door. The father reports becoming angry and taking his first drink in 4 months.

3. *Social pressure* (20% of the relapses): situations in which the individual is responding to the influence of another individual or group of individuals who exert pressure on the individual to engage in the proscribed behavior. Social pressure may be either direct (e.g., interpersonal contact with verbal persuasion) or indirect (e.g., being in the presence of others who are engaging in the same target behavior, even though no direct pressure is involved). The following example of direct social pressure was given by a formerly abstinent problem drinker:

I went to my boss's house for a surprise birthday dinner for him. I got there late, and as I came into the living room everyone had a drink in hand. I froze when my boss's wife asked me what I was drinking. Without thinking, I said, "J & B on the rocks."

Individuals with drug abuse or dependence also frequently report strong social pressures to use drugs.

In our analyses of relapse episodes, these same three high-risk situations are frequently found to be associated with relapse, indicative of a common risk factor for a variety of addictive behaviors (i.e., problem drinking, smoking, gambling, heroin use, or overeating). Other high-risk situations include negative physical states (e.g., withdrawal), testing personal control, and responsivity to substance cues (i.e., craving, urges). This pat-

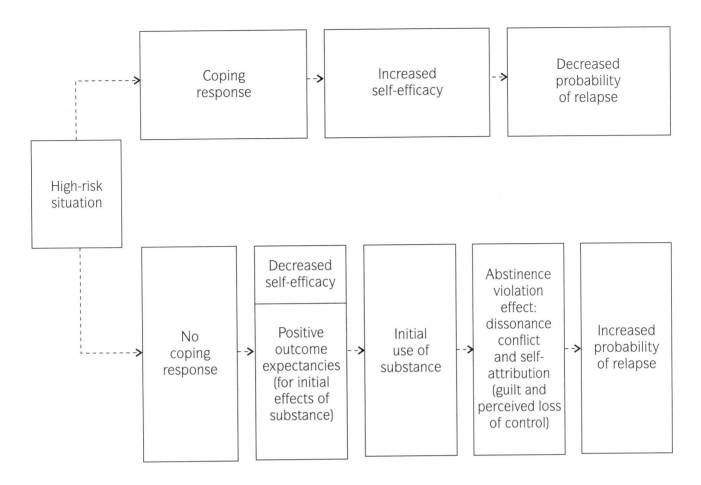

**Figure 31–4.** Cognitive-behavioral model of the relapse process.

tern of findings lends support to our hypothesis that common triggers frequently initiate the relapse process.

If an individual is able to execute an effective coping response in a high-risk situation (e.g., by being assertive in counteracting social pressures), the probability of relapse decreases. An individual who copes successfully with a high-risk situation is likely to experience a sense of mastery or perception of control. Successful mastery of one problematic situation is often associated with an expectation of being able to cope successfully with the next challenging event. The expectancy of being able to cope with successive high-risk situations as they develop is closely associated with Bandura's notion of *self-efficacy* (Bandura 1977), defined as the individual's expectation concerning the capacity to cope with an impending situation or task. A feeling of confidence in one's abilities to cope effectively with a high-risk situation is associated with an increased perception of self-efficacy, a kind of "I know I can handle it" feeling. As the duration of the abstinence (or period of con-

trolled use) increases, and an individual is able to cope effectively with more and more high-risk situations, perception of control increases in a cumulative fashion; the probability of relapse decreases accordingly.

What happens if an individual is unable or unwilling to cope successfully with a high-risk situation? Perhaps the individual has never acquired the coping skills involved, or the appropriate response has been inhibited by fear or anxiety. Or, perhaps the individual fails to recognize and respond to the risk involved before it is too late. For others, the anticipated rewards for indulgence may undermine motivation to resist temptation in the high-risk situation. Motivation can change at any point in recovery, and the individual can become ambivalent about abstinence, even after a period in which motivation to change was quite strong. Whatever the reason, if a coping response is not performed, the individual is likely to experience a decrease in self-efficacy, frequently coupled with a sense of helplessness and a tendency to passively give in to the situation. "It's no use, I can't handle this," is a common reaction. As self-efficacy decreases in the precipitating high-risk situation, one's expectations for coping successfully with subsequent problem situations also suffer. If the situation also involves the temptation to engage in the prohibited behavior (i.e., substance abuse) as a means of attempting to cope with the stress involved, the stage is set for a probable relapse. The probability of relapse is enhanced if the individual holds positive expectancies about the effects of the substance involved. Often the individual will anticipate the euphorogenic effects of the substance, positive effects based on past experience, while simultaneously ignoring or not attending to the delayed negative consequences involved. The lure of immediate gratification looms dominantly as the reality of the full consequences of the act recedes. For many individuals, smoking a marijuana cigarette or taking a drink has long been associated with coping with stress. "A drink would sure help me get through this," or, "If only I could have a joint, I would feel more relaxed," are commonly held beliefs. Positive outcome expectancies are a primary motivational determinant of alcohol and drug use.

Being unable to cope effectively in a high-risk situation coupled with positive outcome expectancies for the effects of the habitual coping behavior (i.e., substance use) greatly increases the probability that an initial lapse will occur. On the one hand, the individual is faced with a high-risk situation with no coping response available; self-efficacy decreases as the individual feels less able to exert control. On the other hand, there is the lure of the old coping response—the drink or the drug. At this point, unless a last-minute coping response or a sudden change of circumstances occurs, the individual may cross over the abstinence border. Whether the first lapse is followed by a total relapse depends in part on the individual's attributions as to the "cause" of the lapse and the reactions that are associated with its occurrence.

The requirement of abstinence is an absolute dictum. Once someone has crossed over the line, there is no going back. From this black-white perspective (see Figure 31–1), a single drink or use of a drug is sufficient to violate the rule of abstinence: once committed, the deed cannot be undone. Unfortunately, many individuals who attempt to stop a habit, such as using drugs or drinking, perceive quitting in this "once and for all" manner. To account for the reaction to the transgression of an absolute rule, we have postulated a mechanism called the *abstinence violation effect* (AVE) (Marlatt and Gordon 1985). The AVE is postulated to

occur under the following conditions. Prior to the first lapse, the individual is personally committed to an extended or indefinite period of abstinence. The intensity of the AVE varies as a function of several factors, including the degrees of prior commitment or effort expended to maintain abstinence, the duration of the abstinence period (the longer the period, the greater the effect), and the subjective value or importance of the prohibited behavior to the individual. We hypothesize that the AVE is characterized by two key cognitive-affective elements: cognitive dissonance (conflict and guilt) and a personal attribution effect (blaming the self as the cause of the relapse). Individuals who experience an intense AVE following a lapse often experience a motivation crisis (demoralization reaction) that undermines their commitment to abstinence goals.

## Covert Antecedents of Relapse

In the foregoing discussion of the immediate determinants and reactions to relapse, the high-risk situation is viewed as the precipitating or triggering situation associated with the initial lapse or first "slip" following a period of abstinence or controlled use. In many of the relapse episodes we have studied, the first lapse is precipitated in a high-risk situation that the individual encounters unexpectedly. In most of these instances, the individual is not expecting the high-risk situation to occur and/or is generally ill-prepared to cope effectively with the circumstances as they arise. Quite often, the individual will suddenly find himself or herself in a rapidly escalating situation that cannot be dealt with effectively. For example, one of our patients who had a serious drinking problem experienced her first lapse after several weeks of abstinence when she treated a new friend to lunch. A last-minute change of plans led them to eat at a restaurant that served alcoholic beverages. Just moments after their arrival, a cocktail waitress approached their table and asked for drink orders. Our patient's friend ordered a cocktail first, and then the waitress turned to the patient saying, "And you?" She too ordered a drink, the first of a series of events that culminated in a full-blown relapse. As the patient said later, "I didn't plan it, and I wasn't prepared for it."

In other relapse episodes, however, the high-risk situation appears to be the last link in a chain of events preceding the first lapse. For example, another patient was a compulsive gambler who came to us for help in controlling his habit, a habit that had caused him numerous marital and financial problems. Before coming to us, he had managed to abstain from all gambling for approximately 6 months, followed by a relapse and an inability to regain abstinence. We asked him to describe this last relapse episode. "There's nothing much to talk about," he began. "I was in Reno and I started gambling again." Obviously, Reno, Nevada, is a high-risk city for any gambler who is trying to maintain abstinence. We then asked him to describe the events preceding his arrival in Reno. A close analysis of this chain of events led us to conclude that this patient had covertly set up or "planned" his relapse. Although he strongly denied his responsibility in this covert planning process, there were a number of choice-points (forks in the road) preceding the relapse where the patient "chose" an alternative that led him closer to the brink of relapse. He finally ended up in a downtown Reno casino putting a dollar in a slot machine, an event that triggered a weekend-long binge of costly gambling. It was as if he had placed himself in a situation so risky that it would take a "moral Superman" to resist the temptation to resume gambling.

Why do some patients appear to set up their own relapse? From a cost-benefit perspective, a relapse can be seen as a rational choice (or a justified gamble). The benefit is swift in coming: a payoff of immediate gratification. The reward of instant gratification is seen to outweigh the cost of potential negative effects that may or may not occur sometime in the distant future. Why not take a chance when this time the outcome might be different? Cognitive distortions such as denial and rationalization make it much easier to set up one's own relapse episode; one may deny both the intent to relapse and the importance of long-range negative consequences. There are also many excuses one can use to rationalize the act of indulgence.

Denial and rationalization are cognitive distortion mechanisms that go hand in hand in the covert planning of a relapse episode. These two defense mechanisms may combine to influence the individual to make certain uninformed choices or decisions as part of a chain of events leading ultimately to relapse. We hypothesize that an individual headed for a relapse often makes a number of mini-decisions over time, each of which brings the individual closer to the brink of succumbing to or creating a high-risk situation. The term *apparently irrelevant decisions* is used to describe these choices. An example is that of the abstinent drinker who buys a bottle of sherry to take home, "just in case guests drop by." In our gambler case study, a last-minute decision was made to expand a driving trip to eastern California to include a visit to Lake Tahoe, a short drive from

Reno. In these examples, the individual sets the stage for relapse through a serious of apparently irrelevant decisions, each moving him or her one step closer to relapse.

A final advantage in setting up a relapse in this manner is that the individual may attempt to avoid assuming personal responsibility for the relapse episode itself. By putting oneself in an impossibly tempting high-risk situation, one can claim being overwhelmed by external circumstances that are impossible to resist. There is almost nothing a gambler can do to resist the temptation of a "downtown Reno" situation, but he or she can accept responsibility for plotting the chain of events that led to Reno. Similarly, a drug-addicted person will have difficulty resisting drugs when in the presence of drug use. For example, smelling crack cocaine or marijuana and watching others get high are powerful motivators to engage in substance use.

By helping the patient review the chain of events leading to the substance use, gambling, or other behavior that he or she was trying to change, an individual may be trained to recognize early warning signs that precede a relapse and to plan and execute a series of intervention strategies before it is too late to do anything. The clinician should be aware that many patients erroneously believe that preparation isn't necessary or that they have "learned their lesson" following a lapse or relapse. By examining irrelevant decisions and warning signs with the patient, the clinician can better prepare him or her for the realities of changing a substance use problem and thus reduce relapse risk.

One of the most tempting rationalizations is that the desire to yield to temptation is justified. Our research findings and clinical experience suggest that the degree of *lifestyle balance* has a significant effect on the individual's desire for indulgence or immediate gratification (Marlatt and Gordon 1985). Here, we are defining *balance* as the degree of equilibrium that exists in one's daily life between those activities perceived as external demands (the *shoulds*) and those perceived as activities engaged in for pleasure or self-fulfillment (the *wants*). Paying bills or performing routine chores or menial tasks at work would count highly as shoulds for many individuals. At the other end of the scale are the wants, activities the individual enjoys or likes to perform (e.g., going fishing, taking time off for lunch with a friend, engaging in a creative work task). Other activities represent a mixture of wants and shoulds. We find that if a patient's lifestyle is encumbered with a preponderance of perceived shoulds, this is often associated with an increased perception of self-deprivation and a corresponding desire for indulgence and gratification. It is as if the individual who spends his or her entire day engaged in activities high in external *should* demands then attempts to balance this disequilibrium by engaging in an excessive want or self-indulgence at the end of the day (e.g., drinking to excess in the evening). The patient may rationalize this behavior by saying, "I owe myself a drink or two—I deserve a break today!" For example, a department manager of a large hospital frequently worked long hours and weekends. In examining a relapse, she stated, "I felt burned out because all I did was work and deal with the demands of my job. I felt totally controlled by my job. I remember thinking to myself when I took my first drink that this was the one thing in my life that my employer couldn't control."

## Assessment and Specific Intervention Strategies

In this section, we discuss strategies designed to teach the patient to recognize and cope with high-risk situations that may precipitate a lapse, and to modify cognitions and other reactions to prevent a single lapse from developing into a full-blown relapse. Explicitly focused on the high-risk situations for relapse, these procedures are referred to collectively as *specific RP intervention strategies*. We also go beyond the microanalysis of the initial lapse and present strategies designed to modify the patient's lifestyle and to identify and cope with covert determinants of relapse. We refer to these procedures as *global RP self-control strategies*. In selecting techniques from the material to be presented in the remaining sections, it should be kept in mind that the RP model can be applied either as an "add-on" program, in which techniques are introduced as an addition to an already existing substance abuse treatment program, or as a general self-control approach designed to develop and maintain a balanced lifestyle. A complete application of the RP model would integrate both specific and global (i.e., lifestyle) intervention techniques.

Specific and global RP strategies can be grouped in three main categories: skill training, cognitive reframing, and lifestyle intervention. *Skill-training* strategies include both behavioral and cognitive responses to help the patient cope with high-risk situations. *Cognitive reframing* procedures are designed to provide the patient with alternative cognitions concerning the nature of the habit-change process (i.e., to view it as a learning process), to introduce coping imagery to deal with urges and early warning signs, and to reframe reactions to the

initial lapse (i.e., restructuring of the AVE). Finally, *lifestyle balancing strategies* (e.g., meditation, mindfulness, and exercise) are designed to strengthen the patient's global coping capacity and to reduce the frequency and intensity of urges and cravings that are often the product of an unbalanced lifestyle.

Which of the various intervention techniques should be applied with a particular patient? It is possible to combine techniques into a standardized package, with each patient receiving identical components, if the purpose is to evaluate the effectiveness of a package RP program. Most therapists, however, will adapt the RP model with patients in an applied clinical setting. In contrast with those who deal with the demands of treatment outcome research, practitioners working in the clinical area typically prefer to develop a tailor-made program of techniques for each patient. We recommend the individualized approach for implementation of RP with most patient problems. Particular techniques should be selected based on a carefully conducted assessment program (Donovan and Marlatt 1988). Therapists are encouraged to select intervention procedures based on their initial evaluation and assessment of the patient's substance abuse problem and general lifestyle pattern.

The possibility of moderation as an alternative to abstinence is the single most controversial issue associated with treatment planning. Resistance to controlled drinking in the treatment of alcohol abuse and dependence has intensified in the traditional *disease model* or *chemical dependency* programs in the United States. Because a complete discussion of the controversy is beyond the scope of this chapter, the reader is referred to other publications on the topic (e.g., Heather and Robertson 1987; Marlatt et al. 1993). As a form of secondary prevention or harm reduction, controlled drinking may work best for those who are beginning to develop problems with their drinking rather than as a remedial treatment program for individuals who have developed a long-term dependence on alcohol (Baer et al. 1992; Kivlahan et al. 1990). Initial reduction of alcohol use rather than abstinence may also be used as a motivational tool (Miller and Rollnick 1991) to motivate otherwise resistant patients to seek help. For example, some college students who exhibit problems with alcohol are able to learn how to monitor their intake and limit the amount and frequency of alcohol use. Those unable to successfully moderate intake would be appropriate for abstinence-oriented approaches.

When abstinence has been identified as the goal of treatment, the overall aim of specific intervention procedures is to teach the patient to anticipate and cope with the possibility of relapse, to recognize and cope with high-risk situations that may precipitate a slip, and to modify cognitions and other reactions to prevent a single lapse from developing into a full-blown relapse. Figure 31–5 shows a schematic overview of the specific RP intervention techniques. The first step in the prevention of relapse is to teach the patient to recognize high-risk situations that may precipitate or trigger a relapse. Here, the earlier one becomes aware of being involved in a chain of events that increases the probability of a slip or lapse, the sooner one can intervene by performing an appropriate coping skill. Patients are taught to recognize and respond to warning signs (*discriminative stimuli*) associated with entering a high-risk situation and to use these signs as reminders to engage in alternative or remedial action.

An essential aspect of teaching patients to better handle high-risk situations is to help them to identify and anticipate these situations. Earlier we discussed prototypic kinds of high-risk situations. Ultimately the identification of high-risk situations is an individualized question requiring ideographic assessment procedures. *Self-monitoring procedures* (e.g., keeping a diary or daily tally) offer an effective method for assessing high-risk situations whenever it is possible to have patients keep a record of their addictive behavior for a baseline period prior to treatment. As little as 10 days of self-monitoring data can often highlight situational influences and skill deficits that underlie an addictive behavior pattern. If the patient is already abstinent, monitoring strong urges or cravings can provide similar information. Reviewing lists of common relapse risk factors to identify personal potential relapse precipitants is another useful way to

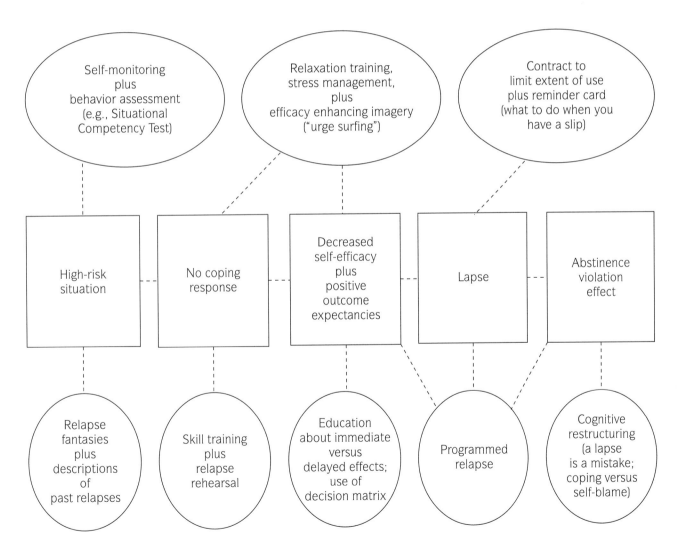

**Figure 31–5.** Relapse prevention: specific intervention strategies.

assess the patient's perceptions of high-risk situations (Daley 1997; Daley and Marlatt 1997a).

Determining the adequacy of preexisting coping abilities is a critical assessment target. In a treatment outcome investigation aimed at teaching alcoholic patients to handle situational temptations, Chaney et al. (1978) devised the Situational Competency Test to measure coping ability. In this technique, the patient is presented with a series of written or audiotaped descriptions of potential relapse situations. Each description ends with a prompt for the patient to respond. Later, the patient's responses to the scenes can be scored on a number of dimensions, including response duration and latency, degree of compliance, and specification of alternative behaviors. A similar technique involves the use of *self-efficacy ratings*, in which the patient, and perhaps his or her spouse, is presented with a list of potential relapse situations (Annis and Davis 1988). For each situation, the patient uses a rating scale to estimate the subjective expectation of successful coping. Ratings across a wide range of situations enable the individual to identify both problematic situations and skill deficits in need of remedial training. Results from these types of assessment tools can later dictate the focus of skill-training procedures.

Carefully administered assessment procedures will enable the individual to identify many high-risk situations. The patient must then learn an alternative approach for responding to these situations. A first step in this new approach is to recognize that high-risk situations are best perceived as discriminative stimuli signaling the need for behavior change in the same way that road signs signal the need for alternative action. Viewed in this way, high-risk situations can be seen as junctures where choices are made rather than as inevitable and uncontrollable challenges that must be endured. In this light, the choice to simply avoid or take a detour around risky situations becomes more available to the individual. However, routine avoidance of particular high-risk situations is unrealistic. Therefore, patients must acquire coping skills that enable them to cope with these situations as they arise. The specific coping skills to be taught will depend on whether the existing deficiencies are due to actual skill deficits or response inhibition. An individual who has never learned or mastered the skills required to better cope with the high-risk situation needs remedial skill training. In response inhibition, an individual has already acquired the skills needed to cope with the situation but is unable to execute them because of inhibiting anxiety and/or conflicted motivation. In this instance, skill training focuses on interven-

tions designed to disinhibit the appropriate behavior, either by reducing anxiety (e.g., relaxation training) or by working on motivational resistance to active coping.

Remedial skill training necessitated by identification of coping skill deficits is the cornerstone of the RP treatment program. When the individual lacks coping skills, a variety of coping skills can be taught. The content of the skill-training program is variable and will depend on the needs of the individual. Possible content areas include assertiveness, stress management, relaxation training, anger management, expression of feelings, enhancement of interpersonal relationships, building of support systems, communication skills, marital therapy, and general social and/or dating skills.

Along with education about the long-range negative effects of excessive substance use on physical health and social well-being, a *decision matrix* allows patients to examine both the immediate and the delayed effects of substance use, which may help counter the tendency of patients to think only of the initial pleasant short-term effects. In skill training, the teaching procedures are based on the work of McFall (1977) and other investigators. The range of methods includes behavior rehearsal, instruction, coaching, evaluative feedback, modeling, and role-playing (Daley and Marlatt 1997b). In addition, cognitive self-instructional methods introduced by Meichenbaum (1977) have been especially valuable. For troubleshooting and consolidating the newly acquired skills, regular homework assignments are an essential ingredient in skill training.

In some instances, it is impractical to rehearse the new coping skills in real-life situations. This problem can be surmounted through *relapse rehearsal methods*. In this procedure, the patient is instructed to imagine being involved in actual high-risk situations and performing more adaptive coping behaviors and thoughts. The emphasis here is on active coping rather than on resisting temptation. The patient is thus encouraged to visualize that he or she is successfully handling the difficult situation through effective coping instead of exercising willpower. To emphasize self-efficacy enhancement, the patient can be instructed to imagine that the rehearsed experience is accompanied by mounting feelings of competence and confidence. For example, a socially anxious patient with alcohol dependence reported numerous social situations in which anxiety was high. During these situations, he often drank alcohol to reduce his social anxiety. On one occasion, he lost a prospective job by showing up for the interview after drinking. The patient was taught breathing and cognitive strategies to control anxiety in social situations.

This helped him cope with social situations without using alcohol. Many patients experience distress over a variety of situations. Because distress and stressful social situations cannot be avoided, learning to tolerate distress and manage it often reduces such problematic feelings and helps the individual cope successfully without using substances. In the case just cited, although the patient's anxiety was reduced, he still experienced it in social situations. The key was learning how to manage his anxious feelings so that they did not lead to alcohol use.

That the patient may fail to effectively use these coping strategies and experience a slip must be anticipated. The patient's postlapse reaction is a pivotal intervention point in the RP model because it determines the degree of escalation from a single, isolated lapse to a full-blown relapse. The first step in anticipating and dealing with this reaction is to devise an explicit therapeutic contract to limit the extent of use if a lapse occurs. The specifications of the contract can be worked out individually with the patient. However, the fundamental method of intervention after a lapse is the use of cognitive restructuring to counteract the cognitive and affective components of the AVE. It may be helpful in this regard to have the patient carry a wallet-sized reminder card with instructions to read and follow in the event of a slip. The text of this card should include the name and telephone number of a therapist or treatment center to be called and the cognitive reframing antidote to the AVE. Because some patients may be reluctant to self-disclose lapses or relapses, it helps to teach them the importance of sharing these experiences with others as a way of reducing the potential of a full-blown relapse. Discussing such experiences provides the patient with an opportunity to understand what occurred and to figure out how to manage the lapse or relapse.

## Global Lifestyle Strategies

The final thrust in the RP self-management program is the development of global intervention procedures for lifestyle change. It is insufficient to teach patients only mechanistic skills for handling high-risk situations and regulating consumption. A comprehensive RP self-management program also should attempt to improve the patient's overall lifestyle to increase his or her capacity to cope with more pervasive stress factors that are antecedents to high-risk situations. To accomplish this training, treatment strategies have been devised to short-circuit the covert antecedents to relapse and promote mental and physical wellness. Figure 31–6 shows

a schematic representation of the global self-control strategies used in the RP approach.

As discussed earlier in this chapter, a persistent and continuing disequilibrium between shoulds and wants can pave the way for relapse by producing a chronic sense of deprivation. As these feelings mount, the individual may experience a growing desire for self-indulgence. For some patients, substance use is viewed as a means of restoring balance in an unfairly lopsided equation. This desire for indulgence translates into urges, cravings, and distortions that permit a patient to "unintentionally" meander closer to the brink of relapse.

An effective way to induce patients to view this disequilibrium as a precursor of relapse is to have them self-monitor wants and shoulds. By keeping a daily record of duties and obligations on the one hand and enjoyable pleasures on the other, the patient becomes aware of the sources of imbalance. Review of this "lifestyle balance worksheet" (Daley and Marlatt 1997a) can help the patient examine all major domains of life (i.e., physical, emotional, intellectual, creative, family, interpersonal, spiritual, occupational, and financial) to determine which areas are out of balance and need attention. The patient can then be encouraged to seek a restoration of balance by engaging daily in healthy lifestyle habits (*positive addictions*) (Glasser 1976) or other pleasant activities. The advantage of this shift from negative addiction (i.e., substance abuse) to positive addiction or pleasant activities lies in the capacity to contribute toward the individual's long-term health and well-being while also providing an adaptive coping response for life stressors and relapse situations. As long-range health benefits accrue, the individual begins to develop more self-confidence and self-efficacy.

Despite the efficacy of these techniques for counteracting feelings of deprivation that would otherwise predispose the individual toward relapse, urges and cravings may still surface from time to time. As indicated in Figure 31–6, various *urge-control procedures* are recommended. Sometimes urges and cravings are triggered directly by external cues such as seeing one's favorite beer mug in the kitchen cabinet, smelling pot or crack cocaine that others are smoking, seeing a needle or other paraphernalia associated with ingestion of drugs, or participating in events previously associated with substance use (e.g., sporting events, parties, gatherings at bars, holiday celebrations, weddings). The frequency of these externally triggered urges can be reduced substantially by using simple *stimulus control techniques* aimed at minimizing exposure to these cues. In some instances, avoidance strategies are the most effective way

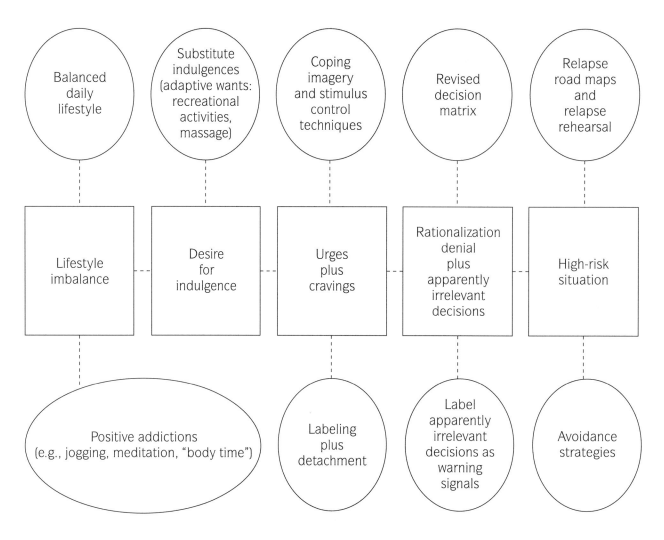

**Figure 31–6.**  Relapse prevention: global lifestyle strategies.

to reduce the frequency of externally triggered urges. In the case of tobacco, alcohol, or other drug problems, removing substances or paraphernalia from the immediate environment often reduces relapse risk. Consider this patient's report of an unexpected craving to use: "I was looking for a sweater and found a bag of weed in the bottom of the drawer. I hadn't smoked pot for several months and figured a joint wouldn't hurt. So I lit one up." Cravings can happen quickly and unexpectedly, leading to impulsive substance use.

In teaching patients to cope with urge and craving experiences, it is important to emphasize that the discomfort associated with these internal events is natural. Indeed, urges can be likened to waves in the sea: they rise, crest, and fall. Using this urge-surfing metaphor, we encourage the patient to wait out the urge, look forward to the downside, and maintain balance when the urge wave is peaking.

Recall that urges and cravings may not always operate at a conscious level but may become masked by cognitive distortions and defense mechanisms. As such, they still exert a potent influence by allowing for apparently irrelevant decisions that inch the individual closer to relapse. To counter this effect, we train the patient to see through these self-deceptions by recognizing their true meanings. Explicit self-talk can help in making apparently irrelevant decisions seem more relevant. By acknowledging to oneself that certain mini-decisions (e.g., keeping a bottle of wine at home for friends dropping over) actually increase the risk of relapse, the patient may be able to identify these decisions as early warning signs. An important objective in these urge-control procedures is to enable the individual to externalize urges and cravings and to view them with objective detachment. Another way to achieve this detachment is to encourage the patient to deliberately label the urge as soon as it registers into consciousness. Urges should be viewed as natural occurrences in response to environmental and lifestyle forces rather than as signs of treatment failure and indicators of future relapse.

## Social Support in Couples and Families

The importance of family and spouse involvement and social support in recovery from substance abuse and in relapse prevention has been emphasized by several authors (Edwards and Steinglass 1995; Maisto et al. 1995; McCrady 1989; O'Farrell et al. 1993).

Myers and Brown (1990) reported improved outcome in adolescent abstinence when social support, situational appraisal, and problem-focused coping skills were used in potential relapse situations. O'Farrell et al. (1993) summarized promising results with couples who were treated with methods that used behavioral marital therapy in conjunction with RP. This combination of interventions with couples can be used to help facilitate the initial motivation to change in the alcoholic individual and to promote the use of problem-solving and communication skills to increase positive interactions between spouses. The program is designed to stabilize the marriage while the alcoholic individual is trying to maintain sobriety and to teach both members of the couple how to recognize and cope with triggers that could lead to relapse. Available data show more days of abstinence and marital gains made in the recovery process when behavioral marital therapy and RP are combined.

Cawthra et al. (1991) discussed the use of family group therapy with RP. Participants included alcoholic patients and their family members, meeting in a format in which emotional warnings of relapse were discussed and using the shared expertise of the group to develop problem-solving skills that focused on emotional, cognitive, and behavioral aspects of the relapse process in families. Patient attendance in the RP program was improved through the use of family involvement in the group.

Steinglass (1987) provided an extensive analysis of variations and similarities in alcoholic family interaction patterns. In an approach that integrates both a family systems and developmental view of alcoholism, Steinglass emphasized the heterogeneous nature of these families while also discussing the discrete, alcohol-centered regulatory mechanisms that govern alcoholic

family interactions and short-term problem-solving efforts. The expression of affect is often a cue that problem solving must occur; however, it is the use of alcohol that provides a means by which both positive and negative affect can be expressed. For example, consider a husband who arrives home late for dinner and complains to his wife and children about his job dissatisfaction. His wife voices her upset about the excessive number of hours that he is working and is thus unavailable to the family. As their parents begin to argue, the children leave the table and disappear to their rooms. The husband opens a bottle of wine. After he has a few drinks, he apologizes to his wife for his frequent evenings away from home. She accepts his apology, and they retire to the living room to talk affectionately about past romantic times when life was not so hectic. The recognition of these distinctive, short-term problem-solving behaviors, and repetitive interactional sequences described in family systems models of alcoholism, provide new directions for helping families to understand, recognize, and change behavioral patterns that lead to relapse and vulnerability to future alcohol use.

## Conclusion

Although significant numbers of individuals with alcohol, tobacco, and other drug problems experience a lapse or relapse to substance use during or after formal treatment, most of them benefit from treatment and stop or reduce substance use and/or improve one or more areas of their functioning. RP strategies are an integral part of treatment for all addictive disorders. RP interventions, although designed primarily for the maintenance stage of recovery, are frequently used in all stages of recovery across the continuum of care in residential, partial hospital, intensive outpatient, outpatient, and aftercare programs. The clinical material presented in this chapter can be adapted for use in individual, family, or group treatment contexts to prepare patients to anticipate and cope with the possibility of posttreatment lapse or relapse. The empirical underpinnings of the RP model have been reviewed by Marlatt and Gordon (1985). Additional applications of the RP model also have been presented. Research is under way on the treatment efficacy of RP, expanding the model to work with couples, families, and adolescents. Research on the role of expectancies (i.e., self-efficacy and outcome expectancies) and coping skills in the habit-change process provide general support for the RP model.

# References

Annis HM, Davis CS: Assessment of expectancies in alcohol dependent clients, in Assessment of Addictive Behaviors: Behavioral, Cognitive, and Physiological Processes. Edited by Donovan DM, Marlatt GA. New York, Guilford, 1988, pp 84–111

Baer JS, Marlatt GA, Kivlahan DR, et al: An experimental test of three methods of alcohol risk-reduction with young adults. J Consult Clin Psychol 60:974–979, 1992

Bandura A: Self-efficacy: toward a unifying theory of behavior change. Psychol Rev 84:191–215, 1977

Carroll KM: Relapse prevention as a psychosocial treatment: a review of controlled clinical trials. Exp Clin Psychopharmacol 4:46–54, 1996

Cawthra E, Borrego N, Emrick C: Involving family members in the prevention of relapse: an innovative approach. Alcoholism Treatment Quarterly 8:101–112, 1991

Chaney EF, O'Leary MR, Marlatt GA: Skills training with alcoholics. J Consult Clin Psychol 46:1092–1104, 1978

Childress RF, McLellan AT, O'Brien CP: Role of conditioning factors in the development of drug dependence. Psychiatr Clin North Am 9:413–425, 1986

Daley DC (ed): Relapse: Conceptual, Research, and Clinical Perspectives. New York, Haworth, 1989

Daley DC: Relapse Prevention Workbook: For Recovery Alcoholics and Drug Dependent Persons. Holmes Beach, FL, Learning Publications, 1997

Daley D, Lis J: Relapse prevention: intervention strategies for mental health clients with comorbid addictive disorders, in Psychotherapy and Substance Abuse: A Practitioner's Handbook. Edited by Washton A. New York, Guilford, 1995, pp 243–263

Daley DC, Marlatt GA: Managing Your Drug or Alcohol Problem. San Antonio, TX, Psychological Corporation, 1997a

Daley DC, Marlatt GA: Managing Your Drug or Alcohol Problem; Therapist Guide. San Antonio, TX, Psychological Corporation, 1997b

Donovan DM, Marlatt GA (eds): Assessment of Addictive Behaviors: Behavioral, Cognitive, and Physiological Processes. New York, Guilford, 1988

Edwards ME, Steinglass P: Family therapy treatment outcomes for alcoholism. J Marital Fam Ther 21:475–509, 1995

Glasser W: Positive Addiction. New York, Harper & Row, 1976

Heather N, Robertson I (eds): Controlled Drinking, 2nd Edition. London, Methuen, 1987

Higgins ST, Budney AJ, Bickel WK, et al: Incentives improve outcome in outpatient behavioral treatment of cocaine dependence. Arch Gen Psychiatry 51:568–576, 1994

Kadden R, Carroll K, Donovan D, et al (eds): Cognitive-behavioral coping skills therapy manual: a clinical research guide for therapists treating individuals with alcohol abuse and dependence, in Project MATCH Monograph Series 3. Rockville, MD, National Institute on Alcohol Abuse and Alcoholism, 1995

Kivlahan DR, Marlatt GA, Fromme K, et al: Secondary prevention with college drinkers: evaluation of an alcohol skills training program. J Consult Clin Psychol 58:805–810, 1990

Maisto SA, McKay JR, O'Farrell TJ: Relapse precipitants and behavioral marital therapy. Addict Behav 20:383–393, 1995

Marlatt GA, Gordon J (eds): Relapse Prevention: Maintenance Strategies in the Treatment of Addictive Behaviors. New York, Guilford, 1985

Marlatt GA, Tapert SF: Harm reduction: reducing the risk of addictive behavior, in Addictive Behaviors Across the Lifespan. Edited by Baer JS, Marlatt GA, McMahon B. Newbury Park, CA, Sage Publications, 1993, pp 243–273

Marlatt GA, Larimer ME, Baer JS, et al: Harm reduction with alcohol problems: moving behind the controlled drinking controversy. Behavior Therapy 24:461–504, 1993

McCrady B: Extending relapse models to couples. Addict Behav 14:69–74, 1989

McFall RM: Parameters of self monitoring, in Behavioral Self-Management: Strategies, Techniques and Outcomes. Edited by Stuart RB. New York, Brunner/Mazel, 1977

Meichenbaum D: Cognitive-Behavioral Modification. New York, Plenum, 1977

Meyers RJ, Smith JE: Clinical Guide to Alcohol Treatment: the Community Reinforcement Approach. New York, Guilford, 1995

Miller WR, Brown JM, Simpson TL, et al: What works? a methodological analysis of the alcohol treatment outcome literature, in Handbook of Alcoholism Treatment Approaches, 2nd Edition. Edited by Hester R, Miller W. Boston, MA, Allyn & Bacon, 1995, pp 12–44

Miller WR, Rollnick S: Motivational Interviewing. New York, Guilford, 1991

Myers MG, Brown SA: Coping responses and relapse among adolescent substance abusers. J Subst Abuse 2:117–189, 1990

O'Farrell TJ, Choquette KA, Cutter HS, et al: Behavioral marital therapy with and without additional couples relapse prevention sessions for alcoholics and their wives. J Stud Alcohol 54:652–666, 1993

Robins LN, Regier DA: Psychiatric Disorders in America: The Epidemiologic Catchment Area Study. New York, Free Press, 1991

Steinglass P: The Alcoholic Family. New York, Basic Books, 1987

Wilson PH (ed): Principles and Practice of Relapse Prevention. New York, Guilford, 1992

# Chapter

## 32 Group Therapy

Edward J. Khantzian, M.D.
Sarah J. Golden, Ph.D.
William E. McAuliffe, Ph.D.

The group therapy approach has traditionally served as the most popular treatment of addiction and is currently the treatment of choice as addictions are increasingly recognized in our society. The suffering and disruption of lives caused by substance abuse and dependence, and the heightened awareness of "hidden" addictive disorders, such as eating, sex, and gambling, and of the comorbidity and substitution of one addiction for another (Flores 1998) have trained our attention anew on the question of what is to be done. Whereas the controversy over the etiology and conceptualizations of addiction continues unabated, there appears to be an often unacknowledged consensus about the advantages of group treatment over individual approaches in addressing this problem. Thus, whereas the origins of addiction to substances may be diversely viewed as physiological, intrapsychic, social and environmental, or moral and volitional, almost all these conceptual rivals have advocated the group approach as a remedy.

Group approaches are as wide ranging in form as the theories that give rise to them. Self-help "fellowships" of Alcoholics Anonymous (AA); time-limited psychoeducational and cognitive-behavioral models; and open-ended, psychodynamic group therapies adhere not only to different assumptions about the nature of addiction but also to different practices in the management of and recovery from addiction.

All group approaches share an appreciation of the healing power of the connection with others, what Herman (1992) has called "the restoration of social bonds" that "begins with the discovery that one is not alone" (p. 215). Psychoanalytic thinking holds that the group experience addresses the "universal need to be-

long, to establish a state of psychological unity with others, [representing] a covert wish to restore an earlier state of unconflicted well-being inherent in the exclusive union with the mother" (Tuttman describing the work of Scheidlinger in Roth et al. 1990, pp. 15–16). Yalom (1983), an existential group theorist, holds that in a group the "disconfirmation of the feeling of uniqueness offers considerable relief and a 'welcome to the human race' experience" (p. 41). Orford (1985) sees the self-help group and therapeutic community as using public testimony, social support, and social coercion to guide the individual through a "moral passage" to forge a new social identity. In the respite from the shame, isolation, and loneliness of addiction that the group offers (Khantzian 1986), and in the possibilities for both support and confrontation that it provides, the group approach continues to hold its own as a force for managing and changing addictive behavior.

## Groups and Addiction

Historically, the most widely accepted approach to addiction is the group, with the kind of group reflecting a particular view of addiction. Orford (1985) attributed the popularity and success of the self-help group, epitomized by AA, to its ability to "fuse the disease and the moral perspectives" (p. 309), to offer both a practical explanation and a corrective spiritual and moral approach to the problem of addiction. Significantly, AA was founded in 1935 by two men, Bill Wilson and Dr. Bob, in an attempt to help each other. Their fledgling organization derived from the model of a Christian fellowship, with its "ideas of self-examination, acknowledgment of character defects, restitution for harm done to others, and working with others" (Orford 1985, p. 309).

In the self-help group, change takes place in a public forum. Orford (1985) emphasized that, beyond support, this forum promotes the expectation to conform to certain values: the group provides this "new set of attitudes and values, and it is to the group's ideology or 'will' that the novice must submit if he or she is to become a successful member" (p. 303). A wider range of group processes are described by Khantzian and Mack (1989) as accomplishing change in the group: they see support, surrender, spirituality, and altruism serving as the therapeutic and transformational elements. After enjoying five decades of growth, AA has more recently served as a model for 12-step programs addressing many other addictive behaviors such as drug taking and gambling.

The concept of the individual's submission to the group's ideology has perhaps found its fullest expression in therapeutic communities for the treatment of addiction. Synanon, established in the 1960s to address heroin addiction, aggressively used the group to change attitudes through confinement, structure, daily work assignments, and often demanding interpersonal confrontation (Cherkas 1965). This "total" group approach, in which every aspect of daily life is regimented, continues to thrive in programs such as Daytop and Phoenix House. The therapeutic community model, with group therapy as its mainstay, is also found in shorter-term "detox" and intensive inpatient treatments for a wide range of addictions, including cocaine, narcotics, eating disorders, and gambling.

Other major group approaches in the treatment of addiction have developed from the cognitive-behavioral and psychoanalytic, psychodynamic clinical traditions. From these schools of thought have emerged both individual and group therapies for addiction. We focus here on the group models.

## Cognitive-Behavioral Group Approaches

Cognitive-behavioral theory holds that addiction is learned behavior that is reinforced by contingencies such as the pleasurable effects of drugs (McAuliffe and Ch'ien 1986). The addictive behavior is conditioned and then generalized to a range of stimuli in the environment that continue to perpetuate it. The treatment of addiction thus involves learning to recognize and avoid these stimuli and to suppress conditioned responses to these stimuli. The aim of cognitive-behavior therapy is to develop alternative thoughts and behaviors to the conditioned, "addictive" responses.

The psychoeducational group is one form of cognitive-behavior group therapy. This model uses the group format to inform and teach addicted individuals about the behavioral, medical, and psychological consequences of their addiction. Such groups are a staple of most rehabilitation programs (Nace 1987) and are often seen as the first step of a more comprehensive treatment program. By raising awareness of the consequences of addictive behavior through informational materials, didactic presentations, and group discussions, this method educates the group members and attempts to show them how the addiction complicates their lives (Drake et al. 1991). Thus, the psychoeducational group intends to prepare the group members to make a commitment to further treatment.

McAuliffe and Ch'ien (1986) developed a cognitive-behavioral group treatment for substance abuse (recovery training and self-help) that uses a curriculum in a highly structured, didactic group format to teach group members about the cognitive and behavioral factors involved in drug use (e.g., to recognize the social and environmental cues that can lead to relapse). Restructuring lifestyles that have been associated with the addictive use of substances, anticipating obstacles to recovery, and finding alternative ways to manage problems that have triggered drug use are systematically addressed in the group. Although the focus of this method is on managing and modifying one's own behavior, the group setting emphasizes the commonality of certain situations and responses in both addicted and recovering lifestyles. This group model was studied experimentally in the Harvard Cocaine Recovery Project (Khantzian et al. 1990).

An outpatient cessation model for early recovery from cocaine addiction, also developed in the Harvard Cocaine Recovery Project, is described by McAuliffe and Albert (1992) in *Clean Start*. "From the initiation of recovery, the model is a group one in which chemical rewards are replaced with social ones" (McAuliffe and Albert 1992, p. 27). The group serves as an arena for social learning and social backing: "Seeing others make changes gives clients a clear picture of how change is accomplished, and provides motivation to try a little harder" (p. 28). Group members experience nonexploitative friendships, perhaps for the first time, and are prepared by this "prosocial abstinent culture" for participation in the larger recovering community (p. 28).

## Psychoanalytic, Psychodynamic Group Approaches

Several group models have emerged from the psychoanalytic, psychodynamic tradition. Most relevant for the treatment of addiction have been groups that have a psychodynamic, interpersonal focus and that address the particular needs of the addicted individual for safety and structure in the group setting (Brown and Yalom 1977; Khantzian et al. 1990; Matano and Yalom 1991; Vannicelli 1982, 1988; Yalom 1974).

In the psychoanalytic, psychodynamic tradition, addiction is understood as the individual's "solution" to the problem of psychological vulnerability. Contemporary psychoanalytic theory has elaborated on these vulnerabilities as defects of self, both intrapsychic and characterological, that can lead to addiction in an attempt to regulate and medicate the distress caused by the defect (Kohut 1977; Meissner 1986; Wurmser 1978). Khantzian's work (1974, 1978, 1985, 1995, 1997) addressed the particular psychological and narcissistic vulnerabilities of the potential addict: his *self-medication* hypothesis holds that addictions result when an individual seeks to relieve the suffering and distress resulting from deficits in ego/self capacities to regulate affects, self-esteem, self-care, and relationships with others as they play themselves out in everyday life. Heightening awareness of self and changing characteristic patterns of handling these vulnerabilities in everyday situations are addressed in the psychodynamic group treatment of addiction.

Perhaps the most important aspect of Khantzian's model is that it is modified dynamic group therapy (MDGT; Khantzian et al. 1990, 1995). The modifications mean that the vulnerabilities and difficulties of the addicted individual are recognized in the format of the treatment: the group model establishes maximum safety for addicted individuals in requiring and helping to maintain abstinence, in providing outreach and support, in using an active style of leadership, and in always addressing the potential for drug and psychological relapse. Structure and containment rather than confrontation are emphasized. This group model also has been studied experimentally as part of the Harvard Cocaine Recovery Project (Khantzian et al. 1990).

### Efficacy

The literature on the efficacy of group therapy for addiction is notably sparse, and controlled studies of treatment outcome are needed. The Harvard Cocaine Recovery Project, a National Institute on Drug Abuse (NIDA)–funded study carried out at Harvard Medical School at the Cambridge Hospital from 1987 to 1990, compared two group treatments (cognitive-behavioral and psychodynamic) and a no-group treatment for cocaine-addicted individuals in a controlled clinical trial. Preliminary findings indicated that both groups had high retention and benefited from treatment. A more detailed analysis of the study is yet to be completed. Other recent studies, although less comprehensive in their conception, shed light on the efficacy issues of abstinence, tenure in treatment, the matching of the patient and the treatment, the type of group, and maintenance of improvement (Carroll et al. 1998; Getter et al. 1992; Martin et al. 1996; Shaffer et al. 1997).

In a study comparing individual and family therapy and group treatment for cocaine use disorders, Kang et al. (1991) found that improvement was most strongly related to abstinence and also concluded that an intense level of therapy is needed to sustain this abstinence. Bowers and al-Redha (1990) studied alcoholic individuals and their spouses and found that group therapy for couples was superior to individual therapy for the couple in lowering alcohol consumption for the alcoholic partner. They also found a trend for the conjointly treated couples to report better marital adjustment and higher relationship ratings than the individually treated couples. Hellerstein and Meehan (1987) reported that group treatment in schizophrenic substance-abusing patients resulted in a marked decrease in days of hospitalization over 1 year. These studies provide evidence for the group modality's need to address the particular addictive behavior and its capacity to address other life issues and problems beyond the addiction.

A study by Yalom et al. (1978) that compared interactional groups of alcoholic patients with groups of neurotic patients found no significant differences in outcome but did find that despite a higher initial number of dropouts from the alcoholic group, their tenure in therapy was greater than that for the neurotic group members. A study by Cooney et al. (1991) comparing outcomes of coping skills groups and interactional group therapies reported that individuals scoring high on sociopathy or global pathology had better outcomes in coping skills groups, whereas patients scoring low on these dimensions did better in interactional groups. Poldrugo and Forti (1988) concluded from their study that group treatment for alcoholic patients is most useful for those with dependent personality disorders and is not beneficial to antisocial patients. These studies begin to address the particular needs of addicted individuals in group therapy and the nature of the group treatment most beneficial to them.

Although more definitive studies of outcome and efficacy of group treatment of addiction are needed, diverse group treatments have conceptually and practically gained prominence in recent years.

## Group Therapy as Treatment of Choice

Group psychotherapy has been described as "the definitive treatment for producing character change" (Alonso 1989, p. 1) because in a group setting, the "cost of character defenses is illuminated and presents a conflict which can render the same traits dystonic and thus available to interpretation and change" (Alonso 1989, p. 8). Similarly, group therapy has been described as "the treatment of choice for chemical dependency" (Matano and Yalom 1991, p. 269). Matano and Yalom attributed this choice to the "power of groups—the power to counter prevailing cultural pressures to drink, to provide effective support to those suffering from the alienation of addiction, to offer role modeling, and to harness the power of peer pressure, an important force against denial and resistance" (pp. 269–270).

The rapidly growing focus of mental health professionals on the patient with a dual diagnosis (i.e., a diagnosis of a major mental illness and an addiction, usually a substance use disorder) has opened up new possibilities in the treatment of these disorders (Minkoff and Drake 1991). In acknowledging that addicted individuals often also have a range of psychological and characterological problems and that both the addiction and the psychological difficulties need to be actively addressed for improvement to occur in either domain, access to adequate treatment becomes available for the first time. Paradoxically, the acceptance of a dual diagnosis may mean that an individual's treatment can be unified, coherent, and integrated rather than fragmented or divided between care systems, systems that have often worked at cross-purposes to each other.

In this context, *dual diagnosis* does not apply only to the severely and chronically mentally ill individual. Klein et al. (1991) asserted that individuals who have severe personality disorders, disorders diagnosed on Axis II of DSM-III-R (American Psychiatric Association 1987), and who are also actively abusing substances are most accurately considered to be dually diagnosed. Klein and colleagues' conceptualization of *Axis II therapy groups* addressed the special problems of providing

group therapy for patients with these severe personality disorders and substance abuse. The supportive holding environment of the group facilitates treatment of the addiction. At the same time, the group is tailored to manage the characterological difficulties of these patients. In the same manner, the MDGT model developed for cocaine-addicted patients by Khantzian et al. (1990) actively addresses both the substance abuse and the psychological and character problems of the group members. Group therapies for substance-abusing patients based on the interpersonal model, variants of this same conceptualization, were described by Vannicelli (1988) and by Matano and Yalom (1991). Here the attempt is to make available to substance-abusing patients in groups "a very powerful therapeutic element: the interactive group process" (Matano and Yalom 1991, p. 270). The group is seen as an adaptation of "regular" interactive group therapy, in which a focus on the here-and-now interpersonal relationships in the group as a "social microcosm" offers a rich source of learning and change.

## Special Needs of Addicted Individuals in Group Therapy

Whether individuals are seen as vulnerable to addiction because they are narcissistically compromised through early experiences of deprivation and damage, with the persistent feelings of shame, loneliness, depression, defectiveness, and emptiness described by Kohut (1977), Wurmser (1978), and Meissner (1986); whether they are understood to be narcissistically vulnerable and impaired *secondary* to the addiction (Vaillant 1983); or whether some common shared factor is responsible for both addiction and character problems (Flores 1998), the addicted individual faces particular difficulties in the therapeutic process. A narcissistically vulnerable individual may on the one hand crave empathy and contact with others yet fear and reject such attention (Liebenberg 1990). The characteristically uneven and inconsistent way in which cocaine-addicted patients relate suggests their dilemma on entering therapy. As Khantzian et al. (1990) reported

> They may be alternately charming, seductive, and passively expectant, or they may act aloof, as if they do not need other people. Their supersensitivity may be evident in deferential attitudes and attempts to gain approval and acceptance, but they may rapidly shift and become ruthless and demanding in their dealings with others. (p. 40)

Klein et al. (1991, p. 99) outlined the relevant issues in providing outpatient group psychotherapy in addicted individuals with character disorders:

- Patients must be viewed as dually diagnosed.
- The "recurrent dangers these individuals pose to themselves and/or to others" must be recognized.
- "Their intense demands, during repeated crises," "their propensity for acting out anxiety and aggression, and tendency to split clinicians and systems," and the difficult countertransference these patients can evoke all must be addressed.

Action, rather than bearing affect or anxiety or talking about things, is the preferred expressive mode, and the acting out may well involve relapsing to the addictive behavior—drinking, using drugs, or gambling. Other characteristic acting-out behaviors may involve splitting, violations of boundaries, and violations of the group contract (e.g., attempting to do group business outside the group either with therapists or with other group members).

Matano and Yalom's (1991) report on the group treatment of alcohol-abusing patients identified their tendency to externalize, to "see themselves as being influenced or controlled primarily by external events," and to compensate by employing the defenses of "defiance, grandiosity, and counterdependency" (pp. 288–289). Because the patients do not see themselves as being effective or in control, they rebel against control experienced as coming from outside. These defenses, or characteristic ways of coping, are taken into account in tailoring group therapy to the needs of the addicted patient.

Khantzian (1985) identified four areas of psychological vulnerability in the addicted individual that may be seen as disturbances or deficits in ego functioning and that potentiate characterological problems: 1) regulation of affects, 2) self-care (the capacity to protect oneself from undue risk or danger), 3) relationships with others, and 4) self-esteem. The difficulty in regulating affects manifests itself in an intensity of unmodulated feeling, often dysphoric, or in being unable to identify one's own emotions. Self-care deficits find their expression in poor attention to health, engaging in risky behaviors such as unsafe sex, and a general lack of concern for emotional and physical self-preservation. Relationships with others can be problematic in many ways—tumultuous, dependent, or lacking because of the individual's isolation and withdrawal. Finally, self-esteem is compromised or shaky and may manifest

as idealization or devaluing of others, feelings of shame and inadequacy, or bravado and grandiosity.

In modifying group treatment for the special needs of the addicted individual, these four dimensions of everyday intrapsychic and social life become the organizing foci for understanding the individual's distress, behavioral difficulties, characteristic ways of handling problems, and possibilities for change. The dimensions provide clarity and structure for handling complex issues with action-oriented, crisis-prone, and affectively constricted or volatile group members.

## The Tradition of Exclusion

Although group therapy has acknowledged advantages in the treatment of addiction in patients with character disorders, the addicted individual has often been excluded from group therapy because he or she is too unstable, disruptive, or unmotivated. His or her difficulty in tolerating affect and managing anxiety; the characteristic postures of self-sufficiency, disavowed need, and bravado (Khantzian 1986); the tendency toward using more primitive defenses (splitting, denial); and the propensity for action rather than reflection have often made the addicted individual an unwelcome group candidate. The addicted individual as candidate for therapy can easily be seen as one of the "difficult" patients described by Rice and Rutan (1987) who can make the therapist feel "puzzled, overwhelmed, depressed, angry, [and] confused" and on whom "all our skill and knowledge has little impact" (p. 131).

Negative countertransference responses, often unacknowledged and resulting in a reluctance to work with addicted individuals, have been a problem in providing adequate individual or group treatment for addicted individuals (Levy 1987). Levy reported, for example, that the therapist may "not be able to tolerate the alcoholic's repeated 'falls off the wagon' and might, in subtle ways, castigate the patient, adding to the alcoholic's already low self-esteem and causing the alcoholic to continue drinking as a way to cope with such feelings" (p. 786). The ongoing possibility of relapse—*both* relapse to the addictive behavior and psychological relapse to the unadaptive, problematic emotional state—must be tolerated and actively addressed. The characteristic "difficult" postures, attitudes, and behaviors of addicted patients must be understood and worked with. The propensity for impulsive action leads to crisis, instability, and lack of safety, continually testing the therapist's empathy, objectivity, and steadiness. As Klein et al.

(1991) pointed out, these difficulties are geometrically increased in a group. The group, like its individual members, can change rapidly, verge on dissolution, and regroup in the nick of time.

The exclusion from treatment can be rationalized from either the viewpoint of the addictions approach or the mental health perspective. A situation develops in which an individual is either excluded from both systems, shuttled back and forth to the other, or receiving parallel—yet potentially uncoordinated—treatments.

Sciacca (1991) distinguished between the characteristics of traditional *addiction* treatment and those of traditional *mental health* treatment approaches. Programs to treat addictions stress willingness and motivation (with the exception of hospitalization for detoxification) and often involve highly confrontational encounters that attempt to break down denial of the problematic consequences of addiction and about one's own behavior. In a similar vein, addiction treatment may emphasize the necessity of "hitting bottom." Sciacca (1991) reported that "patients must experience severe losses or deterioration in order to perceive that they need help for addiction" (p. 72). Otherwise, addicted patients are seen as not ready for treatment. The addicted patient must be willing and motivated by dint of having hit bottom and thus ripe for confrontation.

On the other hand, mental health or psychotherapeutic approaches, according to Sciacca, characteristically require first that the patient have a diagnosable mental illness. If addiction is the most salient presenting feature of the individual coming for treatment, then the patient may be referred for addiction treatment rather than considering a larger, more comprehensive, psychological picture. Mental health approaches, however, are less likely than addiction programs to emphasize motivation or even awareness or acceptance of the addiction as a prerequisite for treatment. This is seen as the work of the therapy itself, and the approach is more likely to be supportive than confrontational; it is less interested in breaking down defenses than in shoring them up (Sciacca 1991, p. 73). Finally, the mental health professional may be unaccepting of addictive problems, either unaware of and unable to easily identify them or judgmental and critical in response to recognizing them.

Thus, the traditional mental health approach to the addicted individual with a character disorder may emphasize outreach and engagement, understanding and tolerance of defensive structures, and support during treatment. However, because of a lack of awareness of the psychological aspects of addictive suffering—the

way in which the addiction expresses the vulnerable, compromised ego or self—the traditional approach may see addiction as *the* problem and be unwilling to provide therapy. Negative prejudices about the addicted individual may result in exclusion from mental health or psychotherapeutic services. Therapy programs specializing in addiction, on the other hand, welcome the most desperate of addicted patients but tend to want them to come to treatment with a degree of preparation and readiness, to underplay the importance of psychological factors and defenses, and to confront rather than support. The addicted individual is assumed to have certain strengths to sustain the treatment and a capacity for individual responsibility or to be just "not ready."

Failure to appreciate the whole of the addicted individual's experience leads to fragmented, exclusionary, and ineffective treatments. Getting caught between two systems is a real possibility. Taking into account the strengths and shortcomings of both traditional addiction and mental health approaches, as in Sciacca's schema, can serve as a guide for developing an integrated treatment. Conceptually and practically, these two traditions can then inform the treatment of choice for the addicted patient with a character disorder—the specially modified group therapy.

## Features of the Group

Specific features of group therapy for the addicted individual derive from the consideration of the addicted person's special needs and have been discussed by several authors in the literature of addiction and group psychotherapy (Brown and Yalom 1977; Flores 1998; Golden et al. 1993; Khantzian 1995; Khantzian et al. 1990, 1992; Matano and Yalom 1991; McAuliffe and Albert 1992; Vannicelli 1982, 1988; Yalom 1974). In addition, the emerging literature of group psychotherapy for the difficult patient, one whose character defenses and acting-out behavior challenge the traditional group therapy format, contributes to our understanding of what is needed (Fenchel and Flapan 1985; Klein et al. 1991; Leszcz 1989; Rice and Rutan 1987; Roth et al. 1990; Stone and Gustafson 1982). Finally, the literature of dual diagnosis of major mental illness and substance use disorder offers guidance in modifying group therapy for this population (Levy and Mann 1988; Minkoff and Drake 1991).

### Pregroup Preparation

Group therapy in the treatment of addiction begins pregroup with outreach and preparation. The goal of this preparation is to provide a welcome that will increase motivation for the treatment, reduce premature dropouts, ease fears of and resistance to the group modality, and increase self-awareness. Sciacca (1991) emphasized the supportive, collaborative nature of the pregroup contacts: the potential group member's level of motivation and readiness is accepted, and he or she is encouraged to keep an open mind regarding himself or herself and others. A clear therapeutic contract is presented, including guidelines for boundaries between group members and between therapist and group member, and "the necessity for therapist communication and collaboration with other treaters" (Klein et al. 1991, p. 99).

Khantzian et al. (1990) stated that the therapist "can play a critical role at this point in establishing optimistic and realistic member expectations regarding the efficacy" of the group. The therapist (in this case for a psychodynamic group treating cocaine addiction) not only "acquaints the new members with the established ground rules, which include strict confidentiality, attendance and promptness, and abstinence from drugs and alcohol," but also discusses the benefits of group therapy, explains the focus of the group, acknowledges the difficulty of joining groups, "explains the work of therapy," and identifies the new members' personal goals (Khantzian et al. 1990, pp. 46–48).

Reaching out to the prospective group member, anticipating what will follow, and concretely outlining the expectations provide necessary structure to allay overwhelming anxiety.

## Structure

Structure in the group for addicted patients is provided in several ways. The group contract serves as an organizing feature initially and as the group progresses. It is a given that the contract will be tested and perhaps hotly debated; this is part of the work of the group. Matano and Yalom (1991) caution against an overly authoritarian stance and advise that the group therapist be sensitive to the addicted patient's feeling of loss of personal control, which evokes defiant and counterdependent reactions.

Shared norms, explicitly stated and reiterated, also provide structure. Abstinence from the problematic, addictive behavior; a commitment to talking about feelings and problems rather than acting on them in the group; and agreement about the goals of the treatment are important. Vannicelli (1988), in describing a group for alcoholic patients, emphasized that the shared un-

derstanding "about what it means to be working on one's drinking problem" and "what it means to be getting better" is necessary to the integrity of the group (Vannicelli 1988, p. 349). These norms are essential for dealing with the regression to the addictive behavior—relapse and "slips"—and for providing a vision of progress, improvement, and recovery.

Didactic and psychoeducational groups, self-help and 12-step programs, and cognitive-behavioral groups are all models with a high degree of inherent structure. This chapter's focus is thus on the less structured, psychodynamic and interpersonal groups and how they can be modified to provide adequate containment and comfort for the addicted group member. Enhanced structure in a psychodynamically oriented group means explicitly endorsing certain group norms, an active leadership style for the therapist, and, as in Khantzian's MDGT model, a focus on specific character and self-regulation problems.

## Safety

Safety considerations in the group setting include ensuring immediate physical safety during the group meetings, ensuring safety for therapeutic exploration and change by establishing the norm of abstinence, and promoting an atmosphere of enough interpersonal comfort and psychological security for the interactive work of the group to proceed. Physical safety is a consideration in selection of the meeting place, the group leadership, and the strongly upheld norm of putting things into words instead of actions.

In the treatment of addiction, especially in the beginning stages, as Matano and Yalom (1991, p. 273) stated, "Nothing takes precedence over recovery—it is a life or death issue." In their interpersonal group model for alcoholic patients, these investigators advocate the active facilitation of achieving and maintaining sobriety. Thus, early on in the group, any interpersonal interaction is "gentle, supportive, and directly supportive of sobriety" (p. 274). Vigilance for any threats to the recovery process is counseled.

Safety is also of paramount importance in MDGT (Khantzian et al. 1992). One of the four foci of MDGT—self-care—addresses the self-defeating, destructive, and dangerous nature of the addictive involvement: the addicted individual's poor capacity for self-preservation plays itself out through the addiction. Cognitive-behavioral and psychoeducational groups emphasize the risks that are external to the individual, such as dangerous companions who are active in their addictive behavior or environments that can stimulate cravings or actual relapse. The individual learns in the group to recognize and avoid these dangers and to find new, safe friends and activities to replace them.

McAuliffe and Albert's model (1992) emphasizes the building of "walls" and a "foundation" by detailing a "system of steps that creates a life space that is free of drugs and that ensures support for recovery" (p. 33). Attention to the real dangers of the addiction and relapse in everyday life and the strengthening of the motivation for abstinence are necessary from the inception of the group therapy.

Discovering what increases the safety for individual group members may lead to directing members to other, concomitant treatments. Some individuals, for example, may need support between weekly group meetings and find the accessibility of AA meetings vitally important. As one group member who attends a weekly Cocaine Anonymous meeting and a psychodynamic group meeting for cocaine-addicted individuals each week put it, "I need to keep seeing guys who are right at the beginning so I don't forget, and some who have a lot of recovery, but I want to talk about *all* the problems in my life." Some may need concurrent individual and group treatment. Others may need to use emergency or crisis intervention services. Developing an individualized combination of services to increase safety is an ongoing aspect of the work of the group therapist for addicted patients.

Within the group, safety is maintained by attending to the ever-possible psychological relapse or relapse to the addictive behavior. In a group for pathological gamblers, for example, the ongoing stress of overwhelming debt, often compounded by the unfamiliar tension of paying back slowly, over time, puts the abstinent gambler at continuing risk that must be monitored in the group. It may be common to find the group struggling with the question of what constitutes gambling (running a game at a carnival, buying a raffle ticket for a good cause, investing in stock for the children's college education) long after "the last bet." The question of openness versus keeping secret the extent of the ongoing debt also persists and may add to the risk. Even as self-awareness grows in the group, new stressors appear (e.g., long-term debt, the family's anger), and the risk of relapse remains high.

The atmosphere of the group also must be maintained as one safe for listening and disclosure: accepting, empathic, respectful of varying amounts of awareness and motivation, encouraging of participation, and understanding of resistance. Modeling this accepting

stance, the group leader maintains safety by protecting members from attack, shame, or premature self-disclosure, such as of traumatic material (Khantzian et al. 1990). Acknowledging the possible discomfort and anxiety of being in a group, the group leader assists the group in managing these feelings and in persisting with abstinence and psychological recovery.

## Confrontation Versus Support

Matano and Yalom (1991) pointed to the dangers of an overly confrontational approach in the group. Although increasing the addicted patient's honesty with himself or herself and others is necessary, the attempt to break down denial can backfire, causing the patient to leave the treatment program or to "dissemble compliance while inwardly retreating" (p. 291). Addicted patients should be treated like other patients—that is, by relating to them in an empathic, supportive, and understanding manner. A central task of the group leader is thus to manage the anxiety that the group process, particularly confrontation, inevitably stimulates in the group members and to keep it at a tolerable level.

Leszcz (1989), in writing about the group treatment of the characterologically difficult patient, saw the group as first providing a holding environment, a place that is reliable, constant, and accepting, a place where group members can "relate in a nonrelated way, until they are able to ascertain that it is safe" (p. 326). The confrontation itself is spelled out as "a forceful, but supportive pressure on the patient to acknowledge something that is conscious or preconscious, but avoided because of the distress that it involves" (p. 327).

The group model of Khantzian et al. (1990) encourages an understanding of addictive behavior as an attempt to deal with feelings and experiences, an adaptation that has outlived its usefulness, and an understanding of resistance to change: group members are guided "to appreciate how their ways of coping and the crises they precipitate are linked to the past; they need to acknowledge their painful feelings from the past and in the present, and to support each other in finding alternative ways to cope with their painful feeling states and problems in living" (p. 76). In other words, the group members, although they are held responsible for their choices and actions and are asked to look squarely at themselves, are not blamed and judged.

The group modality offers a particular advantage when it comes to confrontation: group members are more likely to respond to confrontation by their peers. As Leszcz (1989) put it, "[G]roup members are less restricted in their range of responses and may be better able to use humor, cajole, or shock one another to force attention to a disavowed issue" (p. 327). The following case example is from a psychodynamic group led by one of the authors (S. J. G.):

> Bob, a group member who kept his distance from others and refused to "come clean" with his family about the extent of his addictive behavior, never removed his coat during the group meetings for many months, stating that he was "too cold." After other group members had "worked" on him for a while, he not only began to consider the problem of his secretiveness but also actually shed his coat for the first time, which was greeted by pleased laughter and a fellow group member's remark: "We *must* be hot tonight if Bob is taking off his coat!" Bob's joining in was acknowledged, gladly but lightly, without making him unduly self-conscious.

Perhaps the question of responsibility lies at the heart of the balancing of confrontation and support. Matano and Yalom (1991) distinguished between the *addictive process* (called the *disease* in AA terms) and the *recovery process*. Although they do not hold the alcoholic patient responsible for the addiction itself, for the "psychological loss of control," or for his or her culturally learned beliefs about drinking, they do "demand that patients assume responsibility for their recovery" (pp. 277–278). Clarity about responsibility is crucial in group therapy for addiction, especially because this treatment may represent the confluence of the mental health and the addiction traditions that have so widely diverged on the question.

## Cohesion and the "Addict Identification"

Cohesiveness in group therapy has been likened to the importance of the relationship or therapeutic alliance in individual therapy (Yalom 1985). *Cohesiveness*, or the attraction of the members to the group and their sense of belonging, has been correlated with tenure in the group (prevention of early dropout), with the stability necessary for any kind of long-term therapeutic work to occur (Yalom 1985), and as the central mediator of outcome (Budman et al. 1989). Matano and Yalom (1991), in their work specifically addressing group therapy for the alcoholic patient, linked the individual's identification as an "alcoholic" as well as the emphasis on sameness among the group members with feeling connected to the group and the growth of group cohesion and safety (p. 275). Vannicelli (1988) warned against overdoing the bonding that occurs by talking about the ad-

diction. War stories about the glory days of drinking and how bad things finally got, for example, can also serve as a defense against further development of the group, a way to avoid other emotionally charged issues. Group members, even while seeking mutuality and safety in their identification as "addicts," can withdraw in this way from other contact with their fellow group members.

Khantzian et al. (1990) described the group process in the modified psychodynamic group for substance-abusing individuals as moving toward the discovery of common ground. Initially, the group bonds around the identity as an addict. Many dually diagnosed patients see their addicted status as preferable and more socially acceptable than other labels. To call oneself an alcoholic or a drug addict and to belong to a group for addicted individuals is a less stigmatized identity than that of mental patient, borderline personality disorder patient, or narcissist. The "outlaw" life of the addicted individual and the desperate extremities of addiction bring the group together, idealized even as they are now disavowed. Self-esteem is maintained, and cohesion is established.

However, the group must progress to find common bonds in some larger, universal human experience if the members are to grow and begin to see themselves are part of the human mainstream. For addicted individuals in group therapy, the common ground to seek is the middle ground about which they may be ambivalent, "as if the price of ordinary life were one of unremitting drudgery and joyless obligation" (Khantzian et al. 1990, p. 95). The personal material shared after the initial identification as an addict may be equally extreme or grandiose or may be withheld as not worthy of exposure in the group. Here is where the work of the group on awareness of self and others and on addressing problems of living can proceed.

The very nature of the psychodynamic or interpersonal group, with an emphasis on interpersonal interactions in the here-and-now and on the understanding of individual characterological patterns as they emerge within the group, provides a way to talk about ordinary life. For instance, a member of a group for cocaine-addicted individuals offered her group members a chance for greater involvement with one another when she remarked that she felt closer to them than to her family. This remark led to a discussion of alienation from neglectful or intrusive parents instead of the usual accounts of past ruthless quests for cocaine and the enumeration of the pitfalls of addiction. Ordinary problems, everyday life beyond the addiction, offer the group members a way into the ordinary world.

## The Group Therapist

The therapist in the group therapy for addiction has an active, demanding role to play. Concerns for safety and structure require an alert presence, a readiness to manage and help to modulate anxiety, to address acting-out behavior, and to intervene if necessary by setting limits and upholding the group contract, even as building cohesion and developing the work of the group proceed. This active mode of leadership is important because, as reported by Khantzian et al. (1990), addicted individuals with histories of neglect and trauma "do not respond well to the traditions of therapeutic passivity . . . instead they need therapists who can actively and empathically help to engage them and each other around their vulnerabilities and the self-defeating defenses and behaviors they adopt to avoid their distress and suffering" (p. 162).

The therapist may become the focus of anger and dependency, the mediator of struggles, and the unintentional voice of the superego. Co-therapists are split into good and evil. Countertransference feelings may be difficult, especially when helplessness and fear are evoked, as they often are in these groups (Klein et al. 1991). Supervision, opportunities to share the work, concurrent therapies, or supports for the group members—working as part of a team or a program—all help to make the group therapy for addiction possible and effective.

## Summary

Current group approaches to addiction have emerged from several traditions: self-help fellowships; the psychoeducational, cognitive-behavioral modality; and the psychodynamic, interpersonal tradition. Although the group approach has evolved from these diverse theoretical and ideological viewpoints, there is a dearth of controlled studies of efficacy and outcome that could support a particular school of thought. Conceptually and pragmatically, practitioners working with addicted individuals have reached similar conclusions regarding their special needs in a group setting. If addicted individuals are to receive the full benefit of treatment, their characterological and psychological vulnerabilities must be recognized and addressed. Traditional treatments are then modified, particularly if they do not already provide the high degree of structure and safety necessary for engaging and retaining the addicted individual. The group approach, in its powerful capacity to support and confront, to comfort and to challenge, and to in-

volve its members in encounters that vividly heighten awareness of interpersonal and characterological problems and provide a safe place for change, is now viewed as the treatment of choice for addiction. Special features of group therapy for the treatment of addiction are an emphasis on outreach and preparation for involvement in the group, a high degree of structure and active leadership, a concern for safety (particularly an awareness of the risk for relapse to the addictive behavior), a balance between confrontation and support, and a goal of moving beyond the initial cohesiveness of the group members' identification as addicts to helping them discover common bonds in living ordinary lives.

## References

Alonso A: Character Change in Group Therapy. Paper presented at Psychiatric Grand Rounds, The Cambridge Hospital, Cambridge, MA, September 1989

American Psychiatric Association: Diagnostic and Statistical Manual of Mental Disorders, 3rd Edition, Revised. Washington, DC, American Psychiatric Association, 1987

Bowers TG, al-Redha MR: A comparison of outcome with group/marital and standard/individual therapies with alcoholics. J Stud Alcohol 51:301–309, 1990

Brown S, Yalom ID: Interactional group therapy with alcoholics. J Stud Alcohol 38:426–456, 1977

Budman SH, Soldz S, Demby A, et al: Cohesion, alliance and outcome in group psychotherapy. Psychiatry 52:339–350, 1989

Carroll KM, Nich C, Ball SA, et al: Treatment of cocaine and alcohol dependence with psychotherapy and disulfiram. Addiction 93:713–727, 1998

Cherkas MS: Synanon foundation—a radical approach to the problem of addiction (editorial). Am J Psychiatry 121:1065, 1965

Cooney NL, Kadden RM, Litt MD, et al: Matching alcoholics to coping skills or interactional therapies: two year follow-up results. J Consult Clin Psychol 59:598–601, 1991

Drake RE, Antosca LM, Noordsy DL, et al: New Hampshire's specialized services for the dually diagnosed, in Dual Diagnosis of Major Mental Illness and Substance Disorder. Edited by Minkoff K, Drake RE. San Francisco, CA, Jossey-Bass, 1991, pp 57–67

Fenchel GH, Flapan D: Resistance in group psychotherapy. Group 9:35–47, 1985

Flores PJ: Group Psychotherapy With Addicted Populations. New York, Haworth, 1998

Getter H, Litt MD, Kadden RM: Measuring treatment process in coping skills and interactional group therapies for alcoholism. Int J Group Psychother 42:419–430, 1992

Golden S, Halliday K, Khantzian EJ, et al: Dynamic group therapy for substance abuse patients: a reconceptualization, in Group Therapy in Clinical Practice. Edited by Alonso AA, Swiller HI. Washington, DC, American Psychiatric Press, 1993, pp 271–287

Hellerstein DJ, Meehan B: Outpatient group therapy for schizophrenic substance abusers. Am J Psychiatry 144: 1337–1339, 1987

Herman JL: Trauma and Recovery. New York, Basic Books, 1992

Kang SY, Kleinman PH, Woody GE, et al: Outcomes for cocaine abusers after once-a-week psychosocial therapy. Am J Psychiatry 148:630–635, 1991

Khantzian EJ: Opiate addiction: a critique of theory and some implications for treatment. Am J Psychother 131:160–164, 1974

Khantzian EJ: The ego, the self, and opiate addiction: theoretical and treatment considerations. International Review of Psychoanalysis 5:189–198, 1978

Khantzian EJ: The self-medication hypothesis of addictive disorders: focus on heroin and cocaine dependence. Am J Psychiatry 142:1259–1264, 1985

Khantzian EJ: A contemporary psychodynamic approach to drug abuse treatment. Am J Drug Alcohol Abuse 12:213–222, 1986

Khantzian EJ: Self-regulation vulnerabilities in substance abusers: treatment implications, in The Psychology and Treatment of Addictive Behavior. Edited by Dowling S. New York, International Universities Press, 1995, pp 17–41

Khantzian EJ: The self-medication hypothesis of substance use disorders: a reconsideration and recent applications. Harv Rev Psychiatry 4:231–244, 1997

Khantzian EJ, Mack JE: Alcoholics Anonymous and contemporary psychodynamic theory, in Recent Developments in Alcoholism, Vol 7: Treatment Research. Edited by Galanter M. New York, Plenum, 1989, pp 67–89

Khantzian EJ, Halliday K, McAuliffe WE: Addiction and the Vulnerable Self. New York, Guilford, 1990

Khantzian EJ, Halliday KS, Golden S, et al: Modified group therapy for substance abusers: a psychodynamic approach to relapse prevention. Am J Addict 1:67–76, 1992

Khantzian EJ, Golden SJ, McAuliffe WE: Group therapy for psychoactive substance use disorders, in Treatments of Psychiatric Disorders, 2nd Edition, Vol 1. Gabbard GO, Editor-in-Chief. Washington, DC, American Psychiatric Press, 1995, pp 832–839

Klein RH, Orleans JF, Soule CR: The Axis II group: treating severely characterologically disturbed patients. Int J Group Psychother 41:97–115, 1991

Kohut H: Preface, in Psychodynamics of Drug Dependence (NIDA Res Monogr No 12; DHEW Publ No ADM-77–470). Edited by Blaine JD, Julius DA. Washington, DC, U.S. Government Printing Office, 1977, pp vii–ix

Leszcz M: Group psychotherapy of the characterologically difficult patient. Int J Group Psychother 39:311–335, 1989

Levy MS: A change in orientation: therapeutic strategies for the treatment of alcoholism. Psychotherapy: Research and Practice 24:786–793, 1987

Levy MS, Mann DW: The special treatment team: an inpatient approach to the mentally ill alcoholic patient. J Subst Abuse Treat 5:219–227, 1988

Liebenberg B: The unwanted and unwanting patient: problems in group psychotherapy of the narcissistic patient, in The Difficult Patient in Group. Edited by Roth B, Stone W, Kibel H. Madison, CT, International Universities Press, 1990, pp 311–322

Martin K, Grannandrea P, Rogers B, et al: Group intervention with pre-recovery patients. J Subst Abuse Treat 13:33–41, 1996

Matano RA, Yalom ID: Approaches to chemical dependency: chemical dependency and interactive group therapy—a synthesis. Int J Group Psychother 41:269–293, 1991

McAuliffe WE, Albert J: Clean Start. New York, Guilford, 1992

McAuliffe WE, Ch'ien JMN: Recovery training and self help: relapse prevention program for treated opiate addicts. J Subst Abuse Treat 3:9–20, 1986

Meissner WW: Psychotherapy and the Paranoid Process. New York, Jason Aronson, 1986

Minkoff K, Drake RE (eds): Dual Diagnosis of Major Mental Illness and Substance Disorder. San Francisco, CA, Jossey-Bass, 1991

Nace EP: The Treatment of Alcoholism. New York, Brunner/Mazel, 1987

Orford J: Excessive Appetites: A Psychological View of Addictions. New York, Wiley, 1985

Poldrugo F, Forti B: Personality disorders and alcoholism treatment outcome. Drug Alcohol Depend 21:171–176, 1988

Rice CA, Rutan JS: Inpatient Group Psychotherapy. New York, Macmillan, 1987

Roth B, Stone W, Kibel H (eds): The Difficult Patient in Group. Madison, CT, International Universities Press, 1990

Sciacca K: An integrated treatment approach for severely mentally ill individuals with substance disorders, in Dual Diagnosis of Major Mental Illness and Substance Disorder. Edited by Minkoff K, Drake RE. San Francisco, CA, Jossey-Bass, 1991, pp 69–84

Shaffer HU, LaSalvia TA, Stein JP: Comparing Hatha yoga with dynamic group psychotherapy for enhancing methadone maintenance treatment: a randomized clinical trial. Altern Ther Health Med 3:57–66, 1997

Stone W, Gustafson JP: Technique in group psychotherapy of narcissistic and borderline patients. Int J Group Psychother 32:29–47, 1982

Tuttman S: Principles of psychoanalytic group therapy applied to the treatment of borderline and narcissistic disorders, in The Difficult Patient in Group. Edited by Roth B, Stone W, Kibel H. Madison, CT, International Universities Press, 1990, pp 7–29

Vaillant GE: The Natural History of Alcoholism. Cambridge, MA, Harvard University Press, 1983

Vannicelli M: Group psychotherapy with alcoholics. J Stud Alcohol 43:17–37, 1982

Vannicelli M: Group therapy aftercare for alcoholic patients. Int J Group Psychother 38:337–353, 1988

Wurmser L: The Hidden Dimension: Psychodynamics of Compulsive Drug Use. New York, Jason Aronson, 1978

Yalom ID: Group psychotherapy and alcoholism. Ann N Y Acad Sci 233:85–103, 1974

Yalom ID: Inpatient Group Psychotherapy. New York, Basic Books, 1983

Yalom ID: The Theory and Practice of Group Psychotherapy. New York, Basic Books, 1985

Yalom ID, Bloch S, Bond G, et al: Alcoholics in interactional group therapy: an outcome study. Arch Gen Psychiatry 35:419–425, 1978

# Chapter 33

# Family Therapy: Alcohol

## Peter Steinglass, M.D.

During the past two decades, a growing clinical and research literature on family issues in alcoholism has pointed to the important role of family factors in the onset and clinical course of this condition (Lawson and Lawson 1998; Steinglass and Robertson 1983). Considerable interest has been generated not only in investigating family aspects of alcoholism but also in applying family therapy techniques to its treatment (Edwards and Steinglass 1995). Well into the 1970s, clinicians treating alcoholism by and large ignored families. The current picture is dramatically different. One is now hard pressed to find a credible alcoholism treatment program that does not at least give lip service to the importance of including family members in the treatment plan. Nevertheless, despite this growing interest in the family on the part of alcoholism specialists, and the widespread perception that family therapy is being offered as a standard component of most treatment programs, considerable confusion remains as to how this family component should be implemented.

In this chapter, I discuss alcoholism treatment primarily from the vantage point of a systems-oriented family therapist. At issue here are several questions:

- How does the therapist conceptualize a rationale for a genuine family therapy approach to alcoholism?
- What core issues must therapists be aware of?
- How would assessment issues play themselves out within such a therapy framework?
- What are the central therapeutic components of such an approach?
- To what extent is outcome data available regarding efficacy of these treatment approaches?

I also want to caution the reader that it would be rare to find such an approach practiced in pure form in an alcoholism treatment setting. Instead, the approaches I discuss should be looked on as examples of how treatment for alcoholism has been carried out when a family therapist has taken on this clinical population.

## Family Therapy Treatment Approaches to Alcoholism

### Overview

Family therapists have used a number of conceptual models for designing treatment strategies for alcoholism. The best known approach is the family systems approach, a model that applies principles of general systems theory to families. Particular attention is paid to ways in which families, as behavioral systems, regulate their internal and external environments, and to how patterns of interactional behavior change over time. Structural, strategic, and newer constructivist approaches to family therapy use family system theory as their conceptual bases.

A second, also widely used approach is a family behavioral model that extends classical conditioning principles to interpersonal behavior. Concepts of reciprocity, coercion, and reinforcement are applied to an analysis of the contingencies that help explain patterns of interactional behavior.

A third approach, the network therapy approach, focuses particular attention on constructs of stress and coping, as applied to families rather than just to individuals. Constructs such as social support and social networks, and stressful life events are used to understand the factors that either help or hinder families in solving problems in the face of stressful events.

However, despite their different emphases, these three approaches also share much in common. For example, in each approach the conceptual model has been used both to suggest strategies for assessment in which family data become integral components of the diagnostic process and to guide treatment intervention approaches. Particularly important is the growing conviction that family involvement during the initial assessment phase increases the success rate of engagement of alcoholic patients in treatment programs. Perhaps the best known of these family-based strategies is the family intervention model developed by the Johnson Institute (Johnson 1980). Others worth noting are the ARISE model (Garrett et al. 1997), which combines family systems and network therapy approaches, and a model based on structural-strategic family therapy specifically designed for engaging adolescent substance abusers and their families (Szapocznik et al. 1988).

At the same time, however, family-based conceptual models have not become fully integrated into mainstream thinking about alcoholism, in part because they do not fit well with current conventions for diagnosing alcoholism. Thus, although there is widespread acknowledgment of the importance of family factors in the onset and course of chronic alcoholism, no widely accepted schema exists for integrating a family perspective into DSM-IV (American Psychiatric Association 1994) criteria sets for diagnosing alcohol abuse and alcohol dependence. Instead, descriptive models based on family systems, behavioral, and stress/coping concepts together form the conceptual rationale for the family therapy approaches currently used in alcoholism treatment settings.

With that caveat, let us summarize the main tenets of these conceptual models of alcoholism.

## Family Systems Therapy

The family systems model of alcoholism treatment, as described in greatest detail by Steinglass et al. (1987), centers around the concept of *the alcoholic system*, defined as a behavioral system in which alcohol acquisition and/or consumption is a major organizing principle for patterns of interactional behavior within the system. In tracking this process of reorganization of families around alcoholism, the family systems model focuses particular attention on two aspects of family life: 1) a set of regulatory behaviors that families typically use to structure the pattern of everyday life, to establish fam-

ily priorities, and to ensure stability; and 2) the course of family development. In terms of family regulatory behaviors, the interest is in whether family behavior has been altered by inordinate attention to the demands of alcoholism. Three areas of family life have been suggested as foci for assessing this question: short-term, problem-solving strategies; daily routines; and family rituals (e.g., holidays, vacations, dinnertime). For each area, the central question is the extent to which family behavior patterns have been invaded (i.e., substantively changed) to accommodate the unique demands generated by the family's alcoholic member.

This focus on family regulatory behaviors as vehicles for assessment of the role of alcoholism in family life has also received considerable research validation. Empirical studies of problem-solving behavior in alcoholic families have demonstrated consistently the striking differences between interactional behavior in the presence of alcohol and in its absence (Jacob and Seilhammer 1987)—often referred to as the contrast between *wet* and *dry* family behavior patterns. Detailed studies of family daily routines have demonstrated that these behaviors are linked closely to highly significant clinical course issues related to alcoholism (Steinglass 1981). Finally, studies of alcoholic family rituals have yielded important findings about the relationship between family environmental factors and intergenerational transmission of alcoholism (Wolin et al. 1980).

Regarding the second major focus of systems-oriented models, that of family development, the critical question is whether the inordinate attention being given to alcoholism-related issues within the family is taking the family away from competing developmental issues (e.g., an adolescent family member's needs for differentiation). Within this model, it is posited that family development is often distorted when alcoholism is introduced into family life because the family typically skews its focus toward an emphasis on short-term stability at the expense of long-term growth. This process gives the family the appearance of rigidity or narrowness, a characteristic mentioned frequently in the clinical literature.

A manualized version of a family systems treatment approach, developed by Shoham and her colleagues (Rohrbaugh et al. 1996), has been researched in a controlled clinical trial of family systems versus behavioral treatment approaches for alcoholism (Beutler et al. 1997). Although outcome data are still emerging from this study, this work demonstrates the feasibility of translating systems treatment approaches into clearly defined principles and a standardized treatment protocol.

## Behavioral Family Therapy

As already noted in this chapter, behaviorally oriented marital and family therapy is an extension of the basic constructs of learning theory to behavior in families. Central here is the tenet that behaviors, including interactional behaviors, are learned and maintained via positive and negative reinforcements of these behaviors. In the alcoholism field, behaviorally oriented treatment approaches have been based primarily on social learning theory, a variant of behavior theory that starts with the basic stimulus-response models of operant and classical conditioning but also incorporates the role of cognitive processes.

As outlined by McCrady (1986), one of the major proponents of the use of behavior therapy techniques for the treatment of alcoholism, reinforcement patterns involving families struggling with alcoholism issues take on three major forms (i.e., types of responses or consequences families establish for drinking behavior): 1) reinforcing drinking behavior in the form of attention or caretaking; 2) shielding the alcoholic individual from experiencing the negative consequences; and 3) punishing drinking behavior (p. 310).

Faced with this clinical situation, the behavior therapist would attempt to do the following:

1. Identify specific sequences of behavior toward identifying the stimulus-response patterns associated with repetitive drinking episodes.
2. Categorize these response patterns (consequences) as either positively or negatively reinforcing drinking behavior.
3. Introduce interventions to increase and reinforce positive behavioral interactions at the spousal or family level and concomitantly decrease negative behavioral response patterns related to drinking. The terms positive and negative here connote consequences that seem to further increase drinking behavior (negative reinforcers) or those that reinforce or reward decreased drinking (positive reinforcers).

Toward these goals the assessment phase of treatment focuses on identification of specific behaviors that can be targeted for subsequent interventions. Treatment approaches use the now familiar techniques of monitoring behavior, establishing and rehearsing alternative behavioral sequences, and establishing specific behavioral goals regarding positive reinforcement patterns (O'Farrell and Cutter 1984).

The Beutler et al. (1997) study mentioned earlier in this chapter also included a cognitive-behavioral couples treatment as one of its comparison treatments. A detailed manual describing this approach was prepared as part of the study (Wakefield et al. 1996) and is the clearest explication to date of behavioral principles applied to couples therapy for alcoholism.

## Social Network Therapy

Social network therapy, based on a social systems model (Colletti and Brownell 1982; Galanter 1993; Moos et al. 1989), uses a variety of family interventions in support of a treatment plan targeted at the alcoholic individual as the primary patient. Here, the family's involvement is undertaken with one or more of the following goals in mind:

- To obtain more accurate and complete historical data regarding the identified patient's (IP's) alcoholism history
- To increase the likelihood of engaging the patient in the treatment process
- To increase compliance rates, especially for disulfiram therapy and detoxification strategies
- To increase the social supports available to the alcoholic individual, especially during the postdetoxification period
- To provide independent counseling to family members regarding their own coping strategies and psychological sequelae related to the effect of chronic alcoholism on family life

Typically, these goals are achieved by establishing a concurrent program for family members parallel to and integrated with the treatment program for the IP. For example, family sessions (often without the alcoholic member present) might occur on a regular basis during the time when the alcoholic member is engaged in a residential detoxification program. Another popular approach has been the use of multiple-family group therapy, groups that focus on issues presumably relevant to the nonalcoholic members of the family, including supportive approaches geared to help families deal with common difficulties they face as a result of having an alcoholic member. In some instances, groups for spouses and/or children meet concurrently with groups for the alcoholic family members. In other instances, the alcoholic members are included in the group, but the focus remains a social systems one.

## Al-Anon Groups

It is important to include a word here about the use of self-help groups designed for family members as part of treatment planning. The models of family therapy for alcoholism discussed earlier in this chapter have all been proposed by family therapy specialists. For the most part, they are also designed to be implemented by family therapy clinicians.

However, by far the most active family-oriented program for alcoholism is a self-help one: the Al-Anon family group. Al-Anon is an indigenous self-help movement that arose spontaneously as a parallel but separate movement to Alcoholics Anonymous (AA) in the 1940s. Al-Anon family groups are modeled after AA (i.e., a group fellowship of peers sharing a common problem). In the case of Al-Anon, the peers are spouses, children, and close relatives of alcoholic individuals who are usually, but not necessarily, part of an AA group.

Ablon (1977), who has studied extensively the Al-Anon movement, suggested that successful Al-Anon members must accept one basic didactic lesson and three principles for operating in the groups themselves. The didactic lesson is the acceptance of the AA concept of alcoholism as an obsession of the mind and an allergy of the body, implying that the alcoholic individual has a disease that is totally outside his or her control. The three operating principles are 1) a loving detachment from the alcoholic individual, in which family members accept as a given that they are powerless to intervene constructively in the behavior of the alcoholic family member; 2) the reestablishment of the individual's self-esteem and independence; and 3) a reliance on a higher power, a spiritual emphasis that, of course, also closely parallels AA.

Family therapists are divided about combining traditional family therapy approaches with concurrent involvement in AA or Al-Anon groups. Some therapists have argued that the two approaches work at cross purposes in that AA and Al-Anon clearly see the alcoholic individual, not the family, as the patient. The prevailing view, however, is that participation in self-help groups is a useful adjunctive experience to family therapy for many families, especially as a component of the rehabilitation (relapse prevention) phase of treatment.

## Integration of Models

Although I have separately delineated the main principles of family systems therapy, behavioral family ther-

apy, social network therapy, and self-help approaches, it would be most unusual to find any of these approaches being practiced in pure form in an alcoholism treatment program. In part, this is because major conceptual and technical overlaps exist among these approaches. For example, systems therapists routinely analyze interactional sequences of behaviors as part of their assessment procedures and also use techniques such as behavioral monitoring as part of their treatment armamentarium. In like fashion, behavioral family therapists rely heavily on systems concepts in extending notions of social learning theory to marital and family units. Another factor is that alcoholism treatment programs tend to be eclectic in their organization, with frequent mixing of psychodynamically oriented treatments with 12-step programs, and biomedically oriented detoxification and psychopharmacological approaches side by side with marital sessions and family education.

As research efforts increasingly focus on the development of meaningful clinical typologies of the subtypes of alcoholism (see, for example, Cloninger 1987), a challenge for clinicians will be how to incorporate these ideas into treatment decisions (Beutler et al. 1993). A concomitant research challenge will be the implementation of treatment evaluation research designed to determine which treatment approach seems most efficacious for each alcoholism subtype identified within the different typologies, what has more generally been called *aptitude-treatment interaction research* (Dance and Neufeld 1988). Initial efforts have already begun in this direction (Beutler et al. 1997; Kadden et al. 1989; Longabaugh et al. 1995), but the first large-scale study specifically designed to examine aptitude-treatment interaction in the alcoholism area suggested few if any advantages to matching patients to treatment approaches over generic treatment (Project MATCH Research Group 1997). Nevertheless, the next decade may see an increasing emphasis placed on clarifying the components of each family therapy treatment approach that contribute uniquely to efficacy for a specific pattern or subtype of alcoholism.

## Family Systems Approaches to Assessment and Detoxification

Of the family therapy treatment approaches outlined in this chapter, family systems therapy is perhaps the most unique. In the next sections, I describe in somewhat greater detail how the first two phases of treatment assessment and detoxification are implemented in a family systems therapy approach.

## Assessment Strategies

In the typical clinical situation, therapists are guided in their assessment approaches by the need to answer two fundamental questions: 1) what is wrong here (i.e., the question of diagnosis), and 2) how should the clinical problem be treated? Treatment evaluation typically includes assessment of patient strengths and weaknesses, and a review of treatment options.

Family therapists undertake the same assessment process, but in family systems therapy, particular emphasis is placed on family-level evaluation. Toward that goal, the assessment phase is typically carried out via conjoint interviews of the whole family and/or important subunits (especially the marital dyad). In many regards, the material covered parallels that of an individual assessment of an alcoholic patient. In this approach, however, the therapist has available the multiple perspectives of all family members, and the database therefore tends to be both richer and far more reliable than is the case with assessment of the alcoholic individual alone.

This ability to obtain multiple perspectives is especially valuable in assessing the effect of intoxicated behavior on family regulatory mechanisms (as discussed earlier, these mechanisms include family problem-solving styles, daily routines, and family rituals). A key aspect of family systems therapy in alcoholism treatment posits that differences between patterns of interactional behavior in the presence and in the absence of active drinking must be understood before undertaking detoxification. Otherwise, the complex ways in which alcohol-related behaviors have become incorporated in family life will not be understood, and removal of alcohol may inadvertently destabilize rather than improve family life.

Consequently, an interest has been generated in the development of assessment techniques for addressing these differences. In some instances an opportunity to assess behavior under so-called *wet conditions* is afforded by the alcoholic family member appearing for a treatment session in an intoxicated state. The therapist can use this opportunity to observe differences in interaction patterns regarding variables such as activity and passivity of various family members, interaction rates, range of affective expression, levels of direct conflict, verbal content (especially related to the raising of problem areas not previously mentioned), interactional dis-

tance, prevailing mood, and degree of interpersonal engagement. For example, an observation that a married couple seems more emotionally engaged during such a session might lead to speculations that the couple is inadvertently using this engagement to carry out problem solving during periods of intoxication, a factor that might become a reinforcer of subsequent episodes of drinking.

At the same time, studies of such differences in patterns of interactional behavior under wet versus dry conditions, although having established that such differences do exist, have remained speculative as to the functional or adaptive consequences of this biphasic quality of family life. Also important to underscore here is that individual families differ in their response to the presence of an intoxicated member (e.g., one family might forcefully engage the intoxicated member; another might avoid or isolate the drinker). This observation also suggests that the direction of changes in interactional patterns during wet conditions may vary considerably from family to family as well.

## Family Detoxification

The family systems model of alcoholism treatment shares with virtually all other treatment approaches the belief that meaningful psychotherapeutic work can proceed only after the IP has stopped drinking. However, the model's approach to detoxification is fundamentally different in two regards: 1) the goal for this treatment phase is family-level detoxification (including, of course, abstinence on the part of the IP), and 2) the central technique for accomplishing detoxification is the establishment of a contract with the entire family to achieve an alcohol-free environment at a *family level* as well as at an individual level. (The most complete description of this approach can be found in Steinglass et al. 1987.)

The underlying rationale for family detoxification could be stated as follows: whether or not alcoholism started because of the behavior of one individual within the family, by the time it reaches its chronic phase it has become a central organizer of important aspects of family life. For the marital couple receiving treatment, important aspects of their interaction patterns are likely inexorably linked to patterns of alcohol consumption on the part of the IP. Daily routines may be paced to drinking patterns. Interaction rates, problem solving, and so forth have been shaped by the types of behaviors the couple manifests when drinking is occurring. Each spouse has developed strong opinions and feelings about the reasons for and implications of alcoholic drinking, and these views have become fixed. Associated behaviors (e.g., physical violence, sexual behavior, employment records) and their exigencies have required family attention and responses. These responses may also have placed heavy demands on family emotional and financial resources. In these ways, alcoholism has invaded family life and dictated the shape and flavor of life within the family.

The cessation of drinking by the IP will therefore have profound implications for all family members. Hence, the entire family has a stake in how the detoxification process unfolds. Further, because chronic alcoholism is now driving (organizing) much of family life, detoxification will at least initially be a destabilizing event for the family. For these reasons, it is important that the detoxification process be framed from both a family and an IP perspective—hence, the establishment of the twofold goal of, first, facilitating a cessation of drinking by the alcoholic family member, and, second, establishing an alcohol-free psychosocial environment for the family. This second goal differentiates the family systems approach from more traditional individually oriented treatments. The term *psychosocial environment* as applied to the family refers to all settings in which the family is interacting and behaving as a unit, including its home and relationships with friends and relatives.

To accomplish these goals, Steinglass et al. suggest a multiphase process that centers on the development of a written contract—the family detoxification contract—conjointly constructed by the family and the therapist. The process begins with the therapist explaining to the couple the rationale and need for detoxification as the first step in successful treatment and then proceeds through a series of steps in which the couple identifies what has to be done to achieve an alcohol-free environment and assigns tasks to accomplish these goals.

As a first step, a contract is developed that is intended to ensure that no drinking occurs at home and that the household environment is made totally alcohol free. Once this first step has been accomplished (i.e., a contract has been designed and successfully implemented), the family environment metaphor is expanded to include the environments of the extended family and the family's social and work networks. A simpler way of saying it is that the contract first aims at detoxifying the family's daily routines, then moves on to ensure that the family's external boundaries are protected from any new alcohol invasion, and finally, when the family moves into the outside world it does so within a protective bubble that still keeps it alcohol free (i.e., it takes along the alcohol-free environment as it, as a family unit, ventures out into the world).

However, once the contract discussion begins to focus on family behavior outside the home, it becomes potentially much more complex. The number of possible combinations and permutations exceed the ability of the contract to anticipate all possible situations, so instead the contract focuses on a limited number of model exchanges between the family and the outside world that are examples of how the contract terms should be interpreted in such circumstances. Critical here is the therapist's ability to identify with the family two or three situations that in the past would have been high-risk situations for drinking. Once identified, the family then rehearses with the therapist an alternative way of handling the situation that will protect the alcohol-free family environment.

Finally, the therapist uses two additional techniques throughout the process of contracting that are designed to reinforce and solidify the terms of the contract itself. These techniques are 1) making the terms of the contract public by sharing with friends or relatives that the contract has been established and is in effect, and 2) using rehearsing techniques to anticipate any problems the couple might have implementing the details of the contract.

To summarize, the success of family-level detoxification depends on six integrated components: 1) the detoxification contract; 2) the use of a core set of metaphors around which the detoxification contract is framed; 3) a multistage strategy for implementing the scope of detoxification; 4) the use of public disclosure to reinforce the meaning and importance of the detoxification contract; 5) the use of a prospective, anticipatory stance to identify potential challenges to abstinence; and 6) ample rehearsal of strategies to effectively meet these potential challenges to abstinence.

The family detoxification component is the most unique aspect of the family systems treatment model. By asking the couple to work together on framing the contract, and by establishing as the treatment goals the metaphor of an alcohol-free family environment, the therapist is automatically reframing the entire alcoholism issue in family rather than individual terms. Although the therapist is not disputing that the IP has been consuming the alcohol, he or she is dramatically reinforcing the concept that alcoholism has in important ways taken over family life. Thus, at the same time that this phase of treatment is aimed at the important goal of cessation of drinking (as a necessary prerequisite for further treatment), the therapist is also carrying out essential reframing work to enable the couple to reorganize family life so that the necessary relapse prevention tools and structures are in place.

## Efficacy

Although there are still few controlled clinical trials of family therapy approaches to alcoholism and drug abuse treatment, studies carried out to date have consistently indicated the superiority of marital and/or family therapy over individual therapy approaches (Collins 1990; Edwards and Steinglass 1995; Orford 1984; Steinglass and Robertson 1983). Further, involvement of family members substantially increases patient engagement in both detoxification and rehabilitation phases of treatment (Stark 1992). Thus, the importance of family involvement in substance abuse treatment has solid empirical support.

Reviews of the family therapy literature make it clear that a wide array of family treatment techniques (e.g., family systems therapy, behavioral family therapy, multiple-couples therapy, and multiple-family group therapy) have been used with this population of families, and all techniques have their strong advocates. These family therapy approaches are only beginning to be tested against one another; nevertheless, a body of studies suggest that most family-oriented treatment approaches are efficacious for treatment of alcoholism, and we are just now beginning to see the undertaking of studies using treatment match designs. This new generation of studies, which take advantage of clinical models proposing different typologies of alcoholism, are likely to yield interesting data that would form the basis of informed treatment assignments of different types of alcoholic patients not only to individual versus family-oriented treatments but perhaps even to different types of family treatments.

## Treatment Outcome Literature

A modest literature now exists examining the efficacy of a variety of family therapy approaches for the treatment of alcoholism. The following generalizations about this literature seem warranted:

- Both clinical reports and controlled studies are overwhelmingly favorable to the use of family therapy for the treatment of alcoholism. Put another way, no reports in the literature suggest either that family ther-

apy is less effective than an alternative treatment approach to which it has been compared or that inclusion of family members in a treatment program has had detrimental effects. Further, various family treatment approaches have been tried, including conjoint family therapy, behavioral marital therapy, concurrent group therapy, multiple-couples therapy, and multiple-family group therapy. All approaches have been reported to be efficacious; none has occupied a dominant position in the field.

With rare exceptions, however, all studies published to date must be characterized as pilot in nature. Yet even though in most studies sample sizes are small, random assignment of patients is infrequent, and details regarding treatment programs and qualifications of therapists tend to be scanty, Edwards and Steinglass (1995) identified 21 studies of adequate enough design quality to include in a meta-analysis of treatment effect.

- Based on this meta-analysis, Edwards and Steinglass concluded both that compelling evidence indicates that the involvement of a nonalcoholic spouse in a treatment program significantly improves participation rates of alcoholic family members in treatment and that such involvement also has a positive effect on the likelihood that these individuals will alter their drinking behavior after treatment. This conclusion was based on an examination of three different family-oriented treatment engagement approaches: the intervention method (Liepman et al. 1989), unilateral family therapy (Thomas and Ager 1993), and community reinforcement training (Sisson and Azrin 1986). The Edwards and Steinglass meta-analysis demonstrated that alcoholic individuals whose spouses participate in treatment protocols themselves engage in treatment at rates almost two standard deviations higher than alcoholic individuals whose spouses do not participate in treatment. Alcoholic individuals whose family members are involved in some form of treatment enter treatment at rates ranging from 57% to 86% across the studies reviewed, compared with rates ranging from 0% to 31% in the control groups.

A related theme is that of overall compliance with ongoing treatment, even when the treatment is biomedically oriented. For example, around the critical issue of compliance with disulfiram use, Keane et al. (1984) demonstrated an unusually high rate of compliance with the disulfiram regimen (88%) when the treatment regimen included a contract to take the disulfiram in the presence of the spouse and subsequent positive reinforcement for taking disulfiram. That compliance should improve if spouses can be appropriately involved as active members of treatment planning and implementation would surely have considerable face validity. It is thus encouraging to see the emergence of data supportive of this notion.

- Although family therapy approaches have clear-cut effects on engagement of alcoholic individuals in treatment and also seem efficacious in their short-term effect on drinking behavior, remarkably few studies have examined long-range outcomes for these treatment approaches. Given that alcoholism is a chronic disorder, much more attention will have to be paid to these long-range issues before we can be satisfied that we know how to evaluate the true effect of family-oriented treatment approaches on alcoholism.

- Although most clinicians acknowledge that family issues are relevant to the comprehensive treatment of alcoholism, they often approach alcoholism without a sophisticated sense of family dynamics or family systems principles. Further, little evidence indicates that clinicians fully appreciate the heterogeneity of alcoholic members' families. Instead, the dominant model in clinical practice remains heavily influenced by the AA/Al-Anon philosophy of separate but equal treatment. For example, it would be unusual to find an alcoholism treatment program that incorporates a sophisticated family assessment as a mandatory part of its workup and then designs a treatment program based on the finding of such a workup. Much more likely, a standard program exists and the alcoholic individual and his or her family are pushed and squeezed to fit the preconceived notions, treatment schedule, and goals of this already-established program.

- Overall, the alcoholism field is receptive to the notion that family intervention has an appropriate place in the treatment process, but the field is still struggling to define the scope and form this intervention should take.

## References

Ablon J: Perspectives on Al-Anon family groups, in Alcoholism: Development, Consequences, and Interventions. Edited by Estes NJ, Heinemann ME. St. Louis, MO, CV Mosby, 1977

American Psychiatric Association: Diagnostic and Statistical Manual of Mental Disorders, 4th Edition. Washington, DC, American Psychiatric Association, 1994

Beutler LE, Patterson K, Jacob T, et al: Matching treatment alcoholism subtypes. Psychotherapy 30:463–472, 1993

Beutler LE, Shoham V, Jacob T, et al: Family versus behavioral treatment of alcoholism; a final report on Grant No 1-RO-11108486. Washington, DC, National Institute of Alcoholism and Alcohol Abuse, 1997

Cloninger CR: Neurogenetic adaptive mechanisms in alcoholism. Science 236:410–416, 1987

Colletti G, Brownell KD: The physical and emotional benefits of social support: application to obesity, smoking, and alcoholism, in Progress in Behavior Modification. Edited by Hersen M, Eisler RM, Miller PM. New York, Academic Press, 1982, pp 109–178

Collins RL: Family treatment of alcohol abuse: behavioral and systems perspectives, in Alcohol and the Family: Research and Clinical Perspectives. Edited by Collins RL, Leonard KE, Searles JS. New York, Guilford, 1990, pp 285–308

Dance KA, Neufeld RWJ: Aptitude-treatment interaction research in the clinical setting: a review of attempts to dispel the "patient uniformity" myth. Psychol Bull 104:192–213, 1988

Edwards ME, Steinglass P: Family therapy treatment outcomes for alcoholism. J Marital Fam Ther 21:475–509, 1995

Galanter M: Network Therapy for Alcohol and Drug Abuse. New York, Basic Books, 1993

Garrett J, Landau-Stanton JL, Stanton MD, et al: ARISE: a method for engaging reluctant alcohol- and drug-dependent individuals in treatment. J Subst Abuse Treat 14:235– 248, 1997

Jacob T, Seilhammer R: Alcoholism and family interaction, in Family Interaction and Psychopathology: Theories, Methods and Findings. Edited by Jacob T. New York, Plenum, 1987, pp 535–580

Johnson VE: I'll Quit Tomorrow. San Francisco, CA, Harper & Row, 1980

Kadden RM, Cooney NL, Getter H, et al: Matching alcoholics to coping skills or interactional therapies: posttreatment results. J Consult Clin Psychol 57:698–704, 1989

Keane TM, Foy DW, Nunn B, et al: Spouse contracting to increase Antabuse compliance in alcoholic veterans. J Clin Psychol 40:340–344, 1984

Lawson G, Lawson A: Alcoholism and the Family: A Guide to Treatment and Prevention. Gaithersburg, MD, Aspen, 1998

Liepman MR, Nirenberg TD, Begin AM: Evaluation of a program designed to help families and significant others to motivate resistant alcoholics into recovery. Am J Drug Alcohol Abuse 15:209–221, 1989

Longabaugh R, Wirtz PW, Beattie MC, et al: Matching treatment focus to patient social investment and support: 18-month follow-up results. J Consult Clin Psychol 63: 296–307, 1995

McCrady BS: The family in the change process, in Treating Addictive Behaviors: Processes of Change. Edited by Miller WR, Heather NH. New York, Plenum, 1986, pp 305–318

Moos R, Fenn C, Billings A, et al: Assessing life stressors and social resources: applications to alcoholic patients. J Subst Abuse 1:135–152, 1989

O'Farrell TJ, Cutter HSG: Behavioral marital therapy couples groups for male alcoholics and their wives. J Subst Abuse Treat 1:191–204, 1984

Orford J: The prevention and management of alcohol problems in the family setting: a review of work carried out in English-speaking countries. Alcohol 19:109–122, 1984

Project MATCH Research Group: Matching alcoholism treatments to client heterogeneity: Project MATCH posttreatment drinking outcome. J Stud Alcohol 58:7–29, 1997

Rohrbaugh MJ, Shoham V, Spungen C, et al: Family systems therapy in practice: a systemic couples therapy for problem drinking, in Comprehensive Textbook of Psychotherapy: Theory and Practice. Edited by Bongar B, Beutler LE. New York, Oxford University Press, 1996, pp 228–253

Sisson RW, Azrin NH: Family member involvement to initiate and promote treatment of problem drinkers. J Behav Ther Exp Psychiatry 17:15–21, 1986

Stark MJ: Dropping out of substance abuse treatment: a clinically oriented review. Clin Psychol Rev 12:93–116, 1992

Steinglass P: The alcoholic family at home: patterns of interaction in dry, wet, and transitional stages of alcoholism. Arch Gen Psychiatry 38:578–584, 1981

Steinglass P, Robertson A: The alcoholic family, in The Biology of Alcoholism, Vol 6; The Pathogenesis of Alcoholism: Psychosocial Factors. Edited by Kissin B, Begleiter H. New York, Plenum, 1983, pp 243–307

Steinglass P, Bennett L, Wolin SJ, et al: The Alcoholic Family. New York, Basic Books, 1987

Szapocznik J, Perez-Vidal A, Brickman AL, et al: Engaging adolescent drug abusers and their families in treatment: a strategic structural treatment approach. J Consult Clin Psychol 56:552–557, 1988

Thomas EJ, Ager RD: Unilateral family therapy with spouses of uncooperative alcohol abuser. Journal of Social Service Research 10:145–162, 1993

Wakefield P, Williams RE, Yost E, et al: Couples Therapy for Alcoholism: A Cognitive-Behavioral Treatment Manual. New York, Guilford, 1996

Wolin SJ, Bennett LA, Noonan DL, et al: Disrupted family rituals: a factor in the intergenerational transmission of alcoholism. J Stud Alcohol 41:199–214, 1980

# 34 Family Therapy: Other Drugs

Edward Kaufman, M.D.

**D**rug abuse has a profound effect on the family, and the family is a critical factor in the treatment of drug abuse. In this chapter, I focus on the role of the family in drug abuse treatment. Dealing with the family represents further involvement with the patient's ecosystem, which also includes the treatment team, 12-step groups, sponsors, employers, Employee Assistance Program (EAP) counselors, managed care workers, parole officers, and other members of the legal system. Upon entering treatment, the family is generally the most critical part of this ecosystem. In family therapy, there are three basic phases of the family's involvement in treatment: 1) developing a system for establishing and maintaining a drug-free state, 2) establishing a workable method of family therapy, and 3) dealing with the family's readjustment after the cessation of drug abuse. I discuss these three phases in detail, with an emphasis on variations in treatment techniques to meet the needs of different types of drug-abusing individuals. The variations are based on the following factors: substance(s) abused, family reactivity, stage of disease, and gender of the individual. Before presenting this material, I review the efficacy of family treatment of drug abuse.

## Efficacy of Family Therapy in Drug Abuse Treatment

A major problem in assessing family therapy is that all family therapy is not the same. Thus it is difficult to generalize success or failure from one program or individual to another or to the field in general.

Several family therapy outcome studies, generally characterized by a lack of methodological sophistication, were performed in the 1970s. Silver et al. (1975)

described a methadone program for addicted pregnant women and their addicted spouses; 40% of the women in treatment became drug free, and the employment rate of the spouses increased from 10% to 55%. Both rates are higher than those achieved by traditional methadone programs without family treatment. A problem with this study, as with most evaluations of family approaches to drug abuse, is the lack of follow-up data or control groups.

Hendricks (1971) found at 1-year follow-up that narcotic-addicted subjects who had received $5\frac{1}{2}$ months of multiple-family therapy were twice as likely to remain in continuous therapy as addicted subjects who did not respond to this therapy. Kaufman and Kaufmann's (1977) work has shown that addicted adolescents who receive multiple-family therapy have half the recidivism rate of patients who do not.

Stanton (1979) noted that of 68 studies of the efficacy of family therapy of drug abuse, only 14 quantified their outcome. Only six of these studies provided comparative data with other forms of treatment or control groups. Four of the six studies (Hendricks 1971; M. A. Scopetta et al., unpublished observations, 1979; Stanton and Todd 1982; Wunderlich et al. 1974) showed family treatment to be superior to other modes. Winer et al. (1974) and Ziegler-Driscoll (1977) found no superiority of family treatment. Stanton (1979) concluded that "family treatment shows considerable promise for effectively dealing with problems of drug abuse" (p. 10).

Stanton and Todd (1982) provided the field with an early controlled study of the family therapy of drug abuse. They emphasized concrete behavioral changes, including a focus on family rules about drug-related behavior and the use of weekly urine tests to give tangible indications of progress. They focused on interrupting and altering the repetitive family interactional patterns that maintain drug taking. In their family therapy groups, Stanton and Todd found at 1-year follow-up that days free of methadone, illegal opioids, and marijuana all shifted favorably, compared with a non-family-therapy group. However, there was no significant decrease in alcohol abuse or increase in work or school productivity. They noted a high mortality rate in the non-family-therapy group (10%) compared with only 2% in those who received family therapy. However, lack of success in certain outcome aspects is troubling. Even their best treatment group (i.e., paid family) had 31% of days on methadone, 19% on illegal opioids, 12% on nonopioid illegal drugs, 25% on marijuana, 44% on alcohol, and 63% of possible work or school days not attended or involved (an important parameter of individuation).

McCrady et al. (1986) compared the effectiveness of family therapy on drinking behavior and life satisfaction in three treatment groups: 1) minimal spouse involvement with interventions directed toward the drinker, although the spouse was present; 2) alcohol-focused spouse involvement, in which coping skills for alcohol-related situations were emphasized; and 3) alcohol behavioral marital therapy, in which they addressed the need to modify the marital relationship. Results showed better compliance, a faster decrease in drinking, and a greater likelihood of staying in treatment and marital satisfaction posttreatment in the subjects receiving alcohol behavioral marital therapy.

Cognitive-behavioral skills training has continued to be successful, as evaluated in several studies of the family treatment of drug abuse (Maisto et al. 1995; Monti et al. 1990; Nakamura and Takano 1991; Thomas et al. 1996). Inclusion of the family, particularly in the treatment of drug abuse in adolescents, has been associated consistently with greater improvement regarding drug abuse and family function (Alexander and Gwyther 1995; Enders and Mercier 1993), which is sustained and enhanced 2 years after completion of treatment (Stewart and Brown 1993).

Positive family function predicts success in drug abuse treatment, particularly in "the extent to which family members are encouraged to be assertive, self sufficient" (Friedman et al. 1986). Home-based multisystemic therapy with drug-abusing delinquents greatly enhanced completion of a full course of therapy (98%) as compared with treatment through usual community services, in which completion was minimal (Henggeler et al. 1996).

# Developing a System for Achieving and Maintaining Abstinence

The family treatment of drug abuse begins with development of a system to achieve and maintain abstinence. This system, together with specific family therapeutic techniques and knowledge of family patterns commonly seen in families with a drug-abusing member (also known as the identified patient, or IP), provides a workable, therapeutic approach to drug abuse.

Family treatment of drug abuse must begin with an assessment of the extent of drug dependence and the difficulties it presents for the individual and the family. The quantification of the individual's drug abuse history can take place with the entire family present; the IP often will be honest in this setting, and "confession" is a helpful way to begin communication. Moreover, other family members can often provide more accurate information than the IP. However, some IPs will give an accurate history only when interviewed alone. In taking a drug abuse history, the clinician should determine the IP's current and past use of every type of abusable drug, including alcohol. IPs also should be asked about the quantity and quality of the substances they've used, the duration of use, the expense, the methods used to support and prevent their drug intake, and the presence of physical effects, tolerance, withdrawal, and medical complications. Other past or present drug-abusing family members may be identified, and their drug use and its consequences should be quantified without putting the family on the defensive. It is also essential to document the family's patterns of reactivity, codependency, and enabling of drug use and abuse. The specific method necessary to achieve abstinence can be decided on only after the extent and nature of drug abuse are quantified.

## Establishing a System for Achieving Abstinence

It is critical first to establish a system for enabling the IP to become drug free so that family therapy can take place effectively. The specific methods used to achieve abstinence vary according to the extent of use, abuse, and dependence. Mild to moderate abuse in adolescents can often be controlled if both parents agree on clear limits and expectations and on how to enforce them. Older abusing individuals may also stop if they are aware of the medical or psychological consequences to themselves or the effects on their family.

If drug abuse is moderately severe or intermittent and without physical dependence, such as intermittent use of hallucinogens or weekend cocaine abuse, then the family can be offered a variety of measures, such as regular attendance at Narcotics Anonymous (NA) or Cocaine Anonymous (CA) for the IP, and Al-Anon for family members.

If the abuse pattern is severe, then hospitalization should be set as a requirement very early in therapy.

## Establishing a System for Maintaining Abstinence

The family is urged to adopt some system that will enable the IP to continue to stay drug free. This system is part of the therapeutic contract made early in treatment. A lifetime commitment to abstinence is not required. Rather, the "one day at a time" approach of Alcoholics Anonymous (AA) is recommended. The patient is asked to establish a system for abstinence, which is committed to for only one day at a time but which is renewed daily using the basic principles of NA and CA. When the patient has a history of drug dependence, therapy is most successful when total abstinence is advocated.

Many individuals initially have to shop around for CA or NA groups in which they feel personally comfortable. Every recovering patient is strongly encouraged to attend small study groups, which work on the 12 steps, and larger meetings that often have speakers and are open to anyone including family members. Abstinence can also be achieved in heroin-addicted individuals by drug-aided measures such as methadone maintenance or naltrexone blockade. These medications work quite well in conjunction with family therapy, as work with the family enhances compliance, and the blocking effects on the primary drug of abuse helps calm the family system so that family and individual therapy can take place. Hospitalization also calms an overreactive family system. Another advantage of hospitalization is that it provides an intensive 24-hour-a-day orientation to treatment.

Individuals who have been dependent on illicit drugs for more than a few years generally do not do well in short-term programs, although these programs may buy time so that effective individual and family therapy can occur. For drug-dependent patients who fail in outpatient and short-term hospital programs, insistence on long-term residential treatment is the only workable alternative. Most families, however, will not accept this approach until other methods have failed. To accomplish this end, a therapist must be willing to maintain long-term ties with the family, even through multiple treatment failures. However, it may be more helpful to terminate treatment if the patient continues to abuse drugs, because continued family treatment implies that change is occurring when it is not. One way to continue therapist-family ties while not condoning drug abuse is to work with the family without the patient present (discussed later in this chapter). In other cases, it is more effective to terminate treatment until all family members are willing and able to adopt a workable program for reinforcing abstinence. Families that believe that therapy is being terminated in their best interest often return a few months or years later, ready and willing to commit to abstinence from drugs of abuse (Kaufman 1985).

## Working With Families in Which Drug Abuse Continues

The family therapist is in a unique position in regard to continued drug abuse and other manifestations of the IP's resistance to treatment, including total nonparticipation. The family therapist still has a workable and highly motivated patient: the family. A technique that can be used with an absent or highly resistant patient is the *intervention* (Johnson 1973), which was developed for use with alcoholic patients but can be adapted readily to work with drug-abusing patients, particularly those who are middle class, involved with their nuclear families, and employed.

If the drug-abusing patient does not meet criteria for an intervention or if the intervention has failed, we are left with the problem of dealing with a drug-abusing family. Berenson (1979) offered a workable, three-step therapeutic strategy for dealing with spouses or other family members of individuals who continue to abuse drugs or who are drug dependent.

1. Step 1 involves calming down the family system by explaining problems, solutions, and coping mechanisms.
2. Step 2 involves creating an external supportive network for family members so that the emotional intensity is not concentrated in the relationship with the IP or redirected to the therapist. Two types of support systems are available: 1) a self-help group in the Al-Anon model and 2) a significant others (SO) group led by a trained therapist. In the former, the group and sponsor provide emotional support, reinforce detachment, and help calm down

the family. An SO group may provide more insight and less support for remaining with a drug-abusing spouse.

3. Step 3 involves giving the spouse or other over-involved family member three choices: 1) keep doing exactly what you are doing, 2) detach or emotionally distance yourself from the patient, or 3) separate or physically distance yourself.

As part of the initial contract with a family, the therapist suggests that the patient's spouse continue individual treatment, Al-Anon, Co-Anon, or a spouse group even if the patient drops out. Other family members are also encouraged to continue in family therapy and support groups. It should be reemphasized that whenever the therapist maintains therapy with a family in which serious drug abuse continues, he or she has the responsibility to not maintain the illusion that a family is resolving problems while it is really reinforcing them. In contrast, even when the IP does not participate in treatment, the therapist may be quite helpful to the rest of the family.

## Motivating the Entire Family to Participate

Although I described earlier how to deal with a family when the IP is resistant to treatment participation, it should be obvious that treatment works best when the entire family is available for therapy. Once the family therapist has knowledge of the characteristics of the drug-abusing family, a program for dealing with drug abuse, and a workable personal method of family therapy, it becomes remarkably easy to get the entire family to come in for therapy. The individual who calls for an initial appointment is generally the one who is best able to get the entire household to participate. However, in some cases, the therapist may have to contact one or more family members directly. It then becomes imperative for the therapist to establish a contract with the family that all members feel will relieve the pain that they and the IP are experiencing.

The concept of the family as a multigenerational system necessitates that the entire family be involved in treatment. The family members necessary to perform optimum treatment include the entire household and any relatives who maintain regular contact with the family. Relatively emancipated family members who have less than weekly contact may be very helpful to these families; sessions that include them should be scheduled around their visits home.

The use of a multigenerational approach involving grandparents, parents, spouse, and children at the beginning of family therapy and at certain key points throughout the therapy is advised. However, for IPs younger than about age 24, the critical family unit is the IP and his or her siblings and parents. The critical family unit for married IPs older than 24 is the IP and his or her spouse. However, the more dependent the IP is on his or her parents, the more critical is work with the parents. Most sessions should be held with these family units; the participation of other family members is essential for a more thorough understanding and permanent change in the family.

The most effective drug abuse treatment programs for women with young children are those that house the children jointly, provide child care, and attend directly to parenting and child care issues.

## An Integrated Approach to a Workable System of Family Treatment

### Family Diagnosis

Accurate diagnosis is as important a cornerstone of family therapy as it is in individual therapy. In family diagnosis, we examine family interactional and communication patterns and relationships. In assessing a family, it is helpful to construct a map of its basic alliances and roles (Minuchin 1975). We also examine the family rules, boundaries, and adaptability. We look for coalitions (particularly transgenerational ones), shifting alliances, splits, cutoffs, and triangulation. We observe communication patterns, confirmation and disconfirmation, unclear messages, and conflict resolution. We note the family's stage in the family life cycle. We note *mind reading* (i.e., predicting reactions and reacting to them before they happen, or knowing what someone thinks or wants), double binds, and fighting styles. It is helpful to obtain an abbreviated three-generation genogram that focuses on the IP, his or her parents and progeny, and the IP's spouse's parents.

### Overview of Family Treatment Techniques

In this chapter, I summarize the family therapy systems currently in use, with an emphasis on the application of these techniques to IPs. These systems are classified into four schools: *structural-strategic, psychodynamic, Bowen's systems theory,* and *behavioral.* Any of these types of family therapy can be applied to IPs if their common family patterns are kept in mind and if a method to handle drug abuse is implemented.

## Structural-Strategic Family Therapy

In structural-strategic family therapy, the structural and strategic types of family therapy are combined because they were developed by many of the same practitioners, and shifts between the two types are frequently made by these therapists, depending on the family's needs. The thrust of structural family therapy is to restructure the system by creating interactional change within the session. The therapist actively becomes a part of the family yet retains sufficient autonomy to restructure the family (Stanton 1981).

According to strategic therapists, symptoms are maladaptive attempts to deal with difficulties that develop a homeostatic life of their own and continue to regulate family transactions. The strategic therapist works to substitute new behavior patterns for the destructive repetitive cycles. The therapist is responsible for planning a strategy to solve the family's problems. Techniques used by strategic therapists include the following (Stanton 1981):

- Putting the problem in solvable form.
- Placing considerable emphasis on change outside the sessions.
- Learning to take the path of least resistance so that the family's existing behaviors are used positively.
- Using the paradox (described later in this chapter), including restraining change and exaggerating family roles.
- Allowing the change to occur in stages. The therapist may create a new problem so that solving it leads to solving the original problem. The family hierarchy may be shifted to a different, abnormal one before reorganizing it into a new functional hierarchy.
- Using metaphorical directives in which the family members do not know they have received a directive.

Stanton and Todd (1982) successfully used an integrated structural-strategic approach with heroin-addicted patients who were receiving methadone maintenance.

## Psychodynamic Family Therapy

A psychodynamic family therapy approach has rarely been applied to IPs because such patients usually require a more active, limit-setting emphasis on the here and now than is usually associated with psychodynamic techniques. However, if certain basic limitations are kept in mind, psychodynamic principles can be extremely helpful in the family therapy of drug abuse.

The implementation of psychodynamic techniques has two cornerstones: the therapist's self-knowledge and a detailed family history. Every family member will internalize a therapist's good qualities, such as warmth, trust, trustworthiness, assertion, empathy, and understanding. Likewise, they may incorporate less desirable qualities such as aggression, despair, and emotional distancing. It is essential that a therapist thoroughly understand his or her own emotional reactions and those of the family.

Important elements of psychodynamic family therapy include the following:

**Countertransference.** A fundamental difference in work with families is that the therapist may have a countertransference problem toward the entire family or any individual subsystem or member of the family. We may particularly rally to the defense of our IPs against "oppressive" family members; this can set up power struggles between the therapist and the family.

Judicious expression of countertransference feelings may be helpful in breaking fixed family patterns. For example, sharing anger at a controlling patient may give the family enough support to express its anger at that patient in a manner that finally has an effect.

Family therapists view their emotional reactions to families in a systems framework and in a countertransference context. Thus they must be aware of how families will replay their problems in therapy by attempting to detour or triangulate their problems onto the therapist. The therapist must be particularly sensitive about becoming an enabler who, like the family, protects or rejects the IP.

**The therapist's role in interpretation.** Interpretations can be extremely helpful if they are made in a complementary way, without blaming, guilt induction, or dwelling on the hopelessness of long-standing, fixed patterns. The therapist can point out to each family member repetitive patterns and their maladaptive aspects and can give tasks to these individuals to help them change these patterns. Some families need interpretations before they can fulfill tasks. An emphasis on mutual responsibility when making any interpretation is an example of a beneficial fusion of structural and psychodynamic therapy (Kaufman 1985).

Overcoming resistance.   *Resistance* is defined as behaviors, feelings, patterns, or styles that prevent change (Anderson and Stewart 1983). In drug-abusing families, key resistance behaviors that must be dealt with involve the failure to perform functions that enable the abuser to stay drug free.

Every drug-abusing family has characteristic patterns of resistant behavior in addition to individual resistances. This family style may contribute significantly to resistance. Some families may need to deny all conflict and emotion and are almost totally unable to tolerate any displays of anger or sadness; others may overreact to the slightest disagreement.

The treatment contract can focus on resistance by having each family member agree to cooperate in overcoming resistance. If a family is willing to perform its assigned tasks, then most resistances are irrelevant or can be overcome. The therapist can directly discourage resistances such as blaming, dwelling on past injustices, and scapegoating. He or she may overcome resistance by joining techniques (see section "Joining" later in this chapter), including minimizing demands on the family to change so that the family moves more slowly but in the desired direction.

Working through.   Derived from psychoanalysis, the important concept of *working through* underscores the need to work repeatedly on many different overt issues, all of which stem from the same dysfunctional core. Thus, to have real change, a family must deal with a problem over and over until it has been worked through. If the system later pulls the family's behavior back to old maladaptive ways, then it becomes necessary to work through the conflicts in many different transactions until stable change takes place.

### Bowen's Systems Family Therapy

In Bowen's (1971) approach, the cognitive is emphasized and the use of affect is minimized. Systems theory focuses on triangulation, which implies that whenever emotional distance or conflict occurs between two individuals, tensions will be displaced onto a third party, issue, or drug. Drugs are frequently the subject of triangulation.

### Behavioral Family Therapy

Behavioral family therapy is commonly used with drug-abusing adolescents. Its popularity may be attributed to the fact that it can be elaborated in clear, easily learned steps.

Noel and McCrady (1984) developed seven steps in the therapy of alcoholism in couples that can be applied readily to married drug-abusing adults and their families:

1. *Functional analysis.*   Families are taught to understand the interactions that maintain drug abuse.
2. *Stimulus control.*   Drug use is viewed as a habit triggered by certain antecedents and maintained by certain consequences. The family is taught to avoid or change these triggers.
3. *Rearranging contingencies.*   The family is taught techniques to provide reinforcement for efforts at achieving a drug-free state by frequent reviewing of positive and negative consequences of drug use and by self-contracting for goals and specific rewards for achieving these goals. Covert reinforcement is accomplished by rehearsing in fantasy a scene in which the IP resists a strong urge to use drugs.
4. *Cognitive restructuring.*   IPs are taught to modify their self-derogatory, retaliatory, or guilt-related thoughts. IPs question the logic of these irrational thoughts and replace them with more rational ideation.
5. *Planning alternatives to drug use.*   IPs are taught techniques for refusing drugs through role-playing and covert reinforcement.
6. *Problem solving and assertion.*   IPs and their families are helped to decide if a situation calls for an assertive response and then, through role-playing, to develop effective assertive techniques. IPs are to perform these techniques twice daily and to use them in difficult situations that would have previously triggered the urge to use drugs.
7. *Maintenance planning.*   The entire course of therapy is reviewed, and the new armamentarium of skills emphasized. IPs are encouraged to practice these skills regularly and to reread handout materials that explain and reinforce these skills.

Families can also be taught through behavioral techniques to become aware of their nonverbal communication to make the nonverbal message concordant with the verbal and to learn to express interpersonal warmth nonverbally and verbally (Stuart 1980).

## Specific Structural Techniques

In this section, I emphasize the family therapy techniques I have found most useful in my work with drug-abusing individuals. Many of these techniques evolve from the structural family work of Minuchin (1975) and Haley (1977). My approach also borrows from systems and psychoanalytic techniques and integrates these disparate treatment methods into one system. The reader is advised to choose those methods that are compatible with his or her personality, to learn and practice these techniques by rote at first, and eventually to use them in a spontaneous manner. I describe these techniques individually, although most techniques are a fusion of several others as they are implemented in clinical practice. These techniques include the contract, joining, actualization, marking boundaries, assigning tasks, reframing, the paradox, balancing and unbalancing, and creating intensity.

## The Contract

The *contract* is an agreement to work on mutually agreed on, workable issues. The contract should always promise help with the IP's problem before it is expanded to other issues.

The primary contract is drafted with the family at the end of the first interview. In subsequent sessions, the concept of a contract is always maintained so that family assignments and tasks are agreed on and their implementation contracted by the family. The likelihood that the family will return after the first session is greatly enhanced by a contract that develops measures for problem resolution. In establishing a contract, the family must choose a system to achieve abstinence and agree to pursue that system after it has been agreed on as part of the initial evaluation.

The family should be provided with the beginnings of a system of shifting overreactivity to drug abuse in the initial contract. Family members may be coached to disengage from the IP, using strength gained from support groups and the therapist. At times, this disengagement can be accomplished only by powerful restructuring or paradoxical interventions. Later in therapy, contingency contracting principles can be used to facilitate mutual trust, particularly in areas such as adolescent individuation (e.g., a child agrees to be more respectful if his or her curfew is extended).

## Joining

In *joining*, the therapist adjusts himself or herself in a number of ways to affiliate with the family system. Joining enhances the therapist's leverage to change the system. The therapist alternates between joining that supports the family system and its members and joining that challenges it. Joining with only one part of a family may severely stress or change the rest of the family. The therapist must make contact with all family members so that they will comply with the therapist even when they sense that the therapist is being unfair (Kaufman 1985). The therapist should join by respecting and not challenging the initial defensiveness so common in these families.

Joining begins in the first moment of the session when the therapist makes the family comfortable through social amenities and by chatting with each member. The three types of joining techniques are maintenance, tracking, and mimesis (Minuchin 1975).

### Maintenance

In *maintenance*, the therapist supports the family structures and behaves according to the family rules. In its most extreme form, this includes accepting the family scapegoats as the problem when another family member is much more problematic. Maintenance operations include supporting areas of family strength, rewarding, affiliating with a family member, complimenting or supporting a threatened member, and explaining a problem. The therapist uses the family's metaphors, expressions, and language.

### Tracking

In *tracking*, the therapist follows the content of the family's interactions by listening carefully to what everyone has to say and by providing comments and expressions that help each member know he or she has been heard and understood.

### Mimesis

In *mimesis*, the therapist adopts the family's style and affect. If a family uses humor, then so should the therapist. If a family communicates through touching, then the therapist can also touch. The therapist supports family members or the entire family by means of nonverbal identification.

## Actualization

Patients usually direct their communications to the therapist. They should be trained to talk to one another rather than to the therapist. They should be asked to enact transactional patterns rather than describe them.

Drug-abusing families frequently gravitate to a rehash of past fights, hoping to entrap the therapist into deciding who started the fight, who is wrong and right, and what is the proper decision. The therapist should not be triangulated into such a position but rather should have the family choose an unresolved conflict and actualize its problem-solving methods or lack of them in the session. If a family arrives with an intoxicated member, the family should not be dismissed but its interactions observed, as this will demonstrate how family members interact during a good portion of their time together. If intoxication recurs, then the family must develop a system to end the drug abuse before therapy can continue.

## Marking Boundaries

All individuals and subsystems are encouraged to preserve their appropriate boundaries. Each individual should be spoken to, not about; and no one should talk, feel, think, answer, or act for anyone else. Each family member is encouraged to tell his or her own story and to listen to and acknowledge the communications of others. Nonverbal checking and blocking of communications should also be observed and, when appropriate, pointed out and halted. Mind reading is common but should be strongly discouraged because even if the mind reader is correct, this behavior almost always starts an argument. No one likes his or her reactions to be anticipated.

The most important boundary shift in family therapy is a weakening of ties between an overinvolved parent and a child and a strengthening of the boundary that protects the parents as a unit and supports them in dealing with their own parents, in-laws, potential or actual lovers, and the rest of the world external to the nuclear family.

If a role or tie is removed from a family member, this relationship should be replaced by building ties with other family members or individuals outside of the family. When boundaries are strengthened around a system, its functioning invariably improves.

## Assigning Tasks

Tasks help gather information, intensify the relationship with the therapist, continue the therapy outside of sessions, and give family members the opportunity to behave differently (Haley 1977). Tasks should be chosen that work in the framework of family goals, particularly those involving changing the IP's behaviors. Tasks should involve everyone in the family and bring gains to each member. A task should be completed successfully in session before one is assigned as homework.

Tasks should be specific, clear, and concise. If tasks are performed successfully, they will restructure the family toward optimal functioning. Tasks that fail are used as valuable learning experiences that reveal family dysfunction. Still, the family should not be let off easily, and the reasons for its failing should be explored.

## Reframing

In *reframing* (Minuchin and Fishman 1981), the therapist takes information received from the family and transforms it into a format that will be most helpful to changing the family. Reframing begins at the start of the first session as the therapist receives information from the family, molding it so that family members feel their problems are clear and solvable. Reframing is achieved by focusing material as it is received, selecting the elements that will facilitate change, and organizing the information to give it new meaning. Perhaps the most common use of reframing occurs when an IP's behaviors are broadened to include the entire family system.

## The Paradox

*Paradoxical techniques* work best with chronically rigid, repetitive, circular, highly resistant family systems, particularly ones that have had many prior therapeutic failures (Papp 1981).

The paradox is often used to slow progress so that a family is chafing at the bit to move faster or to exaggerate a behavior to emphasize the family's need to eliminate it. A behavior that is an externalized acting-out of family conflicts (e.g., stealing, secret drug-taking) can be prescribed to be performed within the family (i.e., tell them to behave as they are already behaving) so that the family can deal with it. An individual's behavior is not prescribed without relating it to its function in the family system. At times, psychodynamic interpretations can be made in a paradoxical way that gives greater impact to reach and change the family.

## Balancing and Unbalancing

*Balancing techniques*, which tend to support a family, are conceptually similar to Minuchin and Fishman's (1981) complementary technique. They challenge the family's views of behaviors as part of a linear hierarchy and emphasize the reciprocal involvement of behavior formation while supporting the family. In using balancing as a technique, mutual responsibility is emphasized, and tasks that involve change in all parties should be given.

*Unbalancing* involves changing or stressing the existing hierarchy in a family. The therapist unbalances by affiliating with a family member of low power so that this individual can challenge his or her prescribed family role, or by escalating a crisis, emphasizing differences, blocking typical transactional patterns, developing implicit conflict, and rearranging the hierarchy (Minuchin and Fishman 1981).

## Creating Intensity

Creating intensity techniques are verbal devices used to ensure that the family hears and incorporates the therapist's message . One simple way to be heard is to repeat either the same phrase or different phrases that convey the same concept. Another way to create intensity is through isomorphic transactions that use many different interventions to attack the same underlying dysfunctional pattern.

# Variations in Family Treatment for Different Types of Drug-Abusing Patients

In this section, I consider the modification of treatment typologies necessary for optimal results with abusers of various types of drugs and their families. In family treatment we must consider the needs of at least one other individual, and in most cases many others, as we adapt our treatment techniques to each individual family. It is not the drug of abuse that demands modification in techniques but rather other variables such as extent and severity of drug abuse, psychopathology, ethnicity, family reactivity, stage of disease, and gender (Kaufman 1985).

## Drug Type

Most of the modifications in family treatment that are based on drug type occur in the first phase of treatment when a system is developed for establishing and maintaining a drug-free state. Family self-help support groups are extremely helpful adjuncts to family therapy. Co-Anon is extremely helpful in dealing with the specific problems of the relatives of cocaine-abusing individuals. Some relatives of abusers of minor tranquilizers can participate well in Al-Anon, whereas the relatives of abusers of other types of drugs may find it difficult to relate to the relatives of alcoholic individuals and would work best in a specialized group. In most geographic areas, groups such as Co-Anon and Narc-Anon do not exist, and it is helpful to use groups of significant others that may be organized according to the drug of abuse and according to other factors such as social class and ethnicity.

## Family Reactivity

Drug-abusing families have been categorized according to four types: functional, enmeshed, disintegrated, and absent, each with different needs for family therapy (Kaufman and Pattison 1981).

### Functional Families

Functional families have minimal overt conflict and a limited capacity for insight as they protect their working homeostasis. Thus, the therapist should not be too ambitious about cracking the defensive structure of the family, which is likely to be resistant. The initial use of family education is often well received. Explanation of the medical effects of drugs provides a concrete way for the family to face up to the consequences of drug abuse (Kaufman and Pattison 1981). These families can usually be taught appropriate family rules and roles. Cognitive modes of interaction are usually acceptable; more uncovering and emotional interactions may be resisted. If abstinence and equilibrium are achieved, the therapist should be content even if the family members continue to use a great deal of denial and emotional isolation.

Short-term hospitalization may be required. Drug-abusing patients from functional families are often resistant to long-term residential treatment because they are protected by the family homeostasis.

### Enmeshed Families

The therapeutic approach used with enmeshed families is much more difficult and prolonged than that used with functional families. Educational and behavioral methods may provide some initial relief but are not likely to have much effect on enmeshed neurotic relationships. Often these families are resistant to ending drug abuse, and the therapist is faced with working with the family while drug abuse continues. The more hostile the enmeshed family interactions, the poorer the prognosis.

Although initial hospitalization or detoxification may achieve temporary abstinence, the IP is highly vulnerable to relapse. Therefore, long-term family therapy with substantial restructuring is required to develop an affiliated family system free of drug abuse. An integrated synthesis of several schools of family therapy techniques may be required.

Because of the enmeshment and explosiveness of these families, the therapist usually must reinforce boundaries, define personal roles, and diminish reactivity. The therapist must be active and directive to keep the emotional tensions within workable limits. Disengagement can be assisted by getting family members involved with external support groups.

### Disintegrated Families

Disintegrated families have a history of reasonable vocational function and family life but a progressive deterioration of family function and, finally, separation from the family. The use of family intervention might seem irrelevant in such a case; however, many of these marriages and families have fallen apart only after severe drug-related behavior. Further, there is often only pseudoindividuation (i.e., false individuation by rebellion, which keeps children close to their family of origin through failure) of the patient from marital, family, and kinship ties.

These families cannot and will not reconstitute during the early phases of rehabilitation. Early therapeutic sessions are usually characterized by apathy or by intense hostility toward the IP; thus, the early stages of treatment should focus primarily on the IP. Potential ties to spouse, immediate family, more distant relatives, and friends should be explored early in treatment, and some contact should be initiated. When abstinence and personal stability have been achieved over several months, the therapist can work with the family to reestablish family ties, but reconstitution of the family unit should not be a necessary goal.

### Absent Families

In absent family systems, there is a total loss of the family of origin and a lack of other permanent relationships. Nevertheless, two types of social network intervention are possible. The first is the elaboration of still-existing friend and relative contacts. Often these social relationships can be revitalized and provide meaningful social support. Second, younger patients have a positive response to peer-group approaches, such as long-term therapeutic communities, NA, church fellowships, and recreational and avocational clubs, which draw them into social relationships and vocational rehabilitation.

These patients can develop new skills and the ability to engage in satisfactory marriage and family life.

## Gender

Drug abuse treatment in the United States has traditionally been male oriented. In countering this one-sided approach, family therapists must be aware that the families of chemically dependent women demonstrate much greater disturbance than those of male patients seeking treatment. These disturbances include greater incidence of chemical dependency of other family members, mental illness, suicide, violence, and physical and sexual abuse. Family-related issues also bring far more women than men into treatment: potential loss of custody of minor children heads the list (Sutker 1981).

Because of the differences between the families of drug-abusing men and those of women, family intervention strategies with women must differ from those for men. Family therapy may be more essential for drug-abusing women because of symbolic or often actual losses of spouse and children. The therapist should not impose a stereotyped view of femininity on female patients; this could intensify the conflicts that may have precipitated the drug use (Sandmaier 1980). The therapist should be sensitive to the specific problems of women and drug-abusing women in our society and should address these issues in treatment.

Drug-abusing women have special concerns about their children and child care. Family therapy may help them see how the parenting role fits into their lives and how to establish parenting skills, perhaps for the first time. Many women have been victimized, including through incest, battering, and rape. Catharsis and understanding of these feelings may be essential before a woman can build new relationships or improve her current ties (Kaufman 1985). Several studies have demonstrated that drug abuse treatment programs that address women's needs and accommodate children have better program retention and treatment outcomes.

For male patients, special issues such as pride and acceptance of their own dependency strivings often need to be addressed (Metsch et al. 1995).

## Family Readjustment After Cessation of Drug Abuse

Once the drug abuse has stopped, the family may enter a honeymoon phase in which major conflicts are denied.

The family may maintain a superficial harmony based on relief and suppression of negative feelings. Alternatively, when the IP stops using drugs, other family problems may be uncovered, particularly in the parent's marriage or in other siblings. These problems, which were present all along but obscured by the IP's drug use, will be "resolved" by the IP's return to symptomatic behavior if not dealt with in family therapy. In the latter case, the family then reunites around its problem person, according to its familiar pathological style.

Too many treatment programs in the drug abuse field focus their efforts on an intensive inpatient or partial hospital program, neglecting aftercare. Many of these programs include a brief but intensive family educational and therapeutic experience but with even less focus on the family in aftercare. These intensive short-term programs have great impact on the family system but only temporarily. The pull of the family homeostatic system will draw the IP and/or other family members back to symptomatic behavior. The family must be worked with for months and often years after drug abuse first abates if a drug-free state is to continue. Ongoing family therapy is also necessary for the emotional well-being of the IP and other family members.

In my experience, family therapy, as described in this chapter, reduces the incidence of premature treatment dropouts, acts as a preventive measure for other family members, and creates structural family changes that interdict the return of both drug and alcohol abuse.

## References

Alexander D, Gwyther R: Alcoholism in adolescents and their families. Pediatr Clin North Am 42:217–234, 1995

Anderson CM, Stewart S: Mastering Resistance: A Practical Guide to Family Therapy. New York, Guilford, 1983

Berenson D: The therapist's relationship with couples with an alcoholic member, in Family Therapy of Drug and Alcohol Abuse. Edited by Kaufman E, Kaufmann P. New York, Gardner, 1979, pp 233–242

Bowen M: Family therapy and family group therapy, in Comprehensive Group Psychotherapy. Edited by Kaplan H, Sadock B. Baltimore, MD, Williams & Wilkins, 1971, pp 181–189

Enders L, Mercier J: Treating chemical dependency: the need for including the family. International Journal of the Addictions 28:507–519, 1993

Friedman AS, Utada A, Morrissey MR: Families of adolescent drug abusers; are these families either "disengaged" or "enmeshed" or both? Fam Process 26:131–148, 1986

Haley J: Problem Solving Therapy. San Francisco, CA, Jossey-Bass, 1977

Hendricks WJ: Use of multifamily counseling groups in treatment of male narcotic addicts. Int J Group Psychother 21:34–90, 1971

Henggeler S, Pickrel S, Brondino M, et al: Eliminating (almost) treatment dropout of substance abusing or dependent delinquents through home-based multisystemic therapy. Am J Psychiatry 153:427–428, 1996

Johnson VE: I'll Quit Tomorrow. New York, Harper & Row, 1973

Kaufman E: Substance Abuse and Family Therapy. New York, Grune & Stratton, 1985

Kaufman E, Kaufmann P: Multiple family therapy: a new direction in the treatment of drug abusers. Am J Drug Alcohol Abuse 4:467–468, 1977

Kaufman E, Pattison EM: Different methods of family therapy in the treatment of alcoholism. J Stud Alcohol 42:951–971, 1981

Maisto S, McKay J, O'Farrell T: Relapse precipitants and behavioral marital therapy. Addict Behav 20:383–393, 1995

McCrady B, Noel NE, Abrams DB, et al: Comparative effectiveness of three types of spousal involvement in outpatient behavioral alcoholism treatment. J Stud Alcohol 14:459–467, 1986

Metsch L, Rivers J, Miller M, et al: Implementation of a family centered treatment program for substance abusing women and their children: barriers and resolutions. J Psychoactive Drugs 27:73–83, 1995

Minuchin S: Families and Family Therapy. Cambridge, MA, Harvard University Press, 1975

Minuchin S, Fishman HC: Family Therapy Techniques. Cambridge, MA, Harvard University Press, 1981

Monti P, Abrams D, Binkoff J, et al: Communication skills training, communication skills training with family and cognitive behavioral mood management training for alcoholics. J Stud Alcohol 51:263–270, 1990

Nakamura K, Takano T: Family involvement for improving the abstinence rate in the rehabilitation process of female alcoholics. International Journal of the Addictions 26:1055–1064, 1991

Noel NE, McCrady BS: Behavioral treatment of an alcohol abuser with the spouse present, in Power to Change: Family Case Studies in the Treatment of Alcoholism. Edited by Kaufman E. New York, Gardner, 1984, pp 23–77

Papp P: Paradoxical strategies and countertransference, in Questions and Answers in the Practice of Family Therapy. Edited by Gurman AS. New York, Brunner/Mazel, 1981, pp 38–44

Sandmaier M: The Invisible Alcoholics: Women and Alcohol Abuse in America. New York, McGraw-Hill, 1980

Silver FC, Panepinto WC, Arnon D: A family approach in treating the pregnant addict, in Developments in the Field of Drug Abuse. Edited by Senay E. Cambridge, MA, Schenkman, 1975, pp 212–217

Stanton MD: Family treatment approaches to drug abuse problems: a review. Fam Process 18:251–280, 1979

Stanton MD: An integrated structural/strategic approach to family therapy. J Marital Fam Ther 7:427–439, 1981

Stanton MD, Todd TC (eds): The Family Therapy of Drug Abuse and Addiction. New York, Guilford, 1982

Stewart M, Brown S: Family functioning following adolescent substance abuse treatment. J Subst Abuse 5:327–339, 1993

Stuart RB: Helping Couples Change. New York, Guilford, 1980

Sutker PB: Drug dependent women: an overview of the literature, in Treatment Services for Drug Dependent Women, Vol 1 (NIDA Publ No ADM-81-1177). Edited by Beschner GM, Reed B, Mondanaro J, et al. Rockville, MD, National Institute on Drug Abuse, 1981, pp 25–51

Thomas E, Yoshioka M, Ager R: Spouse enabling of alcohol abuse: conception, assessment, and modification. J Subst Abuse 8:61–80, 1996

Winer LR, Lorio JP, Scrofford I: Effects of Treatment on Drug Abusers and Family. Report to SOADAP, 1974

Wunderlich RA, Lozes J, Lewis J: Recidivism rates of group therapy participants and other adolescents processed by a juvenile court. Psychotherapy: Research and Practice 11:243–245, 1974

Ziegler-Driscoll G: Family research study at Eagleville Hospital and Rehabilitation Center. Fam Process 16:175–189, 1977

# 5

# Special Approaches and Treatment Programs

# Chapter 35

# Alcoholics Anonymous and Other 12-Step Groups

Chad D. Emrick, Ph.D.

Since its founding in 1935, Alcoholics Anonymous (AA) has grown into a worldwide organization with an estimated nearly 2 million active members in almost 97,000 groups in more than 100 countries (C. D. Emrick, personal communication, December 18, 1997). Its success as a social movement is indisputable, with the organization exercising considerable influence on the professional community and government agencies and programs, as well as on the general public. The shape of public policy and opinion has been substantially determined by the depiction in film, on television, and in the print media of AA's primacy and potency in helping "alcoholics" "recover" from "alcoholism." The primary purpose of this chapter is to inform health care providers about pertinent findings from recent quantitative research on AA and to amplify these findings with observations from contemporary clinical writings concerning the organization. On the basis of these findings, suggestions are given for caregivers for making maximum use of AA and other 12-step groups. In this chapter, the term *12-step group* is used to refer to any group whose structure and function are guided by the Twelve Steps and Twelve Traditions of AA (see Appendix).

## Demographics of Current AA Membership

Findings from the most recent triennial survey of AA members in North America reveal the demographics of the current membership (Alcoholics Anonymous World Services 1997). The average age of AA members is 44 years; 13% of members are age 30 years or younger, and 12% are age 61 years or older. Sixty-seven percent of members are men, and 40% of members age 30 years or younger are women. Married persons make up 39% of the membership, and 28% of members are single, 24% are divorced, 6% are widowed, and 3% are separated. Eighty-six percent of members are white, 5% are black, 4% are Hispanic, and 4% are Native American. Only 7% of members are unemployed. Twenty-nine percent hold professional/technical, manager/administrator, or health professional positions.

When given the chance to identify three factors most responsible for joining AA, 51% of members reported that they had sought the support of AA on their own, whereas 48% were influenced to begin participation in AA by an AA member, 40% were influenced by a treatment facility, 16% by a counseling agency, and 8% by an individual health care provider. A total of 73% of members reported that their physicians knew they belonged to AA. Eighty-six percent of members reported that they belonged to a "home group" (a group identified as being primary for the member). Members reported attending an average of more than two AA meetings per week. Seventy-six percent of members had an AA sponsor (an established member who helps the newcomer go through the Twelve Steps of AA), and 67% of members had obtained a sponsor within 90 days of attending

The author wishes to express his appreciation to Keith Humphreys, Dick Longabaugh, Barbara McCrady, Rudolf Moos, and Scott Tonigan for providing him with manuscripts that were in press, in review, in preparation, or difficult to obtain. Valuable assistance in conducting the literature review was also provided by Nancy Harris. The author is indebted to Nancy Moore, who not only brought her expert computer and editing skills to the preparation of the manuscript but also provided invaluable support and encouragement throughout the project. A special note of appreciation goes to Scott Tonigan, who was central to the acquisition of the research reports reviewed in this chapter and who also contributed substantially to the conceptualization of the project.

an AA meeting. A total of 45% of members have been sober for more than 5 years, 28% have been sober for 1–5 years, and 27% have been sober for less than a year. The average duration of sobriety among active members is more than 6 years. Of the 60% of members who reported having received some type of treatment or counseling before attending an AA meeting, 77% said that the treatment or counseling played an important role in directing them to the organization. After beginning participation in AA, 62% of members received some type of treatment or counseling, with 85% of those members indicating that this treatment or counseling played an important part in their recovery.

## Who Attends 12-Step–Group Meetings?

Multiple variables—both individual and social/interpersonal—have an effect on who attends 12-step–group meetings and who does not. Findings concerning the relative severity of drinking problems of those who choose to go to AA meetings depend, at least in part, on the sample being studied. For example, in a meta-analysis of the AA literature, Tonigan et al. (1996b) found that for outpatient samples, measures of drinking severity were modestly predictive of AA meeting attendance, with greater severity predicting attendance. For inpatient samples, no relation between drinking severity and AA meeting attendance was found.

As with data concerning severity of alcohol problems, the data are inconsistent with respect to the role the support system of the person with a drinking problem plays in seeking the resources of AA. Generally, however, research findings indicate that an individual with a drinking problem, particularly when that person is not being treated in a residential setting, is more likely to join and become involved in AA if family and friends provide weak or inconsistent support for overcoming the problem or if familial and friendship networks are impoverished. This observation appears valid, inasmuch as AA is a social network that supports abstinence and encourages the development of helping relationships among its members.

Ethnicity also appears to affect the decision to become involved in AA, although no consistent pattern has been found. In one sample, among those involved in the criminal justice or welfare systems, whites were more likely than blacks or Hispanics to have attended AA meetings. However, in samples drawn from primary health care settings, blacks were more likely than whites or Hispanics to attend AA meetings (Caetano 1993). In another study (Kessler et al. 1997), blacks were less likely than whites to participate in self-help groups for substance abuse (mostly 12-step groups). In an additional study, Hispanics were found to attend AA meetings less frequently than were whites (Arroyo et al. 1998).

Finally, women with substance abuse disorders have been more likely than men with these disorders to participate in self-help (mostly 12-step) groups (Kessler et al. 1997).

The complex and inconsistent findings concerning the relationship between personal and contextual variables and the selection of AA as a resource provide the health care professional with few, if any, clear guidelines for determining who will be a good match for AA or a similar 12-step group. For now, health care practitioners should keep in mind that *any given individual patient may or may not be a suitable candidate for AA or other 12-step group.* Generally, the more severe the individual's drinking or other identified problem and the fewer the individual's interpersonal supports among family and friends (particularly in the case of an outpatient), the more likely the person is to join AA or another 12-step group.

## Frequency of Use of 12-Step Programs by Individuals With Substance Abuse Disorders

Although AA and other 12-step programs appear to be increasingly used, particularly by women, the level of participation in AA and other 12-step groups by individuals with substance use disorders may still be modest. Hasin and Grant (1995) found that less than 6% of a sample of individuals who formerly drank alcohol who responded to the 1988 National Health Interview Survey (about half of whom met DSM-IV [American Psychiatric Association 1994] criteria for a diagnosis of alcohol use disorder) had attended AA meetings. In reporting data from another national survey, Hasin (1994) observed that less than 4% of the sample of individuals who currently or formerly drank alcohol (only a portion of whom were or had been dependent on alcohol) had attended AA meetings. These recent data highlight the opportunity that exists for increased use of AA and other 12-step programs in the treatment of substance use disorders.

Although apparently relatively few individuals who have substance use disorders attend meetings of AA or other 12-step groups, evidence indicates that most of those persons with substance use disorders who do seek treatment go to 12-step–group meetings.

## Attitudes of Health Care Practitioners Toward 12-Step Programs

Most physicians consider participation in AA an effective treatment for alcoholism, yet physicians often lack belief in the benefits of other forms of alcoholism treatment, despite scientific proof that other treatments can be beneficial. Such lack of belief may result in the underuse of effective professionally delivered treatments for individuals with substance abuse disorders.

Mental health treatment providers and substance abuse counselors vary in their endorsement of 12-step groups, although many believe in the effectiveness of these programs. Depending on theoretical orientation, the mental health treatment provider views 12-step groups more or less as salient therapeutic resources. Similarly, substance abuse treatment providers vary in the degree to which they endorse the spiritual thinking found in the philosophy of AA, their level of endorsement varying according to variables such as their own involvement in 12-step groups, their religious affiliation, and their educational background.

## Effectiveness of AA

Ample research data document the effectiveness of AA (and, by extension, other 12-step groups) in helping individuals maintain a lifestyle free of substance abuse. In effect, research evidence substantiates the intuitive knowledge that 12-step–group members and their families and friends (as well as large numbers of health care providers) possess concerning the effectiveness of 12-step programs.

### Outcome Studies

The results of a meta-analysis of 107 studies on AA (Emrick et al. 1993) suggested that "professionally treated patients who attend AA during or after treatment are more likely to improve in drinking behavior than are patients who do not attend AA, although the chances of drinking improvement are not overall a great deal higher" (p. 57). Also, a positive relationship between AA affiliation and psychological health was observed.

Most salient among the recent original research findings on AA's effectiveness are the findings of investigators at the Center for Health Care Evaluation in Menlo Park, CA. In one of these studies (Humphreys et al. 1997), 515 subjects from an original sample of 631 individuals with previously untreated drinking problems were followed up at 1 year. Of those in the sample who attended AA meetings but did not receive inpatient or outpatient professional treatment, significant improvement was found on all measures of drinking problems as well as on several other measures of functioning. A total of 395 subjects in this sample were followed up at 8 years, at which time it was found that the number of AA meetings attended during the first 3 years of follow-up was positively related to suspension of alcohol problems 8 years after the beginning of the project. AA attendance in the first 3 years of the study also predicted, at 8-year follow-up, lower levels of depression as well as higher-quality relationships with friends and partners or spouses. Of particular note is that inpatient professional treatment services, which some in the sample received, failed to predict any measure of outcome at the 8-year follow-up. Although outpatient professional treatment was found to predict drinking outcome at 8-year follow-up, no other benefits of such treatment were observed. This comparison of AA and outpatient professional treatment leads to the obvious conclusion that at least for this sample of persons with previously untreated drinking problems, AA's therapeutic benefits had a broader effect on alcoholic individuals' lives than did outpatient professional treatment. Humphreys et al. (1997) concluded that compared with professionally delivered inpatient or outpatient treatment, "AA probably helped more people more substantially in this sample" (p. 237).

This same research group evaluated the effects of different types of aftercare treatment 1 year after inpatient treatment in a large sample of veterans (Ouimette et al. 1998). Overall, the results led the researchers to conclude that "12-step attendance and involvement were more strongly related to positive outcomes than was outpatient treatment attendance" (p. 519).

### Patient Satisfaction Surveys

AA's effectiveness can also be evaluated by obtaining patient ratings of satisfaction with treatment services received. One study (Mavis and Stoffelmayr 1994) found that for outpatients, the degree of influence by AA on the professional treatment they received was unrelated to patient satisfaction ratings. For inpatients, on the other hand, AA's influence on professional treatment as well as the degree to which AA beliefs were held by staff *were* related to patient treatment satisfaction, although not necessarily to treatment outcome.

## Treatment Cost

Humphreys and Moos (1996) assessed the effectiveness of AA in another way. The per-person treatment costs for individuals with alcohol problems who sought help as outpatients from professional providers of alcoholism treatment were compared with the costs of treatment for individuals with drinking problems who initially chose to go to AA meetings. Costs were assessed for a 3-year period. Over the course of the study, some individuals within both groups required detoxification and inpatient or residential treatment. Furthermore, some persons who initially went to AA meetings also had outpatient treatment and vice versa. When all cost factors were calculated, those individuals who initially attended AA incurred per-person treatment costs that were 45% lower than the costs incurred by those individuals who initially sought outpatient treatment. AA appears to be as effective as professional outpatient treatment, along with being considerably less costly, in helping at least some individuals with alcohol problems.

## Mechanisms of Effectiveness

Clinical writings assert that AA and, by extension, other 12-step groups are effective because these groups (particularly AA) are readily and widely available, provide a philosophy for living, and present a structured community of individuals who are living life without alcohol. Twelve-step groups are normative organizations that help individuals experience, express, and manage feelings, in part through giving members the opportunity to express feelings in group meetings without fear of negative feedback from others. The groups also help members develop the capacity for self-regulation, increase their sense of self-efficacy, perceive the continuity of time, improve a sense of relationship to others, discover their purpose in life or meaning of life, find a way to connect with the unknown reality that exists outside themselves, engage in self-examination and self-expression, increase their ability to listen to others, and repair vulnerabilities in self-care.

Twelve-step groups teach members healthy strategies for interpreting stressful events and experiences and for behaving in response to those events and experi-

ences. For example, participants are taught to distinguish between controllable and uncontrollable events. Active cognitive coping strategies are provided for dealing with uncontrollable events (e.g., members are instructed to think "This too shall pass" when they are faced with a situation they cannot change). For events that are controllable, use of active behavioral coping strategies is encouraged (e.g., members are taught to deal immediately and actively with interpersonal conflict). No matter the controllability of the event, members are urged to reduce their use of avoidant and destructive coping strategies, such as turning to alcohol or drugs.

In several recent research efforts (Humphreys et al. 1994; Morgenstern et al. 1996; Snow et al. 1994), data have been collected pertaining to the operational ingredients in AA's effectiveness. These data indicate that the more current and actively involved an individual is in AA, the more he or she uses a variety of therapeutic or adaptive processes, including behavioral change processes such as avoidance of high-risk situations and the use of active cognitive and behavioral coping strategies.

## Twelve-Step Group Affiliation and Involvement

The research just referred to elucidates an important aspect of membership in AA and other 12-step groups. Namely, individuals may go to AA and other 12-step–group meetings but limit their active participation in the 12-step community. In other words, 12-step–group attendance (affiliation) must be distinguished from 12-step–group involvement (participation and use). This distinction will guide both clinicians and researchers in assessing more precisely individuals' relationships with 12-step groups.

Some evidence suggests that if individuals merely increase the number of meetings they attend, even if they do not necessarily actively participate in the community in other ways, better outcomes may be achieved. These positive relationships may have been mediated, at least in part, by the fact that frequent attendance of meetings is likely to bring about more active involvement in other aspects of the 12-step community. Just as a man who spends much time in a barbershop is likely to get a haircut, individuals who are frequently in attendance at meetings may be pulled by natural psychological and social forces into numerous aspects of the 12-step community. Thus, practitioners may indirectly achieve the goal of facilitating their patients' active participation in the 12-step community by urging their patients to go to meetings with some frequency.

Although attendance of 12-step–group meetings may be positively associated with good outcome, considerable evidence exists in support of the notion that mere attendance of 12-step–group meetings after treatment is not likely to be as helpful as active involvement in the 12-step community. The apparent reason for this is that greater involvement in AA enhances the use of therapeutic processes, which, in turn, improve outcome.

## Measuring Involvement in 12-Step Groups

Inasmuch as attendance of 12-step–group meetings is not tantamount to active involvement in 12-step communities, treatment evaluators would do well to dispense with the practice of assessing the effectiveness of 12-step programs by measuring the outcomes of those persons who are merely affiliated with 12-step groups. As a corollary to this suggestion, professionally delivered treatment should be assessed with regard to its effectiveness in facilitating *active involvement* in 12-step groups.

Given the role active involvement plays in enhancing the effectiveness of AA and other 12-step groups, practitioners may find it helpful to avail themselves of one or more instruments that have been developed for determining the degree to which a patient is actively involved in AA or another 12-step group. Of these instruments, all of which have at least an adequate degree of reliability, the most notable are those developed by Tonigan et al. (1996a) and Humphreys et al. (1998).

## Health Care Providers and 12-Step Groups

### Facilitating Affiliation and Involvement

Because AA and, by extension, other 12-step groups can play a vital part in recovery from chemical dependency, health care practitioners need to prepare their patients for participation in these groups. To be successful in their efforts, professionals must have an accurate understanding of the nature of 12-step groups. Practitioners need to understand, for example, that AA does *not* assert that "(1) there is only one form of alcoholism or alcohol problem; (2) moderate drinking is impossible for everyone with alcohol problems; (3) alcoholics

should be labeled, confronted aggressively or coerced into treatment; (4) alcoholics are riddled with denial and other defense mechanisms; (5) alcoholism is purely a physical disorder; (6) alcoholism is hereditary; (7) there is only one way to recover; or (8) alcoholics are not responsible for their condition or actions" (Miller and Kurtz 1994, p. 165). Also, clinicians must educate their patients about the difference between religion and spirituality, because AA is often perceived to be a form of religion. AA is essentially a "spiritual program of living" (Miller and Kurtz 1994, p. 165) or "a way of life" (Gold 1994, p. 97). This is the case because "there is no dogma, theology, or creed to be learned" in AA (Chappel 1993, p. 181). Knowledgeable clinicians would do well to keep this understanding in mind as they assist their patients in preparing for AA participation.

Practitioners can also assist their patients in becoming beneficially involved in 12-step groups by offering basic instruction about the meaning and purpose of each of the Twelve Steps and Twelve Traditions of AA. Further, professionals may facilitate involvement by having contact with their patients' sponsors, encouraging their patients to choose home groups and to attend 12-step–group meetings frequently (particularly at the beginning of participation), and offering their patients guidance in becoming actively involved in the 12-step community.

### Learning How to Integrate 12-Step Programs and Professional Treatment

Health care professionals can further enhance the effective use of AA and other 12-step programs by acquiring knowledge about how best to integrate these programs and professional treatment. Integration is advised because persons with substance abuse disorders who combine these two systems of care appear to have better outcomes (at least with respect to substance abuse) than do those who avail themselves of only one form of help.

A common theme in writings regarding integrating 12-step programs and professional treatment is the need for professionals to learn the language and culture of such programs in order to understand in what ways the two systems differ and where the commonalities in concepts and processes exist. For example, both systems facilitate the development of cognitive and behavioral change processes; only the language used to foster this development differs. By possessing a working knowledge of the language and culture of both systems, health care providers can become more skilled in aiding their patients to use both forms of help, simultaneously, alternately, or sequentially.

## Tailoring Facilitation Efforts to Specific Groups

Professionals must tailor their facilitation efforts to the unique characteristics of the particular 12-step groups in which their patients are to become involved. Given the fact that heterogeneity has been found to exist among different AA groups, a patient may find one particular group in his or her community to be compatible with individual needs and other groups to be inappropriate. Health care providers are encouraged to help patients understand the heterogeneity of groups and, therefore, the need to attend meetings of several groups before deciding which group (or groups) is most suitable.

## Becoming Knowledgeable About Special-Population Considerations

Recent reports identify points of consideration (as well as guidelines, in some cases) for facilitating AA involvement by individuals with special characteristics. These reports focused on the following special populations: veterans with posttraumatic stress disorder (Satel et al. 1993), lesbians (Hall 1994), adolescents (Kennedy and Minami 1993), persons with dual disorders (Kurtz et al. 1995), women (Sandoz 1995), persons with substance use disorders who do not have a high degree of need to affiliate with others in a group (Smith 1993), and individuals within particular ethnic groups (Caetano 1993). The health care provider needs to become knowledgeable about, and sensitive to, these special-population issues to be maximally effective in facilitating 12-step–group involvement by his or her patients.

## Matching Patients to 12-Step Groups

An intuitively appealing, though practically difficult, approach to facilitating use and increasing effectiveness of 12-step programs is to find appropriate matches for these programs. The study Project MATCH (Project MATCH Research Group 1998) suggests four matching strategies that health care providers need to keep in mind when considering a referral to AA or another 12-step group.

Although not addressing AA per se but rather assessing treatment that orients individuals to AA, using an approach called 12-step facilitation (TSF) therapy, researchers involved in Project MATCH reported that TSF therapy was more effective in terms of drinking outcome than was an approach directed toward helping patients acquire motivation to stop drinking with a method called motivational enhancement therapy (MET). This difference was observed only for a specific group of patients, however. That group was characterized by not having social networks that clearly discourage any drinking of alcoholic beverages. Thus, health care professionals may wish to be particularly assertive in their efforts to get a patient into a 12-step group when that patient is not surrounded by family and friends who strongly support abstinence from alcohol and other drugs of abuse. Also, Project MATCH found that individuals with drinking problems who were angry at the start of treatment had better drinking outcomes if they were initially helped in a nonconfrontational manner to acquire motivation to change their drinking behavior through the use of MET. Further, Project MATCH data showed that persons who had low anger levels at the start of treatment had better drinking outcomes if they were encouraged at the outset to attend AA (through the use of TSF therapy) or were guided in developing skills for coping with thoughts, feelings, and actions (through the use of cognitive-behavioral coping skills therapy [CBT]) than if they were initially assisted in acquiring motivation to give up drinking (through the use of MET). These findings pertaining to intake levels of anger were significant, although the magnitude of significance was small. Level of anger at intake should, therefore, not be used as a significant basis for steering patients toward 12-step groups. Nevertheless, practitioners may wish to be sensitive to the issue of patient anger in determining how actively to urge their patients to join a 12-step community at the start of treatment.

Also, Project MATCH (Tonigan et al., in press b) found that individuals with drinking problems who were seeking meaning in life were more compatible with outpatient treatment that was oriented toward the 12-step–program philosophy (TSF therapy) than they were with treatment based on CBT or MET. However, this difference did not translate into better drinking outcome rates. Even though drinking outcome rates may not be improved, health care providers may wish to provide 12-step–oriented treatment to their outpatients who are in need of and want to find meaning in life. At least, such treatment appears to be a good fit for these individuals.

## Matching AA Members to Professional Treatment

How are health care providers to approach their patients who have been involved previously in 12-step groups but who are now seeking the services of a professional? Does prior 12-step–group involvement affect the efficacy of certain types of treatment? Project MATCH data include relevant information concerning these questions.

Tonigan et al. (in press a) found that patients who had been involved in AA before being treated in inpatient or intensive residential programs did equally well in each of three psychosocial treatments after inpatient treatment (i.e., TSF therapy, MET, and CBT). Thus, it appears that health care providers need not take prior AA involvement into consideration when assigning inpatients or graduates of intensive residential programs to different psychosocial outpatient treatments.

On the other hand, in the case of alcoholic individuals treated only in an outpatient setting, Project MATCH data suggest that consideration might be given to whether these patients had been involved in AA before such treatment. This consideration derives from the finding that for outpatients who have been involved in AA before professional treatment, TSF treatment seems to be a more compatible, though not necessarily a more effective, option than either CBT or MET.

The reader is cautioned against establishing rigid referral practices on the basis of the data presented in this section. In Project MATCH, differences in treatment response between outpatients with prior AA involvement and outpatients without prior AA involvement were of modest proportions. Future research is needed to generate major qualifiers to the matching strategies suggested by Project MATCH.

## Twelve-Step Programs Are Not Always Helpful

The health care practitioner must keep in mind that any intervention having the power to help some people possesses the potential to harm others. Should a health care provider assume that 12-step–group participation "can't hurt," he or she may fail to intervene appropriately if a patient claims to be worsening through his or her involvement in a 12-step community. Quite often, such a complaint is an expression of resistance to a beneficial membership, in which case helping the patient overcome resistance to active membership is appropriate. On the other hand, the organization may truly be having a negative effect on the patient, as evidenced by increased drug use; exacerbation of depressive symptoms such as helplessness, guilt, or inadequacy perceptions; or lack of improvement in family or social relationships.

If the health care practitioner determines that 12-step–group involvement is having negative effects on his or her patient, the practitioner needs to work with the patient to reverse such effects. One obvious course of action is to assist the patient in finding alternative treatments. Insisting a patient continue attending 12-step–group meetings when he or she is being harmed by such attendance is equivalent to instructing a patient to continue taking medication that not only is failing to improve his or her condition but also is causing harmful side effects. Good medical practice proscribes such behavior.

## Alternatives to 12-Step Groups

Given that AA and other 12-step groups are not always effective and may even be harmful to certain individuals, what community group alternatives do persons with substance abuse disorders have for dealing with their disorders? Rational Recovery is one such alternative to 12-step groups (see Galanter et al. 1993), as are Women for Sobriety (see Kaskutas 1996) and Secular Organizations for Sobriety/Save Our Selves (see Connors and Dermen 1996).

Certainly, Rational Recovery and other alternatives to AA are worthy of the health care provider's attention and are organizations to which the practitioner needs to consider making referrals, when appropriate.

## Summary

In this chapter, a wide spectrum of issues has been covered concerning AA and other 12-step groups. Information has been presented regarding the demographics of the current North American membership of AA, the degree to which AA and other 12-step programs are being used, the beliefs and attitudes held by health care providers concerning AA and other 12-step groups, the effectiveness of AA, the distinction between mere attendance of 12-step–group meetings and active involvement in the 12-step community, strategies for measuring involvement in 12-step groups, ways to enhance the use of 12-step programs, matching patients to 12-step groups, referral of patients involved in 12-step groups to appropriate professional treatment, the limits of 12-step groups, and alternatives to 12-step groups.

A virtual explosion of new understandings concerning AA and other 12-step groups has resulted from the research reviewed in this chapter. Health care providers, armed with greater knowledge than ever before about AA and other 12-step groups, can now offer their patients even wiser counsel regarding such groups.

## References

Alcoholics Anonymous World Services: Alcoholics Anonymous 1996 Membership Survey. New York, Alcoholics Anonymous World Services, 1997

American Psychiatric Association: Diagnostic and Statistical Manual of Mental Disorders, 4th Edition. Washington, DC, American Psychiatric Association, 1994

Arroyo JA, Westerberg VS, Tonigan JS: Comparison of treatment utilization and outcome for Hispanics and non-Hispanic whites. J Stud Alcohol 59:286–291, 1998

Caetano R: Ethnic minority groups and Alcoholics Anonymous: a review, in Research on Alcoholics Anonymous: Opportunities and Alternatives. Edited by McCrady BS, Miller WR. New Brunswick, NJ, Rutgers Center of Alcohol Studies, 1993, pp 209–231

Chappel JN: Long-term recovery from alcoholism. Psychiatr Clin North Am 16:177–187, 1993

Connors GJ, Dermen KH: Characteristics of participants in Secular Organizations for Sobriety (SOS). Am J Drug Alcohol Abuse 22:281–295, 1996

Emrick CD, Tonigan JS, Montgomery H, et al: Alcoholics Anonymous: what is currently known? in Research on Alcoholics Anonymous: Opportunities and Alternatives. Edited by McCrady BS, Miller WR. New Brunswick, NJ, Rutgers Center of Alcohol Studies, 1993, pp 41–76

Galanter M, Egelko S, Edwards H: Rational Recovery: alternative to AA for addiction? Am J Drug Alcohol Abuse 19:499–510, 1993

Gold MS: Neurobiology of addiction and recovery: the brain, the drive for the drug, and the 12-step fellowship. J Subst Abuse Treat 11:93–97, 1994

Hall JM: The experiences of lesbians in Alcoholics Anonymous. West J Nurs Res 16:556–576, 1994

Hasin DS: Treatment/self-help for alcohol-related problems: relationship to social pressure and alcohol dependence. J Stud Alcohol 55:660–666, 1994

Hasin DS, Grant BF: AA and other helpseeking for alcohol problems: former drinkers in the US general population. J Subst Abuse 7:281–292, 1995

Humphreys K, Moos RH: Reduced substance-abuse-related health care costs among voluntary participants in Alcoholics Anonymous. Psychiatr Serv 47:709–713, 1996

Humphreys K, Finney JW, Moos RH: Applying a stress and coping framework to research on mutual help organizations. J Community Psychol 22:312–327, 1994

Humphreys K, Moos RH, Cohen C: Social and community resources and long-term recovery from treated and untreated alcoholism. J Stud Alcohol 58:231–238, 1997

Humphreys K, Kaskutas LA, Weisner C: The Alcoholics Anonymous Affiliation Scale: development, reliability, and norms for diverse treated and untreated populations. Alcohol Clin Exp Res 22:974–978, 1998

Kaskutas LA: Pathways to self-help among Women for Sobriety. Am J Drug Alcohol Abuse 22:259–280, 1996

Kennedy BP, Minami M: The Beech Hill Hospital/Outward Bound Adolescent Chemical Dependency Treatment Program. J Subst Abuse Treat 10:395–406, 1993

Kessler RC, Mickelson KD, Zhao S: Patterns and correlates of self-help group membership in the United States. Social Policy 27:27–46, 1997

Kurtz LF, Garvin CD, Hill EM, et al: Involvement in Alcoholics Anonymous by persons with dual disorders. Alcoholism Treatment Quarterly 12:1–18, 1995

Mavis BE, Stöffelmayr BE: Program factors influencing client satisfaction in alcohol treatment. J Subst Abuse 6:345–354, 1994

Miller WR, Kurtz E: Models of alcoholism used in treatment: contrasting AA and other perspectives with which it is often confused. J Stud Alcohol 55:159–166, 1994

Morgenstern J, Kahler CW, Frey RM, et al: Modeling therapeutic response to 12-step treatment: optimal responders, nonresponders, and partial responders. J Subst Abuse 8:45–59, 1996

Ouimette PC, Moos RH, Finney JW: Influence of outpatient treatment and 12-step group involvement on one-year substance abuse treatment outcomes. J Stud Alcohol 59:513–522, 1998

Project MATCH Research Group: Matching alcoholism treatments to client heterogeneity: Project MATCH three-year drinking outcomes. Alcohol Clin Exp Res 22:1300–1311, 1998

Sandoz CJ: Gender issues in recovery from alcoholism. Alcoholism Treatment Quarterly 12:61–69, 1995

Satel SL, Becker BR, Dan E: Reducing obstacles to affiliation with Alcoholics Anonymous among veterans with PTSD and alcoholism. Hosp Community Psychiatry 44:1061–1065, 1993

Smith AR: The social construction of group dependency in Alcoholics Anonymous. J Drug Issues 23:689–704, 1993

Snow MG, Prochaska JO, Rossi JS: Processes of change in Alcoholics Anonymous: maintenance factors in long-term sobriety. J Stud Alcohol 55:362–371, 1994

Tonigan JS, Connors GJ, Miller WR: Alcoholics Anonymous Involvement (AAI) scale: reliability and norms. Psychology of Addictive Behaviors 10:75–80, 1996a

Tonigan JS, Toscova R, Miller WR: Meta-analysis of the literature on Alcoholics Anonymous: sample and study characteristics moderate findings. J Stud Alcohol 57:65–72, 1996b

Tonigan JS, Miller WR, Connors GJ: Prior Alcoholics Anonymous Involvement and Treatment Outcome: Matching Findings and Causal Chain Analyses, Vol 8 (Project MATCH Monogr). Bethesda, MD, NIAAA (in press a)

Tonigan JS, Miller WR, Connors GJ: The Search for Meaning in Life as a Predictor of Alcoholism Treatment Outcome, Vol 8 (Project MATCH Monogr). Bethesda, MD, NIAAA (in press b)

# Appendix

## The Twelve Steps of Alcoholics Anonymous

1. We admitted we were powerless over alcohol—that our lives had become unmanageable.
2. Came to believe that a Power greater than ourselves could restore us to sanity.
3. Made a decision to turn our will and our lives over to the care of God *as we understood Him.*
4. Made a searching and fearless moral inventory of ourselves.
5. Admitted to God, to ourselves and to another human being the exact nature of our wrongs.
6. Were entirely ready to have God remove all these defects of character.
7. Humbly asked Him to remove our shortcomings.
8. Made a list of all persons we had harmed, and became willing to make amends to them all.
9. Made direct amends to such people wherever possible, except when to do so would injure them or others.
10. Continued to take personal inventory and when we were wrong promptly admitted it.
11. Sought through prayer and meditation to improve our conscious contact with God, *as we understood Him*, praying only for knowledge of His will for us and the power to carry that out.
12. Having had a spiritual awakening as the result of these steps, we tried to carry this message to alcoholics, and to practice these principles in all our affairs.

## The Twelve Traditions of Alcoholics Anonymous

1. Our common welfare should come first; personal recovery depends up A.A. unity.
2. For our group purpose, there is but one ultimate authority—a loving God as He may express Himself in our group conscience. Our leaders are but trusted servants; they do not govern.
3. The only requirement for A.A. membership is a desire to stop drinking.
4. Each group should be autonomous except in matters affecting other groups or A.A. as a whole.
5. Each group has but one primary purpose—to carry its message to the alcoholic who still suffers.
6. An A.A. group ought never endorse, finance, or lend the A.A. name to any related facility or outside enterprise, lest problems of money, property, and prestige divert us from our primary purpose.
7. Every A.A. group ought to be fully self-supporting, declining outside contributions.
8. Alcoholics Anonymous should remain forever non-professional, but our service centers may employ special workers.
9. A.A., as such, ought never be organized; but we may create service boards or committees directly responsible to those they serve.
10. Alcoholics Anonymous has no opinion on outside issues; hence the A.A. name ought never be drawn into public controversy.
11. Our public relations policy is based on attraction rather than promotion; we need always maintain personal anonymity at the level of press, radio, and films.
12. Anonymity is the spiritual foundation of all our traditions, ever reminding us to place principles before personalities.

# Chapter 36

# Inpatient Treatment

Roger D. Weiss, M.D.

In recent years, few subjects in the field of addiction research have generated as much debate as the role of inpatient treatment for patients with substance use disorders. This controversy has been fueled, in part, by the enormous cost of alcoholism treatment in the United States. It has been estimated, for example, that in 1993, more than $6 billion was spent on treating substance-related problems in a wide variety of health care settings (Harwood et al. 1994). On the other hand, the cost to society of alcohol- and drug-related problems themselves was estimated at $168 billion for the year 1991 (American Psychiatric Association 1995). Therefore, establishing effective treatment methods for patients with substance use disorders represents both a public health and a financial priority. Moreover, because the resources available to tackle this issue are finite, treatment should be not only effective but also cost-effective. Because the cost differential between inpatient and outpatient treatment is substantial, and because there is wide variation in per diem costs even among inpatient facilities, determining the proper role of hospital treatment is critical.

Unfortunately, discussions regarding inpatient treatment have often been fueled by political and financial considerations rather than clinical research data. This has sometimes led to the promulgation of extremist positions from proponents of various viewpoints. As a result, arguments are alternately presented that support either the extraordinary effectiveness of (McElrath 1988) or the virtual lack of need for (Miller and Hester 1986) inpatient treatment. This debate has been intensified by the fact that in the late 1970s and early 1980s, private sector (much of it for-profit) hospital treatment

of chemically dependent individuals increased dramatically at the same time that the number of public hospital units decreased. By the mid-1980s, however, inpatient treatment of substance use disorders had become the focus of cost-containment efforts. As clinicians, researchers, government officials, and entrepreneurs attempted to develop less costly alternatives to hospitalization, the rationale for inpatient treatment was questioned, and it has remained a subject of considerable controversy.

In this chapter, I present an overview of inpatient treatment, discuss current thinking about the indications for hospital care, and review research on the efficacy of this treatment modality.

## What Is Inpatient Treatment?

The term *inpatient treatment* actually refers to a variety of forms of treatment that may take place in one of many different settings. Inpatient treatment may involve detoxification, rehabilitation, a combination of the two, or one followed by the other. The treatment may take place either in a medical or general psychiatric setting or on a specialized chemical dependency unit, located in a general hospital, a psychiatric hospital, or a freestanding chemical dependency facility. The level and nature of staffing may vary as well, depending on the facility and the patient population. For example, a substance abuse inpatient facility that treats patients with complex medical comorbidity would have more medical staff than would a facility that primarily treats patients who have both substance use disorders and psychiatric illnesses; the latter program, conversely,

Supported by National Institute on Drug Abuse Grant DA00326 and a grant from the Dr. Ralph and Marian C. Falk Medical Research Trust.

would require more psychiatric staff. The American Society of Addiction Medicine Patient Placement Criteria (1996) distinguish between "medically managed" and "medically monitored" intensive inpatient treatment; some facilities refer to the latter as "acute residential" treatment. This form of treatment offers the psychosocial intensity of an inpatient program, with less need for physician and nursing services. Many clinicians who work with substance-dependent patients recommend that they be treated in a specialized setting because of the availability of peer support and confrontation, the presence of a knowledgeable and dedicated clinical staff, and the fact that substance-abusing patients and patients with other psychiatric disorders may feel uncomfortable around each other. However, I am aware of no studies that have compared the effectiveness of treating chemically dependent patients on a specialized unit as opposed to in a general psychiatric setting.

The recognition during the past decade of the frequent comorbidity of addictive disorders and other psychiatric illness (Brooner et al. 1997; Kessler et al. 1997; Mirin et al. 1991; Regier et al. 1990; Ross et al. 1988) has led to the creation of numerous *dual diagnosis* inpatient units, which are devoted to the treatment of patients with coexisting mental illness and chemical dependency. One problem with the use of the term *dual diagnosis patients* is that it connotes more similarities among this population than actually exist (Weiss et al. 1992). In fact, patients with coexisting mental illness and chemical dependency are diverse. Thus, although such patients may be grouped together for the purpose of creating greater cohesion on an inpatient unit, this desired result may not, in fact, occur. For example, a young, bulimic cocaine-dependent patient will not necessarily feel commonality with an elderly, depressed alcoholic patient merely because they each have two disorders. Thus, although treating patients with dual diagnoses together may make programmatic sense in a particular institution, it is important to recognize the potential pitfalls inherent in this approach.

Dual diagnosis treatment may occur on a unit with a primary psychiatric focus, on a substance abuse unit with a psychiatric consultant (who may be either peripherally involved or well integrated), or on a unit that attempts to integrate principles of psychiatric and chemical dependency treatment. Minkoff (1989), for example, argued that substance-abusing patients, psychiatric patients, and individuals with both types of disorders are best treated together in an integrated therapeutic model. He posited that many of the concepts that have traditionally been associated with chemical dependency treatment (e.g., acceptance of and recovery from a chronic illness, the need to overcome denial and shame, the importance of asking for help, active use of treatment, development of new coping skills) are equally useful in the treatment of patients with other primary psychiatric disorders. Kofoed (1993) suggested that for patients with coexisting psychiatric illness and substance use disorders, the choice of setting should be based on stage of illness, level of motivation, and current symptom picture (e.g., acute withdrawal, substance-induced psychiatric symptoms).

In virtually all inpatient substance abuse programs in the United States, abstinence from all drugs of abuse, including alcohol, is considered the cornerstone of successful treatment. The most common form of inpatient treatment in this country is the *Minnesota Model* (Cook 1988a), so named because of its development in that state in the 1950s. A Minnesota Model treatment program often has a standardized, fixed length of stay, commonly 4 weeks (although the latter aspect of such programs has changed in recent years in favor of more flexibility). After initial detoxification, patients attend educational lectures based on the disease concept of chemical dependency. In addition to learning about the harmful psychological and medical consequences of drugs and alcohol, patients are typically taught about the natural history of alcoholism, the effects of substance abuse on the family, conditioned cues and relapse prevention techniques, the importance of making lifestyle changes, and alternative coping mechanisms. Patients are often asked to recount their drug and alcohol histories in front of other patients and staff members in a forum similar to Alcoholics Anonymous (AA) meetings. The purpose of this exercise is to help patients confront and accept the adverse effects of their substance use; minimization or denial of the severity of their problems is common among patients admitted to inpatient units. Minnesota Model programs rely strongly on group therapy and peer confrontation and heavily employ recovering alcoholic individuals as primary counselors. Systems interventions, including involvement of employers and family members, are also frequently used in these programs.

Many therapy groups in Minnesota Model programs are based on principles of AA and Narcotics Anonymous. Indeed, orienting patients to AA and establishing their continued AA and group therapy involvement after discharge are major goals of such programs.

Psychiatrists may be involved to a variable extent in Minnesota Model treatment programs, often playing a consultative role in dealing with patients who have clear coexisting psychiatric disorders. The degree of integration between the psychiatric and counseling staff is variable, with situations ranging from cooperation and integration to mutual distrust.

Minnesota Model programs provide intense immersion in an environment that is dedicated to challenging addictive thoughts and beliefs through group therapy, peer evaluation, and meetings with counselors who themselves are recovering from substance use disorders. One of the most powerful tools in these programs is the instillation of hope, helpful for many individuals who have felt trapped in their addiction. To this end, these programs generally emphasize the importance of spirituality in the recovery process.

Cook (1988b) referred to the "comprehensive and dogmatic ideology" of Minnesota Model programs as one of their most powerful therapeutic tools. This aspect of these programs, however, has also been a target of criticism. For example, some patients who have objected to the spiritual aspects of these programs or who have found AA distasteful, for whatever reason, have believed that treatment staff members have given up on them. Some such patients are accused of being resistant to treatment, when in fact they are merely being resistant to AA. Alternative self-help groups such as SMART Recovery and Secular Organizations for Sobriety have arisen, in part, in response to this complaint. Despite these criticisms, however, Minnesota Model programs remain popular in the United States.

A few hospitals in the United States practice chemical aversion counterconditioning therapy (Institute of Medicine 1990). In this form of treatment, an emetic drug is paired with the patient's favored alcoholic beverage to induce him or her to associate drinking with nausea and vomiting. Although findings of uncontrolled or partial research on this procedure have indicated favorable outcome (Neuberger et al. 1980; Smith et al. 1991), results of controlled investigations have been less encouraging (Richard 1983).

## The Rationale for Inpatient Treatment

Inpatient treatment offers several advantages over less intensive programs. First, a hospital setting permits a high level of medical supervision and safety for individuals who require intensive physical and/or psychiatric monitoring. Thus, for patients with medically dangerous conditions, or for those who represent an acute danger to themselves or others, inpatient treatment in a hospital setting is indicated. The intensity of inpatient treatment may also be helpful for patients who, for whatever reason, do not respond to lesser measures. For example, hospital treatment may benefit those patients who are too discouraged or unmotivated to regularly undergo outpatient treatment on their own. Moreover, inpatient treatment may benefit some individuals by increasing their awareness of the internal triggers that place them at risk for returning to substance abuse. For example, the intensity and degree of discomfort that some patients feel in a 24-hour-per-day treatment setting may precipitate drug urges. Experiencing these urges in a protected setting, where patients are not in danger of acting on them, may help patients learn enough about their vulnerability to either avoid such situations in the future or learn to cope with them effectively. Moreover, inpatient treatment can help to interrupt a cycle of drug use even in the absence of medically dangerous withdrawal symptoms. For some individuals, the safety of an inpatient environment and a period of respite from a barrage of conditioned cues may help them in their attempt to make life decisions that are in their best interest.

The protectiveness of an inpatient treatment unit also represents one of its potential disadvantages, however. Because one of the major determinants of craving is drug availability (Meyer and Mirin 1979), patients admitted to inpatient units may not experience drug urges simply because they are living in a drug-free environment. Therefore, they may not be fully prepared to handle the drug urges that they will surely have after discharge on returning to a setting in which drugs are once again available. As a result, some inpatient programs gradually expose patients to such triggers by granting them brief passes during their hospital stay.

The other disadvantages of inpatient treatment are obvious. First, hospital treatment is expensive, typically costing more than several hundred dollars per day. Second, patients who enter a hospital are unable to work, care for their families, study, or conduct their normal daily activities. Finally, patients may be stigmatized as a result of having been hospitalized. Thus, inpatient treatment should not be recommended lightly and generally should be used only when less intensive treatment methods either have failed or are considered too risky to attempt.

## When Should Patients Be Hospitalized?

The implementation of cost-containment efforts, when combined with data challenging the effectiveness of inpatient treatment, has led clinicians to hospitalize chemically dependent patients less often than previously. Lists of indications for inpatient treatment have been developed by a variety of health care insurers, managed care companies, hospitals, and professional groups. For example, Hoffman et al. (1991) listed six areas that should be assessed in determining whether a patient requires inpatient treatment, partial hospital care, or less intensive ambulatory treatment. The areas recommended for assessment are 1) acute intoxication and/or withdrawal potential, 2) biomedical conditions and complications, 3) emotional and behavioral conditions or complications, 4) treatment acceptance or resistance, 5) relapse potential, and 6) recovery environment. Although one may argue with the emphasis placed on specific criteria in this or any other document, it is important to recognize the importance of a multidimensional assessment in determining the optimal treatment plan for a chemically dependent patient.

When this assessment has been completed, the clinician must ultimately consider two major issues in deciding whether to hospitalize a patient: 1) the danger that the patient might be imminently harmful to himself or herself or others and 2) the likelihood that the patient would achieve treatment success in a less restrictive environment. These issues can sometimes be extremely difficult to evaluate in patients abusing substances. For example, although patients who engage in active homicidal ideation and/or who have made a recent suicide attempt might be considered clear candidates for hospitalization, danger to self or others may occur in substance-abusing patients in the absence of overt threats or self-destructive or violent acts. Patients who regularly drive while intoxicated, share needles with others, or commit violent crimes to finance their drug habits may also represent a substantial risk to themselves and to society. Because one of the functions of inpatient treatment is to protect the chemically dependent patient and/or the people around him or her during a period of acute danger, decisions regarding the timing of hospitalizing those individuals who represent a chronic recurrent danger are complicated.

An inpatient setting may also provide safety during the process of detoxification. This is particularly true for patients who are being detoxified from alcohol and/or sedative-hypnotic drugs, because withdrawal from these agents may be accompanied by serious medical consequences, including grand mal seizures, delirium, and death. A number of studies have shown that outpatient alcohol detoxification can be accomplished safely and effectively in selected settings (Collins et al.

1990; Hayashida et al. 1989). However, inpatient detoxification is still commonly used because of the risk of potentially serious medical sequelae of withdrawal in combination with the potential unreliability of this patient population. For example, some patients undergoing outpatient alcohol detoxification may concomitantly use other drugs, such as cocaine, which lowers seizure threshold. Although detoxification from therapeutic doses of benzodiazepines is frequently done on an outpatient basis, patients with mixed benzodiazepine and alcohol dependence or patients who have been abusing benzodiazepines are often detoxified as inpatients. Moreover, although opioid withdrawal is generally less medically dangerous than sedative-hypnotic or alcohol withdrawal, the discomfort that many opioid-dependent patients experience in attempting detoxification may diminish the effectiveness of outpatient treatment because of frequent relapses. Some patients who are unable to successfully detoxify from opioids on an outpatient basis may thus be admitted as inpatients to complete the withdrawal process. Complicated detoxification regimens such as those prescribed for patients who are dependent on two or more classes of drugs should generally be administered in a hospital because of the need for frequent reevaluation and adjustment of such regimens. Similarly, patients with significant organ (e.g., cardiac, cerebral, hepatic) dysfunction should generally be detoxified in a hospital.

As can be seen in the latter examples of indications for hospitalization, there is frequently an overlap between the use of the hospital as a protective environment and the use of the hospital to reap the benefits of a maximally intensive treatment program. Some individuals are treated as inpatients because of their actual or perceived inability to benefit from less intensive forms of treatment. Although hospitalization was frequently recommended as an initial treatment modality a decade ago, patients currently are recommended for hospital care either in the case of imminent danger (as described earlier) or after previous outpatient or partial hospital treatment efforts have failed. For patients who need to be in a structured and safe environment while undergoing rehabilitation, medically monitored or "residential" treatment programs may be appropriate, whereas patients who represent a more acute level of danger to themselves or others, those who require intensive medical supervision to undergo detoxification, or those who need psychiatric stabilization during detoxification require medically managed hospital-based treatment.

Studies comparing inpatients and outpatients typically show that the former have more severe substance use histories and a greater prevalence of medical, psychosocial, and vocational difficulties, including less social stability, more unemployment, and a greater preponderance of medical and psychiatric disorders (Harrison et al. 1988; Skinner 1981). Of course, these data in part reflect referral patterns and do not necessarily indicate which populations fare best in which settings. Indeed, a number of studies have been undertaken in which alcohol- or drug-dependent patients were randomly assigned to inpatient treatment or a less intensive alternative. Although these studies have generally shown little difference between inpatient treatment and other modalities (Longabaugh 1988; Miller and Hester 1986), methodological flaws in some of these studies may have affected their results (Nace 1990; Pettinati et al. 1993; Sell 1995). For example, one frequently cited study (Longabaugh et al. 1983) concluded that individuals treated as inpatients or in a partial hospital setting had similar outcomes. However, the patients in each of the two groups in this study were initially treated as inpatients. Another well-known study (Edwards et al. 1977) concluded that a session of outpatient "advice" was as effective as inpatient treatment. However, later analysis of the data from this study showed that patients with more severe alcohol dependence responded better to inpatient treatment than to outpatient treatment (Nace 1990).

One of the difficulties with studies that compare inpatient and outpatient treatment for substance use disorders is related to the framing of the question that is frequently asked, namely, "Which is better: inpatient or outpatient treatment?" This type of head-to-head competition has been called "nonsensical" (Weddington and McLellan 1994) because the goals and structure of and overall approach to treatment of substance dependence problems are different in inpatient and outpatient settings. Asking about the place of inpatient treatment in substance use disorders is similar to asking about the use of inpatient treatment for other chronic illnesses such as diabetes or asthma. These are all lifelong, chronic relapsing illnesses, for which inpatient treatment is required for certain complications and to support the long-term outpatient management of the disorders.

Even in studies in which patients were randomly assigned to inpatient treatment or to intensive outpatient or partial hospital treatment, patients were systematically excluded if they had serious medical, psychiatric, or social comorbidity that might make random assignment to anything other than inpatient treatment haz-

ardous (Weddington and McLellan 1994). For example, although McKay et al. (1997) found that the *psychosocial* dimensions of the original American Society of Addiction Medicine Patient Placement Criteria (Hoffman et al. 1991) did not predict who would do well in inpatient compared with intensive outpatient substance abuse rehabilitation, these researchers did not study the two medical problem areas (acute intoxication/withdrawal and physical complications) in these patient placement criteria, because random treatment assignment of patients meeting those criteria would not have been possible.

Results of studies of randomized treatment have been conflicting with regard to the role of inpatient treatment. Walsh et al. (1991) showed inpatient treatment to be more effective than assignment to AA meetings for alcohol-dependent individuals referred for treatment by their employee assistance programs. However, intermediate-level options (e.g., partial hospitalization or intensive outpatient treatment) were not offered in this study. Alterman et al. (1994) found day hospital treatment of cocaine-dependent patients to be as effective as inpatient treatment at 7-month follow-up, although the treatment completion rate among the inpatients was higher. Pettinati et al. (1993) examined the role of psychiatric severity and level of social supports in predicting the rate of early attrition from inpatient or intensive outpatient treatment. These investigators found that outpatients were more likely to experience early treatment failure, regardless of level of psychiatric severity. At this time, studies are needed to determine which groups of patients are most likely to respond best to which specific types of treatment at which stage of their illnesses.

## Inpatient Treatment: Outcome

### General Findings

A number of follow-up studies involving patients treated in hospital programs have shown impressive success rates. For example, Gilmore et al. (1986) conducted 6-month and 12-month follow-up questionnaire assessments of patients who had been treated at the Hazelden Foundation (a well-known Minnesota Model treatment center) and two other facilities. These researchers found that 73% of those patients who completed the questionnaires (approximately half of the total sample) were abstinent from alcohol at the time of the 6-month assessment, and 58% of respondents were abstinent 1 year after discharge. Wallace et al. (1988) presented similarly favorable results among patients treated at Edgehill Newport, an analogous facility that has since closed. They found that 57% of patients interviewed had been continuously abstinent from alcohol and drugs for 6 months after discharge. However, in both treatment samples, patients who were discharged prematurely or (in the case of the latter study) were unmarried were excluded from the follow-up study. In a 4-year follow-up of inpatients treated at the Carrier Foundation, approximately half of the study sample had favorable outcomes (Pettinati et al. 1982). However, fluctuations in outcome status were common, and only one-fourth of patients were continuously abstinent for all 4 years.

In a study of nearly 75,000 alcoholic men identified through the Department of Veterans Affairs computerized database, Bunn et al. (1994) found that patients who completed extended formal inpatient alcoholism treatment had lower mortality rates in the 3 years after discharge than did patients who had shorter inpatient stays (either because they entered a short-term detoxification program or because they did not complete a longer-term program) or patients who were hospitalized without receiving any formal alcoholism treatment.

Unfortunately, all of the studies mentioned here were uncontrolled and were therefore subject to the biases inherent in uncontrolled research. It is because of these concerns that an increasing number of controlled studies have recently been undertaken. However, as explained earlier, controlled studies are also not immune to methodological flaws. Thus, continued research on this topic is needed.

## Patient Characteristics in Inpatient Treatment Outcome Research

Although, as previously mentioned, some authors have written that inpatient treatment of substance-abusing individuals is often not superior to less intensive treatment, some subgroups of patients do appear to respond better than others to hospitalization. In general, most studies of inpatient treatment have found that the following groups have a better prognosis: patients who are older, patients who are married, patients who abuse alcohol rather than other drugs, and patients whose families participate in treatment (Harrison et al. 1991). Individuals with histories of intravenous drug use or antisocial behavior tend to fare less well in inpatient treatment outcome studies (Harrison et al. 1991).

However, these are the same patient characteristics that portend a favorable prognosis in other forms of substance abuse treatment as well.

## Program Characteristics in Inpatient Treatment Outcome Research

Although a number of studies have focused on the contribution of patient factors in substance abuse treatment outcome, there has been a relative paucity of research on characteristics of inpatient treatment programs that affect prognosis. Although some authors have argued that programmatic variables are less important than patient characteristics in determining treatment outcome (Armor et al. 1976), Cronkite and Moos (1978)—who conducted a path analysis of treatment outcome for 429 alcoholic patients treated in five different programs—concluded that program-related characteristics did influence treatment outcome substantially.

Several different characteristics of inpatient substance abuse treatment have been examined to determine their effect on treatment outcome (Adelman and Weiss 1989), but many of these studies either have been uncontrolled or have not included a carefully matched control group. Moreover, these studies were generally performed in the 1970s and 1980s, when hospitalization was often a first-line treatment for patients with substance use disorders.

In a study of the effect of the referral process on outcome, employed alcoholic individuals who were forced by their employers to enter treatment fared better than individuals who volunteered for treatment (Chopra et al. 1979). Moberg et al. (1982) also found that involving a patient's employer during hospitalization had a beneficial effect on treatment outcome.

Some evidence indicates that the level of emphasis on peer group interaction in a treatment center may affect treatment efficacy as well. Stinson et al. (1979) randomly assigned 466 patients to two alcoholism treatment programs: one with an emphasis on intensive individualized treatment and a high staff-to-patient ratio and the other with a lower staff-to-patient ratio and an emphasis on peer group interaction. Patients who entered the latter program had better treatment outcomes, which suggests the potential importance of peer support in alcoholism treatment programs.

Characteristics of staff members have been examined in several studies. Valle (1981) found that the interpersonal skills of alcoholism counselors in an inpatient treatment facility had a marked effect on treatment outcome in their patients. McLellan et al. (1988) obtained similar results in a study of counselors in an outpatient methadone maintenance program. These findings add weight to the argument that characteristics of specific counselors may substantially affect treatment outcome within a given treatment setting. Studies of inpatient substance abuse programs have also shown that degree of medical orientation may affect treatment outcome. Smart and Gray (1978) studied 792 alcoholic patients in five different inpatient treatment programs and attributed 30% of the variance in dropout rates to treatment variables. These investigators found that patients who were treated in facilities that were more medically oriented were most likely to complete treatment.

Psychiatric assessment has also been shown to be an important part of treatment. For example, in a well-known series of studies, McLellan et al. (1986) demonstrated the importance of severity of psychopathology as a predictor of outcome in patients with substance use disorders. These researchers found that patients with moderate levels of psychiatric severity, as measured by the Addiction Severity Index (McLellan et al. 1980), had the best response to inpatient treatment. The recent development of psychological and pharmacological treatment approaches for specific subgroups of patients with coexisting substance use disorder and psychiatric illness (Weiss and Najavits 1998) illustrates the importance of performing careful psychiatric evaluations in substance-dependent patients.

One of the major components of virtually all inpatient treatment programs is the emphasis on group therapy and attendance of AA meetings. Because of the near ubiquity of these aspects of inpatient treatment, little research has actually been done on their relative contribution to treatment outcome. However, some specific types of groups have been examined, and positive results have been reported for patient-centered groups (Ends and Page 1959), groups teaching social skills (Eriksen et al. 1986), and groups teaching coping skills (Vogel et al. 1997). Other specific interventions that have been reported to be beneficial include thermal and electromyographic biofeedback (Denney et al. 1991) and the use of patient-written treatment contracts (as opposed to staff-written or mutually written contracts) in treatment planning (Vannicelli 1979). Physical exercise also was shown in one study to reduce state and trait anxiety and depression in chemically dependent inpatients, although long-term effects of exercise on outcome are not clear (Palmer et al. 1988).

Aftercare has long been considered an essential part of inpatient treatment; several studies have shown the positive effect of aftercare on treatment outcome. Some researchers have questioned whether the aftercare program itself improves treatment outcome or whether the patients who are likely to have good treatment outcome are also those who participate in aftercare more often. Two studies using cross-lagged analyses have supported the former hypothesis (Costello 1980; Vannicelli 1978). However, McLatchie and Lomp (1988) disputed this theory. These investigators randomly assigned 155 patients who had completed a 4-week inpatient alcoholism treatment program to one of three aftercare groups: 1) a mandated aftercare group; 2) a voluntary aftercare group, in which patients could decide on their own whether to participate; and 3) a group in which patients were dissuaded from participating in aftercare. No differences were found among groups with respect to relapse to drinking, lifestyle, satisfaction, or level of anxiety. However, 66% of patients in the voluntary aftercare group did request aftercare.

Finally, the correlation between length of stay and inpatient treatment outcome has long been a controversial subject. Although some research, as mentioned earlier, found that inpatient treatment offered no more benefit than a session of outpatient advice (Edwards et al. 1977), and one study (Rae 1972) correlated longer hospital stays with poorer outcome, other studies (Finney et al. 1981; McLellan et al. 1982) found a positive correlation between length of stay and treatment response. However, many of these results are difficult to evaluate because of lack of randomization or poor comparability of study groups. Gottheil et al. (1992) examined 131 alcoholic male veterans who received inpatient treatment for the recommended 90 days. The authors found that patients with less severe impairment, as measured by the Addiction Severity Index, fared best. Moreover, in these patients, a longer hospital stay resulted in better treatment outcome. Patients with the most severe problems, on the other hand, did not benefit from increased length of stay. The results of this study are similar to those of Simpson (1979), who found that drug-dependent patients who received less than 90 days of treatment in either inpatient or outpatient programs did less well than patients who received 90 days or more of treatment. Indeed, Gottheil et al. (1992) posited that the more severely psychiatrically ill patients may have failed to benefit from treatment because even 90 days of hospitalization were insufficient to meet their needs.

## Future Implications

The role of inpatient treatment for patients with substance use disorders remains a complex and controversial issue, with public health, political, philosophical, financial, and moral implications attached to its discussion. It is clear, however, that attempting to formulate simplistic guidelines about the use of this treatment modality serves no one's best interest. Thus, the question should not be "Is inpatient treatment effective?" but rather "For which patients is inpatient treatment effective, at what time or times, and for how long?" To that end, the emphasis of current research in this area, particularly that being performed by McLellan et al. (1992), is on defining the *active* and *inert* ingredients of inpatient (and outpatient) treatment in order to discern more clearly which aspects of inpatient treatment are truly effective for which subgroups of patients. As future research helps to clarify these issues, it is hoped that inpatient treatment can have a more stable and defined place in the therapeutic approach to patients with substance use disorders.

## References

Adelman SA, Weiss RD: What is therapeutic about inpatient alcoholism treatment? Hosp Community Psychiatry 40:515–519, 1989

Alterman AI, O'Brien CP, McLellan AT, et al: Effectiveness and costs of inpatient versus day hospital cocaine rehabilitation. J Nerv Ment Dis 182:157–163, 1994

American Psychiatric Association: Practice Guideline for Treatment of Patients With Substance Use Disorders: Alcohol, Cocaine, Opioids. Washington, DC, American Psychiatric Association, 1995

American Society of Addiction Medicine: Patient Placement Criteria for the Treatment of Substance-Related Disorders. Chevy Chase, MD, American Society of Addiction Medicine, 1996

Armor DJ, Polich JM, Stambul H: Alcoholism and Treatment. Santa Monica, CA, Rand Corporation, 1976

Brooner RK, King VL, Kidorf M, et al: Psychiatric and substance use comorbidity among treatment-seeking opioid abusers. Arch Gen Psychiatry 54:71–80, 1997

Bunn JY, Booth BM, Cook CAL, et al: The relationship between mortality and intensity of inpatient alcoholism treatment. Am J Public Health 84:211–214, 1994

Chopra KS, Preston DA, Gerson LW: The effect of constructive coercion on the rehabilitative process: a study of the employed alcoholics in an alcoholism treatment program. J Occup Med 21:749–752, 1979

Collins MN, Burns T, Van Den Berk PAH, et al: A structured programme for out-patient alcohol detoxification. Br J Psychiatry 156:871–874, 1990

Cook CCH: The Minnesota Model in the management of drug and alcohol dependence: miracle, method or myth? Part I: the philosophy and the programme. British Journal of Addiction 83:625–634, 1988a

Cook CCH: The Minnesota Model in the management of drug and alcohol dependence: miracle, method or myth? Part II: evidence and conclusions. British Journal of Addiction 83:735–748, 1988b

Costello RM: Alcoholism aftercare and outcome: cross-lagged panel and path analysis. British Journal of Addiction 75: 49–53, 1980

Cronkite RC, Moos RH: Evaluating alcoholism treatment programs: an integrated approach. J Consult Clin Psychol 46:1105–1119, 1978

Denney MR, Baugh JL, Hardt HD: Sobriety outcome after alcoholism treatment with biofeedback participation: a pilot inpatient study. International Journal of the Addictions 26:335–341, 1991

Edwards G, Orford J, Egert S, et al: Alcoholism: a controlled trial of "treatment" and "advice." J Stud Alcohol 38: 1004–1031, 1977

Ends EJ, Page CW: Group Psychotherapy and Concomitant Psychological Change: Psychological Monographs, Vol 73, No 480. Washington, DC, American Psychological Association, 1959

Eriksen L, Bjornstad S, Gotestam KG: Social skills training in groups for alcoholics: one-year treatment outcome for groups and individuals. Addict Behav 11:309–330, 1986

Finney JW, Moos RH, Chan DA: Length of stay and program component effects in the treatment of alcoholism: a comparison of two techniques for process analyses. J Consult Clin Psychol 49:120–131, 1981

Gilmore K, Jones D, Tamble L: Treatment Benchmarks. Center City, MN, Hazelden, 1986

Gottheil E, McLellan AT, Druley KA: Length of stay, patient severity and treatment outcome: sample data from the field of alcoholism. J Stud Alcohol 53:69–75, 1992

Harrison PA, Hoffman NG, Gibb L, et al: Determinants of chemical dependency treatment placement: clinical, economic, and logistic factors. Psychotherapy 25:356–364, 1988

Harrison PA, Hoffmann NG, Streed SG: Drug and alcohol addiction treatment outcome, in Comprehensive Handbook of Drug and Alcohol Addiction. Edited by Miller NS. New York, Marcel Dekker, 1991, pp 1163–1197

Harwood HJ, Thompson M, Nesmith T: Final Report: Healthcare Reform and Substance Abuse Treatment: The Cost of Financing Under Alternative Approaches. Fairfax, VA, Lewin-VHI, 1994

Hayashida M, Alterman AI, McLellan AT, et al: Comparative effectiveness and costs of inpatient and outpatient detoxification of patients with mild-to-moderate alcohol withdrawal syndrome. N Engl J Med 320:358–365, 1989

Hoffman NG, Halikas JA, Mee-Lee D, et al: Patient Placement Criteria for the Treatment of Psychoactive Substance Use Disorders. Washington, DC, American Society of Addiction Medicine, 1991

Institute of Medicine: Broadening the Base of Treatment for Alcohol Problems. Washington, DC, National Academy Press, 1990

Kessler RC, Crum RC, Warner LA, et al: Lifetime co-occurrence of DSM-III-R alcohol abuse and dependence with other psychiatric disorders in the National Comorbidity Survey. Arch Gen Psychiatry 54:313–321, 1997

Kofoed L: Outpatient vs. inpatient treatment for the chronically mentally ill with substance use disorders. J Addict Dis 12:123–137, 1993

Longabaugh R: Longitudinal outcome studies, in Alcoholism: Origins and Outcome. Edited by Rose RM, Barrett J. New York, Raven, 1988, pp 267–280

Longabaugh R, McGrady B, Fink E, et al: Cost effectiveness of alcoholism treatment in partial vs inpatient settings: six-month outcomes. J Stud Alcohol 44:1049–1071, 1983

McElrath D: The Hazelden Treatment Model. Testimony Before the U.S. Senate Committee on Governmental Affairs, Washington, DC, June 16, 1988

McKay JR, Cacciola JS, McLellan AT, et al: An initial evaluation of the psychosocial dimensions of the American Society of Addiction Medicine criteria for inpatient versus intensive outpatient substance abuse rehabilitation. J Stud Alcohol 58:239–252, 1997

McLatchie BH, Lomp KGE: An experimental investigation of the influence of aftercare on alcoholic relapse. British Journal of Addiction 83:1045–1054, 1988

McLellan AT, Luborsky L, Woody GE, et al: An improved diagnostic evaluation instrument for substance abuse patients: the Addiction Severity Index. J Nerv Ment Dis 168:26–33, 1980

McLellan AT, Luborsky L, O'Brien CP, et al: Is treatment for substance abuse effective? JAMA 247:1423–1428, 1982

McLellan AT, Luborsky L, O'Brien CP: Alcohol and drug abuse treatment in three different populations: is there improvement and is it predictable? Am J Drug Alcohol Abuse 12:101–120, 1986

McLellan AT, Woody GE, Luborsky L, et al: Is the counselor an "active ingredient" in substance abuse rehabilitation? An examination of treatment success among four counselors. J Nerv Ment Dis 176:423–430, 1988

McLellan AT, O'Brien CP, Metzger D, et al: Is substance abuse treatment effective—compared to what? in Addictive States. Edited by O'Brien CP, Jaffe JH. New York, Raven, 1992, pp 231–252

Meyer RE, Mirin SM: The Heroin Stimulus: Implications for a Theory of Addiction. New York, Plenum, 1979

Miller WR, Hester R: Inpatient alcoholism treatment: who benefits? Am Psychol 41:794–805, 1986

Minkoff K: An integrated treatment model for dual diagnosis of psychosis and addiction. Hosp Community Psychiatry 40:1031–1036, 1989

Mirin SM, Weiss RD, Griffin ML, et al: Psychopathology in drug abusers and their families. Compr Psychiatry 32:36–51, 1991

Moberg DP, Krause WK, Klein PE: Post-treatment drinking behavior among inpatients from an industrial alcoholism program. International Journal of the Addictions 17:549–567, 1982

Nace EP: Inpatient treatment of alcoholism: a necessary part of the therapeutic armamentarium. The Psychiatric Hospital 21:9–12, 1990

Neuberger OW, Matarazzo JD, Schmitz RE, et al: One-year follow-up of total abstinence in chronic alcoholic patients following emetic counterconditioning. Alcoholism 4:306–312, 1980

Palmer J, Vacc N, Epstein J: Adult inpatient alcoholics: physical exercise as a treatment intervention. J Stud Alcohol 49:418–421, 1988

Pettinati HM, Sugerman AA, DiDonato N, et al: The natural history of alcoholism over four years after treatment. J Stud Alcohol 43:201–215, 1982

Pettinati HM, Meyers K, Jensen JM, et al: Inpatient vs outpatient treatment for substance dependence revisited. Psychiatr Q 64:173–182, 1993

Rae JB: The influence of wives on the treatment outcome of alcoholics: a follow-up study at two years. Br J Psychiatry 120:601–613, 1972

Regier DA, Farmer ME, Rae DS, et al: Co-morbidity of mental disorders with alcohol and other drug abuse: results from the Epidemiologic Catchment Area (ECA) study. JAMA 264:2511–2518, 1990

Richard GP: Behavioral treatment of excessive drinking. Unpublished dissertation, University of New South Wales, 1983

Ross HE, Glaser FB, Germanson T: The prevalence of psychiatric disorders in patients with alcohol and other drug problems. Arch Gen Psychiatry 45:1023–1031, 1988

Sell J: Academic outcome studies: the research and its misapplication to managed care of alcoholism. Alcoholism Treatment Quarterly 13:17–31, 1995

Simpson DD: The relation of time spent in drug abuse treatment to posttreatment outcome. Am J Psychiatry 136:1449–1453, 1979

Skinner HA: Comparison of clients assigned to inpatient and outpatient treatment for alcoholism and drug addiction. Br J Psychiatry 138:312–320, 1981

Smart RG, Gray G: Multiple predictors of dropout from alcoholism treatment. Arch Gen Psychiatry 35:363–367, 1978

Smith JW, Frawley PJ, Polissar L: Six- and twelve-month abstinence rates in inpatient alcoholics treated with aversion therapy compared with matched inpatients from a treatment registry. Alcohol Clin Exp Res 15:862–870, 1991

Stinson DS, Smith WG, Amidjaya I, et al: Systems of care and treatment outcomes for alcoholic patients. Arch Gen Psychiatry 36:535–539, 1979

Valle SK: Interpersonal functioning of alcoholism counselors and treatment outcome. J Stud Alcohol 42:783–790, 1981

Vannicelli M: Impact of aftercare in the treatment of alcoholics: a cross-lagged panel analysis. J Stud Alcohol 39:1875–1886, 1978

Vannicelli M: Treatment contracts in an inpatient alcoholism treatment setting. J Stud Alcohol 40:457–471, 1979

Vogel PA, Eriksen L, Bjornelv S: Skills training and prediction of follow-up status for chronic alcohol dependent inpatients. European Journal of Psychiatry 11:51–63, 1997

Wallace J, McNeill D, Gilfillan D, et al: Six-month treatment outcomes in socially stable alcoholics: abstinence rates. J Subst Abuse Treat 5:247–252, 1988

Walsh DC, Hingson RW, Merrigan DM, et al: A randomized trial of treatment options for alcohol-abusing workers. N Engl J Med 325:775–782, 1991

Weddington WW, McLellan AT: Substance abuse treatment (letter). Hosp Community Psychiatry 45:80, 1994

Weiss RD, Najavits LM: Overview of treatment modalities for dual diagnosis patients: pharmacotherapy, psychotherapy, and twelve-step programs, in Dual Diagnosis: Substance Abuse and Comorbid Medical and Psychiatric Disorders. Edited by Kranzler HR, Rounsaville BJ. New York, Marcel Dekker, 1998, pp 87–105

Weiss RD, Mirin SM, Frances RJ: The myth of the typical dual diagnosis patient. Hosp Community Psychiatry 43:107–108, 1992

# Chapter 37

# Employee Assistance Programs and Other Workplace Interventions

Paul M. Roman, Ph.D.
Terry C. Blum, Ph.D.

Employee Assistance Programs (EAPs) are currently the principal means for dealing with the population of employed individuals with substance abuse problems. These programs have diffused widely in the United States and are growing in importance internationally. They are not, however, the only workplace strategy focused on substance abuse; therefore, in addition to an in-depth discussion of EAPs, this chapter includes a section on complementary strategies for preventing workplace substance abuse problems.

Within a workplace, an EAP should have two main components: 1) access to professional assistance for implementing the EAP technology (i.e., identification, intervention, motivation, referral, and follow-up) and 2) written policies and procedures whereby the core techniques of EAP work are integrated with the bureaucratic features of the workplace. How these services are provided varies considerably. In some work sites, access to professional assistance may be fairly removed, with contractual services being provided by an organization outside the workplace. Such contracts vary greatly in their scope of services and in the relative control over service delivery exercised by the provider and by the contracting work organization. In other instances, fully staffed EAP units are incorporated into the organization's medical department or human resource management function.

The variations in EAP organization are functions of workplace size and of the physical or geographic distribution of employees. Typical in large multisite organizations is an EAP system that includes an internal EAP staffed by corporate employees, the duties of whom include provision of services to employees at corporate headquarters as well as selection and monitoring of contractors servicing programs in other corporate sites.

EAPs are found in most American workplaces, with the proportion of coverage varying directly with workplace size (Hartwell et al. 1996). Within Fortune 500 corporations, there is virtually always some form of EAP. Such a rate of adoption would seem to imply the importance of EAPs within the behavioral health care system. Although EAPs' widespread presence suggests uniform service coverage, they are variable in terms of attention focused on employee substance abuse problems. These observations suggest a confused picture, and clarification may be achieved through the following discussion of how EAPs evolved in the United States.

## The Discovery of Employed Substance-Abusing Individuals

A main ingredient in the growth of the American alcoholism movement during the 1970s was a symbolic reconstruction and expansion of the alcohol-troubled population, accomplished through the definition of the "hidden alcoholic" (Roman 1991; Roman and Blum 1987). This set the stage for using workplaces as settings for the identification of alcohol problems.

The transformation followed this pattern: one of the residues of the repeal of national Prohibition in 1933 was the pervasive characterization of the American alcoholic person as a "skid row bum." Through the 1950s and 1960s, a small but concerted effort centered on the medicalization of alcohol problems, in part through substituting treatment for incarceration (Schneider 1978). This movement never developed a strong constituency, despite the prominence of some of the recovering alcoholic individuals who were leaders of the movement. Custody of public inebriates, decriminalized or not, was a weak basis for attracting public interest, involvement, and support.

Successful mainstreaming of alcoholism treatment into the health care management system in the United States required a refocus of attention. This attention emerged fitfully but in some ways can be said to have institutionalized the model of the course of alcoholism that was implicit in the ideology of Alcoholics Anonymous (AA). With the support of the National Institute on Alcohol Abuse and Alcoholism (NIAAA) after its founding in 1970, the social construction of the "hidden alcoholic" began in earnest (Roman 1991). Still evident today across multiple media is the characterization of the typical American alcoholic individual as employed (or married to an employed person) with a stable residence and family. But unlike the homeless inebriate reclining or panhandling in public view, the new alcoholic individuals are surrounded by systems of enabling that make identification and referral particularly difficult. In many ways, the thematic features of the hidden alcoholic could be found in the stories of successful members of AA. The theme that most hidden alcoholic persons were employed set the stage for the emergence of EAPs.

## EAPs and Mainstreaming of Substance Abuse Treatment

Compared with other substance abuse–related interventions, EAPs have a curious and important history relative to their mainstreaming of substance abuse treatment (Roman and Blum 1987). The concept of an EAP stems from industrial alcoholism programming that began in the early 1940s as a direct spin-off of

knowledge and influence of AA and its members (Trice and Schonbrunn 1981). In fact, the first industrial alcoholism program, founded at the Dupont Chemical Company, stemmed directly from an unplanned and casual conversation between a Dupont executive and Bill Wilson, cofounder of AA, that took place as they rocked on the front porch of a Massachusetts inn where they both happened to be vacationing.

A key idea that has been embellished in various ways over the years is that in the early or early middle (using Jellinek-type concepts) stages of serious dependence, an individual developing alcoholism gradually manifests measurable job performance deterioration that can be used by supervisors as a basis for motivating behavioral change (Sonnenstuhl and Trice 1986). Through its control over continued employment, the workplace possesses unique leverage to motivate behavioral change (Roman and Trice 1968).

Advantages of such interventions center on the savings rendered to employers by the curbing of alcoholic behavior before there are serious shortfalls in quality or quantity of job output. At the same time, the intervention may allow for conservation of employees in whom there may be substantial investment. Through prompt implementation of these interventions, employers may substantially reduce on-the-job safety risks and reduce the effect of alcoholic behavior on fellow employees and supervisors. In addition to these benefits for employers, keeping one's job and reducing unhealthy behaviors should redound to the personal advantage of affected employees and their families.

As attractive as these concepts of the benefits of reaching employed alcoholic individuals may seem, their diffusion to workplaces was limited through the 1950s and 1960s. Clearly there was relatively little public interest in alcohol problem issues during this period. In retrospect, two further barriers to workplace adoption are evident. First, the acceptance of such a program was tacit admission that alcohol problems existed in a given workplace, a stigma that could affect both customer and stockholder relations. Second, employers needed to be convinced of the viability and feasibility of rehabilitation of workers with alcohol problems.

Less evident was a potentially troublesome flaw in program design. The procedures were based on the assumption that supervisors and managers would be able to accurately target those job performance problems that were linked with alcohol abuse. Although this possible flaw was not widely recognized or discussed, it is clear in retrospect that a singular focus on alcohol not only was problematic from a logistical perspective but also might suggest moralism on the part of the employer, a concept that smacked of the ideology of Prohibition.

Through a series of trial-and-error experiences in which the acceptance of the industrial alcoholism model seemed limited, NIAAA ultimately moved toward the promotion of a new strategy that ultimately became embellished as the philosophy of the EAP (Roman 1975, 1981, 1988; Roman and Trice 1976; Wrich 1973). Instead of focusing on the substance-abusing employee per se, this strategy assumed that a wide variety of *behavioral-medical problems* affect employees and in turn bring about costly disruptions and productivity losses. Substance abuse is only one category of these problems, albeit an important category. Thus, whereas an employer's motives might be questioned if the focus of the program is solely on alcohol, it is acceptable for a manager to state concern about employees' problems that affect job performance.

The new approach sidestepped the issue of supervisory identification of alcoholism by refocusing managerial concern on performance problems rather than on behavioral symptoms. The task of diagnosis of problems, a task that required professional expertise, was given to a program coordinator, employed either within the workplace or by an external contractor. On receiving a referral from a supervisor, the EAP expert was to assess, motivate, and direct those employees to the treatment resources in the community most appropriate for their needs.

The EAP represented an early form of mainstreaming of substance abuse treatment into the broader areas of health care and human resource management. A consequence of the adoption of this model was the need for a particular combination of workplace and clinical expertise, to be incorporated in the role of the EAP coordinator. In many ways, the demands of the role parallel those of an effective occupational physician or nurse, although these models did not guide NIAAA's development of training for EAP coordinators. Instead, experience in alcoholism treatment was considered an important part of an EAP coordinator's background, and at first, recovering alcoholic individuals were often chosen as EAP administrators of workplace programs. Although the representation by this group has diminished over the years, there tends to be a stronger emphasis on the clinical demands of EAP work than on skills in human resources management.

Because of the wide range of employee problems that are presented to an EAP, alcohol and drug abuse problems may not receive adequate attention. The broader program model is likely to be evaluated on its level of activity and overall caseload size. Given this fact, there are three reasons for a relatively minor emphasis on employee substance abuse. First, there is likely more attention given to problems that are less stigmatized and thus more readily addressed by the affected individuals, their supervisors, and their co-workers. Second, it is clear that problems will be less resistant to intervention when the key actors are actively seeking solutions; in contrast, substance abuse disorders are characterized by stumbling blocks such as denial, manipulation, enabling, and the expectation of relapse. Finally, because substance abuse treatment has been mainstreamed into EAPs and the training that EAP coordinators receive emphasizes counseling and psychiatric perspectives, there is no assurance that substance abuse problems will be adequately addressed.

## The EAP Process

An EAP is essentially a broad-based employee problem identification policy. Identification and referral to an EAP can occur through supervisory documentation of deteriorated job performance or through self-referral. After entry into the program, it is the task of the designated EAP counselor or coordinator to identify the nature of the presenting problem. Especially important are the coordinator's skills in determining whether 1) the employee's performance difficulties reflect an underlying behavior problem that fits or approximates a diagnostic category, 2) the performance difficulties are an outcome of a poor fit between abilities and job demands, or 3) the referral is a consequence of underlying interpersonal conflicts or work-group politics. Thus, along with clinical expertise, workplace familiarity and knowledge of organizational behavior are critical for the effective performance of EAP coordinator roles.

After the problem is identified, the EAP coordinator links the individual with the community resources most appropriate for dealing with the problem. The EAP coordinator should function as a case manager from this point on. The essence of the "EAP contract" between the employer and the employee (with the EAP coordinator acting as "broker") is as follows: The employee is responsible for cooperating with the prescribed regimen and must work to resolve the job performance problems that precipitated the referral, and the employer is responsible for providing the employee with opportunities to engage in treatment and must not stigmatize or penalize the employee after treatment is completed—that is, the problem is to be treated like any other employee health issue.

In the case of self-referrals that typically do not involve evidence of job performance problems, this "contract" does not apply. In some ways, inviting self-referrals changes the employer's focus from job performance issues to treatment. While the industrial alcoholism model predominated, there was little mention (and probably little likelihood) of self-referrals. With the introduction of the broad EAP model, employers were urged to offer EAP opportunities to everyone (Wrich 1973), both as an added employee benefit and with the assumption that such early interventions might prevent later job performance problems. Self-referrals are defined as problems for which employees desire assistance. The range of individuals' reasons for desiring EAP assistance escalates rapidly. With an increase in self-referrals, EAP staff are hindered from focusing on identifying and dealing with difficult employee alcohol and drug problems.

In many instances today, EAP counselors do not make external referrals but instead offer a limited number of counseling sessions with the expectation that these will result in a resolution of the problem. This approach may be a reasonable adaptation in the face of limits imposed by managed care and may be a cost-effective component of an external EAP contract. But here there can be little question that the employer is in the "treatment business." Offering such counseling through an internal program may create problems because the employer is functioning as both judge and jury for the employee. If an employee who is counseled by a company representative is later punished for continued deviant behavior that might be alleged to reflect failure of this counseling, employer liability is probable. Thus, direct EAP counseling may make sense given the existence of managed care and an overall desire for health care cost containment, but it is not without pitfalls. In any event, it is unlikely that major substance abuse problems of employees could be effectively managed with brief counseling of this sort, but no studies have evaluated this possibility.

After referral of employees to treatment, the EAP coordinator should monitor employees' progress in counseling or treatment. Sometimes this monitoring includes coordinating the involvement of individuals' supervisors if the treatment plans are so designed. Finally, it is a typical responsibility of the EAP coordinator to engage in structured follow-up with employees after treatment. Such follow-up involves not only dealing with the short-term problem of workplace reentry and encouraging affiliation with a self-help group, but also dealing with longer-term issues of successful rehabilitation and relapse prevention. Sustaining long-term follow-up can be difficult.

## Workplace Functions Served by EAPs

For employers concerned about dealing with employee substance abuse, at least five basic functions can be served by EAPs.

The first function dates back to the earliest industrial alcoholism programs and is *the retention of employees who have developed substance abuse problems but in whom the organization has a substantial training investment.* The intervention strategies embedded in EAPs can be used to reduce or eliminate the job performance problems of substance-abusing employees through motivating these employees to change their behavior with the assistance of counseling or treatment. The image that without EAPs workplace management would identify and dismiss all employees with substance abuse problems is inaccurate. Most managements view employee turnover as expensive and undesirable. Especially when dismissals occur, turnover is disruptive to the morale and efficiency of work groups. Thus turnover prevention or employment conservation is valuable for the work organization.

Further, the use of constructive intervention has a humanitarian dimension. Under an EAP policy, the employer's efforts to support the recovery process usually include extending treatment opportunities with benefit coverage, affording use of sick leave when appropriate, and suspending the steps of progressive discipline when employees demonstrate motivation in response to counseling or treatment that may resolve their substance abuse problems. Such support by employers recognizes employees' personal investments, commitments, and contributions to the workplace. As the stories of individual problems and recovery become known in the workplace, the image of the employer who took supportive action may be enhanced.

A second function of EAPs is *the reduction of supervisory and managerial responsibility for and involvement in counseling employees with substance abuse problems* (Roman 1988). It is typically believed that without supportive assistance from an EAP, supervisors and managers facing a substance-abusing employee engage in denial and try their best to cover up and ignore the problem. The EAP community has long promoted this self-serving belief. However, data show that there is a marked degree of co-worker and supervisory activity relative to the problem as it progresses (Roman et al. 1992; cf. Trice and Beyer 1984). What should be emphasized is that in the absence of an EAP and the supportive resources that it offers to supervisors and managers, there is an implicit policy that delegates the responsibilities for troubled employees to these supervisors and managers. In unionized settings, these implicit expectations also devolve on union shop stewards.

In undertaking these counseling responsibilities by default, some supervisors and managers might be effective in leading an employee to rehabilitation. But there is little reason to expect such outcomes. Without assistance from professional expertise, attempts at intervention will be notably inefficient. Without knowing the "right" thing to do, others in the workplace will be hesitant about and often inconsistent in trying to deal with problems that typically become increasingly visible over time. EAP policy implementation should insist that supervisors and managers seek consultative assistance from an EAP specialist when it is evident that they are dealing with such a problem. When supervisors turn over a problem to an EAP specialist, they continue to be central in the focus on performance issues but there is expert backup from the EAP. Supervisors may initially resist what seems to be interference with their prerogatives, but generally they eventually welcome this assistance and use of the EAP becomes routine.

According to Phillips and Older (1977), the supervisor attempting to deal with substance-abusing subordinates on his or her own commonly develops a parallel troubled behavior pattern, marked by doubts and ambivalence that may come to undermine the supervisor's own job performance and his or her relationships with other subordinates. Phillips and Older (1977) suggested that the performance problems of the troubled supervisor could be as costly to the organization as those of the troubled employee.

With regard to the third function that EAPs may serve, it should be recognized that the contemporary environment within which work organizations operate is characterized by the following:

- A multitude of legal protections that have developed around the employment relationship
- Labor-management relationships that are governed by collective bargaining agreements
- The organization's own guidelines regarding employees' rights, benefits, and responsibilities and the steps in the implementation of progressive discipline

The third function is *the provision for due process for those employees whose substance abuse is affecting the quality and/or quantity of their work performance.*

In a broad sense, the provision of offers of assistance for employees with substance abuse problems may protect the employer against subsequent legal action. Part of the logic behind court decisions regarding this issue is that because a health-based technology exists for dealing with substance abuse and mental health problems, employees should be given the opportunity to use such technology before their employment is terminated because of substandard job performance. This principle is becoming more pervasive in court decisions in which employees charge their employers with discriminatory behavior vis-à-vis a substance abuse issue (Sonnenstuhl and Trice 1986). If properly implemented in an appropriate context of employees' rights and responsibilities, EAP policy can also assure that through the offer of assistance through an EAP, an employer is not committed to ensuring employees' recovery or their permanent employment.

More recently, EAPs have demonstrated their value as a referral outlet for employees who produce positive results on random or for-cause urine screening for the use of illegal drugs (Roman and Blum 1992). Firing such employees is not always a reasonable alternative and invites litigation that may serve no one's interest (Blum 1989). The presence of an EAP encourages approaches in which assistance is offered but responsibility for adequate job performance (and continuing negative drug screens) after receiving assistance is placed on the substance-abusing employee. When the EAP is part of written human resource management policy, the likelihood of equitable implementation is enhanced. EAP sensitivity to due process also fosters an atmosphere in which unions can work cooperatively with management in dealing with substance-abusing employees.

A fourth function is *contribution to overall health care cost containment through encouragement of substance abuse treatment among employees and their dependents.* As a group, untreated alcoholic individuals show levels of health care use that markedly exceed the levels of their nonalcoholic peers. This heavy use pattern extends to their families as well (Fein 1984; Holder 1987; Holder and Hallan 1986). These levels of health care use, by both substance-abusing individuals and their family members, decrease substantially after successful interventions to deal with substance abuse problems.

These reductions in service use do not occur immediately but usually require several years. Thus, although the initial investment involved in providing treatment for substance abuse problems may appear high, follow-up studies indicate that these investments have the ultimate effect of health care cost containment (Smith and Mahoney 1989). Unfortunately, managed care firms have not yet recognized these effects of intensive substance abuse treatment.

A fifth function served by EAPs is *the gatekeeping and channeling of employees' use of substance abuse treatment services, including the use of treatment by employee dependents*. It is expected that EAP providers are well situated to evaluate the quality and cost efficiency of community-based substance abuse treatment alternatives. This knowledge may be superior to that of managed care contractors. Many employers have assigned EAPs to treatment selection roles in the cost-containment process. In some instances, employees and their dependents have lower co-payments if their use of substance abuse or mental health services is channeled through the EAP.

However, involvement of the EAP in the managed care "loop" varies from setting to setting, and cost-containment procedures do not always include the EAP in key gatekeeping decisions. Such inclusion varies with the extent to which the EAP is integrated into human resources management, particularly benefits management. Rather than being empowered in the gatekeeping process, the EAP itself can be the subject of gatekeeping review. EAP staff are sometimes outsiders in conflicts over access to care that result from the use of managed care and utilization review devices. Clear lines of communication and coordination, reasonable outcome-oriented databases, and mutual professional respect are all necessary if EAPs and managed care devices are to produce the desired outcomes of the more effective use of care, particularly in the case of substance abuse. There is a need for proactive efforts to educate workplace leaders about the value of full-scale treatments for substance abuse problems, including structured posttreatment follow-up that is effectively managed by the EAP.

A possible sixth function of EAPs is *aiding in transformation of workplaces' organizational cultures in regard to their images of substance abuse*. Specifically, the effective use of an EAP with substance-abusing employees can promote cultural norms within the organization that treatment rather than punishment is the appropriate approach for dealing with these problems. Further, through the presence of employees who are recovering from substance abuse problems, the reality of effective rehabilitation is communicated to those who are skeptical about recovery.

## The Dynamics of EAP Implementation

How effectively can EAPs fulfill these six functions within workplaces? As substance abuse interventions, EAPs are quite new and have diffused rapidly in many different forms. Thus, few research data exist that allow for conclusive generalizations across a wide range of EAP settings. In general terms, evidence suggests that EAPs "work" in relation to resolving problems of employee substance abuse. There is less information on how different combinations of these components work in concert. We shall return to the discussion of efficacy and its appropriate application to understanding EAPs later in this chapter.

EAPs may be seen as a seedbed for role conflict for EAP administrators. As employees of workplaces either directly or through contract, EAP counselors are expected to maximize the extent of "smoothing" of organizational functioning in their dealing with employed substance abusers (i.e., the identification and management of these employees should minimally interfere with ongoing organizational functioning). On the other hand, as human services professionals, many EAP staff members feel bound to their commitments to maximize the welfare of individuals who have sought help. Thus, the macro-level issues associated with the multiple evaluation criteria that might be used to judge EAP effectiveness may be reflected in ethical issues at the level of individual practitioners. We turn now to the individual components of the EAP implementation process.

### Policy Statements

The development and promulgation of a written policy statement is the initial step in a workplace's implementation of an EAP. The policy serves three functions:

1. It introduces the program, explains its purpose and philosophy, and generates support for the EAP at all levels of the work organization.
2. It spells out the roles of individuals who may be faced with dealing with a substance abuser or other troubled employee. Usually the policy urges that supervisors or managers contact the EAP for assistance rather than attempt a referral on their own.
3. It may ensure equity. By providing rules and guidelines, the policy statement ensures that all employees have equal opportunities to use the services of the program if necessary. Further, it ensures confi-

dentiality and the suspension of disciplinary procedures when applicable.

In settings in which unions are present, the development of the components of the policy statement can be an opportunity for labor and management to work together (Trice and Roman 1972). This can be the foundation for cooperation throughout the implementation process. Joint support of the program by labor and management can be important in encouraging utilization; when union stewards and other representatives are directly involved in the EAP and the developing of the policy statement, supervisors and managers are ensured that they will not generate conflict through use of the program.

The written policy statement also provides a vehicle for top management of the organization to indicate both symbolically and tangibly its support for this new program. Ideally, as a personnel policy, the EAP policy is introduced in such a way that it is seen as something that should be used by supervisors in dealing with problem employees. It can signal a shift in organizational culture to the acceptance of substance abuse as a health problem to be dealt with in the same fashion as other health issues.

Some organizations operate without EAP policy statements or ignore the contents of the policy. Routine review, change, and ongoing diffusion of written policy are needed to maintain the EAP's vitality.

## Policy Diffusion and Training

Diffusion of the policy is essential for EAP use. Since the early days of industrial alcoholism programs, specific training of supervisors and managers has been deemed essential for effective program implementation (Trice and Roman 1972).

Training is typically conducted by EAP staff. Training can serve to acquaint company personnel with the staff and reduce "social distance," but carrying out training is time-consuming for EAP staff, who must also continue to perform their direct service functions.

The logic behind training is that the effectiveness of an EAP rests on a reasonable degree of readiness to use the program on the part of supervisors and managers. Interaction between trainers and trainees helps to ferret out and eliminate barriers to program use.

## EAP Referral Routes

There are many barriers within the context of social interaction that prevent or hinder supervisors from taking definitive actions with respect to subordinates whose behavior deviates from organizational standards (Roman et al. 1992). A variety of beliefs may be embedded in organizational cultures:

- The problem will eventually diminish or go away
- A referral to another part of the organization might injure the subordinate
- The referral may reflect badly on the supervisor's ability to manage
- It is easier to put up with the troublesome situation than to get involved in embarrassing and unpredictable referral actions

These beliefs are norms of organizational culture and may be held by supervisors and employees. They tend to lead supervisors to try to resolve the problem themselves. If such attempts persist, the supervisor and subordinate may become enmeshed in a cycle of enabling and denial with regard to the employee's substance abuse. Certainly such a situation is to be discouraged. But regardless of the effectiveness of supervisory training and other means of encouraging referral, it is typical for knowledge of problematic employee behavior to exist for some time before supervisory referrals occur.

The self-referral is, of course, a different matter. Accumulated knowledge about substance abuse suggests that cases of substantial alcohol and drug dependence are well known to supervisors and co-workers as well as to the affected individual long before any kind of referral occurs. Data from a study of EAP referral routes indicate that most cases involving employee substance abuse that are recorded as self-referrals are indeed the result of informal "nudges" by supervisors and other significant others (Blum and Roman 1992; Blum et al. 1995). In these circumstances, the supervisor does not undertake a formal referral of the employee but threatens that a formal referral will be forthcoming unless the employee undertakes a self-referral. This minimizes the likelihood of the supervisor's becoming enmeshed in red tape or interpersonal complications. Furthermore, from the supervisor's perspective, self-referral accomplishes the same thing as a supervisory referral. But from the perspective of the EAP, when the supervisor fails to become formally involved, as in the case of self-referral, there is less motivation for the individual to engage in genuine behavioral change. Nevertheless, it is clear from this research study that the EAP can greatly reduce the distance between substance-abusing individuals and help for their problems. Over time, the existence of the EAP becomes well known to family members, and in contrast to what has been previously assumed, family members play an important role in motivating self-referrals (Blum and Roman 1992; Blum et al. 1995). Within professional and technical occupational groups, peers may also play major roles in the referral process.

## Diagnosis and Use of Treatment

If referrals are to be carried out effectively, accurate and complete diagnosis is essential. Although some EAPs include staff with professional-level diagnostic skills, other EAPs may use central diagnostic and referral agencies. Use of a central agency frees the employer of the critical and potent diagnostic role and prevents the potential conflicts that diagnosis of one organizational employee by another may create. Further, use of a central diagnostic agency allows for an emphasis on different skills in EAP staffing, thus increasing the likelihood that the incumbent will be more skilled in the organizational dynamics vital to EAP success. On the other hand, conducting diagnosis within the work organization allows short steps in the processing of employees and avoids the potential loss of motivation.

After diagnosis, suggestions are made to the employee with regard to the type of counseling or treatment that may be necessary. According to EAP principles, these are suggestions rather than directives to the employee. This ensures that entry into a treatment regimen is an individual choice and that treatment success is heavily dependent on individual responsibility. An employer may mistakenly perceive constructive confrontation after diagnosis as ordering the employee to "go to treatment or else." This type of confrontation is a directive rather than a suggestion and would create an implied contract that the treatment will solve the employee's problems.

Referral should be based on a matching of the employee's treatment needs, the employee's job and family situation, the kinds of third-party coverage available to pay for treatment, the availability of appropriate facilities, and the accessibility of facilities. What the clinical substance abuse literature calls *treatment matching* includes only a tiny part of these considerations, all of which are vital to treatment success. The complexity of these considerations highlights the necessity for having an EAP specialist rather than a human resources staff member who performs the EAP function on a part-time basis. This complexity also lends support to the concept of integration of the EAP into a workplace, as well as the inadequacy of having contracted services that rely

on methods that reveal only the employee's clinical status.

Thus, in making a referral decision, EAP staff need to be highly informed not only in terms of the effectiveness of the external agency but also in terms of the changing provisions in employee insurance coverage. EAP staff must be fully acquainted with the benefits structure of their organization and any changes that occur in benefits provisions. EAP administrators need to remain well acquainted with the providers of services in the community and to be aware of the appropriateness of these services for their particular workforce. EAP staff must monitor the employee's passage through the substance abuse treatment process.

## Posttreatment

In our own research (Blum and Roman 1992; Blum et al. 1995), we have found that effective posttreatment follow-up is an area of weakness in the operation of most EAPs. At the same time, follow-up associated with most substance abuse treatment programs is notably weak.

One of the greatest advantages of EAP policies is their intention to maintain the substance-abusing worker's employment throughout the course of treatment and recovery. Thus, in the EAP process, a structure for follow-up is usually in place; unlike employees in a work organization, patients whose substance abuse problems are addressed at a treatment center may be widely dispersed after treatment. The workplace also provides opportunities for relapse prevention. Follow-up in the form of self-help–group participation (if appropriate) or brief follow-up counseling sessions can be crucial during this first year after treatment and beyond. Follow-up counseling may reveal needs for changes within work role assignments, such changes often being a key step in relapse prevention.

Lack of attention to follow-up is a consequence not of a lack of follow-up skills but rather of a lack of time on the part of EAP staff. Given the obvious value of follow-up as insurance on the investment in treatment, this is regrettable. The neglect stems from the fact that workplace managers most often use rates of intake to monitor EAP effectiveness. Such rates have obvious face validity relative to what most EAPs are supposed to accomplish, and use of these statistics is encouraged by EAP staff members themselves. The unfortunate consequence is that there is minimal emphasis on posttreatment or long-term outcomes of employees who have used EAP services.

## The Efficacy of EAPs

Although much recent effort has been devoted to surveying the extent and structure of EAPs (Hartwell et al. 1996), we must turn to older data in considering outcomes. It is generally agreed that with EAPs, there is 70% "success." This figure is based on the 1985 reports of coordinators of 317 internal programs and the contract monitors of 126 external programs (Blum and Roman 1989; Blum et al. 1992), as well as a range of other summaries of discrete studies of program functioning (Blum and Roman 1995; Roman and Blum 1996; Sonnenstuhl and Trice 1986). Another way to look at outcome is to examine the operation of discrete components of EAPs. In a classic study, Trice and Beyer (1984) established that constructive confrontation was highly efficacious for alcoholic subordinates described by a sample of supervisors in several locations of a large corporation. Some evidence indicates the impact of supervisory training associated with EAPs (Colan and Schneider 1992; Gerstein et al. 1989). Data from several different sources confirm the cost-effectiveness of EAPs (Blum and Roman 1995; Foote et al. 1978; Smith and Mahoney 1989).

There is no answer to the questions of whether EAPs are efficacious or how efficacious they are under different circumstances. These are the wrong questions because they approach EAPs as though they were a treatment modality, which they are not. The outcomes of most substance abuse referrals to EAPs are tied to the treatment and aftercare that are provided, which are completely independent of the EAP. Thus, to examine outcomes associated with EAPs is to focus on the consequences of multiple inputs wherein it is impossible to disentangle the positive or negative influences of EAP inputs, treatment inputs, or aftercare or follow-up inputs.

These questions are also the wrong questions because they presume that EAPs are primarily focused on patient outcomes. Research indicates that EAP personnel spend substantial amounts of their time in resolving problems between supervisors and subordinates that do not lead to referral, in giving advice to individuals that is not recorded in case records, and in attempting to motivate providers to upgrade the quality of treatment services so that treatment efficacy is improved, to cite only a few examples (Blum and Roman 1989; Blum et al. 1992; Roman and Blum 1987).

Asking about the efficacy of EAPs is similar to asking about the efficacy of employer-provided health insurance benefits or the efficacy of pension plans for retirees. Such questions seem absurd; the immediate and obvious responses are "Efficacious for accomplishing what?" and, perhaps, "What kind of health insurance coverage or pension plan?"

What health insurance and pension plans have in common with EAPs is that they are human resource management practices based in the workplace, not free-standing human service programs. These practices do not lend themselves to typical evaluations of efficacy because there is such a broad range of outcomes of interest to different constituency groups and there is such variation in their structure and design. Concepts of program evaluation assume commonalities across programs and program ingredients, coupled with the opportunity for some form of quasi-experimental design to ascertain program impact.

Thus, EAPs' effectiveness is relative to their workplace settings, their integration within these settings, and the extent to which the EAPs attract the investment of organizational resources. It is impossible to determine EAP efficacy in dealing with employee substance abuse or other employee problems without considering the relatively complex context within which given EAPs function.

## Complements to EAPs

Given the dominance and visibility of EAPs as strategies for addressing employee substance abuse, it is easy to overlook interventions that are complementary to EAPs, several of which are well established. Nearly half of the workforce does not have access to EAPs. Some proportion of this group likely has access to these alternative services. Further, these interventions may have important (but largely undocumented) effects on employee substance abuse.

### Workplace Prohibition of Psychoactive Substance Use

Prohibition is a passive primary prevention strategy. Employers do not mandate that their employees actively do anything; rather, employers require that their employees not perform certain acts that in themselves are not directly linked to work.

Alcohol and drug prohibition rules are found in nearly all workplaces, and prohibition rules predate national Prohibition (Staudenmeier 1989). With the emergence of attention to illegal drugs, these substances were included in the general list of intoxicating substances and were recognized and addressed in prohibition policy statements in most workplaces, beginning about 25 years ago.

Alcohol and work have not always been segregated. Drinking breaks and on-the-job drinking were historically part of many occupational settings (Ames 1989). Industrialists' interests and capitalist economic growth in the nineteenth and early twentieth centuries in America brought about changes in the links between alcohol and work (Rumbarger 1989).

Because it is so thoroughly institutionalized, workplace prohibition cannot be easily evaluated. Even without data, however, it is reasonable to conclude that many accidents and injuries would occur if alcohol and drugs were intermingled with the work technologies of today.

## Workplace Drug Testing

Workplace drug testing has been the subject of much debate as it has rapidly spread over the past two decades (Macdonald and Roman 1995). At issue are whether preemployment screening identifies persons with drug problems and whether it is an accurate predictor of job performance. It has been found that drug use does not necessarily mean a drug problem exists and that evidence of drug use does not necessarily mean that persons cannot perform a job. Further, there is no evidence that preemployment drug screening reduces the rate of drug problems that are subsequently identified in workplaces (Blum 1989; Roman 1989). Nonetheless, it appears that preemployment drug testing may become nearly universally adopted. Parallel tests for alcohol are considerably less feasible, but such testing is being adopted in safety-sensitive industries. This is not a new concept; as part of their rules of conduct or fitness-for-duty regulations, many workplaces have reserved the right to test employees for the presence of alcohol either on suspicion of intoxication or after an accident or other disruptive incident.

Random drug screening of current employees might be seen as a "follow-up" to preemployment screening or possibly as a means of screening those employees who were hired before the practice of preemployment screening was instituted. Random drug screening is associated with the same problems as preemployment screening is, in terms of identification of drug abuse and prediction of job performance. For-cause screening (i.e., screening after the occurrence of a major job performance problem) fits more closely with traditional workplace intervention approaches and, like random screening, is sometimes accompanied by referral to an

EAP for assistance—but often with the condition that such an offer of help will not be repeated. Because for-cause screening is linked to a performance problem, which may involve accidents or injury, this form of screening comes closer to the assumptions underlying EAPs.

In some instances, random drug screening protocols are developed for individuals who have undergone treatment for drug problems under EAP auspices. Here also there may be only a single opportunity for an observed "slip," although EAP policies vary in the extent to which they regard relapse as one of the common or even expected features of recovery from a substance dependence problem. There is anecdotal evidence that the use of random testing can be a strong motivator for treated employees who desire to keep their jobs, and thus this form of testing can be an important complement to EAPs.

## Health Promotion and Stress Management

Recent research suggests that health promotion and wellness programs may be effective in preventing substance abuse problems, with educational programs having a measured impact on self-reported drinking behavior (Stolzfus and Benson 1994). As yet, there is no evidence of widespread use of health risk appraisals or widespread impact of health risk appraisals on employee drinking. It is possible, but undocumented, that employees participating in exercise programs or other health-oriented leisure activities may change their drinking behavior because excessive drinking does not fit in with their new healthy regimen. Likewise, although stress management is a widely used intervention in the workplace, its effect on employee substance abuse has not been studied.

## Peer Intervention Programs and Member Assistance Programs

Since the 1970s, in the fields of medicine, law, dentistry, psychology, and nursing, there have been reports of activities oriented toward resolving problems of alcohol abuse and alcoholism through peer intervention programs. Two intertwined concepts underlie such programs.

First, most professionals often have considerable autonomy in determining work hours, techniques, and other aspects of work styles. Indeed, independence of performance often marks highly creative or heroic accomplishments among professionals. Second, there exists a strong sense of community in these professions, with members of a professional group tending to protect one another from external confrontations, interventions, or criticism. This concept relates to the first: to the extent that supervision of professionals occurs at all, it is typically one member of a profession who is supervising other members.

With these characteristics of work, typical organizationally based interventions directed toward substance abuse problems would have a low likelihood of effectiveness. It would be expected that professionals' problematic performance would be minimally visible, that professionals would readily cover up for one another, and that because of their power and autonomy, professionals would be highly resistant to any form of confrontation.

It is likely that the person who is aware of a professional's drinking or drug problem is another professional. Further, because of professionals' shared interest and shared fate, the deviance, misbehavior, or malpractice of one professional may put at risk the reputation and status of professional peers, as well as jeopardize the credibility of the organization employing the professionals. Finally, because most professions are certified or licensed through boards composed of professional peers, the profession itself may be in the position to threaten sanctions against members with substance use problems.

Peer intervention programs reportedly exist in numerous locations, generally within the local or statewide association of a particular professional group. These programs are operated and governed by members of the profession, sometimes by members who have recovered from their own substance abuse problems.

Although private surveys of some "impaired professionals" programs have been conducted, published evidence in scientific journals about how these programs work and how effective they are is almost nonexistent. As might be expected, outsiders are not readily admitted to carry out objective research studies on the profession, particularly studies of potentially threatening behaviors such as patterns of substance abuse. Given the nature of professional power and how it is maintained, this is not surprising. Although there are a number of partially circulated reports on the success of these programs, they were prepared by the program administrators or by others with a clear vested interest in sustaining good public relations for the professional group.

Another complement to EAPs are member assis-

tance programs. A research group at Cornell University has been examining member assistance programs in labor unions for more than a decade. In a first set of studies (summarized in Sonnenstuhl 1996), the focus was on a small, independent union with an intense drinking culture that included on-the-job drinking. With the slow introduction of a union-based program providing recovery assistance to alcoholic union members (a program staffed by a union member who was a recovering alcoholic individual), the workplace drinking culture gradually changed. Recovery and abstinence became accepted as chosen lifestyles, and near-universal pressure to drink with work peers both on and off the job diminished. This was a dramatic example of a change in what appeared to be deeply entrenched drinking norms, and the study findings suggest that it may be possible to prevent worker disability associated with substance abuse through workplace interventions directed toward cultural change.

A second set of studies by the Cornell group (Bacharach et al. 1994) focused on member assistance programs with broader ranges of coverage. The researchers examined programs in the railroad industry and a program organized by flight attendants. The effect of these programs was found to be almost uniformly positive. There were no means for comparing the efficacy of these member assistance programs with that of management-based EAPs. However, the programs did have an effect on substance abuse among union members across these wide-ranging settings within the transportation industry.

The focus on a single type of industry and the lack of comparison with other types of strategies are obvious limitations of this research. The applicability of the findings is also limited by the relatively small proportion of the United States labor force that is unionized.

It has been said that the American workplace is moving away from hierarchical management and toward a model of peer organization, one involving participative management and collective responsibility. Should these predictions prove correct, peer intervention and member assistance programs may be particularly appropriate means for dealing with employee substance abuse. Perhaps the most attractive feature of these programs is their lack of association with authority, power, and accompanying opportunities for coercion and threat.

On the other hand, peer intervention is not without problems. Defining and implementing actions toward deviant behavior within an informal and undocumented framework may lead to abuses that are greater than in a bureaucratic hierarchy. A bureaucratic system offers opportunities for obtaining equitable treatment and for lodging grievances when authority, procedure, and rules are breached.

## Conclusion

In conclusion, the voluntary adoption of EAPs over the past 20 years, to the point where their coverage extends to more than 40% of the workforce, is testimony to their value as perceived by workplace managers and labor unions. That EAPs are better than some alternative is impossible to address because EAPs are essentially "value-added" human resource management practices in the workplace rather than substitutes or replacements for preexisting structures or programs.

Because EAPs are widely involved in the mainstreaming of substance abuse treatment and identify with this "behavioral health" mainstream, the community of EAP workers lies outside the community of substance abuse interventionists. EAPs are not well understood by this broader community, and the fact that they are perceived as work-based treatment programs leads to frustrations for those who demand simple analyses of the program efficacy. As human resource management practices that are adapted to particular workplace settings, EAPs require a different frame of reference if their value in dealing with substance abuse issues is to be understood. EAPs are, however, unique in their access to the employed population, which includes the vast majority of society's recovering, active, and potential substance-abusing individuals. A better understanding of the roles of EAPs by substance abuse interventionists as well as interventionists whose primary focus is on psychiatric and family problems is critical if treatment interventions are to have a substantial effect on consequences of behaviors linked to substance abuse.

## References

Ames G: Alcohol related movements and their effects on drinking policies in American workplaces: an historical review. Journal of Drug Issues 19:489–510, 1989

Bacharach SB, Bamberger P, Sonnenstuhl WJ: Member Assistance Programs in the Workplace. Ithaca, NY, ILR Press of Cornell University, 1994

Blum TC: The presence and integration of drug abuse intervention in human resource management, in Drugs in the Workplace: Research and Evaluation Data (NIDA Res Monogr No 91). Edited by Guste S. Washington, DC, U.S. Government Printing Office, 1989, pp 271–286

Blum TC, Roman PM: Employee assistance and human resources management, in Research in Personnel and Human Resources Management, Vol 7. Edited by Rowland K, Ferris G. Greenwich, CT, JAI Press, 1989, pp 258–312

Blum TC, Roman PM: Identifying alcoholics and persons with alcohol-related problems in the workplace: a description of EAP clients. Alcohol Health Res World 16:120–128, 1992

Blum TC, Roman PM: Cost Effectiveness and Preventive Impact of Employee Assistance Programs (Center for Substance Abuse Prevention Monogr 5). Washington, DC, Department of Health and Human Services, 1995

Blum TC, Martin JK, Roman PM: A research note on EAP prevalence, components and utilization. Journal of Employee Assistance Research 1:209–229, 1992

Blum TC, Roman PM, Harwood E: Employed women with alcohol problems who seek help from employee assistance programs: description and comparisons, in Recent Developments in Alcoholism, Vol 12. Edited by Galanter M. New York, Plenum, 1995, pp 126–161

Colan NB, Schneider R: The effectiveness of supervisor training: one-year follow-up. Journal of Employee Assistance Research 1:83–95, 1992

Fein R: Alcohol in America: The Price We Pay. Minneapolis, MN, Care Institute, 1984

Foote A, Erfurt J, Strauch P, et al: Cost Effectiveness of Occupational Employee Assistance Programs. Ann Arbor, MI, Institute of Labor and Industrial Relations of the University of Michigan, 1978

Gerstein L, Eichenhofer D, Bayer G, et al: EAP referral training and supervisors' beliefs about troubled workers. Employee Assistance Quarterly 4:15–30, 1989

Hartwell TD, Steele PD, French MT, et al: Aiding troubled employees: the prevalence, cost and characteristics of employee assistance programs in the United States. Am J Public Health 86:804–808, 1996

Holder HD: Alcoholism treatment and potential health care cost savings. Med Care 25:52–71, 1987

Holder HD, Hallan JB: Impact of alcoholism treatment on total health care costs: a six-year study. Adv Alcohol Subst Abuse 6:1–15, 1986

Macdonald S, Roman P (eds): Drug Testing in the Workplace. New York, Plenum, 1995

Phillips DA, Older HJ: A model for counseling troubled supervisors. Alcohol, Health and Research World 2:24–30, 1977

Roman PM: Secondary prevention of alcoholism: problems and prospects in occupational programming. Journal of Drug Issues 5:327–343, 1975

Roman PM: From employee alcoholism to employee assistance: an analysis of the de-emphasis on prevention and on alcoholism problems in work-based programs. J Stud Alcohol 42:244–272, 1981

Roman PM: Growth and transformation in workplace alcoholism programming, in Recent Developments in Alcoholism, Vol 6. Edited by Galanter M. New York, Plenum, 1988, pp 131–158

Roman PM: The use of employee assistance programs to deal with drug abuse in the workplace, in Drugs in the Workplace: Research and Evaluation Data (NIDA Res Monogr 91). Edited by Guste S. Washington, DC, U.S. Government Printing Office, 1989, pp 245–270

Roman PM: Problem definitions and social movement strategies: the disease concept and the hidden alcoholic revisited, in Alcohol: The Development of Sociological Perspectives on Use and Abuse. Edited by Roman PM. New Brunswick, NJ, Center of Alcohol Studies, Rutgers University, 1991, pp 235–254

Roman PM, Blum TC: Notes on the new epidemiology of alcoholism in the USA. Journal of Drug Issues 11:321–332, 1987

Roman PM, Blum TC: Employee assistance and drug screening programs, in Treating Drug Problems, Vol 2. Edited by Gerstein DR. Washington, DC, National Academy of Sciences Press, 1992, pp 221–262

Roman PM, Blum TC: Effectiveness of workplace alcohol problem interventions. American Journal of Health Promotion 11:112–128, 1996

Roman PM, Trice HM: The sick role, labeling theory and the deviant drinker. Int J Soc Psychiatry 12:245–251, 1968

Roman PM, Trice HM: Alcohol abuse in work organizations, in The Biology of Alcoholism, Vol 4: Social Aspects of Alcoholism. Edited by Kissin B, Begleiter H. New York, Plenum, 1976, pp 445–518

Roman PM, Blum TC, Martin JK: "Enabling" of male problem drinkers in work groups. British Journal of Addiction 87:275–289, 1992

Rumbarger JJ: Power, Profits and Prohibition: Alcohol Reform and the Industrializing of America, 1800–1930. Albany, NY, State University of New York, 1989

Schneider J: Deviant drinking as disease: alcoholism as a social accomplishment. Social Problems 25:361–372, 1978

Smith D, Mahoney J: McDonnell Douglas Corporation's EAP produces. The ALMACAN 19:18–26, 1989

Sonnenstuhl WJ: Working Sober. Ithaca, NY, ILR Press of Cornell University Press, 1996

Sonnenstuhl W, Trice HM: Strategies for Employee Assistance Programs: The Crucial Balance (Key Issues 30). Ithaca, NY, ILR Press, 1986

Staudenmeier WJ: Contrasting organizational responses to alcohol and illegal drug abuse among employees. Journal of Drug Issues 19:451–472, 1989

Stolzfus JA, Benson PA: The 3M alcohol and other drug prevention program. Journal of Primary Prevention 15:147–159, 1994

Trice HM, Beyer J: Work-related outcomes of constructive confrontation strategies in a job-based alcoholism program. J Stud Alcohol 45:393–404, 1984

Trice HM, Roman PM: Spirits and Demons at Work: Alcohol and Other Drugs on the Job. Ithaca, NY, Publications Divisions of the New York State School of Industrial and Labor Relations at Cornell University, 1972

Trice HM, Schonbrunn M: A history of job-based alcoholism programs, 1900–1955. Journal of Drug Issues 11:171–198, 1981

Wrich J: The Employee Assistance Program. Center City, MN, Hazelden Foundation, 1973

# Chapter 38

## Community-Based Treatment

Jonathan I. Ritvo, M.D.
James H. Shore, M.D.

In this chapter, we discuss two usages of the term *community-based treatment*. The first usage conforms to the concept of the community role in treatment described in the Institute of Medicine's (IOM's) 1990 landmark report, *Broadening the Base of Treatment for Alcohol Problems* (Institute of Medicine 1990). The IOM committee, defining alcohol treatment as all efforts to address alcohol problems, considered identification and intervention by community institutions to be nonspecialist treatment that was appropriate for many mild to moderate alcohol problems. The second usage relates to specialist treatment services that are not hospital based.

The IOM report proposed a systems approach to alcohol treatment. Our adaptation of this approach for substance abuse treatment is shown in Figure 38–1. The left side of Figure 38–1 represents the community role in treatment. In this chapter, we first consider community settings (primary care settings and colleges) in which brief, noncoercive, motivational interventions have proved effective in reducing alcohol problems. We then consider community settings in which interventions are more coercive (the workplace, social service agencies, and the criminal courts) and where identification can be coordinated with referral for specialist treatment (see the right side of Figure 38–1). Finally, we examine some non-hospital-based specialist treatment interventions, including case management and continuity of care. (Other specialist treatment functions and interventions are discussed elsewhere in this volume.)

## Community Intervention

### Brief Intervention in Primary Care Settings

Studies in the primary care setting have repeatedly shown that professional attention, discussion, education, and follow-up regarding alcohol consumption and its consequences reduce heavy drinking (Graham 1994; Institute of Medicine 1990). In a multinational (eight-site) study, the WHO (World Health Organization) Brief Intervention Study Group (1996) found that in men who drank heavily, primary care setting intervention, consisting of either 5 minutes of simple advice or 20 minutes of brief counseling, substantially decreased daily alcohol consumption and intensity of drinking, compared with control subjects. In another recent study (Fleming et al. 1997), researchers screened 17,695 patients in primary care practices in southern Wisconsin. This yielded 774 patients with drinking problems, excluding those individuals who had recently received alcohol treatment or who had symptoms of dependence. The intervention for half of this group consisted of two 15-minute physician advice sessions 1 month apart and telephone follow-up by a nurse 2 weeks after each session. At 1 year, the intervention group showed positive differences from the control group ($P \leq 0.001$) for number of drinks in the previous week, episodes of binge drinking in the previous month, and excessive drinking in the past week. During the year, men in the intervention group also were hospitalized for fewer days (178 vs. 314 days for control subjects).

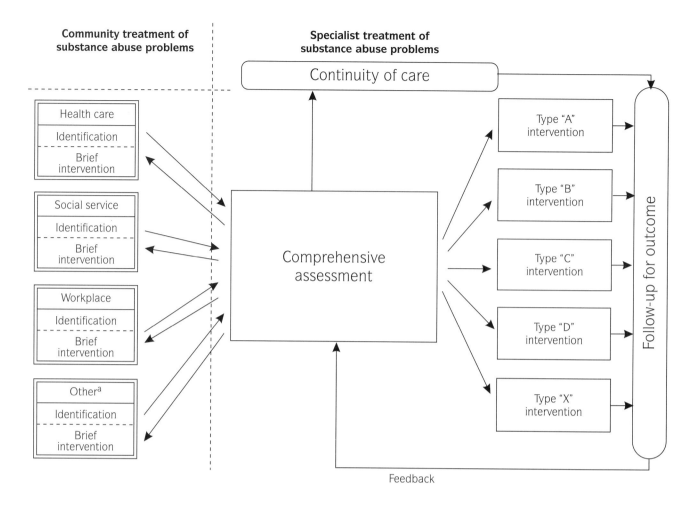

**Figure 38–1.**    Systems model of substance abuse treatment. [a]Education, criminal justice, etc.
*Source.*    Adapted from Institute of Medicine: *Broadening the Base of Treatment for Alcohol Problems.* Washington, DC, National Academy Press, 1990. Copyright 1990, National Academy of Sciences. Courtesy of the National Academy Press. Used with permission.

The screening/brief intervention strategy appears particularly valuable for reducing morbidity in individuals who drink heavily and who may not yet be symptomatic and therefore may not yet be candidates for specialist alcohol treatment. In the current health care system, the primary care physician is well situated to offer brief intervention, continuity of care, and follow-up for this population with mild to moderate alcohol problems, as well as to refer to specialist treatment those persons with increasing alcohol problems who do not respond to brief intervention. Mild to moderate problems are more frequent than dependence. Therefore, the repeatedly replicated findings of brief intervention studies in primary care have profound implications for public health and general medical practice. These findings indicate major cost-effective health consequences from the use of screening instruments to

identify individuals who drink heavily, when combined with the investment of physician time, to inform these patients about the benefits of reducing their drinking.

## Brief Intervention in Colleges

The IOM report (1990) identified college students as a population whose problem drinking is appropriate for a brief intervention approach. The committee recommended a harm-reduction approach designed to foster moderate and safe drinking practices through the use of personalized feedback "containing non-judgmental normative information" and saw this approach as speeding up the normal maturational process of increasing personal responsibility for drinking. G. A. Marlatt's group at the University of Washington described programs for accomplishing this goal with college students who drink heavily (Baer et al. 1992; Dimeff et al. 1995). These programs do not involve diagnosis of alcoholism, labeling of problem drinking, or prescribing of abstinence. Risks, benefits, choices, normative data, and personalized feedback are presented, as are strategies and standards for moderate and safe drinking. Marlatt (1997) reported that first-year students who drank heavily and who received brief, motivational intervention of this type showed greater reductions over 2 years in their drinking rates and drinking problems than did control subjects. Both the intervention and the control groups (as well as their peers who were not considered to drink heavily) showed decreases in drinking and drinking problems over time, consistent with the postulated maturational effect.

## Workplace Drug Testing

The workplace is another site of successful community intervention strategies. Employee Assistance Programs (EAPs) are well suited to providing intervention, follow-up, assessment, and referral for workers. (EAPs are discussed in detail in Roman and Blum, Chapter 37, in this volume.) In this section, we discuss workplace drug testing, an intervention that often originates from management and may be followed up by an EAP. Workplace drug testing can be considered a form of brief intervention because it results in decreased drug use among many employees whose drug use is deterred by the possibility of discovery. For the employee whose drug use is discovered through drug testing, a well-functioning EAP can bring about referral to effective specialist treatment.

Random drug testing has been instituted by some employers, often under federal mandate (e.g., transportation and nuclear power industries). Positive test rates and workplace problems associated with illicit drug use have decreased after random testing has been established (DuPont et al. 1995). DuPont and colleagues (1995) concluded that random drug testing is effective in identifying frequent users and in discouraging casual use in the workplace. Lawental et al. (1996) compared patients coerced into treatment after their drug use was discovered through random drug testing with voluntary patients referred for treatment by the same EAP. The coerced patients were generally negative about entering treatment and reported less problem severity than the self-referred patients did but were more likely to complete treatment. The two groups showed similar improvement at 6 months.

## Social Service Agency Intervention

Child protective services. MacMahon (1997) reviewed the cases of 53 San Mateo County, CA, infants who were reported to child protective services because of urine positive for illicit substances in the newborn nursery. As a result of the hospital report, all mothers were court-ordered to participate in drug rehabilitation programs and undergo urine monitoring. The 44% who complied with treatment had repeatedly drug-free urine. All mothers with repeatedly drug-free urine regained custody of their infants. Forty-six percent of infants were returned to their mothers within a week of birth, and 76% were with a relative within the first month. Seventeen percent were eventually adopted, and another 17% entered long-term guardianship with relatives. Failure of family reunification was most strongly predicted by a history of failed drug treatment, previous involvement with child protective services, or previous removal of a child because of substance abuse and was highly correlated with noncompliance with current treatment and positive urine tests. MacMahon (1997) noted that for a few mothers, the threat of losing custody of the child in the final disposition hearing at 18 months was critical in motivating treatment. In this county with progressive services, the process of identification of maternal substance abuse in the newborn nursery, with intervention and follow-up by child protective services and the courts and referral to specialist treatment, appears to work as intended in the best interest of the child.

Disability and public support. Substance abuse by recipients of public support has been an area of recent societal concern and legislative action. Shaner et al. (1995) documented increased cocaine use, psychiatric symptomatology, and hospitalization among cocaine-dependent schizophrenic individuals around the first of the month, when they received support payments. On the other hand, Frisman and Rosenheck (1997) found no increased drug and alcohol use among homeless mentally ill veterans who received disability payments. Other reports have linked the receipt of large lump-sum retroactive disability payments with negative treatment events, namely premature, abrupt termination of long-term residential substance abuse treatment (Satel et al. 1997) and missed visits and positive urine tests during methadone maintenance (Herbst et al. 1996).

Herbst et al. (1996) also found that use of a representative payee (an agency or individual appointed to receive and manage disability payments for the use and benefit of the disabled individual) protected against the negative effect on treatment of large lump-sum retroactive payments. Rosenheck et al. (1997) found that use of representative payees had a positive effect on homelessness but not on substance abuse in homeless mentally ill individuals. Neither report presented data on the identities or practices of the payees.

Ries and Comtois (1997) described a successful community mental health center program that managed benefits for some of its chronically mentally ill, substance-abusing patients as part of their treatment. Case managers served as representative payees. The form and frequency of disbursement depended on the patient's functional stability, sobriety, and treatment participation. Compared with a control group of patients in the same program who were not on payee status, the payee-managed patients were more likely to be male and to have a diagnosis of schizophrenia, a history of high inpatient utilization, high psychiatric and substance abuse severity, and lower functional stability. However, while they were payee-managed, they showed no difference from the control group in hospitalization, homelessness, or incarceration and attended outpatient services twice as frequently.

Legislative changes in Social Security disability require recipients with alcoholism and/or drug addiction to be referred to treatment, starting with applications filed in July 1996. Benefits based on disability due to alcoholism and/or addiction were terminated on January 1, 1997 (Social Security Administration 1996).

Currently, the Social Security Act (1935) grants the Commissioner of Social Security considerable freedom in appointing representative payees for alcoholic and addicted beneficiaries (with disabilities not based on substance abuse). The act specifies that preference in selection of the payee be given to community-based nonprofit social service agencies and certain agencies of federal, state, and local governments, including those involved in health care activities. We are not aware of any systematic implementation of this aspect of the act. In fact, the Veterans Administration (VA) prohibits its programs and clinicians from serving as payees (Satel 1995). Ries and Dyck (1997) found that most Washington State mental health centers offered payee services but wanted more clearly articulated guidelines. The larger centers were more likely to link the frequency of payments to behavioral goals including goals related to substance abuse. Considering the importance of money in access to substances and in relapses, greater coordination of policy and practice between entitlement/support programs and local treatment services, regarding

the representative payee mechanism, could add considerable leverage to substance abuse treatment.

For the substance-abusing individual, disability benefits may be a mixed blessing. Before supporting an application for disability benefits, the clinician needs to consider potential negative aspects: disincentive to work, ineligibility for many rehabilitation programs, loss of the structuring of time and the rewards for sobriety provided by work, and availability of money for addictive substances. For the substance-abusing patient who is to receive disability payments, the clinician needs to consider a representative payee arrangement as part of the treatment plan.

Adult protective services.    Adult protective services seldom use their guardianship capacity to address the substance abuse/payee problem. In addition, judges are reluctant to appoint conservators for financial incompetence due solely to substance use (Satel 1995). In Denver, even when the substance-abusing individual has dementia, understaffed and underfunded adult protective services often choose not to be involved unless the patient is elderly (J. I. Ritvo, personal observations, 1989–1997). The nonelderly alcoholic patient with dementia needing chronic custodial care who is long estranged from family, unwelcome in nursing homes, and unwanted by adult protective services, the public mental health system, or state hospitals poses a difficult problem and often is left to receive care through emergency and acute hospital services.

## Intervention Through Criminal Courts

Drunk driving.    Alcohol use patterns among drunk drivers range from social drinking to incipient problem drinking to alcohol dependence. In the late 1960s and early 1970s, the Alcohol Safety Action Programs of the National Highway Traffic Safety Administration broadened the response to drunk driving from jail and license actions to education and rehabilitation. Evaluation revealed that social drinkers might benefit from alcohol safety schools, that education and rehabilitation programs had a small effect on recidivism (compared with no intervention) but no effect on subsequent accidents, and that license sanctions were superior to rehabilitation alone in reducing accidents and convictions (Hagen 1985). A recent analysis of California drunk driving convictions supports the last finding (DeYoung 1997). For drunk drivers, specialist interventions such as education and rehabilitation serve as adjuncts to, but not replacements for, community intervention in the form of license sanctions.

Drug abuse.   Because rates of current drug use among arrestees are in the 35%–50% range, the criminal justice system seems a promising setting for substance abuse identification and intervention (Leukefeld et al. 1992). One study in this area found that noncoerced case management offered to arrestees who were using illicit drugs other than marijuana decreased drug use and recidivism and increased use of substance abuse treatment (Rhodes and Gross 1997).

In the past decade, special drug courts around the United States reaffirmed that coerced treatment can be effective and provided a model for cooperation between the criminal justice and specialist treatment systems. Starting in Miami in 1989, specifically designated judges, prosecutors, public defenders, and treatment programs have worked together to divert low-level, nonviolent, drug felony cases (typically crack or cocaine possession) to treatment. The judge monitors progress in treatment and issues bench warrants for relapses and missed court appearances, resulting in jail stays of 2–8 days. Relapse generally does not lead to termination of the treatment program. The daily presence in court of a treatment program representative helps the judge tailor programs flexibly and creatively. Charges are dropped with successful completion of the treatment program. The Miami drug court's 18-month rearrest rate for treatment completers (28%) is about half the rate for comparable offenders at the time the court did not exist (Belenko and Dumanovsky 1993).

Similar surveillance, monitoring, and contingencies for treatment are possible with probation. Currently, 3.2 million Americans, about 58% of the adults in the correctional system, are under probation, and 10% of correctional funding goes to probation programs. Probation officers are stretched thin, with caseloads averaging 258 offenders. Few communities have invested the resources in probation and treatment needed to realize the treatment potential of probation (Petersilia 1997).

## Interventions No Longer Through Criminal Courts

Detoxification.   In *Robinson v. California* (1962), the Supreme Court held that courts could not consider addiction a crime but could require compulsory treatment. The Uniform Alcoholism and Intoxication Treatment Act published by the National Conference of Commissioners on Uniform State Laws in 1971 sought

to replace the criminal justice solution to public drunkenness with medical alternatives. Persons incapacitated by alcohol were to be taken home or to health care or treatment facilities instead of being arrested and held in "drunk tanks." By 1980, more than half of the states had implemented major provisions of the act (Finn 1985).

This legislation led to the development of detoxification centers as the medical alternative to the drunk tank. Detoxification centers developed along two major models, medical and nonmedical or social, the latter relying on rest, comfort, and support, with minimal use of medication or medical examination or supervision (Whitfield et al. 1978). The social model initially predominated because of both low cost and the refusal of some hospitals to provide detoxification services (Finn 1985). Over time the distinction between the two models blurred. As benzodiazepine therapy became the standard treatment for alcohol withdrawal, some nonmedical detoxification centers were "medicalized," in that protocols were adopted by which nurses could administer benzodiazepines. Although the act encouraged voluntary, community-based treatment through a continuum of services, Finn (1985) concluded it did little to rehabilitate the "skid row alcoholic." It replaced one revolving door with another. Although the detoxification center is more hospitable and humane than the drunk tank, decriminalization did little to address the problems essential to rehabilitation, such as inadequate shelter, poverty, and vocational and social handicaps.

Civil commitment.   As part of the decriminalization effort, many states legislated civil commitment procedures, first for alcoholic persons and later for drug-abusing individuals. In 1989, Massachusetts judges frequently initiated commitment as an alternative to criminal prosecution. At that time, the frequency of substance abuse commitment was two-thirds that of mental health commitment (Beane and Beck 1991). Steiner et al. (1995) reviewed 99 consecutive alcohol commitments initiated on patients at Denver General Hospital. They concluded that the commitment procedure offered little benefit for patients with severe medical complications of alcoholism because they found that of the 99 patients, only 2 remained sober after 6 months, whereas 59 had relapsed, and no follow-up was available for 38. Eleven patients died within 2 years of commitment. The Colorado procedure seems to have greater value when initiated by families of alcoholic individuals in the community. In this situation, civil commitment often helps families extricate themselves from enabling positions and apply therapeutic pressure on their alcoholic relatives (J. I. Ritvo, personal observations, 1989–1997).

## Non-Hospital-Based Intervention

The 1990s saw a major change in the paradigm of substance abuse treatment. In the 1980s, the Minnesota Model of 28-day residential treatment followed by aftercare and participation in Alcoholics Anonymous was the treatment standard and was supported by generous reimbursement of inpatient treatment by insurance companies. The pressure to provide less costly, less restrictive treatment has brought about an increase in emphasis on community-based treatment, as opposed to hospital-based treatment, and a restricting of inpatient and intensive residential (Minnesota Model) treatment to cases involving more severe complications or in which "life is in danger or other forms of treatment have failed" (Book et al. 1995). The standard of care now emerging involves individualized treatment determined through the matching of a patient's biopsychosocial needs to a continuum of levels of care and a spectrum of specific services (Gastfriend and McLellan 1997). In this section, we discuss the portion of the continuum of levels of care based in the community.

We conceptualize three types of service components characterizing different levels of care: residential, addiction focused, and comprehensive. Residential services involve provision of room and board. Addiction-focused services encompass the general social support functions of the treatment milieu as well as specific treatments directed toward substance abuse disorders. (For a discussion of many of these treatments, see Zimberg, Chapter 29, and Woody et al., Chapter 30 [individual psychotherapy]; Marlatt et al., Chapter 31 [relapse prevention]; and Emrick, Chapter 35 [self-help groups], in this volume.) Comprehensive services are usually provided by specialized professionals such as psychiatrists, other physicians, nurses, social workers, vocational rehabilitation counselors, or family therapists and address problems that are comorbid with, or secondary to, addiction, problems in areas such as physical and mental health, finances, housing, employment, and family relationships.

### Day Hospital and Intensive Outpatient Treatment

Day or partial hospital programs evolved from inpatient programs through the subtraction of the overnight residential component. In the 1980s, comparisons of day and inpatient programs for alcoholic patients who were physically and psychiatrically stable demonstrated equivalent outcome and 50% cost savings for day programs (Longabaugh et al. 1983; McLachlan and Stein 1982). With cocaine-dependent patients, day programs have had more difficulty with retention in early treatment and inpatient programs have had more difficulty with the transition to aftercare. The net result is equivalent outcome at 6–7 months (Alterman et al. 1994; Schneider et al. 1996). The intense cue reactivity common in cocaine addiction and the lack of a deterrent such as disulfiram may explain why this finding appears specific to cocaine. McKay et al. (1994) described and evaluated a 4-week (27 hours per week) day hospital rehabilitation program at the Philadelphia VA, with most of the features of "Minnesota Model" programs, for individuals who abused alcohol or cocaine. Continuity of care with up to 5 months of twice-weekly aftercare and an emphasis on 12-step–group participation were important features of the program. Alterman et al. (1994) compared the outcome for the cocaine-dependent patients of this day program with the outcome of 28-day inpatient treatment at another Pennsylvania VA, located 35 miles away in Coatesville. After 28 days of inpatient treatment at Coatesville, patients returned to the twice-weekly aftercare program of the Philadelphia VA day program. Although the inpatient program had better treatment retention than the day hospital in the first 28 days, the difference between the groups largely disappeared when the inpatients returned to Philadelphia for aftercare. At 7 months, there was no difference in outcome. Obviously, the goal of facilitating the transition to ongoing self-help–group involvement is more practical for community-based programs than for residential programs at a distance from the patient's community.

The distinction between intensive outpatient (IO) and day or partial hospital programs is not always precise. McKay et al. (1997) used the term *intensive outpatient* when referring to the 27-hour-per-week Philadelphia VA day program (described in the previous paragraph as a day hospital). The American Society of Addiction Medicine's *Patient Placement Criteria for the Treatment of Substance-Related Disorders* (American Society of Addiction Medicine 1996) require 9 hours/week of structured programming for IO programs and 20 hours/week for partial hospital programs. Partial hospital programs are also described as programs having more immediate access to medical and psychiatric services. McLellan et al. (1997) used a similar minimum criterion of 9 hours/week (three sessions per week) to define 10 IO programs and then compared them with 6 "traditional" outpatient programs that offered no more than two 2-hour sessions per week. All programs in both categories were non-hospital-based and oriented toward abstinence. Patients in IO programs engaged in more severe substance use and had more social and health problems. They received more addiction-focused treatment but not more comprehensive services related to medical, employment, family, or social problems. Patients in both kinds of programs showed notable 6-month improvement in substance use, personal health, and social function. These research findings should prompt referring clinicians to examine individual IO programs before assuming they are intensive in terms of comprehensive services. Day or partial hospital programs may better serve patients with substantial need for comprehensive services. IO programs, which often have evening schedules, may better serve patients for whom continued employment or attendance at school is indicated during treatment.

## Treatment in Community Residential Facilities

Community residential facilities (CRFs), often called halfway houses, typically receive patients, from inpatient treatment or detoxification, who are not yet ready for independent living and need the supervision and support of a living environment committed to sobriety. Moos et al. (1995) studied the 127 CRFs to which the VA system referred 10 or more patients in 1991 (4,677 patients were referred). Length of stay in a CRF was associated with a lower rate of readmission to inpatient facilities. Average length of stay was 42 days. Facilities had an average of 30 residents each and generally had a 12-step orientation. Study patients were severely and chronically ill and were more ill than were patients in CRFs in 1987. For one VA hospital, CRF placement improved involvement in aftercare for patients returning from out-of-town inpatient treatment (Hitchcock et al. 1995). In general, halfway houses and CRFs ease the transition between inpatient and independent living for the substance-abusing individual with limited sober social support or limited sober housing resources.

## Outpatient Detoxification

Mild to moderate alcohol withdrawal can be managed on an outpatient basis with safety and efficacy, although the dropout rate is higher than for inpatient detoxifica-

tion (Hayashida et al. 1989). Providing housing and starting psychosocial treatment during detoxification can improve retention (Wiseman et al. 1997). In the study by Wiseman and colleagues (1997), 5% of patients undergoing outpatient detoxification required transfer to inpatient facilities. Outpatient cost can be as low as 10% of inpatient cost (Hayashida et al. 1989).

## Case Management and Continuity of Care

The goals of case management are the assurance of continuity of care and the integration of the other functions of the treatment system (Figure 38–1) (Institute of Medicine 1990). Case management can involve patient advocacy, shepherding of patients through the administrative system, improvising to fill in gaps in services, outreach to involve and retain patients in treatment, provision of basic services such as transportation, and development of an individualized supportive, therapeutic relationship. A wide variety of persons can perform case management or provide continuity of care: psychiatrists, primary care physicians, social workers, case workers, probation officers, college counselors, alcohol or drug counselors and other therapists, Alcoholics Anonymous sponsors, trained laypersons, or even the patient himself or herself (Institute of Medicine 1990). EAPs and physician health programs and similar programs for dentists, nurses, and other health care professionals are community institutions that perform case management and continuity-of-care functions. Physician and other health care professional programs perform this function by integrating community identification, patient advocacy, relations with licensing boards, assessment and referral for specialist treatment, and ongoing monitoring.

Multiple factors determine whether patients will require case management to achieve optimal therapeutic results. On the patient's side, these factors include motivation or resistance, experience, knowledge, intelligence, and other internal and external resources or deficits. On the system's side, relevant variables include the complexity of the system, the accessibility of the relevant components, and how well the components are integrated with one another and match the patient's needs. Perhaps most important, many patients need individualized, caring longitudinal relationships that may not be present elsewhere in treatment. Given the variation in types of case management, and in the settings, populations, and systems in which it is applied, it is not surprising that the literature on the efficacy of case management for substance-abusing patients is inconsistent.

A maximal paradigm for case management is the assertive community treatment (ACT) model that provides a full range of services for the chronically mentally ill through a community-based team operating around the clock (Burns and Santos 1995). The ACT approach has shown impressive results for substance abuse in chronically mentally ill populations (Drake et al. 1993; Ries and Comtois 1997). Another case management approach, described as patient driven and strengths based, proved useful for substance-abusing individuals in a VA rehabilitation program who were interested in employment assistance. In addition to helping patients gain access to resources in other areas, case managers were particularly active and flexible in assisting patients with employment. Techniques included using past successes to identify employment-related strengths and accompanying patients on job searches (Siegal et al. 1996).

For homeless substance-abusing persons seeking treatment, case management approaches that are more office-based, more time-limited, and more directed toward arranging rather than directly providing services have not been shown to have a differential effect beyond the general short-term improvement that accompanies seeking treatment for substance abuse (Braucht et al. 1995; Stahler 1995; Stahler et al. 1995). Case management approaches less intensive than the ACT approach have been effective in engaging and helping substance-abusing individuals who were not seeking treatment, as in the arrestee study mentioned earlier (Rhodes and Gross 1997) and the Chronic Inebriate Case Management (CICM) program in Seattle (Freng et al. 1995). It is noteworthy that the arrestee study attributed its case management effect more to personalized supportive relationships than to referral activity. The CICM program targeted the most frequent users of the county detoxification center. Initially, this program focused on benefits, payee arrangements, and housing rather than on substance abuse treatment. Targeted patients demonstrated improvement in all of these areas, as well as a decrease in detoxification center admissions.

## Summary

In this chapter, we reviewed substance abuse identification and intervention in a variety of community settings and we examined both the community-based portion of the continuum of levels of care and the case management and continuity-of-care approaches that serve to integrate the complex treatment system for the individ- ual patient. As a framework, we used a model for the substance abuse treatment system, which relates the identification and intervention efforts of community institutions to the assessment, intervention, follow-up, and continuity-of-care functions of the specialist portion of the treatment system. We described instances, such as in drug courts and child protective services in some communities, in which the relationship between community institutions and specialist treatment has been fruitful. We identified promising community interventions, in primary care settings and colleges, that we hope will be disseminated, and we identified community institutions, such as probation and public support programs, in which little of the potential for community-based substance abuse treatment has been realized.

## References

Alterman AI, O'Brien CP, McLellan AT: Effectiveness and costs of inpatient versus day hospital rehabilitation. J Nerv Ment Dis 182:157–163, 1994

American Society of Addiction Medicine: Patient Placement Criteria for the Treatment of Substance-Related Disorders, 2nd Edition. Chevy Chase, MD, American Society of Addiction Medicine, 1996

Baer JS, Marlatt GA, Kivlahan DR, et al: An experimental test of three methods of alcohol risk reduction with young adults. J Consult Clin Psychol 60:974–979, 1992

Beane EA, Beck JC: Court based civil commitment of alcoholics and substance abusers. Bull Am Acad Psychiatry Law 19:359–366, 1991

Belenko S, Dumanovsky T: Special Drug Courts: Program Brief. Washington, DC, Bureau of Justice Assistance, 1993. Available at: http://www.ncjrs.org/txtfiles/spdc.txt

Book J, Harbin H, Marques C, et al: The ASAM and Green Spring alcohol and drug detoxification and rehabilitation criteria for utilization review. Am J Addict 4:187–192, 1995

Braucht GN, Reichardt CS, Geissler LJ, et al: Effective services for homeless substance abusers. J Addict Dis 14:87–109, 1995

Burns BJ, Santos AB: Assertive community treatment: an update of randomized trials. Psychiatr Serv 46:669–675, 1995

DeYoung DJ: An evaluation of alcohol treatment, driver license actions and jail terms in reducing drunk driving recidivism in California. Addiction 92:989–997, 1997

Dimeff LA, Kilmer J, Baer JS, et al: Binge drinking in college. JAMA 273:1903–1904, 1995

Drake RE, McHugo GJ, Noordsy DL: Treatment of alcoholism among schizophrenic outpatients: 4-year outcomes. Am J Psychiatry 150:328–329, 1993

DuPont RL, Griffin DW, Siskin BR, et al: Random drug testing at work: the probability of identifying frequent and infrequent users of illicit drugs. J Addict Dis 14:1–17, 1995

Finn P: Decriminalization of public drunkenness: response of the health care system. J Stud Alcohol 46:7–23, 1985

Fleming MF, Barry KL, Manwell LB, et al: Brief physician advice for problem alcohol drinkers. JAMA 277:1039–1045, 1997

Freng SA, Carr DI, Cox GB: Intensive case management for chronic public inebriates: a pilot study. Alcoholism Treatment Quarterly 13:81–90, 1995

Frisman LK, Rosenheck R: The relationship of public support payments to substance abuse among homeless veterans with mental illness. Psychiatr Serv 48:792–795, 1997

Gastfriend DR, McLellan AT: Treatment matching: theoretical basis and practical implications. Med Clin North Am 81:945–966, 1997

Graham A: Brief intervention, in Principles of Addiction Medicine. Edited by Miller NS. Chevy Chase, MD, American Society of Addiction Medicine, 1994, Section 4, Chapter 7, pp 1–7

Hagen RE: Evaluation of the effectiveness of educational and rehabilitation efforts: opportunities for research. J Stud Alcohol 46 (suppl 10):179–183, 1985

Hayashida M, Alterman A, McLellan AT, et al: Comparative effectiveness and cost of inpatient and outpatient detoxification of patients with mild to moderate alcohol withdrawal syndrome. N Engl J Med 320:358–365, 1989

Herbst MD, Batki SL, Manfredi LB, et al: Treatment outcomes for methadone clients receiving lump-sum payments at initiation of disability benefits. Psychiatr Serv 47:119–120, 142, 1996

Hitchcock HC, Stainback RD, Roque GM: Effects of halfway house placement on retention of patients in substance abuse aftercare. Am J Drug Alcohol Abuse 21:379–390, 1995

Institute of Medicine: Broadening the Base of Treatment for Alcohol Problems. Washington, DC, National Academy Press, 1990

Lawental E, McLellan AT, Grissom GR, et al: Coerced treatment for substance abuse problems detected through workplace urine surveillance: is it effective? J Subst Abuse 8:115–128, 1996

Leukefeld C, Mathews T, Clayton R: Treating the drug-abusing offender. Journal of Mental Health Administration 19:76–82, 1992

Longabaugh R, McCrady B, Fink E, et al: Cost effectiveness of alcoholism treatment in partial vs inpatient settings: six-month outcomes. J Stud Alcohol 44:1049–1071, 1983

MacMahon JR: Perinatal substance abuse: the impact of reporting infants to child protective services. Pediatrics (serial online) 100:e1, 1997. Available at: http://www.Pediatrics.org/cgi/content/full/100/5/e1

Marlatt GA: Reducing binge drinking in young adults: a harm reduction approach. Paper presented at the annual meeting of the American Academy of Addiction Psychiatry, San Antonio, TX, December 1997

McKay JR, Alterman AI, McLellan AT, et al: Treatment goals, continuity of care and outcome in a day hospital substance abuse rehabilitation program. Am J Psychiatry 151:254–259, 1994

McKay JR, Cacciola JS, McLellan AT: An initial evaluation of the psychosocial dimensions of the American Society of Addiction Medicine criteria for inpatient versus intensive outpatient substance abuse rehabilitation. J Stud Alcohol 58:239–252, 1997

McLachlan JFC, Stein RL: Evaluation of a day clinic for alcoholics. J Stud Alcohol 43:261–272, 1982

McLellan AT, Hagan TA, Meyers K, et al: "Intensive" outpatient substance abuse treatment: comparison with "traditional" outpatient treatment. J Addict Dis 16:57–84, 1997

Moos RH, Pettit B, Gruber VA: Characteristics and outcomes of three models of community residential care for substance abuse patients. J Subst Abuse 7:99–116, 1995

Petersilia J: Probation in the United States: practices and challenges. National Institute of Justice Journal (serial online) 233:2–8, 1997. Available at: http://www.ncjrs.org/txtfiles/jr000233.txt

Rhodes W, Gross M: Case management reduces drug use and criminality among drug-involved arrestees: an experimental study of an HIV prevention intervention (National Institute of Justice Res Rep). Washington, DC, U.S. Department of Justice, Office of Justice Programs, 1997. Available at: http://www.ncjrs.org/txtfiles/155281.txt

Ries RK, Comtois KA: Managing disability benefits as part of treatment for persons with severe mental illness and comorbid drug/alcohol disorders: a comparative study of payee and non-payee participants. Am J Addict 6:330–338, 1997

Ries RK, Dyck DG: Representative payee practices of community mental health centers in Washington State. Psychiatr Serv 48:811–814, 1997

Robinson v California, 370 US 660 (1962)

Rosenheck R, Lam J, Randolph F: Impact of representative payees on substance use by homeless persons with serious mental illness. Psychiatr Serv 48:800–806, 1997

Satel SL: When disability benefits make patients sicker. N Engl J Med 333:794–796, 1995

Satel S, Reuter P, Hartley D, et al: Influence of retroactive disability payments on recipients' compliance with substance abuse treatment. Psychiatr Serv 48:796–799, 1997

Schneider R, Mittelmeier C, Gadish D: Day versus inpatient treatment for cocaine dependence: an experimental comparison. Journal of Mental Health Administration 23: 234–245, 1996

Shaner A, Eckman TA, Roberts LJ, et al: Disability income, cocaine use and repeated hospitalization among schizophrenic cocaine abusers. N Engl J Med 333:777–783, 1995

Siegal HA, Fisher JH, Rapp RC, et al: Enhancing substance abuse treatment with case management: its impact on employment. J Subst Abuse Treat 13:93–98, 1996

Social Security Act, §1631, 42 USC §1383 (1935), amended through January 1, 1997. Available at: http://www.ssa.gov/OP_Home/ssact/

Social Security Administration: Disability Based on Drug Addiction or Alcoholism (SSA Publ No 05-10047), May 1996. Available at: http://www.ssa.gov/pubs/10047.txt

Stahler GJ: Social interventions for homeless substance abusers: evaluating treatment outcomes (editorial). J Addict Dis 14:xv–xxvi, 1995

Stahler GJ, Shipley TF Jr, Bartelt D, et al: Evaluating alternative treatments for homeless substance-abusing men: outcomes and predictors of success. J Addict Dis 14:151–167, 1995

Steiner C, Lezotte D, Gabow P: Court-ordered treatment of patients with medical problems. Am J Addict 4:127–132, 1995

Whitfield CL, Thompson G, Lamb A, et al: Detoxification of 1,024 alcoholic patients without psychoactive drugs. JAMA 239:1409–1410, 1978

WHO Brief Intervention Study Group: A cross-national trial of brief interventions with heavy drinkers. Am J Public Health 86:948–955, 1996

Wiseman EJ, Henderson KL, Briggs MJ: Outcomes of patients in a VA ambulatory detoxification program. Psychiatr Serv 48:200–203, 1997

# Chapter 39

# Therapeutic Communities

George De Leon, Ph.D.

D rug-free residential programs for substance abuse appeared a decade later than did therapeutic communities (TCs) in psychiatric hospitals pioneered by Jones (1953) and others in the United Kingdom. The name *therapeutic community* evolved in these hospital settings, although the two models arose independently. The TC for substance abuse emerged in the 1960s as a self-help alternative to existing conventional treatments. Recovering alcoholic and drug-addicted individuals were its first participant-developers. Although its modern antecedents can be traced to Alcoholics Anonymous and Synanon, the TC prototype is ancient, existing in all forms of communal healing and support.

Contemporary TCs are sophisticated human services institutions. Today, the term *therapeutic community* is generic, describing a variety of short- and long-term residential programs, as well as day-treatment and ambulatory programs that serve a wide spectrum of drug- and alcohol-abusing patients. Although the TC model has been widely adapted, it is the traditional long-term residential prototype that has documented effectiveness in rehabilitating substance-abusing individuals.

## The Traditional TC

Traditional TCs are similar in planned duration of stay (15–24 months), structure, staffing pattern, perspective, and rehabilitative regimen, although they differ in size (30 to several hundred beds in a facility) and patient demography. Staffs consist of TC-trained clinicians and other human services professionals. Primary clinical staffs usually include former substance-abusing individuals who were rehabilitated in TC programs. Other staffs consist of professionals providing medical, mental health, vocational, educational, family counsel-

ing, fiscal, administrative, and legal services.

TCs accommodate a broad spectrum of drug-abusing patients. Although TCs originally attracted narcotic-addicted individuals, most of their patient populations are non-opioid-abusing persons with different lifestyles; various social, economic, and ethnic or cultural backgrounds; and drug problems of varying severity.

In TCs, drug abuse is viewed as a deviant behavior, reflecting impeded personality development or chronic deficits in social, educational, and economic skills. Such behavior is a result of socioeconomic disadvantage, poor family effectiveness, and psychological factors. Thus, the principal aim of the TC is a global change in lifestyle, involving abstinence from illicit substances, elimination of antisocial activity, development of employability, and development of prosocial attitudes and values. The rehabilitative approach requires multidimensional influence and training, which for most can occur only in a 24-hour residential setting.

The traditional TC can be distinguished from other major drug treatment modalities in three general ways. First, the TC coordinates a comprehensive range of interventions and services in a single treatment setting. Vocational counseling; work therapy; recreation, group, and individual therapy; and educational, medical, family, legal, and social services all are offered within the TC. Second, the primary "therapist" and teacher in the TC is the community itself, consisting of peers and staff who serve as role models of successful personal change. Staff members also serve as rational authorities and guides in the recovery process. Thus, the community as a whole provides a crucial 24-hour context for continued learning in which individual changes in conduct, attitudes, and emotions are monitored and mutually reinforced in the daily regimen. Third, the TC approach to rehabilitation is based on an explicit perspective of the substance use disorder, the patient, the recovery process, and healthy living. It is this perspective that shapes its organizational structure, staffing, and treatment process.

## The TC Perspective

The TC perspective consists of four interrelated views, each of which is briefly outlined here.[1]

### View of the Disorder

Drug abuse is viewed as a disorder of the whole person, affecting some or all areas of functioning. Cognitive and behavior problems are evident, as are mood disturbances. Thinking may be unrealistic or disorganized; values are confused, nonexistent, or antisocial. Frequently there are deficits in verbal, reading, writing, and marketable skills. Moral or even spiritual issues, whether expressed in existential or psychological terms, are apparent.

The problem is the individual, not the drug. Addiction is a symptom, not the essence of the disorder. In the TC, chemical detoxification is a condition of entry, not a goal of treatment. The focus of rehabilitation is on maintaining a drug-free existence.

### View of the Person

In TCs, individuals are distinguished along dimensions of psychological dysfunction and social deficits rather than according to drug use patterns. Vocational and educational problems are marked; middle-class mainstream values are either missing or not sought. Usually these residents emerge from a socially disadvantaged sector, where drug abuse is more a social response than a psychological disturbance. Their TC experience is better termed *habilitation*, development of a socially productive, conventional lifestyle for the first time.

Among patients from more advantaged backgrounds, drug abuse is more directly expressive of psychological disorder or existential malaise. For these, the word *rehabilitation* is more suitable, because the term emphasizes a return to a lifestyle previously lived, known, and perhaps rejected.

Notwithstanding these social differences, substance-abusing individuals in TCs share important similarities. Either as a cause or a consequence of their drug abuse, all such persons exhibit features of personality disturbance and impeded social function (see section "Clinical Characteristics" later in this chapter). Thus, all residents in the TC follow the same regimen. Individual differences are recognized in specific treatment plans that modify the emphasis, not the course, of their experience in the TC.

### View of Recovery

In the TC's view of recovery, the aim of rehabilitation is global, involving both a change in lifestyle and a change in personal identity. The primary psychological goal is to change the negative patterns of behavior, thinking, and feeling that predispose the individual to drug use; the main social goal is to develop the skills, attitudes, and values of a responsible drug-free lifestyle. Stable recovery, however, depends on a successful integration of these social and psychological goals. Behavioral change is unstable without insight, and insight is insufficient without felt experience. Thus, conduct, emotions, skills, attitudes, and values must all be addressed, to ensure enduring change.

#### Motivation

Recovery depends on pressures to change, positive and negative. Some patients seek help, driven by stressful external pressures; others are moved by more intrinsic factors. For all, however, remaining in treatment requires continued motivation to change. Thus, elements of the rehabilitation approach are designed to sustain motivation or to enable detection of early signs of premature termination.

#### Self-Help and Mutual Self-Help

Strictly speaking, treatment is not provided; rather, it is made available to the individual in the TC through its staff and peers and the daily regimen of work, groups, meetings, seminars, and recreation. However, the effectiveness of these elements depends on the individual, who must constantly and fully engage in the treatment regimen. In self-help recovery, the individual

---

[1]Descriptive accounts of the TC for substance-abusing patients, which are less formal than the description presented here, are contained in the literature (e.g., Casriel 1966; Deitch 1972; Yablonsky 1965), and formal accounts of the TC from sociological, anthropological, or psychodynamic perspectives are contained in Sugarman 1986, Frankel 1989, and Kooyman 1993, respectively.

makes the main *contribution* to the change process. In mutual self-help, the main messages of recovery, personal growth, and "right living" are mediated by peers through confrontation and sharing in groups, by example as role models, and as supportive, encouraging friends in daily interactions.

### Social Learning

A lifestyle change occurs in a social context. Negative patterns, attitudes, and roles were not acquired in isolation, nor can they be altered in isolation. Thus, recovery depends not only on what has been learned but on how and where learning occurs. This assumption is the basis for the community's serving collectively as teacher. Learning is active, involving doing and participating. A socially responsible role is acquired by acting the role. What is learned is identified with the individuals involved in the learning process—supportive peers and staff serving as credible role models.

Sustained recovery requires a perspective on self, society, and life that must be continually affirmed by a positive social network of others within and beyond the TC.

### Treatment as an Episode

Residence in the TC is a relatively brief period in an individual's life, and the influence of this period must compete with the influences of the years before and after treatment. For this reason, unhealthy "outside" influences are minimized until the individual is better prepared to deal with these on his or her own. Thus, life in the TC is necessarily intense, the daily regimen is demanding, and the therapeutic confrontations are unmoderated.

## View of Right Living

TCs adhere to certain precepts that constitute a view of healthy, personal, and social living. These precepts concern moral behavior, values, and a social perspective that are intimately related to the TC view of the individual and of recovery. For example, in TCs, unambiguous "moral" positions are held regarding social and sexual conduct. Explicit right and wrong behaviors are identified, for which there are appropriate rewards and sanctions. These include antisocial behaviors and attitudes; the negative values of the street, jails, or negative peers; and irresponsible or exploitative sexual conduct.

Guilts relating to self, significant others, and the larger community outside the TC are central issues in the recovery process. Although they are associated with moral matters, guilts are special psychological experiences that if not addressed maintain the individual's disaffiliation from peers and block the self-acceptance that is necessary for authentic personal change.

Certain values are stressed as being essential to social learning and personal growth. These values include truth and honesty (in word and deed), a work ethic, self-reliance, earned rewards and achievement, personal accountability, responsible concern (being one's brother's or sister's keeper), social manners, and community involvement.

Treatment helps the individual focus on the personal present (here and now) versus the historical past (then and when). Past behavior and circumstances are explored only to illustrate the current patterns of dysfunctional behavior, negative attitudes, and outlook. Residents are encouraged and trained to assume personal responsibility for their present reality and destiny.

## Who Comes for Treatment

Most patients who enter TCs have histories of multiple drug use, including use of marijuana, opioids, alcohol, and prescription medications, although in recent years most residents report cocaine or crack as their primary drug of abuse. However, research has documented that persons admitted to TCs have a considerable degree of psychosocial dysfunction in addition to their substance abuse.

### Social Profiles

Patients in traditional programs are usually men (70%–75%), but the number of admissions of women is increasing. Most community-based TCs are integrated across gender, race or ethnicity, and age, although the demographic proportions differ by geographic regions and in certain programs. In general, Hispanics, Native Americans, and patients younger than 21 years represent smaller proportions of admissions to TCs.

Most patients admitted are from broken homes or have ineffective families, have poor work histories, and have engaged in criminal activities. Among adults who are admitted to TCs, fewer than one-third are employed full-time in the year before treatment, more than two-thirds have been arrested, and 30%–40% have drug treatment histories (e.g., De Leon 1984; Hubbard et al. 1997; Simpson and Sells 1982).

## Psychological Profiles

Patients differ in demographics, socioeconomic background, and drug use patterns, but psychological profiles obtained with the use of standard instruments appear uniform, as has been shown in a number of TC studies (e.g., Biase et al. 1986; Brook and Whitehead 1980; De Leon 1984; De Leon et al. 1973; Holland 1986; Kennard and Wilson 1979; Zuckerman et al. 1975).

Typically, symptom measures on depression and anxiety are deviantly high, socialization scores are poor, and IQ is in the dull-to-normal range. Self-esteem is markedly low and Minnesota Multiphasic Personality Inventory scores are deviant, reflecting confusion (high F), character disorder (Pd), and disturbed thinking and affect (high Sc). Smaller but still deviant peaks are seen on depression (D) and hypomania (Ma).

The psychological profiles mirror features of both psychiatric and criminal populations. For example, the character disorder elements and poor self-concept of delinquent and repeated offenders are present, as are the elements of dysphoria and confused thinking of emotionally unstable or psychiatric populations. Thus, in addition to their substance abuse, patients in TCs have considerable degrees of psychological disability.

### Clinical Characteristics

Regardless of drug preference or severity, most individuals admitted to TCs have shared clinical features that are directly addressed in the TC treatment. These characteristics center around immaturity and/or antisocial dimensions. They include, for example, low tolerance for all forms of discomfort and delay of gratification; problems with authority; inability to manage feelings (particularly hostility, guilt, and anxiety); poor impulse control (particularly sexual or aggressive impulse control); poor judgment and reality testing concerning consequences of actions; unrealistic self-appraisal in terms of a discrepancy between personal resources and aspirations; prominence of lying, manipulation, and deception as coping behaviors; and personal and social irresponsibility (i.e., inconsistency or failures in meeting obligations). Additionally, many TC residents have marked deficits in learning, marketable, and communication skills.

These clinical characteristics are not necessarily indicative of an "addictive personality," although many of these features are typical of conduct disorder in the younger substance-abusing individual, which later evolves into adult character disorder. Nevertheless, whether antecedent or consequent to serious drug involvement, these characteristics are commonly observed to be correlated with chemical dependency. More important, in TCs, a positive change in these characteristics is considered to be essential for stable recovery.

## Psychiatric Diagnoses

In diagnostic studies in which the Diagnostic Interview Schedule was used, more than 70% of patients admitted to TCs had a lifetime (i.e., beginning before the last 30 days) non-drug-related psychiatric disorder in addition to substance-related problems. A third had a current (beginning within the last 30 days) mental disorder in addition to substance-related problems. The most frequent non-drug-related diagnoses were phobias, generalized anxiety, psychosexual dysfunction, and antisocial personality. There were few cases of schizophrenia, but lifetime affective disorders occurred in more than one-third of those studied (De Leon 1993; Jainchill 1994).

That the psychological and psychiatric profiles reveal few psychotic features, and relatively low variability in symptoms or personality characteristics, reflects several factors: the TC exclusionary criteria, the common characteristics among all substance-abusing individuals, and to some degree the self-selection among those who seek admission to residential treatment programs. Nevertheless, patients do differ, as attested by the differences in patient dropout and success rates (discussed later in this chapter).

## Contact and Referral

Voluntary contacts of TCs occur through self-referral, social agencies, treatment providers, and active recruitment by TCs. Outreach teams (usually trained graduates of TCs and selected human services staff) recruit in hospitals, jails, courtrooms, and social agencies and on the street, conducting brief orientations or face-to-face interviews to determine receptivity to the TC.

Among adolescents, 40%–50% have been legally referred to treatment, compared with 25%–30% of adults; in some programs, considerably higher percentages of patients have been legally referred (e.g., Pompi and Resnick 1987).

Although most admissions to TCs are voluntary, many of these patients come to treatment programs under various forms of perceived pressures from family or significant others, employment difficulties, or antici- pated legal consequences (De Leon 1988).

## Detoxification

With few exceptions, admission to residential treat- ment does not require medically supervised detoxifica- tion. Thus, traditional TCs do not usually provide this service on the premises. Most individuals whose pri- mary drugs of abuse are opioids, cocaine, alcohol, barbi- turates, and amphetamines have undergone self- or medical detoxification before seeking admission to the TC. A small proportion require detoxification during the admission evaluation, and these persons are offered the option of detoxification at a nearby hospital. Indi- viduals who use barbiturates are routinely referred for medically supervised detoxification, after which they are assessed for admission. A minor percentage of pa- tients admitted to TCs have been primarily involved with hallucinogens or phencyclidine (PCP). In the case of those who appear compromised, a referral is made for psychiatric service, after which the individuals can return for residential treatment.

## Criteria for Residential Treatment

Traditional TCs maintain an open-door policy with re- spect to admission for residential treatment. This un- derstandably results in a wide range of treatment candi- dates, not all of whom are equally ready for, suited for, or motivated to face the demands of the residential reg- imen. Relatively few are excluded, because the TC pol- icy is to accept individuals who elect residential treat- ment, regardless of the reasons influencing their choice.

One factor that is useful to consider during the pro- cess of deciding whether to admit a patient to a TC is community risk. *Risk* refers to the extent to which pa- tients present a management burden to the staff or pose a threat to the security and health of the community. Specific exclusionary criteria most often include histo- ries of arson, suicide attempts, and serious psychiatric disorder. Psychiatric exclusion is usually based on docu- mented history of psychiatric hospitalizations or evi- dence of psychotic symptoms on interview (e.g., frank delusions, thought disorder, hallucinations, confused orientation, signs of serious affect disorder). An impor- tant differential diagnostic issue concerns drug-related mood or mental states. For example, disorientation, dysphoria, and thought or sensory disorders clearly as- sociated with use of hallucinogens, PCP, and sometimes cocaine may not exclude an otherwise suitable individ-

ual from the TC. When diagnosis remains in question, most TCs will use a psychiatric consultation after ad- mission. Referral, however, is based on the patient's suitability or risk rather than on diagnosis alone.

Generally, patients on regular psychotropic regimens are excluded because use of these regimens usually cor- relates with chronic or severe psychiatric disorder. Pa- tients taking medication for medical conditions can be admitted, as can handicapped individuals or persons who require prosthetics, providing these patients can participate fully in the program. Physical examinations and laboratory workups (blood and urine profiles) are performed after admission. Because of concern about communicable disease in a residential setting, some TCs require tests for conditions such as hepatitis to be performed before patients enter the facility or at least within the first weeks of admission.

Policy and practices concerning testing for HIV and management of AIDS and AIDS-related complex (ARC) emphasize voluntary testing with counseling, special education seminars on health management and sexual practices, and special support groups for resi- dents who are HIV-positive or who have a clinical diag- nosis of AIDS or ARC (e.g., Barton 1994; De Leon 1996b; McCusker and Sorensen 1994).

### Suitability for the TC

A number of those seeking admission to a TC may not be ready for treatment in general or suited for the de- mands of a long-term residential regimen. Assessment of these factors at admission provides a basis for treat- ment planning in the TC or sometimes appropriate re- ferral. Some indicators of motivation and readiness and suitability for TC treatment are acceptance of the se- verity of the drug problem; acceptance of the need for treatment (patient thinks he or she "can't do it alone"); willingness to sever ties with family and friends and halt current lifestyle while in treatment; and willingness to surrender a private life and meet the expectations of a structured community. Although motivation, readiness, and suitability are not criteria for admission to the TC, the importance of these factors often emerges after en- try to treatment, and these factors, if not identified and addressed, are related to early dropout (De Leon et al. 1994).

 ## The TC Approach

The TC uses the diverse elements and activities of com- munity to foster rehabilitative change. These can be organized in terms of the TC structure or social organization and the TC process in terms of the individual's passage through stages of change within the context of community life.

## TC Structure

The TC is composed of relatively few staff along with resident peers, at junior, intermediate, and senior levels, who constitute the community or family in the residence. This peer-to-community structure strengthens the individual's identification with a perceived, ordered network of others. More important, it arranges relationships of mutual responsibility to others at various levels in the program.

The daily operation of the community itself is the task of the residents, who work together under staff supervision. The broad range of resident job assignments illustrates the extent of the self-help process. Residents perform all house services (e.g., cooking, cleaning, kitchen service, minor repair), serve as apprentices, run all departments, and conduct house meetings, certain seminars, and peer-encounter groups.

The TC is managed by staff who monitor and evaluate patient status, supervise resident groups, assign and supervise resident jobs, and oversee house operations. The staff conduct therapeutic groups (other than peer-encounter groups), provide individual counseling, organize social and recreational projects, and confer with significant others. They make decisions relating to resident status, discipline, promotion, transfers, discharges, furloughs, and treatment planning.

The new patient enters a setting of upward mobility. The resident job assignments are arranged in a hierarchy, according to seniority, clinical progress, and productivity. Residents are first assigned the most menial tasks (e.g., mopping the floor) and then work their way up to levels of coordination and management. Indeed, individuals come in as patients and can leave as staff. This social organization of the TC reflects the fundamental aspects of its rehabilitative approach: *work as education and therapy, mutual self-help, peers as role models*, and *staff as rational authorities*.

### Work as Education and Therapy

Work and job changes have clinical relevance for substance-abusing patients in TCs, most of whom have not successfully negotiated the social and occupational world of the larger society. Vertical job movements carry the obvious rewards of status and privilege. How-

ever, lateral job changes are more frequent and permit exposure to all aspects of the community.

Job changes in the TC are singularly effective therapeutic tools, providing both measures of and incentives for behavioral and attitudinal changes. In the vertical structure of the TC, ascendancy marks how well the patient has assimilated what the community teaches and expects; hence, job promotion is an explicit measure of the resident's improvement and growth. Lateral or downward job movements also create situations that require demonstrations of personal growth. These movements are designed to teach new ways of coping with reversals and change that appear to be unfair or arbitrary.

### Mutual Self-Help

The essential dynamic in the TC is mutual self-help. In their jobs, groups, meetings, recreation, and personal and social time, residents continually transmit to one another the main messages and expectations of the community.

### Peers as Role Models

Peers, serving as role models, and staff, serving as role models and rational authorities, are the primary mediators of the recovery process. TC members who demonstrate the expected behaviors and reflect the values and teachings of the community are viewed as role models. Thus, all members of the community—roommates, older and younger residents, and junior, senior, and directorial staff—are expected to be role models. TCs require these multiple role models in order to maintain the integrity of the community and ensure the spread of social learning effects. Two main examples of how role models function in the community are illustrated:

1. *Resident role models "act as if."* The resident behaves as the person that he or she should be, rather than as the person that he or she has been. Despite resistances, perceptions, or feelings to the contrary, residents engage in the expected behaviors and consistently maintain the attitudes and values of the community. These include self-motivation, commitment to work and striving, positive regard for staff as authority, and an optimistic outlook toward the future. In the TC's view, acting as if is not merely an exercise in conformity; it is an essential mechanism for more complete psychological change. Feelings, insights, and altered self-perceptions often follow rather than precede behavioral change.

2. *Role models display responsible concern.* This concept is closely akin to the notion of being one's brother's or sister's keeper. Showing responsible concern involves willingness to confront others whose behavior is not in keeping with the rules of the TC, the spirit of the community, or the community expectations of growth and rehabilitation. Role models are obligated to be aware of the appearance, attitude, moods, and performances of their peers and to confront negative signs in these. In particular, role models are aware of their own behavior in the overall community and the process prescribed for personal growth.

### Staff as Rational Authorities

Staff foster the self-help learning process through performance of the managerial and clinical functions described earlier and through maintenance of psychological relationships with the residents as role models, parental surrogates, and rational authorities. TC residents often have had difficulties with authorities who have not been trusted or who have been perceived as guides and teachers. Thus, they need a positive experience with an authority figure who is viewed as credible (recovered), supportive, corrective, and protective, in order to gain authority over themselves (personal autonomy). As rational authorities, staff provide the *reasons* for their decisions and explain the *meaning* of consequences. They exercise their powers to teach and guide, facilitate and correct, rather than to punish, control, or exploit.

## The TC Process: Basic Program Elements

The recovery process may be defined as the interaction between treatment interventions and patient change. Unlike other treatment approaches, however, the TC treatment intervention is the daily regimen of structured and unstructured activities and social intercourse occurring in formal and informal settings.

The typical day in a TC is highly structured. It begins at 7:00 A.M. and ends at 11:00 P.M. During this time, residents participate in a variety of meetings, encounter and other therapeutic groups, and recreational activities; perform job functions (work therapy); and receive individual counseling. The interplay of these activities is part of the TC process. As interventions they may be divided into three main groups: *therapeutic-educative activities, community enhancement activities,* and *community and clinical management.*

### Therapeutic-Educative Activities

Therapeutic-educative activities consist of various group processes and individual counseling. These activities provide residents with opportunities to express feelings, divert negative acting-out, and resolve personal and social issues. They increase communication and interpersonal skills, bring about examination and confrontation of behavior and attitudes, and offer instruction in alternative modes of behavior.

The four main forms of group activity in the TC are encounters, probes, marathons, and tutorials. These differ somewhat in format, objectives, and method, but all have the goal of fostering trust, personal disclosure, intimacy, and peer solidarity to facilitate therapeutic change. The focus of the *encounter* is behavioral. Its approach is confrontation, and its objective is to modify negative behavior and attitudes directly. *Probes* and *marathons* have as their primary objective substantial emotional change and psychological insight. In *tutorials,* the learning of concepts and specific skills is stressed.

*Encounters* are the cornerstone of group process in the TC. The term *encounter* is generic, describing a variety of forms that use confrontational procedures as their main approach. The basic encounter group is a peer-led group composed of 12–20 residents; it meets at least three times weekly, usually for 2 hours in the evening, and an additional 30-minute period follows for snacking and socializing. The basic objective of each encounter is to heighten individual awareness of specific attitudes or behavioral patterns that should be modified.

*Probes* are staff-led group sessions, involving 10–15 residents, conducted to obtain in-depth clinical information on patients early in their residence (in the first 2–6 months). They are scheduled when needed and usually last from 4 to 8 hours. Their main objectives are to increase staff understanding of individuals' backgrounds for the purposes of treatment planning and to increase openness, trust, and mutual identification. Unlike the encounter, in which confrontation is stressed, the probe involves the use of support, understanding, and the empathy of the other group members. Probes go beyond the here-and-now behavioral incident, which is the material of the encounter, to past events and experiences.

*Marathons* are extended group sessions whose objective is to initiate resolution of life experiences that have impeded individuals' development. During his or her 18 months of residence, every patient participates in several marathons. These sessions are conducted by all staff, who are assisted by senior residents with marathon experience. Marathons usually include large groups of selected residents and last for 18–36 hours. Considerable experience, both personal and professional, is required to ensure safe and effective marathons.

The intimacy, safety, and bonding in the marathon setting facilitate emotional processing ("working through") of a significant life event and encourage the individual to continue to deal with certain life-altering issues of the past. These issues are identified in counseling, probes, or other group sessions and may include violence, sexual abuse, abandonment, illness, and deaths of significant others. A wide variety of techniques are employed, including psychodrama, primal therapy, and pure theater, to produce impact.

*Tutorials* are primarily directed toward training or teaching. Tutorial groups, usually staff led, consist of 10–20 residents. Tutorials are scheduled as needed and focus on certain themes, including personal growth, recovery, and right-living concepts (e.g., self-reliance, maturity, relationships); job skills training (e.g., training in management of the department or the reception desk); and clinical skills training (e.g., training in the use of encounter tools).

The four main groups are supplemented by *other groups* that convene as needed. These vary in focus, format, and composition. For example, gender, ethnic, or age-specific theme groups may use encounter or tutorial formats. Dormitory, room, or departmental encounters may address issues of daily community living. Additionally, sensitivity training, psychodrama, and conventional gestalt and emotionality groups are used to varying extents.

*One-to-one counseling* balances the needs of the individual with those of the community. Peer exchange is ongoing and is the most consistent form of informal counseling in TCs. Staff counseling sessions may be formal or informal and are usually conducted as needed. The staff counseling method in the TC is not conventional, as is evident in its main features: transpersonal sharing, direct support, minimal interpretation, didactic instructions, and concerned confrontation.

## Community Enhancement Activities

Community enhancement activities, which facilitate assimilation into the community, include the four main facility-wide meetings: the morning meeting, the seminar, the house meeting (these three meetings are held each day), and the general meeting (which is called when needed).

All residents of the facility and the staff on the premises attend the *morning meeting*, which takes place after breakfast and usually lasts 30 minutes. The purpose of the meeting is to instill a positive attitude at the beginning of the day, motivate residents, and strengthen unity. This meeting is particularly relevant because most residents of TCs have never adapted to the routine of an ordinary day.

*Seminars* take place every afternoon and usually last 1 hour. Because it brings all residents together, the seminar in the afternoon complements the daily morning meeting and the house meeting in the evening. A clinical aim of the seminar is to balance the individual's emotional and cognitive experience. Most seminars are led by residents, although some are led by staff and outside speakers. The seminar is unique among the various meetings and group processes in the TC in its emphasis on listening, speaking, and conceptual behavior.

*House meetings* take place nightly, after dinner, usually last 1 hour, and are coordinated by a senior resident. The main aim of these meetings is to transact community business, although they also have a clinical objective. In this forum, social pressure through public acknowledgment of positive or negative behaviors is judiciously applied to facilitate individual change.

*General meetings* take place only when needed and are usually called so that negative behavior, attitudes, or incidents in the facility can be addressed. All residents and staff (including those not on duty) are assembled at any time and for an indefinite duration. These meetings, conducted by multiple staff, are designed to identify problem individuals or conditions or to reaffirm motivation and reinforce positive behavior and attitudes in the community.

Community enhancement occurs in a variety of nonscheduled informal activities as well. These include activities related to rituals and traditions, celebrations (e.g., celebrations of birthdays, graduations, phase changes), ceremonies (e.g., those relating to general and cultural holidays), and memorial observances for deceased residents, family members of residents, and staff. These activities reflect humanistic reactions of the membership, which increase cohesiveness of the community.

## Community and Clinical Management Elements

Community and clinical management elements maintain the physical and psychological safety of the environment and ensure that resident life is orderly and productive. They protect the community as a whole and strengthen it as a context for social learning. The main elements are privileges, disciplinary sanctions, surveillance, and urine testing.

### Privileges.

In the TC, privileges are explicit rewards that reinforce the value of achievement. Privileges are accorded with overall clinical progress in the program. Displays of inappropriate behavior or negative attitude can result in loss of privileges, which can be regained through demonstrated improvement.

Privileges range from telephone and letter writing privileges earlier in treatment to overnight furloughs later in treatment. Successful movement through each stage earns privileges that grant wider personal latitude and increased self-responsibility.

Privileges acquire importance because they are earned through investment of time, investment of energy, and self-modification and because residents seeking them risk failure and face disappointment. Thus, the earning process establishes the value of privileges and gives them potency as social reinforcements. Although the privileges offered in the TC are quite ordinary, it is their social and psychological relevance to the patient that enhances their importance.

Moreover, because substance-abusing patients often cannot distinguish between privilege and entitlement, the privilege system in the TC teaches that productive participation or membership in a family or community is based on an earning process.

Finally, privileges are tangible rewards that are contingent on individual change. This concrete feature of privilege is particularly suitable for those with histories of performance failure or incompletion.

### Disciplinary sanctions.

TCs have their own specific rules and regulations that guide the behavior of residents and the management of facilities. The explicit purpose of these rules is to ensure the safety and health of the community. However, their implicit aim is to train and teach residents through the use of discipline.

In the TC, social and physical safety are prerequisites for psychological trust. Therefore, sanctions are invoked against any behavior that threatens the safety of the therapeutic environment. For example, breaking one of the TC's cardinal rules—such as the rule of no violence or threat of violence—can bring immediate expulsion. Even a minor deviance such as the unapproved borrowing of a book is a threat that must be addressed.

Verbal reprimands, rescindment of privileges, or speaking bans may be selected for less severe infractions. Job demotions or loss of accrued time may be invoked for more serious infractions. Expulsion may be appropriate for behavior that is incorrigible or dangerous to others.

Sanctions are implemented as contracts with the resident. Although sanctions are often perceived as punitive, the basic purpose of contracts is to create a learning experience by compelling residents to attend to their own conduct, to reflect on their own motivation, to feel some consequence of their behavior, and to consider alternative forms of acting under similar situations.

The entire facility is made aware of all disciplinary actions. Thus, contracts deter violations. They create vicarious learning experiences for others. As symbols of safety and integrity, they strengthen community cohesiveness.

### Surveillance: the house run.

The TC's most comprehensive method for assessing the overall physical and psychological status of the residential community is the *house run*. Several times a day, staff and senior residents walk through the entire facility, examining its overall condition. This single procedure has clinical implications as well as management goals. House runs provide global snapshot impressions of the facility: its cleanliness, planned routines, safety procedures, morale, and psychological tone. They illuminate the psychological and social functioning of individual residents and peer groups.

### Urine testing.

Most TCs use unannounced random urine testing or incident-related urine-testing procedures. Residents who deny the use of drugs or refuse to undergo urine testing on request are rejecting a fundamental expectation in the TC, which is to trust staff and peers enough to disclose undesirable behavior. The voluntary admission of drug use initiates a learning experience, which includes exploration of conditions precipitating the infraction. Denial of actual drug use, either before or after urine testing, can block the learning process and may lead to termination or dropout.

When urine tests positive for drugs, the action taken depends on the drug used, the resident's time and status in the program, the resident's history of drug and other infractions, and the locus and condition of use. Actions may involve expulsion, loss of accrued time, radical job demotions, or rescinding of privileges for specific periods. Review of the triggers or reasons for drug use is also essential.

## The TC Treatment Process: Program Stages and Phases

Rehabilitation and recovery in the TC are a developmental process, one that occurs in a social learning setting. The developmental process itself can be understood as a passage through stages of learning. The learning that occurs at each stage facilitates change at the next, and each change reflects movement toward the goals of recovery.

Three major program stages characterize change in long-term residential TCs: orientation-induction, primary treatment, and reentry. Additional substages or phases are also discussed.

### Stage 1: Orientation-Induction (0–60 Days)

The main goals of this initial phase of residence are further assessment and orientation to the TC. The aim of orientation in the initial phase of residence is for the individual to be assimilated into the community through full participation and involvement in all of its activities. Rapid assimilation is crucial at this point, when patients are most concerned about the amount of time they are required to spend in the TC.

Formal seminars and informal peer instruction focus on reducing anxiety and uncertainty, accomplished through dissemination of information and instruction concerning cardinal rules (i.e., no use of drugs, no violence or threat of physical violence); house regulations (e.g., no leaving the facility, stealing, borrowing, or lending; maintain manners) or expected conduct (e.g., punctuality, attendance, conduct relating to speaking and dressing); the program itself (e.g., TC structure, job functions, the privilege system, TC process stages, TC philosophy and perspective); and TC tools (e.g., encounter and other groups).

Successful passage through the initial stage is reflected mainly in retention. The fact that patients have remained for 30–60 days indicates that they have adhered to the rules of the program enough to meet the orientation objectives of this stage and have passed through the period of time when they are most vulnerable to drop out.

### Stage 2: Primary Treatment (2–12 Months)

The three phases of primary treatment roughly correlate with time spent in the program (2–4, 5–8, and 9–12 months). These phases are marked by plateaus of stable behavior that signal the need for further change. The daily therapeutic-educational regimen of meetings, groups, job assignments, and peer and staff counseling remains the same throughout the year of primary treatment. However, progress is reflected at the end of each phase in terms of three interrelated dimensions of change: community status, development or maturity,

and overall psychological adjustment. The following brief profile of a resident who has completed 9–12 months of primary treatment serves to illustrate this concept.

Twelve-month residents are established role models in the program. Privileges reflect the increasing degree of personal autonomy. These residents enjoy more privacy and can obtain regular furloughs. Although they cannot hold jobs outside the facility, their positions within the TC indicate that they effectively run the house. As senior coordinators, for example, they are responsible for arranging resident schedules, trips, and seminars, tasks they perform under staff supervision. Similarly, their status in terms of earning power is also increased; they are eligible to be staff-in-training in executive management offices, in special ancillary services, or as junior counselors. They are expected to assist staff in monitoring the facility overnight and on weekends. Those beginning vocational-educational programs experience the pressures and challenges of academics or training. They accept responsibility for themselves and for other members in the community.

The maturity of 12-month residents is most evident in their emotional self-management and increased autonomy. Job performance is consistent, and self-assessment is realistic, as is goal setting. Their social interactions with staff are more spontaneous and relaxed, and they socialize with positive peers during recreational activities and on furlough. Their movement past conformity is evident in their ability to adapt to new situations and teach others TC values.

Twelve-month residents show some insight into their drug problems and personalities. These residents also display paradoxical signs of positive change. Although they are confident and eager to move forward, a certain degree of anxiety and insecurity emerges, associated with their uncertainty about the future. Their openness about anticipated problems is considered a positive psychological sign. After a year, residents are fully trained participants in the group process and often serve as facilitators. A high level of personal disclosure is evident in groups, in peer exchange, and in their increased use of staff counseling.

### Stage 3: Reentry (13–24 Months)

Reentry is the stage at which the patient must strengthen skills for autonomous decision-making and the capacity for self-management and rely less on rational authorities or a well-formed peer network. The two phases of the reentry process are early reentry and later reentry.

*Early reentry phase (13–18 months).* The main objective of the early reentry phase, during which patients continue to live in the facility, is to prepare patients for separation from the community. Emphasis on rational authority decreases, the assumption being that patients in this phase are sufficiently capable of self-management. This capability is reflected in more individual decision-making about privileges, social plans, and life design. Particular emphasis is placed on life-skills seminars, which provide training for life outside the community. Attendance is mandated for sessions on budgeting, job seeking, use of alcohol, sexuality, parenting, use of leisure time, and so on.

During this phase, the development of plans for the individual is a collective task of the patient, a key staff member, and peers. These plans are comprehensive blueprints for long-term psychological, educational, and vocational efforts, which include goal attainment schedules, methods of improving interpersonal and family relationships, and counseling on social and sexual behavior. Patients may be attending school or holding full-time jobs, either within or outside the TC. Still, they are expected to participate in house activities when possible and to have some community responsibilities (e.g., monitoring of the facility at night).

*Later reentry phase (18–24 months).* The objective of the later reentry phase is successful separation from the community. Patients have a "live-out" status; they hold full-time jobs or attend school full-time, and they maintain their own households, usually with live-out peers. They may participate in Alcoholics Anonymous or Narcotics Anonymous or attend family or individual therapy sessions. Contact with the TC is frequent at first and is gradually reduced to weekly telephone calls and monthly visits with a primary counselor.

## Graduation

Completion marks the end of active program involvement. Graduation itself, however, is an annual event conducted in the facility for individuals who have completed the program, usually 1 year after their residence is over. Thus, the TC experience is preparation rather than a cure. Residence in the program facilitates a process of change that must continue throughout life, and what is gained in treatment are tools to guide the individual on a path of continued change. Completion, or graduation, therefore, is not an end but a beginning.

## Aftercare

Until recently, an aftercare period was not formally acknowledged in long-term TC programs as a definable period after program involvement. Nevertheless, in TCs, patients' efforts to maintain sobriety and a positive lifestyle beyond graduation have always been appreciated. In most TCs, key clinical and life adjustment issues of aftercare are addressed during the reentry stages of the 2-year program. However, as discussed in the later section on modifications, many contemporary TCs now have explicit aftercare components within their systems or through linkages with outside agencies.

# Research: Effectiveness and Retention

## Success Rates

A substantial amount of evaluation literature documents the effectiveness of the TC approach in rehabilitating drug-abusing individuals (e.g., Condelli and Hubbard 1994; De Leon 1984, 1985; Hubbard et al. 1997; Simpson and Sells 1982; Tims and Ludford 1984; Tims et al. 1994). The findings of single-program and multiprogram studies regarding short- and long-term posttreatment outcome are summarized in this section.

Substantial improvements are noted on separate outcome variables (i.e., drug use, criminality, and employment) and on composite indices for measuring individual success. Maximally to moderately favorable outcomes (in terms of opioid, nonopioid, and alcohol use; arrest rates; retreatment; and employment) occur in more than half of the sample of patients who have completed programs and dropouts (De Leon 1984; Simpson and Sells 1982).

There is a consistent positive relationship between time spent in residential treatment and posttreatment outcome (De Leon 1984; Simpson and Sells 1982; Simpson et al. 1997). For example, in long-term TC programs, success rates (on composite indices of no drug use and no criminality) at 2 years after completion of treatment approximate 90%, 50%, and 25%, respectively, for graduates or completers, dropouts who remain in residential treatment for more than 1 year, and dropouts who remain in residential treatment for less than 1 year.

In a few studies that investigated psychological outcomes, results uniformly showed marked improvement at follow-up (e.g., Biase et al. 1986; De Leon 1984; Holland 1983). A direct relationship has been demonstrated between posttreatment behavioral success and psychological adjustment (De Leon 1984; De Leon and Jainchill 1981–1982).

Since the early 1980s, most patients admitted to residential TCs have been multiple-drug-abusing individuals—primarily abusing cocaine, crack, and alcohol—and there have been relatively few patients admitted whose primary drug of abuse is heroin (e.g., De Leon 1993). Several large-scale federally funded evaluation efforts have documented the effectiveness of TCs for the changing population of substance-abusing individuals. These studies include the Drug Abuse Treatment Outcome Study (Hubbard et al. 1997) and the multisite program of research carried out in the Center for Therapeutic Community Research (De Leon 1997).

## Retention

Dropout is the general rule for all drug treatment modalities. For TCs, retention is of particular importance because research has established a firm relationship between time spent in treatment and successful outcome. However, most patients admitted to TCs leave the programs, with many leaving before treatment influences are presumed to be effectively rendered.

Research on retention in TCs has been increasing. Reviews of the TC retention research are contained in the literature (e.g., De Leon 1985, 1991; Lewis and Ross 1994). The key findings from these are summarized here.

### Retention Rates

Dropout rates are highest (30%–40%) for the first 30 days of residence but decrease sharply thereafter (De Leon and Schwartz 1984). This temporal pattern of dropout is uniform across TC programs (and other modalities). In long-term residential TC programs, completion rates range from 10% to 25% of all admissions. One-year retention rates range from 20% to 35%, although more recent findings suggest gradual increases in annual retention compared with the period before 1980 (De Leon 1991).

### Predictors of Dropout

No reliable patient characteristics predict retention, the exception being severe criminality and/or severe psychopathology, which are correlated with earlier dropout. Studies point to the importance of dynamic factors in predicting retention in treatment, such as perceived legal pressure, motivation, and readiness for treatment

(e.g., Broome et al. 1997; Condelli and De Leon 1993; Condelli and Dunteman 1993; De Leon 1988; De Leon et al. 1994; Hubbard et al. 1988).

### Enhancing Retention in TCs

Some attempts to enhance retention in TCs have involved supportive individual counseling, improved orientation to treatment by experienced staff ("senior professors"), and family alliance strategies to reduce early dropout (e.g., De Leon 1991). Other efforts involve providing special facilities and programming for mothers and children (e.g., Coletti et al. 1997; Stevens et al. 1997) and teaching curriculum-based relapse-prevention methods (Lewis and Ross 1994) to sustain retention throughout residential treatment. Although results are promising, these efforts require replication in multiple sites.

Although a legitimate concern, retention should not be confused with treatment effectiveness. TCs are effective for those who remain long enough for treatment influences to occur. Obviously, however, a critical issue for TCs is maximizing holding power to benefit more patients.

## Treatment Process

Recent developments have facilitated empirical studies into the hitherto underinvestigated area of treatment process. These developments include formulations of the essential elements of the TC approach and of the stages of recovery in the TC (e.g., De Leon 1995, 1996a). Preliminary findings based on these formulations illuminate some active ingredients in the treatment process (Melnick and De Leon, in press).

## The Evolution of the TC: Modifications and Applications

The traditional TC model described in this chapter is actually the prototype of a variety of TC-oriented programs. Today, the TC modality consists of a wide range of programs serving a diversity of patients who use a variety of drugs and present with complex social-psychological problems in addition to their chemical abuse. Patient differences as well as clinical requirements and funding realities have encouraged the development of modified residential TC programs with shorter planned durations of stay (3, 6, and 12 months) as well as TC-oriented day-treatment and outpatient ambulatory models. Correctional facilities, medical and mental hospitals, and community residences and shelters, overwhelmed with alcohol and drug abuse problems, have implemented TC programs within their institutions. Highlighted in the following sections are some of the key modifications and applications of the TC approach for different patient populations in different settings.

## Current Modifications of the TC Model

Most community-based traditional TCs have expanded their social services or have incorporated new interventions to address the needs of their diverse residents. These changes and additions include family services; primary health care specifically geared toward HIV-positive patients and individuals with AIDS (e.g., Barton 1994; De Leon 1996b; McCusker and Sorensen 1994); aftercare, particularly for special populations such as substance-abusing inmates (e.g., Lockwood and Inciardi 1993); relapse-prevention training (e.g., Lewis and Ross 1994); 12-step–group components (De Leon 1990–1991); and mental health services (e.g., Carroll and Sobel 1986). Mostly these various modifications are additions to the program activities and enhance but do not alter the basic TC regimen. In some cases, these modifications substantially change the TC model itself.

### The Multimodal TC and Patient-Treatment Matching

Traditional TCs are highly effective for a certain segment of the drug-abusing population. However, those who seek assistance in TCs represent a broad spectrum of patients, many of whom may not be suited for a long-term residential stay. Improved diagnostic capability and assessment of individual differences have clarified the need for options other than long-term residential treatment.

Many TC agencies are multimodality treatment centers, which offer services in their residential and nonresidential programs depending on the clinical status and situational needs of the individual. The modalities include short- (less than 90 days), medium- (6–12 months), and long-term (1–2 years) residential components and drug-free outpatient services (6–12 months). Some TC agencies have drug-free day-treatment and methadone maintenance programs. Attempts are made to match the patient to the appropriate modality within the agency. For example, the spread of drug abuse, particularly cocaine use, in the workplace has prompted the development of short-term residential and ambulatory TC models for employed, more socialized patients.

To date, the effectiveness of TC-oriented multimodality programs has not been systematically evaluated, although several relevant studies indicate that positive outcomes are obtained in various shorter-term residential, day-treatment, and outpatient programs (e.g., Bucardo et al. 1997; Karson and Gesumaria 1997; McCusker and Sorensen 1994).

Given what is known about the complexity of the recovery process in addiction and the importance of length of stay in treatment, there is little likelihood that shorter-term treatment components alone will be sufficient to produce stable positive outcomes for individuals with serious substance-abuse problems. In multimodality TCs, for example, combinations of residential and outpatient services are needed for long-term treatment involvement and effect.

## Current Applications to Special Populations

An important sign of the evolution of the TC is its application to special populations and special settings. It is beyond the purview of this chapter to detail the modifications of these adapted TC models. In the main examples of these models, the focus on mutual self-help is retained, along with basic elements of the community approach, meetings, groups, work structure, and perspective on recovery and right living. Examples of these adaptations are more fully described elsewhere (De Leon 1997).

Recent research provides evidence for the effectiveness of modified TCs for special populations. These study populations include adolescents in various adaptations of the community-based TC (Hubbard et al. 1988; Jainchill 1997), inmates in prison TCs (Inciardi et al. 1997; Simpson et al. 1997; Wexler et al., in press), mentally ill chemical-abusing individuals (Sacks et al. 1997), addicted mothers and their children (Coletti et al. 1997; Winick and Evans 1997), and, although not described, patients receiving methadone in a day-treatment TC (De Leon et al. 1995).

## The TC in Human Services

The modifications of the traditional model and its adaptation for special populations and settings are redefining the TC modality within mainstream human services and mental health services. Most contemporary TC programs adhere to the perspective and approach described earlier. However, the basic peer/social learning framework has been enlarged to include additional social, psychological, and health services. Staffing compositions have altered, reflecting the fact that traditional professionals—correctional, mental health, medical and educational, family, and child care specialists; social workers; and case managers—serve along with experientially trained TC professionals.

These changes in patients, services, and staffing have also brought to the surface complex issues, particularly concerning staff divergence and integration. Some issues relate to the TC's philosophy of drug-free living and the TC's self-help perspective, others to differences in therapeutic concepts and terms, staff academic education, staff experience with addiction, and roles and functions within the context of a peer-community model.

The issues of integration have been addressed through vigorous training and orientation efforts guided by a common perspective of recovery (Carroll and Sobel 1986; Deitch and Solit 1993; De Leon 1985; Galanter et al. 1991). Indeed, the cross-fertilization of personnel and methods between traditional TCs and mental health and human services portends the evolution of a new TC: a general treatment model applicable to a broad range of populations for whom affiliation with a self-help community is the foundation for effecting the process of individual change.

## References

Barton E: The adaptation of the therapeutic community to HIV/AIDS. Proceedings of the Therapeutic Communities of America 1992 Planning Conference. Providence, RI, Manisses Communications Group, 1994, pp 66–70

Biase DV, Sullivan AP, Wheeler B: Daytop miniversity—phase 2—college training in a therapeutic community: development of self concept among drug free addict/abusers, in Therapeutic Communities for Addictions: Readings in Theory, Research, and Practice. Edited by De Leon G, Ziegenfuss JT. Springfield, IL, Charles C Thomas, 1986, pp 121–130

Brook RC, Whitehead IC: Drug-Free Therapeutic Community. New York, Human Sciences Press, 1980

Broome KM, Knight DK, Knight R, et al: Peer, family, and motivational influence on drug treatment process and recidivism for probationers. J Clin Psychol 53:387–397, 1997

Bucardo J, Guydish J, Acampora A, et al: The therapeutic community model applied to day treatment of substance abuse, in Community as Method: Therapeutic Communities for Special Populations and Special Settings. Edited by De Leon G. Westport, CT, Greenwood, 1997, pp 213–224

Carroll JFX, Sobel BS: Integrating mental health personnel and practices into a therapeutic community, in Therapeutic Communities for Addictions: Readings in Theory, Research, and Practice. Edited by De Leon G, Ziegenfuss JT. Springfield, IL, Charles C Thomas, 1986, pp 209–226

Casriel D: So Fair a House: The Story of Synanon. New York, Prentice-Hall, 1966

Coletti SD, Schinka JA, Hughs PH, et al: Specialized therapeutic community treatment for chemically dependent women and their children, in Community as Method: Therapeutic Communities for Special Populations and Special Settings. Edited by De Leon G. Westport, CT, Greenwood, 1997, pp 115–128

Condelli WS, De Leon G: Fixed and dynamic predictors of retention in therapeutic communities for substance abusers. J Subst Abuse Treat 10:11–16, 1993

Condelli WS, Dunteman GH: Issues to consider when predicting retention in therapeutic communities. J Psychoactive Drugs 25:239–244, 1993

Condelli WS, Hubbard RL: Client outcomes from therapeutic communities, in Therapeutic Community: Advances in Research and Application (NIDA Res Monogr No 144, NIH Publ No 94-3633). Edited by Tims FM, De Leon G, Jainchill N. Rockville, MD, National Institute on Drug Abuse, 1994, pp 80–98

Deitch DA: Treatment of Drug Abuse in the Therapeutic Community: Historical Influences, Current Considerations, and Future Outlooks, Vol 4. Washington, DC, National Commission on Marihuana and Drug Abuse, 1972, pp 158–175

Deitch DA, Solit R: Training drug abuse treatment personnel in therapeutic community methodologies. Psychotherapy 30 (special issue):305–316, 1993

De Leon G: The Therapeutic Community: Study of Effectiveness (NIDA Treatment Res Monogr ADM-84-1286). Rockville, MD, National Institute on Drug Abuse, 1984

De Leon G: Adolescent Substance Abusers in the Therapeutic Community: Treatment Outcomes. Proceedings of the Ninth World Conference on Therapeutic Communities, Montreal, Canada, 1985

De Leon G: Legal pressure in therapeutic communities, in Compulsory Treatment of Drug Abuse: Research and Clinical Practice (NIDA Res Monogr No 86, DHHS Publ No ADM-88-1578). Edited by Leukefeld CG, Tims FM. Rockville, MD, National Institute on Drug Abuse, 1988, pp 160–177

De Leon G: Aftercare in therapeutic communities. International Journal of the Addictions 25:1225–1237, 1990–1991

De Leon G: Retention in drug free therapeutic communities, in Improving Drug Treatment (NIDA Res Monogr 106). Edited by Pickens RW, Leukefeld CG, Schuster CR. Rockville, MD, National Institute on Drug Abuse, 1991, pp 218–244

De Leon G: Cocaine abusers in therapeutic community treatment, in Advances in Cocaine Treatment: Research and Clinical Perspectives (NIDA Monogr No 135, NIH Publ No 93–3639). Edited by Tims FM. Rockville, MD, National Institute on Drug Abuse, 1993, pp 163–189

De Leon G: Therapeutic communities for addictions: a theoretical framework. International Journal of the Addictions 30:1603–1645, 1995

De Leon G: Integrative recovery: a stage paradigm. Substance Abuse 17:51–63, 1996a

De Leon G: Therapeutic communities: AIDS/HIV risk and harm reduction. J Subst Abuse Treat 13:411–420, 1996b

De Leon G (ed): Community as Method: Therapeutic Communities for Special Populations and Special Settings. Westport, CT, Greenwood, 1997

De Leon G, Jainchill N: Male and female drug abusers: social and psychological status 2 years after treatment in a therapeutic community. Am J Drug Alcohol Abuse 8:465–497, 1981–1982

De Leon G, Schwartz S: The therapeutic community: what are the retention rates? Am J Drug Alcohol Abuse 10:267–284, 1984

De Leon G, Skodol A, Rosenthal MS: Phoenix House: changes in psychopathological signs of resident drug addicts. Arch Gen Psychiatry 23:131–135, 1973

De Leon G, Melnick G, Kressel D, et al: Circumstances, motivation, readiness and suitability (the CMRS scales): predicting retention in therapeutic community treatment. Am J Drug Alcohol Abuse 20:495–515, 1994

De Leon G, Staines G, Perlis PE, et al: Therapeutic community methods in methadone maintenance (Passages): an open clinical trial. Journal of Drug and Alcohol Dependence 37:45–57, 1995

Frankel B: Transforming Identities, Context, Power, and Ideology in a Therapeutic Community. New York, Peter Lang, 1989

Galanter M, Egelko S, De Leon G, et al: Crack/cocaine abusers in the general hospital: assessment and initiation of care. Am J Psychiatry 149:810–815, 1991

Holland S: Evaluating community based treatment programs: a model for strengthening inferences about effectiveness. International Journal of Therapeutic Communities 4:285–306, 1983

Holland S: Measuring process in drug abuse treatment research, in Therapeutic Communities for Addictions: Readings in Theory, Research, and Practice. Edited by De Leon G, Ziegenfuss JT. Springfield, IL, Charles C Thomas, 1986, pp 169–181

Hubbard RL, Collins JJ, Rachal JV, et al: The criminal justice client in drug abuse treatment, in Compulsory Treatment of Drug Abuse: Research and Clinical Practice (NIDA Res Monogr No 86, DHHS Publ No ADM-88-1578). Edited by Leukefeld CG, Tims FM. Rockville, MD, National Institute on Drug Abuse, 1988, pp 57–80

Hubbard RL, Craddock SG, Flynn PM, et al: Overview of 1-year follow-up outcomes in the Drug Abuse Treatment Outcome Study (DATOS). Psychology of Addictive Behaviors 11 (special issue):261–278, 1997

Inciardi JA, Martin SS, Butzin CA, et al: An effective model of prison-based treatment for drug-involved offenders. Journal of Drug Issues 27:261–278, 1997

Jainchill N: Co-morbidity and therapeutic community treatment, in Therapeutic Community: Advances in Research and Application (NIDA Res Monogr No 144, NIH Publ No 94-3633). Edited by Tims FM, De Leon G, Jainchill N. Rockville_,MD, National Institute on Drug Abuse, 1994, pp 209–231

Jainchill N: Therapeutic communities for adolescents: the same and not the same, in Community as Method: Therapeutic Communities for Special Populations and Special Settings. Edited by De Leon G. Westport, CT, Greenwood, 1997, pp 161–178

Jones M: Therapeutic Community: A New Treatment Method in Psychiatry. New York, Basic Books, 1953

Karson JS, Gesumaria RV: Program description and outcome of an enhanced, six-month residential therapeutic community, in Community as Method: Therapeutic Communities for Special Populations and Special Settings. Edited by De Leon G. Westport, CT, Greenwood, 1997, pp 199–212

Kennard D, Wilson S: The modification of personality disturbance in a therapeutic community for drug abusers. Br J Med Psychol 52:215–221, 1979

Kooyman M: The Therapeutic Community for Addicts: Intimacy, Parent Involvement, and Treatment Success. Rotterdam, The Netherlands, Erasmus University, 1993

Lewis BF, Ross R: Retention in therapeutic communities: challenges for the 90s, in Therapeutic Community: Advances in Research and Application (NIDA Res Monogr No 144, NIH Publ No 94-3633). Edited by Tims FM, De Leon G, Jainchill N. Rockville, MD, National Institute on Drug Abuse, 1994, pp 99–116

Lockwood D, Inciardi JA: CREST outreach center: a work release iteration of the TC model, in Innovative Approaches in the Treatment of Drug Abuse: Program Models and Strategies. Edited by Inciardi J, Tims FM, Fletcher BW. Newport, CT, Greenwood, 1993, pp 61–69

McCusker J, Sorensen JL: HIV and therapeutic communities, in Therapeutic Community: Advances in Research and Application (NIDA Res Monogr No 144, NIH Publ No 94-3633). Edited by Tims FM, De Leon G, Jainchill N. Rockville, MD, National Institute on Drug Abuse, 1994, pp 232–258

Melnick G, De Leon G: Clarifying the nature of therapeutic community treatment: a survey of essential elements. J Subst Abuse Treat (in press)

Pompi KF, Resnick J: Retention in a therapeutic community for court referred adolescents and young adults. Am J Drug Alcohol Abuse 13:309–325, 1987

Sacks S, Sacks J, De Leon G, et al: Modified therapeutic community for mentally ill chemical abusers: background; influences; program description; preliminary findings. Substance Use and Misuse 32:1217–1259, 1997

Simpson DD, Sells SB: Effectiveness of treatment for drug abuse: an overview of the DARP research program. Adv Alcohol Subst Abuse 2:7–29, 1982

Simpson DD, Joe GW, Brown BS: Treatment retention and follow-up outcomes in DATOS. Psychology of Addictive Behaviors 11 (special issue):294–307, 1997

Stevens SJ, Arbiter N, McGrath R: Women and children: therapeutic community substance abuse treatment, in Community as Method: Therapeutic Communities for Special Populations and Special Settings. Edited by De Leon G. Westport, CT, Greenwood, 1997, pp 129–142

Sugarman B: Structure, variations, and context: a sociological view of the therapeutic community, in Therapeutic Communities for Addictions: Readings in Theory, Research, and Practice. Edited by De Leon G, Ziegenfuss JT. Springfield, IL, Charles C Thomas, 1986, pp 65–82

Tims FM, Ludford JP (eds): Drug Abuse Treatment Evaluation: Strategies, Progress, and Prospects (NIDA Res Monogr No 51), Special Issue on Research Analysis and Utilization System. Rockville, MD, National Institute on Drug Abuse, 1984

Tims FM, De Leon G, Jainchill N (eds): Therapeutic Community: Advances in Research and Application (NIDA Res Monogr No 144, NIH Publ No 94-3633). Rockville, MD, National Institute on Drug Abuse, 1994

Wexler HK, De Leon G, Thomas G, et al: The Amity Prison TC evaluation: reincarceration outcomes. Criminal Justice and Behavior (in press)

Winick C, Evans JT: A therapeutic community for mothers and their children, in Community as Method: Therapeutic Communities for Special Populations and Special Settings. Edited by De Leon G. Westport, CT, Greenwood, 1997, pp 143–160

Yablonsky L: Synanon: The Tunnel Back. New York, Macmillan, 1965

Zuckerman M, Sola S, Masterson J, et al: MMPI patterns in drug abusers before and after treatment in therapeutic communities. J Consult Clin Psychol 43:286–296, 1975

# 6 Special Populations

# 40 Adolescent Substance Abuse

Yifrah Kaminer, M.D.
Ralph E. Tarter, Ph.D.

Childhood and adolescence are not only critical phases for normal development but also periods when various pathological behaviors or disorders including substance use disorders are first recognized (Kaminer 1994). There is mounting concern regarding the physical and mental health outcomes of adolescents who use psychoactive drugs. This concern among professionals and policy makers is based on epidemiological data demonstrating a continued increase in the incidence of substance use among youth (Johnston et al. 1996), a decrease in the age at first diagnosis of substance use disorder (T. Reich et al. 1988), and an increase in the lifetime prevalence of substance abuse and dependence in the general population (Lewinsohn et al. 1996), as well as on the observation that use of alcohol and other drugs is a leading cause among adolescents of morbidity and mortality from motor vehicle accidents, suicidal behavior, violence, drowning, and unprotected sexual activity (U.S. Department of Vital Statistics 1993).

In this chapter, we review the literature on the development of adolescent substance use, placing particular emphasis on the transition from substance use to substance abuse or dependence. The effect of prevention and treatment on the course of substance use disorders is also addressed. We discuss the difference between substance use and substance use disorders and then review the natural history of substance use disorders among adolescents and the pattern of psychiatric comorbidity. We conclude with a brief evaluation of the efficacy of prevention and treatment of substance use disorders in adolescents.

## Nosology

### Normative Behavior

Although any nonmedical use of drugs (including tobacco and alcohol) by adolescents is illegal and can therefore be viewed as a form of abuse, this perspective ignores some key epidemiological findings. Specifically, the high prevalence of alcohol and tobacco use underscores the fact that use of alcohol and tobacco can be viewed as normative, or at least not extremely deviant. By age 18 years, 79.2% of youth in the United States have drunk alcohol, and 3.7% drink alcohol daily (Johnston et al. 1996); 63.5% have smoked cigarettes, and 13% smoke half a pack a day. Other drugs that are illegal for the whole population also have a high prevalence of use. Marijuana has been used at least once in the lifetime by 44.9% of 18-year-olds; 4.9% use the drug daily. Lifetime exposure rates for inhalants (16.6%), stimulants (15.3%), hallucinogens (14.0%), and cocaine (7.9%) illustrate the extent of drug use in the population of 18-year-old high school students in the United States.

Most adolescents who engage in substance use do not develop substance use disorders as defined by DSM-IV criteria (American Psychiatric Association 1994). It is thus imperative to understand adolescent substance use in the context of changeable patterns of normative behavior and to distinguish this behavior from substance use disorder.

Adolescence has long been recognized as a phase of transition (Erikson 1968). During this period of life, biological and psychological maturation are completed. The social roles of adulthood are increasingly assumed during the final stage of sexual, physical, and psychological maturation. Working, driving, engaging in sexual activity, and using psychoactive substances, particularly alcohol and tobacco, are adultlike activities and behaviors that become increasingly common in persons ages 13–18 years. Alcohol and drug use (particularly tobacco use) can thus be viewed as one facet of adolescent socialization (Newcomb 1995). In one study, adolescents who experimented with psychoactive substances had better psychological outcomes than did adolescents who used substances frequently or adolescents who abstained (Shedler and Block 1990). It should not be concluded from the presentation of this finding that experimentation with psychoactive substances is recommended. However, the finding is evidence that some substance use during adolescence does not necessarily portend an adverse outcome.

## Pathological Behavior

Approximately 8% of the United States population will fulfill the criteria for a diagnosis of a substance use disorder during their lifetimes. The cutoff point for a diagnosis of substance use disorder or dependence is somewhat arbitrary, however, particularly in adolescents (Rohde et al. 1996). In clinical psychiatry, a categorical paradigm (e.g., normal vs. abnormal) has traditionally been used, even though this theoretical perspective has limitations in terms of understanding pathogenesis and improving treatment (Bukstein and Kaminer 1994). In addition, serious negative effects of drugs in adolescents at the subdiagnostic levels have been recognized, although they have not yet been addressed in DSM (Lewinsohn et al. 1996).

In DSM-III-R (American Psychiatric Association 1987), psychoactive substance use disorders were divided into two diagnostic categories: dependence and abuse, a residual disorder. Abuse was considered a less maladaptive disorder than dependence was. However, because abuse was considered a residual disorder, and therefore perhaps not considered severe enough to warrant intensive or professional treatment, availability of treatment for adolescents with this diagnosis was not assured.

The importance of differentiating between substance abuse and dependence in treatment was supported by empirical evidence provided by Hasin and associates (1990). They concluded that most adults with a diagnosis of substance abuse had never progressed to dependence. Abuse and dependence are therefore distinct, and abuse is not always a prodrome and may be developmentally limited in many adolescents.

The DSM-IV diagnostic criteria for substance abuse and dependence are the same for adolescents and adults. Empirical data generally support the validity of the DSM-IV criteria for adolescents (Lewinsohn et al. 1996; Martin et al. 1995).

Studies involving alcoholic patients in which a dimensional approach, rather than a categorical approach, to psychiatric diagnosis was used revealed two main variants, labeled as either Type 1 and Type 2 (Cloninger 1987; Sigvardsson et al. 1996) or Type A and Type B (Babor et al. 1992). The Type 2 or Type B variant is first diagnosed in adolescents and is characterized by an earlier onset of alcohol-seeking behavior, a rapid acceleration of alcohol (and other drug) involvement, severe symptoms, antisocial behavior, and a poor prognosis. Three personality characteristics—high level of novelty seeking, low level of harm avoidance, and low dependence on reward—have been implicated (Cloninger 1987) in this variant, but empirical evidence in support of this profile is inconsistent.

Temperament deviations have also been shown to be associated with psychopathology and substance abuse (W. Reich et al. 1993). Children having a "difficult temperament" commonly manifest externalizing and internalizing behavior problems by middle childhood (Earls and Jung 1987) and in adolescence (Maziade et al. 1990). High levels of behavioral activity have been noted in youth at high risk for substance abuse as well as in those with substance use disorder. High levels of activity also correlate with disorder severity (Tarter et al. 1990a, 1990b). Other temperamental trait deviations found in youth at high risk include reduced attention span (Schaffer et al. 1984), high impulsivity (Noll et al. 1992) and negative affect states such as irritability (Brook et al. 1990), and emotional reactivity (Blackson 1994). Tarter and colleagues (1994) used the difficult-temperament index to classify adolescent alcoholic patients. The obtained clusters were similar to the adult subtypes reported by Cloninger (1987) and Babor et al. (1992). The smaller subset of adolescents manifesting behavioral dyscontrol and hypophoria were included in Cluster 2, whereas those with primarily negative affect were included in Cluster 1. Compared with Cluster 1 subjects, Cluster 2 patients were younger at the time of first substance use, first substance abuse diagnosis, and first psychiatric diagnosis. Moreover, adolescents with a difficult temperament had a high probability of developing psychiatric disorders such as conduct disorder, attention-deficit/hyperactivity disorder (ADHD), anxiety disorders, and mood disorders (Tarter et al. 1994). Recently, Tarter et al. (1997) reported that Cluster 1 and Cluster 2 were identified in both male adolescents and female adolescents.

## Initiation, Maintenance, and Transitions of Substance Use

A number of behavioral dispositions and environmental influences are predictive of age at initiation of drug use, drug use intensity, and the experience of negative consequences during adolescence (Hawkins et al. 1992; Petraitis et al. 1995). Behavioral characteristics most commonly include impulsivity, aggression, sensation seeking, low levels of harm avoidance, inability to delay gratification, low levels of striving to achieve, lack of religiosity, and psychopathology, especially conduct disorder. Contextual or environmental factors that are most common include stressful life events, lack of support from parents, absence of normative peers, perception of high availability of drugs, social norms that facilitate drug use, and relaxed laws and regulatory policies. Clearly, manifold risk factors, each having different salience, determine overall risk for each person. In aggregate, these risk factors determine the slope and momentum of the developmental trajectory into adulthood, culminating in substance use, abuse, or dependence (Bates and Labouvie 1995). Although adolescence is a time of heightened risk, heavy use is often limited to the period of adolescence. That is, substance use does not invariably increase and lead to dependence. Indeed, moderation or even cessation may occur during or after adolescence (Labouvie 1996).

Kandel (1982), the initial proponent of the "gateway" theory, argued that there are at least four distinct developmental stages of drug use: 1) beer or wine consumption, 2) cigarette smoking or hard liquor consumption, 3) marijuana use, and 4) other illicit drug use.

According to Kandel (1982), 26% of adolescents who use illicit drugs progress to the next stage, compared with only 4% who have never used marijuana. A recent study by Golub and Johnson (1994) indicated that alcohol is losing its importance as a prerequisite for progression to marijuana, but marijuana's role as a gateway drug appears to have increased, and marijuana use nearly always precedes use of substances that have less normative attitudes (e.g., heroin).

Kandel et al. (1986) studied the 10-year outcome of adolescent substance use at age 15–16 years. They found that the strongest predictor of drug use is prior drug use. However, the consequences of drug use affect every aspect of life in early adulthood. Illicit drug use begun at an early age has also been found to increase the risk of drug problems during late adolescence. According to the results of a retrospective analysis of the Epidemiologic Catchment Area data (Anthony and Petronis 1995), prior drug use predicts future drug use. However, in a prospective study of adolescents (Bates and Labouvie 1997), age at first use of illicit drugs did not emerge as an independent risk factor for either persistence or severity of drug use in adulthood.

When substance use behaviors at age 18 years are controlled, there is no significant relationship between adolescent risk and adult substance use intensity and consequences (Teichman et al. 1989). In effect, the effect of child and adolescent risk factors on adult substance use may be mediated by the intensity of substance use in late adolescence (Bates and Labouvie 1997).

Temperament precursors such as impulsivity and novelty and sensation seeking tend to peak in late adolescence or early adulthood (Zuckerman 1994) and to decrease toward the fourth decade of life, the decrease accompanied by an increase in cognitive structure. These changes may in part be responsible for the low predictive utility of differences in these and other adolescent risk variables at age 18 years, as reported by Bates and Labouvie (1997). More study is needed to link changes over the long term in both interpersonal and environmental risk and protective factors to long-term use patterns.

The available results suggest that programs aimed at reducing risk factors during adolescence may have more beneficial long-term effects if they can limit drug use during the peak lifetime period, at ages 18–21 years. Programs that focus on postadolescence thus need to concentrate on the concurrent risk factors that are not necessarily the same as those during adolescence. In early adolescence, prevention efforts should be directed at delaying onset and increase of drug use, because drug use predicts future drug use, although not in an invariant fashion.

## Psychiatric Comorbidity

Psychiatric disorders in childhood, particularly the disruptive behavior disorders, confer an increased risk for the development of substance use disorders (Bukstein et al. 1989; Christie et al. 1988; Loeber 1988). However, the etiological mechanisms have not been systematically researched. A number of possible relationships exist between substance use disorders and psychopathology. Psychopathology may precede substance use disorders, may develop as a consequence of preexisting substance use disorders, may moderate the severity of substance use disorders, or may originate from a common vulnerability (Hovens et al. 1994).

A number of psychiatric disorders are commonly associated with substance use disorders in youth. Conduct disorder is commonly associated with adolescent substance use disorders, and if it occurs, it usually precedes the substance use disorder (Loeber 1988; Milin et al. 1991). Rates of conduct disorder range from 50% to 80% in adolescent patients with substance use disorders. Although ADHD is frequently observed in substance-using and substance-abusing youth, such an association is likely due to the high level of comorbidity between conduct disorder and ADHD (Alterman and Tarter 1986; Wilens et al. 1994). An earlier onset of conduct problems and aggressive behavior, in addition to ADHD, increases the risk for substance abuse (Loeber 1988). In a prospective follow-up study, Biederman et al. (1997) found that adolescents with and adolescents without ADHD had similar magnitudes of risk for substance use disorders. Conduct disorder and bipolar disorder mediated the association between childhood ADHD and substance use disorder outcome.

In addition, mood disorders, especially depression, frequently precede substance use and substance use disorders in adolescents (Bukstein et al. 1992; Deykin et al. 1992). The prevalence of depressive disorders ranges from 24% to more than 50%.

The empirical literature also supports an association between substance use disorders and suicidal behavior in adolescents (Kaminer 1996). Adolescents who commit suicide are frequently under the influence of alcohol or other drugs at the time of suicide (Brent et al. 1987). Possible mechanisms underlying this relationship include the direct acute pharmacological and chronic neurological effects of psychoactive substances. Acute intoxication may be experienced as a transient but intense dysphoric state, with behavioral disinhibition and impaired judgment. Substance use may also exacerbate preexisting psychopathology, especially impulse dyscontrol, depression, and anxiety.

Several studies of clinical populations have found a high rate of anxiety disorder among youth with substance use disorders (D. B. Clark and Sayette 1993; D. B. Clark et al. 1995). In adolescent patients with substance use disorders, the prevalence of anxiety disorder ranged from 7% to more than 40% (D. B. Clark et al. 1995; Stowell 1991). The order of appearance of

anxiety and substance use disorders is variable, depending on the specific anxiety disorder. Social phobia usually precedes substance abuse, whereas panic and generalized anxiety disorder more often follow the onset of substance use disorders (Kushner et al. 1990). Adolescents with substance use disorders often have a history of posttraumatic stress disorder from physical or sexual abuse (D. B. Clark et al. 1995; Van Hasselt et al. 1993). Bulimia nervosa (Bulik 1987); pathological gambling (Griffiths 1995); and personality disorders, particularly those in Cluster B (Grilo et al. 1995), are also commonly found in adolescents with substance use disorders.

There are no reports of research regarding the stability of psychiatric disorders in adolescents with dual diagnoses. A study of the stability of comorbid psychiatric disorders in alcoholic men after 1 year of follow-up revealed that the symptoms are stable over time and therefore constitute a potential target for treatment (Penick et al. 1988). On the other hand, Rounsaville and Kleber (1986) reported good stability of comorbid psychiatric disorders at 6-month follow-up among opiate-addicted individuals, and this stability deteriorated by 2.5-year follow-up, resulting in a low rate of stability. Penick and colleagues (1988) attributed these differences to a threshold effect.

## Prevention

Efforts to curtail substance abuse have historically concentrated on modifying the supply-to-demand ratio. However, reduction of supply cannot succeed as long as a demand exists. Hence, reducing demand is an integral component of prevention. Laws and regulations can reduce demand. For example, Coate and Grossman (1987) found that alcohol consumption decreased in youth when the cost of alcoholic beverages or the legal drinking age was increased. O'Malley and Wagenaar (1991) reported a reduction in car accidents among youth after the legal drinking age increased to 21 years.

An overarching goal of prevention is to delay initiation of use of gateway substances such as cigarettes, alcohol, and marijuana. The traditional prevention strategy involves an educational program designed to increase knowledge of the consequences of drug use. That increased knowledge alone prevents drug use is, however, not supported by available evidence (Schinke et al. 1991). Alternative activities programs, and affective education that is designed to increase self-esteem and responsible decision-making, have also been found to be ineffective in preventing drug use (Bangert-Drowns 1988; Tobler 1986). More promising prevention strategies are aimed at enhancing social skills and drug-refusal skills. Botvin et al. (1995) implemented a curriculum involving teaching of general life skills and of skills for resisting social influences to use drugs. This curriculum included classes in the seventh grade and booster sessions during the 2 years after completion of the intervention. The investigators reported a substantial and lasting reduction in drug use 6 years later among more than 2,000 twelfth-graders. These findings need to be replicated to confirm effectiveness for primary as well as secondary prevention.

The challenge confronting health care providers is to identify high-risk individuals before or shortly after initiation of substance use. One of the largest high-risk populations are children who have a biological parent with a diagnosis of substance dependence. The risk of substance use disorders is 4–10 times greater in these children (Goodwin 1985). Children of parents with opioid dependence also have a high rate of psychopathology and more frequently have academic, family, and legal problems (Kolar et al. 1994; Wilens et al. 1995). A balanced view is needed regarding the development and outcomes of children of alcoholic individuals because most children raised by an alcoholic parent do not develop alcoholism (Wilson and Crowe 1991). Moreover, the labeling of children of alcoholic individuals as such is potentially harmful (Burk and Sher 1990). Thus, although children of substance-abusing persons are at an increased risk for developing substance use disorders themselves, prevention efforts need to take into account the adverse effect of labeling while recognizing that most children do not experience the negative outcome. The interaction between risk and protective factors may influence the development or arrest of substance abuse in the vulnerable child. The study of resilience among youth growing up in substance-abusing families is continuing (Wolin and Wolin 1996).

To maximize outcome, an understanding of the heterogeneity of the adolescent population is required. In addition, prevention efforts need to take into account the developmental staging of substance use behavior. In this regard, prevention must address the needs of adolescents in multiple domains of life. Prevention programs that are sensitive to ethnic differences also need to be devised (Catalano et al. 1993).

## Treatment

Most research on substance use disorders in adolescents has focused on the descriptive features, particular

diagnosis, psychiatric comorbidity, and assessment (Kaminer 1994). Most studies on treatment outcome have one or more methodological flaws. Documentation of reliability and validity of diagnostic rating scales to assess substance use disorder severity was often lacking. Personal and demographic variables such as gender, age, race, and socioeconomic factors have not been reported such that a determination of whether specialized treatments program components were needed was not carefully assessed or even considered. Lastly, in the limited number of studies involving a methodologically acceptable number of adolescents within the appropriate age range (12–18 years), the treatment setting, type of interventions, and time in treatment were not controlled. Methodological variability has also hampered the comparability of studies. These shortcomings in the studies conducted to date limit our capacity to draw definitive conclusions.

After reviewing 47 studies on the treatment outcome of adolescents with substance use disorders, we concluded that some treatment is better than no treatment. However, the effects of treatment are not uniform. Substantial variability is observed in posttreatment outcome (Catalano et al. 1990–1991; Kaminer 1994).

Most studies in which prediction of outcome was a goal have focused on patient characteristics measured at the time treatment was initiated. Factors such as age, race, socioeconomic status, severity of drug use, and mental health status have been postulated to be associated with prognosis. Although some studies provide evidence of a relationship between pretreatment patient characteristics and outcome, the findings are not consistent. Variables such as severity of alcohol problems, severity of other drug use, severity of internalizing symptoms, and level of self-esteem are prognostic of treatment completion in American, Canadian, and Irish adolescents (Blood and Cornwall 1994; Doyle et al. 1994; Kaminer et al. 1992). Psychopathology, particularly conduct disorder, is negatively correlated with treatment completion and posttreatment abstinence (Myers et al. 1995).

Most studies on treatment outcome of adolescents with substance use disorders have focused on completion of treatment rather than follow-up status. Reports of follow-up studies indicate that relapse rates are high, ranging between 35% and 85% (Brown et al. 1989; Catalano et al. 1990–1991; Doyle et al. 1994). The high relapse rate is associated with social pressures. Abstinent teens experience decreased interpersonal conflict, improve academically, and demonstrate increased involvement in normative social and occupational activities (Brown et al. 1994; Vik et al. 1992).

Treatment research on adolescents has focused on three general areas: length of time in treatment, staff characteristics, and program environment and treatment services. The most important findings are discussed here.

Length of time in treatment has been shown to be less predictive of treatment outcome than staff characteristics, program environment, and treatment services. However, research has shown that the longer the adolescent remains in treatment, the better the prognosis is (Catalano et al. 1990–1991; Kaminer 1994). Longer time in treatment means more opportunities for improvement. How individual patient characteristics and the various components of treatment interact to affect treatment retention has not yet been studied.

Staff characteristics that affect treatment success include amount of professional experience, competence in taking a problem-solving approach, and availability of volunteers in the program who interact with patients (Friedman et al. 1989). Staff who themselves have recurring addiction problems do not have a positive effect on treatment outcome (Catalano et al. 1990–1991).

Recent findings suggest that the treatment setting (e.g., inpatient, residential, and outpatient settings) is less important than the menu of treatment, with regard to treatment outcome (Kaminer 1994). That is, to improve clinical status, it is imperative to provide adequate dosages and specific interventions. Two interventions have been shown to be particularly useful in the treatment of adolescents with substance use disorders: family therapy and cognitive-behavior therapy (CBT). The involvement of the family increases the likelihood that the patient will complete treatment and reduces problem behavior during treatment (Barrett et al. 1988). Several investigators have demonstrated the benefits of family-based approaches in treating substance use disorders in adolescents (Friedman and Utada 1989; Liddle and Dakof 1995; Szapocznik et al. 1988). The multisystemic therapy model is a successful family-based ecological systems approach in which interventions simultaneously target family functioning and communication, school and peer functioning, and adjustment in the community (Henggeler et al. 1992, 1996).

Behavioral treatment has been reported to be superior to supportive counseling (Azrin et al. 1994). A number of cognitive-behavioral treatment approaches, including many previously used with adults (e.g., relapse prevention), have also shown promise for

treatment in adolescents (Kaminer 1994). Manual-guided therapy has been shown to be helpful in improving drug-refusal, problem-solving, and social skills (Kaminer 1994). Comparison of the effectiveness of two 12-week psychosocial interventions revealed that adolescents enrolled in a CBT program fared better than those who participated in an interactional therapy program. Those assigned to CBT demonstrated a statistically significant reduction in severity of substance use, as determined through the use of the Teen-Addiction Severity Index (Kaminer et al. 1991, 1993) and controlled by the Teen Treatment Services Review (Kaminer et al. 1998b), compared with those assigned to interactional therapy (Kaminer et al. 1998c). Improvements were also observed in the areas of family function, school adjustment, peer or social relationships, legal problems, and psychiatric disturbance in patients receiving CBT, although the difference was not statistically significant (Kaminer et al. 1998c).

Friedman et al. (1989) reported that prognosis is enhanced by the provision of special services, including instruction in relaxation techniques and counseling in the areas of school, work, recreation, and contraception. We are not familiar with studies on the effect of self-help groups on adolescent substance abuse. Finally, pharmacotherapy of adolescent substance use disorders is a neglected therapeutic modality; progress in terms of research has only recently been made, primarily in the form of publication of single-case studies (Kaminer 1995). More studies are needed on the efficacy of this treatment modality.

An emphasis in psychotherapy is on determining the intervention modality that best produces specific changes by particular therapists in specified particular settings (Waltz et al. 1993). One promising treatment strategy for substance-abusing adults involves *patient-treatment matching*—matching the patient to treatment on the basis of specific needs and characteristics of the patient (Kadden et al. 1989; Litt et al. 1992). Research on patient-treatment matching has focused not on main effects of treatment, such as efficacy (a comparison between treatments), but on the effects of interaction between treatment intervention modality and patient variables. Kadden et al. (1989) reported that alcoholic adults scoring high on measures of sociopathy or global psychopathology have better prognoses when the coping-skills approach is used, whereas patients scoring low on either of these measures have better outcomes when interpersonal group treatment is the treatment used. Litt and colleagues (1992) analyzed the data of Kadden et al. (1989), reclassifying subjects with the use of the empirically derived Type A/Type B typology of alcoholism (Babor et al. 1992). They found that type A alcoholic individuals—those with adult onset, rapid progression to severe alcohol dependence, and little or no criminality—fared poorly when a coping-skills training approach was used, whereas type B patients—those with teenage onset and recurrent psychiatric, social, and legal problems—had worse outcomes when interpersonal therapy was used. A review of more than 30 studies indicated that patient-treatment matching may maximize prognosis (Mattson et al. 1994). However, matching effects similar to those reported by Kadden et al. (1989) in alcoholic adults were not found in substance-abusing adolescents (Kaminer et al. 1998c). Use of multivariate typology in studies involving adolescents (Tarter et al. 1997) may be helpful in the investigation of patient-treatment matching.

A comorbid psychiatric disorder may be the primary reason adolescents with substance use disorder seek treatment. Indeed, Friedman and Glickman (1987) reported that 28% of adolescents sought treatment because of an emotional or psychiatric problem. The effect of psychiatric comorbidity on treatment outcome in adolescents with comorbid disorders has been addressed in two studies. Friedman and Glickman (1987) studied court-referred drug-abusing men in a day-treatment program. The findings indicated that the number of psychiatric symptoms negatively correlated with treatment outcome. Kaminer and colleagues (1992) investigated patient variables that may distinguish treatment completers from noncompleters in hospitalized adolescents with dual diagnoses. Significant differences between groups were not found for any of the following variables: age, parent or caregiver level of education, socioeconomic status, gender, race, domicile, legal status on admission, and history of psychiatric and/or substance abuse treatment. Members of the two groups also did not differ with respect to prevalence of psychiatric disorders in their parents. However, the two groups were distinguishable by psychiatric diagnosis. Mood and adjustment disorders were substantially more frequent among the treatment completers, whereas the noncompleters were more likely to have a diagnosis of conduct disorder.

Because existing treatments are generally associated with modest prognosis, there is a need to develop and test innovative psychosocial treatment approaches (Crits-Christoph and Siqueland 1996). The development of manual-guided therapies, as well as measurements that assess treatment type and frequency of treatment provision (e.g., Teen Treatment Services Review) and the treatment process for adolescents with substance use disorders (Kaminer et al. 1998a), ensures honest adherence to protocols in the application of treatment procedures. Another area of interest pertains to efficacy versus effectiveness and the dissemination of the results of clinical research (G. N. Clark 1995).

## Conclusion

Individual differences exist in the etiological pathway to drug abuse. Drug use in most adolescents subsides or stops by adulthood. However, adolescents who have poor social skills and limited social networks and who engage in substance use during late adolescence are at high risk for substance dependence in adulthood. Research is needed to clarify the emergence and interaction of individual and contextual risk factors in relation to intervention modality. When such data are obtained, the patient can be matched with the treatment associated with the best prognosis. This approach maximizes both prevention and treatment outcomes.

## References

Alterman AI, Tarter RE: An Examination of Selected Topologies: Hyperactivity, Familial and Antisocial Alcoholism: Recent Developments in Alcoholism, Vol 4. New York, Plenum, 1986

American Psychiatric Association: Diagnostic and Statistical Manual of Mental Disorders, 3rd Edition, Revised. Washington, DC, American Psychiatric Association, 1987

American Psychiatric Association: Diagnostic and Statistical Manual of Mental Disorders, 4th Edition. Washington, DC, American Psychiatric Association, 1994

Anthony JC, Petronis KR: Early onset drug use and risk of later drug problems. Drug Alcohol Depend 40:9–15, 1995

Azrin NH, Donohue B, Besalel VA: Youth drug abuse treatment: a controlled outcome study. Journal of Child and Adolescent Substance Abuse 3:1–16, 1994

Babor TF, Hoffman M, Del Boca FK, et al: Types of alcoholics, I: evidence for an empirically derived typology based on indicators of vulnerability and severity. Arch Gen Psychiatry 49:599–608, 1992

Bangert-Drowns RL: The effects of school-based substance abuse education: a meta-analysis. J Drug Educ 18:243–264, 1988

Barrett ME, Simpson DD, Lehman WE: Behavioral changes of adolescents in drug abuse intervention programs. J Clin Psychol 44:461–473, 1988

Bates ME, Labouvie EW: Personality-environment constellations and alcohol use: a process-oriented study of intraindividual change during adolescence. Psychology of Addiction Behavior 9:23–35, 1995

Bates ME, Labouvie EW: Adolescent risk factors and the prediction of persistent alcohol and drug use into adulthood. Alcohol Clin Exp Res 21:944–950, 1997

Biederman J, Wilens T, Mick E, et al: Is ADHD a risk factor for psychoactive substance use disorders? Findings from a four-year prospective follow-up study. J Am Acad Child Adolesc Psychiatry 36:21–29, 1997

Blackson TC: Temperament: a salient correlate of risk factors for alcohol and drug abuse. Drug Alcohol Depend 36:205–214, 1994

Blood L, Cornwall A: Pretreatment variables that predict completion of an adolescent substance abuse treatment program. J Nerv Ment Dis 182:14–19, 1994

Botvin GJ, Baker E, Dusenbury I, et al: Long-term follow-up results of a randomized drug abuse prevention trial in a white middle-class population. JAMA 273:1106–1112, 1995

Brent DA, Perper JA, Allman C: Alcohol, firearms and suicide among youth: temporal trends in Allegheny County, Pennsylvania, 1960 to 1983. JAMA 257:3369–3372, 1987

Brook JS, Whiteman M, Gordon AS, et al: The psychosocial etiology of adolescent drug use: a family interactional approach. Genet Soc Gen Psychol Monogr 116:113–267, 1990

Brown SA, Vik PN, Creamer V: Characteristics of relapse following adolescent substance abuse treatment. Addict Behav 14:291–300, 1989

Brown SA, Myers MG, Mott MA, et al: Correlates of success following treatment for adolescent substance abuse. Applied and Preventive Psychology 3:61–73, 1994

Bukstein OG, Kaminer Y: The nosology of adolescent substance abuse. Am J Addict 3:1–13, 1994

Bukstein OG, Brent DA, Kaminer Y: Comorbidity of substance abuse and other psychiatric disorders in adolescents. Am J Psychiatry 146:1131–1141, 1989

Bukstein OG, Glancy LJ, Kaminer Y: Patterns of affective comorbidity in a clinical population of dually diagnosed substance abusers. J Am Acad Child Adolesc Psychiatry 31:1041–1045, 1992

Bulik CM: Drug and alcohol abuse by bulimic women and their families. Am J Psychiatry 144:1604–1606, 1987

Burk JP, Sher KJ: Labeling the child of an alcoholic: negative stereotyping by mental health professionals and peers. J Stud Alcohol 51:156–163, 1990

Catalano RF, Hawkins JD, Wells EA, et al: Evaluation of the effectiveness of adolescent drug abuse treatment, assessment of risks for relapse, and promising approaches for relapse prevention. International Journal of the Addictions 25:1085–1140, 1990–1991

Catalano RF, Hawkins JD, Krenz C, et al: Using research to guide culturally appropriate drug abuse prevention. J Consult Clin Psychol 61:804–811, 1993

Christie KA, Burke JD, Regier DA, et al: Epidemiologic evidence for early onset of mental disorders and higher risk of drug abuse in young adults. Am J Psychiatry 145:971–975, 1988

Clark DB, Sayette MA: Anxiety and the development of alcoholism. Am J Addict 2:56–76, 1993

Clark DB, Bukstein OG, Smith MG, et al: Identifying anxiety disorders in adolescents hospitalized for alcohol abuse or dependence. Psychiatr Serv 46:618–620, 1995

Clark GN: Improving the transition from basic efficacy research to effectiveness studies: methodological issues and procedures. J Consult Clin Psychol 63:718–725, 1995

Cloninger CR: Neurogenetic adaptive mechanisms in alcoholism. Science 236:410–415, 1987

Coate D, Grossman N: Change in alcoholic beverage prices and legal drinking age. Alcohol Health Res World Fall: 22–25, 1987

Crits-Christoph P, Siqueland L: Psychosocial treatment for drug abuse: selected review and recommendations for national health care. Arch Gen Psychiatry 53:749–756, 1996

Deykin EY, Buka SL, Zeena TH: Depressive illness among chemically dependent adolescents. Am J Psychiatry 149:1341–1347, 1992

Doyle H, Delaney W, Trobin J: Follow-up study of young attendees at an alcohol unit. Addiction 89:183–189, 1994

Earls F, Jung K: Temperament and home environment characteristics in the early development of child psychopathology. J Am Acad Child Adolesc Psychiatry 26:491–498, 1987

Erikson EH: Identity: Youth and Crisis. New York, Plenum, 1968

Friedman AS, Glickman NW: Program characteristics for successful treatment of adolescent drug abuse. J Nerv Ment Dis 174:669–679, 1987

Friedman AS, Utada A: A method for diagnosing and planning the treatment of adolescent drug abusers (the Adolescent Drug Abuse Diagnosis [ADAD] instrument). J Drug Educ 19:285–312, 1989

Friedman AS, Schwartz R, Utada A: Outcome of a unique youth drug abuse program: a follow-up study of clients of Straight, Inc. J Subst Abuse Treat 6:259–268, 1989

Golub A, Johnson BD: The shifting importance of alcohol and marijuana as gateway substances among serious drug abusers. J Stud Alcohol 55:607–614, 1994

Goodwin DW: Alcoholism and genetics: the sins of the fathers. Arch Gen Psychiatry 42:171–174, 1985

Griffiths M: Adolescent Gambling. London, Routledge, 1995

Grilo CM, Becker DF, Walker ML, et al: Psychiatric comorbidity in adolescent inpatients with substance use disorders. J Am Acad Child Adolesc Psychiatry 34:1085–1091, 1995

Hasin DS, Grant B, Endicott J: The natural history of alcohol abuse: implications for definitions of alcohol use disorders. Am J Psychiatry 147:337–341, 1990

Hawkins JD, Catalano RF, Miller JY: Risk and protective factors for alcohol and other drug problems in adolescence and early adulthood: implications for substance abuse prevention. Psychol Bull 112:64–105, 1992

Henggeler SW, Melton GB, Smith LA: Family preservation using multi-systemic therapy: an effective alternative to incarcerating serious juvenile offenders. J Consult Clin Psychol 66:953–961, 1992

Henggeler SW, Pickrel SG, Brondino MJ, et al: Eliminating treatment dropout of substance abusing or dependent delinquents through home-based multisystemic therapy. Am J Psychiatry 153:427–428, 1996

Hovens J, Cantwell DP, Kiriakos R: Psychiatric comorbidity in hospitalized adolescent substance abusers. J Am Acad Child Adolesc Psychiatry 33:476–483, 1994

Johnston LD, O'Malley IM, Bachman JG: News and Information (press release), The University of Michigan (21st national survey), December 11, 1996

Kadden RM, Cooney NL, Getter H, et al: Matching alcoholics to coping skills or interactional therapies: posttreatment results. J Consult Clin Psychol 57:698–704, 1989

Kaminer Y: Adolescent Substance Abuse: A Comprehensive Guide to Theory and Practice. New York, Plenum, 1994

Kaminer Y: Issues in pharmacological treatment of adolescent substance abuse. Journal of Child and Adolescent Psychopharmacology 5:93–106, 1995

Kaminer Y: Adolescent substance abuse and suicidal behavior, in Adolescent Substance Abuse and Dual Disorders (Child Adolescent Psychiatric Clinics in North America series). Edited by Jaffe SL. Philadelphia, PA, WB Saunders, 1996, pp 59–71

Kaminer Y, Bukstein OG, Tarter TE: The Teen Addiction Severity Index: rationale and reliability. International Journal of the Addictions 26:219–226, 1991

Kaminer Y, Tarter RE, Bukstein OG, et al: Comparison between treatment completers and noncompleters among dual-diagnosed substance-abusing adolescents. J Am Acad Child Adolesc Psychiatry 31:1046–1049, 1992

Kaminer Y, Wagner E, Plummer B, et al: Validation of the Teen Addiction Severity Index: preliminary findings. Am J Addict 2:221–224, 1993

Kaminer Y, Blitz C, Burleson JA, et al: Measuring treatment process in cognitive-behavioral and interactional group therapies for adolescent substance abusers. J Nerv Ment Dis 186:407–413, 1998a

Kaminer Y, Blitz C, Burleson JA, et al: The Teen Treatment Services Review (T-TSR): rational and reliability. J Subst Abuse Treat 15:291–300, 1998b

Kaminer Y, Burleson JA, Blitz C, et al: Psychotherapies for adolescent substance abusers: treatment outcomes. J Nerv Ment Dis 186:684–690, 1998c

Kandel DB: Epidemiological and psychosocial perspective on adolescent drug use. J Am Acad Child Adolesc Psychiatry 20:328–347, 1982

Kandel DB, Davies M, Karus D, et al: The consequences in young adulthood of adolescent drug involvement. Arch Gen Psychiatry 43:746–754, 1986

Kolar AF, Brown BS, Haertzen CA, et al: Children of substance abusers: the life experiences of children of opiate addicts in methadone maintenance. Am J Drug Alcohol Abuse 20:159–171, 1994

Kushner MG, Sher KJ, Beitman BD: The relation between alcohol problems and anxiety disorders. Am J Psychiatry 147:685–695, 1990

Labouvie E: Maturing out of substance use: selection and self-correction. Journal of Drug Issues 26:455–474, 1996

Lewinsohn PM, Rohde P, Seeley J: Alcohol consumption in high school adolescents: frequency of use and dimensional structure of associated problems. Addiction 91: 375–390, 1996

Liddle HA, Dakof GA: Family based treatment for adolescent drug use: state of the science, in Adolescent Drug Abuse: Clinical Assessment and Therapeutic Interventions (NIH Publ No 95-3908). Edited by Rahdert E, Czechowicz D. Rockville, MD, National Institute on Drug Abuse, 1995, pp 218–254

Litt MD, Babor TF, DelBoca FK, et al: Types of alcoholics, II: application of an empirically derived typology to treatment matching. Arch Gen Psychiatry 49:609–614, 1992

Loeber R: Natural histories of conduct problems, delinquency and associated substance use, in Advances in Clinical Child Psychology. Edited by Lahey BB, Kazdin AE. New York, Plenum, 1988, pp 73–124

Martin CS, Kaczynski NA, Maisto SA, et al: Patterns of DSM-IV alcohol abuse and dependence symptoms in adolescent drinkers. J Stud Alcohol 56:672–680, 1995

Mattson ME, Allen JP, Longabaugh R, et al: A chronological review of empirical studies matching alcoholic clients to treatment. J Stud Alcohol Suppl 12:16–29, 1994

Maziade M, Caron C, Cote P, et al: Extreme temperament and diagnosis: a study in a psychiatric sample of consecutive children. Arch Gen Psychiatry 47:477–484, 1990

Milin R, Halikas JA, Meller JE, et al: Psychopathology among substance abusing juvenile offenders. J Am Acad Child Adolesc Psychiatry 30:569–574, 1991

Myers MG, Brown SA, Mott MA: Preadolescent conduct disorder behaviors predict relapse and progression of addiction for adolescent alcohol and drug abusers. Alcohol Clin Exp Res 19:1528–1536, 1995

Newcomb MD: Identifying high-risk youth: prevalence and patterns of adolescent drug abuse, in Adolescent Drug Abuse: Clinical Assessment and Therapeutic Interventions (NIH Publ No 95-3908). Edited by Rahdert E, Czechowicz D. Rockville, MD, National Institute on Drug Abuse, 1995, pp 7–38

Noll RB, Zucker RA, Fitzgerald HE, et al: Cognitive and motoric functioning of sons of alcoholic fathers and controls: the early childhood years. Dev Psychol 28:665–675, 1992

O'Malley PM, Wagenaar AC: Effects of minimum drinking age laws on alcohol use, related behaviors and traffic crash involvement among American youth: 1976–1987. J Stud Alcohol 52:478–491, 1991

Penick EC, Powell B, Liskow BI, et al: The stability of coexisting psychiatric syndromes in alcoholic men after 1 year. J Stud Alcohol 49:395–405, 1988

Petraitis J, Flay BR, Miller TQ: Reviewing theories of adolescent substance use: organizing pieces of the puzzle. Psychol Bull 117:67–86, 1995

Reich T, Cloninger CR, Van Eerdewegh P, et al: Secular trends in the familial transmission of alcoholism. Alcohol Clin Exp Res 12:458–464, 1988

Reich W, Earls F, Frankel O, et al: Psychopathology in children of alcoholics. J Am Acad Child Adolesc Psychiatry 32:995–1002, 1993

Rohde P, Lewinsohn PM, Seeley JR: Psychiatric comorbidity with problematic alcohol use in high school students. J Am Acad Child Adolesc Psychiatry 35:101–109, 1996

Rounsaville BJ, Kleber HD: Psychiatric disorders in opiate addicts: preliminary findings on course and interaction with program type, in Psychopathology and Addictive Disorders. Edited by Meyer RE. New York, Guilford, 1986, pp 140–168

Schaffer K, Parson O, Yohman J: Neuropsychological differences between male familial alcoholics and nonalcoholics. Alcohol Clin Exp Res 8:347–351, 1984

Schinke SP, Botvin GJ, Orlani MA: Substance Abuse in Children and Adolescents: Evaluation and Intervention. Newbury Park, CA, Sage, 1991

Shedler J, Block J: Adolescent drug use and psychological health: a longitudinal inquiry. Am Psychol 45:612–630, 1990

Sigvardsson S, Bohman M, Cloninger CR: Replication of the Stockholm adoption study of alcoholism: confirmatory cross-fostering analysis. Arch Gen Psychiatry 53:681–688, 1996

Stowell RJ: Dual diagnosis issues. Psychiatric Annals 21:98–104, 1991

Szapocznik J, Perez-Vidal A, Briskman AL, et al: Engaging adolescent drug abusers and their families in treatment. J Consult Clin Psychol 56:552–557, 1988

Tarter RE, Laird SB, Mostefa K, et al: Drug abuse severity in adolescents is associated with magnitude of deviation in temperamental traits. British Journal of Addiction 85:1501–1504, 1990a

Tarter RE, Laird SB, Moss HB: Neuropsychological and neurophysiological characteristics of children of alcoholics, in Children of Alcoholics: Critical Perspectives. Edited by Windel M, Searles JS. New York, Guilford, 1990b, pp 73–98

Tarter RE, Kirisci L, Hegedus A, et al: Heterogeneity of adolescent alcoholism, in Types of Alcoholics: Evidence from Clinical, Experimental and Genetic Research. Edited by Babor TF, Hesselbrock V, Meyer RE, et al. New York, Annals of the New York Academy of Science, 1994, pp 172–180

Tarter RE, Kirisci L, Mezzich A: Multivariate typology of adolescents with alcohol use disorder. Am J Addict 6:150–158, 1997

Teichman M, Barnea Z, Ravav G: Personality and substance use among adolescents: a longitudinal study. British Journal of Addiction 84:181–190, 1989

Tobler NS: Meta-analysis of 143 adolescent drug prevention programs: quantitative outcome results of program participants compared to a control or comparison group. Journal of Drug Issues 16:537–567, 1986

U.S. Department of Vital Statistics. Washington, DC, Bureau of Mortality Statistics, 1993

Van Hasselt VB, Null JA, Kempton T: Social skills and depression in adolescent substance abusers. Addict Behav 18:9–18, 1993

Vik PW, Grisel K, Brown SA: Social resource characteristics and adolescent substance abuse relapse. Journal of Adolescent Chemical Dependency 2:59–74, 1992

Waltz J, Addis ME, Koerner K, et al: Testing the integrity of a psychotherapy protocol: assessment of adherence and competence. J Consult Clin Psychol 61:620–630, 1993

Wilens TE, Biederman J, Spencer TJ: Comorbidity of attention-deficit disorder and psychoactive substance use disorders. Hosp Community Psychiatry 45:421–435, 1994

Wilens TE, Biederman J, Kiely K: Pilot study of behavioral and emotional disturbances in the high-risk children of parents with opioid dependence. J Am Acad Child Adolesc Psychiatry 34:779–785, 1995

Wilson JR, Crowe L: Genetics of alcoholism: can and should youth at risk be identified? Alcohol Health Res World 15:11–17, 1991

Wolin S, Wolin SJ: The challenge model: working with strengths in children of substance-abusing parents, in Adolescent Substance Abuse and Dual Disorders (Child Adolescent Psychiatric Clinics in North America series). Edited by Jaffe SL. Philadelphia, PA, WB Saunders, 1996, pp 243–255

Zuckerman M: Behavioral Expressions and Biosocial Bases of Sensation Seeking. New York, Cambridge University Press, 1994

# Chapter

# Dual Diagnosis

Kathleen T. Brady, M.D., Ph.D.
Patricia Halligan, M.D.
Robert J. Malcolm, M.D.

The term *dual diagnosis* in the context of substance use disorders has generally been used to refer to the co-occurrence of a psychiatric disorder with a substance use disorder. The relationship between substance use and psychiatric disorders is a complex one, and co-occurrence may manifest in several ways: 1) substance use and psychiatric disorders may co-occur by coincidence, 2) substance use may cause psychiatric conditions or increase the severity of psychiatric symptoms, 3) psychiatric disorders may cause or increase the severity of substance use disorders, 4) both disorders may be caused by a third condition, and 5) substance use and withdrawal may produce symptoms that mimic those of a psychiatric disorder (Meyer 1989). In any individual case, different aspects of this complex relationship may be operating. This complexity can lead to difficulties in diagnosis and management of comorbid conditions.

Two epidemiological surveys emphasized the prevalence of comorbid psychiatric and substance use disorders in community samples: the National Institute of Mental Health Epidemiologic Catchment Area (ECA) Study (Reiger et al. 1990) and the National Comorbidity Survey (NCS) (Kessler et al. 1994). In the ECA study, an estimated 45% of individuals with an alcohol use disorder and 72% of individuals with a drug use disorder had at least one co-occurring psychiatric disorder (Reiger et al. 1990). In the NCS, approximately 78% of alcohol-dependent men and 86% of alcohol-dependent women met lifetime criteria for another psychiatric disorder, including drug dependence (Kessler et al. 1994).

## General Diagnostic Considerations

One of the most difficult challenges in the area of comorbidity is diagnosis. Manifestations of substance use and withdrawal can mimic nearly every psychiatric disorder. Substances of abuse have profound effects on neurotransmitter systems involved in the pathophysiology of most psychiatric disorders and, with chronic use, may unmask a vulnerability or lead to organic changes that manifest as psychiatric disorder. The best way to differentiate substance-induced, transient psychiatric symptoms from psychiatric disorders that warrant treatment is through observation of symptoms during a period of abstinence. It is likely that the minimum amount of time necessary for diagnosis will vary depending on the comorbid condition being diagnosed. In the case of depression and many anxiety symptoms, there appears to be symptom resolution for 2–4 weeks after last use (Brown and Schuckit 1988; Thevos et al. 1991). Other psychiatric disorders are less well studied in this regard. A family history of psychiatric illness, clear onset of psychiatric symptoms before onset of the substance use disorder, and sustained psychiatric symptoms during lengthy periods of abstinence in the past can all weigh in favor of making a psychiatric diagnosis in cases that are unclear.

## General Treatment Considerations

In general, treatment efforts addressing psychiatric and substance use disorders have developed in parallel. Determination of the appropriate integration of treatment modalities from both fields is necessary to design treatments specifically tailored for patients with comorbidity. Psychosocial treatments are powerful interventions for both substance use and psychiatric disorders. There are common themes in the psychosocial treatments from both fields, themes that can be built on to optimize outcome.

Research in pharmacotherapies for both substance use and psychiatric disorders is progressing rapidly. Integration of information from both the psychiatric and the substance abuse fields has led to the testing of strategies targeting individuals with both disorders. Specific comorbid disorders are discussed in detail later in this chapter, but general principles of choosing a pharmacological agent include paying particular attention to potential toxic interactions of the agent with drugs and alcohol should relapse occur and assessing the abuse potential of the agent being used.

Because of space limitations, this chapter contains an overview of the most common and clinically relevant comorbidities of Axis I psychiatric disorders and substance use disorders. For every category of psychiatric diagnosis discussed, prevalence rates, differential diagnosis, and information on pharmacotherapeutic and psychotherapeutic treatment options are briefly reviewed.

## Psychotic Disorders

### Prevalence

Psychotic symptoms may occur with substance use disorders as a direct result of chemical intoxication and/or withdrawal or because of a primary underlying psychotic disorder. As many as 50% of treatment-seeking schizophrenic patients have alcohol or illicit drug dependence, and more than 70% are nicotine dependent (Dixon et al. 1991; Shaner et al. 1993; Ziedonis et al. 1994). Epidemiological surveys indicate that individuals with schizophrenia are at substantial risk (odds ratio, 4–5) for having a substance use disorder, compared with the general population (Kessler et al. 1994; Reiger

et al. 1990). The relationship between psychosis and substance use is complex. Individuals with schizophrenia may use substances to decrease the negative symptoms of schizophrenia (depression, apathy, anhedonia, passivity, social withdrawal), to combat the overwhelming positive symptoms of schizophrenia (typically auditory hallucinations and paranoid delusions), or as an attempt to ameliorate the adverse effects of neuroleptic medication (dysphoria, akathisia, and sedation).

### Diagnosis

Differential diagnosis frequently involves differentiating a substance-induced psychotic disorder from a primary psychotic disorder. Findings that might support a diagnosis of substance-induced psychotic disorder rather than primary psychotic disorder are younger age at onset of psychosis, family history of drug use, male gender, and good premorbid adjustment (Kosten and Ziedonis 1997). Obtaining a thorough history concerning symptoms during abstinent periods and observation during monitored abstinence are essential to accurate diagnosis.

### Treatment

The optimal management of patients with comorbid schizophrenia and substance use involves both pharmacotherapy and psychotherapy. There are few empirical data concerning specific pharmacotherapeutic strategies, but atypical antipsychotic agents such as clozapine and olanzapine may better target the negative symptoms of schizophrenia and may also have fewer neuroleptic-induced side effects than the more traditional antipsychotics, thereby reducing patient tendency to self-medicate with substances of abuse (Wilkins 1997). There are several small case-series reports of positive response by patients with schizophrenia and substance use disorders to clozapine (Buckley et al. 1994; George et al. 1995). Management of dysphoric affect in substance abuse in patients may be an important step in successful treatment. One group of investigators studying adjunctive desipramine treatment in a small group of cocaine-abusing schizophrenic individuals found that the desipramine-treated group stayed in treatment longer and had fewer cocaine-positive urine drug screens (Ziedonis et al. 1992). Disulfiram must be used with caution in this comorbid population because it may increase central levels of dopamine by blocking dopamine β-hydroxylase and thereby exacerbate psychosis (Wilkins 1997). The use of naltrexone to decrease alcohol consumption in individuals with schizophrenia is an intriguing idea that has not been explored in a systematic manner.

The psychotherapeutic management of comorbid schizophrenia and substance abuse is critical. Patients must be closely monitored with urinalysis and Breathalyzer, and clear limits must be set. Feedback should be given in an empathic and nonjudgmental manner. The confrontational group process approach often used for substance-abusing persons has little value in the treatment of the substance-abusing schizophrenic individual (Kosten and Ziedonis 1997) and may exacerbate psychosis. Ziedonis and Trudeau (1997) noted the problem of poor motivation to quit substance use with many schizophrenic patients and suggested a dual-diagnosis, treatment-matching strategy based on motivation levels, substance of abuse, and illness severity.

## Affective Disorders

### Prevalence

Symptoms of mood instability and depression are among the most common psychiatric symptoms seen in individuals with substance use disorders. In the ECA study, 32% of individuals with an affective disorder also had a comorbid substance use disorder (Reiger et al. 1990). Of the individuals with major depression, 16.5% had an alcohol use disorder and 18% had a drug use disorder; and 56.1% of individuals with bipolar disorder had a substance use disorder. In both the ECA study and the NCS, bipolar disorder was the Axis I condition most likely to occur with a substance use disorder.

Studies in treatment-seeking samples have resulted in variable estimates of the comorbidity of affective illness with substance use disorders. As discussed later, the likely reason for this is that diagnostic issues at the interface of affective illness and substance use disorders are particularly complex. Estimates of the prevalence of depressive disorders in treatment-seeking alcoholic individuals range from 15% to 67% (Hasin et al. 1988; Powell et al. 1982). In studies of cocaine-dependent individuals, estimates of affective comorbidity range from 33% to 53% (Nunes et al. 1991; Rounsaville et al. 1991; Weiss et al. 1988). Bipolar disorders appear to be more prevalent (20%–30%) among cocaine-dependent individuals than among alcoholic individuals. In opiate-dependent samples, rates of lifetime affective disorder (primarily depressive disorders) range from 16% to 75% (Brooner et al. 1997; Milby et al. 1996; Rounsaville et al. 1982).

### Diagnosis

Up to 98% of individuals presenting for substance abuse treatment have some symptom of depression (Jaffe and Ciraulo 1986). Many of these symptoms resolve with abstinence alone. Obviously, assessment done too early in recovery may lead to overdiagnosis and unnecessary treatment. Underdiagnosis also presents a risk because new evidence indicates that appropriate treatment of depression can improve substance-related outcomes. Affective symptoms that predate the onset of substance use, a strong family history of affective disorder, and/or symptoms that have persisted during abstinent periods in the past are clinical features that should influence treatment decisions.

### Treatment

Studies of tricyclic antidepressant (TCA) treatment of major depressive episodes and alcoholism indicate that such treatment modestly decreases alcohol use and the symptoms of depression (Mason et al. 1996; McGrath et al. 1996). Serotonin has been implicated in the control of alcohol intake (Amit et al. 1991). A number of serotonin reuptake inhibitors (SRIs) have been shown to modestly decrease alcohol consumption in persons with drinking problems and in alcoholic individuals (Gorelick 1989). In a recent study investigating the use of fluoxetine in a group of alcoholic persons with major depression (Cornelius et al. 1997), individuals who received fluoxetine had significantly greater reduction in both depressive symptoms and alcohol consumption, compared with the placebo group. This study is particularly important because the clinical improvement was more substantial than that seen with the studies involving TCAs, and SRIs have less potential for toxicity and interaction with drugs of abuse than do TCAs.

Several trials of TCAs have been performed with opioid-dependent patients. Nunes and colleagues (1998) found that imipramine significantly decreased depression in a group of depressed patients receiving methadone maintenance. The effect of imipramine on drug use was less marked, however, and although self-report measures indicated significantly less craving and drug use, there were no differences in positive urine drug screens. Monitoring of TCA plasma levels is important in methadone-maintained patients because patients receiving methadone and desipramine have been found to have increased plasma desipramine levels (Weiss and Mirin 1989).

The primary focus of use of TCAs in cocaine-dependent patients has been on treatment of cocaine dependence, rather than on treatment of depression. Several studies involving desipramine have shown improvement in anhedonia and cocaine craving and increased initial abstinence in nondepressed patients, and one small study showed improvement in depressed patients (Rao et al. 1995). Clinicians should be aware, however, that desipramine may have an activating effect in cocaine-dependent individuals, which can precipitate relapse, and, should relapse occur, desipramine may have additive cardiotoxicity in combination with cocaine (Weiss and Mirin 1989).

There are few published data on the treatment of bipolar disorder complicated by substance abuse. Lithium has been the standard treatment for bipolar disorder for several decades; however, substance abuse may be a predictor of poor response to lithium (Bowden 1995; O'Connell et al. 1991). Patients with mixed manic episodes and/or rapid-cycling disorder have a better response to anticonvulsant drugs compared with lithium. Patients with bipolar disorder and concomitant substance use disorders appear to have more mixed and/or rapid-cycling episodes and therefore may have a stronger response with anticonvulsant mood-stabilizing medications (Calabrese et al. 1992; Freeman et al. 1992). In an open-label pilot study, Brady and colleagues (1995b) found valproate to be safe and effective in patients with bipolar disorder and concurrent substance dependence. Weiss et al. (1998) reported better medication compliance with valproate, compared with lithium, in a group of substance-abusing patients with bipolar disorder.

The psychotherapeutic/psychosocial strategies used in the treatment of comorbid conditions should be specifically tailored and contain elements of effective treatment from the areas of both substance abuse and affective disorders. Many of the principles of cognitive-behavior therapy are common to the treatment of affective disorder as well as substance use disorders. Alcoholics Anonymous and Narcotics Anonymous are found in all communities, and active participation can be a major factor in an individual's recovery. Further work is needed in developing therapies specifically geared toward individuals with comorbid affective and substance use disorders, therapies in which therapeutic techniques for each type of disorder are combined.

## Anxiety Disorders

### Prevalence

Data from the NCS indicate that approximately 36% of individuals with anxiety disorders also have a substance use disorder (Kessler et al. 1994). Because the anxiety disorders are so heterogeneous and the issues concerning diagnosis, treatment, and prevalence differ substantially between disorders, each disorder is discussed in separate subsections.

### Panic Disorder

In the ECA survey, 36% of individuals with panic disorder had lifetime substance use disorder (Reiger et al. 1990). In the NCS, the odds ratio for co-occurring drug and alcohol dependence and panic disorder was 2.0 (Kessler et al. 1996). The estimated prevalence of panic disorder and agoraphobia in treatment-seeking samples of alcoholic persons is variable, with estimates ranging from 5% to 42% (Kushner et al. 1990). This variability is, in part, related to diagnostic difficulties. Anxiety symptoms in general and panic attacks in particular are commonly seen in withdrawal periods. Alcohol, sedative-hypnotic, and opiate withdrawal are all marked by hyperexcitability of the noradrenergic systems, which also occurs with panic attacks. Other drugs of abuse (cocaine, marijuana, other stimulants) may induce panic attacks in cases of acute intoxication (Aronson and Craig 1986; Louie et al. 1989).

The most widely used classes of pharmacotherapeutic agents for the treatment of panic disorder are the TCAs, SRIs, monoamine oxidase inhibitors (MAOIs), and benzodiazepines (Lydiard et al. 1988). TCAs have been the mainstay of treatment in the non-substance-abusing patient with panic disorder, but controlled trials in substance-using patients have not been reported. Benzodiazepines are generally contraindicated in substance-using populations because of their abuse potential. This is a controversial issue, however, and some investigators have reported successful use of benzodiazepines in patients with comorbid panic disorder and substance use disorders in remission without evidence of any abuse of the drug by the patients (Adinoff 1992). Benzodiazepines may be considered as adjuncts during the early treatment phase when activation and latency of onset of the antidepressants are issues of concern. When a benzodiazepine is being prescribed to a patient with comorbid substance use, limited amounts of medication should be given, and the patient should be closely monitored for relapse.

MAOIs are also difficult to use in patients with comorbid substance use disorders. Dietary restrictions are necessary because of the interaction with tyramine in the diet, which may result in a hypertensive crisis. Moreover, MAOIs in combination with stimulant drugs may precipitate a hypertensive crisis.

Clinical trials have demonstrated the efficacy of SRIs in the treatment of panic disorder in non-substance-using patients (Lydiard et al. 1988). Recently, paroxetine was approved by the U.S. Food and Drug Administration for use in the treatment of panic disorder. As mentioned earlier, SRIs have been shown by some investigators to modestly decrease alcohol consumption. These drugs, therefore, are a logical choice for the patient with comorbid panic disorder and alcoholism, but controlled clinical trials have not been conducted.

Panic disorder is responsive to nonpharmacological treatment. Cognitive-behavioral techniques, such as exposure and systematic desensitization, have been shown to be particularly effective in the treatment of panic disorder (Barlow 1988; Barlow and Lehman 1996). It is particularly important to maximize these nonpharmacological treatments in patients with substance use disorders. The ability to self-regulate subjective states and the confidence that can result from successful mastery through therapy can be helpful to individuals in recovery. Many of the techniques used in anxiety disorders overlap with therapies known to be successful in the treatment of substance use disorders. Therefore, combination therapy is feasible. Finally, by learning therapeutic anxiety-reducing strategies, patients may be able to acquire alternative coping strategies and break out of the mind-set of using external agents to combat intolerable subjective states.

## Generalized Anxiety Disorder

For generalized anxiety disorder (GAD) and substance use disorders, diagnostic issues are particularly complex. The DSM-IV (American Psychiatric Association 1994) criteria for GAD specify that symptoms must occur for 6 months, without being directly related to physiological effects of a substance. Symptoms of GAD substantially overlap with symptoms of acute intoxication with stimulants and withdrawal from alcohol, sedative-hypnotics, and opiates, and often the 6-month period of abstinence may be difficult to ascertain. Although many substance-using individuals report anxiety symptoms consistent with GAD, they may not meet diagnostic criteria for GAD because of difficulty in distinguishing symptoms of anxiety from substance-related symptoms.

The treatment of GAD complicated by a substance use disorder is challenging. Benzodiazepines are effective in the treatment of GAD; however, as previously discussed, their abuse potential limits utility in the substance-abusing population. Buspirone is a nonbenzo-

diazepine anxiolytic with no abuse potential that has been shown in several studies of alcoholic individuals with anxiety to decrease alcohol consumption and improve symptoms of anxiety (Kranzler et al. 1994; Tollefson et al. 1992). Because of the low abuse potential and reports of success in well-controlled studies, buspirone remains a good choice in individuals with comorbid GAD and substance use disorders. Although there are no reported systematic trials of TCAs or SRIs in the treatment of GAD in individuals with substance use disorders, these agents have been useful in non-substance-abusing populations (Lydiard et al. 1988).

As mentioned in the section on panic disorder, nonpharmacological treatments for anxiety disorder can be useful. GAD can be effectively managed with the use of relaxation, coping, and cognitive-behavior therapy techniques (Barlow 1988; Barlow and Lehman 1996; Jansson and Ost 1982). Pharmacotherapy and psychotherapy are likely to complement each other with regard to maximizing of patient outcomes. Nonpharmacological treatment strategies in conjunction with judicious pharmacotherapeutic management should be encouraged.

## Social Phobia

Studies examining the interface of alcohol abuse and dependence with social phobia have found rates of comorbidity ranging from 8% to 56% (Kushner et al. 1990). Social phobia in drug dependence has not been well studied, but in one study (Myrick and Brady 1996), the lifetime prevalence of social phobia in a cocaine-dependent population was 13.9%.

Because social phobia may interfere with an individual's ability to engage in treatment effectively, early recognition is paramount. A lengthy period of abstinence may not be needed, because fear of interaction in a social situation is not a specific feature of substance use or withdrawal. However, the social fears that arise only during periods of intoxication with marijuana or stimulants should not be considered sufficient for diagnosis of social phobia.

MAOIs, reversible inhibitors of monoamine oxidase, SRIs, and benzodiazepines have documented efficacy (Lydiard et al. 1988) in the treatment of uncomplicated social phobia, but there are no studies of psychopharmacological treatment of individuals with comorbid social phobia and substance use. SRIs are often the first choice of medication for treatment of comorbid social phobia and substance abuse because these agents are efficacious, necessitate no dietary restrictions, and may produce modest decreases in alcohol consumption.

Psychotherapeutic treatment is important. It may be difficult for socially phobic patients to participate in group therapy or 12-step programs. A treatment plan with an emphasis on cognitive-behavior therapy may prove to be more effective. Although there are no published studies that have systematically examined these treatments in patients with comorbid social phobia and substance use, several types of nonpharmacological treatments, such as systematic desensitization, imaginal flooding, graduated exposure, social skills training, and cognitive approaches, have proven effective in non-substance-using individuals with social phobia (Heimberg et al. 1990).

## Posttraumatic Stress Disorder

The prevalence of comorbid posttraumatic stress disorder (PTSD) and substance use disorders is high. In the NCS study, approximately 30%–50% of men and 25%–30% of women with lifetime PTSD had a co-occurring substance use disorder (Kessler et al. 1995). In substance-abusing individuals who seek treatment, the lifetime prevalence of PTSD is between 36% and 50%, and the current prevalence is between 25% and 42% (Dansky et al. 1994; Grice et al. 1995; Triffleman et al. 1993).

TCAs, MAOIs, and SRIs have been shown in double-blind, placebo-controlled trials to improve symptoms of PTSD (Davidson 1992; van der Kolk et al. 1994). Unfortunately, none of the trials included individuals with substance use disorders. There is one report of an open trial of sertraline treatment in a small group of individuals with comorbid PTSD and alcohol dependence that resulted in decreased alcohol consumption and decreased symptoms of PTSD (Brady et al. 1995a).

The appropriate psychotherapeutic approach to comorbid PTSD and substance use disorders remains unclear. Cognitive-behavior therapies have shown efficacy in the treatment of PTSD, but a widely accepted treatment approach in substance abuse treatment settings has been to defer treatment of trauma-related conditions until the substance use disorder is in remission. However, a number of case studies in the literature indicate that successful treatment of symptoms of PTSD can lead to reductions in alcohol and drug abuse (Fairbank and Keane 1982; Polles and Smith 1995). For some patients, relief of PTSD symptoms may improve the chances of recovery from substance abuse. This area warrants further investigation.

## Attention-Deficit/Hyperactivity Disorder

The co-occurrence of attention-deficit/hyperactivity disorder (ADHD) and psychoactive substance use disorders has received much recent attention. When data were summarized from several studies of adults and adolescents with substance use disorders, the mean percentage of subjects with a comorbid diagnosis of ADHD was determined to be 23% (Wilens et al. 1994). In investigations of substance use disorders in adults with ADHD, rates of alcohol use disorders have been estimated to be between 17% and 45%, and rates of drug use disorders have been estimated to be between 9% and 50% (Wilens et al. 1994).

As with many comorbid conditions, diagnostic issues with ADHD in substance use disorders are problematic. Because attentional problems may be a common occurrence during withdrawal and acute intoxication, symptoms must be assessed during abstinence. Because the symptoms of ADHD must first occur in childhood and then persist over time, careful screening for childhood symptoms may be of help in differentiating withdrawal and ADHD.

Pharmacotherapy plays an important role in the treatment of ADHD. Stimulants are ordinarily the first-line drug of choice for uncomplicated ADHD in children and adults. However, because of the abuse potential of the stimulants, the risks may outweigh potential benefits. Several case studies, however, indicate that appropriate treatment of the ADHD can abate the substance use (Cocores et al. 1987; Khantzian 1983). Prospective, controlled trials of stimulant treatment in this subgroup of substance-abusing individuals are needed. Pemoline, because of its longer half-life, may have less abuse potential than methylphenidate or dextroamphetamine. However, there is recent evidence concerning hepatotoxicity with pemoline. TCAs and bupropion may be helpful in treating ADHD, as well as any coexisting depression. Antihypertensive medications such as clonidine and propranolol have been helpful in decreasing impulsivity and aggression (Wilens et al. 1994).

Psychotherapy should address psychoeducation surrounding ADHD, substance use disorders, interpersonal difficulties, low self-esteem, impulsivity, and time management. Behavioral treatments to improve focus and attention can be helpful in the treatment of childhood ADHD but have not been adequately studied in the treatment of adult ADHD. As with other comorbid conditions, it is important to maximize nonpharmacological treatment approaches.

## Conclusion

Evidence from multiple lines of investigation is converging to indicate that substance use disorders and psychiatric disorders commonly co-occur. This co-occurrence presents challenges for diagnosis as well as optimal patient management. In terms of diagnosis, strategies designed to focus on features of the disorder or history most likely to be useful in making early diagnosis will be helpful. General principles emerging from the literature to guide treatment efforts include the combining of psychotherapeutic techniques from the psychiatric and substance use fields to design specifically tailored strategies for comorbid populations. Although much work remains to be done with regard to pharmacotherapeutic treatment for individuals with comorbid psychiatric and substance use disorders, the development of scientific techniques capable of elucidating the common neurobiological pathways in both disorders is promising for the development of specifically targeted pharmacotherapeutic strategies. Recent studies have provided helpful information concerning diagnosis and pharmacotherapeutic and psychotherapeutic treatment strategies tailored for this population, but developing the optimal treatment for this prevalent group of disorders will require further work.

## References

Adinoff B: Long-term therapy with benzodiazepines despite alcohol dependence disorder: seven case reports. Am J Addict 1:288–293, 1992

American Psychiatric Association: Diagnostic and Statistical Manual of Mental Disorders, 4th Edition. Washington, DC, American Psychiatric Association, 1994

Amit Z, Smith BR, Gill K: Serotonin uptake inhibitors: effects on motivated consummatory behaviors. J Clin Psychiatry 55 (suppl):55–60, 1991

Aronson TA, Craig TJ: Cocaine precipitation of panic disorder. Am J Psychiatry 143:643–645, 1986

Barlow DH: Anxiety and Its Disorders: The Nature and Treatment of Anxiety and Panic. New York, Guilford, 1988

Barlow DH, Lehman CL: Advances in the psychosocial treatment of anxiety disorders: implications for national health care. Arch Gen Psychiatry 53:727–735, 1996

Bowden CL: Predictors of response to divalproex and lithium. J Clin Psychiatry 56:25–30, 1995

Brady KT, Sonne SC, Roberts JM: Sertraline treatment of comorbid posttraumatic stress disorder and alcohol dependence. J Clin Psychiatry 56:502–505, 1995a

Brady KT, Sonne SC, Anton R, et al: Valproate in the treatment of acute bipolar affective episodes complicated by substance abuse: a pilot study. J Clin Psychiatry 56:118–121, 1995b

Brooner RK, King VL, Kidorf M, et al: Psychiatric and substance comorbidity among treatment-seeking opioid abusers. Arch Gen Psychiatry 54:71–80, 1997

Brown WE, Schuckit M: Changes in depression among abstinent alcoholics. J Stud Alcohol 49:412–417, 1988

Buckley P, Thompson P, Way L, et al: Substance abuse among patients with treatment-resistant schizophrenia: characteristics and implications for clozapine therapy. Am J Psychiatry 151:385–389, 1994

Calabrese JR, Markovitz PJ, Kimmel SE, et al: Spectrum of efficacy of valproate in 78 rapid-cycling bipolar patients. J Clin Psychopharmacol 12 (suppl 1):53S–56S, 1992

Cocores JA, Davies RK, Mueller PS, et al: Cocaine abuse and adult attention deficit disorder. J Clin Psychiatry 48:376–377, 1987

Cornelius JR, Salloum IM, Ehler JG, et al: Fluoxetine in depressed alcoholics: a double-blind, placebo-controlled trial. Arch Gen Psychiatry 54:700–705, 1997

Dansky BS, Brady KT, Roberts JT: Post-traumatic stress disorder and substance abuse: empirical findings and clinical issues. Substance Abuse 15:247–257, 1994

Davidson J: Drug therapy of post-traumatic stress disorder. Br J Psychiatry 160:309–314, 1992

Dixon L, Haas G, Weiden PJ, et al: Drug abuse in schizophrenic patients: clinical correlates and reasons for use. Am J Psychiatry 148:224–230, 1991

Fairbank JA, Keane TM: Flooding for combat-related stress disorders: assessment of anxiety reduction across traumatic memories. Behavior Therapy 62:499–510, 1982

Freeman TW, Clothier JL, Pazzaglia P, et al: A double-blind comparison of valproate and lithium in the treatment of acute mania. Am J Psychiatry 149:108–111, 1992

George TP, Sernyak MJ, Ziedonis DM, et al: Effects of clozapine on smoking in chronic schizophrenic outpatients. J Clin Psychiatry 56:344–346, 1995

Gorelick DA: Serotonin uptake blockers and the treatment of alcoholism. Recent Dev Alcohol 7:267–281, 1989

Grice DE, Dustan LR, Brady KT: Victimization and PTSD in substance dependent individuals. Am J Addict 44:297–305, 1995

Hasin DS, Grant BF, Endicott J: Lifetime psychiatric comorbidity in hospitalized alcoholics: subject and familial correlates. International Journal of the Addictions 23:827–850, 1988

Heimberg RG, Dodge CS, Hope DA, et al: Cognitive-behavioral group treatment of social phobia: comparison to a credible placebo control. Cognitive Therapy Research 14:1–23, 1990

Jaffe JH, Ciraulo KA: Alcoholism and depression, in Psychopathology and Addictive Disorders. Edited by Meyer RE. New York, Guilford, 1986, pp 293–320

Jansson L, Ost LG: Behavioral treatments for agoraphobia: an evaluative review. Clinical Psychology Review 2:311–336, 1982

Kessler RC, McGonagle KA, Zhao S, et al: Lifetime and 12-month prevalence of DSM-III-R psychiatric disorders in the United States: results from the National Comorbidity Survey. Arch Gen Psychiatry 51:8–19, 1994

Kessler RC, Sonnega A, Bromet E, et al: Posttraumatic stress disorder in the National Comorbidity Survey. Arch Gen Psychiatry 52:1048–1060, 1995

Kessler RC, Nelson CB, McGonagle KA, et al: The epidemiology of co-occurring addictive and mental disorders: implications for prevention and service utilization. Am J Orthopsychiatry 66:17–31, 1996

Khantzian EJ: An extreme case of cocaine dependence and marked improvement with methylphenidate treatment. Am J Psychiatry 140:784–785, 1983

Kosten TR, Ziedonis DM: Substance abuse and schizophrenia: editors' introduction. Schizophr Bull 23:181–186, 1997

Kranzler HR, Burleson JA, DelBoca FK, et al: Buspirone treatment of anxious alcoholics: a placebo-controlled trial. Arch Gen Psychiatry 51:720–731, 1994

Kushner MG, Sher KJ, Beitman BD: The relation between alcohol problems and the anxiety disorders. Am J Psychiatry 147:685–695, 1990

Louie AK, Lannon RA, Ketter TA: Treatment of cocaine-induced panic disorder. Am J Psychiatry 146:40–44, 1989

Lydiard RB, Roy-Byrne PP, Ballenger JC: Recent advances in the psychopharmacological treatment of anxiety disorders. Hosp Community Psychiatry 39:1157–1165, 1988

Mason BJ, Kocsis JH, Ritvo EC, et al: A double-blind, placebo-controlled trial of desipramine for primary alcohol dependence stratified on the presence or absence of major depression. JAMA 275:761–767, 1996

McGrath PJ, Nunes EV, Stewart JW, et al: Imipramine treatment of alcoholics with primary depression: a placebo-controlled clinical trial. Arch Gen Psychiatry 53:232–240, 1996

Meyer RE: Prospects for a rational pharmacotherapy of alcoholism. J Clin Psychiatry 50:403–412, 1989

Milby JB, Sims MK, Khuder S, et al: Psychiatric comorbidity: prevalence in methadone maintenance treatment. Am J Drug Alcohol Abuse 22:95–107, 1996

Myrick DH, Brady KT: Social phobia in cocaine-dependent individuals. Am J Addict 6:99–104, 1996

Nunes EV, Quitkin FM, Brady R, et al: Imipramine treatment of methadone maintenance patients with affective disorder and illicit drug use. Am J Psychiatry 148:667–669, 1991

Nunes EV, Quitkin FM, Donoval SJ, et al: Imipramine treatment of opiate-dependent patients with depressive disorders. Arch Gen Psychiatry 55:153–160, 1998

O'Connell RA, Mayo JA, Flatow L, et al: Outcome of bipolar disorder on long-term treatment with lithium. Br J Psychiatry 159:123–129, 1991

Polles AG, Smith PO: Treatment of coexisting substance dependence and post traumatic stress disorder. Psychiatr Serv 46:729–730, 1995

Powell BJ, Penick EC, Othmer E, et al: Prevalence of additional psychiatric syndromes among male alcoholics. J Clin Psychiatry 43:404–407, 1982

Rao S, Ziedonis D, Kosten T: The pharmacotherapy of cocaine dependence. Psychiatric Annals 25:363–368, 1995

Reiger DA, Farmer ME, Rae DS, et al: Comorbidity of mental disorders with alcohol and other drug abuse: results from the Epidemiologic Catchment Area (ECA) Study. JAMA 264:2511–2518, 1990

Rounsaville BJ, Weissman MM, Kleber H, et al: Heterogeneity of psychiatric diagnosis in treated opiate addicts. Arch Gen Psychiatry 39:161–168, 1982

Rounsaville BJ, Anton SF, Carroll K, et al: Psychiatric diagnoses of treatment-seeking cocaine abusers. Arch Gen Psychiatry 48:43–51, 1991

Shaner A, Khalsa ME, Roberts L, et al: Unrecognized cocaine use among schizophrenic patients. Am J Psychiatry 150:758–762, 1993

Thevos AK, Johnston AL, Latham PK, et al: Symptoms of anxiety in inpatient alcoholics with and without DSM-III-R anxiety diagnoses. Alcohol Clin Exp Res 15:102–105, 1991

Tollefson GD, Montague-Clouse J, Tollefson SL: Treatment of comorbid generalized anxiety in a recently detoxified alcoholic population with a selective serotonergic drug (buspirone). J Clin Psychopharmacol 12:19–26, 1992

Triffleman E, Marmer C, Delvechi K: Childhood trauma and PTSD in substance abuse inpatients. Paper presented at the annual College on Problems Drug Dependence, Phoenix, AZ, June 1993

van der Kolk BA, Dreyfuss D, Michaels M, et al: Fluoxetine in posttraumatic stress disorder. J Clin Psychiatry 55:517–522, 1994

Weiss RD, Mirin SM: Tricyclic antidepressants in the treatment of alcoholism and drug abuse. J Clin Psychiatry 50 (suppl):4–11, 1989

Weiss RD, Mirin SM, Griffin ML, et al: Psychopathology in cocaine abusers: changing trends. J Nerv Ment Dis 176:719–725, 1988

Weiss RD, Greenfield SF, Najavits LM, et al: Medication compliance among patients with bipolar disorder and substance use disorder. J Clin Psychiatry 59:172–174, 1998

Wilens TE, Biederman J, Spencer TJ, et al: Comorbidity of attention-deficit hyperactivity and substance use disorders. Hosp Community Psychiatry 45:421–435, 1994

Wilkins JN: Pharmacotherapy of schizophrenia patients with comorbid substance abuse. Schizophr Bull 23:215–228, 1997

Ziedonis DM, Trudeau K: Motivation to quit using substances among individuals with schizophrenia: implications for a motivation-based treatment model. Schizophr Bull 23:229–238, 1997

Ziedonis D, Richardson T, Lee E, et al: Adjunctive desipramine in the treatment of cocaine abusing schizophrenics. Psychopharmacol Bull 28:309–314, 1992

Ziedonis DM, Kosten TR, Glazer WM, et al: Nicotine dependence and schizophrenia. Hosp Community Psychiatry 45:204–206, 1994

# *42* Addiction in Women

## Sheila B. Blume, M.D., C.A.C.

## Why Study Addiction in Women?

Addiction has traditionally been considered a disease of men. Although it is true that males are more likely than females to abuse or be dependent on alcohol or other drugs, the addictive disorders are a major cause of mortality and morbidity in American women. Furthermore, because of the important gender-related differences in the nature and progression of these diseases, gender-specific approaches to case finding, diagnosis, and treatment are required (Blume 1997b, 1998). Historically, research in addiction has concentrated on male subjects, and models of treatment were developed to meet the needs of male patients. The women's movement and renewed interest in women's health converged to bring about more recent studies on gender differences. Unfortunately, these findings have not yet sufficiently influenced the addiction treatment service network so that adolescent girls and adult women are provided the services they need (Blume 1997a).

## Physiological Factors

Women are more sensitive to alcohol than men are. That is, a measured amount of absolute alcohol (even when adjusted for body weight) will lead to a higher blood alcohol concentration in a female than a male subject (Schenker 1997). This difference is based in part on the higher proportion of fat and lower proportion of water in women's bodies. Because alcohol absorbed through the gastrointestinal tract is distributed in total body water, less water leads to a higher concentration. In addition, evidence has accumulated that men

have substantially more alcohol dehydrogenase in the gastric mucosa, which results in a higher rate of first-pass metabolism. Therefore, women absorb more of the alcohol they drink. This greater sensitivity may explain, at least in part, why alcohol dependence progresses more rapidly in women. Both alcohol-related symptoms and physical complications such as fatty liver, cirrhosis, hypertension, anemia, malnutrition, gastrointestinal hemorrhage, peptic ulcer requiring surgery (Ashley et al. 1977), peripheral myopathy, and cardiomyopathy (Urbano-Marquez et al. 1995) develop and worsen more rapidly in women. In addition, mortality is higher for females with alcoholism (Blume 1998).

Physiological differences in the effects of other addictive drugs have been less studied. It is known that methadone-maintained opiate-addicted individuals require an increased dose during pregnancy, perhaps because of metabolic differences as well as increased body mass (Blume 1998). Pregnancy in any addicted woman is a time of particular risk because serious and irreversible damage to the developing fetus can result from a combination of direct effects on fetal growth and development (especially established for alcohol); reduction in the supply of blood to the placenta, caused by alcohol, cocaine, and other drugs; effects of impaired nutrition; and a variety of other factors common in these women's lives, such as smoking, faulty diet, and inadequate exercise (Hoegerman et al. 1990). Smoking itself during pregnancy has been correlated with lowered birth weight, an increased risk of sudden infant death syndrome, and hyperactivity (Wakschlag et al. 1997).

Although alcohol is believed by the general public to be a sexual stimulant for women, it actually depresses female sexual arousal and orgasm in a dose-response relationship (Blume 1991). Chronic heavy drinking is a major factor in female infertility and other sexual dysfunctions (Blume 1998). The mistaken notion that alcohol improves their sexual responsiveness causes many alcoholic women to fear sexual intercourse in early recovery. In fact, most alcoholic women report improved responsiveness and pleasure in their sexual relationships once abstinence from alcohol is established (Blume 1998).

HIV infection is a growing problem among females. Nearly 80% of affected girls and women are between ages 13 and 39 years. About half are injection-drug users, and an additional 15% are identified as nonusing sexual partners of male injection-drug users. When these women and girls become pregnant, they run the risk of passing the disease to their offspring unless an accurate diagnosis is made and they are appropriately treated. Much research has shown that successful treatment of drug-dependent women is associated with improved health-related behaviors, including safer sexual practices and more appropriate treatment-seeking.

Studies of the genetics of addiction have focused almost entirely on alcoholism. Although the evidence is mixed, there is some indication that greater genetic influence exists in males, specifically in the form of a highly heritable male-limited variant of alcoholism (Sigvardsson et al. 1996).

## Psychological Factors

Few longitudinal studies examining psychological predictors of alcoholism have included women (Blume 1997b, 1998). A 27-year follow-up study of college women found that the best predictors of later drinking problems were drinking to relieve shyness, drinking to feel high, and drinking to get along better on dates. These patterns predicted later problems even better than did actual drinking problems in college. The pattern was distinctly different from that in college men (K. M. Filmore, S. D. Bacon, M. Hyman: "The 27-Year Longitudinal Panel Study of Drinking by Students in College." 1979 Report to National Institute of Alcoholism and Alcohol Abuse [Contract No ADM 281-76-0015]. Washington, DC, 1979). Several shorter-term longitudinal studies have found that women who reported depression or sexual dysfunction when first interviewed reported increases in drinking and/or drinking problems several years later (Blume 1997b, 1998). Retrospective studies have found that a history of being sexually abused substantially increases the risk for both

drug (including alcohol) abuse and dependence in women (Wilsnack et al. 1997).

Epidemiological data, especially from the National Comorbidity Survey (Kessler et al. 1994), indicate a higher lifetime prevalence of comorbid psychiatric disorders in females than males who meet diagnostic criteria for drug (including alcohol) abuse or dependence. Furthermore, these diagnoses are more often primary (i.e., the psychiatric disorder precedes the addictive disorder or occurs during a prolonged period of abstinence) in women. For example, the odds ratio for later developing alcohol abuse or dependence is 4.10 for a female subject with major depression, compared with 2.67 for a male with the same disorder (Kessler et al. 1997). Other studies in general, clinical, and research volunteer populations of alcohol-dependent adults have found that in women who meet diagnostic criteria for both major depression and alcohol dependence, the major depression is independent or primary approximately two-thirds of the time, whereas in alcoholic men who meet depression criteria, the alcohol diagnosis is primary about two-thirds of the time and depression is predominantly alcohol-related (Blume 1997b, 1998). The high prevalence of psychiatric comorbidity in addicted women makes careful psychiatric evaluation important; and in the evaluation, the psychiatrist should determine which disorder occurred first, because a primary disorder is less likely to improve spontaneously with the establishment of abstinence from substances of abuse and is more likely to require specific treatment. However, it must be stressed that treatment of a primary psychiatric disorder will not automatically lead to remission of the patient's substance use disorder. Both require treatment for stable recovery to occur.

## Sociocultural Factors

Whether or not addictive disorders turn out to be determined less by nature and more by nurture in women, the importance of sociocultural factors in shaping the etiology and course of these disorders is clearly established. The traditional expectations that women will drink less than men and will drink only on special occasions protect women from developing alcohol problems. Societal changes in women's roles have been associated with an increase in drinking and alcohol problems. Research has demonstrated that compared with men's drinking patterns, women's drinking patterns are more influenced by those of spouses or significant others (Blume 1997b, 1998).

Although societal norms protect women to some degree, they can also be destructive. The social stigma attached to heavy drinking and to drug use by women (a stigma that is associated with the incorrect expectation of sexual arousal and promiscuity) brands such individuals as "fallen women." When alcoholic women do not fit the societal stereotype, their disease is not recognized. Thus, the stigma reinforces denial in the affected women as well as their families and in professionals, who might otherwise diagnose and treat the disease early. The probability that a diagnosis of alcoholism will be missed in a general medical and surgical hospital population is highest when the patient is better educated, of higher socioeconomic status, privately insured, and female (Moore et al. 1989).

This societal stereotyping also encourages sexual assault, including date rape, against women who drink. A woman who is drinking is assumed to be sexually available. In our society, a rapist who is intoxicated is considered less responsible for his behavior, whereas a victim who is intoxicated is blamed for the assault (Blume 1991).

There is a recent trend in many states to prosecute pregnant or postpartum women for use of alcohol or other drugs during their pregnancy (Blume 1997a). In some jurisdictions, a positive urine test in a newborn leads to automatic removal of the child, without any effort to make a diagnosis or treat the mother or to help the family unit. In others, criminal charges of "prenatal child abuse" have been pressed, even when the accused woman had tried to obtain treatment during her pregnancy and had been unsuccessful because of a lack of facilities (Blume 1997a). Such policies are widely publicized and tend to further erode the addicted woman's tenuous trust in the public medical system. By deterring such women from seeking either addiction treatment or prenatal care, these policies have the potential to increase the numbers of alcohol- and drug-affected newborns rather than improve infant health.

## Treatment

As mentioned earlier, the continuum of treatment modalities and settings that has evolved over the past half century was initially developed to help alcoholic and addicted men. Common sense dictates that treatment professionals and programs tailor their treatment to women's needs. However, this is not always done. For example, the so-called boot-camp treatment model of military-style discipline and physical challenge for con-

victed drug-addicted men has been applied, unchanged (even with regard to male-style clothing and haircuts), to young women. The Twelve Steps of Alcoholics Anonymous (AA), also used in some form by other self-help groups for addicted individuals and their families, were originally written as a distillation of the recovery experience of the first hundred or so AA members, most of them middle-class white men (White and Chaney 1993). Many women have indeed recovered through participation in 12-step programs, and at present, fully one-third of total AA members are women (40% of members age 30 years or younger). An understanding of gender differences can enhance the ability of health professionals to recommend these steps to and interpret these steps for women. For example, admitting powerlessness over alcohol (the first step in AA) often represents a spiritual crisis for a culturally empowered male who is accustomed to running his own life. In contrast, an unmarried mother who lives in urban poverty and has been sexually abused might think that to admit she is powerless and that her life is unmanageable is merely to describe her situation. For such women, learning to take control rather than give it up will be a major goal of treatment.

National data show that women are currently underrepresented in addiction treatment, particularly at alcoholism treatment facilities. Barriers to treatment for women include lack of child care (virtually no residential programs accommodate both women and their children), reluctance on the part of many addiction programs to accept pregnant patients (Blume 1997a), and lack of health insurance (more women than men are employed in low-paying jobs that do not provide health insurance). In addition, the most common organized referral programs (Employee Assistance Programs in the workplace and drunk-driver or other criminal justice–based programs) are more effective at identifying addicted men than addicted women. For example, among convicted drunk drivers, men outnumber women by about nine to one. What case-finding methods would work better for women? When male and female patients in alcoholism facilities are asked to identify the problems that brought them into treatment, they reply differently. Among men, the problems most frequently cited are problems related to work and those involving the justice system, reflecting current intervention techniques. Among women, the most frequently mentioned problems relate to health and family. Simple screening programs in health facilities would identify a large number of women with addictive disorders. Research using pencil-and-paper screening tools found serious alcohol problems in 11%–17% of female ambulatory primary care and gynecological patients and 12.5%–14% of female medical and surgical inpatients, percentages well above the general population prevalence (Blume 1998). However, such screening is rarely done. Likewise, screening among clients of divorce lawyers and family service agencies could uncover addictive disorders in earlier stages than are now generally recognized.

Once a female patient begins treatment, she should be carefully evaluated for additional psychiatric and substance use disorders. Many alcoholic and drug-addicted women develop iatrogenic dependence on sedatives, benzodiazepines, and/or opiates, prescribed symptomatically for a variety of complaints by clinicians who have failed to recognize the underlying addictive disorder. Such dependencies must be treated along with the primary alcohol or drug dependence.

When comorbid psychiatric disorders are discovered, it is helpful to determine whether the disorder preceded the addiction or had its onset during a prolonged period of abstinence and therefore may be regarded as primary. In these latter cases particularly, the patient should be prepared to recognize early indications of recurrence of the disorder during her recovery from addiction. Prompt treatment—of recurrent major depression, for example—can relieve symptoms and avert a relapse of addiction. Primary psychiatric disorders are less likely than secondary ones (such as depression with onset during active addiction) to be relieved without specific treatment during early recovery. Whether primary or secondary, however, some disorders—such as anorexia nervosa, bulimia, severe depression, or psychosis—will require treatment along with the addictive disorder.

In evaluating an addicted woman, it is important to obtain an adequate history of physical and/or sexual abuse. Women in a currently abusive relationship may need help in obtaining safe shelter before treatment can be successfully undertaken. An additional effort should be made to assess the female patient's children for problems related to intrauterine exposure or to living with an addicted parent. Such children can often profit from programs designed for school-age children of alcoholic and addicted individuals. Parenting programs and programs that offer assistance for single parents are particularly helpful in the long-term rehabilitation of addicted women. Often from families made dysfunctional by the alcohol or drug dependence of their own parents, these women commonly feel overwhelmed by the parental role. Family members should be involved in the female patient's treatment whenever possible and should be encouraged to participate in self-help groups such as Al-Anon, Narc-Anon, Alateen, and Adult Children of Alcoholics.

Vocational rehabilitation is also a useful adjunct in women's treatment. Often unemployed or underemployed and restricted in outlook by narrow gender-stereotyped role choices, recovering women can gain a feeling of competence and control through job training and adequately paid employment. Care must be taken to avoid maintenance of sexist attitudes within the treatment program itself (Blume, in press). In mixed-gender programs, women should not be role stereotyped, assigned only "women's work," or allowed to defer to male group members without challenge. On the other hand, women's stereotyping of men (e.g., all men are batterers) should also be challenged, to enlarge such women's understanding of the world and the opportunities that are open to them in recovery.

To avoid the problem of gender stereotyping, a number of all-female treatment programs have been developed, both as residential and as outpatient models (Dahlgren and Willander 1989). These programs tend to employ female staff members and apply feminist principles to their treatment. Other programs that serve both sexes have developed woman-led women's groups of various types, either as primary therapy groups or as supplements to mixed-sex groups. It is often easier for women to discuss sexual and abuse problems in all-female settings. Female staff members provide role models for patients, as do recovering women encountered in self-help groups. An all-women self-help group, Women for Sobriety, meets in some parts of the United States, as do some all-women AA and Narcotics Anonymous groups.

Special populations of addicted women, including lesbians; Native American, African American, and Hispanic women; women in the military; and female health care professionals require special approaches that recognize the specific cultural context in which their addictive disorders developed (and in which their recovery will be played out) (Howard et al. 1996).

## Prevention

Little effort has been devoted to the development of prevention methods specifically geared toward women. Of those methods designed, most have as their focus the prevention of alcohol-related birth defects and involve educating pregnant women, health care professionals, and the public (e.g., through warning labels on alcoholic beverage containers) about the danger of drinking during pregnancy. Evaluations of such measures have revealed a decrease in light and moderate drinking during pregnancy. However, individuals who drink heavily are often unable to stop in response to education. Screening, case identification, intervention, and treatment are critical to prevention of fetal alcohol syndrome, because most women who give birth to such children are alcohol dependent. Similarly, fetal damage due to other drug use can be prevented through screening, intervention, and treatment. A urine toxicology survey of obstetric practices in one Florida county found a similar prevalence of positive tests for illegal drugs in public (16%) and private (13%) prenatal care settings (Chasnoff et al. 1990).

Primary prevention in children and adolescents has tended to focus on a combination of education and life-skills training. However, these programs seldom include information about the special sensitivity of women to alcohol. Delaying or preventing the initiation of cigarette and alcohol use is among the primary goals of these programs. Recent studies have found that smoking is in danger of becoming a predominantly female habit; more teenage girls than boys now begin smoking, and more men than women quit. Primary prevention efforts geared toward girls should therefore cover all drugs of dependence and might profitably include measures to combat gender stereotyping, raise self-esteem, decrease emphasis on thinness (many girls begin smoking to lose weight), and offer help to girls who have been abused. For adult women, primary prevention can be accomplished through group support for women involved in separation, divorce, or widowhood and through support for single mothers, caregivers of elderly or chronically ill persons, battered women, and other women in stressful situations. Helping these women to cope with their problems without the use of alcohol or other drugs will prevent abuse and dependence. Helping society to see addicted women as people with treatable illnesses will bring about an end to the prejudice that now keeps those in need from receiving help.

## ◾ References

Ashley MJ, Olin JS, LeRiche WH, et al: Morbidity in alcoholics: evidence for accelerated development of physical disease in women. Arch Intern Med 137:883–887, 1977

Blume SB: Sexuality and stigma: the alcoholic woman. Alcohol Health Res World 15:139–146, 1991

Blume SB: Women and alcohol: issues in social policy, in Gender and Alcohol: Individual and Social Perspectives. Edited by Wilsnack RW, Wilsnack SC. New Brunswick, NJ, Rutgers Center of Alcohol Studies, 1997a, pp 462–489

Blume SB: Women: clinical aspects, in Substance Abuse: A Comprehensive Textbook, 3rd Edition. Edited by Lowinson JH, Ruiz P, Millman RB, et al. New York, Williams & Wilkins, 1997b, pp 645–654

Blume SB: Women and addictive disorders, in Principles of Addiction Medicine, 2nd Edition. Edited by Graham A, Schultz P. Chevy Chase, MD, American Society of Addiction Medicine, 1998, pp 15.1.1–15.1.30

Blume SB: Common myths and misconceptions in the treatment of addicted women, in Problems, Mistakes and Failures in the Care of Alcoholics and Addicts. Edited by Westermeyer J. Group for the Advancement of Psychiatry (in press)

Chasnoff IJ, Landress HJ, Barrett ME: The prevalence of illicit drug or alcohol use during pregnancy and discrepancies in mandatory reporting in Pinellas County, Florida. N Engl J Med 322:1202–1206, 1990

Dahlgren L, Willander A: Are special treatment facilities for female alcoholics needed? A controlled 2-year follow-up study from a specialized female unit (EWA) versus a mixed male/female treatment facility. Alcohol Clin Exp Res 13:499–504, 1989

Hoegerman G, Wilson CA, Thurmond E, et al: Drug-exposed neonates. West J Med 152 (special issue):559–564, 1990

Howard JM, Martin SE, Mail PD, et al (eds): Women and alcohol: issues for prevention research (NIAAA Res Monogr 32, NIH Publ No 96-3817). Bethesda, MD, National Institutes of Health, 1996

Kessler RC, McGonagle KA, Zhao S, et al: Lifetime and 12-month prevalence of DSM-III-R psychiatric disorders in the United States: results from the National Comorbidity Survey. Arch Gen Psychiatry 51:8–19, 1994

Kessler RC, Crum RM, Warner LA, et al: Lifetime co-occurrence of DSM-III-R alcohol abuse and dependence with other psychiatric disorders in the National Comorbidity Survey. Arch Gen Psychiatry 54:313–321, 1997

Moore RD, Bone LR, Geller G, et al: Prevalence, detection and treatment of alcoholism in hospitalized patients. JAMA 261:403–408, 1989

Schenker S: Medical consequences of alcohol abuse: is gender a factor? Alcohol Clin Exp Res 21:179–181, 1997

Sigvardsson S, Bohman M, Cloninger CR: Replication of the Stockholm adoption study of alcoholism: confirmatory cross-fostering analysis. Arch Gen Psychiatry 53:681–687, 1996

Urbano-Marquez A, Ramon E, Fernandez-Sola J, et al: The greater risk of alcoholic cardiomyopathy and myopathy in women compared with men. JAMA 274:149–154, 1995

Wakschlag LS, Lahey BB, Loeber R, et al: Maternal smoking during pregnancy and the risk of conduct disorder in boys. Arch Gen Psychiatry 54:670–676, 1997

White W, Chaney R: Metaphors of Transformation: Feminine and Masculine. Bloomington, IL, Lighthouse Training Institute, 1993

Wilsnack SC, Vogeltanz ND, Klassen AD, et al: Childhood sexual abuse and women's substance abuse: national survey findings. J Stud Alcohol 58:264–271, 1997

# Chapter 43

# Perinatal Substance Use

Beth Glover Reed, Ph.D.

The perinatal period is defined narrowly as the period from 26 weeks' gestation to 1 week postpartum (Imaizumi 1992) and more broadly as the months of pregnancy to 3 months to a year afterward. Thus, it is approximately 1 year of a woman's life, and this period is repeated with each additional pregnancy. Risks and opportunities are created by the physiological, psychological, and relationship changes that occur. Environmental factors either add to or mitigate risk and protective factors arising from other sources, and all are important in understanding current and potential policies and practices with regard to use of alcohol, tobacco, and other drugs during the perinatal period.

Public policy and research on perinatal substance use (in this chapter, the term *substance* or *drug* encompasses alcohol, tobacco, and other drugs) have focused heavily on the health and welfare of the developing fetus and the newborn, and some attention has been paid to the challenges of mother-child attachment and early parenting. Interventions in the United States have usually been concerned with infant mortality, fetal alcohol syndrome, and heroin-involved or crack babies. These interventions have often been associated with moral judgments, uninformed by empirical knowledge and clinical experience, and uncoordinated. Sources of attention to perinatal use of substances include administrative, legislative, and judicial branches of government; the criminal justice and child welfare systems; and public health and women's advocates. Some interventions have the goals of reducing alcohol and tobacco consumption during pregnancy, but the major legal emphases have been on illicit drugs. Practices differ widely in different locations, and approaches to prenatal care and addiction treatment often conflict (Puentes 1993).

Punitive approaches tend to focus on and blame women, with little concern shown for their lives before and after pregnancy. With these approaches, little attention is paid to fathers' parenting skills and responsibilities and to longer-term issues concerning the child (or children), and punitive approaches allow many risk factors for mother and child to continue. Past and many current policies contribute to the increase in numbers of women in jails and prisons, separated from their children, with large numbers of children in unstable substitute care. Too often, debates are framed as the rights of the mother versus the rights of the child, although multiple efforts are being made to develop legal theory and policies that do not dichotomize these two sets of interests (Garcia 1997; Keys 1992).

Pregnancy is an opportunity for positive interventions, if conflicting approaches can be reconciled. Those concerned about gender-sensitive prevention and treatment have taken advantage of waves of public concern about infants to increase resources and broaden policies and service options for all women; much has been learned about what works (Substance Abuse and Mental Health Services Administration 1997a).

In this chapter, I summarize some critical issues arising from substance use during the perinatal period and describe briefly how they have been addressed in research, policy, and practice. The chapter is organized according to policy, treatment, and services options at different levels and stages of substance use and pregnancy. All substance use and all types of preventive interventions, not merely those usually defined as treatment, are discussed, because during pregnancy, levels of use lower than levels considered indicative of addictive disorder, drug abuse, or drug dependence can have negative consequences, especially when other health or lifestyle stressors are present.

## Prevalence of Substance Use and Co-Occurring Problems During Pregnancy

Accurately estimating the prevalence of high-risk use during pregnancy is difficult for multiple reasons, including underreporting because of stigma and negative attitudes (Substance Abuse and Mental Health Services Administration 1997c), use of drug combinations that are difficult to assess (S. C. Allen 1994; Allgulander et al. 1990; Substance Abuse and Mental Health Services Administration 1997c), and inconsistencies in screening for substance use (Zellman et al. 1990, 1993). Despite this, some data are available. Two years (1994–1995) of National Household Survey data were combined for women and girls ages 15–44 years (U.S. Department of Health and Human Services 1997). Some findings are given here: 31.7% reported tobacco use in the last month (21.5% while pregnant), almost half reported drinking alcohol (Substance Abuse and Mental Health Services Administration 1997c) and 18.5% reported binge drinking (2.9% while pregnant), and 9.3% reported current use of illicit drugs (2.3% while pregnant). This suggests that many women can reduce use while pregnant, but among women with a child under 2 years, rates were only slightly lower than those before pregnancy. Thus, women do not sustain reductions in use postpartum (U.S. Department of Health and Human Services 1997). Results from a national survey of pregnant women (National Institute on Drug Abuse 1994) were similar, except that illicit drug use was reported by only 5.5% during pregnancy.

Other reviews suggest that women of childbearing age have used alcohol, marijuana, and heroin in relatively stable patterns over the past 10 years, although use of cocaine, and especially crack, became more common in the 1980s (Hutchins 1997; Laken and Hutchins 1996). Subpopulations of women vary substantially. For example, white, non-Hispanic women are most likely to drink, and younger women (ages 15–25 years) are more likely to use all drugs (U.S. Department of Health and Human Services 1997). Although comparative studies are scarce, drug use during pregnancy appears to occur at all economic levels. One study screened women in both public and private health care practices, and about 15% of women tested positive for drugs, although the mix of substances in the two settings differed somewhat (Chasnoff et al. 1990). Women who use one substance are also likely to use others. For instance, in 1995, 12.6% of smokers drank heavily (2.7% of nonsmokers) and 13.6% used illicit drugs (3.0% of nonsmokers) (U.S. Department of Health and Human Services 1997); 32% of women who reported use of one drug also smoked cigarettes and drank alcohol (National Institute on Drug Abuse 1994).

In terms of substance abuse disorders, 3% of women in household studies report heavy use of alcohol, whereas 2% report problematic illicit drug use (Substance Abuse and Mental Health Services Administration 1997c). In subgroups, the rates of substance abuse disorders are higher. For instance, studies show that from 16% to 67% of homeless women have one or more substance abuse disorders (Smith et al. 1993). Forty-three percent of women with substance abuse disorders have high-risk pregnancies. In addition, they often seek prenatal care later than other women and receive less adequate health care (Marcenko et al. 1994).

Women also experience many co-occurring problems before and during pregnancy. These include psychiatric problems (Beal and Redlener 1995; Jessup 1996; Ziedonis et al. 1994), domestic violence (Miller et al. 1993), childhood sexual abuse and/or adult rape (Boyd 1993; Liebschutz et al. 1997), and eating disorders (Holderness et al. 1994). Violence often escalates during pregnancy (Amaro et al. 1990).

## Risks Associated With Substance Use During Pregnancy

Pregnancy can pose risks for a woman even when she receives good health care and has optimal social supports; risks are considerably higher in the absence of such care and support. Substance use and life-threatening conditions that are common among persons who use drugs add additional risks. The effects on the fetus or newborn of most drugs used by a pregnant woman are short-term (e.g., withdrawal symptoms) because infants must metabolize the drugs they receive through the umbilical cord (Zuckerman et al. 1995). Knowledge about longer-term effects of many drugs on children is limited and contradictory. Some studies report various behavioral and learning difficulties, whereas others show few or none, especially if the study controls for other life conditions and health problems. Longitudinal studies are needed that measure multiple aspects of a mother's (and father's) use and lifestyle and many aspects of a child's life circumstances, behavior, and health (Mallouh 1996).

Alcohol use is associated with many complications in the mother, including endocarditis, hepatitis, pneumonia, and sexually transmitted diseases (Mallouh 1996).

Cocaine use is associated with preeclampsia, pulmonary edema, seizures, and cardiac arrhythmias (Fox 1994). Alcohol and cocaine use can also interrupt pregnancies, resulting in spontaneous abortion, preterm delivery, bleeding, and stillbirth (Fox 1994; Sanchez 1992). Fetal alcohol syndrome or fetal alcohol effects can leave a child substantially and permanently impaired, physically and mentally (Streissguth et al. 1994). Tobacco use is probably the single largest contributor to reduced birth weight, which in turn contributes to infant mortality and development of many other complications (Floyd et al. 1993; Ker et al. 1996). Tobacco appears to have addictive and sometimes synergistic effects with alcohol or other drugs, increasing the impact of alcohol or other drugs on fetal growth and fetal problems (Ker et al. 1996).

## Interventions in the Extended Perinatal Period

### Prevention and Treatment of Drug Problems: Stages and Levels

Outlined in Table 43–1 is a public health approach to drug use and problems during pregnancy. Drug-related needs and types of interventions are arrayed on the horizontal axis, and the time frames before, during, and af-

ter the perinatal period are listed on the vertical axis. Listed below a continuum of drug use, risks, and needs for interventions are the types of preventive and treatment interventions suggested for each level of risks and needs (Mrazek and Haggerty 1994; Substance Abuse and Mental Health Services Administration 1997b). The goals of the examples discussed in the following section are low-risk pregnancies and optimally healthy women and infants.

To maintain and strengthen healthy conditions, universal preventive measures are used, which target everyone regardless of risk (Table 43–1, far right column). Some risk factors for substance use include lack of knowledge about the effects of drugs in pregnancy, unplanned pregnancies, absence of prenatal care, environmental hazards or stressors (e.g., poverty, violence), and barriers to adequate health care (e.g., no health care benefits). Related interventions include warning labels on cigarette packages and liquor bottles about the risks of smoking and drinking in pregnancy, as well as broad-based education about family planning and nutrition so that pregnancies are wanted and women are well nourished.

In cases in which risk factors are present but problems related to drug use are not yet evident, selective preventive interventions are warranted (Table 43–1, second column from right). Risk factors may be biologi-

**Table 43–1.** Levels of drug use (including alcohol and tobacco use) or risks for drug use and types of treatment or prevention in the perinatal period

| | Level of drug use or risk for drug use | | | | |
|---|---|---|---|---|---|
| | Drug problems interrupted | Drug use present and severe | Drug problems developing | Risk factors present | No or unknown risk factors |
| | Type of treatment or prevention | | | | |
| Pregnancy stage | Maintenance, rehabilitation | Treatment, case identification | Indicated preventive measures | Selective preventive measures | Universal preventive measures |
| Prepregnancy | | | | | |
| First trimester | | | | | |
| Second trimester | | | | | |
| Third trimester | | | | | |
| 3 months postpartum | | | | | |
| 1 year postpartum | | | | | |
| 3 years postpartum | | | | | |
| Ongoing | | | | | |

cal or health related (e.g., genetic predispositions, depression, or particular health conditions), historical (e.g., a problematic family of origin), related to current life situations (e.g., a violent relationship or an unsafe living situation with easy access to drugs), or social or economic (e.g., poverty or racism). Selective prevention approaches are designed to reduce risk factors or strengthen protective factors for those with particular risks. Examples of such approaches include increasing access to prenatal care in high-risk neighborhoods and providing special education and support for young people whose parents abuse or formerly abused drugs. Child sexual abuse appears to be a risk factor for all types of problems in women, including substance abuse and mental illness (Boyd 1993; Ratner 1993; Wilsnack et al. 1997).

When signs of problems are present, but problems are not yet severe or ongoing (Table 43–1, third column from right), indicated preventive approaches are appropriate. These identify people or situations with signs of problems and intervene to interrupt the development of problems and/or decrease their negative consequences. Examples of such approaches include screening programs for pregnant women to identify those who are using potentially harmful substances and refer them for assistance (Gillogley et al. 1990), brief treatment (Sanchez-Craig et al. 1991), and parenting support groups for individuals with insufficient knowledge about effective parenting or evidence of neglect. A number of studies have shown that women respond more than men to health messages and to programs that give them the tools to reduce their use and the consequences of that use (Sanchez-Craig et al. 1991). Violence and stigma are major barriers to seeking early assistance.

Interventions in this category might also target those in a position to recognize early signs of trouble—pediatricians, significant others, people women talk with and trust. Professionals often maintain negative societal attitudes about women with drug problems and are undertrained in recognizing drug use or problems and the options available (Dawson et al. 1992). Urine, blood, or hair testing and effective screening interviews are not conducted routinely with pregnant women by health professionals, except in some locations, and the women who are screened are most often poor women who must rely on public clinics (Zellman et al. 1993). The accuracy of different screening methods varies, screening requires resources that may not be available, and many health care professionals believe that screening may disrupt their relationships with their patients

(Zellman et al. 1997). Numerous screening tools are available to help pregnant women and others around them to identify signs of problems (Center for Substance Abuse Treatment 1993b; Morse et al. 1997; Ostrea 1992; Russell et al. 1991).

When drug problems are present and severe—that is, when women are using psychoactive substances, with potentially negative consequences for themselves and their infants—the appropriate interventions are therapeutic treatments, with assessment to determine what type and what level of treatment are required (Table 43–1, second column from left). Techniques for safely managing pregnancy and delivery in high-risk women with substance abuse problems also fall into this category. A number of protocols are available to guide the management of pregnancy in women with drug problems (P. M. Allen and Sandler 1993; Center for Substance Abuse Treatment 1993a; Chiang and Finnegan 1995; Mitchell 1993/5; Sanchez 1992; Zuckerman et al. 1995).

Pregnant women with substance use problems face many barriers to treatment, including fear of loss of their children; family responsibilities; insufficient financial resources and health insurance; unsafe living conditions; transportation difficulties; lack of support and even opposition from partners, families, and friends; shame; low self-esteem; chaotic lifestyles; and treatment programs that are geared more toward men or that do not treat pregnant women (K. Allen 1994; Gehshan 1993; Reed 1987; Robin et al. 1997). All contribute to difficulties in seeking treatment and following through on appointments and health care regimens.

Multiple efforts have been made to increase services and access to drug treatment for women, especially pregnant women (Schmidt and Weisner 1995; Somon et al. 1996). Public Law 102-321 (1993) requires states to ensure that pregnant women have first priority for drug treatment, are not put on waiting lists, have timely access to health care, and are provided with child care and transportation assistance. Access to treatment and health care seems to be improving for pregnant women (Breitbart et al. 1994), although difficulties are still reported in many locations.

During the 1990s, many federally funded demonstration programs added to the knowledge about the needs of women with drug problems (Center for Substance Abuse Treatment 1994; Finkelstein 1994) and how treatment must be modified to address issues for women (National Women's Resource Center 1997a). Special issues include shame, guilt, depression (O'Connor et al. 1993); current or past domestic and sexual violence (Fazzone et al. 1997; Fullilove and Fullilove 1994; Harvey et al. 1994); and relationships and sexuality (Beckman and Ackerman 1995; Finkelstein 1993, 1994). Ignoring these issues can exacerbate the problems of women (National Women's Resource Center 1997a; Reed 1991). Women who are heavily burdened with multiple life problems and have little social support are more likely to drop out of treatment and have the most need for intensive, coordinated services (Brown et al. 1995; Lanehart et al. 1996). Gaps in knowledge still exist concerning how to integrate the psychological tasks necessary for pregnancy and motherhood with what is needed for sobriety and a stable lifestyle.

Resources are also available for assisting women to care for their infants (Bays 1992; Camp and Finkelstein 1995; VanBremen and Chasnoff 1994). These infants are often irritable and demanding; they need attention and consistency while their mothers are struggling to resist cravings and maintain sobriety or abstinence. The mother's ability to prepare for and bond with the infant may be seriously disrupted by the work required either to sustain her drug use or to develop and maintain a stable recovery (Mallouh 1996). Evidence is increasing that parenting training and support and well-baby services increase treatment retention and success in high-risk women (Brown et al. 1995; Hughes et al. 1995; Lanehart et al. 1996; National Women's Resource Center 1997b; Szuster et al. 1996).

Individuals who have had substance abuse problems but have interrupted the progression of these problems require maintenance and rehabilitation (Table 43–1, first column from left). Women in this category need assistance to maintain progress, consolidate recovery, and avoid relapse. Habilitation may also be required, involving the development of skills for daily living, of positive relationships, and of communication skills; and basic education and job readiness training. Attention should be paid to trauma symptoms over time, as well as to tobacco use, in addition to drugs that disrupt daily life, because of tobacco's interactions with other drugs and the extensive health consequences of use (Campbell et al. 1995; Ker et al. 1996).

It is possible to locate particular programs and approaches in different places in the schema outlined in Table 43–1, depending on target populations and goals. For instance, if the goal is a healthy pregnancy, pregnancy testing within drug treatment programs might be considered a selective or indicated preventive measure because special assistance is likely to be needed during pregnancy and potential relapse endangers pregnancy.

## Interventions According to Stages in the Extended Perinatal Period

Time frames before, during, and after the perinatal period are listed on the vertical axis of Table 43–1. What procedures are followed depends partially on when the particular woman begins prenatal care or substance abuse treatment (Mitchell 1993/5). Key issues before pregnancy are a woman's general health status and health practices, relationships, and knowledge of family planning, the goals being that pregnancy is planned and wanted and that the woman is healthy at conception. Universal and selective interventions can be accomplished through public education or the broad-based public health system. These approaches can target women themselves, their families and friends, potential gatekeepers, or public attitudes and knowledge. Prohealth, health promotion, and family planning activities are also important for women in treatment or receiving aftercare for substance abuse problems, and models for delivering such services are available (Ker et al. 1996; Nelson and Mondanaro 1982).

Women may be unaware for at least part of the first trimester that they are pregnant, especially women who are heavy users of alcohol or other drugs. Menses are disrupted by many types of use and by nutritional imbalances, and sleep disruptions are common among those who drink or use drugs heavily. By the middle trimester, a woman's pregnancy becomes more obvious to others, who are then in a position to encourage her to seek prenatal care and substance treatment. Blood volume dramatically increases during the third trimester, which causes a decrease in the concentration of drugs in the mother and an increase in the delivery of drugs to the fetus through the umbilical cord (Imaizumi 1992).

Good prenatal care is important at all stages of pregnancy to monitor progress and to identify, prevent, or manage problems (Imaizumi 1992). Guidelines for prenatal care for persons who use substances outline what is needed at different stages (Center for Substance Abuse Prevention 1993; Chiang and Finnegan 1995; Farkas and Parran 1993; Mitchell 1993/5). Medical personnel in drug treatment settings and prenatal care settings often have different perspectives and knowledge and may present a woman with conflicting instructions (Puentes 1993). Health care providers focus on both the fetus and the mother and maintain efforts toward goals of good health care even if the mother is not always cooperative or continues to use drugs. Nutritional and pharmacological interventions are frequent. Traditional approaches to addiction treatment most often focus on the adult and emphasize the substance-using individual's motivation and compliance. The drug treatment system may insist on abstinence, as may the state's legal system.

A critical time is labor and delivery and the period of stabilization of both the mother and the child after delivery. Some women who use drugs arrive at emergency rooms at the time of delivery without having had any previous prenatal care. This is especially true when women fear prosecution for their drug use and have no positive relationships with health care providers. A woman may use drugs immediately before she delivers because she fears the anticipated pain (Zuckerman et al. 1995). Health care providers may need to manage flashbacks and other reactions associated with post-traumatic stress that may be triggered by medical procedures during pregnancy and delivery (Mallouh 1996).

Often a mother's drug use is not detected until the infant's meconium or blood is tested or the pediatrician identifies withdrawal symptoms in the neonate (Zellman et al. 1997). Important requirements after delivery include strengthening of mother-infant attachment, early infant care, well-baby check-ups and immunizations, and promotion of growth and self-regulation of the infant. Over the longer term, new mothers need adequate financial and other resources, safe living spaces, support for parenting, child care, health care, and often other social services.

Interventions designed to sustain reduced use are important, especially in the postpartum period. These interventions are likely to be important for all women, whether or not they test or screen positive for use or have risk factors at delivery. Many women resume use after pregnancy. Parenting is stressful, and some women may develop drug problems *after* delivery as a way to cope with new stressors. Strategies could involve self-assessment tools and behavioral prevention methods women can use to identify relapse triggers and practice alternative responses.

Special risks include little experience with positive parenting because of problems in families of origin, health risks during pregnancy related to age, and domestic violence. Pregnancy and parenting interventions must be culturally sensitive; interventions with strong scientific foundations will be rejected if they are not respectful of a woman's cultural beliefs and traditions.

## Arenas and Contexts for Prevention and Treatment Interventions

Some arenas and contexts for preventive and treatment interventions are shown in Table 43–2. The social-cultural-political context helps shape funding and regulatory legislation and has an effect on enforcement of laws and the willingness of potential interveners to enforce these laws and intervene in other ways. Pregnant women must seek services within these environments, and they often internalize societal attitudes. Health care, welfare, and child welfare reform can result in new opportunities and risks during the perinatal period, depending on the criteria used to determine access to services (N. K. Young and Gardner 1996).

Currently, many differences of opinion exist about drug use and problems and how best to intervene during pregnancy (Chavkin 1990; Dobson and Eby 1992; Ferguson and Kaplan 1994; I. M. Young 1994). Those who believe that drug use is primarily a moral problem stress legal or moral sanctions. Public health approaches seek to define perinatal substance use as a health problem—a chronic and relapsing disease that can be prevented and managed once it has developed. Empowerment approaches target women's stigma and lower status in society, compared with men. These approaches endeavor to build on women's strengths and to provide women with the knowledge, skills, and support to advocate for and make healthy decisions for themselves and their children.

The legal environment at the international, national, state, and local levels both reflects public attitudes and helps to shape them (Weber 1992). Many different legislative and legal strategies have been pursued, sometimes punitive and sometimes intended to force or persuade a woman to go into treatment (Glink 1991; Roper 1992). These strategies include laws mandating drug testing, treatment (Chavkin 1991), reporting to child protective services (Besharov 1992), or arrest and prosecution of pregnant women for child maltreatment, delivery of drugs to a minor, and other infractions (Petro 1991). As of 1997, only 20 states had no evidence of any legal attention to substance abuse during pregnancy (P. D. Jacobson, personal communication, April 1997).

Professional and community-based organizations are also important. The actual day-to-day messages and knowledge that a woman receives from those around her are strongly affected by local environments. How available are psychoactive substances (this relates to prescribing practices, sale and serving of alcohol, and accessibility of tobacco and acceptability of tobacco smoking)? What types of early interventions are available? How hard have local organizations worked to develop gender-sensitive approaches, remove barriers to treatment, or enforce laws equitably?

**Table 43–2.** Arenas and contexts for preventive interventions targeting drug use (including alcohol and tobacco use) in the perinatal period

| Context or focus of preventive interventions | Example of intervention arena |
|---|---|
| Social-cultural-political | Overall attitudes toward and resources for |
|  |     Women in general |
|  |     Parenting |
|  |     Drug use interventions |
| Legal environment | Laws about |
|   Federal |     Use of different substances during pregnancy |
|   State |     Screening for use during pregnancy |
|   Local |     Reporting (to whom, with what consequences) |
|  |   Prosecutor behavior, court interpretations |
| Availability and accessibility of local resources | Availability of women-friendly programs |
|  | Special outreach for women and persons who use drugs |
|  | Parenting programs and options |
| Policies and practices in community-based organizations | Policies about access to services, range of services, reporting, mechanisms, outreach processes |
|   Health care providers | |
|   Drug use prevention/treatment organizations | Drug use–detection practices (prenatal) |
|   Other service providers, gatekeeper organizations | Ready access to drug use–related services for pregnant women |
|   Schools, churches, social organizations | Strong referral linkages, joint programs |
| Service providers | Training and education for service providers on women and drug use, mother-child attachment issues |
|   Attitudes, knowledge, behavior | |
| Families and friends | Outreach and education for general community in locations of women and significant others and in forms that will reach women and significant others |
| Women themselves | |

Communities vary widely in availability of a continuum of care and women-sensitive coordinated comprehensive services (Weisner and Schmidt 1992). Until recently, many drug treatment programs refused to work with pregnant women, apparently because of liability concerns and lack of knowledge. Mechanisms for collaboration across multiple systems, interdisciplinary responses, and comprehensive case management are essential (Grella 1997; Jessup 1996; Puentes 1993). Drug treatment programs also need linkages (often not in place) to address violence against women (child sexual abuse, battering, rape) (Fazzone et al. 1997).

At the service provider level, recurrent training is likely to be needed in multiple settings to address negative attitudes, increase knowledge, and inform the practices of those in a position to identify potential problems and help a woman to locate assistance. These settings include women's health care settings, Lamaze classes and other childbirth-preparation settings, domestic violence shelters, and employability programs. Also needing training are other community gatekeepers

(clergy, child care workers, pharmacists, educators, workers in child welfare and criminal justice systems, and others who frequently interact with women—for instance, hairstylists). Training should include opportunities to develop shared knowledge and linkages across the multiple systems of services a woman is likely to need, as well as opportunities to reduce barriers to prenatal care and to substance abuse treatment. Approaches can also target families and friends directly to increase knowledge and support and reduce stigma. In many cases, women with substance abuse problems must create new support systems to initiate and sustain recovery, and programs that can facilitate this should be helpful in many ways.

Finally, the woman herself must be considered an important target of all types of interventions. Health messages need to be presented where women go—laundromats, work sites, health and beauty establishments, grocery stores, entertainment sites, buses and other forms of transportation, and child-related locations. Most women are highly motivated to have healthy infants and be good mothers, even when their own behavior is actively putting attainment of these goals at risk. The most common reason women with children give for entering treatment is concern for their children.

## Summary and Recommendations

Most experts believe that punitive approaches alone deter prenatal care. Some types of mandatory testing and reporting appear to increase use of prenatal care and substance abuse treatment when they are combined with incentives for treatment, women-appropriate treatment, and adequate and well-informed prenatal care. Pregnant women need immediate entry into appropriate programs, and states appear to be making progress toward meeting this need.

Emphases in policies and practices should reflect the high proportions of women using drugs, including alcohol and tobacco, and the multiple risks these drugs pose to pregnant women and neonates. Within health care sectors, better detection is needed at all stages of pregnancy, as are more-informed staff. Within substance use programs, pregnancy testing for all women is important, as are procedures that do not stop provision of health care and support for risk reduction even when program rules are violated. Substance use programs need strong ties with health care systems and to other services women are likely to need.

Reduction of stigma is important at all levels of intervention. If gender-sensitive preventive and treatment interventions were available throughout women's lives, less attention might be necessary during the perinatal period, although the opportunities a pregnancy represents are important. Parenting education and support are also important for men, and women need to be able to earn living wages and not merely receive education and training for parenting. Communities need to have a mix of gender-sensitive and nonpunitive policies and programs at all levels of intervention. Policy conflicts need to be resolved with approaches that are concerned with both mother and infant and that coordinate multiple systems.

## References

Allen K: Development of an instrument to identify barriers to treatment for addicted women, from their perspective. International Journal of the Addictions 29:429–444, 1994

Allen PM, Sandler M: Critical components of obstetric management of chemically dependent women. Clin Obstet Gynecol 26:347–360, 1993

Allen SC: Risk versus gain: the use of psychotropic medication in women of child-bearing age. Paper presented at the Young Adult Institute Conference, New York, April 1994

Allgulander C, Nowak J, Rice JP: Psychopathology and treatment of 30,344 twins in Sweden, I: the appropriateness of psychoactive drug treatment. Acta Psychiatr Scand 82: 420–426, 1990

Amaro H, Fried LE, Cabral H, et al: Violence during pregnancy and substance abuse. Am J Public Health 80:575–579, 1990

Bays J: The care of alcohol- and drug-affected infants. Pediatr Ann 21:485–495, 1992

Beal AC, Redlener I: Enhancing perinatal outcome in homeless women: the challenge of providing comprehensive health care. Semin Perinatol 19:307–313, 1995

Beckman LJ, Ackerman KT: Women, alcohol and sexuality, in Recent Developments in Alcoholism, Vol 12: Women and Alcohol. Edited by Galanter M. New York, Plenum, 1995, pp 267–285

Besharov DJ: Mandatory reporting of child abuse and research on the effects of prenatal drug exposure, in Methodological Issues in Epidemiological, Prevention, and Treatment Research on Drug-Exposed Women and Their Children (NIDA Res Monogr 117, DHHS Publ No ADM-92-1881). Edited by Kilbey MM, Asghar K. Rockville, MD, National Institute on Drug Abuse, 1992, pp 366–384

Boyd CJ: The antecedents of women's crack cocaine abuse: family substance abuse, sexual abuse, depression and illicit drug use. J Subst Abuse Treat 10:433–438, 1993

Breitbart V, Chavkin W, Wise PH: The accessibility of drug treatment for pregnant women: a survey of programs in five cities. Am J Public Health 84:1658–1661, 1994

Brown VB, Huba GJ, Melchoir LA: Level of burden: women with more than one co-occurring disorder. J Psychoactive Drugs 27:339–346, 1995

Camp JM, Finkelstein N: Fostering Effective Parenting Skills and Healthy Child Development Within Residential Substance Abuse Treatment Settings. Cambridge, MA, Coalition on Addiction, Pregnancy and Parenting, 1995

Campbell B, Wander N, Stark MJ, et al: Treating cigarette smoking in drug abusing clients. J Subst Abuse Treat 12: 89–94, 1995

Center for Substance Abuse Prevention: Pregnancy and Exposure to Alcohol and Other Drug Use (CSAP Technical Rep 7, DHHS Publ No SMA-93-2040). Rockville, MD, Center for Substance Abuse Prevention, 1993

Center for Substance Abuse Treatment: Improving Treatment for Drug-Exposed Infants (Treatment Improvement Protocol No 5). Rockville, MD, Center for Substance Abuse Treatment, 1993a

Center for Substance Abuse Treatment: Maternal Substance Use Assessment Methods Reference Manual: A Review of Screening and Clinical Assessment Instruments for Examining Maternal Use of Alcohol, Tobacco, and Other Drugs. Rockville, MD, Center for Substance Abuse Treatment, 1993b

Center for Substance Abuse Treatment: Practical Approaches in the Treatment of Women Who Abuse Alcohol and Other Drugs. Rockville, MD, U.S. Department of Health and Human Services, 1994

Chasnoff IJ, Griffin DR, MacGregor S, et al: The prevalence of illicit drug or alcohol use during pregnancy and discrepancies in mandatory reporting in Pinellas County, Florida. N Engl J Med 322:1202–1206, 1990

Chavkin W: Drug addiction and pregnancy: policy crossroads. Am J Public Health 80:483–487, 1990

Chavkin W: Mandatory treatment for drug use during pregnancy. JAMA 266:1556–1561, 1991

Chiang CN, Finnegan LP (eds): Medications Development for the Treatment of Pregnant Addicts and Their Infants (NIDA Res Monogr 149, NIH Publ No 95-3891). Rockville, MD, National Institute on Drug Abuse, 1995

Dawson N, Dadheech G, Speroff T, et al: The effect of patient gender on the prevalence and recognition of alcoholism on a general medicine inpatient service. J Gen Intern Med 7:38–45, 1992

Dobson T, Eby KK: Criminal liability for substance abuse during pregnancy: the controversy of maternal v. fetal rights. St. Louis University Law Journal 36:655–694, 1992

Farkas KJ, Parran TV: Treatment of cocaine addiction during pregnancy. Clin Perinatol 20:29–45, 1993

Fazzone PA, Holton JK, Reed BG: Substance Abuse Treatment and Domestic Violence (Treatment Improvement Protocol No 25, DHHS Publ No SMA-97-3163). Rockville, MD, Substance Abuse and Mental Health Services Administration, 1997

Ferguson SK, Kaplan MS: Women and drug policy: implications of normalization. Affilia 9:129–144, 1994

Finkelstein N: The relational model, in Pregnancy and Exposure to Alcohol and Other Drug Use (CSAP Technical Rep 7, DHHS Publ No SMA-93-2040). Rockville, MD, Center for Substance Abuse Prevention, 1993, pp 47–60

Finkelstein N: Treatment issues of alcohol and drug dependent pregnant and parenting women. Health Soc Work 19:7–15, 1994

Floyd RL, Rimer BK, Giovino GA, et al: A review of smoking in pregnancy: effects on pregnancy outcomes and cessation efforts. Annu Rev Public Health 14:379–411, 1993

Fox CH: Cocaine use in pregnancy. J Am Board Fam Pract 7:225–228, 1994

Fullilove M, Fullilove J: Post-traumatic stress disorders in women recovering from substance abuse, in Anxiety Disorders in African Americans. Edited by Friedman S. New York, Springer, 1994, pp 89–101

Garcia SA: Ethical and legal issues associated with substance abuse by pregnant and parenting women. J Psychoactive Drugs 29:101–111, 1997

Gehshan S: A Step Toward Recovery: Improving Access to Substance Abuse Treatment for Pregnant and Parenting Women. Washington, DC, Southern Regional Project on Infant Mortality, 1993

Gillogley KM, Evana AT, Hansen RL, et al: The perinatal impact of cocaine, amphetamine and opiate use detected by universal intrapartum screening. Am J Obstet Gynecol 163:1535–1542, 1990

Glink SB: The prosecution of maternal fetal abuse: is this the answer? University of Illinois Law Review 1991:533–580, 1991

Grella CE: Services for perinatal women with substance abuse and mental health disorders: the unmet need. J Psychoactive Drugs 29:67–78, 1997

Harvey EM, Rawson RA, Obert JL: History of sexual assault and the treatment of substance abuse disorders. J Psychoactive Drugs 26:361–367, 1994

Holderness CC, Brooks-Gunn J, Warren MP: Comorbidity of eating disorders and substance abuse: review of the literature. Int J Eat Disord 16:1–34, 1994

Hughes PH, Coletti SD, Neri RL, et al: Retaining cocaine-abusing women in a therapeutic community: the effect of a child live-in program. Am J Public Health 85:1149–1152, 1995

Hutchins E: Drug use during pregnancy. Journal of Drug Issues 27:463–485, 1997

Imaizumi S: Perinatal factors that influence neonatal outcome, in Identifying the Needs of Drug-Affected Children: Public Policy Issues. Rockville, MD, Office of Substance Abuse Prevention, 1992, pp 11–23

Jessup M: Coexisting mental illness and alcohol and other drug dependencies in pregnant and parenting women. J Psychoactive Drugs 28:311–317, 1996

Ker M, Leischow S, Markowitz IB, et al: Involuntary smoking cessation: a treatment option in chemical dependency programs for women and children. J Psychoactive Drugs 28:47–60, 1996

Keys LJ: Rethinking the aim of the "war on drugs": states' roles in preventing substance abuse by pregnant women. Wisconsin Law Review 1:197–232, 1992

Laken MP, Hutchins E: Recruitment and Retention of Substance-Using Pregnant and Parenting Women: Lessons Learned. Arlington, VA, National Center for Education in Maternal and Child Health, 1996

Lanehart R, Clark H, Rollings J, et al: Impact of intensive case-managed intervention on substance-using pregnant and postpartum women. J Subst Abuse 8:487–495, 1996

Liebschutz JM, Mulvey KP, Samet JH: Victimization among substance-abusing women: worse health outcomes. Arch Intern Med 157:1093–1097, 1997

Mallouh C: The effects of dual diagnosis on pregnancy and parenting. J Psychoactive Drugs 28:367–380, 1996

Marcenko MO, Spence M, Rohweder C: Psychosocial characteristics of pregnant women with and without a history of substance abuse. Health Soc Work 19:17–22, 1994

Miller BA, Downs WR, Testa M: Interrelationships between victimization experiences and women's alcohol use. J Stud Alcohol Suppl 11:109–117, 1993

Mitchell JL: Pregnant, Substance-Using Women (Treatment Improvement Protocol No 2, DHHS Publ No SMA-95-3056). Rockville, MD, Center for Substance Abuse Treatment, 1993/5

Morse B, Gehshan S, Hutchins E: Screening for Substance Abuse During Pregnancy: Improving Care, Improving Health. Arlington, VA, National Center for Education in Maternal and Child Health, 1997

Mrazek PJ, Haggerty RJ (eds): Reducing Risks for Mental Disorders. Washington, DC, National Academy Press, 1994

National Institute on Drug Abuse: National Pregnancy and Health Survey. Rockville, MD, National Institute on Drug Abuse, 1994

National Women's Resource Center for the Prevention and Treatment of Alcohol, Tobacco, and Other Drug Abuse and Mental Illness: Gender Specific Substance Abuse Treatment. Alexandria, VA, National Women's Resource Center for the Prevention and Treatment of Alcohol, Tobacco, and Other Drug Abuse and Mental Illness, 1997a

National Women's Resource Center for the Prevention and Treatment of Alcohol, Tobacco, and Other Drug Abuse and Mental Illness: A Reason for Hope: Substance Abuse Treatment During Pregnancy Has Long-Term Benefits. Alexandria, VA, National Women's Resource Center for the Prevention and Treatment of Alcohol, Tobacco, and Other Drug Abuse and Mental Illness, 1997b

Nelson MB, Mondanaro J: Health promotion for drug dependent women, in Treatment Services for Drug Dependent Women, Vol II (DHHS Publ No ADM-82-1219). Edited by Reed BG, Beschner GM, Mondanaro J. Rockville, MD, National Institute on Drug Abuse, 1982, pp 247–302

O'Connor LE, Berry J, Inaba D, et al: Shame, guilt and depression in men and women in recovery from addiction. J Subst Abuse Treat 11:503–510, 1993

Ostrea EM: Detection of prenatal drug exposure in the pregnant woman and her newborn infant, in Methodological Issues in Epidemiological, Prevention, and Treatment Research on Drug-Exposed Women and Their Children (NIDA Res Monogr 117, DHHS Publ No ADM-92-1881). Edited by Kilbey MM, Asghar K. Rockville, MD, National Institute on Drug Abuse, 1992, pp 61–79

Petro J: Addicted mothers, drug-exposed babies: the unprecedented prosecution of mothers under drug-trafficking statutes. New York Law School Review 36:573–607, 1991

Public Law 102–321. ADAMHA Reorganization Act of 1992. Regulation 45CFR Part 96, Section 1922 (C)(A)(B)(C), July 10, 1992. Interim Final Rules and Regulations. Federal Register 58(60), March 31, 1993

Puentes AJ: System responses to perinatal addiction, in Pregnancy and Exposure to Alcohol and Other Drug Use (CSAP Technical Rep 7, DHHS Publ No SMA-93-2040). Rockville, MD, Center for Substance Abuse Prevention, 1993, pp 7–45

Ratner PA: The incidence of wife abuse and mental health status in abused wives in Edmonton, Alberta. Can J Pub Health 84:246–249, 1993

Reed BG: Developing women-sensitive drug dependency treatment services: why so difficult? J Psychoactive Drugs 19:151–164, 1987

Reed BG: Linkages: battering, sexual assault, incest, child sexual abuse, teen pregnancy, dropping out of school and the alcohol and drug connection, in Alcohol and Drugs Are Women's Issues, Vol 1. Edited by Roth P. Metuchen, NJ, Scarecrow, 1991, pp 130–149

Robin RW, Chester B, Rasmussen JK, et al: Factors influencing utilization of mental health and substance abuse services by American Indian men and women. Psychiatr Serv 48:826–832, 1997

Roper ME: Reaching the babies through the mothers: the effects of prosecution on pregnant substance abusers. Law and Psychology Review 16:171–188, 1992

Russell M, Martier SS, Sokol RJ, et al: Screening for pregnancy risk-drinking: TWEAKing the tests. Alcohol Clin Exp Res 15:368, 1991

Sanchez LT: Withdrawal in the pregnant alcoholic, in Drug Dependency in Pregnancy: Managing Withdrawal. Edited by Jessup M. Sacramento, California Department of Health Services, 1992, pp 15–21

Sanchez-Craig M, Spivak K, Davila R: Superior outcome of females over males after brief treatment for the reduction of heavy drinking: replication and report of therapist effects. British Journal of Addiction 86:867–876, 1991

Schmidt L, Weisner C: The emergence of problem-drinking women as a special population in need of treatment, in Recent Developments in Alcoholism, Vol 12: Women and Alcohol. Edited by Galanter M. New York, Plenum, 1995, pp 309–334

Smith EM, North CS, Spitznagel EL: Alcohol, drugs, and psychiatric comorbidity among homeless women: an epidemiological study. J Clin Psychiatry Mar:82–87, 1993

Somon LA, Brindis C, Dunn-Malhotra E: The interplay of national, state, and local policy in financing care for drug-affected women and children in California. J Psychoactive Drugs 28:3–15, 1996

Streissguth AP, Barr HM, Sampson PD, et al: Prenatal alcohol and offspring development: the first fourteen years. Drug Alcohol Depend 36:89–99, 1994

Substance Abuse and Mental Health Services Administration: Substance Use Among Women in the United States (DHHS Publ No SMA-97-3162). Rockville, MD, Substance Abuse and Mental Health Services Administration, 1997a

Substance Abuse and Mental Health Services Administration: How to Build a Perinatal Addiction Program. SAMHSA News 2:12–14, 1997b

Substance Abuse and Mental Health Services Administration: SAMHSA works to prevent substance abuse through managed care. SAMHSA News 4:6–9, 1997c

Szuster RR, Rich LL, Chung A, et al: Treatment retention in women's residential chemical dependency treatment: effect of admission with children. Subst Use Misuse 31: 1001–1013, 1996

U.S. Department of Health and Human Services, Substance Abuse and Mental Health Services Administration, Office of Applied Studies: National Household Survey of Drug Abuse Advance Report #18. Centers for Disease Control and Prevention Web site. November 1997

VanBremen JR, Chasnoff IJ: Policy issues for integrating parenting interventions and addiction treatment for women. Topics in Early Childhood Special Education 14:254–274, 1994

Weber EM: Alcohol- and drug-dependent pregnant women: laws and public policies that promote and inhibit research and the delivery of services, in Methodological Issues in Epidemiological, Prevention, and Treatment Research on Drug-Exposed Women and Their Children (NIDA Res Monogr 117, DHHS Publ No ADM-92-1881). Edited by Kilbey MM, Asghar K. Rockville, MD, National Institute on Drug Abuse, 1992, pp 349–365

Weisner C, Schmidt L: Gender disparities in treatment for alcohol problems. JAMA 268:1872–1876, 1992

Wilsnack SC, Vogeltanz ND, Klassen AD, et al: Childhood sexual abuse and women's substance abuse: national survey findings. J Stud Alcohol 58:264–271, 1997

Young IM: Punishment, treatment, empowerment: three approaches to policy for pregnant addicts. Feminist Studies 20:33–57, 1994

Young NK, Gardner SL: Implementing Welfare Reform: Solutions to the Substance Abuse Problem. Irvine, CA, Children and Family Futures, 1996

Zellman GL, Jacobson PD, DuPlessis H, et al: Detecting prenatal substance exposure: an exploratory analysis and policy discussion. Journal of Drug Issues 23:375–387, 1993

Zellman GL, Jacobson PD, Bell RM: Influencing physician response to prenatal substance exposure through state legislation and work-place policies. Addiction 92:1123–1131, 1997

Ziedonis D, Rayford B, Bryant K, et al: Psychiatric comorbidity in white and African-American cocaine addicts seeking substance abuse treatment. Hosp Community Psychiatry 45:43–49, 1994

Zuckerman B, Frank D, Brown E: Overview of the effects of abuse and drugs on pregnancy and offspring, in Medications Development for the Treatment of Pregnant Addicts and Their Infants (NIDA Res Monogr 149, NIH Publ No 95-3891). Edited by Chiang CN, Finnegan LP. Rockville, MD, National Institute on Drug Abuse, 1995, pp 16–38

# 44 HIV/AIDS and Substance Use Disorders

Steven L. Batki, M.D.
Kalpana I. Nathan, M.D.

HIV disease has become one of the defining features on the landscape of substance use disorders. The connection between HIV infection and substance use is especially important in that injection-drug use, directly or indirectly, is the main conduit for HIV transmission to heterosexual adults, women, minorities, and children. Persons with drug problems who are infected with HIV make up a rapidly growing group of patients for whom adequate assessment and treatment of their substance use disorders are required for optimal medical and psychiatric care. HIV infection complicates the treatment of substance use disorders in several ways. HIV-related public health concerns are increasingly influencing traditional addiction treatment. The HIV epidemic has lent special urgency to the need to provide treatment for substance use disorders and has also given treatment added importance. The most salient public health issues are primary prevention of HIV infection (prevention of transmission to uninfected individuals) and secondary and tertiary prevention (reducing HIV- and injection-related morbidity). Substance use disorders may make the medical management of HIV infection more difficult because the behavioral disturbances that accompany drug dependence may complicate administration of treatment for the infection. The triple diagnosis of HIV infection, substance use, and other comorbid psychiatric disorders creates diagnostic problems and requires novel treatment approaches.

In this chapter, we review the epidemiology of HIV infection among persons who use drugs; included in the review is a summary of the effect of HIV infection on psychiatric and medical morbidity. We also describe the assessment and treatment of HIV-infected patients with substance use disorders and review various models for integrating the treatments for these two diseases.

## Epidemiology

The total number of AIDS cases in the United States through June 1998 was 665,357, continuing the pattern of decrease in incidence since 1995–1996 (Centers for Disease Control and Prevention 1997, 1998). The number of new cases of AIDS peaked in 1993, at the time of the change in the case definition for AIDS ("1993 Revised Classification System" 1992). Deaths among persons with AIDS have decreased (42% decrease between 1996 and 1997), more so than the decrease in AIDS incidence between 1996 and 1997 (15%), which has led to a corresponding increase in AIDS prevalence in the United States.

Persons who use injection drugs were among the first HIV risk groups to be identified. Injection-drug use is a major route of HIV infection in much of the world, including the United States, western and eastern Europe, the former Soviet Union, and parts of Asia. In the United States, 32% of the total AIDS cases through June 1998 involved injection-drug use (26% solely injection-drug use, and 6% men who have sex with men and inject drugs). There is wide variation in HIV seroprevalence by geography and demographic variables. In the United States, seroprevalence among samples of street-recruited individuals who used injection drugs ranged from 1% in Flagstaff, Arizona, to 48% in

Miami (Kral et al. 1998). African Americans and Latinos are overrepresented among those with HIV and AIDS. In 1996, for the first time, AIDS incidence was highest among African Americans, who made up 41% of new AIDS cases, whereas whites made up 38% and Hispanics made up 19% of cases ("Update" 1997).

## Prevention of HIV Transmission Among and by Drug-Using Individuals

### HIV Risk Assessment and HIV Testing

Health care providers should routinely ask patients about their risk for HIV infection and offer HIV counseling and voluntary testing services to those at risk ("Recommendations for HIV Testing Services" 1993). Voluntary and confidential HIV testing is useful in clarifying differential diagnosis of medical conditions, initiating early medical management of HIV infection, and informing infected persons or those at risk for infection about how to prevent HIV transmission. HIV testing of individuals who use drugs does not appear to be associated with major psychological or behavioral deterioration (Casadonte et al. 1990). Informing those with drug problems about HIV-positive serostatus is not associated with worse outcome in addiction treatment (Weddington et al. 1991). No evidence exists to indicate that there is a sustained increase in psychological distress (Davis et al. 1995) or suicide risk (van Haastrecht et al. 1994) among drug-using individuals after notification of presence of HIV infection. However, the severity of psychiatric symptoms after HIV testing may be greater in persons who use drugs than in those who do not (Perry et al. 1993).

### Risk-Reduction Education

Teaching how to reduce HIV risk is important, given recent evidence that HIV-infected individuals who use drugs often continue to practice risky behaviors (Centers for Disease Control and Prevention 1996). In general, risk reduction among drug-using individuals has been greater in the area of drug use than in risky sexual behavior, although there is evidence of reduction of both risk behaviors (Booth and Watters 1994). Risk-reduction counseling focuses on safer sexual behavior and drug use. Ideally, counseling is culturally appropriate, is sensitive to issues of sexual identity, and provides information at a level consistent with the person's age,

learning skills, language, and style of communication. Instruction regarding condom use and the use of clean injection equipment is essential, as is information about syringe exchange. If clean syringes are unavailable to patients, information about disinfecting syringes should be provided. However, bleach and other agents are unreliable as disinfectants (Normand et al. 1995), and disinfection does not offer complete protection against HIV transmission.

Various models for psychoeducational HIV counseling exist, but it is unclear whether any one technique, such as teaching relapse prevention, is superior (Baker et al. 1993). Small-group intervention is commonly used to share information and build social support for changing both drug use and sexual behaviors. An example of risk-reduction counseling methods is the "levels of defense" approach that focuses on both drug use and sexual behavior (Sorensen and Batki 1997). In this approach, patients are counseled about the range of risk severity associated with various behaviors. For example, drug-using behaviors in order of increasing risk are abstinence, using drugs but not injecting, injecting drugs but not sharing injecting equipment, and injecting and sharing. Patients who are already infected with HIV are informed that continued drug use may contribute to medical morbidity and that continued needle sharing and unsafe sex increase the risks of infection with other retroviruses (such as more virulent strains of HIV or human T-cell lymphotropic virus type II [HTLV-II]). Decreased needle use may be associated with decreased morbidity in HIV-infected persons who use drugs (Des Jarlais et al. 1987), although this conclusion is by no means unanimous (Selwyn et al. 1992).

### Harm Reduction

The term *harm reduction* refers to a wide range of activities whose aim is to reduce the adverse health consequences of drug use (Des Jarlais 1995). The harm-reduction perspective is essentially pragmatic and nonjudgmental, and harm reduction is often presented as an alternative to abstinence-oriented approaches to addiction treatment. Examples of harm-reduction approaches include making methadone maintenance (MM) readily available, teaching those who inject drugs how to inject more safely, and providing syringe-exchange opportunities. Syringe-exchange programs (SEPs) offer more than a supply of clean injecting equipment. A 1996 survey of SEPs in the United States showed that all SEPs provided drug-using individuals with information about safer injection techniques and/or use of bleach to disinfect injection equipment ("Update" 1997). Other services included referral to substance abuse programs, instruction in the use of condoms, and education about prevention of sexually transmitted diseases. Health services offered on site included HIV counseling and testing, primary health care, tuberculosis skin testing, and screening for sexually transmitted diseases ("Update" 1997). Studies of SEPs have so far shown no increase in illicit-drug injection associated with the exchanges and have shown marked decreases in drug-related risk behavior (Paone et al. 1995).

## Treatment

### Treatment of Substance Use Disorders in HIV-Infected Patients

The treatment of substance use disorders is an important part of the overall care of HIV-infected patients and requires more flexibility than is customary in traditional substance abuse programs (Batki 1990b; Sorensen and Batki 1997). Addiction treatment may need to be adapted to the varying levels of HIV disease severity so that patients remain in treatment and public health risks are reduced. For example, for desired reductions in drug use to be achieved, sicker patients may need to be given more leeway in treatment than less impaired patients (Center for Substance Abuse Treatment 1995).

Providing treatment such as MM to HIV-infected individuals is crucial because it can prevent transmission by reducing needle use and needle sharing (Ball et al. 1988). In addition to reducing needle sharing, drug abuse treatment has the potential to prevent HIV transmission by reducing the number of impulsive and possibly unsafe sex acts associated with the intoxication and disinhibition that result from drug use. Treatment programs can also provide a setting to deliver other services needed by HIV-infected patients, including HIV-related medical care, psychiatric treatment, social services, and education about HIV disease.

### Methadone Maintenance

MM is of particular value for HIV-infected individuals with drug problems because opioid dependence is common among those who use injection drugs (Center for Substance Abuse Treatment 1995). This form of treatment is particularly effective for HIV-infected persons who inject drugs because it affords nearly daily contact with patients and provides a stable setting for the provision of medical and psychiatric care (Sorensen and Batki 1997). Despite concerns about the potential of opioids to depress immune function (Carballo-Dieguez et al. 1994), studies of individuals who use injection drugs have found that MM is associated with normalization of the alterations in immune function that accompany heroin abuse (Ayuso 1994). Furthermore, MM is protective against the spread of HIV (Metzger et al. 1993) and may be somewhat effective in slowing the progression of HIV disease (Weber et al. 1990).

Treatment can be provided to HIV-infected patients with the use of standard methadone doses, although dosing may be affected by some important interactions between methadone and other medications used in treating HIV disease. Methadone is extensively metabolized by cytochrome P450 3A4, and methadone level may decrease with use of potent P450 3A4 inducers such as carbamazepine and rifampin, necessitating higher doses. Conversely, the potential exists for methadone levels to be increased by potent P450 3A4 inhibitors such as the protease inhibitor ritonavir (Iribarne et al. 1997). Methadone, in turn, inhibits the metabolism of zidovudine (AZT) and can increase AZT levels (Schwartz et al. 1992). Additional analgesics are needed to treat acute or chronic pain in HIV-infected patients with drug problems who are receiving methadone, because patients do not obtain adequate pain relief from their usual daily dose of methadone, to which they have become tolerant.

MM programs offer a number of benefits, including a long-term, stable treatment setting and a variety of medical, psychiatric, and social services. HIV-related medical care may be more effective if it is provided on site in MM programs (Goosby et al. 1992; Selwyn et al. 1989, 1993). The effectiveness of MM in reducing injection-drug use, along with its utility as a medical service delivery platform, gives it a special role in the treatment of drug-using individuals at risk for HIV disease. MM is generally associated with improved health status in persons who use heroin, and it may be helpful in reducing the morbidity associated with HIV infection (Des Jarlais et al. 1987). Furthermore, MM may have the potential to reduce use of medical services by HIV-infected patients who use drugs (Batki et al. 1996a).

### Counseling

Counseling specifically for HIV disease is a necessary part of substance abuse treatment. In addition to risk-reduction counseling, family and couples counseling may help patients and their families come to terms with the stresses associated with HIV disease. Grief counseling may help patients adjust to the effect of the deaths of significant others. Counseling may also help patients cope with grief about other sorts of losses, such as loss of physical or mental ability. Patients may require specialized support groups—such as those for heterosexual persons who use drugs, for women, or for minorities—in addition to individual counseling.

## Residential Treatment

Residential addiction-treatment programs have begun to address the special problems of treating HIV-infected patients (Galea et al. 1988; Goldstein and Yuen 1988). Patients with HIV disease, especially those whose symptoms are advanced, may be reluctant to commit themselves to long periods of residential treatment. Shortened residential treatments may be more acceptable to these patients.

Residential programs that attempt to work with HIV-infected individuals must also come to terms with the medical aspects of HIV disease. Programs usually are not set up to provide the medical monitoring, evaluation, and treatment sick residents require. Related problems include the problem of determining how and when to move deteriorating therapeutic community residents to a hospital or hospice and the problem of determining to what degree the needs of the residential treatment community should be subordinated to the medical needs of individuals.

## Psychiatric Care

### HIV Infection, Psychiatric Disorders, and Substance Use Disorders

The complexities presented by the triple diagnosis of HIV infection, psychiatric disorder, and substance use disorder are difficult to tease apart (Batki 1990b). Lyketsos et al. (1996) studied a series of 222 HIV-infected patients in a medical clinic and found that a comorbid substance use disorder was the most powerful and consistent predictor of psychiatric distress, whereas HIV illness variables and psychiatric history were not strong predictors. In a study of HIV-infected patients receiving methadone, 79% were found to have current DSM-III-R (American Psychiatric Association 1987) Axis I psychiatric disorders (Batki et al. 1996b).

Nearly two-thirds of these individuals had two or more current Axis I disorders. Although this high rate of current psychiatric disorders is similar to rates found among in-treatment opioid-dependent patients in studies done before the AIDS epidemic, it is higher than the rates documented among HIV-infected homosexual and bisexual men (Lyketsos and Federman 1995). Most psychiatric disorders (e.g., depression, anxiety, and insomnia) may be related to drug use or to medical illness (Batki et al. 1996b). For example, insomnia and anxiety may be caused by medications such as AZT or methadone or by stimulants such as cocaine and amphetamine. The use of stimulants by HIV- infected persons who use drugs is also a common cause of psychotic symptoms such as delusions and hallucinations (Sewell et al. 1994).

No reliable evidence exists to suggest that HIV-infected individuals who use drugs are more likely than other HIV-infected patients to develop cognitive decline. In a number of studies, however, drug abuse has been found to be a major contributing factor to psychiatric disorders and neuropsychological impairment in drug-using patients who are seropositive. Overall, the bulk of the evidence suggests that the high rate of psychiatric disorders seen in HIV-infected persons who use drugs reflects the background rate of these disorders found in drug-using individuals without HIV infection. In addition, at least in the early stages of HIV infection, drug use appears to be a more important cause of psychopathology than HIV infection itself (Egan et al. 1990; Lipsitz et al. 1994; McKegney et al. 1990).

### Treatment of Psychiatric Disorders

Both psychological and pharmacological treatments are necessary to treat comorbid psychiatric disorders in patients with HIV infection and drug problems. Support groups and self-help groups can help patients feel less isolated and teach patients about the basics of HIV-related health care. Day-treatment programs may become necessary as cognitive decline sets in and patients are less able to independently perform or engage in activities of daily living, such as meal preparation or socialization. Inpatient psychiatric treatment may be required for acute exacerbations of mood disorders or if symptoms of psychosis develop. Occasionally, inpatient detoxification may be required to manage a severe relapse into drug use. Supportive psychotherapy by substance abuse counselors can help to improve patients' coping abilities (Center for Substance Abuse Treatment 1995).

## Pharmacotherapy in HIV-Infected Individuals Who Use Drugs

Safety and abuse liability are two key clinical issues that affect the pharmacological treatment of HIV-infected, drug-using patients with psychiatric disorders. Safety (in terms of adverse effects, drug interactions, and overdose lethality) varies widely among pharmacotherapeutic agents. Little systematic study has been undertaken to assess the safety of psychiatric medications, or the efficacy of their use, in drug-using patients with HIV infection. A controlled study of the serotonin reuptake inhibitor (SRI) fluoxetine in HIV-infected, cocaine-dependent patients receiving methadone showed that when given in doses of up to 40 mg/day, fluoxetine was well tolerated and was associated with reductions in both depression and cocaine use (Batki et al. 1993). However, fluoxetine has not been shown to be effective in reducing cocaine abuse in other studies. For most other psychopharmacological agents, available recommendations are based on findings of studies that involved HIV-infected patients who did not use drugs (Center for Substance Abuse Treatment 1995). The treatment of anxiety and insomnia is particularly problematic because of abuse liability associated with benzodiazepines and other sedative-hypnotics (Friedman et al. 1996). It is best to initiate pharmacotherapy for anxiety disorders with a medication that has little or no abuse liability, such as buspirone. In an open trial of buspirone in doses of 30–40 mg/day in drug-using patients with HIV infection, most patients showed improvements in anxiety levels and experienced few adverse effects (Batki 1990a).

To reduce the possible risks associated with medication, a stepwise, hierarchical approach to the pharmacological treatment of psychiatric disorders in drug-using patients infected with HIV has been proposed (Center for Substance Abuse Treatment 1995). This approach involves using medications with lower abuse liability and lower overdose risk first (e.g., trazodone for insomnia or buspirone or SRI antidepressants for anxiety disorders), before proceeding to medications with higher abuse liability (e.g., benzodiazepines) or overdose risk (e.g., lithium or tricyclic antidepressants).

## Medical Care for HIV-Infected Individuals Who Use Drugs

### Behavioral Aspects of Care

Although little evidence exists of substantial differences between drug-using patients with HIV infection and other HIV-infected patients in the rate of progression of HIV disease, some behavioral issues presented by drug-using patients affect HIV-related medical care. Persons who abuse drugs or alcohol tend to have behavior problems associated with their substance use. These problems may at times interfere with the ability of a patient to adhere to medical regimens (Wall et al. 1995).

Without routine HIV-antibody screening, HIV infection is often diagnosed later in the course of illness among drug-using individuals than in other HIV-infected patients—typically after the onset of AIDS (Hu et al. 1995). Furthermore, persons who use injection drugs may delay initiating medical treatment, such as antiretroviral therapy (Broers et al. 1994). This may contribute to greater use of expensive emergency medical services and more frequent hospitalization (rather than use of more cost-effective routine outpatient care) (Solomon et al. 1991). Drug-using individuals with AIDS have been found to be more likely to be without a source of primary care and more likely to use emergency medical services than patients with AIDS who do not use drugs (Mauskopf et al. 1994). Because of such problems, innovative treatment approaches have been implemented to provide integrated medical and substance abuse services.

There is no consistent evidence that HIV disease progresses more rapidly in drug-using individuals than in those who do not use drugs, although some evidence exists to the contrary (Eskild et al. 1994). When HIV-infected patients with drug problems receive the same level of HIV care in the same clinic as those who do not use drugs, no differences in disease progression or survival are seen (Chaisson et al. 1995).

### Settings for Medical Care

It is a complex task to coordinate medical services for injection drug–using patients with HIV infection, who may have a variety of medical problems. There are a number of current models for providing primary medical care to HIV-infected patients who are receiving addiction treatment. In one model medical care is provided by referral of patients to a nearby HIV clinic. This approach may be most effective for patients who are stable, but it may be less appropriate, for example, for patients who are actively using drugs, who may have minimal or strained relationships with health care providers. Also, patients with drug problems often require ongoing adjunctive care for coexisting psychiatric problems (Batki 1990b; Brettle and Nells 1988). Untreated behavior problems can interfere with medical care. Patients with drug problems may have difficulty keeping appointments and may be fearful of or ambivalent about medical care (Solomon et al. 1991). Medical staff in HIV or primary care clinics may not be fully equipped to manage the psychiatric and substance use problems that can interfere with administration of medical care. However, if the medical clinic is conveniently situated, the referral model can work effectively (O'Connor et al. 1992).

A second model of primary medical care for HIV-infected patients with drug problems involves establishing a substance abuse treatment component at an AIDS clinic. This model would allow drug-using patients with HIV infection to obtain methadone or other treatment for substance use disorders on site in a primary care HIV medical clinic. One limitation of this model, however, is the difficulty of responding to the regulatory requirements for MM. In addition, some primary care physicians may not be fully comfortable with treating injection drug–using patients in their practice (Gerbert et al. 1991).

In a third model, on-site primary medical care for patients who use injection drugs is provided in an addiction treatment facility, such as the site of an MM program (Goosby et al. 1992; Selwyn et al. 1989, 1993). The MM program setting permits "one-stop shopping" for medical services. Referral of patients to off-site primary care clinics can sometimes result in patients' failing to obtain medical care. In a study by Umbricht-Schneiter et al. (1994), 92% of injection drug–using patients in MM programs who were assigned to on-site primary care actually received ongoing medical care, compared with only 35% of patients who received a referral. Continued primary medical care for HIV-infected patients who use injection drugs is critical. For example, Selwyn et al. (1992) found that the incidence of AIDS was 62% lower among injection drug–using patients who received antiretroviral treatment than among those patients who did not.

## Summary

HIV-infected patients who use drugs have complex medical, psychiatric, and drug-related problems that require careful assessment and management. HIV disease and its associated neurocognitive problems do not appear to progress more rapidly in patients who use drugs, and these patients' psychiatric disorders are more often caused by drug use than by HIV infection. Because of the behavior problems associated with drug use, provision of medical, psychiatric, and substance abuse treat-

ment services in a common site is a useful model of service delivery. The combined treatment of substance use and psychiatric disorders may improve the likelihood that patients will receive adequate medical treatment for HIV disease, particularly if integrated systems of care are in place.

## References

American Psychiatric Association: Diagnostic and Statistical Manual of Mental Disorders, 3rd Edition, Revised. Washington, DC, American Psychiatric Association, 1987

Ayuso JL: Use of psychotropic drugs in patients with HIV infection. Drugs 47: 599–610, 1994

Baker A, Heather N, Wodak A, et al: Evaluation of a cognitive-behavioral intervention for HIV prevention among injecting drug users. AIDS 7:247–256, 1993

Ball JC, Lange WR, Myers CP, et al: Reducing the risk of AIDS through methadone maintenance treatment. J Health Soc Behav 29:214–226, 1988

Batki SL: Buspirone in drug users with AIDS or AIDS-related complex. J Clin Psychopharmacol 10 (3 suppl):111S–115S, 1990a

Batki SL: Drug abuse, psychiatric disorders, and AIDS: dual and triple diagnosis. West J Med 152:547–552, 1990b

Batki SL, Manfredi LB, Jacob P 3rd, et al: Fluoxetine for cocaine dependence in methadone maintenance: quantitative plasma and urine cocaine/benzoylecgonine concentrations. J Clin Psychopharmacol 13:243–250, 1993

Batki SL, Sorensen JL, Young V: Effects of methadone treatment on hospital utilization in HIV+ and HIV– injection drug users (Abstract Mo.B.1173). Paper presented at the XI International Conference on AIDS, Vancouver, Canada, July 1996a

Batki SL, Ferrando SJ, Manfredi LB, et al: Psychiatric disorders, drug use, and medical status in injection drug users with HIV disease. Am J Addict 5:249–258, 1996b

Booth RE, Watters JK: How effective are risk-reduction interventions targeting injecting drug users? AIDS 8:1515–1524, 1994

Brettle RP, Nelles B: Special problems of injecting drug-misusers. Br Med Bull 44:149–160, 1988

Broers B, Morabia A, Hirschel B: A cohort study of drug users' compliance with zidovudine treatment. Arch Intern Med 154:1121–1127, 1994

Carballo-Dieguez AJ, Goetz R, El Sadr W, et al: The effect of methadone on immunological parameters among HIV-positive and HIV-negative drug users. Am J Drug Alcohol Abuse 20:317–329, 1994

Casadonte PP, Des Jarlais DC, Friedman SR, et al: Psychological and behavioral impact among intravenous drug users learning HIV test results. International Journal of the Addictions 25:409–426, 1990

Center for Substance Abuse Treatment: Treatment for HIV-Infected Alcohol and Other Drug Users (DHHS Publ No SMA-95-3038). Washington, DC, U.S. Government Printing Office, 1995

Centers for Disease Control and Prevention: Continued sexual risk behavior among HIV-seropositive, drug-using men—Atlanta, Washington, D.C., and San Juan, Puerto Rico. MMWR Morb Mortal Wkly Rep 45:151–152, 1996

Centers for Disease Control and Prevention: HIV/AIDS Surveillance Report, Vol 9. Atlanta, GA, U.S. Department of Health and Human Services, Public Health Service, 1997, pp 1–39

Centers for Disease Control and Prevention: HIV/AIDS Surveillance Report, Vol 10. Atlanta, GA, U.S. Department of Health and Human Services, Public Health Service, 1998, pp 1–40

Chaisson RE, Keruly JC, Moore RD: Race, sex, drug use, and progression of human immunodeficiency virus disease. N Engl J Med 333:751–756, 1995

Davis RF, Metzger DS, Meyers K, et al: Long-term changes in psychological symptomatology associated with HIV serostatus among male injecting drug users. AIDS 9:73–79, 1995

Des Jarlais DC: Harm reduction—a framework for incorporating science into drug policy. Am J Public Health 85:10–11, 1995

Des Jarlais DC, Friedman SR, Marmor M, et al: Development of AIDS, HIV seroconversion, and potential co-factors for T4 cell loss in a cohort of intravenous drug users. AIDS 1:105–111, 1987

Egan VG, Crawford J, Brettle RP, et al: The Edinburgh cohort of HIV-positive drug users: current intellectual function is impaired but not due to early AIDS dementia complex. AIDS 4:651–656, 1990

Eskild A, Magnus P, Sohlberg C, et al: Slow progression to AIDS in intravenous drug users infected with HIV in Norway. J Epidemiol Community Health 48:383–387, 1994

Friedman JB, O'Dowd MA, McKegney FP: Managing diazepam abuse in an AIDS-related psychiatric clinic with a high percentage of substance abusers. Psychosomatics 37:43–47, 1996

Galea RP, Lewis BF, Baker LA: A model for implementing AIDS education in a drug abuse treatment setting. Hosp Community Psychiatry 39:886–888, 1988

Gerbert B, Maguire BT, Bleecker T, et al: Primary care physicians and structural barriers to care. JAMA 266:2837–2842, 1991

Goldstein MJ, Yuen FM: Coping with AIDS: an approach to training and education in a therapeutic community—The Samaritan Village Program. J Subst Abuse Treat 5:45–50, 1988

Goosby E, Batki SL, London J, et al: Medical care of HIV disease in methadone maintenance treatment, in Problems of Drug Dependence 1991 (DHHS Publ No ADM-92-1888). Edited by Harris LS. Washington, DC, U.S. Government Printing Office, 1992, p 431

Hu DJ, Byers R Jr, Fleming PL, et al: Characteristics of persons with late AIDS diagnosis in the United States. Am J Prev Med 11:114–119, 1995

Iribarne C, Dreano Y, Bardou LG: Interaction of methadone with substrates of human hepatic cytochrome P450 3A4. Toxicology 117:13–23, 1997

Kral AH, Bluthenthal RN, Booth RE, et al: HIV seroprevalence among street-recruited injection drug and crack cocaine users in 16 US municipalities. Am J Public Health 88:108–113, 1998

Lipsitz JD, Williams JB, Rabkin JG, et al: Psychopathology in male and female intravenous drug users with and without HIV infection. Am J Psychiatry 151:1662–1668, 1994

Lyketsos CG, Federman EB: Psychiatric disorders and HIV infection: impact on one another. Epidemiol Rev 17:152–164, 1995

Lyketsos CG, Hutton H, Fishman M, et al: Psychiatric morbidity on entry to an HIV primary care clinic. AIDS 10:1033–1039, 1996

Mauskopf J, Turner BJ, Markson LE, et al: Patterns of ambulatory care for AIDS patients, and association with emergency room use. Health Serv Res 29:489–510, 1994

McKegney FP, O'Dowd MA, Feiner C, et al: A prospective comparison of neuropsychologic function in HIV-seropositive and seronegative methadone-maintained patients. AIDS 4:565–569, 1990

Metzger DS, Woody GE, McLellan AT, et al: Human immunodeficiency virus seroconversion among intravenous drug users in- and out-of-treatment: an 18-month prospective follow-up. J Acquir Immune Defic Syndr 6:1049–1056, 1993

Normand J, Vlahov D, Moses LE (eds): Preventing HIV Transmission: The Role of Sterile Needles and Bleach. Washington, DC, National Academy Press, 1995

O'Connor PG, Molde S, Henry S, et al: Human immunodeficiency virus infection in intravenous drug users: a model for primary care. Am J Med 8:382–385, 1992

Paone D, Des Jarlais DC, Gangloff R, et al: Syringe exchange: HIV prevention, key findings, and future directions. International Journal of the Addictions 30:1647–1683, 1995

Perry S, Jacobsberg L, Card CA, et al: Severity of psychiatric symptoms after HIV testing. Am J Psychiatry 150:775–779, 1993

Recommendations for HIV testing services for inpatients and outpatients in acute-care hospital settings. MMWR Morb Mortal Wkly Rep 42(RR-2):1–6, 1993

1993 Revised classification system for HIV infection and expanded surveillance case definition for AIDS among adolescents and adults. MMWR Morb Mortal Wkly Rep 41(RR-17):1–19, 1992

Schwartz EL, Brechbul AB, Kahl P, et al: Pharmacokinetic interactions of zidovudine and methadone in intravenous drug using patients with HIV infection. J Acquir Immune Defic Syndr 5:619–626, 1992

Selwyn PA, Feingold AR, Iezza A, et al: Primary care for patients with human immunodeficiency virus (HIV) infection in a methadone maintenance treatment program. Ann Intern Med 111:761–763, 1989

Selwyn PA, Alcabes P, Hartel D, et al: Clinical manifestations and predictors of disease progression in drug users with human immunodeficiency virus infection. N Engl J Med 327:1697–1703, 1992

Selwyn PA, Budner NS, Wasserman WC, et al: Utilization of on-site primary care services by HIV-seropositive and seronegative drug users in a methadone maintenance program. Public Health Rep 108:492–500, 1993

Sewell DD, Jeste DV, Atkinson JH, et al: HIV-associated psychosis: a study of 20 cases. Am J Psychiatry 151:237–242, 1994

Solomon L, Frank R, Vlahov D, et al: Utilization of health services in a cohort of intravenous drug users with known HIV-1 serostatus. Am J Public Health 81:1285–1289, 1991

Sorensen JL, Batki SL: Management of the psychosocial sequelae of HIV infection among drug abusers, in Substance Abuse: A Comprehensive Textbook, 2nd Edition. Edited by Lowinson JH, Ruiz P, Millman R, et al. Baltimore, MD, Williams & Wilkins, 1997, pp 788–792

Umbricht-Schneiter A, Ginn DH, Pabst KM, et al: Providing medical care to methadone clinic patients: referral versus on-site care. Am J Public Health 84:207–210, 1994

Update: syringe-exchange programs—United States, 1996. MMWR Morb Mortal Wkly Rep 46:565–568, 1997

van Haastrecht MJ, Mientjes GH, van den Hoek AJ, et al: Death from suicide and overdose among drug injectors after disclosure of first HIV test result. AIDS 8:1721–1725, 1994

Wall TL, Sorensen JL, Batki SL, et al: Adherence to zidovudine (AZT) among HIV-infected methadone patients: a pilot study of supervised therapy and dispensing compared to usual care. Drug Alcohol Depend 37:261–269, 1995

Weber R, Ledergerber B, Opravil M, et al: Progression of HIV infection in misusers of injected drugs who stop injecting or follow a program of maintenance treatment with methadone. BMJ 301:1362–1365, 1990

Weddington WW, Haertzen CA, Hess JM, et al: Psychological reactions and retention by cocaine addicts during treatment according to HIV-serostatus: a matched-control study. Am J Drug Alcohol Abuse 17:355–368, 1991

# Chapter 45

# Treatment of Pain in Drug-Addicted Persons

Barry Stimmel, M.D.

The treatment of pain has always been problematic. Surveys have consistently demonstrated that pain is most often inadequately relieved, resulting in needless suffering and loss of function. Although the principles physicians should adhere to in relieving pain have been published in numerous journals and monographs (Acute Pain Management Guideline Panel 1992; Jacox et al. 1994; Stimmel 1997), for reasons not yet clearly defined, these principles, and even their specific guidelines offering protocols for relief of pain with the use of opioids, are most often honored in the breach. Various explanations have been offered to explain this phenomenon (Table 45–1). The reasons that seem to dominate are the physicians' fears of promoting addiction, or of being accused of such activity, and the often unstated concern that a person's pain may not be as severe as proclaimed.

It is of interest that the fear of addiction is focused on the use of opioids, with relatively little anxiety demonstrated by physicians in prescribing hypnotics, sedatives, or tranquilizers, despite the ability of these drugs to cause dependence equal to, if not greater than, that seen with the opioids. The irrationality of this "opiophobia" (Morgan 1985–1986) in physicians is emphasized by the observation that drugs not considered narcotic but that act on the same receptors as pure opioid agonists, such as propoxyphene, or mixed agonist-antagonists, such as pentazocine and buprenorphine, are freely prescribed without any apparent concern over their misuse or potential to promote addictive behaviors. Fear of sanctions has also been demonstrated by the institution of multiple-copy prescription programs, usually followed by a considerable decrease in the prescription of these drugs, although not necessarily by a decrease in their abuse (Jacob 1990; U.S. Department of Justice 1987; Weintraub et al. 1991). That this fear is not entirely misplaced has been demonstrated by a survey of state medical board members, many of whom stated that they would recommend investigation of a physician solely on his or her having prescribed an opioid for malignant pain in excess of 6 months (Joranson et al. 1992).

In view of a physician's hesitancy to provide appropriate analgesic relief to patients, it is not at all surprising that persons in pain who are also known to use either prescribed or nonprescribed, licit or illicit mood-altering substances are at particular risk for failing to have their pain relieved, even when the cause of the pain is undeniable (Cleeland et al. 1994). This in turn results in increased anxiety and stress in the patient, accompanied by an increase in the intensity of the pain and the development of a clear adversarial relationship with the physician. Not infrequently, the psychiatrist is called on to arbitrate the needs of the patient and the desires and beliefs of the treating physician, a task for which he or she is usually ill suited. Unfortunately, the disciplines of both psychiatry and pain management have developed in isolation not only from each other but from addiction medicine (Portenoy et al. 1997). This has served neither medicine nor the public well.

In this chapter, I focus on the pharmacological treatment of pain in persons who intermittently or consistently use mood-altering substances, be they licit, illicit, prescribed for recognized medical disorders, or taken in the belief that they are beneficial. In addressing this issue, I pay little attention to the biology of pain, the specific pharmacological dose of available analgesics, or the nonpharmacological methods of treatment. These sub-

**Table 45–1.**    Reasons for inadequate prescription of opioids

Insufficient knowledge

Fear of producing an addiction

Excessive paperwork (triplicate prescriptions)

Concern over being manipulated

Cultural biases

Fear of sanctions

jects are far from unimportant; however, so many reviews have been published that to repeat such information would be less than productive. What follows then is a pragmatic approach to pain relief in persons who are concurrently dependent on or addicted to mood-altering substances, with an emphasis on the basic principles to be followed in their evaluation and management.

## Guidelines for Relieving Pain

The specific approach to relief of pain depends on whether the pain is acute, intermittent, or chronic and, if chronic, whether the pain is due to a malignant or nonmalignant disorder. However, in an assessment of a person in pain, certain general principles always apply (Table 45–2). These principles are especially important in dealing with a person who may have a concurrent drug dependence.

### Define the Cause of Pain

It belabors the obvious to state that a comprehensive history and physical examination are essential. A frequent assumption is that a person taking mood-altering drugs, especially opioids, is fabricating symptoms to obtain medication. Although at times this may be so, it is also equally if not more likely that a specific cause of pain exists, which may have been relieved or hidden by the use of other mood-altering drugs. In persons who use drugs parenterally, underlying afflictions can often go undetected until breakthrough pain occurs. Failure

**Table 45–2.**    Initial assessment of a patient in pain

Define the cause of pain

Assess severity of pain

Identify existing modifying psychological and environmental factors

Determine prior successful means of pain relief

Determine whether drug therapy is needed

to recognize the existence of such conditions may have severe consequences. In persons using stimulants, pain may be a concomitant symptom heralding the onset of a cardiac or pulmonary event that must be appropriately addressed. A person who uses hallucinogens may have experienced unrecognized physical trauma that resulted in a painful injury. Coexisting, well-defined medical conditions may exist that are responsible for the existing pain, such as a sickle cell crisis, ileitis, migraine headaches, neuropathy, gastritis, or pancreatitis. Unless a careful medical evaluation is carried out, these conditions may go unrecognized, with the physician assuming that the patient is exhibiting manipulative behavior to obtain additional mood-altering drugs.

In addition to well-defined sources of pain, Savage (1994) described a syndrome of pain facilitation or dissipation in currently dependent persons. This state is characterized by a relatively constant level of pain that can be relieved only by a drug in the same group on which the individual is dependent. Individuals undergoing withdrawal may experience nonspecific pain symptoms as part of the withdrawal process due to either sympathetic stimulation, which may intensify the painful experience, or increased muscle activity (seen in withdrawal from sedatives and opioids). These symptoms may be relieved by provision of appropriate medication, with a subsequent slow detoxification from the primary drug.

### Assess Severity of Pain

It is always important to obtain a comprehensive description of the painful experience. Although various standardized questionnaires can be used to assess pain intensity, asking the person to assess its severity on a scale of 1–10 and establishing its intensity based on previous painful experiences can be helpful and will be essential in monitoring the effectiveness of subsequent therapy. Toward this end, when analgesic therapy is started, it is important to assess its effect on pain relief at least every 8 hours—as frequently as every 2 hours when the pain is acute and severe.

### Identify Existing Modifying Psychological and Environmental Factors

Many factors are known to modulate the pain threshold (Table 45–3). With persons using mood-altering drugs, the presence of such factors becomes important in assessing and subsequently relieving the severity of the

**Table 45–3.** Factors affecting the pain threshold

| Threshold-lowering factors | Threshold-increasing factors |
|---|---|
| Anxiety | Sleep |
| Depression | Sympathy |
| Discomfort | Understanding |
| Fatigue | Mood elevation |
| Fear | |
| Isolation | |
| Recalling of last painful experience | |

pain. Drug craving and its associated anxiety lower the pain threshold, making one more susceptible to the pain experience. Withdrawal, as noted earlier, heightens an individual's sensations and awareness of pain, with the actual withdrawal state producing increased sympathetic, muscular, abdominal, and neuropathic pain. Stimulant use and its associated lack of sleep also serve to lower the pain threshold, making the pain experience more intense. Fatigue, common with abuse of many mood-altering drugs, also can heighten a painful experience, as can the depression so commonly seen in those persons using mood-altering drugs. Finally, fear or anger over the inability to have the pain relieved or the feeling that the pain is not being taken seriously will increase intensity of pain. Secondary pain may also play a role in promoting pain. It is therefore important to identify such factors so that they can be effectively addressed.

## Determine Prior Successful Means of Pain Relief

A simple but often forgotten way of maximizing pain relief is to ask the patient what has worked in the past. Although people are more than willing to recount their past painful experiences and to describe ways of providing relief that were effective for them, not infrequently physicians fail either to elicit this information or to believe it when it is given. A prime example is the acute, painful crises of sickle cell disease. Persons with recurrent sickle cell crises are well aware of the exact strength of opioid needed to relieve their pain and, if allowed to use patient-controlled analgesia, relieve their pain quickly and shorten their hospital stay. Yet more often than not, physicians do not prescribe the requested medication, causing increasing anxiety and in the end a greater use of opioids.

## Determine Whether Drug Therapy Is Needed

In many instances, pain may be relieved without any pharmacological intervention. Indeed, for various types of pain, nonpharmacological treatment may be more effective and can usually be easily provided (Table 45–4). The use of a nonpharmacological treatment, when indicated, allows an individual using mood-altering drugs to address those factors related to inappropriate drug use and the issues that may be causing the pain. Indeed, as noted later in this chapter, in individuals with chronic pain both pharmacological and nonpharmacological therapies, including psychotherapy, may be warranted in the attempt to assist an individual to function at maximum capacity.

 **Pharmacological Guidelines for Providing Analgesia**

If it is decided that pharmacological therapy is needed, guidelines also exist to enable the physician to choose appropriately (Table 45–5).

### Define the Cause of Pain

Knowledge of the etiology of the pain will always direct a physician to the type of drug needed. In many cases,

**Table 45–4.** Nonpharmacological means of relieving pain

| Behavioral | Physical |
|---|---|
| Biofeedback | Active and passive exercises |
| Imagery | Acupuncture |
| Meditation | Application of heat or cold |
| Relaxation | Transcutaneous nerve stimulation |
| Psychotherapy | Surgical nerve block |

**Table 45–5.** Guidelines for pharmacological treatment of pain

Define the cause of pain

Start with an analgesic that is least likely to cause dependence

Understand the concepts of dependence, tolerance, and withdrawal

Use equivalent doses when changing an analgesic

Use drug combinations carefully

analgesics not only may be contraindicated but may actually prevent the physician from appropriately relieving the pain. If it is determined that a specific state does not exist that can be relieved by drugs specifically targeted to the existing pathophysiology, then general analgesic therapy is warranted.

## Start With the Least-Potent Analgesic Least Likely to Cause Dependence

A person who uses opioids will have a tolerance threshold to other opioids. Also, someone dependent on drugs in the alcohol-hypnotic sedative group may require, because of stimulation of the hepatic microsomal system, an increased dose of opioids to obtain pain relief. However, not infrequently, pain can be relieved with the use of a nonopioid, such as acetaminophen, aspirin, or a nonsteroidal anti-inflammatory drug (NSAID) (Table 45–6). These drugs have therapeutic ceilings, do not cross-react with opioids, and on an individual basis may enhance opioid analgesia when given concurrently. In cases of mild to moderate pain, these nonopioids should be the first line of medication. It is important to note that NSAIDs available as over-the-counter (OTC) medications are packaged in the lowest possible dose. Failure of a person to relieve pain with an OTC medication does not mean that the same drug, given in appropriate doses, will be ineffective. As an example, ibuprofen is sold as an OTC medication in 200-mg pills, whereas the effective analgesic dosage may be up to 800 mg four times daily. If neuropathic pain is present, the first line of drugs may be those antidepressants

found effective for neuropathy, rather than the opioid analgesics. In patients with moderate or severe pain, not infrequently opioids will be needed to relieve the pain and in such cases should be prescribed appropriately.

## Understand the Concepts of Dependence, Tolerance, and Withdrawal as Applied to Analgesia

In relieving pain in individuals already taking dependence-producing drugs, it is essential to understand completely the concepts of dependence, tolerance, withdrawal, and addiction, which have been discussed elsewhere. In reviewing the common classification of mood-altering drugs (Table 45–7), it is important to remember that although virtually any drug within a group can be substituted in equivalent doses for any other drug, such substitution cannot occur across groups. In addition, combining drugs from group 1 and group 5 not only will not enhance analgesia but also will increase the potential for central nervous system depression.

If an individual has been taking an opioid, regardless of the reason, a tolerance threshold will have developed to the analgesic effects of the opioids, requiring a greater-than-usual dose to provide relief. It is therefore important, if opioid analgesia is warranted, to estimate the average opioid dose needed to meet the baseline requirement and then to provide an additional dose for analgesia. In addition, if a person has been taking drugs in the sedative-hypnotic group, as well as opioids, the physician must also be aware of the possibility of withdrawal from this group of drugs, which, if untreated,

**Table 45–6.**    Nonopioid analgesics

| Generic name | Trade name |
| --- | --- |
| Acetaminophen | (various brands) |
| Aspirin | (various brands) |
| Diclofenac | Voltaren, Cataflam |
| Diflunisal | Dolobid |
| Etodolac | Lodine |
| Ibuprofen | Advil, Motrin, Nuprin, Saleto-200–600, Genpril |
| Ketoprofen | Orudis, Actron |
| Ketorolac | Toradol |
| Meclofenamate | Meclomen |
| Naproxen | Anaprox, Naprosyn, Aleve |
| Tramadol | Ultram |

**Table 45–7.**    Classification of mood-altering drugs

| Group | Drugs |
| --- | --- |
| 1: Alcohol, sedative-hypnotics, minor tranquilizers | Alcohol, barbiturates, other drugs with sedative effects (e.g., chloral hydrate, chlordiazepoxide, diazepam, meprobamate, methaqualone) |
| 2: Cannabis | All preparations of *Cannabis sativa* |
| 3: Hallucinogens | Lysergic acid, hallucinogenic amphetamine |
| 4: Khat | All preparations of *Catha edulis* Forsk |
| 5: Opiates and opioids | Including narcotics with effects like those of morphine |
| 6: Stimulants | Amphetamines, certain other stimulants, cocaine and coca leaves, nicotine |
| 7: Volatile solvents | Glue, some cleaning fluids |

can result in severe morbidity or mortality. The importance of obtaining a complete drug history cannot be overemphasized, and appropriate medication should be prescribed if a risk of withdrawal exists.

## Use Equivalent Doses When Changing Analgesics

Although there may be a number of reasons for switching analgesics, it is always important to use equivalent doses. However, when changing from one opioid to another, to account for individual differences in cross-tolerance, it is safest to begin by dividing the dose of the second opiate in half and then titrating the dose upward for the first 24 hours to obtain analgesia.

This rule must be modified in persons dependent on opioids when a change is made from a nonopioid to an opioid analgesic, to account for the presence of tolerance. When converting to an opioid for analgesia, it is simplest to calculate the total baseline opioid dose taken over 24 hours and then prescribe an opioid analgesic dose in excess of the baseline requirement. To diminish the chances of individual variability, two-thirds of the calculated total dose can initially be administered, with adjustment upward as needed.

It is always important, however, to be aware of the pharmacokinetics of the drug used. For example, use of a long-acting opioid, such as methadone, is initially accompanied by a consistent increase in plasma levels over several days. On the other extreme, meperidine has an extremely short duration of action, and its metabolite, normeperidine, in increasing plasma concentrations can cause seizures. Because meperidine is excreted by the kidneys, use of this drug in individuals with renal disease can be exceptionally hazardous and should be avoided.

Partial agonists, such as buprenorphine, and agonist-antagonists, such as nalbuphine and butorphanol, should be avoided. Their use in high doses is associated at times with cognitive side effects, and in a patient dependent on opioids, withdrawal can be produced.

## Use Drug Combinations Carefully

Combinations of drugs should be used only when specific effects are desired. It is important to avoid excessive sedation through use of drugs in the alcohol-barbiturate-benzodiazepine group. These drugs should never be used to enhance analgesia. However, there are drugs that can enhance analgesia when used in combination with opioids (Table 45–8). Antidepressants have

**Table 45–8.**   Drugs used to enhance opioid analgesia

| | |
|---|---|
| Acetaminophen | Carbamazepine |
| Amphetamines | Chlorpromazine |
| Antidepressants | Fluphenazine |
| Aspirin | Gabapentin |
| Baclofen | Hydroxyzine |

been found an effective adjunctive therapy in persons in pain who are also depressed and as effective as a single agent in relief of neuropathic pain. Effective analgesia can also be obtained through combinations of opioids and amphetamines, hydroxyzine, clonidine, and baclofen. Concurrent use of anti-inflammatory drugs with opioid analgesics may also result in a decrease in musculoskeletal pain.

## Pain Management According to Type of Pain

Pain can generally be classified as acute, intermittent, or chronic. Chronic pain can be further subdivided into malignant pain, nonmalignant pain, and pain of undefined etiology. Although the general guidelines to be followed in pain management are the same, regardless of the type of pain, specific differences exist, based on whether the pain is acute or chronic. Acute pain is usually associated with an identifiable injury of limited duration; however, it is also markedly affected by psychological and environmental factors. Chronic pain may be frequently initiated by local tissue injury; however, it can also be related to an injury of the central nervous system and usually has a concurrent psychogenic component, which must be addressed if optimal relief is to be provided.

### Management of Acute Pain

In managing acute pain in an individual who is concurrently using mood-altering drugs, the general guidelines mentioned earlier should be followed. However, certain guidelines need emphasis. The administration of opioids in individuals dependent on these drugs must be in effective doses, in excess of a person's baseline requirement. In addition, the medication should be prescribed on an ongoing basis, consistent with the particular opioid's pharmacological action. Prescribing medication as needed should be avoided, because the use of as-needed orders is consistently associated with increased anxiety on the part of the patient and ultimately with a need for a greater analgesic dose of opioid. Once the acute painful episode is resolved, if the opioid has been prescribed for 48–72 hours, it can be abruptly stopped. In individuals who have had a tolerance threshold, however, doses of the opioid should be decreased only to the individual's baseline opioid requirement.

Although meperidine is most often the drug preferred for treatment of acute pain, it has no advantage over other opioids. In fact, it has considerable disadvantages because of its short duration of action, its frequent irritation of subcutaneous tissues when it is given intramuscularly, its association with delirium in postoperative patients, and its metabolite, normeperidine, which can also cause irritability, confusion, and convulsions, especially in the presence of compromised renal function. For this reason, the U.S. Public Health Service recommended that meperidine not be used for acute pain unless other opioids cannot be tolerated (Carr et al. 1992).

Use of patient-controlled analgesia (PCA) has become an increasingly acceptable way of relieving acute pain, and the efficacy of PCA has been documented. PCA, contrary to common belief, allows an individual to self-administer intravenous doses of narcotics as needed. Limits can be set on frequency of dose-dispensing and amount of dose dispensed, and PCA is associated with a lower total dose of analgesia and a shorter time of hospitalization. Overdose rarely occurs, because the person must be alert to administer the analgesic. Intermittent, nonscheduled administration of medications may be appropriate in relieving acute pain, if the precipitating causes of the pain are known, and the drugs are administered before the pain occurs.

The relief of acute pain in persons on methadone maintenance regimens has become problematic. This is not because of the difficulty of relieving pain but because of the lack of physician knowledge regarding the appropriate way to provide analgesia. Persons receiving methadone do not have an impaired perception of pain. In the presence of inflammation, the use of a nonopioid, such as an NSAID, is appropriate. Opioid agonist-antagonists should be avoided at all costs, because these will precipitate withdrawal symptoms. A mild opioid analgesic will probably be ineffective because of the tolerance accompanying methadone maintenance, although the actual degree of tolerance is dependent on the daily methadone dose.

Parenteral narcotics can be effective in relieving pain in persons on methadone maintenance regimens, if given in appropriate doses. The tolerance threshold to methadone is based on a single oral dose of methadone given every 24 hours. The administration of parenteral, short-acting opioids in doses slightly greater than those usually recommended may be effective. Depending on the tolerance threshold, however, this dose must be increased until analgesia is obtained. If a person receiving methadone is admitted and not able to take any medication by mouth, intramuscular methadone may be given to maintain baseline requirements in divided doses. Alternatively, the patient's daily methadone dose may be converted to an equivalent dose of morphine sulfate to provide baseline needs, with the dose then increased to provide analgesia. Although this method will relieve pain and prevent withdrawal, it does disturb the steady-state methadone plasma level. Therefore, administering parenteral methadone intramuscularly every 8–12 hours is preferred by many physicians.

## Management of Chronic Pain

Unlike acute pain, which serves as a warning of impending danger, chronic pain has little if any useful biological function, serving to restrict one's daily activities and productivity. In addition, the constant presence of pain results in depression, anxiety, and a marked disturbance in interpersonal relationships. Defining the etiology of chronic pain is especially important, because if it is of malignant origin, other therapies may be instituted, which might be effective in providing pain relief and perhaps in producing a cure or a remission. The use of opioids to relieve pain of malignant origin is well accepted in medical practice, even in persons with a history of drug abuse. Unfortunately, most often relief of pain is not obtained, because physicians fail to follow the guidelines discussed earlier in this chapter.

Treatment of chronic pain of nonmalignant origin with opioids has been somewhat more controversial. However, many physicians now believe that if an etiology for the pain exists, relief of pain should be the primary goal. Analgesia should not be the only goal in such settings. In addition, a therapeutic plan with well-defined objectives should be developed and agreed on by both physician and patient. The presence of a chronic, debilitative disease may never allow one to be completely free from discomfort. This has to be realized and addressed not only by physician and patient but by family members as well. Available, nonpharmacological modalities, both invasive and noninvasive, can be effective in providing pain relief, depending on the etiology. If an opioid is decided on, it should be one with a long duration of action, because tolerance, which will develop with time, will occur more slowly (Table 45–9). Unlike other analgesics, opioids do not have a ceiling on their effectiveness. Increasing the dose is usually accompanied by increasing analgesia. Pain relief, however, should be accompanied by an increase in function. Use of sedatives should be avoided. Breakthrough pain, when seen, can be managed with short-acting opioids until the dose of the long-acting opioid can be adjusted upward.

Because a variety of pharmacological and nonpharmacological modalities may be helpful in relieving chronic pain, referral to a center devoted to pain management can often provide a needed team approach by a staff who are both interested in and knowledgeable about the relief of chronic pain as well as comfortable in dealing with the specific demands of patients with chronic pain. However, if a person wishes treatment outside a pain center, it is essential that analgesic care be provided by a single physician, with ongoing review and assessment carefully documented in the medical record.

Finally, it must be noted that there will be persons with chronic pain in which a demonstrative cause cannot be found. This presents a physician with a moral dilemma: whether it is appropriate to prescribe opioid medications when the reason for these drugs is not fully defined. Because in most instances patients are dependent on many medications when seen by a physician, it is often difficult to establish whether a primary addictive disorder exists or the dependence is related to an attempt to provide relief. Guidelines have been suggested for developing an approach for these patients (Table 45–10).

If it can be documented that long-term opioid therapy is not being abused and is providing pain relief and allowing maintenance of daily functions without adverse consequences, many physicians believe that the use of opioids should be continued. This is obviously an individual decision that each physician must make. However, it is essential that the treating physician set

| **Table 45–9.** | Long-acting opioids |
| --- | --- |
| Generic name | Trade name |
| Levorphanol | Levo-Dromoran |
| Morphine, controlled-release | MS Contin |
| Methadone | Dolophine |
| Oxycodone, controlled-release | OxyContin |
| Fentanyl, transdermal | Duragesic |

**Table 45–10.** Approach for patients with chronic pain syndrome without identifiable cause

Make certain an organic-based etiology has not been overlooked

Identify associated factors, such as secondary gain, depression, insomnia, anxiety

Attempt appropriate slow, long-term detoxification with use of nonopioid if mild pain occurs

Determine whether pattern of use of opioids or other mood-altering drugs is consistent with pharmacological action for pain relief or erratic, consistent with addiction

Determine whether function has been completely restored when person is taking opioids

*Source.* Modified from Savage 1994.

definite boundaries with respect to development of a reasonable analgesic regimen, discussing the matter fully with the patient and the family in a nonconfrontational manner. A clear message should be provided that the physician will not function merely as a supplier of drugs but will work with the patient to enable functioning. If it is believed that addictive behavior is present, referral should be made to an appropriate treatment facility.

 **Summary**

There is no reason individuals dependent on or using licit or illicit mood-altering substances cannot obtain adequate relief when pain is experienced. The assessment of pain in such persons should be little different from assessment in the general population. If the physician can overcome the cultural biases not infrequently present in dealing with those who abuse drugs, adequate relief from pain can be obtained, and a solid, long-lasting physician-patient relationship can be developed. It is this relationship that may be the most important factor in addressing the presence of the "addictive behaviors" that may exist.

**References**

Carr DB, Jacox AK, Chapman CR, et al: Acute Pain Management: Operative or Medical Procedures and Trauma (Clinical Practice Guideline, AHCPR Publ No 92-0032). Rockville, MD, U.S. Department of Health and Human Services, Public Health Service, Agency for Health Care Policy and Research, 1992

Cleeland CS, Gonin R, Hatfield AK, et al: Pain and its treatment in outpatients with metastatic cancer. N Engl J Med 330:592–596, 1994

Jacob TR: Multiple copy prescription regulation and drug abuse: evidence from the DAWN Network, in Balancing the Response to Prescription Drug Abuse. Edited by Wilfred BB. Chicago, IL, American Medical Association, 1990, pp 205–217

Jacox AK, Carr DB, Payne R, et al: Management of Cancer Pain (Clinical Practice Guideline, AHCPR Publ No 94-0592). Rockville, MD, U.S. Department of Health and Human Services, Public Health Service, Agency for Health Care Policy and Research, 1994

Joranson DE, Cleeland CS, Weissman DE, et al: Opioids for chronic cancer and non-cancer pain: a survey of state medical board members. Federal Bulletin 4:415–449, 1992

Morgan JP: American opiophobia: customary underutilization of opioid analgesics. Adv Alcohol Subst Abuse 5:163–173, 1985–1986

Portenoy RK, Dole V, Joseph H, et al: Pain management and chemical dependency: evolving perspectives. JAMA 278:592–593, 1997

Savage SR: Management of acute and chronic pain and cancer pain in the addicted patient, in Principles of Addiction Medicine. Edited by Miller NS, Doot MC. Chevy Chase, MD, American Society of Addiction Medicine, 1994, Section 8, pp 1–16

Stimmel B: Pain and Its Relief Without Addiction: Clinical Issues in the Use of Opioids and Other Analgesics. Binghamton, NY, Haworth, 1997

U.S. Department of Justice, Drug Enforcement Administration: Multiple Copy Prescription Program Resource Guide. Washington, DC, U.S. Government Printing Office, 1987

Weintraub M, Singh S, Byrne L, et al: Consequences of the 1989 New York State triplicate benzodiazepine prescription regulations. JAMA 266:2392–2397, 1991

# 7 Special Topics

# 46 Diagnostic Testing— Laboratory and Psychological

## Robert L. DuPont, M.D.

The diagnosis of substance use disorder, like most other medical diagnoses, is primarily clinical. Laboratory and psychological testing play a supportive role (Brostoff 1994). Nevertheless, laboratory and psychological testing are increasingly important in the identification of both addiction and comorbid medical and mental disorders, as well as in the assessment of the severity of these disorders and treatment planning (DuPont 1994).

## Laboratory Testing

Laboratory testing in addiction medicine can be divided into tests that identify recent drug use and tests that identify common correlates of alcohol and other drug use, such as infectious diseases and abnormal liver function. Laboratory tests cannot detect impairment, physical dependence, or addiction to alcohol and/or other drugs (DuPont 1997a).

### Identifying Recent Drug Use

Alcohol and other nonmedical drugs (such as marijuana, cocaine, and heroin) are used because they produce brain reward mediated by the neurotransmitter dopamine primarily in the ventral tegmental area and the nucleus accumbens, the brain's pleasure centers (DuPont 1997b; DuPont and Gold 1995). Drugs and their metabolites are identifiable in virtually all fluids in the body, including urine, blood, sweat, and saliva. Drugs also can be identified in all tissues of the body, including hair and finger- and toenails. Because alcohol is volatilized in the lungs, it is the only abused drug that can be

identified easily in breath (DuPont 1997a; Schwartz 1988).

Two decades ago, drug testing technology was relatively primitive, and the only commonly used sample for drug testing was urine, in which drugs and drug metabolites are relatively concentrated and easily identified. The exception was breath and blood testing for alcohol, which has been common for several decades. In more recent years, as drug detection technology has improved and as more reliable procedures for collection and sample handling have been developed, it has become more practical to test sweat, saliva, and hair for recent drug use.

The sample selected for alcohol and other drug testing reflects many factors, including ease of access, cost of the test, and the most appropriate detection window (i.e., the period of time that is sampled to identify drug use). Breath, saliva, and hair samples are the most easily collected, whereas blood and organ samples (such as liver biopsies) are the most difficult to obtain. Urine is easier to obtain than blood in most settings. Costs of analysis are similar, although hair, sweat, and blood testing are somewhat more expensive than urine testing. Sweat and hair testing are done only at specialized laboratories at present, but urine testing is done at most clinical laboratories. More recently, urine testing kits have become available for on-site screening, which produces results within a few minutes of collection. If the alcohol and other drug testing relates to the workplace, then legal regulations are important considerations, including secure collection with forensic standards of specimen handling and laboratory confirmation (U.S. Department of Health and Human Services 1988).

Blood has the shortest window of detection; most drugs are cleared from the blood at measurable levels in 12 hours or less. Urine has a detection window of about 1–3 days, as most drugs are cleared within this time after the most recent use of the drug. This is true even for marijuana, unless the tested individual has been a chronic heavy smoker of marijuana, in which case the urine results may remain positive for up to a month or longer after use stops. After smoking one or two marijuana cigarettes, in the absence of prior heavy chronic marijuana use, results are negative in many subjects within 24 hours, and all results will be negative at the 100-ng cutoff within 3 days. After smoking one or two marijuana cigarettes, urine test results will be negative in all subjects at the more sensitive 20-ng cutoff within 5 days of last marijuana use (Schwartz 1988).

Hair grows at the rate of about 0.5 inch (or a bit more than 1 cm) a month. Drugs are laid down in the hair matrix when it is created in the follicle. It takes about a week for the hair to grow long enough to be sampled in routine clipping of head hair. Thus, a standard 1.5-inch sample of head hair contains drug residuals from the prior 90 days, minus the week immediately before sample collection. Hair testing is particularly useful and superior to urine testing in various situations in which the longer detection window is important (DuPont and Baumgartner 1995). Because preemployment urine drug testing is a scheduled test, a drug user has to refrain from nonmedical drug use for only 3–5 days prior to submitting a urine sample in order to pass a urine test for abused drugs. It is much harder for most drug abusers to refrain from drug use for 90 days prior to preemployment testing, the period covered by a hair sample.

In contrast to urine samples, hair samples do not cause problems with sample substitution, adulteration, or dilution. However, hair treatments, such as perming, bleaching, and straightening, may reduce drug levels in hair in a way that can convert borderline positive results to negative results. Hair is less offensive to collect than urine. However, substantial drug use in the 90 days prior to sample collection is required to create a positive hair test result. This higher threshold for a positive hair test result means that eating poppy seeds will not produce a positive hair laboratory test result for opiates, as it commonly does in urine tests. Positive laboratory results for opiates on urine tests are routinely reversed by medical review officers (MROs), making opiate testing of urine samples in the workplace all but worthless because of the poppy seed problem.

Workplace drug testing conducted under federal guidelines is limited to a small number of drugs (codeine/morphine, amphetamine/methamphetamine, phencyclidine [PCP], marijuana, and cocaine) with urine tests. This means that the use of any other drug is not detected, including lysergic acid diethylamide (LSD), methylenedioxymethamphetamine (MDMA), synthetic opioids, and stimulants (such as hydromorphone hydrochloride, oxycodone hydrochloride, and methylphenidate hydrochloride).

Sweat patch testing is the newest of the commonly used techniques for drug testing. The person wears a patch, similar to a nicotine patch worn by people attempting to quit smoking, which, once removed, cannot be replaced without noticeable puckering of the edges of the patch. Sweat is continuously absorbed into the patch, with the water in the sweat evaporating through the outer patch membrane while the drug substance is affixed to the absorbent patch. Because skin normally desquamates, patches can be worn only for 2–4 weeks before they fall off. Drug detection sweat patches can be worn for periods of a few hours to a few weeks. During that time, they reliably identify any substantial drug use that occurs. Once removed, the patches are sent to a laboratory for testing.

Patches are commercially available for the detection of cocaine, opiates, marijuana, PCP, and amphetamine/methamphetamine. Sweat patches are not yet marketed for the detection of alcohol use, but alcohol detection patches are in the final stages of clinical testing and are expected to be available soon. Sweat patch testing is especially useful for follow-up testing, for example, in return-to-work settings when daily urine testing for drug use and virtually hourly breath testing for alcohol are impractical.

Hair testing and sweat patches offer important advantages over urine testing for abused drugs in many settings. Both are far more resistant to cheating, both offer rough quantitation (enabling the separation of heavy users from light users), and neither produces positive test results for opiates after poppy seed ingestion. See Table 46–1 for a comparison of blood, urine, hair, and sweat patch testing for abused drugs.

Saliva testing for drugs of abuse is now commonly used by the insurance industry to detect nicotine (cotinine), cocaine, and other drug use. Saliva testing for abused drugs soon will be used in the workplace and other settings. Saliva is in equilibrium with blood; therefore, saliva testing can detect only very recent use of drugs, often within the prior 6–12 hours. Saliva testing for alcohol is now available. Because saliva is easily obtained (unlike urine and blood) and can be screened

**Table 46–1.** Blood, urine, hair, and sweat patch testing for drugs of abuse

| | Blood | Urine | Hair | Sweat patch |
|---|---|---|---|---|
| Immunoassay screen | Yes | Yes | Yes | Yes |
| GC/MS confirmation option | Yes | Yes | Yes | Yes |
| Chain-of-custody option | Yes | Yes | Yes | Yes |
| Retained positives for retest option | Yes | Yes | Yes | Yes |
| Medical review officer option | Yes | Yes | Yes | Yes |
| Surveillance window | 3–12 hours | 1–3 days | 7–90 days | 1–21 days |
| Intrusiveness of collection | Severe | Moderate | None | Slight |
| Retest of same sample | Yes | Yes | Yes | Yes |
| Retest of new sample if original test disputed | No | No | Yes | No |
| Number of drugs screened | Unlimited[a] | Unlimited | 5[b] | 5[c] |
| Cost/sample (NIDA-5) | About $200 | About $15–$30 | About $40–$65 | About $20 |
| Permits distinction between light, moderate, and heavy use | Yes, acutely | No, chronically | Yes, chronically | Yes |
| Resistance to cheating | High | Low | High | High |
| Best applications | Postaccident and overdose testing for alcohol and other drugs | Reasonable cause and random testing | Preemployment testing | Posttreatment testing follow-up |
| | Blood alcohol concentration level | Frequent testing of high-risk groups such as post-treatment follow-up and criminal justice system | Random and periodic testing | Maintaining absti-nence |
| | | | Testing to determine severity of drug use for referral to treatment | Opiate-addicted per-sons claiming poppy seed "false positive" |
| | | | Testing subjects sus-pected of seeking to evade urine test detection | |
| | | | Opiate-addicted per-sons claiming poppy seed "false positive" | |

*Note.* GC/MS = gas chromatography/mass spectrometry.
[a]Blood testing for alcohol is routine, costing about $25 per sample, but blood testing for drugs is done by only a few laboratories in the United States. Blood testing for drugs is relatively expensive, costing about $60 for each drug detected.
[b]Currently, hair testing is available only for HHS-5 (cocaine, opiates, marijuana, amphetamines, and phencyclidine).
[c]HHS-5. Additional sweat patch tests will become available for alcohol.

on site (unlike hair samples), it is especially useful in postaccident and highway testing and in other settings in which immediate results and easy collection are important.

## Identifying Common Correlates of Alcohol and Other Drug Use

Clinical chemistry tests can be useful in identifying and following alcohol use because of the wide range of adverse biological effects of chronic heavy drinking (Allen and Litten 1994). Laboratory tests are neither as specific nor as sensitive as clinical assessment for diagnosing alcoholism (DuPont 1994). Nevertheless, it is useful to have a clear picture of the common laboratory results seen after heavy drinking. Abnormal laboratory results are more common in older drinkers, reflecting years of negative health effects of alcohol. Clinical chemistry test results are less likely to be abnormal in younger people, even if they heavily use alcohol.

γ-Glutamyltransferase (GGT) is elevated in about two-thirds of chronic heavy drinkers. GGT sensitively but nonspecifically reflects alcohol and, to a lesser extent, drug damage to the liver as well as infiltrative liver disorders and biliary obstruction. GGT reflects both liver damage and enzyme induction secondary to heavy drinking over extended periods of time. GGT is induced not only by alcohol but also by phenobarbital, dilantin, and many other drugs. GGT levels return to normal after about 3 weeks of abstinence from alcohol use.

Mean corpuscular volume (MCV) is elevated in about one-quarter of alcoholic patients. Elevation of the MCV is a relatively late manifestation of alcoholism and can result from both direct toxic effects of alcohol on the bone marrow and disruptions in folate metabolism. Unlike GGT elevations, MCV elevations persist for several months after abstinence from alcohol. The specificity of GGT elevation in identifying alcoholism is enhanced when it occurs in conjunction with MCV elevation because the nonalcohol factors that raise GGT levels do not raise MCV levels.

Alanine aminotransferase (ALT) and aspartate aminotransferase (AST) are elevated in about one-half of chronic heavy drinkers. Elevations of these transaminase levels are nonspecific signs of liver damage. ALT (formerly serum glutamate pyruvate transaminase [SGPT]) and AST (formerly serum glutamic-oxaloacetic transaminase [SGOT]) are elevated in many conditions, including various liver disorders such as cirrhosis, fatty liver, and alcoholic hepatitis; myocardial infarction; circulatory dysfunction; muscle injury; central nervous system disorders; and other diseases unrelated to the liver. The ratio of mitochondrial AST to total AST is more specific to alcoholic liver damage than is the AST level itself. AST levels may be greater than ALT levels in alcoholism because of the toxicity of alcohol on ALT synthesis. Although ALT is equally sensitive and possibly more specific to liver damage than is AST, it adds little of clinical value to AST levels alone.

Carbohydrate-deficient transferrin (CDT) is elevated in about 80% of people who drink heavily every day for 1 week or longer. CDT returns to normal during periods of abstinence from alcohol consumption, with values declining by about 50% after every 2 weeks of abstinence. Unlike transaminase levels, CDT is not commonly elevated in liver diseases unrelated to heavy alcohol consumption. CDT may be elevated in severe hepatic failure unrelated to heavy drinking and in individuals with rare genetic variants of transferrin, a β-globulin in the blood that transports iron. CDT can be a useful marker of heavy drinking in follow-up studies and in the clinical management of recovering alcoholic patients.

Other laboratory findings that are associated with heavy drinking include the following:

- Uric acid is elevated in about one-tenth of alcoholic patients because alcohol produces excessive levels of lactic acid, which competes with uric acid in the kidney and may produce elevations in serum uric acid levels.
- Triglycerides are elevated in about one-fourth of alcoholic patients.
- Bilirubin is elevated in about one-seventh of alcoholic patients. Bilirubin levels may be elevated for many reasons other than alcoholism; it is common in many chronic and acute liver diseases.
- Alkaline phosphatase is elevated in about one-sixth of alcoholic patients.
- Glucose levels are depressed in many alcoholic patients.

Other common abnormal laboratory findings in alcoholism include lowered potassium, magnesium, calcium, phosphate, and zinc levels; lowered red and white blood cell counts; and lowered platelet levels. Amylase is elevated in alcoholic pancreatitis.

## Psychological Testing

Psychological testing in addiction medicine today comprises two broad areas: 1) screening tests that are used to identify people at risk for addiction and 2) assessment tests that quantitatively evaluate people undergoing addiction treatment.

## Screening Tests

Psychological tests can augment clinical interviews and help to overcome the low rates at which clinicians recognize addiction to alcohol and other drugs. The simplest psychological screening test, and still one of the best, is the CAGE test. In this test, the interviewer asks patients whether they have attempted to **C**ut down on drinking, whether they have been **A**nnoyed by people's comments about their drinking, whether they have felt **G**uilty about any aspect of their drinking, and whether they have used alcohol early in the day as an **E**ye-opener to get going. Although this screening test is certainly simple, it is remarkably effective in identifying drinking problems. Even a single positive answer is ample reason to explore drinking and its consequences more fully.

Another psychological test is the Michigan Alcoholism Screening Test (MAST), which has several versions. The original MAST is a 25-item, self-administered questionnaire. The Short MAST (SMAST) has 13 items, whereas the Brief MAST (BMAST) has only 10 items. Both CAGE and MAST are related to drinking but not to drug use; therefore, problems related to nonmedical drug use are overlooked. Three other screening tests enjoy wide support: the Alcohol Use Disorders Identification Test (AUDIT), the Self-Administered Alcoholism Screen Test (SAAST), and the Adolescent Drinking Inventory (ADI) (Allen and Litten 1994).

The AUDIT alcohol-problem screening test was developed by the World Health Organization (WHO) as a short, structured questionnaire and brief clinical examination that included 10 questions on alcohol use (frequency of drinking, average amount of alcohol used, and peak levels of alcohol use), symptoms of alcohol dependence, and alcohol-related difficulties. The AUDIT covers the prior year rather than the subject's lifetime, and, unlike most alcohol-problem screening tests, the AUDIT is designed for international use and to detect alcohol-related problems even in the early stages of alcoholism (Babor et al. 1989).

The SAAST is longer than the CAGE but can still be administered in less than 10 minutes. The SAAST is a variant of the MAST with these differences: 1) it is more comprehensive in the domains sampled, 2) it can be self-administered, and 3) each item correlates equally to the total score.

The ADI is a 24-item screening test, with results tab-

ulated into four domains related to teenage drinking behavior: loss of control, social effects of drinking, psychological difficulties, and physical symptoms. Like the SAAST, the ADI is a self-administered test that can be used to screen large numbers of people at risk for alcohol abuse.

Positive results on screening tests should be followed by more intensive clinical evaluation to identify alcohol and other drug problems and to develop effective plans for intervention and treatment. Screening tests are flags for generalists, designating individuals who need more intensive attention from specialists in addiction medicine or from other clinicians who can handle substance use disorders in their practices.

## Assessment Tests

Because clinicians in addiction medicine feel pressure from third-party payers to reduce health care costs and to raise the quality of care, the past decade has seen a powerful new movement to establish formal and systematic approaches to diagnosis and treatment of addictive disorders. In particular, the controversies over the use of inpatient treatment for addiction to alcohol and other drugs, which were especially intense in the 1980s when inpatient addiction treatment was one of the most rapidly growing health care costs, have encouraged a more systematic assessment of patients' problems with alcohol and other drugs and an effort to match these problems to specific addiction treatments. Psychological instruments can provide standardization and credibility for systematic treatment selection and can facilitate the study of treatment outcomes (Gastfriend et al. 1994).

Patient Placement Criteria, published by the American Society of Addiction Medicine (ASAM; 1991), was one of the earliest and most influential efforts to standardize data collection related to treatment selection. These criteria have had a major effect on treatment decisions since their publication in 1991. ASAM criteria divide addiction treatment into four levels of care defined by the settings of that treatment: 1) hospital, 2) nonhospital inpatient, 3) day treatment, and 4) outpatient. The criteria were expanded in 1996 (American Society of Addiction Medicine 1996) to include a broader range of addiction treatment programs within each of the four major levels of care. ASAM criteria assess six patient-related dimensions, including

1. Acute intoxication and/or withdrawal
2. Medical diagnoses or complications

3. Emotional/behavioral disorders or complications
4. Treatment acceptance or resistance
5. Relapse or continuing use
6. Recovery/living environment

**Diagnosis of substance use disorder.**    The Structured Clinical Interview for DSM-IV (SCID) is suitable for both clinical and research uses (First et al. 1996). It is the most highly developed of the currently used assessment instruments to establish the diagnosis of alcohol or drug abuse or dependence. The SCID, evolved from research practice, is tied to formal DSM diagnoses to standardize the results of research studies.

The SCID is not easily administered by clinicians. The SCID is administered by specially trained clinical evaluators from the masters to the doctorate level. The SCID is labor intensive. It does not work the more intuitive, subjective way that clinicians approach patients in practice. Detailing both Axis I and Axis II diagnoses, the SCID requires more than 2 hours to administer, whereas the Psychoactive Use Disorders module of the SCID can be administered alone in about 30–60 minutes, depending on the extent of the subject's substance use history and the current intensity of substance use and related problems. This module, like the total SCID, now has questions specifically related to each item in the DSM-IV (American Psychiatric Association 1994) diagnostic criteria so that data are collected to establish lifetime and current diagnoses and age at onset of first abuse and first dependence for each category of drug.

SCID diagnoses have shown good interrater reliability for substance use disorders but less good reliability for comorbid conditions such as anxiety and depression (Skre et al. 1991).

The SCID is systematic and comprehensive. It gathers the information required to fit the DSM-IV diagnostic criteria. Several other diagnostic tests are available, but the SCID has the advantage of having been widely used for more than a decade in psychiatric research. Modern psychiatric research has relied to such an extent on the SCID to establish diagnoses that clinicians may one day be required to meet this standard of diagnosis for insurance and managed care purposes. More intensive, and therefore more expensive, addiction treatments will be the first to apply this systematic diagnostic instrument in addiction medicine.

**Substance abuse and dependence severity.**    The most widely used instrument to assess the severity of substance use disorders is the Addiction Severity Index (ASI; McLellan et al. 1992). The ASI uses a 30-minute semistructured interview to assess seven areas that are typically affected by dimensions of substance use: 1) medical problems, 2) employment/support, 3) drug/alcohol use, 4) legal status, 5) family history, 6) family/social relationships, and 7) psychiatric problems. Information is obtained about drug and alcohol use in the prior 30 days and during the subject's lifetime. The ASI can be administered by a trained technician (not necessarily a licensed clinician, as is required for the SCID). The ASI has been widely used for clinical, administrative, and research purposes. A smaller subset of ASI items has been used in follow-up studies.

The ASI is based on patient report without independent verification or review of collateral material such as workplace, criminal justice, or family sources. The ASI uses a rater assessment of the patient's reliability and the rater's own assessment of the severity of the patient's overall substance use disorder on a 10-point scale so that it is not totally dependent on what the patient says about his or her own problem. The ASI was developed and initially used in the methadone treatment of heroin addiction, but it has now been used in a wide variety of settings, including drug-free treatment, homeless shelters, and inpatient psychiatric hospitals (McLellan et al. 1980). Reflecting its origins, the ASI identifies severe alcohol- and other drug-related impairments but is not as good at characterizing less severely impaired patients, including those commonly seen in outpatient alcohol treatment programs and in many drug-free outpatient treatment settings.

The ASI has recently been enhanced for female populations in the ASI-F (Brown et al. 1995). The ASI-F captures dimensions that are unique to women, such as those related to pregnancy, and new items that also may apply to men, such as a history of trauma, child care responsibilities, partner abuse, and homelessness. This new version of the ASI can also be used for male patients.

**Motivation for recovery and treatment readiness.**    The Recovery Attitude and Treatment Evaluator Clinical Evaluation (RAATE-CE) is the most promising of the instruments for assessing treatment readiness (Mee-Lee 1988). The RAATE-CE assesses in a systematic and quantifiable way the patient's resistance and impediments to addiction treatment. This clinician-rated structured interview (like the SCID) assesses five dimensions related to substance treatment planning: 1) resistance to treatment; 2) resistance to continuing care; 3) severity of medical problems; 4) severity of psychiatric problems; and 5) extent of unsupportive family, social, and environmental factors. The RAATE-CE has 35 items scored from 1 to 4, with the higher scores corresponding to greater resistance and impediments to recovery.

**Summary.** Results of these tests are becoming the language of managed care with respect to addiction treatment decisions. In many settings, particularly inpatient addiction treatment, it is becoming standard to complete all three of these assessment tests (SCID, ASI, and RAATE-CE) in patients to make—and to defend—treatment placement decisions.

These three assessments are now widely used to make patient assessment more systematic and quantifiable. Therefore, clinicians must understand these tests and become familiar with their uses. Whether this approach produces better results and/or lower costs than the earlier purely clinical approaches to patient treatment decisions remains to be determined. Many clinicians have found these or similar instruments important in their everyday patient assessments and in managing long-term addiction treatment.

# References

Allen JP, Litten RZ: Biochemical and psychometric tests, in Principles of Addiction Medicine. Edited by Miller NS. Chevy Chase, MD, American Society of Addiction Medicine, 1994, Section IV, Chapter 3, pp 1–8

American Psychiatric Association: Diagnostic and Statistical Manual of Mental Disorders, 4th Edition. Washington, DC, American Psychiatric Association, 1994

American Society of Addiction Medicine: Patient Placement Criteria. Washington, DC, American Society of Addiction Medicine, 1991

American Society of Addiction Medicine: Patient Placement Criteria, 2nd Edition. Chevy Chase, MD, American Society of Addiction Medicine, 1996

Babor TF, de la Fuente JR, Saunders J, et al: AUDIT: The Alcohol Use Disorders Identification Test: Guidelines for Use in Primary Health Care. Geneva, Switzerland, World Health Organization, 1989

Brostoff WS: Clinical diagnosis, in Principles of Addiction Medicine. Edited by Miller NS. Chevy Chase, MD, American Society of Addiction Medicine, 1994, Section IV, Chapter 1, pp 1–5

Brown E, Frank D, Friedman A: Supplementary Administration Manual for the Expanded Female Version of the Addiction Severity Index (ASI) Instrument, The ASI-F. Herndon, VA, Head and Co, 1995

DuPont RL: Laboratory diagnosis, in Principles of Addiction Medicine. Edited by Miller NS. Chevy Chase, MD, American Society of Addiction Medicine, 1994, Section IV, Chapter 2, pp 1–8

DuPont RL: Drug testing, in Manual of Therapeutics for Addictions. Edited by Miller NS, Gold MS, Smith DE. New York, Wiley-Liss, 1997a, pp 86–94

DuPont RL: The Selfish Brain: Learning From Addiction. Washington, DC, American Psychiatric Press, 1997b

DuPont RL, Baumgartner WA: Drug testing by urine and hair analysis: complementary features and scientific issues. Forensic Sci Int 70:63–76, 1995

DuPont RL, Gold MS: Withdrawal and reward: implications for detoxification and relapse prevention. Psychiatric Annals 25:663–668, 1995

First M, Gibbon M, Spitzer R, et al: Users Guide for the Structured Clinical Interview for DSM-IV Axis I Disorders—Research Version (SCID I, Version 2.0, February 1996). New York, Biometrics Research Department, New York State Psychiatric Institute, 1996

Gastfriend DR, Najavits LM, Reif S: Assessment instruments, in Principles of Addiction Medicine. Edited by Miller NS. Chevy Chase, MD, American Society of Addiction Medicine, 1994, Section IV, Chapter 4, pp 1–8

McLellan AT, Luborsky L, Woody GE: An improved diagnostic evaluation instrument for substance abuse patients: the Addiction Severity Index. J Nerv Ment Dis 168: 26–33, 1980

McLellan AT, Kushner H, Metzger D, et al: The fifth edition of the Addiction Severity Index. J Subst Abuse Treat 9: 199–213, 1992

Mee-Lee D: An instrument for treatment progress and matching: the Recovery Attitude and Treatment Evaluator (RAATE). J Subst Abuse Treat 5:183–186, 1988

Schwartz RH: Urine testing in the detection of drugs of abuse. Arch Intern Med 148:2407–2412, 1988

Skre I, Onstad S, Torgersen S, et al: High interrater reliability for the Structured Clinical Interview for DSM-III-R Axis I. Acta Psychiatr Scand 84:167–173, 1991

U.S. Department of Health and Human Services: Mandatory guidelines for federal workplace drug testing programs. Federal Register, April 11, 1988, pp 11979–11989

# *47* Medical Education

John N. Chappel, M.D.
David C. Lewis, M.D.

> It is becoming unacceptable to ignore alcohol and drug related issues in clinical settings. Performing an alcohol and drug history on every patient seen in a clinical setting and providing specific treatment plans for those identified as abusers is likely to become the new standard of care.
>
> Fleming et al. 1994a, p. 368

**R**esistance to medical education about addiction has been slowly eroding in the past two decades. When the Career Teacher Program in Alcohol and Other Drug Abuse began in 1972 (Labs 1981), it was both acceptable and common practice to ignore addiction in medical education and in medical settings. Furthermore, physicians often reacted negatively to a patient once his or her addiction became known. Those practicing addiction psychiatry and addiction medicine in the 1970s were often told by patients of rejection or mistreatment by the primary care or specialist physicians who had discovered their addiction. These negative reactions, shared by many people in our culture, are based on the moral model of addiction, which views both addicting drugs and the people addicted to them as bad (Miller and Kurtz 1994).

These attitudes toward drug addiction have made the changes reflected in the above quote by Fleming and colleagues slow in coming. Despite the ubiquity of alcohol and other drug problems in medical and psychiatric patients (see Anthony, Chapter 6, in this volume), very little addiction medicine and addiction psychiatry was taught in medical schools before 1970. The Career Teacher Program led to significant, but insufficient, additions to medical school curricula (Pokorny and Solomon 1983).

Since then research has led to two profound changes that affect medical education. The first change is the move away from a 28-day intensive inpatient or residential treatment followed by variably structured, but usually not intensive, aftercare. The American Society of Addiction Medicine Patient Placement II Criteria describe a continuum of care from medically managed inpatient; through residential, partial, or day care; to outpatient in varying degrees of intensity and of sufficient length to develop stable sobriety (American Society of Addiction Medicine 1996). Three new dimensions of addiction severity have been added to the usual medical and psychiatric criteria:

1. *Resistance to treatment:* inability to recognize the severity of the addiction
2. *Relapse potential:* based on actual or near relapses in the community
3. Absence of a *recovery supportive environment* for the patient in the community

Any of these dimensions may necessitate a move to residential or inpatient treatment. The result of these changes is that medical education must now take place across all levels of treatment and use the new dimensions of care, which can be of great help in altering managed care reviewers' focus on medical necessity from a strictly physical point of view.

The second change is the inclusion of primary care physicians in addiction medicine. Efforts to involve both family and internal medicine in addiction medicine were made in the 1980s by small dedicated groups of physicians (Bigby and Barnes 1993; Fleming et al. 1992). Research support for the efficacy and cost-effectiveness of brief interventions by primary care physicians continued to grow (Fleming et al. 1997; Moore et al. 1989; Walsh et al. 1991). In 1994, a Macy

Conference brought together leaders in primary care education (Macy Conference Proceedings 1995). Subsequent meetings led to action by the Residency Review Committee (RRC) in Internal Medicine, which issued the following requirements in 1997: "All residents should receive instruction in diagnosis and management of alcoholism and other substance abuse. The instruction should include the principles of addiction medicine and intervention techniques. Residents should have clinical experience in managing patients with alcoholism and substance abuse disorders" (Accreditation Council for Graduate Medical Education Residency Review Committee 1997, p. 5.J.10).

This change should be matched by similar, if not more intensive, requirements in psychiatric residency training and bring about a much closer working relationship between psychiatrists and primary care physicians in providing better addiction treatment.

## What Should Be Taught, and When?

A growing body of knowledge in addiction medicine and addiction psychiatry has been captured in textbooks such as this one (American Society of Addiction Medicine 1994, 1998; Lowinson et al. 1997). A smaller, less extensive textbook has reached four editions (Schuckit 1994). With this information, faculty assigned to develop curricula have a wealth of material from which to select.

A useful outline for organizing a curriculum in addiction medicine is contained in the "Practice Guidelines for the Treatment of Patients With Substance Use Disorders" developed by the American Psychiatric Association (1995). This outline has the advantage of being applicable to medical school, residency, and continuing medical education.

Despite a substantial and rapidly growing knowledge base and a clear outline of addiction treatment, finding a place for addiction medicine in undergraduate and graduate medical education has not been easy. Part of the problem is the compartmentalization that has occurred with the development of basic science and clinical departments and disciplines. No one department is responsible for addiction medicine. Even psychiatry, which claims substance use disorders in the *Diagnostic and Statistical Manual of Mental Disorders*, has been a reluctant "parent." It was not until 1980, with the publication of DSM-III (American Psychiatric Association 1980), that the addictive disorders were moved from

the personality disorders section of the manual. Only in 1989 were psychiatry residencies required to provide "structured training" in the area of substance abuse (American Psychiatric Association 1989).

In the most recent study of medical education in addiction medicine, Fleming et al. (1994a) defined a "curriculum unit" as "any formal teaching activity, including a lecture, grand rounds, or a workshop, as well as clinical experiences in a treatment program or a detoxification unit" (p. 364). By 1992, only 93% of medical schools had "at least one curriculum unit in substance abuse." Table 47–1 shows the small number of curriculum units offered in the different departments. Although a total average of 7.2 curriculum units in all medical schools is better than the one lecture received by many who graduated in the 1950s and 1960s, it is still much too little for a group of disorders that account for 20% or more of hospital admissions and 25% of the actual causes of death (McGinnis and Foege 1993).

## The Basic Science Years

Medical students should be introduced to addiction medicine within the first year of medical training. Courses in pharmacology, neurobiology, and introductions to clinical medicine provide opportunities for introducing students to the fundamentals of addictive disorders.

We believe that the best results are obtained when a schoolwide committee or task force is responsible for developing an integrated curriculum in addiction medicine. One example is the Johns Hopkins Alcohol/Drug Project, which began in 1985 (Gopalan et al. 1992). Courses on alcohol and other drug problems were inserted into the required undergraduate curriculum for freshmen and sophomores, including the course in clini-

**Table 47–1.** Medical school curriculum units in 1992

|  | At least one unit (%) | Average curriculum units |
|---|---|---|
| Psychiatry | 95 | 4.3 |
| Family medicine | 87 | 3.0 |
| Pediatrics | 59 | 3.5 |
| Internal medicine | 47 | 3.9 |
| Obstetrics/gynecology | 45 | NA |
| All medical schools | 93 | 7.2 |

*Note.* NA = not available.

cal skills that prepares students for the clinical years. The result of this enhanced curriculum was a significant improvement in knowledge, acceptance of role responsibility, and positive attitudes between freshman and sophomore years.

Another example of innovation in this area is the model curriculum developed by Brown University for use in the basic science years. Project ADEPT contains five core curriculum modules, which require between 7 and 13 hours of curriculum time (Dube et al. 1989–1990). The material in the modules is inexpensive and uses a classroom or seminar structure, which experienced clinicians will find easily adaptable to their style of teaching.

Central to the introductory material in the basic science years is the increasing recognition that addiction is a chronic, primary, relapsing disease of the brain (American Psychiatric Association 1994; Leshner 1997; Morse and Flavin 1992). The response to treatment is comparable to that of hypertension, diabetes, and asthma rather than that of infectious diseases (O'Brien and McLellan 1996). Research in both the neurobiology and the treatment of addiction, combined with the influence of managed care, has changed the practice of addiction medicine. Much greater emphasis is now placed on outpatient treatment with long-term monitoring.

## The Clinical Years

The integrated approach that may be used in the classroom during the basic science years is lost during the clinical clerkships and electives. Many career teachers have observed this experience at Johns Hopkins University. Research at Johns Hopkins University found that medical student acceptance of role responsibility for screening, counseling, and following up patients with addiction problems decreased significantly during the clinical years (Gopalan et al. 1992). This reduction is probably because attending physician faculty in the various clerkships have had little training and even less interest in addiction medicine (Bander et al. 1987; Moore et al. 1989). Gopalan et al. (1992) noted that the reluctance of faculty to teach addiction diagnosis and treatment "may be related to a lack of technical expertise, teaching skill, or academic interest" (p. 265).

At Johns Hopkins University, the best antidote to the negative effect of the clerkship years was a 1-week elective that immersed the students in interactions with recovering alcoholic and drug-addicted patients by requiring attendance at Alcoholics Anonymous (AA), Narcotics Anonymous (NA), and Al-Anon meetings (Gopalan et al. 1992). This course is similar to the Physicians in Residence (PIR) programs at Hazelden and the Betty Ford Center (Levin et al. 1996). The participants in the elective course had significantly more positive attitudes, endorsed higher levels of role responsibility, and attained higher levels of applied knowledge score than did those who took only the required curriculum.

In every medical school, both addiction faculty and addiction treatment programs that serve the clinical training sites are needed. Gopalan and colleagues recommend an institutionwide effort aimed at house staff and faculty. The provision of curriculum units in addiction medicine in all medical school departments should be combined with systematic exposure to the 12-step programs. This interaction can best be done with members of AA. Each medical student and each faculty member should be taken to an open AA meeting by an AA member in good recovery. Scientific support for the efficacy of 12-step programs of recovery in AA justifies making this activity a required part of the medical school curriculum (Chappel 1993; Project MATCH Research Group 1997; Vaillant 1983, 1995).

This early exposure to AA has several benefits:

- Students learn how to contact AA and other 12-step programs to make effective patient referrals.
- Students meet alcoholic persons in good recovery, which helps them develop optimism to counter the pessimism produced by experience with alcoholic and addicted patients in emergency departments and acute-care hospital wards.
- Students develop history-taking skills with alcoholic persons who are willing to be interviewed, share their stories of addiction and recovery, and make suggestions about how to interview more effectively active alcoholic patients in denial.

These experiences are highly rated by medical students at all levels.

## Residency Training

Residency training is a crucial arena of medical education during which physician practice patterns are formed. Unfortunately, it has been the least affected by the changes that have taken place in addiction medicine and addiction psychiatry. The percentage of residency programs offering at least one curriculum unit in addiction medicine in 1992 can be seen in Table 47–1. Most required units were lectures and seminars. The elective experiences were usually 2- to 8-week clinical rotations in alcohol and drug treatment programs.

Change, even when required, has been slow. In 1989, the RRC in Psychiatry required training in addiction treatment for all residencies (American Psychiatric Association 1989). Most programs have complied, but they have complied minimally. This lack of enthusiasm is a very short-sighted position for psychiatry residency directors to take. Changes in primary care training are happening now. Similar changes will soon occur in surgery and its subspecialties, including anesthesiology. As these physicians screen, diagnose, attempt brief interventions, and ultimately refer their patients for more intensive treatments, their logical consultants will be psychiatrists trained in addiction medicine and addiction psychiatry.

Some psychiatry residencies now are providing excellent training. In 1992, Halikas described a model curriculum based on the adult psychiatry residency at the University of Minnesota. Westreich and Galanter (1997) have added to this model, emphasizing the importance of managed care, outpatient treatment, and dual diagnoses.

Primary care residency training has become a major focus of attention in recent years. Small, dedicated groups of primary care physicians have been working to improve residency training in addiction medicine. By 1993, the Society of General Internal Medicine had trained 87 primary care faculty in a 1-week course (Bigby and Barnes 1993). The Society of Teachers in Family Medicine had also trained 165 faculty participants in a similar course (Fleming et al. 1994b). A catalytic event was the Macy Conference on Training About Alcohol and Substance Abuse for All Primary Care Physicians in 1994 (Macy Conference Proceedings 1995). This conference, and the publication of the proceedings, was followed by a series of meetings involving leaders in primary care education. The new addition by the RRC in Internal Medicine, quoted at the beginning of this chapter, is the first of a series of actions that we hope will add training in addiction medicine to all residencies. Also, a recent Substance Abuse and Mental Health Services Administration (1997) guide attends to the growth of the educational needs of primary care physicians.

The case for the addition of addiction medicine training to surgical residencies also is substantial. Studies have shown that surgeons are less interested in addiction (Bander et al. 1987), diagnose it less often (Moore et al. 1989), and counsel patients less (Wells et al. 1984) than do other physicians. However, trauma patients, who are seen often by surgeons, frequently have addictive disorders. One study of 45 trauma center patients found that 76% of those with a positive blood alcohol concentration (BAC) met criteria for an addictive disorder, whereas 63% of those with a *negative* BAC also met the same criteria (Soderstrom et al. 1992). Interventions, arranged by surgeons, on alcoholic trauma patients have been highly effective in getting those patients into addiction treatment (Gentilello et al. 1988).

Models for addiction medicine training in primary care and other residency programs have not been developed yet. Many of the elements described above in psychiatric residency training will be needed. At minimum, a seminar series, supervised clinical experience in an addiction treatment program, and supervised experience doing brief interventions and following up patients in hospital and ambulatory settings will be needed (Warburg et al. 1987). A useful summary of physician competencies was developed for the Macy Foundation Conference (see Table 47–2) (Fleming 1995).

## Who Will Teach Addiction Medicine?

The interest in expanding and improving medical education in addiction treatment has led to the development of subspecialties in addiction medicine and addiction psychiatry. The American Society of Addiction Medicine developed a certification examination in 1983, which has been taken by more than 3,000 physicians (Schnoll et al. 1993). Initial credentialing for this examination did not require other specialty board certification or fellowship training. In contrast, the CAQ in addiction psychiatry, which was first offered in 1993, does require board certification (ABPN). Since 1998, only those who have taken a fellowship in addiction psychiatry have been able to take the examination.

Addiction fellowships began in 1973 (Galanter and Burns 1993). By 1992, 45 programs had graduated 161 addiction fellows. If the American Society of Addiction Medicine certification examination were accepted as the basis for a CAQ in other medical specialties, there would be a major stimulus for the continued development of fellowships in addiction medicine. The need is clear, as documented by Lewis (1997). At present, funding for fellowships is questionable as academic medical centers adjust to a new economic climate. However, "generalist and specialist training centers re-

**Table 47–2.** Recommended physician competencies for treating substance abuse disorders

Screening patients for alcohol and drug use

Assessment for problems related to alcohol and drug use

Office-based treatment

Pharmacology

   Withdrawal

   Symptom relief postwithdrawal

   Comorbid conditions

Referral to treatment programs

Pain management

   Acute pain

   Chronic pain

Drug testing

   Breath

   Urine

   Blood

Care of affected family members

Physician impairment

   Prevention

   Recognition

   Monitoring recovery

*Source.* Reprinted from Fleming MF: "Competencies for Substance Abuse Training," in *Training About Alcohol and Substance Abuse for All Primary Care Physicians: The Macy Foundation Conference Proceedings.* New York, Josiah Macy Jr Foundation, 1995, pp. 213–248. Used with permission.

alize that they need each other to survive in this new economic climate. The expertise of medical disciplines, including the ready access to consultation from psychiatry and addiction medicine, is part of a truly integrated system of care" (Lewis 1997, p. 840).

## Conclusion

Addiction medicine and addiction psychiatry belong in the mainstream of medical care. Integration of these systems requires changes in both medical education and practice. Data contained in this book and in the references to this chapter provide a powerful argument for including addiction medicine in all residency training. As physicians in all areas of medical practice become more skilled in identifying and intervening in the addictive disorders of their patients, the opportunity for addiction psychiatrists and addiction medicine specialists to work together is growing. When harm reduction through reduced use of addicting drugs does not work,

then abstinence, with or without opioid maintenance and other pharmacological support, accompanied by proven psychosocial therapies and relapse prevention, must be initiated. As a step in this direction, the American Society of Addiction Medicine and the American Managed Behavioral Health Care Association, representing more than 80 million enrollees, made the following joint statement in 1997: "Health plan coverage for the treatment of alcohol, nicotine and other drug dependencies should be non-discriminatory . . . and addictive disorders benefits plans should have the same provisions, lifetime benefits, and catastrophic coverage as any other physical illness" (Mee-Lee 1997).

## References

Accreditation Council for Graduate Medical Education Residency Review Committee: Essentials of Accredited Residency in Graduate Medical Education: Institutional and Program Requirements. Program Requirements for Residency Education in Internal Medicine, 1997, p. 5.J.10

American Psychiatric Association: Special essentials (requirements) for graduate education in psychiatry. Washington, DC, Residency Review Committee, November 1989

American Psychiatric Association: Diagnostic and Statistical Manual of Mental Disorders, 3rd Edition. Washington, DC, American Psychiatric Association, 1980

American Psychiatric Association: Diagnostic and Statistical Manual of Mental Disorders, 4th Edition. Washington, DC, American Psychiatric Association, 1994

American Psychiatric Association: Work Group on Substance Use Disorders. Practice guidelines for the treatment of patients with substance use disorders: alcohol, cocaine, opioids. Am J Psychiatry 152 (11 suppl):1–59, 1995

American Society of Addiction Medicine: Principles of Addiction Medicine, 1st Edition. Chevy Chase, MD, American Society of Addiction Medicine, 1994

American Society of Addiction Medicine: Patient Placement Criteria for the Treatment of Substance Related Disorders, 2nd Edition. Chevy Chase, MD, American Society of Addiction Medicine, 1996

American Society of Addiction Medicine: Principles of Addiction Medicine, 2nd Edition. Chevy Chase, MD, American Society of Addiction Medicine, 1998

Bander KW, Goldman DS, Schwartz MA, et al: Survey of attitudes among three specialties in a teaching hospital toward alcoholics. Journal of Medical Education 62:17–24, 1987

Bigby J, Barnes H: Evaluation of a faculty development program in substance abuse education. J Gen Intern Med 8:301–305, 1993

Chappel JN: Long term recovery from alcoholism. Psychiatr Clin North Am 16:177–187, 1993

Dube CE, Goldstein MD, Lewis DC, et al: Project ADEPT: Curriculum for Primary Care Physician Training, Vol 1: Core Modules, 1989; Vol 2: Special Topics and Videotape, 1990. Providence, RI, Brown University Center for Alcohol and Addiction Studies, 1989–1990

Fleming MF: Competencies for substance abuse training, in Training About Alcohol and Substance Abuse for All Primary Care Physicians: The Macy Foundation Conference Proceedings. Edited by Sirica C. New York, Josiah Macy Jr Foundation, 1995, pp 213–248

Fleming MF, Clark K, Davis A, et al: A national model of faculty development. Addiction Medicine 67:691–693, 1992

Fleming M, Barry K, Davis A, et al: Medical education about substance abuse: changes in curriculum and faculty between 1976 and 1992. Acad Med 69:362–369, 1994a

Fleming MF, Barry KL, Davis A, et al: Faculty development in addiction medicine: project SAEFP, a one-year follow-up study. Fam Med 26:221–225, 1994b

Fleming MF, Barry KL, Manwell LB, et al: Brief physician advice for problem alcohol drinkers: a randomized controlled trial in community based primary care practices. JAMA 277:1039–1045, 1997

Galanter M, Burns J: The status of fellowships in addiction psychiatry. Am J Addict 2:4–8, 1993

Gentilello LM, Duggan P, Drummond D, et al: Major injury as a unique opportunity to initiate treatment in the alcoholic. Am J Surg 156:558–561, 1988

Gopalan R, Santora P, Stokes EJ, et al: Evaluation of a model curriculum on substance abuse at the Johns Hopkins University School of Medicine. Acad Med 67:260–266, 1992

Halikas J: Model curriculum for alcohol and drug abuse training and experience during the adult psychiatry residency. Am J Addict 1:222–229, 1992

Labs SM: The Career Teacher Grant Program: alcohol and drug abuse education for the health professions. Journal of Medical Education 56:202–204, 1981

Leshner AI: Addiction is a brain disease, and it matters. Science 278:45–47, 1997

Levin FR, Owen P, Rabinowitz E, et al: Physicians in Residence Program. Substance Abuse 17:5–18, 1996

Lewis DC: The role of the generalist in the care of the substance-abusing patient. Med Clin North Am 81:831–843, 1997

Lowinson JH, Ruiz P, Millman RB, et al: Substance Abuse: A Comprehensive Textbook, 3rd Edition. Baltimore, MD, Williams & Wilkins, 1997

Macy Conference Proceedings: Training About Alcohol and Substance Abuse for All Primary Care Physicians. New York, Josiah Macy Jr Foundation, 1995

McGinnis JM, Foege WH: Actual causes of death in the United States. JAMA 270:2202–2212, 1993

Mee-Lee D: ASAM and AMBHA: striving toward agreement. Behavioral Health Management 19–23, 1997

Miller WR, Kurtz E: Models of alcoholism used in treatment. J Stud Alcohol 55:159–166, 1994

Moore RD, Bone LR, Geller G, et al: Prevalence, detection, and treatment of alcoholism in hospitalized patients. JAMA 261:403–407, 1989

Morse RM, Flavin DK: The definition of alcoholism. JAMA 268:1012–1014, 1992

O'Brien CP, McLellan AT: Myths about the treatment of addiction. Lancet 347:237–240, 1996

Pokorny AD, Solomon JA: Follow-up survey of drug abuse and alcoholism teaching in medical schools. Journal of Medical Education 58:316–321, 1983

Project MATCH Research Group: Matching alcoholism treatments to client heterogeneity. J Stud Alcohol 58:7–29, 1997

Schnoll S, Durburg J, Griffin J, et al: Physician certification in addiction medicine 1986–1990: a four-year experience. The Examination Committee of ASAM. J Addict Dis 12:123–133, 1993

Schuckit MA: Drug and Alcohol Abuse: A Clinical Guide to Diagnosis and Treatment, 4th Edition. New York, Plenum, 1994

Soderstrom CA, Dischinger PC, Smith GS, et al: Psychoactive substance dependence among trauma center patients. JAMA 267:2756–2759, 1992

Substance Abuse and Mental Health Services Administration: A Guide to Substance Abuse Services for Primary Care Clinicians. Rockville, MD, Substance Abuse and Mental Health Services Administration, 1997

Vaillant GE: The Natural History of Alcoholism. Cambridge, MA, Harvard University Press, 1983

Vaillant GE: The Natural History of Alcoholism: Revisited. Cambridge, MA, Harvard University Press, 1995

Walsh DC, Hingson RW, Merrigan DM, et al: A randomized trial of treatment options for alcohol abusing workers. N Engl J Med 325:775–782, 1991

Warburg MM, Cleary PD, Rohman M, et al: Residents' attitudes, knowledge, and behavior regarding diagnosis and treatment of alcoholism. Journal of Medical Education 62:497–503, 1987

Wells KB, Lewis CE, Leake B, et al: Do physicians preach what they practice? A study of physicians' health habits and counseling practices. JAMA 252:2846–2848, 1984

Westreich L, Galanter M: Training psychiatric residents in addiction. Substance Abuse 18:13–25, 1997

# Chapter

## 48 Prevention

### Mary Anne Pentz, Ph.D.

Prevention of drug abuse in youth, particularly primary prevention, is worthy of increased attention because drug use among youth has been rising about 1%–3% per year since 1991, with only a slight decline in 1996 (Johnston et al. 1997). In this chapter, I review types of prevention and principles of effective preventive interventions for youth. I then describe specific intervention modalities, followed by a summary of outcomes for each modality. The chapter concludes with a rationale for a comprehensive, multimodality approach to drug abuse prevention.

## What Is Prevention?

In the broadest terms, prevention refers to preventing or blocking the progression of use to abuse, whether in adults or youth. In the strictest terms, prevention refers to preventing onset of *any* use, usually in children and adolescents. Because defining what constitutes abuse in youth is difficult, and permanently preventing onset or experimentation is probably not realistic, prevention researchers and practitioners have adopted a more practical working definition of prevention that includes any program that has as its goal either delay of onset, delay of progression from lower to higher use prevalence (frequency) or consumption (amount), or decrease in use prevalence and consumption.

In the prevention field, use levels are arbitrarily defined by the frequency or the relative proportion of the youth population that uses at a particular level rather than by levels that reflect dysfunction. Most commonly, these levels refer to experimental use (first or second occasion), occasional use (less than monthly), and "regular use" for the youth population, the latter usually defined as once a month to once a week, or statistically as 10% or less of the population that uses more than monthly (Pentz 1998). Prevention, then, is most relevant to DSM criteria for nonpathological child and adolescent substance use (Kaminer 1994). Prevention efforts do not usually address dependence, withdrawal, or intoxication other than briefly in programs that include weighing the benefits and negative social and physical consequences of use (Hansen 1992).

Prevention in childhood and early adolescence focuses heavily on tobacco, alcohol, and marijuana, substances referred to as *gateway* drugs for their temporal, if not causal, relationship to the use of other substances in later adolescence and adulthood. As such, prevention is relevant to DSM criteria for tobacco and alcohol dependence as well as dependence on other drugs (Martin et al. 1996).

## Types of Prevention

Preventive efforts can be characterized by approach to drug abuse control (demand vs. supply reduction), level of prevention (primary, secondary, tertiary; more recently referred to as universal, selective, indicated) (Kumpfer 1989), and focus (direct focus on drug use resistance and risk reduction vs. indirect focus on life skills and protective factors).

### Approach to Drug Abuse Control

In general, drug abuse control efforts—including prevention—can be categorized as demand or supply reduction. Most prevention programs focus on demand reduction—that is, changing the demand for drugs by changing attitudes, perceptions, and behaviors toward drug use. In contrast, supply reduction efforts are typically aimed at systems or environments rather than individuals and are focused primarily on changing supply or access to drugs (Holder and Wallack 1986).

## Level of Prevention

Prevention programs have been characterized on a continuum from primary to selective to indicated prevention, depending on the level of drug use involvement by the target youth population at the point of intervention (Aktan et al. 1996).

Primary, or universal, prevention involves whole populations of youth and typically is accomplished through education by teachers or peers in school settings. *Selective* prevention programs are for high-risk youth (e.g., student assistance programs) (McGovern and DuPont 1991). This type of intervention consists of individual counseling, small group counseling, and support groups aimed at youth who are at risk for or already experiencing academic difficulties, drug use, and/or mental distress caused by poor personal or social functioning, adverse family environment, or adverse peer social environment. *Indicated* prevention programs focus on youth who are considered at high risk for drug use and already have one or more problem behaviors associated with later use, including truancy, school achievement problems, stealing, gang involvement, and conduct disorder. Prevention at this level is considered early intervention and may consist of outpatient programs or counseling, or even brief inpatient treatment. The more comprehensive indicated prevention programs will link prevention services offered within the school to community clinics, agencies, or hospitals outside the school (Bruininks et al. 1994; Council on Scientific Affairs 1990).

## Focus

Prevention efforts can be roughly categorized according to whether they *directly* address youth drug use by focusing on skills and strategies to resist drug use and avoid drug use environments or *indirectly* address use by focusing on early risk factors for problem behavior or early protective factors against later drug use. Risk factors for other problem behaviors include school failure, peer pressure, and lack of positive parent-child communication and support (Brook et al. 1989; Dryfoos and Dryfoos 1993; Hawkins et al. 1992). Protective factors include social bonding, academic competence, and support-seeking and communication skills, as well as general life skills such as decision making (Hawkins et al. 1992). The selection of a program that focuses on risk

or protective factors depends on the age and level of drug involvement of youth at the point of or prior to intervention. For example, children in elementary school may benefit more from a program that focuses on building protective factors of age-appropriate, prosocial bonding to peers and adults, play-relevant skills of sharing and communicating, and school-relevant skills of asking for help than from a program that teaches youth how to refuse a drug use offer, if drugs are not available at this age level. Alternatively, early and mid-adolescents may benefit from age-appropriate protective skills of assertiveness and decision making combined with specific drug use resistance skills or resistance skills alone.

## What We Know and Do Not Know About Prevention

Several reviews of the prevention literature have shown the following in terms of what we know does *not* work (Dusenbury and Falco 1995; Hansen 1992; Tobler 1992). Prevention programs that are primarily didactic in delivery, focus primarily on changing knowledge about drugs or consequences of drug use, and target affect or self-esteem have no significant effects on changing adolescent drug use. Programs that are atheoretical, or focused on activities rather than cognitive and behavioral skills, also show no effects. No evidence indicates that drug use events, such as Red Ribbon Days or testimonials by former drug users, have an effect on drug use behavior. A basis in theory does not ensure effectiveness. Some programs that have been based on sound theories of behavior change, such as the popular police-delivered program DARE (Ennett et al. 1994), have shown no substantial effects on adolescent drug use behavior. Poor program implementation and failure to change risk mediators (e.g., resistance skills) are major reasons for program failure or weak effects on drug use (Donaldson et al. 1994; Dusenbury and Falco 1995; MacKinnon et al. 1991; Pentz and Trebow 1991; Resnicow and Botvin 1993). Some possibilities may involve the type of individual(s), instructional method, or support available to implement programs (Ellickson et al. 1993; Ennett et al. 1994).

Multiple questions remain concerning what we do not know about prevention:

1. Relatively little research information exists on what constitutes effective indicated prevention for youth who are already using drugs, outside of the school, agency, or hospital setting.

2. Why most communities and schools in the United States continue to opt for prevention programs and activities that have shown no effects on changing drug use behavior (e.g., DARE) or have not been evaluated sufficiently to determine effects (e.g., the use of testimonials by former drug users) is unknown (Rogers 1992).

3. The capability of even the most comprehensive, well-designed, and well-implemented prevention programs to prevent drug abuse morbidity and mortality over the long term is not yet known.

4. Other than a few pilot studies on office- or clinic-based interventions involving advice or feedback about risk or media programs (e.g., Klitzner et al. 1987), little is known about what role a psychiatrist or other types of physicians might take in the prevention of drug use (Pentz 1993a).

## How Do Effective Prevention Programs Work?

Effective prevention programs share at least three common features (Dusenbury and Falco 1995; Hansen 1992; Pentz 1998): 1) a focus on counteracting risk factors and promoting protective factors, shown in epidemiological research to affect drug use; 2) a basis in theories of behavior change; and 3) use of specific program implementation strategies that enhance youth-provider interaction, quality of program implementation, and youth participation in and exposure to programming (dose-response).

### Counteracting Risk Factors and Promoting Protective Factors From Epidemiological Research

Risk factors have been identified at three levels: 1) the person (intrapersonal cognitions, affect, behavior), 2) the social situation (interpersonal or group norms, attitudes, and behavior), and 3) the environment (organizational, systems, community, or larger influences) (Pentz, in press).

At the intrapersonal level, a combination of prior use, positive beliefs about use, positive appraisal of the drug use experience, and lower perceived risk or consequences of use contributes to drug use (Bachman et al. 1991; Pentz, in press). Ironically, most prevention efforts aimed at individuals that focus on knowledge of drug use alone or are limited to single intrapersonal factors such as decision making, without regard to social context, are not effective (Tobler 1992).

At the social level, risk factors include exposure to drug use models, access and attachment to users, and positive perceived social norms for use (Pentz, in press). Prevention programs focused on counteracting social situational risk factors typically include training in avoidance, peer pressure resistance, and/or assertiveness skills; weighing positive and negative consequences of drug use; and correcting perceived social norms for use (Hansen 1992; Tobler 1992). Most of these are implemented in schools during the early adolescent years. A few programs implemented during the elementary school years have focused on bonding with nonusing peers (e.g., Hawkins et al. 1992). These programs are considered primary or universal prevention programs because they include whole populations of school-attending youth. Selective or indicated prevention programs (Aktan et al. 1996) have typically included social support-seeking and selection of nonuse alternatives along with skills training (e.g., Aktan et al. 1996; Eggert et al. 1994). With a few exceptions, social influences programs have been effective in delaying and reducing adolescent drug use, for periods of 5 years or more, when compared with either control or standard health education conditions (Ary et al. 1990; Botvin et al. 1995; Hansen 1992; Tobler 1992).

At the environmental level, risk factors include exposure to and positive beliefs about media portrayals of drug use, exposure to drug use environment, access to drugs, low exposure to prevention programs and resources, and positive perceived environmental norms for drug use (Pentz, in press). Prevention programs that counteract these influences may include organizing and empowering community leaders to change drug use, enforce policy, and institutionalize prevention programs and resources. Programs that address environmental influences have consisted of either mass media programs or campaigns, policy enforcement or policy change intervention, community coalitions or partnerships organized for drug abuse prevention, or a combination. In general, mass media programs have produced small effects on changing attitudes toward drug use and beliefs about consequences and intentions to use drugs in the future (Donohew et al. 1991; Flay et al. 1985; Flynn et al. 1992). Restricted access policies that involve youth in enforcement, for example, through activism or "sting" operations, have an effect on decreasing tobacco sales and purchases by youth and may decrease alcohol consumption (Forster et al. 1998; Jason et al. 1991; Perry and Jessor 1985). Community coalitions tend to show a trend toward decreasing adolescent drug use, but the effects are small or not significant (Saxe et al., in press; Yin and Kaftarian 1997). Effects of environmental interventions appear to be stronger to the extent that they are combined—for example, a community no-smoking ordinance with youth sting operations and mass media programming (Jason et al. 1991). In a recent study, relative reductions of up to 20% in youth tobacco use prevalence were achieved by combining community and youth activism to promote restricted access policy and local mass media support (Forster et al. 1998).

Intrapersonal, social, and environmental risk factors interact to affect youth drug use, including the decision, immediate opportunity, and access to drugs. Comprehensive community-based programs attempt to address and integrate these risk factors. All of these comprehensive programs have included multiple components representing personal, social, and environmental risk counteractive strategies, usually by combining school programs with parent, mass media, and/or community organization training. All have shown significant (20%–60%) reductions in use prevalence by youth compared with control conditions; several of those evaluated over the long term have shown maintenance of effects of 8 years or more (Pentz 1998, in press; Perry et al. 1996; Vartiainen et al. 1990).

## Basis in Theories of Behavior Change

Basing prevention programs on sound theories of behavior change enables researchers to determine whether a program, if effective, changed behavior according to the mechanisms proposed by the theory or, if ineffective, failed to change behavior because the mechanisms themselves were not implemented or did not change.

Several theories help to explain how counteracting risk factors should work to change drug use behavior.

- *Problem behavior theory* posits that adolescents experience transition periods that make them feel vulnerable (Jessor 1982). Trying a drug is an attempt to appear older and more confident in the face of vulnerability. Teaching skills such as decision making and resistance is an alternative way to build confidence.
- *Expectancy theory* posits that the perceived social norms for drug use, the expectancy of use, and the positive value of a drug use experience will interact to contribute to drug use (Fishbein and Ajzen 1975). The extent to which a prevention program can promote negative rather than positive norms and expectancies will help curb drug use experimentation.

- *Social learning theory* posits that available, credible peer models for drug use behavior combined with social reinforcement for drug use will contribute to drug use experimentation (Bandura 1977). Alternatively, the extent to which youth can be taught to emulate and bond with nonusing models will help decrease drug use. First, a credible model or trainer (e.g., teacher) provides students with the general organizing principles (overview) about what training will involve, a credible peer models the skill, youths role-play or try out the skill, the group provides discussion and feedback about the role-play, and then the group continues to practice the skill in real-life settings (e.g., through homework or at the next party). This learning process is the same as that used in behavioral group therapy. Some prevention programs also incorporate, to a limited extent, principles from cognitive therapy such as guided imagery.
- *Diffusion of innovation theory* posits that a social norm making drug use acceptable will develop if the early users are considered innovative and the trial drug use experience is easy. Alternatively, the extent to which a new prevention program or prevention skill is communicated from models to peers, and from programs to other settings, will determine how rapidly skills are adopted and nonuse norms are established.
- *Transactional theories* posit that the three levels of risk factor strategies to counteract personal, social, and environmental risk factors should interact in a prevention program. Programs that have shown the strongest and most immediate effects on drug use behavior are those that include social learning theory and at least one other theory of behavior change (Hansen 1992). Programs with the most sustained effects tend to include transactional theories (Tobler 1992).

## Program Implementation Strategies

Effective drug abuse prevention programs share several features related to program implementation (Dusenbury and Falco 1995; Hansen 1992; Tobler 1992).

1. The use of standardized training or teaching materials and procedures for program implementors, who may be teachers, peers, counselors, parents, or service agency staff: A typical training session consists of at least a day of training that follows the same process outlined in social learning theory (Bandura 1977) to train youth: an overview of general princi-

ples, modeling, role-playing, group discussion with feedback, and extended practice through homework assignments, or initiation of program implementation with observation.

2. The use of social learning theory methods of implementation with youth: Trainer-youth interaction is enhanced, often with the assistance of peer leaders (Perry et al. 1996).

3. Attention to quality of implementation: Included is adherence to program materials and procedures as designed, delivery of the full amount of contact hours of programming, and flexibility for "reinvention" (i.e., some tailoring of the program to the specific needs of youth without sacrificing adherence) (Pentz and Trebow 1997).

4. The use of periodic booster programming (Dusenbury and Falco 1995)

5. The use of techniques, settings, or individuals that can extend prevention beyond the program setting: Included is the use of interactive homework with parents and agreement to practice prevention skills outside of the program setting (Pentz 1993b).

## Program Modalities, or Channels for Program Delivery

Major settings for counteracting drug use, thus settings for prevention programming and program implementors, include the school (teachers), the home (parents), mass media (television and news programmers), community organizations (either existing youth serving organizations or new organizations developed for the express purpose of drug abuse prevention planning), and local school and community policy settings (school and community leaders).

### School Programs

Most school programs are demand reduction prevention programs concentrating on primary prevention. The fewest have focused on selective and indicated prevention programs, such as student assistant programs. Most are delivered by teachers, some with assistance of trained peer leaders.

Overall, the pattern of school-based studies suggests strong 1- to 3-year effects on experimental use rates of gateway drugs; few effects on regular gateway drug use rates; and no effects at 5-year follow-up, with one exception, which required 30 sessions of instruction (Botvin et al. 1995). The magnitude of effect overall

appears to be larger than that achieved from school health education programs—20%–67% versus 7% (Pentz 1998)—perhaps attributable to the shift from didactic to interactive education (Hansen 1992).

### Parent Programs

Relatively few prevention programs have focused primarily or solely on parents. Primary prevention programs include those delivered in or under the auspices of elementary schools, which focus on promoting positive parent-child communication and bonding (Hawkins et al. 1992; Kosterman et al. 1997); take-home assignments that involve parent-child interaction, which are distributed typically in middle school to early adolescents as part of a media program (e.g., Flay et al. 1985; Flynn et al. 1992); take-home assignments as part of a middle school prevention program or multi-component community programs (e.g., Botvin et al. 1995; Hansen 1992; Pentz 1998; Perry et al. 1996); and parent prevention focused on parent involvement in school policy, parent-child communication skills, and prevention support skills as part of a multicomponent community program (e.g., Pentz 1998). All of these have shown some effects of parent participation in prevention and on parent-child communication. Parent programming delivered as part of a multicomponent school or community intervention has had effects on parent use behavior, as well as communication and participation in prevention (Rohrbach et al. 1994).

Programs for parents of children with conduct disorder have focused on increasing positive parent-child interaction and working with educators to maximize child learning in school (e.g., Dishion and Andrews 1995; Kosterman et al. 1997). These types of programs have some effect on changing child aggressive behavior and attention in school.

### Mass Media Programs

Mass media programs include primary prevention programs targeted at a general adolescent population (e.g., Flay et al. 1985; Flynn et al. 1992), advertising campaigns and small-scale interventions involving exposure of high-risk youth to different types of counter-advertising (e.g., Donohew et al. 1991; Lorch et al. 1994), antiuse and antiuse policy advocacy campaigns aimed at the general youth population (e.g., Hingson et al. 1996; Jason et al. 1991; Murray et al. 1994), and media literacy programs or sessions, usually delivered through a program modality other than media (e.g., counteradvertising lessons as part of a school program) (e.g., Flay et al. 1985). Overall, effects of mass media programs, if not combined with other programs such as school programs, have been limited to changing adolescent attitudes toward drug use and intentions to use (Flay et al. 1985; Flynn et al. 1992), with some suggestion of behavioral change (Flynn et al. 1992). Advertising campaigns and interventions aimed at high-risk youth have changed attention to counteradvertising messages, attitudes toward drug use, and sensation seeking (Donohew et al. 1991; Lorch et al. 1994). General antiuse campaigns have shown no effects on adolescent use (e.g., Pierce et al. 1994), although antiuse policy advocacy campaigns have shown effects on both alcohol and cigarette use (e.g., Jason et al. 1991). Media literacy appears to have an effect of recognition of mass media influences on drug use (e.g., Johnson et al. 1990).

## Community Programs

Social influences programs conducted in community settings, such as Boys & Girls Clubs, have shown significant short-term decreases in gateway drug use comparable to short-term decreases reported for school-based programs (St. Pierre et al. 1992). Other community programs consist of public education or community organization for prevention. Neither of these approaches, by themselves, have produced large or significant changes in adolescent drug use behavior (Saxe et al., in press; Yin and Kaftarian 1997). However, they do show an overall trend toward effects on drug use behavior (usually changes of less than 1% in prevalence; e.g., Yin and Kaftarian 1997) and significant changes in community leader prevention planning behavior (e.g., Mansergh et al. 1996).

## Policy Programs

Most studies of policy as a program modality for youth tend to emphasize tobacco or alcohol policy change at the local level of community or school. Lower adolescent smoking is associated with prevention rather than punishment orientation of school policy (Pentz et al. 1989a). Restricted access policy has an effect on decreasing adolescent smoking (A. Biglan, D. V. Ary, T. E. Duncan, et al: "A Randomized Control Trial of a Community Intervention to Prevent Adolescent Tobacco Use," manuscript under review). Policy change, in conjunction with a school program, mass media campaign, community activism or organization, or multicomponent community program, has produced significant re-

ductions in youth and young adult tobacco or alcohol use (A. Biglan, D. V. Ary, T. E. Duncan, et al: "A Randomized Control Trial of a Community Intervention to Prevent Adolescent Tobacco Use," manuscript under review; Hingson et al. 1996; Jason et al. 1991; Pentz 1998; Perry 1987; Perry et al. 1996; Yin and Kaftarian 1997).

## Multicomponent Programs

Multicomponent community-based programs should include substantial school programming to initiate behavior change, in conjunction with a community organization structure and process that promotes mass media programming and coverage, parent and adult education, and informal or formal policy change (Pentz 1998). Overall, results of school programs that included one or more additional program components have shown short-term effects on monthly smoking and drug use similar to those of comprehensive school programs that included a large number of sessions and boosters; however, effects of school plus community programs appeared to have a greater range of effects and larger long-term effects on heavier use rates, averaging 8% net reductions (Pentz 1995). Multicomponent programs are the only programs to have any effects on parent behavior.

Combining parent involvement through education or homework with a school program increases effects on parent involvement and youth behavior and parent behavior (Flay and Petraitis 1994). Overall, multicomponent prevention programs that include a school program may be more likely than school programs alone to produce a larger, synergistic or interactive effect rather than a simple additive effect on reducing drug use risk and subsequently drug use behavior.

## Comprehensive Community Programs

A comprehensive community-based prevention program attempts to incorporate all of the modalities that are hypothesized to affect youth drug use: school, parent, mass media, community organization, and community policy. Using all modalities, usually in a staggered sequence rather than simultaneously, maintains novelty and interest by a community over the long term, increases the potential to change community social norms for drug use, and generally provides greater dose-response and booster effects than would be expected to occur from single or nonsequenced modality programs (Pentz 1993a).

A tobacco prevention program in Oregon integrated school and parent tobacco education, community activism, local media campaigns, and restricted access policies; results showed effects on both adolescent use and prevention support behaviors of adults (A. Biglan, D. V. Ary, T. E. Duncan, et al: "A Randomized Control Trial of a Community Intervention to Prevent Adolescent Tobacco Use," manuscript under review). Two adult heart disease prevention programs that had a youth component incorporated school programming, parent involvement, policy change, community organization, and mass media campaigns and programming; both showed sustained effects on adolescent tobacco use through 5-year follow-up in Minnesota (Perry et al. 1992) and 8-year follow-up in Finland (Vartiainen et al. 1990). Two recent comprehensive programs focused on restricting youth access to tobacco (Forster et al. 1998) and alcohol (Perry et al. 1996). Both incorporated school and parent education, youth and community activism, and mass media coverage and campaigns to change policy and then to evaluate effects of policy on use. Both showed significant effects on adolescent use through early follow-ups. Finally, a comprehensive community program for drug abuse prevention staggered school, parent, mass media, community organization, and policy change programs over a 5-year period (Pentz et al. 1989b). Separate trials of this program in 26 communities in two metropolitan areas found sustained intervention effects on gateway and illicit drug use from early adolescence through early adulthood (age 23; Pentz 1998).

What does a comprehensive program look like? Taking the latter drug abuse prevention intervention as an example, each program component can be summarized. The school program consisted of 18 sessions delivered over 2 years in middle school by teachers with student peer leader assistance. Sessions were delivered in an interactive style, based on social learning theory (Bandura 1977). Sessions included resistance skills and assertiveness training, counteraction of social influences and perceived social norms, recognition of policy, and public commitment to avoid drug use. The parent program consisted of a 2-hour parent training session on building parent-child communication and prevention support skills and establishing clear family rules about drug use prevention. The parent program also included a school parent committee of principals, peer leaders, and trained parents who met regularly to plan enforcement and support activities for school drug-free zone policies. Community organization consisted of drug use epidemiology and prevention training of identified community leaders from the areas of business, mass media, youth service agencies, schools, parent groups, health care and treatment agencies, recreation, and policy/law enforcement, followed by their development of prevention campaigns, activities, referral services, and funding to support the other prevention programs. Policy change consisted of lobbying and initiatives developed by the community organization to revise and support restricted access and taxation policies for tobacco and alcohol. On average, an adolescent was exposed to approximately 30 hours of direct intervention over a 5-year period. If an adolescent's family included a community leader, the potential for direct contact was estimated to be up to 80 hours over a 5-year period. Results of this intervention have shown sustained net reductions of 2%–8% in tobacco, alcohol, marijuana, amphetamine, lysergic acid diethylamide (LSD), and cocaine use (Pentz 1998).

## Summary

The types of prevention programs are summarized in Table 48–1. Overall, the prevention literature suggests that most prevention programs are primary or universal. Fewer programs have been implemented with high-risk or drug-using youth. Specifically, there are gaps in research on policy, community organization, and comprehensive programs for high-risk and drug-using youth. Virtually no systematic studies of physician-delivered prevention programs have been done. However, using physicians as advisors to give feedback about drug use risk, models or trainers in a mass media program, or community leaders as part of community organization for drug use prevention may contribute to participation in prevention and recall of prevention messages, perhaps related to credibility of the physician as a model (Pentz 1993a). As a start, some research has been conducted on factors related to effective physician screening for drug use risk (e.g., Gabel et al. 1993).

In terms of effectiveness, social influences prevention programs produce significant effects on youth drug use. Programs aimed at protective factors affect parent-child communication, bonding, and intentions to use drugs; programs aimed at risk factors affect drug use resistance, drug use, and intentions. Approximately 30 hours of a well-implemented school program with boosters can yield sustained effects similar to those of 30 hours of a multicomponent or comprehensive community program, but the latter may have more generalizable effects across substances (cf, Botvin et al.

**Table 48–1.**    Summary of types of prevention programs

| Type | Risk | Primary modality | Summary of effectiveness |
|------|------|------------------|--------------------------|
| Universal | Protective and risk | School | Most prevalent type; social influences program effects last up to 5 years; 2%–6% net reduction in drug use |
| | Protective | Parent | Effects on parent-child interaction, communications; no effects on use as isolated program |
| | Risk | Media | Limited effects on attitude, intent to use; no effects on behavior as isolated program |
| | Risk | Community | Nonsignificant trend toward less use (0.1%) as isolated program |
| | Risk | Policy | No effects on youth in isolation from community organization |
| | Risk | Comprehensive | Program effects last 8 years or more; 2%–8% net reduction in gateway and hard drug use |
| Selective | Risk | School | 25%–40% reduction in use from programs; no experiential evidence of student assistance programs |
| | Protective | Parent | Effects on parent-child communication |
| | Risk | Media | Effects on recall, attitudes |
| | Risk | Community (recreational) | Short-term significant effects of social influences programs delivered in youth recreational settings |
| Indicated | Risk | School | 25%–40% reductions in use from behavioral skills/training or counseling |
| | Risk | Parent | No evidence of effect |
| | Risk | Media | No evidence of effect |
| | Direct | Community (Agency) | Suggestive evidence of reduced smoking from hospital- or clinic-based programs |

*Note.*    Most modalities reported here are based on studies that included one or more theories from P, S, or E levels. A missing modality or effectiveness reported as no evidence indicates a lack of research in the category.

1995; Perry et al. 1992). A single or multimodality program without a school program appears to have little or no effect on youth drug use. Results of research argue strongly for the use of comprehensive community-based prevention programs that include school programming and more research on the potential role of the physician in drug abuse prevention.

# References

Aktan GB, Kumpfer KL, Turner C: Effectiveness of a family skills training program for substance use prevention with inner city African-American families. Subst Use Misuse 31:157–175, 1996

Ary DV, Biglan A, Glasgow R, et al: The efficacy of social-influence prevention programs versus "standard care": are new initiatives needed? J Behav Med 13:281–296, 1990

Bachman JG, Johnston LD, O'Malley PM: Explaining the recent decline in cocaine use among young adults: further evidence that perceived risk and disapproval lead to reduced drug use. J Health Soc Behav 31:173–184, 1991

Bandura A: Social Learning Theory. Englewood Cliffs, NJ, Prentice-Hall, 1977

Botvin GJ, Baker E, Dusenbury L, et al: Long-term follow-up results of a randomized drug abuse prevention trial in a white middle-class population. JAMA 273:1106–1112, 1995

Brook JS, Nomura C, Cohen P: A network of influences on adolescent drug involvement: neighborhood, school, peer, and family. Genetic, Social, and General Psychology Monographs 115:123–145, 1989

Bruininks RH, Frenzel M, Kelly A: Integrating services: the case for better links to schools. J Sch Health 64:242–248, 1994

Council on Scientific Affairs: Providing medical services through school-based health programs. J Sch Health 60:87–91, 1990

Dishion TJ, Andrews DW: Preventing escalation in problem behaviors with high-risk young adolescents: immediate and 1-year outcomes. J Consult Clin Psychol 63:538–548, 1995

Donaldson SI, Graham JW, Hansen WB: Testing the generalizability of intervening mechanism theories: understanding the effects of adolescent drug use prevention interventions. J Behav Med 17:195–216, 1994

Donohew J, Sypher HE, Bukowski WJ: Persuasive communication and drug abuse prevention. Hillsdale, NJ, Lawrence Erlbaum, 1991

Dryfoos JG, Dryfoos G: Preventing substance use: rethinking strategies. Am J Public Health 83:793–795, 1993

Dusenbury L, Falco M: Eleven components of effective drug abuse prevention curricula. J Sch Health 65:420–425, 1995

Eggert LL, Thompson EA, Herting JR, et al: Preventing adolescent drug abuse and high school dropout through an intensive school-based social network development program. American Journal of Health Promotion 8(3):202–215, 1994

Ellickson PL, Bell RM, McGuigan K: Preventing adolescent drug use: long-term results of a junior high program. Am J Public Health 83:856–861, 1993

Ennett ST, Tobler NS, Ringwalt CL, et al: How effective is drug abuse resistance education? A meta-analysis of Project DARE outcome evaluations. Am J Public Health 84:1394–1401, 1994

Fishbein M, Ajzen I: Belief, Attitude, Intention, and Behavior: An Introduction to Theory and Research. Reading, MA, Addison-Wesley, 1975

Flay BR, Petraitis J: The theory of triadic influence: a new theory of health behavior with implications for preventive interventions. Advances in Medical Sociology 4:19–44, 1994

Flay BR, Pentz MA, Johnson CA, et al: Reaching children with mass media health promotion programs: the relative effectiveness of an advertising campaign, a community-based program, and a school-based program, in Health Education and the Media, Vol 2. Edited by Leather DS. Oxford, England, Pergamon, 1985

Flynn BS, Worden JK, Secker-Walker RH, et al: Prevention of cigarette smoking through mass media intervention and school programs. Am J Public Health 82:827–834, 1992

Forster JL, Murray D, Wolfson M, et al: The effects of community policies to reduce youth access to tobacco. Am J Public Health 88:1193–1198, 1998

Gabel LL, Siegal HA, Hostetler J: Preventing substance abuse: an interview paradigm. J Fam Pract 37:503–505, 1993

Hansen WB: School-based substance abuse prevention: a review of the state of the art in curriculum, 1980–1990. Health Education Research 7:403–430, 1992

Hawkins JD, Catalano RF, Morrison DM, et al: The Seattle Social Development Project: effects of the first four years on protective factors and problem behaviors, in The Prevention of Antisocial Behavior in Children. Edited by McCord J, Tremblay R. New York, Guilford, 1992, pp 139–161

Hingson R, McGovern T, Howland J, et al: Reducing alcohol-impaired driving in Massachusetts: the Saving Lives program. Am J Public Health 86:791–797, 1996

Holder HD, Wallack L: Contemporary perspectives for preventing alcohol problems: an empirically-derived model. Journal on Public Health Policy 7:324, 1986

Jason LA, Li PY, Anes MD, et al: Active enforcement of cigarette control laws in the prevention of cigarette sales to minors. JAMA 266:3159–3161, 1991

Jessor R: Problem behavior and developmental transition in adolescence. J Sch Health 52:295–300, 1982

Johnson CA, Pentz M, Weber MD, et al: The relative effectiveness of comprehensive community programming for drug abuse prevention with risk and low risk adolescents. J Consult Clin Psychol 58:447–456, 1990

Johnston LD, O'Malley PM, Bachman JG: National Survey Results on Drug Use From the Monitoring the Future Study, 1975–1996, Vol 1: Secondary School Students (NIH Publ No 94-3809). Rockville, MD, U.S. Department of Health and Human Services, 1997

Kaminer Y: Adolescent substance abuse, in The American Psychiatric Press Textbook of Substance Abuse Treatment. Edited by Galanter M, Kleber H. Washington, DC, American Psychiatric Press, 1994, pp 415–437

Klitzner M, Schwartz RH, Gruenewald P, et al: Screening for risk factors for adolescent alcohol and drug use. American Journal of Diseases of Children 141:45–49, 1987

Kosterman R, Hawkins JD, Spoth R, et al: Effects of a preventive parent-training intervention on observed family interactions: proximal outcomes from preparing for the drug free years. Journal of Community Psychology 25:277–292, 1997

Kumpfer KL: Prevention of alcohol and drug abuse: a critical review of risk factors and prevention strategies, in Prevention of Mental Disorders, Alcohol and Other Drug Use in Children and Adolescents (Monograph 2). Edited by Shaffer D, Philips I, Enzer NB. Rockville, MD, Office of Substance Abuse Prevention, 1989

Lorch E, Palmgreen P, Donohew L, et al: Program context, sensation seeking, and attention to televised anti-drug public service announcements. Human Communication Research 20:390–412, 1994

MacKinnon DP, Johnson CA, Pentz MA, et al: Mediating mechanisms in a school-based drug prevention program: first year effects of the Midwestern Prevention Project. Health Psychol 10:164–172, 1991

Mansergh G, Rohrbach L, Montgomery SB, et al: Process evaluation of community coalitions for alcohol and other drug prevention: comparison of two models. Journal of Community Psychology 24:118–135, 1996

Martin CS, Kaczynski NA, Maisto SA, et al: Polydrug use in adolescent drinkers with and without DSM-IV alcohol abuse and dependence. Alcohol Clin Exp Res 20:1099–1108, 1996

McGovern JP, DuPont RL: Student assistance programs: an important approach to drug abuse prevention. J Sch Health 61:260–264, 1991

Murray DM, Prokhorov AV, Harty KC: Effects of a statewide antismoking campaign on mass media messages and smoking beliefs. Prev Med 23:54–60, 1994

Pentz MA: Benefits of integrating strategies in different settings, in American Medical Association State-of-the-Art Conference on Adolescent Health Promotion: Proceedings (NCEMCH Res Monogr). Edited by Elster A, Panzarine S, Holt K. Arlington, VA, National Center for Education in Maternal and Child Health, 1993a, pp 15–34

Pentz MA: Primary prevention of adolescent drug abuse, in Applied Developmental Psychology. Edited by Fisher CB, Lerner RM. New York, McGraw-Hill, 1993b, pp 435–474

Pentz MA: The school-community interface in comprehensive school health education, in Institute of Medicine Annual Report, Committee on Comprehensive School Health Programs, Institute of Medicine, Bethesda, MD. Edited by Stansfield S. Washington, DC, National Academy Press, 1995

Pentz MA: Preventing Drug Abuse Through the Community: Multi-Component Programs Make the Difference (NIDA Res Monogr). Edited by Sloboda Z, Hansen WB. Washington, DC, National Institute on Drug Abuse, 1998

Pentz MA: Prevention aimed at individuals: an integrative transactional perspective, in Addictions: A Comprehensive Guidebook for Practitioners. Edited by McCrady BS, Epstein EE. New York, Oxford University Press (in press)

Pentz MA, Trebow E: Implementation issues in drug abuse prevention research, in Drug Abuse Prevention Intervention Research: Methodological Issues (NIDA Res Monogr Ser 107; DHHS Publ No ADM-91-1761). Edited by Leukfeld C, Bukoski WJ. Washington, DC, National Institute on Drug Abuse, 1991, pp 123–139

Pentz MA, Trebow E: Implementation issues in drug abuse prevention research. Subst Use Misuse 32:1655–1660, 1997

Pentz MA, Brannon BR, Charlin CV, et al: The power of policy: the relationship of smoking policy to adolescent smoking. Am J Public Health 79:857–862, 1989a

Pentz MA, Dwyer JH, MacKinnon DP, et al: A multi-community trial for primary prevention of adolescent drug abuse: effects on drug use prevalence. JAMA 261:3259–3266, 1989b

Perry CL: Results of prevention programs with adolescents. Drug Alcohol Depend 20:13–19, 1987

Perry CL, Jessor R: The concept of health promotion and the prevention of adolescent drug abuse. Health Educ Quarterly 12:170–184, 1985

Perry CL, Kelder SH, Murray DM, et al: Community-wide smoking prevention: long-term outcomes of the Minnesota Heart Health Program and the Class of 1989 Study. Am J Public Health 82:1210–1216, 1992

Perry CL, Williams CL, Veblen-Mortenson S, et al: Project Northland: outcomes of a community wide alcohol use prevention program during early adolescence. Am J Public Health 86:956–965, 1996

Pierce JP, Evans N, Farkas AJ, et al: Tobacco Use in California: An Evaluation of the Tobacco Control Program 1989–1993. La Jolla, University of California, San Diego, 1994

Resnicow K, Botvin G: School-based substance use prevention programs: why do effects decay? Prev Med 22:484–490, 1993

Rogers EV: The impact of drug abuse prevention programs: Project Star in Kansas City, in Organizational Aspects of Health Campaigns. Edited by Backer TE, Rogers EM. Newbury Park, CA, Sage Publications, 1992

Rohrbach LA, Hodgson CS, Broder BI, et al: Parental participation in drug abuse prevention: results from the Midwestern Prevention Project. Journal of Research on Adolescence 4:295–317, 1994

Saxe L, Reber E, Hallfors D, et al: Think global, act local: assessing the impact of community-based substance abuse prevention. Evaluation and Program Planning (in press)

St. Pierre TL, Kaltreider DL, Mark NN, et al: Drug prevention in a community setting: a longitudinal study of the relative effectiveness of a three-year primary prevention program in boys and girls clubs across the nation. Am J Community Psychol 20:673–706, 1992

Tobler NS: Drug prevention programs can work: research findings. J Addict Dis 11:1–28, 1992

Vartiainen E, Fallonen U, McAllister A-L, et al: Eight-year follow-up results of an adolescent smoking prevention program: the North Karelia Youth Project. Am J Public Health 60:76–78, 1990

Yin RK, Kaftarian SJ: What the national cross-site evaluation is learning about CSAP's community partnerships, in Secretary's Youth Substance Abuse Prevention Initiative: Resource Papers (SAMHSA Prepublication Documents). Edited by Chavez NR, O'Neill SJ. Washington, DC, U.S. Department of Health and Human Services, 1997, pp 179–196

# Substance Abuse Treatment Under Managed Care: A Provider Perspective

Arnold M. Washton, Ph.D.
Richard A. Rawson, Ph.D.

A tidal wave of managed care is reshaping the landscape of health care delivery systems in the United States, and the substance abuse treatment system is certainly no exception. Substance abuse treatment providers everywhere are scrambling to adapt their services to the new managed care environment, especially with the rapid expansion of managed care from commercially insured populations into publicly funded programs such as Medicaid and Medicare (Moss 1995). The driving force behind these changes is the unwillingness and/or inability of private industry and government to pay the current cost of behavioral health care services.

Managed care became a clearly visible force in the substance abuse treatment arena in the late 1980s, primarily in the private sector delivery system. The stated goals of managed care are to improve access to and quality of care and to reduce costs. But exactly how this can be accomplished without dismantling or destroying the current substance abuse treatment delivery system is unclear. Certainly, some positive changes have occurred as a result of managed care's influence on the delivery system. However, managed care has also created serious problems for both providers and patients.

In this chapter, we describe selected aspects of managed care's effects—both positive and negative—on the substance abuse treatment provider system. Although we have attempted to present a balanced view, we do not portend to be impartial because we are substance abuse treatment services providers, and our perspec-

tives are unavoidably influenced by our experiences with managed care and those of numerous colleagues.

## Strategies and Structure of Managed Behavioral Care

One difficulty in describing the effect of managed care on the treatment delivery system is defining the term *managed care* because managed care organizations exist in various forms. In this chapter, the term *managed care* is used to describe organizations that directly influence access to care, appropriateness of care, type and level of care, and the overall amount and cost of care delivered to patients. The most common forms of managed care in behavioral health care (i.e., substance abuse and mental health delivery systems) are 1) health maintenance organizations (HMOs) and 2) specialized managed behavioral health care companies. The latter are frequently hired by HMOs, private employers, or government agencies to manage all aspects of the utilization, delivery, and payment of behavioral health care services for a defined population of enrollees. Strategies used by managed care organizations to exert influence on service delivery include

1. Selecting providers in a specific geographic area to be included on their panel of preferred providers, who are eligible to receive patient referrals and financial reimbursement for their services

2. Establishing procedures that govern patient assessment, referral, and placement into treatment
3. Monitoring the delivery of ongoing care with utilization management, quality improvement, and concurrent (ongoing) case review procedures
4. Using various authorization and reimbursement strategies that determine whether and how providers are compensated for care delivery

These strategies are common to virtually all managed care models, although the extent to which they are used may vary greatly among managed care organizations.

Financing strategies used by managed care organizations are designed to reduce treatment costs presumably without reducing the quality of care. In *discounted fee-for-service* (FFS) arrangements, managed care organizations reimburse providers according to a predetermined schedule of fees for agreed-on services. Often, provider fees are reduced 20%–40% below standard rates to establish a contractual agreement. In FFS agreements, managed care assumes all of the financial risk, and the provider assumes none. The provider's compensation in an FFS contract is directly related to volume: the more services delivered, the larger the provider's revenues. Accordingly, in FFS contracts, managed care organizations usually exert the most vigilant and aggressive control over service delivery, and with their inherently opposing financial incentives, it is not surprising that FFS arrangements engender the most conflict and disagreement between providers and managed care organizations. A provider's request for managed care organization authorization of what he or she perceives as clinically necessary treatment services for a given patient may be at odds with the managed care organization's utilization management criteria and the managed care organization's desire to contain costs.

In *risk-sharing arrangements*, the managed care organization and the provider each accept partial responsibility for both the financial risks and the potential rewards involved in providing care to a defined population. These arrangements more closely align the incentives of the provider with those of the managed care organization and may engender more synergistic (less adversarial) interaction between the parties. One type of partial risk-sharing arrangement is a *case rate*, in which the provider receives a fixed fee (case rate) for an episode of care regardless of the type, intensity, length, and amount of treatment that the patient receives in that episode of care. If the provider is able to treat the patient in less time than the average length of stay on which the case rate is based, the provider bene-

fits from the cost savings. On the other hand, if treatment exceeds the average length of stay–based case rate, the provider absorbs the additional cost. This arrangement gives the provider a financial incentive to contain costs. To prevent or discourage delivery of inadequate care, case rates typically include a "warranty" provision stipulating that if, after completing a defined episode of care, the patient reenters treatment within a specified postdischarge time span (e.g., 6–12 months), the provider receives no additional compensation for treating that patient.

Another form of risk sharing is the *capitation* arrangement. In a capitation agreement, the provider assumes some degree of financial risk with the managed care organization, or in some cases the provider takes virtually all of the risk. The provider typically receives a fixed fee "per member per month" as ongoing compensation for making care available to a defined member population that resides within a specified geographic area (usually defined by zip codes). The managed care organization may partially protect the capitated provider with a financial stop-loss contingency that limits the provider's maximum financial outlay in the event that utilization rates unexpectedly exceed a predefined level.

## Effect of Managed Care on the Structure of the Delivery System

Managed care has significantly affected the structure of the substance abuse treatment delivery system in several important respects. Some of the most visible and noteworthy of these changes are outlined below.

### Outpatient Services as the Hub of the New Delivery System

Before managed care, inpatient programs, including free-standing rehabilitation facilities and hospital-based specialty units, were the focal point of the substance abuse delivery system. These inpatient programs were accepted by many as the de facto standard of care for the treatment of substance abuse disorders. Outpatient programs were viewed as aftercare support services and/or less effective substitutes for the preferred residentially based programs.

Under managed care, the centerpiece of the new substance abuse delivery system and treatment site of first choice is the outpatient facility. With expanded access to a variety of outpatient services, including intensive outpatient programs and outpatient detoxification services, managed care can more effectively reduce inpatient admissions and shorten inpatient stays. The essential role of outpatient substance abuse services in the reconfigured delivery system represents a dramatic turnabout from pre–managed care days when these services were not only scarce but also rarely recognized or reimbursed by third-party payers (Washton 1997).

## Integrated Delivery Systems

Whether created by a single provider organization or by a partnership between two or more providers, an integrated delivery system is a horizontally integrated continuum or network of care that offers "one-stop shopping" for managed care organizations and other purchasers of behavioral health care services (Moss 1995). An "ideal" integrated delivery system has centralized intake and case management; easy access to crisis intervention services; and clinical protocols for matching patients to the most appropriate, least restrictive level of care and for determining length of stay in each level. The integrated delivery system not only ensures that patients have easy access to treatment but also enhances continuity between different levels of care. The reduced fragmentation between different services prevents patients from "falling between the cracks" when, for example, they are transferred (stepped up or down) from one level of care to the next. An integrated delivery system for substance abuse treatment should incorporate a variety of modalities and levels of care, including

- Outpatient assessment and crisis intervention services
- Outpatient medical detoxification services
- Low-, intermediate-, and high-intensity outpatient programs
- Preparatory motivational counseling
- Outpatient relapse prevention program
- Outpatient dual-diagnosis programs that combine substance abuse and psychiatric services
- Day treatment or partial hospitalization programs for both substance abuse and dual diagnosis
- Inpatient assessment and crisis stabilization services
- Inpatient medical detoxification services
- Inpatient dual-diagnosis services
- Adolescent and family treatment services

It is conceivable that if highly efficient and effective integrated delivery systems become widely available,

this system of care will replace the existing patchwork of nonintegrated providers and programs.

## Integration of Substance Abuse and Mental Health Services

There is increasing recognition of the need for specialized treatment services for patients with concurrent (coexisting) substance abuse and mental health problems. Historically, these so-called dual-diagnosis patients have not been especially welcomed or treated appropriately as a result of rigid separation of substance abuse and mental health treatment systems and because of a general lack of cross-training by clinicians in those systems. Recently, both clinical and financial pressure has increased to integrate substance abuse and mental health services and to create specialized dual-diagnosis services. Clinical studies continue to document the strikingly high comorbidity of substance abuse and mental health disorders and the increased effectiveness of an integrated multidisciplinary treatment that addresses both problems (Beeder and Millman 1995; Mirin and Weiss 1991; Ross et al. 1988). On the financial side, contracts in which the managed care organization is at risk for both substance abuse and mental health services (an increasingly common occurrence) provide greater incentive to identify and competently address the needs of patients with co-occurring disorders, preferably within a single facility and by a single well-coordinated team of cross-trained clinicians who can appropriately treat both problems simultaneously.

## Linkage Between Substance Abuse and Medical Services

Studies have shown repeatedly that alcohol and substance abuse contribute to increased use of many different types of health care services and, more important, that early identification and treatment of these problems significantly reduce unnecessary overutilization of medical services and resulting elevated costs (Holder and Blose 1992; Institute of Medicine 1990). There is heightened interest, particularly among HMOs, in linking primary health care with behavioral health care services, including substance abuse treatment. In the public sector, government-sponsored initiatives are actively encouraging linkages between substance abuse treatment and medical care services to facilitate access to essential services such as prenatal care, AIDS treatment, and screening for infectious diseases. A key to improved linkage is more reliable identification and screening of substance abuse problems in primary health care settings. Primary care physicians have a pivotal role to play in prevention and treatment of alcohol and drug abuse problems and, with specific training, are in an excellent position to identify and clinically manage current or emerging problems with alcohol or drugs. Making substance abuse treatment services more available in primary health care settings (e.g., hospitals, clinics, and group practices) as well as making general medical services more available in specialized substance abuse treatment facilities may help to achieve the desired integration.

## Partnerships Between Public and Private Sector Providers

The boundaries between historically separate public and private sector substance abuse delivery systems are becoming blurred as a result of the nationwide movement by state governments to place Medicaid and other publicly funded health care services under the control of managed care. Substance abuse treatment providers in both the public and the private sectors have much to offer one another because they have complementary strengths and skills, all of which are increasingly needed for survival in the rapidly changing managed care environment (Rawson et al. 1996). For example, private sector providers typically have extensive experience with managed care, with computerized billing and collection procedures, and with services geared mainly toward employed patients who have commercial insurance plans. Their facilities are typically located in middle- or working-class neighborhoods, business districts, or corporate and professional environments. Conversely, public sector providers have extensive experience serving chronically unemployed, chronically ill, homeless, and other underserved populations covered by Medicaid, Medicare, and other public funding sources. They also have experience coordinating medical, legal, child care, vocational, and other essential "wraparound" services with their substance abuse treatment services. Their facilities are typically located in inner-city or rural poverty areas where persons requiring these types of services reside. Increasing recognition of these complementary strengths, coupled with mounting financial pressure to serve both populations, is rapidly giving rise to various types of partnership and joint-venture arrangements between public and private sector substance abuse providers.

## Treatment Innovations

Managed care has been a strong catalyst for the development of clinical innovations aimed at improving both the effectiveness and the efficiency of substance abuse treatment delivery. The process has been accelerated by a growing need to deliver more accessible, clinically efficacious, and cost-effective treatment to an increasingly heterogeneous patient population, especially in outpatient settings. Several noteworthy treatment innovations to appear in recent years are described below. Some have developed as a direct result of managed care's influence on the delivery system, whereas others have emerged independently of managed care but appear to be particularly well suited to meet the demands of the managed care environment.

### Flexible Patient-Driven Models of Care

A "one size fits all" mentality and rigid program configurations have dominated substance abuse treatment for decades. Traditionally, patients have been required to fit the program rather than vice versa. Under pressure from managed care, these models are giving way to the development of variable-length and multiple-intensity services with defined criteria for placement of patients into the clinically most appropriate level of care along with objective indicators of patient progress.

### Outpatient Crisis Intervention Services to Reduce Unnecessary Hospitalization

Patients in acute crises are those most likely to end up unnecessarily in a hospital bed or other inpatient facility. Rapid access to outpatient crisis services, such as face-to-face evaluation, outpatient medical detoxification, and outpatient psychiatric intervention, increases the likelihood of averting a more costly hospital stay. These rapid response services are very attractive to managed care organizations because they offer the potential for substantially reducing hospital admissions and associated costs, while providing timely crisis management services.

Under pressure from managed care organizations to reduce inpatient admissions and costs wherever possible, medical detoxification from alcohol and other substances in outpatient settings is increasingly being used. Careful patient selection criteria and ongoing coordination of medical and psychosocial interventions are essential to ensure that outpatient detoxification is both safe and effective. Recently, practice guidelines and clinical protocols for outpatient medical detoxification have been published by the American Society of Addiction Medicine (1997), the American Psychiatric Association (1995), and the federal Center for Substance Abuse Treatment (1995).

## Brief Treatment Approaches

Recent evidence suggests that many substance abusers do not require intensive or protracted treatment (Hester and Bien 1995; Miller 1990). Clearly, some substance-using individuals can and do show significant clinical benefit from short-term, time-limited interventions that are much briefer and less intense than the most commonly used substance abuse treatment regimens. The key to successful use of brief interventions is proper patient selection. Brief treatment approaches have been developed primarily for use with problem drinkers who do not meet clinical criteria for alcohol dependence. Similarly, brief approaches do not appear to be well suited for cocaine- or heroin-dependent patients, except perhaps as preparatory strategies to engage and motivate patients who might need, but are not yet ready to accept, more intensive treatment (Martin et al. 1996; Obert et al. 1997; Washton, in press).

## Motivation-Enhancement Techniques

The cost-effectiveness of substance abuse services is adversely affected by failure to engage patients in treatment and by premature dropout before the patient has received a clinically adequate "dose" of treatment. Studies of motivation enhancement (Miller and Rollnick 1991) indicate that the traditional confrontation-of-denial approach may actually cause or exacerbate dropout. Motivational techniques are designed to maximize the likelihood that patients will enter into, participate in, and complete an agreed-on episode of treatment. These strategies provide substance abuse clinicians with a useful way to reconceptualize and revamp their approach to patients previously viewed as "resistant," "unmotivated," "noncompliant," or "just not ready" for change.

## Stage-Specific Treatment Interventions

There is increasing recognition that the types of therapeutic interventions that work best in substance abuse treatment often depend on where the patient is in the process of change (recovery). Treatment interventions that are mismatched to the patient's stage of recovery

are likely to be ineffective and perhaps even harmful (i.e., countertherapeutic). Individuals who are attempting to give up alcohol and other substances progress through a series of definable stages as they move from active use toward sustained abstinence and recovery. Accordingly, it is becoming common practice to segment substance abuse treatment programs into several components or stages, each focusing on specific tasks and goals most relevant to that particular stage, especially in outpatient programs in which the natural progression is from stopping all substance use, to securing abstinence, and eventually to prolonging or maintaining abstinence. Guidelines and procedures for delivering preparatory (prerecovery) and other stage-specific interventions are described elsewhere (Martin et al. 1996; Washton, in press).

## Pharmacological Treatments

At least several new pharmacological treatments may increase the potential for improved clinical outcomes. Studies indicate that naltrexone, an opioid antagonist, can reduce relapse rates in alcoholic individuals (O'Malley et al. 1992; Volpicelli et al. 1992). The 1993 U.S. Food and Drug Administration (FDA) approval of the long-acting opiate agonist or L-$\alpha$-acetylmethadol (LAAM) offers a new therapeutic option for opioid maintenance therapy (Ling et al. 1994). For many patients, LAAM is as clinically efficacious as methadone, and its 72-hour half-life eliminates the need for daily medication ingestion and daily clinic visits. Buprenorphine, although not yet approved by the FDA for routine clinical use, may offer another effective treatment option for both opioid maintenance and detoxification (Ling et al. 1994). Developing medications that can suppress cocaine cravings has been designated as a high priority for government-funded addiction research, and investigators are optimistic that new agents will be available in the near future to enhance the clinical efficacy of cocaine treatment (Leshner 1997).

## Problems Between Managed Care and Treatment Providers

### Provider Resistance to Change

Before managed care appeared, providers controlled where, when, how, and for how long treatment was delivered. When managed care organizations began requiring providers to share with them control of clinical decision making, many providers found this loss of total control unacceptable. Provider resistance to change can be attributed in part to a fundamental clash of ideology and financial incentives with managed care and to providers' tenaciously held traditions and deeply entrenched belief systems about how to treat substance abuse disorders. Accordingly, acceptance and implementation of treatment innovations have been relatively slow. Providers who have resisted collaborative work with managed care organizations to reengineer the delivery of substance abuse treatment services have contributed substantially to antagonism between providers and managed care. Additional problems in the managed care–provider interface, such as those mentioned below, have further exacerbated these joint feelings of antagonism.

## Provider Concerns About Managed Care Organizations' Overemphasis on Cost

Providers routinely complain that although managed care organizations claim that their primary goal is to improve quality and reduce costs, the actual behavior of managed care organizations indicates that their overriding concern is cost. There is ample reason to characterize the current managed care–dominated marketplace as price-driven. When the managed care organization has multiple providers to choose from in a geographic area, referrals often go to the lowest bidder with little, if any, concern about quality of care beyond minimally acceptable standards. To maintain a stream of patients and revenue, providers often enter into managed care contracts in which they are actually paid *less* than it costs them to deliver a clinically viable service (i.e., the provider agrees to operate at a financial loss and essentially subsidizes each patient's treatment). Providers accept these financially self-defeating agreements because they are typically offered these rates by managed care organizations on a "take it or leave it" basis. Although managed care organization representatives tout the professional expertise and quality of their provider network to their customers, there is little indication in contract negotiations that quality of care rivals concerns about cost. Many providers have found it difficult to adjust to working in a delivery system that places such heavy emphasis on cost. To date, very few treatment providers have been asked by managed care to document their clinical outcomes or have been chosen to join a preferred provider panel based on empirical evidence documenting the clinical efficacy of their services.

## Managed Care Organizations' Negative Attitudes and Behavior Toward Providers

Many providers feel bullied, devalued, and disrespected by managed care as a result of not only severe cost-containment pressures but also the way they are treated by managed care organization case managers with whom they must frequently interact. Highly experienced, competent, well-trained clinicians frequently have their clinical judgment called into question and have their treatment recommendations substantially altered or flatly denied by managed care organization case managers who have no clinical or graduate training whatsoever (in many managed care organizations, the minimum qualification for a case manager position is a bachelor's degree in a health-related field). Even when the case manager does happen to be a licensed mental health professional, this person typically has little or no training or clinical experience in substance abuse treatment per se. Furthermore, it is not uncommon for managed care organization case managers to be abrupt, rude, and impatient in their interactions with clinicians. Certainly, the reverse happens as well (i.e., frustrated clinicians are quite capable of venting their hostility toward managed care on case managers).

## Claims Payment Problems

Long delays in obtaining reimbursement for services, the norm for providers working with managed care organizations, put severe strains on providers' cash flow and contribute to their financial duress. Time-consuming preauthorization, reauthorization, and case review procedures requiring repeated telephone conversations and mounds of supporting paperwork drive up the cost of delivering care. The lethal combination of increased overhead, reduced fees, and strained cash flow is a prescription for disaster that can and does send many providers into financial crisis and, in some cases, insolvency. When providers inquire about unpaid, long-overdue claims, managed care organizations often tell them that the claims either were never received or are held up in a review process. Claims are frequently lost or remain chronically unpaid in an abyss of inefficient, bureaucratic claims processing. Ironically, these highly inefficient claims processing operations (seemingly incapable of issuing timely payments) are nonetheless very efficient at finding reasons to deny requests for reimbursement. Especially frustrating is retroactive denial of payment: the provider is informed after the fact and despite having procured the required preauthorization from the managed care company to admit a patient into treatment that the patient's benefits were retroactively canceled by his or her employer and that no reimbursement will be forthcoming for any treatment that has already been delivered. The managed care company typically takes no responsibility for this problem and offers no recourse, blaming the patient's employer for delays in providing updated information on employee benefit eligibility. The provider is left in the untenable position of having to ask the patient to pay for the services (usually a futile endeavor), to treat the patient at no charge (a financial strain), or to terminate the patient's treatment (an ethical dilemma). Usually, the provider ends up absorbing the unreimbursed costs.

## Final Comment

Improved access to treatment and quality of care cannot be realized if competent substance abuse providers are forced either to operate under severe financial duress with inadequate resources or to close their doors. Meanwhile, substance abuse providers who hope to survive under managed care must work hard and fast to reengineer both clinical and administrative aspects of their service delivery system. This is no small task, considering that the typical substance abuse provider (whether public or private) lacks the financial resources and/or business savvy needed to implement the necessary changes rapidly.

The managed care industry is largely unregulated and thus has almost unlimited control over provider delivery systems. Ideally, managed care and treatment providers should be able to work cooperatively and synergistically with each other to achieve the ultimate goal of highly accessible, efficient, and effective treatment at reduced cost. Proliferation of integrated delivery systems in combination with more widespread use of risk-sharing financial arrangements appears to hold promise for accomplishing this goal.

## References

American Psychiatric Association: Practice guideline for the treatment of patients with substance use disorders: alcohol, cocaine, opioids. Am J Psychiatry 152 (11 suppl): 1–59, 1995

American Society of Addiction Medicine: Detoxification: principles and protocols, in Topics in Addiction Medicine, Vol 1, No 2. Chevy Chase, MD, American Society of Addiction Medicine, 1997

Beeder AB, Millman RB: Treatment strategies for comorbid disorders: psychopathology and substance abuse, in Psychotherapy and Substance Abuse: A Practitioner's Handbook. Edited by Washton AM. New York, Guilford, 1995, pp 76–102

Center for Substance Abuse Treatment: Detoxification From Alcohol and Other Drugs (Treatment Improvement Protocol Series [TIPS], No 19; DHHS Publ No SMA 93). Rockville, MD, U.S. Department of Health and Human Services, 1995

Hester RK, Bien TH: Brief treatment, in Psychotherapy and Substance Abuse: A Practitioner's Handbook. Edited by Washton AM. New York, Guilford, 1995, pp 204–222

Holder HD, Blose JO: The reduction of health care costs associated with alcoholism treatment. J Stud Alcohol 53: 293–302, 1992

Institute of Medicine, National Academy of Sciences: Broadening the Base of Treatment for Alcohol Problems. Washington, DC, National Academy Press, 1990

Leshner AI: Drug abuse and addiction treatment research: the next generation. Arch Gen Psychiatry 54:105–108, 1997

Ling W, Rawson RA, Compton MA: Substitution pharmacotherapies for opioid addiction: from methadone to LAAM to buprenorphine. J Psychoactive Drugs 26:119–128, 1994

Martin K, Giannandrea P, Rogers B, et al: Group intervention with pre-recovery patients. J Subst Abuse Treat 13:31–41, 1996

Miller WR: Alcoholism treatment alternatives: what works?, in Treatment Choices for Alcoholism and Substance Abuse. Edited by Milkman HB, Sederer HI. Lexington, MA, Lexington Books, 1990, pp 253–264

Miller WR, Rollnick S (eds): Motivational Interviewing: Preparing People to Change Addictive Behaviors. New York, Guilford, 1991

Mirin SM, Weiss RD: Substance abuse and mental illness, in Clinical Textbook of Addictive Disorders. Edited by Francis RJ, Miller SI. New York, Guilford, 1991, pp 271–298

Moss S: Managed care and substance abuse treatment: trends into the 21st century. The Counselor, September/October 1995, pp 8–11

Obert JL, Rawson RA, Miotto K: Substance abuse treatment for "hazardous" users. J Subst Abuse Treat 29:291–298, 1997

O'Malley SS, Jaffe A, Chang G, et al: Naltrexone and coping skills therapy for alcohol dependence: a controlled study. Arch Gen Psychiatry 49:881–887, 1992

Rawson RA, Marinelli-Casey P, Washton AM: Integrating the delivery of privately and publicly funded substance abuse services. Behavioral Healthcare Tomorrow, April 1996, pp 32–36

Ross HE, Glaser FB, Germanson T: The prevalence of psychiatric disorders in patients with alcohol and other drug problems. Arch Gen Psychiatry 45:1023–1031, 1988

Volpicelli JR, Alterman AI, Hagashida M, et al: Naltrexone in the treatment of alcohol dependence. Arch Gen Psychiatry 49:876–880, 1992

Washton AM: Evolution of intensive outpatient treatment (IOP) as a "legitimate" treatment modality, in Intensive Outpatient Treatment for the Addictions. Edited by Gottheil E. New York, Haworth Medical Press, 1997, pp xix–xxv

Washton AM: Outpatient groups at different stages of substance abuse treatment: preparation, initial abstinence, and relapse prevention, in The Group Psychotherapy of Substance Abuse. Edited by Brook DW, Spitz HI. Washington, DC, American Psychiatric Press (in press)

# Index

*Page numbers printed in **boldface** type refer to figures or tables.*

## A

AA. *See* Alcoholics Anonymous
Abortion, 493
Abscesses, 256
Abstinence
    effects in adolescents, 469–470
    family systems to achieve and
        maintain, 390–391
    as goal of relapse prevention, 354,
        358, 360–361
    as goal of therapeutic communities,
        447, 448
    after inpatient treatment, 417–418
    maximizing motivation for, 89–90
    network therapy for maintenance of,
        330
    pharmacotherapy for alcoholic
        patient during, 155–160
    protracted abstinence syndrome,
        90
    psychiatric disorders persisting after,
        91, 475, 477
    rebuilding substance-free lifestyle,
        90
    as requirement for psychodynamic
        psychotherapy, 311, 314, 315
    sense of perceived control
        experienced during, 355
    as treatment goal, 89, 353, 414
Abstinence model, 353
Abstinence violation effect (AVE),
    358, **361**, 363
ABT-431, 26
Abusive behavior, alcoholism and, 162
Acamprosate, 94, 130, 156, 337
Acceptance
    of diagnosis of substance abuse,
        316, 317
    maintaining accepting atmosphere
        for group therapy, 374
    of responsibility for one's own
        actions, 314, 375
    of self in recovery, 317

Access to treatment, 80
Acetaldehyde, 285
Acetaminophen, 514, **514, 515**
Acetorphan, 267
Acetylcholine, 206
L-α-Acetylmethadol (LAAM), 12, 77,
    277–278, 549
    active metabolites of, 278
    analgesics for patients on, 278
    compared with methadone
        maintenance, 136–137,
        278, 549
    compliance with, 137
    dosage and administration of,
        277–278
    drug interactions with, 278
    eligibility criteria for treatment with,
        278
    overdose of, 18
    pharmacology of, 277–278
    during pregnancy, 278
    remissions during therapy with,
        111
    side effects of, 278
    withdrawal from, 278
Acquired immunodeficiency syndrome.
    *See* Human immunodeficiency
    virus infection
ACT (assertive community treatment),
    444
ACTH. *See* Adrenocorticotropic
    hormone
Actron (ketoprofen), **514**
Actualization techniques, 395–396
Acupuncture
    for alcohol abuse, 132, 156
    for opioid detoxification, 267–268
    for pain management, **513**
Adam, 295. *See also* Methylenedioxy-
    methamphetamine
"Addict identification," 376
Addiction counseling, 136, 331, 343,
    349, 372, 437, 454, 505–506

Addiction medicine, 529–533. *See also*
    Medical education in addiction
    medicine
Addiction psychiatry, 532
Addiction Severity Index (ASI), 100,
    114, 124, 277, 419, 526
    for women (ASI-F), 526
Addictive behaviors, 353
Addictive process, 375
Adenylyl cyclase
    alcohol effects and, 4, 5
    cannabinoid effects and, 40, 43
    opioid effects and, 15–16, **16**
ADHD. *See* Attention-deficit/
    hyperactivity disorder
Adolescent Drinking Inventory (ADI),
    525
Adolescent substance abuse,
    465–471
    addiction typology and, 466
    adult substance use and, 467
    affiliation with deviant peers and, 53,
        56
    alcoholism, 101
    behavioral characteristics associated
        with, 467
    club drugs, 295
    cocaine, 465
    developmental phases of drug use,
        467 (*See also* Gateway
        drugs)
    in DSM, 466
    environmental factors associated
        with, 467
    hallucinogens, 53, 168, 196, 465
    identifying persons at high risk for,
        469
    inhalants, 168, 465
    initiation, maintenance, and
        transitions of substance use,
        467
    marijuana, 165–168, **166, 168,**
        174–175, 465, 467

Adolescent substance abuse
    *(continued)*
    nosology of, 465–467
        normative behavior, 465–466
        pathological behavior, 466–467
    pandemics of, 76–77
    parental substance dependence and,
        469
    personality traits associated with,
        466, 467
    phencyclidine, 205, 206
    physical and mental health outcomes
        of, 465
    prevalence of, 168
    prevention of, 468–469, 535–542
    prior drug use as predictor of future
        drug use, 467
    psychopathology and, 467–468
        anxiety disorders, 468
        attention-deficit/hyperactivity
            disorder, 468
        conduct disorder, 54, 56, 59, 99,
            468
        depression, 468
        personality disorders, 468
        as reason for seeking treatment,
            471
        stability of, 468
        suicidal behavior, 468
    at rave parties, 295
    relapses of, 469
    risk factors for, 467, 537–538
    stimulants, 168, 465
    temperament and, 53, 60, 466, 467
    treatment interventions for
        assessment of, 471
        cognitive-behavioral therapy, 470
        family therapy, 380, 389, 390,
            470
        manual-guided therapy, 470, 471
        methadone maintenance, 272
        psychodynamic psychotherapy,
            312
        relapse prevention, 365, 470
        special services, 470
        in therapeutic communities,
            450, 459
    treatment outcome for, 469–471
        disseminating research results on,
            471
        effect of family involvement on,
            389
        effects of abstinence, 469–470
        length of treatment and, 470
        limitations of studies of, 469

    patient-treatment matching and,
        470–471
    pretreatment patient
        characteristics and, 469
    staff characteristics and, 470
    treatment completion and, 469
Adoption studies, 59–60, **60,** 100–101
α-Adrenergic agonists. *See also*
        Clonidine; Lofexidine
    for alcohol withdrawal, 152
    for opioid withdrawal, 259, 261–263
    for smoking cessation, 230
$\alpha_2$-Adrenergic receptor, 263
Adrenocorticotropic hormone (ACTH)
    hallucinogen effects on, 196
    opioid abuse and, 12, 14–15
Adult Children of Alcoholics, 488
Adult protective services, 440
Advertising campaigns for substance
        abuse prevention, 539–540
Advil. *See* Ibuprofen
Advocacy, 443
Affect regression, 324
Affect regulation, 310, 313
Affective disorders, 477–478
    adolescent substance use and,
        467, 468
    alcohol abuse and, 90, 98–99,
        115–116, 132, 477
    cocaine dependence and, 477
    prevalence among substance-abusing
        persons, 477
    psychodynamic psychotherapy for,
        312
    among women substance abusers,
        486
Affective flooding, 324
Affective state and drug seeking,
        324, 355
    in adolescents, 466
Aftercare, 92, 142, 529
    in Employee Assistance Programs,
        426, 430
    focus on family in, 399
    inpatient treatment and, 419
    therapeutic communities and,
        457, 459
Age at onset of substance abuse, 61, **61**
Age distribution of substance abuse, 49,
        **55**
    alcohol, 49
    cocaine, **55**
    hallucinogens, 53, **55**
    marijuana, **55,** 165–167, **166**
    phencyclidine, 205, 206

Agency for Health Care Policy and
        Research (AHCPR), 225–228, 230
Aggressive and agitated behavior, 99.
        *See also* Criminality
    alcoholism and, 101, 102, 162
    inpatient treatment for patients
        exhibiting, 415, 416
    phencyclidine-induced, 206, 210
Agoraphobia, alcoholism and, 313, 316,
        478
AHCPR (Agency for Health Care Policy
        and Research), 225–228, 230
AIDS. *See* Human immunodeficiency
        virus infection
Akathisia, 159
Al-Anon, 177, 338, 382, 391, 392, 397,
        488, 531
Alanine aminotransferase (ALT), 290,
        524
Alateen, 488
Alcohol (ethanol), 3–9, 110, **514**
    acute effects of, 3–4
    blood level of, 3, 152, 153, 161, 532
    chemical structure of, 3
    consumption by adolescents,
        465–466
    consumption during pregnancy,
        487–488, 492
        fetal effects of, 491, 493
    dopamine and, 7, 8
    driving under the influence of, 161
    effects of chronic ingestion of, 3
    effects on endogenous opioids, 291
    effects on $GABA_A$ receptor, 3–5, 7–8
    effects on NMDA receptor system,
        6–8
    glycine receptor protein studies of
        effects of, 4
    hepatotoxicity of, 115, 160, 524
    interaction with disulfiram, 337
    intoxication with, 113
        legal blood alcohol level for, 161
    legal age for drinking, 468
    neuroadaptive phenomena associated
        with dependence on, 7–9
    neurobiology of, 3–9
    neuronal membrane lipid
        perturbation hypothesis of
        effects of, 3, 4
    pathogenic use patterns for, 78–79
    physiological effects in women,
        485–486, 489
    Ro 15-4513 effects on central
        nervous system depression
        due to, 4

role of receptor-gated ion channels in reinforcing properties of, 7
serotonin and, 6–7, 101, 130–131, 477
taxes on beverages containing, 161
Alcohol abuse treatment, 151–162
  acupuncture, 132, 156
  Alcoholics Anonymous, 403–411
  biofeedback, 133, 161, 339
  brief interventions, 129–130, 437–439
  *Broadening the Base of Treatment for Alcohol Problems*, 437
  cognitive-behavioral approaches, 129, 131, 161, 338–339, 408–409
  for college students, 438–439
  community-based, 437–444
  community reinforcement approach, 70–71, 129, 130
  detoxification, 151–155
    danger of inadequate treatment, 152
    before diagnosis of psychiatric disorder, 336
    inpatient, 153, 416
    for mild to moderate alcohol withdrawal, 152–153
    outpatient, 152–153, 416
    for severe alcohol withdrawal, 153–155
    "symptom-triggered therapy," 152
  Employee Assistance Programs, 423–434
  family therapy, 323, 325, 379–386
  goals of, 152
  group therapy, 323, 369
  individual psychotherapy, 335–341, 348
  inpatient, 153, 413–420
  liver transplantation, 160
  marital therapy, 326
  motivational enhancement therapy, 103–104, 129, 130, 133, 348, 408–409, 549
  network therapy, 323–332
  outcome research on, 129–133, 320, 385–386 (*See also* Treatment outcomes)
  outpatient, 152–153, 416
  patient-treatment matching strategies, 97, 100, 103–104, 124–125, 133, 151, 382, 470–471

for patient with comorbid cocaine abuse, 151, 187
peer intervention programs and member assistance programs, 432–434
pharmacological, 6–7, 94, 130–131
  β-blockers, 153
  buspirone, 6–7, 131
  carbamazepine, 154–155
  clomethiazole, 154
  clonidine, 153
  guanabenz, 153
  γ-hydroxybutyrate, 154
  indications for, 152
  in individual therapy, 337
  serotonergic drugs, 6–7, 130–131, 477
pharmacotherapy during abstinence phase, 155–160
  acamprosate, 94, 130, 156, 337
  for comorbid psychopathology, 157–160
    antidepressants, 6–7, 99, 115–116, 131, 132, 157–158
    anxiolytics, 132, 158–159
    neuroleptics, 159
  disulfiram, 94, 129, 130, 155, 326, 337
  γ-hydroxybutyrate, 156
  lithium, 131, 156
  nalmefene, 337
  naltrexone, 7, 94, 130, 155–156, 291–292, 337, 549
  as part of psychosocial-behavioral treatment program, 156
  for patients with organ damage secondary to ethanol intake, 160
  vitamins, 159–160
psychodynamic psychotherapy, 312–321, 335
psychological interventions, 160
relapse prevention, 131, 132, 354
scaffolding therapy, 338–339
social interventions, 161–162
  educational approaches, 132–133, 161–162
  legal approaches, 161
teaching "controlled" use, 89–90, 360
Alcohol dehydrogenase, 63, 485
Alcohol Dependence Scale, 114
Alcohol Safety Action Programs, 440
Alcohol Use Disorders Identification Test (AUDIT), 114, 525

Alcohol withdrawal, 111
  Alcohol Withdrawal Scale, 152
  benzodiazepine self-medication to ameliorate effects of, 240
  Clinical Institute Withdrawal Assessment for Alcohol Scale, 123
  combined alcohol-benzodiazepine withdrawal syndrome, 154–155
  decreased dopamine release during, 8
  inpatient treatment during, 416
  mild to moderate, 152–153
  NMDA receptor–induced neuronal excitability during, 8
  panic attacks during, 478
  protracted withdrawal syndrome, 157
  screening instruments for, 151–152
  severe, 153–155
  social phobic–like symptoms or panic attacks during, 90
  symptoms of, 8, 113, 152, 153
Alcohol withdrawal delirium, 153–155, 416
  benzodiazepines for, 153–154
  carbamazepine for, 154–155
  criteria for, 153
  duration of, 153
  hospitalization for, 153
Alcohol Withdrawal Scale (AWS), 152
Alcoholic system, 380
Alcoholics Anonymous (AA), 91, 97, 142, 177, 323, 367, 382, 403–411, 424, 442, 447
  alternatives to, 409, 415
  attendance at meetings of
    compliance with, 328
    difficulty for persons with social phobia, 311, 480
    during early stage of treatment, 338–339
    encouragement of, 338
    frequency of, 403, 406–407
    during inpatient treatment, 419
    long-term, 340
    mandated, 132
    during middle stage of treatment, 339
    patients' willingness and, 323
  attitudes of health care practitioners toward, 405
  bias against psychiatry by members of, 335

Alcoholics Anonymous (AA)
  *(continued)*
  demographics of current
      membership of, 403–404
  duration of sobriety among members
      of, 404
  effectiveness of, 336, 367, 405–406
    AA is not always helpful, 409
    mechanisms of, 406
    outcome studies of, 405
    patient satisfaction surveys of,
        405–406
    treatment cost and, 406
  ethnicity of members of, 403, 404
  exposing medical students to, 531
  facilitating affiliation and
      involvement in, 407
    tailoring to specific groups, 408
  frequency of use by persons with
      substance abuse disorders,
      404–405
  group affiliation and involvement in,
      406–407
  health care provider's knowledge
      about special-population issues
      related to, 408
  history of, 367–368, 403
  "home groups" of, 403
  individual psychotherapy and, 338
  integrating professional treatment
      with, 407–408
  matching members to professional
      treatment, 409
  measuring involvement in, 407
  media portrayals of, 403
  Minnesota Model programs based on
      principles of, 414
  network therapy and, 328
  "one day at a time" approach of, 391
  "professionalization" of, 135
  psychodynamics applied to,
        309–311, 314, 318–320, 367,
        369, 375
  reasons for participation in, 403, 404
  when to refer to, 404
  as social support network, 404
  speaking at meetings of, 339
  sponsors in, 403
  success as a social movement, 403
  Twelve Steps and Twelve Traditions
      of, 403, 407, 411
  women's participation in, 404, 487
Alcoholism
  adolescent, 101
  adoption study of, 60, **60**, 100–101

age at onset of, 100–102
  antisocial personality disorder and,
      99
  early-onset versus late-onset,
      101–102
  in Type 1 versus Type 2
      alcoholics, 100–102
age distribution of, 49
amblyopia and, 160
annual incidence of, 48
antisocial, 101
benzodiazepine abuse and,
      240–241
causes of, 335
children of patients with, 315–316,
      318, 469
cluster analyses of patients with,
      102–103
criminality and, 101
developmentally cumulative, 101
developmentally limited, 101
disease model of, 360
drinking cues and, 133, 323–326
  among elderly persons, 336
family factors associated with, 380
gender distribution of, 49
genetics of, 5, 14, 50, 59,
      61, 100–102
    Collaborative Study of the
        Genetics of Alcoholism,
        61, **62**, 65, **65**, 66
    genome scans for detecting
        linkage, 65
geographical distribution of, 50, **51**
heterogeneity of patients with, 336
history taking for, 112–113
identification in workplace, 424
identification of "hidden alcoholics,"
      424
industrial alcoholism model,
      424–425
intergenerational transmission
      of, 380
laboratory findings in, 115, 155, 161,
      521, 524
methadone maintenance and, 273
negative-affect, 101
neuroadaptive phenomena associated
      with, 7–9
patient's acceptance of diagnosis of,
      316, 317
peripheral neuropathies and, 160
personality traits and, 60–62, **62**, 65,
      **65**, 101, 102
prevalence of, 48–49

psychiatric disorders and, 98–100,
      336–337
    abusive behavior, 162
    agoraphobia, 313, 316, 478
    antisocial personality disorder, 60,
        61, 98–100, 102, 105
    anxiety disorders, 90, 98, 102,
        158, 313, 316
    attention-deficit/hyperactivity
        disorder, 158–159, 480
    bipolar disorder, 102
    depression, 90, 98–99, 115–116,
        132, 157–158, 477
    differential diagnosis and
        treatment of, 336
    drug abuse, 98, 102
    dual-diagnosis typology, 336–337
    mania, 98
    obsessive-compulsive disorder, 98
    panic disorder, 90, 98, 102, 158,
        316, 478
    posttraumatic stress disorder, 480
    prevalence of, 475
    primary/secondary distinction for,
        98–99, 157
    schizophrenia, 159
    social phobia, 90, 158, 313, 479–480
    suicidality, 102
  psychodynamics of, 309, 335–336
  psychosis induced by, 159
  screening tests for, 61, 114,
      152–153, 161, 525
  self-destructiveness and, 312
  severity of, 98
  sleep disturbances and, 113–114
  smoking and, 217, 218
  social learning factors and, 68
  subtypes of, 97–105 (*See also*
      Typologies of addiction)
    Types 1 and 2, 59–61, 101–102,
        151
    Types A and B, 103, 151
  twin studies of, 50
  vitamin deficiencies and, 159–160
  warning signs for relapse, 354
  in women, 485–489
Aldehyde dehydrogenase, 63
Alendronate, 160
Aleve (naproxen), **514**
Alexithymia, 310
Alkaline phosphatase, 524
Alpidem, 240
Alprazolam (Xanax)
  phenobarbital withdrawal equivalent
      for, **246**

use by alcoholic persons, 158,
240–241
withdrawal from, 241
ALT (alanine aminotransferase), 290,
524
Amandamide, 42
Amantadine, 186
Ambien (zolpidem), 240
Amblyopia
alcoholic, 160
opioid-induced, 18
Amenorrhea, marijuana-induced, 174
American Cancer Society, 232
American Lung Association, 232–233
American Managed Behavioral Health
Care Association, 533
American Society of Addiction
Medicine (ASAM), 533, 549
certification examination of, 532
Patient Placement Criteria for the
Treatment of Psychoactive
Substance Use Disorders, 121,
**122,** 123, 414, 417, 442,
525–526, 529
levels of care in, 525
patient-related dimensions
assessed by, 525–526,
529
second edition of, 124
α-Amino-3-hydroxy-5-methyl-4-
isoxazolepropionate (AMPA)
receptors, 6, 17, 156
γ-Aminobutyric acid (GABA)
alcohol and, 4
carbamazepine and, 248
γ-hydroxybutyrate and, 301
stimulants and, 22
valproate and, 248
γ-Aminobutyric acid (GABA) agonists
for alcohol problems, 129, 130
benzodiazepines, 239
γ-Aminobutyric acid (GABA) receptors
alcohol effects on GABA$_A$ receptor,
3–5, 7–8
barbiturate effects on, 4
benzodiazepine effects on, 4,
239–240
subunits of GABA$_A$ receptor, 5
Amitriptyline, 158
Ammonium chloride, 208–210
Amobarbital (Amytal), **247**
Amotivational syndrome, 175
AMPA (α-amino-3-hydroxy-5-methyl-
4-isoxazolepropionate) receptors,
6, 17, 156

Amphetamine use, 21–27, 110. *See also*
Stimulant use
administration routes for, 184
by adolescents, 168
for attention-deficit/hyperactivity
disorder, 159, 480
behavioral effects of, 21–22
consequences of repeated exposure,
22–26
sensitization, 23–24
tolerance, 24–25
toxicity, 25–26
drug discrimination paradigm for,
34
to enhance opioid analgesia, **515**
epidemics of, 77, 183
historical cycles of, 21
mechanism of action for, 21
methylenedioxymethamphetamine,
295–299
patient assessment for, 112
prevalence of, 21
psychosis induced by, 23, 33, 36,
185
reinforcing effects of, 22, 183–184
similarities and differences between
cocaine use and, 27
withdrawal from, 111, 185
depressive symptoms during, 90
Amytal (amobarbital), **247**
ANA (anandamide), 41–42, 171, 174
Analgesic effects of drugs
clonidine, 263
marijuana, 39
opioids, 12, 13, 344, 514–515
phencyclidine, 206, 208
Analgesic therapy. *See* Pain management
in drug-addicted persons
Anandamide (ANA), 41–42, 171, 174
Anaprox (naproxen), **514**
Anesthesia
ketamine for, 299
phencyclidine for, 299–300
ultrarapid detoxification under,
264–266
Angel dust, 33, 206, 299. *See also*
Phencyclidine
Anger, 355–356
Anhedonia
during alcohol withdrawal, 8
methylenedioxymethamphetamine-
induced, 297
Animal models
of drug self-administration, 22,
67–68, 70

of novelty-seeking, 64
of opioid dependence, 14
Annual incidence of drug dependence,
48–49
Anomie, 79
Anorectics, for smoking cessation, 230
Anorexia nervosa, 488
Antabuse. *See* Disulfiram
Antacids, 210
Anticholinergic crisis, 200
Anticonvulsant effects
of alcohol, 4
of benzodiazepines, 153
of marijuana, 39
Anticonvulsants
for bipolar disorder, 478
for methylenedioxymeth-
amphetamine intoxication,
298
use with methadone, 273
Antidepressants, 91, 93, 477–478
for alcoholic persons, 6–7, 99, 131,
132, 157–158, 477
delaying initiation of, 115–116,
132
for attention-deficit/hyperactivity
disorder, 480
for cocaine abuse, 27, 186–187, 189,
477–478
to enhance opioid analgesia, **515**
for generalized anxiety disorder,
479
for HIV-infected persons who abuse
drugs, 507
interaction with lysergic acid
diethylamide, 197
for neuropathic pain, 514, 515
for opioid addicts, 99, 477
for panic disorder, 478–479
for posttraumatic stress disorder,
480
for smoking cessation, 230
use with methadone, 273
use with naltrexone, 290
Antihypertensive agents
for attention-deficit/hyperactivity
disorder, 480
for phencyclidine-intoxicated
persons, 209
Antiparkinsonian drugs, 159
Antipsychotics. *See* Neuroleptics
Antiretroviral therapy, 507–508
insomnia and anxiety induced by,
506
interaction with methadone, 505

Antisocial personality disorder (ASPD),
54, 59, **60, 61,** 62
alcoholism and, 60, 61, 98–100,
102, 105
conduct disorder and, 99
diagnostic criteria for, 99
effect of methadone maintenance on,
277
effect on substance abuse treatment
outcome, 99–100
novelty-seeking and, 61
opioid dependence and, 99, 277
Oregon Social Learning Center
model for, 54–56
among patients entering therapeutic
communities, 450
psychodynamic psychotherapy
contraindicated for, 313
risk of substance abuse in persons
with, 91, 94
stimulant abuse and, 188
subtypes of, 99
Anxiety
during benzodiazepine withdrawal,
241–243
during detoxification, 328
hallucinogen-induced, 197,
199–201
marijuana-induced, 170
medications contraindicated for, 93
methylenedioxymethamphetamine-
induced, 297
among patients entering therapeutic
communities, 450
relapse and, 355
Anxiety disorders, 344, 478–480
adolescent substance use and,
467, 468
alcoholism and, 90, 98, 102, 158,
313, 316
generalized anxiety disorder, 479
among HIV-infected
substance-abusing persons,
506, 507
independent of substance abuse,
90–91
opioid dependence and, 277
panic disorder, 478–479
posttraumatic stress disorder, 480
prevalence among substance-abusing
persons, 478
psychodynamic psychotherapy for,
312, 313
severity of opioid withdrawal
symptoms related to, 253

social phobia, 479–480
withdrawal-related, 90
Anxiolytic effects
of alcohol, 3–5
of opioids, 12
Anxiolytics, 110. *See also*
Benzodiazepines
for alcoholic persons, 132,
158–159
patient assessment for use of, 112
sedative-hypnotics and
benzodiazepines, 239–248
for smoking cessation, 230
use with methadone, 273
withdrawal from, 111
Apnea aversion therapy, 129, 131
Appetite disturbances, 113
Aptitude-treatment interaction
research, 382
Arachidonic acid, 40
Arachidonyl ethanol-amide
(anandamide), 41–42, 171, 174
2-Arachidonyl glycerol, 42
ARISE model, 380
Arrhythmias, drug-induced
marijuana, 173
phencyclidine, 209
Arylcyclohexylamines, 205–212.
*See also* Phencyclidine
ASAM. *See* American Society of
Addiction Medicine
Ascorbic acid, 209, 210
ASI (Addiction Severity Index), 100,
114, 124, 277, 419, 526
for women (ASI-F), 526
Asian opium epidemic, 76
Aspartate, 301
Aspartate aminotransferase (AST), 115,
290, 524
ASPD. *See* Antisocial personality
disorder
Aspirin, 514, **514**
Assertive community treatment (ACT),
444
Assessment of family, 383, 390, 392
Assessment of patient, 109–117
ability to cope with high-risk
situations, 362
for admission to therapeutic
community, 451
for comorbid psychiatric disorders,
115–116
components of, 109
to determine necessity for inpatient
treatment, 416

diagnosis of substance-related
disorders, 110–111, 526
eliciting patient's history, 111–113
factors that interfere with, 109
failure to diagnose substance abuse,
109
with family present, 390
goals of, 109
interviews with significant others, 114
laboratory testing, 114–115,
521–524
for pain management, **512,** 512–513,
**513**
physical and mental status
examination, 113–114
psychological testing, 524–527
for risk of HIV infection, 504
screening instruments and structured
interviews, 114, 123, 525–527
(*See also* Screening and
assessment instruments)
AST (aspartate aminotransferase), 115,
290, 524
Atenolol, 152
Atheism, 312
Ativan. *See* Lorazepam
Atropine poisoning, 198
Attention-deficit/hyperactivity disorder
(ADHD), 467, 480–481
adolescent substance use and, 468
alcoholism and, 158–159, 480
conduct disorder and, 468
criteria for diagnosis in adults,
158–159
diagnosis in substance-abusing
persons, 480
pharmacological therapy for, 480
prevalence among substance-abusing
persons, 480
stimulant abuse and, 188
treating cocaine abuse in persons
with, 186
Attitudes
about smoking, 63, 224
about use of hallucinogens, 196
of health care practitioners about
12-step groups, 405
maintaining accepting attitude for
group therapy, 374
managed care organizations' negative
attitudes and behavior toward
providers, 550
of physicians toward
substance-abusing persons,
109, 529

AUDIT (Alcohol Use Disorders Identification Test), 114
Autohemotherapy, 252
Availability of drugs, 52, 80, 196, 251
AVE (abstinence violation effect), 358, **361,** 363
Aversive techniques, 353
    nausea aversion therapy for alcohol abuse, 129, 131, 415 (*See also* Disulfiram)
    for smoking cessation, 231
Avoidant personality disorder, 312
AWS (Alcohol Withdrawal Scale), 152
AZT (zidovudine), 505, 506

## B

Baclofen, **515**
"Bad trips," 199
BAL (blood alcohol level), 3, 152, 153, 161
Balancing techniques, 396–397
Barbiturates, 77, 112
    abuse of, 241
    effects on GABA$_A$ receptors, 4
    interaction with methadone, 273
    for phencyclidine intoxication, 209
    phenobarbital withdrawal equivalents, 245–247, **246, 247**
    withdrawal from, 241, 451
Barriers to treatment of women, 487, 494
Basal ganglia, 42
Beck's cognitive theory, 313
Behavior change theories, 538
Behavioral approaches, 93, 353–354
    for adolescents, 470
    for alcohol abuse, 129, 131, 161, 379, 381
    behavioral family therapy, 379, 381, 394
    contracting (*See* Contracting)
    for smoking cessation, 230–231
    for stimulant abuse, 187–188
Behavioral factors and substance abuse, 54
    conditioned drug seeking, 324–325
    therapeutic community view of right living, 449
Benzodiazepine receptor, 4, 239–240
Benzodiazepine withdrawal, 111, 241–244
    combined alcohol-benzodiazepine withdrawal syndrome, 154–155

dependence/withdrawal cycle, **243,** 243–244
    pretreatment phase, 243
    resolution phase, 244
    symptom escape and dosage escalation phase, 244
    therapeutic phase, 243
    withdrawal phase, 244
effects of abrupt discontinuation, 241, 242
high-dose withdrawal syndrome, 241, **245**
inpatient treatment for, 416
low-dose withdrawal syndrome, 241–243, **245**
    clinical studies of, 242
    malpractice claims related to, 242
    protracted, 242–243, **245**
    risk factors for, 243
    symptom rebound, 242, **245**
    symptom reemergence, 243, **245**
    terminology for, 241
onset of, 241
pharmacological treatment of, 244–248
    high-dose withdrawal, 245–247
        phenobarbital substitution, 245–247, **246, 247**
        strategies for, 245
        individualization of, 245
    low-dose withdrawal, 247–248
        gradual reduction of benzodiazepine, 248
        valproate and carbamazepine, 248
    outpatient treatment, 248
signs and symptoms of, 241
Benzodiazepines, 112, 239–248
    abuse and dependence on, 240–241
        among alcohol and prescription drug abusers, 240–241
        biological predisposition to, 240
        as part of polydrug abuse pattern, 240
        potential for, 478, 479
    for acute hallucinogen reactions, 200
    agonists, inverse agonists, and antagonists, 239
    for alcohol withdrawal, 152
        mild to moderate, 152
        severe, 153–154
    for anxiety reduction in alcoholic persons, 158
    contraindications to, 241
    effects on GABA$_A$ receptors, 4

    for generalized anxiety disorder, 479
    for HIV-infected persons who abuse drugs, 507
    for ketamine intoxication, 301
    mechanism of action of, 239
    memory impairment due to, 244
    for methylenedioxymeth-amphetamine intoxication, 298
    for opioid withdrawal, 15
    overdose of, 239
    for panic disorder, 478
    for phencyclidine reactions, 209, 210
    safety of, 239
    for social phobia, 479
    for stimulant overdose, 185
    tapering of, 242
    tolerance to, 240
    for ultrarapid detoxification under anesthesia/sedation, 264–265
Betty Ford Center, 531
Bilirubin, 524
Biofeedback
    for alcohol abuse, 133, 161, 339
    during inpatient treatment, 419
    for pain management, **513**
Biomarkers, 52, 115
Biopsychosocial model, 317
Bipolar disorder, 355
    alcoholism and, 102
    anticonvulsants for, 478
    cocaine dependence and, 477
    effect of methadone maintenance on, 277
    lithium for, 91, 93, 478
    prevalence among substance-abusing persons, 477
    risk of substance abuse in persons with, 91
    treatment in substance-abusing persons, 478
Bismuth subsalicylate (Pepto Bismol), 259
Blaming, 111
Bleuler, Eugen, 309
β-Blockers
    for akathisia, 159
    for alcohol withdrawal symptoms, 152
    for attention-deficit/hyperactivity disorder, 480
    for esophageal variceal bleeding, 160
    for phencyclidine delirium, 210
Blocking, phencyclidine-induced, 211
Blood alcohol level (BAL), 3, 152, 153, 161, 532
    in women, 485

Blood toxicology testing, 114–115, 521, 522, **523**. *See also* Laboratory testing
BMAST (Brief Michigan Alcohol Screening Test), 525
Boot camps, 487
Borderline personality disorder, 312–313, 315
Boredom, 355
Boston Target Cities Project, 123
Boundary preservation, 396
Bowen's systems family therapy, 394
Bowman, Karl, 97
Boys & Girls Clubs, 540
Brain
    distribution of cannabinoid receptors in, 42, 172, 174
    mesolimbic reward system, 310, 312, 521
Breast milk, Δ-tetrahydrocannabinol in, 174
Breathalyzer test, 115, 273, 477
Brief interventions, 71, 549
    for alcohol problems, 129–130, 437–439
    in colleges, 438–439
    FRAMES acronym for, 130
    in primary care settings, 437–438, 529–530
Brief Michigan Alcohol Screening Test (BMAST), 525
*Broadening the Base of Treatment for Alcohol Problems*, 437
2-(4-Bromo-2,5-dimethoxyphenyl)-1-aminoethane (Nexus), **34, 35,** 36
1-(4-Bromo-2,5-dimethoxyphenyl)-2-aminopropane (DOB), **34, 35,** 36
Bromocriptine
    for cocaine abuse, 26, 186
    for methylenedioxymeth-amphetamine intoxication, 298
Bronchitis, 172–173, 216
Bulimia nervosa, 488
Buprenorphine, 12, 511
    abrupt discontinuation of, 266
    ceiling effect with, 266
    for cocaine abuse, 26–27, 187
    combined with naloxone, 266, 291
    compared with naltrexone and methadone, 291
    disadvantages of, 291
    effect on regional cerebral blood flow in cocaine abusers, 184
    maintenance therapy with, 251, 266, 277, 291

opiate partial agonist effects of, 281, 282, 291
    for opioid withdrawal, 12, 266–267
    overdose of, 18, 291
    for rapid detoxification, 266–267
    reducing abuse potential of, 291
    sublingual form of, 266
    withdrawal from, 291
Bupropion
    for attention-deficit/hyperactivity disorder, 159, 480
    for cocaine abuse, 187
    interaction with monoamine oxidase inhibitors, 229
    side effects of, 228
    for smoking cessation (Zyban), 220, **222–223,** 226, 228
        combined with use of nicotine patch, 229
        contraindications to, 229
        dosage of, 228
        efficacy of, 228
Burns, 256
Buspirone (BuSpar)
    for alcohol abuse, 6–7, 131
    contraindicated for patients with history of benzodiazepine abuse, 241
    for generalized anxiety disorder, 479
    for HIV-infected persons who abuse drugs, 507
    low abuse potential for, 241, 479
    onset of anxiolytic effects of, 241
    for opioid detoxification, 267
    phenobarbital withdrawal equivalent for, **247**
Butabarbital (Butisol), **247**
Butalbital (Fiorinal, Sedapap), **247**
Butisol (butabarbital), **247**
Butorphanol, 12

# C

CA. *See* Cocaine Anonymous
Caffeine, 110, 112
CAGE questionnaire, 114, 161, 175–176, 525
Calcium acetyl homotaurinate (acamprosate), 94, 130, 156, 337
Calcium carbimide, 132
Calcium channels, voltage-sensitive, 7
Calcium level in alcoholism, 524
cAMP. *See* Cyclic adenosine monophosphate
cAMP response element binding protein (CREB), 16, **16**

Cancer, smoking-related, 173, 216–217
Candidate genes, 63–64, **64, 65**
Cannabidiol (CBD), 39
Cannabinoid agonists, 40–41
Cannabinoid antagonists, 42, 172
Cannabinoid receptors, 39–44, 172
    brain distribution of, 42, 172, 174
    CB₁ receptor, 40–42
    CB₂ receptor, 40
    effects of chronic cannabinoid exposure on function of, 43
    endogenous ligands for, 41–42
    regulation of expression of, 42–43
    relationship between pharmacological effects and activation of, 42
Cannabinoids, 39–44, 169
    endogenous system of, 39, 41–44
        anandamide, 41–42, 171, 174
        2-arachidonyl glycerol, 42
        functional significance of, 42
    fat solubility of, 39, 169–170, 172
    neurobiology of, 39–44
    relationship between receptor activation and pharmacological effects of, 42
    signal transduction and, 40–41
Cannabinol (CBN), 39, 40
Cannabis dependence treatment, 175–178
    crisis intervention, 177
    detoxification, 176
    family therapy, 177–178
    group therapy, 177, 348
    individual psychotherapy, 177–178, 348
    individualization of, 176
    inpatient treatment, 177
    overview of, 176–177
    phases of, 176–177
    presentation for, 175
    research on, 175
    12-step groups, 176–177
Cannabis use, 33, 39–44, 110, 165–179, **514**
    acute effects of, 39, 166, 169–171, **170**
    administration routes for, 165–166, 169
        oral ingestion, 165, 169
        smoking, 165–166, 169
    by adolescents, 165–168, **166, 168,** 174–175, 295, 465, 467
        mixed messages about, 168
        parental expectations and, 168

protective and risk factors associated with, 178, **178**
adverse psychiatric reactions to, 170–171
age distribution of, **55**, 165
analgesic effects of, 39
"brand" names, 167
chronic cannabis syndrome due to, 175
cocaine use and, 166, 170
cost of, 165, 197
cultural influences on, 168
dependence on, 43, 171
    diagnosis of, 175–176
    prevalence of, 50, 171
drug forms and types of, 165–166
drug potency and, 165–168
dysphoria produced by, 170
educating youths about, 178
effects on college students and adolescents, 174–175
    behavioral, 174–175
    neuropsychological, 174
emergency presentations of, 170
epidemiology of, 166–169
euphoria produced by, 39, 165, 169
factors associated with, 167–168, **168**
as gateway drug, 169, 467, 535
gender distribution of, 165
history of, 166
ingredients in marijuana smoke, 166, 169, 173 (*See also* Δ⁹-Tetrahydrocannabinol)
intoxication due to, 169–170, **170**
laboratory testing for, 175, 176, 522
medical implications of, 172–174
    carcinogenic, 173
    cardiovascular, 173
    immunological, 173
    respiratory, 172–173
    sexual dysfunction and related issues, 173–174
medicinal, 167
memory impairment induced by, 39, 42, 171
neurobiology of, 39–44
overdose due to, 172
panic attacks induced by, 170, 478
patient assessment for, 112
patterns of, 166–167
during pregnancy and lactation, 174
prevalence of, 165
proponents of legalization of, 167
reasons for, 165

social context for, 167
social fears induced by, 479
therapeutic effects of, 39
tobacco use and, 168–169
    effect on marijuana-induced effects, 170
    learning how to smoke, 168
tolerance to, 43, 171
twin studies of, 59, **60**
withdrawal from, 171–172
CAP (Civil Addict Program), 144
Capitation, 546
Carbamazepine
    for alcohol-benzodiazepine withdrawal syndrome, 154–155
    for alcohol withdrawal, 154–155, 248
    antikindling effects of, 154
    for cocaine abuse, 187
    to enhance opioid analgesia, **515**
    interaction with methadone, 505
    for low-dose benzodiazepine withdrawal, 248
Carbohydrate-deficient transferrin (CDT), 115, 524
Carbon monoxide in cigarette smoke, 216
Carboximide hydrochloride (SR141716A), 41–43
Carcinogenicity
    of cigarette smoking, 173
    of marijuana, 173
Cardiovascular effects. *See also* Hypertension
    alcoholic cardiomyopathy, 163
    of cigarette smoking, 216–217, 219
    of marijuana, 173
    of phencyclidine, 206, 209
CareUnit system, 143
Career Teacher Program in Alcohol and Other Drug Abuse, 529
Carrier Foundation, 418
Case management, 443–444
    assertive community treatment model for, 444
    Chronic Inebriate Case Management program for, 444
    components of, 443
    efficacy of, 443
    goals of, 443
    for homeless substance-abusing persons, 444
    in integrated service delivery system, 547

for mentally ill, substance-abusing persons, 440
    patient driven and strengths based, 444
    patient selection for, 443
    providers of, 443
    for substance-abusing arrestees, 441
Case rates, 546
Cataflam (diclofenac), **514**
Cataleptoid anesthetics, 205, 299. *See also* Ketamine; Phencyclidine
Catapres. *See* Clonidine
Causes of substance abuse, 50–54
    cultural risk factors, 78–79
    drug availability, 52, 80
    effective contact, 51
    genetic factors, 59–66
    Human Envirome Project, 52–53
    individual vulnerabilities and their consequences, 14–15, 53–54, 70
    social causation versus social selection, 52
    twin studies, 50–51
CBD (cannabidiol), 39
CBF (cerebral blood flow), 174, 184
CBI (Cumulative Block Increment) Model of treatment matching, 125
CBN (cannabinol), 39, 40
CDT (carbohydrate-deficient transferrin), 115, 524
Center for Health Care Evaluation, 405
Centrax (prazepam), **246**
Cerebellum, 5, 42
Cerebral blood flow (CBF), 174, 184
Cerebrospinal fluid findings in alcoholic persons, 101
Certification in addiction medicine, 532
CES (Cumulative Evidence Score), 129
Change
    assessing patient's readiness for, 116–117, 549
        related to smoking cessation, 225–226
    global lifestyle change strategies, 360, 363–365, **364**
    process in therapeutic communities, 455–456
    resistance to, 394
    theories of behavior change, 538
    University of Rhode Island Change Assessment, 116
CHD (coronary heart disease), smoking-related, 216–217, 219
Cheilosis, 256

Chemical Abuse/Addiction Treatment
    Outcome Registry, 143
Chemical aversion counterconditioning
    therapy, 415
Chemical dependency treatment, 142,
    360. *See also* Short-term inpatient
    treatment
Child abuse, alcoholism and, 162
Child protective services, 439
Chloral hydrate (Noctec), 152, **247**
Chlordiazepoxide (Librium), 154, 241,
    **246**
Chloroform, 77
*m*-Chlorophenylpiperazine, 101
Chlorpromazine
    for acute hallucinogen reactions,
        200
    to enhance opioid analgesia, **515**
    for neonates of methadone-
        maintained mothers, 275
Cholinergic receptors, nicotinic, 4
Chronic cannabis syndrome, 175
Chronic Inebriate Case Management
    (CICM), 444
Chronic obstructive pulmonary disease
    (COPD)
    alcoholism and, 163
    cigarette smoking and, 216–217
    marijuana smoking and, 172–173
CICM (Chronic Inebriate Case
    Management), 444
Cigarette burns, 256
Circuit parties, 295–303
Cirrhosis, 160, 485
Civil Addict Program (CAP), 144
Civil commitment, 441–442
CIWA-Ar (Clinical Institute
    Withdrawal Assessment for
    Alcohol Scale), 123, 151–154
Claims payment problems, 550–551
Classification of mood-altering drugs,
    110, 514, **514**
*Clean Start*, 368
*Clearing the Air*, 225
Cleveland Criteria, 123
Clinical Institute Withdrawal
    Assessment for Alcohol Scale
    (CIWA-Ar), 123, 151–154
Clomethiazole, 154
Clonazepam (Klonopin), **246**
Clonidine (Catapres)
    administered via transdermal patch,
        263
    for alcohol withdrawal, 152
    analgesic effects of, 263

for attention-deficit/hyperactivity
        disorder, 480
    contraindications to, 262
    to enhance opioid analgesia, **515**
    insomnia during treatment with,
        262–263
    interaction with methadone, 273
    mechanism of action of, 261
    for opioid withdrawal, 15, 16, 259,
        261–263
        clonidine-naltrexone ultrarapid
            detoxification, 264, **265,**
            287
        ultrarapid detoxification under
            anesthesia/sedation,
            264–266
    side effects of, 152, 261
    for smoking cessation, 230
Clorazepate (Tranxene), **246**
Clozapine, 200, 476
Club drugs, 295–303
Cluster analyses of alcoholic persons,
    102–103
Co-Anon, 392, 397
Coalition for National Treatment
    Criteria, 124
Cocaine abuse treatment, 185–189
    ambulatory clinical trials of, 136
    behavioral therapy, 187–188
        contingency contracting, 328
        community reinforcement approach,
            70–71, 347
    effect of therapist characteristics on,
        345
    group therapy, 369
    individual psychotherapy, 347, 348
    partial hospitalization, 442
    for patient with comorbid alcohol
        abuse, 151, 187
    pharmacological, 26–27, 549
        animal self-administration testing
            for, 70
        antidepressants, 27, 186–187,
            189, 477–478
        buprenorphine, 187
        carbamazepine, 187
        cocaine vaccine, 187
        disulfiram, 187
        dopaminergic agonists, 26,
            185–186
        drug interactions affecting, 189
        for HIV-infected persons, 507
        opiates, 26–27
    for patients with psychiatric
        comorbidity, 188

    relapse prevention, 347
    therapeutic communities, 138
Cocaine Anonymous (CA), 135, 142,
    328, 391
Cocaine use, 21–27, 110
    administration routes for, 184
    by adolescents, 465
    affective disorders and, 477
    age distribution of, **55**
    behavioral effects of, 21–22
    benzodiazepine self-medication to
        ameliorate effects of, 240
    cognitive effects of, 184
    consequences of repeated exposure,
        22–26
        sensitization, 23–24
        tolerance, 24–25
        toxicity, 25–26
    cost of, 197
    crack cocaine, 184, 185, 348
        crack babies, 491
        overdose of, 185
        during pregnancy, 492
    $D_2$ dopamine receptor polymorphism
        related to, 64, **65**
    historical cycles of, 21, 183
    laboratory testing for, 115
    marijuana use and, 166, 170
    mechanism of action of, 21
    neurobiology of chronic abuse, 184
    panic attacks induced by, 478
    patient assessment for, 112, 189
    during pregnancy, 492–493
    prevalence of, 50
    psychosis induced by, 23, 185
    reinforcing effects of, 22,
        183–184
    related to public support payments
        in schizophrenic patients,
        439
    similarities and differences between
        amphetamine and, 27
    social phobia and, 479
    vulnerability to dependence on, 14
    withdrawal from, 111, 136, 185
        depressive symptoms during, 90
Cocktail lounge culture, 75
Codeine, 11, 12
    withdrawal from, **254,** 257, **257**
COGA (Collaborative Study of the
    Genetics of Alcoholism), 61, **62,**
    65, **65, 66**
Cognitive-behavioral approaches, 91
    for adolescents, 470
    for affective disorders, 478

for alcohol abuse, 129, 131, 161, 338–339, 408–409
  behavioral family therapy, 379, 381
in family therapy, 379, 381, 390
for generalized anxiety disorder, 479
in group therapy, 367, 368
for panic disorder, 479
for posttraumatic stress disorder, 480
for relapse prevention, 353–365
for smoking cessation, 225, 230–231
  behavior change strategies, 230
  contracts, 231
  rewards, 230
for social phobia, 480
Cognitive distortion, 359, 364
Cognitive functioning assessment, 113, 115
Cognitive labeling, 325
Cognitive reframing, 360, 396
Cognitive restructuring, 394
Cohesiveness in group therapy, 375
Cold therapy, **513**
Collaborative Study of the Genetics of Alcoholism (COGA), 61, **62**, 65, **65, 66**
Colleges, brief interventions in, 438–439
Coma, drug-induced
  γ-hydroxybutyrate, 302
  phencyclidine, 207, **207**, 208
Community-based prevention programs, 540–541, **542**
Community-based treatment, 437–444
  community interventions, 437–442
    brief intervention in colleges, 438–439
    brief intervention in primary care settings, 437–438, 529–530
    interventions no longer through criminal courts, 441–442
      civil commitment, 441–442
      detoxification, 441
    interventions through criminal courts, 440–441
      drug abuse, 441
      drunk driving, 161, 440–441
    for perinatal substance use, 496–497, **497**
    social service agency intervention, 439–440
      adult protective services, 440
      child protective services, 439
      disability and public support, 439–440
    workplace drug testing, 439

non-hospital-based interventions, 442–444
  case management and continuity of care, 443–444
  community residential facilities, 443
  day hospital and intensive outpatient treatment, 442–443
  outpatient detoxification, 443
role in systems model of substance abuse treatment, 437, **438**
usages of term, 437
Community reinforcement approach (CRA), 70–71, 354
  for alcohol problems, 70–71, 129, 130
  for cocaine abuse, 70–71, 347
Community residential facilities (CRFs), 443
Comorbidity
  among different forms of substance abuse, 59
  learning-based treatments and, 71
  of psychopathology and substance abuse, 90–91, 98–100, 109, 114, 336, 344, 475–481 (*See also* Psychiatric disorders)
Compensatory effects, 324
Compliance with treatment
  L-α-acetylmethadol, 137
  Alcoholics Anonymous attendance, 328
  disulfiram, 155, 326, 385–386
  effect of network therapy on, 326, 328
  effect of spouse's involvement on, 326, 385–386, 390
  impact of therapeutic alliance on, 345
  nicotine-containing gum, 227
  nicotine transdermal patch, 227
Compulsions, 310
Conditioned drug seeking, 324–325
Conduct disorder, 54, 56, 59
  adolescent substance use and, 54, 56, 59, 99, 468
  antisocial personality disorder and, 99
  attention-deficit/hyperactivity disorder and, 468
  effect on treatment completion, 469
  programs for parents of children with, 539
Conflict theory, 313, 315

Confrontational approaches, 93, 372
  for alcohol abuse, 132, 160
  contraindicated for substance-abusing schizophrenic persons, 477
  encounters in therapeutic communities, 454
  family intervention, 391
  in group therapy, 374–375
  for marijuana dependence, 176
  in psychodynamic psychotherapy, 314
Contact dermatitis, 256
Contemplation Ladder, 116
Contingency-management interventions, 70
  for stimulant abuse, 187–188
Continuity of care, 443–444. *See also* Case management
Continuum of care, 121–124, **122**, 525, 529, 547. *See also* Patient placement criteria
Contracting, 354
  adapted to network therapy, 328
  for alcohol abuse, 129, 131
  definition of, 395
  within family of alcohol-abusing person, 384
  within family of drug-abusing person, 394, 395
  during inpatient treatment, 419
  for smoking cessation, 226, 231
  for stimulant abuse, 187–188
  in therapeutic communities, 455
"Controlled" substance use, 89–90, 114, 360
Cooperativeness, 62
COPD. *See* Chronic obstructive pulmonary disease
Coping skills training, 362
  for alcoholism, 103–104
Coping with high-risk situations, 357–358
  assessing abilities for, 362
Cornerstone, 143–144
Coronary heart disease (CHD), smoking-related, 216–217, 219
Correctional treatment programs, 143–144
  Civil Addict Program, 144
  compulsory treatment of paroled criminal alcoholics, 161
  Cornerstone, 143–144
  effectiveness of, 145
  elements of successful programs, 143

Correctional treatment programs
    (*continued*)
    individual psychotherapy, 344
    methadone maintenance, 272
    naltrexone for probationers in
        work-release program, 286
    Stay'n Out, 143, 144
    therapeutic communities, 459
Corticosteroids, 14–15
Corticotropin-releasing factor (CRF)
    effect of substance withdrawal on,
        171–172
    opioid abuse and, 12, 14–15
Cortisol, 196
Cost containment, 121, 545, 550.
    *See also* Managed care
Cost-effectiveness of treatment, 93,
    121, 320, 413, 549
    needs-to-services matching, 125
    related to Alcoholics Anonymous
        participation, 406
Cost of substance abuse, 69, 413
Cottage industry techniques, 77
Countertransference reactions, 313,
    318, 340
    definition of, 340
    in group therapy, 371
    in psychodynamic family therapy,
        393
Couples' therapy. *See* Marital therapy
Covert reinforcement, 394
Covert sensitization, 129, 131, 353
CP 55,940, 40, 41, 43
CRA. *See* Community reinforcement
    approach
Crack cocaine, 184, 185, 348. *See also*
    Cocaine use
    crack babies, 491
    overdose of, 185
    use during pregnancy, 492
"Crash," after stimulant withdrawal,
    22, 185
Craving
    effect of naltrexone on, 283
    relapse and, 324
    teaching patients to cope with,
        363–364
Creating intensity techniques, 397
CREB (cAMP response element binding
    protein), 16, **16**
CRF. *See* Corticotropin-releasing factor
CRFs (community residential facilities),
    443
Criminal courts. *See* Legal
    interventions

Criminality, 60, 61, **61**
    alcoholism and, 101, 102
    decriminalization of substance abuse,
        441
    methadone maintenance and, 137
Crisis intervention
    for cannabis dependence, 177
    outpatient services for, 548–549
Cross-cultural aspects of substance
    abuse, 75–82
    consequences of addiction on
        ethnicity, 80
    from cottage industry to high-tech
        industry, 77–78
        concentration of traditional
            substances, 77
        smuggling, 78, 80
        synthetic psychoactive substances,
            77–78
    cultural risk factors, 78–79
    culturally prescribed or taboo drug
        use, 78
    definitions related to, 75
    ethnic identity and substance use, 78
    ethnic minority patients, 81
    ethnicity and treatment, 80–81
        access to treatment, 80
        cultural recovery, 81
        cultural reentry, 81
        recovery subcultures, 81
    factors affecting ethnic distribution
        of substance abuse, 79–80
    historical descriptions of substance-
        related pathology, 76–77
    influences on marijuana use, 168
    prehistory, 75–76
        routes of drug administration, 75
        social controls, 75–76
    prevention, 82
    travelers, foreign students,
        immigrants, and refugees,
        81–82
    victimized persons, 82
Cross-national comparisons of drug
    dependence, 50
Cue exposure, 353
    alcoholism and, 133, 323–326
    conditioned drug seeking and,
        324–325
    techniques to minimize, 363–364
Culture. *See* Cross-cultural aspects of
    substance abuse
Cumulative Block Increment (CBI)
    Model of treatment matching, 125
Cumulative Evidence Score (CES), 129

Cutaneous signs of drug abuse, 256
Cyclic adenosine monophosphate
    (cAMP)
    alcohol and, 5
    cannabinoids and, 40
    opioids and, 15–16, **16**
Cyclothymia, 188

**D**

DA. *See* Dopamine
Dalmane (flurazepam), **246**
Dangerous patients, 415, 416
Dantrolene sodium, 298
DARE program, 536–537
DARP (Drug Abuse Reporting
    Program), 140, 141, 143
"Date rape drug," 240, 303
DATOS (Drug Abuse Treatment
    Outcome Study), 138, 140–143
Day hospitals. *See* Partial hospitalization
    programs
Daytop Village, 138, 140, 368
Decriminalization of substance abuse,
    441
Defense mechanisms, 109, 111
    during alcohol abuse treatment, 339
    psychodynamic psychotherapy and,
        309–318
    relapse and, 359
Delirium, drug-induced
    during alcohol withdrawal, 153–155,
        416
    during benzodiazepine withdrawal,
        241
    hallucinogens, 195
    marijuana, 170, 198
    phencyclidine, 206, 209–211
    stimulants, 185
Delirium tremens, 195
Delusions, drug-induced
    alcohol, 159
    hallucinogens, 195
    stimulants, 185
Denial, 109, 111, 115, 117, 276, 312,
    314, 315, 317–318, 326, 359, 414
Depersonalization, drug-induced
    hallucinogens, 198
    marijuana, 170
    phencyclidine, 206
Depression, 344
    adolescent substance use and, 468
    alcoholism and, 90, 98–99, 115–116,
        132, 157–158, 477
    antidepressants for, 90, 93
    benzodiazepine abuse and, 240, 241

diagnosis in substance-abusing
  persons, 477
effect of methadone maintenance on,
  277
among HIV-infected
  substance-abusing persons,
  506
independent of substance abuse, 90
medications contraindicated for, 93
methylenedioxymethamphetamine
  use and, 297
opioid dependence and, 277
among patients entering therapeutic
  communities, 450
phencyclidine use and, 211
prevalence among substance-abusing
  persons, 477
psychodynamic psychotherapy for,
  312
relapse and, 355
smoking and, 218, 219
stimulant abuse and, 188
during stimulant withdrawal, 90
treatment in substance-abusing
  persons, 477–478
in women substance abusers,
  486, 488
Deprol (meprobamate), 241, **247**
Derealization, marijuana-induced, 170
Dermatological signs of drug abuse, 256
Desensitization techniques, 479, 480
Designer drugs, 36, **36,** 77
Desipramine
  for alcoholic persons, 99
  for cocaine abuse, 27, 186–187
    in schizophrenic persons, 476
DET (*N,N*-diethyltryptamine), **34, 35**
Detoxification
  from alcohol, 151–155, 416
  anxiety during, 328
  community-based centers for, 441
  definition of, 251
  of family, 383–385
    advantages of, 384–385
    contracting, 384
    factors affecting success of, 384
    goals of, 383
    multiphase process of, 384
    rationale for, 383–384
  inpatient, 252, 258–259, 261, 413,
    416
  from opioids, 251–268
  outpatient, 443, 548–549
    from alcohol, 152–153, 416, 443
    from opioids, 252, 258–259, 261

reasons addicts enter programs for,
  251
as route into treatment, 251
from sedative-hypnotics, 416
serious medical consequences of,
  416
therapeutic communities and, 451
Development of family, 380
Developmental causal model of
  substance abuse, 54–56
Developmental phases of drug use, 467.
  *See also* Gateway drugs
Dextroamphetamine, 21, 24, 25.
  *See also* Amphetamine
  for attention-deficit/hyperactivity
    disorder, 480
Dextromethorphan, 17, 267
Dezocine, 12
Diagnosis of substance abuse, 110–111.
  *See also* Assessment of patient
  cannabis, 175–176
  comorbid with psychopathology,
    475–476, 481
  hallucinogens, 198–199
  laboratory testing for, 114–115,
    521–524
  patient's acceptance of, 316, 317
  phencyclidine, 211
  psychological testing for, 524–527
  smoking, 112, 219–225
  using Structured Clinical Interview
    for DSM-IV, 114, 526
*Diagnostic and Statistical Manual of
  Mental Disorders* (DSM), 344
  antisocial personality disorder in, 99
  cannabis intoxication in, 169–170,
    **170**
  generalized anxiety disorder in, 479
  nicotine dependence in, 215
  reemergence of descriptive
    psychiatry in, 105
  substance-induced disorders in, 110
  substance use disorders in, 69, 97,
    98, 110, 466
Diagnostic Interview Schedule (DIS),
  49, 450
Diarrhea, 154, 254
Diazepam (Valium)
  for alcohol withdrawal, 153–154
  for anxiety reduction in alcoholic
    persons, 158
  low abuse potential of, 240
  memory impairment due to, 244
  for neonates of methadone-
    maintained mothers, 275

for phencyclidine-intoxicated
  persons, 209
phenobarbital withdrawal equivalent
  for, **246**
withdrawal from, 241
Diclofenac (Voltaren, Cataflam), **514**
Dicyclomine, 259
*N,N*-Diethyltryptamine (DET), **34, 35**
Diffusion of innovation theory, 538
Diflunisal (Dolobid), **514**
Dihydrocodeine, 253
Dilaudid (hydromorphone), 12, 112
  withdrawal from, 253, **254,** 257,
  **257**
1-(2,5-Dimethoxy-4-iodophenyl)-2-
  aminopropane (DOI), **34, 35**
Dimethoxymethylamphetamine (DOM,
  "STP"), 33, 34, **34, 35,** 195, 197,
  200
Dimethyltryptamine (DMT), **34, 35,**
  195, 196
DIS (Diagnostic Interview Schedule),
  49, 450
Disability payments, 439–440
Disciplinary sanctions in therapeutic
  communities, 455
Dissociative anesthetics, 205, 299.
  *See also* Ketamine; Phencyclidine
Disulfiram (Antabuse), 94, 129, 130,
  155, 281, 284–285
  for comorbid alcoholism and cocaine
    abuse, 187
  compliance with, 155, 326
    effect of spouse's involvement on,
      326, 385–386
  discontinuation of, 339
  dosage of, 155
  efficacy of, 129, 130, 155
  hepatotoxicity of, 155
  indications for discontinuation of,
    155
  initiation of, 329
  interaction with alcohol, 337
  mechanism of action of, 285, 337
  onset and duration of clinical effect
    of, 337
  placebo effect of, 130
  use in Employee Assistance
    Programs, 337
  use in individual therapy, 337
  use in patients with schizophrenia,
    155, 159, 476
  use with methadone, 273
  use with naltrexone, 290
Diuresis, 210

DMT (dimethyltryptamine), **34, 35,** 195, 196
DOB (1-(4-bromo-2,5-dimethoxyphenyl)-2-aminopropane), **34, 35,** 36
DOI (1-(2,5-dimethoxy-4-iodophenyl)-2-aminopropane), **34, 35**
Dolobid (diflunisal), **514**
Dolophine. *See* Methadone
DOM (dimethoxymethyl-amphetamine), 33, 34, **34, 35,** 195, 197, 200
Dopamine-β-hydroxylase, 155
Dopamine (DA), 521
    alcohol and, 7, 8
    cannabinoid receptor expression and, 43
    drug dependence and dopamine receptor polymorphisms, 64, **65**
    γ-hydroxybutyrate effects on, 302
    opioids and, 13–14
    phencyclidine and, 206
    smoking and, 218
    stimulants and, 21–23, 25, 183–184
Dopaminergic drugs, 26, 185–186
Doral (quazepam), **246**
Doriden (glutethimide), **247**
Doxepin, 99, 158
Dream interpretation, 315
Drives, 309–310
Driving
    accidents related to marijuana use, 169–170
    drunk, 161, 440–441
    under the influence of alcohol (DUI), 161
    while on methadone maintenance, 273
Dromoran, **257**
Dronabinol (Marinol), 165–166
Dropouts
    from therapeutic communities, 458
    from 12-step groups, 323
Drug Abuse Reporting Program (DARP), 140, 141, 143
Drug Abuse Treatment Outcome Study (DATOS), 138, 140–143
Drug courts, 441
Drug discrimination paradigm, 34
Drug Enforcement Administration, 70, 196
Drug experimentation, 465–466

Drug interactions
    between chlorpromazine and hallucinogens, 200
    with cocaine, 189
    with hallucinogens, 197
    with L-α-acetylmethadol, 278
    with methadone, 273, 505
    with naltrexone, 290
    with phencyclidine, 206
Drug-refusal skills, 469
Drug-seeking behavior, 12, 14, 276, 324
Drug smuggling, 78, 80
Drug testing. *See* Laboratory testing
Drunk driving, 161, 440–441
"Drunk tanks," 441
Dual-diagnosis patients, 90–91, 98–100, 109, 114, 311, 336, 414, 475–481. *See also* Psychiatric disorders
DUI (driving under the influence of alcohol), 161, 440–441
Duragesic (fentanyl), **517**
Dynorphin peptides, 13, 17
Dysphoria, drug-induced
    hallucinogens, 199
    marijuana, 170
    naltrexone, 282–283
    during opioid withdrawal, 254
    opioids, 14, 15
    sedative-hypnotics, 241
    during stimulant withdrawal, 185
Dysthymia, 312, 344
Dystonia, 209

**E**

EAPs. *See* Employee Assistance Programs
Eating disorders, 353, 355, 356, 367, 488, 492
ECA (Epidemiologic Catchment Area) surveys, 48–49, 56, 467, 475, 477, 478
ECG (electrocardiogram), 173
Ecosystem of patient, 389
Ecstasy, 36, 54, 195, 295. *See also* Methylenedioxymethamphetamine
Edgehill Newport, 418
Education, professional. *See* Medical education in addiction medicine
Educational approaches, 132–133, 161–162
    about Alcoholics Anonymous, 407
    about dangers of substance abuse, 90
    during pregnancy, 488–489, 493
    about marijuana, 178

in group therapy, 367, 368
    psychodynamic psychotherapy and, 315
    to reduce risk of HIV infection, 504
    for relapse prevention, 92, 362
    in short-term inpatient treatment programs, 142
    for substance abuse prevention, 468, 535–542
    in therapeutic communities, 454
EEG. *See* Electroencephalogram
Effective contact, 52
Effectiveness of treatment. *See* Treatment outcomes
Ego, 309, 312, 313
    hallucinogen effects on functioning of, 198, 199
Ego psychology, 309, 311, 315, 317–318
Eicosanoids, 40
Elderly persons
    adult protective services for, 440
    alcoholism among, 336
Electrical aversion therapy, 131
Electro-acupuncture, 267
Electrocardiogram (ECG), 173
Electroconvulsive therapy, for phencyclidine delirium, 210–211
Electroencephalogram (EEG)
    during benzodiazepine withdrawal, 241
    hallucinogen effects on, 198
    phencyclidine effects on, 207
Embalming fluid, 169
Emergency treatment
    for cannabis use, 170
    for lysergic acid diethylamide reactions, 199
Empathy of therapist, 133
Emphysema, 173, 216
Employee Assistance Programs (EAPs), 389, 423–434, 439
    access to professional assistance in, 423
    advantages of, 424
    compared with industrial alcoholism model, 424–425
    complements to, 431–434
        health promotion and stress management, 432
        peer intervention programs and member assistance programs, 432–434
        workplace drug testing, 432, 439, 521, 522

workplace prohibition of
    psychoactive substance use,
    431–432
components of, 423
contract between employee and
    employer in, 425–426
definition of, 425
discovery of employed
    substance-abusing persons,
    423–424
dynamics of implementation of,
    428–430
    diagnosis and use of treatment,
        430
    policy diffusion and training, 429
    policy statements, 428–429
    posttreatment, 430
    referral routes, 429–430
efficacy of, 431
follow-up after treatment in,
    426, 430
history of, 424–425
identification of women substance
    abusers by, 487
mainstreaming of substance abuse
    treatment and, 424–425
percentage of workforce covered by,
    434
process of, 425–426
range of problems presented to, 425
referral to, 425–426, 429–430
role conflicts affecting administrators
    of, 428
use of disulfiram in, 337
variations in organization of, 423
widespread presence of, 423
workplace functions served by,
    426–428
    contribution to health care cost
        containment, 427–428
    provision of due process for
        employees, 427
    provision of gatekeeping and
        channeling of employees'
        use of treatment services,
        428
    reduction of supervisory and
        managerial responsibility,
        426–427
    retention of employees, 426
    transformation of workplace
        organizational culture,
        428
written policies and procedures of,
    423, 428–429

Enabling behaviors, 338, 390
Encephalopathy
    hepatic, 160
    Wernicke's, 154, 160
Encounters, in therapeutic
    communities, 453
Endocarditis, 18, 492
Endocrine effects
    of cocaine, 184
    of hallucinogens, 196
    of marijuana, 173–174
    of opioids, 12
Endogenous opioid peptides, 11, 13
    effect of opioid antagonists on, 282,
        288–289
Endomorphin peptides, 13
β-Endorphin, 13–14
    during opioid withdrawal, 14–15
    during smoking, 218
Enebriants. *See* Hallucinogens
Enkephalin peptides, 13
Environmental context of substance
    abuse, 50–53, 69
Epidemics of substance abuse, 76
Epidemiologic Catchment Area (ECA)
    surveys, 48–49, 56, 467, 475, 477,
    478
Epidemiology of drug dependence,
    47–56
    cannabis use, 166–169
    causes, 50–54
        drug availability, 52, 80
        effective contact, 51
        genetic factors, 59–66
        Human Envirome Project, 52–53,
            56
        individual vulnerabilities and their
            consequences, 14–15,
            53–54, 70
        social causation versus social
            selection, 52
        twin studies, 50–51
    genetic epidemiology, 59–62
    "iceberg" phenomenon of treated
        and untreated cases, 47, **48**
    location, 49–50
        age and gender distribution,
            49–50
        geographical distribution, 50, **51,**
            79
    mechanisms, 54–56, **55**
    prevention and intervention, 56
    primary rubrics for, 47
    quantity, 48–49
        annual incidence rate, 48–49

lifetime prevalence, 48
population frequency, 48
prevalence of recently active drug
    dependence, 49
Equagesic (meprobamate), 241, **247**
Equanil (meprobamate), 241, **247**
Esophageal varices, 160
Estazolam (ProSom), **246**
Ethanol. *See* Alcohol
Ethchlorvynol (Placidyl), **247**
Ether, 77
Ethnicity. *See also* Cross-cultural
    aspects of substance abuse
    of Alcoholics Anonymous members,
        403, 404
    definition of, 75
    effects of addiction on, 80
    ethnic identity and substance use,
        78
    ethnic minority patients, 81
    HIV infection and, 504
    treatment and, 80–81
        access to treatment, 80
        cultural recovery, 81
        cultural reentry, 81
*N*-Ethyl-1-phencyclohexalamine (PCE),
    205
Etodolac (Lodine), **514**
Euphoria, drug-induced
    alcohol, 3
    hallucinogens, 197
    γ-hydroxybutyrate, 302
    marijuana, 39, 165, 169
    nicotine, 218
    opioids, 12, 14
    sedative-hypnotics, 241
    stimulants, 21, 183, 184
Eve, 298. *See also*
    Methylenedioxyamphetamine
Evoked potentials, **61,** 62, 65, **66**
Exercise
    during inpatient treatment, 419
    for pain management, **513**
    for phencyclidine-abusing persons,
        212
Expectancy theory, 538
Exposure therapy, 479, 480
Extrapyramidal symptoms, 159

**F**

Fagerstrom Test for Nicotine
    Dependence (FTND), 110, 218,
    220
Fagerstrom Tolerance Questionnaire,
    220

Family, 380
  absent, 398
  aftercare for, 399
  Al-Anon groups for, 177, 338, 382, 391, 392, 397, 488
  alcoholic, 380
    heterogeneity of, 386
    involvement during initial assessment phase of treatment, 380
    wet and dry behavior patterns in, 380
  assessment of, 383, 390, 392
  assigning tasks in, 396
  Co-Anon groups for, 392, 397
  creating supportive network for, 391–392
  daily routines in, 380
  detoxification of, 383–385
  development of, 380
  disengagement from substance-abusing member of, 395
  disintegrated, 398
  drug-abusing, 391–392
  enabling behaviors of, 338, 390
  enmeshed, 397–398
  functional, 397
  functional analysis of, 394
  genogram of, 392
  impact of parental substance dependence on adolescent substance use, 469
  interactional patterns in, 380, 381, 392
  interviews with, 114, 383
  involvement in relapse prevention, 365
  marking boundaries in, 396
  mind reading in, 392, 396
  participation in intervention, 391
  participation in network therapy, 323, 379–381
  phases of involvement in treatment process, 389
  problem solving and assertion in, 394
  pseudoindividuation in, 398
  readjustment after cessation of drug abuse, 398–399
  regulatory behaviors of, 380
  relationships in, 91
  reluctance to disclose information about patient's substance abuse, 109
  resistance in, 394, 397

  reunification after removal of infant by child protective services, 439
  stimulus control in, 394
  therapist's emotional reactions to, 393
Family history of substance abuse, 112
Family studies, 59, 100
Family therapy, 91, 313, 344
  for adolescent substance abusers, 380, 389, 390, 470
  for alcohol problems, 323, 325, 379–386
    advantages of, 385–386
    Al-Anon groups, 382
    behavioral family therapy, 379, 381
    common features of treatment approaches for, 380
    confusion about implementation of, 379
    effect on treatment compliance, 385–386
    efficacy of, 385, 390
    family systems therapy, 379, 380
      assessment strategies, 383
      family detoxification, 383–385
    integration of models for, 380, 382
    overview of treatment models for, 379–380
    reasons for increasing interest in, 379
    related to alcoholism subtype, 382
    social network therapy, 379–381
    treatment outcome literature on, 385–386
  effect on treatment compliance, 385–386, 390
  network therapy and, 328–329, 379–380
  for other drug abuse, 389–399
    cannabis dependence, 177–178
    developing system for achieving and maintaining abstinence, 390–392
    achieving abstinence, 390–391
    dealing with continued drug abuse, 391–392
    maintaining abstinence, 391
    motivating entire family to participate, 392
    efficacy of, 389–390
    family diagnosis for, 392

    family reactivity and, 397–398
      absent families, 398
      disintegrated families, 398
      enmeshed families, 397–398
      functional families, 397
    family readjustment after cessation of drug abuse, 398–399
    impact on patient mortality, 390
    overview of techniques for, 392–394
      behavioral family therapy, 394
      Bowen's systems family therapy, 394
      psychodynamic therapy, 393–394
      structural-strategic therapy, 393
    related to drug type, 397
    related to gender of identified patient, 398
    specific structural techniques for, 394–397
      actualization, 395–396
      assigning tasks, 396
      balancing and unbalancing, 396–397
      contracting, 395
      creating intensity, 397
      joining, 395
      marking boundaries, 396
      paradoxical techniques, 396
      reframing, 396
    variations of, 397–398
  for relapse prevention, 365
  strategic family approach for, 329
  for women substance abusers, 398, 488
Fee-for-service (FFS) arrangements, 546
Fellowships in addiction medicine, 532
Fenfluramine, 101
Fentanyl, 12, 77, 253
  transdermal (Duragesic), **517**
Fetal alcohol effects, 493
Fetal alcohol syndrome, 491, 493
Fetal effects of drugs. *See* Perinatal substance use
Fever, during opioid withdrawal, 260
FFS (fee-for-service) arrangements, 546
Field surveys of drug dependence, 48
Financial management guidance, 91
Financial resources, 92
Financing strategies of managed care organizations, 546

Fiorinal (butalbital), **247**
Flashbacks, 201
Flexible patient-driven models of care, 548
Flumazenil (Romazicon), 4, 239–240
  for hepatic encephalopathy, 160
  phenobarbital withdrawal equivalent for, **246**
Flunitrazepam (Rohypnol), 240, **246,** 303
Fluoxetine
  for alcoholic persons, 99, 477
  for cocaine abuse, 27, 187
    in HIV-infected persons, 507
  interaction with lysergic acid diethylamide, 197
Flupenthixol, 26
Fluphenazine, **515**
Flurazepam (Dalmane), **246**
Follicle-stimulating hormone (FSH), 174
Ford, Betty, 317, 531
Foreign students, 81–82. *See also* Cross-cultural aspects of substance abuse
Fortune 500 corporations, 423
Free association, 315
Freud, Sigmund, 309
Frustration, 355
"Fry," 169
FSH (follicle-stimulating hormone), 174
FTND (Fagerstrom Test for Nicotine Dependence), 110, 218, 220
Functional analysis, 131
Funding for substance abuse treatment, 92
Furosemide, 210
Fyn kinase, 6

**G**

G proteins. *See* Guanine nucleotide-binding proteins
GABA. *See* γ-Aminobutyric acid
Gabapentin (Neurontin), 248, **515**
GAD. *See* Generalized anxiety disorder
GAF (global adaptive functioning), 61, **61**
Galactorrhea, 174
Gambling, 353, 355–357, 367, 468
Gastric lavage, 208, 298
Gastrointestinal complications, 160
Gateway drugs, 54, 169, 467, 468, 535
Gay men's circuit parties, 295–303

Gender distribution of substance abuse, 49, 50, 109, 165. *See also* Women substance abusers
Generalized anxiety disorder (GAD), 479
  alcoholism and, 158
  diagnosis in substance-abusing persons, 479
  treatment in substance-abusing persons, 479
Genetics of substance abuse, 59–66, 70
  adoption study, 59–60, **60,** 100–101
  alcoholism, 5, 14, 50, 59, 61, 100–102
    Collaborative Study of the Genetics of Alcoholism, 61, **62,** 65, **65, 66**
  candidate gene approaches, 63–64, **64, 65**
  clinical observations guiding candidate gene searches in polysubstance abusers, 61, **61**
  genetic epidemiology, 59–62
  genome scans for detecting linkage, 65, **65, 66**
  Human Genome Project, 53, 56
  opioid dependence, 14–15
  personality traits, 53–54, 59–63
  twin studies, 50–52, 59, **60**
Genogram, 392
Genpril. *See* Ibuprofen
Geographical distribution of drug dependence, 50, **51,** 79
GGT ( γ-glutamyltransferase), 115, 155, 161, 290, 524
GH. *See* Growth hormone
GHB. *See* γ-Hydroxybutyrate
Gin epidemic, 76
Global adaptive functioning (GAF), 61, **61**
Global lifestyle change strategies, 360, 363–365, **364**
Globus pallidus, 18
Glucocorticoids, 14
Glucose
  cocaine effects on metabolism of, 184
  levels in alcoholic patients, 524
  use during alcohol withdrawal, 154
Glutamate
  ketamine and, 301
  phencyclidine and, 206
  stimulants and, 25–26
Glutamate receptors
  alcohol and, 6
  opioids and, 17
  stimulants and, 24

γ-Glutamyltransferase (GGT), 115, 155, 161, 290, 524
Glutethimide (Doriden), **247**
Glycine receptor proteins, 4
Goals of treatment. *See* Treatment goals
Going geographic, 81
Grandiosity, 109, 335–336
"Grievous bodily harm." *See* γ-Hydroxybutyrate
"Groucho eyes," 208
Group therapy, 313, 367–376
  addiction and, 367–368
  advantages of, 367
  for alcohol problems, 323, 369
  as arena for social learning and social backing, 368
  for cannabis dependence, 177, 348
  for cocaine use disorders, 369
  cognitive-behavioral, 368
  cohesion and "addict identification" in, 376
  confrontation versus support in, 374–375
  efficacy of, 369–370
  features of groups for addicted persons, 372–376
  individual's submission to group's ideology in, 368
  during inpatient treatment, 419
  maintaining accepting attitude for, 374
  negative countertransference reactions in, 371
  network therapy, 323–332
  for patients with DSM Axis II diagnoses, 370
  pregroup preparation for, 372–373
  psychodynamics applied to, 311, 314, 318, 367, 369, 375
    modified dynamic group therapy, 369, 370, 373
  psychoeducational, 367, 368
  for relapse prevention, 365
  safety issues in, 373–374
  for schizophrenic substance-abusing patients, 369
  for smoking cessation, 225, 226, 232–233
  special needs of addicted persons in, 370–371
  structure for, 373
  therapeutic communities and, 368
  therapist for, 376
  tradition of exclusion from, 371–372
  as treatment of choice, 367, 370
  variations of, 367

Growth hormone (GH)
    cocaine effects on, 184
    γ-hydroxybutyrate effects on,
        301, 302
    marijuana effects on, 174
Guanabenz, 153
Guanfacine, 261
Guanine nucleotide-binding proteins
    (G proteins)
    alcohol and, 4
    cannabinoids and, 41
    opioids and, 11
Guia Para Dejar de Fumar (Guide for
    Quitting Smoking), 225
Guilt, 335, 449

## H

Habilitation, 448
Habitrol. See Nicotine transdermal
    patch
Hair toxicology testing, 114–115, 208,
    521, 522, **523**. See also Laboratory
    testing
Halazepam (Paxipam), **246**
Halcion (triazolam), 241, **246**
Halfway houses, 143, 344, 443
Hallucinations, 113, 159, 195, 199
Hallucinogens, 33–37, 110, 195–201,
    **514**. See also specific drugs
    adolescent use of, 53, 168, 196, 465
    age distribution of use of, 53, **55**
    attitudes toward use of, 196
    availability as street drugs, 196
    classical, 33–37
        chemical structures of, **35**
        classification of, 33–36, **34**
        definition of, 33
        mechanism of action of, 36
        stimulus generalization and
            stimulus antagonism tests
            of, 34
    clinical research on, 195–196
    contaminated with phencyclidine,
        205
    definition of, 33, 195
    designer drugs, 36, **36**
    diagnosis of use of, 198–199
    drug interactions with, 197
    dysphoria induced by, 199
    effects on ego functioning, 198, 199
    emotional responses to, 197
    euphoria induced by, 197
    flashbacks induced by, 201
    neurobiology of, 33–37
    onset and duration of action of, 197

patient assessment for use of, 112
personality changes due to, 198
physiological effects of, 33, 196–197
potency of, 197
prevalence of use of, 195, 196
psychological effects of, 33, 197–198
street names for, 195
terminology for, 33
treatment for abuse of, 199–201
    acute adverse reactions, 199–200
    chronic adverse reactions, 200–201
    psychotherapy, 201
twin studies of abuse of, **60**
use in 1960s culture, 196, 198
Haloperidol, 200, 209, 210
Hand edema, 256
Hangover effects, 297
Harm-avoidance, 60–62, **62, 65,** 101,
    466
Harm reduction, 220, 229, 353, 354,
    360, 438
    definition of, 504
    for HIV infection, 504–505
    syringe-exchange programs, 504–505
Harmaline, **34, 35**
Harvard Cocaine Recovery Project,
    368, 369
Hashish, 112, 165
Hashish oil, 165
Hazelden, 142, 143, 417, 531
The Health Benefits of Smoking
    Cessation, 217
Health care professionals who abuse
    drugs
    "impaired professionals" programs
        for, 433
    naltrexone therapy for, 282, 284,
        285
    peer intervention programs for,
        432–434
    12-step groups for, 405, 407–408
Health maintenance organizations
    (HMOs), 545, 547. See also
    Managed care
Health promotion programs in
    workplace, 432
Heanta, 267
Heart disease. See Cardiovascular
    effects
Heat therapy, **513**
Helplessness, 310
Hemiplegia, 197
Hepatic effects of drugs
    alcohol, 115, 160, 524
    dantrolene sodium, 298

disulfiram, 155
monoamine oxidase inhibitors, 155
naltrexone, 289–290, 337
pemoline, 480
Hepatic encephalopathy, 160
Hepatitis, 18, 492
    alcoholic, 160
Heritability. See Genetics
Heroin, 12, 112, 281
    administration routes for, 251
    age distribution of use of, **55**
    availability of, 251
    cost of, 251
    dependence on
        among Vietnam veterans, 52
        vulnerability to, 14
    detoxification from, 251–268 (See
        also Opioid detoxification)
    development of, 77
    genetic influences on abuse of, 14
    immunological effects of, 505
    long-term residential treatment for
        users of, 138–141
    methadone maintenance for users of,
        136–138
    naltrexone for users of, 286–287
    purity of, 251, 257
    use during pregnancy, 492
    withdrawal from, 291
        benzodiazepine self-medication to
            ameliorate effects of, 240
        glucocorticoid levels during, 14
        methadone for, 257, **257**
        onset and duration of symptoms
            of, 15, 253–254, **254**
5-HIAA (5-hydroxyindoleacetic acid),
    101
High-risk situations, 355–358
    abstinence violation effect and,
        358
    assessing patient's ability to cope
        with, 362
    coping effectively with, 357
    definition of, 355
    inability to cope with, 357–358
    interpersonal conflict, 355–356
    negative emotional states, 355
    social pressure, 356
Hippocampus, 4–5, 42
Historical overview of substance abuse,
    75–78
    hallucinogens, 196, 198
    γ-hydroxybutyrate, 302
    ketamine, 299–300
    marijuana, 166

methylenedioxymethamphetamine, 296
phencyclidine, 205, 299–300
History taking
with family present, 390
for opioid-addicted persons, 255
for smoking, 112, 219
strategies for, 111–113
HIV. *See* Human immunodeficiency virus infection
HMOs (health maintenance organizations), 545, 547. *See also* Managed care
"Home" drug tests for marijuana, 176
Homelessness, 91, 439, 444
House runs in therapeutic communities, 455
HPA (hypothalamic-pituitary-adrenal) axis, 14–15
5-HT. *See* Serotonin
Human Envirome Project, 52–53, 56
Human Genome Project, 53, 56
Human immunodeficiency virus (HIV) infection, 18, 251, 256, 271, 503–508
assessing risk for, 504
comorbid with substance use disorders and psychiatric disorders, 506
pharmacotherapy for patients with, 507
treatment of psychiatric disorders in patients with, 506
effect on tuberculin skin test, 256
epidemiology of, 503–504
ethnicity and, 504
incidence of, 503
injection-drug use and, 503, 507–508
medical care for substance-abusing persons with, 507–508
behavioral aspects of, 507
settings for, 507–508
mortality from, 503
during pregnancy, 486
preventing transmission of, 504–505
harm reduction, 504–505
syringe-exchange programs, 504–505
risk-reduction education, 504
condom use, 504
disinfection of syringes, 504
"levels of defense" approach, 504
relationship between substance abuse and, 503

stimulant abuse and, 183, 506
testing for, 504
treatment of substance use disorders in persons with, 505–506
counseling, 505–506
methadone maintenance, 505, 508
residential treatment/therapeutic communities, 451, 459, 506
in women, 486
Huntington's disease, 289
Hydralazine, 209
Hydromorphone (Dilaudid), 12, 112
withdrawal from, 253, **254**, 257, **257**
5-Hydroxy-α-methyltryptamine, **34, 35**
4-Hydroxy-*N,N*-dimethyltryptamine (Psilocin), **34, 35**
γ-Hydroxybutyrate (GHB), 295, 301–303
for alcoholic persons, 154, 156
γ-aminobutyric acid and, 301
brain distribution of, 301
deaths associated with use of, 301
dependence on, 303
history of use of, 302
legal status of, 301
manufacture of, 301
mechanism of action of, 302
for narcolepsy, 301
physiological effects of, 302
recreational dosage of, 302
respiratory depression induced by, 301, 302
side effects of, 302
stimulation of growth hormone release by, 301, 302
street names of, 301
therapeutic index for, 301, 302
treating intoxication with, 302–303
use of alcohol or sedatives with, 303
withdrawal from, 303
6-Hydroxydopamine, 25
5-Hydroxyindoleacetic acid (5-HIAA), 101
Hydroxyzine, **515**
Hypertension
alcohol withdrawal, 153
hypertensive crisis in patients on monoamine oxidase inhibitors, 478
induced by interaction between cocaine and tricyclic antidepressant, 189

phencyclidine-induced, 206, 208, 209
Hyperthermia, 209
Hypertriglyceridemia, 524
Hypnosis
for alcohol abuse, 132, 339
for smoking cessation, 231, 232
Hypoglycemia, 153
Hypotension, 262, 263
Hypothalamic-pituitary-adrenal (HPA) axis, 14–15

**I**

Ibogaine, 267
Ibuprofen
marijuana use and, 172
for pain, 514, **514**
use during opioid detoxification, 259
ICD *(International Classification of Diseases)*, 97
Ice amphetamine, 184
"Iceberg" phenomenon, 47, **48**
ICS 205-930 (tropisetron), 7
Id, 309, 313
Illusionogenic drugs. *See* Hallucinogens
Imagery, for pain management, **513**
Imaginal flooding, 480
Imidazopyridines, 240
Imipramine
for alcoholic persons, 99
for cocaine abuse, 187
for patients on methadone maintenance, 477
Immigrants, 81–82. *See also* Cross-cultural aspects of substance abuse
Immunological effects of drugs
marijuana, 173
opioids, 505
"Impaired professionals" programs, 433
Impulsivity
adolescent substance use and, 466, 467
in attention-deficit/hyperactivity disorder, 480
among patients entering therapeutic communities, 450
In utero drug exposure. *See* Perinatal substance use
Incidence of drug dependence, 48–49
Incoordination, 4, 5
Indicated prevention of substance abuse, 536, **542**

Individual psychotherapy
    for alcoholism, 335–341, 348
        advantages of, 337–338
        Alcoholics Anonymous
            participation and, 338
        central problem in, 335
        during early stage of treatment,
            338–339
        indications for, 338
        during late stage of treatment, 339
        during middle stage of treatment,
            339
        outcome studies of, 340–341
        pharmacotherapy and, 337
        termination of, 340
        transference and
            countertransference
            reactions during, 340
    for other drug abuse, 343–349
        availability of, 343
        cocaine use disorders, 347, 348
        compared with addiction
            counseling, 343
        definition of, 343
        efficacy of, 346–348
        frequency and intensity of,
            348–349
        guidelines for, 346, 349
        knowledge required for, 344
        marijuana use disorders, 177–178,
            348
        opioid dependence, 346, 348
        rational for use of, 343–344
        settings for, 344
        smoking, 225, 226, 232–233
        techniques of, 346
        therapeutic alliance and, 345–346
        therapist qualities for, 345
Individual vulnerabilities to substance
        abuse, 14–15, 53–54, 70
    genetic factors, 59–66
Indolealkylamines, **34, 35,** 195
Infections and injection-drug use,
        18, 77
    HIV infection, 503–508
Infertility, 486
Inhalant use, 110, **514**
    by adolescents, 168, 465
    patient assessment for, 112
Injection-drug use, 77
    HIV infection and, 503, 507–508
    infections due to, 18, 77
Inpatient treatment, 413–420, 529
    advantages of, 323, 415
    aftercare and, 419

for alcohol withdrawal, 153
assessment of patient for, 416
attending Alcoholics Anonymous
        during, 419
for benzodiazepine withdrawal, 248
for cannabis dependence, 177
chemical aversion
        counterconditioning therapy,
        415
comparison of inpatients and
        outpatients, 416–417
controversy about, 413
cost of, 415
couples' therapy, 326
for dangerous patients, 415, 416
definition of, 413
determining active and inert
        ingredients of, 420
for detoxification, 413, 416
    from alcohol, 153, 416
    from opioids, 252, 258–259, 261
    from sedative-hypnotics, 416
disadvantages of, 323, 415
for drug abuse, 135
for dual-diagnosis patients, 414
exercise and, 419
facilities for, 413–414
    private sector versus public
        hospital units, 413
    proliferation of, 323
    staff of, 413–414, 418–419
future implications for, 420
group therapy during, 419
for HIV-infected persons, 506
importance of peer support during,
        418
indications for, 415–417
individual psychotherapy during, 344
to initiate methadone maintenance,
        273
intensity of, 415
length of stay in, 419
long-term residential treatment,
        138–141, 391
before managed care, 546
"medically managed" versus
        "medically monitored," 414
Minnesota Model of, 142, 414–415,
        442
outcome of, 417–419
    flaws in studies of, 417
    general findings of, 417–418
    patient characteristics and, 418
    program characteristics and,
        418–419

for phencyclidine abuser, 210–212
psychiatric assessment during, 419
psychodynamic psychotherapy
        during, 314
rationale for, 415
safe environment of, 415, 416
short-term, 142–143
for smoking cessation, 219
stigma associated with, 415
use of contracts in, 419
Insight-oriented therapy. *See*
        Psychodynamic psychotherapy
Insomnia
    antidepressants for alcoholic persons
        with, 158
    during benzodiazepine withdrawal,
        241, 243
    among HIV-infected persons with
        substance use disorders, 506
    medications contraindicated for, 93
    during opioid withdrawal, 259
        clonidine effects on, 262–263
    sedative-hypnotics for, 239
    zolpidem for, 240
Instant gratification, 359
Institute of Medicine (IOM), 437, 438
Integrated service delivery systems, 547
Integrated substance abuse and mental
        health services, 547
Intellectualization, 317
Intensive outpatient (IO) treatment,
        442–443
    compared with partial
        hospitalization, 442
    compared with traditional outpatient
        treatment, 443
    minimum criterion for, 442–443
    patient selection for, 443
*International Classification of Diseases*
        (ICD), 97
Internet, 331–332
Interpersonal conflict, 355–356, 469
Interpersonal psychotherapy, for alcohol
        persons, 160
Intervention by family, 391
Interview. *See also* Assessment of
        patient
    to determine need for opioid
        detoxification, 255
    to elicit patient history, 111–113
    motivational, 109–110, 116–117,
        549
    with significant others, 114–115,
        383
    structured, 114, 526

Intoxicants. *See* Hallucinogens
Intoxication
  with alcohol, 113, 161
  with cannabis, 169–170, **170**
  examination for signs of, 113
  Freud's theory of, 309
  with methylenedioxymeth-
    amphetamine, 298
  with phencyclidine, 206–209, **207**
  with sedative-hypnotics, 241
  with stimulants, 113, 185
Intraocular pressure elevation, 39
Inverse exponential withdrawal method,
  258
IO programs. *See* Intensive outpatient
  treatment
IOM (Institute of Medicine), 437,
  438
Ion channels, receptor-gated, 6–9

**J**

Jaundice, 256
Jellinek, E.M., 97
Jews, 78
Job functioning, 91
Johns Hopkins Alcohol/Drug Project,
  530–531
Johnson Institute, 380
Joining techniques, 395
  maintenance, 395
  mimesis, 395
  tracking, 395

**K**

K, 299. *See also* Ketamine
K-hole, 300
Ketamine, 195, 205, 295, 299–301,
  303
  administration routes for, 300
  central nervous system effects of,
    206, 301
  dissociation produced by, 299
  history of use of, 299–300
  liquid form of, 300
  mechanism of action of, 300–301
  physiological effects of, 300
    emergence state, 300
    onset of, 300
  recreational dosage of, 300
  reinforcing effects of, 301
  street names for, 299
  tolerance to, 300
  treatment for abuse of, 301
  veterinary use of, 299
Ketanserin, 36

Ketoprofen (Orudis, Actron), **514**
Ketorolac (Toradol), 259, **514**
Khat, **514**
"Kicking the habit," 15
Kindling, 152, 154
Klonopin (clonazepam), **246**

**L**

LAAM. *See* L-α-Acetylmethadol
"Labeling" patients, 109
Labor and delivery, 496
Laboratory testing, 114–115, 521–524
  to assess effects of naltrexone on
    blood chemistry, 289–290
  to identify common correlates of
    alcohol and other drug use,
    115, 155, 161, 524
  to identify recent drug use, 521–524,
    **523**
    blood testing, 114–115, 521,
      522
    body fluids in which drugs can be
      identified, 521
    comparison of methods for, **523**
    costs of, 521
    hair testing, 114–115, 521, 522
    hallucinogens, 198
    legal regulations affecting, 521
    marijuana, 175, 176, 522
    opioids, 256, 522
    phencyclidine, 207, 208
    preemployment testing, 176, 432,
      522
    in pregnant women, 494
    saliva testing, 521–524
    sample selected for, 521
    sweat patch testing, 522
    urine testing, 114–115, 521,
      522
    workplace testing, 432, 439, 521,
      522
  purposes of, 521
Lactic acid, 524
Lamotrigine (Lamictal), 248
Lapse, 354–355, **355**. *See also* Relapse
Laudanum, **257**
LC (locus coeruleus), 16, **16,** 218, 261
Learning principles, 67–71
  in behavioral family therapy,
    379, 381
  clinical applications of, 70–71
    brief interventions, 71
    community reinforcement
      approach, 70–71
    contingency management, 70

  learning-based treatments and
    comorbidity, 71
  skills training, 70
conditioned drug seeking,
  324–325
drugs as reinforcers, 67–68
learning-based conceptual
  framework, 69–70
preclinical applications of, 70
social learning theory, 68, 449, 539
theoretical implications of, 68–69
therapeutic community view of
  recovery based on social
  learning, 449
Legal interventions
  for alcohol abuse, 161
  to curb tobacco use, 215
  for drug abuse, 441
    drug courts, 441
    probation, 441
  for drunk driving, 161, 440–441
  interventions no longer through
    criminal courts, 441–442
    civil commitment, 441–442
    detoxification, 441
  for perinatal substance use, 491,
    496, **497**
  referral to therapeutic communities,
    450
Legalization of marijuana, 167
Leu-enkephalin, 13
Levels of care, 121–124, **122,** 525, 529,
  547. *See also* Patient placement
  criteria
Levels of prevention, 536, **542**
Levorphanol (Levo-Dromoran), **257,**
  **517**
LH (luteinizing hormone), 174
Librium (chlordiazepoxide), 154, 241,
  **246**
Lifestyle, substance-free. *See also*
  Abstinence
  as goal of therapeutic communities,
    447–449
  motivation to achieve, 89–90
  rebuilding of, 90
Lifestyle balance, 359–360, 363
Lifestyle change strategies, 360,
  363–365, **364**
Lifetime prevalence of drug
  dependence, 48
Linear withdrawal method, 258
Liquid Ecstasy, 301. *See also*
  γ-Hydroxybutyrate
Liquor taxes, 161

Lithium
   for alcohol abuse, 131, 156
   for bipolar disorder, 91, 93, 478
   for cocaine addicts with
         attention-deficit/hyperactivity
         disorder, 188
   for HIV-infected persons who abuse
         drugs, 507
   interaction with lysergic acid
         diethylamide, 197
   use with methadone, 273
   use with naltrexone, 290
Liver enzymes, 115, 290, 524
Liver transplantation, 160
Living situations, 91
Locus coeruleus (LC), 16, **16,** 218, 261
Lodine (etodolac), **514**
Lofexidine, 16, 261, 263–264
Long-term residential treatment (LRT),
      138–141, 391. *See also* Therapeutic
      communities
   for cocaine dependence, 138
   compared with methadone
         maintenance therapy, 138, 139
   continued involvement after
         graduation from, 139
   duration of, 139
   effectiveness of, 139–140, 144–145,
         457–458
   methods of, 138
   modifications from older therapeutic
         community practices, 139
   patient population receiving, 138
   reasons for varying results of, 141
   retention rates in, 139, 140, 145
   staffing for, 141
   in therapeutic communities, 447–460
Lorazepam (Ativan)
   for acute hallucinogen reactions, 200
   for alcohol withdrawal
         mild to moderate, 152
         severe, 153–154
   for phencyclidine-intoxicated
         persons, 209
   phenobarbital withdrawal equivalent
         for, **246**
Loss of control, 323–325
"Lost weekend," 312
Love Drug, **34, 35**
LRT. *See* Long-term residential
      treatment
LSD. *See* Lysergic acid diethylamide
Lung cancer, 173, 216–217
Luteinizing hormone (LH), 174
Lying, 111

Lysergic acid diethylamide (LSD), 33,
      34, **34,** 37, 54, 112, 195–201.
      *See also* Hallucinogens
   absorption of, 197
   adolescent use of, 168, 196
   age distribution of use of, 53
   attitudes toward use of, 196
   availability as street drug, 196
   "bad trips" on, 199
   "businessman's," 197
   cost of, 197
   differentiating paranoid
         schizophrenia from psychosis
         induced by, 199
   differentiating phencyclidine
         intoxication from intoxication
         with, 208
   drug interactions with, 197
   flashbacks induced by, 201
   as model of schizophrenia, 198–199
   onset and duration of action of, 197
   overdose of, 197
   personality changes due to, 200
   physiological effects of, 196–197
   potency of, 197
   prevalence of use of, 196
   psychological effects of, 197–198
   street doses of, 197
   structure of, **35**
   therapeutic index for, 197
   tolerance to, 196
   treatment interventions for abuse of,
         199–201
      acute adverse reactions, 199–200
      chronic adverse reactions,
            200–201
   use at rave parties, 295
   use in 1960s culture, 196, 198

# M

Macy Conference on Training About
      Alcohol and Substance Abuse for
      All Primary Care Physicians,
      529–530, 532
"Magic mushrooms," 195
Magical thinking, 198
Magnesium level in alcoholism, 524
Magnesium pemoline, 480
Malnutrition of alcoholic persons,
      159–160
Malpractice claims, 242
Managed care, 320, 545–551
   adapting treatment services to
         environment of, 545
   definition of, 545

   effect on short-term inpatient
         treatment programs, 143
   effect on structure of delivery
         system, 546–548
      integrated delivery systems, 547
      integration of substance abuse and
            mental health services, 547
      linkage between substance abuse
            and medical services,
            547–548
      outpatient services as hub of new
            delivery system, 546–547
      partnerships between public and
            private sector providers,
            548
   goals of, 545
   patient placement criteria and,
         121–124
   problems between treatment
         providers and, 549–551
      claims payment problems,
            550–551
      managed care organizations'
            negative attitudes and
            behavior toward providers,
            550
      provider concerns about managed
            care organizations'
            overemphasis on cost, 550
      provider resistance to change,
            549–550
   strategies and structure of, 545–546
      financing strategies, 546
         capitation, 546
         discounted fee-for-service
               arrangements, 546
         risk-sharing arrangements, 546
         health maintenance organizations,
               545
         service delivery strategies, 545–546
   treatment innovations under,
         548–549
      brief interventions, 549
      flexible patient-driven models of
            care, 548
      motivation-enhancement
            techniques, 549
      outpatient crisis intervention,
            548–549
      pharmacological treatments, 549
      stage-specific treatment
            interventions, 549
Mania. *See also* Bipolar disorder
   alcoholism and, 98
   due to stimulant intoxication, 185

Manufacture of illicit drugs, 18
MAOIs. *See* Monoamine oxidase
    inhibitors
Marathons, in therapeutic communities,
    453–454
Marijuana, 165–179. *See also* Cannabis
    use
Marijuana Tax Act of 1937, 166
Marinol (dronabinol), 165–166
Marital therapy, 91, 326. *See also*
    Family therapy
    for alcohol abuse, 129, 131–132,
        369, 379–386
    in groups, 369
    for relapse prevention, 365
Mass media
    portrayals of Alcoholics Anonymous
        in, 403
    programs for substance abuse
        prevention, 539–540, **542**
MAST (Michigan Alcohol Screening
    Test), 61, 114, 161, 525
Mazindol, 186
MCV (mean corpuscular volume),
    115, 524
MDA (methylenedioxyamphetamine),
    **34, 35,** 195, 298
MDGT (modified dynamic group
    therapy), 369, 370, 373
MDMA. *See* Methylenedioxy-
    methamphetamine
Mean corpuscular volume (MCV), 115,
    524
Mecamylamine, 230
Mechanisms of drug dependence,
    54–56, **55**
Meclofenamate (Meclomen), **514**
Medicaid, 124, 545, 548
Medical education in addiction
    medicine, 529–533
    Career Teacher Program in Alcohol
        and Other Drug Abuse, 529
    determining what should be taught
        and when, 530–532
        basic science years, 530–531
            Johns Hopkins Alcohol/Drug
                Project, 530–531
            Project ADEPT, 531
        clinical years, 531
        curriculum units, 530, **530**
        "Practice Guidelines for the
            Treatment of Patients With
            Substance Use Disorders,"
            117, 530
        residency training, 531–532

factors affecting changes in, 529
    continuum of care, 124, 529
    role of primary care physicians,
        437–438, 529–530
    recommended physician
        competencies for treating
        substance abuse disorders, **533**
    training teachers for, 532–533
Medical status, 90
    laboratory evaluation of, 115
    of persons on methadone
        maintenance therapy, 136
Medically ill patients
    with HIV infection, 503–508
    linkage between substance abuse and
        medical services for, 547–548
    methadone maintenance for, 276
    pain management for, 511–517
    smoking cessation for, 219
    therapeutic community treatment
        for, 451
Medicare, 545, 548
Meditation, 339, **513**
Memantine, 267
Member assistance programs, 433
Memory impairment, drug-induced
    benzodiazepines, 244
    cocaine, 184
    marijuana, 39, 42, 171
    phencyclidine, 211
Mental health approach to addiction,
    372
Mental status examination, 113–114,
    255
Mentally ill chemical abusers (MICA),
    336. *See also* Psychiatric disorders
Meperidine, 18
    disadvantages for acute pain, 516
    withdrawal from, 253, 254, **254,**
        257, **257**
Meprobamate (Miltown), 241, **247**
Mescaline, 33, 34, **34, 35,** 37, 112, 195,
    199
Mesolimbic reward system, 310, 312,
    521
α-MeT (α-methyltryptamine), **34, 35**
Met-enkephalin, 13
MET (motivational enhancement
    therapy), 103–104, 129, 130, 133,
    348, 408–409, 549
Methadone (Dolophine), 12, 77, 94,
    112, **517**
    benzodiazepines to enhance effects
        of, 240
    blocking of NMDA receptor by, 17

drug interactions with, 273, 505
for neonates of methadone-
    maintained mothers, 275
for opioid withdrawal, 256–261
    dosage of, **257,** 257–258
    guidelines for, 261
    length of regimen for, 258–259
    during pregnancy, 261, 389
overdose of, 18
pharmacology of, 136, 272–273,
    505
side effects of, 272
withdrawal from, 15, 253, 254,
    **254**
Methadone maintenance (MM),
    136–138, 251, 271–278, 281, 391
    for adolescents, 272
    alcohol use and, 273
    alternatives to, 277–278
        L-α-acetylmethadol, 136–137,
            277–278, 549
        buprenorphine, 277
    behavior modification techniques
        and, 275
    characteristics of programs offering,
        136
    compared with other therapies,
        136–139
        L-α-acetylmethadol, 136–137
        naltrexone, 284
        outpatient nonmethadone
            treatment, 137
        therapeutic communities, 138,
            139
    counseling and, 136
    definition of, 136
    dosage for, 136, 138, 144, 273–275
        federal regulation of, 274
        individualization of, 273
        initial dose, 273
        maintenance dose, 273–275
        making adjustments in, 274
    driving while on, 273
    effect on criminal behavior, 137
    effectiveness of, 137, 144, 271, 274
    federal and state eligibility criteria
        for, 271–272
        current physiological dependence
            on opioids, 272
        persons in penal institutions, 272
        persons under age 18 years, 272
        pregnant persons, 272
        previously treated patients, 272
    health and nutritional status of
        persons on, 136

Methadone maintenance (MM)
    (continued)
    for HIV-infected patients, 505, 508
        benefits of, 505
        drug interactions affecting, 505
        pain management and, 505
    long-term toxic effects of, 136
    medical maintenance model for,
        275
    monitoring and adjustment features
        of programs offering, 136
    optimal blood levels for, 272
    pain management for persons on,
        516
    as part of comprehensive treatment
        program, 271, 275
    for persons with medical or surgical
        illness, 276
    during pregnancy, 261, 272,
        275–276, 485
    psychiatric aspects of, 276–277
    reasons for varying results of,
        137–138
    remissions associated with, 111
    retention rates in programs for, 137,
        138, 144, 275
    safety of, 272
    supportive-expressive psychotherapy
        for persons on, 309
    sweating among patients on, 15
    tricyclic antidepressants for persons
        on, 99, 477
    withdrawal from, 259
        blind (without patient consent),
            274
        metyrapone stimulation of
            withdrawal symptoms,
            15
Methamphetamine, 21–26, 240.
    See also Amphetamine
Methaqualone, 241
Methcathinone, 36
5-Methoxy-N,N-dimethyltryptamine,
    34, **34, 35**
1-Methyl, 4 phenyl,
    1,2,3,6-tetrahydropyridine
    (MPTP), 18
N-Methyl-D-aspartate (NMDA)
    receptor antagonists
    effect on alcohol actions, 7, 8
    effect on cannabinoid receptor
        expression, 43
    effect on stimulant actions, 22, 24,
        27
    for opioid detoxification, 267

N-Methyl-D-aspartate (NMDA)
    receptors
    alcohol and, 4, 6–8
    ketamine and, 301
    opioids and, 17
    phencyclidine and, 206
    similarities to GABA$_A$ receptor, 6
    stimulants and, 24
Methylenedioxyamphetamine (MDA),
    **34, 35,** 195, 196, 298
Methylenedioxymethamphetamine
    (MDMA), 36, 54, 195, 295–299,
        303
    administration routes for, 296
    cost of, 296
    deaths associated with, 299
    diagnosis of intoxication with, 298
    history of use of, 296
    illegal status of, 295, 296
    manufacture of, 296
    mechanism of action of, 297
    neurotoxicity of, 296–298
    physiological effects of, 296–297
        hangover effects, 297
        onset of, 296
        plateau stage, 296–297
        short-term and long-term effects,
            297
    prevalence of use of, 295
    psychiatric illness precipitated by,
        297
    psychiatric symptoms of intoxication
        with, 298
    psychological effects of, 296
    street names for, 36, 195, 295
    treatment for abuse of, 298–299
        acute reactions, 298
        dependence, 298–299
    varying purity of, 296
α-Methylmescaline (3,4,5-TMA),
    **34, 35**
Methylphenidate
    for alcoholic persons, 159
    for attention-deficit/hyperactivity
        disorder, 480
    for cocaine addicts, 186, 188
α-Methyltryptamine (α-MeT), **34, 35**
Methyprylon (Noludar), **247**
Metronidazole, 132
Metropolitan areas, 52
Metyrapone, 15
MICA (mentally ill chemical abusers),
    336. See also Psychiatric disorders
Michigan Alcohol Screening Test
    (MAST), 61, 114, 161, 525

Midazolam (Versed), 240, **246,** 265
Miltown (meprobamate), 241, **247**
Mimesis, 395
Mind-manifesting drugs.
    See Hallucinogens
Mind reading in families, 392, 396
Minimization, 109, 111, 414
Minnesota Model, 142, 414–415, 442.
    See also Short-term inpatient
        treatment
Minnesota Multiphasic Personality
    Inventory (MMPI), 102, 450
Minority patients, 81. See also Cross-
    cultural aspects of substance abuse
Miosis, 12, 18
MK-801, 17, 43
MM. See Methadone maintenance
MMPI (Minnesota Multiphasic
    Personality Inventory), 102, 450
Moderation in substance use, 89–90,
    114, 360
Modified dynamic group therapy
    (MDGT), 369, 370, 373
Modified Selective Severity Assessment
    Scale (MSSA), 152
Mogadon (nitrazepam), **246**
Moniliasis, 256
Monitoring the Future Study, 165, 166,
    **166,** 205
Monoamine oxidase inhibitors (MAOIs)
    dietary tyramine and, 478
    drug interactions with
        bupropion, 229
        lysergic acid diethylamide, 197
    hepatotoxicity of, 158
    hypertensive crisis in patients on,
        478
    for panic disorder, 158, 478
    for posttraumatic stress disorder, 480
    for social phobia, 479
Moral model of addiction, 529
Morality, 449
Mormons, 78
Morphine, 11, 12, 14, 112
    controlled-release (MS Contin), **517**
    development of, 77
    dextromethorphan combined with,
        17
    withdrawal from, 257, **257**
        onset and duration of, 15, **254**
Mortality rate
    for females with alcoholism, 485
    impact of family therapy on, 390
    impact of inpatient treatment on,
        418

Motivation
    to achieve abstinence, 89–90, 109
    assessing patient's readiness for
        change, 116–117
        theories of behavior change, 538
    of behavioral change in workplace,
        424
    of family to participate in treatment,
        392
    inpatient treatment for unmotivated
        patients, 415
    to quit smoking, **221,** 224–226
    therapeutic community view of,
        448
Motivational enhancement therapy
    (MET), 103–104, 129, 130, 133,
    348, 408–409, 549
Motivational interviewing, 109–110,
    116–117, 133
Motrin. *See* Ibuprofen
MPTP (1-methyl, 4 phenyl,
    1,2,3,6-tetrahydropyridine), 18
MS Contin (morphine), **517**
MSSA (Modified Selective Severity
    Assessment Scale), 152
Muscimol, 8
Muslims, 78
Myocardial infarction, 260
Myoglobinuria, 209

## N

NA. *See* Narcotics Anonymous
NAATP (National Association of
    Addiction Treatment Providers)
    Patient Placement Criteria, 123
Nalbuphine, 12
Nalmefene, 12
    for acute overdose, 18
    for alcoholism, 337
    for ultrarapid detoxification under
        anesthesia/sedation, 265
Nalorphine, 282
Naloxone, 281
    for acute overdose, 18, 283
    combined with buprenorphine,
        266, 291
    compared with naltrexone, 283
    to diagnose opioid dependence, 282
    dosage of, 18
    effects on opioid receptors, 282,
        289
    medical uses of, 282
    for neonates whose mothers received
        opioids during labor, 282

opioid withdrawal syndrome
    precipitated by, 282
    to test for residual dependence
        before initiating naltrexone,
        287–288
Naloxone challenge test, 15, 208, 258
Naltrexone, 12, 141, 281–292, 391
    absence of dependence on, 284
    for alcoholism, 7, 94, 130, 155–156,
        282, 291–292, 337, 549
        in persons with schizophrenia,
            476–477
    benefits of, 283–284
    clinical use of, 283–287
    compared with naloxone, 283
    compared with other treatment
        approaches, 284–285
        buprenorphine, 291
        methadone maintenance, 284
    depot, 290–291
    drug interactions with, 290
    effectiveness of, 284
    effects of, 282–283
        on blood chemistry, 289–290
        dysphoria, 282–283
        on opioid receptors, 282, 289
        reduced drug craving, 283
    mechanism of action of, 281, 337
    opioid withdrawal syndrome
        precipitated by, 282
    as part of comprehensive treatment
        program, 281, 284, 287–288
        detoxification, 287
            clonidine-naltrexone ultrarapid
                detoxification, 264, **265**
            ultrarapid detoxification under
                anesthesia/sedation,
                264–266
        naloxone testing for residual
            dependence, 287–288
        for relapse prevention, 288
    for patients dependent on both
        opioids and cocaine, 282
    safety of, 156
        during pregnancy, 290
        in women and children, 290
    side effects of, 288–289, 337
    for smoking cessation, 230
    target populations for, 282, 285–287
        employed persons, 285–286
        health care professionals, 282,
            284, 285
        heroin-addicted persons, 286–287
        probationers in work-release
            program, 286

treating pain during maintenance
    with, 290
use in individual therapy, 337
use in liver disease, 289–290
Naproxen (Anaprox, Naprosyn, Aleve),
    **514**
Narc-Anon, 397, 488
Narcissism, 310, 313, 317, 324, 335,
    336, 370
    malignant, 310
Narcissistic collapse, 310, 324
Narcissistic personality disorder,
    312–313
Narcissistic vulnerability, 310, 324, 370
Narcolepsy, 301
Narcotic Withdrawal Scale, 123
Narcotics. *See* Opioids
Narcotics Anonymous (NA), 135, 142,
    177, 265, 328, 391
    difficulty of attending for persons
        with social phobia, 311
    exposing medical students to, 531
    groups for women, 488
    Minnesota Model programs based on
        principles of, 414
    for phencyclidine-abusing persons,
        212
    psychodynamics applied to, 318
Nasal septum ulceration or perforation,
    256
National Association of Addiction
    Treatment Providers (NAATP)
    Patient Placement Criteria, 123
National Association of State Drug and
    Alcohol Directors, 166
National Cancer Institute, 225
National Center on Addiction and
    Substance Abuse, 166
National Comorbidity Survey (NCS),
    14, 49, 56, 475, 477, 478, 480,
    486
National Health Interview Survey, 404
National Highway Traffic Safety
    Administration, 440
National Household Surveys on Drug
    Abuse (NHSDA), 50, **51, 55,** 56,
    125, 166, 169, 492
National Institute on Alcohol Abuse and
    Alcoholism (NIAAA), 103, 424,
    425
National Institute on Drug Abuse
    (NIDA), 165, 166, 205, 292, 347,
    369
Native Americans, 78, 79, 195
Natural history of drug dependence, 54

Nausea and vomiting
    during alcohol withdrawal, 154
    during benzodiazepine withdrawal,
        241
    lysergic acid diethylamide–induced,
        196–197
    marijuana for, 39
    methylenedioxymethamphetamine-
        induced, 296
    naltrexone-induced, 283
    opioid-induced, 12
    during opioid withdrawal, 254, 260
Nausea aversion therapy, 129, 131, 415
NCS (National Comorbidity Survey),
    14, 49, 56, 475, 477, 478, 480, 486
Needle puncture marks, 256, 258
Needs-to-services treatment matching,
    124–125
Nembutal (pentobarbital), 240, 241,
    **247**
Nerve blocks, **513**
Network therapy, 323–332
    acknowledging contributions of
        network members, 327
    addressing problems of relapse and
        loss of control, 323–325
    for alcohol problems, 379–381
    cohabiting couple as network, 326
    contingency contracting and, 328
    definition of, 323
    duration of, 330
    effect on patient's treatment
        compliance, 326, 328
    when family of origin is absent, 398
    family therapy and, 328–329,
        379–380
    frequency of sessions for, 330
    goals of, 323, 327, 381
    initiation of, 329–330
    membership of network, 323,
        326–327
    outcome of, 325–326
    patient selection for, 329
    priorities during, 330
    rationale for, 323
    research on, 330–332
        office-based clinical trial,
            330–331
        treatment by addiction counselors,
            331
        treatment by psychiatry residents,
            331
        use of Internet, 331–332
    specific techniques for, 327–328
    termination of, 330

therapist's relationship to network,
    327
training in use of, 331–332
use of Alcoholics Anonymous in, 328
Neurobiology, 310
    of alcohol, 3–9
    of hallucinogens, 33–37
    of marijuana, 39–44
    of opioids, 11–18
    of stimulants, 21–27, 184
Neuroimaging
    after administration of
        $\Delta^9$-tetrahydrocannabinol, 174
    after administration of mescaline,
        199
    in cocaine abusers, 184
    in phencyclidine users, 206
    in schizophrenia, 199
Neuroleptic malignant syndrome
    (NMS), 185, 298, 299
Neuroleptics, 91, 93, 476
    for acute hallucinogen reactions, 200
    for alcoholic persons, 159
        disulfiram and, 155, 159
        extrapyramidal side effects of, 159
    for phencyclidine reactions, 209, 210
    for stimulant-induced drug states,
        185, 189
    use in methylenedioxymeth-
        amphetamine intoxication, 298
    use with methadone, 273
    use with naltrexone, 290
Neuronal membrane lipid perturbation
    hypothesis, 3, 4
Neurontin (gabapentin), 248, **515**
Neurotoxic effects of drugs
    methylenedioxymethamphetamine,
        296–298
    opioids, 18
    stimulants, 25–26
Nexus (2-(4-bromo-2,5-
    dimethoxyphenyl)-1-
    aminoethane), **34, 35,** 36
NHSDA (National Household Surveys
    on Drug Abuse), 50, **51, 55,** 56,
    125, 166, 169, 492
NIAAA (National Institute on Alcohol
    Abuse and Alcoholism), 103, 424,
    425
Nicoderm. *See* Nicotine transdermal
    patch
NicoDerm CQ. *See* Nicotine
    transdermal patch
Nicotine, 110, 215–234. *See also*
    Smoking

Nicotine-containing gum, 220,
    **222–223,** 226–227
    combined with use of nicotine patch,
        229
    compliance with use of, 227
    contraindications to, **223,** 229
    dosage and administration of, 227
    duration of use of, 227
    efficacy of, 226–227
    errors in use of, 227
Nicotine fading, 226, 230
    brand switching, 230
    tapering, 230
Nicotine inhaler, 220, **222–223,** 228
    side effects of, 228
    technique for use of, 228
    underdosing with, 228
Nicotine maintenance devices, 229
Nicotine nasal spray, 220, **222–223,**
    227–228
    absorption of, 228
    administration of, 228
    advantages of, 228
    contraindications to, **223,** 229
    duration of use of, 228
    side effects of, 228
Nicotine replacement therapy (NRT),
    219, **222–223,** 225–229
    adverse reactions to, **222**
    for alcohol and drug abusers, 229
    combined therapy, 229
    contraindications to, **223,** 229
    cost of, **223**
    duration of use of, **222**
    group therapy and, 232–233
    "harm-reduction" option for, 220,
        229
    over-the-counter availability of, 220
    predicting value for particular
        patients, 220
    setting quit date for patient using,
        233
Nicotine transdermal patch, 220,
    **222–223,** 227
    advantages of, 227
    combined with use of bupropion,
        229
    combined with use of nicotine gum,
        229
    compliance with use of, 227
    contraindications to, **223,** 229
    dosage administered by, 227
    duration of use of, 227
    efficacy of, 227
    skin reactions to, 227

Nicotine withdrawal symptoms, 111, 112, 220, 233. *See also* Smoking cessation
  onset and duration of, 233
  patients' desire to avoid, 218
  percentage of smokers experiencing, 217, 233
  preparing patient to cope with, 233
  relapses among smokers experiencing, 220
  related to heaviness of smoking, 220
  weight gain, 233
NIDA (National Institute on Drug Abuse), 165, 166, 205, 292, 347, 369
Nitrazepam (Mogadon), **246**
Nitrendipine, 7
Nitric oxide (NO), 17, 24
Nitrous oxide, 77
NMDA receptors. *See* N-Methyl-D-aspartate receptors
NMS (neuroleptic malignant syndrome), 185, 298, 299
NO (nitric oxide), 17, 24
Nociceptin, 13
Noctec (chloral hydrate), 152, **247**
Noludar (methyprylon), **247**
Noncompliance. *See* Compliance with treatment
Nonsteroidal anti-inflammatory drugs (NSAIDs)
  marijuana use and, 172
  for pain, 514, **514**
  use during opioid detoxification, 259
Norepinephrine
  phencyclidine and, 206
  smoking and, 218
  stimulants and, 21, 183
Norm conflict, 78
Normeperidine, 18
Novelty-seeking, 54, 60–64, **62, 65**
  among adolescents, 466
  alcoholism and, 101
NRT. *See* Nicotine replacement therapy
NSAIDs. *See* Nonsteroidal anti-inflammatory drugs
Nucleus accumbens, 310, 521
  alcohol effects in, 5
  opioid effects in, 13, 16
  stimulant effects in, 22, 24
Nuprin. *See* Ibuprofen
Nystagmus, drug-induced
  phencyclidine, 206, 208, 210
  sedative-hypnotics, 241

**O**

Object relations, 313, 315, 317
Obsessive-compulsive disorder, 90, 98, 313
Obsessive Compulsive Drinking Scale, 156
Octreotide, 264
Olanzapine
  for acute hallucinogen reactions, 200
  for alcoholic persons, 159
Ondansetron
  for alcoholism, 6, 131
  for ultrarapid detoxification under anesthesia/sedation, 264
ONT. *See* Outpatient nonmethadone treatment
Operant conditioning, 68
Opioid agonists, 11–13, 281, 282, 511. *See also* Methadone
Opioid antagonists, 11, 12, 15, 281–292, 324. *See also* Naloxone; Naltrexone
  for acute overdose, 18
  for alcoholism, 7, 94, 130, 155–156, 282, 291–292, 337
  to diagnose opioid dependence, 282
  effects of, 282–283
    on opioid receptors, 282, 289
  medical uses for, 282
  opioid withdrawal syndrome precipitated by, 282
  during pregnancy, 261
Opioid dependence, 12, 15–17, 281
  affective disorders and, 477
  animal studies of, 14
  antidepressants for persons with, 99, 477
  antisocial personality disorder and, 99
  as criteria for methadone maintenance treatment, 272
  D4 dopamine receptor polymorphism and, 64, **65**
  future directions for treatment of, 18
  genetics and vulnerability factors for, 14–15
  individual psychotherapy for, 346, 348
  mechanisms of, 15–17, **16**
  methadone for, 94
  psychiatric aspects of, 276–277
  related to drug availability, 52
  twin studies of, 14, 59, **60**
  verifying before initiation of detoxification regimen, 258
  among Vietnam veterans, 52
Opioid detoxification, 251–268
  acupuncture for, 267–268
  avoiding intoxication during, 260
  benzodiazepines for, 15
  buprenorphine-aided, 12, 266–267
  choice of narcotic agent for, 257
  clonidine-aided, 15, 16, 259, 261–263
    administered via transdermal patch, 263
    advantages and disadvantages of, 263
    analgesic effects of, 263
    clonidine-naltrexone ultrarapid detoxification, 264, **265, 287**
    compared with methadone, 261–262
    contraindications to, 262
    dosage for, 261, 262, **262**
    effectiveness of, 261
    insomnia during, 262–263
    mechanism of action of, 261
    side effects of, 261
    techniques for, 262, **262**
    time to antiwithdrawal effects of, 262
  definition of, 251
  determining success of, 252
  effect of family involvement on outcome of, 389
  evaluation and diagnosis for, 254–256
    interview, 255
      drug history, 255
      other medical history, 255
      psychological status, 255
      social functioning, 255
    laboratory testing, 256, 522
    physical examination, 255–256
      cutaneous signs, 256
  experimental medications for, 267
  goals of, 251–252
  guidelines for, 261
  historical overview of, 252–253
  initiation of, 257–258
    dosage for, 257–258
    naloxone challenge test before, 258
    reasons for delaying, 258
    verifying physical dependence before, 258

Opioid detoxification (continued)
    insomnia during, 259
    length of withdrawal for, 258–259
        inpatient versus outpatient
            withdrawal, 258–259
        linear versus inverse exponential
            withdrawal methods, 258
    lofexidine-aided, 16, 261, 263–264
    long-term residential treatment
        after, 138
    from methadone maintenance, 259
    for mixed addictions, 260
    naltrexone for, 287
        clonidine-naltrexone ultrarapid
            detoxification, 264, **265,**
            287
    options for, 251
    other drugs and supportive measures
        for, 259
    other medical conditions associated
        with, 260
    during pregnancy, 260–261, 389
    reasons addicts enter programs for,
        251
    repetitive withdrawal, 260
    seizures during, 260
    settings for, 252
    short-term versus long-term, 257
    ultrarapid detoxification under
        anesthesia/sedation, 264–266
    use of methadone for, 256–261,
        **257**
    visitors during, 259
    vomiting during, 260
    without subsequent treatment,
        135–136
Opioid receptors, 11–12, 281
    alcohol actions and, 7
    changes after exposure to opioid
        agonists or antagonists, 17
    effects of opioid antagonists on,
        282, 289
    endogenous opioid peptide binding
        to, 13
    intracellular changes due to
        activation of, 11
    orphan receptor, 13
    phencyclidine actions and, 206
    preferential binding to, 12
    selective antagonists for, 12
    types of, 11–12
Opioid withdrawal syndrome, 11, 111,
    253–254
    addicts' efforts to avoid, 14, 15
    benzodiazepines for, 15

conditioned cues and, 324
factors influencing severity of, 15,
    253
    duration and regularity of use,
        253
    psychological factors, 253
    specific drug used, 253
    total daily amount used, 253
glucocorticoid levels during, 14–15
hypothalamic-pituitary-adrenal axis
    function during, 14–15
locus coeruleus hyperactivity during,
    16
metyrapone stimulation of, 15
Narcotic Withdrawal Scale, 123
in neonates of methadone-
    maintained mothers, 275
onset and duration of, 15, 253–254,
    **254**
panic attacks during, 478
precipitated by opioid antagonists,
    282
signs and symptoms of, 113,
    253–254, **254**
Opioids, 21–27, 110, **514.** See also
    specific drugs
    actions of, 11
    agonists, antagonists, and partial
        agonists, 12–13, 281–292
    analgesic effects of, 12, 13, 344
    for cocaine abuse, 26–27
    definition of, 11
    effect on stimulant sensitization,
        24
    endogenous, 11, 13
        alcohol effects on, 291
        opioid antagonist effects on, 282,
            288–289
        role in postwithdrawal
            functioning, 17
    high produced by, 12
    immunological effects of, 505
    long-acting, 516–517, **517**
    methadone maintenance for users of,
        136–138, 271–278
    neurobiology of, 11–18
    overdose of, 17–18
    for pain, 511–517
    patient assessment for use of, 112
    pharmacokinetics and likelihood of
        abuse of, 12
    reinforcing properties of, 13–14
    rush produced by, 12
    signs of intoxication with, 113
    tolerance to, 11, 12, 15–16, 514

toxicity of, 17–18
    from contaminants in drug, 18
    infections among injection-drug
        users, 18, 77
    neurological lesions, 18
    toxic metabolites, 18
use during pregnancy, 261, 492
"Opiophobia," 511
Opisthotonos, 209
Opium, 11, 253
Opium den culture, 75
Opium epidemic, 76
Opium tincture, **257**
Orbitofrontal cortex, 310
Organ damage secondary to ethanol
    intake, 160
Organic brain syndromes, 195, 199, 211
Orphanin FQ, 13
Orudis (ketoprofen), **514**
Osteoporosis, alcoholic, 160
Outcome studies. See Treatment
    outcomes
Outpatient nonmethadone treatment
    (ONT), 141–142
    compared with methadone
        maintenance, 137
    diversity of, 141
    duration of, 141
    effectiveness of, 141–142, 145
    medications used in, 141
    patient populations receiving, 141
    reasons for varying results of, 142
    retention rates in, 141–142
Outpatient treatment, 529
    for alcohol withdrawal, 152–153,
        416, 443
    for benzodiazepine withdrawal, 248
    comparison of inpatients and
        outpatients, 416–417
    couples' therapy, 326
    crisis intervention services, 548–549
    as hub of new service delivery
        system under managed care,
        546–547
    individual psychotherapy, 344
    intensive, 442–443
    for opioid detoxification, 252,
        258–259, 261
    for phencyclidine abuse, 212
    psychodynamic psychotherapy, 314
Ovarian function, 174
Overdose of drugs
    benzodiazepines, 239
    cannabis, 172
    crack cocaine, 185

ketamine, 301
lysergic acid diethylamide, 197
opioids, 17–18
phencyclidine, 209
stimulants, 185
Overeating, 353, 355, 356
Oxazepam (Serax)
for alcohol withdrawal, 152–154
mild to moderate, 152
severe, 153
phenobarbital withdrawal equivalent
for, **246**
use during clonidine-naltrexone
ultrarapid detoxification,
264, **265**
withdrawal from, 241
Oxford Houses, 135
Oxycodone, 112
controlled-release (OxyContin), **517**
withdrawal from, 257

**P**

P300 voltage, **61,** 62, 65, **66**
PAG (periaqueductal gray), 16
Pain management in drug-addicted
persons, 511–517
according to type of pain, 515–517
acute pain, 515–516
patient-controlled analgesia, 516
chronic pain, 516–517, **517**
for HIV-infected patients who are
receiving methadone, 505
during naltrexone maintenance, 290
nonpharmacological, 513, **513**
patient assessment guidelines for,
**512,** 512–513
assessing severity of pain, 512
defining cause of pain, 512
determining prior successful
means of pain relief, 513
determining whether drug therapy
is needed, 513, **513**
identifying modifying
psychological and
environmental factors,
512–513, **513**
for patients on L-α-acetylmethadol,
278
for patients on methadone
maintenance, 516
pharmacological guidelines for, **513,**
513–515
defining cause of pain, 513–514
starting with least-potent
analgesic, 514, **514**

understanding concepts of
dependence, tolerance, and
withdrawal, **514,** 514–515
using drug combinations carefully,
515, **515**
using equivalent doses when
changing analgesics, 515
reasons for inadequate prescription
of opioids, 511, **512**
Panic attacks, drug-induced, 478
cocaine, 478
hallucinogens, 199
marijuana, 170, 478
phencyclidine, 206
stimulants, 478
during substance withdrawal, 478
Panic disorder, 478–479
alcoholism and, 90, 98, 102, 158,
316, 478
benzodiazepine abuse and, 240, 241
prevalence among substance-abusing
persons, 91, 478
treatment in substance-abusing
persons, 478–479
antidepressants, 478–479
benzodiazepines, 478
nonpharmacological, 479
Pantothenic acid deficiency, 160
Paradoxical techniques, 396
Paranoia, drug-induced
hallucinogens, 197, 198, 199
ketamine, 301
marijuana, 170
phencyclidine, 206
stimulants, 185
Paregoric, **257,** 275
Parent programs for substance abuse
prevention, 539
Parenting support groups, 494
Parenting training, 495, 496
Parents. *See* Family
Parkinsonism, 18
Paroxetine, 479
Partial hospitalization programs, 313,
442–443, 529
assessment of patients for, 416
for cocaine-abusing persons, 442
compared with inpatient
hospitalization, 442
compared with intensive outpatient
treatment, 442–443
for HIV-infected persons, 506
individual psychotherapy in, 344
for opioid detoxification, 252
Patient-centered therapy, 129, 130

Patient-controlled analgesia (PCA), 516
Patient placement criteria, 121–125
computerized algorithm for, 125
definition of, 121
level-of-care matching, 121–123,
**122,** 525, 529, 547
needs-to-services matching,
124–125
origins of, 123–124
American Society of Addiction
Medicine Criteria, 121,
**122,** 123, 525
Boston Target Cities Project, 123
Cleveland Criteria, 123
National Association of Addiction
Treatment Providers
Criteria, 123
structured interviews, 123
rationale for, 121–123
revision of American Society of
Addiction Medicine Criteria,
124, 414, 417, 442, 525–526,
529
Patient-treatment matching, 116, 121,
442
for adolescents, 470–471
for alcohol problems, 97, 100,
103–104, 124–125, 133, 151,
382, 470–471
criteria for, 121–125
in Employee Assistance Programs,
430
history of, 123
Project MATCH, 103–104, 133,
345, 347, 348, 382, 408–409
for schizophrenic substance-abusing
persons, 477
in therapeutic communities, 459
for 12-step groups, 404, 408–409
Patterns of substance use, 112
alcohol, 78–79
in women, 486
cigarette smoking, 217
marijuana, 166–167
phencyclidine, 205
stimulants, 184–185
Paxipam (halazepam), **246**
PCA (patient-controlled analgesia), 516
PCC (1-piperidinocyclohexane
carbonitrile), 205
PCE (*N*-ethyl-1-phencyclohexalamine),
205
PCP. *See* Phencyclidine
Peer influence and substance abuse,
53, 56, 69, 537

Peer intervention programs, 432–434
    advantages of, 433
    history of, 432
    lack of research on, 433
    problems with, 433–434
    underlying concepts of, 432–433
Peer role models in therapeutic
        communities, 447, 452–453
Pemoline, 480
Pentazocine, 12, 18, 257, 511
Pentobarbital (Nembutal), 240, 241, **247**
Pepto Bismol (bismuth subsalicylate), 259
Perceptual alterations, 170, 197
Pergolide mesylate, for cocaine abuse, 26
Periaqueductal gray (PAG), 16
Perinatal substance use, 485, 491–498.
        *See also* Women substance abusers
    L-α-acetylmethadol, 278
    alcohol, 487–488, 492
    as cause of newborn referral to child
        protective services, 439
    cocaine, 492–493
    definition of perinatal period, 491
    educating women about dangers of,
        488–489, 493
    focus of public policy and research
        on, 491
    marijuana, 174, 492
    methadone for opioid withdrawal,
        261, 389
    methadone maintenance, 261, 272,
        275–276, 485
    naltrexone, 290
    opioids, 261, 492
    parent-child attachment and, 491
    phencyclidine, 209
    prevalence of, 492
    prevention and treatment
        interventions for, 488–489,
        493–498, 496
        according to stages in extended
            perinatal period, 495–496
        arenas and contexts for, 496–498,
            **497**
        barriers to, 494
        identifying exposed infants, 496
        during labor and delivery, 496
        parenting training, 495, 496
        prenatal care, 495
        punitive approaches, 491, 496
        recommendations for, 498
        stages and levels of, **493,** 493–495
    problems co-occurring with, 492
    risk factors for, 493
    risks associated with, 492–493

screening women for, 487–488, 494
    smoking, 216–217, 485, 493
    sources of attention to, 491
    underreporting of, 492
    violence against women and, 492
Peripheral neuropathies, 160
Persistence, **65**
Personality disorders, 98, 312–313. *See
    also specific personality disorders*
    adolescent substance use and, 468
    group therapy for substance-abusing
        patients with, 370
    psychodynamic psychotherapy for,
        312–313
Personality traits and substance abuse,
        53–54, 59–63, **62, 63**
    in adolescents, 466, 467
    alcoholism, 60–62, **62,** 65, **65,** 101,
        102, 369
    cooperativeness, 62
    determining cause of personality
        changes during treatment, 313
    hallucinogens, 198, 200
    harm-avoidance, 60–62, 101, 466
    inappropriateness of trying to change
        personality style, 94
    novelty-seeking, 54, 60–64, **64,** 101,
        466
    in patients entering therapeutic
        communities, 450
    reward-dependence, 61, 62, 101, 466
    self-directedness, 62
    smoking, 62–63, **63**
PET. *See* Positron-emission tomography
Petroleum chemicals, 77
Peyote, 78, 195
Pharmacotherapy, 549
    for acute hallucinogen reactions, 200
    for alcoholism, 6–7, 94, 130–131,
        152, 549
    animal self-administration models for
        development of, 70
    for benzodiazepine withdrawal,
        244–248, **246, 247**
    for cocaine dependence, 26–27, 549
    for HIV-infected persons with
        substance use disorders, 507
    methadone maintenance, 94,
        136–138, 271–278
    in outpatient nonmethadone
        treatment, 141
    for pain management in drug-
        addicted persons, 511–517
    for smoking cessation, 220,
        **222–223,** 226–230

for stimulant abuse, 26–27, 185–187
    for substance-abusing patients with
        comorbid psychopathology, 91
    affective disorders, 115–116, 132,
        477–478
    attention-deficit/hyperactivity
        disorder, 480
    generalized anxiety disorder, 479
    panic disorder, 478–479
    posttraumatic stress disorder, 480
    schizophrenia, 476–477
    social phobia, 479
    for withdrawal symptoms, 93
Phenalkylamines, **34, 35,** 195
Phencyclidine (PCP), 17, 33, 34, 110,
        112, 195, 198, 205–212, 299
    administration routes for, 205
    adolescent users of, 205, 206
    analgesic effects of, 206, 208
    central nervous system effects of,
        206
    as contaminant in other drugs, 169,
        205, 206
    contaminants in, 205, 206
    dependence on, 211
    diagnosing abuse of, 211
    drug interactions with, 206
        chlorpromazine, 200
    duration of action of, 205
    epidemiology of, 205
    "Fry" laced with, 169
    history of use of, 205, 299–300
    intoxication with, 206–209
        coma due to, 207, 208
        complications of, 209
        diagnosis of, 206–207
        differential diagnosis of, 207–208
        laboratory evaluation for, 207, 208
        management of, 208–209
        signs and symptoms of, 206–208
        stages of, 207, **207**
    managing abuse and dependence on,
        211–212
        difficulties in, 211
        length of treatment, 212
        outpatient therapy, 212
        self-help groups, 212
        settings for, 212
        strategies for, 211–212
        therapeutic communities, 212
    manufacture of, 205
    as model to study schizophrenia, 206
    organic mental disorder induced by,
        211
        management of, 211

overdose of, 209
patterns of use of, 205
pH effects on tissue concentration of, 208
pharmacokinetics of, 205
physiological effects of, 206, 299–300
profile of users of, 206
psychosis (delirium) induced by, 206, 209–211, 300
  clinical features of, 209–210
  diagnostic workup of, 210
  duration of, 209
  management of, 210–211
  phases of, 210
street names for, 206
tolerance to, 211
twin studies of abuse of, **60**
unpredictability of response to, 206
use as anesthetic, 299–300
withdrawal from, 211
1-(1-Phencyclohexyl)pyrrolidine (PHP), 205
Phenelzine, 158
Phenobarbital substitution, 245–247
  for neonates of methadone-maintained mothers, 275
  rationale for, 245–246
  in stabilization phase, 246–247
  withdrawal equivalents for benzodiazepines, **246**
  withdrawal equivalents for sedative-hypnotics, **247**
  in withdrawal phase, 247
Phentolamine, 209
Phenylalkylamines, **34, 35**
Phenylisopropylamines (PIAs), 36, **36**
Philosophy of treatment, 92
Phobias
  alcoholism and, 90, 98
  among patients entering therapeutic communities, 450
Phoenix House, 138, 140, 143, 368
Phosphate level in alcoholism, 524
PHP (1-(1-phencyclohexyl)pyrrolidine), 205
Physical examination, 113
  for cannabis use, 112
  cutaneous signs of drug abuse, 256
  of opioid-addicted persons, 255–256
  for phencyclidine intoxication, 206–207
Physicians in Residence (PIR) programs, 531
PIAs (phenylisopropylamines), 36, **36**

Pills Anonymous, 328
Piloerection, 256
"Pink cloud," 339
Pinpoint pupils, 12, 18
1-Piperidinocyclohexane carbonitrile (PCC), 205
PIR (Physicians in Residence) programs, 531
Pirenperone, 36
PKA (protein kinase A), 5
PKC (protein kinase C), 5, 6
Placebo therapy, for alcohol abuse, 131
Placidyl (ethchlorvynol), **247**
Plexitis, 18
Pneumonia, 492
Pneumothorax, 173
Policy substance abuse prevention programs, 540
Polysubstance abuse, 59, 111, 189, 198, 240
  clinical observations guiding candidate gene searches in, 61, **61**
  methadone maintenance and, 273
  novelty-seeking and, 63–64, **64**
  among participants of circuit parties, 295
  withdrawal from, 260
POMC (proopiomelanocortin), 13, 14
Population frequency of drug dependence, 48
Portal hypertensive gastropathy, 160
Positron-emission tomography (PET)
  after administration of $\Delta^9$-tetrahydrocannabinol, 174
  in cocaine abusers, 184
  in phencyclidine users, 206
Posthallucinogenic perception disorder, 299
Posttraumatic stress disorder (PTSD), 82, 480
  adolescent substance use and, 468
  alcoholism and, 480
  prevalence among substance-abusing persons, 480
  treatment in substance-abusing persons, 480
Potassium
  levels in alcoholism, 524
  for phencyclidine psychosis, 210
Powerlessness, 310
"Practice Guidelines for the Treatment of Patients With Substance Use Disorders," 117, 530
Prazepam (Centrax), **246**

Preemployment drug testing, 176, 432, 522
Prefrontal cortex, 22, 24
Pregnancy, 491–498. *See also* Perinatal substance use; Women substance abusers
  opioid withdrawal during, 260–261
  prenatal care during, 495
  reluctance of treatment programs to accept women during, 487
  vertical transmission of HIV infection during, 486
Preterm delivery, 493
Prevalence of drug dependence, 48–49
Prevention of substance abuse, 56, 535–542. *See also* Relapse prevention
  in adolescents, 468–469, 535–542
  cross-cultural aspects of, 82
  definition of, 535
  effectiveness of programs for, **542**
  features of effective programs for, 537–539
    basis in theories of behavior change, 538
    counteracting risk factors and promoting protective factors from epidemiological research, 537–538
    program implementation strategies, 538–539
  gateway drugs and, 54, 169, 467, 468, 535
  marijuana, 178
  by modifying supply-to-demand ratio, 468, 535–536
  program modalities for, 539–541
    community programs, 540
    comprehensive community programs, 540–541
    mass media programs, 539–540
    multicomponent programs, 540
    parent programs, 539
    policy programs, 540
    school programs, 539
  related to use levels, 535
  smoking, 178, 541
  types of, 535–536
    approach to drug abuse control, 468, 535–536
    focus, 536
    primary, selected, and indicated levels of prevention, 536
  summary of, **542**

Prevention of substance abuse
(continued)
    what is known and not known about,
        536–537
    in women, 488–489
        during perinatal period, 488–489,
            493–498
Primary care interventions, 437–438,
    529–530
Primary care residency training, 532
Prison-based treatment. See
    Correctional treatment programs
Private sector health care services,
    413, 548
Probes, in therapeutic communities, 453
Problem behavior theory, 538
Prochlorperazine, 154
Prodynorphin, 13
Proenkephalin, 13
Prognostic factors
    comorbid psychopathology, 116, 344
    positive prognostic indicators for
        psychodynamic psychotherapy,
        311
    primary/secondary distinction, 99
    Type A/Type B alcoholism subtypes,
        103–104
    unidimensional typologies of
        addiction, 98
Project ADEPT, 531
Project MATCH, 103–104, 133, 345,
    347, 348, 382, 408–409
Projection, 109, 111, 312, 314, 317–318
Projective identification, 312, 317
Prolactin
    cocaine and, 184
    hallucinogens and, 196
    marijuana and, 174
Proopiomelanocortin (POMC), 13, 14
Propofol, 264–266
Propoxyphene, 257, 511
Propranolol
    for akathisia, 159
    for alcohol withdrawal symptoms,
        152
    for attention-deficit/hyperactivity
        disorder, 480
    for esophageal variceal bleeding, 160
Propylthiouracil, 160
ProSom (estazolam), **246**
Prostaglandins, 40
Prostep. See Nicotine transdermal patch
Protective services
    for adults, 440
    for children, 439

Protein kinase A (PKA), 5
Protein kinase C (PKC), 5, 6
Protracted abstinence syndrome, 90
Protracted withdrawal syndrome (PWS)
    from alcohol, 157
    from low-dose benzodiazepines,
        242–243, **245**
Pseudoindividuation, 398
Psilocin (4-hydroxy-N,N-
    dimethyltryptamine), **34, 35**
Psilocybin, 195
Psychedelics. See Hallucinogens
Psychiatric disorders. See also specific
    disorders
    comorbid with substance abuse,
        90–91, 98–100, 109, 114, 336,
        344, 475–481
    in adolescents, 467–468
    affective disorders, 477–478
    alcoholism, 98–100, 336–337
    anxiety disorders, 478–480
        generalized anxiety disorder,
            479
        panic disorder, 478–479
        posttraumatic stress disorder,
            480
        social phobia, 479–480
    assessment of, 115–116
    attention-deficit/hyperactivity
        disorder, 480–481
    cannabis use, 170
    diagnosis of, 475–476, 481
    documented in mental status
        examination, 114
    epidemiological surveys of, 475
    group therapy for, 370
    in HIV-infected persons, 506–507
    inpatient treatment for, 414
    integrated substance abuse and
        mental health services for,
        547
    manifestations of, 475
    opioid dependence, 276–277
    among patients entering
        therapeutic communities,
        450, 451, 459
    pharmacotherapy for, 481
    prevalence of, 355, 475
    primary/secondary distinction and,
        98–99
    prognostic significance of, 116,
        344
    psychodynamic psychotherapy for,
        312–313
    psychotic disorders, 476–477

    smoking, 218
    stimulant abuse, 188
    temporary psychiatric conditions,
        90
    treatment considerations for,
        476, 481
    in women, 486, 488
    distinguishing primary psychiatric
        disorders from substance-
        induced disorders, 115–116,
        344, 475
    effect of methadone maintenance on,
        277
    effect of severity on outcome of
        inpatient treatment, 419
    identification and treatment of,
        90–91
    independent of substance abuse,
        90–91
    medications contraindicated for, 93
    methylenedioxymethamphetamine-
        induced, 297
    negative emotional states due to, 355
    relationship between substance abuse
        and, 475
    during stimulant withdrawal, 90
Psychoanalytic psychotherapy, 311,
    315, 320, 335
Psychodynamic psychotherapy,
    309–321, 323
    abstinence required for, 311, 314,
        315
    acceptance of self in recovery, 317
    for adolescents and young adults,
        312
    application to groups and self-help,
        309–311, 314, 318–320, 367,
        369, 375
    characteristics of patients choosing,
        311–312
    combined with other treatments, 311
    compared with psychoanalysis, 311
    confrontational approaches in, 314
    contraindications to, 313
    danger of reductionism in, 313
    determining focus of, 316
    ego psychological model of
        rehabilitation, 317–318
    for family of drug-abusing person,
        393–394
        countertransference, 393
        overcoming resistance, 394
        therapist's role in interpretation,
            393
        working through, 394

frequency of sessions for, 311, 314
goals for, 314
indications and rationale for, 311–313
initiation of, 314
myths about, 319
as part of combined treatment
approach, 315–316
patient-therapist relationship for,
311, 318–319
for patients with personality
disorders, 312–313
phases of, 316
pitfalls in, 319–320
positive prognostic indicators for,
311
for relapse prevention, 311, 312, 317
research implications for, 320
settings for, 314
technical aspects of, 315
timing of interpretations during, 314
transference and countertransference
reactions during, 313, 318–319
treatment parameters for, 315
usefulness of treatment outcome
research on, 320
watching for relapse during, 316–317
Psychodynamic theory, 309–311
of alcoholism, 309, 335–336
applied to treatment, 311
early development of, 309
outcome research on, 309
recent developments in, 309–311
Psychoeducation. *See* Educational
approaches
Psychological testing, 524–527
assessment tests, 525–527
to assess motivation for recovery
and treatment readiness,
526
to determine substance abuse and
dependence severity, 526
to diagnose substance use
disorder, 526
of opioid-addicted persons, 255
screening tests, 525
Psychosis, 111, 476–477. *See also*
Schizophrenia
alcohol-induced, 159
as contraindication for therapeutic
community treatment, 451
differentiating phencyclidine
intoxication from, 207–208
hallucinogen-induced, 198, 200
among HIV-infected persons, 506
marijuana-induced, 170, 198

phencyclidine-induced, 206,
209–211
prevalence among substance-abusing
persons, 476
during protracted benzodiazepine
withdrawal syndrome, 243
psychodynamic psychotherapy
contraindicated for, 313
stimulant-induced, 185
amphetamine, 23, 33, 36
cocaine, 23, 185
among women substance abusers,
488
Psychotherapy. *See also* Family therapy;
Group therapy; Individual
Psychotherapy; Psychodynamic
psychotherapy
compared with addiction counseling,
343
definition of, 343
for dual-diagnosis patients, 476, 481
affective disorders, 478
generalized anxiety disorder, 479
panic disorder, 479
posttraumatic stress disorder, 480
schizophrenia, 477
social phobia, 480
family
for alcohol problems, 323, 325,
379–386
for other drug abuse, 389–399
group, 367–376
for HIV-infected persons, 506
individual
for alcoholism, 132, 160,
335–341, 348
for other drug abuse, 343–349
cannabis, 177–178
hallucinogens, 201
smoking, 225, 232
for pain management, **513**
psychoanalytic, 311, 315, 320, 335
psychodynamic, 309–321
Psychotomimetic drugs.
*See* Hallucinogens
PTSD. *See* Posttraumatic stress disorder
Public health issues, 47
Public support payments, 439–440
Publicly funded health care services,
413, 548
Pulmonary edema, 18
Purkinje cells, 5
PWS. *See* Protracted withdrawal
syndrome
Pyridoxine deficiency, 160

**Q**

Quazepam (Doral), **246**

**R**

RAATE (Recovery Attitude and
Treatment Evaluation), 123
RAATE-CE (Recovery Attitude and
Treatment Evaluator Clinical
Evaluation), 526–527
Randomized studies of drug
dependence, 52
Rape, 162
Rational Recovery, 409
Rationalization, 111, 112, 317, 359
Rave parties, 172, 196, 295–303
Reaction formation, 317
Receptor-gated ion channels, 6–9
Recovery Attitude and Treatment
Evaluation (RAATE), 123
Recovery Attitude and Treatment
Evaluator Clinical Evaluation
(RAATE-CE), 526–527
Recovery process, 375
Recovery subcultures, 81
Red Ribbon Days, 536
Reductionism, 313
Referral
to Employee Assistance Programs,
425–426, 429–430
of newborn to child protective
services, 439
to therapeutic community, 450–451
to 12-step groups, 404
Reframing, 360, 396
Refugees, 81–82. *See also* Cross-cultural
aspects of substance abuse
Regression, 309
Reimbursement for services, 550–551
Reinforcing effects of drugs, 67–68, 70,
353
alcohol, 7
benzodiazepines, 240
ketamine, 301
marijuana, 165
nicotine, 218
opioids, 13–14
stimulants, 22, 183–184
Relapse, 354–360, 529
among adolescents, 469
apparently irrelevant decisions
leading to, 359
avoiding responsibility for, 359
cognitive-behavioral model of, **357**
cognitive distortion mechanisms and,
359

Relapse *(continued)*
  covert antecedents of, 358–360
  definition of, 354
  drug craving and, 324
  high-risk situations for, 355–358
    abstinence violation effect and,
      358
    coping effectively with, 357
    definition of, 355
    inability to cope with, 357–358
    interpersonal conflict, 355–356
    negative emotional states, 355
    social pressure, 356
  instant gratification and, 359
  lapse and, 354–355, **355**
    patient's reaction to, 363
  lifestyle balance and, 359–360
  network therapy and, 323–325
  observing patient for, 316–317
  viewed as transitional process,
    354–355, **356**
  warning signs for, 354, 361
Relapse prevention (RP), 353–365
  for adolescents, 365, 470
  for alcohol abuse, 131, 132, 354
  behaviors to which model is applied,
    353
  for cannabis dependence, 177
  for cocaine abuse, 347
  controlled substance use and, 360
  definition of, 325, 353
  global lifestyle strategies for, 360,
    363–365, **364**
    lifestyle balance worksheet, 363
    stimulus control techniques,
      363–364
    urge-control strategies, 363–365
  goals and philosophy of, 353–354
    abstinence, 354, 360–361
    harm reduction, 354
  naltrexone for, 288
  psychodynamic psychotherapy for,
    311, 312, 317
  skill training for, 354
  after smoking cessation, 226,
    233–234
  social support for, 365
  specific intervention strategies for,
    360–363, **361**
    assessing coping abilities, 362
    choice of, 360
    cognitive reframing, 360
    coping skills training, 362
    education, 92, 362
    lifestyle balancing, 360

  recognizing and coping with
    high-risk situations,
    361–362
  relapse rehearsal methods,
    362–363
  self-monitoring procedures, 361
  skill training, 354, 360, 362
  for stimulant abuse, 187–188
  in therapeutic communities, 459
  as treatment goal, 91–92
Relaxation training, 354
  for alcohol abuse, 132, 339
  for pain management, **513**
  for phencyclidine abuse, 212
  for smoking cessation, 226, 231–232
Religious beliefs, 91, 407. *See also*
  Spirituality
Religious experiences,
  phencyclidine-induced, 206
Remission, 110–111
Renal colic, 260
Renal failure, 209
Repression, 317
Residency Review Committee (RRC)
  in Internal Medicine, 530, 532
  in Psychiatry, 532
Residency training, 531–532. *See also*
  Medical education
Resistance to treatment, 394, 397,
  415, 529
Resource allocation, 92
Respiratory depression, drug-induced,
  239
  γ-hydroxybutyrate, 301, 302
  opioids, 12, 17–18
    naloxone for neonates with, 282
Respiratory effects of marijuana
  smoking, 172–173
REST (restricted environmental
  stimulation therapy), 232
Restoril (temazepam), **246**
Restraints, 208
Restricted environmental stimulation
  therapy (REST), 232
Retention in treatment
  inpatient treatment, 419
  long-term residential treatment, 139,
    140, 145, 458
  methadone maintenance, 137, 138,
    144, 275
  outpatient nonmethadone treatment,
    141–142
Reward-dependence, 61, **62, 65**
  among adolescents, 466
  alcoholism and, 101

Rewards
  privileges in therapeutic
    communities, 455
  for smoking cessation, 230
Rhabdomyolysis, 208, 209
Rifampin, 273, 505
Risk factors for substance abuse
  in adolescents, 467, 537–538
    marijuana, 178, **178**
  antisocial personality disorder,
    91, 94
  bipolar disorder, 91
  comorbid psychopathology, 116,
    344
  cultural, 78–79
  high-risk situations for relapses,
    355–358
  in perinatal period, 493
Risk-sharing arrangements, 546
  capitation, 546
  case rates, 546
Risperidone, 159, 200
Ritonavir, 505
"Ro," 303. *See also* Flunitrazepam
Ro 15-4513, 4
*Robinson v. California*, 441
Rohypnol (flunitrazepam), 240, **246,**
  303
Romazicon. *See* Flumazenil
"Roofies," 303. *See also* Flunitrazepam
RP. *See* Relapse prevention
RRC. *See* Residency Review Committee

**S**

S-TT ("symptom-triggered therapy"),
  152
SAAST (Self-Administered Alcoholism
  Screen Test), 525
Safety issues, 92–93
  avoiding use of restraints for
    phencyclidine-intoxicated
    persons, 208
  drunk driving, 161, 440–441
  in group therapy, 373–374
  pharmacotherapy for HIV-infected
    substance-abusing persons,
    507
  safe environment of inpatient
    settings, 415, 416
  substance abuse in workplace,
    424
Saleto-200-600. *See* Ibuprofen
Saliva toxicology testing, 521–524.
    *See also* Laboratory testing
Scaffolding therapy, 338–339

Schizophrenia, 476–477
    alcoholism among persons with, 159, 476
        disulfiram for, 155, 159, 476
        naltrexone for, 476–477
    antipsychotics for, 91, 93, 476
    case management for substance-abusing persons with, 440
    cocaine use related to public support payments in patients with, 439
    differential diagnosis of, 476
        hallucinogen-induced psychosis, 198–199
        phencyclidine intoxication, 207–208
    effects of hallucinogens in persons predisposed to, 199
    effects of methadone maintenance on, 277
    group therapy for substance-abusing persons with, 369
    hallucinations in, 199
    lysergic acid diethylamide as model of, 198–199
    marijuana use and, 170
    neuroimaging in, 199
    occurring in persons who were previously treated for phencyclidine psychosis, 210
    patient-treatment matching for substance-abusing persons with, 477
    phencyclidine as model of, 206
    prevalence among substance-abusing persons, 91, 476
    psychotherapy for substance-abusing persons with, 477
    reasons for substance use in persons with, 476
    smoking and, 218, 476
    treatment for comorbid psychopathology and, 476–477
Schizophreniform reactions, 200
Schools
    academic performance and substance abuse, 53–54
    alcohol abuse education in, 161–162
    substance abuse prevention programs in, 536, 539, **542**
    teaching general life skills and drug-refusal skills in, 469
SCID (Structured Clinical Interview for DSM-IV), 114, 526

SCL-90-R (Symptom Checklist-90—Revised), 154, 219
Screening and assessment instruments, 109, 114, 525–527
    Addiction Severity Index, 100, 114, 124, 277, 419, 526
    Adolescent Drinking Inventory, 525
    Alcohol Dependence Scale, 114
    Alcohol Use Disorders Identification Test, 114, 525
    Alcohol Withdrawal Scale, 152
    for alcoholism, 61, 114, 152–153, 161, 525
    CAGE questionnaire, 114, 161, 175–176, 525
    Clinical Institute Withdrawal Assessment for Alcohol Scale, 123, 151–154
    Contemplation Ladder, 116
    to determine patient involvement in 12-step group, 407
    Diagnostic Interview Schedule, 49, 450
    Fagerstrom Test for Nicotine Dependence, 110, 218, 220
    Fagerstrom Tolerance Questionnaire, 220
    Michigan Alcohol Screening Test, 61, 114, 161, 525
    Minnesota Multiphasic Personality Inventory, 102, 450
    Modified Selective Severity Assessment Scale, 152
    Narcotic Withdrawal Scale, 123
    Obsessive Compulsive Drinking Scale, 156
    for pregnant women, 487–488, 494
    Recovery Attitude and Treatment Evaluation, 123
    Recovery Attitude and Treatment Evaluator Clinical Evaluation, 526–527
    Self-Administered Alcoholism Screen Test, 525
    Situational Competency Test, **361**, 362
    Structured Clinical Interview for DSM-IV, 114, 526
    Symptom Checklist-90—Revised, 154, 219
    T-ACE questionnaire, 114
    Temperament and Character Inventory, 60, 62, **62**
    Tridimensional Personality Questionnaire, 60

TWEAK questionnaire, 114
University of Rhode Island Change Assessment, 116
Secobarbital (Seconal), 241, **247**
Second messengers
    alcohol effects and, 5
    for cannabinoids, 40
    opioid receptors and, 11, 281
Secular Organizations for Sobriety/Save Our Selves, 409, 415
Sedapap (butalbital), **247**
Sedative-hypnotics, 110, 239–248, **514.** *See also* Benzodiazepines
    for alcohol withdrawal, 152–153
    benzodiazepine abuse and dependence, 240–241
    benzodiazepine withdrawal syndromes, 111, 241–244
        pharmacological treatment of, 244–248
    buspirone, 241
    inpatient treatment for withdrawal from, 416
    intoxication with, 241
        differentiating phencyclidine intoxication from, 208
    panic attacks during withdrawal from, 478
    patient assessment for use of, 112
    short-acting, 241
    synthetic, 77
    twin studies of abuse of, **60**
    use with methadone, 273
Seizures
    during alcohol withdrawal, 8, 152, 153, 154, 416
    during benzodiazepine withdrawal, 241
    benzodiazepines for, 239
    due to crack cocaine overdose, 185
    in hallucinogen abusers, 200
    $\gamma$-hydroxybutyrate-induced, 302, 303
    during opioid withdrawal, 260
    phencyclidine-induced, 206, 209
Selective prevention of substance abuse, 536, **542**
Selective serotonin reuptake inhibitors (SSRIs)
    for alcohol abuse, 6–7, 131, 477
    for cocaine abuse, 27
    compared with tricyclic antidepressants for substance-abusing persons, 477
    flashbacks induced by, 201

Selective serotonin reuptake inhibitors (SSRIs) *(continued)*
　for generalized anxiety disorder, 479
　for HIV-infected persons who abuse drugs, 507
　interaction with lysergic acid diethylamide, 197
　for panic disorder, 479
　for posttraumatic stress disorder, 480
　for social phobia, 479–480
Self-Administered Alcoholism Screen Test (SAAST), 525
Self-administration paradigm, 22, 67–68, 70. *See also* Reinforcing effects of drugs
Self-care deficits, 371
Self-control, perception of, 355
Self-control training, 360
　for alcohol abuse, 129, 131
Self-deprivation, 359, 363
Self-destructiveness, 312
Self-directedness, 62
Self-efficacy, 175, 177, 224, 357, 362
Self-esteem deficits, 335–336, 371, 450
Self-help programs. *See* Alcoholics Anonymous; Cocaine Anonymous; Narcotics Anonymous; Twelve-step groups
Self-hypnosis, 339
Self-medication, 240, 324, 369
Self-monitoring
　of drinking, 131
　for relapse prevention, 361, **361**
　of smoking behavior, 220, 224
Self psychology, 313
Self-report questionnaires. *See* Screening and assessment instruments
Sensory deprivation, 133
SEPs (syringe-exchange programs), 504–505
Serax. *See* Oxazepam
Serotonergic drugs, for alcoholism, 6–7, 130–131, 477
Serotonin (5-HT)
　alcohol and, 101, 130–131, 477
　methylenedioxymethamphetamine and, 296–299
　phencyclidine and, 206
　receptors for, 6–7, 36
　stimulants and, 21, 23–24, 183
Serotonin antagonists, 36, 200
Serotonin syndrome, 298, 299

Sertraline
　for alcohol abuse, 131
　for cocaine abuse, 187
　for posttraumatic stress disorder, 480
Serum glutamate pyruvate transaminase (SGPT). *See* Alanine aminotransferase
Serum glutamic-oxaloacetic transaminase (SGOT). *See* Aspartate aminotransferase
Severity of substance use, 98, 110
　Addiction Severity Index, 100, 114, 124, 277, 419, 526
　effect on treatment outcome, 98
　needs-to-services matching based on, 124–125
Sexual abuse, 486
Sexual behavior, high-risk, 353
Sexual dysfunction
　induced by alcohol in women, 485–486
　marijuana-induced, 173–174
　among patients entering therapeutic communities, 450
Sexually transmitted diseases, 492
SGOT (serum glutamic-oxaloacetic transaminase). *See* Aspartate aminotransferase
SGPT (serum glutamate pyruvate transaminase). *See* Alanine aminotransferase
Short Michigan Alcohol Screening Test (SMAST), 525
Short-term inpatient treatment (SIT), 142–143
　compared with therapeutic communities, 142
　components of, 142
　definition of, 142
　duration of, 142
　effectiveness of, 142–143, 145
　follow-up after, 142
　patient populations receiving, 142
　reasons for varying results of, 143
Sidewalk ashram culture, 75
Signal transduction, cannabinoids and, 40–41
Significant others. *See also* Family
　interviews with, 114–115, 383
Silver acetate, 230
Single photon emission computed tomography (SPECT)
　in cocaine abusers, 184
　after mescaline administration, 199
　in schizophrenia, 199

SIT. *See* Short-term inpatient treatment
Situational Competency Test, **361,** 362
Skills-training interventions, 70, 353, 354, 362
　in family therapy, 390
Skin signs of drug abuse, 18, 256
Sleep disturbances, 113–114, 254
"Slip." *See* Relapse
SMART Recovery, 415
SMAST (Short Michigan Alcohol Screening Test), 525
Smoked substances
　crack cocaine, 184
　ice amphetamine, 184
　marijuana, 165–179
　phencyclidine, 205
Smoking (tobacco), 76, 110, 215–234
　addictive nature of, 217–218
　among adolescents, 465–466
　alcohol use and, 217
　alcoholism and, 217, 218
　behavioral self-monitoring of, 220, 224
　carcinogenicity of, 173, 216
　central nervous system effects of, 215
　changing social attitudes toward, 63
　commonalities with other addictive substances, 215
　depression and, 218, 219
　diagnosis and assessment of, 112, 219–225
　　comprehensiveness of, 219
　　evaluation of physiological addiction, 220
　　flowchart for, **221**
　　psychological assessment, 220–224
　　　attitudes and cognitions, 224
　　　behavior, 220, 224
　　　emotional meaning of cigarettes, 224
　　social assessment, 224–225
　　standardized instruments for, 219–220
　in DSM, 215
　factors supporting smoking behavior, 217–219
　　etiology and stages of smoking, 217–218
　　physiological factors, 218
　　psychological factors, 218
　　social, demographic, and medical factors, 218–219
　health risks of, 215–217

initiation of, 217
learning how to smoke, 168
personality correlates of, 62–63, **63**
physiological effects of cigarette
smoke, 216–217
carbon monoxide, 216
medical impact, 216–217
nicotine, 216
tar, 216
during pregnancy, 216–217, 485,
493
prevalence of tobacco dependence,
49–50
prevention of, 178, 541
recognition as serious medical
problem, 215–216
schizophrenia and, 218, 476
stress-related, 218
tobacco/marijuana connection,
168–169
among women, 489
Smoking cessation
adolescents' desire for, 217
factors affecting success of,
217–219, 226
comorbid psychopathology, 218
heaviness of smoking, 218
life stress, 218
medical illness, 219
physiological factors, 218
social support, 218–219, 224–225
health benefits of, 217, 225
outcome of interventions for, 225
patient education materials about,
225
patient's motivation for, **221,**
224–226
pharmacological approaches to, 220,
**222–223**
reasons for, 215–217, 225–226
reviewing patients' past attempts at,
220, 226
stage 1: commitment to change and
goal setting, 225–226
stage 2: action, 226–233
group versus individual therapy,
232–233
setting quit date, 233
social support and number of
contacts, 232
techniques to decrease
physiological addiction,
226–230 (*See also* Nicotine
replacement therapy)
bupropion, 228

combined therapy, 229
health and safety risks of, 229
nicotine fading, 230
nicotine maintenance, 229
nicotine replacement therapy,
226–228
other pharmacotherapies, 230
pharmacotherapy for alcohol
and drug abusers, 229
techniques to decrease
psychological dependency,
230–232
aversive techniques, 231
cognitive-behavioral treatment,
230–231
hypnosis, 231
relaxation training, 231–232
stage 3: maintenance of nonsmoking,
233–234
coping with withdrawal effects,
233
prevalence of relapses, 218, 233
relapse prevention, 233–234
stages of, 217, 225
summary of recommendations for,
234
treatment in mental health facility,
219
types of interventions for, 225
related to assessment outcomes,
**221**
work-site programs for, 219
"Smoking Cessation Clinical Practice
Guideline," 225–228, 230
*Smoking Facts and Quitting Tips for
African-Americans*, 225
Smuggling of drugs, 78, 80
Snide-E, 296. *See also* Methylenedioxymethamphetamine
Social causation and social selection
hypotheses of drug dependence, 52
Social controls on drug use, 75–76
Social functioning of opioid addicts,
255
Social learning theory, 68, 449, 538
Social phobia, 311, 479–480
adolescent substance use and, 468
alcohol abuse and, 90, 158, 313,
479–480
cocaine dependence and, 479
differentiation from social fears
arising during marijuana or
stimulant intoxication, 479
difficulty in attending 12-step groups
due to, 480

importance of early recognition of,
479
treatment in substance-abusing
persons, 479–480
Social pressure, 356
Social role conflicts, 80
Social Security Act, 440
Social service agency intervention,
439–440
adult protective services, 440
child protective services, 439
disability and public support,
439–440
Social skills training
for alcohol problems, 129, 130
for social phobia, 480
Social support, 53, 529
network therapy, 323–332
provided by Alcoholics Anonymous,
404
for relapse prevention, 365
for smoking cessation, 218–219,
224–225, 232
Society of General Internal Medicine,
532
Society of Teachers in Family Medicine,
532
Special K, 299. *See also* Ketamine
Special populations of substance abusers
adolescents, 465–471
dual-diagnosis patients, 475–481
HIV-infected patients, 503–508
patients requiring pain management,
511–517
therapeutic communities for, 459
12-step groups for, 408
women, 485–489
during perinatal period, 491–498
SPECT. *See* Single photon emission
computed tomography
Spinal gray matter necrosis, 18
Spirituality, 91, 312, 407, 411, 415
Splitting, 312, 314, 317
SR-95531, 5
SR141716A (carboximide
hydrochloride), 41–43
SSRIs. *See* Selective serotonin reuptake
inhibitors
Standard of care, 442
Status conflict, 79–80
Status epilepticus, 209. *See also*
Seizures
Stay'n Out, 143, 144
Steppingstone hypothesis, 54. *See also*
Gateway drugs

Stigmatization, 109, 415, 498
Stillbirth, 493
Stimulant abuse treatment, 185–189
   behavioral therapy, 187–188
   guidelines for, 189
   for overdose, 185
   pharmacological, 26–27, 185–187
      antidepressants, 27, 186–187, 189
      buprenorphine, 187
      carbamazepine, 187
      cocaine vaccine, 187
      disulfiram, 187
      dopaminergic agonists, 26,
         185–186
      neuroleptics, 185, 189
      opiates, 26–27
      for patients with psychiatric
         comorbidity, 188
Stimulant-hallucinogens, **34, 35,** 195
Stimulant use, 21–27, 110, 183–189,
   **514.** See also Amphetamine;
   Cocaine
   abuse potential for, 480
   administration routes for, 184
   by adolescents, 168, 465
   for attention-deficit/hyperactivity
      disorder, 480
   binge-crash cycles of, 22, 185
   comparison of amphetamine and
      cocaine, 27
   consequences of repeated exposure,
      22–26
      sensitization, 23–24
      tolerance, 24–25
      toxicity, 25–26
   dangers associated with, 183
   delirium due to, 185
   differentiating phencyclidine
      intoxication from, 208
   euphoria produced by, 21, 183, 184
   historical cycles of, 21
   among HIV-infected persons,
      183, 506
   intoxication, 113, 185
   mechanism of action for, 21
   neurobiology of, 21–27
      chronic stimulant abuse, 184
   panic attacks induced by, 478
   patient assessment for, 112, 189
   patterns of, 184–185
   psychiatric comorbidity with, 188
   psychosis induced by, 23, 33, 36,
      185
   reinforcing effects of, 22, 183–184
   for smoking cessation, 230

social fears induced by, 479
subjective and discriminative
   stimulus effects of, 21–22
synthetic drugs, 77
twin studies of, 59, **60**
withdrawal from, 185
   "crash," 22, 185
   depressive symptoms during, 90
   phases of, 185
Stimulus antagonism tests, 34
Stimulus control techniques, 363–364
Stimulus generalization tests, 34
"STP," 195
Strategic family approach, 329
Stress and drug-seeking behavior, 324
Stress management training, 354
   for alcohol abuse, 131, 132,
      338–339
   in workplace, 432
Stria terminalis, 5
Stroke, 209
Structural-strategic family therapy, 393
Structured Clinical Interview for
   DSM-IV (SCID), 114, 526
Structured interviews, 114, 123
Sublimation, 317–318
Substance abuse
   in adolescents, 465–471
   adoption study of, 59–60, **60,**
      100–101
   age distribution of, 49, **55**
   comorbidity among different forms
      of, 59
   "controlled" substance use and,
      89–90, 114, 360
   cost of, 69, 413
   cross-cultural aspects of, 75–82
   decriminalization of, 441
   definition of, 110
   diagnosis of, 110–111 (See also
      Assessment of patient)
   educating patient and family about
      dangers of, 90
   environmental context of, 50–53,
      69
   epidemics of, 76
   epidemiology of, 47–56
   gateway theory of, 54, 169, 467,
      468, 535
   gender distribution of, 49, 50, 109
   genetics of, 59–66, 70
   geographical distribution of, 50, **51,**
      79
   history of, 75–78
   HIV infection and, 503–508

incidence of, 48–49
individual vulnerabilities to, 14–15,
   53–54, 70
medical education about, 529–533
perinatal, 491–498
personality traits and, 53–54, 59–63,
   **62, 63**
planning alternatives to, 394
prevalence of, 48–49
prevention of, 56, 535–542
primary versus secondary, 98–99
psychiatric disorders and, 90–91,
   98–100, 109, 114, 336, 344,
   475–481
psychodynamic theory of, 309–311
symptoms of, 110
in women, 485–489
Substance Abuse and Mental Health
   Services Administration, 532
Substance dependence
   DSM-IV criteria for, 110
   epidemiology of, 47–56
   on opioids, 12, 15–17
   physical or physiological, 110
   polysubstance dependence, 111
   rating severity of, 98, 110
   symptoms of, 110
Substance-induced disorders, 110
Substance use disorders
   in adolescents, 466
   in DSM, 69, 97, 98, 110, 466
   lifetime prevalence of, 466
   subtypes of persons with, 97–105
      (See also Typologies of
      addiction)
Substances of abuse
   classification of mood-altering drugs,
      110, 514, **514**
   club drugs, 295–303
   development of concentrates of
      traditional substances, 77
   synthetic, 77–78
Subtypes of substance abuse.
   See Typologies of addiction
Sudden infant death syndrome, 485
Suicidality, 90, 312
   adolescent substance use and, 468
   alcoholism and, 102
Super K, 299. See also Ketamine
Superego, 309, 312, 313, 317, 335
Sweat patch testing, 521, 522, **523.**
   See also Laboratory testing
Symbolic meanings of drug use, 78
Symptom Checklist-90—Revised
   (SCL-90-R), 154, 219

"Symptom-triggered therapy" (S-TT), 152
Synanon, 138, 368, 447
Synesthesia, 197
Synthetic psychoactive substances, 77–78
Syringe-exchange programs (SEPs), 504–505
Systematic desensitization, 479, 480
Systems model of substance abuse treatment, 437, **438**

## T

T-ACE questionnaire, 114
Taboo drug use, 78
*Taking Charge of Your Smoking*, 230
Talking-down technique
    for acute hallucinogen reactions, 199–200
    avoiding in phencyclidine-intoxicated persons, 208
Tar in cigarette smoke, 216
Tardive dyskinesia, 159
Tattoos, 256
Tavern culture, 75
Taxes
    on alcoholic beverages, 161
    Marijuana Tax Act of 1937, 166
TCI (Temperament and Character Inventory), 60, 62, **62**
TCP (1-(1-2-thienyl-cyclohexyl)piperidine), 205
TCs. *See* Therapeutic communities
Teen Treatment Services Review, 471
Temazepam (Restoril), **246**
Temperament, 53, 60–61, **61**, 312, 313. *See also* Personality traits and substance abuse
    adolescent substance use and, 53, 60, 466, 467
Temperament and Character Inventory (TCI), 60, 62, **62**
Testimonials by former drug users, 536
Testosterone, 174
Δ⁹-Tetrahydrocannabinol (THC), 33, 34, 39–43, 165–167, 198. *See also* Cannabis use
    acute effects of, 166
    anandamide compared with, 41
    in breast milk, 174
    cerebral blood flow response to, 174
    concentration in cannabinoids, 165–168
    contaminated with phencyclidine, 169, 205

effects on sexual hormones, 173–174
    fat solubility of, 39, 169–170, 172
    immunological effects of, 173
    memory impairment due to, 39, 42, 171
    novel synthetic analogs of, 40
    oral form of, 165–166
    pharmacological effects of, 169
    positron-emission tomography scanning after administration of, 174
    in pregnancy, 174
    psychosis induced by, 170, 198
    respiratory effects of, 173
    role of cAMP in mediating effects of, 40
    structure-activity relationships for, 39–40
    tolerance to, 43, 171
Therapeutic communities (TCs), 138, 447–460. *See also* Long-term residential treatment
    for adolescents, 450, 459
    aftercare and, 457, 459
    approach of, 451–457
    basic program elements of, 453–455
        community and clinical management elements, 454–455
            disciplinary sanctions, 455
            privileges, 455
            surveillance: house runs, 455
            urine testing, 455
        community enhancement activities, 454
            general meetings, 454
            house meetings, 454
            morning meetings, 454
            during nonscheduled informal activities, 454
            seminars, 454
        definition of recovery process, 453
        therapeutic-educative activities, 453–454
            ad hoc groups, 454
            encounters, 453
            goals of, 453
            marathons, 453–454
            one-to-one counseling, 454
            probes, 453
            tutorials, 454
        typical day, 453
    change process in, 455–456

compared with other treatment modalities, 447–448
        methadone maintenance, 138, 139
        short-term inpatient treatment, 142
    contact and referral to, 450–451
    criteria for residential treatment in, 451
        community risk, 451
        suitability, 451
    current modifications of, 139, 459
        multimodal treatment and patient-treatment matching, 459
    definition of, 447
    duration of treatment in, 447
    effectiveness of, 139–140, 144–145, 457–458
    evolution of, 458–460
    exclusionary criteria of, 451
    expulsion from, 455
    for former prisoners, 143
    goals of, 447
    graduation from, 457
    history of, 447
    for HIV-infected persons, 451, 459, 506
    in human services, 459–460
    individual psychotherapy in, 344
    individual's submission to group's ideology in, 368
    job assignments in, 453
    open-door policy of, 451
    outreach teams from, 450
    patient populations of, 447, 449–451
        clinical characteristics of, 448, 450
        detoxification of, 451
        gender distribution of, 449
        psychiatric diagnoses of, 450
        psychological profiles of, 450
        social profiles of, 448, 449
        special populations, 459
    perspective of, 448–449
        view of disorder, 447, 448
        view of person, 448
        view of recovery, 448–449
            motivation, 448
            self-help and mutual self-help, 448–449
            social learning, 449
            treatment as an episode, 449
        view of right living, 449
    for phencyclidine-abusing persons, 212

Therapeutic communities (TCs)
(continued)
program stages and phases in,
455–457
stage 1: orientation-induction, 456
stage 2: primary treatment, 456
stage 3: reentry, 456–457
early phase, 457
later phase, 457
range of services in, 447
rehabilitative approach of, 447, 448
research on treatment process of,
458
retention in, 139, 140, 145, 458
enhancement of, 458
predictors of dropout, 458
rates of, 458
size of, 447
staff of, 447, 452, 453
structure of, 452–453
mutual self-help, 452
peers as role models, 447,
452–453
staff as rational authorities, 453
work as education and therapy,
452
traditional prototype for, 447–448
Therapist characteristics
empathy, 133
for group therapy, 376
impact on treatment outcome, 133,
345
Therapist-patient relationship, 311,
318–319, 345–346
Thiamine, 153, 154, 159–160
1-(1-2-Thienyl-cyclohexyl)piperidine
(TCP), 205
Thioridazine, 290
Thrombophlebitis, 256
Thrush, 256
3,4,5-TMA (α-methylmescaline), **34, 35**
Tobacco use, 215–234. *See also*
Smoking
Tolerance to drug effects, 69, 110
cannabis, 43, 171
definition of, 110
effect on pain management, 514
ketamine, 300
lysergic acid diethylamide, 196
midazolam, 240
opioids, 11, 12, 15–16, 514
phencyclidine, 211
questioning patient about, 112
stimulants, 24–25
zolpidem, 240

TOPS (Treatment Outcome
Prospective Study), 138, 140,
141, 143
Toradol (ketorolac), 259, **514**
Toxicology testing. *See* Laboratory
testing
TPQ (Tridimensional Personality
Questionnaire), 60
Tracking, 395
"Tracks," 256
Training, professional
medical education in addiction
medicine, 529–533
in use of network therapy, 331–332
Tramadol (Ultram), **514**
Transactional theories, 538
Transcutaneous nerve stimulation, **513**
Transference reactions, 318–319, 340
Transferrin, carbohydrate-deficient
(CDT), 115, 524
Transverse myelitis, 18
Tranxene (clorazepate), **246**
Travelers, 81–82. *See also* Cross-
cultural aspects of substance abuse
Trazodone, 158, 187, 507
Treatment goals, 89–94
categories of, 89
patient-oriented, 89–92
achieving substance-free lifestyle,
89–90
maximizing motivation for
abstinence, 89–90
rebuilding substance-free life,
90
maximizing multiple aspects of
life functioning, 90–91
addressing relevant spiritual
issues, 91
dealing with homelessness, 91
dealing with marital and other
family issues, 91
enriching job functioning and
financial management, 91
identifying and treating
psychiatric symptoms and
disorders, 90–91
optimizing medical functioning,
90
preventing relapse, 91–92
potentially inappropriate, 93–94
programmatic, 92–93
to carefully use financial and staff
resources, 92
to clearly state philosophy of staff,
92

to consider fiscal and political
realities, 92
to determine that treatment
approaches being
considered are more
effective than no treatment
at all, 93
to remember that no treatment is
totally safe, 92–93
Treatment interventions, 56, 309–460
for adolescents, 469–471
for alcohol abuse, 151–162
based on patient assessment, 109,
110, 117
for cannabis dependence, 175–178
community-based, 437–444
compliance with (*See* Compliance
with treatment)
cost-effectiveness of, 93, 121, 125,
320, 406, 413
for dual-diagnosis patients, 475–481
(*See also* Psychiatric disorders)
effectiveness of (*See* Treatment
outcomes)
Employee Assistance Programs and
other workplace interventions,
423–434
ethnicity and, 80–81
family therapy
for alcoholism, 379–386
for other drug abuse, 389–399
goals of, 353
abstinence model, 353
harm-reduction model, 353
group therapy, 367–376
for hallucinogen abuse, 195–201,
199–201
for HIV-infected patients, 505–508
individual psychotherapy
for alcoholism, 335–341
for other drug abuse, 343–349
inpatient treatment, 413–420
learning-based, 70–71
under managed care, 545–551
for methylenedioxymeth-
amphetamine abuse, 298–299
network therapy, 323–332
for opioid abuse
detoxification, 251–268
methadone maintenance,
271–278
opioid antagonists and partial
agonists, 281–292
pain management in drug-addicted
persons, 511–517

patient placement criteria for, 121–125
  levels of care, 121–124, **122**
  needs-to-services matching, 124–125
patient's ecosystem for, 389
pharmacological, 549 (*See also* Pharmacotherapy)
for phencyclidine abuse, 208–212
"Practice Guideline for Treatment of Patients With Substance Use Disorders," 117, 530
psychodynamic psychotherapy, 309–321
relapse prevention, 353–365
for sedative-hypnotic abuse, 239–248
for smoking cessation, 215–234
stage-specific, 549
for stimulant abuse, 185–189
systems model of, 437, **438**
therapeutic communities, 447–460
12-step groups, 403–411
for women, 487–489
  in perinatal period, 493–498
Treatment Outcome Prospective Study (TOPS), 138, 140, 141, 143
Treatment outcomes, 121, 323
  for adolescents, 469–471
  for alcohol problems, 129–133, 153, 320
    Alcoholics Anonymous, 336, 367, 405–406, 409
    effect of comorbid psychopathology on, 98–100, 116
      antisocial personality disorder, 99–100
      depression, 99
      related to primary/secondary distinction, 98–99
    effect of dependence severity on, 98
    effect of patient-treatment matching on, 97, 100, 103–104, 124–125, 133, 151
    family therapy, 385–386, 390
    individual psychotherapy, 340–341, 348
    methodology for rating treatment effectiveness, 129
    therapies with indeterminate evidence of effectiveness, 131–132

therapies with insufficient evidence of effectiveness, 132–133
    therapies with potential effectiveness, 133
    therapies with strong evidence of effectiveness, 129–131
    in Type 1 versus Type 2 alcoholics, 100–102, 151
    in Type A versus Type B alcoholics, 103–104, 151
  for drug abuse, 135–145
    conclusions about treatment effectiveness, 144–145
    correctional treatment programs, 143–144
    family therapy, 389–390
    individual psychotherapy, 346–348
    long-term residential treatment, 138–141
    methadone maintenance, 136–138, 271, 275
    outpatient nonmethadone treatment, 141–142
    paradigm for analysis of, 135
    short-term inpatient treatment, 142–143
    therapies excluded from analysis of, 135
  effect of therapist characteristics on, 133, 345
  for Employee Assistance Programs, 431
  for group therapy, 369–370
  for inpatient treatment, 417–419
  with needs-to-services matching, 124–125
  for network therapy, 325–326, 330–331
  for partial hospitalization programs, 442
  for psychodynamic psychotherapy, 309
  for therapeutic communities, 139–140, 144–145, 457–458
Treatment philosophy, 92
Triazolam (Halcion), 241, **246**
Tridimensional Personality Questionnaire (TPQ), 60
Triglycerides, 524
Tropisetron (ICS 205-930), 7
TSF (twelve-step facilitation therapy), 408

Tuberculin skin test, 256
Tuberculosis, 251
Tutorials, in therapeutic communities, 454
TWEAK questionnaire, 114
Twelve-step facilitation therapy (TSF), 408–409
Twelve-step groups, 403–411. *See also* Alcoholics Anonymous; Cocaine Anonymous; Narcotics Anonymous; Pills Anonymous
  for alcoholism, 103–104, 132, 133, 403–411
  alternatives to, 409, 415
  attendance at meetings of
    compliance with, 328
    difficulty for persons with social phobia, 311, 480
    patients' willingness and, 323
  attitudes of health care practitioners toward, 405
  definition of, 403
  dropouts from, 323
  effectiveness of, 405–406
  exposing medical students to, 531
  facilitating affiliation and involvement in, 407
    tailoring to specific groups, 408
  frequency of use by persons with substance abuse disorders, 404–405
  group affiliation and involvement in, 406–407
  health care provider's knowledge about special-population issues related to, 408
  integrating professional treatment with, 407–408
  lack of formal evaluation of, 135
  for marijuana dependence, 176–177
  matching members to professional treatment, 409
  matching patients to, 404, 408
  measuring involvement in, 407
  Minnesota Model programs based on principles of, 414
  network therapy and, 328
  psychodynamics applied to, 309–311, 314, 318–320, 367, 369, 375
  when to refer to, 404
  during short-term inpatient treatment, 142
  women's participation in, 404, 487

Twin studies, 50–52, 59, **60**
 of alcoholism, 50
 of hallucinogen abuse, **60**
 of marijuana abuse, 59, **60**
 of novelty-seeking, 63
 of opioid dependence, 14, 59, **60**
 of sedative abuse, **60**
 of stimulant abuse, 59, **60**
Typologies of addiction, 97–105
 adolescent substance abuse and, 466
 based on familial substance abuse,
  100–102
 gamma and delta alcoholics, 97
 historical overview of, 97
 patient-treatment matching and,
  103–104
 statistical approaches to classification
  of, 102–103
 unidimensional, 97–100
  coexisting psychopathology,
   98–100
  dependence severity, 98
  prognostic utility of, 98, 99
  range of criteria for, 97–98
  shortcomings of, 100
Tyramine, dietary, 478
Tyrosine kinases, 6

**U**

Ultram (tramadol), **514**
Unbalancing techniques, 397
Uniform Alcoholism and Intoxication
 Treatment Act, 441
United Kingdom, 50
Universal prevention of substance
 abuse, 536, **542**
University of Rhode Island Change
 Assessment (URICA), 116
Urban drug use, 52, 79
Urge-control procedures, 363–365
Uric acid, 524
URICA (University of Rhode Island
 Change Assessment), 116
Urine acidification, 208–210
Urine toxicology testing, 114–115, 521,
 522, **523**. *See also* Laboratory
  testing
 for hallucinogens, 198
 kits for on-site screening, 521
 for marijuana, 175, 176
 for opioids, 256
 for phencyclidine, 207, 208
 preemployment, 176, 432
 in therapeutic communities, 455
 in workplace, 432, 439, 521, 522

 **V**

Vaccines against substance abuse, 70
Valium. *See* Diazepam
Valproate, 248
Values, 449
Ventral tegmental area (VTA), 310, 521
 opioid effects in, 13, 16
 stimulant effects in, 22–24, 183
Verbomarkers, 52
Versed (midazolam), 240, **246,** 265
Victimization, 82, 398, 486–488
Videotape self-confrontation, 132
Vietnam veterans, 52
Violent behavior, 99. *See also*
 Criminality
 alcoholism and, 101, 102, 162
 phencyclidine-induced, 206, 210
Visual disturbances, drug-induced
 hallucinogens, 197, 201
 marijuana, 170
 phencyclidine, 211
Vitamin K, 299. *See also* Ketamine
Vitamin supplements
 for alcoholic persons, 159–160
 vitamin C for phencyclidine
  intoxication, 209, 210
Vocational education, 91, 488
Voltage-sensitive calcium channels
 (VSCC), 7
Voltaren (diclofenac), **514**
Vomiting. *See* Nausea and vomiting
VSCC (voltage-sensitive calcium
 channels), 7
VTA. *See* Ventral tegmental area
Vulnerabilities to substance abuse,
 14–15, 53–54, 70
 genetic factors, 59–66

**W**

Warning signs for relapse, 354, 361
Water balance therapy, 252
Wellness programs in workplace, 432
Wernicke's encephalopathy, 154, 160
WHO (World Health Organization),
 437, 525
Withdrawal symptoms, 110, 111
 from alcohol, 151–155
 from benzodiazepines, 241–244
 from cannabis, 171–172
 from cocaine, 111, 136, 185
 conditioned, 324–325
 delirium, 111, 113
 examination for, 113
 medications for, 93
 from methadone maintenance, 259

from nicotine, 217, 218, 220, 233
from opioids, 14–15, 253–254
pain, 512, 513
from phencyclidine, 211
protracted withdrawal syndrome
 from alcohol, 157
 from low-dose benzodiazepines,
  242–243, **245**
psychiatric symptoms and, 90
questioning patient about, 112
from stimulants, 185
Women for Sobriety, 409, 488
Women substance abusers, 485–489.
 *See also* Perinatal substance use;
  Pregnancy
 Addiction Severity Index-F for, 526
 assessing children of, 488
 concerns about children and child
  care, 398
 disturbances in families of, 398
 family therapy for, 398, 488
 gender distribution of drug
  dependence, 49, 50
 HIV infection among, 486
 iatrogenic dependence on prescribed
  drugs among, 488
 identification of, 487
 marijuana use by, 165
 physiological factors affecting,
  485–486
 preventive strategies for, 488–489
 psychiatric comorbidity among, 486,
  488
 psychological factors affecting, 486
 reasons for studying, 485
 smoking, 489
 sociocultural factors affecting,
  486–487
 treatment of, 487–488
  all-female programs, 488
  barriers to, 487, 494
  expanding outreach and treatment
   services, 50
  issues affecting, 494–495
  parenting training, 495, 496
  therapeutic communities, 459
  12-step groups, 404, 487
  vocational rehabilitation, 488
 victimization of, 398, 486–488
Women's movement, 485
Work-release programs, 286
Working through, 394, 454
Workplace
 advantages of interventions in, 424
 behavioral-medical problems in, 425

drug testing in, 432, 439, 521, 522
  federally mandated, 439
  preemployment, 176, 432, 522
Employee Assistance Programs in,
  423–434
health promotion and stress
  management in, 432
industrial alcoholism model,
  424–425
involvement of patient's employer
  during inpatient treatment,
  418
motivating behavioral change in, 424
naltrexone for employed persons,
  285–286

peer intervention programs and
  member assistance programs
  in, 432–434
prohibition of psychoactive
  substance use in, 431–432
safety risks of substance abuse in,
  424
smoking cessation programs in, 219
World Health Organization (WHO),
  437, 525
Worthlessness, 335

 **X**

X, 195, 295. *See also*
  Methylenedioxymethamphetamine

Xanax. *See* Alprazolam
XTC, 36, 295. *See also*
  Methylenedioxymethamphetamine

 **Y**

Youth culture, 77

 **Z**

Zidovudine (AZT), 505, 506
Zimeldine, 6
Zinc, alcoholism and, 160, 524
Zolpidem (Ambien), 240
Zopiclone, 240
Zyban. *See* Bupropion, for smoking
  cessation